Nick - congratulations! What a
excellent job you ~ 6/01

lonely p

D0378433

Japan

P.S. Please
don't forget
where you
live.

Chris Rowthorn
John Ashburne
Sara Benson
Mason Florence

LONELY PLANET PUBLICATIONS
Melbourne • Oakland • London • Paris

JAPAN

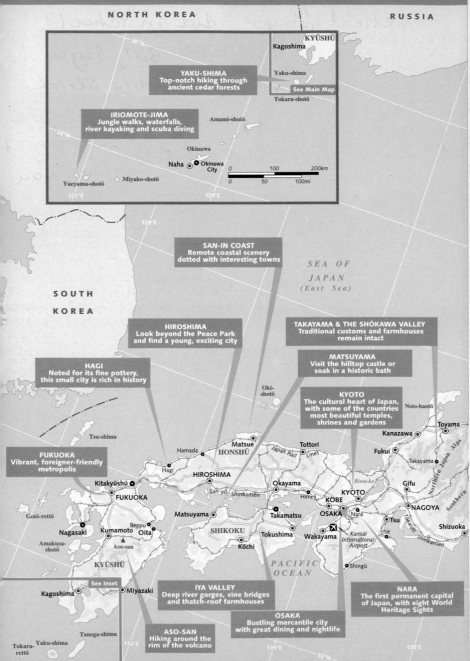

NORTH KOREA

RUSSIA

KYŪSHŪ

Kagoshima

Yaku-shima

See Main Map

Tokara-shotō

YAKU-SHIMA
Top-notch hiking through
ancient cedar forests

30°N

Amami-shotō

IRIOMOTE-JIMA
Jungle walks, waterfalls,
river kayaking and scuba diving

26°N

Okinawa

Naha   Okinawa
        City

Yaeyama-shotō   Miyako-shotō

0   100   200km

0   50   100mi

123°E   129°E

129°E

SAN-IN COAST
Remote coastal scenery
dotted with interesting towns

SEA OF

JAPAN

(East Sea)

SOUTH
KOREA

HIROSHIMA
Look beyond the Peace Park
and find a young, exciting city

TAKAYAMA & THE SHŌKAWA VALLEY
Traditional customs and farmhouses
remain intact

MATSUYAMA
Visit the hilltop castle or
soak in a historic bath

HAGI
Noted for its fine pottery,
this small city is rich in history

KYOTO
The cultural heart of Japan,
with some of the countries
most beautiful temples,
shrines and gardens

Noto-hantō

Oki-
shotō

Toyama

FUKUOKA
Vibrant, foreigner-friendly
metropolis

Tsu-shima

Matsue

HONSHŪ

Tottori

Kanazawa

Fukui

Japan Rail
Lines

Takayama

Hamada

Biwa-ko

Gifu

Hagi

HIROSHIMA

Kitakyūshū

FUKUOKA

San-yō Shinkansen

Okayama

KYOTO

KOBE

Himeji

NAGOYA

Gotō-rettō

Matsuyama

Nagasaki

Kumamoto

Beppu
Oita

SHIKOKU

Takamatsu

Tokushima

OSAKA

Nara

Tsu

Ise

Shizuoka

Northern Japan Alps

Southern

Tōkaido Shinkansen

Kansai
International
Airport

Aso-san

KYŪSHŪ

Amakusa-
shotō

Kōchi

Wakayama

PACIFIC

OCEAN

Shingū

See Inset

Kagoshima

Miyazaki

IYA VALLEY
Deep river gorges, vine bridges
and thatch-roof farmhouses

NARA
The first permanent capital
of Japan, with eight World
Heritage Sights

Tokara-
rettō

Yaku-shima

Tanega-shima

132°E

ASO-SAN
Hiking around the
rim of the volcano

OSAKA
Bustling mercantile city
with great dining and nightlife

135°E

32°N

138°E

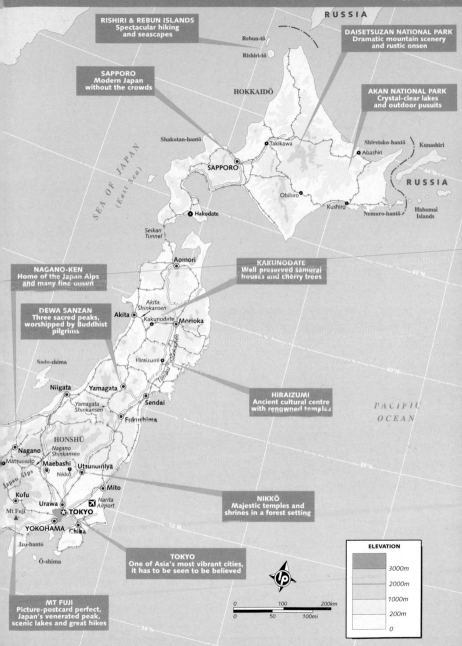

JAPAN

RUSSIA

RISHIRI & REBUN ISLANDS
Spectacular hiking
and seascapes

Rebun-tō
Rishiri-tō

DAISETSUZAN NATIONAL PARK
Dramatic mountain scenery
and rustic onsen

SAPPORO
Modern Japan
without the crowds

HOKKAIDŌ

AKAN NATIONAL PARK
Crystal-clear lakes
and outdoor pusuits

Shakotan-hantō
Takikawa

Shiretoko-hantō   Kunashiri

SAPPORO
Abashiri

RUSSIA

SEA OF JAPAN
(East Sea)

Obihiro

Kushiro   Nemuro-hantō   Habomai
Islands

Hakodate

Seikan
Tunnel

Aomori

KAKUNODATE
Well preserved samurai
houses and cherry trees

NAGANO-KEN
Home of the Japan Alps
and many fine onsen

Akita
Shinkansen

DEWA SANZAN
Three sacred peaks,
worshipped by Buddhist
pilgrims

Akita
Kakunodate   Morioka

Hiraizumi

Sado-shima

Niigata   Yamagata

Yamagata
Shinkansen

Sendai

HIRAIZUMI
Ancient cultural centre
with renowned temples

PACIFIC
OCEAN

Fukushima

HONSHŪ

Nagano
Shinkansen

Nagano

Matsumoto   Maebashi

Utsunomiya

Japan Alps   Nikkō

Kofu   Mito

Urawa   Narita
Airport

Mt Fuji   TOKYO

NIKKŌ
Majestic temples and
shrines in a forest setting

YOKOHAMA   Chiba

Izu-hantō

Ō-shima

TOKYO
One of Asia's most vibrant cities,
it has to be seen to be believed

MT FUJI
Picture-postcard perfect,
Japan's venerated peak,
scenic lakes and great hikes

ELEVATION

3000m
2000m
1000m
200m
0

0   100   200km
0   50   100mi

Japan
7th edition – October 2000
First published – October 1981

Published by
Lonely Planet Publications Pty Ltd ABN 36 005 607 983
90 Maribyrnong St, Footscray, Victoria 3011, Australia

Lonely Planet Offices
Australia Locked Bag 1, Footscray, Victoria 3011
USA 150 Linden St, Oakland, CA 94607
UK 10a Spring Place, London NW5 3BH
France 1 rue du Dahomey, 75011 Paris

Photographs
Many of the images in this guide are available for licensing from
Lonely Planet Images.
email: lpi@lonelyplanet.com.au

Front cover photograph
Detail of a geisha wearing traditional *tabi* (split-toed socks) and *geta*
(sandles), Kyoto. Photograph by Frank Carter

ISBN 0 86442 693 3

text & maps © Lonely Planet 2000
photos © photographers as indicated 2000

Printed by The Bookmaker International Ltd
Printed in China

Contents – Text

1

PERFORMING ARTS 265

AROUND TOKYO 273

CENTRAL HONSHŪ 323

KANSAI REGION 399

WESTERN HONSHŪ   523

NORTHERN HONSHŪ (TŌHOKU)   597

4 Contents – Text

OKINAWA & THE SOUTH-WEST ISLANDS   853

LANGUAGE   889

GLOSSARY   895

THANKS   902

INDEX   910

MAP LEGEND   back page

METRIC CONVERSION   inside back cover

Contents – Maps

The Authors

Chris Rowthorn
Chris was born in England and grew up in the USA. Since 1992 he's been based in Kyoto. He's worked on a total of nine books for Lonely Planet, including *Malaysia, Singapore & Brunei, Tokyo, Hiking in Japan* and *Asia & India: Read This First*. When he's not on the road for Lonely Planet, Chris enjoys trekking in Nepal, diving in Thailand and relaxing in Japanese hot springs.

John Ashburne
John Ashburne grew up in Yorkshire, flirted with English Literature and Education at Durham and Cambridge Universities, and worked as a private tutor in the Caribbean. Thereafter he attempted office work with Robert Maxwell's publishing company in Oxford, fleeing two seconds ahead of his dismissal notice, ending up in the rural hinterlands of Japan. Fourteen years later he resides in Kyoto, where he roots out noodle restaurants, when he's not off to Vietnam, Cambodia or Italy – in search of more noodle restaurants. He is author of several books on Japan, and twice winner of the Mazda International Photo Contest.

Sara 'Sam' Benson
After one summer as an exchange student in Hiroshima, Sam Benson knew she'd end up back in Japan someday. After graduating from university in Chicago, she worked across Japan for two years before returning to the US, via a long backpacking detour through Asia, to a number of not quite fulfilling jobs as an editor, writer, graphic designer and teacher. In 1999, Japan called her back once more to walk the narrow road to the deep north for Lonely Planet. Sam now lives most of her life out of one rucksack but calls San Fransisco her home.

Mason Florence
A native New Yorker, Mason migrated west to the Rocky Mountains to pursue his childhood dream of becoming a cowboy. After barely graduating from the University of Colorado, he gave up a budding career on the rodeo circuit, traded in his boots and spurs for a Nikon and a laptop, and relocated to Asia. Now a Kyoto-based photo-journalist and correspondent for *The Japan Times*, he spends around half the year on the road in South-East Asia, and free moments restoring a 300-year-old thatched-roof farmhouse in rural Shikoku. As well as *Japan*, Mason has worked on Lonely Planet's *Kyoto, Hiking in Japan, Vietnam, Hanoi, Ho Chi Minh City & South-East Asia on a shoestring*, and his articles and photographs appear frequently in newspapers and magazines worldwide.

FROM THE AUTHORS

Chris Rowthorn Chris would like to thank Chiori for all the help. He would also like to thank Inuishi Tomoko and Kimura Hiroko of JNTO for their invaluable assistance. Other thanks are due to John Ashburne, Sam Benson, Mason Florence, Ralph Saunders and Nakata Chika, Katoh Shiho and Suzuki Hirotaka, Robert Neff, Francesco Baldessari, Robb Satterwhite, Eric Johnston of *The Japan Times*, Cheryl Aldridge, Dan Grunebaum, Neelu Kaur and Peter MacIntosh.

John Ashburne First and foremost John would like to thank Sasha. He would also like to thank JKA, Eiko Setoyama, Micah Gampel for the photo, Jeroen Veldhuizen, Akira Hata, Ikuyo Kamada, Kumiko Simpson, Arai Nobue, Sachiko Miyairi, Mikiko Ogawa, Mac & Yuri, Yuko & Miyuki, Chris Rowthorn, Chris Taylor (whichever trail he's on), and the countless people who helped him 'on the road'.

Sara 'Sam' Benson Over half of my thanks go to Justin Bales, whose logistical and moral support made all things possible, and Masahiro Kikuchi for truly last-minute translations that solved the mysteries of the Seikan tunnel (and bike warriors). For special favors in times of need, I am grateful to the Niseko Annupuri Youth Hostel and the Wakkanai post office. Thank you also to the many JETs of Hokkaidō and Tōhoku, the Sapporo International Communication Plaza Foundation, Junko Hirai of the Japan Eurasia Association, Julia Morse, Lynnika Butler and Ed Talmadge.

Mason Florence I'd like to thank first and foremost Luka Weng, a faithful travel partner and patient friend. Also hats off to Chris & Lauren Shannon, Kazuhiko Miyazaki, Tim Reiner, Don Weiss, Alex Kerr, John Benson, Justin Giffin, Junji Sugita and Andy Couturier; a special note of thanks to 'Princess Dirtball' for coordinating the JETS! As always, a deep bow of gratitude to the folks at JNTO, and to the countless staff at the various tourist offices. Finally a big *otsukare-sama deshita* to the whole Japan 7 crew at Lonely Planet.

Special Thanks

The authors of this edition would like to say a special thank you to all the members of the JET (Japan Exchange & Teaching) program (including some former JETs & JET friends) who took the time to enlighten us with local travel tips and information. Domo arigato! Apologies to anyone that was left off this list – gomen ne!

Adrian J. Tanner (Hokkaido), Aimee E. Elliott (Kagawa-ken), Alan Casey (Miyazaki-ken), Andrew M Lea (Niigata-ken), Andrew Shoolbread

(Kagawa-ken), Austin Keys (Ehime-ken), Biana Hitt (Ehime-ken), Big Jen Biggers (Kagawa-ken), Brian Cundieff (Miyazaki-ken), Cathy Eberst (Oita-ken), Chad Sowards (Kochi-ken), Chio Hatakeyama (Ehime-ken), Chris Lightfoot (Miyako-jima), Clair James (Ehime-ken), Claire Skipper (Tokushima-ken), Claudia Macedo (Miyazaki-ken), Daryl Beres (Kagawa-ken), Dave Aldwinckle (Hokkaido), Dave and Beca (Kagawa-ken), Debbie Griffith (Hokkaido), Eileen Ellis (Ehime-ken), EM & Michelle (Kiso-Fukushima), Eric Lindblom (Nagano-ken), Fleur Kics, Frankie Vinelott (Miyazaki-ken), Grant Mitchell and Mary Hamblyn., Howard Gilbert (Oita-ken), Ian Speakman (Okayama-ken), Jean Christophe Helary (Kagawa-ken), Jenny Ruthensteiner (Kagawa-ken), Jerry Keys (Okayama-ken), Jess Kawachi (Ehime-ken), Jessica Kennett (Hiroshima-ken), Jim Cork & Jess Kennett (Hiroshima-ken), Jon Fairbanks (Miyazaki-ken), Jon Hinze (Shimane-ken), Joseph Geruntino (Ehime-ken), Joshua Beatty (Saga-ken), Joy Sakurai (Okinawa-ken), Julanne Morris (Tokushima-ken), Kirsty Hamson (Kyushu), Laura Cook (Ehime-ken), Lauren Shannon (Kagawa-ken), Lisa Asahina (Hiroshima-ken), Lynnika Butler (Yamagata-ken), Mandali Khalesi (Miyazaki-ken), Marcos Benevides (Okinawa-ken), Maria Christina Lim (Okayama-ken), Marie Mincks (Kochi-ken), Mary Jane McKitterick (Kagawa-ken), Masumi Tomiyama (Miyako-jima), Maya Ileto (Tokushima-ken), Michael Mahon (Ehime-ken), Mike Liska (Ehime-ken), Morgan C. Benton (Hokkaido), Nic Hopkins (Nagano-ken), Nicola Finkle (Kochi-ken), Owen Phillips (Miyako-jima), Scott Boslow (Okayama-ken), Scott Cohen (Akita-ken), Scott McKeeman, Sean Chamberlain (Ehime-ken), Sean Conlon (Kagoshima-ken), Seth Renquist (Ishigaki-jima), Shannon Disney (Okayama-ken), Shivaun Gleeson (Akita-ken), Stella Durdin (Yamaguchi-ken), Steve Maki (Hokkaido), Suparna Guha (Miyazaki-ken), Tania Kyriakides (Toyama-ken), Tom and Mary (Kochi-ken), Wendy Myers (Oita-ken), Whei Ru Cheng (Kochi-ken), Will Jasprizza (Ehime-ken), Yuuta Sasaki (Miyazaki-ken).

This Book

The first three editions of this book were written by Ian L McQueen. The 4th edition was rewritten by Chris Taylor, Robert Strauss and Tony Wheeler. Chris Taylor updated the 5th edition. The 6th edition was updated by Chris Taylor, Nicko Goncharoff, Mason Florence and Chris Rowthorn.

This fine edition, the seventh, was ably coordinated by Chris Rowthorn, who also took on the gargantuan task of updating the introductory chapters, not to mention Tokyo, Around Tokyo and Kansai. John Ashburne's wit now graces the Central Honshū, Western Honshū and Kyūshū chapters. Sam Benson's meticulous research speaks for itself in the Northern Honshū and Hokkaidō chapters and, last but not least, Mason Florence did it his way in Shikoku and Okinawa.

Special section contributors include John Ashburne for the Onsen Mania! section, Merrilee Lewis and Jane Thompson for the Performing Arts section, Kieran Grogan for the Contemporary Architecture section and Chris Rowthorn for the Matsuri Magic section. Merrilee Lewis also contributed to the Cinema entry in the Facts About Japan chapter.

Thanks also go to Jane Thompson for delving back into the dark days of having her 'smalls' pinched from her Tokyo clothes-line, to Tim Fitzgerald for getting down and denki whilst wandering the paths of the great Zen garden masters, to Liz Filleul for her aside on the World Cup, to Jennifer Swanton for telling the world about the Yamagata International Documentary Film Festival, and to Kate Watson, Yuko Florence Yunokawa and Justin Giffin for insider information.

From the Publisher

This seventh edition of Japan was edited in the Melbourne office by Kate Daly, Jane Thompson, Lyn McGaurr, Joanne Newell and Lucy Williams, with additional proofing assistance from Evan Jones, Lara Morcombe, Fiona Meiers and Darren O'Connell. Yoshi Abe ably provided translation and script assistance, and Megan Fraser provided final script checking. Jenny Jones and Sonya Brooke shared the helm of design and mapping, with assistance from Barbara Benson, Kusnandar, Meredith Mail, Neb Milic and Paul Piaia. Illustrations were drawn by Mick Weldon. Valerie Tellini sourced photographs from LPI, and Margaret Jung designed the cover. Quentin Frayne co-ordinated the language chapter. A monumental thanks to Tim Uden and Errol Hunt for indexing. Thanks also to the Lonely Planet team of seniors including Martin Heng, Jocelyn Harewood, Tim Fitzgerald and Jane Hart.

One last thanks to Tim Uden for demanding that the Hello Kitty Web site URL be included in this guide.

Foreword

ABOUT LONELY PLANET GUIDEBOOKS

The story begins with a classic travel adventure: Tony and Maureen Wheeler's 1972 journey across Europe and Asia to Australia. Useful information about the overland trail did not exist at that time, so Tony and Maureen published the first Lonely Planet guidebook to meet a growing need.

From a kitchen table, then from a tiny office in Melbourne (Australia), Lonely Planet has become the largest independent travel publisher in the world, an international company with offices in Melbourne, Oakland (USA), London (UK) and Paris (France).

Today Lonely Planet guidebooks cover the globe. There is an ever-growing list of books and there's information in a variety of forms and media. Some things haven't changed. The main aim is still to help make it possible for adventurous travellers to get out there – to explore and better understand the world.

At Lonely Planet we believe travellers can make a positive contribution to the countries they visit – if they respect their host communities and spend their money wisely. Since 1986 a percentage of the income from each book has been donated to aid projects and human rights campaigns.

Updates Lonely Planet thoroughly updates each guidebook as often as possible. This usually means there are around two years between editions, although for more unusual or more stable destinations the gap can be longer. Check the imprint page (following the colour map at the beginning of the book) for publication dates.

Between editions up-to-date information is available in two free newsletters – the paper *Planet Talk* and email *Comet* (to subscribe, contact any Lonely Planet office) – and on our Web site at www.lonelyplanet.com. The *Upgrades* section of the Web site covers a number of important and volatile destinations and is regularly updated by Lonely Planet authors. *Scoop* covers news and current affairs relevant to travellers. And, lastly, the *Thorn Tree* bulletin board and *Postcards* section of the site carry unverified, but fascinating, reports from travellers.

Correspondence The process of creating new editions begins with the letters, postcards and emails received from travellers. This correspondence often includes suggestions, criticisms and comments about the current editions. Interesting excerpts are immediately passed on via newsletters and the Web site, and everything goes to our authors to be verified when they're researching on the road. We're keen to get more feedback from organisations or individuals who represent communities visited by travellers.

Lonely Planet gathers information for everyone who's curious about the planet – and especially for those who explore it first-hand. Through guidebooks, phrasebooks, activity guides, maps, literature, newsletters, image library, TV series and Web site we act as an information exchange for a worldwide community of travellers.

Research Authors aim to gather sufficient practical information to enable travellers to make informed choices and to make the mechanics of a journey run smoothly. They also research historical and cultural background to help enrich the travel experience and allow travellers to understand and respond appropriately to cultural and environmental issues.

Authors don't stay in every hotel because that would mean spending a couple of months in each medium-sized city and, no, they don't eat at every restaurant because that would mean stretching belts beyond capacity. They do visit hotels and restaurants to check standards and prices, but feedback based on readers' direct experiences can be very helpful.

Many of our authors work undercover, others aren't so secretive. None of them accept freebies in exchange for positive write-ups. And none of our guidebooks contain any advertising.

Production Authors submit their raw manuscripts and maps to offices in Australia, USA, UK or France. Editors and cartographers – all experienced travellers themselves – then begin the process of assembling the pieces. When the book finally hits the shops, some things are already out of date, we start getting feedback from readers and the process begins again...

WARNING & REQUEST

Things change – prices go up, schedules change, good places go bad and bad places go bankrupt – nothing stays the same. So, if you find things better or worse, recently opened or long since closed, please tell us and help make the next edition even more accurate and useful. We genuinely value all the feedback we receive. Julie Young coordinates a well travelled team that reads and acknowledges every letter, postcard and email and ensures that every morsel of information finds its way to the appropriate authors, editors and cartographers for verification.

Everyone who writes to us will find their name in the next edition of the appropriate guidebook. They will also receive the latest issue of *Planet Talk*, our quarterly printed newsletter, or *Comet*, our monthly email newsletter. Subscriptions to both newsletters are free. The very best contributions will be rewarded with a free guidebook.

Excerpts from your correspondence may appear in new editions of Lonely Planet guidebooks, the Lonely Planet Web site, *Planet Talk* or *Comet*, so please let us know if you *don't* want your letter published or your name acknowledged.

Send all correspondence to the Lonely Planet office closest to you:

Australia: Locked Bag 1, Footscray, Victoria 3011
USA: 150 Linden St, Oakland, CA 94607
UK: 10A Spring Place, London NW5 3BH
France: 1 rue du Dahomey, 75011 Paris

Or email us at: talk2us@lonelyplanet.com.au

For news, views and updates see our Web site: www.lonelyplanet.com

HOW TO USE A LONELY PLANET GUIDEBOOK

The best way to use a Lonely Planet guidebook is any way you choose. At Lonely Planet we believe the most memorable travel experiences are often those that are unexpected, and the finest discoveries are those you make yourself. Guidebooks are not intended to be used as if they provide a detailed set of infallible instructions!

Contents All Lonely Planet guidebooks follow roughly the same format. The Facts about the Destination chapters or sections give background information ranging from history to weather. Facts for the Visitor gives practical information on issues like visas and health. Getting There & Away gives a brief starting point for researching travel to and from the destination. Getting Around gives an overview of the transport options when you arrive.

The peculiar demands of each destination determine how subsequent chapters are broken up, but some things remain constant. We always start with background, then proceed to sights, places to stay, places to eat, entertainment, getting there and away, and getting around information – in that order.

Heading Hierarchy Lonely Planet headings are used in a strict hierarchical structure that can be visualised as a set of Russian dolls. Each heading (and its following text) is encompassed by any preceding heading that is higher on the hierarchical ladder.

Entry Points We do not assume guidebooks will be read from beginning to end, but that people will dip into them. The traditional entry points are the list of contents and the index. In addition, however, some books have a complete list of maps and an index map illustrating map coverage.

There may also be a colour map that shows highlights. These highlights are dealt with in greater detail in the Facts for the Visitor chapter, along with planning questions and suggested itineraries. Each chapter covering a geographical region usually begins with a locator map and another list of highlights. Once you find something of interest in a list of highlights, turn to the index.

Maps Maps play a crucial role in Lonely Planet guidebooks and include a huge amount of information. A legend is printed on the back page. We seek to have complete consistency between maps and text, and to have every important place in the text captured on a map. Map key numbers usually start in the top left corner.

Although inclusion in a guidebook usually implies a recommendation we cannot list every good place. Exclusion does not necessarily imply criticism. In fact there are a number of reasons why we might exclude a place – sometimes it is simply inappropriate to encourage an influx of travellers.

Introduction

Contemporary Japan is a land of extremes. But then, arguably, it has always been that way. After centuries of bloodshed and social upheaval as warlords struggled to gain control of the nation, the country was shut tight from 1600 to 1867 under a policy of *sakoku* or 'national seclusion'. The arrival of Commodore Perry's 'black ships' in 1853 set the insular nation a-jitter with speculation about the changing world outside its locked doors. By 1868 the doors had been flung open, an emperor was restored to his throne and the Japanese rushed to greet an incoming tide of Western technology and ideas that would turn their traditional world upside down.

Today, after having their economy and country ravaged by WWII and having spectacularly bounced back to become an economic superpower, it's surprising just how much of that traditional world still lingers. It's this, as much as anything else, that gives the visitor the sensation of having strayed into a land of startling opposites, a land where suburban sprawl gives way to the sensuous contours of a temple roof, where rustic red-lantern restaurants nestle in the shadow of the high-rise future.

The extremes never end. You could splurge your life savings on a week in Tokyo, but then again you could just as easily maintain a diet of youth hostels and country inns, filling yourself up in cheap noodle shops, and come away spending no more than you would on a holiday at home. Cities such as Tokyo and Osaka can sometimes seem like congested, hi-tech visions of the future, but the national parks of Hokkaidō and the Alps of central Honshū

offer some sparsely populated vistas that very few foreigners set their eyes on.

All this, perhaps, adds to the mythology of Japan, a country which is the subject of more gullible and misguided musings than any other place in the world. The best way to approach Japan is by discarding your preconceptions. Somewhere between the elegant formality of Japanese manners and the candid, sometimes boisterous exchanges that take place over a few drinks, between the sanitised shopping malls and the unexpected rural festival, everyone finds their own vision of Japan.

Come with an open mind and be prepared to be surprised.

15

Facts about Japan

HISTORY
Prehistory

The origin of Japan's earliest inhabitants is obscure. There was certainly emigration via land bridges that once connected Japan with Siberia and Korea, but it is also thought that seafaring migrants from Polynesia may have landed on Kyūshū and Okinawa. The truth is probably that the Japanese people are a result of emigration from Siberia in the north, China and Korea to the west and, perhaps, Polynesian stock from the south.

The first recorded signs of civilisation in Japan are found in the Neolithic period around 10,000 BC. This is called the Jōmon (Rope Mark) period after the discovery of pottery fragments with rope marks. The people at this time lived as fishers, hunters and food-gatherers.

This period was gradually superseded by the Yayoi era, which dates from around 300 BC and is named after the site near modern Tokyo where pottery fragments were found. The Yayoi people are considered to have had a strong connection with Korea and their most important developments were the wet cultivation of rice and the use of bronze and iron implements.

The period following the Yayoi era has been called the Kofun (Burial Mound) period by archaeologists who discovered thousands of grave mounds concentrated mostly in central and western Japan. Judging by their size and elaborate construction, these mounds must have required immense resources of labour. It seems likely that the custom of building these tombs was brought to an end by the arrival of Buddhism, which favoured cremation.

As more and more settlements banded together to defend their land, groups became larger until, by AD 300, the Yamato clan had loosely unified the nation through conquest or alliance. The Yamato leaders claimed descent from the sun goddess, Amaterasu, and introduced the title of *tennō* (emperor) around the 5th century. With the ascendancy of the Yamato emperors, Japan for the first time became a true nation, stretching from the islands south of Kyūshū to the northern wilds of Honshū.

Buddhism & Early Chinese Influence

In the mid-6th century, Buddhism was introduced from China via the Korean kingdom of Paekche. The decline of the Yamato court was halted by Prince Shōtoku (573–620), who set up a constitution and laid the guidelines for a centralised state headed by a single ruler. He also instituted Buddhism as a state religion.

Despite family feuds and coups d'etat, subsequent rulers continued to reform the country's administration and laws. Previously, it had been the custom to avoid the pollution of imperial death by changing the site of the capital for each successive emperor.

From the earliest days of the Yamato court, it had been the custom to relocate the capital following the death of an emperor. However, in 710, this long-held custom was altered and the capital was shifted to Nara, where it remained for the next 75 years.

Historical Periods

Period	Date
Jōmon	10,000–300 BC
Yayoi	300 BC–AD 300
Kofun	300–710
Nara	710–94
Heian	794–1185
Kamakura	1185–1333
Muromachi	1333–1576
Momoyama	1576–1600
Edo	1600–1867
Meiji	1868–1912
Taishō	1912–26
Shōwa	1926–89
Heisei	1989 to the present

During the Nara period (710–94) there was strong promotion of Buddhism, particularly under Emperor Shōmu, who ordered the construction of Tōdai-ji and the casting of its Daibutsu (Great Buddha) as supreme guardian deity of the nation. Both the temple and Buddha image can still be seen in Nara.

Establishment of a Native Culture: Heian Period (794–1185)

By the end of the 8th century, the Buddhist clergy in Nara had become so politically meddlesome that Emperor Kammu decided to relocate the capital to insulate it against their growing influence. The site eventually chosen was Heian (modern-day Kyoto).

Like Nara, Heian was modelled on Chang-an (present-day Xi'an), the capital of the Tang dynasty in China, and it was to continue as the capital of Japan until 1868. This was a period that saw a great flourishing in the arts and important developments in religious thinking, as the Chinese imported ideas and institutions and adapted them to the needs of their new homeland.

Rivalry between Buddhism and Shintō, which is the traditional religion of Japan, was reduced by presenting Shintō deities as manifestations of Buddha. Religion was assigned a role separated from politics; and Japanese monks returning from China established two new sects, Tendai and Shingon, which became the mainstays of Japanese Buddhism.

During the late Heian period, emperors began to devote more time to leisure and scholarly pursuit and less time to government. This created an opening for the Fujiwara, a noble family, to capture important court posts and become the chief power brokers, a role the clan was able to maintain for several centuries.

The Heian period is considered the apogee of Japanese courtly elegance, but out in the provinces a new power was on the rise, that of the *samurai*, or 'warrior class', which built up its own armed forces and readily turned to arms to defend its autonomy. Samurai families moved into the capital, where they muscled in on the court.

The corrupt Fujiwara were eventually eclipsed by the Taira clan, who ruled briefly before being ousted by the Minamoto family (also known as the Genji) at the battle of Dannoura (Shimonoseki) in 1185.

Domination through Military Rule: Kamakura Period (1185–1333)

In 1192 Minamoto Yoritomo conquered the inhabitants of what is now Aomori-ken or pro, thereby extending his rule to the tip of northern Honshū. For the first time in its history, all of Japan proper was now under unified rule. After assuming the rank of *shōgun* (military leader), Yoritomo set up his headquarters in Kamakura, while the emperor remained the nominal ruler in Kyoto. It was the beginning of a long period of feudal rule by successive samurai families. In fact, this feudal system was effectively to linger on until imperial power was restored in 1868.

Yoritomo purged members of his own family who stood in his way, but after his death in 1199 after falling from a horse, his wife's family (the Hōjō) eliminated all of Yoritomo's potential successors and became the true wielders of power behind the figureheads of shōguns and warrior lords.

During this era, the popularity of Buddhism spread to all levels of society. From the late 12th century, Japanese monks returning from China introduced a new sect called Zen, the austerity of which offered a particular appeal to the samurai.

The Mongols, under their leader Kublai Khan, reached Korea in 1259 and sent envoys to Japan seeking Japanese submission. In response, the envoys were expelled. The Mongols reacted by sending an invasion fleet, which arrived near present-day Fukuoka in 1274. This first attack was only just repulsed with a little help from a typhoon. Further envoys sent by Kublai Khan were promptly beheaded.

In 1281 the Mongols dispatched a huge army of over 100,000 soldiers to Japan to make a second attempt at invasion. After initial success, the Mongol fleet was almost completely destroyed by yet another typhoon. Ever since, this lucky typhoon has been

Samurai

The prime duty of a *samurai*, a member of the warrior class, was to give faithful service to his feudal lord or *daimyō*. In fact, the origin of the term samurai is closely linked to a word meaning 'to serve', and this overlap can be seen in the *kanji* (Chinese script used for writing Japanese) for the word. Over the centuries, the samurai established a code of conduct that came to be known as *bushidō* (the way of the warrior). This code was drawn from Confucianism, Shinto and Buddhism.

Confucianism required a samurai to show absolute loyalty to his lord. Toward the oppressed a samurai was expected to show benevolence and exercise justice. Subterfuge was to be despised, as were all commercial and financial transactions. A real samurai had endless endurance and total self-control, spoke only the truth and displayed no emotion. Since his honour was his life, disgrace and shame were to be avoided above all else and all insults were to be avenged.

From Buddhism, the samurai learnt the lesson that life is impermanent – a handy reason to face death with serenity. Shinto provided the samurai with patriotic beliefs in the divine status both of the emperor and of Japan, the abode of the gods.

Seppuku (ritual suicide), also known as *hara-kiri*, was a practice to which Japanese Buddhism conveniently turned a blind eye and was an accepted means of avoiding dishonour. Seppuku required the samurai to ritually disembowel himself, watched by an aide, who then drew his own sword and lopped off the samurai's head. One reason for this ritual was the requirement that a samurai should never surrender but always go down fighting. Since surrender was considered a disgrace, prisoners received scant mercy. During WWII this attitude was reflected in the Japanese treatment of prisoners of war – still a source of bitter memories for those involved.

UNBEATEN TRACKS IN JAPAN, J.F. BISHOP

In quiet moments, a samurai dressed simply but was easily recognisable by his triangular *eboshi*, a hat made from rigid black cloth.

The samurai's standard battle dress or armour (usually made of leather or maybe lacquered steel) consisted of a breastplate, a similar covering for his back, a steel helmet with a visor and more body armour for his shoulders and lower body. Samurai weaponry – his pride and joy – included a bow and arrows (in a quiver), swords and a dagger; and he wasn't complete without his trusty steed.

Before entering the fray, a samurai was expected to be freshly washed and groomed. The classic samurai battle took the form of duelling between individuals rather than the clashing of massed armies.

Not all samurai were capable of adhering to their code of conduct – samurai indulging in double-crossing or subterfuge, or displaying outright cowardice, were popular themes in Japanese theatre.

known to the Japanese as the *kamikaze* (divine wind) – a name later given to the suicide pilots of WWII.

Although the Kamakura government emerged victorious, it was unable to pay its soldiers and lost the support of the samurai class. In an attempt to take advantage of popular discontent, Emperor Go-Daigo led an unsuccessful rebellion against the government and was exiled to the Oki Islands near Matsue in Western Honshū, where he waited a year before trying again. The second attempt successfully toppled the government.

Country at War: Muromachi Period (1333–1576)

Emperor Go-Daigo refused to reward his warriors, favouring the aristocracy and priesthood instead. This led to the revolt of Ashikaga Takauji, who had previously changed sides to support Emperor Go-Daigo. Ashikaga defeated Go-Daigo at Kyoto, then installed a new emperor and appointed himself shōgun; the Ashikaga family later settled at Muromachi, an area of Kyoto. Go-Daigo escaped to set up a rival court at Yoshino, a mountainous region near Nara. Rivalry between the two courts continued for 60 years until the Ashikaga made a promise (which was not kept) that the imperial lines would alternate.

The Ashikaga ruled with gradually diminishing effectiveness in a land slipping steadily into civil war and chaos. Despite this, there was a flourishing of those arts now considered typically Japanese, such as landscape painting, classical *nō* (stylised dance-drama), *ikebana* (flower arranging) and *chanoyu* (the tea ceremony). Many of Kyoto's famous gardens date from this period, as do such well-known monuments as Kinkaku-ji (Golden Temple) and Ginkaku-ji (Silver Temple). Formal trade was re-established with Ming-dynasty China and Korea, although Japanese piracy continued to strain these relationships.

The Ōnin War, which broke out in 1467, developed into a full-scale civil war and marked the rapid decline of the Ashikaga family. *Daimyō* (domain lords) and local leaders fought for power in bitter territorial disputes that were to last for a century. This period, from 1467 to around the start of the Momoyama period in 1576, is known as the Warring States period (Sengoku-jigai).

Politically, the Japan of the Warring States period resembled pre-Yamato Japan: the country was merely a collection of disparate groups vying for control of local areas without any centralised authority. It was up to the next generation of leaders to reverse this situation and bring the country under the control of a powerful centralised government once more.

Return to Unity: Momoyama Period (1576–1600)

In 1568 Oda Nobunaga, the son of a daimyō, seized power from the imperial court in Kyoto and used his military genius to initiate a process of pacification and unification in central Japan. His efforts were cut short when he was betrayed by one of his own generals, Akechi Mitsuhide, in 1582. Under attack from Akechi and seeing all was lost, he disembowelled himself in Kyoto's Honnō-ji.

Oda was succeeded by his ablest commander, Toyotomi Hideyoshi, who was reputedly the son of a farmer, although his origins are not clear. His diminutive size and pop-eyed features earned him the nickname of Saru-san (Mr Monkey). Toyotomi extended unification so that by 1590 the whole country was under his rule. He then became fascinated with grandiose schemes to invade China and Korea. The first invasion was repulsed in 1593 and the second was aborted on the death of Toyotomi in 1598.

The arts of this period are noted for their flamboyant use of colour and gold-leaf embellishment. There was also a vogue for building castles on a extravagant scale; the most impressive example was Osaka-jō, which reputedly required three years of labour by up to 100,000 men.

The Christian Century (1543–1640)

In the mid-16th century, when the Europeans first made their appearance, foreign trade was little regulated by Japan's central government. The first Portuguese to be ship-wrecked off southern Kyūshū in 1543 found an appreciative reception for their skills in firearm manufacture, skills which were soon adopted by Japanese. The Jesuit missionary Francis Xavier arrived in Kagoshima in 1549 and was followed by more missionaries, who quickly converted local lords keen to profit from foreign trade and assistance with military supplies. The new religion spread rapidly, gaining several hundred thousand converts, particularly in Nagasaki.

At first Oda Nobunaga saw the advantages of trading with Europeans and tolerated the arrival of Christianity as a counterbalance to Buddhism. Once Toyotomi Hideyoshi had assumed power, however, this tolerance gradually gave way to a suspicion that an alien religion would subvert his rule. Edicts against Christianity were followed in 1597 by the crucifixion of 26 foreign priests and Japanese converts.

Proscription and persecution of Christianity continued under the Tokugawa government until it reached its peak in 1637, with the ferocious quelling of the Christian-led Shimabara Rebellion. This brought the Christian century to an abrupt close, although the religion continued to be practised in secret until it was officially allowed to resurface at the end of the 19th century.

Peace & Seclusion: Edo or Tokugawa Period (1600–1867)

The supporters of Toyotomi Hideyoshi's young heir, Toyotomi Hideyori, were defeated in 1600 by his former ally, Tokugawa Ieyasu, at the battle of Sekigahara. Tokugawa set up his field headquarters (*bakufu*) at Edo, now Tokyo, and assumed the title of shōgun. The emperor and court continued to exercise purely nominal authority in Kyoto.

A strict political regime was introduced. The Tokugawa family, besides retaining large estates, also took control of major cities, ports and mines; the remainder of the country was allocated to autonomous daimyō. In descending order of importance, society consisted of the nobility, who had nominal power; the daimyō and

their samurai; the farmers; and at the bottom of the list, artisans and merchants. To ensure political security, the daimyō were required to make ceremonial visits to Edo every alternate year, and their wives and children were kept in permanent residence in Edo as virtual hostages of the government. The cost of this constant movement and the family ties in Edo made it difficult for the daimyō to remain anything but loyal. At the lower end of society, farmers were subject to a severe system of rules that dictated in the minutest detail their food, clothing and housing. Social mobility from one class to another was blocked as social standing was determined by birth.

Under Tokugawa rule, Japan entered a period of *sakoku* (national seclusion). Japanese were forbidden on pain of death to travel abroad or engage in trade with foreign countries. Only the Dutch, Chinese and Koreans were allowed to remain, and they were placed under strict supervision. The Dutch were confined to the island of Dejima, near Nagasaki, and their contacts restricted to merchants and prostitutes.

The rigid emphasis of these times on submitting unquestioningly to rules of obedience and loyalty has lasted to the present day. One effect of strict rule during the Tokugawa period was the creation of an atmosphere of relative peace and security in which the arts thrived. There were great advances, for example, in *haiku* (17-syllable poems), *bunraku* (classical puppet theatre) and *kabuki* (stylised Japanese theatre). Weaving, pottery, ceramics and lacquerware became widely appreciated by the privileged classes for their refined quality.

By the turn of the 19th century, the Tokugawa government was falling into stagnation and corruption. Famines and poverty among the peasants and samurai further weakened the system. Foreign ships started to challenge Japan's isolation with increasing insistence, and the Japanese soon realised that their outmoded defences were ineffectual. Russian contacts in the north were followed by British and American visits. In 1853 Commodore Matthew Perry of the US Navy arrived with a squadron of 'black ships' to demand the opening up of Japan to trade. Other countries moved in to demand the opening of treaty ports and the relaxation of restrictions on trade barriers.

The arrival of foreigners proved to be the decisive blow to an already shaky Tokugawa regime. Upset by the shogunate's handling of the foreign incursion, two large daimyō areas in western Japan, the Satsuma and the Chōshū, allied themselves with disenchanted samurai and succeeded in capturing the emperor in 1868, declaring a restoration of imperial rule and an end to the power of the shōgun. A brief counterattack by Tokugawa guards in Kyoto in the same year failed and in 1867 the ruling shōgun, Tokugawa Yoshinobu, resigned, allowing Emperor Meiji to resume control of state affairs.

Emergence from Isolation: Meiji Restoration (1868–1912)

The initial stages of this restoration were resisted in a state of virtual civil war. The abolition of the shogunate was followed by the surrender of the daimyō, whose lands were divided into the prefectures that exist today. Edo became Japan's new capital and was renamed Tokyo (Eastern Capital). The

Emperor Meiji oversaw
Japan's modernisation

government became centralised again and Western-style ministries were appointed for specific tasks. A series of revolts by the samurai against the erosion of their status culminated in the Saigō Uprising, where the samurai were finally beaten and stripped of their power.

Despite nationalist support for the emperor under the slogan of *sonnō-jōi* ('Revere the emperor; repel the barbarians'), the new government soon realised it would have to meet the West on its own terms. Under the slogan *fukoku kyōhei* ('Rich country; strong military'), the economy underwent a crash course in Westernisation and industrialisation. An influx of Western experts was encouraged and Japanese students were sent abroad to acquire expertise in modern technologies. In 1889 Japan created a Western-style constitution which, like the military revival, owed much to Prussian influences.

By the 1890s government leaders were concerned by the spread of liberal Western ideas and encouraged a swing back to nationalism and traditional values.

Japan's growing confidence was demonstrated by the abolition of foreign treaty rights and by the ease with which it trounced China in the Sino-Japanese War (1894–95). The subsequent treaty recognised Korean independence and ceded Taiwan to Japan. Friction with Russia led to the Russo-Japanese War (1904–05), in which the Japanese army attacked the Russians in Manchuria and Korea. The Japanese Navy stunned the Russians by inflicting a crushing defeat on their Baltic fleet at the battle of Tsu-shima. For the first time, the Japanese were able to consider that they had drawn level with the Western powers.

Industrialisation & Asian Dominance

On his death in 1912, Emperor Meiji was succeeded by his son, Yoshihito, whose period of rule was named the Taishō era. The later stages of his life were dogged by ill health that was probably attributable to meningitis.

When WWI broke out, Japan sided against Germany but did not become deeply involved in the conflict. While the Allies were occupied with war, Japan took the opportunity, through shipping and trade, to expand its economy at top speed. At the same time, Japan gained a strong foothold in China, thereby giving Japan a dominant position in Asia.

Social unrest led the government to pursue a more democratic, liberal line; the right to vote was extended, and Japan joined the League of Nations in 1920. Under the influence of the *zaibatsu* (financial cliques of industrialists and bankers), a moderate and pacific foreign policy was followed.

Nationalism & the Pursuit of Empire

The Shōwa era commenced when Emperor Hirohito ascended the throne in 1926. He had toured extensively in Europe, mixed with European nobility and developed a liking for the British lifestyle.

A rising tide of nationalism was quickened by the world economic depression that began in 1930. Popular unrest was marked by plots to overthrow the government and political assassinations. This led to a strong increase in the power of the militarists, who approved the invasion of Manchuria in 1931 and the installation of a Japanese puppet regime. In 1933 Japan withdrew from the League of Nations and in 1937 entered into full-scale hostilities against China.

As the leader of a new order for Asia, Japan signed a tripartite pact with Germany and Italy in 1940. The Japanese military leaders saw their main opponents to this new order for Asia, the so-called 'Greater East Asia Co-prosperity Sphere', in the USA.

World War II

When diplomatic attempts to gain US neutrality failed, Japan launched itself into WWII with a surprise attack on Pearl Harbor on 7 December 1941.

At first, Japan scored rapid successes, pushing its battle fronts across to India, down to the fringes of Australia and out into the mid-Pacific. The Battle of Midway opened the US counterattack, puncturing Japanese naval superiority and turning the tide of the war against Japan. Exhausted by submarine blockades and aerial bombing, by 1945 Japan had been driven back on all fronts. In August of the same year, the declaration of war by the Soviet Union and the atomic bombs dropped by the USA on Hiroshima and Nagasaki proved to be the final straws: Emperor Hirohito announced unconditional surrender.

Having surrendered, Japan was occupied by Allied forces under the command of General Douglas MacArthur. The chief aim was a thorough reform of Japanese government through demilitarisation, the trial of war criminals and the weeding out of militarists and ultranationalists from the government. A new constitution was introduced that dismantled the political power of the emperor, who completely stunned his subjects by publicly renouncing any claim to divine origins. This left him a mere figurehead.

The occupation was terminated in 1952, although the island of Okinawa was only returned to Japan in 1972.

Post-war Reconstruction

At the end of the war, the Japanese economy was in ruins and inflation was rampant. A program of recovery provided loans, restricted imports and encouraged capital investment and personal saving.

By the late 1950s, trade was again flourishing, and the economy continued to expand rapidly. From textiles and the manufacture of labour-intensive goods, such as cameras, the Japanese 'economic miracle' branched out into virtually every sector of economic activity. Economic recession and inflation surfaced in 1974 and again in 1980, mostly as a result of steep increases in the price of imported oil, on which Japan is dependent. But despite these setbacks, Japan became the world's most successful export economy, generating massive trade surpluses and dominating such fields as electronics, robotics, computer technology, car manufacturing and banking.

The Giant Falters

For a long time, Japan seemed unstoppable. The term 'Japan Inc' came to be used with suspicion by commentators who saw Japan as some huge well-oiled machine. It seemed a nation of unassailable job security and endless economic growth.

But in the 1990s the so-called 'Bubble Economy' burst, and the old certainties seemed to vanish. Japan's legendary economic growth slowed to a standstill, and the economy actually started to contract. In 1993, after 38 years at the helm, the conservative Liberal Democratic Party (LDP) succumbed to a spate of scandals and was swept from power by an eight-party coalition of reformers. In January 1995 a massive earthquake struck Kōbe; the government was confused and slow to react, and confidence in Japan's much vaunted earthquake preparedness was shattered. And to top it all off, just months later, a millennial cult with doomsday ambitions the Aum Shinrikyō (Aum Supreme Truth Sect) – engineered a poison gas attack on the Tokyo subway system.

In the wake of all this, the situation in Japan remains unclear. The economy remains mired in recession, the government appears unable to make any significant changes, the population is ageing at an alarming rate, and, as its economic competitors surge ahead, Japan experiments with a series of short-term fixes and dubious public works projects to stimulate growth.

However, all is not lost. Japan has more than once come back from seeming ruin to claim astonishing success. It is difficult to anticipate how this will happen, but one thing is certain: the next few years will be an interesting time for Japan.

GEOGRAPHY

Japan is an island nation. Much of its cultural heritage has been drawn from nearby Asian countries, but it is this 'apartness' from the Asian mainland that is defining for many Japanese. Both China and Korea are close enough to have been decisive influences, but at the same time they are too distant to have dominated Japan.

Japan has not always been physically isolated. At the end of the last ice age, around 10,000 years ago, the level of the sea rose enough to flood a land bridge connecting Japan with the Asian continent. Today, Japan consists of a chain of islands that rides the back of a 3000km-long arc of mountains along the eastern rim of the continent. It stretches from around 25°N at the southern islands of Okinawa to 45°N at the northern end of Hokkaidō. Cities at comparable latitudes are Miami and Cairo in the south and Montreal and Milan in the north. Japan's total land area is 377,435 sq km, and more than 80% of it is mountainous.

Japan consists of some 1000 small islands and four major ones: Honshū (slightly larger than Britain), Hokkaidō, Kyūshū and Shikoku. Okinawa, the largest and most significant of Japan's many smaller islands, is about halfway along an archipelago that stretches from the western tip of Honshū almost all the way to Taiwan. It is far enough from the rest of Japan to have developed a culture that differs from that of the 'mainland' in many respects.

GEOLOGY

If Japanese culture has been influenced by isolation, it has equally been shaped by the country's mountainous topography. Many of the mountains are volcanic, and more than 40 of these are presently active. As a result, the islands are blessed with numerous hot springs and spectacular scenery. At the same time, there is a danger of frequent eruptions and intense seismic activity. Indeed, it is possible that the rough and tumble of earthquakes, volcanic eruptions and *tsunami* (tidal waves), along with a monsoonal climate, have contributed to Japanese industriousness. The Japanese are used to rebuilding their world every 20 or 30 years.

Japan has the dubious distinction of being one of the most seismically active regions of the world. It is calculated that the country is on the receiving end of around 1000 earthquakes a year, most of them too small to notice without sophisticated seismic equipment. This seismic activity is particularly concentrated in the Kantō region, in which Tokyo is situated. But earthquakes can strike just about any part of the archipelago, as the citizens of Kōbe discovered in the disastrous earthquake of January 1995, which killed more than 6000 people.

CLIMATE

The combination of Japan's mountainous territory and the length of the archipelago (covering about 20° of latitude) makes for a complex climate. There are significant climatic differences between Hokkaidō in the north, which has short summers and lengthy winters with heavy snowfalls, and the southern islands such as Okinawa in the Nansei-shotō (South-West Islands), which enjoy a subtropical climate. At the same time, Japan's proximity to the continental landmass also has significant climatic implications, producing a high degree of seasonal variation.

In the winter months (December to February), cold, dry air masses from Siberia move down over Japan, where they meet warmer, moister air masses from the Pacific. The resulting precipitation results in huge snowfalls on the side of the country that faces the Sea of Japan. The Pacific side of Japan receives less snow but can still be very cold; Tokyo has colder average January temperatures than Reykjavík in Iceland, but snow, when it does fall on the capital, rarely lasts long.

The summer months (June to August) are dominated by warm, moist air currents from the Pacific, and produce high temperatures and humidity throughout most of Japan (with the blissful exception of Hokkaidō). In the early part of summer, usually mid-May to June, there is a rainy season lasting a few weeks that starts in the south and gradually works its way northwards. Although it can be inconvenient, this rainy

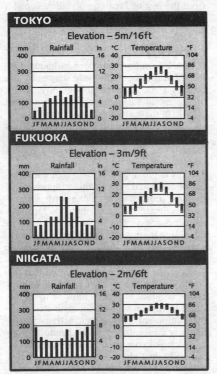

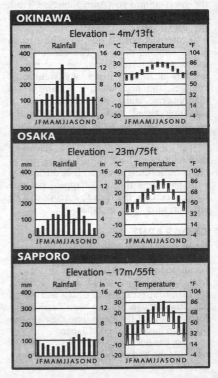

season is not usually a significant barrier to travel. Further heavy rains can occur in late summer when the country is visited by typhoons bringing torrential rains and strong winds that can have devastating effects, particularly on coastal regions.

In contrast to the extremes of summer and winter, spring and autumn are comparatively mild. Rainfall is relatively low and the days are often clear.

ECOLOGY & ENVIRONMENT

Japan was the first Asian nation to industrialise. It has also been one of the most successful at cleaning up the resulting mess, though problems remain. In the early post-war years, when Japan was frantically rebuilding its economy, there was widespread public ignorance of the problems of pollution and government did little to enlighten the public.

Industrial pollution was at its worst from the mid-1960s to the mid-1970s. But public awareness of the issue had already been awakened by an outbreak of what came to be called Minamata disease (after the town of the same name), in which up to 6000 people were affected by organomercury poisoning in 1953. It was not until 1968 that the government officially acknowledged the cause of the disease.

By the late 1960s public consciousness of environmental problems had reached levels that the government could only ignore at its risk. Laws were passed to curb air and water pollution. These have been reasonably successful, though critics are quick to point out that whereas toxic matter has been mostly removed from Japanese waters, organic pollution remains a problem. Similarly, controls on air pollution have had mixed results: photochemical smog emerged as a problem in Tokyo in the early 1970s; it remains a problem and now affects other urban centres around Japan.

In 1972 the government passed the Nature Conservation Law, which aimed to protect the natural environment and provide recreational space for the public. National parks, quasi-national parks and prefectural parks were established, and it appears that such measures have been successful in raising wildlife numbers.

More recently, Japan has been facing a new set of problems, including dioxin given off by waste incineration plants and a series of accidents at nuclear reactors and nuclear fuel processing facilities. The only up side is that these accidents have forced the government to revise its safety guidelines for the industry and to consider phasing out nuclear power altogether.

FLORA & FAUNA

The latitudinal spread of the islands of Japan makes for a wide diversity of flora and fauna. The Nansei and Ogasawara island groups in the far south are subtropical, and flora and fauna in this region are related to those found on the Malaysian peninsula. Mainland Japan (Honshū, Kyūshū and Shikoku), on the other hand, shows more similarities with Korea and China, while subarctic northern and central Hokkaidō has features of its own.

Flora

The flora of Japan today is not what the Japanese saw hundreds of years ago. This is not just because much of Japan's natural landscape has succumbed to modern urban culture, but because much of Japan's flora is naturalised, not indigenous. It is thought that some 200 to 500 plant species have been introduced to Japan since the Meiji period (1868–1912), mainly from Europe but with the USA becoming a major source in recent years. Japanese gardens laid out in the Edo period and earlier are good places to see native Japanese flora, even though you won't be seeing it there as it might have flourished naturally.

Much of Japan was once heavily forested. The cool-temperate zones of central and northern Honshū and southern Hokkaidō were home to broad-leaved deciduous forests and still are to a certain extent. Nevertheless, large-scale deforestation is a feature of contemporary Japan. Pollution and acid rain have also taken their toll. Fortunately, the sheer inaccessibility of much of Japan's mountainous topography has preserved areas of great natural beauty – in

What Happened to the Hills?

Visitors to Japan are often shocked at the state of the Japanese landscape. It seems that no matter where you look, the hills, rivers, coastline and fields bear the unmistakable imprint of human activity. Indeed, it is only in the highest, most remote mountains that one finds nature untouched by human hands. Why is this?

Undoubtedly, population density is the crucial factor here. With so many people packed into such a small space, it is only natural that the landscape should be worked to the hilt. However, it is not just simple population pressure that accounts for Japan's scarred and battered landscape; misguided land management policies and pork-barrel politics also play a role.

Almost 70% of Japan's total land area is wooded. Of this area, almost 40% is planted, most of it with uniform rows of conifers, known as *sugi* (cryptomeria). Even national forests are not exempt from tree farming and these forests account for 33% of Japan's total lumber output. The end result of this widespread tree farming is a rather ugly patchwork effect over most of Japan's mountains – monotonous stands of sugi interspersed with occasional swaths of bare, clear-cut hillside.

To make matters worse, the planting of monoculture forests and clear cutting reduces the stability of mountain topsoil, resulting in frequent landslides. To combat this, land engineers erect unsightly concrete retaining walls over huge stretches of hillside, particularly along roadsides or near human habitations. These, combined with high-tension wire towers and patchwork forests, result in a landscape that is quite unlike anything elsewhere in the world.

As if this weren't enough, it is estimated that only three of Japan's 30,000 rivers and streams are undammed. In addition to dams, concrete channels and embankments are built around even the most inaccessible mountain streams. Although some of this river work serves to prevent flooding downstream, much of it is clearly gratuitous and can only be understood as the unfortunate result of Japanese pork-barrel politics.

In Japan, rural areas yield enormous power in national politics, as representation is determined more by area than by population. In order to insure the support of their constituencies, rural politicians have little choice but to lobby hard for government spending on public work projects, as there is little other work available in these areas. Despite the negative effects this has on the Japanese landscape and economy, Japanese politicians seem unable to break this habit.

The upshot of all this is a landscape that looks, in many places, like a giant construction site. Perhaps the writer Alex Kerr put it best in his book *Lost Japan*: 'Japan has become a huge and terrifying machine, a Moloch tearing apart its own land with teeth of steel, and there is absolutely nothing anyone can do to stop it.' For the sake of the beauty that remains in Japan, let's hope he is wrong.

particular the alpine regions of central Honshū and the lovely natural parks of Hokkaidō.

Fauna

Japan's one-time conjunction with the Asian continent allowed the migration of animals from Korea and China, and the fauna of Japan has much in common with these regions, though there are species that are unique to Japan, such as the Japanese giant salamander and the Japanese macaque. The Nansei-shotō, which has been separated from the mainland for longer than the rest of Japan, has a few examples of fauna (for example the Iriomote cat) that are classified by experts as 'living fossils'.

Japan's largest carnivorous mammals are its bears. Two species are found in Japan – the *higuma* (brown bear) of Hokkaidō and the *tsukinowaguma* (Asiatic brown bear) of Honshū, Shikoku and Kyūshū. The brown bear can grow to a height of 2m and weigh up to 400kg. The Asiatic brown bear is smaller at an average height of 1.4m and a weight of 200kg.

Japanese macaques are medium-sized monkeys that are found in Honshū, Shikoku and Kyūshū. They average around 60cm in length and have short tails. The last survey of their numbers was taken in 1962, at which time there were some 30,000. They are found in groups of 20 to 150 members.

A survey carried out in 1986 by the Japanese government's Environment Agency found that 136 species of mammals were in need of protection and that 15 species were already extinct. Endangered species include the Iriomote cat, the Tsushima cat, Blakiston's fish owl and the Japanese river otter.

National Parks
Japan has 28 *kokuritsu kōen* (national parks) and 55 *kokutei koen* (quasi-national parks). Ranging from the far south (Iriomote National Park is the southernmost of Japan's national parks) to the northern tip of Hokkaidō (Rishiri Rebun-Sarobetsu National Park), the parks represent an effort to preserve as much as possible of Japan's natural environment. The parks are administered either directly (in the case of national parks) or indirectly (in the case of quasi-national parks) by the Environment Agency of the Prime Minister's Office.

The highest concentration of national parks and quasi-national parks is in the Tōhoku (Northern Honshū) and Hokkaidō regions, where population density is relatively low. But there are also national parks and quasi-national parks, such as Chichibu-Tama and Nikkō, within easy striking distance of Tokyo. The largest of Japan's national parks is the Seto Naikai Kokuritsu-kōen (Inland Sea National Park), which extends some 400km east to west, reaches a maximum width of 70km and encompasses over 1000 islands.

GOVERNMENT & POLITICS
Japan's governmental system is more similar to the British parliamentary system than the US presidential one. Just as the British parliament has two houses, so the Japanese Diet has the lower House of Representatives and the upper House of Councillors. The party that controls the majority of seats in the Diet is the party in power and has the right to appoint the prime minister – usually

the party's president. The prime minister then appoints his cabinet, which is usually constituted entirely of Diet members.

The members of Japan's Diet are elected by popular election, making the country, in principle, a democracy. In fact, real power is wielded by powerful political cliques in conjunction with the country's dominant *keiretsu* (business cartels). Together, these two groups make almost all of the country's important policy decisions behind closed doors. Until quite recently, this seemed to suit Japanese voters just fine, but the present economic difficulties have given rise to calls for a more transparent and representative form of government.

In addition to the elected government, Japan retains its emperor, who holds a curious position within the nation. For centuries under the shogunate the role was purely symbolic, but during the Meiji Restoration, the emperor was 'restored' to power. In fact, he was merely brought out of the closet, dusted off and given a new figurehead position. The close of WWII brought further changes when it was announced that the emperor was no longer divine; despite this, he is still a figure of enormous respect in Japan and criticism of the emperor is almost unheard of.

Since its formation in 1955, the conservative LDP has been almost continuously in power, shaking off scandal after scandal. Elections in 1993 pushed the LDP out into the cold for a brief spell, but it quickly recaptured political power under the leadership of Hashimoto Ryutaro.

The LDP was re-elected in 1998 under Obuchi Keizo, who governed as part of a three-party coalition, sharing power with the Liberal Party and the Kōmeito (Clean Government Party). There was already some doubt that he would last, politically at least, until the general election of mid-October 2000. However, in April 2000, Obuchi suffered a massive stroke and lapsed into a coma. In accordance with Japanese law, the cabinet resigned.

Mori Yoshiro – previously secretary-general of the ruling Liberal Democratic Party – was elected as prime minister, following his instalment earlier in the day as

POLITICAL & ADMINISTRATIVE BOUNDARIES

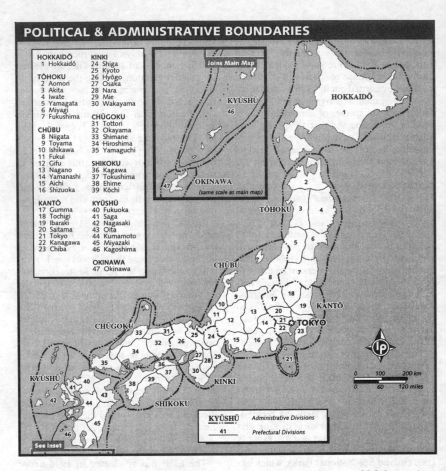

HOKKAIDŌ
1 Hokkaidō

TŌHOKU
2 Aomori
3 Akita
4 Iwate
5 Yamagata
6 Miyagi
7 Fukushima

CHŪBU
8 Niigata
9 Toyama
10 Ishikawa
11 Fukui
12 Gifu
13 Nagano
14 Yamanashi
15 Aichi
16 Shizuoka

KANTŌ
17 Gumma
18 Tochigi
19 Ibaraki
20 Saitama
21 Tokyo
22 Kanagawa
23 Chiba

KINKI
24 Shiga
25 Kyoto
26 Hyōgo
27 Osaka
28 Nara
29 Mie
30 Wakayama

CHŪGOKU
31 Tottori
32 Okayama
33 Shimane
34 Hiroshima
35 Yamaguchi

SHIKOKU
36 Kagawa
37 Tokushima
38 Ehime
39 Kōchi

KYŪSHŪ
40 Fukuoka
41 Saga
42 Nagasaki
43 Oita
44 Kumamoto
45 Miyazaki
46 Kagoshima

OKINAWA
47 Okinawa

KYŪSHŪ — Administrative Divisions

41 — Prefectural Divisions

president of the LDP. He pledged to persist with the economic policies set in motion by Obuchi (who died in May 2000), and promised he'd not back-pedal on reforms.

Geographical, Political & Administrative Divisions

Japan is divided up into nine political regions and subdivided into 47 divisions (see the Political & Administrative Boundaries map). *Ken* (prefectures) make up 43 of these divisions, and their names are written as, for example, 'Okayama-ken' or 'Chiba-ken'. The remaining four are Hokkaidō, which is a *dō* (district); Tokyo-to, which is a *to* (metropolis); and Osaka-fu and Kyoto-fu, which are *fu* (urban prefectures). Each of the three city areas incorporates the named city but is otherwise similar in land area to a ken.

Ken are subdivided into *gun* (county), *mura* (village) and *chō* (neighbourhood or village), while *to* and *fu* are subdivided into *shi* (city), *ku* (ward) and *chō*. Hokkaidō is the exception to all this, being subdivided into 14 *shichō*, which are prefecture-like 'districts'.

There are also traditional names for each region of the country. Thus, Chūgoku, or

Western Honshū, consists of the San-in, or North Coast, region and the San-yō, or South Coast, region. Other traditional names you may come across in tourist literature or other sources include Hokuriku (Fukui, Ishikawa and Toyama Prefectures), Sanriku (Aomori, Iwate and Miyagi), Shinetsu (Nagano and Niigata) and Tokai (Aichi, Gifu, Mie and Shizuoka). In addition, the Tokyo area is often referred to as Kantō, while the area around Osaka is known as Kansai or Kinki.

ECONOMY

The Japanese economic phenomenon is a rags to riches story that has left commentators around the world searching for its whys and wherefores. In the short space of just 50 or so years, Japan has gone from a defeated nation to the world's largest creditor nation. The reason for this success is complex, but to a large part it can be credited to the industriousness of the Japanese, the export orientation of the economy, controls on imports, and the boost given to the economy by the Korean War (Japan served as both a base and supplier for much of the US war effort).

The Japanese economy was devastated at the end of WWII. The MacArthur government of occupation restored the competitiveness of Japanese products by drastically devaluing the yen. From a prewar yen-dollar exchange rate of ¥4 to the US$1, the yen plummeted to ¥360 to the US$1. Before long, Japanese products were filling the 'cheap and nasty' bins of supermarkets and stores around the world.

It might have stayed that way except that Japanese industry reinvested profits into research and development, so that by the mid-1970s Japan was filing more patents than the USA. The Japanese began to make products that were cheap but also skilfully produced and of great usefulness. Even a potentially disastrous event, such as the unstable oil prices of the 1970s, which vastly increased the costs of Japan's imported energy needs, conspired to cooperate with Japanese export ambitions. It pushed the yen down further still, increasing the competitiveness of Japanese goods, and made Japanese fuel-efficient cars suddenly seem a lot more attractive than they had been before.

Faced with an increasingly successful export economy, the US Reagan administration introduced the Yen-Dollar Agreement in 1984. The yen was internationalised, and in theory this was to force up the value of the yen and make Japanese products more expensive. What wasn't taken into account was Japan's immense savings reserves and the willingness of Japanese industry to tighten belts and endure hardship. Rise the yen did, but as the yen doubled in value so did Japanese reserves of savings. Japanese industry countered with investments that offset the losses in exports. When the yen shouldered its way to an all-time post-war high of ¥130 to the US$1, exports increased in price by just 20%, and the Japanese economy became stronger than ever.

Until 1990, it looked as though the Japan economic juggernaut was unstoppable. But there was trouble in paradise. During the 1980s, escalating property values, a bullish stock market and easy credit led to what is now known as the 'Bubble Economy'. With a seemingly endless supply of easy money to hand, developers and investors threw their money into one grand scheme after another, on the assumption that the Japanese stock prices and land values would continue rising indefinitely.

In January 1990, however, the Tokyo stock market began to slide. By October of the same year it had lost 48% of its value – the bubble had sprung a leak. In 1991, Japanese banks, hit by the fall in stock market values, could no longer afford to be so free with their money and raised their interest rates. In turn, land prices came crashing back to earth. The sudden economic slowdown led to the failure of many of the speculative development ventures initiated during the 1980s, leaving the country's banks with a mountain of bad loans. The repercussions were felt in every sector of the economy and the country plunged into a recession from which it has yet to recover.

The South-East Asian currency crisis of 1997 worsened the recession. In 1998 Japan recorded its second year of negative economic growth and in 1999 Japan's unemployment rate topped 5% for the first time since WWII. In an effort to stimulate the economy, the government has responded with a series of vast public works projects, most of them financed by borrowing, swelling an already huge government debt. While some critics hold that these pump-priming measures will eventually pay off, most argue that the only way for Japan to pull out of the current crisis is radically to reorder its economy. For the time being at least the government seems to lack the necessary resolve to do this.

POPULATION & PEOPLE

Japan has a population of approximately 126 million people (the ninth largest in the world) and, with 75% of it concentrated in urban centres, population density is extremely high. Areas such as the Tokyo-Kawasaki-Yokohama conurbation are so densely populated that they have almost ceased to be separate cities, running into each other and forming a vast coalescence that, if considered as a whole, would constitute the world's largest city.

While this high urban population density is tough on the Japanese, it has the advantage of leaving other parts of the country reasonably sparsely populated. Travellers visiting Japan are still able to enjoy large national parks, mountainous regions and, in places like Hokkaidō, near-wilderness.

The other notable feature of Japan's population is its ethnic and cultural homogeneity. This is particularly striking for visitors from the USA, Australia and other multicultural nations. The main reason for this ethnic homogeneity is Japan's strict immigration laws, which have ensured that only a small number of foreigners settle in the country.

The largest non-Japanese group in the country is made up of 650,000 *zai-nichi kankoku-jin* (resident Koreans). For outsiders, Koreans are an invisible minority. Indeed, even the Japanese themselves have no way of knowing that someone is of Korean descent if he or she adopts a Japanese name. Nevertheless, Japanese-born Koreans, who in some cases speak no language other than

Japanese, were only very recently released from the obligation to carry thumb-printed ID cards at all times, and still face discrimination in the workplace and other aspects of their daily lives.

Aside from Koreans, most foreigners in Japan are temporary workers from China, South-East Asia, South America and Western countries. Indigenous groups such as the Ainu have been reduced to very small numbers and are concentrated mostly in Hokkaidō.

Burakumin

The Burakumin are a mysterious minority. They are racially the same as other Japanese, and yet history has made them an outcast class. Traditionally, the Burakumin belonged to communities whose work brought them into contact with the contamination of death – butchering, leatherworking and the disposing of corpses.

There are thought to be around three million hereditary Burakumin nowadays. While discrimination against Burakumin is now against the law, there continues to be significant discrimination against Burakumin in such important aspects of Japanese social life as work and marriage. It is common knowledge, though rarely alluded to, that information about any given individual's possible Burakumin origin is available to anyone (generally employers and prospective fathers-in-law) who is prepared to make certain discreet investigations. Many Japanese dislike discussing this topic with foreigners, and unless you are on very familiar terms or in enlightened company it is probably bad taste to bring it up.

Ainu

The indigenous populations of Hokkaidō originally included a variety of ethnic groups, but the most dominant of these still residing on the island are the Ainu. In Ainu language, the word 'Ainu' means 'man' or 'human being'. There is a possible link between the Ainu and the people known in ancient records as the Ezo, who lived in Tōhoku. Other experts theorise that the Ainu are a Caucasian race who pushed into Japan from Siberia. Although the Ainu have more body hair and tend towards lighter skin colouring, the physical differences between Ainu and Japanese are slight. Intermarriage has further reduced these differences, and it's calculated that there are now probably less than 200 pure-blood Ainu left.

Estimates of the total Ainu population in Hokkaidō range from 24,000 to 77,000, with the largest communities of Ainu residing in Shiraoi, Asahikawa, the Hidaka district and Akan National Park. There are also a few thousand Ainu living on Honshū (mostly in Tokyo) and Russia's Sakhalin Island. The exact population figures are hard to pin down since many people choose not to identify themselves as Ainu out of fear of continuing social discrimination.

Traditionally, the Ainu people are animists who ceremonially worship the deities incarnate in rivers, forests, fire, animals etc. The most well-known Ainu religious ceremony is *iyomante*, for which a village will

UNBEATEN TRACKS IN JAPAN, I F BISHOP

A 19th-century illustration of the Ainu, the indigenous people of Hokkaidō

trap a young bear (regarded as the earthly form of a deity, which has come to visit the Ainu) and then feed and care for it as an honoured guest. After a time, usually in midwinter, the bear will be ritually sacrificed to send the deity back to *kamuy-moshir* (the land of the gods). Rarely performed nowadays, this central rite has long been outlawed by the Japanese government in a rare (and convenient) fit of ecological consciousness.

Culturally, the Ainu have suffered a historical experience similar to Native Americans in North America. As far back as the 7th century, Ainu were known to have inhabited northern Japan, Hokkaidō and Russia's Sakhalin and Kuril Islands. Over the centuries, Japanese traders, farmers and military expeditions made repeated incursions into southern Hokkaidō. In the 16th century, the Matsumae clan arrived in force and negotiated formal trading treaties with the Ainu, but by the end of the 19th century the Tokugawa shogunate and the successive Meiji government had taken back direct control and accelerated the colonisation of Hokkaidō.

At that time, many Ainu customs, including women's tattoos and the burning of a house where a person had died, were outlawed. Land and hunting rights were severely curtailed in an attempt to force the Ainu, who were traditionally hunters and gatherers, into becoming settled agriculturists. The Japanese government did provide limited social welfare and public education, but this system fostered a disempowering reliance by Ainu communities on government aid that continues to some extent today.

Some Japanese still exercise racial discrimination against people of Ainu descent, though Ainu are usually only distinguishable from their Japanese neighbours when they choose to identify themselves. As recently as 1986, the government maintained that Japan was a 'mono-ethnic nation', but this was contradicted by the international community when an Ainu representative gave the inaugural speech for the United Nations (UN) Year of Indigenous People in 1992. After increasing pressure, the Japanese Diet passed a new law in 1997 that mandated nationwide promotion of Ainu culture and traditions. This law also provided funds and increased support for Ainu research, private Ainu cultural associations and, most importantly, Ainu language classes, as only a few of the older generation are fluent and able to pass on the rich tradition of *yukar* (epic poems).

Most Japanese tourists seem comfortable at seeing Ainu culture only in the context of pseudo 'Ainu villages', with souvenir shops selling cheap replicas of traditional crafts. Ainu traditions are re-enacted by sometimes listless performers and these tourist circuses can be depressing – they are often combined with caged bears in a debased imitation of this sacred iyomante festival. It is worth keeping in mind, however, that that these tourist sites were often created and are still managed by Ainu communities, in which much of the profits are reinvested. For a long time, these sites were the only evidence of Ainu culture left in Japan. Many souvenir shops, if you look carefully, actually do sell good-quality woodcarving, as well as other traditional items, such as those made from sturdy woven elm-bark cloth.

If you want to see how the Ainu wish to portray themselves, make a point of visiting any of the several museums of Ainu culture in Hokkaidō, most notably at Niputani (Biratori) and Shiraoi. There are also several other smaller museums with exhibits on Ainu culture and the other indigenous peoples of Hokkaidō, the best of which are at Abashiri and Hakodate. For more information on Ainu cultural events and related reading, see the Hokkaidō chapter.

Ageing Japan

WWII left Japan with a very young population that, at the time, had a relatively short average lifespan compared with the average lifespan of people in advanced Western nations. Now, Japan's astonishingly low birth rate of 1.4 births per woman and extreme longevity are turning this situation around. From being a nation of youngsters Japan is rapidly becoming a nation of oldsters. Taken together with Japan's strict rules on immigration this will inevitably result in a shrinking population. Experts predict that the present population of 126 million will grow slightly until 2007, after which it will rapidly decline, to 100 million in 2050 and 67 million in 2100. Needless to say, such demographic change will have a major influence on the economy in coming decades.

EDUCATION

Japanese often describe their society as a *gaku-reki shakai*, a society in which a person's future is almost completely determined by their academic record. It is not surprising, then, that Japanese take education very seriously. Indeed, it is fair to say that education is the defining force in Japanese society.

It all starts at a very young age: after a blissful two or three years of freedom in infancy, Japanese children are thrown into one of the most gruelling education systems in the world. Competition is fierce from the beginning, since getting into the right school can mean an important head start when it comes to the university exams. These exams, of legendary difficulty, are so demanding that any student preparing for them and getting more than four hours sleep a night, is said to have no hope of passing.

To help coach students through the exams, *juku* (evening cram schools) teach students those things that they might have missed in their regular schools. Students who fail to gain entry to the university of their choice frequently spend one or two years repeating the final year of school and sitting the exams again. These students, known as *rōnin*, or 'masterless samurai', are in a kind of limbo between the school education system and the higher education system, the key to employment in Japan.

The intense pressure of this system derives in no small part from the fact that 12 years of education culminates in just two examinations that effectively determine whether or not the student will enter university. One exam is sat by all Japanese final-year high school students on the same day; the other exam is specific to the university the student wishes to attend

Continued on page 61

JAPANESE ARTS

THE CREATIVE MIND

Until the 19th century, the major influences on Japanese art came from China and Korea. Japan was still living in the Stone Age, when China had a well-developed technological culture. It's hardly surprising, then, that when frequent contact was established that Japan would be hungry for whatever skills and knowledge the Chinese had to give. In borrowing many aspects of Chinese culture, Japan also absorbed influences from distant cultures, such as Persia, Afghanistan and even ancient Rome, as China had maintained an active trade along the Silk Road. Perhaps the most important influence of all came from India, via China, in the form of Buddhism, which entered Japan in the 6th century.

Looking beyond these outside influences, the Japanese always add something of their own to their arts. There is a fascination with the ephemeral, with the unadorned, with forms that echo the randomness of nature. A gift for caricature is also present, from early Zen ink paintings right up to the *manga*, or comics, of contemporary Japan. There also exists a wildness and passion that is less evident in the arts of China. An interest in the grotesque or bizarre is also often visible, from Buddhist scrolls depicting the horrors of hell to the stylised depictions of body parts in the *ukiyo-e*, or wood-block, prints of the Edo period.

When asked to define their aesthetic principles, Japanese artists reach for words like *wabi*, *sabi* and *shibui*, words which have no real English-language equivalent. These concepts tend to overlap, and are often used more emotively than descriptively. Together they refer to a kind of rustic simplicity and to a restrained, quiet and cultivated sense of beauty. These ideals can be found, for example, in the measured proceedings of the tea ceremony. They are by no means, though, the final summation of a long and vibrant artistic tradition that actively seeks new inspirations and produces surprising new forms.

The distinction between art and craft is foreign to Japan – works of art are used in daily life, such as painted screens, while a range of crafts are produced purely as works of art, such as *shikki*, or lacquerware. Beyond these subjective definitions, the arts of Japan are founded on creative ability, coupled with a tremendous technical facility.

Art Periods

The Japanese arts are heavily influenced by mainland culture, and it is natural that the evolution of the Japanese arts continuously reflects the state of relations between Japan, China and Korea. During periods of frequent contact, new ideas and techniques were rapidly assimilated, resulting in art that was sometimes indistinguishable from that of the mainland. During periods of isolation, native ideas and sensibilities were allowed to come to the fore and the Japanese arts developed their own personality.

Title Page: Detail from a *fusuma* (sliding panel) from Tenryū-ji (Heavenly Dragon Temple), Kyoto (photograph by Matthias Ley).

Left: The prints used in this special section are, unless otherwise stated, taken from *Ehon Sakae-Gusa* (The Illustrated Book of Family Prosperity), Katsukawa (Shuncho), 1790.

Archaeologists have unearthed a range of artefacts from Japan's earliest historical periods. The Jōmon period (10,000–300 BC) takes its name from the decorative 'coiled rope' pottery produced by Japan's early hunters and gatherers. Similarly, the Yayoi period (300 BC–AD 300), which saw the introduction of wet-rice farming and bronze and iron use from the mainland, has left many examples of simple, refined earthenware pottery and clay figurines. The Kofun period (AD 300–710) is named after the *kofun* – the round or keyhole-shaped burial mounds of Japan's earliest emperors. *Haniwa* (clay ring) earthenware cylinders and sculptures, some as tall as 1.5m, surrounded these burial mounds.

The Asuka (552–645) and Hakuhō (645–710) periods mark an important turning point. The arrival of Mahayana, or Greater Vehicle, Buddhism introduced religious themes that would inspire the Japanese arts for over five hundred years. The earliest works of sculpture were produced by Korean artisans – notable examples can be seen at the temples Hōryū-ji in Nara and Kōryū-ji in Kyoto. However, by the Nara period (710–794) a golden age of Japanese sculpture had arrived. Japanese sculptors produced masterpieces, such as the Shō-Kannon statue and the Yakushi Triad (both on display at Yakushi ji in southern Nara) as well as the Ganjin statue at Tōshōdai-ji. Also during this period, outstanding religious murals were painted, very much in the vein of Indian religious cave paintings.

It was difficult in these early days for Japan to shrug off the influence of China; however, by the early Heian period (794–1185), as Tang-dynasty China faltered and Japan distanced itself from its mainland neighbour, a truly native culture began to emerge. For Japanese, this period is the apogee of elegant courtly life. The imperial capital moved from Nara to Heian (modern-day Kyoto); and the literary arts flourished. The break with Chinese tradition can be seen in the development of the 31-syllable *waka* poem, precursor to the 17-syllable haiku, and in narrative epics like *Genji Monogatari* (The Tale of Genji) by Murasaki Shikibu. In the visual arts, *yamato-e* (Japanese painting) broke with Chinese landscape tradition by depicting imperial court scenes on folding panels. The graceful lines of the temple, Byōdō-in, in Kyoto, one of the few remaining structures from this period, are also testament to the beauty of Heian architecture.

After a period of brutal internecine warfare a military government was established in Kamakura. The early art of the Kamakura period (1185–1333) was filled with a wild energy, though later art of the period became more subdued under the influence of a military government that eschewed vibrancy in the arts for a more spartan aesthetic. During this period, Zen Buddhism became popular in Japan. Its disavowal of Buddha images gave rise to a new tradition of human portraits and statues, and marked the beginning of a secularisation of the arts which would gain momentum in the following centuries.

In 1336 the centre of power moved back to Kyoto. During the Muromachi period (1333–1576), Zen had an enormous impact on the arts in Japan, exemplified by the ink paintings of Sesshū, the tea ceremony of the master Sen no Rikyū and the garden of Ginkaku-ji in Kyoto. The period was marked by a spirit of contemplation. However in 1467, the 11-year Ōnin War broke out, which essentially destroyed the country. This 'brush with the void' left a deep impact on Japan, and the idea of *wabi*, or stark simplicity, was born.

After another period of internal struggle, a powerful *shōgun*, Toyotomi Hideyoshi, took control and presided over an era of unprecedented grandeur and flamboyance in the arts. The new elite encouraged artists to produce elaborate works to decorate their palaces. The Momoyama period (1576–1600) was typified by huge gardens, gilded screen paintings and brilliant textile work. Also during this period, the first Westerners arrived, bringing with them technology and treasures unlike anything yet seen in Japan.

During the Edo period (1600–1867) of *sakoku*, or national seclusion, the Japanese arts coalesced into the forms we recognise today. With the rise of the merchant class, the arts were no longer the province of emperors and nobles and this had a tonic effect on Japanese artists, who could now sell their work to a much wider audience. The most important development during this time was *ukiyo-e*, or the wood-block print, depicting the 'floating world' of Edo courtesans and *kabuki* performers. Ukiyo-e marks the end of a long progression in the Japanese arts, which began with depictions of the Buddha and ended with depictions of normal people in everyday situations.

Since the Meiji Restoration, the arts in Japan have been revolutionised by contact with the West. As was the case with early Chinese influences, Japanese artists have swiftly moved from imitation to innovation: from film to fashion, architecture to literature, Japanese artists have made and continue to make unique international contributions (see also the Music, Literature and Cinema entries under Arts in Facts about Japan).

Architecture

Japan's traditional architecture, encompassing domestic, military and religious buildings, is full of contradictions. Characterised by extremes in size and scale, a diversity of influences and a tension between tradition and renewal, there are, however, strong underlying principles that define traditional Japanese architecture as a whole. For example, wood is the material of choice for nearly all traditional structures no matter what their function, teamed often with paper, straw and clay. This preference for timber has led to the across-the-board adoption of a post-and-beam framing system, and a preference for rectilinear forms. The post-and-beam system, because of its geometric nature, encourages the use of modules and allows for a more flexible interior partitioning system. This concept of flexible space, one of the most characteristic aspects of Japanese architecture, is often achieved through the use of movable interior walls and is carried across all building types.

This fluidity applies not just to interior spaces, but also to the boundary between the inside and outside of a building, which is often not clearly defined. There may be direct openings to the outside, or perhaps a series of transitional spaces, such as verandahs. There is a sense of responsiveness and harmony with the natural world in many traditional Japanese buildings – an important theme that later resonates in more modern architecture (see the special 'Contemporary Architecture' colour section).

Traditional Secular Architecture

Houses With the exception of the northern island of Hokkaidō, traditional Japanese houses are built with the broiling heat of summer in mind. They are made of flimsy materials designed to take advantage of even the slightest breeze. The reasoning behind this is that it is easier to bundle up in winter than it is to cool down in summer. Before the

advent of air-conditioning, this was certainly the case. Another reason behind the gossamer construction of Japanese houses is the relative frequency of earthquakes in the country, which precludes the use of heavier building materials such as stone or brick. Principally very simple and refined, the typical house is constructed of post-and-beam timber, with sliding panels of wood or rice paper (for warmer weather) making up the exterior walls. Movable screens, or *shoji*, divide the interior of the house. There may be a separate area for the tea ceremony – the harmonious atmosphere of this space is of the utmost importance and is usually achieved through the use of natural materials and the careful arrangement of furniture and utensils.

A particularly traditional type of Japanese house is the *machiya* (townhouse) built by merchants in cities like Kyoto and Tokyo. Until very recently, the older neighbourhoods of Kyoto and some areas of Tokyo were lined with neat, narrow rows of these houses, but most have fallen victim to the current frenzy of construction. These days, the best place to see *machiya* is in eastern Kyoto, near the temple, Kiyomizu-dera. Takayama, as well as the post towns along the Kiso Valley, are also good spots to view traditional machiya architecture. The more elegant mansions of the noble classes and warriors, with their elaborate receiving rooms, sculptured gardens and teahouses, can also be viewed in places like Kyoto, Nara and Kanazawa and former feudal cities scattered around Japan.

Farmhouses The most distinctive type of Japanese farmhouse is the thatched-roof *gasshō-zukuri*, so named for the shape of the rafters, which resemble a pair of praying hands. While these farmhouses look cosy and romantic, bear in mind that they were often home for up to 40 people and occasionally farm animals as well. Furthermore, the black floorboards, soot-covered ceiling and the lack of windows guaranteed a cave-like atmosphere. The only weapon against this darkness was a fire built in a central fireplace in the floor, known as an *irori*, which also provided warmth in the cooler months and hot coals for cooking. Multi-storey farmhouses were also built to house silkworms for silk production (particularly prevalent during the Meiji era) in the airy upper gables.

Kura Japan's traditional *kura* (storehouses) are instantly recognisable by their white plaster walls. The use of a thick coat of plaster was not merely decorative but was designed to protect the building and the valuables stored inside from the frequent fires that plagued Japanese cities. The plaster seems to have done its job, and many kura survive to this day in villages like Imai-cho in Nara, Kurashiki in Western Honshū and Kitakata in Northern Honshū.

Castles Japan seems to have an abundance of castles. Few of them are originals, however, and even the copies represent a small proportion of the number that once dotted the country. The first Japanese castles were simple mountain forts that relied more on natural terrain than on structural innovations for defence. The great disadvantage of these structures was that they were as inaccessible to the defenders as to the enemy.

The 'plains castle' *(hira-jiro)*, the kind mostly seen in Japan today, evolved from the fortified residences of *daimyō*, or domain lords, which were built on flatter terrain. By the Momoyama period (1576–1600), castle architecture had reached a level of sophistication, producing masterworks of impregnability and grace, such as Himeji-jō, Osaka-jō and Fushimi-jō. Defences became ever more elaborate, with the addition of stone walls, moats, earthworks and labyrinthine halls and tunnels within the castles. *Jōka-machi*, or castle towns, grew around the castles.

The central feature of the castle was the donjon, a tower or keep. The larger castles had several donjons ranged around the central one, and the various gates were also mounted with fortifications. The buildings atop stone ramparts were mostly built of wood, but the wood was covered with plaster to protect it against fire and firearms.

The wide-ranging wars of the 16th and 17th centuries left Japan with a huge number of castles. In 1615 the Edo government, seeking

Right: Built in 1595 during the Momoyama period, Matsumoto-jō exhibits the grace and sophistication of Japan's peak castle architecture period. The three-turreted donjon is built in contrasting black and white, and at the very top is a *tsukimi yagura* or 'moon viewing platform', designed not for defense but simply to survey the natural world.

STUART WASSERMAN

to rein in the power of local daimyō, ordered that there be only one castle to each domain. In the years of peace that followed, the castle fell into disuse. During the Meiji era more castles were destroyed, leaving only 39 originals. By the end of WWII this had further been reduced to 12. The 1960s saw an enormous spate of castle reconstructions, most built of concrete and steel, but these were all rebuilt like Hollywood movie sets – authentic when viewed from a distance but distinctly modern in appearance when viewed from up close.

Some of the best castles to visit include Himeji-jō, which is often described as the most dramatic original castle still standing in Japan. Also known as White Egret Castle because of its white colour, it was situated on a major route to the western provinces and originally had three moats, along with a five-storey donjon and three smaller donjons. Edo-jō, which modern Tokyo has grown around, was built in 1457 by Oota Doukan. Some thirty years later, the Edo-period shōgun Tokugawa Ieyasu gained control of the castle and began a massive rebuilding project – the main compound at one stage covered an amazing 357,000 square metres. It was to remain the Tokugawa shogunate's headquarters until 1868. The last of the surviving original castles is Matsuyama-jō, which was rebuilt in 1854 after a fire 70 years earlier. It was again restored in 1969, with many of the original structures, including the main donjon and three lesser donjons, now rebuilt.

Traditional Religious Architecture

Japan's two major religions are Shintō, the indigenous religion of Japan, and Buddhism, which first came to Japan from China in the 6th century.

Shrines Shintō translates as the 'way of the gods'. Japanese *kami* (gods) inhabit all natural phenomena – from towering volcanoes to curiously misshapen rocks – and the earliest Shintō shrines were simply sacred places marked off with a special plaited rope called a *shimenawa* and strips of *gohei*, or white paper. From this rope evolved fences and eventually the *torii*, or Shintō shrine gate, which is now one of the most obvious features of a shrine.

Shrine buildings come in many varieties, but the architecture of most probably evolved from the storehouses and dwellings of prehistoric Japan: many of their now ornamental features were once functional in nature. Pairs of stone lion-like creatures called *komainu* often flank the main path to a shrine; one usually has its mouth open in a roar and the other has its mouth closed. Farther along the approach is an *chōzuya* (ablution basin) where visitors use the *hishaku*, or ladle, to rinse both hands before pouring water into a cupped hand to rinse their mouths. The shrine's main building is the *honden*, which enshrines the resident kami. The honden is off limits to layfolk, and only occasionally entered by Shintō priests. In front of the honden is the *haiden*, or hall of worship. In smaller shrines, these may share one roof. In front of the haiden is an *saisen-bako* (offering box), above which hangs a gong and a long piece of rope. Visitors throw a coin into the box, then sound the gong twice, make two deep bows, clap loudly twice, bow again twice (once deeply, once lightly) and then step back to the side.

The oldest Japanese shrines were built in a 'pure' native style. But with the introduction of Buddhism to Japan, shrine buildings started to incorporate elements of Chinese temple architecture. The 'pure' style is marked by features such as natural wood columns and walls (as opposed to red and white), *chigi* (horns) protruding over the ridge of the roof, and free-standing columns that support the ridge of the roof at either gabled end. Look too for *katsuogi* – short logs that lie horizontally across the ridge of the roof.

Right: Yōmei-mon, the spectacular entrance gate leading to the *haiden* (hall of worship) of Tōshō-gū in Nikkō is in contrast with the very essense of the minimalist approach generally associated with Japanese art. It is crowded with detail – and its gold leaf and red lacquerwork walls are decorated with intricate patterning, coloured relief-carvings and paintings. The shrine is dedicated to the shōgun, Tokugawa Ieyasu.

The three major Shintō shrine styles are the Shimmei, Taisha, and Sumiyoshi. The Naikū (Inner Shrine), a pre-Buddhist, Japanese-style shrine that forms part of the Ise-jingū Grand Shrine at Ise in Mie-ken, is a stunning example of the Shimmei. The shrine, Izumo-taisha, in Shimane-ken is a notable example of the Taisha style; as is Sumiyoshi-jinja, in Osaka city, of the Sumiyoshi style.

As part of an ideal of renewal and purity, shrines are traditionally rebuilt on the same spot every twenty years. This practice is extremely lengthy and costly and, as a result, Ise is the only shrine that is still regularly rebuilt. It has been rebuilt 60 times, the last time being in 1973, whilst Izumo-taisha has been rebuilt 25 times.

Temples Along with Buddhism itself, Japan also imported the architectual styles of the Buddhist temples of China and Korea. China's temple architecture strongly influenced the Japanese until the 8th century, when a native Japanese style emerged. Temples are divided into three broad architectural categories: *wayō*, or Japanese style; *daibutsuyō*, or Great Buddha style; and *karayō*, or Chinese style.

Distinguishing a Buddhist temple from a Shintō shrine is simply a matter of examining the entrance. While shrines are entered through an arched torii, a temple is entered through a gateway, usually flanked by guardian figures.

In early Japanese temples, the principal structure was the pagoda, a building that evolved from the Indian stupa (a reliquary for enshrining sacred remains of the Buddha). The Japanese variety, a graceful terraced structure of rooves capped with a spire, is Chinese-influenced. In time the pagoda became just one of many buildings that could typically be found in a temple complex, with accessory structures including the drum tower and the holy font. Temples vary widely in their construction depending on the type of school and the historical era of construction, although wood has always been a favourite material and the framing is generally of post-and-beam form.

MARTIN MOOS

Left: Dating from 1651 this shrine, like its counterpart in Nikkō, is dedicated to Tokugawa Ieyasu.

Buddhist temples can be found the length and breadth of Japan, but a selection of the finest Buddhist temples would include many in and around Kyoto, Nara and Kōya-san, as well as Eihei-ji near Fukui in Chūbu; Chūson-ji at Hiraizumi in Tōhoku; Zenkō-ji in Nagano; and, close to Tokyo, the temple complexes of Nikkō and Kamakura.

The Japanese Garden

Garden design is considered a form of high art in Japan, and many gardens are counted among the most impressive and internationally respected artistic outputs of the country. Japanese artists have long had an appreciation of abstract and minimalist forms. The ancient Chinese collected rocks that resembled mythical creatures or geographical features, such as dragons and mountains; the Japanese took this one step further, and collected rocks that looked like nothing, and so could succumb to a plethora of interpretations – a garden that could be meditated upon indefinitely.

Japanese gardens are epitomised by *kare sansui*, or gardens that set these ambiguously shaped rocks in raked gravel. The best known of these is Ryōan-ji in north-western Kyoto, but this type of garden can be seen at other Zen Buddhist temples around Japan, and in other forms around the globe.

Although some Japanese gardens are very formal, and all are carefully arranged, the Japanese garden does not use straight lines or symmetry to achieve this formality. Instead, the gardens are a miniaturisation of the Japanese landscape, albeit a very refined version. *Tsukiyama* gardens, as these are called, often incorporate meandering paths which lead the viewer through a carefully controlled set of scenes. This control is achieved in ways such as slowing a viewer by placing stepping stones or rough paving where a certain detail is in need of appreciation, or creating mystery by partially concealing garden features. Views will often

Right: The garden, Ittekikaino-niwa in the grounds of Kōmyōzen-ji in Kyūshū is a beautiful example of a *kare sansui* garden.

TONY WHEELER

include 'borrowed' landscape, a common concept in Japanese garden design. Vistas to distant mountains and other features beyond the garden boundary are carefully framed, becoming an integral part of the garden.

The third basic type of garden is the tea garden, or *chaniwa*. This garden supports the traditional Japanese tea ceremony, both as a backdrop, and as a functional facility. Water-features in chaniwa, for instance, are used for washing prior to entering the tea ceremony pavillion.

Japanese gardens can also be categorised according to how they are viewed. *Funa asobi* gardens, such as Byōdō-in in southern Kyoto, are set around a lake, and are best viewed from a boat; *shūyū* gardens, such as Ginkaku-ji in Kyoto, are revealed along a winding path; *kanshō* gardens are viewed from a single viewpoint (such as the kare sansui meditation gardens, where a walk in the garden might result in a confrontation with a rake-wielding Zen monk!); and *kaiyū* gardens, such as Katsura Rikyū Imperial Villa in western Kyoto, which are formed by many smaller gardens that are often set around a central pond and a teahouse.

Much contemporary landscape design follows some of the basic principles of the traditional ways. Variations mostly impose more obvious human intervention in the scene, reflecting contemporary Japanese society's technological slant. Abstract granite blocks are more likely to be carefully composed alongside a stainless steel lightpost than a stone lantern. Raked gravel gardens abound, as they do throughout the world, but they rarely achieve anything like the standards set over 500 years ago.

Sculpture

Fine art in Japan begins with the introduction of Mahayana Buddhism in the 6th century. At this time the nation turned its nascent artistic skill, already manifest in its production of fine pottery and metalwork, to the production of Buddhist images. Early works of this time are heavily continental in influence, many of them actually made by Korean or Chinese immigrants. These sculptors were brought over from the mainland to furnish Japan's new temples with Buddhist images. Later, when contacts with China evaporated during the late Heian era, native sculpture techniques were allowed to flourish and a distinct Japanese style began to appear.

A knowledge of the different types of Buddhist sculptures found in Japanese temples is a good step to understanding Buddhism itself. The images fall into four main groups, each of which represents a different level of being in the Buddhist cosmology. This cosmology, of course, comes to Japan from India, via China and Korea, and Japanese Buddhist art naturally reflects this rich inheritance.

At the head of Japanese Buddhism's hierarchy of deities are *nyorai*, or Buddhas. These are beings who have attained enlightenment and freed themselves from the cycle of rebirth. Nyorai images are most

Left: The stone Dainichi Buddha head, near Usuki in Kyūshū is part of a collection of superb 10th to 13th-century Buddha images (photograph by Martin Moos).

conspicuous by their simple robes, a weight of stone on the head that symbolises wisdom and a head of tight 'snail shell' curls.

The major nyorai are: Shaka (the Historical Buddha), recognisable by one hand raised in a preaching gesture; Yakushi (the Healing Buddha), with one hand also raised in a preaching gesture and the other hand clutching a vial of medicine; Amida (the Buddha of Western Paradise or of Light), usually seen sitting with knuckles together in a meditative posture; and Dainichi (the Cosmic Buddha), usually portrayed in princely attire, sitting with one hand clasped around a raised finger of the other hand (a sexual gesture indicating the unity of being). Nyorai are usually portrayed with two bodhisattvas in a triad configuration.

The next most important beings are *bosatsu* (bodhisattvas). These are beings who have put off their own personal entry into nirvana in order to help others attain enlightenment. Images of bosatsu are more human in appearance than nyorai and are most easily distinguished from the latter by a topknot of hair or a crowned headpiece, sometimes with smaller figures built into the crown. The most common bosatsu in Japanese temples is Kannon, the goddess of mercy. Also common, both in temples and scattered around the countryside, are images of Jizo, the bodhisattva assigned to aid travellers and children. Jizō are often depicted carrying children in their arms.

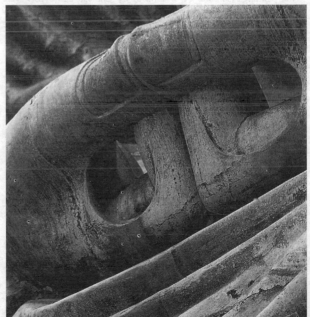

Right: Detail of a meditative Amida Buddha – Kamakura.

JOHN HAY

The next group of beings are not native to Buddhism, but were borrowed from Hinduism to serve particular purposes in the Buddhist cosmology. These beings are called *ten* (heavenly beings or deva). While some appear as beastly ogres, others are human in appearance. The most common of these are *niō* (guardians), which are often found in the gates leading up to temples. The giant Kongō guardians at Nara's Toōdai-ji are perhaps the most famous of these images.

Finally, there are the *myō-ō* (kings of wisdom or light). These beings serve as protectors of Buddhism and were introduced to Japan along with esoteric Buddhism in the 9th century. The most common myō-ō image is Fudō Myō-ō who is usually depicted as a wrathful being clutching an upright sword.

Painting

The techniques and materials used in the early stages of Japanese painting owe much to Chinese influence. By the end of the Heian period (794–1185), the emphasis on painting religious themes following Chinese conventions gave way to a purely Japanese style of painting. Known as *yamato-e*, this style covered local subjects and was frequently used in scroll paintings and on screens.

Ink paintings *(suiboku-ga* or *sumi-e)* by Chinese Zen artists were introduced to Japan during the Muromachi period and copied by Japanese artists, who produced hanging pictures *(kakemono)*, scrolls *(emaki)* and decorated screens and sliding doors.

During the Momoyama period, Japan's daimyō flaunted their wealth and power by commissioning artists who painted in flamboyant colours and used copious gold leaf embellishment. The most popular themes depicted Japanese nature or characters from Chinese legends. The Kanō school was the most famous follower of these painting styles.

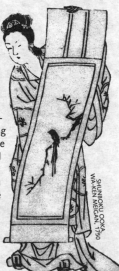

SHUNBOKU OOKA,
WA-KEN MEIGAN, 1750

Western techniques of painting, including the use of oils, were introduced during the 16th century by the Jesuits. Japanese painters who combined Western and Japanese styles sometimes produced interesting results: portraits of Westerners thoughtfully included a sloe incline to the eyes.

The Edo period was marked by the enthusiastic patronage of a wide range of painting styles. The Kanō school continued to be in demand for the depiction of subjects connected with Confucianism, mythical Chinese creatures or scenes from nature. The Tosa school, whose members followed the yamato-e style of painting, was kept busy with commissions from the nobility to paint scenes from the ancient classics of Japanese literature.

The Rimpa school not only absorbed the style of other schools (Chinese, Kanō and Tosa), but progressed beyond their conventions to produce strikingly original decorative painting. The works of art produced by a trio of outstanding artists from this school (Tawaraya Sōtatsu, Hon'ami Kōetsu and Ogata Kōrin) rank among the finest of this period.

Calligraphy

Shodō (the way of writing) is one of Japan's most valued arts, cultivated by nobles, priests and *samurai* alike, and still studied by Japanese schoolchildren today as *shūji*. Like the characters of the Japanese language itself, the art of shodō was imported from China. In the Heian period, a distinctly Japanese style of shodō evolved called *wayō*. This is more fluid and cursive than the purely Chinese style, which is referred to as *karayō*. The Chinese style remained popular in Japan among Zen priests and the literati even after the Heian period.

In both Chinese and Japanese shodō there are three important types. Most common is *kaisho*, or block-style script. Due to its clarity, this style is favoured in the media and in applications where readability is a must. *Gyōsho*, or running hand, is semi-cursive, and often used in informal correspondence. *Sōsho*, or grass hand, is a truly cursive style. Sōsho abbreviates and links the characters together to create a flowing, graceful effect.

Ukiyo-e

If there is one art form that Westerners instantly associate with Japan, it is ukiyo-e, or wood-block print. Ukiyo-e (pictures of the floating world) comes from the term 'ukiyo' – a Buddhist metaphor for the transient world of fleeting pleasures. The subjects chosen by artists were characters and scenes from the 'floating world' of the entertainment quarters in Edo (modern-day Tokyo), Kyoto and Osaka.

The floating world, centred in pleasure districts like Edo's Yoshiwara, was a topsy-turvy kingdom, an inversion of all the usual social hierarchies that were held in place by the power of the Tokugawa shogunate. Here, money counted for more than rank, actors and artists were the arbiters of style, and prostitutes elevated their art to such a level that their social and artistic accomplishments matched those of the ladies of noble families. Added to this was an element of spectacle. Both kabuki

and *sumō*, with their ritualised visual opulence, found large popular audiences in this period.

The vivid colours, novel composition and flowing lines of ukiyo-e caused great excitement in the West, sparking a vogue which a French art critic dubbed 'Japonisme'. Ukiyo-e became a key influence on impressionists (for example, Toulouse-Lautrec, Manet and Degas) and post-impressionist artists. Among the Japanese the prints were hardly given more than passing consideration – millions were produced annually in Edo. They were cheap items, often thrown away or used as wrapping paper for pottery. For many years, the Japanese continued to be perplexed by the keen interest foreigners took in this art form which they considered of ephemeral value.

The first ukiyo-e prints in the early 17th century were black and white; the technique for colour printing was only developed in the middle of the

Right: A drawing by the ukiyo-e master, Hokusai.

HOKUSAI MANGA, HOKUSAI KATSUSHIKAI

Manga – Japanese Comics

 The Japanese are insatiable readers of manga – a catch-all word covering cartoons, magazine and newspaper comic strips, and the ubiquitous comic book. Even high art *ukiyo-e* prints were once a form of manga, evolving with the *kibyōshi* (yellow cover) wood blocks that were used to create adult story books. The great ukiyo-e artist Hokusai actually coined the word 'manga' by combining the characters for 'frivolous' and 'picture'.

The father of modern manga was Tezuka Osamu who, in the late 1940s, began working cinematic effects based on European movies into his cartoons – pioneering multi-panel movements, perspectives that brought the reader into the action, close-ups, curious angles and a host of movie-like techniques. His adventurous stories quickly became movie-length comic strips – essentially films drawn on paper. What Tezuka started took off in a big way once weekly magazines realised that they could boost sales by including manga in their pages. As a result of Tezuka's innovations, Japanese comics are rarely slim affairs (weekly comics as thick as phone directories are not unusual). And with this popularity came recognition – Japanese comic-strip artists are often elevated to celebrity status becoming as wealthy and well known as pop *idoru* (idols).

Many manga also spin off into popular, cutting-edge *anime* (animation films) that can make Disney creations look like goofy doodling (to say nothing of the soundtracks). Mamoro Oshii's 1995 anime version of the Shirow Masamune manga *Ghost in the Shell* is a good example (see the Cinema entry in the Arts section of Facts About Japan).

Manga text is in Japanese, but there's usually an English subtitle on the cover announcing whether it's a 'Lady's Comic', a 'Comic for Business Boys' or even an 'Exciting Comic for Men' ('exciting' is generally a lame euphemism for soft porn). Japanese censors may entertainingly blur the pubic hair in imported porn, but it's all on view in comic books. You only have to peer over a shoulder on the train and you may catch a schoolgirl quietly following the progress of a 2km-long penis as it ravages Tokyo – even *shōjo manga* ('girls comics') are jumping with sexual activity. Manga isn't all 'frivolous', however. It also tackles straight subjects: *jitsuma manga* (practical comics) and *benkyō manga* (study comics) set out to teach everything from high school subjects to ikebana and international finance.

Those interested in Japanese comics can join the crowds leafing through recent issues in bookshops. A good introduction to manga is *Dreamland Japan Writings on Modern Manga* by Frederik Schodt (1996). If you're really keen, make a trip to the Hiroshima City Manga Library, which has a small Comic Museum.

Left: Illustration by Mick Weldon.

18th century. The success of a print lay in close cooperation between the artist, engraver and printer through all stages of production.

The first stage required the artist *(eshi)* to draw a design on transparent paper and indicate the colouring needed. The engraver *(horishi)* then pasted the design face down on a block of cherry wood and carved out the lines of the design in relief. The printer *(surishi)* inked the block and took a proof. Each colour required a separate block; it was up to the printer to use his skill to obtain accurate alignment and subtle colour effects that depended on the colour mixture and pressure applied.

The reputed founder of ukiyo-e was Iwa Matabei. The genre was later developed by Hishikawa Moronobu, who rose to fame with his illustrations for erotic tales. His wood-block prints of scenes from the entertainment district of Yoshiwara introduced the theme of *bijin-e* (paintings of beautiful women), which later became a standard subject. Early themes also covered scenes from the theatre (including the actors), and erotic *shunga*. Kitagawa Utamarō is famed for his bijin-e, which emphasise the erotic and sensual beauty of his subjects. All that is known about Tōshūsai Sharaku, a painting prodigy whose life is a mystery, is that he produced 145 superb portraits of kabuki actors between 1794–95.

Towards the end of the Edo period, two painters produced outstanding ukiyo-e works. Hokusai Katsushika was a prolific artist who observed his fellow inhabitants of Edo with a keen sense of humour. His most famous works include manga, *Fugaku Sanjūrokkei* (Thirty-Six Views of Mt Fuji) and *Fugaku Hyakkei* (One Hundred Views of Mt Fuji). As Hokusai approached the end of his life (he died at the age of 89) he delighted in signing his works with the pen name *gakyōrōjin* (literally, 'old man mad with painting'). Andō Hiroshige followed Hokusai, specialising in landscapes, although he also created splendid prints of plants and birds. His most celebrated works include *Tōkaidō Gojūsan-tsugi* (Fifty-Three Stations of the Tōkaidō), *Meisho Edo Hyakukei* (One Hundred Views of Famous Places in Edo) and *Omi Hakkei* (Eight Views of Lake Omi) – Omi is now known as Biwa-ko.

Ikebana

The art of flower arranging developed in the 15th century and can be grouped into four main styles: *rikka* (standing flowers), *nageire* (throwing-in), *shōkai* (living flowers) and *moribana* (heaped flowers). There are several thousand different schools at present, the top three of which are Ikenobō, Ōhara and Sōgetsu, but they share one aim – to arrange flowers to represent heaven, earth and humanity. Ikebana displays were originally used as part of the tea ceremony but can now be found in private homes – in the *tokonoma* (display alcove) – and even in large hotels. Apart from its cultural associations, *ikebana* is also a lucrative business – today its schools have millions of students, including many young women who view proficiency in the art as a means to improve their marriage prospects.

Tea Ceremony

Chanoyu also known as *sadō*, or 'the way of tea', dates back to the Nara period, when it was used by meditating Buddhist monks to promote alertness. By the 14th century the tea ceremony had developed into a highly elaborate and expensive pursuit for the aristocracy. The turning point for the ceremony took place in the 16th century. The tea master Sen no Rikkyū (1522–91) established a spartan aesthetic, using utensils that echoed the irregularities of the natural world. Other tea masters took different approaches, and today the tea ceremony can be divided into the three Senke schools (Ura, Omote and Mushakoji) and other influential schools such as Enshu, Yabunouchi and Sohen.

The traditional setting for the tea ceremony is a thatched teahouse in the setting of a landscaped garden. The preparation and drinking of the tea is conducted according to a highly stylised etiquette and the mental discipline involved was once an essential part of the training of a samurai. Novices tend to find the proceedings fatiguing, and connoisseurs maintain that full appreciation of the art takes years of training and reflection.

For a demonstration of chanoyu in Tokyo or Kyoto ask for details at the TIC or check with the large hotels. A classic treatment of this subject, written with precision and devotion, is *The Book of Tea* by Okakura Kakuzō.

Ceramics

The ceramic arts in Japan are usually considered to have started around the 13th century, with the introduction of Chinese ceramic techniques and the founding of a kiln in 1242 at Seto in Central Honshū by Tōshirō. The Japanese term for pottery and porcelain, *setomono* (literally, 'things from Seto'), clearly derives from this still thriving ceramics centre. During the 14th century, another five kilns were established: Tokoname, Shigaraki, Bizen, Echizen and Tamba. Together with Seto, these were known as the 'Six Ancient Kilns' and acquired a reputation for high-quality stoneware.

The popularity of the tea ceremony in the 16th century stimulated further ceramic development. The great tea masters, Furuta Oribe and Sen no Rikyū, promoted production of exquisite Oribe and Shino wares in Gifu. The powerful shōgun Toyotomi Hideyoshi, who thought nothing of plastering the walls of his tearoom with gold, encouraged the master potter Chōjiro to create works of art from clay found near Hideyoshi's palace. Chōjiro was allowed to embellish the tea bowls he created with the Chinese character *'raku'* (enjoyment). This was the beginning of Kyoto's famous *raku-yaki* style of pottery. Tea bowls became highly prized objects commanding inflated prices. Even today, connoisseurs of the tradition of the tea ceremony are happy to pay as much as US$30,000 for a tea bowl.

Hideyoshi's invasion of Korea at the end of the 16th century was a military disaster, but it proved to be a boon to Japanese ceramics when captured Korean potters introduced Japan to the art of manufacturing porcelain. In 1598, a Korean master potter, Ri Sampei, built the first porcelain kiln at Arita in Kyūshū. During the Edo period, many daimyō encouraged the founding of kilns and the production of superbly designed ceramics. The 'climbing kiln' *(noborigama)* was widely used. Constructed on a slope, the kiln had as many as 20 chambers and the capability to achieve temperatures as high as 1400°C.

During the Meiji period, ceramics waned in popularity, but were later included in a general revival of interest in folk arts *(mingei-hin)* headed by Yanagi Sōetsu, who encouraged famous potters such as Kawai Kanjirō, Tomimoto Kenkichi and Hamada Shōji. The English potter Bernard Leach studied in Japan under Hamada and contributed to the folk art revival. On his return to Cornwall in England, Leach maintained his interest in Japanese ceramics and promoted their appreciation in the West.

There are now over 100 pottery centres in Japan with large numbers of artisans producing everything from exclusive tea utensils to souvenir folklore creatures, such as Kitsune (the fox) or Tanuki (the badger). Department stores regularly organise exhibitions of ceramics. Master potters are highly revered and the government designates the finest as 'Living National Treasures' (see the boxed text later).

Famous Ceramic Centres

Arita-yaki porcelain is still produced in the town where the first Japanese porcelain was made – Arita in Kyūshū. In the mid-17th century, the Dutch East India Company exported these wares to Europe, where they were soon copied in ceramics factories such as those of the Germans (Meissen), the Dutch (Delft) and the English (Worcester). It is commonly known to Westerners as 'Imari' after the name of the port from which it was shipped. The Kakiemon style uses designs of birds and flowers in bright colours. Another popular style is executed in blue and white and incorporates scenes from legends and daily life. Some famous styles include:

Satsuma-yaki The most common style of this porcelain, from Kagoshima in Kyūshū, has a cloudy white, crackled glaze enamelled with gold, red, green and blue.

Karatsu-yaki Karatsu, near Fukuoka in northern Kyūshū, produces tea ceremony utensils that are Korean in style and have a characteristic greyish, crackled glaze.

Hagi-yaki The town of Hagi in Western Honshū is renowned for Hagi-yaki, a type of porcelain made with a pallid yellow or pinkish crackled glaze.

Bizen-yaki The ancient ceramics centre of Bizen in Okayama-ken, Honshū, is famed for its solid unglazed bowls, which turn red through oxidation. Bizen also produces roofing tiles.

Mashiko-yaki The town of Mashiko in Tochigi-ken, Northern Honshū, is renowned as a folk craft centre, producing wares with a distinctive reddish glaze.

Mino-yaki From Toki, in Gifu-ken in Central Honshū, come pieces executed in the Oribe style, which have a greenish glaze and are decorated with creatures and flowers. The Shino style, greatly prized by connoisseurs of tea ceremony utensils, employs a heavy white glaze.

Temmoku-yaki Seto city in Aichi-ken, Central Honshū, has a long tradition as a ceramics centre. The standard product is ash-glazed, heavy stoneware, but Seto also produces special ceramic wares such as *temmoku*, an ancient Chinese style with a brown and black glaze.

Kiyomizu-yaki The approach road to the temple, Kiyomizu-dera, in Kyoto is lined with shops selling Kiyomizu-yaki, a style of pottery that can be enamelled, blue-painted or red-painted in appearance.

Kutani-yaki The porcelain from Ishikawa-ken in Central Honshū is usually green or painted.

The Tourist Information Center's (TIC) useful *Ceramic Art & Crafts in Japan* leaflet is published by the Japan National Tourist Organization (JNTO) and provides full details of pottery centres, kilns and pottery fairs in Japan.

Lacquerware

The Japanese have been using lacquer to protect and enhance the beauty of wood since the Jōmon period In the Meiji era, lacquerware became very popular abroad and remains one of Japan's best known products. Known in Japan as *shikki* or *nurimono*, lacquerware is made using the sap from the lacquer tree *(urushi)*. Raw lacquer is actually toxic and causes a severe irritation of the skin in those who have not developed an immunity. Once hardened, however, it becomes inert and extraordinarily durable. The most common colour of lacquer is an amber or brown colour, but additives have been used to produce black, violet, blue, yellow and even white lacquer. In the better pieces, multiple layers of lacquer are painstakingly applied and left to dry, and finally polished to a luxurious shine. Japanese artisans have devised various ways to further enhance the beauty of lacquer. The most common method is called *maki-e*, which was developed in the 8th century. Here, silver and gold powders are sprinkled onto the liquid lacquer to form a picture. After the lacquer dries, another coat of lacquer is applied to seal the picture. The final effect is often dazzling and some of the better pieces of lacquerware made using this method are now National Treasures.

Right: A deceptively simple *maki-e* wave design on a laquer box, Sanzen-in, Kyoto.

FRANK CARTER

Handmade Paper

Traditional Japanese handmade paper, known as *washi*, was introduced from China in the 5th century. Its golden age was the Heian era, when washi was highly prized by members of the Kyoto court for writing poetry and diaries. Colours were added to produce patterns (silver and gold leaf was often applied), and sometimes paper was made to especially complement the mood of a particular poem. Washi continued to be made in large quantities until the introduction of Western paper in the 1870s. After that time, the number of families involved in papermaking plummeted to only 851 in 1973. Recently, washi has enjoyed something of a revival and a large variety of colourful, patterned paper is widely available.

Textiles

Textiles have always played an important role in Japanese society: the fabric used in a *kimono* was an indication of class status. Until the introduction of cotton to Japan in the 16th century, Japanese textiles were made mostly of bast fibres or silk. Of all Japanese textiles, intricately embroidered brocades have always been the most highly prized, but sumptuary laws imposed on the merchant class in the Edo period prohibited the wearing of these kimono. To circumvent these laws, new techniques of kimono decoration were devised – the most

The Decorated Skin

Japanese *irezumi*, or tattooing, is widely considered the best of its kind. Usually completed in blue and red natural dyes, the tattoos often cover the whole body, with intricate designs featuring auspicious animals, flowers, Buddhist deities or folktale characters. In feudal times, the authorities tattooed criminals, thus stigmatising them as 'branded'. In due course, those who had been tattooed exhibited a defiant pride in these markings that set them apart from the rest of society. As a sop to foreign sensibilities, tattooing was banned during the Meiji era, but was promptly reinstated after the Prince of Wales (later to become King George V) took a liking to the art and had a dragon tattooed on his arm in 1881. Today, the *yakuza*, or Japanese mafia, are the only ones to stand out with magnificent *irezumi*, though to have a chance to see their exquisite body art you may have to visit *onsen* regularly!

important being the technique of *yūzen* dyeing. In this technique, rice paste is applied to the fabric like a stencil to prevent a colour from bleeding onto other areas of the fabric. By repeatedly changing the pattern of the rice paste, very complex designs can be achieved.

At the other end of the spectrum, *aizome* (the technique of dyeing fabrics in vats of fermented indigo plants) gave Japan one of its most distinctive colours. Used traditionally in making hardy work clothes for the fields, Japan's beautiful indigo-blue can still be seen in many modern-day textile goods.

Furniture Design

If jade is the perfect medium for the expression of the Chinese artistic genius, then for the Japanese it is wood; perhaps nowhere in the world has the art of joinery been lifted to such high levels. This genius for joinery translates well to the art of cabinetmaking. Chests called *tansu* are particularly prized by collectors of Japanese antiques. Perhaps the most prized of all *tansu* is the *kaidan dansu*, so named because it resembles a flight of stairs (*kaidan* is the Japanese word for 'stairs'). These are becoming increasingly difficult to find, but determined hunting at flea markets and antique stores may still turn up the occasional good piece, but don't expect any bargains.

Living National Treasures

Beat Takeshi, an irreverent local comedian, once presented himself at the Agency for Cultural Affairs with a request that he be designated a 'Living National Treasure'. He was unsuccessful. However, he wasn't attempting the impossible. In Japan it is not a requirement that you be an inanimate work of art to be designated a national treasure.

'Living National Treasure' has a nice ring to it and would certainly look impressive on a business card. How do you become one? Well, for a start, you need to be Japanese. Secondly you need to be involved in the traditional arts or performing arts of Japan, more specifically to be a 'Bearer of Important Intangible Cultural Assets', which is, for the record, how Living National Treasures are more properly addressed.

Living National Treasures first came into being in 1955 as a result of the Law for the Protection of Cultural Assets of 1950. It is difficult to see how appointing people Living National Treasures protects them in any way but, by 1990, 97 individuals had been officially 'treasured' in the fields of *kabuki*, *nō*, *bunraku* and traditional music and dance, and a further 92 in ceramics, paper making, weaving and lacquerware. New appointments and new categories are made annually.

Perhaps Beat still has a chance...

Japanese Dolls

Dolls, or *ningyō*, have played a part in Japanese society from prehistoric times, when the rites of burial demanded that clay figures be buried along with the dead. During the Kofun period of ancient Japan, burial mounds of emperors and nobles were usually surrounded by hundreds of *haniwa* clay figures, some in human form.

Today, dolls still figure prominently in two Japanese festivals: the Hina Matsuri (Doll Festival, 3 March), when girls display ornamental *hina-ningyō* on tiered platforms as part of the festivities; and on

Right: An elaborately dressed *ningyō*.

MASON FLORENCE

JAPANESE ARTS

Kodomo-no-hi (Children's Day, 5 May), when both boys and girls display special dolls. Some of the more common dolls today are: *daruma*, which are based on the figure of Bodhidarma, who brought Buddhism to China from India; *gosho-ningyō*, chubby plaster dolls sometimes dressed as figures in *nō* dramas; *kyō-ningyō*, elaborate dolls made in Kyoto, dressed in fine brocade fabrics; *kiku-ningyō*, large dolls covered by real chrysanthemum flowers; and *ishō-ningyō*, which is a general term for elaborately costumed dolls, sometimes based on kabuki characters.

Bamboo Objects

Japanese bamboo baskets are among the finest in the world, and are remarkable for their complexity and delicacy (as well as their price). Tools used in the tea ceremony, like ladles and tea whisks, are also made of bamboo and make interesting souvenirs. However, be careful when buying bamboo crafts in Japan as many are not Japanese at all, but cheap imitations imported from other parts of Asia.

FRANK CARTER

Left: Bamboo *hishaku*, o ladles, are used to rinse both hands before entering a temple.

Continued from p32

Once exams have been completed and a student gains a university place, it is time to let loose a little. University or college is considered a transitional stage between the worlds of education and employment, a stage in which one spends more time in drinking bouts with other students than in the halls of higher learning. In a sense, the university years, for those who make it, are a time to recover from the struggles of the previous 12 years.

It is also worth noting that male and female students often take different paths in the Japanese educational system. Not only do far more male students go on to the top-level universities, but the academic majors chosen by male and female students are often different: male students tend to major in economics or engineering, while female students tend to major in foreign languages or literature. As a result, Japanese female graduates are in the vanguard of the country's push toward internationalisation, accounting for the majority of interpreters, translators and bilingual workers, while the majority of male graduates go on to become 'salarymen' in the nation's large companies.

ARTS

For information on traditional architecture, art history, painting and other Japanese arts, see the special section 'Japanese Arts'.

Music

Ancient Music *Gagaku* is 'elegant' classical music of the Japanese imperial court, which was derived from Chinese models. It flourished between the 8th and 12th centuries, then declined for several centuries until a revival of interest in national traditions during the Meiji period. Court orchestras were divided into two sections, with formally prescribed functions. The orchestra of the 'right' played Korean music. The orchestra of the 'left' played Chinese, Indian or Japanese music. The repertoire of an orchestra included *kangen* (instrumental) pieces and *bugaku* (dance) pieces.

Today, a gagaku ensemble usually consists of 16 players performing on drums and kettle drums, string instruments such as the *biwa* (lute) and *koto* (plucked zither) and wind instruments such as the *hichiriki* (Japanese oboe) and various types of flute.

Traditional Instruments Several traditional Japanese instruments continue to play a part in Japanese life, both publicly and privately. Some are used in orchestras or the theatre, while others are used for solo performances.

The *shamisen* is a three-stringed instrument, resembling a banjo with an extended neck. It was very popular during the Edo period, particularly in the entertainment districts of Osaka and Edo. It is still used as formal accompaniment in kabuki and bunraku, and the ability to perform on the shamisen remains one of the essential skills of a geisha.

The koto is a type of plucked zither with 13 strings. It was adapted from a Chinese instrument sometime before the 8th century and the number of strings gradually increased from five to 13. A bass koto, with 17 strings, was created in the 20th century – leading to an even greater musical range for this ancient instrument.

The biwa, which resembles a lute, was also derived from a Chinese instrument and appeared in Japan in the 8th century. It was played by travelling musicians, often blind, who recited Buddhist sutras (collections of dialogues and discourses) to the accompaniment of the instrument. During the Heian period, the biwa was used in court orchestras. In the succeeding Kamakura period, storytellers created a different style for the biwa to accompany tales from medieval war epics, the most famous of which are the *Tales of Heike*. Although biwa ballads were in vogue during the 16th century, the instrument later fell out of favour. More recently, the composer Takemitsu Tōru has found a new niche for the biwa in a Western orchestra.

The *shakuhachi* is a wind instrument imported from China in the 7th century. The shakuhachi was popularised by wandering Komusō monks in the 16th and 17th centuries, who played it as a means to enlightenment as they walked alone through the woods.

Taiko refers to any of a number of large Japanese drums often played at festivals or in parades. Perhaps most famous of all taiko music is performed during the Earth Celebration festival on Sado-ga-shima, near Niigata (see the boxed text 'Festive Sado'). The drummers who perform this music train year-round to endure the rigours of playing these enormous drums. Check with the Tourist Information Center (TIC) about occasional special taiko festivals which are held on the island.

Contemporary Music Japan has a huge domestic market. More than any other nation in Asia, the Japanese have taken to Western music, and you can meet fans of every type of music from Bach to acid jazz. An overwhelming feature of the local music scene is the *aidoru* (idol singer). The popularity of idols is generated largely through media appearances and is centred on a cute, girl-next-door image.

The predominance of Western-style imitation is probably the main reason why few Japanese acts have had any popularity in the West. Notable exceptions are electronic music performers, such as Kitarō, whose oriental synthesised sounds have had considerable success, and Ryūichi Sakamoto, a former member of Yellow Magic Orchestra and composer of the score for *The Last Emperor* (for which he won an Oscar). See the boxed text 'Denki Download' for more information.

A perhaps surprising music export was Orqesta de la Luz, a salsa band composed entirely of Japanese musicians. The band regularly played to ecstatic Hispanic audiences at stadium-sized venues across the USA and Latin America in the 1990s. In 1993 they became the first group ever to receive an award for cultural achievement from the United Nations. Still, no Japanese act has as yet been able to match the success of one Sakamoto Kyū, who made it to the top of the American hit parade in 1963 singing 'Sukiyaki'.

In addition to his growing popularity in Japan, Okinawan music maverick Kina Shokichi has been a driving force in placing Okinawan music on the world circuit. He is one of the few Japanese musicians to develop a true following in the West (his fans include David Byrne and Ry Cooder). His electric-traditional crossovers make for fascinating, often haunting listening.

The peninsula, Tsugaru-hantō, at the tip of Tōhoku in Northern Honshū, has its own brand of music called Tsugaru-jamisen, which is a fun combination of racing banjos and wailing songs.

Literature

Like the other arts, Japanese literature has always been heavily influenced by outside sources. For most of Japan's history, this influence came from China. Japan's first real literature, the *Kojiki* (Record of Ancient Matters) and *Nihon Shoki* (Chronicle of Japan) were written in the 8th century in emulation of Chinese accounts of the country's history. It was only during times of relative isolation from the mainland that Japanese literature developed its own voice.

Interestingly, much of Japan's early literature was written by women. One reason for this was that men wrote in *kanji* (imported Chinese characters), while women wrote in *hiragana* (Japanese script). Thus, while the men were busy copying Chinese styles and texts, the women of the country were producing the first authentic Japanese literature. Among these early female authors is Murasaki Shikibu, who wrote one of Japan's all time classics, *Genji Monogatari* (The Tale of Genji). Now available in translation, this novel documents the intrigues and romances of early Japanese court life. Although it is perhaps Japan's most important work of literature, its extreme length probably limits its appeal to all but the most ardent Japanophile. *The Narrow Road to the Deep North* is a famous travel classic by the revered Japanese poet Matsuo Bashō.

Kokoro by Natsume Sōseki is a modern classic depicting the conflict between old and new Japan in the mind and heart of an aged scholar. The modern and the traditional also clash in the lives of two couples in *Some Prefer Nettles* by Tanizaki Junichirō. *The Makioka Sisters*, also by

Denki Download

Electronic music is alive and well in Japan, supported by a large band of technologically savvy and image-conscious listeners. Japanese electronic music has also been well received internationally; this may owe something to the Western view of Japan as a technology-obsessed nation, but is also probably due to the stress electronic music places on sounds, rather than lyrics. However, it has to be noted that some Japanese bands have twisted the English language into forms exotic enough to appeal without musical accompaniment, for example, *What's the Trouble With My Silver Turkey?*, by Buffalo Daughter, or *The Homerun Tiger in a Bush*, by Denki Groove.

It all started with the advent of synthesisers. Yellow Magic Orchestra (later simply YMO), a synth-pop group, was formed in 1978. They were among the first wave of mainstream electronic musicians, though they were preceded and influenced by the German group, Kraftwerk. YMO split in 1983. One of the trio, Ryuichi Sakamoto is now a composer with an eclectic output, and has composed music for almost everything, including film scores. Another member, Haruomi Hosono, remains a respected composer and producer in Japan.

Masanori Takahashi also dabbled in electronic music in the early days, though he is now more commonly known by his recording alias, Kitarō. He, like YMO, began experimenting with synthesisers in the 1970s, but from a New Age rather than pop angle. Albums have been coming thick and fast since the mid-1980s, when Kitarō gained international attention. Rumour has it that every year in reverence of nature, he beats a *taiko* (Japanese drum) from dusk till dawn under a full moon – despite his hands becoming bloodied. In a slightly different vein again, Isao Tomita used the new synth-technology to reinterpret works by classical composers, producing some interesting results.

Since the 1980s synthesisers have been replaced by samplers, computers and turntables as the instruments of choice. Japan has a number of internationally successful DJs and dance music producers, and many others who continue to perform and record for home audiences.

Ken Ishii creates music that is a mix of ambient techno and experimental sounds. Look out for *Innerelements* (R&S, 1994), his debut release, and his international breakthrough LP, *Jelly Tones* (R&S, 1995). Satoshi Tomiie started as a DJ in the Tokyo club scene in the late 1980s, and has gone on to pump out his brand of Japanese house music in clubs around the world. If you miss him live, check out his debut album, *Full Lick* (Sony, 1999).

Other Japanese DJs to watch out for include Yasuharu Konishi (a member of the cheery lounge/pop/electronica group, Pizzicato Five), Takkyu Ishino (half of the dancey Denki Groove duo) and DJ Krush.

However, DJs are not the only contemporary exponents of electronic music in Japan. Many bands mix traditional instruments and vocals with a decent serve of electronic noise, such as Denki Groove, Pizzicato Five and Buffalo Daughter. Legend has it that Buffalo Daughter were 'discovered' at a Luscious Jackson concert in Tokyo, which secured them a deal with Grand Royal, the record label run by Mike D (of Beastie Boys fame). They have since released a string of cutely named albums including *Captain Vapour Athletes* (Grand Royal, 1996) and the remixed *Socks, Drugs and Rock 'N' Roll* (Grand Royal, 1997). Their music is experimental rather than catchy, but well worth a listen.

If you like your electronic music mixed with a big spoonful of sugar-sweet pop, have a listen to Kahimi Karie. Or try Pizzicato Five or Cornelius (aka Keigo Oyamada).

Tokyo is the best place to sample contemporary electronic music. The Liquid Room in Shinjuku is an institution, regularly featuring Japanese as well as international artists. Also check the listings in *Tokyo Classified* or *Tokyo Journal*.

The Japanese music scene also has sizeable Web prescence – most of the musicians mentioned have official pages or fan sites, with details on new releases, appearances and free downloadable music!

Tim Fitzgerald

Tanizaki, is a famous family chronicle that has been likened to a modern-day *The Tale of Genji*. Ibuse Masuji's *Black Rain* is a response to Japan's defeat in WWII. (Although made into a film in Japan, the book bears no relation to the Hollywood movie of the same name.)

Snow Country by Kawabata Yasunari is a famous story set in Japan's northern regions. Endō Shūsaku's *Silence* is a historical story of the plight of Japanese Christians following Tokugawa Ieyasu's unification of the country.

Mishima Yukio's *The Golden Pavilion* reconstructs the life of a novice monk who burned down Kyoto's famous golden temple, Kinkaku-ji, in 1950. Although Mishima is probably the most controversial of Japan's modern writers and is considered unrepresentative of Japanese culture by many Japanese, his work still makes for very interesting reading. Abe Kōbō's *Woman of the Dunes* is a classic tale by one of Japan's more respected avant-garde writers.

Of course not all Japanese fiction can be classified as literature. Murakami Ryū's *Almost Transparent Blue* is strictly sex and drugs, and was a blockbuster in the Japan of the 1970s. Murakami has written another provocative bestseller for the 1990s in *Coin Locker Babies*. Murakami Haruki is another bestselling author; novels available in English include *A Wild Sheep Chase* and *Dance, Dance, Dance* – both touch on sheep and Hokkaidō. Banana Yoshimoto has had unaccountable international success for her novel *Kitchen*.

Ōe Kenzaburō is Japan's Nobel laureate. Look out for *Pluck the Buds, Shoot the Kids* – which must rate alongside Mishima's *The Sailor Who Fell from Grace with the Sea* as one of the best titles in modern Japanese fiction. Ōe's semi-autobiographical *A Personal Matter*, tells the story of how the birth of a brain-damaged child affects his father.

Cinema

Japan has a vibrant film industry and proud, critically acclaimed cinematic and cinematographic traditions. Renewed international attention since the mid-1990s has reinforced interest in domestic films, which account for an estimated 40% of box office receipts, nearly double the level in most European countries. Of course, this includes not only artistically important works, but also films in the science fiction, horror and 'monster-stomps-Tokyo' genres for which Japan is also known.

At the time cinema first developed in the West, Japan was in the throes of the Meiji Restoration and was enthusiastically embracing everything associated with modernity. Cinema was first introduced to Japan in 1896 and, in characteristic fashion, the Japanese were making their own films by 1899. Until the advent of talkies, dialogue and general explanations were provided by a *benshi,* or narrator. This was necessary for foreign films, but even with Japanese silent films the benshi quickly became as important a part of the cinematic experience as the film itself. It was the narrator who brought the characters to life for the audience, and in essence became the star of early Japanese cinema.

At first, Japanese films were merely cinematic versions of traditional theatrical performances, but the Tokyo earthquake in 1923 prompted a split between *jidaigeki* (period films) and new *gendaigeki* films, which followed modern themes. The more realistic storylines of the new films soon reflected back on the traditional films with the introduction of *shin jidaigeki* (new period films). During this era, samurai themes became an enduring staple of Japanese cinema.

As the government became increasingly authoritarian in the years leading up to WWII, cinema was largely used for propaganda purposes. After the war, feudal films, with their emphasis on blind loyalty and martial themes, were banned by the Allied authorities, but cinematic energy soon turned to new pursuits, including *anime* (animated films), monster movies and comedies.

The decade of the 1950s was the golden age of Japanese cinema, beginning with the release in 1950 of Kurosawa Akira's *Rashōmon,* winner of the Golden Lion at the 1951 Venice International Film Festival and an Oscar for best foreign film.

Continued on page 73

Contemporary Architecture

CONTEMPORARY ARCHITECTURE

MARTIN MOOS

CHRIS ROWTHORN

Title page: Towering achievement – the Tokyo Metropolitan Government Offices (Photograph by Izzet Keribar)

Top: Tokyo Dome

Bottom: The Glass Hall of the Tokyo International Forum

MOVEMENTS AND CURRENTS

Contemporary Japanese architecture is currently among the world's most exciting and influential. The traditional Japanese leaning towards simple, natural and harmonious spaces is still evident in the work of modern architects – but this style is now combined with high-tech materials and the building techniques of the West.

The departure away from timber as the major traditional building material is perhaps the most noticeable difference between the old and the new, along with a dramatically rocketing skyline. Tradition has always been of extreme importance to the Japanese, but this does not necessarily imply permanence. This attitude has allowed Japanese architecture to incorporate new influences without losing the essence of its origins. A unique set of circumstances, including strong economic growth and the devastation wrought on the landscape by WWII, has meant many chances to move in new directions, and the resulting changes to the urban fabric have been extreme.

Japan first opened its doors to Western architecture in 1868 with the Meiji Restoration. Japan's architects immediately reacted to these new influences, combining traditional Japanese methods of wood construction with Western designs; but some 20 years later, a nationalistic push against the new influence of the West saw a resurgence in the popularity of traditional Japanese building styles.

Bottom:
Urban sprawl – Tokyo

JOHN HAY

The Coming of the West

This ambivalence towards Western architecture continued until after WWI, when foreign architects, like Frank Lloyd Wright and his assistant Antonin Raymond, came to build the Imperial Hotel in Tokyo. Wright introduced the International Style, characterised by sleek lines, cubic forms and materials such as glass, steel and brick.

By WWII many Japanese architects were using Western techniques and materials and blending old styles with the new. Later, the aggressively sculptural work in concrete and stone of French architect Le Corbusier was to exert a strong influence on Japanese architects. By the mid 1960s, Japanese architects had developed a unique style and were beginning to attract attention on the world stage.

First Generation: Modern

Japan's most famous postwar architect, Kenzo Tange, was strongly influenced by Le Corbusier. Tange's buildings, including the **Kagawa Prefectural Offices** at Takamatsu (1958) and the **National Gymnasium** (completed 1964), fuse the sculptural influences and materials of Le Corbusier with traditional Japanese characteristics such as post-and-beam construction and strong geometry. His **Tokyo Metropolitan Government Offices** (1991), located in Nishi-Shinjuku (West Shinjuku), is the tallest building in Tokyo. It may look a little sinister and has been criticised as totalitarian, but it is a remarkable achievement and pulls in around 6000 visitors daily. Those with an interest in Tange's work should also look out for the **United Nations University**, close to Omote-sando subway station in Tokyo.

In the 1960s, architects such as Kazuo Shinohara, Kisho Kurokawa, Fumihiko Maki and Kiyonori Kikutake, began a movement known as Metabolism that promoted flexible spaces and functions at the expense of fixed forms in building. Shinohara finally came to design

BY PERMISSION OF THE JAPANESE CONSULATE, MELBOURNE

Left: Tokyo Metropolitan Government Offices

MARTIN MOOS

in a style he called Modern Next, incorporating both modern and post-modern design ideas combined with Japanese influences. This style can be seen in his **Centennial Hall** at **Tokyo Institute of Technology**, an elegant and uplifting synthesis of clashing forms in a shiny metal cladding. Kurokawa's architecture blends Buddhist building traditions with modern influences; while Maki, the master of minimalism, pursued design in a modernist style whilst still emphasising the elements of nature – like the roof of his **Tokyo Metropolitan Gymnasium** (nearby Sendagaya Station), which takes on the form of a sleek metal insect. Another Maki design, the **Spiral Building**, built in Aoyama in 1985, is a favourite with Tokyo residents and is also an interior treat.

Arata Isozaki, an architect who originally worked under Kenzo Tange, also promoted the Metabolist style before later becoming interested in geometry and post-modernism. His work includes the **Gunma Museum** (1974) in Takasaki and the **Cultural Centre** in Mito (1990), which contains a striking geometrical snake-like tower clad in different metals. Situated about an hour's travelling time from Tokyo, the trip to Mito is a popular one for day trippers and well worth the effort.

A contemporary of Isozaka's, Kikutake, went on to design the **Edo-Tokyo Museum** (1992) in Sumida-ku, which charts the history of the Edo period (1600–1867), and is arguably his best known building. It is a truly enormous structure, encompassing almost 50,000 square metres of built space and reaching 62.2 metres (the height of the castle, Edo-jō) at its peak. It has been likened in form to a crouching giant and easily dwarfs its surroundings.

Right: Edo-Tokyo Museum

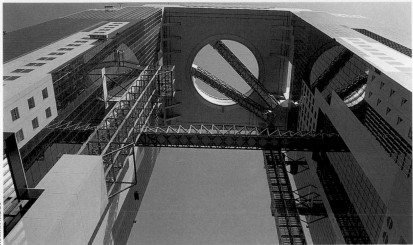

Another influential architect of this generation is Hiroshi Hara. Hara's style defies definition, but the one constant theme is nature. His **Umeda Building** (1993), in Kita, Osaka, is a sleek, towering structure designed to resemble a garden in the sky. The **Yamamoto International Building** (1993) on the outskirts of Tokyo, is the headquarters of a textile factory. Both these buildings, though monumental in scale, dissolve down into many smaller units upon closer inspection – just like nature itself.

Second Generation: Modern

In the 1980s, a second generation of Japanese architects began to gain recognition within the international architecture scene, including Tadao Ando, Itsuko Hatsegawa and Toyo Ito. This younger group has continued to explore both modernism and post-modernism, while they have been incorporating the renewed interest in Japan's architectural heritage.

Tadao Ando's architecture in particular blends classical modern and native Japanese styles. His buildings often combine materials like concrete together with the strong geometric patterns that have so regularly appeared in Japan's traditional architecture. Ando's restrained and sensitive use of materials often lends itself to the design of reflective or religious spaces.

Itsuko Hatsegawa is one of the few female Japanese architects to gain international recognition – in a breathtaking mix of old and new, she creates artificial landscapes from modern materials such as glass and steel. Her **Shonandai Cultural Centre** (1990) in Fujisawa, includes a space-age forest of steel trees with huge spheres representing the planets.

Left: The Umeda Building, Osaka

MARTIN MOOS

Similarly Toyo Ito uses high-tech materials to express things usually found in nature. However, while Hasegawa's vision is a literal interpretation of what we see around us in the natural world, Ito's architecture is more reflective – his **Tower of Winds** (in front of JR Yokohama Station) is covered by a skin of over a thousand lamps that modulate their glow according to the winds.

Foreign Architects

Foreign architects have had a strong influence on the modern Japanese landscape. Many Western architects following on from Frank Lloyd Wright have come to Japan to practise over the years, particularly during the economic boom of the 1980s. Visitors to Asakusa in search of 'lost Japan' might pause and take a look at **Asahi Flamme D'or**, an eccentric Philippe Starck design that celebrates Asahi beer in an upside down building complete with a 'golden flame' up top – supposedly representing the frothy head of a beer, but also affectionately known as the 'golden turd'. The interior is as remarkable as the exterior.

Top: A futuristic temple in Kamiyachō.

Bottom: An intriguing monument to Asahi's brewing success, Asakusa's Super Dry Hall is topped by Phillippe Starck's La Flamme d'Or (The Golden Flame), otherwise known to local expats as 'the golden turd'.

CHRIS ROWTHORN

CONTEMPORARY ARCHITECTURE

The Urban Fabric

One overwhelming architectural feature of modern Tokyo is the Tokyo Metropolitan Expressway – 220km of it girds the city. For many it is such an eyesore that it tends to get overlooked, but as Tajima Noriyuki points out in his pocket guide *Tokyo – A Guide to Recent Architecture*: 'The scale and monumentality, weight and strength of the expressway – like ancient Roman city walls – easily overwhelms any of the city's buildings, and striking contrasts are formed against its backdrop.' Take a look at how the expressway interacts with street scenes in central Tokyo (particularly Yūraku-chō and Nihombashi) and you'll see what he means.

JOHN HAY

In central Tokyo the **Tokyo International Forum** was the product of an international competition held in 1989, and was completed in 1996; Tokyo Dome forms part of this building. To some it stands as a last reminder of the boom in expressive public architecture during the 1980s. New York architect's Rafael Vinoly's vision of an urban forum to facilitate the exchange of culture and information, takes shape in the form of a 60m-high hull-shaped glass and steel atrium. Public seating is interspersed among cafes, trees and public sculptures.

21st Century Japan

The collapse of the 'bubble economy' in the 1990s saw an end to the favourable conditions that had allowed so much exciting architecture to arise. Even so, constantly surprising and dynamic architecture is still produced in Japan, continually changing the landscape, whilst at the same time reflecting it.

Kieran Grogan

Continued from page 64

The increasing realism and high artistic standards of the period are evident in such landmark films as *Tōkyō Monogatari* (Tokyo Story, 1953), by the legendary Ōzu Yasujirō; Mizoguchi Kenji's classics *Ugetsu Monogatari* (Tales of Ugetsu, 1953), winner of the 1953 Venice International Film Festival, and *Saikaku Ichidai Onna* (The Life of Oharu, 1952), a best foreign film prizewinner at Venice in 1952; and Kurosawa's 1954 masterpiece *Shichinin no Samurai* (Seven Samurai). Annual attendance at the country's cinemas reached 1.1 billion in 1958; and Kyoto, with its large film studios, such as Shōchiku, Daiei and Toei, and its more than 60 cinemas, enjoyed a heyday as Japan's own 'cinecity'.

As it did elsewhere in the world, television spurred a rapid drop in the number of cinema-goers in Japan in the high-growth decades of the 1960s and 1970s. Despite falling attendance, Japanese cinema remained a major artistic force: these decades gave the world such landmark works as Ichikawa Kon's *Chushingura* (47 Samurai, 1962), and Kurosawa's *Yōjimbo* (1961).

The decline continued through the 1980s, reinforced by the popularisation of videos in the 1980s, with annual attendance at cinemas bottoming out at just over 100 million. Yet Japan's cinema was far from dead. Kurosawa garnered acclaim worldwide for *Kagemusha* (1980), which shared the Palme d'Or at Cannes, and *Ran* (1985). Imamura Shōhei's heartrending *Narayama Bushiko* (The Ballad of Narayama) won the Grand Prix at Cannes in 1983. Itami Jūzō became perhaps the most widely known Japanese director outside Japan after Kurosawa with such biting satires as *Osōshiki* (The Funeral, 1985), *Tampopo* (Dandelion, 1986) and *Marusa no Onna* (A Taxing Woman, 1988). Ōshima Nagisa, best known for controversial films such as *Ai no Corrida* (In the Realm of the Senses, 1976), scored a critical and popular success with *Senjo no Merry Christmas* (Merry Christmas, Mr. Lawrence) in 1983.

In the 1990s popular interest in Japan seemed to catch up with international attention as attendance rates began to rise once again. In 1997 Japanese directors received top honours at two of the world's three most prestigious film festivals: *Unagi* (Eel), Imamura Shohei's black-humoured look at human nature's dark side won the Palme d'Or in Cannes – making him the only Japanese director to win this award twice – while Kitano Takeshi, originally an actor and comedian, took the Golden Lion in Venice for *Hana-bi*, a tale of life and death, and the violence and honour that links them.

A new generation of directors has also emerged to carry on the tradition, including Koreeda Hirokazu, with *Maboroshi no Hikari* (Wonderful Life) and Kurosawa Kiyoshi *(Cure)*; and Ichikawa Jun, winner of the Best Director's prize at the Montreal Film Festival in 1997 for *Tōkyō Yukyoku* (Tokyo Drugstore).

Anime The term anime, a Japanese word derived from French and English, is used worldwide to refer to Japan's highly sophisticated animated films. Unlike its counterparts in other countries, anime occupies a position very near the forefront of the film industry in Japan. Anime films encompass all genres, from science fiction and action adventure to romance and historical drama, and while anime is supported by three key media: television, original video animation and full-length feature films, it is the stunning animation of the last that has brought anime critical acclaim worldwide.

Unlike its counterparts in many other countries, anime targets all ages and social groups. Anime films include deep explorations of philosophical questions and social issues, humorous entertainment and bizarre fantasies. The films offer breathtakingly realistic visuals, exquisite attention to detail, complex and expressive characters and elaborate plots. Leading directors and voice actors are accorded fame and respect, while characters become popular idols.

Japan's most famous anime genius is Miyazaki Hayao, creative head of Studio Ghibli since 1984. Miyazaki's films include

Kaze no Tani no Nausicaa (Nausicaa of the Valley of the Winds, 1984), *Tonari no To-toro* (My Neighbour Totoro, 1988) and *Majō no Takkyubin* (Kiki's Delivery Service, 1989). During 1997, Miyazaki's *Mononoke-hime* (The Princess Mononoke), a fantasy about a 14th-century princess who fights the destruction of the forests, opened at 250 theatres across Japan, the largest opening in Japanese cinema history. History was made again in 1998 when *Mononoke-hime* broke the Japanese box-office record set by E.T. in 1982. In 1998, the film opened to a tremendous reception in the United States after Disney signed an agreement to release subtitled and dubbed versions of Miyazaki films.

Other leading anime masters who have gained recognition worldwide include Mamoru Oishii, whose 1995 masterpiece *Ghost in the Shell* has become a cult classic in Japan and overseas, and Katsuhiro Otomo, creator of the science-fiction action adventure classic *Akira*.

SOCIETY & CONDUCT

The Japanese are so convinced that they are different from everyone else that it's easy to find yourself agreeing with them. A complex mythology of uniqueness has grown up

Urban Anthropology

Visitors to Japan expecting to find a nation of suit-wearing conformists are often shocked by the sheer variety of subcultures they discover. Indeed, in places like Tokyo's Shibuya or Osaka's Shinsaibashi, ordinary street traffic on a Friday night approaches a kind of gaudy street theatre, and people-watching is half the fun of being there. The following guide delineates some of the more common types that you're likely to encounter in the big cities. Also check out this Web page, *Fashion of the Moment*, part of the Gay Scene Japan Web site for monthly updates and pictures: http://members.tripod.co.jp/GSJ/FASHION2000/fashion_menu.html.

Bosozoku These are motorcycle gangs, who dye their hair and wear bright, flashy clothes. Typically, they'll spend a night loudly revving their motorcycle engines and speeding off tailed by the police, who never catch them. Like *chimpira*, some of the wilder bosozoku go on to become *yakuza*.

Chimpira This is often a *yanqui* who has taken rebellion a step further and hopes to attract the attention of yakuza and be asked to join the gang as a junior yakuza.

Furyou gaijin Foreigners (often misfits in their own country) who have become so taken with being a celebrity in Japan that they never leave, dating a string of *gyaru* and hanging out in Roppongi bars. The word furyou literally means 'no-good' or 'the antithesis of good'.

Ko Gyaru 'Ko' comes from either 'kōkō', the Japanese word for high school, or *ko*, the word for girl/small, while 'gyaru' comes from the English word 'girl/gal'. This is a high-school girl who favours day-glo colours, miniskirts, towering high-heel boots, a dark suntan, blonde hair and, of course, a portable phone. She is sometimes just called a gyaru.

Obattalion This word is derived from the Japanese word 'obaasan' (grandmother) and the English word 'battalion'. Perhaps best translated as 'battle axe', an *obattalion* is an elderly woman known for shouldering her way onto trains and buses, terrorising shop clerks and generally getting her way in any situation.

Office Ladies Also known as OLs, these women may be secretaries but may equally be women who do the same work as their male bosses for half the pay. OLs usually travel in small groups wearing matching uniforms of skirts, white blouses and vests.

Ojōsan This is a young woman, usually a college student or graduate, who is middle class and headed for marriage to a young salaryman. An ojōsan's dress is conservative, with the exception of the occasional miniskirt.

Salarymen These are just what you'd expect: businessmen, always clad in suits, often in matching groups.

around the Japanese, and one of the challenges of discovering Japan for yourself is putting the myths straight.

The Group

One of the most cherished ideas about the Japanese is that the group is more important than the individual. The image of loyal company workers bellowing out the company anthem and attending collective exercise sessions is synonymous with Japan Inc – itself a corporate metaphor.

It's easy to start seeing Japan's business-suited workers as members of a collectivised society that rigorously suppresses individual tendencies. But remember that the Japanese are no less individual than their Western counterparts: they experience the same frustrations and joys as Westerners do, and are just as likely to complain about their work conditions, the way their boss treats them and so on. The difference is that while these individual concerns have a place, they are less likely to be seen as defining.

The tension between group and individual interests has been a rich source of inspiration for Japanese art. Traditional values emphasise conflict between *honne* (the individual's personal views) and *tatemae* (the views that are demanded by the individual's position in

---

Urban Anthropology

Yakuza These are the real thing. They used to stand out, with tight 'punch-perms' and loud suits, but modern yakuza are hardly noticeable, except perhaps for their swagger and black Mercedes with tinted windows.

Yan-mama This word is formed from the English word 'young' or the Japanese 'yan-qui', and 'mama' (mother). A yan-mama is a woman who has married and had children at a very young age (usually high school students) and continues to dress in miniskirts and platform shoes, to the great horror of conservative weekly magazines in Japan.

Yanqui Pronounced 'yankee', a member of this tribe prefers brown or blond hair, sports flashy clothes and has a portable phone permanently glued to his ear. Male yanqui often work in the construction industry, where their penchant for loud clothes is expressed in the brightly coloured *nikka-bokka* pants that they wear (from the English word 'knickerbockers').

Yamamba These girls in their late teens (20 would be considered too old) get their name from a witch-like figure with long white hair who appears in Japanese *mukashi-banashi* (fairly tales). Not only is their hair white, but their make-up (lipstick and eye-shadow) is also white, contrasting with their salon-tanned faces, giving a ghostly appearance. See also the boxed text 'Trends' in the Tokyo chapter.

MICK WELDON

the group). The same conflict is expressed in the terms *ninjō* (human feelings) and *giri* (social obligations). Salaried workers who spend long hours at the office away from the families they love are giving priority to giri over ninjō.

All this is deeply rooted in Japanese history. Until very recently, almost all Japanese lived in small villages, many of them engaged in rice farming. In order to live in harmony and produce a successful harvest, a high degree of cooperation was vital – there was little room for free-thinking individualists. Perhaps more importantly, with so many people packed into so little space, the Japanese learned long ago that the only way to live together was to put the needs of the group before those of the individual.

Men & Women

Traditional Japanese society restricted the woman's role to the home, where as housekeeper she wielded considerable power, overseeing all financial matters, monitoring the children's education and, in some ways, acting as the head of the household. Even in the early Meiji period, however, the ideal was rarely matched by reality: labour shortfalls often resulted in women taking on factory work; even before that, women often worked side by side with men in the fields.

As might be expected, the contemporary situation is complex. There are, of course, those who stick to established roles. They tend to opt for shorter college courses, often at women's colleges, and see education as an asset in the marriage market. Once married, they leave the role of breadwinner to their husbands.

Increasingly, however, Japanese women are choosing to forgo or delay marriage in favour of pursuing their own career ambitions. Of course, changing aspirations do not necessarily translate into changing realities, and Japanese women are still significantly under-represented in upper-management and political positions, but over-represented as office fodder, such as OLs (office ladies). Part of the reason for this is the prevalence of gender discrimination and sexual harassment in Japanese companies. Societal expectations, however, also play a role: Japanese women are forced to choose between having a career and having a family. Not only do most companies refuse to hire women for career-track positions, the majority of Japanese men are simply not interested in having a career woman as a spouse. This makes it very intimidating for a Japanese woman to step out of her traditional gender role and follow a career path.

Although much of this is hidden to the casual visitor, it will be hard to miss certain aspects of the male-female dynamic in Japan. On television shows, for example, the male host invariably has a female sidekick whose job it is to agree with everything he says and laugh at his jokes. This is, of course, relatively benign, and not hugely different from many Western television programs, but darker aspects of the male-female dynamic are out there as well, from the sadistic imagery in Japanese *manga* (comics) to the degrading images of women in the media and the widespread acceptance of all forms of prostitution.

The Japanese & Gaijin

As a foreign visitor to Japan, you are a *gaijin*, literally, an 'outside person'. Some foreigners insist (correctly in fact) that the term *gaikokujin* (literally, 'outside country person') is more polite than the contraction gaijin, but the latter is so widely used that you will be knocking your head against a brick wall if you try to change it.

Away from the big cities it's not unusual to hear whispered exclamations of *gaijin da* ('it's a foreigner!'); even in suburban Tokyo, where gaijin are a dime a dozen, many school children are still unable to resist erupting into giggles at the sight of a foreign face.

Long-term visitors to Japan are prone to develop a love-hate relationship with the Japanese. After initially being overwhelmed by Japanese courtesy, many foreigners who feel that they have been in Japan long enough to deserve to be on a more intimate footing with their hosts come to the conclusion that Japanese politeness and helpfulness mask a morbid ethnocentricity.

Fortunately, most short-term visitors come away with miracle stories of Japanese courtesy. If you approach the Japanese with an open mind and a smile on your face, it's almost certain that you too will be the recipient of countless acts of spontaneous kindness, and this, more than anything else, is one of the great joys of travelling in Japan.

Etiquette

One of the most enduring Western notions about Japan is that of Japanese courtesy and rigid social etiquette. However, with a little sensitivity, there is almost no chance of offending anyone, and the visitor to Japan should rest easy in the knowledge that the Japanese are very forgiving when it comes to the little slip-ups of foreign visitors.

To be sure, many things are different: the Japanese bow and indulge in a ritualised exchange of *meishi* (business cards) when they meet; they exchange their shoes for slippers before entering the home; and social occasions involve sitting on the floor in positions that will put the legs of an ill-bred foreigner to sleep within five minutes. But, overall, most of the complex aspects of Japanese social interaction are functions of the language and only pose problems for the advanced student who's trying to get as close to the culture as possible.

Sitting When visiting a Japanese home or eating in certain types of restaurants, you will be expected to sit on the floor. In very formal situations, this is done by tucking your legs directly beneath you in what is known as the *seza* position. However, in ordinary situations, it is perfectly acceptable to sit in whatever manner is comfortable, as long as you don't point your feet at anyone. Indeed, the Japanese themselves are unlikely to sit in seza pose for very long and are quick to adopt a more comfortable position. If you are unsure of what to do, simply emulate your Japanese hosts.

Bowing & Shaking Hands There is a distinct etiquette to bowing. The general rule is that the deepness of a bow depends on the status (relative to oneself) of the person to

whom one is bowing. Fortunately, no-one expects foreigners to understand this and the polite thing to do when meeting Japanese is to incline your head slightly and perhaps bow very slightly from the waist. Nowadays, of course, many Japanese have taken to shaking hands. Since the practice is still a little unusual, it's probably better not to offer your hand – let the other party take the lead.

Business Cards If you intend to find work in Japan, make sure you get some business cards printed. All introductions and meetings in Japan involve an exchange of business cards – handing out yours to the right people can make things happen. Cards should be exchanged and accepted with some ceremony, studied carefully and referred to often. It's polite to accept a card with two hands. Do not simply stuff a proffered card into your pocket. Also, never write anything on a card you are given.

Gift Giving The exchange of gifts, the return of one kindness with another, is an important part of Japanese social life. If you visit somebody at their home, you should bring them a gift. It needn't be anything big – chocolates, flowers or other items similar to those given as gifts in the West will do. Ideally, bring something from your own country. Gifts used for cementing friendships and for paying off small obligations are usually small and unostentatious. If money is given, it is presented in an envelope.

As a foreigner, it's quite likely that you will sometimes be given gifts 'for your travels'. You may not be able to reciprocate in these situations. The polite thing to do is to refuse a couple of times when the gift is offered. The other party will probably keep pushing as long as you keep refusing. A couple of refusals should be enough to ensure that you will not seem too grasping if you finally make off with the spoils.

Flattery What passes for flattery in the West is often perceived as quite natural in Japan. The Japanese rarely pass up the opportunity to praise each other in company.

Omiyage Obligation

Gifts are the grease that keeps the wheels of Japanese society turning. A gift can serve as a token of appreciation, a sign of respect, a guarantee of continued favour or even a bribe (just think of Japanese politics).

Perhaps the most troublesome and time-consuming gift of all is *omiyage* – a souvenir given to friends, family and colleagues upon return from travel. In most Japanese companies, leaving for a vacation naturally entails a sense of shame, of letting down the team. To make up for this betrayal, an armful of omiyage is required. Of course, shopping for all these gifts can eat up an entire vacation (particularly a Japanese vacation, which usually lasts only a few days anyway).

Ever resourceful, the Japanese have come up with a unique solution to this problem – the train station regional speciality store. These stores are located in the passageways around major city train stations. In the space of a few hundred metres you can pick up crab from Hokkaidō, dolls from Kyūshū and pickled vegetables from Shikoku. Even if everybody knows that their souvenir was picked up at the local train station, the obligation is fulfilled and everybody is happy.

Recently, these stores have sprung up in airports as well, selling souvenir gifts from Japan's favourite international destinations: Hawaii, Disneyworld and Paris.

People have also thought of new ways to make use of gifts purchased at these stores. The story goes that they are commonly used as alibis: after a weekend spent at the local love hotel, a gift purchased at a regional speciality store is face-saving proof that a wayward salaryman was actually on a business trip.

The foreigner who has made an effort to learn a few sentences of Japanese or to get by with chopsticks is likely to receive regular dollops of praise. The correct response to praise is to decline it with something like 'Not at all' *(sono koto wa arimasen)*. Try to reciprocate if you can.

Directness Japanese do not make a virtue of being direct. Indeed, directness is seen as vulgar. The Japanese prefer to feel their way through a situation when dealing with others. There is an expression for this that translates as 'stomach talk' – where both sides tentatively edge around an issue, feeling out the other's point of view until it is clear which direction negotiations can go. This can often result in what for many Westerners is a seemingly interminable toing and froing that only ever seems to yield ambiguous results. But don't be deceived, the Japanese can usually read the situation just as clearly as if both sides were clearly stating their interests.

Try to avoid direct statements that may be seen as confrontational. If someone ventures an opinion, however stupid it may seem, try not to crush it with a 'No, I disagree completely', or something similar. And remember, silence has a very distinct meaning in Japan and it almost never signifies agreement.

Calls of Nature It's not unusual to find men urinating in crowded streets; on the other hand, the public use of handkerchiefs for blowing your nose is definitely frowned upon. The polite thing to do if you have a cold in public is to keep sniffing until you can get to a private place to have a good honk!

Avoiding Offence

Japanese are tolerant of foreigners' customs for the most part; there's little chance of committing any grave faux pas. But there are certain situations where it is important to follow the Japanese example. Shoes should be removed, for example, when entering a Japanese home or entering a *tatami* (woven floor matting) room of any kind, even when entering a change room – Japanese will not make allowances for foreign customs in this case.

Bathing in Japan also conforms to fairly strict rules and you should follow them. Whether it's a Japanese-style bath in a private home, a *sentō* (public bath) or an *onsen* (mineral bath/spa bath), remember that body washing takes place *before* entering the water. Showers or taps and plastic tubs are provided for this purpose. Baths and onsen are for soaking in *after* you have washed.

As in other parts of Asia, the respectful way to indicate that someone should approach you is to wave your fingers with the palm downwards.

Japanese don't eat food in the street unless there are seats provided for them to sit on while they do so. Ice creams are an exception to this rule. It's up to you whether you want to abide by this custom: no-one's going to be particularly upset if they see you wandering down the street munching on a Big Mac.

Meeting the Japanese

In general, it is quite easy to meet with the Japanese, at least on a superficial basis. You'll find that Japanese are very curious about other countries and people and are keenly interested in how Japan is perceived by outsiders. By far the best place to meet Japanese is in an *izakaya* (Japanese pub/ eatery). Here, after a few drinks, you'll find people just about queuing up to talk to you. Indeed, you might even find the attention cloying after a while. If you prefer a more formal introduction, you can also try the Home Visit System (see later in this section).

Shyness The Japanese are a relatively shy lot, especially when it comes to dealing with foreigners. There are two main reasons for this. Firstly, Japanese tend to speak limited English and are deathly afraid of making mistakes when speaking the language. Secondly, most Japanese have had precious little interaction with foreigners and simply aren't sure how to handle the situation. Thus, when you deal with Japanese you should always speak slowly and clearly and approach everyone with a smile on your face.

Home Visit System The Home Visit System is publicised in JNTO (Japan National Tourist Organization) pamphlets and gives visitors to some of Japan's larger cities the opportunity to visit a Japanese family in their home. Visits take place in the evening and, while dinner is usually not served, the hosts will often provide tea and sweets. It is polite to bring a small gift with you when you visit to show your appreciation of your hosts' thoughtfulness and hospitality. Contact the nearest JNTO office for details (see Tourist Offices in the Facts for the Visitor chapter).

RELIGION

In many respects, the term 'religion' can be misleading for Westerners when it is applied to either Japan or China. In the West and in Islamic culture, religion is connected with the idea of an exclusive faith. Religions in Japan, for the most part, are not exclusive of each other.

Shintō (the native 'religion' of Japan), Buddhism, Confucianism and even Christianity all play a role in contemporary Japanese social life, and are defining in some way of the Japanese world view. If you are sceptical of the inclusion of Christianity, you need only attend a Japanese wedding to find certain Christian elements mingling happily with more traditional practices.

Shintō and Buddhism, the major religions in Japan, have coexisted for many centuries in relative harmony. A notable break in this amicable relationship occurred during the Meiji period, when nationalist fervour introduced 'State Shintō' as the state religion. Severe restraints were placed on Buddhism, which came under attack from nationalist zealots. The balance was restored with the abolition of State Shintō after the Allied occupation in 1945.

Shintō

Shintō is an indigenous religion that acquired its name, 'the way of the gods', to distinguish it from Buddhism, a later import. It seems to have grown out of an awe for manifestations of nature that included the sun, water, rock formations, trees and even sounds. All such manifestations were felt to have their *kami* (god), a belief that led to a complex pantheon of gods and a rich mythology. In particularly sacred spots, shrines were erected. Important to Shintō is the concept of purification before entering such sacred domains.

Shintō is a religion without a founder and without a canon; indeed it is not a religion in the sense that you could convert to it. It encompasses myths of the origin of Japan and the Japanese people, beliefs and practices in local communities and the highly structured rituals associated with the imperial family. Shintō tradition held that the emperor was a kami, or divine being, until 1945, when the emperor was officially disabused of his divine status under the American occupation of Japan.

Japanese Myths The chief sources for Japanese myths are the *Kojiki* (Records of Ancient Matters), and the *Nihon Shoki* (Chronicle of Japan). The myths contained in these 8th-century works have much in common with those of neighbouring countries and the South-East Asian and Mongolian area.

The creation of Japan is ascribed to Izanagi-no-Mikoto and Izanami-no-Mikoto. Standing on the Floating Bridge of Heaven, they dipped the Heavenly Jewelled Spear into the ocean. Brine dripped from the spear and created the island of Onogoro-jima, where the two were married. Izanami gave birth to the islands of Japan and to its deities.

Izanami gave birth to 35 gods, but in giving birth to the fire deity she was burned and died. Izanagi ventured into the Land of the Dead (Yomi-no-Kuni). There he found Izanami, horribly transfigured by death, who joined with the Eighty Ugly Females to pursue her former mate. He escaped only by blocking the entry to Yomi with a huge boulder, thus separating the lands of the living and the dead. On his return to the Land of the Living, Izanami purified himself in a stream. This act created more deities, the three most important being Amaterasu Ōmikami (the sun goddess, from whom the imperial family later claimed descent),

Tsukuyomi-no-Mikoto (the Moon God) and Susano-ō-no-Mikoto (the God of Oceans).

According to the legend, Amaterasu ruled the High Plain of Heaven and Susano-ō was given charge of the oceans. Susano-ō missed his mother and stormed around causing general destruction for which he was exiled by his father. In a fit of pique, Susano-ō visited his sister and they had such a quarrel that Amaterasu rushed off to hide in a cave, plunging the world into darkness. All the gods assembled round the cave entrance to find a way to make Amaterasu return.

Finally, Ame-no-Uzume-no-Mikoto performed a ribald dance causing much laughter among the onlookers. Amaterasu, attracted by the commotion, peeped out of her cave and was quickly hauled out to restore light to the High Plain of Heaven. The site of these events is near Takachihō in Kyūshū. Susano-ō was deprived of his beard, toenails and fingernails and banished to earth, where he landed in Korea before heading to Izumo in Japan.

Okuninushi, a descendant of Susano-ō, took control of Japan but passed it on to Ninigi, a grandson of Amaterasu. Myth merges into history with Ninigi's grandson, Jimmu, who became the first emperor of Japan. Amaterasu is credited with having supplied the emperor with the Three Treasures (mirror, sword and beads) – symbols of the emperor's authority.

Shintō & Buddhism With the introduction of Buddhism in the 6th century, the Japanese formed a connection between the religions by considering Buddha as a kami from neighbouring China. In the 8th century the kami were included in Buddhist temples as protectors of the Buddhas. Assimilation progressed with the belief that kami, like human beings, were subject to the suffering of rebirth and similarly in need of Buddhist intercession to achieve liberation from this cycle. Buddhist temples were built close to Shintō shrines and Buddhist sutras were recited for the kami. Later, the kami were considered incarnations of Bodhisattvas (Buddhas who delay liberation to help others). Buddhist statues were included on

Visiting a Shrine

Entering a Japanese shrine can be a bewildering experience for travellers. In order to make the most of the experience, follow these guidelines and do as the Japanese do.

Just past the *torii* (shrine gate), you'll find a *chōzuya* (trough of water) with long-handled ladles perched on a *hishaku* (rack) above. This is for purifying yourself before entering the sacred precincts of the shrine. Some Japanese do forgo this ritual and head directly for the main hall. If you choose to purify yourself, however, take a ladle, fill it with fresh water from the spigot, pour some over one hand, transfer the spoon and pour water over the other hand, then pour a little water into a cupped hand and rinse your mouth, spitting the water onto the ground beside the trough, *not* into the trough.

Next, head to the *haiden* (hall of worship), which sits in front of the *honden* (main hall) enshrining the *kami* (god of the shrine). Here you'll find a thick rope hanging from a gong, in front of which is an offerings box. Toss a coin into the box, ring the gong by pulling on the rope (to summon the deity), pray, then clap your hands twice, bow and then back away from the shrine. Some Japanese believe that a ¥5 coin is the best for an offering at a temple or shrine, and that the luck engendered by the offering of a ¥10 coin will come further in the future (since 10 can be pronounced *tō* in Japanese, which can mean 'far').

If photography is forbidden at a shrine, it will be posted as such; otherwise, it is permitted and you should simply use your discretion when taking photos.

Shintō altars or statues of kami were made to represent Buddhist priests.

State Shintō There had been something of a revival of interest in Shintō during the Edo period, particularly by neo-Confucian scholars interested in Japan's past. Some of them called for a return to imperial rule, with Shintō as the state religion. This is exactly what happened with the advent of the Meiji Restoration.

During the Meiji period, Shintō shrines were supported by the government, Shintō doctrines were taught in school and the religion became increasingly nationalistic. It was a relatively brief affair. After Japan's WWII defeat, the Allied forces dismantled the mechanisms of State Shintō and forced the emperor to refute his divine status, a principal tenet of Shintō.

The main training centres for priests are Kokugakuin University in Tokyo and Kōgakukan University in Ise. Priests are allowed to marry, and most of the posts are commonly patrilineal.

Shintō Rites & Festivals These events are important components of Japanese life. For newborn children the first shrine visit occurs on the 30th or 100th day after birth. On 15 November, the Shichigosan rite is celebrated by taking children aged *shichi* (seven), *go* (five) and *san* (three) to the shrine to be blessed. Seijin-no-hi, the day of adulthood, is celebrated on the second Sunday in January by young people who have reached the age of 20.

Virtually all marriages are performed according to Shintō ritual by taking a vow before the kami. Funerals, however, are almost always Buddhist. Both religions coexist in traditional Japanese homes, where there are two altars: a Shintō *kamidana* (a shelf shrine) and a Buddhist *butsudan* (Buddha stand).

Shintō also plays a role in professional and daily life. A new car can be blessed for accident-free driving, a purification rite is often held for a building site or the shell of a new building, and completed buildings are similarly blessed. One of the most common purification rites is *oharai*, when the priest waves a wand to which are attached thin strips of paper.

Amulets are popular purchases at Japan's shrines. Special talismans (*omamori*) are purchased at shrines to ensure good luck or ward off evil – taxi-drivers often have a 'traffic-safety' with one dangling from the rear-view mirror. Votive plaques (ema) made of wood with a picture on one side and a blank space on the other are also common. On the blank side visitors write a wish: a hope for success in exams, luck in finding a sweetheart or safe delivery of a healthy child. Dozens of these plaques can be seen attached to boards in the shrine precincts.

Fortunes (omikuji) are selected by drawing a bamboo stick at random from a box and picking out a fortune slip according to the number indicated on the stick. Luck is classified as dai-kichi (great good fortune); kichi (good fortune); shō-kichi (middling good fortune); and kyō (bad luck). If you like the fortune slip you've been given, you can take it home. If you've drawn bad luck, you can tie it to the branch of a tree in the shrine grounds – presumably some other force can then worry about it.

The kannushi (chief priest) of the shrine is responsible for religious rites and the administration of the shrine. The priests dress in blue and white; on special occasions they don more ornate clothes and wear an eboshi (a black cap with a protruding, folded tip). The miko (shrine maidens) dress in red and white. The ceremonial kagura dances performed by the miko can be traced back to shamanistic trances.

Shintō matsuri (festivals) occur on an annual or occasional basis and are classed as grand, middle-size or minor. See the special colour section 'Matsuri Magic' for more information on festivals.

Buddhism

Japanese Buddhism has evolved in a unique fashion with some decisive differences from other forms of the religion.

Origins of Buddhism The founder of Buddhism, Siddhartha Gautama, was born around 563 BC at Lumbini on the border of present-day Nepal and India.

In his 20s, Prince Siddhartha left his wife and newborn son to follow the path of an ascetic. Despite studying under several masters, he remained dissatisfied and spent another six years undergoing the most severe austerities. During this period he gave

a graphic account of himself: 'Because of so little nourishment, all my bones became like some withered creepers with knotted joints; my buttocks like a buffalo's hoof; my backbone protruding like a string of balls ...' Realising that this was not the right path for him, he gave up fasting and decided to follow his own path to enlightenment. He sat cross-legged under a Bodhi tree at Bodhgaya and went into deep meditation for 49 days. During the night of the full moon in May, at the age of 35, he became 'the enlightened one' or 'awakened one'.

Shortly afterwards, Buddha delivered his first sermon, 'Setting in Motion the Wheel of Truth', at Deer Park near Sarnath. Then, as the number of his followers grew, he founded a monastic community and codified the principles according to which the monks should live. The Buddha continued to preach and travel for 45 years until his death at the age of 80 in 483 BC. To his followers, Buddha was also known as Sakyamuni (the sage of the Sakya clan, or 'Shaka' in Japanese). Buddhists believe that he is one of the many Buddhas who appeared in the past and that more will appear in the future.

Approximately 140 years after Buddha's death, the Buddhist community diverged into two schools: Hinayana (the Lesser Vehicle) and Mahayana (the Greater Vehicle). The essential difference between the two was that Hinayana supported those who strove for the salvation of the individual, whereas Mahayana supported those who strove for the salvation of all beings. Hinayana prospered in South India and later spread to Sri Lanka, Burma, Thailand, Cambodia, Indonesia and Malaysia. Mahayana spread to inner Asia, Mongolia, Siberia, Japan, China and Tibet.

The basis of Buddhism is that all suffering in life comes from desire. Suppression of desire will eventually lead to a state of nirvana where desire is extinct and we are free from its delusion.

Buddha, who was not a god and did not even claim to be the only enlightened one, taught that the way to nirvana was to follow an eight-fold path of right behaviour and thinking.

Zen Buddhism

Japan's most famous brand of Buddhism actually arose in China, though its origins lie in India. The word zen is the Japanese reading of the Chinese ch'an (from Sanskrit dhyana). Legend has it that Bodidharma, a 6th-century Indian monk, introduced Zen to China, but most historians credit this to Huineng (638–713), a Chinese monk.

It took another 200 years for Zen to take root in Japan. It did so in two major schools: Rinzai and Sōtō. The differences between the schools are not easily explained, but at a simple level the Sōtō school places more emphasis on zazen (seated meditation), and the Rinzai school on kōan (riddles). The object of meditative practice for both schools is satori (enlightenment).

The practice of zazen has its roots in Indian yoga. Its posture is the lotus position: the legs are crossed and tucked beneath the sitter, the back ramrod straight, the breathing rhythmical. The idea is to block out all sensation and empty the mind of thought – much harder than you might imagine.

A kōan is a riddle that lacks a rational answer. Most are set pieces that owe their existence to the early evolution of Zen Buddhism in China. In the course of meditating on an insoluble problem, the mind eventually returns to a form of primal consciousness. The most famous kōan was created by the Japanese monk Hakuin: 'What is the sound of one hand clapping?' Fans of The Simpsons will already know the answer to this one, and are already enlightened.

Although Zen emphasises the direct, intuitive approach to enlightenment rather than rational analysis, there are dozens of books available on the subject. Two favourites are Zen & Japanese Culture by DT Suzuki and Zen Flesh, Zen Bones compiled by Paul Reps.

Development of Buddhism in Japan

Buddhism was introduced to Japan via Korea in the 6th century. Shōtoku Taishi, acknowledged as the 'father of Japanese Buddhism', drew heavily on Chinese culture to form a centralised state and gave official recognition to Buddhism by constructing temples in and around the capital. Horyū-ji, close to Nara, is the most celebrated temple in Japan from this period.

Nara Period The establishment of the first permanent capital at Heijō-kyō (present-day Nara) in AD 710 also marked the consolidation of Buddhism and Chinese culture in Japan.

In 741, Emperor Shōmu issued a decree for a network of state temples (kokubun-ji) to be established in each province. The centrepiece of this network was Tōdai-ji, with its gigantic Vairocana Buddha (Daibutsu).

Nara Buddhism revolved around six schools – Ritsu, Jōjitsu, Kusha, Sanron, Hossō and Kegon – which covered the whole range of Buddhist thought as received from China. Three of these schools have continued to this day: the Kegon school, based at the Tōdai-ji; the Hossō school, based at the Kōfuku-ji and Yakushi-ji; and the Ritsu school, based at the Tōshōdai-ji.

Heian Period In 794, the capital was moved from Nara to Heian-kyō (present-day Kyoto). During the Heian period, political power drifted away from centralised government into the hands of aristocrats and their clans, who became a major source of Buddhist support.

The new schools, which introduced Mikkyō (Esoteric Buddhism) from China, were founded by separate leaders on sacred mountains away from the orthodox pressures of the Nara schools.

The Tendai school (derived from a Chinese school on Mt Tian-tai in China) was founded by Saichō (762–822), also known as Dengyō Daishi, who established a base at the Enryaku-ji on Hiei-zan, near Kyoto.

Saichō travelled to Mt Tian-tai in China, where he studied meditation and the Lotus Sutra. On his return, he expanded his studies to include Zen meditation and Tantric ritual. The Tendai school was only officially recognised a few days after his death, but the

Enryaku-ji developed into one of Japan's key Buddhist centres and was the source of all the important schools (Pure Land, Zen and Nichiren) in the following Kamakura period.

The Shingon school (derived from the Chinese term for 'mantra') was established by Kūkai (714–835), often referred to as Kōbō Daishi, at the Kongōbu-ji on Kōyasan and the Tō-ji in Kyoto.

Kūkai trained for government service but decided at the age of 18 to switch his studies from Confucianism and Taoism to Buddhism. He travelled as part of a mission to Chang-an (present-day Xi'an) in China, where he immersed himself in Esoteric Buddhism. On his return, he made a broad impact on cultural life, not only spreading and sponsoring the study of Mikkyō, but also compiling the first Chinese-Japanese dictionary and the hiragana syllabary, which made it much easier for Japanese to put their language into writing.

During this period, assimilation with Shintō continued. Many *jingū-ji* (shrine temples) were built for Buddhist rituals in the grounds of Shintō shrines. Theories were propounded that held the Shintō kami to be manifestations of Buddhas or Bodhisattvas. The collapse of law and order during these times inspired a general feeling of pessimism in society and encouraged belief in the Mappō, or End of the Law, theory, which predicted an age of darkness with a decline in Buddhist religion. This set the stage for subsequent Buddhist schools to introduce the notion of Buddhist saviour figures such as Amida.

Kamakura Period In this period, marked by savage clan warfare and the transfer of the capital to Kamakura, three schools emerged from Tendai tradition.

The Jōdo (Pure Land) school, founded by Hōnen (1133–1212), shunned scholasticism in favour of the Nembutsu, a simple prayer that required the believer to recite '*namu amida butsu*' ('Hail Amida Buddha'), as a path to salvation. This 'no-frills' approach – easy to practise and easy to understand – was popular with the common folk.

Shinran (1173–1262), a disciple of Hōnen, took a more radical step with his master's teaching and broke away to form the Jōdo Shin (True Pure Land) school. The core belief of this school considered that Amida had *already* saved everyone and hence to recite the Nembutsu was an expression of gratitude, not a petition for salvation.

The Nichiren school bears the name of its founder, Nichiren (1222–82), a fiery character who spurned traditional teachings to embrace the Lotus Sutra as the 'right' teaching. Followers learned to recite '*namu myōhō rengekyō*' ('Hail the Miraculous Law of the Lotus Sutra'). Nichiren's strident demands for religious reform of government caused antagonism all round and he was frequently booted into exile.

The Nichiren school increased its influence in later centuries; the now famous Hokke-ikki uprising in the 15th century was led by Nichiren adherents. Many of the new religious movements in present-day Japan – Sōka Gakkai, for example – can be linked to Nichiren.

Later Developments During the Tokugawa period (1600–1867), Buddhism was consolidated as a state institution. When the shogunate banned Christianity, a parallel regulation rigidly required every Japanese to become a certified member of the local temple.

During the Meiji period, Shintō was given priority and separated from Buddhism, which suffered a backlash of resentment. Today, Buddhism prospers in Japan both in the form of traditional schools and in a variety of new movements.

Buddhist Gods There are dozens of gods in the Japanese Buddhist pantheon. Images vary from temple to temple, depending on the religious schools or period of construction, but three of the most common images are those of Shaka (in Sanskrit 'Sakyamuni'), the Historical Buddha; Amida (in Sanskrit 'Amitabha'), the Buddha of the Western Paradise; and Miroku (in Sanskrit 'Maitreya'), the Buddha of the Future.

Kannon (in Sanskrit 'Avalokitesvara') is the 'one who hears their cries' and is available in no less than 33 different versions, including the goddess of mercy, a female form popular with expectant mothers. When Christianity was banned, Japanese believers ingeniously kept faith with the Holy Virgin by creating a clone 'Maria Kannon'.

Jizō is often depicted as a monk with a staff in one hand and a jewel in the other. Pieces of clothing or red bibs draped around Jizō figures are an attempt to cover the souls of dead children. According to legend, this patron of travellers, children and expectant mothers helps the souls of dead children perform their task of building walls of pebbles on the banks of Sai-no-kawara, the river of the underworld. Believers place stones on or around Jizō statues as additional help.

For information on Buddhist temples see the Traditional Architecture section in the special 'Japanese Arts' section.

Shugendō

This somewhat offbeat Buddhist school incorporates ancient Shamanistic rites, Shintō beliefs and ascetic Buddhist traditions. The founder was En-no-Gyōja, to whom legendary powers of exorcism and magic are ascribed. He is credited with the enlightenment of kami, converting them to gongen (manifestations of Buddhas). Practitioners of Shugendō, called yamabushi (mountain priests), train both body and spirit with arduous exercises in the mountains.

Until the Meiji era, many of Japan's mountains were the domain of yamabushi who proved popular with the locals for their skills in sorcery and exorcism. During the Meiji era, Shintō was elevated to a state religion and Shugendō was barred as being culturally debased. Today, yamabushi are more common on tourist brochures than in the flesh, but Shugendō survives on mountains such as Dewa Sanzan in Yamagata-ken and Omine-san in Nara-ken.

Confucianism

Although Confucianism is essentially a code of ethics, it has exerted a strong enough influence to become part of Japanese religion. Confucianism entered Japan via Korea in the 5th century. To regulate social behaviour, Confucius took the family unit as his starting point and stressed the importance of the five

human relationships: master and subject, father and son, elder brother and younger brother, husband and wife, friend and friend.

The strict observance of this social 'pecking order', radiating from individual families to encompass the whole of society, has evolved over centuries to become a core concept in Japanese life. The influence of Confucianism can be seen in such disparate examples as the absolute loyalty demanded in bushidō (the way of the warrior), the extreme allegiance to the emperor in WWII, the low status of women, and the hierarchical ties in modern Japanese companies.

Folklore & Gods

Japan has a curious medley of folk gods. Common ones include the following:

Benzaiten The goddess of art is skilled in eloquence, music, literature and wisdom. She holds a biwa (Japanese lute) and is often escorted by a sea snake.

Bishamon The god of war wears a helmet and a suit of armour and brandishes a spear. As a protector of Buddhism, he can be seen carrying a pagoda.

Daikoku The god of wealth has a bag full of treasures slung over his left shoulder and a lucky mallet in his right hand.

Ebisu The patron of seafarers and a symbol for prosperity in business, Ebisu carries a fishing rod with a large red sea bream dangling on the line and can be recognised by his beaming, bearded face.

Fukurokuju This god looks after wealth and longevity. He has a bald, dome-shaped head, and a dumpy body and wears long, flowing robes.

Jurojin This god also covers longevity. He sports a distinguished white beard and holds a cane to which is attached a scroll listing the life span of all living beings.

Hotei The god of happiness is instantly recognisable (in Japan and elsewhere in Asia) by his large paunch and Cheshire-cat grin. Originally a Chinese beggar-priest, he is the only god in this group whose antecedents can be traced to a human being. His bulging bag provides for the needy and is never empty.

Shichifuku-jin The Seven Gods of Luck are a happy band of well-wishers plucked from Indian, Chinese and Japanese sources. Their images are popular at New Year, when they are, more often than not, depicted as a group on a takarabune (treasure ship).

A variety of fabulous creatures inhabit Japanese folklore and crop up regularly in shops, festivals and shrines:

Kappa These are amphibious creatures about the size of a 12- or 13-year-old boy. They have webbed hands and feet. They have a reputation for mischief, such as dragging horses into rivers or stealing cucumbers. The source of their power is a depression on top of their heads that must always contain water. A crafty method to outwit a kappa is to bow to it. When the kappa – Japanese to the core – bows back, it empties the water from its head and loses its power. The alternatives are not pleasant. Kappa are said to enjoy ripping out their victim's liver through the anus!

Kitsune This creature is a fox, but for the Japanese it also has strong connections with the supernatural and is worshipped in Japan at over 30,000 Inari shrines as the messenger of the harvest god. The shrine, Fushimi Inari Taisha near Kyoto is the largest of its kind and is crammed with fox statues.

Maneki-neko The Beckoning Cat is a very common sight outside shops or restaurants. The raised left paw attracts customers – and their money.

Tanuki This creature is often translated as 'badger', but bears a closer resemblance to a North American raccoon. Like the fox, the tanuki is thought of as a mischievous creature and is credited with supernatural powers, but it is more a figure of fun than the fox. Statues usually depict the tanuki in an upright position with straw headgear, clasping a bottle of sake.

Tengu The mountain goblin has a capricious nature – sometimes abducting children, sometimes returning those who were missing. Its unmistakable feature is a long nose, like that of a proboscis monkey.

Christianity

Portuguese missionaries introduced Christianity to Japan in the 16th century. In 1549 Francis Xavier landed at Kagoshima in Kyūshū. At first, the daimyō seemed eager to convert, together with their subjects. However, the motivation was probably less faith and more an interest in gaining trade advantages.

The initial tolerance shown by Oda Nobunaga was soon reversed by his successor, Toyotomi Hideyoshi, who considered the Jesuits a colonial threat. The religion

was banned in 1587 and 26 Christians were crucified in Nagasaki 10 years later. After expelling the remaining missionaries in 1614, Japan closed itself off from the outside world for several centuries. During this time a small number of Christians kept their faith active as a type of 'back-room Buddhism'. Christian missions were allowed back at an early stage during the Meiji era to build churches and found hospitals and schools, many of which still exist.

Despite these efforts, Christianity has not met with wide acceptance among the Japanese, who tend to feel more at home with Shintō and Buddhism. There are very few Christians in Japan – possibly one million.

New Religions

A variety of new religions has taken root in Japan. They cover a wide range of beliefs, from founder cults to faith healing. Easily the largest of these new religions is Sōka Gakkai (Creative Education Society). Founded in the 1930s, it follows Nichiren's teachings and boasts over 20 million followers. (Kōmeito, which is now part of the ruling coalition in Japan, was founded in 1964 as a political offshoot of Sōka Gakkai, but now tends to play down the association).

More recently, Aum Shinrikyō drew attention to the existence of cults in Japan with its 1995 subway gas attack in downtown Tokyo. Since the attack, cult members have been hounded out of one community after another but have stubbornly refused to disband. Another new religious group, Hō-No-Hana (The Flower of the Way), recently made headlines in Japan for bilking millions of yen from a group of housewives by promising to deliver miracle cures for a variety of illnesses.

LANGUAGE

Japanese is the language spoken across almost all of Japan. The only exceptions are some elderly residents of the Nansei-shotō (around Okinawa), some of whom may still speak the old language of the Ryūkyū Kingdom, and some elderly members of the Ainu community who may still speak and understand Ainu (although Japanese is the lingua franca for almost all modern Ainu).

While standard Japanese, or *hyōjungo,* is understood by almost all Japanese, whether educated or not, many Japanese, particularly in rural areas speak strong local dialects (known as *ben,* as in the famous dialect of Kansai, *kansai-ben*). These dialects can be quite impenetrable, even for Japanese from other parts of the country. Luckily, you can always get your point across in hyōjungo (understanding the answer may be another issue).

For a complete selection of useful Japanese words and phrases, including Japanese script, see the Language chapter. The 'Japanese Cuisine & Menu Glossary' special section also has a listing of common menu items. For a useful Japanese train glossary, see the boxed text in the Getting Around chapter.

Facts for the Visitor

HIGHLIGHTS

With the notable exception of Mt Fuji (Fuji-san), Japan has few sights known the world over. Nonetheless, the country is overflowing with first-class attractions. Discovering them for the first time is half the fun of travelling in Japan.

Castles

Japan has an abundance of castles (*shiro, jō*), though few of them are originals; however, even the copies represent a small proportion of the number that once dotted the country. In the 17th century, the Tokugawa shogunate decreed that each domain maintain just one castle, which led to the destruction of many minor castles. In 1873, the sixth year of the Meiji era, the government, in a paroxysm of anti-feudalism, ordered that another 144 castles be destroyed, leaving 39 originals. By the end of WWII this had further been reduced to 12. By general agreement, the greatest survivor is Himeji-jō, an easy day trip from Kyoto.

Combining elegance and impregnability the castle soars above the Himeji plain, earning it the name 'White Egret'. Running a close second place is Shikoku's Matsuyama-jō.

Matsumoto-jō in Central Honshū is another fascinating castle that has withstood the march of the years remarkably well. Hirosaki-jō (Northern Honshū) is not quite in the same league as the others, but it does have the added attraction of well-preserved *samurai* quarters.

Conveniently near Kyoto are the pretty lakeside Hikone-jō and the small Inuyama-jō. Elsewhere, Matsue-jō has a fine setting and some interesting nearby streets. Bitchū-Matsuyama, in Takahashi, represents an earlier era; it's hidden away on a high hilltop rather than standing proudly at the centre of its town.

In Kyūshū, Kumamoto-jō is a modern reconstruction, but its design is very interesting and the museum has informative displays about castle construction. Edo-jō was once the largest castle in the world; today its huge moats and walls surround the Tokyo Imperial Palace.

Gardens

Japan is famed for its beautiful gardens, and whether they are the larger Edo 'stroll gardens' or the small contemplative Zen gardens, there is always exquisite attention to detail. Gardens are known as *-en*, *-kōen*, or *-teien*.

The Japanese love to rate things: the 'big three' in the garden category are Kairaku-en (Kansai), Kenroku-en (Central Honshū) and Kōraku-en (Western Honshū). Not all visitors are likely to agree with the official listings; Kairaku-en, for example, simply has lots of lawn.

Kyoto has almost too many gardens to mention, including gardens that virtually define the rock garden and the Zen *kare-sansui* (dry-landscape garden). Among the best of the smaller Zen gardens outside Kyoto are the beautiful temple gardens of Kōmyō-ji at Dazaifu, Jōei-ji in Yamaguchi and Raikyū-ji at Takahashi.

Other large gardens include Ritsurin-kōen in Shikoku; Suizenji-kōen in Kumamoto (Kyūshū), with its miniature Mt Fuji; and Iso-teien in Kagoshima (Kyūshū), with a real smoking volcano as 'borrowed scenery'. Hikone in Kansai has the very beautiful Genkyū-en and one of Japan's few surviving original castles. The Sankei-en in Yokohama is also very fine.

Scenery & Natural Attractions

Expressways, railways, factories, skyscrapers and a teeming population would scarcely seem to leave room for natural attractions. Yet, despite its population density, Japan is a mountainous country with many areas of great natural beauty.

Just as the Japanese rate the three best gardens, they also rate the three best views. These are the 'floating' *torii* (Shintō shrine gates) of the island, Miya-jima; the long sandspit of Amanohashidate (Bridge to Heaven) in Western Honshū; and the bay, Matsushima-wan in Northern Honshū, with its pine-covered islands. The misty, island-dotted waters of the Inland Sea would also have to be one of the most beautiful sights.

Some of the most spectacular mountain scenery in Japan is found in Nagano-ken (Kamikōchi and Hakuba) and northern Gifu-ken (Takayama and the Shōkawa-dani region).

Mt Fuji, the much-climbed symbol of Japan, can actually seem like Tokyo's busiest station at rush hour when you're climbing it, but from a distance it's as beautiful as it has ever been. Bandai-san and its lakes in Northern Honshū offer more superb scenery.

Hokkaidō, the second-largest but least densely populated island, offers wonderful mountain scenery around the lake areas of Mashu-ko, in the Daisetsuzan National Park, and Tōya-ko and Shikotsu-ko in the west. The Shiretoko-hantō and Shakotan-hantō peninsulas have fine coastal scenery. If you can fit in an extra few days on Hokkaidō, the islands of Rishiri tō and Rebun-tō in the north offer superb hiking.

Kyūshū has some wonderful volcanic scenery, particularly in the immense caldera of Aso-san, the bleak, volcano-studded Kirishima National Park, and rumbling Sakurajima near Kagoshima.

At the extreme western end of the country, the island, Iriomote-jima, has dense jungle and good scuba diving.

Historical Japan

Feudal castles are not the only symbols of 'old Japan' that have disappeared over the years. The destruction caused during WWII, the Japanese penchant for knocking down the old and putting up the new, plus the often flimsy and inflammable construction of so many old Japanese buildings, have combined to leave few reminders of an earlier Japan. However, some highlights remain.

Hakodate in Hokkaidō is a fascinating old port town with some very interesting Western-style Meiji-era buildings. Similar buildings can be seen in the port towns of Nagasaki and Kōbe. Hakone, near Tokyo, was a post town (way station) on the Tōkaidō Highway and preserves a short stretch of that road. Tsumago and Magome also maintain a post town atmosphere.

Takayama, north of Nagoya in Central Honshū, has many fine old buildings and a farmhouse village (Hida Folk Village) consisting of more than a dozen houses of the *gasshō-zukuri* (literally 'hands in prayer') architectural style. The houses were all dismantled and reconstructed as a village after a huge dam was built in the region. Similar farmhouse villages can be found at Kawasaki and Takamatsu (Shikoku). Kanazawa (Central Honshū), which escaped bombing during WWII, is another town with many reminders of an earlier era.

Kurashiki (Western Honshū) is famed for its canal district and old warehouses, many of which have been converted into museums. Further along the San-yō coast is Tomo-no-Ura, a small port, easily explored by bicycle. On the opposite San-in coast, the town of Hagi exemplifies the kind of contradiction so typical of Japan. While the town is famous for its role in the ending of the Edo period and the beginning of the Meiji Restoration, it is also famous for its finely preserved Edo-period buildings. Uchiko in Shikoku has a single old street, Yōkaichi, where wealthy wax merchants once lived. The small town of Chiran, near Kagoshima in southern Kyūshū, has an old street of well-preserved samurai buildings and a *kamikaze* (literally 'divine wind') museum.

Shrines

Shrines are known as *jinja*, though you will also come across the terms *jingū, taisha* and *gū*. Shrines are the focus of Japan's indigenous Shintō faith and appear in many styles, but there are clues that distinguish shrines from Buddhist temples. Generally, a red torii (or perhaps a series of them) marks the entrance to a shrine; inside the entrance you will find a *temizuya* – a small pavilion with a basin for ritual purification of the hands and mouth.

The three great shrine centres are Ise, Nikkō and Izumo. Ise has the imperial shrine to Amaterasu, the mythical ancestor of the Japanese imperial line. Nikkō has the shrine to Tokugawa Ieyasu, founder of the Tokugawa shogunate. Izumo has the largest and, it is claimed, oldest shrine hall in Japan. Kyoto is, of course, particularly well-endowed with impressive shrines.

Other important or interesting shrines include Meiji-jingū in Tokyo, the Itsukushima-jinja on Miya-jima, with its much photographed floating torii, and the hilltop Kotohira-gū in Shikoku. Kyūshū has two particularly interesting shrines. The Tenmangū at Dazaifu near Fukuoka is dedicated to the legendary Sugawara-no-Michizane, who was exiled there from Kyoto. Just outside Takachiho the Ama-no-Iwato-jinja has the very cave where Amaterasu once hid. In Northern Honshū, you can see shrines frequented by worshippers of Shugendō in the spectacular surroundings of the sacred mountains of Dewa Sanzan, near Tsuruoka.

Temples

Temples are known as *ji*, though you will also come across the terms *dera*, *tera*, *dō* and *in*. The most important temples in Japan are found in Kyoto and Nara and the surrounding Kansai region.

Kyoto highlights include Daitoku-ji, with its gardens; the ancient Kiyomizu-dera with its superb hillside site; the 13th-century Sanjūsangen-dō and the Tō-ji, founded by the Buddhist saint Kōbō Daishi. Nara has the fine Tōshōdai-ji and the Tōdai-ji, with its Daibutsu (Great Buddha). Also in the Kansai region is Kōbō Daishi's mountain-top Kōya-san, the wonderful Hōryū-ji and the Byōdō-in in Uji, one of the most famous buildings in Japan.

Close to Tokyo, Kamakura offers some of the best temple tramping in Japan; Kō-toku-in has the best known Daibutsu statue in Japan. Although the 88 temples in Kōbō Daishi's circuit of Shikoku have no great significance individually; taken together they represent the most important pilgrimage route in Japan. The Kōsan-ji, at nearby Setoda in the Inland Sea, is a Disneyland of

temples – all modern reproductions of important temples crammed together in one location. Onomichi, on the Honshū coast near Setoda, has an interesting temple walk.

Modern Japan

Ancient temples and shrines, feudal castles and Zen gardens are all very well, but Japan is also the land of *pachinko* (pinball gambling game) parlours, love hotels, robot-operated production lines and multi storey buildings filled with nothing but bars. It's also the only place in the world to have suffered atomic destruction, and the atomic bomb museums at Hiroshima and Nagasaki should be on your list of places to visit.

Hiroshima is also a good place to see the modern Japanese industrial machine in peak form. It's easy to arrange a factory visit at many centres in Japan, but the huge Mazda car factory in Hiroshima is certainly worth a visit. After work, Japanese salarymen head for the huge entertainment districts, where the neon burns bright and the bill at the end of the evening would bankrupt the average Third World country. Even if you don't venture inside a single bar, these colourful areas are fascinating to wander around. Interesting ones include Tokyo's lively Roppongi area and, in the Shinjuku district, the decidedly raunchier Kabuki-chō area. Shinjuku in Tokyo is also the face of 'modern Japan'; with two million people passing through its railway station every day, it is probably the busiest transport hub in the world.

Osaka's Namba district is another good example of a busy entertainment district, while Nakasu Island in Fukuoka is said to have a higher concentration of bars than anywhere else in Japan – hence the world? If you travel north in search of bars and nightlife, try Kokubun-chō in Sendai (Northern Honshū) and the Susukino entertainment district in Sapporo (Hokkaidō).

Love hotels are another side of Japan and it's surprising that an enterprising publisher hasn't yet produced a coffee-table book on love hotel architecture. In some places there are major enclaves of love hotels – the Dō-genzaka area of Tokyo's Shibuya district is a good example.

SUGGESTED ITINERARIES

Given the high costs of touring Japan, most travellers keep to fairly tight itineraries. Fortunately, with a little forethought this is easy to do: Japan's excellent road and rail network allow you to get around quickly, and public transport almost unfailingly runs to schedule. If you want to see as much of Japan as possible in a short time, don't forget to organise a Japan Rail (JR) Rail Pass before you go (see the Japan Rail Pass entry under Train in the Getting Around chapter).

Individual destination chapters contain more detailed Suggested Itinerary entries.

Tokyo-Kyoto

The Tokyo-Kyoto route is the most popular Japan primer. For first-time visitors with only a week or so to look around, a few days in Tokyo sampling the modern Japanese experience and four or five days in the Kansai region exploring the historical sites of Kyoto and Nara is a recommended option. It allows you take in some of Japan's most famous attractions while not attempting to cover too much ground. The journey between Tokyo and Kyoto might be broken half way at Nagoya in order to take an overnight trip to Takayama, a delightful rural town.

Tokyo & South-West

Travellers with more time to spend in Japan tend to head west and south before considering Northern Honshū and Hokkaidō. The reason is that Kansai, Western Honshū and Kyūshū are richer in sights than the northern regions of Japan. If you're a nature buff, you should consider dropping these regions in favour of the Japan Alps and Northern Honshū and Hokkaidō, where there is superb hiking.

Assuming you fly into Tokyo, it's worth spending a few days exploring the city before heading off to the Kansai area (notably Kyoto and Nara). A possible side trip enroute would be to Takayama from Nagoya and then on to Kanazawa, a culturally interesting city that gets neglected by many travellers. An interesting overnight trip out of Kyoto or Osaka is to the Buddhist mountain sanctuary of Kōya-san with its atmospheric temple lodgings.

From Kansai, many Rail Pass travellers take a *shinkansen* (bullet train) straight down to Fukuoka in Kyūshū. From there, regular trains continue on to Nagasaki, a city with an interesting, cosmopolitan history and a moving and fascinating museum about the atomic blast of 1945. From Nagasaki it is possible to do a loop through northern Kyūshū that takes in Kumamoto, the volcanic Aso-san (some good hiking in this area) and the penultimate in tacky hot spring resorts, Beppu. To the south is the balmy port city of Kagoshima, complete with the ash-spewing volcanic island of Sakurajima, just offshore.

The fastest way to return to Kansai or Tokyo is by shinkansen along the Inland Sea side of Western Honshū. Possible stopovers include Hiroshima and Himeji, a famous castle town. From Okayama, the seldom visited island of Shikoku is easily accessible. The Japan Sea side of Western Honshū is less touristed and more rural – notable attractions are the shrine at Izumo and the small cities of Matsue and Tottori.

Tokyo/Kansai & Northern Japan

A good approach to northern Japan from either Tokyo or Kansai is via Matsumoto and Nagano, which are excellent bases for hikes and visits to rural communities such as Kamikōchi. From Nagano, you might travel up to Niigata and from there to the seldom visited island of Sado-ga-shima, famous for its *taiko* drummers and August Earth Celebration. On the other side of Honshū, the city of Sendai provides easy access to Matsushima, one of Japan's most celebrated scenic outlooks.

Highlights north of Sendai include peaceful Kinkazan-jima; Tazawa-ko, the deepest lake in Japan; and the nearby hot springs of Nūtō Onsen, with its fantastic *rotemburo* (outdoor bath). Hiraizumi and Towada-Hachimantai National Park are also worth a visit.

From northern Honshū to Hokkaidō by train involves a journey through the world's longest underwater tunnel, the Seikan Tunnel. If you're short of time it might make sense to stick to the southern and central regions of Hokkaidō: Hakodate, Tōya-ko, Niseko, Biei and Biratori. And don't miss the capital of Hokkaidō, Sapporo, which is famous for its annual February snow festival, the Sapporo Yuki Matsuri.

The real treasures of Hokkaidō, however, are its national parks which require either more time or your own transport. If you've only got three or four days you might hit Shiretoko and Akan National Parks. If you've got at least a week, head to Daisetsuzan National Park. More distant but rewarding destinations include the scenic islands of Rebun-tō and Rishiri-tō.

PLANNING
When to Go

Without a doubt, the best times to visit Japan are the climatically stable seasons of spring and autumn. The only drawback during spring (March to May) is that the cherry blossom season, Hanami, is a holiday period for the Japanese, and many of the more popular travel destinations tend to be flooded with Japanese tourists, who head out of the cities in droves. Popular tourist attractions become congested at this time of year and it is wise to book ahead for your accommodation.

If it's the cherry blossoms you want to see, bear in mind that the blossoms are notoriously fickle, blooming any time from early to late April. Moreover, when the blossoms do come, their moment of glory is brief, lasting generally a mere week. Still, if you're going to be travelling in Japan during April, chances are you'll come across cherry blossoms somewhere, as they bloom first in the south and then bloom progressively northward.

Autumn (September to November) is an equally good time to travel, with pleasant temperatures and soothing autumn colours out in the country – the shrines and temples of historical centres such as Kamakura or Kyoto look stunning against a backdrop of russet leaves.

Travelling in either winter or summer is a mixed bag. Mid-winter (December to February) weather can be bitterly cold, particularly on the Japan Sea coast of Honshū and Hokkaidō, while the sticky summer months (June to August) can turn even the briefest excursion out of the air-conditioning into a soup bath. June is also the month of Japan's brief rainy season, which while not enough to prevent travel, frequent downpours can make things difficult. On the plus side, you will generally find major tourist attractions to be quieter during the winter and summer months.

Also keep in mind that peak holiday seasons, particularly 'Golden Week', which takes place in late April to early May, and the mid-summer O-bon (Festival of the Dead) can cause travel problems. Likewise, almost everything in Japan shuts down from 29 December to 3 January because of Shōgatsu (New Year celebrations) and you may find yourself surviving on fast food and convenience store rations if you're not prepared. See Public Holidays & Special Events later in this chapter for more information.

Maps

If you'd like to buy a map of Japan before arriving, both Nelles and Periplus produce reasonable maps of the whole country. For more detailed maps it's probably better to wait until you arrive. You'll find a good selection of English mapping materials in the bookshops of Tokyo, Osaka and Kyoto.

The Japan National Tourist Organization's (JNTO) free *Tourist Map of Japan*, available at all JNTO-operated tourist information centers, is a reasonable 1:2,000,000 English-language map of the whole country that is quite adequate for general route planning. If you'd like something a little more

Using This Guide

! Japan's streets are a maze of small alleys interconnected by wider streets. Many of the maps in this guide only *approximate* an area's actual layout. Many small lanes or narrow streets have not been drawn on the map. Keep this in mind when navigating your way around.

detailed, both Shobunsha and Kodansha (Japanese publishers) publish a series of bilingual fold-out maps with prices starting from around ¥700.

The *Japan Road Atlas* (Shobunsha) covers all of Japan at 1:250,000 except for Hokkaidō, which is covered at 1:600,000. Most towns are shown in *kanji* (Chinese ideographic script used for writing Japanese) as well as *romaji* (transliteration of Japanese into Roman alphabet script). However, mountains, passes, lakes, rivers and so on are only shown in romaji, and it is not unusual for small towns and villages to be left off altogether. Despite these drawbacks, the atlas is the best English-language map available for detailed exploration of the country, both by car and rail, as every railway station is marked. Those looking for something less bulky should pick up a copy of the *Bilingual Atlas of Japan* (Kodansha).

If you can read a little Japanese, you'll have much more choice. The best all-round Japanese atlases and maps are published by Shobunsha. If you intend to drive around Japan, pick up one of their excellent *Super Mapple* road atlases. Also, check the Service & Parking Area (SAPA) maps which are available free at expressway service centres.

What to Bring

The number one rule in Japan, as anywhere else, is travel light. Bulky luggage can be a hassle in Japan, as often the coin lockers at train stations are only large enough to hold a day-pack – not ideal if you wish to stop en route and go exploring.

What clothing you bring will depend not only on the season, but on where you are planning to go. Japan extends a long way from north to south: the north of Hokkaidō can be under deep snow at the same time as the Okinawa and the Nansei-shotō (South-West Islands) are basking in tropical sunshine. If you're going anywhere near the mountains, or intent on climbing Mt Fuji, you'll need good cold-weather gear at most times of the year, even in the height of summer. Generally, however, Japan's climate is somewhat similar to that of continental USA. The main islands of Japan can be quite cold in winter, particularly in the north of Honshū and in Hokkaidō. In the summer though, things can get uncomfortably hot and humid, particularly in the big cities. If you find yourself in Japan during the sticky months of July and August, you might want to head to Hokkaidō, which remains relatively cool and dry. Outside of summer and winter, much of Japan enjoys mild temperatures and relatively clear skies.

There is a distinct wet season between June and July, but rain is a possibility at any time of year, and an umbrella or wet-weather clothing is well worth having. Almost every shop and hotel in Japan seems to have an umbrella stand outside, sometimes with a neat locking arrangement so that umbrellas can be stowed safely.

Unless you're in Japan on business, you are unlikely to meet situations where 'coat and tie' standards are enforced. Casual clothing is all you'll need. Men should keep in mind, however, that trousers are preferable to shorts, especially in restaurants. There is no need to bring too many clothes as laundrettes are reasonably common, so you can count on recirculating your wardrobe fairly regularly. Some hotels, hostels and other accommodation have laundry facilities for guest use.

Choose your shoes carefully – you want shoes which are not only comfortable for walking but which are also easy to slip on and off for the frequent indoor occasions where they must be abandoned. Remember that slippers are almost always provided for indoor and bathroom use, so you don't really need to bring anything other than your outdoor shoes. And if your feet aren't small, make sure your shoes will outlast your stay in Japan – you probably won't be able to find your size in Japan. The top sizes for men are American size 9 and for women, size 7.

Bring a towel – even in an expensive *ryokan* (traditional Japanese inn), a towel is not necessarily provided or it may be of a size Westerners will consider more like a washcloth.

Other than large-size shoes, clothes and undergarments, you'll be able to buy whatever you need in Japan. Perhaps the only exception to this is English-language books, which are only available in big cities, such as Tokyo, Osaka and Kyoto – if you're a voracious reader, you might want to buy up big there or bring a few books from home.

See the Health section later in this chapter for advice regarding health-related items to bring with you.

TOURIST OFFICES

The Japan National Tourist Organization (JNTO) produces a great deal of literature, which is available both from its overseas offices and Tourist Information Centers (TIC; see below). Publications include *Your Guide to Japan*, a handy booklet giving information on places of interest, calendar events and travel data; the *Tourist Map of Japan* and *Your Travelling Companion Japan – with tips for budget travel*, which has money-saving tips on travel, accommodation and places to eat. Also worth picking up is *The Tourist's Language Handbook – Practical Ways to Help You Communicate*, which has a lists of useful phrases written in both Japanese and romaji, with their English equivalents. Most publications are available in English and, in some cases, other European and Asian languages. Separate brochures are available on a number of important tourist destinations. The JNTO also has an Internet homepage which features travel updates: http://www.jnto.go.jp.

A note on language difficulties. Foreign travellers are well catered for at major tourist destinations, but outside these areas some Japanese language ability will certainly come in handy. JNTO-operated Tourist Information Centers are operated specifically for foreign travellers and offer a wide range of information in English as well as some other major European languages. At other tourist offices you'll find varying degrees of English ability; in big cities and at major tourist attractions there will almost always be an English speaker on hand; in rural areas and small towns you may find yourself relying more on one word communication and hand signals. Nonetheless, with a little patience and a smile on your face you can usually get the information you need even from the smallest local tourist information office.

Tourist Information Centers (TIC)

JNTO operates five Tourist Information Centers:

Kansai
(☎ 0724-56-6025) Kansai international airport, Passenger Terminal Bldg, 1st floor, Izumi-Sano, Osaka 549-0011 (9 am to 9 pm)
Kyoto
(☎ 075-371-5649) 1st floor, Kyoto Tower Bldg, Higashi-Shiokoji-chō, Shimogyō-ku, Kyoto 600-8216 (9 am to 5 pm weekdays, 9 am to noon on Saturday, closed on Sunday and national holidays)
Tokyo
(☎ 03-3201-3331) B1F, Tokyo International Forum, 3-5-1, Marunouchi, Chiyoda-ku, Tokyo 100 (9 am to 5 pm weekdays, 9 am to noon Saturday, closed Sunday and national holidays)
New Tokyo international airport (Narita)
Main office: (☎ 0476-34-6251)
Passenger Terminal 2, 1st floor, Narita airport, Chiba 282-0004 (9 am to 8 pm)
Branch office: (☎ 0476-30-3383) Passenger Terminal 1, 1st floor, Narita airport, Chiba 282-0004 (9 am to 8 pm)

The Welcome Inn Reservation Center works closely with the JNTO and their staff at TICs can make reservations for you at member hotels and ryokan. TIC staff cannot make transport bookings; they can, however, direct you to agencies that can, such as the Japan Travel Bureau (JTB) or the Nippon Travel Agency (NTA).

JNTO also operates Goodwill Guides, a volunteer program with over 30,000 members, who wear a blue-and-white badge with a dove and globe logo.

Japan Travel-Phone

JNTO operates the Japan Travel-Phone, a service that provides travel-related information and language assistance in English. From within most of Japan the number can be dialled toll-free (☎ 0088-22-4800). Within Kyoto (☎ 371-5649) and Tokyo (☎ 3201-3331) it's a local call. The service is available seven days a week (9 am to 5 pm).

Teletourist Service

'Teletourist' (☎ 03-3201-2911) is a round-the-clock recorded information service on current events in and around Tokyo, operated by Tokyo TIC.

Tourist Information System

JNTO's Tourist Information System operates English-language tourist information offices throughout Japan (92 offices in 62 cities at the last count). The centres are usually located in the main railway stations of major Japanese cities. Look for the red question mark with the word 'information' printed beneath it.

Other Information Offices

Away from Tokyo or Kyoto there are tourist information offices *(kankō annai-jo – 観光案内所)* in almost all the major railway stations, but the further you venture into outlying regions, the less chance you have of finding English-speaking staff. If you want a licensed, professional tourist guide try TIC or a large travel agency such as JTB, or phone the Japan Guide Association (☎ 03-3213-2706) in Tokyo.

Tourist Offices Abroad

JNTO has a number of overseas offices including the following:

Australia
(☎ 02-9232-4522) Level 33, The Chifley Tower, 2 Chifley Square, Sydney, NSW 2000
Canada
(☎ 416-366-7140) 165 University Ave, Toronto, Ontario M5H 3B8
France
(☎ 01-42-96-20-29) 4-8 Rue Sainte-Anne, 75001 Paris
Germany
(☎ 069-20353) Kaiserstrasse 11, 60311 Frankfurt am Main 1
Hong Kong
(☎ 2968-5688) Suite 3704-05, 37th floor, Dorset House, Taikoo Place, Quarry Bay
South Korea
(☎ 02-732-7525) 10th floor, Press Centre Bldg, 25 Taipyongno 1-ga, Chung-gu, Seoul
Thailand
(☎ 02-233-5108) Wall Street Tower Bldg, 33/61, Suriwong Rd, Bangkok 10500

UK
(☎ 0171-734-9638) Heathcoat House, 20 Savile Row, London W1X 1AE
USA
Chicago: (☎ 312-222-0874) 401 North Michigan Ave, Suite 770, IL 60611
Los Angeles: (☎ 213-623-1952) 515 South Figueroa St, Suite 1470, CA 90071
New York: (☎ 212-757-5640) One Rockefeller Plaza, Suite 1250, NY 10020
San Francisco: (☎ 415-989-7140) 360 Post St, Suite 601, CA 94108

VISAS & DOCUMENTS

Passport

A passport is essential. If yours is within a few months of expiry, get a new one now – many countries will not issue a visa if your passport has less than six months of validity remaining. Also, ensure that your passport still has several empty pages for visa, entry and exit stamps. Even in modern Japan, losing a passport is a hassle. It's sensible to keep a photocopy of the information page of your passport in a separate place from your passport; at the very least ensure that you carry some photo ID apart from your passport.

Visas

Tourist and business visitors of many nationalities are not required to obtain a visa if staying in Japan less than 90 days. Visits involving employment or other remunerated activity require an appropriate visa.

Stays of up to six months are permitted for citizens of Austria, Germany, Ireland, Mexico, Switzerland and the UK. Citizens of these countries will almost always be given a 90-day Short Stay Visa upon arrival, which can be extended for another 90 days at immigration bureaus inside Japan (see Visa Extensions later in this chapter). Citizens of the USA, Australia and New Zealand may be granted 90-day Short Stay Visas, while stays of up to three months are permitted for citizens of Argentina, Belgium, Canada, Denmark, Finland, France, Iceland, Israel, Italy, The Netherlands, Norway, Singapore, Spain, Sweden and a number of other countries.

Visitors from other countries must acquire a visa (typically a Short Stay Visa) before coming to Japan. The visa is usually issued free, but passport photographs are required and a return or onward ticket must be shown. Visas are valid for 90 days.

Visa Extensions It has become difficult to extend visas. With the exception of nationals of the few countries whose reciprocal visa exemptions allow for stays of six months, 90 days is the limit for most visitors. Those who do apply should obtain two copies of an Application for Extension of Stay (available at immigration bureaus), a letter stating the reasons for the extension (along with any supporting documentation) and your passport. There is a processing fee of ¥4000. You will also need to complete an Alien Registration Card (see the entry later in this section).

It is possible to get around the extension problem by briefly leaving the country, usually going to Hong Kong, South Korea or Taiwan, and re-entering on a new 90-day Short Stay Visa. However, if immigration authorities suspect that you're working illegally in Japan, you may be detained at the airport and sent back to your home country at your own expense. If you do decide to return to Japan after a brief spell abroad, you should be prepared to show that you have adequate funds to live in Japan for three months without working, and a credible reason why you want to do so.

In early 2000, the revised immigration law cracked down on those who overstay their visa. Violators may be imprisoned for up to three years, or fined up to ¥300,000. Deportees will be refused entry into the country for at least five years. The new law is primarily directed at repeat offenders, but you should check your visa expiry dates carefully.

Working Holiday Visas Australians, Canadians and New Zealanders between the ages of 18 and 25 (the age limit can be pushed up to 30 in some cases) can apply for a Working Holiday Visa. This visa allows a six-month stay and two six-month extensions. The visa's aim is to enable young people to travel extensively during their stay and for this reason part-time or temporary employment options are stipulated in the visa conditions, although in practice, many people work full time.

A Working Holiday Visa is much easier to obtain than a regular Working Visa and is popular with Japanese employers as it can save them a great deal of inconvenience. Single applicants must have the equivalent of A$2500 (C$2005) of funds and a married couple A$5000 (C$4010), and all applicants must have an onward ticket from Japan. For details, inquire at the nearest Japanese embassy or consulate.

Work Visas It is not as easy as it once was to get a Work Visa for Japan. Ever-increasing demand has prompted much stricter working visa requirements. Arriving in Japan and looking for a job is quite a tough proposition these days, though people still do it. There are legal employment categories for foreigners that specify standards of experience and qualifications.

Once you find an employer in Japan who is willing to sponsor you it is necessary for you to obtain a Certificate of Eligibility. You must then take this certificate to any Japanese embassy or consulate overseas, not in Japan itself, where the actual visa will be issued. The whole procedure usually takes two to three months.

Alien Registration Card Anyone, and this includes tourists, who stays for more than 90 days is required to obtain an Alien Registration Card (*gaikokujin torokushō*). This card can be obtained at the municipal office of the city, town or ward in which you're living but moving to another area requires that you re-register within 14 days.

You must carry your Alien Registration Card at all times as the police can stop you and ask to see the card. If you don't have the card, you will be taken back to the station and will have to wait there until someone fetches it for you.

Onward Tickets

Japan requires that visitors to the country entering on a Short Stay Visa possess an ongoing air or sea ticket or evidence thereof. In practice, few travellers are asked to produce such documents, but to avoid surprises it pays to be on the safe side. Particularly if you look like you're at the end of the road, you may be asked to show that you have sufficient funds to finance your visit and fly out of the country.

Travel Insurance

Even in a country as safe as Japan, you should arrange for a travel insurance policy that covers theft, property loss and medical expenses. Theft may be very rare, but in the event of serious medical problems or an accident, it is unlikely that your travel budget would meet the bill in Japan.

There are a wide variety of travel insurance policies available, and it is wise to check with a reliable travel agent about which will best suit you in Japan and other countries in the region. The policies handled by STA Travel, which has branches in Japan, are usually good value.

Wherever you buy your travel insurance, always check the small print. Some policies specifically exclude 'dangerous activities' such as scuba diving and motorcycling. If you are going to be doing dangerous activities in Japan, check the policy coverage.

Some policies offer a choice between lower and higher medical expense options; choose the high-cost option for Japan. Also check whether your medical coverage requires you to pay first and claim later (if this is the case you will need to keep all documentation). Be sure to bring your insurance card or other certificate of insurance with you to Japan; Japanese hospitals have been known to refuse treatment to foreign patients with no proof of medical insurance.

Driving Licence

To drive in Japan, you will need an International Driving Permit backed up by your national licence. See the Car section of the Getting Around chapter for more details.

Hostel Cards

Youth hostel accommodation is plentiful in Japan. See the Youth Hostels entry under Accommodation later in this chapter for information about obtaining a membership card.

Student & Youth Cards

Japan is one of the few places left in Asia where a student card can be useful. Officially, you should be carrying an ISIC (International Student Identity Card) to qualify for a discount (usually for entry to places of interest), but in practice you will often find that any youth or student card will do the trick.

Seniors' Cards

There are a variety of discounts available for seniors over the age 65 in Japan. In almost all cases a passport will be sufficient proof of age, so seniors' cards are rarely worth bringing.

International Health Certificate

Japan is scrupulous about the risks of travellers arriving from countries where there is a risk of becoming infected with yellow fever or an epidemic of, say, cholera. If you are arriving from a high-risk area, it would be a good idea to come prepared with an International Health Certificate that indicates you have had all the necessary jabs.

An example of Japan's scrupulousness can be seen in the comment below:

When travellers fill out the yellow quarantine forms on arrival, they should be careful with their answers. A friend arriving from Thailand admitted to stomach problems and after being sent for a medical checkup, was isolated in quarantine for 10 days without a translator or any appropriate food (she was a vegetarian).

Dennis Nielsen

Other Documents

Extra passport photographs are easy to organise in Japan. Those arriving on a Working Holiday Visa should bring their educational certificates and work references. Those hoping to arrange a Work Visa should take their degree (not a copy) and documentation of work experience.

Copies

All important documents (passport data page and visa page, credit cards, travel insurance policy, air/bus/train tickets, driving licence etc) should be photocopied before you leave home. Leave one copy with someone at home and keep another with you, separate from the originals.

It's also a good idea to store details of your vital travel documents in Lonely Planet's free online Travel Vault in case you lose the photocopies or can't be bothered with them. Your password-protected Travel Vault is accessible online anywhere in the world – create it at www.ekno.lonelyplanet.com.

EMBASSIES & CONSULATES

Japanese Embassies & Consulates

Diplomatic representation abroad includes:

Australia (☎ 02-6273-3244) 112 Empire Circuit, Yarralumla, Canberra, ACT 2600
   Consulate in Brisbane: (☎ 07-3221-5188)
   Consulate in Melbourne: (☎ 03-9639-3244)
   Consulate in Perth: (☎ 08-9321-7816)
   Consulate in Sydney: (☎ 02-9231-3455)
Canada (☎ 613-241-8541) 255 Sussex Drive, Ottawa, Ontario K1N 9E6
   Consulate in Edmonton: (☎ 403-422-3752)
   Consulate in Montreal: (☎ 514-866-3429)
   Consulate in Toronto: (☎ 416-363-7038)
   Consulate in Vancouver: (☎ 604-684-5868)
France (☎ 01-48-88-62-00) 7 Ave Hoche, 75008-Paris
Germany (☎ 0228-81910) Godesberger Allee 102-104, 53175 Bonn
Hong Kong (☎ 852-2522-1184) 47th floor, One Exchange Square, 8 Connaught Place, Central
Ireland (☎ 01-269-4033) Nutley Bldg, Merrion Centre, Nutley Lane, Dublin 4
Netherlands (☎ 70-346-9544) Tobias Asserlaan 2, 2517 KC, The Hague
New Zealand (☎ 04-473-1540) 7th floor, Norwich Insurance House, 3-11 Hunter St, Wellington 1
   Consulate in Auckland: (☎ 09-303-4106)
South Korea (☎ 822-739-7400) 9th floor, Kyobo Bldg, Chongro 1-KA, Chongro-ku, Seoul
Thailand (☎ 02-252-6151) 1674 New Petchburi Rd, Bangkok 10310
UK (☎ 020-7465-6500) 101-104 Piccadilly, London, W1V 9FN
USA (☎ 202-238-6700) 2520 Massachusetts Ave, NW Washington DC 20008-2869
There are several Japanese consulates in the states (check with the embassy), including:
   Consulate in Los Angeles: (☎ 213-617-6700)
   Consulate in New York: (☎ 212-371-8222)

Embassies & Consulates in Japan

Australia
   Embassy: (☎ 03-5232-4111) 2-1-14 Mita, Minato-ku, Tokyo
   Consulate: (☎ 06-6941-9271) 2-1-61 Shiromi, Chūō-ku, Osaka
   Consulate: (☎ 092-734-5055), Tsurutakeyaki Bldg, 7F, 1-1-5 Akasaka, Chuo-ku, Fukuoka
Canada
   Embassy: (☎ 03-3408-2101) 7-3-38 Akasaka, Minato-ku, Tokyo
   Consulate: (☎ 06-6212-4910) 2-2-3 Nishi Shinsaibashi, Chūō-ku, Osaka
   Consulate: (☎ 092-752-6055) F.T. Bldg, 7F, 4-8-28 Watanabe-dori, Chuo-ku, Fukuoka
China
   Embassy: (☎ 03-3403-3380) 3-4-33 Moto Azabu, Minato-ku, Tokyo
   Consulate: (☎ 06-6445-9473) 3-9-2 Utsubo Honmachi, Nishi ku, Osaka
   Consulate: (☎ 092-713-1121) 1-3-3 Jigyo-hama, Chuo-ku, Fukuoka
France
   Embassy: (☎ 03-5420-8800) 4-11-44 Minami Azabu, Minato-ku, Tokyo
   Consulate: (☎ 06-4790-1500) 1-2-27 Shiromi, Chūō-ku, Osaka
Germany
   Embassy: (☎ 03-3473-0151) 4-5-10 Minami Azabu, Minato-ku, Tokyo
   Consulate: (☎ 06-6440-5070) 1-1-88 Oyodo-naka, Kita-ku, Osaka
Ireland
   Embassy: (☎ 03-3263-0695) 2-10-7 Koji-machi, Chiyoda-ku, Tokyo
   Consulate: (☎ 06-6309-0055) 4-7-4 Nishi-nakajima, Yodogawa-ku, Osaka
Netherlands
   Embassy: (☎ 03-5401-0411) 3-6-3 Shiba-kōen, Minato-ku, Tokyo
   Consulate: (☎ 06-6944-7272) 2-1-61 Shiromi, Chūō-ku, Osaka
New Zealand
   Embassy: (☎ 03-3467-2271) 20-40 Kamiyama-chō, Shibuya-ku, Tokyo
   Consulate: (☎ 06-6942-9016) 2-1-61 Shiromi, Chūō-ku, Osaka
South Korea
   Embassy: (☎ 3-3452-7611) 1-2-5 Minami Azabu, Minato-ku, Tokyo
   Consulate: (☎ 092-771-0461) 1-1-3 Jigyo-hama, Chuo-ku, Fukuoka
Thailand
   Embassy: (☎ 03-3441-7352) 3-14-6, Kami Ōsaki, Shinagawa-ku, Tokyo
   Consulate: (☎ 06-6243-5563) 3-6-9 Kita Kyuhojimachi, Chūō-ku, Osaka

UK

Embassy: (☎ 03-3265-5511) 1 Ichiban-chō, Chiyoda-ku, Tokyo

Consulate: (☎ 06-6281-1616) 3-5-1 Bakuro-machi, Chūō-ku, Osaka

Consulate: (☎ 092-476-2525) c/o Nishi Nippon Bank, Ltd, 1-3-6 Hakataekimae, Hakata-ku, Fukuoka

USA

Embassy: (☎ 03-3224-5000) 1-10-5 Akasaka, Minato-ku, Tokyo

Consulate: (☎ 06-6315-5900) 2-11-5 Nishitenma, Kita-ku, Osaka

Consulate: (☎ 092-751-9331) 2-5-26 Ohori, Chuo-ku, Fukuoka

Vietnam

Embassy: (☎ 03-3466-3313) 50-11 Moto-yoyogi, Shibuya-ku, Tokyo

Consulate: (☎ 06-263-1600) 10F Estate Bakuro-cho Bldg, 1-4-10, Bakuro-cho, Chuo-ku 541, Osaka

Your Own Embassy It's important to realise what your own embassy – the embassy of the country of which you are a citizen – can and can't do to help you if you get into trouble.

Generally speaking, it won't be much help in emergencies if the trouble you're in is remotely your own fault. Remember that you are bound by the laws of the country you are in. Your embassy will not be sympathetic if you end up in jail after committing a crime locally, even if such actions are legal in your own country.

In genuine emergencies you might get some assistance, but only if other channels have been exhausted. For example, if you need to get home urgently, a free ticket home is exceedingly unlikely – the embassy would expect you to have insurance. If you have all your money and documents stolen, it might assist with getting a new passport, but a loan for onward travel is out of the question.

Some embassies used to keep letters for travellers or have a small reading room with home newspapers, but these days the mail holding service has usually been stopped and even newspapers tend to be out of date.

CUSTOMS

Customs allowances include the usual tobacco products plus three 760mL bottles of alcoholic beverages, 57g of perfume, and gifts and souvenirs up to a value of ¥200,000 or its equivalent. The alcohol and tobacco allowances are available only for those who are 20 or older. Spirits have come down in price in Japan over recent years, but a good bottle of duty-free will still be appreciated as a gift. The penalties for importing drugs are very severe.

Pornography (magazines, videos etc) in which pubic hair or genitalia are visible is illegal in Japan and will be confiscated by customs officers.

There are no limits on the import of foreign or Japanese currency. The export of foreign currency is also unlimited but a ¥5 million limit exists for Japanese currency.

MONEY
Currency

The currency in Japan is the yen (¥) and banknotes and coins are easily identifiable. There are ¥1, ¥5, ¥10, ¥50, ¥100 and ¥500 coins; ¥1000, ¥5000 and ¥10,000 banknotes. The ¥1 coin is an aluminium lightweight coin, the ¥5 and ¥50 coins have a punched hole in the middle. The Japanese pronounce yen as 'en', with no 'y' sound. The kanji for yen is: 円

Exchange Rates

All major currencies are accepted by banks in Japan. The currencies of neighbouring Taiwan and Korea, however, are not easy to offload – change NT dollars and Korean won into yen or US dollars before arriving in Japan.

As of mid-2000, currency exchange rates were:

country	unit		yen
Australia	A$1	=	¥63.31
Canada	C$1	=	¥73.77
euro	€1	=	¥99.09
France	10FF	=	¥15.11
Germany	DM1	=	¥50.66
Hong Kong	HK$1	=	¥14.07
New Zealand	NZ$1	=	¥48.99
Singapore	S$1	=	¥63.26
United Kingdom	UK£1	=	¥161.72
United States	US$1	=	¥107.21

It's always risky to pin down a currency on paper (or on screen), so try this currency converter on the Web to give you the current value of the yen (www.oanda.com).

Exchanging Money

You can change cash or travellers cheques at an 'Authorised Foreign Exchange Bank' (signs are always displayed in English), major post offices, some large hotels and most big department stores. These are easy to find in cities, but much less common elsewhere. The safest and most practical way to carry your money is in travellers cheques, which also provide slightly more favourable rates.

Banking Hours As a general rule, always change more money than you think you will need. Banking hours are 9 am to 3 pm weekdays, closed weekends and national holidays. Japan may be a hi-tech place, but to change money you have to show your passport, fill in forms and (sometimes) wait until your number is called, all of which can take anything up to half an hour. If you're

---

Warning! ATM Access

The spread of international ATMs has been remarkably slow in Japan – Nagasaki, for example, still has no international ATM. The vast majority of ATMs in Japan *do not* accept foreign-issued credit and bank cards. In fact, in recent years, the number of ATMs that accept foreign-issued cards has actually decreased – a testament, if nothing else, to the astonishing insularity of the Japanese banking system.

ATMs that accept foreign-issued cards can only be found in areas frequented by foreign tourists, such as Tokyo, Osaka, Kyoto and a few other large cities. The machines can usually be distinguished by the presence of English instructions and advertising stickers for international networks such as Cirrus and Plus.

Other Japanese ATMs may be festooned with stickers from dozens of networks, but close inspection will reveal that these are all domestic networks. Even if you see stickers for VISA and MasterCard you may not be able to withdraw money – more often than not you must have a Japanese VISA card or MasterCard to use these machines.

Citibank, which is aggressively expanding across Japan, also has machines that accept cards which are part of the Cirrus or Plus networks. Many of these Citibank ATMs are open 24 hours a day, seven days a week.

Card holders would be wise to visit the Global ATM Locators for Citibank and VISA and make hard copies of the information before they leave home.

Citibank Global ATM locator
   http://www.webdata.com/dbForward.htf?ID=1174001&CLID=220
VISA Global ATM locator
   http://www.visa.com/pd/atm/main.html

Although it may be inconvenient, travellers cheques are still the safest and most reliable option in Japan.

If you don't want to be bothered with travellers cheques there are a couple of options:

- Use international ATMs in the big cities and carry lots of extra cash into the countryside
- Use visa cards for cash advances at Sumitomo banks around Japan
- Open a postal account (see Bank & Post Office Accounts in this chapter), deposit enough for all your travels in Japan and withdraw Japanese currency from post offices as you make your way around the country. Your initial deposit can come from cashed travellers' cheques or from an international ATM in one of Japan's big cities.

caught without cash outside regular banking hours, try a large department store or a major hotel.

Credit Cards

Do not rely on credit cards in Japan. While department stores, top-end hotels and *some* fancy restaurants do accept cards, most businesses in Japan do not. Cash-and-carry is still very much the rule in Japan. If you do bring a credit card, you'll find VISA most useful, followed by MasterCard, American Express and Diners Club.

The main credit card offices in Tokyo and their emergency numbers are:

American Express (toll-free ☎ 0120-020-120, 24 hours) American Express Tower, 4-30-16 Ogikubo, Suginami-ku

MasterCard (☎ 00531-11-3886) Dai Tokyo Kasai Shinjuku Bldg, 16F, 3-25-3 Yoyogi, Shibuya-ku

VISA (☎ 03-5251-0633, toll-free ☎ 0120-133-173) Nissho Bldg, 4F, 2-7-9 Kita-Aoyama, Minato-ku

International Transfers In order to make an international transfer you'll have to find a Japanese bank associated with the bank from which the money will be sent. Start by asking at the central branch of any major Japanese bank. If they don't have a relationship with your bank, they can usually refer you to a bank that does. Once you find a related bank in Japan, you'll have to give your home bank the exact details of where to send the money: the bank, branch and location. Telex or telegraphic transfers are much faster, though more expensive, than mail transfers. A credit-card cash advance is a worthwhile alternative.

Bank & Post Office Accounts Opening a regular bank account is difficult for foreign visitors on a Tourist Visa (most banks ask to see an Alien Registration Card) and some may also require a name stamp (*hanko* or *inkan*, easily available at speciality stores in most towns). A much better option for long-term visitors or those who don't want to bother with changing money all the time is a postal savings account (*yūbin chokin*). You can open these at any

major post office in Japan. With a postal savings account you'll be issued a cash card that enables you to withdraw funds from any post office in Japan (and these are everywhere). You should be able to get things started by using the phrase: '*yūbin chokin no kōza o hirakitai desu*' ('I would like to open a post office savings account').

Security

The Japanese are used to a very low crime rate and often carry wads of cash for the almost sacred ritual of cash payment. Foreign travellers in Japan can safely copy the cash habit, but should still take the usual precautions – don't, for example, leave large amounts of cash in your back pocket; always keep your travellers' cheques, credit cards etc in a safe place.

Costs

However you look at it, Japan is a very expensive place to travel. A skeleton daily budget, assuming you spend ¥2800 a night for accommodation at a youth hostel, eat modestly for ¥2000 per day and spend ¥1500 on short-distance transport, all works out at ¥6300 (US$60). Add at least ¥1000 (US$10) for extras like snacks, drinks, admission fees and entertainment. Mid-range accommodation costs around ¥4500 to ¥6000 for a *minshuku* (Japanese-style B&B), cheap ryokan or business hotel.

Food costs can be kept within reasonable limits by ordering set meals *(setto)*. A fixed 'morning service' breakfast *(mōningu sābisu* or *setto)* is available in most coffee shops for around ¥400. At lunch time there are set meals *(teishoku)* for about ¥700. Cheap noodle places, often found at stations or in department stores, charge around ¥400 for a filling bowl of noodles. For an evening meal, there's the option of a set course again or a single order – ¥700 to ¥900 should cover this. Average prices at youth hostels are ¥500 for breakfast and ¥900 for dinner.

Transport is a major expense, although there are ways to limit the damage. The Japan Rail Pass or regional rail passes are well worth the money if you intend to travel widely in a short space of time (see Getting Around). Overnight buses are cheaper than the train, and enable you to save on accommodation. Hitching is not only easy, it also puts you in touch with a cross section of Japanese society (see Hitching in the Getting Around chapter for warnings on solo hitchhiking and general information). If you want to avoid emptying your wallet at an alarming rate, you should only use taxis as a last resort. Most cities in Japan have fast, efficient public transport, so you rarely need to rely on taxis anyway.

Tipping & Bargaining

There is little of either in Japan. If you want to show your gratitude to someone, give them a gift rather than a tip. Bargaining is largely restricted to flea markets (where anything goes) and discount electronics districts (where a polite request will often bring the price down by around 10%).

Consumer Taxes

Japan has a 5% consumer tax. If you eat at expensive restaurants and stay in top-end accommodation you will encounter a service charge which varies from 10% to 15%. A local tax of 5% is added for restaurant bills exceeding ¥5000 or for hotel bills exceeding ¥10,000. This means it is sometimes cheaper to ask for separate bills. You can ask for separate bills by saying *'betsu-betsu de onegaishimasu'* when they are tallying your bill.

POST & COMMUNICATIONS

The symbol for post offices is a red T with a bar across the top on a white background. Red mailboxes are for ordinary mail, blue ones are for special deliveries. The Japanese postal system is reliable and efficient and, for regular postcards and airmail letters, not markedly more expensive than other developed countries.

Addresses in Japan

In Japan, finding a place from its address can be a near impossibility, even for the Japanese. The problem is twofold: firstly, the address is given by an area rather than a street; and secondly, the numbers are not necessarily consecutive: prior to the mid-1950s numbers were assigned by date of construction. During the occupation after WWII, an attempt was made to bring some 'logic' to Japanese addresses, and many streets were assigned names, but the Japanese reverted to their own system as soon as the Americans left.

To find an address, the usual process is to ask directions – even taxi drivers often have to do this. The numerous local police boxes are there, in part, to give directions. Businesses often include a small map in their advertisements or on their business cards to show their location.

Starting from the largest area and working down to an individual address, first comes the *ken* (prefecture) as in Okayama-ken or Akita-ken. Four areas in Japan do not follow this rule – Tokyo-to, Kyoto-fu, Osaka-fu (those cities and the areas around them) and the island of Hokkaidō. After the prefecture comes the *shi* or city. Thus Okayama city in Okayama Prefecture is properly Okayama-shi, Okayama-ken. In country areas, there are also *gun*, which are like counties, and *mura* or 'villages'.

Large cities are then subdivided first into *ku* (wards), then into *chō* or *machi* and then into *chōme*, an area of just a few blocks. The chōme is the smallest division, so an address like 4-4 3-chōme should locate the actual place you want. For the bewildered *gaijin* (foreigner), the system often seems to be changed back and forth without rhyme or reason and an address like 2-4-8 Nishi Meguro can also be written 4-8 Nishi Meguro 2-chōme. The building number is either a single numeric or a hyphenated double numeric. When there are three hyphenated numerals the first one is the chōme, so 1-2-3 is building 2-3 in 1-chōme.

You can buy maps that show every building in every chōme and there are often streetside signs indicating building locations, but they are very hard to interpret.

Postal Rates

The airmail rate for postcards is ¥70 to any overseas destination; aerograms cost ¥90. Letters weighing less than 10g are ¥90 to other countries within Asia, ¥110 to North America, Europe or Oceania (including Australia and New Zealand) and ¥130 to Africa and South America. One peculiarity of the Japanese postal system is that you will be charged extra if your writing runs over onto the address side (the right side) of a postcard.

Sending Mail

District post offices (the main post office in a ward, or *ku*), are normally open from 9 am to 7 pm weekdays, 9 am to 3 pm Saturday, and closed Sunday and public holidays. Local post offices are open 9 am to 5 pm weekdays, closed Saturday, Sunday and public holidays. Main post offices in the larger cities may have an after-hours window open 24 hours a day, seven days a week.

Mail can be sent to Japan, from Japan or within Japan when addressed in Roman script (*romaji*) but it should, of course, be written as clearly as possible.

Receiving Mail

Although any post office will hold mail for collection, the poste restante concept is not well known and can cause confusion in smaller places. It is probably better to have mail addressed to you at a larger central post office. Letters are usually only held for 30 days before being returned to sender. When inquiring about mail for collection ask for *'kyoku dome yubin'*.

Telephone

The Japanese public telephone system is very well developed; there are a great many public phones and they work almost 100% of the time. It is very unusual to see a vandalised phone in Japan. Local calls cost ¥10 for three minutes; long-distance or overseas calls require a handful of coins which are used up as the call progresses. Unused ¥10 coins are returned after the call is completed, but no change is given on ¥100 coins.

Most payphones will also accept prepaid phonecards (*terefon kādo*), though probably not for international calls. It's much easier to buy one of these than worry about having coins to hand; they are readily available from vending machines and convenience stores in ¥500 and ¥1000 denominations. Phonecards are magnetically encoded, and after each call a small hole is punched to show the remaining yen value. The phone also displays the remaining value of your card when you insert it. Since phonecards come in a huge variety of designs, card collecting is a popular activity.

International Calls Due to the proliferation of counterfeit telephone cards, it is no longer possible to make international direct dial calls from regular green pay phones.

Paid and reverse-charge (collect) overseas calls can be made from grey ISDN phones and green phones which have a gold metal plate around the buttons. These are usually found in phone booths marked 'International & Domestic Card/Coin Phone'. Unfortunately, these are rather rare; try looking in the lobbies of top-end hotels and in airports.

In hotel lobbies and airports, you will also find KDD 'Credit Phones' which allow you to make international calls with credit cards issued outside Japan. In some youth

Japan Area Codes

The country code for Japan is ☎ 81. When dialling from outside Japan, drop the zero from the beginning of area codes.

Fukuoka	☎ 092
Hiroshima	☎ 082
Kōbe	☎ 078
Kyoto	☎ 075
Matsuyama	☎ 0899
Nagasaki	☎ 0958
Nagoya	☎ 052
Nara	☎ 0742
Narita	☎ 0476
Osaka	☎ 06
Sapporo	☎ 011
Sendai	☎ 022
Tokyo	☎ 03
Yokohama	☎ 045

hostels and 'gaijin houses', you will also find pink coin-only phones from which you cannot make international calls (though you can receive them).

Calls are charged by the unit, each of which is six seconds, so if you don't have much to say you could phone home for just ¥100.

You can save money by dialling late at night. Economy rates, with a discount of 20%, apply from 7 to 11 pm weekdays and to 11 pm on weekends and holidays. From 11 pm to 8 am a discount rate brings the price of international calls down by 40%. Note that it is also cheaper to make domestic calls by dialling outside the standard hours.

To place an international call through the operator, dial ☎ 0051 (international operators all seem to speak English). To make the call yourself, dial ☎ 001 (KDD), ☎ 0041 (ITJ) or ☎ 0061 (IDC) – there's very little difference in their rates – then the international country code, the local code and the number.

Another option is to dial ☎ 0039 for home country direct, which takes you straight through to a local operator in the country dialled (your home country direct code can be found in phone books or by calling ☎ 0051). You can then make a reverse-charge call or a credit-card call with a telephone credit card valid in that country. In some hotels or other tourist locations, you may find a home country direct phone where you simply press the button labelled USA, UK, Canada etc, to be put through to your operator. You need to arrange the home country direct service with your home telephone company before you leave for Japan.

Another phonecard option is Lonely Planet's eKno Communication Card. It's aimed specifically at independent travellers and provides budget international calls (for local calls, you're usually better off with a local card), a range of message services, free email and travel information. Accessing its Web site is the easiest way to find out more or to join (www.ekno.lonely planet.com). To join by phone from within Japan call Customer Service toll free on ☎ 00531-21-2039 or toll free from anywhere

else worldwide on USA ☎ +1-213-927-0101. Once you've joined you can use the phone or the Internet to contact your friends and family and manage your account.

Check the eKno Web site for joining and access numbers from other countries and updates on super budget local access numbers and new features.

One more option for making international calls is prepaid phone cards, such as the KDD Superworld Card, which provides ¥3200 worth of calls for ¥3000. Unlike conventional phonecards, this one operates via a 'secret' number that lasts as long as the charge remains on the card. There is no need to insert the card into a phone, and you can make international calls from any touchtone phone. These cards can be purchased in hotels and ryokan that cater to foreigners, otherwise try a convenience store. Dialling codes include:

country	direct dial	home country direct
Australia	001-61	0039-611
Canada	001-1	0039-161
Hong Kong	001-852	0039-852
Netherlands	001-31	0039-311
New Zealand	001-64	0039-641
Singapore	001-65	0039-651
Taiwan	001-886	0039-886
UK	001-44	0039-441
USA	001-1	0039-111 or 0039-121

Directory Assistance For local directory assistance dial ☎ 104, or for assistance in English ring ☎ 0120-364-463 (9 am to 5 pm weekdays). For international directory assistance dial ☎ 0057. An English telephone directory is available in City Source, available free at any NTT (Japan's largest phone company) office or the Tokyo TIC. To place a domestic collect call, dial ☎ 106. For orders and inquiries about phone installation, ring the NTT English Service Section toll-free on ☎ 0120-364-463.

Fax
Most convenience stores in Japan have fax machines where you can send and sometimes receive faxes. If you can't understand

how to operate the machine, ask the shop assistant for assistance – *'fakusu o okuritai desu'* ('I want to send a fax'). To receive one ask: *'kochira de fakusu o uketoru kota ga dekimasu ka'* ('Can I receive a fax here?'). You can also send and receive faxes at most top-end hotels, although some places only allow paying guests to use their facilities. The main offices of NTT also have fax machines. Facility locations are on some maps, otherwise you can check *City Source* or ask at your lodgings.

Email & Internet Access

If you plan on bringing your laptop with you to Japan, first make sure that it is compatible with Japanese current (100V AC; 50Hz in eastern Japan and 60Hz in western Japan). Most laptops function reasonably well on Japanese current. Second, check to see if your plug will fit Japanese wall sockets (Japanese plugs are flat two pin, identical to most ungrounded North American plugs). Both transformers and plug adapters are readily available in electronics districts like Tokyo's Akihabara or Osaka's Den-Den Town.

Modems and phone jacks are similar to those used in the USA (RJ11 phone jacks). If you have any misgivings about whether your modem will function in Japan, you can always pick up a 'global modem'. Conveniently, many of the grey IDD pay phones in Japan have a standard phone jack and an infrared port so that you can log on to the Internet just about anywhere in the country.

Major Internet service providers such as AOL (www.aol.com), CompuServe (www.compuserve.com) and IBM Net (www.ibm.net) have dial-in nodes in most big Japanese cities like Osaka and Tokyo. It's best to download a list of the dial-in numbers before you leave home. If you access your Internet email account at home through a smaller internet service provider (ISP) or your office or school network, your best option is either to open account with a global ISP, like those mentioned above, or to rely on cybercafes and other public access points to collect your email.

If you do intend to rely on cybercafes, you'll need to carry three pieces of information with you to enable you to access your home email account: your incoming (POP or IMAP) mail server name, your account name and your password. Your ISP or network supervisor will be able to give you these. Armed with this information, you should be able to access your home email account from any Net-connected machine in the world, provided it runs some kind of email software (remember that Netscape and Internet Explorer both have mail modules). It pays to become familiar with the process for doing this before you leave home.

A final cybercafe email collection option is to open a free Web-based email account such as HotMail (www.hotmail.com) or Yahoo! Mail (mail.yahoo.com). You can then access your mail from anywhere in the world from any Net-connected machine running a standard Web browser.

You'll find cybercafes only in the big cities of Japan (we list these in the appropriate sections wherever possible). Rates are steep in most places – ¥500 for 30 minutes is the norm. For a more up-to-date list of cybercafes, check out www.netcafeguide.com.

INTERNET RESOURCES

The World Wide Web (WWW) is a rich resource for travellers. You can research your trip, hunt down bargain air fares, book hotels, check on weather conditions or chat with locals and other travellers about the best places to visit (or avoid!).

There's no better place to start your Web explorations than the Lonely Planet Web site (www.lonelyplanet.com). Here you'll find succinct summaries on travelling to most places on earth, postcards from other travellers and the Thorn Tree bulletin board, where you can ask questions before you go or dispense advice when you get back. You can also find travel news and updates to many of our most popular guidebooks, and the subWWWay section links you to the most useful travel resources elsewhere on the Web.

Other Web sites with useful Japan information and links include:

Japanese-English Dictionary Gateway A really useful site for Japanese-English or English-Japanese translations.
http://enterprise.dsi.crc.ca/cgi-bin/j-e/
Japan National Tourist Organization (JNTO) Great information on all aspects of travel in Japan.
www.jnto.go.jp
J Cult Magazine An refreshingly alternative look at Japan.
www.jcult.com/
Japan Rail Passes Good information on rail travel in Japan with details on the Japan Rail Pass. www.jreast.co.jp/jrp/index.htm
Jin Japan A useful index of Japan links.
www.jinjapan.org/
Japan Ministry of Foreign Affairs Covers Japan's foreign policy and has useful links to embassies and consulates under 'MOFA info'.
www.infojapan.org/
Japan Echo Scholarly essays, interviews and discussions by noted commentators on topics of interest in Japan today.
www.japanecho.co.jp/
Sanrio Come And Join Us! This Web site is dedicated to *kawai*, or cute, culture. It's worth visiting regularly during your stay in Japan for the 'Weekly Character Spotlight'.
http://www.sanrio.co.jp/english/welcome.html
Tokyo Tokyo Tokyo Select Japanese language/ESL learning Web sites, guides to Tokyo and greater Japan, and links to Japanese cross-cultural understanding organisations, eg, pen-pals.
www.asahi-net.or.jp/~tx2h-mtok/
Townpage, Japan Telephone Directory is an English-language telephone directory published in Japan. It includes the Japan Yellow Pages, city maps and useful information on touring and living in Japan.
http://townpage.pearnet.org/jtd/

BOOKS

Most books are published in different editions by different publishers in different countries. As a result, a book might be a hardcover rarity in one country while it's readily available in paperback in another. Fortunately, bookshops and libraries search by title or author, so your local bookshop or library is best placed to advise you on the availability of the following recommendations. If you can't find these books at home,

you should definitely be able to find them in Tokyo, Osaka or Kyoto. Outside these cities, however, you may have a hard time locating English-language books. For this reason, it's a good idea to stock up before heading out into the countryside.

Lonely Planet

If you'd like to explore Tokyo or Kyoto in real depth, pick up a copy of Lonely Planet's *Tokyo* or *Kyoto* city guides. Likewise, if you feel like taking the plunge into Japanese, Lonely Planet's *Japanese phrasebook* is a good place to start. This handy little book has phrases and vocabulary to cover most situations you're likely to encounter in Japan.

For an intimate look at Japan, pick up a copy of Alex Kerr's *Lost Japan* (Lonely Planet Journeys). Originally written in Japanese, the book draws on the author's experiences in Japan over 30 years. Kerr explores the ritualised world of *kabuki* (a form of Japanese theatre), retraces his initiation into Tokyo's boardrooms, and exposes the environmental and cultural destruction that is the other face of contemporary Japan.

Hiking in Japan is a must for anyone wishing to explore Japan's woods and mountains. It contains a balance of convenient one-day hikes near major cities and extended hikes in more remote areas.

Guidebooks

There are two excellent books available devoted exclusively to hot springs. *A Guide to Japanese Hot Springs* by Anne Hotta with Yoko Ishiguro (Kodansha, 1986) details over 160 springs, and *Japan's Hidden Hot Springs* by Robert Neff (Tuttle, 1995) takes an even more selective approach in introducing *onsen* and memorable inns located off the conventional tourist routes, though Neff was clearly not on a tight budget.

Wild Flowers of Japan (Kodansha) by Ron Levy is a good field-guide to the many different types of flowers you're likely to spot along hiking trails. In a similar vein, Betty Richards' and Anne Kaneko's *Japanese Plants* (Shufunomoto) covers the most common flowers, as well as trees and grasses.

The best all-around guide to the wonders of Japanese cuisine is Robb Satterwhite's *What's What in Japanese Restaurants: A Guide to Ordering, Eating and Enjoying* (Kodansha). With detailed introductions to each major type of Japanese cuisine and detailed Japanese and English menus, this book makes it possible for non-Japanese-speakers to enter any Japanese restaurant with confidence.

Travel
Travel books about Japan often end up turning into extended reflections on the eccentricities or uniqueness of the Japanese. One writer who does not fall prey to this temptation is Alan Booth. *The Roads to Sata* (Penguin) is the best of his writings about Japan, and traces a four-month journey on foot from the northern tip of Hokkaidō to Sata, the southern tip of Kyūshū. Booth's *Looking for the Lost – Journeys Through a Vanishing Japan* (Kodansha) was his last book, and again recounts walks in rural Japan. A more recent account of a tramp across the length of Japan is Craig McLachlan's enjoyable *Four Pairs of Boots* (Yohan).

The *Inland Sea* (Weatherhill) by Donald Richie is another memorable Japanese travelogue, this time about a journey through the little-visited islands between Western Honshū and Shikoku.

Oliver Statler's *Japanese Inn* is an excellent introduction to Japanese history, as seen from the perspective of a post town. He has also penned a fascinating account of a walking tour of the Shikoku temple circuit in *Japanese Pilgrimage* (Picador).

Okubo Diary (Stanford University Press), by the British anthropologist Brian Moeran, is a memoir of his stay in a tiny Kyūshū village.

History
Those looking for a brief and readable account of how modern Japan got to be the way it is should grab a copy of Ann Waswo's *Modern Japanese Society – 1868–1994* (Oxford University Press). It is a no-nonsense round-up of recent events that has little truck with the accepted cliches, and in this sense it makes for a refreshing read. Other recommended reads in a similar vein include Richard Storey's *A History of Modern Japan* (Penguin) and *The Japanese Achievement* (Sidgwick & Jackson) by Hugh Cortazzi which spans earliest Japanese history to the present.

Japan: A Short Cultural History (Stanford University Press) by George B Sansom, though written some 40 years ago, is still among the best wide-ranging introductions to Japanese history. Sansom is also author of the more scholarly, three-volume *A History of Japan* (Stanford University Press). Those who get hooked should seek out the six-volume *Cambridge History of Japan*.

Edward Seidensticker's *Low City, High City* (Knopf) traces the history of Tokyo from 1867 to 1923 – the tumultuous years from the Edo period to the great earthquake. *Tokyo Rising: The City Since the Great Earthquake* (Knopf) continues the story from the 1920s, through the destruction of WWII and the period of explosive growth to today's super-city status. Paul Waley's *City of Stories* (Weatherhill) is another good historical account of Tokyo.

Religion
The role of religion in Japanese society is a complex one, but there are several good primers that are readily available in good Japanese bookshops. The best of these include: *Japanese Religion: A Cultural Perspective* by Robert S Elwood & Richard Pilgrim (Prentice-Hall); *Religions of Japan – Many Traditions within One Sacred Way* by H Byron Earhart (Harper & Row); *Shintō: The Kami Way* by Ono Sokyo (Tuttle); and *Japanese Religion – A Survey by the Agency for Cultural Affairs* (Kodansha).

Probably the best introduction to Zen is *Zen & Japanese Culture* by Daisetsu T Suzuki (Routledge & Kegan Paul). Peter Matthiessen, author of the *Snow Leopard* and many other fine books, gives a personal account of his Zen experiences in Japan and elsewhere in *Nine-Headed Dragon River* (Shambala).

The Cult at the End of the World – the Incredible Story of Aum (Arrow), by David E

Kaplan & Andrew Marshall, as its subtitle helpfully explains, tells the incredible story of the Aum cult. This extremely readable piece of investigative journalism follows Shoko Asahara's journey from small-time charismatic to the head of a cult that attempted to bring the world to its knees by gassing central Tokyo.

Culture & Society

Although it's a little dated, Ruth Benedict's *The Chrysanthemum & the Sword* is considered by many Japanese and foreigners to be the definitive study of Japanese culture and attitudes. Written in the USA during WWII, this groundbreaking book explains the complex underpinning of the Japanese moral world. Remarkably, Benedict was a cultural anthropologist who had never visited Japan or studied the language. Her book has been translated into Japanese and remains something of a classic despite the difficult circumstances under which it was written.

The Japanese Today (Belknap) by Edwin O Reischauer, is a standard textbook on Japanese society and a useful primer for anyone planning to spend time in Japan.

For a witty look at life inside one of Japan's government bureaucracies, pick up a copy of *Straightjacket Society* by Miyamoto Masoo. The author uses his experience as an employee at Japan's Ministry of Health and Welfare to comment on Japanese society at large. By the end of the book, you won't be surprised to learn that Miyamoto is no longer employed by the ministry.

Donald Richie's *Japanese Cinema – An Introduction* (Oxford University Press, Hong Kong, 1990) is a brief, but useful guide for the beginner.

Business

There is no shortage of books that purport to describe the secrets of Japanese business. Two notable books to start with are *The Art of Japanese Management – Applications for American Executives* (Simon & Schuster) and *Japan in the Passing Lane – An Insider's Account of Life in a Japanese Auto Factory* by Satoshi Kamata (Pantheon).

The *Townpage English Telephone Directory* is an essential reference source for those thinking of starting a business in Japan. It has over 1000 pages of telephone numbers and a wealth of useful practical information. Copies are available at the main Tokyo TIC and NTT offices across Japan.

For more nuts-and-bolts information on doing business in Japan, contact the Japan External Trade Organization in Tokyo on ☎ 03-5562-3131 or your country's chamber of commerce in Tokyo (check the *Townpage* English directory).

Cookbooks

Food of Japan by Shirley Booth offers a richly personal but very practical guide to cooking Japanese food. It's also entertaining with chapter headings such as 'Meat – Food of the Hairy Barbarians'.

General

Foreign authors have also tackled Japan in their writings, the most recent example being Arthur Golden's wildly successful *Memoirs of a Geisha*. This book sparked something of a mini-geisha boom in the States. James Clavell has also contributed to the genre with *Shogun* an account of an Englishman who finds himself involved with the 17th-century Tokugawa shogunate. William Gibson's *Idoru* covers a completely different Japan, that of the 21st century, where computers and computer-generated idols are the name of the game. A much more realistic novel is Alan Brown's *Audrey Hepburn's Neck*, the story of a simple Hokkaidō lad who falls for a reckless Western woman. It's notable because it attempts to portray the Japanese as human beings instead of walking stereotypes.

Among the more interesting recent books to appear about Japan is Ian Buruma's *Wages of Guilt – Memories of War in Germany & Japan* (Littlebrown). It explores the effects of Japan's (and Germany's) involvement in WWII on the contemporary psyche of the nation. Ian Buruma is also the author of one of the best introductions to Japan's sleazy 'water trade' and the overall cultural implications of what goes on there in *A Japanese Mirror* (Penguin).

In the Realm of a Dying Emperor (Vintage), by Norma Field, is a lyrical combination of memoir and reportage, as the author's past mingles with her account of three Japanese whose lives have been lived at odds with mainstream Japanese society. It gives pause to thought for all those who see Japanese culture as monolithic and depersonalising. Karl Taro Greenfield attempts the same in his racy *Speedtribes – Children of the Japanese Bubble*, a book which stretches the reader's credulity somewhat, but still makes for an entertaining foray into the drug-peddling, computer-hacking underworld of disaffected Japanese youth.

Jonathan Rauch's *Outnation – A Search for the Soul of Japan* (Littlebrown) is an intelligent and penetrating account of his six months in Japan. Pico Iyer's *The Lady and the Monk* (Vintage) is an unabashed romanticisation of Japan (mainly Kyoto) by a writer whose primary strength is as an essayist. It still makes for a great read, even if you might want to balance some of his reflections with the reality of modern Japan. One of the earliest writers to grapple with the difficulty of presenting Japan to a foreign audience was the 19th-century Japanophile, Lafcadio Hearn (also known as Koizumi Yakumo). *Writings From Japan* (Penguin) is a good sampler that follows Hearn's deepening affection for the country he visited and never left.

NEWSPAPERS & MAGAZINES

On the English-language front, Japan produces several good newspapers and a small clutch of decent magazines. You can buy these, along with the big-name foreign magazines like *Time* and *Newsweek*, in most major urban centres. Out in the country, however, there may not be anything but Japanese publications. And in Okinawa, Kyūshū and Hokkaidō, the English dailies sometimes arrive a day late, if they arrive at all.

The *Japan Times*, with its good international news section and unbiased coverage of local Japanese news is read by most newcomers looking for work because of its employment section – the Monday edition has the most extensive listings. The *Daily Yomiuri* rates alongside the *Japan Times* in its coverage of local and international news, and is particularly worth picking up on Saturday when a 'World Report' from the *Los Angeles Times* is included, and on Sunday when it has an eight-page supplement, 'View From Europe', culled from the British *Independent*.

The *Mainichi Daily News* is another good English-language newspaper widely available in Tokyo and its environs. If you oversleep and miss the morning papers, the *Asahi Evening News* is better than nothing – look out for the Entertainment section on Thursday if you're in Tokyo. All these newspapers can be picked up from newsstands in the major cities, particularly at train stations, or at hotels that cater to foreign tourists and businesspeople.

Foreign magazines and newspapers are available in the major bookshops in major cities, though they tend to be very expensive. US magazines such as *Newsweek* and *Time* are popular and widely available. For specialist magazines, such as *The Face* or *Wired*, you'll need to visit the big bookshops in Tokyo, Osaka and Kyoto.

Resident expats also produce a number of interesting monthly magazines that provide information on what's on, details about various cultural events, as well as classifieds for anything from marriage partners to used cars. In Tokyo, the best of these is the free magazine *Tokyo Classified*, followed by the slick *Tokyo Journal*. Kansai residents are much better served by the excellent *Kansai Time Out*.

Students of Japanese should look out for *Nihongo Journal* and the *Hiragana Times*, monthly bilingual magazines for Japanese learners. The *Nihongo Journal* is particularly good, with its accompanying tape for pronunciation and listening comprehension practice, and good listings of Japanese-language schools. Both magazines require that you have some basic Japanese-language skills and can at least read *hiragana* (phonetic syllabary used to write Japanese words) and a smattering of kanji.

RADIO
Recent years have seen an increase in stations aimed specifically at Japan's foreign population. Many of these play surprisingly cosmopolitan music and give news updates in several languages, including English.

InterFM (76.1 FM) is a favourite of Tokyo's foreign population. The station broadcasts news and useful day-to-day information mainly in English, but also in seven other languages, including Spanish and Chinese. The play list is more cosmopolitan than most other stations, too.

The Kansai equivalent of InterFM is FM Co Co Lo (76.5 FM) which broadcasts in English and several other languages including Portuguese, Thai, Chinese and Tagalog. In addition to useful news programs, the station plays a wide variety of multi-ethnic music.

TV
Some TVs have a bilingual function so that you can listen to certain English-language programs and movies in either Japanese or English. The Japan Broadcasting Corporation (NHK) has a nightly bilingual news report and on Sunday nights you can catch fairly recent Hollywood movies with a simultaneous bilingual broadcast. Ask the owner of the place where you're staying to see if the TV has the bilingual feature. The more upmarket hotels also have English-language satellite services, including BBC and CNN.

Apart from bilingual broadcasts and satellite TV, you're going to have to content yourself with regular Japanese-language programming. Although Japanese TV programs are frequently criticised as inane, childish, cruel or downright stupid (and let's face it, there are plenty that fit this description), there are some blissful exceptions to this rule. NHK airs some excellent documentaries and variety shows, as well as insightful news shows. Of course, without a decent command of Japanese these may be of very little use to you.

Even if you don't understand Japanese, it's worth turning on the TV to see what's on – it's a great window into the culture!

VIDEO SYSTEMS
Japan is the world's leading producer of VCRs and video recorders. The local system is the American NTSC standard. If you are using a PAL or SECAM system video camera, bring your own video cartridges with you. In electronics meccas such as Tokyo's Akihabara, it is possible to buy duty-free video equipment that switches between the three systems.

PHOTOGRAPHY
Film & Equipment
The Japanese are a nation of photographers. No social occasion is complete without a few snaps and an exchange of photos taken at the last get-together. This, combined with the fact that the Japanese are major producers of camera equipment and film, means there is no problem obtaining photographic equipment or print film. Slide film is readily available but cheaper in other places around Asia.

A 36-exposure Kodachrome 64ASA-slide film costs about ¥850 without processing; Fuji slide film, such as Velvia and Provia, is similarly priced. The very popular disposable cameras are even sold from vending machines. They typically cost from ¥1000 to ¥2000; more expensive ones have a built-in flash.

Processing
Processing print film is fast and economical in Japan, although standards are not always high and prices vary (¥2000 for a 36-exposure film is typical). In the big cities it is usually possible to have Fuji slide film processed within 24 hours (¥1000 for 36 exposures) and the final results are of a consistently high standard.

TIME
Despite Japan's east-west distance, the country is all on the same time, nine hours ahead of Greenwich Mean Time (GMT). So if it's noon in Japan, it's 5 pm the previous day in Honolulu, 7 pm the previous day in San Francisco, 10 pm the previous day in New York, 3 am in London, 11 am in Hong Kong, 1 pm in Sydney and 3 pm in Auckland. Japan does not have daylight saving.

Calendars & Dates

In 1873, the Japanese switched from the lunar calendar to the Gregorian calendar used in the West. As is the case throughout Asia, the result has been that official public holidays are dated according to the Gregorian calendar, while traditional festivals and events still follow the lunar calendar.

Years are counted in Japan according to two systems: Western and Imperial. The Western system sets the date from the birth of Christ. The Imperial system calculates the years from the accession of the emperor. The reign of each emperor is assigned a special name.

The reign of the previous emperor, Hirohito (1926–89), is known as the Shōwa (Enlightened Peace) era. Thus 1988 was Shōwa 63. The present emperor, Akihito, reigns in the Heisei era, so 1999 was Heisei 11, and 2000 was Heisei 12.

ELECTRICITY
Voltage & Cycles

The Japanese electric current is 100V AC, an odd voltage found almost nowhere else in the world. Furthermore, Tokyo and eastern Japan are on 50Hz, western Japan including Nagoya, Kyoto and Osaka is on 60Hz. Most North American electrical items, designed to run on 117V, will function reasonably well on Japanese current.

Plugs & Sockets

Japanese plugs are the flat two-pin type, which are identical to North American plugs. If you have a three-pin plug, you'll have to buy an adaptor at one of Japan's many electronics stores.

WEIGHTS & MEASURES

Japan uses the international metric system. One odd exception is the size of rooms, which is often given in *tatami* (tightly woven floor matting) measurements known as *jō*. Tatami sizes vary regionally in Japan, which tends to complicate things. In Tokyo a tatami mat measures 1.76 by 0.88m, while in Kyoto a mat measures 1.91 by 0.96m (see the Long-Term Accommodation entry

under Accommodation later in this chapter for more information).

LAUNDRY

Some youth hostels and ryokan have washing facilities but, failing this, the best option is to seek out a *koin rāndori* (coin laundry). In suburban Japan there is almost always one within easy walking distance. Costs range from ¥200 to ¥300 for a load of washing and ¥100 for every seven to 10 minutes of drying time. Those staying in business hotels or top-end accommodation can use the hotel laundry service.

TOILETS

In Japan you will come across both Western-style toilets and Asian squat toilets. When you are compelled to squat, the correct position is facing the hood, away from the door. This is the opposite to squat toilets in most other places in Asia. Make sure the contents of your pockets don't spill out. Toilet paper isn't always provided so carry tissues with you. You may be given small packets of tissue on the street in Japan – a common form of advertising for advertising for *tere-kura* (telephone clubs), the phone dating services that have been implicated in *enjo-kosai* (a euphemism for prostitution, mostly by school-age girls). However, not all the tissues given out are for sleazy services. In homes and ryokan, separate toilet slippers are often provided just inside the toilet door. These are for use in the toilet only, so remember to change out of them when you leave.

It's quite common to see men urinating in public – the unspoken rule is that it's acceptable at night time if you happen to be drunk. Public toilets are free in Japan. The katakana script for 'toilet' is トイレ, and the kanji script is お手洗い. You'll often also see these kanji:

男	女
Male	Female

HEALTH

Travel health depends on your predeparture preparations, your day-to-day health care while travelling and how you handle any medical problem or emergency that may develop. However, looking after your health in Japan should pose few problems as hygiene standards are high and medical facilities widely available. The average life expectancy in Japan is now 80 years for women and 74 years for men, a sure sign that the Japanese are doing something right.

Predeparture Preparations

Immunisations No immunisations are required for Japan, however, be aware that Japan is scrupulous with visitors who arrive from countries where there is a risk of yellow fever and other diseases. Vaccinations you should consider in consultation with your doctor include the following.

Hepatitis A The vaccine for hepatitis A (eg, Avaxim, Havrix 1440 or VAQTA) provides long-term immunity (possibly more than 10 years) after an initial injection and a booster at six to 12 months.

Alternatively, an injection of gamma globulin can provide short-term protection against hepatitis A – two to six months, depending on the dose given. It is not a vaccine, but a ready-made antibody collected from blood donations. It is reasonably effective and, unlike the vaccine, it is protective immediately, but because it is a blood product, there are current concerns about its long-term safety.

Hepatitis A vaccine is also available in a combined form, Twinrix, with hepatitis B vaccine. Three injections over a six-month period are required; the first two providing substantial protection against hepatitis A.

Hepatitis B Travellers who should consider vaccination against hepatitis B include those on a long trip, as well as those visiting countries where there are high levels of hepatitis B infection, where blood transfusions may not be adequately screened or where sexual contact or needle sharing is a possibility. Vaccination involves three injections, with a booster at 12 months. More rapid courses are available if necessary.

Health Insurance Make sure that you have adequate health insurance. See Travel

Insurance under Visas & Documents earlier in this chapter.

Travel Health Guides The most useful book on health and medicine in Japan is the *Japan Health Handbook* by Meredith Maruyama, Louise Picon Shimizu and Nancy Smith Tsurumaki (Kodansha). More general guides to health on the road include *Travellers' Health* by Dr Richard Dawood (Oxford University Press); and Lonely Planet's *Healthy Travel Asia & India*, a handy pocket-size guide packed with useful information including pretrip planning, emergency first aid, immunisation and disease information and what to do if you get sick on the road. *Travel with Children* from Lonely Planet also includes advice on travel health for younger children.

There are also a number of excellent travel health sites on the Internet. From the Lonely Planet home page there are links at www.lonelyplanet.com/weblinks/wlprep.htm #heal to the World Health Organization and the US Centers for Disease Control & Prevention.

Other Preparations Make sure you're healthy before you start travelling. Dental treatment in Japan is expensive. If you're short-sighted bring a spare pair of glasses and your prescription. If you require a particular medication bring an adequate supply as it may not be available in Japan, but also remember to bring the prescription – it may be illegal in Japan. Another idea, if you need particular medication, is to bring the packaging showing the generic rather than the brand name (which may not be available locally), as it will make getting replacements easier.

Basic Rules

Care in what you eat and drink is the most important health rule; stomach upsets are the most likely travel health problem (between 30% and 50% of travellers in a two-week stay experience this), but such problems are unusual in Japan.

Water Tap water is safe to drink all over Japan, but drinking from mountain streams should be done with caution. On the island of Rebun-tō (Hokkaidō), travellers have been warned that the springs could be contaminated with fox faeces, which contain tapeworm cysts. There have been reports of the schistosomiasis parasite still lurking in rice paddies or stagnant water – avoid wading around barefoot in these places.

Medical Kit Check List

Following is a list of items to consider including in your medical kit – consult your pharmacist for brands available in your country.

☐ **Aspirin or paracetamol (acetaminophen in the USA)** – for pain or fever

☐ **Antihistamine** – for allergies, eg, hay fever; to ease the itch from insect bites or stings; and to prevent motion sickness

☐ **Cold and flu tablets, throat lozenges and nasal decongestant**

☐ **Multivitamins** – consider for long trips, when dietary vitamin intake may be inadequate

☐ **Antibiotics** – consider including these if you're travelling well off the beaten track; see your doctor, as they must be prescribed, and carry the prescription with you

☐ **Loperamide or diphenoxylate** –'blockers' for diarrhoea

☐ **Prochlorperazine or metaclopramide** – for nausea and vomiting

☐ **Rehydration mixture** – to prevent dehydration, which may occur, for example, during bouts of diarrhoea; particularly important when travelling with children

☐ **Insect repellent, sunscreen, lip balm and eye drops**

☐ **Calamine lotion, sting relief spray or aloe vera** – to ease irritation from sunburn and insect bites or stings

☐ **Antifungal cream or powder** – for fungal skin infections and thrush

☐ **Antiseptic (such as povidone-iodine)** – for cuts and grazes

☐ **Bandages, Band-Aids (plasters) and other wound dressings**

☐ **Water purification tablets or iodine**

☐ **Scissors, tweezers and a thermometer** – note that mercury thermometers are prohibited by airlines

Food Hygiene in Japan rarely causes complaints. Most of the raw food can be eaten without health worries, although raw freshwater fish and raw wild boar meat should be avoided. The consumption of *fugu* (globefish) – not for the budget traveller – can famously result in death, but the dangers are absurdly exaggerated. (See the special Japanese Cuisine section for more details.)

Medical Problems & Treatment

Self-diagnosis and treatment can be risky, so you should always seek medical help. An embassy, consulate or top-end hotel can usually recommend a local doctor or clinic. Although we do give drug dosages in this section, they are for emergency use only. Correct diagnosis is vital. In this section we have used the generic names for medications – check with a pharmacist for brands available locally.

Note that antibiotics should ideally be administered only under medical supervision. Take only the recommended dose at the prescribed intervals and use the whole course, even if the illness seems to be cured earlier. Stop immediately if there are any serious reactions and don't use the antibiotic at all if you are unsure that you have the correct one. Some people are allergic to prescribed antibiotics such as penicillin; carry this information (eg on a bracelet) when travelling.

Medical Assistance The TIC has lists of English-speaking hospitals, doctors and dentists in the large cities. Dental care is widely available at steep prices. If you need a medicine that isn't readily available try the American Pharmacy (☎ 03-3271-4034) close to the main TIC in Tokyo. A peculiarity of the Japanese medical system is that most pharmaceuticals are supplied not by pharmacies but by doctors. Critics say that as a result, doctors are prone to over-prescribe and choose the most expensive drugs.

Counselling & Advice If you're staying on a long-term basis, adjusting to life in Japan can be tough, but there are several places to turn to for help. The phone service Tokyo English Life Line (TELL; ☎ 03-5721-4347) offers confidential and anonymous help.

There is also the Foreign Residents Advisory Center (☎ 03-5320-7744), which is operated by the Tokyo metropolitan government (weekdays). Otherwise, try the 24-hour Japan Helpline (see Emergencies later in this chapter).

Environmental Hazards

Altitude Sickness Lack of oxygen at high altitudes (over 2500m) affects most people to some extent. The effect may be mild or severe and occurs because less oxygen reaches the muscles and the brain at high altitude, requiring the heart and lungs to compensate by working harder. Symptoms of acute mountain sickness (AMS) usually develop during the first 24 hours at altitude but may be delayed up to three weeks. Mild symptoms include headache, lethargy, dizziness, difficulty sleeping and loss of appetite. AMS may become more severe without warning and can be fatal. Severe symptoms include breathlessness, a dry, irritative cough (which may progress to the production of pink, frothy sputum), severe headache, lack of coordination and balance, confusion, irrational behaviour, vomiting, drowsiness and unconsciousness. There is no hard-and-fast rule as to what is too high: AMS has been fatal at 3000m, although 3500 to 4500m is the usual range.

Treat mild symptoms by resting at the same altitude until recovery, usually a day or two. Paracetamol or aspirin can be taken for headaches. If symptoms persist or become worse, however, immediate descent is necessary; even 500m can help. Drug treatments should never be used to avoid descent or to enable further ascent.

The drugs acetazolamide and dexamethasone are recommended by some doctors for the prevention of AMS; however, their use is controversial. They can reduce the symptoms, but they may also mask warning signs; severe and fatal AMS has occurred in people taking these drugs. In general we do not recommend them for travellers. To try to prevent acute mountain sickness:

Ascend slowly Have frequent rest days, spending two to three nights at each rise of 1000m. If you reach a high altitude by trekking, acclimatisation takes place gradually and you are less likely to be affected than if you fly directly to high altitude.

Sleep at a lower altitude It is wise to sleep at a lower altitude than the greatest height reached during the day if possible. Also, once above 3000m, care should be taken not to increase the sleeping altitude by more than 300m per day.

Drink extra fluids The mountain air is dry and cold and moisture is lost as you breathe. Evaporation of sweat may occur unnoticed and result in dehydration.

Meals Eat light, high-carbohydrate meals for more energy.

Drugs Avoid alcohol as it may increase the risk of dehydration; also avoid sedatives.

Hypothermia Too much cold can be just as dangerous as too much heat. If you are trekking at high altitudes or simply taking a long bus trip over mountains, particularly at night, be prepared.

Hypothermia occurs when the body loses heat faster than it can produce it and the core temperature of the body falls. It is surprisingly easy to progress from very cold to dangerously cold due to a combination of wind, wet clothing, fatigue and hunger, even if the air temperature is above freezing. It is best to dress in layers; silk, wool and some of the new artificial fibres are all good insulating materials. A hat is important, as a lot of heat is lost through the head. A strong, waterproof outer layer (and a 'space' blanket for emergencies) is essential. Carry basic supplies, including food containing simple sugars to generate heat quickly and fluid to drink.

Symptoms of hypothermia are exhaustion, numb skin (particularly toes and fingers), shivering, slurred speech, irrational or violent behaviour, lethargy, stumbling, dizzy spells, muscle cramps and violent bursts of energy. Irrationality may take the form of sufferers claiming they are warm and trying to take off their clothes.

To treat mild hypothermia, first get the person out of the wind and/or rain, remove their clothing if it's wet and replace it with dry, warm clothing. Give them hot liquids - not alcohol and some high-kilojoule, easily digestible food. Do not rub victims: instead, allow them to slowly warm themselves. This should be enough to treat the early stages of hypothermia. The early recognition and treatment of mild hypothermia is the only way to prevent severe hypothermia, which is a critical condition.

Motion Sickness Eating lightly before and during a trip will reduce the chances of motion sickness. If you are prone to motion sickness, try to find a place that minimises disturbance – near the wing on aircraft, close to midship on boats or near the centre on buses. Fresh air usually helps; reading and cigarette smoke don't. Commercial antimotion sickness preparations, which can cause drowsiness, have to be taken before the trip commences. Ginger is a natural preventative and is available in capsule form.

Prickly Heat Prickly heat is an itchy rash caused by excessive perspiration trapped under the skin. Keeping cool but bathing often, using a mild talcum powder or opting to use air conditioning might help you to acclimatise.

Sunburn Severe sunburn is possible in Japan, particularly in the South-West Islands. Bring a good sunblock lotion and a hat if you are going to be outdoors for long hours in the summer. Also be sun-smart if you're hiking at high altitudes – sunburn can be a risk at almost any time of year. Use a sunscreen, hat and barrier cream for your nose and lips. Calamine lotion is good for mild sunburn.

Protect your eyes with good quality sunglasses, particularly if you will be near water, sand or snow.

Infectious Diseases

Diarrhoea Simple things like a change of water, food or climate can all cause a mild bout of diarrhoea, but a few rushed toilet trips with no other symptoms is not indicative of a major problem.

Dehydration is the main danger with any diarrhoea, particularly in children or the elderly as dehydration can occur quite

quickly. Under all circumstances fluid replacement (at least equal to the volume being lost) is the most important thing to remember. Weak black tea with a little sugar, soda water, or soft drinks allowed to go flat and diluted 50% with clean water are all good. With severe diarrhoea a rehydrating solution is preferable to replace minerals and salts lost. Commercially available oral rehydration salts (ORS) are very useful; add them to boiled or bottled water. In an emergency you can make up a solution of six teaspoons of sugar and a half teaspoon of salt to a litre of boiled or bottled water. You need to drink at least the same volume of fluid that you are losing in bowel movements and vomiting. Urine is the best guide to the adequacy of replacement - if you have small amounts of concentrated urine, you need to drink more. Keep drinking small amounts often. Stick to a bland, fat-free diet as you recover.

Fungal Infections Fungal infections, which occur with greater frequency in hot weather, are most likely to occur on the scalp, between the toes or fingers, in the groin and on the body (ringworm). You get ringworm, which is a fungal infection not a worm, from infected animals or by walking on damp areas, like shower floors.

To prevent fungal infections wear loose, comfortable clothes, avoid artificial fibres, wash frequently and dry carefully. If you do get an infection, wash the infected area daily with a disinfectant or medicated soap and water, and rinse and dry well. Apply an antifungal cream or powder like Tinaderm. Try to expose the infected area to air or sunlight as much as possible, and wash all towels and underwear in hot water as well as changing them often.

Hepatitis Hepatitis is a general term for inflammation of the liver. It is a common disease worldwide. There are several different viruses that cause hepatitis, and they differ in the way that they are transmitted. The symptoms are similar in all forms of the illness, and include fever, chills, headache, fatigue, feelings of weakness, and aches and pains, followed by loss of appetite, nausea, vomiting, abdominal pain, dark urine, light-coloured faeces, jaundiced (yellow) skin and yellowing of the whites of the eyes. People who have had hepatitis should avoid alcohol for some time after the illness, as the liver needs time to recover.

Hepatitis A is transmitted by contaminated food and water. You should seek medical advice, but there is not much you can do apart from resting, drinking lots of fluids, eating lightly and avoiding fatty foods. **Hepatitis E** is transmitted in the same way as hepatitis A; it can be particularly serious in pregnant women.

There are almost 300 million chronic carriers of **hepatitis B** in the world. It is spread through contact with infected blood, blood products or body fluids, for example through sexual contact, unsterilised needles and blood transfusions, or contact with blood via small breaks in the skin. Other risk situations include having a shave, tattoo or body piercing with contaminated equipment. The symptoms of hepatitis B may be more severe than type A and the disease can lead to long-term problems such as chronic liver damage, liver cancer or a long term carrier state. **Hepatitis C** and **D** are spread in the same way as hepatitis B and can also lead to long-term complications.

There are vaccines against hepatitis A and B, but there are currently no vaccines against the other types of hepatitis. Following the basic rules about food and water (hepatitis A and E) and avoiding risky situations (hepatitis B, C and D) are important preventative measures.

HIV/AIDS HIV, the Human Immunodeficiency Virus, may develop into AIDS, Acquired Immune Deficiency Syndrome. HIV is a major problem in many countries. Any exposure to blood, blood products or bodily fluids may put the individual at risk. The disease is often transmitted through sexual contact or dirty needles – vaccinations, acupuncture, tattooing and ear or nose (or any other) piercing can be potentially just as dangerous as intravenous drug use. HIV/AIDs can also be spread through infected blood transmission. You may want to take a couple of syringes with you, in case of emergency.

Sexually Transmitted Diseases Gonorrhoea and syphilis are the most common of these diseases; sores, blisters or rashes around the genitals, discharges or pain when urinating are common symptoms. Symptoms may be less marked or not observed at all in women. Syphilis symptoms eventually disappear completely but the disease continues and can cause severe problems in later years. While abstinence is the only 100% preventative, using condoms is also effective. The treatment of gonorrhoea and syphilis is by antibiotics.

There are numerous other sexually transmitted diseases, for most of which effective treatment is available. However, there is no cure for herpes and there is also currently no cure for AIDS.

Condoms Condoms are widely available in Japan, but generally only locally produced varieties, which tend to be on the small side. It's a good idea to bring your own, since foreign-made condoms are all but impossible to find in Japan.

Cuts, Bites & Stings

Cuts & Scratches Wash well and treat any cut with an antiseptic such as povidone-iodine. Where possible avoid bandages and Band-Aids, which can keep wounds wet. Coral cuts are notoriously slow to heal and if they are not adequately cleaned, small pieces of coral can become embedded in the wound.

Bites & Stings Bee and wasp stings are usually painful rather than dangerous. However, in people who are allergic to them severe breathing difficulties may occur and require urgent medical care. Calamine lotion or a sting relief spray will give relief and ice packs will reduce the pain and swelling. There are some spiders with dangerous bites but antivenins are usually available. Scorpion stings are notoriously painful and in some parts of Asia, the Middle East and Central America can actually be fatal. Scorpions often shelter in shoes or clothing.

Certain cone shells found in the Pacific can sting dangerously or even fatally. There are various fish and other sea creatures which can sting or bite dangerously or which are dangerous to eat – seek local advice.

Jellyfish If stung by these sea creatures seek local advice. Stings from most jellyfish are simply rather painful. Dousing in vinegar will deactivate any stingers which have not 'fired'. Calamine lotion, antihistamines and analgesics may reduce the reaction and relieve the pain.

Snakes To minimise your chances of being bitten always wear boots, socks and long trousers when walking through undergrowth where snakes may be present. Don't put your hands into holes and crevices, and be careful when collecting firewood.

Snake bites do not cause instantaneous death and antivenins are usually available. Immediately wrap the bitten limb tightly, as you would for a sprained ankle, and then attach a splint to immobilise it. Keep the victim still and seek medical help, if possible with the dead snake for identification. Don't attempt to catch the snake if there is a possibility of being bitten again. Tourniquets and sucking out the poison are now comprehensively discredited.

Women's Health

Gynaecological Problems Antibiotic use, synthetic underwear, sweating and contraceptive pills can lead to fungal vaginal infections, especially when travelling in hot climates. Fungal infections are characterised by a rash, itch and discharge and can be treated with a vinegar or lemon-juice douche, or with yoghurt. Nystatin, miconazole or clotrimazole pessaries or vaginal cream are the usual treatment. Maintaining good personal hygiene and wearing loose-fitting clothes and cotton underwear may help prevent these infections.

Sexually transmitted diseases are a major cause of vaginal problems. Symptoms include a smelly discharge, painful intercourse and sometimes a burning sensation when urinating. Medical attention should be sought and male sexual partners must also be treated. For more details see the section on Sexually Transmitted Diseases earlier. Besides abstinence, the best thing is to practise safer sex using condoms.

Pregnancy Most miscarriages occur during the first three months of pregnancy, so this is the most risky time to travel as far as your own health is concerned. Miscarriage is not uncommon, and can occasionally lead to severe bleeding. The last three months should also be spent within reasonable distance of good medical care. A baby born as early as 24 weeks stands a chance of survival, but only in a good modern hospital. Pregnant women should avoid all unnecessary medication, but vaccinations and malarial prophylactics should still be taken where possible. Additional care should be taken to prevent illness and particular attention should be paid to diet

Contraceptive Control

In June 1999, after years of stalling, the Health Ministry approved the sale of the low-dose contraceptive pill. Until that time, Japanese women had three choices – the male condom, abortion or the rhythm method. It was only when the Health Ministry expedited the approval of the impotence drug Viagra in early 1999 that female lobbyists were able to expose the double standards in operation. Viagra's side-effects were deemed acceptable to American men, and therefore the same risk level applied to Japanese men. In contrast, it was argued that the pill would have different side effects on Japanese women than on Western women.

Other delaying arguments included issues relating to 'public hygiene', meaning the containment of HIV infection; while discussions in the public domain focused on the pill's effect on the lucrative abortion industry. Female lobbyists felt that the real issue blocking approval was the potential it would allow women for sexual equality. Sales of the pill have yet to take off – after years of scaremongering Japanese women are unconvinced that the pill is safe.

and nutrition. Alcohol and nicotine, for example, should be avoided.

WOMEN TRAVELLERS

The major concern, 'Will I be physically safe?' is less of a worry in Japan than many other countries. Statistics show low rates of violent crimes against women, although some Japanese women's organisations and media attribute this to under-reporting.

Jam-packed trains or buses during rush hour, or late-hour services heaving with the inebriated masses, can still bring out the worst in the Japanese male. When movement is impossible, roving hands are sometimes at work and women often put up with this harassment because, in Japan, it would simply be impolite or unseemly to make a fuss. In some cases, a loud complaint will shame the perpetrator into withdrawing his hand. Failing this, you may be able to push your way through to another part of even the most crowded train, especially if other passengers realise what is happening. Finally, some women suggest that the offending hand should be grabbed, held up and the whereabouts of its owner inquired about.

The biggest hazard for many women travellers is that of adopting a too casual disregard for normal safety precautions while in Japan. Many women reason that based on Japan's reputation for safety, nothing will happen to them. This is, unfortunately, false. Although some expats will assure you that it's safe to walk the streets of any Japanese city alone at night, ignore this and follow your common sense: keep to streets with heavier foot traffic, stay in groups etc. Western women who are alone on foot are easy targets for verbal harassment or worse by passing male motorists. Walking solo along highways in remote rural areas at any time of day and hitchhiking are definitely advised against. One Japan resident warned:

I agree that crimes are rare, but after being followed by drunk salarymen and men wanting 'a good time' Western style, I'm not sure being safe is not a worry. I have feared for my personal safety far more often than I ever did at home in Canada.
Jody Marshall

It is the rare (or super streetwise) woman who stays in Japan for any length of time without encountering some type of sexual harassment. Apparently some men find that words are not enough to express how they feel, as flashers and cruder exhibitionists are not uncommon. These men target women in isolated positions (say, making a call from a phone box alone after dark) and may publicly expose themselves or even masturbate directly in front of you. They are, however, unlikely to be shamed into stopping by only a stern look; the best thing you can do is quickly walk away.

Statistics on reported rape are low, but it is estimated that actual rates are significantly higher. If you or someone you know is raped and you attempt to seek help, be forewarned that police and medical personnel can be quite unhelpful, even accusatory. Insist on receiving the appropriate medical care (STD tests, antibiotic booster shot, morning after pill) and, as appropriate, filing a police report.

If you do have a problem and find the local police unhelpful, you can call the Human Rights Center Information Line in Tokyo (☎ 03-3581-2303).

Some aspects of Japanese life may strike women as peculiar on first encounter. For example, in rural areas public toilets are not always sex segregated and it can be a real shock for a Western woman when she enters and finds a row of urinals with men lined up at them. Remote onsen may have *rotemburo* (outdoor baths) for mixed bathing or, when the pools are sex-segregated, their location may involve a bit more exposure than some women are prepared for, say in full view of the highway.

GAY & LESBIAN TRAVELLERS

With the possible exception of Thailand, Japan is Asia's most enlightened nation with regard to the sexual preferences of foreigners. Tokyo, in particular, has an active gay scene, with clubs and support groups and a small but very lively gay quarter (Shinjuku-ni-chōme). Check *Tokyo Classified* or *Tokyo Journal* for listings of gay and lesbian clubs. Outside Tokyo, however, you will find it difficult to break into the local scene unless you spend considerable time in a place or have local contacts who can show you around.

Same-sex couples probably won't encounter too many problems travelling in Japan. However, some travellers have reported problems when checking into love hotels with a partner of the same sex; some have been turned away, others have been grossly overcharged. Apart from this, it's unlikely that you'll run into difficulties, but it does pay to be discreet in rural areas.

Organisations

The following Web site may be of help when planning your trip:

Gay Scene Japan A fun and useful site with information specifically for gay and lesbian travellers.
http://members.tripod.co.jp/GSJ/

DISABLED TRAVELLERS

Many new buildings have access ramps, traffic lights have speakers playing melodies when it is safe to cross, train platforms have raised dots and lines to provide guidance and some ticket machines in Tokyo have Braille. On the other hand there is much in Tokyo that is downright dangerous, depending on your disability.

If you are going to travel by train and need assistance, ask one of the station workers as you enter the station. Try asking: *'karada no fujiyuu no kata no tame no sharyō wa arimasu desho ka?'*

There are carriages on most lines that have areas set aside for those in wheelchairs. Those with other physical disabilities can use one of the seats set aside near the train exits, called *yūsen-zaseki*. You'll also find these seats near the front of buses; usually they're a different colour from the regular seats.

One indispensable guide is *Accessible Tokyo,* published by the Japanese Red Cross. To obtain a copy, write or phone: Japanese Red Cross Language Service Volunteers (☎ 03-3438-1311, fax 3432-5507) c/o Volunteers Division, Japanese Red Cross Society, 1-1-3 Shiba Daimon, Minato-ku, Tokyo 105, Japan

SENIOR TRAVELLERS

Japan is an excellent place for senior travellers. To qualify for widely available senior discounts, you have to be over 60 or 65, depending upon the place/company.

Japanese domestic airlines (JAS, JAL and ANA) offer senior discounts of about 25% on some flights. For more information, contact the airlines. JR offers a variety of discounts and special passes, including the 'Full Moon Green Pass', which is good for travel in Green Cars on shinkansen, regular JR trains and sleeper trains. The pass is available to couples whose combined age exceeds 88 years (passports can prove this). A five-day pass, good for two people, costs ¥79,000. Several restrictions apply to these passes, so it's best to inquire at a TIC for details.

In addition to travel discounts, discounts are available on entry fees to many temples, museums and cinemas.

TRAVEL WITH CHILDREN

Japan is a great place to travel with kids. It's safe and there's never a shortage of places to keep them amused – the only drawback is the expense of it all. Look out for *Japan for Kids* (Kodansha) by Diane Wiltshire Kanagawa and Jeane Huey Erickson, an excellent introduction to Japan's highlights from a child's perspective. Lonely Planet publishes *Travel with Children,* which gives the lowdown on getting out and about with your children.

DANGERS & ANNOYANCES
Theft

The low incidence of theft and crime in general in Japan is frequently commented on, though of course, theft does exist and its rarity is no reason for carelessness. In airports and on the crowded Tokyo rail network it's sensible to take the normal precautions, but there's definitely no need for paranoia.

Lost and found services do seem to work; if you leave something behind on a train or other transport, it's always worth inquiring if it has been turned in.

Yakuza

The *yakuza*, perhaps because they are often referred to as the 'Japanese mafia', are much misunderstood by foreign visitors to Japan. Enjoying deep penetration into Japanese society, powerful right-wing political support, operating as vast syndicates with interests in everything from real estate to hospitals (plus, of course, obvious business activities such as prostitution, drugs and gambling), the yakuza is a highly organised and widely tolerated component of Japan's hierarchical society.

The yakuza occupy (at least nominally) a lowly position in this hierarchy, but they compensate for this with a bravado that looks to historical antecedents. Many yakuza see themselves as custodians of honour and chivalry, traditional values that are all but vanished in contemporary Japan. Japan's ultra-nationalist right – which also looks for a return to 'traditional values' – enjoys yakuza support, and the black propaganda vans you will encounter cruising urban Japan are often driven by yakuza.

There are thought to be close to 90,000 yakuza members in Japan and yakuza earnings are probably over US$10 billion annually. The largest of the groups is the Yamaguchi-gumi, based in Kōbe. It claims over 20,000 'employees' and pulls in about a fifth of total yakuza annual earnings.

How do you pick a yakuza? Short-cropped permed hair is à la mode among the lower orders. Those with money often drive a big black Mercedes with tinted windows and will also affect an arrogant swagger *(iburi)* and a gruff manner of speech *(aragoto)*. A body covered in tattoos is *de rigeur* (cherry blossoms signify the brief but cheerful life of an ardent criminal), but don't forget to look out for that telling detail: failure in one's obligations to the group is punished by the amputation of a little finger at the first joint. On repeated convictions they move to the next joint and so on until, presumably, there are no fingers left – a sign of the honourable but bumbling custodian of Japan's *samurai* past.

Earthquakes

Japan is a very earthquake-prone country, although most can only be detected by sensitive instrumentation. If you experience a strong earthquake, head for a doorway or supporting pillar. Small rooms, like a bathroom or cupboard, are often stronger than large rooms but even a table or desk can provide some protection from falling debris. If you're in an urban area, do not run outside as this could expose you to falling debris.

All Japanese hotels have maps indicating emergency exits, and local area wards have emergency evacuation areas (fires frequently follow major earthquakes). In the event of a major earthquake, stay calm and follow the locals, who should be heading for a designated safe area.

In the event of a serious earthquake, the radio stations listed under Radio will broadcast emergency information in English and several other languages.

Fire

Although modern hotels are subject to high safety standards, traditional Japanese buildings with their wooden construction and tightly packed surroundings can be real firetraps. Fortunately, most old buildings are low-rise – you're unlikely to be trapped on the 40th floor – but it's wise to check fire exits and escape routes.

Beaches & Swimming

Few public beaches have lifeguards and summer weekends bring many drowning accidents. Watch for undertows or other dangers. See Environmental Hazards under Health for information on sunburn.

Noise

In Japanese cities the assault on the auditory senses can be overwhelming, so it's no wonder so many pedestrians are plugged in to Walkmans. Pedestrian crossings are serenaded by electronic playtime music, loudspeaker systems broadcast muzak or advertisements, bus passengers are bombarded with running commentaries in Mickey Mouse tones and accommodation may include TVs turned up full volume in dining rooms or lounges. Earplugs can help, particularly when you're trying to sleep.

Size
Even medium-sized foreigners need to mind their head in Japanese dwellings. The Western frame may find it hard to fit into some seats and those with long legs will often find themselves wedged tight. Toilets in cramped accommodation necessitate contortions and careful aim (be warned!).

Wildlife
Japan is hardly a high danger region when it comes to wildlife, although in Okinawa much fuss is made about the 'deadly' *habu* snake. To avoid an unhappy encounter with a deadly habu, don't go traipsing barefoot through the undergrowth. On the mainland islands the *mamushi* is also poisonous.

There are still bears in remote areas of Hokkaidō and they can be fiercely protective of their cubs. Japan also has wasps, mosquitoes and other biting or stinging insects but not in extraordinary numbers or of unusual danger. Jellyfish and other marine dangers also exist and local advice should be heeded before entering the water. See the entry Cuts, Bites & Stings in the Health section earlier in this chapter for information on related medical treatment.

EMERGENCIES
The emergency telephone number for the police is ☎ 110, and for fire/ambulance emergency services it's ☎ 119. You should be able to get your point across in simple English; however, if you do have problems communicating, ring the Japan Helpline (☎ 0120-461-997), an emergency number that operates 24 hours a day, seven days a week.

See Medical Problems & Treatment under Health earlier in this chapter for more information on dealing with a medical emergency.

LEGAL MATTERS
Japanese police have extraordinary powers in comparison with their Western counterparts. For starters, Japanese police have the right to detain a suspect without charging them for up to three days, after which a prosecutor can decide to extend this period for another 20 days. Police can also choose whether to allow a suspect to phone his or her embassy or lawyer, though if you find yourself in police custody you should insist that you will not cooperate in any way until allowed to make such a call. Your embassy is the first place you should call if given the chance.

Police will speak almost no English; insist that an interpreter *(tsuyakusha)* be summoned. Police are legally bound to provide one before proceeding with any questioning. However, if you do speak Japanese, it's best to deny it and stay with your native language.

For legal counselling in English and some other languages, call the Human Rights Center Information Line (☎ 03-3581-2302) from noon to 5 pm on weekdays. The Gaikokujin Komarigoto Sōdan (Foreigners' Crisis Consultation, ☎ 03-3503-8484) can provide telephone interpretation with police if necessary.

BUSINESS HOURS
Department stores usually open at 10 am and close at 6.30 or 7 pm, seven days a week (with one or two days off each month). Smaller shops are open similar hours but may close on Sunday. Large companies usually work from 9 am to 5 pm, Monday to Friday and some also operate on Saturday morning. (See Banking under Money for banking hours, and the Post & Communications section for post office hours.)

PUBLIC HOLIDAYS & SPECIAL EVENTS
Japan has 14 national holidays. When a public holiday falls on a Sunday, the following Monday is taken as a holiday. You can expect a total sell-out for travel and lodging during the New Year (29 December to 6 January), Golden Week (27 April to 6 May) and the mid-August O-Bon festival.

National Holidays

Ganjitsu (New Year's Day) 1 January
Seijin-no-hi (Coming-of-Age Day) 2nd Sunday in January
Kenkoku Kinem-bi (National Foundation Day) 11 February
Shumbun-no-hi (Spring Equinox) 20 or 21 March
Midori-no-hi (Green Day) 29 April
Kempō Kinem-bi (Constitution Day) 3 May
Kodomo-no-hi (Children's Day) 5 May
Umi-no-hi (Marine Day) 20 July
Keirō-no-hi (Respect-for-the-Aged Day) 15 September
Shūbun-no-hi (Autumn Equinox) 23 or 24 September
Taiiku-no-hi (Sports Day) 2nd Monday in October
Bunka-no-hi (Culture Day) 3 November
Kinrō Kansha-no-hi (Labour Thanksgiving Day) 23 November
Tennō Tanjōbi (Emperor's Birthday) 23 December

CULTURAL EVENTS

Japan has a large number of *matsuri* (festivals) and annual events. Festivals are mainly of Shintō origin and related to the seasonal planting, growing and harvesting of rice. Annual events, on the other hand, are often Buddhist imports from China or more recent imports from the West, as in Valentine's day. Some of the most important events are:

January

Shōgatsu (New Year) – New Year celebrations from 1 to 3 January include much eating and drinking, visits to shrines or temples and the paying of respects to relatives and business associates.
Seijin-no-hi (Coming-of-Age Day) – Ceremonies are held for boys and girls who have reached the age of majority (20).

February–May

Setsubun (Last day of winter according to lunar calendar), 3 or 4 February – To celebrate the end of winter and drive out evil spirits, the Japanese indulge in *setsubun* (bean throwing) while chanting *'fuku wa uchi oni wa soto'* ('in with good fortune, out with the devils').
Hanami (Blossom Viewing) – The Japanese delight in the brief blossom-viewing seasons from February to April. The usual sequence is plum in February, peach in March and cherry in late March or early April.

Hina Matsuri (Doll Festival), 3 March – During this festival old dolls are displayed and young girls are presented with special dolls *(hina)* which represent ancient figures from the imperial court.
Golden Week 29 April–5 May – Golden Week is so called because it takes in Green Day (29 April), Constitution Day (3 May) and Children's Day (5 May). This is definitely not a time to be on the move since transport and lodging in popular holiday areas can be booked solid.
Kodomo-no-hi (Children's Day) – This is a holiday dedicated to children, especially boys. Families fly paper streamers of carp *(koi)*, which symbolise male strength.

July–August

Tanabata Matsuri (Star Festival), 7 July – The two stars Vega and Altair meet in the Milky Way on this night. According to a myth (originally Chinese), a princess and a peasant shepherd were forbidden to meet, but this was the only time in the year when the two star-crossed lovers could organise a tryst. Children copy out poems on streamers and love poems are written on banners that are hung out on display. An especially ornate version of this festival is celebrated from 6 to 8 August in Sendai.
O-Bon (Festival of the Dead) 13–16 July and August – According to Buddhist tradition, this is a time when ancestors return to earth. Lanterns are lit and floated on rivers, lakes or the sea to signify the return of the departed to the underworld. Since most Japanese try to return to their native village at this time of year, this is one of the most crowded times of year to travel or look for accommodation.

November

Shichi-Go-San (Seven-Five-Three Festival), 15 November – Traditionally, this is a festival in honour of girls who are aged three and seven and boys who are five. Children are dressed in their finest clothes and taken to shrines or temples where prayers are offered for good fortune.

ACTIVITIES

Cycling

Although much of Japan is mountainous, the coastal regions are popular with cyclists. See Bicycle in the Getting Around chapter for more information about cycling in Japan. See also Cycling Terminals under Accommodation later in this chapter for information on places to stay.

Skiing

Skiing developed in Japan in the 1950s and there are now more than 300 ski resorts, many with high-standard runs and snow-making equipment. The majority of resorts are concentrated on the island of Honshū, where the crowds are huge, the vertical drops rarely more than 400m and all runs start at altitudes of less than 2000m. Snow cover in southern and eastern Honshū is generally adequate, but can be sparse and icy.

Skiers on Hokkaidō, however, can look forward to powder skiing that rivals anything in the European Alps or the Rockies in the USA. Niseko and Furano, two of Hokkaidō's best resorts, have excellent facilities (Niseko has 43 lifts) and neither suffers from extreme crowding.

JNTO's *Skiing in Japan* pamphlet covers 20 resorts on Honshū and Hokkaidō, with travel information, ski season dates, accommodation details, resort facilities and costs. Japan Airlines offers special ski tour-packages including air fares, transportation, meals and accommodation.

Skiing is normally possible from December to April, though the season can be shorter in some of Honshū's lower-altitude resorts. Akakura, which is within easy reach of Tokyo, is known for its deep snow that thaws quickly by the end of March. Shiga and Zaō, on Honshū, are best for early April skiing. The best time for cross-country skiing is March or April, when the snow is firmer and deeper; January and February are often very cold and stormy.

Resort accommodation ranges from hostels to expensive hotels but is heavily booked during the ski season. There are many resorts at hot springs that double as onsen or bathing spas. Avoid weekends and holidays when lift lines are long and accommodation and transportation are heavily booked.

Lift passes cost ¥3000 to ¥4500 a day. Daily rental of skis, stocks and boots can cost up to ¥5000 but finding larger-size ski boots may be difficult. Equipment can only be hired at resorts and is usually old and of a low standard; advanced equipment for the more experienced skier is rare. Ski gear and clothing can be hired at most resorts. For those with plenty of cash it is possible to buy it in Japan – many ski shops hold sales from September to November and package-deal bargains can be found with skis, bindings and stocks included. Tokyo's Jimbōchō, Shinjuku, Shibuya and Ikebukuro areas have good ski shops.

As well as downhill skiing, Japan also offers good terrain for cross-country skiing and touring, especially in the Hakodate region of Hokkaidō – a good way to get away from the crowds. The Japanese are very hospitable and foreigners are welcome to join in races and festivities organised by the local authorities. One of the most famous is the Sapporo Marathon cross-country ski race.

For more information on skiing in Japan, pick up a copy of T R Reid's *Ski Japan* (Kodansha). Each winter, *Kansai Time Out* magazine also features articles on ski fields within easy reach of Kansai.

Hiking

The Japanese are keen hikers, and many of the national parks of Japan have hiking routes. Around Tokyo, the popular hiking areas are Nikkō and Chichibu-Tama National Park. If you want to get away from it all, Gunma-ken offers hikes where you are very unlikely to happen across other foreigners. In the Kansai region, Nara, Shiga and Kyoto all have pleasant hikes.

Japan comes into its own as a hiking destination in the Central Alps, in Northern Honshū and in Hokkaidō. In these less populated and mountainous regions of Japan, there may be the added incentive of an onsen soak at the end of a long day's walk. Hikers who trek into the mountains see a side of Japan that few foreigners ever experience.

While some rudimentary English-language hiking maps may be available from local tourism authorities, it's better to seek out proper Japanese maps and decipher the kanji. Shobunsha's *Yama-to-Kōgen No Chizu* series covers all of Japan's most popular hiking areas in exquisite detail. The maps are available in all major bookshops in Japan.

Serious hikers will also want to pick up a copy of Lonely Planet's *Hiking in Japan*,

Enjoy Your Trip

Japan's draconian drug laws have long meant that the country has rarely been a stopover on the psychotropically inclined traveller's trail, other than as a place to earn some almighty Japanese yen before hopping off to more fertile stoner grounds in Goa, Ko Phi-Phi or Kathmandu. However, for those wishing an inner voyage to match the outer one, Japan has one excellent means of 'transport' that seems to enjoy semi-legal status – magic mushrooms.

Note: Lonely Planet does not advise or condone recreational drug use. In the case of mushrooms, it is very easy to mistake a poisonous toadstool for a mushroom, and severe poisoning or even death could be the result of consumption. Additionally, the effects of psychotropic substances found in the mushrooms mentioned in this boxed text can be unpredictable, and can include hallucinations, nightmares, and panic and anxiety attacks, as well as the risk of overdose.

The shaman of North-East Asia have long recognised the hallucinogenic and spiritual power of edible fungi, and in particular of *Amanita muscaria*, commonly known as Fly Agaric, which was once commonplace through the Tōhoku and Hokkaidō regions. Psychotropic rituals are rumoured to be still practised today in parts of Siberia, and the Russian-held islands north of Hokkaidō.

More contemporary adepts are the youth of Tokyo's Shibuya and Roppongi, and Osaka's Amerika-mura, where psilocybin, or hallucinogenic mushrooms, are intermittently available in markets and psychedelic stores for around ¥2500 to ¥4500 a shot. Denizens of the Osaka club world even benefit from the nation's love affair with convenience – reports tell of a 24-hour mushroom vending machine.

The legality of mushroom possession and consumption seems to be a nebulous issue. Conflicting stories come from consumers and law-enforcement agencies alike. While street folklore suggests that mushrooms are fully legal, a more likely explanation is that spores are illegal while the mushrooms themselves are not. Thus shops can retail dried mushrooms with impunity, but expect to be nabbed if you walk down the mountain clutching armfuls of psychoactive fungi. However, even the unusually long arm of the Japanese constabulary fails to reach most habitats of *Psilocybe venanata* and co.

A Brief Field Guide to Japanese Magic Mushrooms

Japan boasts several dozen varieties of *doku-kinoko* (poisonous mushroom). Mountain-climbing ethnobotanists are most likely to bump into a few of the following:

Benitengu-dake (Red Long-Nosed Goblin Mushroom)

Amanita muscaria is commonly known as Fly Agaric, or the White-warted Red-capped toadstool. It has a vivid red or orange cap, and can be from 6cm to 15cm wide. A white universal veil will entirely cover the youngest mushrooms, and will form whitish spots or warts on mature mushrooms that may eventually wash or wear off with age. These spots often form concentric circles, although they can also appear randomly. The white- to cream-coloured rather scaly stalk is 10cm to 25cm in length, has a ring and a bulbous base with rows of cottony patches and is 1cm to 3cm in diameter at the base, narrowing slightly towards the cap. Benitengu-dake are found on the ground, in pine and broad-leafed forests, especially in *shirakaba-bayashi* (silver birch woodland). For a visual, check this home page: http://www.snowspr.isp.ntt.co.jp/nature/animal/kinoko/163-163.html

Tengu-dake (Long-Nosed Goblin Mushroom), Haetori-take (Flycatcher Mushroom)

Amanita pantherina is commonly known as Panther Amanita. The 4cm to 25cm roundish or convex-to-flat cap ranges in colour from dark to light brown, tan to dull yellowish. Its edges may be

Enjoy Your Trip

blackish, sooty, or a brownish yellow. It is dark in the centre, lightening towards the outside, and its surface may be sticky when wet. The white (or buff) stalk is 5cm to 30cm long, has a ring and a bulbous base, and is 0.6cm to 3.0cm in diameter at the base, narrowing slightly towards the cap. Tengu-dake are commonly found in *matsubayashi* (pine forests). For a visual, check the Web site dbs.p.kanazawa-u.ac.jp/%7Eohta/tengutake.html

Owarai-take (Great Laughing Mushroom)

Gymnopilus spectabilis is commonly known as Big Laughing Jim. Its cap is 5cm to 15cm wide, and is a golden-yellow or orange colour. Gills vary in colour from yellow to a light rust colour. The stalk is 5cm to 15cm long, and 5mm to 30mm wide. It is found from summer to autumn around broad-leaved trees, in particular *mizunara* oak. The mushroom has the unique property of turning green on cooking. For a visual, see www.cx.sakura.ne.jp/~kinoko/00jap/ohwaraitake.htm

Oshibire-take (Great Numbing Mushroom)

Psilocybe subaeruginascens. Found nationwide, but especially prevalent on the islands of Ishigaki and Yakushima, this mushroom has a whitish cap with a smoke-brown centre. The cap is 1cm to 6cm in width, and is either flat or slightly convex. It surface is smooth and free of hair, and can be sticky in wet or humid weather. The white stem is 1.5mm to 3mm wide, 3cm to 4cm long, and the widely spaced gills are greyish brown and slightly paler at the edges.

If tempted by this mushroom, think twice. It is hallucinogenic in reasonable doses, but unlike most other hallucinogenic fungi, it's also toxic and can be lethal in higher doses. A jpeg is at dbs.p .kanazawau.ac.jp/%7Eohta/ooshibiretake.html.

Warai-take (Laughing Mushroom)

Panaeolus papilonaceus. With a smooth, olive brown to grey brown cap that is generally 1.5cm to 6.0cm in width, cone-like at the top and bell-shaped at the bottom, this mushroom is commonly seen on horse manure from spring to autumn. Sticky when humid or damp, it has close packed, broad, pale grey gills. The stem is 8cm to 15cm long, 2mm to 4mm thick, and is grey-brown, thin, fragile and hollow. For a visual, check this Web site at www.sue.shiga-u .ac.jp/kinoko/k2e.htm

For further information about psychoactive fungi, the extensive Web site at www.erowid.org/ is an excellent place to start.

MICK WELDON

John Ashburne

which covers convenient one-day hikes near major cities and extended hikes in more remote areas.

Golf

Golf equals prestige in Japan. If you want to set foot on a green, a fat wallet and corporate clout are handy assets. Membership fees are rarely less than US$5000, can easily reach US$25,000 and often soar higher. Of course, it is usually the company that takes out corporate membership and thus pays for its employees to go golfing. Green fees usually start at around US$100 a day. If you just need a quick golf fix, you can try one of the many driving ranges located in most Japanese cities.

Diving

The Okinawan islands in the far south-west of Japan and the Izu-shotō (Izu Seven Islands) south of Tokyo are popular among Japanese as diving destinations. Other dive sites in Japan include the waters around Sado-ga-shima, off northern Honshū, and the peninsula, Izu-hantō, south-west of Tokyo.

As you would expect, diving in Japan is expensive. Typical rates are ¥12,000 per day for two boat-dives and lunch. Courses for beginners are available in places such as Ishigaki and Iriomote islands, but starting costs are around ¥80,000. Instruction will usually be in Japanese.

COURSES

There are courses for almost every aspect of Japanese culture. The Tokyo TIC has a wealth of printed information available. Applicants for Cultural Visas should note that attendance at 20 class-hours per week are required. Those wishing to work while studying need to apply for permission to do so.

Japanese Language

There is no shortage of Japanese-language schools in Japan, most of them found in the bigger cities of Tokyo, Osaka, Nagoya, Kōbe and Kyoto. Some offer only part-time instruction, while others offer full-time and intensive courses and may sponsor you for

a Cultural Visa, which will allow you to work up to 20 hours a week while you study (after receiving permission). The best place to look for Japanese language schools is in *Kansai Time Out* magazine and *Tokyo Classified*. Schools also advertise in the four English-language newspapers.

Costs at private Japanese-language schools vary enormously depending on the school's status and facilities. There is usually an application fee of ¥5000 to ¥30,000, plus an administration charge of ¥50,000 to ¥100,000 and then the annual tuition fees of ¥350,000 to ¥600,000. Add accommodation and food, and it is easy to see why it may be necessary to work while you study.

Martial Arts

Aikidō, judō, karate and *kendō* can be studied in Japan. Less popular disciplines, such as *kyūdō* (Japanese archery) and *sumō*, also attract devotees from overseas. Relevant addresses include:

All-Japan Judō Federation (☎ 03-3818-4199) c/o Kodokan, 1-16-30 Kasuga, Bukyō-ku, Tokyo
Amateur Archery Federation of Japan (☎ 03-3481-2387) Kishi Memorial Hall, 4th floor, 1-1-1 Jinan, Shibuya-ku, Tokyo
International Aikidō Federation (☎ 03-3203-9236) 17-18 Wakamatsu-chō, Shinjuku-ku, Tokyo
Japan Kendō Federation (☎ 03-3211-5804/5) c/o Nippon Budokan, 2-3 Kitanomaru-kōen, Chiyoda-ku, Tokyo
Nihon Sumō Kyokai (☎ 03-3623-5111) c/o Kokugikan Sumō Hall, 1-3-28 Yokoami, Sumida-ku, Tokyo
World Union of Karate-dō Organisation (☎ 03-3503-6640) 4th floor, Sempaku Shinkokaikan Bldg, 1-15-16 Toranomon, Minato-ku, Tokyo

Traditional Arts

Many local cultural centres and tourist offices can arrange short courses in Japanese arts, such as ceramics, *washi* (Japanese papermaking), *aizome* (indigo dyeing), woodworking, calligraphy, ink painting and *ikebana* (flower arranging). The best place to pursue these interests is in Kyoto, where the TIC or the International Community

House can put you in touch with qualified teachers.

If you're interested in learning about the art of flower arranging, contact Ikebana International (☎ 03-3293-8188), Ochanomizu Square Building, 1-6 Surugadai, Kanda, Chiyoda-ku, Tokyo. Some schools provide instruction in English.

WORK

Finding work in Japan is still possible but it's nowhere near as easy or as lucrative as it used to be. Teaching English is still the most common job for Westerners, but bartending, hostessing, modelling and various editorial jobs are also possible.

Whatever line of work you choose, it's essential to look neat and tidy for interviews – appearances are *very* important in Japan. You'll also need to be determined, and you should have a sizeable sum of money to carry you through while you are looking for work, and possibly to get you out of the country if you don't find any (it happens). Foreigners who have set up in Japan over the last few years maintain that a figure of around US$5000 or more is necessary to make a go of it in Japan. People do it with less, but they are taking the risk of ending up penniless and homeless before they find a job.

English Teaching

Teaching English has always been the most popular job for native English speakers in Japan. While it's still a fairly common option, competition for the good jobs is now very tight since many schools have failed as a result of Japan's weakened economy. A university degree is an absolute essential as you cannot qualify for a Work Visa without one. Actual teaching qualifications and some teaching experience will be a huge plus when job hunting.

Consider lining up a job before arriving in Japan. Big schools, like Nova for example, now have recruitment programs in the USA and the UK. One downside to the big 'factory schools' that recruit overseas is that working conditions are often pretty dire compared to smaller schools that recruit within Japan.

Australians, New Zealanders and Canadians, who can take advantage of the Japanese Working Holiday Visa (see Visas under Visas & Documents earlier in this chapter), are in a slightly better position. Schools are happier about taking on unqualified teachers if they don't have to bother with sponsoring a teacher for a Work Visa.

Private Schools The classifieds section of the Monday edition of the *Japan Times* is the best place to look for teaching positions. Some larger schools rely on direct inquiries from would-be teachers.

Tokyo is the easiest place to find teaching jobs; schools across Japan advertise or recruit in the capital. Heading straight to another of Japan's major population centres (say Osaka, Fukuoka, Hiroshima or Sapporo), where there are smaller numbers of competing foreigners, is also a good bet.

Check the fine print carefully once you have an offer. Find out how many hours you will teach, whether class preparation time is included and whether you receive sick leave and paid holidays. Find out how and when you will be paid and if the school will sponsor your visa. It's worth checking conditions with other foreign staff. Check also whether your school is prepared to serve as a guarantor in the event that you rent an apartment.

Government Schools The Japan Exchange & Teaching (JET) program provides 2000 teaching assistant positions for foreign teachers. The job operates on a yearly contract and must be organised in your home country. The program gets very good reports from many of the teachers involved with it.

Teachers employed by the JET program are known as Assistant English Teachers (AETs). Although you will have to apply in your home country in order to work as an AET with JET, it's worth bearing in mind that many local governments in Japan are also employing AETs for their schools. Such work can be obtained within Japan.

Contact your nearest Japanese embassy or consulate for more details (see Embassies & Consulates earlier in this chapter).

International Schools

Major cities like Tokyo and Yokohama with large foreign populations have a number of international schools for the children of foreign residents. Work is available for qualified, Western-trained teachers in all disciplines; the schools will usually organise your visa.

Proofreading & Editing

There is ample work, particularly in the Tokyo area, for editors, proofreaders and translators (Japanese to English and vice-versa). Needless to say, it is difficult for the casual visitor to simply waltz into these jobs – you'll need to have the proper qualifications and experience. And even for proofreading and editing, some Japanese ability is a huge plus, if only for dealing with clients. If you think you've got what it takes, check the Monday edition of the *Japan Times* for openings.

Hostessing

A hostess is a woman who is paid to pour drinks for salarymen, listen to their troubles and generally provide an amiable atmosphere. Although hostessing does involve a lot of thinly veiled sexual innuendos and the occasional furtive grab at thighs or breasts, it is not a form of prostitution, however, at some of the seedier places, there may be some pressure to perform 'extracurricular activities'. Hostessing involves late hours, frequent pressure to drink and exposure to astonishing amounts of cigarette smoke. Hostesses should avoid adopting too casual an approach to safety precautions if seeing clients outside working hours. See the Women Travellers section earlier for more information on safety issues.

Work Visas are not issued for hostessing – it is an illegal activity to which the authorities seem to turn a blind eye. An introduction is usually required. Rates for Western women working as hostesses typically range from ¥3000 to ¥5000 per hour (plus tips), with bonuses for bringing customers to the club. An ability to speak Japanese is an asset, but not essential – many Japanese salarymen want to practise their English.

Bartending

Bartending does not qualify you for a Work Visa; most of the foreign bartenders in Japan are either working illegally or on another kind of visa. Some bars in big Japanese cities hire foreign bartenders; most are strict about visas but others don't seem to care. The best places to look are 'gaijin bars', although a few Japanese-oriented places also employ foreign bartenders for 'ambience'. The pay is barely enough to survive on – usually about ¥1000 per hour.

Modelling

Modelling jobs for foreigners are increasingly dominated by professional models; you will need a proper portfolio of photographs. Nonprofessionals are more likely to pick up casual work as extras in advertising or film.

ACCOMMODATION

Japan offers an interesting range of accommodation, from cheap guesthouses to swank hotels, with almost everything in between. Although most options are more expensive than what you'd expect to pay in other Asian countries, you can still find some bargains.

Youth hostels are among the bottom of the range. The typical cost is ¥2400 to ¥3000. But by staying only at youth hostels, you will cut yourself off from an essential part of the Japan experience. Try to vary your accommodation, and try a traditional ryokan (Japanese-style inn), a *shukubō* (temple lodging) and a minshuku (Japanese B&B).

Cheap places to stay are often on the outskirts of town, which can mean an expensive taxi ride if you arrive late. If you get really stuck in the late hours, the nearest *kōban* (police box) should be able to point you in the right direction for a place to stay. Business hotels are often close to the station, but you're generally looking at a minimum of ¥5000 per person in one of these. Capsule hotels or love hotels are useful late-night alternatives.

Reservations

It is quite feasible to look for a room after arriving in a new town, though reservations are best made a few days in advance. During peak holiday seasons, you should book as far ahead as possible, particularly if you have a special choice. Out of season, calling a day in advance is usually sufficient.

Kankō annai-jo (tourist information offices) at main train stations can usually help with reservations, and are often open until about 6.30 pm or later. Even if you are travelling by car, the train station is a good first stop in town for information, reservations and even cheap car parking. The Japanese run their accommodation according to an established rhythm that favours checkouts at around 10 am and check-ins between 5 and 7 pm; unannounced latecomers disturb this pattern.

Making phone reservations in English is usually possible in most major cities. Providing you speak clearly and simply, there will usually be someone around who can get the gist of what you want. There will also be frequent occasions when hotel staff understand no English. If you really get stuck, try asking the desk staff at the last place you stayed to phone your reservation through.

It is possible to make bookings at the Welcome Inn Reservation Centers found in the TIC offices in Tokyo and Kyoto, and at Narita and Kansai airports. JNTO offices abroad and TIC offices in Tokyo and Kyoto stock some useful magazines, such as *Reasonable Accommodations in Japan*, which has details of 200 hotels, ryokan and business hotels in 50 major cities in Japan. Other useful publications include *Directory of Welcome Inns*, a very extensive listing, and *Japanese Inn Group*, which has a number of ryokan throughout Japan that are used to dealing with foreigners.

Camping Grounds & Mountain Huts

Camping is one of the cheapest forms of accommodation, but official camping grounds are often only open during the Japanese 'camping season' (July and August), when you can expect an avalanche of students. Facilities range from bare essentials to deluxe. JNTO publishes *Camping in Japan*, a limited selection of camping grounds with details of prices and facilities.

In some restricted areas and national parks, camping wild is forbidden, but elsewhere, foreigners have reported consistent success. Even if there is no officially designated camping ground, campers are often directed to the nearest large patch of grass. Provided you set up camp late in the afternoon and leave early, nobody seems to mind, though it is common courtesy to ask permission first (assuming you can find the person responsible). Public toilets, usually spotless, and water taps are very common, even in remote parts of Japan.

The best areas for camping are Hokkaidō, the Japan Alps, Tōhoku and Okinawa.

Mountain huts *(yama-goya)* are common in many of the hiking and mountain climbing areas. Unoccupied huts provide a free roof over your head. Other huts, in the Japan Alps for example, are run privately and offer bed and board (two meals) at around ¥5000 to ¥8000 per person; if you prepare your own meal that figure drops to ¥3000 to ¥5000 per person.

Youth Hostels

For budget travellers youth hostels are the best option, and it is quite feasible to plan an entire itinerary using them. Most dorms are single sex. The best source of information on hostels is the *Japan Youth Hostel Handbook* available for ¥580 from the Japan Youth Hostel Association (JYHA, ☎ 03-3288-1417), Suidobashi Nishi-guchi Kaikan, 2-20-7 Misaki-chō, Chiyoda-ku, Tokyo 101-0061.

There is a branch office in Tokyo that stocks the handbook and can supply information. It's on the 2nd level basement of Sogo department store, Yūraku-chō (two minutes on foot from the TIC). Many hostels throughout Japan also sell the handbook.

The *Youth Hostels Map of Japan* is a useful map with one-line entries on each hostel. It's published jointly with JNTO, and is available free from JNTO and TICs in Japan.

The JYHA handbook is mostly in Japanese, though there is some English in the symbol key at the front and on the locater map keys. The hostels on each map are identified by name (in kanji) and a page number. Each hostel is accompanied by a mini-map, photo, address in Japanese, fax and phone details, a row of symbols, access instructions in Japanese, open dates, bed numbers and prices for bed and meals.

By looking at the photos and the symbols it is quite easy to single out hostels which might be interesting. The reversed swastika symbol means that the hostel is a temple. Pay careful attention to the closing and opening dates: many hostels – particularly those in rural areas – close over New Year's or shut down in winter.

The *Youth Hostel Map of Japan* has hostel addresses in English, but it can still be a struggle trying to work out a romaji version of the address. The *IYHF (International Youth Hostel Federation) Handbook* has a ridiculously skimpy set of entries for Japan and is not worth considering for a Japan trip.

Advantages & Disadvantages Youth hostels are comfortable, inexpensive by Japanese standards, and usually good sources of information when used as a base for touring. They are also a good way to meet Japanese travellers and other foreigners. By carefully studying the JYHA handbook, you can select interesting places and weed out possible duds. Many hostels have superb sites: some are farms, remote temples, outstanding private homes or elegant inns.

Some hostels, however, have very early closing hours, often 9 pm, and a routine strongly reminiscent of school or perhaps even prison. In the high season you are likely to encounter waves of school children or throngs of students. Some hostels organise meetings in the evening with games, songs and dances, which any resident gaijin may find difficult to decline. The novelty of these can wear thin. If you are reliant on public transport, access to some youth hostels is complicated and time-consuming.

Membership & Regulations You can stay at over 70 municipal hostels without a youth-hostel membership card. Elsewhere, you will need a JYHA membership card or

one from an affiliate of the IYHF, otherwise you must pay an extra charge. It is much simpler if you become a member in your own country, as JYHA registration requires that members have lived in Japan for a year, have an Alien Registration Card and pay a ¥2000 joining fee.

Nonmembers must pay an additional ¥600 per night for a 'welcome stamp'. Six welcome stamps plus a photograph entitles you to an IYHF International Guest Card valid worldwide for the rest of the year. If you purchase all six stamps at once the price is reduced to ¥2800, a saving of ¥800.

Youth hostel membership has a minimum age limit of four years but no maximum age – you will meet plenty of Japanese seniors and often a few foreign ones approaching their 70s as well.

Hostel charges currently average ¥2800 per night; some also add the 5% *shōhizei* (consumption tax). Private rooms are also available in some hostels at ¥3500 per night upwards. As a friendly gesture, some hostels have introduced a special reduction – sometimes as much as ¥500 per night – for foreign hostellers.

Average prices for meals are ¥500 for breakfast and ¥900 for dinner. Almost all hostels require you to use a regulation sleeping sheet, which you can rent for ¥100 if you do not have your own. Although official regulations state that you can only stay at one hostel for three consecutive nights, this probably depends on the season.

Hostellers are expected to check in between 3 pm and 8 or 9 pm. There is usually a curfew of 10 or 11 pm. Checkout is usually required before 10 am and dormitories are closed between 10 am and 3 pm. Bath time is usually between 5 and 9 pm, dinner time is between 6 and 7.30 pm, breakfast time is between 7 and 8 am.

Hostel Food The food at hostels varies widely: some places provide stodgy and unimaginative fare while others pull out all the stops to offer excellent value. At consecutive hostels in Hokkaidō, you may be served a luscious Jenghis Khan hotpot one night, *sukiyaki* (quick-cooked beef and vegetable stew) the next and *sashimi* the following night.

The hostel breakfast is usually Japanese style, for which it takes a little time to acquire a taste. Some travellers skip *nattō* (sticky, fermented soybeans), *nori* (dried seaweed) and raw egg and head off in search of a *mōningu* (morning) set breakfast of coffee, toast and a boiled egg from a nearby coffee shop. It can even work out cheaper doing it this way. Some hostels require you to help with the washing-up; others prefer to keep you out of the kitchen.

Reservations Advance reservations are essential for the New Year holiday weeks, the late April/early May Golden Week period, and July and August. You should state the arrival date and time, number of nights, number and sex of the people for whom beds are to be reserved and which meals are required. When corresponding from abroad *always* include two International Reply Coupons.

In Japan, computer bookings can be made in Tokyo and Osaka, and increasing numbers of youth hostels are plugging into the system. Some hostels also have fax numbers. For confirmation, return postage-paid postcards are available from post offices or to make things even simpler, use the pre-printed cards available from JYHA headquarters in Tokyo.

Telephone bookings are fine if you can muster enough Japanese. One way to simplify things is to ask a local, perhaps a fellow hosteller or a member of the youth hostel staff, to make the booking for you.

Out of season you can probably get away with booking a day or so in advance. Hostels definitely prefer you to phone, even if it's from across the street, rather than simply rolling up without warning. If you arrive without warning, you shouldn't expect any meals.

Guesthouses

Guesthouses are often old Japanese houses that have been converted into cheap inns, many expressly aimed at foreign travellers. Some also double as 'gaijin houses' (see the Gaijin Houses entry later in this section).

Guesthouses are particularly common in Kyoto but you'll also find a few scattered about Tokyo. The advantage of guesthouses is that they offer youth hostel prices without all the accompanying regimentation. Of course, some guesthouses can be pretty run down, and it's well worth taking a look around before paying your money. Where possible, we list guesthouses in the appropriate Places to Stay sections; otherwise, the best way to find guesthouses is by checking in magazines like *Kansai Time Out* and *Tokyo Classified* or by word of mouth.

Shukubō

Staying in a shukubō or temple lodging is one way to experience another facet of traditional Japan. Sometimes you are allocated a simple room in the temple precincts and left to your own devices. You may also be asked to participate in prayers, services or *zazen* (sitting) meditation. At many temples exquisite vegetarian meals *(shōjin ryōri)* are served.

The TICs in Tokyo and Kyoto both produce leaflets on temple lodgings in their regions. Kōya-san, a renowned religious centre in the Kansai region, includes over 50 shukubō and is one of the best places in Japan to try this type of accommodation.

Over 70 youth hostels are temples or shrines – look for the reverse swastika symbol in the JYHA handbook. The suffixes *-ji*, *-in* or *-dera* are also clues that the hostel is a temple.

Toho

The Toho network is a diverse collection of places that has banded loosely together to offer a more flexible alternative to youth hostels. Toho network inns ascribe to a common philosophy of informal hospitality at reasonable prices. Most of the network's 90 members are in Hokkaidō, although there are a few scattered around Honshū and other islands farther south. The owners may not speak much (if any) English and you should *definitely* phone ahead to make reservations, even if it's just from a phone box down the street. The main drawback (or attraction for some travellers) of these places is that many of them are difficult to reach. Many owners, however, will provide a free pick-up service from the nearest train or bus station if you make arrangements in advance.

For dormitory-style accommodation, prices average ¥3500, or ¥5000 with two meals. Private rooms are sometimes available for about ¥1000 extra. A comprehensive Japanese-language Toho network guide (¥200) with detailed directions is available at bookshops in Hokkaidō or from Toho network inns, including the founding member, Sapporo Inn NADA. You can find limited English-language information on the Toho network at www.toho.net, which features an increasing number of helpful links to individual member inn homepages.

Rider Houses

Catering mainly to touring motorcyclists, *raidā hausu* (rider houses) provide extremely basic shared accommodation from around ¥1000 per night. Some rider houses are attached to local *rāmen* (noodles) shops or other eateries, and may also offer discounted rates if you agree to eat there. You should bring your own sleeping bag or ask to rent bedding from the owner. For bathing facilities, you will often be directed to the local *sentō* (bathhouse). Although rider houses may not be the most comfortable places, they are generally safe for both sexes and a good place to meet alternative, independent Japanese travellers, including bicyclists, hitchhikers and other shoestring travellers.

There are innumerable rider houses throughout Hokkaidō, as well a few in southern Japan, mainly Kyūshū and Okinawa. If you ask around town or at the local tourist information office for a 'raidā hausu', someone will probably point you in the right direction. Unfortunately, many rider houses are located out of town and are hard to reach on public transport. If you can read some Japanese, spiral-bound *Touring Mapple* maps (Shobunsha) mark almost all of the rider houses in a specific region, as well as cheap places to eat along the way. These maps are available at most Japanese bookshops.

Cycling Terminals

Cycling terminals *(saikuringu tāminaru)* provide low-priced accommodation of the bunk-bed or tatami-mat variety and are usually found in scenic areas suited to cycling. If you don't have your own bike, you can rent one at the terminal.

At around ¥2500 per person per night or ¥4000 including two meals, terminal prices compare favourably with those of a youth hostel. For more information contact the Japan Bicycle Promotion Institute (☎ 03-3583-5444), Nihon Jitensha Kaikan Bldg, 1-9-3 Akasaka, Minato-ku, Tokyo.

Kokumin-shukusha

Kokumin-shukusha (people's lodges) are government-supported institutions offering affordable accommodation in scenic areas. Private Japanese-style rooms are the norm, though some places offer Western-style rooms. Prices average ¥5500 to ¥6500 per person per night including two meals. The best way to find kokumin-shukusha is to ask at local tourist offices or kōban.

Minshuku

A minshuku is usually a family-run private lodging, rather like a Western-style B&B. Minshuku can be found throughout Japan and offer an experience of daily Japanese life. The average price per-person, per-night with two meals is around ¥6000. You are expected to lay out and put away your bedding and provide your own towel.

The Japan Minshuku Association (☎ 03-3364-1855), Suegawa Bldg, 4-10-15, Takadanobaba, Shinjuku-ku Tokyo 169-0075, has a leaflet in English describing the minshuku concept and providing advice on staying at one; a list of minshuku is also available. The Nihon Minshuku Center (☎ 03-3216-6556), Tokyo Kōtsū Kaikan Bldg, 2-10-1 Yūraku-chō, Chiyoda-ku, Tokyo 100-0006 can help with computer bookings; a similar office operates in Kyoto. Some of the places listed in the Japanese Inn Group's handy little booklet (see the Ryokan entry) are really minshuku rather than ryokan. The line between the two accommodation categories can be fuzzy.

Ryokan

For a taste of traditional Japanese life, a stay at a ryokan is mandatory. Ryokan range from ultra-exclusive establishments to reasonably priced places with a homey atmosphere, and there are corresponding fluctuations in what you get for your money. Prices start at around ¥4000 (per person, per night) for a 'no-frills' ryokan without meals. For a classier ryokan, expect prices to start at ¥8000. Exclusive establishments – Kyoto is a prime centre for these – charge ¥25,000 and often much more.

Ryokan owners prefer to charge on a room and board (breakfast and dinner) basis

---

Everything You Need to Know about Staying at a Ryokan

On arrival at a *ryokan* (traditional Japanese inn), you leave your shoes at the entrance, don a pair of slippers, and are shown by a maid to your room, which has a *tatami* (reed mat) floor. Slippers are taken off before entering tatami rooms. Instead of using numbers, rooms are named after auspicious flowers, plants or trees.

The interior of the room will contain a *tokonoma* (alcove), probably decorated with a flower display or a calligraphy scroll. Do not step into or place any objects in the tokonoma. One side of the room will contain a cupboard with sliding doors for the bedding; the other side will have sliding screens covered with rice paper and perhaps open onto a verandah with a garden view.

The room maid then serves tea with a Japanese sweet on a low table surrounded by *zabuton* (cushions) in the centre of the room. At the same time you are asked to sign the register. A tray is provided with a towel, *yukata* (cotton kimono) and *obi* (belt) which you put on before taking your bath. Remember to wrap the left side over the right – the reverse order is used for dressing the dead. In colder weather, there will also be a *tanzen* (outer jacket). Your clothes can be put away in a closet or left on a hanger.

Dressed in your yukata, you will be shown to the *o-furo* (bath). At some ryokan, there are rooms with private baths, but the communal ones are often designed with natural pools or a window looking out into a garden. Bathing is communal, but sexes are segregated. Make sure you can differentiate between the bathroom signs for men and women (see the Toilets section in this chapter – it lists the kanji for 'male' and 'female'), although ryokan used to catering for foreigners will often have signs in English. Many inns will have family bathrooms for couples or families.

Dressed in your yukata after your bath, you return to your room where the maid will have laid out dinner – in some ryokan, dinner is provided in a separate room but you still wear your yukata for dining. Dinner usually includes standard dishes such as *miso shiru* (miso-flavoured soup), *tsukemono* (pickles), *sunomono* (vegetables in vinegar), *zensai* (appetisers), fish – either grilled or *sashimi*, and perhaps *tempura* (lightly battered fried seafood and vegetables) and *nabe* (a quickly cooked stew). There will also be bowls for rice, dips and sauces. Depending on the price, meals at a ryokan can become flamboyant displays of local cuisine or refined arrangements of *kaiseki* – a cuisine which obeys strict rules of form and etiquette for every detail of the meal and setting.

After dinner, while you are pottering around or out for a stroll admiring the garden, the maid will clear the dishes and prepare your bedding. A *futon* is placed on the tatami floor and a quilt put on top. In colder weather, you can also add a *mōfu* (blanket).

In the morning, the maid will knock to make sure you are awake and then come in to put away the bedding before serving breakfast – sometimes this is served in a separate room. Breakfast usually consists of tsukemono, *nori* (dried seaweed), *nama tamago* (raw egg), *hoshi-zakana* (dried fish), miso shiru and rice. It can take a while for foreign stomachs to accept this novel fare early in the morning.

Although ryokan etiquette can seem rather complicated at first, and some ryokan are a little wary of foreigners, once you grasp the basics you'll find yourself looking forward to the nights you spend in one. Truly, they are welcome havens for the weary traveller.

per person. If, like many foreigners, you find yourself overwhelmed by the unusual offerings of a Japanese breakfast, it should be possible to have dinner only, but in many ryokan, opting out of both meals is unacceptable. The bill is reduced by about 10% if you decline breakfast.

A service charge or consumption tax may be added to your bill in some establishments. Because this is not always the case and the amount may vary, it's best to ask when making reservations or checking in.

Ryokan Guides & Addresses Welcome Inn Reservation Center (☎ 03-3211-4201, fax 3211-9009), B1, Tokyo International Forum, 3-5-1 Marunouchi, Chiyoda-ku, Tokyo 100-0005, publishes regional guides to ryokan and hotels that welcome foreigners. The *Directory of Welcome Inns* pamphlets are available at TICs, where bookings can also be made. Prices quoted start from ¥4000.

JNTO publishes the *Japan Ryokan Guide*, a listing of government-registered members of the Japan Ryokan Association (JRA). Prices quoted start around ¥8000 and rise to astronomical heights.

Pensions
Pensions are usually run by young couples offering Western-style accommodation based on the European pension concept, and many offer sports and leisure facilities. They are common in rural areas. Pensions seem to specialise in quaint names like Pension Fruit Juice, Pension Pheasant or Pension Morning Salada and often have decidedly quaint decor as well, at times like a romanticised Japanese dream of a European country cottage.

Prices average ¥6000 per person per night or ¥8500 including two meals. Food is often excellent, typically a French dinner and an American breakfast.

Capsule Hotels
In the 1970s, the Japanese architect Kurokawa Kisho, came up with the idea of modifying a shipping container to hold a bed, bath and all 'mod cons'. A site was found for his construction which can still be seen on the outskirts of Tokyo's Ginza area.

Capseru hoteru (capsule hotels) have reduced the original concept to a capsule measuring two metres by one metre by one metre – about the size of a coffin. Inside is a bed, a TV, a reading light, a radio and an alarm clock. Personal belongings are kept in a locker room.

This type of hotel is common in the major cities and often caters to travellers who have partied too hard to make it home or have missed the last train. The majority are only for men but some also accept women; the women's quarters are usually in a separate part of the building. Most capsule hotels have the added attraction of a sauna and a large communal bath.

An average price is ¥3800 per night or ¥1400 for a three-hour stay. You could try one as a novelty, but it's not an experience recommended to those who become claustrophobic easily.

Hotels
Business Hotels These are economical and practical places geared to the single traveller, usually lesser-ranking business types who want to stay somewhere close to the station. Rooms are clean, Western style, just big enough for you to turn around in and include a miniature bath/WC unit. A standard fitting for the stressed businessman is a coin-operated TV with a porno channel. Vending machines replace room service.

Cheap single rooms can sometimes be found for ¥4500, though the average rate is around ¥7000; most business hotels also have twin rooms and doubles. Cheaper business hotels usually do not have a service charge, though places costing ¥7000 or more often add a 10% charge.

Popular business hotel chains include Green Hotel, which are often near train stations, Sun Route, Washington, Tōkyū Inns and Hokke Club. The Hokke Club hotels are unusual in their conveniently early check-in and late checkout times. Most Japanese hotels kick you out by 10 or 11 am and won't let you check in until 3 or 4 pm.

Top-End Hotels Deluxe and 1st class hotels offering the usual array of frills and comforts have sprung up in most of Japan's major cities and are comparable to the best worldwide. Singles start at around ¥8000 and rise to a cool ¥20,000 or way beyond if you fancy a suite. The Japan Hotel Association has 445 government-registered members, all neatly listed in an informative JNTO leaflet, *Hotels in Japan*.

Some of the leading hotel chains, such as ANA, Holiday Inn, New Otani, Prince and Tōkyū have overseas offices. Bookings can also be made through the overseas offices of major Japanese travel agencies such as JTB, Kintetsu International, Tōkyū Tourist Corporation, Nippon Travel Agency (NTA), Japan Airlines (JAL) and All Nippon Airways (ANA). Most of these agencies also have schemes for discount hotel coupons such as JTB's 'Sunrise Super Saver', NTA's 'NTA Hotel Pass' or JAL's 'Room & Rail'.

Expect to pay 10% or more as a service charge plus a 5% consumer tax; add another 3% local tax if the bill exceeds ¥10,000. Asking for separate bills for meals can sometimes reduce the amount of tax.

Love Hotels

Love hotels are one of the wild cards of Japanese accommodation. They are there as a short-time base for couples to enjoy some privacy.

To find one on the street, just look for flamboyant facades with rococo architecture, turrets, battlements and imitation statuary. The design of the hotels emphasises discretion: entrances and exits are kept separate; keys are provided through a small opening without contact between desk clerk and guest; photos of the rooms are displayed to make the choice easy for the customer. There's often a discreetly curtained parking area so your car cannot be seen once inside.

The rooms can fulfil most fantasies, with themes ranging from harem extravaganza to sci-fi. Further choices can include vibrating beds, wall-to-wall mirrors, bondage equipment and video recorders to recall the experience (don't forget to take the video cassette with you when you leave).

During the day, you can stay for a two- or three-hour 'rest' for about ¥4000 (rates are for the whole room, not per person). Love hotels are of more interest to foreign visitors after 10 pm, when it's possible to stay the night for about ¥6500, but you should check out early enough in the morning to avoid a return to peak-hour rates. Outside love hotels there will usually be a sign in Japanese (occasionally in English) announcing the rates for a 'rest' (short stay in the daytime) or a 'stay' (overnight stay).

In theory, you can cram as many people as you like into a love hotel room; in practice you may be limited to two people and same-sex couples may be asked to pay more or may even be rejected outright.

Long-Term Accommodation

If you're intending to stay longer in Japan, a job offer which appears lucrative at first sight may seem markedly less so when you work out your rent and other living costs. Ideally, you can avoid many hassles by negotiating decent accommodation as part of your work contract.

If at all possible, get a Japanese friend to help you with your search and negotiations as Japanese landlords are notoriously wary of foreign tenants and often prefer to do business with a local go-between. If you are on good terms with a Japanese friend, this person may offer to act as a *hoshō-nin* (guarantor). This represents considerable commitment and the guarantor's *hanko* (seal) is usually required on your rental contract.

A pitfall that is often overlooked is that you may have to lay out the equivalent of several months' rent up-front. For starters, there's the equivalent of one to two months' rent payable as *reikin* (key money). This is a non-refundable gift that goes into the pocket of the landlord. Then there's a *shikikin* (damage deposit) equal to one to three months' rent. This is refundable at a later date as long as both sides agree there's no damage. Avoid later squabbles over shikikin by making duplicate inventories, signed by both parties, before you move in. The *fudōsan-yasan* (real estate agent) will of course want *tesūryō* – the equivalent of one month's rent as a non-refundable handling fee. Finally, you may have to pay *maekin* which is equal to one month's rent in advance and this may also be non-refundable.

These high up-front costs are cogent reasons why foreigners looking for long-term employment in Japan should arrive with a sizeable financial float. This will allow more time to choose a decent job and avoid the scenario – assuming your stay was mostly motivated by financial gain – of leaving Japan with very little to show for your stay and an embittered feeling about the place.

Standard rental contracts often run for two years and some *ōya-san* (landowners) may require the additional payment of maintenance fees and fire insurance. When *kōshin* (renewal) comes up, there may be an increase in your *yachin* (monthly rent). When you decide to move on, make absolutely sure you give notice *at least* one month in advance. Otherwise you will be landed with payment of an extra month's rent.

Of course, after all this is said, there are ways around all the above costs. If you get in with the local foreigners' scene in a particular city, you may get tipped off to open apartments and houses for which nothing more than monthly rent is required (this is particularly true outside Tokyo). If you just can't afford to pay all the usual fees for an apartment or house in Japan, try looking a little harder and you may be able to locate a special deal.

What to Look For Inner city rentals are obviously high, as are those for chic suburban areas. Commuting costs often reduce the apparent gain of lower rental costs outside town and you may not like your nightlife being curtailed by transport timetables.

It's usually best for budget travellers to find their feet in a gaijin house before putting out feelers for other accommodation. In major cities like Tokyo and Kyoto, gaijin houses are the cheapest options for long-term stays, but you should be prepared for basic tatami rooms and a communal kitchen. Prices for the cheapest houses start around ¥1600 per night. Outside of Tokyo, if you

negotiate for a monthly price you may be able to reduce the rent to ¥30,000 per month.

At the top end of the housing market are *manshon*, which are modern concrete condominiums or rental apartments. At the lower end are *danchi*, functional concrete blocks of public flats, which are sought after by those with moderate or low incomes.

Japanese are often amazed at the spaciousness of Western housing, since the average Japanese family in the city makes do with much less space in their apartment. If you want a house or apartment similar to urban sizes in the West, you can expect to pay several million yen a month.

Where to Look There are several methods to hunt for housing – it depends what you want and how long you intend to stay.

Asking other foreigners at work or play in schools, clubs, bars, gaijin houses etc is one way of locating long-term accommodation. If you strike it lucky, you may find somebody leaving the country or moving on who is willing to dump their job contacts, housing and effects in one friendly package.

Notice boards are another good source and are often found at tourist information offices, international clubs, conversation clubs etc. Even if there's nothing on the board, ask someone in charge for a few tips.

Regional and city magazines aimed at foreigners often have classified ads offering or seeking accommodation. In Tokyo, you should look at *Tokyo Flea Market* or *Tokyo Classified*; for the Kansai area you should check out *Kansai Time Out*. There are plenty of other magazines all over Japan with suitable ads. The TIC or the local tourist office should know which publications are best, particularly if you decide to live somewhere more remote, such as Hokkaidō or Okinawa.

Common abbreviations in rental ads include D – dining room, K – kitchen, L – living room, UB – unit bath (combined bathroom and toilet). An ad specifying 3LDK, for example, means three bedrooms and one living room combined with dining room and kitchen. The size of rooms is usually given in *jō*, a standard tatami mat

Continued on page 159

JAPANESE CUISINE & MENU GLOSSARY

Nihon Ryōri (Japanese Food)

Those familiar with *nihon ryōri* know that eating is half the fun of travelling in Japan. Even if you've already tried some of Japan's better known specialities in Japanese restaurants in your own country, you're likely to be surprised by how delicious the original is when served on its home turf. More importantly, the adventurous eater will be delighted to find that Japanese food is far more than just sushi, tempura or sukiyaki. Indeed, it could be possible to spend a month in Japan and sample a different speciality restaurant every night.

Variety, though, is fairly new to Japan. Until the beginning of the 20th century, Japanese food was basic at best (at least among the farming masses); a typical meal consisted of a bowl of rice, some *miso-shiru* (miso soup), a few pickled vegetables and, if one was lucky, some preserved fish. As a Buddhist nation, meat was not eaten until the Meiji Restoration of 1868. Even then, it took some getting used to. Early accounts of Japan's first foreign residents are rife with horrified stories of the grotesque dietary practices of 'the barbarians' including the 'unthinkable' consumption of milk!

These days the Japanese have gone to the opposite extreme and have heartily embraced foreign cuisine. Unfortunately this often means a glut of fast-food restaurants in the downtown areas of cities. In fact, there are so many McDonald's that the president of McDonald's Japan once remarked that it was only a matter of time before Japanese youth start growing blonde hair.

Those in search of a truly Japanese experience will probably want to avoid Western-style fast food to sample authentic Japanese cuisine. Luckily this is quite easy to do, although some may baulk at charging into a restaurant where both the language and the menu are likely to be incomprehensible. The best way to get over this fear is to familiarise yourself with the main types of Japanese restaurants so that you have some idea of what's on offer and how to order it. Those timid of heart should take solace in the fact that the Japanese will go to extraordinary lengths to understand what you want and will help you to order.

With the exception of *shokudō* (all-round restaurants) and *izakaya* (pub-style restaurants), most Japanese restaurants concentrate on a speciality cuisine. This naturally makes for delicious eating, but does limit your choice. The following will introduce the main types of Japanese restaurants, along with a menu sample of some of the most common dishes served. With a little courage and effort you will soon discover that Japan is a gourmet paradise where good food is taken seriously.

Eating in a Japanese Restaurant

When you enter a restaurant, you'll be greeted with a hearty *'irasshaimase!'* ('Welcome!'). In all but the most casual places the waiter or waitress will next ask you *'nan-mei sama?'* ('How many people?'). Answer with your fingers, which is what the Japanese do. You will then be led to a table, a place at the counter or a *tatami* room.

At this point you will be given an *oshibori* (hot towel), a cup of tea and a menu. The oshibori is for wiping your hands and face. When you're done with it, just roll it up and leave it next to your place. Now comes the hard part: ordering. If you don't read Japanese you can use the romanised translations in this section to help you, or direct the waiter's attention to the Japanese script. If this doesn't work there are two phrases which may help: *'o-susume wa nan desu ka?'* ('What do you recommend?') and *'o-makase shimasu'* ('Please decide for me'). If you're still having problems, you can try pointing at other diners' food or, if the restaurant has them, dragging the waiter outside to point at the plastic food displays in the window.

When you've finished eating, you can signal for the bill by crossing one index finger over the other to form the sign of an 'X'. This is the standard sign for 'cheque please'. You can also say *'o-kanjō kudasai'*. Remember there is no tipping in Japan and tea is free of charge. Usually you will be given a bill to take to the cashier at the front of the restaurant. At more upmarket places, the host of the party will discreetly excuse him or herself to pay before the group leaves. Unlike some places in the West, one doesn't usually leave cash on the table by way of payment. Only the bigger and more international places take credit cards, so cash is always the surer option.

When leaving, it is polite to say to the restaurant staff *'gochisō-sama deshita'*, which means 'It was a real feast'.

Shokudō

A *shokudō* (eating place) is the most common type of restaurant, and is found near train stations, tourist spots and just about any other place where people congregate. Easily distinguished by the presence of plastic models of dishes in the window, these inexpensive places usually serve a variety of *washoku* (Japanese) and *yoshoku* (Western) foods.

At lunch, and sometimes dinner, the easiest way to order at a shokudō is to order a *teishoku* (set course meal), which is sometimes also called *ranchi setto* (lunch set), or *kōsu*. This usually includes a main dish of meat or fish, a bowl of rice, miso, shredded cabbage and a few Japanese pickles called *tsukemono*. In addition, most shokudō serve a fairly standard selection of *donburi-mono* (rice dishes) and *menrui* (noodle dishes). When you order noodles, you can choose between *soba* and *udon*, both of which are served with a variety of toppings. If you're at a loss as to what to order, simply tell the waiter *'kyō-no-ranchi'* ('Today's lunch') and they'll do the rest. Expect to spend about ¥800 to ¥1000 for a meal at a shokudō.

Eating Etiquette

When it comes to eating in Japan, there is quite a number of implicit rules, but they're fairly easy to remember. If you're worried about putting your foot in it, relax – the Japanese almost expect foreigners to make fools of themselves in formal situations and are unlikely to be offended as long as you follow the standard rules of politeness in your own country.

Among the more important eating 'rules' are those regarding chopsticks. Sticking them upright in your rice is considered bad form – that's how rice is offered to the dead! It's also bad form to pass food from your chopsticks to someone else's – this is also a Buddhist funeral rite. It involves passing the remains of the cremated deceased among members of the family using chopsticks.

It's worth remembering that a lot of effort has gone into the preparation of the food so don't pour *shōyu* (soy sauce) all over it (especially the rice) and don't mix it up with your chopsticks. Also, if possible, eat everything you are given. And don't forget to slurp your noodles!

When eating with other people, especially when you're a guest, it is polite to say *'itadakimasu'* (literally, 'I will receive') before digging in. This is as close as the Japanese come to saying grace. Similarly, at the end of the meal, you should thank your host by saying *'gochisō-sama deshita'*, which means 'It was a real feast'.

When drinking with Japanese people remember that it is bad form to fill your own drink; fill the glass of the person next to you and wait for them to reciprocate. Filling your own glass amounts to admitting to everyone at the table that you're an alcoholic. It is polite to raise your glass a little off the table while it is being filled. Once everyone's glass has been filled, the usual starting signal is a chorus of *'kampai'* which means 'Cheers!'. Constant topping up means a bottomless glass – just put your hand over your glass if you've had enough.

There is also a definite etiquette to bill-paying. If someone invites you to eat or drink with them, they will be paying. Even among groups eating together it is unusual for bills to be split. The exception to this is found among young people and close friends and is called *warikan* (each person paying their own share). Generally, at the end of the meal something of a struggle will ensue to see who gets the privilege of paying the bill. If this happens, it is polite to at least make an effort to pay the bill – it is extremely unlikely that your Japanese 'hosts' will acquiesce.

Rice Dishes

katsu-don	かつ丼	rice topped with a fried pork cutlet
oyako-don	親子丼	rice topped with egg and chicken
niku-don	牛丼	rice topped with thin slices of cooked beef
ten-don	天丼	rice topped with tempura shrimp and vegetables

Noodle Dishes

soba	そば	buckwheat noodles
udon	うどん	thick, white wheat noodles
kake	かけそば/うどん	soba/udon noodles in broth
kitsune	きつねそば/うどん	soba/udon noodles with fried tofu
tempura	てんぷらそば/うどん	soba/udon noodles with tempura shrimp
tsukimi	月見そば/うどん	soba/udon noodles with raw egg on top

Izakaya

An izakaya is the Japanese equivalent of a pub. It's a good place to visit when you want a casual meal, a wide selection of food, a hearty atmosphere and, of course, plenty of beer and sake. When you enter an izakaya, you are given the choice of sitting around the counter, at a table or on a *tatami* floor. You usually order a bit at a time, choosing from a selection of typical Japanese foods like *yakitori*, *sashimi* and grilled fish, as well as Japanese interpretations of Western foods like French fries and beef stew.

Izakaya can be identified by their rustic facades, and the red lanterns outside their doors bearing the *kanji* for izakaya. Since izakaya food is casual fare to go with drinking, it is usually fairly inexpensive. Depending on how much you drink, you can expect to get away with ¥2500 to ¥5000 per person. See also the Yakitori and Sushi entries for more dishes available at an izakaya.

agedashi-dōfu	揚げだし豆腐	deep fried tofu in a fish stock soup
jaga-batā	ジャガバター	baked potatoes with butter
niku-jaga	肉ジャガ	beef and potato stew
shio-yaki-zakana	塩焼魚	a whole fish grilled with salt

yaki-onigiri	焼きおにぎり	a triangle of grilled rice with yakitori sauce
poteto furai	ポテトフライ	french fries
chiizu-age	チーズ揚げ	deep fried cheese
hiya-yakko	冷ややっこ	a cold block of tofu with soy sauce and scallions
tsuna sarada	ツナサラダ	tuna salad over cabbage
yaki-soba	焼きそば	fried noodles with meat and vegetables
kata yaki-soba	固焼きそば	hard fried noodles with meat and vegetables
sashimi mori-awase	刺身盛り合わせ	a selection of sliced sashimi

Robatayaki

Similar to an izakaya, a *robatayaki* is a rustic drinking restaurant serving a wide variety of foods grilled over charcoal. The name means 'hearthside cooking' and every effort is made to re-create the atmosphere of an old country house – which was always centred around a large hearth or *irori*.

Eating at a robatayaki restaurant is a feast for the eyes as well as the taste buds; you sit around a counter with the food spread out in front of you on a layer of ice, behind which is a large charcoal grill. You don't need a word of Japanese to order, just point at whatever looks good. The chef will grill your selection and then pass it to you on a long wooden paddle – grab your food quickly before he snatches it back. Some of the best robatayaki chefs are real performers and make a show of cooking the food and serving customers. You'll wonder how no one winds up getting injured by flying food.

The fare at a robatayaki restaurant is largely the same as that at an izakaya. They have menus, but no one uses them – just point and eat. The drink of choice is beer or sake. Expect to spend about ¥3000 per head. Not as common as izakaya, robatayaki usually have rustic wooden facades modelled on traditional Japanese farmhouses.

Okonomiyaki

The name means 'cook what you like', and an *okonomiyaki* restaurant provides you with an inexpensive opportunity to do just that. Sometimes described as Japanese pizza or pancake, the resemblance is in form only. At an okonomiyaki restaurant you sit around a *teppan* (an iron hotplate) armed with a spatula and chopsticks to cook your choice of meat, seafood and vegetables in a cabbage and vegetable batter.

Some places will do most of the cooking and bring the nearly finished product over to your hotplate for you to season with *katsuo bushi* (bonito flakes), *shōyu* (soy sauce), parsley, Japanese Worcestershire-style sauce and mayonnaise. Cheaper places will simply hand you a bowl filled with the ingredients and expect you to cook it for yourself. If this happens, don't panic. First, mix the batter and filling thoroughly, then place it on the hot grill, flattening it into a pancake shape. After five minutes or so, use the spatulas to flip it and cook for another five minutes. Then dig in.

Most okonomiyaki places also serve *yaki-soba* (fried noodles) and *yasai-itame* (stir-fried vegetables). All of this is washed down with mugs of draft beer. One final word: don't worry too much about preparation of the food – as a foreigner you'll be expected to be awkward and the waiter will keep a sharp eye on you to make sure no real disasters occur.

mikkusu okonomiyaki	ミックスお好み焼き	mixed fillings of seafood, meat and vegetables
modan-yaki	モダン焼き	okonomiyaki with fried egg
ika okonomiyaki	いかお好み焼き	squid okonomiyaki
gyu okonomiyaki	牛お好み焼き	beef okonomiyaki
yasai okonomiyaki	野菜お好み焼き	vegetable okonomiyaki
negi okonomiyaki	ネギお好み焼き	thin okonomiyaki with scallions

Yakitori

Yakitori means 'skewers of grilled chicken', a popular after-work meal. Yakitori is not so much a full meal as it is an accompaniment for beer and sake. At a *yakitori-ya* (yakitori restaurant) you sit around a counter with the other patrons and watch the chef grill your selections over charcoal. The best way to eat here is to order a few skewers of several varieties and then order seconds of the ones you really like. Ordering can be a little confusing since one serving often means two or three skewers (be careful – the price listed on the menu is usually that of a single skewer).

In summer, the beverage of choice at a yakitori restaurant is beer or cold sake, while in winter it's hot sake. A few drinks and enough skewers to fill you up should run from ¥3000 to ¥4000 per person. Yakitori restaurants are usually small places, often near train stations, and are best identified by a red lantern outside and the smell of grilling chicken.

yakitori	やきとり	plain, grilled white meat
hasami/negima	はさみ・ねぎま	pieces of white meat alternating with leek
sasami	ささみ	skinless chicken breast pieces
kawa	かわ	chicken skin

tsukune	つくね	chicken meat balls
gyū-niku	牛肉	pieces of beef
rebā	レバー	chicken livers
tebasaki	手羽先	chicken wings
shiitake	しいたけ	Japanese mushrooms
piiman	ピーマン	small green peppers
tama-negi	たまねぎ	round, white onions
yaki-onigiri	焼きおにぎり	a triangle of rice grilled with yakitori sauce

Sushi & Sashimi

Like yakitori, sushi is considered an accompaniment for beer and sake. Nonetheless, both the Japanese and foreigners often make a meal of it and it's one of the healthiest meals around. Although sushi is now popular in the West, few foreigners are prepared for the delicacy and taste of the real thing. Without a doubt, this is one dish that the visitor to Japan should sample at least once.

There are two main types of sushi: *nigiri-zushi* (served on a small bed of rice – the most common variety) and *maki-zushi* (served in a seaweed roll). Lesser known varieties include *chirashi-zushi* (a layer of rice covered in egg and fish toppings), *oshi-zushi* (fish pressed in a mould over rice) and *inari-zushi* (rice in a pocket of sweet, fried tofu). Whatever kind of sushi you try, it will be served with lightly vinegared rice. In the case of nigiri-zushi and maki-zushi, it will contain a bit of *wasabi* (hot, green horseradish).

Sushi is not difficult to order. If you sit at the counter of a sushi restaurant you can simply point at what you want, as most of the selections are visible in a refrigerated glass case between you and the sushi chef. You can also order a la carte from the menu. When ordering, you usually order *ichi-nin mae* (one portion), which usually means two pieces of sushi. Be careful since the price on the menu will be that of only one piece. If ordering a la carte is too daunting, you can take care of your whole order with one or two words by ordering an assortment plate of nigiri-zushi called a *mori-awase*. These usually come in three grades: *futsū nigiri* (regular nigiri), *jō nigiri* (special nigiri) and *toku-jō nigiri* (extra special nigiri). The difference is in the type of fish used. Most mori-awase contain six or seven pieces of sushi. Of course you can order fish without the rice, in which case it is called sashimi.

Be warned that a good sushi restaurant can cost upwards of ¥10,000, while an average place can run to ¥3000 to ¥5000 per person. One way to sample the joy of sushi on the cheap is to try an automatic sushi place, usually called *kaiten-zushi*, where the sushi is served on a conveyor belt which runs along a counter. Here you simply reach up and grab whatever looks good (which certainly takes the pain out of ordering). You're charged according to how many plates of sushi you've eaten. Plates are colour-coded according to their price and the cost is written either somewhere on the plate itself or on a sign on the wall. You can usually fill yourself up in one of these places for ¥1000 to ¥2000 per person. Kaiten-zushi places are often distinguished by miniature conveyor belts in the window while regular sushi restaurants often can be identified by fish tanks in the window or a white lantern with the characters for sushi written in black letters.

Before popping the sushi into your mouth, dip it in *shōyu* (soy sauce) which you pour from a small decanter into a low dish specially provided for the purpose. If you're not good at using chopsticks, don't worry, sushi is one of the few foods in Japan that is perfectly acceptable to eat with your hands. Slices of *gari* (pickled ginger) will also be served to help refresh the palate. The beverage of choice with sushi is beer or sake (hot in the winter and cold in the summer), with a cup of green tea at the end of the meal.

ama-ebi	甘海老	sweet shrimp
awabi	あわび	abalone
ebi	海老	prawn or shrimp
hamachi	はまち	yellowtail
ika	いか	squid
ikura	イクラ	salmon roe
kai-bashira	貝柱	scallop
kani	かに	crab
katsuo	かつお	bonito
maguro	まぐろ	tuna
tai	鯛	sea bream
tamago	たまご	sweetened egg
toro	とろ	the choicest cut of fatty tuna belly
unagi	うなぎ	eel with a sweet sauce
uni	うに	sea urchin roe

Sukiyaki & Shabu-shabu

Restaurants usually specialise in both these dishes. Popular in the West, sukiyaki is a favourite of most foreign visitors to Japan. When made with high-quality beef, like Kōbe beef, it is a sublime experience. Sukiyaki consists of thin slices of beef cooked in a broth of soy sauce, sugar and sake and is accompanied by a variety of vegetables and tofu. After cooking, all the ingredients are dipped in raw egg (the heat of the ingredients tends to lightly cook the egg) before being eaten.

Shabu-shabu consists of thin slices of beef and vegetables cooked by swirling the ingredients in a light broth and then dipping them in a variety of special sesame seed and citrus-based sauces. Both of these dishes are prepared in a pot over a fire at your private table, but don't fret about preparation – the waiter or waitress will usually help you get started and then keep a close watch as you proceed. The key is to take your time and add the ingredients a little at a time, savouring the flavours as you go.

Sukiyaki and shabu-shabu restaurants usually have a traditional Japanese decor and sometimes a picture of a cow to help you recognise them. Ordering is not difficult. Simply say sukiyaki or shabu-shabu and indicate how many people's worth of food is required. Expect to pay between ¥3000 to ¥10,000 per person.

Tempura

One of the most famous of all Japanese foods, tempura's origins aren't Japanese at all; in fact, the cooking style was borrowed from Portuguese traders and missionaries of the 16th century. Since then, the Japanese have refined the speciality into something uniquely their own. Good tempura is portions of fish, prawns and vegetables cooked in fluffy, non-greasy batter.

When you sit down at a tempura restaurant, you will be given a small bowl filled with *ten-tsuyu* (a light brown sauce) and a plate of grated *daikon* (white radish); you mix this into the sauce. Dip each piece of tempura into this sauce before eating it. Tempura is best when it's hot, so don't wait too long – use the sauce to cool each piece and dig in.

While it's possible to order a la carte, most diners choose to order a teishoku (full set), which includes rice, miso-shiru and Japanese pickles. Some tempura restaurants also offer courses of tempura which include different numbers of tempura pieces.

Expect to pay between ¥2000 and ¥10,000 for a full tempura meal. Finding these restaurants is tricky as they have no distinctive facade or decor. If you look through the window you'll see customers around the counter watching the chefs as they work over large woks filled with oil.

tempura moriawase	てんぷら盛り合わせ	a selection of tempura
shōjin age	精進揚げ	vegetarian tempura
kaki age	かき揚げ	tempura with shredded vegetables or fish

Rāmen

The Japanese imported this dish from China and put their own spin on it to make what is one of the world's most delicious fast foods. *Rāmen* dishes are big bowls of noodles in a meat broth served with a variety of toppings, such as sliced pork, bean sprouts and leeks. In some restaurants, particularly in Kansai, you may be asked if you'd prefer *kotteri* (thick) or *assari* (thin) soup. Other than this, ordering is simple:

just sidle up to the counter and say 'Rāmen', or ask for any of the other choices usually on offer (a list follows). Expect to pay between ¥500 and ¥900 for a bowl. Since rāmen is originally Chinese food, some rāmen restaurants also serve chāhan or yaki-meshi (fried rice), gyōza (dumplings) and kara-age (deep-fried chicken pieces).

Rāmen restaurants are easily distinguished by their long counters lined with customers hunched over steaming bowls. You can sometimes hear a rāmen shop as you wander by – it's considered polite to slurp the noodles and aficionados claim that slurping brings out the full flavour of the broth.

rāmen	ラーメン	soup and noodles with a sprinkling of meat and vegetables
chāshū-men	チャーシュー麺	rāmen topped with slices of roasted pork
wantan-men	ワンタン麺	rāmen with meat dumplings
miso-rāmen	みそラーメン	rāmen with miso-flavoured broth
chānpon-men	ちゃんぽん麺	Nagasaki-style rāmen

Soba & Udon

Soba and udon are Japan's answer to Chinese-style rāmen. Soba noodles are thin, brown, buckwheat noodles, while udon noodles are thick, white, wheat noodles. Most Japanese noodle shops serve both soba and udon prepared in a variety of ways. Noodles are usually served in a bowl containing a light, bonito-flavoured broth, but you can also order them served cold and piled on a bamboo screen with a cold broth for dipping.

By far the most popular type of cold noodles is zaru soba, which is served with bits of nori (seaweed) on top. If you order these noodles you'll receive a small plate of wasabi and sliced scallions – put these into the cup of broth and eat the noodles by dipping them in this mixture. At the end of your meal, the waiter will give you some hot broth to mix with the leftover sauce which you drink like a kind of tea. As with rāmen, you should feel free to slurp as loudly as you please.

Soba and udon places are usually quite cheap (about ¥900), but some fancy places can be significantly more expensive (the decor is a good indication of the price). See the Noodles entry under Shokudō for more soba and udon dishes.

| zaru soba | ざるそば | cold noodles with seaweed strips served on a bamboo tray |

Unagi

Unagi, or 'eel', is an expensive and popular delicacy in Japan. Even if you can't stand the creature back home, you owe it to yourself to try unagi at least once while in Japan. It's cooked over hot coals and brushed with a rich sauce of soy sauce and sake. Full unagi dinners can be expensive, but many unagi restaurants offer *unagi bentō* (boxed lunches) and lunch sets for around ¥1500. Most unagi restaurants display plastic models of their sets in their front windows and have barrels of live eels to entice passers-by.

unagi teishoku	うなぎ定食	full-set unagi meal with rice, grilled eel, eel-liver soup and pickles
unadon	うな丼	grilled eel over a bowl of rice

Fast-Food Chains in Japan

Fast food has made big inroads into Japanese culture, and you may be surprised by the number of times you run across the 'golden arches' or Colonel Sanders in Japan. Of course, it was only a matter of time before the Japanese responded with some of their own:

Yoshinoya This chain specialises in *gyūdon* (sukiyaki-flavoured beef over a bowl of rice). They also do good and healthy Japanese-style breakfasts for as little as ¥400. Look for the orange, black and white sign (some have English writing).

Mos Burger Some of their dishes are pretty tasty and they've got a few veggie choices like rice-burgers. Look for the red sign with English writing.

Lotteria There's not much to recommend this nondescript fast-food chain except perhaps the price – they're dirt cheap. Look for the red and white sign, sometimes with English writing.

Mr Donut Cheap donuts and the only bottomless cup of coffee in the land. And now they've taken to serving dim-sum! We advise sticking to the donuts. Look for the yellow and orange signs with English writing.

Tenya This chain serves up cheap bowls of *ten-don* (tempura shrimp over a bowl of rice). Okay, it's not the best tempura you'll ever eat but the price is right. Look for the yellow and blue sign.

Tengu & Yōrōnotaki These are two similar izakaya chains with picture menus and reasonable prices. They don't have the atmosphere of a traditional izakaya, but they're easier to enter and usually comfortable with foreigners. Unfortunately, neither chain has English signs; look for black on red signs or ask at a *kōban* (police box).

unajū	うな重	grilled eel over a flat tray of rice
kabayaki	蒲焼き	skewers of grilled eel without rice

Nabemono

A *nabe* is a large cast-iron cooking pot and *nabemono* refers to any of a variety of dishes cooked in these pots. Like sukiyaki and shabu-shabu, nabemono are cooked at your table on a small gas burner or a clay *hibachi*. Eating nabemono is a participatory experience, with each diner putting in ingredients from trays of prepared, raw food. The most famous nabemono is called *chanko-nabe*, the high-calorie stew eaten by sumo wrestlers during training. Chanko-nabe restaurants are often run by retired sumo wrestlers and the walls of such restaurants may be festooned with sumo arcana.

Since nabemono are filling and hot, they are usually eaten during winter. They are also popular as banquet and party dishes since the eating of a nabe dish is a very communal experience. It is difficult to pick out a nabe restaurant — the best way is to ask a Japanese friend for a recommendation.

mizutaki	水炊き	clear soup stew with chicken, fish and vegetables
sukiyaki	すき焼き	soy sauce based stew with thinly sliced beef and vegetables; often dipped in raw egg
chanko-nabe	ちゃんこ鍋	sumō wrestler's stew of meat and vegetables
botan-nabe	ぼたん鍋	wild boar stew with vegetables
yose-nabe	寄せ鍋	seafood and chicken stew with vegetables

Fugu

The deadly *fugu*, or globefish, is eaten more for the thrill than the taste. It's actually rather bland – most people liken the taste to chicken – but acclaimed for its fine texture. Nonetheless, if you have the money to lay out for a fugu dinner (around ¥10,000), it makes a good 'been there, done that' story back home.

Although the danger of fugu poisoning is negligible, some Japanese joke that you should always let the other person try the first piece – if they are still talking after five minutes, consider it safe and have some yourself. If you need a shot of liquid courage to get started, try a glass of *hirezake* (toasted fugu tail in hot sake) – the traditional accompaniment to a fugu dinner.

Fugu is a seasonal delicacy best eaten in winter. Fugu restaurants usually serve only fugu and can be identified by a picture of a fugu on the sign out the front.

fugu teishoku	ふぐ定食	a set course of fugu served several ways, plus rice and soup
fugu chiri	ふぐちり	a stew made from fugu and vegetables
fugu sashimi	ふぐ刺身	thinly sliced raw fugu
yaki fugu	焼きふぐ	fugu grilled on a hibachi at your table

Tonkatsu

Tonkatsu is a deep-fried breaded pork cutlet served with a special sauce, usually as part of a set meal *(tonkatsu teishoku)*. Tonkatsu is served both at speciality restaurants and at shokudō. Naturally, the best tonkatsu is to be found at the speciality places, where a full set will run from ¥1500 to ¥2500. When ordering, you can choose between *rōsu*, a fatter cut and *hire*, a leaner cut of pork.

tonkatsu teishoku	とんかつ定食	a set meal of tonkatsu, rice, miso shiru and shredded cabbage
minchi katsu	ミンチカツ	minced pork cutlet
hire katsu	ヒレかつ	tonkatsu fillet
kushi katsu	串かつ	deep-fried pork and vegetables on skewers

Kushiage & Kushikatsu

Dieters beware, this is the fried food to beat all fried foods. *Kushiage* and *kushikatsu* are deep-fried skewers of meat, seafood and vegetables eaten as an accompaniment to beer. *Kushi* means 'skewer' and if food can be fitted on to one, it's probably on the menu. Cabbage is often eaten with the meal, a clever way to ease the guilt of eating all that grease.

You order kushiage and kushikatsu by the skewer (one skewer is *ippon*, but you can always use your fingers to indicate how many you want). Like yakitori, this food is popular with after-work salarymen and students and is therefore fairly inexpensive, though upmarket places exist. Expect to pay from ¥2000 to ¥5000 for a full meal and a couple of beers. Not particularly distinctive in appearance, the best way to find a kushiage and kushikatsu place is to ask a Japanese friend.

ebi	海老	shrimp
ika	いか	squid
renkon	レンコン	lotus root
tama-negi	たまねぎ	white onion
gyū-niku	牛肉	beef pieces
shiitake	しいたけ	Japanese mushrooms
ginnan	銀杏	ginkgo nuts
imo	いも	potato

Kaiseki

Kaiseki is the pinnacle of Japanese cuisine where ingredients, preparation, setting and presentation come together to create a dining experience quite unlike any other. Born as an adjunct to the tea ceremony, kaiseki is a largely vegetarian affair (though fish is often served, meat never appears on the kaiseki menu). One usually eats kaiseki in the private room of a *ryōtei* (an especially elegant style of traditional restaurant), often overlooking a private, tranquil garden. The meal is served in several small courses, giving one the opportunity to admire the plates and bowls which are carefully chosen to complement the food and seasons. Rice is eaten last (usually with an assortment of pickles) and the drink of choice is sake or beer.

This all comes at a steep price – a good kaiseki dinner costs upwards of ¥10,000 per person. One way to sample the delights of kaiseki without breaking the bank is to visit a kaiseki restaurant for lunch. Most places offer a boxed lunch *(bentō)* containing a sampling of their dinner fare for around ¥2500.

Unfortunately for foreigners, kaiseki restaurants can be intimidating places to enter. If possible, bring along a Japanese friend or ask a Japanese friend to call ahead and make arrangements. There is usually only one set course, but some places offer a choice of three courses – graded *ume* (regular), *take* (special) and *matsu* (extra special).

kaiseki	懐石	traditional, expensive Kyoto style cuisine
ryōtei	料亭	a restaurant serving a variety of traditional Japanese dishes
bentō	弁当	boxed lunch
ume	梅	regular course
take	竹	special course
matsu	松	extra-special course

A World of Things to Eat

On the upper floors of most big department stores, in shopping malls and on the basement floors of some large office buildings you'll find what the Japanese call *resutoran-gai* (literally, 'restaurant towns'). Within the space of a few hundred metres, these places contain almost every major type of Japanese restaurant plus a variety of Western favourites like Italian, French and the inevitable fast-food joints.

At lunch and dinner most eateries within a resutoran-gai display their specials outside for all to see; otherwise, most eateries will have the usual plastic food displays for you to choose from – all of which makes ordering a snap. So, when you find yourself at a loss for where to eat in a Japanese city, you can always do what the locals do and head for a resutoran-gai.

Sweets

Although most restaurants don't serve dessert (plates of sliced fruit are usually served at the end of a meal), there is no lack of sweets in Japan. Most sweets (known generically as *wagashi*) are sold in speciality stores for you to eat at home. Many of the more delicate-looking ones are made to balance the strong, bitter taste of the special *matcha* tea served during the tea ceremony.

Although pleasant to look at, some Westerners may find Japanese sweets unappealing – perhaps because many of them contain the unfamiliar sweet, red adzuki-bean paste called *anko*. This unusual filling turns up in even the most innocuous looking pastries. But don't let anyone make up your mind for you; try a Japanese sweet for yourself.

With such a wide variety of sweets it's difficult to specify names. However, you'll probably find many variations on the anko-covered-by-glutinous rice *(mochi)* theme. Another sweet to look out for is the *yōkan* – a sweet, bean jelly slice. For confectionery aficiondos, Kyoto is undisputedly the place to head.

Sweet shops are easy to spot; they usually have open fronts with their wares laid out in wooden trays to entice passers-by. Buying sweets is simple – just point at what you want and indicate how many you'd like with your fingers.

wagashi	和菓子	Japanese-style sweets
anko	あんこ	sweet paste or jam made from adzuki beans
mochi	もち	pounded rice cakes made of glutinous rice
yōkan	ようかん	sweet red bean jelly

MARTIN MOOS

MARTIN MOOS

Top: If you consider Japanese food bland, you probably haven't made use of the many spices available.

Bottom: Takoyaki (fried octopus) surrounded by garnishes and condiments

JOHN HAY

JOHN HAY

Top: Fast-moving trolley – Tsukiji Fish Market. Put Tsukiji at the top of your must-see places in Tokyo (and don't forget to guard your ankles with care).

Bottom: *Iso-yaki* – grilled, skewered fish (literally 'shore grill')

SIMON ROWE

MARTIN MOOS

JOHN HAY

Top Left: Drying starfish from Seto, one of the 3000 islands of the Inland Sea in Western Honshū

Top Right: A mass of cherry-coloured *sakura-ebi* (shrimp)

Middle: The next step out from the ocean – a fish processing plant.

Bottom Left: A simple dish of prawn, squid and seaweed, Tokyo

Bottom Right: Sign for a seafood restaurant, Hokkaidō

JOHN HAY

JOHN HAY

ERIC L WHEATER

JOHN HAY

MASON FLORENCE

SIMON ROWE

Top: Persimmons hanging from a length of bamboo, Kyoto

Middle Left: Apricot pie, Tokyo

Middle Right: *Sake* comes in a huge range of brands, grades and prices. There's also a range of customs apply when drinking sake – the first and most important is that one shouldn't pour for oneself.

Bottom: Fruits for sale, Nagano

Eating on the Cheap

Japan can be an expensive place to eat, however, with a little effort you should be able to get away with a daily food budget of ¥1800, perhaps less.

Like anywhere else, the cheapest way to fill yourself up in Japan is to do your own cooking. Unfortunately, apart from some youth hostels, there are not many places where this is possible. If you're really strapped, however, you can fix instant noodles just about anywhere. Failing that, you can purchase food from supermarkets and convenience stores which involves little or no preparation.

If you have to stick to restaurants, there are a variety of options. Fast food is an obvious contender, but most people haven't come all the way to Japan to eat what they can get at home. Your best bet is probably the humble shokudō. This is where your average working man eats his lunch and maybe his dinner. Noodle and rice dishes in such places usually start at around ¥550. A good option is the lunch set (ranchi setto) served at shokudō, coffee shops and many other restaurants They usually start at ¥600.

Another possible option is the cafeterias of major universities, many of which are open to all and serve government-subsidised meals for around ¥500.

Drinking in Japan

What you pay for your drink depends on where you drink and, in the case of a hostess bar, with whom you drink. As a rule, hostess bars are the most expensive places to drink (up to ¥10,000 per drink), followed by upmarket traditional Japanese bars, hotel bars, beer halls and casual pubs. If you are not sure about a place, ask about prices and cover charges before sitting down.

As a rule, if you are served a small snack with your first round, you'll be paying a cover charge (usually a few hundred yen, but sometimes much more).

Izakaya and *yakitori-ya* are cheap places for beer, sake and food in a casual atmosphere resembling that of a pub. All Japanese cities, whether large or small, will have a few informal bars with reasonable prices. Such places are popular with young Japanese and resident gaijin, who usually refer to such places as 'gaijin bars'. In summer, many department stores open up beer gardens on the roof. They are a popular spot to cool off with an inexpensive beer. Many rooftop gardens offer all-you-can-eat/drink specials for around ¥3000 per person. Beer halls are affordable and popular places to swill your beer in a faux-German atmosphere.

The bars which are found in their hundreds, jammed into tiny rooms of large buildings in the entertainment districts of many cities, are often used by their customers as a type of club – if you drop in unexpectedly the reception may be cool or, more likely, you'll simply be told that they're full.

Hostess bars are inevitably expensive, often exorbitant and, without an introduction, best avoided. They cater mainly to those entertaining on business accounts. Hostesses pamper customers with compliments or lend a sympathetic ear to their problems. The best way to visit is in the company of a Japanese friend who knows the routine – and may pick up the tab.

Japan, of course, is also where karaoke got its beginnings. If you've never sung in a karaoke bar, it's worth a try at least once. The uninitiated usually find that a few stiff drinks beforehand helps. Customers sing to the accompaniment of taped music and, as the evening wears on, voices get progressively more ragged. Sobbing, mournful *enka* (folk ballads) are the norm, although more and more Western hits are finding their way into karaoke 'menus'. If you visit a karaoke place with a Japanese friend, it's unlikely that you'll escape without singing at least one song – a version of *Yesterday* or *My Way* will usually satisfy the crowd.

izakaya	居酒屋	pub-style restaurant
yakitori-ya	焼鳥屋	yakitori restaurant

Alcoholic Drinks

Drinking is the glue that holds Japanese society together. It is practised by almost every adult, and a good number of teenagers (alcohol is sold from vending machines and underage drinking is not nearly as frowned upon as it is in some countries). Going out for a few rounds after work with co-workers is both the joy and bane of the Japanese worker's life. After a few drinks, Japanese workers feel secure enough to vent their frustrations and speak their minds, confident that all will be forgiven by the time they arrive at the office in the morning. Occasionally, Japanese drinking crosses the boundary between good-natured fun and ugly inebriation, as anyone who has been in a public park during cherry blossom season can attest; however, drunkenness rarely leads to violence in Japan.

Beer Introduced at the end of last century, *biiru* (beer) is now the favourite tipple of the Japanese. The quality is generally excellent and

Japanese Cuisine & Menu Glossary 155

the most popular type is the light lager, although recently some breweries have been experimenting with darker brews. The major breweries are Kirin, Asahi, Sapporo and Suntory. Beer is dispensed everywhere, from vending machines to beer halls and even in some temple lodgings. A standard can of beer from a vending machine is about ¥250, although some of the monstrous cans cost over ¥1000. At bars, a beer starts at ¥500 and climbs upward depending on the establishment. *Nama biiru* (draft beer) is widely available, as are imported beers.

| biiru | ビール | beer |
| nama biiru | 生ビール | draft beer |

Sake Rice wine has been brewed for centuries in Japan. Once restricted to imperial brewers, it was later produced at temples and shrines across the country. In recent years, consumption of beer has overtaken that of sake, but it's still a standard item in homes, restaurants and drinking places. Large casks of sake are often seen piled up as offerings outside temples and shrines, and it plays an important part in most celebrations and festivals.

Most Westerners come to Japan with a bad image of sake; the result of having consumed low grade brands overseas. Although it won't appeal to all palates, some of the higher grades are actually very good and a trip to a restaurant specialising in sake is a great way to sample some of the better brews.

There are several major types of sake, including *nigori* (cloudy), *nama* (unrefined) and regular, clear sake. Of these, the clear sake is by far the most common. Clear sake is usually divided into three grades: *tokkyū* (premium), *ikkyū* (first grade) and *nikyū* (second grade). Nikyū is the routine choice. Sake can be further divided into *karakuchi* (dry) and *amakuchi* (sweet). Apart from the national brewing giants, there are thousands of provincial brewers producing local brews called *jizake*.

Sake is served *atsukan* (warm) and *reishu* (cold), with warm sake not surprisingly being more popular in the winter. When you order sake, it will usually be served in a small flask called a *tokkuri*. These come in two sizes, so you should specify whether you want an *ichigō* (small) or a *nigō* (large). From these flasks you pour the sake into small ceramic cups called *o-choko* or *sakazuki*. Another way to sample sake is to drink it from a small wooden box called a *masu*, with a bit of salt on the rim.

However you drink it, with a 17% alcohol content, sake is likely to go right to your head, particularly the warm stuff. After a few bouts with sake you'll come to understand why the Japanese drink it in such small cups. Particularly memorable is a real sake hangover born of too much cheap sake. The best advice is not to indulge the day before you have to get on a plane.

sake	酒	Japanese rice wine
nigori	にごり	cloudy sake
nama	なま	regular clear sake
tokkyū	特級	premium grade sake
ikkyū	一級	first grade sake
nikkyū	二級	second grade sake
karakuchi	辛口	dry sake
amakuchi	甘口	sweet sake
jizake	地酒	local brew
atsukan	あつかん	warm sake
reishu	冷酒	cold sake
o-choko	おちょこ	ceramic sake cup
sakazuki	さかづき	ceramic sake cup

Shōchū For those looking for a quick and cheap escape route from the world of sorrows, *shōchū* is the answer. It's a distilled spirit, with an alcohol content of about 30%, which has been resurrected from its previous low-class esteem (it was used as a disinfectant in the Edo period) to the status of a trendy drink. You can drink it as a *oyu-wari* (with hot water) or as a *chūhai* (a highball with soda and lemon). A 720ml bottle sells for about ¥600 which makes it a relatively cheap option compared to other spirits.

shōchū	焼酎	distilled grain liquor
oyu-wari	お湯割り	shōchū with hot water
chūhai	チューハイ	shōchū with soda and lemon

Wine, Imported Drinks & Whiskey Japanese wines are available from areas such as Yamanashi, Nagano, Tōhoku and Hokkaidō. Standard wines are often blended with imports from South America or Eastern Europe. The major producers are Suntory, Mann's and Mercian. Prices are high – expect to pay at least ¥1000 for a bottle of something drinkable. Imported wines are often stocked by large liquor stores or department stores in the cities. Bargains are sometimes available at ¥600, but most of the quaffable imports are considerably more expensive.

Prices of imported spirits have been coming down in recent years and bargain liquor stores have been popping up in the bigger cities. However, if you really like imported spirits, it is probably a good idea to pick up a duty-free bottle or two on your way through the airport. Whiskey is available at most drinking establishments and is usually drunk *mizu-wari* (with water and ice) or *onzarokku* (on the rocks). Local brands, such as Suntory and Nikka, are sensibly priced and most measure up to foreign standards. Expensive foreign labels are popular as gifts.

Most other imported spirits can be had at drinking establishments in Japan. Bars with a large foreign clientele, including hotel bars, can usually mix anything at your request. If not, they will certainly tailor a drink to your specifications.

whiskey	ウィスキー	whiskey
mizu-wari	水割り	whiskey, ice and water
onzarokku	オンザロック	whiskey with ice

Nonalcoholic Drinks

Most of the drinks you're used to at home will be available in Japan, with a few colourfully named additions like Pocari Sweat and Calpis Water. One convenient aspect of Japan is the presence of drink machines on virtually every street corner, and at ¥120 refreshment is rarely more than a few steps away.

Coffee & Tea *Kōhii* (coffee) served in a *kisaten* (coffee shop), tends to be expensive in Japan, costing between ¥350 and ¥500 a cup, with some places charging up to ¥1000. A cheap alternative is some of the newer chains of coffee restaurants like Doutor or Pronto or donut shops like Mr Donut (which offers free refills). An even cheaper alternative is a can of coffee, hot or cold, from a vending machine. Although unpleasantly sweet, at ¥120 the price is hard to beat.

When ordering coffee at a coffee shop in Japan, you'll be asked whether you like it *hotto* (hot) or *aisu* (cold). Black tea also comes hot or cold, with *miruku* (milk) or *remon* (lemon). A good way to start a day of sightseeing in Japan is with a *mōningu setto* (morning set) of tea or coffee, toast and eggs, which costs around ¥400.

kōhii	コーヒー	regular coffee
burendo kohii	ブレンドコーヒー	blended coffee, fairly strong
american kōhii	アメリカンコーヒー	weak coffee
kōcha	紅茶	black, British-style tea
kafe ōre	カフェオレ	café au lait, hot or cold
orenji jūsu	オレンジジュース	orange juice

Japanese Tea Unlike black tea which Westerners are familiar with, Japanese tea is green and contains a lot of vitamin C and caffeine. The powdered form used in the tea ceremony is called *matcha* and is drunk after being whipped into a frothy consistency. The more common form is *o-cha* (a leafy green tea), which is drunk after being steeped in a pot. While *sencha* is one popular variety of green tea, most restaurants will serve a free cup of brownish tea called *bancha*. In summer a cold beverage called *mugicha* (roasted barley tea) is served in private homes.

Although not particularly popular in the West, Japanese tea is very healthy and refreshing and is said by some to prevent cancer. Most department stores carry a wide selection of Japanese teas.

o-cha	お茶	green tea
sencha	煎茶	medium grade green tea
matcha	抹茶	powdered green tea used in the tea ceremony
bancha	番茶	ordinary grade green tea, has a brownish colour
mugicha	麦茶	roasted barley tea

Continued from page 136

measurements. There are several tatami sizes, but as a general rule of thumb, one tatami mat equals one jō which is 1.8 metres by 0.9 metres (1.62 sq metres). A room described as being 4.5 *jō*, for example, is 7.29 sq metres: a medium-sized room by Japanese standards but pokey by Western standards.

Using a real estate agent is the most expensive option and really only feasible if you intend to stay a long time and need to determine exactly the type and location of your housing. English-language magazines such as *Tokyo Classified* and *Kansai Time Out* carry ads from estate agents specialising in accommodation for foreigners.

Additional Costs Before you sign your contract, ask the landlord for precise details about gas, electricity and water. Check if a telephone is already installed since installation of a new telephone is a costly business. You can expect to pay around ¥75,000 but you've then purchased the right to have a phone line anywhere in Japan. This right is negotiable, either privately or through private agencies that deal in phone rights. If you move and want to take your phone line with you, the charge for transferral is around ¥13,000.

ENTERTAINMENT

Japan offers visitors a wealth of entertainment opportunities, including everything from kabuki to electronica. Tokyo, Osaka and Kyoto are the best places for entertainment, but provincial cities and rural tourist destinations often turn up a surprise find.

The only complaint most visitors have with entertainment in Japan is the expense involved. Cinema tickets, for example, range from ¥1800 to ¥2400, which probably makes Japan the most expensive place in the world to catch a movie. Live music prices are also high, ranging from around ¥1500 for a local act to ¥6000 and upwards for international performers.

In Tokyo, the best place to find out about cinema and live music info is *Tokyo Classified* or *Tokyo Journal*. *Kansai Time Out* has info on movie screenings and music for the Kansai area.

Izakaya

Izakaya are traditional pub-style restaurants where Japanese workers (mostly male) congregate to drink beer and *sake*. The drinks are usually accompanied by simple but hearty dishes like *niku jagga* (meat and potato stew) and plates of sashimi. Izakaya are great places to meet the locals, and you'll find that a few glasses of sake breaks down language barriers faster than years of intensive language study. For more on izakaya, see the special Japanese Food section.

Live Houses & Bars

Live houses and bars are among the cheapest nightlife option for travellers and foreign residents in Japan. It's well worth making a point of at least calling into one 'gaijin bar' while you're in Japan – like izakaya, they are great places to meet young Japanese and a few resident expats while you're at it.

Very few of the gaijin bars recommended in this book have entry charges, and where they do they are usually the price of a drink ticket just to ensure that you do spend some money while you are there. Drink prices generally average out at ¥550 for a beer to ¥800 for spirits.

Live houses are venues for local bands and are often worth checking out. Performances tend to start and finish early (say 7.30 to 10 pm).

Clubs & Discos

Before you think about heading off to a club, bear in mind that you are probably going to be hit for a ¥2000 to ¥5000 cover charge. This will usually include two or three drinks, but it still makes for an expensive night out. In the big cities like Tokyo, Osaka, Kyoto, Fukuoka and Sapporo there are usually a few bars around with no cover charge that have dancing on Friday and Saturday nights.

Cinemas

If you are willing to fork out a fistful of yen for your movie-going pleasure, Japan's major cities (in particular Tokyo) offer the opportunity to catch up with everything from the latest Hollywood blockbusters to rare art-house releases.

Traditional Entertainment

Kabuki is one of the most popular traditional entertainments, and the best place to see it is Tokyo. This is true too of *nō* (classical theatre), though tickets tend to sell out quickly and performance schedules vary – check with the TIC. Bunraku is an Osaka tradition. In Kyoto there are tourist performances that include a little of everything, including *kyogen* (comic interludes) and *gagaku* (court orchestral music).

Geisha entertainment is too expensive for most travellers. Some operators offer 'geisha night tours' of Tokyo. The real thing will cost around ¥50,000 per head (or more) and will require an introduction by well-connected Japanese.

SPECTATOR SPORT
Sumō

Japanese wrestling is a simple sport; it's the ritual surrounding it that is complicated. The rules of the game are deceptively simple – the *higashi* (east) wrestler tries either to push his *nishi* (west) opponent out of the

Sumō moves by the famous artist Hokusai.

ring or unbalance him so that some part of his body other than his feet touch the ground. The 4.55m-diameter ring *(dohyō)* is on a raised platform, much like a boxing ring, but there the similarity ends. Sumō matches do not go 10 rounds, they are brief and often spectacular and the ritual and build up to the brief encounter is just as important as the clash itself.

There are no weight classes in sumō; they're all big, and in a nation of trim people, sumō wrestlers certainly stand out. Gargantuan bulk is the order of the day and sumō wrestlers achieve their pigged-out look through diet (or lack of it from the weight-watcher's point of view). Large quantities of an especially fattening stew called *chanko-nabe* are supplemented with esoteric activities, such as masseurs who manipulate the wrestler's intestines so they can pack more food in. Would-be sumō wrestlers, usually 15-year-olds from rural areas, traditionally join one of the 28 *heya* (stables) of wrestlers, often run by retired fighters, and work their way up through the ranks.

Sumō still retains traces of its connections to Shintō fertility rites, including the shrine-like roof which hangs over the ring and the *gyōji* (referee) in his wizard-like outfit. It is said that the dagger worn by the referee was to allow him to commit instant *seppuku* (ritual suicide) if he made a bad refereeing decision! The wrestlers wear a *mawashi* with a broad leather belt; it's rather like a *fundoshi*, the traditional loincloth drawn between the buttocks. A good grasp on the belt is a favourite hold but there are 48 recognised holds and throws.

The pre-game preliminaries often last far longer than the actual struggle, as the opponents first hurl salt into the dohyō to purify it and then put great effort into psyching each other out with malevolent looks and baleful stares. A series of false starts often follows before two immovable objects finally collide with an earth-shaking wallop. Sometimes that initial collision is enough to tip one wrestler out of the ring, but usually there's a brief interlude of pushing, shoving, lifting and tripping. Sometimes neither opponent is able to get a grip on the other and they stand there, slapping at each other like two angry and very overweight infants.

The Tokyo sumō stables are in Ryōgoku, near the new Kokugikan sumō arena. Six major sumō *basho* (tournaments) are held each year: January (Tokyo – Kokugikan Stadium), March (Osaka – Furitsu Taiik-aikan Gymnasium), May (Tokyo – Kokugikan Stadium), July (Nagoya – Aichi Ken-ritsu Taiikukan Gymnasium), September (Tokyo – Kokugikan Stadium) and November (Fukuoka – Kokusai Center Sogo Hall).

Each tournament commences on the Sunday closest to the 10th of the month and lasts a fortnight, during which each wrestler competes in one bout a day. The big crowds arrive in the late afternoon to watch the top-ranking wrestlers; the earlier part of the day is reserved for the lower-ranking fighters.

At a sumō tournament, prices start at ¥1000 for a bench seat at the back, but if you can afford ¥7000 for a balcony seat, you will not only be closer to the action but will also be able to delve into the mysteries of the refreshment bag that comes with the ticket. Ringside seats are highly prized and virtually unobtainable unless you have inside contacts. Tune in to Far East Network (FEN) on 810kHz for simultaneous radio coverage of the action in English. TV coverage is extensive and most of the English-language newspapers devote a section to sumō.

If you want to see a sumo bout, but arrive in Japan at a time when no tournament is being held, you can visit one of the sumō stables to watch training. JNTO publishes the leaflet *Traditional Sports,* which has a sumō section with full details of tournaments, purchase of tickets, visits to sumō stables and even a bibliography of books and magazines in English on the subject. Contact the TIC for more information.

Baseball

Sumō may be the most Japanese of sporting activities, but baseball is Japan's number one sport both for spectators and participants. Baseball bounced into Japan in 1873 with the US teacher Horace Wilson, who taught at Tokyo University. There have been professional teams since the 1930s and, just as in the USA, there are little-league teams, school teams, work teams and 'bunch of friends in the local park' teams. At the professional level, however, baseball is big business and the nightly televised games draw huge audiences.

Despite the similarity to American baseball – even many of the terms are carried over without translation – baseball has been cleverly altered to fit the Japanese mood. Read Robert Whiting's *You've Got to Have Wa* for the full story on baseball Japanese-style; even the Japanese emphasis on the group over the individual has played its part in fitting baseball into the Japanese mould – *wa* means something like 'team spirit'.

Japanese professional baseball is divided into two leagues: Central and Pacific. Each league has six teams, which are usually given highly original names such as Tigers or Giants (although the Hiroshima Carp do sound distinctly Japanese) and are mostly supported or owned by large corporations. Each team is allowed two gaijin players, usually Americans past their prime or facing some sort of contractual difficulty in the USA. They often have trouble adapting to the Japanese requirements that they be just another member of the team, not rock the boat and definitely not show up the local stars!

The season lasts from April to October and is followed by the Japan Series, a seven-match contest between the top two teams. In Tokyo, the centre of the baseball universe is Kōrakuen Stadium. Expect to pay around ¥1000 for a basic seat.

The All-Japan High School Baseball Championship Tournaments are taken very seriously in Japan. These are the major annual sporting events when the flower of youthful vitality goes on display. During August, when the summer tournament is in progress, baseball seems to be the only topic on anyone's mind.

Soccer

Japan's J-League comprises 16 teams. Excitement about the sport has died since the inaugural year of 1993, when it seemed that soccer was poised to sweep away all other sports and become a national obsession.

The sport is still popular though, and the ruling that teams are allowed to employ up to five foreign players means that some of the world's best goal scorers are lifting the standards of play. In Tokyo, matches are played at the National Stadium.

MARTIAL ARTS

Japan is renowned for its martial arts, many of which filtered through from China and were then adapted by the Japanese. During feudal times, these arts were highly valued by ruling families as a means of buttressing their power.

After WWII, martial arts were perceived as contributing to the aggressive stance which had led to hostilities and their teaching was discouraged. Within a decade, however, they had returned to favour and are now popular both in Japan and abroad.

For more information contact the TIC or the associations listed in the Martial Arts entry under Courses in this chapter. JNTO also publishes a leaflet entitled *Traditional Sports*, which covers this subject.

Kendō

Kendō, or the 'way of the sword', is the oldest of the martial arts and was favoured by the samurai to acquire skills in swordsmanship as well as the development of mental poise. Today, it is practised with a bamboo stave and protective body armour, gauntlets and a face mask. The winner of a bout succeeds in landing blows to the face, arms, upper body or throat of an opponent.

Iaijutsu, the art of drawing a sword, is closely related to kendō. One of the few martial arts developed specifically for women was the art of wielding *naginata*, a type of halberd.

Karate

Karate (literally, 'empty hands') may have originated in India, but was refined in China and travelled from there to Okinawa, where it took hold as a local martial art. It began in the 14th century and only continued on to the rest of Japan in the first half of this century. For this reason it is not considered a traditional Japanese martial art.

The emphasis is on unarmed combat, as the name of the sport implies. Blows are delivered with the fists or feet. For optimum performance, all movements require intense discipline of the mind. There are two methods of practising karate. The first is *kumite*, when two or more people spar together. The second is *kata*, when one person performs formal exercises.

Aikidō

The roots of this solely defensive art can be traced to the Minamoto clan in the 10th century, but the modern form of aikidō was started in the 1920s by Ueshiba Morihei.

Aikidō draws on many different techniques, including shintō, karate and kendō. Breathing and meditation form an integral part of training, as does the concentration on movement derived from classical Japanese dance and the awareness of *ki* (life force or will) flowing from the fingertips.

Judō

This is probably the most well known martial art; it has become a popular sport worldwide and regularly features in the Olympic Games. The origins of this art are found in *jūjutsu*, a means of self-defence favoured by the samurai, which was modernised into judō (the 'gentle way') by Kano Jigoro in 1882. The basic principles and subtle skills of the art lie in defeating opponents simply by redirecting the opponents' strength against themselves.

SHOPPING

Although Japan is one world's most expensive countries, there are some good bargains out there, and you can certainly return home with a bag full of goodies without breaking the bank. As well as all the electronic gadgetry available in Japan, there is a wide range of traditional crafts to choose from, though for good stuff you really need to spend big money. It pays to shop around if you have anything particular in mind. The big department stores, which often have the best selections of Japanese gift items, can vary enormously in their prices from one store to another. In some shops, you are paying for extras such as the high level of service (a feature of all Japanese shops anyway), location and interior decor, all of which are very important to the well-heeled Japanese.

Tax-Free Shopping
Shopping tax-free in Japan is not necessarily the bargain you might expect. Although tax-free shops enable foreigners to receive an exemption from the 5% sales tax levied on most items, these still may not always be the cheapest places to shop. Other bulk-buying shops are often a better deal. The best advice is to shop around and compare prices before making a purchase.

Photographic Equipment
Tokyo is an excellent hunting ground for photographic equipment. Almost all the big-name brands in camera equipment are Japanese, and for these locally produced items, prices can be very competitive. The prices for accessories, such as motor drives and flash units, can even be competitive with Singapore and Hong Kong. In addition, shopping in Japan presents the shopper with none of the rip-off risks that abound in other Asian discount capitals.

As always, be prepared to shop around. Tokyo's Shinjuku area is the best place for buying camera equipment, although Ginza too has a good selection of camera shops. Second-hand camera equipment is worth checking out too. In Tokyo, both Shinjuku and Ginza have a fair number of second-hand shops where camera and lens quality is usually very good and prices are around half what you would pay for new equipment. In Osaka, the area just south of Osaka station has quite a few used camera shops as well.

Electronics
Nowhere in the world will you find a better selection of electronics than in Tokyo's Akihabara district and Osaka's Den-Den Town. Keep in mind though that much of the electrical gadgetry on sale in Japan is designed for Japan's curious power supply (100V at 50 or 60Hz) and may require a transformer for use overseas. The safest bet

is to go for export models – the prices may be slightly higher, but in the long run you'll save the expense of converting the equipment to suit the conditions in your own country. Big electronics stores in Japan are about the only places where a little bargaining (don't get too carried away – this is not India!) will bring prices down around 10% or so.

Computers
Computers, computer accessories and software are widely available. Unfortunately for the foreign traveller, most of what's out there is intended for use by Japanese, meaning that operating systems, keyboards and software are in Japanese – and not of any use unless you intend to work with the Japanese language. However, if you're after hardware like peripherals, chips and the like, where language isn't a factor, you will find lots to choose from, including second-hand goods at unbelievably low prices (check the Sofmap store in Osaka's Den-Den Town).

Pearls
The Japanese firm Mikimoto developed the technique of producing cultured pearls by artificially introducing an irritant into the pearl oyster. Pearls and pearl jewellery are still popular buys for foreign visitors, but it would be wise to check prices in your own country. Size, quality and colour will all have a bearing on the price. Toba, in the Ise area (Kansai region) is a centre for the production of cultured pearls.

Cars, Motorcycles & Bicycles
Information on purchasing these vehicles can be found in the Getting Around chapter.

Clothes
Japanese-made clothes and shoes are of excellent quality and needn't cost the earth. It really is a matter of looking around and finding something that suits your budget, taste and – here's the hard part – your size! In up market and fashionable districts, many of the clothes shops are exclusive boutiques with exclusive prices, although

there are always clusters of stores nearby that are more affordable. In less fashionable areas, there are countless retail outlets for an industry providing economical, mass-produced versions of designer clothes. If you fit into the smaller sizes in your home country, you shouldn't have any problems finding clothes to fit (although pant/trouser length may be cutting it fine). Shoe size can be a problem; for women don't expect to find anything over size 7 (36½), while mens' shoes go up to size 9.

Toys
Tokyo has some remarkable toy shops. See Kids' Stuff under Shopping in the Tokyo chapter for more information. Elsewhere, look out for some of the traditional wooden toys produced as regional specialities – they make good souvenirs for adults and children alike.

Japanese Arts & Crafts
As well as all the hi-tech knick-knacks produced by the Japanese, it is also possible to go home loaded down with traditional Japanese arts and crafts. Anything from carp banners to *kimono* can make good souvenirs for the converted Japanophile. If you visit Tokyo, a one-stop traditional arts and crafts shopping experience can be had at the Oriental Bazaar in Harajuku in Tokyo.

Ningyō Japanese dolls are usually intended for display, not for playing with. Often quite exquisite, with coiffured hair and dressed in kimono, they make excellent souvenirs or gifts. Also available are the *gogatsu-ningyō*, dolls dressed in samurai suits used as gifts on *Kodomo-no-hi* (Children's Day). The most famous dolls are made in Kyoto and are known as *kyō-ningyō*.

Ningyō can be bought in tourist shops, department stores and special doll shops. In Tokyo, Edo-dōri in Asakusa is well known for its many doll shops (see Japanese Dolls under Shopping in the Tokyo chapter).

Kasa Japanese umbrellas are another classic souvenir item. They come in two forms: *higasa*, which are made of paper, cotton or silk and serve as a sunshade; and *bangasa*, which are made of oiled paper and keep the rain off. Again, department stores and tourist shops are your best bet for finding *kasa*.

Koinobori These are the carp banners that you see flying from poles in Japan. The carp is much revered for its tenacity and perseverance, but you might like the banners for their simple elegance.

Katana Japanese swords make a fantastic souvenir – it's just that good ones are going to cost more than all your other travel expenses put together! The reason for their expense is both the mystique attached to them as the symbols of samurai power and the great care that went into making them. Sword shops that sell the real thing will also stock *tsuba* (sword guards), and complete sets of samurai armour. Department stores, on the other hand, stock realistic (to the untrained eye at least) imitations at affordable prices.

Shikki Lacquerware is another Japanese craft that has been mastered to a superlative degree. The lacquer-making process, involving as many as 15 layers of lacquer, is used to create objects as diverse as dishes and furniture. As you might expect, examples of good lacquerware cannot be had for a song, but smaller items can be bought at affordable prices from department stores. Popular, easily transportable items include bowls, trays and small boxes.

Washi Japanese paper has been famous for more than 1000 years as the finest handmade paper in the world. Special shops stock sheets of washi and products made from it, such as notebooks, wallets and so on. As they're generally inexpensive and light, washi products make excellent gifts and souvenirs. Again, you'll find them in the big department stores. See Shopping under Kyoto in the Kansai chapter for suggestions on places to buy washi.

Pottery Numerous pottery villages still exist in Japan. Many of them feature pottery museums and working kilns that are open to the public. Of course, it is also possible to buy examples of stoneware and porcelain. Some villages include: Mashiko, north of Tokyo (see the Around Tokyo chapter); Imbe, near Okayama in Western Honshū, which is famed for its *bizen-yaki* pottery; Tamba Sasayama in the Kansai region, known for its Tamba pottery; Koishiwara, Karatsu, Imari and Arita (in Kyūshū, the home of Japanese pottery) are all sources of different pottery styles.

Department stores are a surprisingly good place to look for Japanese pottery, and Takashimaya often has bargain bins where you can score some real deals. For even better prices try some of Japan's flea markets (see the Kyoto and Tokyo Shopping sections for details).

Ukiyo-e Wood block prints originated in the 18th century as one of Japan's earliest manifestations of mass culture – they were used in advertising and posters. It was only later that *ukiyo-e* was considered an art form. The name (literally 'pictures from the floating world') derives from a Buddhist term indicating the transient world of daily pleasures. Ukiyo-e uniquely depicts such things as street scenes, actors and courtesans.

Today, tourist shops in Japan stock modern reproductions of the work of famous ukiyo-e masters such as Hokusai whose scenes of Fuji-san (Mt Fuji) are favourites.

It is also possible to come across originals by lesser-known artists at prices ranging from ¥5000 to ¥40,000.

Kimono & Yukata Kimono are worn most commonly on ceremonial occasions such as university graduation or on a wedding day. For most non-Japanese, the cost of a kimono is prohibitively expensive. For a 'bottom of the range' kimono, prices start at around ¥60,000 and soar to ¥1 million or more. The best option for those interested in owning their own kimono is to head to a used clothing shop like the Chicago thrift shop in Tokyo's Harajuku area. Used clothing shops usually stock a variety of kimono ranging in price from ¥1500 to ¥9000 depending on quality. The Oriental Bazaar also stocks a limited selection of antique kimono. Alternatively, if you're in Japan during March or September, these are the months that the Daimaru store has sales of its rental kimono. Be warned, however, these sales are also popular with local Japanese.

For those not in the kimono league, another option might be to look for a yukata (the cotton bathrobes worn in ryokan and at summer festivals). These have a distinctively Japanese look and are not only affordable (from around ¥3500 up) but also highly usable. These are also available at the Chicago thrift shop in Tokyo.

Getting There & Away

Flying into Tokyo is only one of a diverse range of ways of getting to Japan and only a tiny part of the whole story. For a start there are many other airports in Japan, some of which make better entry points than Tokyo's somewhat inconvenient New Tokyo international airport (commonly known as Narita international airport). It's also possible to arrive in Japan by sea from a number of nearby countries, particularly South Korea. Japan can also serve as the starting or finishing point for the popular Trans-Siberian Railway trip across Russia.

AIR

There are flights to Japan from all over the world, usually to Tokyo but also to a number of other Japanese airports. Although Tokyo may seem the obvious arrival and departure point in Japan, for many visitors this may not be the case. If you plan on exploring western Japan or the Kansai region,

---

WARNING

The information in this chapter is particularly vulnerable to change: prices for international travel are volatile, routes are introduced and cancelled, schedules change, special deals come and go, and rules and visa requirements are amended. Airlines and governments seem to take a perverse pleasure in making price structures and regulations as complicated as possible. You should check directly with the airline or a travel agency to make sure you understand how a fare (and ticket you may buy) works. In addition, the travel industry is highly competitive and there are many lurks and perks.

The upshot of this is that you should get opinions, quotes and advice from as many airlines and travel agencies as possible before you part with your hard-earned cash. The details given in this chapter should be regarded as pointers and are not a substitute for your own careful, up-to-date research.

---

it might be more convenient to fly into Kansai international airport (KIX) near Osaka.

Airports

There are international airports on the main island of Honshū (Nagoya, Niigata, Osaka/Kansai and Tokyo), Kyūshū (Fukuoka, Kagoshima, Kumamoto and Nagasaki), Okinawa (Naha) and Hokkaidō (Sapporo).

New Tokyo International Airport (Narita) With the exception of China Airlines, all international flights to Tokyo use the somewhat inconveniently located New Tokyo international airport, better known as Narita airport. Since Narita is the most popular arrival/departure point in Japan, flights via Narita are usually cheaper than those using other airports. You'll also get the widest range of choices if you fly via Narita. Of course, if you can get a cheap flight to another airport, particularly one close to your area of interest, then there's no reason not to use another airport.

Osaka/Kansai International Airport (KIX) Almost all of Osaka's international flights now go via the new Kansai international airport. Kansai international airport is the first Japanese airport to function 24 hours a day. It serves the key Kansai cities of Kyoto, Osaka and Kōbe. Airport transport to any of these cities is fast and reliable (though it can be expensive if you're going all the way to Kyoto).

Nagoya Nagoya may have few attractions in its own right, but it's conveniently located between Tokyo and Osaka. From Nagoya, flights connect with Australia, Canada, China, Guam, Hong Kong, Indonesia, Malaysia, New Zealand, the Philippines, Singapore, South Korea, Taiwan, Thailand and the USA.

Fukuoka Fukuoka, at the northern end of Kyūshū, is the main arrival point for western

Japan. The airport, conveniently located near the city, has flight connections with Australia, North America and a number of Asian destinations.

Naha (Okinawa) Okinawa-hontō (the main island of Okinawa), south-west of the main islands of Japan, is a convenient arrival or departure point for Hong Kong and Taiwan.

Niigata Niigata, north of Tokyo, is connected with Seoul in South Korea and with Irkutsk, Vladivostok and Khabarovsk in Russia. From Khabarovsk, Aeroflot and the Trans-Siberian Express operate to Moscow. A *shinkansen* (bullet train) line connects Niigata with Tokyo.

Other Airports On the island of Kyūshū, Kagoshima airport has flights to Hong Kong, Kumamoto airport has flights to South Korea, and Nagasaki has flights to Shanghai and Seoul.

On Hokkaidō, Sapporo airport has connections with South Korea.

Buying Tickets

In most of Japan's major cities there are travel agencies where English is spoken. Most of these places sell a wide range of discount tickets and can advise on the best routes and times for travel. For an idea of the latest prices in Tokyo check the travel ads in *Tokyo Classified* and in Kansai check the *Kansai Time Out*. In other parts of Japan, check the *Japan Times*. For more details on travel agencies, see the Tokyo chapter and the Osaka and Kyoto sections in the Kansai chapter.

Travellers with Special Needs

If you have a special need – a broken leg, a wheelchair, a baby, dietary restrictions, fear of flying – let the airline know early so that it can make arrangements. Remind them when you reconfirm your booking (at least 72 hours prior to departure) and again when you check in at the airport.

Airports and airlines can be quite accommodating to passengers in wheelchairs, but they do need advance warning. Most international airports will provide escorts from the check-in desk to the aeroplane, and there should be ramps, lift-accessible toilets and accessible phones. Aircraft toilets, however, are likely to present a problem; travellers should discuss this with the airline at an early stage and, if necessary, with their doctor.

Hearing-impaired travellers can request airport and in-flight announcements to be written down for them.

Children under the age of two travel for 10% of the standard fare (or free on some airlines), as long as they don't occupy a seat. (They don't get a baggage allowance.) 'Skycots' should be provided by the airline if requested in advance; these take children weighing up to 10kg. Children between the ages of two and 12 usually occupy a seat for half to two-thirds of the full fare, and do get a baggage allowance. Strollers can often be taken on as hand luggage.

Guide dogs for the visually impaired will often have to travel in a specially pressurised baggage compartment with other animals, though smaller guide dogs may be admitted to the cabin.

Japanese regulations on the importation of live animals are very strict, and are not waived for guide dogs. Dogs brought from countries in which rabies has been eradicated need not be quarantined, provided their owners can show an exportation certification (*yūshutsu shomeisho*). Dogs arriving from countries in which rabies occurs will be placed into quarantine for up to six months, unless their owners can supply an exportation certificate, veterinary examination certification and written proof of rabies vaccination.

Departure Tax

Kansai international airport charges a departure tax of ¥2650, which you must pay at the airport (credit cards are accepted). Tokyo's Narita international airport charges a departure tax of ¥2040 but this is almost always figured into the price of your ticket. Departure tax is not charged at the other international airports.

Air Travel Glossary

Cancellation Penalties If you have to cancel or change a discounted ticket, there are often heavy penalties involved; insurance can sometimes be taken out against these penalties. Some airlines impose penalties on regular tickets as well, particularly against 'no-show' passengers.

Courier Fares Businesses often need to send urgent documents or freight securely and quickly. Courier companies hire people to accompany the package through customs and, in return, offer a discount ticket which is sometimes a phenomenal bargain. However, you may have to surrender all your baggage allowance and take only carry-on luggage.

Full Fares Airlines traditionally offer 1st class (coded F), business class (coded J) and economy class (coded Y) tickets. These days there are so many promotional and discounted fares available that few passengers pay full economy fare.

Lost Tickets If you lose your airline ticket an airline will usually treat it like a travellers cheque and, after inquiries, issue you with another one. Legally, however, an airline is entitled to treat it like cash and if you lose it then it's gone forever. Take good care of your tickets.

Onward Tickets An entry requirement for many countries is that you have a ticket out of the country. If you're unsure of your next move, the easiest solution is to buy the cheapest onward ticket to a neighbouring country or a ticket from a reliable airline which can later be refunded if you do not use it.

Open-Jaw Tickets These are return tickets where you fly out to one place but return from another. If available, this can save you backtracking to your arrival point.

Overbooking Since every flight has some passengers who fail to show up, airlines often book more passengers than they have seats. Usually excess passengers make up for the no-shows, but occasionally somebody gets 'bumped' onto the next available flight. Guess who it is most likely to be? The passengers who check in late.

Promotional Fares These are officially discounted fares, available from travel agencies or direct from the airline.

Reconfirmation If you don't reconfirm your flight at least 72 hours prior to departure, the airline may delete your name from the passenger list. Ring to find out if your airline requires reconfirmation.

Restrictions Discounted tickets often have various restrictions on them – such as needing to be paid for in advance and incurring a penalty to be altered. Others are restrictions on the minimum and maximum period you must be away.

Round-the-World Tickets RTW tickets give you a limited period (usually a year) in which to circumnavigate the globe. You can go anywhere the carrying airlines go, as long as you don't backtrack. The number of stopovers or total number of separate flights is decided before you set off and they usually cost a bit more than a basic return flight.

Transferred Tickets Airline tickets cannot be transferred from one person to another. Travellers sometimes try to sell the return half of their ticket, but officials can ask you to prove that you are the person named on the ticket. On an international flight tickets are compared with passports.

Travel Periods Ticket prices vary with the time of year. There is a low (off-peak) season and a high (peak) season, and often a low-shoulder season and a high-shoulder season as well. Usually the fare depends on your outward flight – if you depart in the high season and return in the low season, you pay the high-season fare.

Travel Seasons

The price of your ticket will depend to a great extent on when you fly. High season prices are determined by two sets of holidays and popular travel times: those in the country you're flying from and those in Japan. Generally, high season for travel between Japan and Western countries is in late December (around Christmas and New Year's), late April to early May (around Japan's Golden Week holiday), and July and August. Flights during these periods can be booked out months in advance and tickets may be unavailable at almost any price. If you must fly during these periods, book well in advance. Obviously, you'll save a lot of money by flying outside these times. When you're talking to your travel agency, be sure to ask the exact cut-off dates for high, shoulder and low season travel.

The USA

Recent years have seen huge drops in prices for tickets between North America and Japan. From New York, in the low season you can find discount return fares for as low as US$650, sometimes less. Carriers to check include United Airlines, Northwest Airlines, Korean Air, Japan Airlines (JAL) and All Nippon Airways (ANA). From the US west coast, low season discount return fares can start as low as US$450. High-season discount fares will just about double these figures.

United Airlines is one of the better price bets from the USA to Japan; its schedule and routes are hard to beat for convenience, and its frequent flier program is among the best around. United also has great Japan-USA (four stops)-Japan tickets for as low as ¥80,000, and Japan-USA (four stops)-Europe (one stop)-Japan tickets for as low as ¥120,000.

Check the Sunday travel sections of papers like the *Los Angeles Times* or the *New York Times* for travel bargains. Council Travel and STA Travel are two good discount operations specialising in student fares and cheap deals. They have offices all across North America (check the yellow pages). IACE Travel New York (☎ 212-972-3200, email iace@interport.com) is a travel agency specialising in travel between the USA and Japan and they can often dig up the cheapest fares around.

Canada

Canadian Airlines International, which operates out of Vancouver, often matches or beats the best fares available from the USA. Low season return fares from Vancouver to Tokyo start as low as C$928. Likewise, Air Canada offers some very competitive fares from eastern Canada to Japan. Low season return fares from Ottawa to Tokyo start at around C$1240. Other airlines to try from Canada include JAL, Northwest and United.

Travel Cuts, the Canadian student travel organisation, offers cheap one-way and return Vancouver to Tokyo flights (as low as C$800/C$1000), depending on the season. Check their Web site at www.travelcuts.com.

Australia

Two well-known agents for cheap fares are STA Travel and Flight Centre. STA Travel has offices in all major cities and on many university campuses. Call ☎ 131-776 Australia-wide for the location of your nearest branch or visit its Web site at www.statravel.com.au. Flight Centre (☎ 131-600 Australia-wide) has dozens of offices throughout Australia. Its Web address is www.flightcentre.com.au.

Garuda, Malaysian Airlines and Cathay Pacific have some good deals for travel between Australia and Japan, but these fares will often have a number of restrictions on them. Return fares start from A$1161 with Garuda, which allows a stopover in Bali. Direct flights with airlines including Qantas, Air New Zealand and JAL are more expensive, expect to pay around A$1530 for a return fare.

New Zealand

From New Zealand, Malaysian Airlines, Thai International and Qantas have return fares from around NZ$1489. Flight Centre (☎ 09-309-6171) has a large central office in Auckland at National Bank Towers (corner Queen and Darby Sts) and many branches throughout the country. STA Travel (☎ 09-309-0458) has its main office at 10 High St, Auckland, and has other offices in Auckland as well as in Hamilton, Palmerston North, Wellington, Christchurch and Dunedin. Check out the Web site at www.statravel.co.nz.

The UK

Expect to pay around £500 to £600 for a one-year open return ticket with a good airline via a fast route. Air France is a reliable choice for flights to Japan, but you'll have to change in Paris. British Airways, ANA and JAL also offer frequent flights between London and Tokyo and the latter two also fly into Kansai. For a less convenient trans-Asian route, count on UK£350 or lower and about half that for one-way tickets.

Check STA travel, Campus travel, or the weekly listings magazine *Time Out* for the latest deals. STA, in particular, can put together round-the-world routes incorporating Tokyo on the itinerary.

An alternative route to Japan from Europe is to fly to Hong Kong and buy an onward ticket from one of Hong Kong's very competitive travel agencies. London-Hong Kong flights are much more competitively priced than London-Tokyo ones. If you have to go to Hong Kong en route to Tokyo, a London-Hong Kong-London ticket plus a Hong Kong-Tokyo-Hong Kong ticket may be cheaper than a London-Hong Kong-Tokyo-London ticket.

Continental Europe

Most direct flights between Europe and Japan fly into Tokyo but there are also some flights into Kansai. Typical low-season return fares from major European cities are as follows: Berlin to Tokyo 900DM (Aeroflot); Rome to Tokyo L1,400,000 (Egypt Air); Paris to Tokyo 3800FF (KLM). For flights from France, check the Anyway travel site at www.anyway.fr. For flights from Germany, check the Just Travel site at www.justtravel.de.

Asia

Most Asian nations have air links with Japan. South Korea is particularly popular because it's used by many English teachers

as a place to take a short holiday from Japan when their visas are close to expiring. However, for this reason, immigration authorities treat travellers returning to Japan after a short break in South Korea with great suspicion.

South Korea Numerous flights link Seoul and Pusan with Tokyo. A one-way/return Seoul-Tokyo flight purchased in Seoul costs around US$180/340. From Tokyo, flights to Seoul are the cheapest way out of Japan. Low-season return fares start as low as ¥18,000; there are several departures daily. Getting seats is usually not a problem, even during peak flying season. See the Sea section later in this chapter for information on sea-travel bargains between Korea and Japan.

China Of the Asian air links, Hong Kong has the highest frequency of daily flights to Japan. There are several daily flights on Cathay Pacific, as well as on JAL, ANA and JAS (Japan Air System). Hong Kong-Tokyo return costs around US$900. Check with agents like the Hong Kong Student Travel Bureau or Phoenix Travel.

There are also flights between Japan and Beijing, Shanghai, Guangzhou and Dalian on all the Japanese carriers as well as on Air China, China Eastern Airways and China Southern Air. Beijing-Tokyo costs around US$800 return.

Taiwan Agents handling discounted tickets advertise in the English-language *China News* and *China Post*. There are flights from Taipei to Fukuoka, Naha, Osaka or Tokyo. If you are stopping off in Taiwan between Hong Kong and Japan, check on China Air tickets, which allow a stopover in Taipei before continuing on to Tokyo's very convenient Haneda airport.

Flights also operate between Kaohsiung and Osaka or Tokyo.

Other Asian Centres There are daily flights from Bangkok to Japan on both Thai and ANA with fares costing about US$450 return in the low season. From Singapore on Singapore Airlines, JAL or ANA tickets are about US$600 return; from Indonesia (Jakarta/Denpasar) on Garuda, Continental or Japan Asia Airlines (JAA), a return flight will cost around US$800.

From the Philippines (Manila) a return flight to Japan is around US$600 and from Malaysia (Kuala Lumpur) it's US$700 return. From Vietnam (Ho Chi Minh City) a return flight costs US$660.

Other Asian countries with limited weekly flights to Japan include India, Nepal and Myanmar (Burma).

Other Regions

There are also flights between Japan and South America, Africa and the Middle East.

Round-the-World & Circle Pacific Tickets

Round-the-world (RTW) fares are put together by two or more airlines and allow you to make a circuit of the world using their combined routes. A typical RTW ticket is valid from 90 days to one year, allows for a number of stopovers along the way and costs about UK£1480, A$3700 or US$2500. An example, including Tokyo in Japan, would be a British Airways/United Airways combination flying London-New York-Tokyo-Singapore-London. There are many versions involving different combinations of airlines and routes. Generally, routes which stay north of the equator are cheaper than routes that include countries like Australia or South America.

Circle Pacific fares are a similar idea and allow you to make a circuit of the Pacific. A typical combination is Los Angeles-Tokyo-Bangkok-Sydney-Auckland-Honolulu-Los Angeles (around US$2000). Sydney can generally be interchanged with Brisbane or Cairns.

Enterprising travel agencies put together their own RTW and Circle Pacific fares at much lower prices than the joint airline deals but, of course, the cheapest fares will involve unpopular airlines and less popular routes. It's possible to put together a RTW from London for as little as UK£700. Travel agencies in London have also come up with another variation on these combination fares

– the Circle Asia fare. A possible route would include London-Hong Kong-Tokyo-Manila-Singapore-Bangkok-London.

SEA
South Korea

South Korea is the closest country to Japan and a very popular visa-renewal point. Many long-term visitors to Japan who are teaching English or who are engaged in some other kind of work, drop over to Korea when their permitted period of stay in Japan is about to expire, then come back to start a fresh stay. For this reason you can expect to have your passport rigorously inspected.

Pusan-Shimonoseki The Kampu Ferry Service operates the Shimonoseki-Pusan ferry service. There are daily departures of the Hamayū or the Pukwan at 6 pm from Shimonoseki and Pusan, arriving at the other end at 8.30 am (the next morning). One-way fares start from ¥6800 for students and continue up through ¥8500 for an open, tatami-mat area, ¥10,500 (six-berth cabin), ¥12,000 (four-berth cabin) and ¥14,000 (two-berth cabin). There's a 10% discount on return fares. See the Shimonoseki section of the Western Honshū chapter for more details.

Pusan-Fukuoka Fukuoka has an international high-speed hydrofoil service connecting the city with Pusan in Korea (¥13,000/¥24,000 one-way/return, three hours, daily). The Camelia line also runs a ferry service to Pusan (¥9000/¥17,100 one-way/return, around 15 hours). See the Fukuoka section of the Kyūshū chapter for more details.

China

The Japan-China International Ferry service connects Shanghai and Osaka/Kōbe. The number of departures varies with the seasons. Off-season it's nearly empty, but can be crowded during summer. A 2nd-class ticket is around US$180. For further information in Japan about Shanghai-bound ferries you can ring the Nitchū Kokusai Ferry company (☎ 06-6536-6541, in Japanese).

Ships from Kōbe to Tanggu (near Tianjin) leave from Kōbe every Thursday at noon, arriving in Tanggu the next day. Economy/1st-class tickets cost US$200/US$300. The food on this boat gets poor reviews so bring a few emergency munchies. Tickets can be bought in Tianjin from the shipping office (☎ 22-31-2243) at 89 Munan Dao, Heping District. In Kōbe, the office is at the port (☎ 078-321-5791).

Taiwan

Arimura Sangyō (☎ 098-869-1320 in Naha, 03-3562-2091 in Tokyo) operates a weekly ferry service between Okinawa and Taiwan, sometimes via Ishigaki and Miyako in Okinawa-ken (Okinawa Prefecture). The Taiwan port alternates between Keelung and Kaohsiung. Departure from Okinawa is on Thursday or Friday; departure from Taiwan is usually on Monday. It takes 16 to 19 hours. Fares from Okinawa cost from ¥15,750 in economy class; fares are slightly cheaper from Taiwan than from Japan.

In Taiwan you can buy tickets from Yeong An Maritime Company (☎ 02-771-5911) in Taipei, or in Kaohsiung (☎ 07-551-0281) and Keelung (☎ 02-424-8151).

Russia

For travellers intending to take the Trans-Siberian Railway to/from Moscow, there's a weekly ferry service between Niigata and the Russian port of Nakhodka near Vladivostok (¥27,600, 41½ hours). See the Niigata section in the Northern Honshū chapter for details.

TRANS-SIBERIAN RAILWAY

A little-used option of approaching or leaving Japan is the Trans-Siberian Railway. It won't be particularly attractive to those looking at

getting out of Japan in a hurry – visas and bookings take time – but for those with time to spare and an interest in avoiding expensive flights, it might be an attractive option.

There are three Trans-Siberian Railway options, one of which is to travel on the railway to/from Vladivostok and fly between Vladivostok and Niigata – an expensive option. The cheaper options are the Chinese Trans-Mongolia and Russian Trans-Manchuria routes, which start/finish in China, from where there are ferry connections to/from Japan via Tianjin and Shanghai.

Information on ferry connections between Japan and China is included in the Sea section of this chapter. Air connections with Vladivostok are via Niigata in Northern Honshū. There are also ferry connections between Nakhodka (near Vladivostok) and Niigata. (For details on air and sea connections between Niigata and Vladivostok, see the Niigata section in the Northern Honshū chapter.)

For more information contact national tourist agencies such as the Japan National Tourist Organization (JNTO); see Tourist Offices in the Facts for the Visitor chapter. In Japan the Tourist Information Centers (TIC) in Tokyo and Kyoto and the Japan-Soviet Tourist Bureau (JSTB) should have more information. The JSTB has offices in Tokyo (☎ 03-3432-6161) and Osaka (☎ 06-6531-7416).

More detailed information is also available in a good number of publications – see Robert Strauss' *Trans-Siberian Handbook* in particular. Those making their way to Japan via China (or vice versa) should pick up a copy of Lonely Planet's *China* guide, which has invaluable information on travel in China as well as information on Trans-Siberian travel.

Getting Around

Japan is justifiably famous for its extensive, well-organised and efficient transportation network. Schedules are strictly adhered to and late or cancelled services are almost unheard of. All this convenience comes at a price – you'd be well advised to look into money saving deals whenever possible.

Timetables

In many popular areas of Japan, transport schedules are so frequent that timetables hardly matter – does it really make any difference if the train departs at 10.30 or 10.40 am? If, however, you really want to know what goes where and when, then you need a *jikokuhyō* (book of timetables).

These come in a variety of forms, including a completely comprehensive monthly *JR Jikokuhyō*, which lists just about every passenger vehicle that moves. This can be useful if you're exploring the back blocks of Japan and need to know about buses to remote villages or ferries between small islands. The drawbacks? It's the size and weight of a telephone directory and is completely in Japanese. Deciphering a 1000-page *kanji* (Chinese script) timetable is not most people's idea of fun travel! In any case, the *JR Jikokuhyō* is always available at stations (often tied to the ticket-office counter with a piece of string) and at most *ryokan* (traditional inn) youth hostels, *minshuku* (B&B) and other accommodation.

An easier alternative is the Japan Travel Bureau's (JTB) *Mini-Timetable* which costs ¥310 and is issued monthly. It's about the size of a pocket dictionary and lists JR *shinkansen* (bullet train) services, limited and ordinary expresses, intercity and express trains in the Tokyo, Nagoya and Osaka areas, limited express services on the main private lines, long-distance buses and all the domestic airline schedules. Other advantages of the mini guide are that it has some explanations in English and place names are shown in *romaji* (Japanese roman script) on maps and main timetables.

Travel Agencies

Information and tickets can also be obtained from travel agencies, of which there are a great number in Japan. Nearly every railway station of any size will have at least one travel agency in the station building to handle all sorts of bookings in addition to train services. JTB (Japan Travel Bureau) is the big daddy of Japanese travel agencies. You can also make train and long-distance bus reservations at the Green Window ticket counters ('Midori-no-Madoguchi' in Japanese) of major train stations.

Discount Ticket Shops Known as *kakuyasu-kippu uriba* in Japanese, these stores deal in discounted tickets for trains, buses, domestic plane flights, ferries and a host of other things like cut-rate stamps and phone cards. Typical savings on shinkansen tickets is between 5% and 10%, which is good news for long-term residents who are not eligible for Japan Rail Passes. Discount ticket agencies are found around train stations in medium and large cities. The best way to find one is to ask at the *kōban* (police box) outside the station.

Baggage Forwarding

The average traveller should have no problems stowing their luggage on Japanese trains – there's plenty of storage space overhead. But if you have too much baggage, highly efficient forwarding services are available. Prices are surprisingly reasonable and overnight service is the norm. Perhaps the most convenient service is Yamato Takyūbin, which operates from most convenience stores. Simply pack your luggage and bring it to the store, they'll help with the paperwork and arrange for pick-up.

AIR

Rail travel has such a pervasive image in Japan that it's easy to forget there's a comprehensive network of air routes. In many cases, flying can be much faster than even shinkansen travel and not that much more expensive. Flying is also an efficient way to travel from the main islands to the many small islands around the coast of Japan. As well as numerous small local operators, there are five major domestic airlines.

Domestic Air Services

Japan Air Lines (JAL) is the major international carrier and also has a domestic network linking the major cities. All Nippon Airways (ANA) is the second largest international carrier and operates a more extensive domestic system. Japan Air Systems (JAS) only does a couple of overseas routes but flies to many destinations in Japan. Air Nippon Koku (ANK) and Japan Trans Ocean Air (JTA) are smaller domestic carriers. ANK links many smaller towns all over Japan, while JTA is particularly good for connections through Okinawa and the South-West Islands. In addition to these, Skymark is a recent start-up airline which

undercuts the prices of the more established airlines (check with a travel agency to see if it operates on your intended route).

The 'Domestic Airfares' chart shows some of the major connections and the one-way fares. There's a 10% discount on round-trip fares if the return flight is made within seven to 10 days. The airlines have some weird and wonderful discounts if you know what to ask for. JAL, for example, has a women's group discount available for groups of three or more women. Or a husband and wife discount if their combined age totals 88 years or more! More useful for most people are advance-purchase price reductions: both ANA and JAL offer tickets at up to 50% off if you purchase a month or more in advance, with smaller discounts for purchases made one to three weeks in advance.

ANA also offers the Visit Japan Fare for foreign travellers. Provided you reside outside Japan, purchase your tickets outside Japan and carry a valid international ticket

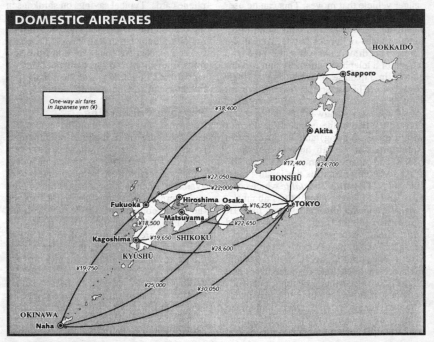

DOMESTIC AIRFARES

One-way air fares in Japanese yen (¥)

HOKKAIDŌ
Sapporo
¥38,400
Akita
¥17,400   ¥24,700
HONSHŪ
¥27,050
¥22,000
Fukuoka   Hiroshima   Osaka
¥16,250   TOKYO
Matsuyama
¥18,500
¥22,650
Kagoshima   ¥19,650   SHIKOKU
KYŪSHŪ   ¥28,600
¥19,750
¥25,000   ¥30,050
OKINAWA
Naha

on any airline, you can fly up to five times within 60 days on any ANA domestic route for only ¥12,000 per flight (a huge saving on some routes). For more details, visit the ANA site at svc.ana.co.jp/eng.

If you're flying to or from Tokyo, note that most domestic airlines use the more convenient Haneda airport, while all international flights, except those with China Airlines, use New Tokyo international airport (commonly known as Narita airport). If you're flying to Tokyo to make an international connection out of Narita airport it would be rather embarrassing to end up at Haneda – make sure you're on a domestic flight to Narita or that you have plenty of time (around three hours) to make the transfer from Haneda to Narita.

TRAIN

As in India, rail is *the* way to travel in Japan but that's where the similarity ends. Japanese rail travel is usually fast, frequent, clean, comfortable and often very expensive. The services range from small local lines to the shinkansen super-expresses or 'bullet trains' which have become a symbol of modern Japan.

Schedules & Information

The most complete timetables can be found in jikokuhyō (timetable books), but the Japan National Tourist Organization (JNTO) produces a handy English-language *Railway Timetable* booklet which explains a great deal about the services in Japan and gives timetables for the shinkansen services, JR limited tokkyū (expresses) and major private lines. If your visit to Japan is a short one and you will not be straying far from the major tourist destinations, this booklet may well be all you need.

The TIC offices at Narita airport, Tokyo and Kyoto can also supply information on specific schedules. Major JR stations all have JR train information counters, and you can usually get your point across in simplified English.

If you need to know anything about JR, such as time schedules, fares, fastest routes, lost baggage, discounts on rail travel, hotels

and car rental, call the JR East-Infoline in Tokyo (☎ 03-3423-0111). The service is available in English (10 am to 6 pm, Monday to Friday, closed holidays).

Train Stations

Train stations in Japan are usually very well equipped. The main station is often literally the town centre and, in many cases, will be part of a large shopping centre with a wide variety of restaurants, bars, fast-food outlets and other facilities.

Meals The Japanese rail system is not renowned for its high-class cuisine, though you may find that the shinkansen dining cars turn out pretty good food. Anyway, you certainly won't starve, as apart from the

---

Ekiben – Lunch In Locomotion

Ekiben are one of those delightful Japanese institutions. A contraction of the words *eki* (train station) and *bentō* (lunch box), every train station worth its salt has an ekiben stand, and some stations are famous for their ekiben.

Legend has it that the first ekiben were served in 1885 at Utsunomiya station, not far from Tokyo. Back in those days an ekiben was a humble offering – pickles and rice balls were standard fare. How times change. There are close to 3000 varieties nowadays; stations vie with each other to produce ever more delectable take away lunch boxes. It must be said, not all of them are successful, and anyone who makes a habit of eating ekiben on their travels is going to come across the occasional dud.

However, as a rule standards are high. This is no surprise because Japanese are obsessive gourmets; some of them travel the country just to savour a regional speciality, and a particular station along the way might be favoured for its mushroom or marinated boar or trout ekiben. Prices are reasonable, once you get used to the idea that you're not buying a hastily flung together takeaway. Famous ekiben tend to range from ¥1000 upwards, although cheaper ones are often available on trains.

dining cars, there are snacks, drinks, ice creams and meals sold from the aisles. A good bet is to come prepared with a *bentō* (boxed lunch). At almost every station there will be a shop selling bentō, typically for ¥1000 or less. Some towns and stations have a particular bentō speciality.

Left Luggage Only major stations have left-luggage facilities, but there are almost always coin-operated storage lockers which cost ¥100 to ¥500 per day, depending on their size. The lockers work until midnight (not for 24 hours) so, after that time, you have to insert more money before your key will work. If your bag is simply too large to fit in the locker, ask someone *'tenimotsu azukai doko desu ka'* ('Where is the left-luggage office?'). If you are directed back to the lockers, just point at your oversized luggage, shake your head and say *'ōki-sugi masu'* ('It's too big!').

Japan Railways
Japan Railways (JR) is actually a number of separate private train systems which provide

---

Train Vocabulary

Train Types

shinkansen	新幹線	bullet train
tokkyū	特急	limited express
shin-kaisoku	新快速	JR special rapid train
kyūkō	急行	express
kaisoku	快速	JR rapid or express
futsū	普通	local
kaku-eki -teisha	各駅停車	local

Other Useful Words

jiyū-seki	自由席	unreserved seat
shitei-seki	指定席	reserved seat
green-sha	グリーン車	first-class car
ōfuku	往復	round trip
katamichi	片道	one way
kin'en-sha	禁煙車	nonsmoking car
kitsuen-sha	喫煙車	smoking car

---

one linked service. For the train user, JR gives every impression of being a single operation which indeed it was for more than a century. In 1987, it was decided that the accumulated losses of the government-run JNR (JR's predecessor) had simply gone too far and the government privatised it.

The JR system covers the country from one end to the other and also provides local services around major cities like Tokyo and Osaka. There is more than 20,000km of railway line and about 20,000 services daily. Shinkansen lines are totally separate from the regular railways and, in some places, the shinkansen stations are a fair distance from the main JR station (as is the case in Osaka). JR also operates buses and ferries, and ticketing can combine more than one form of transport.

Private Railways
The private train lines usually operate short routes, often no more than 100km in length. Local commuter services are often on private train lines. The Kansai region around Kōbe, Kyoto, Nagoya, Nara and Osaka is an area particularly well-served by private train lines.

Unlike JR stations, the private line stations do not usually form the central focus of a town. In Tokyo, the various private lines into the city all terminate on or near the Yamanote loop which forms a neat outer ring around central Tokyo.

Shinkansen
The fastest and best known train services in Japan are the 'bullet trains'. Nobody knows them by that name in Japan, they're simply called shinkansen (which translates as 'new trunk line'). The shinkansen reach speeds of up to 300km/h, running on continuously welded lines which totally eliminate the old railway clickety-clack of wheels rolling over joints. The Nozomi super express is the fastest shinkansen service. In more than 30 years of operation, there has never been a fatality.

The service efficiency starts even before you board the train. Your ticket indicates your carriage and seat number, and platform

Shinkansen Routes

On two of Japan's main shinkansen routes, the Tōkaidō/San-yō route and the Tōhoku route, there are three different services available. Although all of these are 'super express' services, some are faster than others and stop at fewer stations; and one, the Nozomi, requires a special surcharge. Be careful when boarding to ensure that you get on the right shinkansen! Luckily, all are marked in both Japanese and English.

Tōkaidō/San-yō Shinkansen (Tokyo-Hakata)

Nozomi	Super express service (reserved seats only, with surcharge)
Hikari	Express service
Kodama	Local service

Tōhoku Shinkansen (Tokyo-Morioka)

MAX Yamabiko	Super express service
Yamabiko	Express service
Nasuno	Local service

Akita Shinkansen (Morioka-Akita)*

Komachi	Express service

Yamagata Shinkansen (Fukushima-Yamagata)*

Tsubasa	Express service

Jōetsu Shinkansen (Tokyo-Niigata)

Asahi	Express service

Nagano Shinkansen (Tokyo-Nagano)

Asama	Express service

*These services sometimes originate/terminate in Tokyo.

signs indicate where you should stand for that carriage entrance. The train pulls in precisely to the scheduled minute and, sure enough, the carriage door you want is right beside where you're standing. Your departure from the train is equally well organised.

On most shinkansen routes, there are two or three types of services: faster express services stopping at a limited number of stations and slower local services stopping at all shinkansen stations. There is no difference in fare with the exception of the super-express

Nozomi service on the Tōkaidō/San-yō shinkansen line. There are, however, regular and Green Car (1st class) carriages. If you don't share the Japanese passion for cigarettes, there are a limited number of nonsmoking carriages *(kin'en-sha)*; request one when booking or ask on the platform for the unreserved nonsmoking cars *(kin'en-sha-jiyū-seki)*. Unreserved carriages are available on all but the super-express Nozomi service, but at peak holiday periods they can be very crowded and you may have to stand for the entire trip.

Other Train Services

While the shinkansen routes run most of the length of Honshū, a network of JR lines, supplemented by a scattering of shorter private lines, cover much of the rest of Japan. Although these services are efficient, they are nowhere near as fast as the shinkansen, and typically take about twice as long. (See the following section on Classes for more information about non-shinkansen trains.)

JR's steam locomotive (SL) services, though slower even than regular trains, are enormously popular. After retiring its last steam trains in 1975, JR has now revived several services as special holiday attractions. On the Yamaguchi line from Ogōri to Tsuwano in Western Honshū, there's a steam train service operating throughout the summer and autumn months. Other SL services operate on the Hōhi line from Kumamoto to Aso-san in Kyūshū and on the private Oigawa line from Kanaya, near Shizuoka, about 200km south-west of Tokyo, to Senzu. SL services are very popular, so make inquiries and reservations ahead of time.

Classes

All JR trains, including the shinkansen, have regular and Green Car (1st class) carriages. The seating is slightly more spacious in 1st class, but most people will find the regular carriages perfectly acceptable.

The slowest trains stopping at all stations are called *futsū* or *kaku-eki-teisha*. A step up from this is the *kyūkō* (ordinary express), which stops at only a limited number of stations. A variation on the kyūkō trains is the *kaisoku* (rapid) service. Finally, the fastest regular (non-shinkansen) trains are the *tokkyū* (limited express) services, which are sometimes known as *shin-kaisoku*.

The longer the route, the more likely you are to find faster train services. Local futsū trains are mainly limited to routes of less than 100km.

Reservations

Tickets can be bought at any JR station to any other JR station. Tickets for local services are usually dispensed from a vending machine but for longer distances you must go to a ticket window. For reservations, complicated tickets, Japan Rail Pass validations and the like, you will need to visit a JR Travel Service Centre. These are found at Narita and Kansai airports and at the main JR stations including Hakata, Hiroshima, Kyoto, Kumamoto, Nagoya, Niigata, Nishi-Kagoshima, Osaka, Sapporo, Sendai, Shimonoseki, Tokyo (Tokyo, Ueno, Ikebukuro, Shinjuku and Shibuya stations) and Yokohama. Large stations that don't have a Travel Service Centre will have a Green Window ticket counter (Midori-no-Madoguchi); look for the counter with the green band across the glass.

Major travel agencies in Japan also sell reserved-seat tickets, and you can buy shinkansen tickets through JAL offices overseas if you will be flying JAL to Japan.

On futsū services, there are no reserved seats. On the faster tokkyū and shinkansen services you can choose to travel reserved or unreserved. However, if you travel unreserved, there's always the risk of not getting a seat and having to stand, possibly for the entire trip. This is a particular danger at weekends, peak travel seasons and on holidays. Reserved-seat tickets can be bought any time from a month in advance to the day of departure.

Costs

JR fares are calculated on the basis of *futsū-unchin* (basic fare), *tokkyū-ryōkin* (an express surcharge levied only on express services) and *shinkansen-ryōkin* (a special charge for shinkansen services); see the Surcharges entry. The following are some typical fares

from Tokyo or Ueno, not including the new Nozomi super express (prices given for shinkansen are the total price of the ticket):

destination	basic fare (¥)	shinkansen (¥)
Fukushima	4620	8700
Hakata	13,440	21,720
Hiroshima	11,340	18,050
Kyoto	7980	13,220
Morioka	8190	13,840
Nagoya	6090	10,580
Niigata	5640	10,450
Okayama	10,190	16,360
Osaka	8510	13,750
Sendai	5780	10,590
Shimonoseki	12,810	20,570

Surcharges Various surcharges may be added to the basic fare. These include reserved seat, Green Car (1st class), express service and shinkansen surcharges. You may also have to pay a surcharge for special trains to resort areas or for a seat in an observation car. The express surcharges (but not the shinkansen super express surcharge) can be paid to the train conductor on board the train.

Further surcharges apply for overnight sleepers and these vary with the berth type from ¥5250 for a regular three-tier bunk, ¥6300 to ¥10,500 for various types of two-tier bunks, and up to ¥13,350 to ¥17,180 for a standard or 'royal' compartment. Note that there are no sleepers on the shinkansen services as none of these run overnight. Japan Rail Pass users must still pay the sleeper surcharge. Sleeper services mainly operate on trains from Tokyo or Osaka to destinations in Western Honshū and Kyūshū.

The Nozomi super express has higher surcharges than other shinkansen services and cannot be used with a Japan Rail Pass. As a guideline, the Nozomi surcharge for Tokyo-Kyoto is ¥6210 as opposed to ¥5240 by other shinkansen; for Tokyo-Hakata ¥10,120 as opposed to ¥8280 by other shinkansen.

Travel Seasons Some of the fare surcharges are slightly higher (5% to 10%) during peak travel seasons. This applies mainly to reserved seat tickets. Peak season dates are as follows: 21 March to 5 April,

28 April to 6 May, 21 July to 31 August, and 25 December to 10 January.

Discounts & Special Fares If you buy a return ticket for a trip which is more than 600km each way, you qualify for a 20% discount on the return leg. You can also get coupons for discounted accommodation and tours combined with your rail travel. Other special deals are as follows.

Shūyū-ken & Furii Kippu There are a number of excursion tickets, known as *shūyū-ken* or *furii kippu* ('furii' is Japanese for 'free'). These tickets include the return fare to your destination and give you unlimited JR local travel within the destination area. There are shūyū-ken available to travel from Tokyo to Hokkaidō and then around Hokkaidō for up to seven days. A Kyūshū or Shikoku shūyū-ken gets you to and from either island and gives you four or five days of travel around them. You can even go to Kyūshū one way by rail and one way by ferry.

Seishun Jūhachi Kippu If you don't have a Japan Rail Pass, one of the best deals going is a five-day Seishun Jūhachi Kippu, literally a 'Youth 18 Ticket'. These can be used by anyone of any age but are only valid during university vacation periods (2 February to 20 April, 20 July to 10 September, 10 December to 20 January). Basically, for ¥11,500 you get five one-day tickets valid for travel anywhere in Japan on JR lines. The only catches are that you can't travel on tokkyū (express) or shinkansen trains and each ticket must be used within 24 hours. However, even if you only have to make a return trip, say, between Tokyo and Kyoto, you'll be saving a lot of money. If you don't want to buy the whole book of five tickets, you can sometimes purchase separate tickets at discount ticket shops around train stations.

Train Passes

If you plan to do any extended travel in Japan, a Japan Rail Pass is almost essential. Not only will it save you lots of money, it will also spare you the hassle of buying tickets each time you want to board a train.

Japan Rail Pass One of Japan's few real travel bargains is the Japan Rail Pass. The pass lets you use any JR service for seven days for ¥28,300, 14 days for ¥45,100 or 21 days for ¥57,700. Green Car (1st class) passes are ¥37,800, ¥61,200 and ¥79,600, respectively. The pass cannot be used for the new super express Nozomi shinkansen service, but is OK for everything else. The only surcharge levied on the Japan Rail Pass is for overnight sleepers. Since a reserved seat Tokyo-Kyoto shinkansen ticket costs ¥13,220, you only have to travel Tokyo-Kyoto-Tokyo to make a seven-day pass come close to paying off.

The pass can only be bought overseas at JAL and ANA offices and major travel agencies. It can only be used by those with a Short Stay Visa (you'll need to show your passport), which means it cannot be used by foreign residents of Japan.

The clock starts to tick on the pass as soon as you validate it, which can be done at JR Travel Service Centres located in most major train stations and at Narita and Kansai airports if you're intending to jump on a JR train immediately. Don't validate it if you're just going into Tokyo and intend to hang around the city for a few days. The pass is valid *only* on JR services; you will still have to pay for private train services.

For more details on the pass and overseas purchase locations, visit the JR East Web site at www.jreast.co.jp/jrp.

JR East Pass This is a great deal for those who only want to travel in east Japan. The passes are good on all JR lines in east Japan (including Tōhoku, Yamagata, Akita, Jōetsu and Nagano shinkansen but not including the Tōkaidō shinkansen). This includes the area around Tokyo and everything north of Tokyo to the tip of Honshū, but doesn't include Hokkaidō. Prices for five-day passes are ¥20,000/16,000/10,000 for adults over 26, youths between 16 and 25, and children between six and 11, respectively. Ten-day passes are ¥32,000/25,000/16,000 for the same age groups. Four-day 'Flexible' passes are also available which allow travel on any four consecutive or nonconsecutive days within any one-month period. These cost ¥20,000/16,000/10,000 for the age groups listed above. As with the Japan Rail Pass, this can only be purchased outside Japan (in the same locations as the Japan Rail Pass) and can only be used by those with Short Stay Visas (you'll need to show your passport).

JR-West San-yō Area Pass Similar to the JR East Pass, this pass allows unlimited travel on the San-yō shinkansen line (including the Nozomi super express) between Osaka and Hakata, as well as local trains running between the same cities. A four-day pass costs ¥20,000 and an eight-day pass costs ¥30,000 (children are half-price). These can be purchased both inside Japan (at major train stations, travel agencies and Kansai airport) and outside Japan (same locations as the Japan Rail Pass) but can only be used by those with a Short Stay Visa. The pass also entitles you to discounts on car rentals at station rent-a-car offices.

JR-West Kansai Area Pass A great deal for those who only want to explore the Kansai area, this pass covers unlimited travel on JR lines between most major Kansai cities, such as Himeji, Kōbe, Osaka, Kyoto and Nara. It also covers JR trains to/from Kansai airport but does not cover any shinkansen lines. A one-day pass costs ¥2000 and a four-day pass costs ¥6000 (children are half-price). These can be purchased at the same places as the San-yō area rail pass and also entitle you to discounts on station rent-a-car offices.

JR-Kyūshū Rail Pass This pass is valid on all JR lines in Kyūshū with the exception of the shinkansen line. It costs ¥15,000 for a five-day pass and ¥20,000 for a seven-day pass. Like the Japan Rail Pass, it must be purchased outside Japan (see the Japan Rail Pass entry earlier for purchase details). The pass can be activated at major train stations in Kyūshū.

BUS

In addition to its local city bus services, Japan also has a comprehensive network of long-distance buses. These 'highway buses' are

nowhere near as fast as the shinkansen and heavy traffic can delay them even further, but the fares are comparable with those of the futsū (local train) without any reservation or express surcharges. The trip between Tokyo and Sendai (Northern Honshū), for example, takes about two hours by shinkansen, four hours by tokkyū (limited express) and nearly eight hours by bus. Tokyo-Kyoto is less than three hours by shinkansen and more than eight hours by bus.

Bus services have been growing in recent years, partly because of the gradual extension of the expressway network, partly because of the closure of uneconomical JR lines and partly because of escalating rail fares. Of course, there are also many places in Japan where trains do not run and bus travel is the only public transport option.

The main intercity bus services run on the expressways and usually stop at expressway bus stops where local transport is available to adjacent centres. The main expressway bus route runs between Tokyo, Nagoya, Kyoto and Osaka and stops are made at each city's main train station. There are also overnight services – the comfortable reclining seats are better for a night's sleep than sitting up in an overnight train.

Bookings can be made through any travel agency in Japan or at the Green Window in large JR stations. The Japan Rail Pass is valid on some highway buses although, of course, the shinkansen would be far preferable! Note, however, that the storage racks on most buses are generally too small for large backpacks, but on most buses you can stow them in the luggage compartment underneath the bus. Other popular bus services include routes from Tokyo to Sendai, Yamagata and Hirosaki in Northern Honshū and to Niigata and areas around Mt Fuji in Central Honshū. There are extensive networks from Osaka and Hiroshima into areas of Western Honshū and around the smaller islands of Hokkaidō, Kyūshū and Shikoku.

Night Services

An option that is becoming increasingly popular among travellers is the network of night buses. They are relatively cheap, spacious (allowing room to stretch out and get some sleep) and they also save on a night's accommodation. They typically leave at around 10 or 11 pm and arrive the following day at around 6 or 7 am.

Costs

Some typical long-distance prices out of Tokyo include:

destination	fare (¥)
Aomori	10,190
Hakata	15,000
Hiroshima	12,060
Kyoto	8180
Nagoya	6420
Niigata	5250
Osaka	8610
Sendai	6210

CAR

One of the common myths about travel in Japan is that it's virtually impossible for a *gaijin* (foreigner) to travel by car: the roads are narrow and congested making travel incredibly slow; getting lost is a constant fear since the signs are in Japanese; the driving is suicidal; fuel is prohibitively expensive; parking is impossible; and foreigners are altogether better off sticking to the trains.

None of this is necessarily true. Of course, driving in Tokyo is a near impossibility but not many visitors rent cars to get around New York or London either. The roads are actually fairly well signposted in English so, on the major roads, getting lost is unlikely. The minor roads are more likely to test your navigational ability, but Japan is compact so you can never be lost for long. The driving is a long way from suicidal – polite and cautious is probably a better description. Fuel is expensive but no more so than most of Europe, in fact it's cheaper than many countries in Europe. As for parking, it is rarely free, but neither is it impossibly expensive.

All in all, driving in Japan is quite feasible, even for the just mildly adventurous. In some areas of the country it can prove much more convenient than other forms of travel and, between a group of people (two adults and a couple of children for example), it can

also prove quite economical. You will certainly see more of the country than all but the most energetic public transport users.

On the Road

Driver's Licence You will need an International Driving Permit backed up by your own national licence. The international permit is issued by your national automobile association and costs around US$5 in most countries. Make sure it's endorsed for cars and motorcycles if you're licensed for both.

Foreign licences and International Driving Permits are only valid in Japan for six months. If you are staying longer you will have to get a Japanese licence from the *unten-menkyosho* (licence office) To do this, you will need to provide your own licence, passport photos, Alien Registration Card, the fee, and there's also a simple eyesight test.

Fuel There's no shortage of petrol (gas) stations, the cost of petrol is about ¥110 to ¥150 per litre, and the driveway service will bring a tear to the eye of any driver who resents the Western trend to self-service. In Japan, not only does your windscreen get washed but you may even find your floor mats being vacuumed and the whole staff coming out, at the trot, to usher you back into the traffic and bow respectfully as you depart.

Maps & Navigation Get yourself a copy of the *Japan Road Atlas* (Shobunsha, ¥2890). It's all in romaji with enough names in kanji to make navigation possible even off the major roads. If you're really intent on making your way through the back blocks, a Japanese map will prove useful even if your knowledge of kanji is nil. When you really get lost, a signposted junction will offer some clues if you've got a good map to compare the symbols. By far the best Japanese road atlases are the Super Mapple series (Shobunsha), which is available in bookshops and some convenience stores.

These days, there is a great deal of signposting in romaji so getting around is not a great feat. Road route numbers also help; for example, if you know you want to follow Route 9 until you get to Route 36 the frequent roadside numbers make navigation child's play. If you are attempting tricky navigation, use your maps imaginatively – watch out for the railway line, the rivers, the landmarks. They're all useful ways of locating yourself when you can't read the signs. A compass will also come in handy when navigating.

If you're a member of an automobile association in your home country you're eligible for reciprocal rights at the Japan Automobile Federation (JAF). Its office is directly opposite the entrance to Tokyo Tower at Kikaishinkō Kaikan Biru, 3-5-8 Shiba-kōen, Minato-ku, Tokyo 105. JAF publishes a variety of publications, and will make up strip maps for its members.

Road Rules

Driving in Japan is on the left. Apart from being on the wrong side of the road from the European or North American perspective, there are no real problems with driving in Japan. There are no unusual rules or interpretations of them and most signposts follow international conventions. JAF has an English-language *Rules of the Road* book for ¥1860 (slightly discounted if you're a member of an overseas association). See Maps & Navigation earlier for more information about JAF.

Rental

There are a lot of car rental companies in Japan and though you'll find many of them represented at Narita airport, renting a car at Narita to drive into Tokyo is not a good idea. Heading off in the opposite direction towards Hokkaidō makes a lot of sense. Car rental offices cluster round train stations and the best way to use rental cars in Japan is to take a train for the long-distance part of your trip, then rent a car when you get to the area you want to explore. For example, the northern San-in coast of Western Honshū is a good place to drive – but don't drive there from Tokyo, take the train to Kyoto and rent a car from there.

Japanese car rental companies are set up for this type of operation and offer lots of short-term rates – such as for people who just want a car for half a day. However, they're not much good at one-way rentals; you'll usually have to pay a repositioning charge and if the car has to be brought back from another island, the cost can be very high indeed. Typical one-way charges within the island of Honshū are ¥6000 for 100km and ¥2400 for each additional 50km. It makes a lot of sense to make your trip a loop one and return the car to the original renting office. Some of the main Japanese car rental companies and their Tokyo phone numbers are:

Dollar Rent-a-Car	☎ 03-3567-2818
Hertz	☎ 0120-489-882
Toyota Rent-a-Lease	☎ 03-3264-0100

Typical rental rates for a small car is ¥6500 to ¥9000 for the first day and ¥4500 to ¥7000 per day thereafter. Move up a bracket and you're looking at ¥9000 to ¥13,500 for the first day and ¥7000 to ¥9000 thereafter. On top of the rental charge there's a ¥1000 per day insurance cost.

Many rental places offer unlimited kilometres but you should check before heading out, especially in Hokkaidō. Toyota has no limits currently, and Orix (another big rental company in Japan) usually waives theirs. It's also a good idea to check prices at local rent-a-car places. These places can usually match the rates of the big chains and are a good choice when you just want to rent for three or six hours to get around an island or obscure peninsula.

It's also worth bearing in mind that rental costs go up during peak seasons – 28 April to 6 May, 20 July to 31 August, and 28 December to 5 January. The increase can make quite a difference to costs. A car that costs ¥8800 a day usually will go up to ¥9700 during any of the peak seasons.

Communication can be a major problem when renting a car. Some of the offices will have a rent-a-car phrasebook, with questions you might need to ask in English. If you find that you can't communicate adequately with the person at the desk, try calling one of the Tokyo numbers listed above or suggest that the car rental company do so.

Check over your car carefully before hitting the road – perhaps it's an expectation that cars will only be used locally, but rental cars in Japan don't seem to be checked as thoroughly as those in the West. Check that all the tyres are in good order and that the jack and tool kit are in place.

Apart from maps and a phrasebook, other essentials are a compass (see the Maps & Navigation under the On the Road entry earlier) and your favourite music tapes. Non-Japanese speakers will find very little to listen to on Japanese radio and the music will help pass time in traffic jams.

Purchase

While it is possible for foreigners to purchase new cars in Japan, most long-term visitors or residents are more likely to be looking for a second-hand vehicle to use for a while and then sell on departure. However, think carefully before making this decision. There are so many drawbacks to running a car in Japan's crowded cities that the alternative of renting a car on the odd occasion when you really need one may be preferable.

Buying used cars in Japan is subject to the same pitfalls as anywhere else, but stringent safety inspections mean that you're unlikely to buy an unsafe vehicle. Once a car is three years old, every car has to go through a *shaken* (inspection) every two years, which is so severe that it quickly becomes cheaper to junk your car. The shaken costs about ¥100,000 and once the car reaches nine years of age it has to be inspected every year. This is the major reason you see so few old cars on the road in Japan. A car approaching an unpassable shaken drops in value very rapidly and, if you can find one, it could make a good short-term purchase.

Another obstacle to buying a car in Japan is that you must have an off-street parking space before you can complete the registration formalities. Exemption from this requirement is one reason why the little microcars are so popular in Japan. To qualify as a microcar, a vehicle must have an engine of less than 660cc, be less than 140cm wide and less than 330cm long.

Language is likely to be the major handicap in buying a car, so it's very useful to have a Japanese speaker to help with the negotiations. Foreign residents often sell their cars through the English-language papers and international centre message boards.

Types of Roads

If you're going to drive in Japan, do it sensibly. There's absolutely no reason to drive in the big cities or to drive in the heavily built-up areas. If you're simply going from town A to town B and then stopping for a while, you're much better off taking the train.

In the less urbanised areas, however, a car can be useful. The northern San-in coast of Western Honshū, for example, is a world apart from the congested southern coast and slow public transport makes a car a much more attractive option. Hokkaidō is another good area for a drive-yourself trip. There are also many areas where a car can be useful for a short excursion into the surrounding countryside, such as the loop from Kagoshima in Kyūshū down to Chiran and Ibusuki on Satsuma hantō peninsula, or for a couple of days to make a circuit, for example, of Okinawa. Car rental companies cater to this with short rental periods of a day or half day.

Expressways The expressway system will get you from one end of the country to another but it is not particularly extensive. Also, since all the expressways charge tolls, it is uniformly expensive – about ¥27 per kilometre. Tokyo to Kyoto, for example, will cost about ¥9000 in tolls. This does have the benefit of keeping most people off the expressways so they are often delightfully uncrowded. The speed limit on expressways is 80km/h but seems to be uniformly ignored. At a steady 100km/h, you will still find as many cars overtaking you as you overtake, some of them going very fast indeed.

There are good rest stops and service centres at regular intervals. A prepaid highway card, available from tollbooths or at the service areas, saves you having to carry so much cash and gives you a 4% to 8% discount in

Road Distances (km)

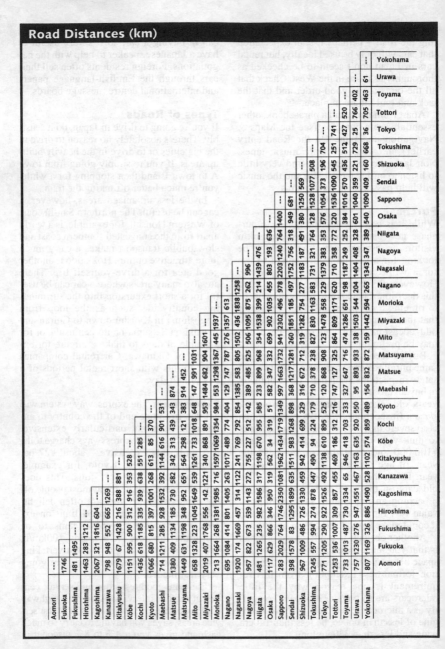

From ↓ \ To →	Aomori	Fukuoka	Fukushima	Hiroshima	Kagoshima	Kanazawa	Kitakyushu	Kōbe	Kochi	Kyoto	Maebashi	Matsue	Matsuyama	Mito	Miyazaki	Morioka	Nagano	Nagasaki	Nagoya	Niigata	Osaka	Sapporo	Sendai	Shizuoka	Tokushima	Tokyo	Tottori	Toyama	Urawa
Fukuoka	1746																												
Fukushima	481	1495																											
Hiroshima	1463	283	1212																										
Kagoshima	2067	321	1816	604																									
Kanazawa	798	948	552	665	1269																								
Kitakyushu	1679	67	1428	216	388	881																							
Kōbe	1151	595	900	312	916	353	638																						
Kochi	1436	618	1185	335	939	551	613	285																					
Kyoto	1066	680	815	397	1001	268	851	85	370																				
Maebashi	714	1211	285	928	1532	459	1144	616	901	531																			
Matsue	1380	409	1134	185	730	582	342	313	439	343	874																		
Matsuyama	1449	631	1198	348	952	651	564	298	121	383	914	452																	
Mito	658	1328	223	1045	1649	539	1261	733	1018	648	147	991	1385																
Miyazaki	2019	407	1768	556	142	1221	340	868	891	953	1484	682	854	1502															
Morioka	213	1664	268	1381	1985	716	1597	1069	1354	984	553	1298	1367	445	1937														
Nagano	695	1084	414	801	1405	263	1017	489	774	404	129	747	613	276	1357	613													
Nagasaki	1920	174	1669	457	314	1122	241	769	792	854	1385	583	229	1478	558	1838	1258												
Nagoya	957	822	673	539	1143	272	755	227	512	142	389	485	389	383	875	506	214	996											
Niigata	481	1265	235	982	1586	670	1198	670	955	585	233	899	968	354	1538	399	214	1538	476										
Osaka	1117	629	866	346	950	319	562	34	319	51	582	347	332	699	902	1035	455	803	193	636									
Sapporo	283	2029	764	1746	2350	1081	1962	1434	1719	1349	997	1732	1663	941	2302	496	978	2203	764	1240	1400								
Sendai	398	1578	83	1295	1899	635	1511	983	1268	898	368	1217	1281	260	1851	185	497	1752	756	318	949	681							
Shizuoka	967	1013	487	730	1334	65	946	418	703	333	327	647	716	127	1286	319	187	1284	277	380	262	1250	569						
Tokushima	1245	557	994	274	878	447	490	94	224	179	550	95	156	710	893	933	138	1503	544	204	1404	408	328	601					
Tokyo	771	1205	290	922	1526	492	1138	610	895	525	120	868	908	123	1478	558	229	1379	383	345	558	1536	373	196	569				
Tottori	1253	536	1007	309	857	455	469	186	312	216	747	127	220	772	955	968	325	864	358	252	384	1250	220	545	741				
Toyama	733	1230	276	947	1551	467	1163	635	920	550	252	716	474	1286	651	198	1404	408	328	601	1040	359	221	729	25	402			
Urawa	757	1230	276	947	1551	467	1163	635	920	550	95	893	933	138	1503	544	204	1404	408	328	601	1040	359	221	160	36	705	463	
Yokohama	807	1169	326	1490	886	528	1102	574	859	489	156	832	872	159	1442	594	265	1343	347	540	1090	409	359	160	409	36	705	463	61

the larger card denominations. You can also pay tolls with most major credit cards, although some toll-booth operators seem unaware of this. Exits are usually fairly well-signposted in romaji but make sure you know the name of your exit as it may not necessarily be the same as the city you're heading towards.

Other Roads On Japan's lesser roads, the speed limit is usually 50km/h, and you can often drive for hours without ever getting up to that speed! The roads are narrow, traffic is usually heavy, opportunities to overtake are limited and often no-overtaking restrictions apply in the few areas where you could overtake safely. Sometimes you never seem to get out of built-up areas and the heavy traffic and frequent traffic lights can make covering 300km in a long day's drive quite a feat. It's worth contemplating that just after WWII, only 1.5% of the roads in Japan were paved.

Generally, however, the traffic does keep moving, slow though that movement may be. The farther you travel from the main highways, the more interesting the countryside becomes. Occasionally you'll come to stretches that are a wonderful surprise. Along a beautiful winding mountain road without a car in sight, it's easy to appreciate why the Japanese have come to make such nice sports cars.

Parking
In most big cities, free curbside parking spots are almost non-existent, while in rural areas you'll be able to park your car just about wherever you want to. If you do have the nerve to drive into a big Japanese city, you'll find that you usually have to pay ¥200 per hour for metered street parking, or anywhere from ¥300 to ¥600 per hour for a spot in a multistorey car park. You'll find car parks around most department stores and near some train stations. Fortunately, most hotels have free parking for guests, as do some restaurants and almost all department stores (you'll have to get a stamp inside the store to show that you've actually been shopping there).

MOTORCYCLE
Japan is the home of the modern motorcycle and you certainly see a lot of them on the road. Once upon a time they were all small displacement machines but now there are plenty of larger motorcycles as well. During the holidays you'll see groups of touring motorcyclists and, as usual in Japan, they will all be superbly equipped with shiny new machines, and top of the range riding leathers, wet-weather gear and equipment.

Rental & Purchase
Renting a motorcycle for long-distance touring is not as easy as renting a car, although small scooters are available in many places for local sightseeing.

If you enjoy motorcycles and you're staying long enough to make buying and selling a motorcycle worthwhile, then this can be a great way of getting around the country. A motorcycle provides the advantages of your own transport without the automotive drawback of finding a place to park. Nor do you suffer so badly from the congested traffic.

Although Japan is famed for its large-capacity road burners, most bikes on the road are 400cc or less. This is because a special licence is required to ride a bike larger than 400cc and few Japanese and even fewer foreigners pass the test necessary to get this licence.

The 400cc machines are the most popular large motorcycles in Japan but, for general touring, a 250cc machine is probably the best bet. Apart from being quite large enough for a compact country like Japan, machines up to 250cc are also exempt from the expensive shaken (inspections).

Smaller machines are banned from expressways and are generally less suitable for long-distance touring but people have ridden from one end of Japan to another on little 50cc 'step-thrus'. An advantage of these is that you can ride them with just a driving licence, and don't need to get a motorcycle licence.

Buying a new machine is no problem, though you will find a better choice of large capacity machines in the big cities. Used motorcycles are often not much cheaper than new ones and, unless you buy from another foreigner, you will face the usual language problems in finding and buying one. As with everything else in Japan, you rarely see a motorcycle more than a couple of years old.

The best place to look for motorcycles in Japan is the Korin-chō motorcycle neighbourhood in Tokyo's Ueno district. There are over 20 motorcycle shops in the area and some employ foreign salespeople who speak both Japanese and English. For used bikes in Tokyo check *Tokyo Classified* and in Kansai check *Kansai Time Out*. In Kyoto, the International Community House message board is also a good place to look for used bikes.

On the Road

As with car driving, your overseas licence and International Driving Permit are all you need to ride a motorcycle in Japan. Crash helmets are compulsory and you should also ensure your riding gear is adequate to cope with the weather, particularly rain. For much

Cycling in Japan

In 1899, the British adventurer John Foster Frazer, cycling across the country en route from Europe to the USA, declared Japan 'the wheelman's paradise'. Foster may not have had to contend with the traffic on Route 1 or the bewildering complexities of Tokyo's expressways, but his original judgement remains sound. Japan is still a great country to explore on two wheels.

Unchanged since Foster's day are the topography and the climate, both important considerations for the would-be bicycle tourer. Japan's topographical wild card is its mountains. Even the coastal roads can have their hilly moments. (I cursed a former edition of this book atop a very large hill on the Niigata coastline for describing the area as 'ideal for cycling' – well, perhaps it was and my legs weren't.)

The Tōkaidō coastline, stretching south-west from Tokyo through Nagoya and past Osaka, is mostly flat, but it is also polluted, congested and unrelievedly boring. Avoid Route 1 at all costs. On the other hand, the Japan Sea coastline – windswept, sometimes hilly but rarely congested – is a cyclist's delight. It provides the cyclist with good roads, abundant wildlife and some of the freshest seafood in Japan. Hokkaidō, Shikoku and Kyūshū offer more of the same on even quieter roads.

That said, my own favourite cycling territory is in the mountains of Central Honshū – hard work but rewarded by spectacular scenery, delicious hot springs in which to soothe aching bones and, best of all, a glimpse of rural Japan that few city dwellers get a chance to see.

Climatic conditions require some serious consideration, particularly for cyclists planning a lengthy tour of Japan. Winter is something of a mixed bag. November and December are often sunny though cold and can be good months for touring Japan's coastal regions. In January and February, however, snowfalls, rain and cold conditions make much of Japan – particularly the Japan Alps, Northern Honshū and Hokkaidō – unattractive to all but the most masochistic of cyclists. Summer, on the other hand, is swelteringly hot and humid, a good time to stick to the coast or the cooler latitudes of Hokkaidō.

The rainy season is best avoided for obvious reasons. While it generally arrives in May and lingers for just a few weeks, it can't always be relied on to end on time, as I discovered on one sodden trip from Niigata to Kyoto. Typhoons blow up with immense ferocity in late summer and can play havoc with a tight itinerary. This leaves spring and autumn, the best seasons to be cycling in Japan: both are blessed with cool weather and minimal rainfall and see the Japanese countryside at its best.

The single biggest frustration for the cyclist in Japan is probably the lack of Romanised street names. This situation is improving gradually, but it can still be maddeningly difficult to find your way out of urban centres onto the road of your choice. (On one memorable occasion, I managed a 90-minute circumnavigation of the Kanazawa ring road that brought me back to where I'd started.) A handy way of avoiding such confusion and the frustration of inner-city traffic is to put your bike on a train.

of the year the climate is ideal for motorcycle touring, but when it rains it really rains.

Touring equipment – panniers, carrier racks, straps and the like – are readily available from dealers. Remember to pack clothing in plastic bags to ensure it stays dry, even if you don't. An adequate supply of tools and a puncture repair kit can prove invaluable.

Riding in Japan is no more dangerous than anywhere else in the world, which is to say it is not very safe and great care should be taken at all times. Japan has the full range of worldwide motorcycle hazards from single-minded taxi drivers to unexpected changes in road surface, heedless car-door openers to runaway dogs.

BICYCLE

Exploring Japan by bicycle is perfectly feasible. Although the slow average speed of traffic on Japanese roads is no problem for a bike rider, pedalling along in a constant stream of heavy traffic is no fun at all. Japanese cyclists seem to have a higher tolerance of heavy traffic and doggedly follow routes down major highways.

Cycling in Japan

To do this, a carry bag is required. Specialist carry bags, known in Japanese as *rinko bukuro* or *rinko baggu*, are available in bike shops, though I have made do with a blanket, two garbage bags and some sticky tape without any hassle. Strictly speaking, a ticket is required for your bike on the train (though it is rarely checked). Ask for a *temawarihin kippu*, a bargain at ¥260 and valid for any single journey. Ferries are also an opportunity to rest aching legs, and taking your bike aboard is no problem, though sometimes an extra charge will be required.

The best machine for touring Japan is a lightweight touring road machine or else a suitably equipped hybrid or cross bike. While mountain bikes are all the rage they are hardly required for Japan's well-paved roads. If you do bring a mountain bike, be sure to fit slimmer profile, preferably slick tyres, unless you're planning to spend all your time on mountain trails. Bikes with suspension forks require too much maintenance to consider as viable touring machines.

Perhaps the most important question for the cyclist looking at a holiday in Japan is costs. However you look at it, Japan is not cheap. Try to bring your own bike and accessories – even though Japan produces some of the world's best cycling equipment, prices will be cheaper at home. Camping is a good antidote to Japan's high accommodation costs, and many cyclists sustain themselves on a diet of instant noodles and sandwiches. Bear in mind, however, that after a long rainy day a comfortable inn with home cooking becomes a great temptation and it's easy to stray from a tight budget. Worst of all, if you're really pinching the pennies you'll never get into the bars, restaurants and hot springs where you can meet the Japanese at their most relaxed and welcoming. Even if you're planning to camp out and eat cheaply, it would be wise to budget US$30 per day.

Japan is a reasonably safe country to cycle in but, on a cautionary note, accidents happen more frequently than you might imagine. Comprehensive insurance is a must, as is a decent lightweight helmet. Also, despite Japan's reputation as a crime-free country, bicycles do get stolen and, of late, professional gangs of bike thieves have been targeting big cities, especially around train stations. I have lost no less than three expensive bikes over the last eight years. Bring a lock.

An essential purchase for those planning to tour Japan by bike is a copy of *Cycling Japan* (Kodansha, 1993), edited by Brian Harrell, long-term resident of Japan. *Cycling Japan* is packed with information on everything from where to buy a large-frame bike to insurance policies to the best *onsen* accommodation. The rest of the book suggests itineraries, from Hokkaidō to Kyūshū. For off-road aficionados the wilderness of the Oku-Shiga forest trail sounds particularly inviting, not least because it passes through the Shiojiri vineyards. Fill your drink bottle with a Honshū muscat or a drop of Chardonnay?

John Ashburne

The secret of enjoyable touring is to get off the busy main highways and onto the minor roads. This requires careful route planning, good maps and either some ability with kanji or the patience to decipher country road signs, where romaji is much less likely to be used. Favourite touring areas for foreign cyclists include Kyūshū, Shikoku, the Japan Alps (if you like steep hills!), Noto-hantō and definitely Hokkaidō. Valiant Japanese cyclists have been known to ride as far up Mt Fuji as the road permits and then shoulder their steeds so that they can conquer the peak together.

There's no point in fighting your way out of big cities by bicycle. Put your bike on the train or bus and get out to the country before you start pedalling. To take a bicycle on a train you may be required to use a bicycle carrying bag: they're available from good bicycle shops.

Maps & Navigation under the Road Rules entry for car travel also applies to bicycles but there is also a series of Bridgestone cycling maps (saikuringu mapu). They identify many places in romaji as well as kanji but, as yet, only cover Central Honshū. The cycling maps show where bicycles can be rented, identify special bicycle tracks and accommodation, which is popular with cyclists and even show steep road gradients. For other areas, try the Touring Mapple (Shobunsha) series, which are aimed at motorcyclists, but are also very useful for bicyclists.

Purchase & Rental

A number of adventure travel companies operate bicycle tours in Japan. It is not easy to rent a touring bike for a long trip but, in many towns, you can rent bicycles to explore the town. Look for bicycle-rental outlets near the railway station; typical charges are around ¥200 per hour or ¥1000 per day. Kyoto, for example, is ideally suited to bicycle exploration and there are plenty of cheap rental shops to choose from.

Many youth hostels also have bicycles to rent – there's a symbol identifying them in the Japan Youth Hostel Handbook. The so-called cycling terminals found in various locations around the country (see the

Discarded Bikes

! Many foreigners who have just arrived in Japan, on seeing the piles of discarded bicycles that litter most Japanese cities, make the assumption that you can just pick one up and ride into the sunset. Theoretically, yes...but Japan doesn't really work that way.

Japanese police are zealous about checking bike registrations. If you get picked up with a bike that is not registered in your name, you'll be hauled down to the local kōban (police box) and have to wait while they trace the original owner and check that the bike in question wasn't stolen (which it very well may have been). If the bike was stolen, it's going to be difficult to convince the police that you weren't the culprit.

Accommodation section in the Facts for the Visitor chapter) also rent bicycles.

If you already have some experience of bicycle touring you will, no doubt, have your own bicycle and should bring this with you. Most airlines these days will accommodate bikes, sometimes as part of your baggage allowance, sometimes free.

Touring cycles are available in Japan but prices tend to be significantly higher than you'd pay back home. And if you're tall, you may not find any suitably sized bikes in stock. One solution for tall riders, or anyone who wants to save money, is to buy a used bike; in Tokyo check the Tokyo Classified and in Kansai check the Kansai Time Out. In Kyoto, the International Community House message board is also a good place to look for used bikes.

HITCHING

Hitching is never entirely safe in any country in the world, and we don't recommend it. Travellers who decide to hitch should understand that they are taking a small but potentially serious risk. In particular, Japan is a very dangerous place for solitary female hitchhikers; there have been countless cases of solitary female hitchers being attacked, molested and raped. People who do choose to hitch will be safer if they travel in pairs and let someone know where they are planning to go.

Provided you understand the risks and take appropriate precautions, Japan can be an excellent country for hitchhiking. Many hitchhikers have tales of extraordinary kindness from motorists who have picked them up. There are equally numerous tales of motorists who think the hitchhiker has simply lost his or her way to the nearest train station, and accordingly takes them there.

The rules for hitchhiking are similar to anywhere else in the world. Make it clear where you want to go – carry cardboard and a marker pen to write your destination in kanji. Write it in romaji as well, as a car-driving foreigner may just be coming by. Look for a good place to hitch; it's no good starting from the middle of town though. Unfortunately, in Japan many towns only seem to end as they merge into the next one. Expressway entrance roads are probably your best bet.

Truck drivers are particularly good for long-distance travel as they often head out on the expressways at night. If a driver is exiting before your intended destination, try to get dropped off at one of the expressway service centres. The Service Area Parking Area (SAPA) guide maps are excellent for hitchers. They're available free from expressway service areas and show full details of each interchange (IC) and rest stop. These are important orientation points if you have a limited knowledge of Japanese.

For more on hitching in Japan pick up a copy of the excellent *Hitchhiker's Guide to Japan* (Tuttle) by Will Ferguson. In addition to lots of general advice, this book details suggested routes and places to stay on the road. All in all, it's just about invaluable for anyone contemplating a long hitch around Japan.

WALKING

There are many opportunities for hiking and mountain climbing in Japan but few visitors set out to get from place to place on foot. Alan Booth did, all the way from Hokkaidō to Kyūshū, and wrote of the four-month journey in *The Roads to Sata*.

It would be quite feasible to base an itinerary on walks, preferably out of season to avoid day-trippers. JNTO publishes several regional walking guides including: *Walking Tour Courses in Tokyo*, *Walking Tour Courses in Nara* and *Walking Tour Courses in Kyoto*.

In the Japan Alps region, Kamikōchi is one of several bases for walks; and Takayama has a pleasant extended walking trail for several hours round the temple district. In the Kiso Valley, there's a very good walk between Magome and Tsumago. On Rebun-tō, at the northern tip of Hokkaidō, there is plenty of scope to spend several days doing different walks in spectacular scenery, and the same applies to the other Hokkaidō national parks, especially Daisetsuzan. Shikoku has some fine walks, particularly up Ishizuchi-san. In Kyūshū there are some excellent walks through areas of volcanic activity, such as on Ebino-kōgen (Ebino Plateau) near Kirishima-yama.

For more on hiking in Japan, see Hiking in the Facts for the Visitor chapter.

BOAT

Japan is an island nation and there are a great many ferry services both between islands and between ports on the same island. Ferries can be an excellent way of getting from one place to another and seeing parts of Japan you might otherwise miss. Taking a ferry between Ōsaka (Honshū) and Beppu (Kyūshū), for example, is a good way of getting to Kyūshū and – if you choose the right departure time – seeing some of the Inland Sea on the way.

The routes vary widely from two-hour services between adjacent islands to 1½-day trips in what are in fact small ocean liners. The cheapest fares on the longer trips are in *tatami*-mat rooms where you simply unroll your *futon* on the floor and hope, if the ship is crowded, that your fellow passengers aren't too intent on knocking back the booze all night. In this basic class, fares will usually be lower than equivalent land travel, but there are also more expensive private cabins. Bicycles can always be brought along and most ferries also carry cars and motorcycles.

There are long-distance routes from Honshū to Hokkaidō and many services from Osaka and Tokyo to ports all over Japan, but the most comprehensive network of ferry routes connects Kyūshū, Shikoku and the southern (San-yō) coast of Western Honshū, across the waters of the Inland Sea. Apart from services connecting A to B, there are many cruise ships operating in these waters. Ferries also connect the mainland islands with the many smaller islands off the coast and those dotted down to Okinawa and beyond to Taiwan.

Information on ferry routes, schedules and fares can be found in the comprehensive *JR Jikokuhyō* timetable and on information sheets from TIC offices. Ask for a copy of the Japan Long Distance Ferry Association's excellent English-language brochure. Some ferry services and their lowest one-way fares include:

Hokkaidō-Honshū	fare (¥)
Muroran-Oarai	9750
Otaru-Maizuru	6710
Otaru-Niigata	5250
Otaru-Tsuruga	7420
Tomakomai-Nagoya	10,200
Tomakomai-Ōarai	6000
Tomakomai-Sendai	7600

departing from Tokyo	fare (¥)
Kōchi (Shikoku)	10,600
Kokura (Kyūshū)	12,600
Kushiro (Hokkaidō)	14,700
Nachi-Katsuura (Honshū)	8800
Naha (Okinawa)	20,050
Tokushima (Shikoku)	8610
Tomakomai (Hokkaidō)	6000

departing from Osaka	fare (¥)
Beppu (Kyūshū)	7030
Imabari (Shikoku)	4170
Kōchi (Shikoku)	4610
Matsuyama (Shikoku)	5000
Naha (Okinawa)	15,750
Shin-Moji (Kyūshū)	5700
Takamatsu (Shikoku)	1320

departing from Honshū	fare (¥)
Kawasaki-Miyazaki (Kyūshū)	18,050
Kōbe-Beppu (Kyūshū)	7030
Kōbe-Matsuyama (Shikoku)	4890
Kōbe-Naha (Okinawa)	15,750
Kōbe-Oita (Kyūshū)	7020
Nagoya-Sendai (Honshū)	4900

departing from Kyūshū	fare (¥)
Hakata-Naha (Okinawa)	13,220
Kagoshima-Naha (Okinawa)	12,070

LOCAL TRANSPORT

All the major cities offer a wide variety of public transport. In many cities you can get day passes for unlimited travel on bus, tram or subway systems. The pass is called an Ichi-Nichi-Jōsha-Ken. If you're staying for an extended period in one city, commuter passes are available for regular travel.

Train & Subway

Several cities, especially Osaka and Tokyo, have mass transit rail systems comprising a loop line around the city centre and radial lines into the central stations and the subway system. Subway systems operate in Fukuoka, Kōbe, Kyoto, Nagoya, Osaka, Sapporo, Sendai, Tokyo and Yokohama. They are usually the fastest and most convenient ways of getting around the city.

For subways and local trains you will probably have to buy your ticket from a machine. Usually they're relatively easy to understand even if you can't read kanji as there will be a diagram explaining the routes, and from this you can find what your fare should be. However, if you can't work the fare out, an easy solution is to buy a ticket for the lowest fare on the machine. When you finish your trip, go to the fare adjustment machine or fare adjustment office before you reach the exit gate and pay the excess. JR train stations and most subway stations not only have their names posted above the platform in kanji and romaji but also the names of the preceding and following stations.

Bus

Almost every Japanese city will have a bus service but it's usually the most difficult public transport system for gaijin to use.

The destination names will almost inevitably be in kanji and often there are no numbers to identify which bus you want. Buses are also subject to the usual traffic delays.

Fares are either paid to the driver on entering or as you leave the bus and usually operate on one of two systems. In Tokyo and some other cities, there's a flat fare irrespective of distance. In the other system, you take a ticket as you board which indicates the zone number at your starting point. When you get off, an electric sign at the front of the bus indicates the fare charged at that point for each starting zone number. You simply pay the driver the fare that matches your zone number. There is often a change machine in the bus that can change ¥100 and 500 coins and ¥1000 notes.

In almost any town of even remote tourist interest, there will be *teiki kankō basu* (tour buses), usually operating from the main railway station. The tour will usually be conducted in Japanese but English-language tours are available in popular sightseeing areas like Kyoto and Tokyo. In places where the attractions are widespread or hard to reach by public transport, tours can be a good bet.

Tram

A number of cities have tram routes – particularly Nagasaki, Kumamoto and Kagoshima in Kyushū, Kōchi and Matsuyama in Shikoku, and Hakodate in Hokkaidō. These are excellent ways of getting around as they combine many of the advantages of bus travel (particularly the good views) with those of subways (it's easy to work out where you're going). Fares work on similar systems to bus travel and there are also unlimited-travel day tickets available.

Taxi

Taxis are convenient but expensive and are found in even quite small towns; the train station is the best place to look. Drivers are often reluctant to stop and pick you up near a station taxi stand, so either wait at the correct spot for a taxi off the rank or flag one down a couple of streets away. Fares vary very little throughout the country – flagfall (posted on the nearside windows) is ¥600 to ¥660 for the first 2km, after which it's around ¥100 for each 350m (approximately). There's also a time charge if the speed drops below 10km/h. During the day, it's almost impossible to tell if a moving taxi is occupied (just wave at it and it will stop if it's free); at night, vacant taxis are distinguishable by an illuminated light on the roof – an occupied taxi will have its light turned off.

Don't whistle for a taxi, a straightforward wave should bring one politely to a halt. Don't open the door when it stops, the driver does that with a remote release. The driver will also shut the door when you leave the taxi.

Drivers are normally as polite as anybody else in Japan but, like the majority of Japanese, they are not linguists. If you can't tell the driver where you want to go, it's useful to have the name written down in Japanese. At hotel front desks there will usually be business cards complete with name and location, which are used for just this purpose. Note that business names, including hotels, are often quite different in Japanese and English.

Taxi drivers have just as much trouble finding Japanese addresses as anyone else. Just because you've gone round the block five times does not necessarily mean your driver is a country boy fresh in from the sticks. Asking directions and stopping at police boxes for help in finding the address is standard practice.

Tipping is not necessary. A 20% surcharge is added after 11 pm or for taxis summoned by radio.

ORGANISED TOURS

Though there are fewer tour operators running speciality trips to Japan from abroad than to places like South-East Asia, the Himalayas and Africa, there are a handful well worth looking into. JNTO publishes an extensive list of US-based, Japan-bound operators in a pamphlet entitled *Japan & The*

Orient – Tour Listing, which can be picked up at JNTO offices in the USA.

Other tour companies either based in Japan or overseas that are worth checking out include:

Esprit Travel (☎ 800-377-7481, 310-289-6060) 2101 Wilshire Blvd, Suite 101, Santa Monica, CA 90403. This US-based Japan specialist tour operator is well worth looking at. As with Journeys East, it runs unique, small group tours, and tends to cater toward upmarket travellers.

Green Tour (☎/fax 03-3447-2560, email midori @pcom.net) 5-15-9 3B Kitashinagawa, Shinagawa-ku, Tokyo 141. This local outfit caters to non-Japanese travellers and specialises in back-country itineraries featuring hiking and *onsen*

(mineral hot-spring spa) visits. Check out their Web site at www2.pcom.net/midori/.

Journeys East (☎ 800-527-2612, email JEin@ aol.com) PO Box 1161, Middletown, CA 95461,USA.

Konichi Walks (email trips@konichiwalks.com) This Canadian-run tour operator is headquartered in the high-mountain prefecture of Nagano-ken. The nature-loving outfit offers a variety of hiking, cycling and walking tours to places like Fuji-san and other more 'off the beaten track' regions in the Japan Alps. Check out their Web site at www.konichiwalks.com.

Intrepid Travel This well-established Australian-based outfit leads noteworthy small-group tours to Japan. Information on trips and a list of Intrepid's international booking agents can be found on their Web site at www.intrepidtravel.com.au/.

Tokyo

With a population of 8.12 million in the central metropolitan area alone, Japan's capital is a city of vast proportions. Like London or Paris or New York or Bangkok, you might spend a lifetime exploring it and never run out of new things to discover. Indeed, it's almost better not to think of Tokyo as one city at all, but as a collection of separate cities connected by the Japan Rail (JR) Yamanote loop-line. And each of these 'cities' has its own distinct character; from funky old Ueno with its fine park and wonderful museums, to ultra-modern Shinjuku with its towering skyscrapers and endless department stores.

And as might be expected of the capital city of the world's second largest economy, what confronts the visitor more than anything else is the sheer level of energy in Tokyo. On the busy train lines, even at 11 pm on a Monday, it's standing room only. Crowds sweep you up, carry you in their wake and deposit you halfway across unfamiliar train stations. And the noise of it all! From train station announcements and *pachinko* (vertical pinball) parlours to store anthems to sirens and car horns, a barrage of noise assaults the visitor at every turn.

And by night, Tokyo really comes into its own: mazes of blazing neon fill every available nook and cranny of city's streets and alleys. Tiny street stalls and expensive hostess bars compete with karaoke boxes, *yakitori* joints, bars and *izakaya* (Japanese-style pubs) to lure the city's tired workers and dazzled travellers. And the party goes on until the first trains roll out, making Tokyo Asia's undisputed nightlife champion.

Above all, Tokyo is an experience. Some of Tokyo's best sights are not the kind of things you can put into a guidebook. They jump out at you unexpectedly on a crowded street: the woman dressed in *kimono* buying a hamburger at McDonald's; and the Buddhist monk with an alms bowl, standing serenely in the midst of jostling crowds of shoppers in Shinjuku. All in all, Tokyo has

Highlights

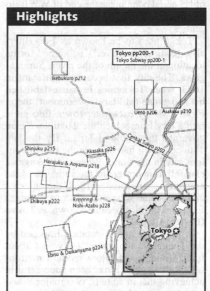

- Wander the streets of Shinjuku, home to Tokyo's busiest train station, rowdiest entertainment district, and some of the best shopping and dining in the country.

- Retreat to the calm of Meiji-jingū, one of Japan's finest shrines.

- Dip into the old-world hustle and bustle of Asakusa's Sensō-ji, probably the liveliest place of Buddhist worship in all Japan.

- Spend a day in Ueno-kōen exploring the museums, including the fine Tokyo National Museum.

- Make the morning trip to Tsukiji Fish Market and top it off with a sushi lunch in nearby Ginza.

to be considered one of Japan's must-see destinations, the perfect counterpoint to the country's other must-see destination, the cultural capital of Kyoto.

TOKYO

HISTORY

Tokyo is something of a miracle; a city that has literally risen from the ashes (the result of US aerial bombing at the end of WWII) to become one of the world's leading economic centres.

Tokyo used to be known as Edo (literally, 'Gate of the River'), so named for its location at the mouth of the river, Sumidagawa. The city first became significant in 1603, when Tokugawa Ieyasu established his shogunate (military government) there. From a sleepy backwater town, Edo grew into a city from which the Tokugawa clan governed the whole of Japan. By the late 18th century it had become the most populous city in the world. When the Tokugawa clan fell from power and the authority of the emperor was restored in 1868, the emperor and the capital were moved from Kyoto to Edo, and the city became known as Tokyo (Eastern Capital).

After 250 years of isolation imposed by the Tokugawa shogunate, Tokyo set about transforming itself into a modern metropolis. Remarkably, it has been successful in achieving this in spite of two major disasters that, in each case, practically levelled the whole city – the great earthquake and ensuing fires of 1923, and the US air raids of 1944 and 1945.

Not much of the old Japan is evident in Tokyo. Indeed, given the violence of the city's history – the periodic conflagrations (known to the locals as the 'flowers of Edo' – see the boxed text), the earthquakes and the destruction brought about through war – it's a wonder that anything is left at all. What you find today is a uniquely Japanese version of a 21st-century city – the bustling heart of the Japanese economic dynamo.

ORIENTATION

Tokyo is a vast conurbation spreading out across the Kantō Plain from Tokyo Bay (Tokyo-wan). The central metropolitan area is made up of 23 *ku* (wards), while outlying areas are divided into 27 separate *shi* (cities), a *gun* (county) and four island-districts. Nearly everything of interest to visitors lies on or near the JR Yamanote line, the rail loop that circles central Tokyo. Those areas not on the Yamanote line, like Roppongi, Tsukiji and Asakusa, are nonetheless within easy reach, as the whole area is crisscrossed by Tokyo's excellent subway system.

In Edo times, Yamanote referred to 'Uptown': the estates and residences of feudal

The Flowers of Edo

Today there is little left of Shitamachi, the old 'downtown', and the only way to get some idea of the circumstances in which the lower classes of old Edo lived is by visiting somewhere like Ueno's Shitamachi History Museum. Edo was a city of wood, and its natural stained-wood frontages and dark-tiled roofs gave the city an attractiveness that is little in evidence in modern Tokyo. Nevertheless, the poor lived in horribly crowded conditions, in flimsy wooden constructions, often with earthen floors. Huge fires regularly swept great swaths through the wooden buildings of the congested city. In a perverse attempt to make the best of misfortune, Edo-dwellers seemed almost to take pride in the fires that periodically purged the city, calling them *Edo-no-hana*, (literally 'flowers of Edo').

The flowers of Edo bloomed with such frequency that it has been estimated that any Shitamachi structure could reckon on a life span of around 20 years, often less, before being destroyed by fire. Preventative measures included building houses that could be completely sealed at the approach of a fire; candles would be left burning inside, starving the houses' interior of oxygen. Private fire brigades operated with standard-bearers who would stake out their territory close to a burning building and exact payment if they managed to save it.

Modern building techniques have eliminated most of Edo's 'flowers', but you can still see the occasional wooden structure that has miraculously survived into the 21st century.

barons, military aristocracy and other Edo elite, in the hilly regions of the city. Shitamachi, or 'Downtown', was home to the working classes, merchants and artisans. Even today the distinction persists. The areas west of the Imperial Palace (Kōkyo) are the more modernised, housing the commercial and business centres of modern Tokyo; the areas east of the palace, like Asakusa and Ueno, retain more of the character of old Edo.

A trip around the JR Yamanote line makes a good introduction to the city. You might start at Tokyo station, the first point of arrival for many travellers. Near to the station are the Marunouchi and Otemachi office districts and the high-class shopping district of Ginza. Continuing north from Tokyo station brings you to Akihabara, the discount electronics centre of Tokyo. Farther along is Ueno, home to many of the city's museums. After rounding the top of the loop you descend into Ikebukuro, a bawdy shopping and entertainment district. A few stops farther on is Shinjuku, a massive shopping, entertainment and business district considered by many the heart of modern Tokyo. From there, trains continue through to the teen-oriented, fashionable shopping areas of Harajuku, Shibuya and Ebisu. A swing through Shinagawa at the bottom of the loop then brings you back to Tokyo station and completes the loop.

The information in this chapter is presented in the order described above (working anti-clockwise around the Yamanote line), with areas not on the Yamanote line covered last.

Maps

We strongly recommend that you pick up a copy of the free *Tourist Map of Tokyo* from one of the Tourist Information Centers (TICs – see Tourist Offices later). This excellent map has detailed insets of Tokyo's major neighbourhoods as well as subway and rail maps. For more in-depth exploration of the city, pick up a copy of *Tokyo City Atlas: A Bilingual Atlas* (Kodansha), which includes *banchi* (street address) numbers essential for finding addresses.

Tokyo's train and subway lines are much easier to navigate with the excellent colour-coded map that is available free at subway stations and tourist information counters around town. We've included it in this guide – see the Tokyo Subway map.

Books

There are a number of publications that might supplement the one you have in your hands, particularly if you are planning to become a resident of Tokyo. For a comprehensive guide to the city, pick up Lonely Planet's *Tokyo*.

The Best of Tokyo by Don Morton and Tsunoi Naoko (Tuttle) is a light-hearted look at the city, with recommendations ranging variously from 'best traditional Japanese dolls' to 'best toilet'. *Tokyo for Free* by Susan Pompian (Kodansha) lists more than 400 things that you can do for free in a very expensive city.

Old Tokyo: Walks in the City of the Shogun by Enbutsu Sumiko (Tuttle) details walking tours in Tokyo with fascinating historical and cultural detail. *Little Adventures in Tokyo* (Kodansha) by Rick Kennedy, one of Tokyo's most famous expats, introduces some of his secret finds in and around Tokyo.

Tokyo: A Guide to Recent Architecture by Tajima Noriyuki (Elipsis Könemann) is a great guide to Tokyo's architectural masterpieces and oddities.

INFORMATION

See the Facts for the Visitor chapter for information on foreign embassies and consulates in Tokyo.

Tourist Offices

The Japan National Tourist Organization (JNTO) operates two TICs in the Tokyo area – one on the 1st floor of Terminal 2, Narita airport (☎ 0476-34-6251), open from 9 am to 8 pm; and one in the basement of the Tokyo International Forum near Tokyo station (☎ 3201-3331), which is open from 9 am to 5 pm (to noon Saturday, closed Sunday and national holidays) – see the Central Tokyo map.

TIC offices will make accommodation reservations, but only for hotels and *ryokan* (traditional Japanese inns) that are members of the Welcome Inn group. The Tokyo TIC also offers Teletourist (☎ 3201-2911), a round-the-clock taped information service on current events in town. It can also arrange for tours of the city with volunteer guides.

The Information Bureau of Tokyo operates two information counters (9 am to 6 pm, closed Sunday and holidays) for foreign travellers; one on the ground floor of Tokyo station near the central Yaesu exit and one on the ground floor of Shinjuku station near the My City exit.

Immigration Offices

The Tokyo Regional Immigration Bureau (☎ 3213-8523) is best reached from Ōtemachi subway station on the Chiyoda line. Take the C2 exit, cross the street at the corner and turn left. Walk past the Japan Development Building; the immigration bureau is the next building on your right.

Money

Banks are open weekdays from 9 am to 3 pm. Look for the 'Foreign Exchange' sign outside. Some post offices also offer foreign-exchange services. See the Facts for the Visitor chapter for more information on changing money.

International ATMs

Unlike other parts of Japan, Tokyo has a reasonable number of automated teller machines (ATMs) that accept foreign-issued cards. The best bet for foreign travellers is Citibank, which has 24-hour English-language ATMs, open every day. There are branches in Ōtemachi, Ginza, Akasaka, East and West Shinjuku, Aoyama, Shibuya and Ikebukuro (see the relevant maps for precise locations). There are other ATMs that accept foreign-issued cards at Sunny's Card Plaza in the Yaesu Underground Mall beneath Tokyo station; on the 1st floor of the Yūraku-chō Mullion Building (see the Central Tokyo map); and on the 1st floor of the Goto Planetarium Building (see the Shibuya map).

Credit Cards The main credit-card offices in Tokyo are:

American Express (☎ 0120-02-0120 – 24 hours) American Express Tower, 4-30-16 Ogikubo, Suginami-ku
MasterCard (☎ 00531-11-3886) 16th floor, Dai Tokyo Kasai Shinjuku Bldg, 3-25-3 Yoyogi, Shibuya-ku
VISA (☎ 5251-0633, 0120-13-3173) 4th floor, Nissho Bldg, 2-7-9 Kita-Aoyama, Minato-ku

Post

The Tokyo central post office is outside Tokyo station (take the Marunouchi exit and then cross the street to the south). Call ☎ 5472-5851 for postal information in English. Poste restante mail will be held at the central post office for 30 days. It should be addressed as follows:

Jane THOMPSON
Poste Restante
Central Post Office
Tokyo, JAPAN

Telephone

Almost all public phones in Tokyo take prepaid phone cards. For domestic directory assistance, call ☎ 104 and ask to be transferred to an English speaker. For details on making international calls from a public phone see the Facts for the Visitor chapter.

Fax

You can send faxes from the front desks of many hotels (some allow nonguests to use their services for a fee), some convenience stores and from Kinko's copy stores (its basic rate to send an international fax is ¥200 plus phone charges). See the Email & Internet Access section later for the locations of some Kinko's stores in Tokyo (and note that there is a Kinko's *without* Internet access inside Tokyo station, on the Yaesu side).

At the Kimi Information Center (☎ 3986-1604) in Ikebukuro you can send faxes for ¥300 plus telephone charges. To receive faxes you must pay a ¥1000 fee (good for six months) and ¥200 for each fax. It also has telephone-answering, mailbox and Internet services.

Email & Internet Access

The following two places offered free Internet access at the time of writing:

NTT Intercommunication Center (☎ 0120-14-4199) 4th floor, Tokyo Opera City, West Shinjuku (¥800 entry, free Internet access once inside, 10 am to 6 pm, closed Monday). See the off-map arrow on the Shinjuku map.
Marunouchi Café (☎ 3215-5025) 1st floor, Fuji Bldg, 3-2-3 Marunouchi, Chiyoda-ku (8 am to 8 pm weekdays). See the Central Tokyo map.

If these free places no longer exist or aren't convenient, the following Internet cafes are a good bet:

Click On Internet Café (☎ 5489-2282) 5th floor, Koike Bldg, 2-23-1 Dōgen-zaka, Shibuya-ku (¥500 for 30 minutes, 11 am to 10 pm). See the Shibuya map.
Cyber Scholé Internet Café (☎ 5330-7219) 10th floor, T-Zone Bldg, 7-11-1 Nishi-Shinjuku, Shinjuku-ku (¥500 for 30 minutes, 11 am to 8.30 pm weekdays, to 7.30 pm weekends and holidays). See the Shinjuku map
Cyberia (☎ 3423-0318) 1st floor, Scala Bldg, 1-14-17 Nishi-Azabu (¥200 for 10 minutes, 11 am to 11 pm). See the Roppongi & Nishi-Azabu map.
Hard Internet Cafe T and T (☎ 5950-9983) B1 floor, Liberty Ikebukuro Bldg, 2-18-1 Ikebukuro, Toshima-ku (¥1000 hourly, or ¥5000 per month unlimited usage, noon to 10 pm, closed Wednesday and 1st and 3rd Sunday of the month). See the Ikebukuro map.

You can also log on at most Kinko's copy stores (¥200 for 10 minutes, 24 hours daily). There are branches in the Hotel Century Southern Tower Building in Shinjuku, and in Ikebukuro (see those maps).

Internet Resources

There are thousands of Web sites about Tokyo. Here are three of the most useful:

Tokyo Classified The best all-round site for Tokyo. Lots of events and jobs listings.
www.tokyoclassified.com
Tokyo Journal Not the best of these sites, but interesting articles and interviews from time to time.
www.tokyo.to

Tokyo Q Another great all-round Tokyo site. Plenty of listings of current and upcoming events.
www.so-net.ne.jp/tokyoq

Travel Agencies

In Tokyo there are a number of travel agencies where English is spoken and where discounting on flights and domestic travel is the norm. For an idea of current prices check the *Japan Times* or *Tokyo Classified*.

Four well-established agencies where English is spoken are: No 1 Travel in Shinjuku (☎ 3200-8871), Shibuya (☎ 3770-1381) and Ikebukuro (☎ 3986-4291); STA Travel, which is represented in Yotsuya (☎ 5269-0751), Shibuya (☎ 5485-8380) and Ikebukuro (☎ 5391-2922); Across Traveller's Bureau in Shibuya (☎ 5467-0077); and Just Travel in Takadanobaba (☎ 3362-3441).

Bookshops

Tower Books (☎ 3496-3661), on the 7th floor of the new Tower Records building in Shibuya, has a large selection of English-language books and a fabulous array of magazines and newspapers from around the world. Its magazines are considerably cheaper than elsewhere around town. It's open daily.

One of Japan's better bookshop chains, Kinokuniya, has two branches in Shinjuku. The old branch is on Shinjuku-dōri (☎ 3354-0131) and the new branch (☎ 5361-3301) in the annex of the Takashimaya Times Square Complex. The new branch has one of the largest selections of English-language books in Tokyo, on the 6th floor.

Maruzen (☎ 3272-7211), in Nihombashi near Ginza, has a collection of books almost equal to Kinokuniya's and is always a lot quieter. It's closed on Sunday.

The 3rd floor of Jena (☎ 3571-2980) in Ginza doesn't carry quite the range of some other foreign-language bookshops but it does have a good selection of fiction and art books, and stocks a large number of newspapers and magazines. It's closed on public holidays.

Some other notable English bookshops around Tokyo include Biblos (☎ 3200-4531), across from JR Takadanobaba station; the Aoyama Book Center (☎ 3442-1651), near Roppongi subway station; and the Yaesu Book Center (☎ 3281-1811), next to JR Tokyo station in Nihombashi.

The best used English-language books are in Ebisu at Good Day Books (☎ 5421-0957). In addition to a wide range of paperbacks, there are some hardcover books and magazines. It also accepts books for exchange, and (very) occasionally will purchase used books. It's closed Tuesday.

Tokyo's traditional bookshop area is Jimbō-chō. Although most in this area cater only to Japanese-readers, there are a couple of foreign-language bookshops scattered around.

Libraries

The National Diet Library (☎ 3581-2331) is the largest library in Japan, with 1.3 million books in Western languages. The library (9.30 am to 5 pm, closed Sunday) is close to Nagata-chō subway station on the Yūraku-chō and Hanzōmon lines.

The British Council (☎ 3235-8031), in Iidabashi, has a library of books and magazines, open from 11 am to 8 pm weekdays. The American Center (☎ 3436-0901) in Shiba-kōen, has a similar set-up (noon to 6.30 pm weekdays).

The Japan Foundation Library (☎ 5562-3527) is close to Kojimachi station on the Yūraku-chō line. It has some 30,000 English-language publications and is open only to foreigners (9.30 am to 5 pm, Tuesday to Saturday).

For languages other than English, go to the Bibliotheque de la Maison Franco-Japonaise (☎ 5424-1141), open from 10 am to noon and 1 to 6 pm, closed Saturday, and is close to Ochanomizu station on the JR Chūō line. The Goethe Institut Tokyo Bibliotek (☎ 3584-3201) has around 15,000 volumes (noon to 6 pm, to 8 pm Friday, closed weekends). It is close to Aoyama Itchōme station on the Ginza line.

In Ginza, Magazine House (☎ 3545-7227) has a good selection of magazines from all corners of the world (11 am to 7 pm).

Newspapers & Magazines

There's plenty of English-language information on Tokyo, starting with the four English-language newspapers (see the Facts for the Visitor chapter for details). The best listings of Tokyo events can be found in Saturday's *Japan Times*.

The *Tokyo Journal* has recently undergone a change of ownership and is not the stand-by it once was. Although its Cityscope listings section still makes it worth the purchase price, the magazine is cursed by its hipper-than-thou attitude and annoying graphics style.

These days, the free weekly *Tokyo Classified* is the magazine of choice for most Tokyo residents, although its cultural listings are not as detailed as those in the *Tokyo Journal*. However, for club events and concerts, this is the best magazine.

Cultural Centres

Cultural centres in Tokyo generally act as focal points of the national groups they represent, and usually have good bulletin boards, events, small libraries and language classes.

The British Council (☎ 3235-8031) 1-2 Kagurazaka, Shinjuku-ku (Iidabashi station)
Goethe Institut Tokyo (☎ 3584-3201) 7-5-56 Akasaka, Minato-ku (Akasaka station)
Institute Franco-Japonais du Tokyo (☎ 5261-3933) 15 Ichigaya Funagawarachō, Shinjuku-ku (Iidabashi station)

Conversation Lounges

Mickey House (☎ 3209-9686) is an 'English bar' that serves ¥350 all-you-can-drink coffee and tea as well as reasonably priced beer and food. Entry is free for English-speaking foreigners. Take the main exit at JR Takadanobaba, go east on to Wasedadōri and look for the Tōzai-line subway station entrance on your left; Mickey House (5 to 11 pm, closed Sunday) is on the 4th floor of the Yashiro Building.

Useful Organisations & Services

There are innumerable associations for foreign residents and travellers. For the one most suited to your needs and interests, we recommend checking the listings sections of *Tokyo Classified* and *Tokyo Journal*.

There is a lot of information and support available to foreign residents and travellers in Tokyo, including several useful telephone services. For general information try the Foreign Residents' Advisory Center (☎ 5320-7744), which operates weekdays (9.30 am to noon and 1 to 4 pm). JR English Information (☎ 3423-0111) offers information on train schedules and fares (10 am to 6 pm weekdays). Tokyo English Lifeline (☎ 3968-4099) can help with information and counselling (9.30 am to 4 pm and 7 to 11 pm).

Laundry

Most hotels, mid-range and up, have laundry services. If you are in a budget ryokan, ask the staff for the nearest *koin randorii* (laundrette). Costs range from ¥150 for a load of washing, and drying costs about ¥100 for 10 minutes.

Kuriningu-yasan (drycleaners) are in almost every neighbourhood. The standards are high and some offer rush service. It's about ¥200 for your basic business shirt.

Left Luggage

There are coin lockers in all train and bus stations in Tokyo. Smaller lockers start at ¥300 (you can leave luggage for up to three days). Otherwise, the Akaboshi (Red Cap) luggage service on the Yaesu side of Tokyo station will store small/large bags during the day for ¥300/400 (you must pick up your luggage by the end of the day you leave it). For longer periods, there is an overnight luggage-storage service in Tokyo station that will hold luggage for up to two weeks, with rates starting at ¥500 per bag per day. Ask at the main information counter on the Yaesu side for a map to both of these services.

Medical Services

There are foreign doctors at the Tokyo Medical and Surgical Clinic (☎ 3436-3028), near Roppongi in Kamiyachō, on the Hibiya subway line. Appointments can be made weekdays from 9 am to 5 pm and

until 1 pm on Saturday. The International Clinic (☎ 3583-7831) in Roppongi also provides services in English (9 am to 5 pm weekdays, to noon Saturday). Both clinics are closed Sunday and holidays.

You can also call the Tokyo Medical Information Service (☎ 5285-8181) for advice about which hospital or clinic can best address your needs. The service operates for non-emergency cases on weekdays from 9 am to 5 pm. For emergency or after-hours cases, call the Tokyo Metropolitan Emergency Translation Service on ☎ 5285-8185 (5 to 10 pm weekdays, 9 am to 10 pm weekends and holidays).

International Pharmacies The American Pharmacy (☎ 3271-4034) is just around the corner from Tokyo International Forum branch of the TIC, near Yūraku-chō station and Hibiya subway station (9.30 am to 7.30 pm, to 6.30 pm Sunday and holidays). Another option is the pharmacy at the National Azabu Supermarket (☎ 3442-3181), close to Hiro-o subway station (9.30 am to 7 pm).

Emergency

Emergency numbers are: police ☎ 110; and fire and ambulance ☎ 119. You should be able to get your point across in simple English. If you have problems communicating, ring the Japan Helpline (☎ 0120-461-997), an emergency number that operates 24 hours a day, seven days a week. See Medical Services earlier for more information on dealing with a medical emergency.

Dangers & Annoyances

Tokyo can be annoying at times but it is rarely dangerous. If possible, avoid the rail network during peak hours – around 8 to 9.30 am and 5 to 7 pm – when the surging crowds would try anyone's patience. The noise can be aggravating in some of the busy commercial districts.

Some travellers may also be disturbed by the overtly sexual nature of some of the signs and sights in Tokyo's red-light districts, like Shinjuku's Kabuki-chō and parts of Ikebukuro.

The Knicker Knock-off

My threadbare underwear was, apparently, an irresistible temptation. So irresistible, in fact, that late one suburban-Tokyo night it inspired someone to scale a wall, leap onto my 2nd-floor balcony and liberate the motley collection from the clothesline.

Anyone who has ever tried to find *gaijin*-sized undergarments in Japan will understand the certain practical considerations that magnified my distress. 'My underwear has...disappeared,' I told my landlady, pale-faced, unable to come up with the Japanese for 'stolen'. She cottoned on at once – and called the police. Under the watchful eye of eight (!) police officers, I spent a good hour or so fielding questions about the colour, size and texture of the missing articles. They'd keep an eye out, they told me, but I really should be more careful.

More careful? My Japanese friends were shocked and horrified – that I'd been so stupid as to peg my bras and undies on an *outdoor* clothesline in the first place. Every nation has its share of knicker-snatchers, but Japan, it seems, may have more than the usual sprinkling.

Jane Thompson

Earthquakes Check the locations of emergency exits in your hotel and be aware of earthquake safety procedures (see Earthquakes under Dangers & Annoyances in the Facts for the Visitor chapter). If an earthquake occurs, the Japan Broadcasting Corporation (NHK) will broadcast information and instructions in English on all its TV and radio networks. Tune to channel 1 on your TV, or to NHK (639 kHz AM), FEN (810 kHz AM) or InterFM (76.1 FM) on your radio.

CENTRAL TOKYO 東京中心部
Imperial Palace 皇居

The Imperial Palace, or Kōkyo, is the home of Japan's emperor and the imperial family. The palace itself is closed to the public for all but two days of the year, 2 January and 23 December (the emperor's birthday).

Even if you can't enter the palace itself, it is possible to wander around its outskirts and visit the gardens, where you can at least get a view of the palace with the bridge, Nijū-bashi, in the foreground.

The present palace was completed in 1968. It replaced the palace built in 1888, which was destroyed by Allied bombing in WWII. It occupies the site of the castle, Edo-jō, from which the Tokugawa shogunate ruled all Japan. In its time the castle was the largest in the world, though apart from the massive moat and walls, virtually nothing remains of it today.

It is an easy walk from Tokyo station, or from Hibiya or Nijūbashi-mae subway stations, to the Nijū-bashi. The walk involves crossing Babasaki Moat and the expansive Imperial Palace Plaza (Kōkyo-mae Hiroba). The vantage point, which is popular with photographers, gives you a picture-postcard view of the palace peeking over its fortifications, with the Nijū-bashi in the foreground.

Imperial Palace East Garden
皇居東御苑

Imperial Palace East Garden (Kōkyo Higashi-gyoen) is the only quarter of the palace proper that is open to the public. The main entrance is through the Ōte-mon, a 10-minute walk north of Nijū-bashi. This was once the principal gate of Edo-jō; the garden itself lies at what was once the heart of the old castle. Entry is free and you'll be given a numbered plastic token to turn in when you depart (9 am to 4 pm, last entry 3 pm, closed Monday and Friday). The store inside the garden sells a good map of the garden for ¥150.

Kitanomaru-kōen

The park, Kitanomaru-kōen, is quite pleasant, and is a good spot for a leisurely stroll or summer picnic. You can get there from Kudanshita or Takebashi subway stations. Alternatively, if you're walking from Kōkyo Higashi-gyoen, go through the Kitahanebashi-mon, turn left and look for Kitanomaru-kōen on the other side of the road.

Kitanomaru-kōen contains the **Nihon Budōkan**, a hall located at the northern end

Tokyo Tower and Zōjō-ji.

Riders making sure they're noticed on their way through Shibuya.

Tracks through the snow in the Imperial Palace East Garden, with Otemachi in the background.

Neon Tokyo – Shinjuku's discount shopping arcades at dusk.

Tips for riding the Yamanote.

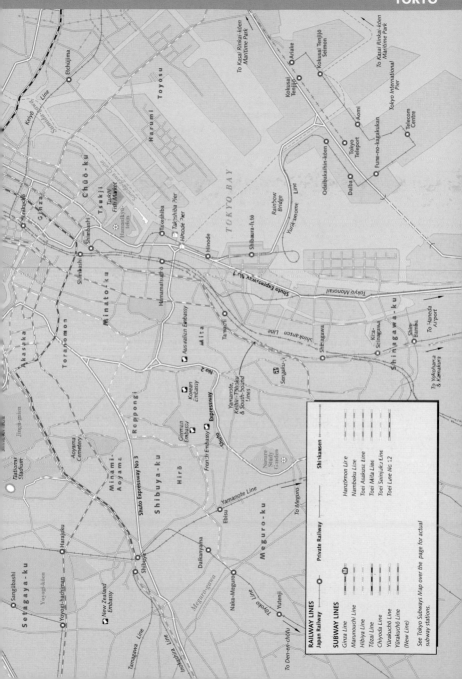

TOKYO BAY

Etchūjima
Harumi
Toyosu
Tsukiji
Chūō-ku
Ginza
Arakuchō
Shinbashi
Shinbashi
Hamamatsuchō
Takeshiba Pier
Hinode Pier
Tsukiji Fish Market
Hamashikyūkien
Hinode
Shibaura-itō
Rainbow Bridge
Ariake
Kokusai Tenjijō Seimon
Kokusai Tenjijō
Aomi
Telecom Centre
Fune-no-kagakukan
Tokyo Teleport
Daiba
Odaibakaihin-koen
To Kasai Rinkai-kōen Maritime Park
To Kasai Rinkai-kōen Maritime Park
Tokyo International Pier
Yurikamome Line

Keiyō Line
Shinsuidō Line

Minato-ku
Akasaka
Toranomon
Australian Embassy
Mita
No 2
Korean Embassy
German Embassy
French Embassy
Shuto Expressway No 3
Shuto Expressway No 3
Shuto Expressway
Minami-Aoyama
Aoyama Cemetery
Roppongi
Hirō
National Stadium
Jingū-gaien
Shuto Expressway No 1
Shinkansen Line
Tamachi
Sengaku-ji
Shinagawa
Shibaugawa
Yamanote, Keihin-Tōhoku & South-bound lines
Kita-Shinagawa
Shin-Banba
Shinagawa-ku
Tokyo Monorail
To Haneda Airport
To Yokohama & Kamakura

Shibuya-ku
New Zealand Embassy
Yamanote Line
Ebisu
Daikanyama
Naka-Meguro
Meguro-ku
Nature Study Garden
To Meguro

Setagaya-ku
Sangūbashi
Harajuku
Yoyogi-hachiman
Yoyogi-kōen
Shibuya
Yūtenji
Naka-Meguro
Tōyoko Line
Meguro-gawa
Tamagawa Line
Inokashira Line
To Den-en-chōfu

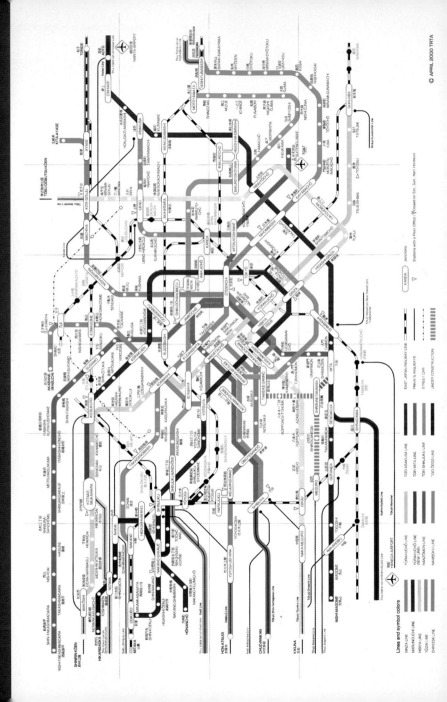

of the park. South of the Budōkan is the **Science Museum** (¥600, 9.30 am to 4.50 pm), which is a decent rainy-day stop for science buffs or those with children in tow. An English booklet is included with the entry fee.

Continuing south from the Science Museum brings you to the **National Museum of Modern Art** (¥515, 10 am to 5 pm, closed Monday). The permanent exhibition here features Japanese art from the Meiji period (1868–1912) onwards. It's worth checking in the *Tokyo Journal* or *Tokyo Classified* to see if any special exhibitions are being held. Your ticket (hold onto the stub) gives you free admission to the nearby **Craft Museum** (same opening hours), which houses a good display of crafts such as ceramics, lacquerware and dolls.

Yasukuni-jinja 靖国神社

If you take the Tayasu-mon exit (just past the Budōkan) of Kitanomaru-kōen, across the road and to your left is Yasukuni-jinja, the Shrine for Establishing Peace in the Empire. Dedicated to the 2.4 million Japanese war-dead since 1853, it is the most controversial shrine in all Japan.

The Japanese constitutional separation of religion and politics and the renunciation of militarism didn't stop a group of class-A war criminals being enshrined here in 1979; it also doesn't stop annual visits by politicians on the anniversary of Japan's defeat in WWII (15 August). The loudest protests are from Japan's Asian neighbours, who suffered most from Japanese aggression. This is not to say you should boycott the shrine; it is well worth a visit. Black vans blasting right-wing propaganda (in Japanese) are often there to remind you where you are, however.

Once you've taken a look at the handsome main hall of the shrine, walk to the rear of the building to check out the pleasant carp pond.

Yūshūkan Museum Next to the Yasukuni-jinja is the Yūshūkan Museum (¥300, 9 am to 5 pm), with treasures from Yasukuni-jinja and other items commemorating Japanese war-dead. There are limited English explanations, but an English pamphlet is also available. Interesting exhibits include the long torpedo in the large exhibition hall that is actually a *kaiten* (human torpedo), a submarine version of the *kamikaze* (WWII suicide pilots). There are also displays of military uniforms, *samurai* armour and paintings of famous battles. Perhaps most interesting of all are the excerpts from books (some in English) arguing that America forced Japan into bombing Pearl Harbor.

Tokyo International Forum 東京国際フォーラム

Located in Yūraku-chō, midway between Tokyo station and Ginza, this wonderful building (8 am to 11 pm) is well worth a visit. The prominent glass wing of this convention centre looks like a glass ship plying the urban waters of central Tokyo. In contrast, the west wing is a boxy affair of cantilevered, overhanging spaces and cavernous atria. The B1 floor of this building holds the main Tokyo TIC.

Ginza 銀座

Ginza is the shopping area in Tokyo that *everyone* has heard of. Back in the 1870s, Ginza was one of the first areas to modernise, featuring a large number of novel (for Tokyoites of that time) Western-style brick buildings. Ginza was also home to Tokyo's first department stores and other harbingers of the modern world, such as gas lamps.

Today, other shopping districts rival Ginza in opulence, vitality and popularity, but Ginza retains a distinct snob value. It is still the place to go and be seen emptying the contents of a bulging wallet. Even if you are on a tight budget, Ginza is an interesting area in which to browse – the galleries are usually free and there are lots of discount coffee shops.

Sunday is the best day for a stroll in Ginza, as the smaller streets are closed to vehicles. Start your exploration at the Sukiyabashi crossing, a 10-minute walk from the Kōkyo, directly above Ginza subway station.

Sony Building Right on Sukiyabashi Crossing is the Sony Building (free, 11 am to 7 pm), which has fascinating hands-on

CENTRAL TOKYO

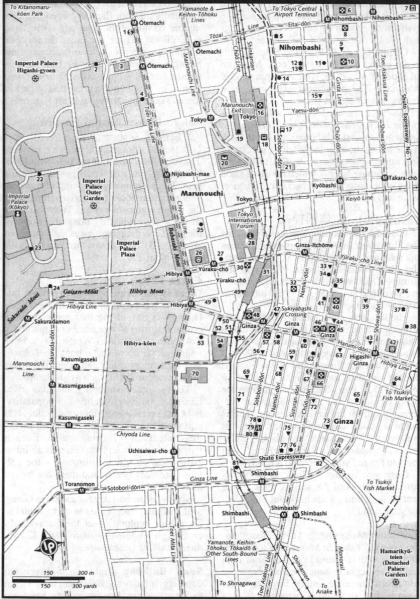

To Kitanomaru-kōen Park

Yamanote &
Keihin-Tōhoku
Lines

To Tokyo Central
Airport Terminal

Ōtemachi

Nihombashi Nihombashi

Eitai-dōri

Tōzai

Shinkansen

Chūō Line

Line

Nihombashi

Ōtemachi

Ōtemachi

Marunouchi Line

Imperial Palace
Higashi-gyoen

Imperial Palace
(Kōkyo)

Imperial
Palace
Outer
Garden

Imperial
Palace
Plaza

Marunouchi
Exit
Tokyo

Tokyo

Nijūbashi-mae

Marunouchi

Tokyo

Tokyo
International
Forum

Toei Mita Line

Chiyoda Line

Babasaki Moat

Yūraku-chō

Hibiya

Sakurada Moat

Gaisen-Mōat

Hibiya Moat

Sakuradamon

Hibiya Line

Hibiya-kōen

Marunouchi
Line

Kasumigaseki

Kasumigaseki

Kasumigaseki

Chiyoda Line

Uchisaiwai-cho

Ginza Line

Toranomon

Sotobori-dōri

Toei Mita Line

Yamanote, Keihin-
Tōhoku, Tōkaidō &
Other South-Bound
Lines

To Shinagawa

Shinkansen

To
Ariake

Yaesu-dōri

Ginza Line

Showa-dōri

Chūō-dōri

Sotobori-dōri

Kyōbashi

Keiyō Line

Takara-chō

Ginza-Itchōme

Yūraku-chō Line

Namiki-dōri

Yūraku-chō

Yūraku-chō

Hibiya

Sukiyabashi
Crossing

Ginza

Ginza

Ginza

Ginza

Higashi-
Ginza

Harumi-dōri

Sotobori-dōri

Namiki-dōri

Suzuran-dōri

Chūō-dōri

Hibiya Line

Showa-dōri

To Tsukiji
Fish Market

Ginza

Shuto Expressway

Shimbashi

Shimbashi

Shimbashi Shimbashi

Monorail

To Tsukiji
Fish Market

Hamarikyū-
teien
(Detached
Palace
Garden)

Shuto Expressway No 1

Toei Asakusa Line

Shuto Expressway No 1

Shinkansen

0   150   300 m
0   150   300 yards

CENTRAL TOKYO

PLACES TO STAY
3 Palace Hotel
　パレスホテル
5 Hotel Yaesu-Ryūmeikan
　ホテル八重洲龍名館
12 Yaesu Terminal Hotel
　八重洲ターミナルホテル
19 Tokyo Station Hotel
　東京ステーションホテル
29 Hotel Seiyo Ginza
　ホテル西洋銀座
37 Hotel Ginza Daiei
　ホテル銀座ダイエー
64 Ginza Tokyu Hotel
　銀座東急ホテル
65 Renaissance Tokyo Hotel
　Ginza Tōbu
　ルネッサンス東京ホテル
　銀座東武
70 Imperial Hotel
　帝国ホテル
74 Ginza Dai-Ichi Hotel
　銀座第一ホテル
77 Ginza International Hotel
　銀座国際ホテル
80 Ginza Nikkō Hotel
　銀座日航ホテル

PLACES TO EAT
9 Mikuniya
　美国屋
15 Sushi Tetsu
　すし鉄
33 Hina Sushi
　ひな寿司
36 Chichibu Nishiki
　ちちぶにしき
39 Tenya
　天屋
43 Nair's
　ナイル
44 Zakuro
　ざくろ
47 Hina Sushi
　ひな寿司
49 Shin-Hi-No-Moto
　新日の基
50 Dondo
　どんど
51 Robata
　炉端

55 Yakitori Alley
　やきとりアリー
56 Ginza Palmy Building
　銀座パルミビル
59 New Torigin
　ニュー鳥銀
63 Maharaja
68 Ten'ichi
　天一
69 Doutor Coffee
71 Restaurant Indonesia
72 Sapporo Lion Beer Hall
73 Jangara Rāmen
　じゃんがらラーメン
75 Kyubei
　久兵衛
82 Farm Grill

OTHER
1 Citibank
2 Ōte-mon
　大手門
4 Wadakura-mon
　和田蔵門
6 Tōkyū Department Store
　東急百貨店
7 Yamatane Museum of Art
　山種美術館
8 Haibara
　はいばら
10 Takashimaya
　Department Store
　高島屋百貨店
11 Maruzen Bookshop
　丸善書店
13 Discount Ticket Shop
　格安チケット売り場
14 Discount Ticket Shops
　格安チケット売り場
16 Daimaru
　Department Store
　大丸百貨店
17 Airport Limousine
　Bus Stop
　空港リムジンバス停
18 JR Highway Bus Station
　ＪＲ高速バスターミナル
20 Central Post Office;
　Tokyo Station Plaza
　東京ステーションプラザ；
　中央郵便局

21 Yaesu
　Book Center
　八重洲ブックセンター
22 Sakashita-mon
　坂下門
23 Nijū-bashi
　二重橋
24 Sakurada-mon
　桜田門
25 Marunouchi Café
　丸の内カフェ
26 Imperial Theatre
　帝国劇場
27 Kokusai Building
　国際ビル
28 TIC
30 Sogo
　Department Store
　そごう百貨店
31 Kōtsū Buildg
　交通会館
32 Printemps
　Department Store
　プランタン百貨店
34 Meldiya International
　Supermarket
　明治屋
35 Itō-ya Stationery Shop
　伊東屋
38 Magazine House
　マガジンハウス
40 Matsuya
　Department Store
　松屋百貨店
41 Nikon Salon
　ニコンギャラリー
42 Kabuki-za Theatre
　歌舞伎座
45 Mitsukoshi
　Department Store
　三越百貨店
46 Wakō
　Department Store
　和光百貨店
48 Hankyū & Seibu
　Department Stores
　阪急／西武百貨店
49 American Pharmacy
　アメリカンファーマシー
52 Godzilla Statue
　ゴジラ像

CENTRAL TOKYO

displays of Sony's many products, including some that have yet to be released. Although there's often a wait, kids love the free video and virtual-reality games on the 6th floor. If nothing else, you can put your feet up and relax for a while in one of the building's two Hi-Vision theatres.

Galleries Ginza is overflowing with galleries, many of them so small that they can be viewed in two or three minutes. Others feature work by unknown artists who have hired the exhibition space themselves. Wander around and visit any galleries that seem particularly interesting. They are scattered throughout Ginza but are concentrated in the area south of Harumi-dōri, between Ginza-dōri and Chūō-dōri.

Idemitsu Art Museum (¥500, 10 am to 5 pm, closed Monday) holds Japanese and Chinese art and is famous for its collection of work by the Zen monk Sengai. It's a five-minute walk from either Hibiya or Yūraku-chō station, on the 9th floor of the Kokusai Building, next door to the Imperial Theatre.

Probably the best of the photographic galleries in the area are **Nikon Salon** (10 am to 6 pm, closed Monday) and **Contax Salon** (10.30 am to 7 pm, closed Monday).

Kabuki-za Theatre Even if you don't plan to attend a *kabuki* performance, it's worth taking a look at the Kabuki-za Theatre (☎ 5565-6000). Performances take place twice daily (usually from 11 am and 4 pm) and tickets range from ¥2520 to ¥16,800, depending on the seat. If you only

want to see one act of a performance you can ask about a restricted ticket (¥500 to ¥1200) for the 4th floor. These tickets must be purchased at the theatre itself. For ¥600, plus a deposit of ¥1000, you can get an earphone guide that explains the kabuki performance in English as you watch – it is not available with restricted tickets. For phone bookings, ring at least a day ahead; they won't take bookings for the same day.

Magazine House Just around the corner from Kabuki-za is Magazine House (11 am to 7 pm weekdays), which stocks about 1200 magazines from around the world, and although loans cannot be made, you are free to sit down and read anything you please. It also has a coffee shop where you can enjoy a drink while you read.

Hamarikyū-teien
Often referred to in English as the Detached Palace Garden (¥300, 9 am to 5 pm), a visit can be combined either with a visit to Ginza or, via the Sumida-gawa Cruise, with a visit to Asakusa (see that section in this chapter). The garden has walks, ponds and tea houses.

Tsukiji Fish Market 築地市場
This is where all that seafood comes after it has been fished out of the sea and before it turns up as *sushi* and *sashimi*. The day begins very early, with the arrival of fish and its wholesale auctioning. The wholesale market is not open to the general public, which is probably a blessing, given that you'd have to be there before 5 am to see

the action. You are free to visit the outer market and wander around the wholesalers' and intermediaries' stalls that sell directly to restaurants, retail stores and other buyers. It is a fun place to visit, and you don't have to arrive *that* early: as long as you're there sometime before 10 am there'll be something going on. Watch out for your shoes – there's a lot of muck and water on the floor.

Hibiya-kōen 日比谷公園

If Ginza has left you yearning for greenery, retrace your steps along Harumi-dōri, back through Sukiyabashi Crossing to Hibiya-kōen. This was Tokyo's first Western-style park, and it makes for a pleasant break, especially if you head for the benches overlooking the pond on the park's eastern side. Also on the park's eastern side, about midway down, is a small restaurant where you can pause for coffee or ice cream.

Godzilla Statue ゴジラ像

This tiny statue, in Hibiya's cinema district, is Tokyo's tribute to the creature that destroyed the city so many times. The sign on the statue warns that we haven't heard the last of Godzilla – keep your eyes peeled.

AKIHABARA 秋葉原

Akihabara is Tokyo's discount electrical and electronics centre, with countless shops ranging from tiny specialist stores to electrical department stores. Nowhere in the world will you find such a range of electrical appliances, and you can easily spend half a day wandering from store to store. Some larger stores (Laox is a reliable option) have tax-free sections with export models for sale (don't forget to ask for duty-free).

While prices may be competitive with those you are used to at home, it's unusual to find prices that match those of dealers in Hong Kong or Singapore. You should be able to knock 10% off the marked prices by bargaining, though this is often not the case with the tax-free items in the bigger stores. To find the shops, take the Electric Town exit of Akihabara station. You'll see the sign on the platform if you come in on the JR Yamanote line.

UENO 上野

Ueno is one of the last places in Tokyo where the old Shitamachi spirit lingers on. Like Asakusa, it is a place where you can catch a glimpse of what life was like in the city before the economic miracle of the 1970s and 80s. The heart of Ueno is crusty old Ameya-yokochō Arcade, a bustling market that feels worlds away from the hyper-trendy shopping meccas of Shibuya and Harajuku. The main reason to visit Ueno, however, is Ueno-kōen, which has the highest concentration of museums and galleries anywhere in Japan. A trip to Ueno, perhaps paired with a jaunt to nearby Asakusa, is the perfect counterpoint to a day spent in ultra-modern Shinjuku.

Ueno-kōen 上野公園

Ueno Hill was the site of a last-ditch defence of the Tokugawa shogunate by about 2000 Tokugawa loyalists in 1868. They were duly dispatched by the imperial army, and the new Meiji government decreed that Ueno Hill would be transformed into Tokyo's first public park. Today, Ueno-kōen may not be the best of Tokyo's parks, but it certainly packs in more attractions than any of the others.

The park is famous as Tokyo's most popular site for *hanami* (blossom viewing) in early to mid-April. Of course, this doesn't mean that Ueno-kōen is the *best* place to see the blossoms (see Shinjuku-gyoen in the Shinjuku section later for an altogether quieter hanami spot). In addition to the cherry blossoms, check out the lotuses in the pond, Shinobazu-ike, at the southern end of the park. It's also worth noting that Ueno-kōen is the centre of Tokyo's surprisingly large population of homeless people; their blue tents fill almost every inch of available land in the northern reaches of the park.

Saigō Takamori Statue This slightly unusual statue of a samurai walking his dog, near the southern entrance to the park, is a favourite meeting place. Saigō Takamori started out supporting the Meiji Restoration but ended up ritually disembowelling himself in defeated opposition to it. The turnabout in his loyalties occurred when the Meiji government withdrew the powers of

TOKYO

UENO

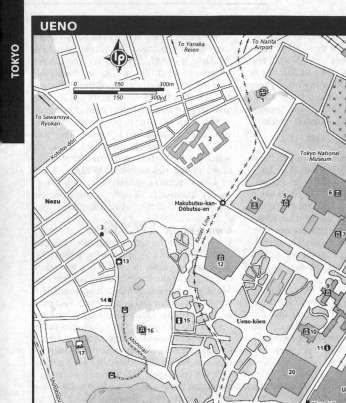

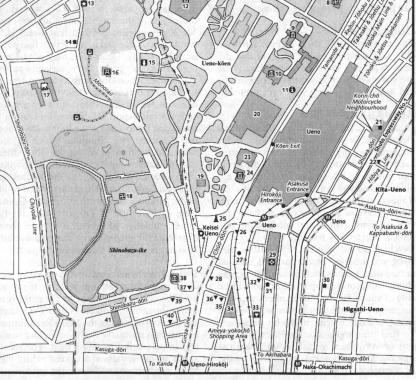

To Yanaka Reien

To Narita Airport

Kototoi-dōri

Uguisudani

0   150   300m
0   150   300yd

Tokugawa Shogun Cemetery

Tokyo National Museum

To Sawanoya Ryokan

Kototoi-dōri

Nezu

Hakubutsu-kan-Dōbutsu-en

Keisei Line

Keihin-Tōhoku Lines
Takasaki & Jōetsu Lines
Tōhoku Main Line & Jōban Line
Tōhoku & Jōetsu Shinkansen

Ueno-kōen

Yamanote &

Korin-chō Motorcycle Neighbourhood

Monorail

Ueno

Shinobazu-dōri

Shōwa-dōri
Shuto Expressway No.1

Hibiya Line

Kōen Exit

Kita-Ueno

Chiyoda Line

Asakusa Entrance

Hirokōji Entrance

Asakusa-dōri

Ueno

Ueno

To Asakusa & Kappabashi-dōri

Keisei Ueno

Chūō-dōri

Shinobazu-ike

Higashi-Ueno

Shinobazu-dōri

Ginza Line

Ameya-yokochō Shopping Area

Kasuga-dōri

To Kanda

Ueno-Hirokōji

To Akihabara

Kasuga-dōri

Naka-Okachimachi

UENO

PLACES TO STAY

3 Ryokan Katsutarō 旅館勝太郎
14 Suigetsu Hotel Ōgaisō 水月ホテル鴎外荘
21 Hotel Green Capital ホテルグリーンキャピタＢ 侠
30 Hotel Sun Targas ホテルサンターガス
31 Ueno Kineya Hotel 上野きめやホテル
41 Hotel Parkside ホテルパークサイド

PLACES TO EAT

22 Maguroyasan まぐろ家さん
26 Pronto プロント
28 Ganko Sushi がんこ寿司
32 Ueno Yabu Soba 上匁絎蕎麦
35 Doutor Coffee
36 Samrat サムラート
37 McDonald's
39 Izu-ei 伊豆栄
40 Musashino 武蔵野

OTHER

1 Kanei-ji 寛永寺
2 Tokyo University of Fine Arts 東京芸術大学
4 Gallery of Hōryūji Treasures 法隆寺宝物館
5 Hyōkei-kan 表慶館
6 Tokyo National Museum Main Hall 東京国立博物館本館
7 Gallery of Eastern Antiquities 東洋館
8 Rinnō-ji 輪王寺
9 National Science Museum 国立科学博物館
10 National Museum of Western Art 国立西洋美術博物館
11 Ueno-kōen Information Centre 上野公園インフォメーションセンター
12 Tokyo Metropolitan Museum of Art 東京都美術館
13 Police 交番
15 Five-Storeyed Pagoda 五重塔
16 Tōshō-gū 東照宮
17 Ueno Zoo 上野動物園
18 Benzaiten 弁財天
19 Kiyomizu Kannon-dō 清水観音堂
20 Tokyo Metropolitan Festival Hall 東京文化会館
23 Japan Art Academy 芸術院会館
24 Ueno-no Mori Art Museum 上野の森美術館
25 Saigō Takamori Statue 西郷隆盛像
27 Ameya-yokochō Arcade アメヤ横丁
29 Marui Department Store 丸井百貨店
33 Warrior Celt
34 Ameyoko Centre Building アメヨコセンタービル
38 Shitamachi History Museum 下町風俗資料館

the military class to which he belonged. See the 'Saigō Takamori' boxed text under Kagoshima in the Kyūshū chapter.

Tokyo National Museum The Tokyo National Museum (9 am to 4.30 pm, to 8 pm Friday from April to September, closed Monday) is the one museum in Tokyo that is worth going out of your way to visit. Not only is it Japan's largest museum, housing some 87,000 items, it also has the world's largest collection of Japanese art. Only a portion of the museum's huge collection is displayed at any one time. Entry is ¥420 (free on the second Saturday of each month).

The museum has four galleries, the most important of which is the Main Hall (Honkan). It's straight ahead as you enter, and houses a very impressive collection of Japanese art, from sculpture and swords to lacquerware and calligraphy. The Gallery of Eastern Antiquities (Tōyō kan), to the right of the ticket booth, has a collection of art and archaeological finds from all of Asia east of Egypt. The Hyōkei-kan, to the left of the ticket booth, has a collection of Japanese archaeological finds. There is a room devoted to artefacts once used by the Ainu, the indigenous people of Japan who now live only in Hokkaidō.

Finally, there is the newly reopened Gallery of Hōryūji Treasures (Hōryūji Hōmotsu-kan), which houses some of Japan's most important Buddhist artworks, all from Hōryū-ji in Nara.

A nice way to cap off a visit to the museum is with a stroll in the Tokugawa Shōgun Cemetery, behind the museum.

Tokyo Metropolitan Museum of Art
The Metropolitan Museum of Art (free, 9 am to 5 pm, closed Monday) has a number of different galleries that run temporary displays (admission varies) of contemporary Japanese art. Galleries feature both Western-style art such as oil paintings and Japanese-style art such as *sumi-e* (ink brush) and *ikebana* (flower arrangement). Unfortunately, there's a lot of wasted space here and exhibits are not always up to snuff.

National Science Museum
This museum (¥420, 9 am to 4.30 pm, closed Monday) is not particularly special: displays are limited in scope and quality, and can be covered in less than an hour. However, excellent special exhibitions are often held, and these cost extra (usually around ¥500). Signs out front of the museum announce special exhibits; you can also ask at the park information centre. Most regular exhibits aren't labelled in English, though you can buy a pamphlet (a few hundred yen). At least stop by to see the life-sized model of the blue whale outside.

National Museum of Western Art
The National Museum of Western Art (¥420, 9.30 am to 4.30 pm, closed Monday) has an impressive, though rather indifferently displayed, permanent collection. It is also frequently host to special exhibits (you may have to pay extra) on loan from other museums of international repute. There is a special emphasis on the French Impressionists, with originals by Rodin, including *The Thinker*, and paintings and sketches by, among others, Renoir and Monet. It's worth checking in the *Tokyo Journal* to see if the special exhibit of the moment warrants a visit.

Shitamachi History Museum
The Shitamachi History Museum (¥200, 9.30 am to 4.30 pm, closed Monday) re-creates life in Edo's Shitamachi, the plebeian downtown quarter of old Tokyo. Exhibits include a merchant's shop, sweet shop, the home and business of a copper-boiler maker, and a tenement house; take off your shoes and look around inside. Upstairs, the museum exhibits utensils and items from the daily life of the average Shitamachi resident. You are free to pick many of them up and have a closer look.

Ueno Zoo
Established in 1882, Ueno Zoo (9.30 am to 4.30 pm, closed Monday) was the first of its kind in Japan. It's a good outing if you have children; otherwise, it can be safely dropped from a busy itinerary. The zoo is very popular with Japanese visitors for its pandas (not on view on Friday). Entry is ¥500 for adults, ¥200 for children junior high-school age and up and free for younger kids.

Tōshō-gū
Dating from 1651 this shrine, like its counterpart in Nikkō, is dedicated to Tokugawa Ieyasu, who unified Japan. You'll find more information under History in the Facts about Japan chapter. The shrine (¥200, 9 am to 5.30 pm, to 4.30 pm in winter) is one of the few extant early-Edo structures, having fortunately survived Tokyo's innumerable disasters.

Ameya-yokochō Arcade アメヤ横丁
Ameya-yokochō was famous as a black-market district after WWII, and is still a lively shopping area where many bargains can be found. Shopkeepers are much less restrained than elsewhere in Tokyo, attracting customers with raucous cries that rattle down the crowded alleyways like the trains overhead. Look for the big *romaji* (Japanese roman script) sign opposite Ueno station.

AROUND UENO 上野周辺
Korin-chō Motorcycle Neighbourhood 上野バイク街
See the Motorcycle section of the Getting Around chapter for information about the busy Korin-chō area, or Ueno Baiku-gai (Bike St), the motorcycle shopping centre in the shadow of Ueno station. There's an interesting motorcycle museum on the 3rd and 4th floors of the clothing shop of Corin Motors.

Kappabashi-dōri かっぱ橋通り
At Tawaramachi, just two stops from Ueno subway station on the Ginza line, is

Kappabashi-dōri. This is where you go if you're setting up a restaurant. You can get flags that advertise the food in your restaurant, personalised cushions, crockery and, most importantly, all the plastic food you'll ever need. Whether you want a plate of spaghetti bolognaise with an upright fork, a plastic steak and chips, a lurid pizza or a bowl of *rāmen* (Chinese-style noodles), it's all there. Items aren't particularly cheap, but some of them are very convincing and could make unusual Japanese mementos.

Kappabashi-dōri is five minutes' walk north-west of any of Tawaramachi subway station's exits; look for the giant chef's head atop the Niomi utensil shop.

ASAKUSA 浅草

Long considered the heart of old Shitamachi, Asakusa is an interesting area to explore on foot. The big attraction is the temple, Sensō-ji, also known as Asakusa Kannon-dō. In Edo times, Asakusa was a halfway stop between the city and its most infamous pleasure district, Yoshiwara. In time, however, Asakusa developed into a pleasure quarter in its own right, eventually becoming the centre for that most loved of Edo entertainments, kabuki. In the very shadow of Sensō-ji a fairground spirit prevailed and a whole range of very secular entertainments were provided, from kabuki theatres to brothels.

When Japan ended its self-imposed isolation with the commencement of the Meiji Restoration, it was in Asakusa that the first cinemas opened, in Asakusa that the first music halls appeared and in Asakusa's Teikoku Gekijo (Imperial Theatre) that Western opera was first performed before Japanese audiences. It was also in Asakusa that another Western cultural import – the striptease – was introduced. A few clubs still operate in the area.

Unfortunately, Asakusa never quite recovered from the bombing at the end of WWII. Although Sensō-ji was rebuilt, other areas of Tokyo assumed Asakusa's pleasure-district role. Asakusa may be one of the few areas of Tokyo to have retained something of the spirit of Shitamachi, but the bright lights have shifted elsewhere – notably to Shinjuku.

Sensō-ji 浅草寺

Sensō-ji enshrines a golden image of Kannon (the Buddhist Goddess of Mercy) which, according to legend, was miraculously fished out of the nearby Sumida-gawa by two fishermen in 628. The image has remained on the spot ever since, through successive rebuildings of the temple. The present temple dates from 1950.

If you approach Sensō-ji from Asakusa subway station, the entrance is via Kaminari-mon (Thunder Gate). The gate's protector gods are Fujin, the god of wind, on the right; and Raijin, the god of thunder, on the left.

Straight ahead is Nakamise-dōri, the temple precinct's shopping street, where everything from tourist trinkets to genuine Edo-style crafts is sold. There's even a shop selling wigs to be worn with kimono. Try the *sembei* (crackers) that a few shops specialise in – you'll have to queue as they are very popular with Japanese visitors.

Nakamise-dōri leads to the main temple compound. Whether the ancient image of Kannon actually exists is a secret – it's not on public display. Not that this stops a steady stream of worshippers making their way to the top of the stairs to bow and clap. In front of the temple is a large incense cauldron: the smoke is said to bestow health and you will see visitors rubbing it into their bodies through their clothes.

Dembō-in Garden 伝法院

To the left of the temple precinct is Dembō-in (Dembō Garden). Although it is not open to the public, it is possible to obtain a pass by calling in to the main office (☎ 3842-0181) to the left of Sensō-ji's Five-Storeyed Pagoda. The garden is one of Tokyo's best, containing a picturesque pond and a replica of a famous Kyoto tea-house. It's closed on Sunday, holidays and whenever a ceremony is being held in the garden. To avoid disappointment, it's best to call a few days in advance to see if it will be open when you visit.

TOKYO

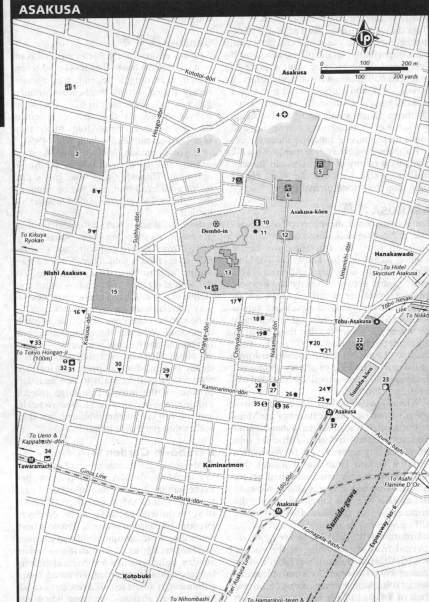

ASAKUSA

Asakusa

Kototoi-dōri

Hisago-dōri

Asakusa-kōen

Dembō-in

Hanakawado

To Kikuya
Ryokan

To Hotel
Skycourt Asakusa

Nishi Asakusa

Sushiya-dōri

Tōbu-Iesaki
Line

To Nikkō

Tōbu-Asakusa

Kokusai-dōri

Orange-dōri

Chinyoko-dōri

Nakamise-dōri

Umamichi-dōri

Sumida-kōen

To Tokyo Hongan-ji
(100m)

Kaminarimon-dōri

Asakusa

To Ueno &
Kappabashi-dōri

Tawaramachi

Ginza Line

Kaminarimon

To Asahi
Flamme D'Or

Asakusa-dōri

Asakusa

Komagata-bashi

Azuma-bashi

Sumida-gawa

Expressway-No-6

Edo-dōri

Kotobuki

Toei Asakusa Line

To Nihombashi

To Hamarikyū-teien &
Hinode Pier

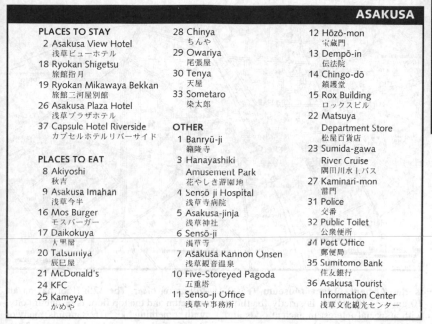

ASAKUSA

PLACES TO STAY
2 Asakusa View Hotel
浅草ビューホテル
18 Ryokan Shigetsu
旅館指月
19 Ryokan Mikawaya Bekkan
旅館三河屋別館
26 Asakusa Plaza Hotel
浅草プラザホテル
37 Capsule Hotel Riverside
カプセルホテルリバーサイド

PLACES TO EAT
8 Akiyoshi
秋吉
9 Asakusa Imahan
浅草今半
16 Mos Burger
モスバーガー
17 Daikokuya
大黒屋
20 Tatsumiya
辰巳屋
21 McDonald's
24 KFC
25 Kameya
かめや

28 Chinya
ちんや
29 Owariya
尾張屋
30 Tenya
天屋
33 Sometaro
染太郎

OTHER
1 Banryū-ji
籍隆寺
3 Hanayashiki
Amusement Park
花やしき遊園地
4 Sensō ji Hospital
浅草寺病院
5 Asakusa-jinja
浅草神社
6 Sensō-ji
浅草寺
7 Asakusa Kannon Onsen
浅草観音温泉
10 Five-Storeyed Pagoda
五重塔
11 Senso-ji Office
浅草寺事務所

12 Hōzō-mon
宝蔵門
13 Dempō-in
伝法院
14 Chingo-dō
鎮護堂
15 Rox Building
ロックスビル
22 Matsuya
Department Store
松屋百貨店
23 Sumida-gawa
River Cruise
隅田川水上バス
27 Kaminari-mon
雷門
31 Police
交番
32 Public Toilet
公衆便所
34 Post Office
郵便局
35 Sumitomo Bank
住友銀行
36 Asakusa Tourist
Information Center
浅草文化観光センター

Sumida-gawa Cruise
隅田川クルーズ

It may not be the most scenic river cruise you've ever experienced, but the *suijō basu* (water bus) is a great way to get to or from Asakusa.

The cruise departs from next to the bridge, Azuma-bashi, in Asakusa and goes to Hamarikyū-teien (see that entry under Ginza, earlier) and Hinode Pier. Probably the best option is to buy a ticket to Hamarikyū-teien (¥620; you'll have to pay an additional ¥300 entry fee for the garden). After looking around the garden it is possible to walk into Ginza in about 10 to 15 minutes. Boats leave every 20 to 30 minutes from 9.50 am to 6.15 pm. The fare to Hinode Pier is ¥660.

IKEBUKURO 池袋

Traditionally Shinjuku's poor cousin, bawdy Ikebukuro has been treated to something of a facelift in recent years. Agreed, it shouldn't be high on a busy itinerary, but

it's worth noting that its attractions include two of the world's largest department stores (Seibu and Tōbu – the world's largest is Yokohama Seibu), one of the tallest buildings in Asia (the Sunshine City building), the second-busiest station in Tokyo, the world's largest automobile showroom (Toyota Amlux), and the escalator experience of a lifetime (Tokyo Metropolitan Art Space). Like Shinjuku, Ikebukuro divides into an east side and a west side.

East Side 東池袋
Sunshine City Billed as a 'city in a building', Sunshine City is essentially 60 floors of office space and shopping malls, with a few overpriced cultural and entertainment options thrown in. If you've got ¥620 to burn, you can take a lift to the lookout (10 am to 6 pm) on the 60th floor and gaze out on Tokyo's murky skyline.

Not in the Sunshine City building itself, but in the Bunka Kaikan of Sunshine City,

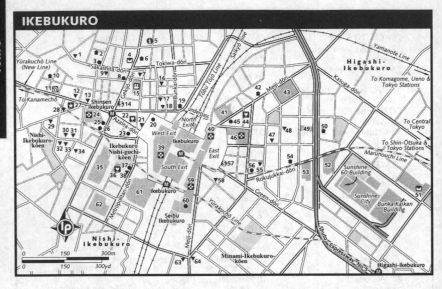

is the **Ancient Orient Museum** (¥500, 10 am to 4.30 pm). It is strictly for those with a special interest in ancient odds and ends such as coins and beads.

Also of interest to some might be **Sunshine Planetarium** (¥800) and **Sunshine International Aquarium** (¥1600).

Toyota Amlux Even if you are not an auto buff, Toyota Amlux (free, 11 am to 8 pm Tuesday to Saturday, 10 am to 7.30 pm Sunday and public holidays) may be worth a visit, particularly on a rainy day. There are auto display areas, features on auto production, good historical displays, and a unique 'sensurround', smellorama cinema. But best of all is the building itself, with its subterranean lighting and ambient sound effects.

Department Stores Just why Ikebukuro should have two of the world's largest department stores is a mystery. **Tōbu** is the bigger of the two, but **Seibu** (for many years the world's biggest) still feels bigger and busier. You can easily spend an entire afternoon just wandering around the basement food-floor of Seibu sampling the little

tidbits on offer. The 12th floor has an art museum and the top floor is restaurant city, with something like 50 restaurants, many of them offering great lunch specials. Tōbu closes on varying days twice monthly, Seibu on Thursday.

Art Galleries In the annexe of the Seibu department store is **Seibu Art Gallery**, which has changing art exhibits, usually of fairly high standard. In Tōbu's Metropolitan Plaza is **Tōbu Art Museum**, which also features changing art exhibits. Admission to both galleries varies according to the exhibit.

West Side 西池袋

There's not really a lot to see on the west side, but anyone who hasn't been to Ikebukuro for a couple of years should check out the area between Tokyo Metropolitan Art Space and the southern end of the station. **Metropolitan Plaza** is packed with classy boutiques, restaurants (8th floor) and a massive HMV (6th floor – great browsing). Just across the road is the **Spice 2** building, which does a repeat performance of Metropolitan Plaza.

IKEBUKURO

PLACES TO STAY
2 Kimi Ryokan
  貴美旅館
6 Ikebukuro
  Royal Hotel
  池袋ロイヤルホテル
10 House Ikebukuro
  ハウス池袋
19 Hotel Sun City
  Ikebukuro
  ホテルサンシティ池袋
42 Hotel Sunroute
  Ikebukuro
  ホテルサンルート池袋
49 Hotel Grand City
  ホテルグランドシティー
50 Ark Hotel
  アークホテル
54 Hotel Theatre
  ホテルシアター
62 Hotel Metropolitan
  ホテルメトロポリタン

PLACES TO EAT
1 Taiwan Hsiao Tiao
  台湾小調
7 Tonerian
  舎人庵
9 Sushi Kazu
  寿司和
12 Doutor Coffee
  ドトールコーヒー
13 Subway
  サブウェイ
16 Doutor Coffee;
  Tenka Ippin Rāmen
  ドトールコーヒー；
  天下一品ラーメン
17 Matsukaze
  松風
18 KFC; Yoshinoya
  KFC；吉野屋
21 McDonald's
  マクドナルド
28 Myun
  ミュン
29 Starbucks
  スターバックス

30 Akiyoshi
  秋吉
31 Capricciosa
  カプリチョーザ
32 Malaychan
  マレーチャン
33 Chez Kibeau
  シェ・キーボウ
34 Tonbo
  とんぼ
37 Cafe du Monde
  カフェドゥモンドゥ
47 Tapa
  タパ
48 Oriental Kitchen
  オリエンタルキッチン
55 Komazushi
  こま寿司
58 Yamabuki
  山吹
63 McDonald's
  マクドナルド
64 Mawaru Sushi Hana Kan
  まわる寿し花館

OTHER
3 Pharmacy
  薬局
4 Ikebukuro Post Office
  池袋郵便局
5 Kimi Information Center
  貴美インフォメーション
  センター
8 Pachinko Parlor
  パチンコパーラ
11 Hard Internet Cafe
  T and T
  ハードインターネット
  カフェ T and T
14 Sumitomo Bank
  住友銀行
15 Cinema Rosa
  シネマロサ
20 Discount Ticket Shop
  格安チケット売り場
22 Bobby's Bar
  ボビーズバー
23 Marui Field Sports Store
  丸井フィールド池袋

24 Marui
  Department Store
  丸井百貨店
25 Virgin Megastore
  バージンメガストアー
26 Kinko's
  キンコーズ
27 Police
  交番
35 Tokyo Metropolitan
  Art Space
  東京芸術会館
36 The Dubliners
  ザダブリナーズ
38 Spice2
  スパイス2
39 Tōbu Department Store
  東武百貨店
40 Parco Department Store
  パルコ
41 Bic Camera (main store)
  ビックカメラ（本店）
43 Toshima-ku Office
  豊島区役所
44 The Black Sheep
  ザブラックシープ
45 Bic Personal
  Computer Store
  ビックカメラパソコン館
46 Mitsukoshi
  Department Store
  三越百貨店
51 Toshima Post Office
  豊島郵便局
52 Toyota Amlux
  トヨタアムラックス
53 Tōkyū Hands
  東急ハンズ
56 Bic Camera
  ビックカメラ
57 Fuji Bank
  富士銀行
59 Seibu
  Department Store
  西武百貨店
60 Seibu Art Gallery
  西武ギャラリー
61 Metropolitan Plaza
  メトロポリタンプラザ

Tokyo Metropolitan Art Space Part of the 'Tokyo Renaissance' plan launched by the Department of Education, this huge cultural bunker was plonked down just where Tokyo needed it most – on Ikebukuro's west side. Designed to host performance art, the building has four halls. Those without a ticket for anything should treat themselves to the soaring escalator ride (it's said to be the world's longest escalator) – it doesn't get much more exciting than this in Ikebukuro!

AROUND IKEBUKURO
池袋周辺
Rikugi-en 六義園

Just three stops from Ikebukuro, near JR Komagome station (Yamanote line), Rikugi-en (¥300, 9 am to 5 pm) is one of Tokyo's better gardens. It's a 10-hectare (25-acre) Edo-style *kaiyū*, or 'many pleasure' garden, built around a tranquil, carp-filled pond. The landscaped views here are said to evoke famous scenes from Chinese and Japanese literature. The garden was established in the late 17th century by Yanagisawa Yoshiyasu and, after falling into disuse, was restored by the founder of the Mitsubishi group, Iwasaki Yataro.

SHINJUKU 新宿

If you had only a day in Tokyo and wanted to dive headfirst into the modern Japanese phenomenon, Shinjuku would be the place to go. Nearly everything that makes Tokyo interesting rubs elbows here: high-class department stores, discount shopping arcades, flashing neon, government offices, swarming push-and-shove crowds, street-side video screens, stand-up noodle bars, hostess clubs, tucked-away shrines and sleazy strip bars.

Shinjuku is a sprawling business, commercial and entertainment centre that never lets up. Every day approximately two million people pass through the station alone, making it one of the busiest in the world. On the western side of the station is Tokyo's highest concentration of skyscrapers and, presiding over them, Tange Kenzō's Tokyo Metropolitan Government Offices – massive awe-inspiring structures. The eastern side of the station – the more interesting by far – is a warren of department stores, restaurants, boutiques, neon and sleaze.

East Side 東新宿

Shinjuku's east side is an area to wander through and get lost in rather than an area in which to search out particular sights.

Kabuki-chō Tokyo's most notorious red-light district lies east of Seibu Shinjuku station, north of Yasukuni-dōri. This is one of the world's more imaginative red-light areas, with 'soaplands' (massage parlours), love hotels, peep shows, pink cabarets ('pink' is the Japanese equivalent of 'blue' in English), porno-video booths and strip shows that involve audience participation. The streets here are all crackling neon and drunken salarymen. High-pitched female voices wail out invitations to enter their establishments through distorting sound-systems, and Japanese punks earn a few extra yen passing out advertisements for karaoke boxes.

Most of what goes on is very much off-limits to foreigners, but it's still an interesting area for a stroll. If you do want to get a peek at the action, try one of the strip bars that deploy foreign touts on the street – count on at least ¥7000 for a show and a drink or two.

Kabuki-chō is not wall-to-wall sex; there are also some very straight entertainment options, including cinemas and some good restaurants.

Hanazono-jinja Nestled in the shadow of Kabuki-chō is this quiet, unassuming shrine. It only takes around 10 minutes to stroll around the grounds, but it's a fine place to sit down and take a break. You hardly know you are in Shinjuku. The shrine is particularly pleasant when it's lit up in the evening.

Shinjuku-gyoen This park (¥200, 9 am to 4 pm, closed Monday) is one of Tokyo's best escapes and, at 57.6 hectares (144

SHINJUKU

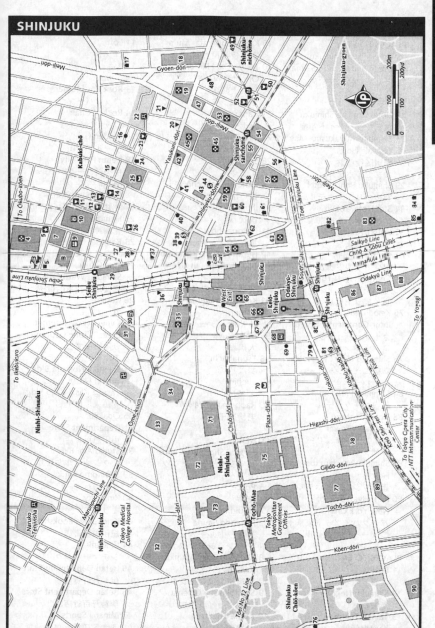

Gyoen-dōri

Meiji-dōri

Shinjuku-nichōme

Shinjuku-gyoen

200m
200yd

0 100

Kabuki-chō

Yasukuni-dōri

Meiji-dōri

Shinjuku-sanchōme

Shinjuku-sanchōme

To Ōkubo-eki

Shinjuku-dōri

Toei Shinjuku Line

Saikyō Line
Chūō & Sōbu Lines
Yamanote Line

Odakyū Line

To Ikebukuro

Seibu Shinjuku Line

Seibu
Shinjuku

Shinjuku

West
Exit

Shinjuku

Keiō-
Shinjuku

Odakyū-
Shinjuku

Shinjuku

South Exit

Shinjuku

Keiō Line

To Yoyogi

Ōme-kaidō

Marunouchi Line

Nishi-Shinjuku

Naruko
Tenjinsha

Nishi-Shinjuku

Tokyo Medical
College Hospital

Chūō-dōri

Plaza-dōri

Kōshū-kaidō

Kōshū-kaidō

Keiō Shin-sen Line

To Tokyo Opera City;
NTT Intercommunication
Center

Higashi-dōri

Nishi-
Shinjuku

Kita-dōri

Tochō-Mae

Tokyo
Metropolitan
Government
Offices

Gijidō-dōri

Tochō-dōri

Kōen-dōri

Toei No 12 Line

Shinjuku
Chūō-kōen

SHINJUKU

PLACES TO STAY

6 Green Plaza Shinjuku;
Green Plaza Ladies Sauna
グリーンプラザ新宿；
グリーンプラザ
レディースサウナ
17 Hotel Sun Lite Shinjuku
ホテルサンライト新宿
24 Shinjuku-Kuyakusho-Mae
Capsule Hotel
新宿区役所前
カプセルホテル
29 Shinjuku Prince Hotel
新宿プリンスホテル
31 Star Hotel Tokyo
スターホテル東京
32 Hilton Tokyo
ヒルトン東京
61 Central Hotel
セントラルホテル
74 Century Hyatt Tokyo
センチュリー
ハイアット東京
75 Keiō Plaza
Inter-Continental Hotel
京王プラザインター
コンチネンタルホテル
76 Shinjuku New City Hotel
新宿ニューシティー
ホテル
84 Shinjuku Park Hotel
新宿パークホテル
88 Hotel Century
Southern Tower
ホテルセンチュリー
サザンタワー
89 Shinjuku Washington
Hotel
新宿ワシントンホテル
90 Park Hyatt Tokyo;
New York Grill
パークハイアット東京；
ニューヨークグリル

PLACES TO EAT

1 Peking
北京
2 Shinjuku Negishi
新宿ねぎし
3 Tainan Taami
台南担仔麺

15 Kabukichō Yatai Mura
歌舞伎町屋台村
20 Tokyo Dai Hanten;
Oriental Wave
東京大飯店；
オリエンタルウェーブ
21 Canard
カナール
27 Ban Thai
バンタイ
28 Suzuya
すずや
36 Omoide Yokochō
思い出横丁
37 Ibuki
伊吹
41 El Borracho
エルブラッチョ
42 Isetan Kaikan; Kushinobō
伊勢丹会館；串の坊
48 Starbucks
スターバックス
51 Keika Kumamoto
Rāmen
桂花熊本ラーメン
56 Daikokuya
大黒屋
58 Tsunahachi
つな八
62 Suehiro
スエヒロ
80 Raobian Gyozakan
老伏鵝子館

OTHER

4 Hygeai Shopping Centre
ハイジヤショッピング
センター
5 Police
交番
7 Liquid Room;
Finlando Sauna
リキッドルーム；
フィンランドサウナ
8 Shinjuku Tōkyū Bunka
Kaikan
新宿東急文化センター
9 Shinjuku Joy Cinema
新宿ジョイシネマ
10 Koma Theatre
コマ劇場

11 Loft
ロフト
12 Asa
アサ
13 Rock Bar Mother
ロックバーマザー
14 Rockin' Chair
ロッキングチェアー
16 Golden Gai
ゴールデン街
18 Isetan Park City
伊勢丹パークシティー
19 Marui
Department Store
丸井百貨店
22 Hanazono-jinja
花園神社
23 Bon's
ボンズ
25 Post Office;
Shinjuku Ward Office
郵便局；新宿区役所
26 Garam
ガラム
30 Cyber Scholé Internet
Café; T-Zone Computers
サイバースコレ；
Tゾーン
33 Shinjuku Nomura Bldg
新宿野村ビル
34 Yasuda Kasai Kaijo Bldg
安田火災海上ビル
35 Odakyū
Department Store
小田急百貨店
38 Studio Alta Bldg
スタジオアルタビル
39 Sumitomo Bank
住友銀行
40 Kirin City
キリンシティー
43 Kinokuniya Bookshop
紀伊国屋書店
44 Citibank
シティーバンク
45 Isetan Department Store
伊勢丹百貨店
46 Isetan Department Store
伊勢丹百貨店
47 Minami Sports
ミナミスポーツ

acres), one of Tokyo's largest parks. It dates back to 1906 and was designed as a European-style park, though a Japanese garden is also included. Other features are a French garden, a hothouse containing tropical plants and, near the hothouse, a pond with giant carp.

West Side 西新宿

Shinjuku's west side is mainly administrative, but the area behind the Keiō department store is home to **Tokyo's largest camera stores**: Yodobashi Camera and Sakuraya Camera. Yodobashi Camera has practically everything you could possibly want that relates to photography, all at very reasonable prices. It even has a limited selection of second-hand photographic equipment.

Elsewhere, the attractions of Shinjuku's west side are mainly the interiors of buildings and the observation floors of the impressive Tokyo Metropolitan Government Offices.

Metropolitan Government Offices
Known as Tokyo Tochō, these two adjoining buildings are worth a visit for their stunning architecture and for the great views from the twin observation floors (free, 9.30 am to 5.30 pm, to 7.30 pm weekends and holidays, closed Monday) of the 202m-tall No 1 building. On really clear days, you might even spot Fuji-san (Mt Fuji) to the west.

Despite its critics, most visitors are won over by the buildings' complex symmetry and computer-chip appearance. Particularly impressive is the spacious Citizen's Plaza in front of the No 1 building – more reminiscent of a Roman amphitheatre than anything Japanese.

To reach the No 1 building's observation floors, take one of the two 1st floor lifts.

Shinjuku NS Building The interior of this building is hollow, featuring a 1600 sq metre atrium illuminated by sunlight, which comes in through the glass roof. Overhead, at 110m, is a 'sky bridge'. The atrium itself features a

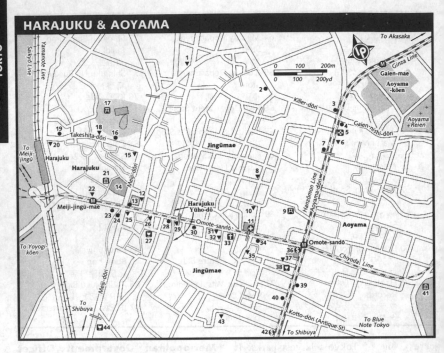

HARAJUKU & AOYAMA

29m-tall pendulum-clock that is said to be the largest in the world. The 29th and 30th floors have a large number of restaurants, all of which sport excellent views over Tokyo.

Shinjuku Sumitomo Building The Sumitomo Building bills itself as 'a building that's actually a city', a concept that the Japanese seem to find particularly appealing (Sunshine City in Ikebukuro – see under Ikebukuro's East Side, earlier – is another 'city' building). Like the Shinjuku NS Building, the Sumitomo Building has a hollow core. There is an observation platform (free) on the 51st floor.

Pentax Forum On the 1st floor of the Shinjuku Mitsui Building is Pentax Forum (free, 10.30 am to 6.30 pm), a must for photography buffs. The exhibition space has changing exhibits by photographers sponsored by Pentax. Undoubtedly the best part of Pentax Forum, however, is the vast array of Pentax cameras, lenses and other optical equipment on display. It is completely hands-on – you can snap away with the cameras and use the huge 1000mm lenses to look through the windows of the neighbouring buildings.

HARAJUKU & AOYAMA
原宿と青山

Harajuku and Aoyama are Tokyo in loafers. They're pleasant areas to stroll in and watch locals spend their money in boutiques and bistros. The big attraction for foreign visitors used to be the Sunday subculture parade at Yoyogi-kōen. The authorities have put a stop to that, and Yoyogi-kōen nowadays is just an average park. But Harajuku and Aoyama still have a lot going for them. Takeshita-dōri still swarms with bubble-gum teenagers shopping for illiterate T-shirts and fishnet stockings; Omote-sandō, with its alfresco cafes and boutiques, is still the closest Tokyo

HARAJUKU & AOYAMA

PLACES TO EAT
1 Mominoki House
モミノキハウス
6 Tony Roma's;
Doutor Coffee
トニーロマーズ；
ドトールコーヒー
8 Maisen
まい泉
10 Apetito
アペティート
12 Tacos del Amigo
タコスデルアミーゴ
15 Son of Dragon Chinese
Restaurant
龍の子
18 Shūtarō
しゅうたろう
20 Doutor Coffee
ドトールコーヒー
22 Stage Y2
ステージY2
25 Lotteria
ロッテリア
26 Cafe de Rope
カフェドロペ
29 Ferbecco; Vivre
ビブレ；フェルバッコ
31 Genroku
元禄
32 Bamboo Cafe
バンブー カフェ
35 Hiroba; Organic
Restaurant Home;
Crayon House
広場；自然食レストラン
HOME；クレヨンハウス

37 News Deli
ニューズデリ
43 Las Chicas
ラスチカス

OTHER
2 Watari-um
Gallery
リタリウム美術館
3 Bell Commons
ベルコモンズ
4 Japan Traditional
Craft Centre
日本伝統工芸センター
5 Daimaru Peacock
Department Store
大丸ピーコック百貨店
7 Cycland
リイクランド
9 Zenkō-ji
善光寺
11 Itō Hospital
伊東病院
13 Gap
ギャップ
14 Laforet
ラフォーレ
16 Get Back
ゲットバック
17 Tōgō-jinja
東郷神社
19 Taurus Vintage
Clothing
21 Ota Memorial
Art Museum
大田記念美術館

23 Chicago Thrift Shop
シカゴ
24 Condomania
コンドマニア
27 Oh God; Zest
オーガット；ゼスト
28 Kiddyland
キティーランド
30 Oriental Bazaar
オリエンタルバザール
33 Tokyo Union Church
東京ユニオンチャーチ
34 Hanae Mori Building;
Citibank;
Le Papillon de Paris;
Antique Mall
森英恵ビル；
シティバンク；
ルパピ゚インドゥパリ；
骨董街
36 Fuji Bank
富士銀行
38 Mix
ミックス
39 Spiral Bldg
スパイラルビル
40 Kinokuniya
International
Supermarket
紀ノ国屋
41 Nezu Fine Art
Museum
根津美術館
42 Citibank
シティバンク
44 Crocodile
クロコダイル

gets to Paris; the bistro alleys of Aoyama sport some of the best international cuisine in town; and Meiji-jingū is Tokyo's most splendid shrine.

Meiji-jingū 明治神宮
Completed in 1920, the shrine was built in memory of Emperor Meiji and Empress Shōken, under whose rule Japan ended its long isolation from the outside world. Unfortunately, like much else in Tokyo, the shrine was destroyed in the bombing at the end of WWII. Rebuilding was completed in 1958.

Meiji-jingū might be a reconstruction of the original but, unlike so many of Japan's postwar reconstructions, it is altogether authentic. The shrine itself was built with Japanese cypress, while the cypress for the huge *torii* (gates) came from Alishan in Taiwan. Entry is free.

Meiji-jingū-neien This garden (¥500, 9 am to 4.30 pm) offers peaceful strolls, being almost deserted on weekdays. It's particularly beautiful in June, when the irises are in bloom.

Meiji-jingū Treasure Museum As you approach Meiji-jingū, there are so many signs indicating the way to the treasure museum (¥500, 9 am to 4.30 pm, closed on the third Friday of each month) that you tend to feel obliged to go there. In fact, the collection of items from the lives of the emperor and empress is a minor attraction. It includes official garments, portraits and other imperial odds and ends.

Yoyogi-kōen 代々木公園

This is not one of Tokyo's best but, at 53.2 hectares (133 acres), its wooded grounds make for a relaxing walk. The Sunday performances of live music, mime and dance are now a thing of the past, though two or three bands may set up of an afternoon, weather permitting.

Ota Memorial Art Museum 太田記念美術館

The Ota Memorial Art Museum (¥500, 10.30 am to 5.30 pm, closed Monday and from the 27th to the end of each month) has an excellent collection of *ukiyo-e* (woodblock prints) and offers a good opportunity to see works by Japanese masters of the art, including Hiroshige. Unfortunately, space is limited and not much of the collection can be displayed. There is an extra charge for special exhibits.

Nezu Fine Art Museum 根津美術館

This museum (¥1000, 9.30 am to 4.30 pm, closed Monday) houses a well-known collection of Japanese art including paintings, calligraphy and sculpture. Also on display are Chinese and Korean art exhibits, and teahouses where tea ceremonies are performed. The exhibits are well displayed and of high quality, though rather small in number. However, the reason many folks visit this museum is to savour its wonderful garden, which contains a pond and several teahouses.

Galleries

Aoyama is packed with tiny galleries, most of which are free. Up Killer-dōri, in particular, look out for **Watari-um** (11 am to 7 pm, closed Monday), an adventuristic display space with a great art bookshop and probably the best supply of postcards in Tokyo. Exhibits are advertised in the lobby/store area and entry averages ¥700. The futuristic **Spiral Garden** (11 am to 8 pm) features changing exhibits, shows, dining and live music.

Kotto-dōri, or 'Antique Street' as it's called in the tourist literature, is a good place to seek out both galleries and souvenirs.

Aoyama Reien 青山霊園

Better known as Aoyama Botchi, this cemetery is perfect for a stroll and provides a nice break from the crowds of Omote-sandō and nearby Roppongi. It's also a good alternative to Ueno-kōen during hanami season.

SHIBUYA 渋谷

Shibuya is a bustling, youth-oriented shopping district where its easy to get the feeling that everyone over the age of 35 has been sent back to Ueno or Ikebukuro from the station. Like Shinjuku, Shibuya is not exactly rich in sights but it is a good area to stroll around and there's some of the best department-store browsing to be had in all Tokyo. You may want to avoid the area on weekends, when the streets are jammed with fashionable Tokyo kids.

Hachiko Statue ハチ公像

If you leave JR Shibuya station by the north-west (Hachiko) exit, you'll see one of Shibuya's main sights and the exit's namesake: a statue of the dog Hachiko. The story of this dog is rather touching: in the 1920s, a professor who lived near Shibuya station kept a small Akita dog, who would come to the station every day to await his master's return. The professor died in 1925, but the dog continued to show up and wait at the station until his own death 11 years later. The poor dog's faithfulness was not lost on the Japanese, and they built a statue to honour his memory.

Tobacco & Salt Museum
たばこと塩の博物館

This small museum (¥100, 10 am to 6 pm, closed Monday) has some fairly interesting exhibits detailing the history of tobacco and the methods of salt production practised in premodern Japan (Japan has no salt mines and until recently harvested salt from the sea). As usual, there's little in the way of English explanations, but a lot of the material is self-explanatory.

TEPCO Electric Energy Museum
電力館

Folks with kids in tow and an interest in electric power might want to stop by the TEPCO Electric Energy Museum (Denryoku-kan). It may be seven floors of advertising for Tokyo Electric Power, but the displays are well presented and cover a lot of ground. Anything and everything associated with electricity gets the treatment. Admission is free (10 am to 6 pm, closed Wednesday).

Goto Planetarium
五島プラネタリウム

The Gotō Planetarium (¥900/500 adults/children) is directly to the east of Shibuya station, on the 8th floor of the Tōkyū Bunka Kaikan cinema complex. Its great drawback is the fact that it is all in Japanese. All the same, the heavens projected onto the 20m-high overhead dome look very impressive. There are generally six one-hour showings (11.20 am to 7.10 pm weekdays, 10.30 am to 6 pm weekends, closed Monday).

Love Hotel Hill

The area around the top of Dōgen-zaka hill is probably the world capital of love hotels. There are love hotels to suit all tastes, from miniature Gothic castles to Middle-Eastern temples (and wait – these are just the buildings – the rooms are even more varied). It's OK to wander in and take a look at the screen with illuminated pictures of the various rooms available.

This area is gradually being invaded by other entertainment options such as al-fresco cafes, restaurants, performance halls and so on. **Dr Jeekhan's** is an upmarket video-game parlour, of a kind that is quite common in Tokyo and elsewhere nowadays. There are two popular nightclubs in the same building (see Shibuya under Bars & Clubs in the Entertainment section, later). Just down the road is the On Air Theatre (east and west branches are on either side of the road), which has a streetside cafe.

EBISU & DAIKANYAMA
恵比寿と代官山

Ebisu and Daikanyama are pleasant alternatives to the crowds and madness of nearby Shibuya and Shinjuku. Daikanyama, in particular, is a great spot for a casual afternoon stroll, with its almost Western ambience and abundant sidewalk cates. However, most folks come to Ebisu and Daikanyama by night to sample some of Tokyo's better clubs and bars. If you do come during the day, most sights worth seeing are in the new Ebisu Garden Place, easily reached from JR Ebisu station by an aerial walkway.

Ebisu Garden Place
恵比寿ガーデンプレイス

This is a complex of shops, restaurants and a 39-floor tower, surrounded by an open mall area – perfect for hanging out on warmer days. Garden Place also features the headquarters of Sapporo Breweries, which contains the **Beer Museum Yebisu** (free, 10 am to 6 pm, closed Monday). There are lots of good exhibits, the best of which is the 'Tasting Lounge', where you can sample Sapporo's various brews in a pleasant space decorated with rare European beer steins (beer is ¥200 a glass).

There are lots of outdoor cafes scattered around the complex. If you're hungry, most serve light meals as well. The restaurants on the 38th and 39th floors of **Ebisu Garden Place Tower** offer excellent views.

Tokyo Metropolitan Museum of Photography
Japan's first large-scale museum devoted entirely to photography

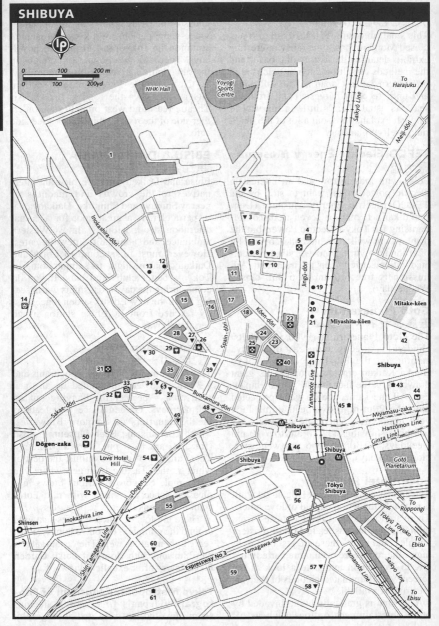

SHIBUYA

0   100   200 m
0   100   200yd

To Harajuku

NHK Hall

Yoyogi Sports Centre

Inokashira-dōri

1

2
3
6
5
4
7
8   9
10
13   12
11
14
15   16   17
18
Kōen-dōri
22
28   27   26
24   25   23
29
30
31   35   38   39   40
33   34   36   37
32
Spain-dōri
Bunkamura-dōri
49   48   47
Sakae-dōri
Dōgen-zaka
50
Love Hotel Hill   54
51   53
52
55
Shinsen
Inokashira Line
60
59
61
Shin-Tamagawa Line
Expressway No 3
Tamagawa-dōri

Jingū-dōri
19
20
21   Miyashita-kōen
Yamanote Line
41
45
46   Shibuya

Saikyō Line
Meiji-dōri

Mitake-kōen
42
Shibuya
43   44
Miyamasu-zaka
Hanzōmon Line
Ginza Line
Shibuya
Gotō Planetarium
Tōkyū Shibuya
56
To Roppongi
Tōkyū Tōyoko Line
To Ebisu
Yamanote Line
Saikyō Line
57
58
To Ebisu

SHIBUYA

PLACES TO STAY

7 Shibuya Tōbu Hotel
渋谷東武ホテル
43 Shibuya Business Hotel
渋谷ビジネスホテル
45 Shibuya Tōkyū Inn
渋谷東急イン
61 Hotel Sun Route Shibuya
ホテルサンルート渋谷

PLACES TO EAT

3 Siam Thai
サイエムタイ
9 New York Kitchen
ニューヨークキッチン
10 Jūnikagetsu Restaurant
Building
月レストランビル
27 Ryūnohige
りゅうのひげ
30 Kushinobō
串の坊
34 Bougainvillea
ブーゲンビリア
37 Segufredo Zanetti
セゴフレートザネティ
39 Samrat
サムラート
42 Myōkō
妙高
48 Tamakyū
玉九
49 Reikyō
麗郷
57 Kantipur
カンティブール
58 Akiyoshi
秋吉
60 Tainan Taami
台南担仔麺

OTHER

1 NHK Broadcasting
Centre
ＮＨＫ放送センター
2 Eggman
エッグマン

4 Tepco Electric
Energy Museum
電力館
5 Marui One
Department Store
丸井ワールド
6 Tobacco & Salt Museum
たばこと塩の博物館
8 Frontier Shibuya
フロンティア渋谷
11 Parco Part II
パルコパート2
12 Cisco Records
シスコレコード
13 Manhattan Records
マンハッタンレコード
14 Kanze Nō-gakudō
観世能楽堂
15 Tōkyū Hands
東急ハンズ
16 Parco Part III
パルコパート3
17 Parco Part I
パルコパート1
18 The Gap
ギャップ
19 Doi Camera
カメラのドイ
20 Tower Records
タワーレコード
21 H.I.S. Travel
エイチアイエストラベル
22 Marui Department Store
丸井日貨店
23 Disney Store;
Humax Pavilion
ディズニーストアー；
ヒューマックス
パビリオン
24 Seibu Seed
西武ＳＥＥＤ
25 Loft Department Store;
Wave Record Shop
ロフト；
ウェーブレコード
26 Police
交番
28 The Beam; Inti Shibuya
ザビーム；
インティ渋谷

29 Club Quattro
クラブクアトロ
31 Tōkyū Department Store;
Bunkamura
東急百貨店；文化村
32 Bar, Isn't It?
バーイズントイット
33 Click On Internet Cafe
クリックオン
35 Book 1st
ブックファースト
36 Citibank
シティバンク
38 One-Oh-Nine Building;
Maruhan Pachinko Tower
１０９ビル；
まるはんパチンコタワー
40 Seibu Department Store
西武百貨店
41 Marui Young
Department Store
丸井ヤング
44 Shibuya Post Office
渋谷郵便局
46 Hachikō Statue
ハチ公像
47 109 Bldg, Natural Station
１０９ビル；
ナチュラルステーション
50 Club Asia
クラブアジア
51 On Air West
オンエアーウエスト
52 Dr Jeekhan's; Pylon;
Harlem
ドクタージーカンズ；
パイロン；ハーレム
53 On Air East
オンエアーイースト
54 Sugar High
シュガーハイ
55 Dōgen-zaka
Itchi-chome Building
道玄坂１丁目ビル
56 South Exit
Bus Station
南口バス停
59 Tōkyū Bldg
東急ビル

(¥500/600/1000 permanent/special/all exhibits, 10 am to 6 pm, to 8 pm Thursday and Friday, closed Monday) is in new premises in Ebisu Garden Place. The emphasis is on Japanese photography, but international work is also displayed. From JR Ebisu station take the covered walkway to Ebisu Garden Place.

TOKYO

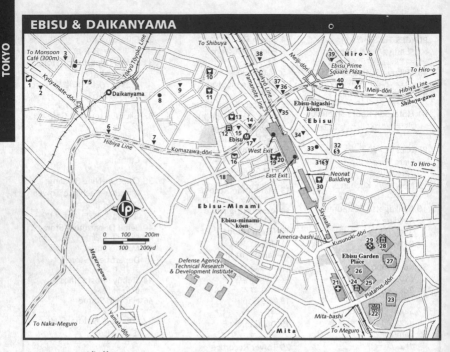

EBISU & DAIKANYAMA

AKASAKA 浅草
Akasaka is home to Tokyo's heaviest concentration of top-notch hotels and a good selection of mid-range restaurants. Its sights, however, are low-key.

Hie-jinja 日枝神社
The shrine itself is not one of Tokyo's major attractions; it's modern, drab and largely cement. The highlight is the walk up to the shrine through a 'tunnel' of orange torii (shrine gates), particularly pretty during cherry-blossom season. Unfortunately, Tokyo is now in the process of building a garish new promenade to the shrine and this will add to its unfortunately modern feel.

Hotel Sights
Some of Akasaka's luxury hotels are sights in themselves. Hotel New Otani, for example, has preserved part of a **400-year-old garden** that was once the property of a Tokugawa regent. You don't have to be a

guest of the hotel to visit the garden; just enter the hotel and ask directions. It's worth a visit to see the enormous and greedy carp that inhabit the central pond.

For views over the area (forget the expensive Tokyo Tower), ANA Hotel Tokyo and Akasaka Prince Hotel both offer **skyline spectacles** from their lofty upper reaches.

Aoyama-dōri 青山通り
Aoyama-dōri runs from Akasaka down to Shibuya, taking in the Akasaka Palace grounds (not a major attraction) and Harajuku en route. About halfway between Akasaka and Aoyama-Itchōme station, on the left-hand side, is the Sōgetsu Kaikan building, headquarters of the **Sōgetsu school of avant-garde flower arrangement**. If you have an interest in ikebana, this is an interesting place to visit. There are displays, a bookshop, and a coffee shop.

On the 6th floor of the same building is the **Sōgetsu Art Museum** (¥500, 10 am to

EBISU & DAIKANYAMA

PLACES TO EAT

2 Caffe Michelangelo
カフェミケランジェロ
3 Bombay Bazar
ボンベイバザール
5 Café Artifagose
カフェアルトファゴス
6 Gazebo Café
ガゼボカフェ
7 Freshness Burger
フレッシュネスバーガー
9 Café Juliet; KM Fils
カフェジュリエット；
カーエムフィス
14 Wendy's
ウェンディーズ
15 Nanaki Soba
なな樹そば
17 Doutor Coffee
ドトールコーヒー
34 Subway
サブウェイ
35 Saboten; Tentsu
Tonkatsu
天津とんかつ
36 KFC
ケンタッキー
フライドチキン
37 Fujii
藤井
38 An An
杏庵
39 Shunsenbō
旬泉坊
41 Ippūdō Rāmen
一風堂らーめん

OTHER

1 Danish Embassy
デンマーク大使館
4 Kamawanu
かまわぬ
8 7-Eleven
セブンイレブン
10 Enjoy House
エンジョイハウス
11 Guest
ゲスト
12 Ebisu-jinja
恵比寿神社
13 What the Dickens;
Milk
ワットザディケンズ；
みるく
16 Ebisu Eki-mae
Post Office
恵比寿駅前郵便局
18 Matsuzakaya
Department Store
松坂屋百貨店
19 Bodeguita
ボデギタ
20 Shanghai
シャンハイ
21 Kōseichūō Hospital
厚生中央病院
22 Ebisu View Tower
恵比寿ビュータワー

23 Ebisu Garden Terrace
Ichiban-kan Building
恵比寿ガーデンテラス
壱番館
24 Tokyo Metropolitan
Museum of Photography
東京都写真美術館
25 Garden Hall
ガーデンホール
26 Ebisu Garden Place
Tower
ガーデンパレスタワー
27 Ebisu Garden Terrace
Niban-kan Building
恵比寿ガーデンテラス
弐番館
28 Beer Museum Yebisu;
Sapporo Breweries HQ
恵比寿麦酒記念館；
サッポロビール本社
29 Mitsukoshi Department
Store
三越百貨店
30 Lust
ラスト
31 Sumitomo Bank
住友銀行
32 Fuji Bank
富士銀行
33 Good Day Books
グッデイブックス
40 Post Office
郵便局

5 pm, closed Sunday), notable for its highly idiosyncratic and eclectic collection of art treasures from across the centuries and from the four corners of the globe. Exhibits range from Indian Buddhas to works by Matisse.

ROPPONGI 六本木

Roppongi is restaurants and nightlife, but mainly nightlife. There's no compelling reason to visit by day, though there are a couple of nearby tourist attractions.

Tokyo Tower 東京タワー

Tokyo's Eiffel-Tower-lookalike is more impressive from a distance; up close, the 330m tower is a tourist trap. The Grand Observation Platform (¥820) is only 150m high; if you want to peer through the smog at Tokyo's uninspiring skyline from 250m, it will cost you a further ¥600 to get to the Special Observation Platform. The platforms are open from 9 am to 8 pm from 16 March to 15 November, to 9 pm in August, and to 6 pm the rest of the year. The tower also features an overpriced aquarium (¥1000), a wax museum (¥850), the Holographic Mystery Zone (¥400) and showrooms.

Tokyo Tower is a fair trudge from Roppongi; take the Hibiya subway line one stop to Kamiyachō station.

Zōjō-ji 増上寺

Behind Tokyo Tower, Zōjō-ji was the family temple of the Tokugawas. It has had a

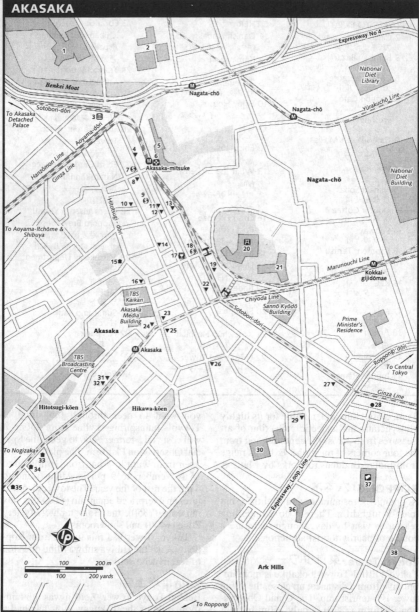

AKASAKA

Expressway No 4

National Diet Library

Benkei Moat

Sotobori-dōri

To Akasaka Detached Palace

Nagata-chō

Nagata-chō

Yūrakuchō Line

3 🏛

Aoyama-dōri

Hanzōmon Line

Ginza Line

Nagata-chō

National Diet Building

4 ▼

5 ▼

6 ✕
Akasaka-mitsuke

7 Ⓢ

8 ▼

9 Ⓢ

10 ▼

11 ▼

12 ▼

13 ▼

To Aoyama-Itchōme & Shibuya

Hitotsugi-dōri

14 ▼

18 ▼

17 ▼ Ⓢ

15 ■

16 ▼

TBS Kaikan

Akasaka Media Building

19 ▼

20 ⛩

21

Marunouchi Line

Kokkai-gijidōmae Ⓜ

22 ▼

Chiyoda Line

Sotobori-dōri

Sannō Kyōdō Building

Prime Minister's Residence

23 ▼

24 ▼   25 ▼

Akasaka

TBS Broadcasting Centre

Ⓜ Akasaka

26 ▼

Roppongi-dōri

To Central Tokyo

31 ▼
32 ▼

27 ▼

Ginza Line

● 28

Hitotsugi-kōen

Hikawa-kōen

29 ▼

30

To Nogizaka

33 ■

34 ■

35 ■

Expressway Loop Line

37 🏢

36

38

Ark Hills

0   100   200 m
0   100   200 yards

To Roppongi

TOKYO

AKASAKA

PLACES TO STAY
1 Hotel New Otani
 ホテルニューオータニ
2 Akasaka Prince Hotel
 赤坂プリンスホテル
5 Akasaka Tōkyū Hotel;
 Kushinobō
 赤坂東急ホテル；
 串の坊
15 Capsule Hotel
 Fontaine Akasaka
 カプセルホテル
 フォンテーメ赤阪
21 Capitol Tōkyū Hotel
 キャピタル東急ホテル
33 Capsule Inn Akasaka
 かぷせるイン赤坂
34 Akasaka Yōkō Hotel
 赤坂陽光ホテル
35 Marroad Inn Akasaka
 マロウド イン赤阪
36 ANA Hotel Tokyo
 全日空ホテル東京
38 Hotel Ōkura
 ホテルオー クラ

PLACES TO EAT
4 Tsunahachi
 つな八

8 Subway
 サブウェイ
10 Tenichi
 天一
11 Trattoria
 Marumo
 トラットリアマルーモ
12 Moti
 モティ
13 The Taj
 ザタージ
14 Sushi-sei
 寿司清
16 Tenya
 大屋
19 Jangara Rāmen
 じゃんがららあめん
22 Tofu-ya
 豆腐屋
23 KFC
24 Starbucks
 スターバック
25 Moti
 モティ
26 Mugyodon
 ムギョドン
27 Tony Roma's
 トニーロマーズ

29 Doutor Coffee
 ドトールコーヒー
31 Aozai
 アオザイ
32 Yakitori Luis
 焼き鳥ルイス

OTHER
3 Suntory Museum of
 Art
 サントリー美術館
6 Tōkyū Plaza
 東急プラザ
7 International ATM
 キャッシュコーナー
9 Citibank
 シティバンク
17 Goose Bar
 グースバー
18 Sumitomo Bank
 住友銀行
20 Hie-jinja
 日枝神社
28 Inachū Lacquerware
 いなちゅう漆器
30 Akasaka Twin Tower
 赤坂ツインタワー
37 US Embassy
 アメリカ大使館

calamitous history, even by Tokyo's standards, having been rebuilt three times in recent history, most recently in 1974. It's still a pleasant place to visit if you're in the vicinity. The main gates date from 1605 and are included among the nation's 'Important Cultural Properties'. On the grounds there is a large collection of statues of Jizō, the patron saint of travellers and the souls of departed children.

ODAIBA/TOKYO BAY
お台場／東京湾

Tokyo is rediscovering that it's a waterfront city and recent years have seen a spate of development in and around Tokyo Bay. Perhaps the most popular spot in the bay is the Odaiba/Ariake area, accessible from downtown Tokyo via the Yurikamome monorail line, which operates from Shim-

bashi station on the JR Yamanote line. While Tokyo Bay is not as beautiful as some city bays around the world, it does make a nice change from the congestion of central Tokyo. See the boxed text 'Odaiba/Tokyo Bay Walking Tour' for details on some of the area's attractions.

OTHER ATTRACTIONS
Parks & Gardens

If you've been hitting the bitumen and haven't seen a tree for days, there are several parks and gardens to cure what ails you. (Many of these are listed in the relevant area sections earlier in this chapter.) **Koishikawa Kōraku-en** (¥300, 9 am to 5 pm) has to be one of the least-visited (by foreigners at least) and best gardens in Tokyo. A stroll-garden with a strong Chinese influence, it was established in the

TOKYO

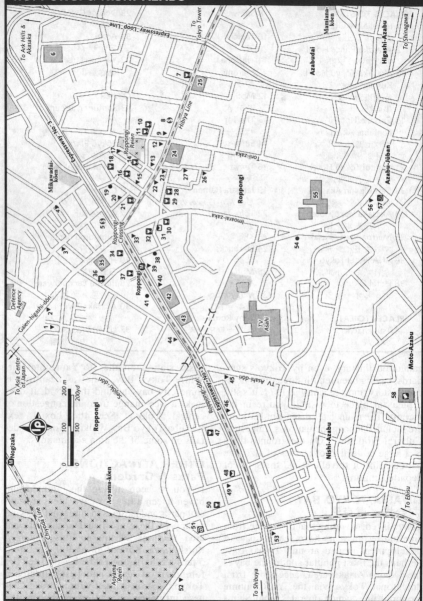

ROPPONGI & NISHI-AZABU

ROPPONGI & NISHI-AZABU

PLACES TO STAY
6 Roppongi Prince Hotel
六本木プリンスホテル
35 Hotel Ibis
ホテルアイビス

PLACES TO EAT
1 Bourbon Street
バーボンストリート
2 Inakaya
田舎屋
3 Havana Café
ハバナカフェ
4 Namban-tei
南蛮亭
9 Hamburger Inn
ハンバーガーイン
12 Bikkuri Sushi; Propaganda
びっくり寿司
13 Bellini's Pizza Kitchen
ベリニーズピッツァ
キッチン
15 Seryna
瀬理奈
17 Kushimura
串村
20 Tainan Taami
台南胆仔麺
22 Starbucks
スターバックス
23 McDonald's
26 Fukuzushi; Spago
福寿司；スパゴ
27 Hard Rock Café;
Tony Roma's
ハードロックカフェ；
トニーロマーズ
33 Almond
アーモンド
39 Hina Sushi
ひな寿司
40 Moti
モティ
44 Bengawan Solo
ベンガワンソロ

45 Little Tribeca
リトルトライベッカ
46 Maenam
メナム
49 Salty Box Grill
ソルティーボックス
グリル
52 Monsoon Café
モンスーンカフェ
53 Hobson's
ホブソンズ
56 Homework's
ホームワークス

OTHER
5 International ATM
キャッシュコーナー
7 Roppongi Pit Inn
六本木ピットイン
8 Sumitomo Bank
住友銀行
10 Déja Vu
デジャブ
11 Gas Panic Café; Gas Panic
Bar, Club 99 Gaspanic
ガスパニックカフェ；
ガスパニックバー；
クラブ99ガスパニック
14 Charleston Club
チャールストンクラブ
16 Lexington Queen
レクシントンクイーン
18 Bar, Isn't It?
バーイズントイット
19 Square Building
スクエアービル
21 Motown House
モータウンハウス
24 Roi Bldg; Paddy Foley's
ロイビル；
パディーフォーリーズ
25 Axis Bldg; Kisso
アクシスビル；吉左右
28 Cavern Club
カバーンクラブ

29 Pints Sportscafé;
Kento's
パインツスポーツバー；
ケントーズ
30 Sweet Basil 139
スイートベイジル139
31 Post Office
郵便局
32 Mogambo; Castillo
モガンボ；カスティロ
34 Geronimo
ジェロニモ
36 Velfarre
ベルファーレ
37 Bauhaus
バウハウス
38 Aoyama Book Center
41 Meidiya International
Supermarket
明治屋
42 Tōnichi Building
東日ビル
43 Wave
ウェーブ
47 Bul -Let's
48 Nishi-Azabu
Post Office
西麻布郵便局
50 Yellow
イエロー
51 Cyberia
サイベリア
54 Swedish Centre;
Stockholm
スウェーデンセンター；
ストックホルム
55 International House
of Japan
国際文化会館
57 Azabu Jūban Onsen;
Koshi-No-Yu Sento
麻布十番温泉；
越の湯銭湯
58 Chinese Embassy
中国大使館

mid-17th century. It's next to Kōraku-en Amusement Park (see Amusement Parks later) and Tokyo Dome, near Kōraku-en subway station on the Marunouchi line.

Museums & Galleries

There's an enormous number of museums and galleries in Tokyo. In many cases their exhibits are small and specialised and the admission charges prohibitively expensive for travellers with a limited budget and a tight schedule. For a more complete listing, get hold of the TIC's *Museums & Art Galleries* pamphlet. Better still, look out for *Tokyo Museums – A Complete Guide* (Tut-

tle) by Thomas & Ellen Flannigan, which covers everything from the Tombstone Museum to the Button Museum.

Edo-Tokyo Museum This is the best of Tokyo's new museums, without a doubt.

ODAIBA/TOKYO BAY WALKING TOUR

This walking tour is a great way to get some fresh sea air and check out the most interesting spots around Tokyo Bay (Tokyo-wan). You can manage this tour in the course of one long afternoon – less if you use the Yurikamome line to cover some of the longer distances (a one-day pass on the line costs ¥800).

Starting from Shimbashi or Shibaura, the first sight on any tour of Odaiba is the **Rainbow Bridge**, which stretches 570m from tower to tower. Immediately after the bridge, near the Odaibakaihin-kōen Yurikamome stop, is **Odaiba Kaihin Kōen Beach**. It's not nearly as bad as you might imagine for a beach located right in the middle of Tokyo Bay, and it's popular with windsurfers, waders and sunbathers in the summer months. Overlooking the beach are two popular restaurant areas: **Restaurant Row** and **Decks Tokyo Beach**. The latter also has a variety of stores and a branch of the **Sega Joypolis** entertainment centre. See the Places to Eat section for details on restaurants in these two areas.

Next along is the futuristic **Fuji Television Japan Broadcast Center**, which offers a studio tour and observation platform (¥500, 10 am to 5 pm, closed Monday), which is inside the distinctive ball-shaped structure on its upper floors. On clear days, it affords good views of the bay and Rainbow Bridge. A ticket to the observatory also gets you into the Fuji Studio Tour, although this is probably of little interest to foreign visitors as it is all in Japanese.

A 15-minute walk along the edge of the island brings you to the ship-shaped **Museum of Maritime Science** (Fune-no-kagakukan), one of the better museums in Tokyo. There are scores of excellent ship models and displays. See the entry in the Other Attractions section of this chapter for details.

From the Museum of Maritime Science you have the option of taking the train or walking to the next stop, **Tokyo International Exhibition Center**, better known as 'Tokyo Big Sight' ('Kokusai Tenjijō Big Sight' in Japanese), with its distinctive inverted-pyramid main hall. If you choose to walk (about 20 minutes), follow the Center Promenade walkway. This leads across the flat middle of the island, with the monolithic towers of the bay area rising on all sides (the most distinctive of these is **Telecom Center**, another building with an observatory from which to view the bay).

On the way to Big Sight, you'll pass the **Toyota T-Gaiku** entertainment, shopping and gallery complex, which was under construction at the time of writing but will be open by the time of publication. Check with the TIC for details on this facility.

From Tokyo Big Sight, there are two ways to return to central Tokyo: you can either get back on the Yurikamome line and retrace your steps to Shimbashi, or you can walk over to the Rinkai Fukutoshin line and go two stops to Shin-Kiba station. At Shin-Kiba you can transfer to the JR Keiyō line, which will take you to Tokyo station in less than 10 minutes.

Another interesting option from Shin-Kiba is take the JR Keiyō line one stop east to Kasai Rinkai-kōen station and check out **Kasai Rinkai-kōen Maritime Park**. This seaside park is good for a stroll or perhaps a picnic, although it's not the most picturesque spot. Those with kids in tow might want to stop off at **Kasai Rinkai Suizoku-en Aquarium** (¥700, 9.30 am to 5 pm, closed Monday). The big draw-cards here are the giant tuna- and shark-tanks that make up the centre of the aquarium.

An interesting way to return to Tokyo from here is on the **Suijō Bus** (Water Bus; ¥800, one hour, last sailing 5 pm), which sails to Hinode Pier, from where it's a 500m walk back to JR Hamamatsu-chō station.

Just the building itself, which looks like it has been spirited from the set of *Star Wars*, is a wonder. The Nihom-bashi divides this vast display into re-creations of Edo-period Tokyo and Meiji-period Tokyo. The museum (¥600, 10 am to 6 pm, to 8 pm Thursday and Friday, closed Monday) is close to Ryōgoku station on the JR Sōbu line, and can be combined with a visit to the Sumō Museum.

Sumō Museum Close to the main entrance to Kokugikan Sumō Stadium, the Sumō Museum (free, 10 am to 4.30 pm weekdays) is quite a treat, but unfortunately there is nothing in the way of English explanations. See Edo-Tokyo Museum earlier for details on getting there.

Tokyo Metropolitan Teien Museum
This museum from (10 am to 6 pm, closed the second and fourth Wednesday of the month) lacks a permanent display of its own, but the building itself was designed by French architect Henri Rapin and it lies in pleasant gardens. Take the east exit of Meguro station (on the Yamanote line), walk straight ahead along Meguro-dōri for around five minutes and look out for the museum on the left. Entry averages ¥600 (depending on the exhibition).

Museum of Maritime Science Down in the Odaiba/Tokyo Bay area, this large, ship-shaped museum (10 am to 5 pm, to 6 pm weekends and holidays) is one of Tokyo's better museums. Known as Fune-no-kagakukan, it has four floors of excellent displays dealing with every aspect of ships and shipping, with loads of highly detailed models. The 4m-long version of the largest battleship ever built, the *Yamato*, is stunning in detail and craftsmanship. There are also lots of hands-on exhibits that kids will love.

To get to the museum, take the Yurikamome New Transit line from Shimbashi station and get off at the Fune-no-kagakukan stop. Admission is ¥700 for adults, ¥400 for children junior high-school age and younger.

Amusement Parks
Tokyo Disneyland Only the Japanese signs reveal that you're a long way from Orange County – Tokyo Disneyland is a near-perfect replica of the original in Anaheim, California. Its opening hours vary seasonally (8.30 am to 10 pm in summer, 10 am to 6 pm in winter) – phone ☎ 047-354-0001 to be sure. It's open daily, except for about a dozen days a year (most of them in January). A variety of tickets are available, including an all-inclusive 'passport' that gives you unlimited access to all the rides for ¥5200 (¥4590/3570 children aged 12 to 17/aged 4 to 11). As at the original Disneyland, there are often long queues at popular rides (30 minutes to one hour is normal). Tokyo Disneyland has a ticket office (☎ 3595-1777) in Hibiya (see the Central Tokyo map), open from 10 am to 7 pm.

There is now a direct train service to Disneyland: take the Keiyō line from Tokyo station to Maihama station (¥210, 15 minutes).

Kōraku-en Amusement Park Next to Kōraku-en subway station on the Marunouchi subway line, the Kōraku-en Amusement Park (¥1500/700 adults/children, ¥600 for most rides, 10 am to 8 pm varying seasonally) is of the old rattle-and-shake school, and is popular precisely for that reason. The Ultra Twister roller coaster takes first prize for most of the visitors. Geopolis is a new hi-tech addition to the amusement park, with attractions like the Geopanic indoor roller coaster and Zombie Zone.

Baths
A nice hot bath is a great way to relax after a day pounding the pavements of Tokyo. Here are a few of Tokyo's more interesting *sento* (public baths), *onsen* (mineral hot spring spa) and spas.

Azabu-Jūban Onsen & Koshi-No-Yu Sento You wouldn't expect to find an onsen in the middle of Tokyo, but here it is. The dark, tea-coloured water here is scalding hot. Downstairs is a sento (¥385, 3 to 10 pm, closed

Tuesday) and upstairs an onsen (¥1260, 11 am to 9 pm, closed Tuesday). The water comes from the same source; the only difference is the price and the fact that upstairs there's a room to hang around in after your bath. See the Roppongi & Nishi-Azabu map.

Asakusa Kannon Onsen It calls itself an onsen, but we don't believe it. Nonetheless, this bath (¥700, 6.30 am to 6 pm, closed Thursday), next to Sensō-ji, is worth a try. See the Asakusa map.

Finlando Sauna A huge 24-hour complex of baths and steam rooms (¥1900/2100/2600 after 5 am/5 pm/midnight) right in the middle of Shinjuku's Kabuki-chō, this is a good place to escape the madness of the streets outside. Massages (¥3060 for an hour) come highly recommended. This complex is men-only. See the Shinjuku map.

Green Plaza Ladies Sauna This decent 24-hour bath and spa (¥27001500 normal/70-minute entry) for women is also in Shinjuku's Kabuki-chō. A 40-minute massage costs ¥3260. See the Shinjuku map.

ORGANISED TOURS

One of the most reliable Tokyo-tour operators is Hato Bus Tours (☎ 3435-6081). Its Panoramic Tour (¥9450 including lunch) takes in most of Tokyo's major sights. Probably the widest range of Tokyo tours is available from the JTB's Sunrise Tours office (☎ 5260-9500). Sunrise offers general sightseeing tours, such as morning tours (¥4500) and afternoon tours (¥4950). Both Hato and Sunrise offer English-speaking guides and/or taped explanations and headsets.

Night tours of the city are offered by Sunrise Tours and by Gray Line (☎ 3433-5745). Sunrise's Kabuki Night tour (¥10,800) includes a *sukiyaki* and *sake* dinner, kabuki at Ginza's Kabuki-za Theatre and a *geisha* show.

All of these tours pick up guests at various major hotels around town. Sunrise and Gray Line also offer tours to sightseeing spots around Tokyo.

SPECIAL EVENTS

These are some of Tokyo's main festivals. For more details on some of these events, see the Facts for the Visitor chapter.

January

Ganjitsu (New Year) 1 January. This is the one day of the year (well, the night before is, anyway) that the trains run all night. For the first shrine-visit of the year, Tokyoites head to Meiji-jingū, Sensō-ji or Yasukuni-jinja. The day after New Year's Day is one of the two occasions each year when the Kōkyo is open to the public. Enter the palace's inner gardens by the Nijū-bashi between 9 am and 3.30 pm.

Dezome-shiki 6 January. Firemen dressed in Edo-period costumes put on a parade involving acrobatic stunts on top of bamboo ladders. The parade takes place on Chūō-dōri in Harumi (Tokyo Bay area) from 10 am onwards. Take the Yūraku-chō line to Tsukushima subway station.

February

Setsubun 3 or 4 February. In Tokyo, ceremonies celebrating the lunar calendar's last day of winter are held at Zōjō-ji, Kanda-myōjin (Kanda Shrine). and Sensō-ji. Sensō-ji offers the added attraction of a classical dance performance.

March

Kinryū-no-Mai 18 March. A golden-dragon dance is held at Sensō-ji to celebrate the discovery of the golden image of Kannon that now rests there. Two or three performances are performed during the day.

April

Hanami (Blossom Viewing) Early to mid-April. In Tokyo, *the* place to go for hanami is Ueno-kōen; if you want some peace, however, go to Shinjuku-gyoen, where the blossoms are better and the crowds smaller. Other famous hanami spots around Tokyo include Yasukuni-jinja and Koishikawa Kōraku-en.

May

Kanda Matsuri Mid-May. This festival is held in odd-numbered years on the Saturday and Sunday closest to 15 May, and is a traditional Edo festival that celebrates a Tokugawa battle victory. A whole range of activities take place at Kanda-myōjin. The nearest subway station is Ochanomizu on the Marunouchi line.

Sanja Matsuri The 3rd Friday, Saturday and Sunday of May. Up to 100 *mikoshi* (portable shrines), carried by participants dressed in traditional clothes, are paraded through the area in the vicinity of Sensō-ji in Asakusa.

June

Sannō-sai 10 to 16 June. Street stalls, traditional music and dancing, and processions of mikoshi

A Tokyo summer festival.

A celebration at Meiji-Jingū.

Cute as – schoolchildren in uniform.

Vitamin drinks – a multimillion dollar hangover-cure industry.

Sumō wrestlers – fully clothed.

People traffic – crossing a busy Ginza intersection.

A little bit of history – Tokyo station.

A water bus, or *suijō basu*, on the Sumida-gawa.

An astonishingly neat set of bicycles parked outside a Tokyo train station.

Kanji decorates paper lanterns.

Wooden amulets for sale at a shrine.

A golden dragon is spectacular

You'll see fish in one form or another in Japan...

Votive plaques, or *ema*, covered with wishes.

A purification ritual precedes entering a shrine.

A springtime view of Mt Fuji from Kawaguchi-ko, the most popular arrival point from Tokyo.

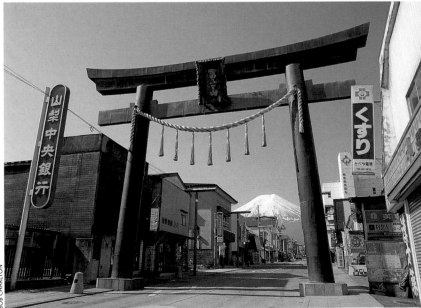

The *torii* leading to Sengen-jinja – a visit to the shrine was once a necessary preliminary to climbing Fuji.

are all part of this Edo Festival, held at Sannō Hie-jinja, near the Akasaka-mitsuke subway station.

July
Sumida-gawa Hanabi Taikai (Sumida River Fireworks Festival) Late July. The biggest fireworks display of its kind in Tokyo is held on the Sumida-gawa in Asakusa. Ask at the TIC for details on the exact date of this and other late-summer fireworks festivals.

August
Fukagawa Hachiman Matsuri 13 to 15 August. In this triennial, three day Edo festival, fool-hardy mikoshi-bearers charge through 8km of frenzied crowds, who dash water on them. The action takes place at Tomioka Hachiman-gū, next to Monzen-Naka-chō subway station on the Tōzai line. The next one should take place in 2002.

Asakusa Samba Matsuri Late August. Japan's least-Japanese festival is also one of its most fun. A parade of scantily clad domestic and international samba teams make their way down Asakusa's Kamanarimon-dōri, to the delight of bemused Tokyoites. Don't miss it!

October & November
Oeshiki 12 October. This festival is held in commemoration of Nichiren (1222–82), founder of the Nichiren sect of Buddhism. On the night of the 12th, people bearing large lanterns and paper flower arrangements make their way to Hommon-ji. The nearest station is Ikegami, on the Tōkyū Ikegami line.

Meiji Reidaisai 30 October to 3 November. A series of events is held at Meiji-jingū in commemoration of the Meiji emperor's birthday. Particularly interesting to watch are displays of horseback archery by riders in traditional clothes. Other events include classical music and dance.

Shichi-go-san (Seven-Five-Three Festival) 15 November. The best places to see the young ones decked out in their best kimono are Meiji-jingū, Yasukuni-jinja and Sannō Hie-jinja.

December
Gishi-sai 14 December. The day's events commemorate the deaths of the 47 *rōnin* (masterless samurai) who committed *seppuku* (ritual suicide) after avenging the death of their master. The activities involve a parade of warriors to Sengaku-ji – the rōnin's burial place – and a memorial service from 7.30 pm onwards. The temple is directly west of Sengaku-ji subway station on the TOEI Asakusa line.

Bōnen-kai Season Late December. Okay, this isn't an official festival at all, but the period leading up to New Year's, when the Japanese hold their year-end parties, is one of the wildest times of the year (matched only by hanami season). Join the fun in any of the city's nightlife areas but be prepared for some very public drunkenness.

PLACES TO STAY
In Tokyo you can choose from the whole range of Japanese accommodation, from capsule hotels to ryokan. Where you end up will mainly be determined by your budget – and budget accommodation in Tokyo can be a bit pricier than elsewhere. Hotels are expensive however you look at it. Business hotels are a good compromise solution, with rates in Tokyo from ¥7000 for singles and around ¥10,000 for doubles. Ryokan and *minshuku* (Japanese-style budget B&B) are better still, if you can make a few concessions to Japanese etiquette, with rates from around ¥4500 per person. At youth hostels and so-called 'gaijin houses' (foreigner houses) you can get single rates down to ¥2500 per person (which is about as low as it gets in Tokyo). There are two caveats however: the youth hostels impose an early evening curfew; and the gaijin houses are generally way out in the boondocks and only take long-termers.

Reservations & Information
The Welcome Inn Reservation Center, at Narita airport and at the TIC in Tokyo, is a free booking service that will make reservations for you at hotels and ryokan in the Japan Welcome Inn hotel group. Hours are the same as the TIC (see Tourist Offices under Information earlier in this chapter). If you wish to book from overseas, you will have to get a Welcome Inn Group reservation form from your nearest JNTO office (see Tourist Offices Abroad in the Facts for the Visitor chapter). Bookings need to be made at least two weeks before departure, and you will need a confirmed air ticket.

Places to Stay – Budget
If it is imperative that you find inexpensive accommodation, be certain to make a

TOKYO

booking before you arrive. Flying into Narita (particularly at night) without accommodation lined up can be nightmarish.

Youth Hostels Tokyo has two standard youth hostels: Tokyo International Youth Hostel in Iidabashi; and Yoyogi Youth Hostel. The usual regulations apply – you have to be out of the building between 10 am and 3 pm (9 am and 5 pm at Yoyogi), and you have to be in by 10 pm; the latter is a real drawback in a late-night city like Tokyo. There's a three-night limit to your stay and the hostels can often be booked right out during peak holiday periods.

The *Tokyo International Youth Hostel* (☎ 3235-1107) doesn't require that you be a member but does ask that you book ahead and provide some identification (a passport will do) when you arrive. To get there, take the west exit (when coming by JR) or the B2b exit (when coming by subway) out of Iidabashi station. It's on the 18th floor of the Central Plaza building, one minute from the station (look for the tall, glass-fronted building). Rates are ¥3100 per person (you may be charged an extra fee for air-con in summer and heating in winter), and breakfast/dinner costs ¥400/800. Check-in is from 3 to 9.30 pm. The Narita airport TIC (see Tourist Offices in the Information section earlier) has a step-by-step instruction sheet on how to get to the hostel from the airport most cheaply.

Yoyogi Youth Hostel (☎ 3467-9163), which charges ¥3000/3600 for members/nonmembers, is the less appealing choice. There are no meals and no cooking facilities. However, all the rooms are singles and are clean. Check-in is from 5 to 8 pm. To get there, take the Odakyū line to Sangūbashi station. Exit the station, turn left and walk 200m, then cross the tracks and turn right. Walk 150m and cross the pedestrian bridge. Continue on in the same direction and enter the National Olympics Memorial Youth Center compound. The guards at the gate have a map to the hostel.

In addition to these, *Hotel Skycourt Asakusa* (☎ 3875-4411, 6-35-8 Asakusa, Taitō-ku) is a clean, new business-hotel that also functions as a youth hostel. The rate for members is ¥5000 per person. Nonmember rates are ¥7000/10,500/13,000 for singles/doubles/twins. All rooms have baths, TVs and air-con. To get there from Asakusa, walk up Edo-dōri past the Tōbu station (keeping it on your left – see the off-map arrow on the Asakusa map) to the third set of lights. Take the street just to the left of the *kōban* (police box) and walk 100m past the first set of lights.

Ryokan & Guesthouses *Kimi Ryokan* (☎ 3971-3766) is the best budget-category choice in Tokyo, with a good location and clean, inexpensive Japanese-style rooms. Of all the ryokan in Tokyo, the Kimi has the most convivial lounge area. There's a notice board, and the constantly changing ikebana adds cheer to the place. Be sure to book ahead; there's nearly always a waiting list. The Kimi is on the western side of Ikebukuro station. Prices start from ¥4500/6500 for singles/doubles.

Also in Ikebukuro, *House Ikebukuro* (☎ 3984-3399) has a variety of rooms including singles/doubles/triples from ¥4000/8000/10,500, all with shared bath and a common kitchen. The best, however, are the apartment-like rooms in the annexe, with en suite shower, fridge and microwave, which go for ¥8500/10,500 for two/three people.

The cheapest place to stay in Tokyo is *New Kōyō (3873-0343)*, a guesthouse two stops north of Ueno on the Hibiya subway line. Small, very basic Western/Japanese-style singles with shared bath cost ¥2500/2700 (the latter are slightly larger). There are also two doubles that go for ¥4800. To get there, take a left out of Minowa station's No 3 exit and walk to the first set of lights. Take a left, walk past three sets of lights and take a right just before the Lawson convenience store; it's on the right in the second block.

Asia Center of Japan (☎ 3402-6111, 8-10-32 Asakusa, Minato-ku), near Aoyama-Itchōme subway station (Ginza line), is a popular option in the upper reaches of the budget category. This place attracts many long-term stayers and is often fully booked (call ahead). The station is under the easily recognisable Aoyama Twin Tower building on Aoyama-dōri. Walk past the building towards Akasaka-mitsuke, turn right on Gaien-Higashi-dōri (towards Roppongi), and the Asia Centre is a short walk up the second street on the left. Rooms have pay-TV, and singles/twins/doubles start at ¥5100/6800/9500 (rooms with bathrooms are more expensive). Breakfast/lunch/dinner costs ¥580/800/1200.

Sakura Hotel (☎ 3261-3939, 2-21-4 Kanda-Jimbōchō, Chiyoda-ku) is a good guesthouse in Jimbōchō, on the Hanzōmon subway line. A bed in a shared two- or four-person room costs ¥3600. Private singles/doubles are ¥6800/8000. There's a small restaurant/bar on the premises with a small outside terrace. To get there from Jimbōchō station, take the A6 exit and turn right, walk two blocks and turn right at the kōban; the hotel is 200m on the right.

Close to JR Gotanda station on the Yamanote line is *Ryokan Sansui-sō* (☎ 3441-7475, 2-9-5 Higashi-Gotanda, Shinagawa-ku). It's not an ideal location, still, it's only a few stops from Shibuya station, the nearest main station. Take the east exit out of Gotanda station. Turn right, take the first right after the big Tōkyū department store and then the first left. Turn left and then right, walk past the bowling centre and look for the sign on the right directing you down the side-street to the ryokan. Singles/twins/triples without bath are ¥4900/8600/12,000; twins with bath cost ¥9000.

Ueno may be a bit of a trek from the bright lights, but it's a good sightseeing base and there are several budget ryokan in the area. *Sawanoya Ryokan* (☎ 3822-2251, 2-3-11 Yanaka, Taitō-ku) is a good choice within walking distance of Nezu subway station on the Chiyoda line (call for walking directions from the station). If you're coming from Narita airport, it will probably be easier and just as cheap (if there are more than one of you) to catch a taxi from Ueno station. Singles cost ¥4700 to ¥5000 without bath; doubles cost ¥8800/9400 without/with bath, and triples without/with bath cost ¥12,000/13,500.

Ryokan Katsutarō (☎ 3821-9808) is another good option in the vicinity. Singles/doubles/triples cost ¥4500/8400/12,300 without bath; doubles/triples with bath cost ¥9000/13,200.

One stop away from Ueno on the JR Yamanote line (Uguisudani station) is *Sakura Ryokan* (☎ 3876-8118, 2-6-2 Iriya, Taitō-ku). Singles/doubles without bath cost ¥5300/9600; triples cost ¥12,600 to ¥13,500. There are also Western-style singles/twins with bath for ¥6300/10,600. It's tricky to find; we suggest calling from the station for directions.

Three stops away from Ueno on the Ginza line is Asakusa, which also has a few reasonably priced ryokan. *Ryokan Shigetsu* (☎ 3843-2345) is a clean, comfortable place around the corner from Sensō-ji. Western-style singles/doubles with bath start at ¥7300/14,000; Japanese-style singles/doubles go for ¥9000/15,000. There is a good Japanese bath on the top floor (see Baths earlier in this chapter), which overlooks Sensō-ji.

Another good option in Asakusa is *Ryokan Mikawaya Bekkan* (☎ 3841-7130). If you reserve through the Welcome Inn Center (see Reservations & Information earlier in this section), prices for Japanese-style singles/doubles are ¥5500/10,000.

In Nishi Asakusa (near Tawaramachi subway station; see off-map arrow on the Asakusa map) is *Kikuya Ryokan* (☎ 3841-6404/4051, 2-18-9 Nishi-Asakusa, Taitō-ku). It's just off Kappabashi-dōri and singles/doubles/triples cost ¥4800/8000/11,000. This ryokan gets good reports as a quiet and friendly place to stay.

Capsule Hotels Capsule hotels are generally a male domain (we list two here that accept women), and you find them in large hubs and nightlife districts. Most are open from 5 pm to 10 am.

Just down the road from the Shinjuku Prince Hotel on Shinjuku's east side is *Green Plaza Shinjuku* (☎ 3207-5411). Your own personal capsule is ¥4200 and this includes admission to the hotel's sauna (see Baths earlier). The front desk of this hotel is on the 3rd floor; take the lift from the basement.

Right in Shinjuku's sleazy Kabuki-chō is **Shinjuku-Kuyakusho-Mae Capsule Hotel** (☎ 3232-1110), which costs ¥4000 per night.

In Akasaka, not far from Akasaka station, is **Capsule Inn Akasaka** (☎ 3588-1811). It costs ¥4000 per night. Closer to Akasaka-mitsuke station is an upmarket capsule hotel, **Capsule Hotel Fontaine Akasaka** (☎ 3583-6554). An overnight stay here costs ¥4800. This is one of the few capsule hotels in Tokyo that accepts women, but it does only on Friday, Saturday and Sunday.

Another capsule hotel that accepts women is **Capsule Hotel Riverside** (3844-1155), near Asakusa station. Capsules here are a bargain at ¥3300. The entrance is around the back of the building.

Gaijin Houses Gaijin houses are more an option for those planning to stay long-term in Tokyo. Some offer nightly or weekly rates, but many are geared to foreigners working in Tokyo and charge by the month. If you just want a cheap place to crash and don't mind commuting into town to do your sightseeing, try ringing around the gaijin houses when you get to Tokyo.

Long-termers can expect to pay from ¥40,000 to ¥70,000 a month for a tiny private room, with no deposits or key money (a nonrefundable gift to the landlord of one or two months' rent) required. The best ways to find a gaijin house are by word of mouth from other foreigners, looking in the *Tokyo Classified*, or going through an agency. Agencies are generally the fastest and easiest way to go, as they have extensive listings and will handle all the arrangements with the landlord. The Tokyo agency with the most listings and best rates is Fontana (☎ 3382-0151). For more on gaijin houses, see the Facts for the Visitor chapter.

Places to Stay – Mid-Range

Mid-range hotels in Tokyo are mostly business hotels. These cost from ¥7000 for singles and from ¥10,000 for doubles. Since there is little to distinguish one business hotel from another, we recommend choosing one

in an area convenient to the sights you'd like to see. Always check what time your hotel locks its doors before heading out at night. Some hotels stay open all night, but many lock up at midnight or 1 am.

An adventurous late-night alternative is a love hotel. These can be found in any of Tokyo's entertainment districts – particularly in Shinjuku, Shibuya, Roppongi and Ikebukuro. All-night rooms range in price from ¥6500 to ¥8000, but 'all night' doesn't start until 10 or 11 pm, when the regular hour-by-hour customers have run out of energy.

Central Tokyo This is a convenient but expensive area in which to be based. If you're in Tokyo on business or need to be near Tokyo station for an early morning train, then this is probably your best bet.

The cheapest deal in the area is **Hotel Yaesu-Ryumeikan** (☎ 3271-0971), with Japanese-style rooms from ¥8600 for one person and ¥15,400 for two. It's a five-minute walk from Tokyo station.

Between Tokyo station and Takashimaya department store is the fairly economical **Yaesu Terminal Hotel** (☎ 3281-3771). It has a business-hotel feel and the rooms are quite small, but the prices are good for this area. Singles/doubles/twins are ¥10,800/15,800/15,800.

If you can't face any more travel upon arriving at Tokyo station, you can try **Tokyo Station Hotel** (☎ 3231-2511), on the Marunouchi (west) side of the station. The rooms are pretty basic, but you can't beat the location. Room prices start at ¥13,000/19,000/19,000.

Hotel Ginza Daiei (☎ 3545-1111), north of Kabuki-za Theatre in Ginza, is a slightly scruffy business hotel. Singles/doubles/twins start at ¥11,400/15,600/17,500.

Right on Sotobori-dōri between Ginza and Shimbashi is a quality hotel, **Ginza Nikkō Hotel** (☎ 3571-4911) in a prime location. Rooms cost from ¥10,000/20,000/24,000.

In a similar class to the Ginza Nikko and located nearby, **Ginza International Hotel** (☎ 3574-1121) offers rooms priced from ¥13,000/18,000/20,000.

Ueno The ryokan (see Ryokan & Guest-houses earlier) in this area are better value but if they're all full, the business hotels here are generally cheaper than those in other areas around Tokyo.

Hotel Green Capital (☎ 3842-2411) is a typical business hotel quite close to Ueno station. The rooms are clean and new, and the staff polite. Prices are also competitive, at ¥7500/10,000/9000 for singles/doubles/twins.

Overlooking the park itself, *Hotel Park-side* (☎ 3836-5711) is another good choice, particularly if you can get a room at the front. The place is pleasant, clean and new. Room prices start from ¥9200/16,100/16,100. Japanese-style rooms are available for ¥16,600 for two people.

If these options are full, try *Ueno Ki-nuya Hotel* (☎ 3838-1921), which has decent Japanese-style singles/doubles from ¥5500/9300 without bath. Slightly less appealing is *Hotel Sun Targas* (☎ 3833-8686), another business hotel not far from the station.

Those who want a change from the typical Western-style hotel may want to try *Suigetsu Hotel Ōgaisō* (☎ 3822-4611), on the western side of the park. This hotel mostly has Japanese-style *tatami* (woven floor-mat) rooms, and there are several large Japanese-style baths. Rooms, including Japanese breakfast, start at ¥16,000 for two people. Western-style rooms start at ¥9300 for a single, with breakfast.

Asakusa Asakusa is an interesting place to stay, if you don't mind sacrificing central location for a funky Shitamachi atmosphere.

Asakusa Plaza Hotel (☎ 3845-2621) is a standard-issue business hotel convenient to the sights. Singles/doubles/twins are priced from ¥6000/9500/11,000.

Another good option is *Hotel Skycourt Asakusa*, a business hotel that doubles as a youth hostel (see the Youth Hostels section earlier).

Ikebukuro There are innumerable business hotels, love hotels and capsule hotels in the Ikebukuro area. Be warned, however,

that the capsule hotels in this neighbour-hood are not nearly as accustomed to foreign guests as their cousins in Akasaka and Shinjuku.

On the east side of Ikebukuro, *Hotel Grand City* (☎ 3984-5121) is a standard business hotel with relatively inexpensive rates. Singles/twins start at ¥7300/11,800.

Also to the east of the station, *Hotel The-atre* (☎ 3988-2251) is centrally located and clean, and has singles/doubles starting at ¥7700/12,700.

Ikebukuro Royal Hotel (☎ 5396-0333) is another basic business hotel not too far from the station, with a nice communal bath. The rooms are nothing special; sin-gles/doubles start at ¥8500/¥11,800.

Hotel Sun City Ikebukuro (☎ 3986-1101) has basic rooms with a few on-premises drinking and dining options. Singles/doubles start at ¥7800/12,600.

Ark Hotel (☎ 3590-0111) has clean, newish rooms and polite staff. Singles/doubles/twins start at ¥8800/16,000/17,000, and Japanese-style rooms are available for ¥17,000 for two people.

Just along the street from the main Bic Camera store, *Hotel Sunroute Ikebukuro* (☎ 3980-1911) has pleasant, clean rooms and friendly staff, some of whom speak English. Prices for singles/doubles/twins start at ¥9000/15,600/15,600.

Shinjuku Shinjuku is a good hunting ground if you're after business hotels accustomed to foreign guests. Moreover, the intense competition in the area helps keep prices down. It's also a pretty convenient area in which to be based.

In east Shinjuku, *Hotel Sun Lite Shin-juku* (☎ 3356-0391) is a good choice. The place is clean and new with small but well-maintained rooms. Singles/doubles/twins cost ¥8300/11,500/13,500.

Just south of the Takashimaya Times Square complex is *Shinjuku Park Hotel* (☎ 3356-0241). While it gets no raves for warm, friendly service, the rooms are a little larger than at most business hotels and the prices are competitive, starting at ¥7900/13,800 for singles/twins.

The newly redecorated *Central Hotel* (☎ 3354-6611) is another decent choice in the heart of east Shinjuku. Pleasant, clean singles/doubles/twins start at ¥11,000/17,000/17,000.

In west Shinjuku, the very conveniently located *Star Hotel Tokyo* (☎ 3361-1111) offers rooms starting at ¥9000/17,000/18,000. The rooms and service are average.

On the far side of Shinjuku's Chūō-kōen, *Shinjuku New City Hotel* (☎ 3375-6511) has rooms slightly larger than usual for a business hotel, starting from ¥8800/16,200/17,600.

Shinjuku Washington Hotel (☎ 3343-3111) offers business-hotel accommodation with lots of restaurants and amenities. Rooms and windows are small, but the views from the upper floors are excellent. Room prices start at ¥11,300/17,000/17,500.

Shibuya Shibuya is an expensive area to base yourself in and the pickings are slim. If you're looking for less expensive business hotels, Ueno, Ikebukuro and even Shinjuku represent much better value for money.

Shibuya Business Hotel (☎ 3409-9300), on a backstreet behind Shibuya post office, is the cheapest choice in the area. Rooms are small but sufficient. Singles/doubles/twins start at ¥7900/11,400/12,900.

Hotel Sun Route Shibuya (☎ 3464-6411) has singles for ¥6700, if you're willing to make do with a shared bath. Otherwise, rooms start at ¥10,000/13,000/17,500.

Shibuya Tōbu Hotel (☎ 3476-0111) is probably the nicest place to stay in Shibuya. The rooms are clean, the common areas are pleasant, there are loads of in-house restaurants and the staff speak English. Rooms here start at ¥12,000/14,400/17,000.

Shibuya Tōkyū Inn (☎ 3462-0109) has rooms from ¥14,700/21,200/22,600. Although it's closer to Shibuya station, it's really not worth paying this much for rooms similar to those at Shibuya Tōbu Hotel.

Roppongi & Akasaka These are good areas in which to be based if you want access to central Tokyo and a lively nightlife (it's possible to walk down to Roppongi from Akasaka).

In Roppongi, right near the famous Roppongi crossing, *Hotel Ibis* (☎ 3403-4411) is a clean, modern hotel with a few restaurants and bars in the building. This being Roppongi, you can count on the staff being used to foreign guests. Singles/doubles/twins start at ¥11,500/14,100/19,000.

Akasaka Yōkō Hotel (☎ 3586-4050), in Akasaka, is a reasonably priced business hotel about midway between Akasaka and Roppongi. Although it's quite simple, the rooms are clean and the staff are friendly. Singles/doubles start at ¥8900/14,000.

On the same street, 100m closer to Roppongi, *Marroad Inn Akasaka* (☎ 3585-7611) is another standard business hotel with features similar to the Yōkō Hotel; singles/doubles/twins start at ¥9400/10,300/15,000.

Places to Stay – Top End

Although Tokyo is one of the world's most expensive cities, its top-end hotels are no more expensive than similar hotels anywhere else, and you get Japan's legendary high standard of service.

Top-end hotels are found mostly in central Tokyo. Given that all such hotels have very high standards, location should be a prime factor in deciding where you stay. The areas around Ginza and the palace have a certain snob-appeal, but the Akasaka area, which combines a good central location with nearby entertainment options, is an equally good choice. The west side of Shinjuku has a concentration of top-notch hotels, and is a good area in which to see Tokyo at its liveliest.

Among Tokyo's best are: Hotel Seiyo Ginza (which also happens to be the most expensive), Akasaka Prince, the Hotel New Otani and Hotel Ōkura. The following prices are for the least expensive rooms available in each hotel.

Central Tokyo Along with Akasaka, Ginza is home to the thickest concentration of elite hotels anywhere in Tokyo. Prices here reflect the glamorous surroundings and proximity to Tokyo station, great shopping, good restaurants, and the political and financial districts of the city.

Ginza Tōkyū Hotel (☎ 3541-2411) is a spacious hotel not far from Tsukiji Fish Market. Singles/doubles/twins start from ¥16,000/26,000/26,000.

Ginza Dai-Ichi Hotel (☎ 3542-5311) is similar to Tōkyū Hotel, but the advantage here is the array of good restaurants and bars that grace its upper and lower floors. Room prices start at ¥17,000/26,000/25,000.

A clean, new hotel just south of Kabuki-za Theatre is *Renaissance Tokyo Hotel Ginza Tōbu* (☎ 3546-0111). The restaurants and bars are excellent and its spacious rooms are priced at ¥23,000/28,000/28,000.

One of Tokyo's grand old hotels, *Imperial Hotel* (☎ 3504-1111) is within walking distance of the sights of Ginza and Hibiya-kōen. It has all the standard amenities in a very elegant setting, and rooms are large and tastefully appointed. In the main building, singles/doubles start at ¥30,000/35,000.

For an experience of over-the-top service in impossibly dignified surroundings, try *Hotel Seiyo Ginza* (☎ 3535-1111). Room prices range from ¥48,000 to ¥72,000.

Finally, directly alongside the Kōkyo, *Palace Hotel* (☎ 3211-5211) is in the running for the best location in Tokyo. Many rooms here command impressive views over the palace. The service is wonderful and the hotel's restaurants are among the best in Tokyo; rooms start at ¥24,000/29,000/28,000.

Asakusa *Asakusa View Hotel* (☎ 3847-1111) is just about Asakusa's only luxury hotel. The 28-storey building boasts an assortment of restaurants, a swimming pool, one storey with Japanese-style rooms, and a shopping area. Singles/doubles/twins start at ¥13,000/21,000/25,000.

Ikebukuro Unless you have a good reason to be based here, there seems little point in paying top-end prices to stay in bawdy Ikebukuro. However, if Ikebukuro is where you want to be, you can try *Hotel Metropolitan* (☎ 3980-1111), on Ikebukuro's west side. This hotel has all the amenities you'd expect, including ample dining and entertainment options, some of which are located on the 27th floor, affording good views over Tokyo and beyond. Singles/doubles/twins here start at ¥16,500/22,000/22,000.

Shinjuku In east Shinjuku, next to Seibu Shinjuku station, *Shinjuku Prince Hotel* (☎ 3205-1111) is a rather drab choice in this price bracket. Singles/doubles/twins start at ¥15,000/17,000/26,000.

In west Shinjuku, the 47-floor *Keiō Plaza Inter-Continental Hotel* (☎ 3344-0111) provides excellent views of the area and quick access to the station. Rooms here start at ¥20/000/24,000/24,000.

Hilton Tokyo (☎ 3344-5111) offers great service, sports facilities, a convenient location and a variety of good restaurants. Its room prices start at ¥23,000/27,000/27,000.

Nearby, *Century Hyatt Hotel* (☎ 3349-0111) offers a similar level of service and spacious rooms, both Western- and Japanese-style, and a 28th-floor pool. Rooms are priced at ¥23,000/32,000/30,000.

A new place in west Shinjuku is *Hotel Century Southern Tower* (☎ 5354-0111), on the upper floors of the Odakyū Southern Tower building. Clean and modest rooms with good views start at ¥16,000/22,000/22,000.

Lastly, for a hotel experience unlike any other, check out the breathtaking *Park Hyatt Tokyo* (☎ 5322-1234), on the upper floors of the new 53-floor Shinjuku Park Tower – it's an island of luxury in the sky. The rooms are new, clean, very stylish, and complemented by some of the most impressive bars and restaurants in Tokyo. Add to this the rooftop pool, the exercise studio overlooking the city, and a great spa-bath and sauna room, and you've got one of the city's best top-end hotels. Singles/doubles are ¥47,000/52,000. Even if you don't stay here, at least stop by for a drink in the New York Bar.

Akasaka & Roppongi Akasaka has a high concentration of luxury hotels because it is a great area in which to be based: there are loads of good restaurants nearby, the political and business centres are within walking distance and Roppongi's nightlife is just down the road.

Akasaka Tōkyū Hotel (☎ 3580-2311) is right in the heart of Akasaka, just above Akasaka-mitsuke subway station. There are lots of good bars and restaurants scattered throughout the building. Singles/doubles/twins start at ¥16,000/28,000/23,000.

Capitol Tōkyū Hotel (☎ 3581-4511) is an elegant place up on the same hill as Hie-jinja. The hotel is built around a fine Japanese garden, with good restaurants and bars from which to take in the view. In warmer months, you can make use of the outdoor swimming pool. Rooms start at ¥23,000/35,500/35,500.

Another skyscraper hotel, *Akasaka Prince Hotel (☎ 3234-1111)* is something of a landmark. The rooms provide excellent views and spaciousness, a commodity in short supply in Tokyo. Western-style rooms start at ¥27,000/37,000/34,000. Japanese-style suites start at ¥95,000.

Hotel New Otani (☎ 3265-1111), not far from the Akasaka Prince, is renowned for the Japanese garden around which it is constructed (see Hotel Sights under Akasaka, earlier). The hotel itself is massive, with all the amenities you'd expect from a hotel of this class, including extensive shopping areas, restaurants and private meeting rooms. Rooms here are priced from ¥28,500/33,500/41,000.

At the top of a very exclusive bunch, *Hotel Ōkura (☎ 3582-0111)*, near the US embassy, is the home of visiting dignitaries and businesspeople. With a fine Japanese garden, elegant common areas and some of Tokyo's best restaurants, there's little reason to leave the hotel. Prices start at ¥28,500/37,000/40,000.

ANA Hotel Tokyo (☎ 3505-1111), midway between Akasaka and Roppongi in the fashionable Ark Hills area, is an excellent choice. Rooms in this modern 37-storey hotel start at ¥24,000/31,000/28,000, and all the amenities are on offer – fitness clubs, an outdoor pool, saunas, salons, shopping, and lots of good bars and restaurants.

In Roppongi itself, *Roppongi Prince Hotel (☎ 3587-1111)* is a good, modern choice. It's built around a huge atrium with an outdoor, heated swimming pool at its centre. If you run out of things to do inside the hotel, the nightlife of Roppongi is only 10 minutes' walk away. Room prices start at ¥19,500/24,500/23,000.

Near Narita Airport For hotels near Narita airport, see the Narita section of the Around Tokyo chapter.

PLACES TO EAT

No city in Asia can match Tokyo for the sheer variety and quality of its restaurants. As well as refined Japanese cuisine, Tokyo is loaded with great international restaurants – everything from Cambodian to African. One thing to keep in mind is that Japanese food tends to be cheaper than international food. For ¥750 you can get a good bowl of noodles in a *shokudō* (all-round eatery); the same money will buy you a plate of spaghetti in one of Tokyo's many cheap Italian places, but it's sure to be a disappointment. If you fancy international food, be prepared to pay a little extra for the good stuff.

Whatever you choose to eat, you rarely have to look far for a restaurant in Tokyo. Check out the basements and upper floors of the big department stores for *resutoran-gai* (restaurant streets) – these invariably have a good selection of Japanese, Chinese and Italian restaurants with inexpensive lunchtime specials. Train stations are the home of rāmen shops, *obentō* (boxed meal) stands and *kareraisu* (curry rice) restaurants. Big commercial districts like the east side of Shinjuku simply brim with restaurants – serving everything from *kaiten-zushi* (revolving, or 'conveyor-belt' sushi) to pizza.

During the day, the best eating areas are the big shopping districts like Shibuya, Shinjuku, Harajuku and Ginza. By night, try Aoyama and Roppongi for some of Tokyo's best international and Japanese food. For something more traditional, try an izakaya or Yakitori Alley in central Tokyo, or the down-at-the-heels eating arcade of Omoide-Yokochō in Shinjuku.

If you are going to be in Tokyo for some time, pick up a copy of John Kennerdell's *Tokyo Restaurant Guide* (Yohan) or Rick

Kennedy's *Good Tokyo Restaurants*. Alternately, check out the Tokyo Food Page Web site at www.bento.com/tokyofood.html, or Tokyo Q's food section at www.so-net.jp/tokyoq, for some up-to-the-minute picks.

Vegetarian

Vegetarian food is less common than you might expect in Tokyo. Luckily, many places that aren't strictly vegetarian, such as Japanese noodle and *tōfu* (bean curd) shops, serve a good variety of no-meat and no-fish dishes. For more information, pick up the TIC's *Vegetarian & Macrobiotic Restaurants in Tokyo* handout. This lists strictly vegetarian restaurants, wholefood shops, *shōjin-ryōri* (Buddhist-temple fare) restaurants, and Indian restaurants that offer a good selection of vegetarian dishes. Also, see the Harajuku & Aoyama entry later in this section for details on three of the city's more popular vegetarian restaurants.

Central Tokyo

Japanese If all you need is a quick bite, you'll find plenty of decent places to eat in the underground mall below Tokyo station. Outside the station, on the Yaesu side, there are some more-interesting choices. *Mikuniya* is a great place to sample *unagi* (eel) in pleasant surroundings. Its standard unagi set is ¥1800 and includes soup and pickles. Nearby, *Sushi Tetsu* is a proper sushi-restaurant where everything is ¥180 except *toro* (tuna belly; ¥350) and *uni* (sea-urchin roe; ¥400). Give this place a try if you're tired of bad kaiten-zushi.

If these spots don't tempt you, then we suggest heading south to Ginza, where restaurants are more plentiful. Although it's expensive in the evening, lunch deals are competitive with those in other areas of town. A few resutoran-gai to check are *Restaurant City*, on the 8th floor of the Matsuya department store; B2 floor of the *Matsuzakaya department store;* and the basement floors of the Ginza Palmy Building, where ¥400 buys a good bowl of rāmen at *Naokyū Rāmen*.

For inexpensive noodle and rice dishes, try *Dondo*, on the other side of the tracks

from Ginza in the direction of Hibiya. Lunch sets start at ¥800. For tastier noodles, head down to *Jangara Rāmen* and order *zenbu iri* (all-in) rāmen for ¥1000.

For a taste of pre-economic-miracle Tokyo, it's worth taking a look around Yūraku-chō's *Yakitori Alley* in the evening. This under-the-tracks litter of scruffy bars is gradually being squeezed out by more genteel establishments, but what's left is still old-time earthy Tokyo at its best – figure on spending ¥1500 per head on beer and some yakitori.

Another great spot under the tracks is *Shin-Hi-No-Moto*, a lively izakaya just around the corner from Yūraku-chō station. The manager, an English expat by the name of Andy, makes the daily trip to Tsukiji and serves delicious sashimi and cooked fish. This is a good chance to try a real izakaya without any language hassles. Count on about ¥2500 for a good feed and some beer.

Ginza is also a good place to dip into Japanese beer-hall culture. *Sapporo Lion Beer Hall* is the biggest, and a good place to start. The extensive menu includes everything from Japanese snacks to German sausages – food and beers will set you back ¥2000 to ¥2500.

Just south of Harumi-dōri is *New Torigin*, hidden away down a very narrow back-alley but signposted in English. There's an English menu too, and this authentic, very popular little place does excellent yakitori at ¥120 to ¥200 per stick, and the steamed-rice dish known as *kamameshi* for ¥700. A complete meal with a beer costs about ¥1500.

Back near the railway tracks is one of Tokyo's most celebrated izakaya, *Robata*. Most of the offerings here are laid out on big plates so it's simply a matter of pointing at what looks good. Plan on about ¥2500 per head for dinner. It's hard to spot the sign, even if you can read Japanese; it's better just to look for the rustic, weathered facade.

Another atmospheric spot in the same price range is *Chichibu Nishiki*, a traditional izakaya with good, cheap food in a very authentic setting. It's tucked away a few blocks behind Kabuki-za, north of the Ginza Dai-Ichi Hotel.

Everywhere Vendors

There are no prizes for guessing that Japan has the largest number of vending machines per capita in the world – about 4.5 million and counting. You cannot walk for five minutes without bumping into one. A major reason must be that they go unmolested in Japan. In most countries, plonking a beer-vending machine down on a suburban street-corner would be unthinkable.

You can buy almost anything from vending machines. Soft drinks, coffee, cigarettes and beer are the most common products. Less common machines sell goods ranging from rice and vegetables to neckties and computer software. Sometimes there are condom vending machines outside pharmacies, and pornography (magazines and videos) machines are found in some areas.

Probably the most controversial vending-machine venture in recent years has been the sale of used panties. Ostensibly once owned and worn by female high-school students, the panties come in vacuum-sealed packs of three (with a photo of the erstwhile owner) and are targeted at the average fetishistic man about town. The cost? Around ¥3000 to ¥5000, making them the perfect, reasonably priced Japanese souvenir for the folks at home.

Ginza is home to two branches of the excellent sushi chain *Hina Sushi*, one of which is located on the 2nd floor of the Nishi Ginza department store. The all-you-can-eat sushi deal for ¥4300 makes a good splurge for lovers of raw fish.

Of course, Ginza is the place for establishment upmarket dining too. Assuming you want to splash out, *Ten'ichi* (☎ 3571-1949) is *the* place for *tempura* (lightly battered portions of seafood or vegetables). Lunch will start at ¥3500, dinner at ¥8000.

Another good spot for a splurge on traditional Japanese food is *Zakuro*, on the B1 floor of the Ginza Saison Restaurant Plaza, behind Mitsukoshi department store. The speciality here is *shabu-shabu* (thin slices of beef and vegetables cooked in a broth at

the table), sets of which start at around ¥5000 at dinner.

Finally, for a truly elegant meal of sushi, try *Kyubei*, in southern Ginza near Shimbashi, an elegant place where sushi dinners easily cost ¥10,000.

International The popular *Nair's* Indian restaurant (in eastern Ginza towards Tsukiji) always seems to have a queue at lunch, because the restaurant's small scale allows the proper attention to be paid to the food. Expect to pay about ¥1500 for lunch.

Another Indian place worth a try is *Maharaja*, a short walk from Sukiyabashi crossing. The ¥950 all-you-can-eat lunch buffet includes rice, *nan* and four kinds of curry. A good Asian spot is *Restaurant Indonesia*, which usually has lunch specials on display out front for around ¥1000.

Without a doubt, the best value in Ginza is *Farm Grill*, which puts out an enormous all-you-can-eat spread of typical Western favourites for ¥1500 at lunch (from 11.30 am to 5 pm) and ¥2300/1900 for men/women at dinner (from 5 to 11 pm). The quality here is better than at most of Tokyo's all-you-can-eat places, and the desserts and salad bar are excellent by Japanese standards. It's under the highway, across the street from the Ginza Dai-Ichi Hotel.

In another price range entirely is *Maxim's de Paris* (☎ 3572-3621), in the Sony Building. The interior and the menu are dead ringers for the original in Paris. Plan on around ¥5000 for lunch and ¥20,000 for dinner (with wine).

In the same building, *Sabatine di Firenze* (☎ 3573-0013) serves over-the-top Italian fare for that special night out. Expect prices in the same league as those at Maxim's de Paris.

Ueno

Japanese The Ueno area is a happy hunting ground for cheap food. You'll find a good variety of cheap Japanese places in and around Ameya-yokochō arcade, where you can also pick up takeaway foods like yakitori, rice balls and fruit from vendors.

Near the arcade, **Ueno Yabu Soba** is a famous *soba* (thin, brown buckwheat noodles) shop that sells the basic article for only ¥600. To really fill up, however, get the *tenseiro* set, which includes tempura for ¥1800. The black-on-white sign is in Japanese but the large picture menu makes ordering a snap.

An excellent place across from the station is **Maguroyāsan**. 'Maguro' means tuna, and if it can be made from tuna, it's probably on the menu. Exotic and tasty *maguro gyōza* (tuna-filled dumplings) cost ¥400. The lunch sets are great: a large bowl of tuna-topped rice (seafood *donburi*), with salad for ¥880, or cold *udon* (thick, white, wheat noodles) for ¥950. The restaurant is nonsmoking during lunch hours.

For decent sushi and *teishoku* (set-course meal) deals at lunch and dinner, try **Ganko Sushi**, on the 6th floor of the Nagafuji Building. It has a picture menu and seems fairly accustomed to foreign customers. Try the sushi *mori-awase* (assortment) for ¥1400 or the tempura *bentō* (¥1100) for lunch or dinner.

Musashino is a *tonkatsu* (deep-fried breaded pork cutlet, served with a special sauce) specialist worth going out of your way for (although the staff do seem a little surprised by the odd foreign customer). The *hire katsu* (lean cutlet) teishoku is ¥1500; the slightly fattier *rōsu katsu* teishoku is ¥1400.

Izu-ei is an elegant choice for authentic Japanese food. The speciality here is unagi and it's tasty. The Izu-ei unagi *bentō* (eel lunch box) costs ¥2500 and includes tempura. Other choices cost from ¥2000 to ¥4000. There is a limited picture menu.

International Old Ueno is not the place to look for international cuisine. That said, you can gorge on decent Indian food at **Samrat**, which does an all-you-can-eat lunch special for ¥890. Otherwise, you'll be looking at the usual cheap fast-food places, all of which are represented in Ueno.

Asakusa

Japanese The area between Sensō-ji and Kaminarimon-dōri is the best place in Asakusa to seek out Japanese food.

A speciality in Asakusa is tempura, and the place to get it is **Daikokuya**, near Nakamise arcade. The place is authentic and the tempura is excellent. Expect to pay about ¥1800 for a meal at lunch (try the tempura donburi) and at least ¥3000 for dinner.

In a similar vein, **Owariya**, on Kaminari-mon-dōri, serves tempura and a variety of noodle dishes. Try the tempura donburi for ¥1300.

For good *okonomiyaki* (meat, seafood and vegetables in a cabbage-and-vegetable batter) in really funky surroundings, try **Sometaro** in Nishi-Asakusa. The standard item here costs ¥400 and you cook it up yourself on a griddle built into your table. Look for the rustic, overgrown facade.

Tatsumiya is an old Edo-period restaurant, full of interesting bric-a-brac, that specialises in *nabe ryōri* (stew; literally, 'pot cuisine') during the winter months. Prices for this speciality average ¥2500. At midday, bentō are available for ¥850. Evening courses that allow you to sample a wide range of goodies cost ¥4200. It's closed on Monday.

For good yakitori and a picture menu, check out **Akiyoshi**, near the Asakusa View Hotel. In addition to standard yakitori, try some *kushi-katsu* (skewers of deep-fried meat, vegetables and seafood) and rice dishes. A full meal and a couple of beers is about ¥3000 per head.

Just down the street, **Asakusa Imahan** is a great place to try sukiyaki or shabu-shabu. The meat is high quality, the preparation excellent and the atmosphere dignified. You're going to have to pay for it, though; sukiyaki sets cost about ¥7000 per person.

A cheaper place to sample sukiyaki and shabu-shabu is **Chinya**, where sukiyaki sets start at ¥1800. Look for the plastic food models in the window.

Close to Asakusa subway station is **Kameya**, said to be the oldest bar in Japan. There's a beer hall on the ground floor, where you order and pay for beer and food as you enter. Upstairs, Western and Japanese food is served. It's closed Tuesday.

International Apart from the standard fast-food offerings, the only decent international

TOKYO

choices in Asakusa are just across Azuma-bashi in the *Asahi Beer Flamme d'Or* complex (you can't miss it – it's got the giant 'golden turd' on top). There are three eateries in the main black building and a brew-pub/restaurant in the nearby circular glass annex. At lunch, the restaurant on the 1st floor of the main building has an all-you-can-eat buffet for ¥1020, including salad, bread, some Chinese and Western fare, and a variety of drinks. None of it is very special, but it's worth paying the price to check out the decor (especially the bathroom).

Ikebukuro

Japanese Ikebukuro is perhaps not the place for a serious Japanese meal but there are plenty of fine places to fill up. At lunchtime, don't forget to check out the restaurant floors in Seibu, Tōbu and Marui department stores.

On the station's eastern side, look for revolving sushi restaurants. Worth recommending is *Komazushi*, a popular place with a friendly atmosphere, where plates start at ¥120. It's near a giant pachinko parlour. A similar automatic sushi place on the same side of the station is *Mawaru Sushi Hana Kan*.

On the west side, *Tonbo* serves good tonkatsu, fried shrimp and related fare. The Tonbo tonkatsu teishoku is ¥850, but a better choice is the hire katsu teishoku for ¥1250.

For a tasty yakitori dinner in approachable, laid-back surroundings, try *Akiyoshi*. There's a large picture menu to help you order and you'll be able to fill up here for between ¥2500 and ¥4000. There's no English sign, but you can easily spot the long counters and smoky grills from out on the street.

Sushi Kazu is a good, standard-issue sushi bar that is definitely a step up from all those revolving sushi bars in the neighbourhood. Whatever you choose, a decent amount of sushi and some beer or sake to wash it down will cost between ¥3000 and ¥5000 per head.

Ikebukuro has plenty of izakaya, like *Tonerian*, a busy place with friendly staff who are used to the occasional gaijin calling in. This is the place to learn about good sake and the master, who speaks English, will be glad to make some suggestions. Count on about ¥3000 for a dinner with drinks. Look for all the empty sake bottles piled up outside.

In a similar vein and right nearby, *Matsukaze* is a rustic izakaya that serves interesting twists on all the standard izakaya favourites. Count on about ¥3500 for dinner. Look for the wooden facade.

Back on the east side, not far from Tōkyū Hands, *Tapa* is cross between an izakaya and a Spanish tapas bar. Count on spending about ¥3000 at dinner to sample a variety of dishes. There's another branch on the 13th floor of Tōbu department store.

Finally, for that wonderful Japanese delicacy, unagi, why not call into *Yamabuki*, which serves *unadon* (unagi over rice) at lunch for ¥980 and dinner for ¥1100. There is a picture menu. Look for all the eel in the window.

International There are lots of cheap international places to eat in Ikebukuro. Some of the deals can be found on department-store restaurant floors. In particular, try the 11–17th floors of Tōbu and the 8th floor of Tōbu's Metropolitan Plaza, where the Italian restaurant *Domani* serves good lunches for around ¥1000 and dinners for ¥2500.

Outside of the department stores, *Oriental Kitchen* serves a vast all-you-can-eat buffet of just about every major Asian food you'd care to name, although none of it is very special. A one-hour lunch binge costs ¥980; a two-hour dinner feast runs to ¥1980. It's on the 2nd floor of its building; look for the large karaoke-box sign.

For large portions of cheap Italian food, head to *Capricciosa*. At lunch you can eat for around ¥1000. Count on double that for dinner.

On a corner across from Nishi-Ikebukuro-kōen is one of Tokyo's few Malaysian restaurants, *Malaychan*. The food is so-so, but it's easy to order from the big picture menu and the drinks are good. *Nasi lemak* (rice with assorted dishes) is a filling introduction to Malaysian food at ¥1070. Lunch sets here start at ¥700.

For reasonable Vietnamese food, try *Myun*, which serves a good lunch set for ¥1500 and a dinner set with seven items for ¥3000. The only drawback is the music: Japanese pop music. Look for the green sign, streetside.

You might want to give *Jembatan Merah* a try for decent Indonesian fare at similar prices. It's on the B1 floor of the Sunshine 60 Building in east Ikebukuro.

Very near Kimi Ryokan, *Taiwan Hsiao Tiao* serves good Taiwanese fare in casual surroundings. Try the steamed *gyōza* (dumplings), the 'healthy' Chinese sake and the crispy duck dishes. At dinner you'll pay around ¥3000. Lunch sets are a bargain at less than ¥1000.

Chez Kibeau serves excellent continental cuisine in a pleasant basement that feels far removed from the chaos on the streets above. The owner speaks English and can help with ordering. Expect to pay around ¥5000 per head for dinner with drinks.

Shinjuku

Japanese Shinjuku is a good place to hunt for bargain meals. Some of the cheaper offerings are pretty grim, including some leathery kaiten-zushi, but a little searching turns up some pleasant surprises.

Don't forget to check the offerings on the restaurant floors of east Shinjuku's many department stores. In particular, Isetan Kaikan has eight floors of restaurants including a branch of *Kushinobo*, a kushi-katsu specialist that serves lunch sets for as low as ¥1000. *Takashimaya Times Square* also has a restaurant park on its 12th–14th floors, with 28 restaurants to choose from.

Outside of the department stores you'll also find plenty to choose from. For excellent tempura at reasonable prices, try *Tsunahachi*, behind Mitsukoshi department store. Its ¥2500 tempura teishoku is highly recommended for dinner. Best of all, there's an English menu and the staff seem accustomed to foreign customers.

For good tonkatsu, head to *Suzuya*, on Yasukuni-dōri. The katsu here are high quality (not greasy) and come in filling sets that include rice and miso soup. We suggest the

hire katsu teishoku (¥1450). It's on the 2nd floor, with signs at street level on the corner.

Also in Kabuki-chō, *Shinjuku Negishi* serves beef tongue and beef stew sets for around ¥1000. It's tasty stuff, and the set meal it comes with is healthy. This cosy little spot is sandwiched between Beijing Rāmen and Tainan Taami Taiwanese restaurant (see the International entry later).

Daikokuya is a good place for hungry, budget-minded travellers, with its all-you-can-eat *yaki-niku* (grilled meat; ¥1500), shabu-shabu (¥1950) and sukiyaki (¥3500) courses – add ¥1300 and it's all-you-can-drink too.

In a similar vein, *Suehiro* specialises in cheap lunch and dinner sets (Japanese versions of Western favourites like steak and hamburger). Expect to pay around ¥1000 for lunch.

Ibuki, an excellent sukiyaki and shabu-shabu restaurant, has an English menu and sign, and gets a lot of foreign visitors. Pop in and try a sukiyaki course for ¥2500 or shabu-shabu for ¥3200.

For authentic rāmen, try *Keika Ku mamoto Rāmen*, out towards Shinjuku-sanchōme. The noodles are distinctively chewy and the broth is thick. Try the *chashūmen* (rāmen with roast pork) for ¥800. You order and pay as you enter.

Lastly, for a taste of Occupation-era Tokyo – tiny restaurants packed willy-nilly into a wonderfully atmospheric old alley – try *Omoide-yokochō*, street beside the JR tracks just north-west of Shinjuku station. Here, local workers stop off for yakitori, *oden* (fishcakes, tōfu, vegetables and eggs simmered for hours in a kelp-flavoured broth), noodles and beer before braving the trains back home. It's pointless to make recommendations; most of the places serve the same thing and few have names. What they serve will be piled high on the counters; just point and eat. Expect to pay about ¥2500 per person for a memorable time.

International This is a good place to look for good deals on international food. However, there's a lot of junk mixed in with the bargains in Shinjuku. Beware of all-you-can-eat specials and other such deals – there's a reason why the food is so cheap. In addition to the places listed here, see the Clubhouse entry under Bars & Clubs in the Entertainment section later.

For good Chinese-style rāmen, head to **Peking** in Kabuki-chō. It gets no awards for warm and friendly service, but the noodles are authentic, and so are the Chinese staff. Rāmen starts at ¥800 and six gyōza go for ¥300.

The closest thing you'll get to a South-East Asian night-market is **Kabukichō Yatai Mura** (Street Stall Village), behind the Shinjuku ward office. The quality here varies, but for around ¥1500 you can put together a meal of Thai, Korean, Japanese and Chinese food.

Better Thai can be had at **Ban Thai**, Kabuki-chō fixture. Lunches here go for less than ¥1000 but aren't very special. You'd do better to go at dinner and order a la carte, which will run to about ¥2000 a head.

For great Taiwanese cuisine in a rowdy izakaya atmosphere, try **Tainan Taami**. The menu comes complete with photographs of the dishes, which are small, ranging in price from ¥300 to ¥600.

For inexpensive Mexican food in a real hole-in-the-wall atmosphere, check out **El Borracho**. As with most Japanese versions of Mexican food, it's none too authentic, but this place isn't bad. El Borracho is next to Mos Burger; look for the Aztec motif.

For yum cha or dim sum, one of the few possibilities is **Tokyo Dai Hanten**, on the 3rd floor of the unfortunately named Oriental Wave building. For Sunday brunch it serves dim sum a la Hong Kong, bringing it around on trolleys. With a pot or two of good Chinese tea, expect to fill up for about ¥4000 a head.

Canard, tucked into a tiny alley near Hanazono-jinja, serves good French food in cosy surroundings. Lunch courses here start at ¥1500 and dinner courses at ¥2500 (but plan on ¥10,000 for two with a good bottle of wine).

Over in west Shinjuku, a good spot for a light lunch is **Royal Deli**, under the Shinjuku Mitsui Building. It does a whole range of

sandwiches and other deli fare and there's a nice outdoor patio for the warmer months. Count on about ¥900 for lunch. You can also pick up a good takeaway lunch here.

For authentic thick-skinned Beijing-style gyōza and other Chinese fare, try **Raobian Gyozakan**. The gyōza here are so good that you don't need sauce for dipping. However, the portions are small and you'll have to pay at least ¥3000 to fill up.

Among all the fine restaurants in the hotels of west Shinjuku, one place worth going out of your way for is the **New York Grill** (☎ 5323-3458), on the 52nd floor of the Park Hyatt Tower. This is power dining at its best – hearty portions of steak and seafood and a drop-dead view. One bargain worth mentioning is the ¥3900 Sunday brunch. On the way in, you can warm up with a few drinks at the adjoining New York Bar.

Harajuku & Aoyama

Japanese In trendy Harajuku and Aoyama there aren't many Japanese places; international cuisine is the rule here. However, there are a few spots worth recommending.

Maisen is a shrine dedicated to that classic Japanese dish, tonkatsu. If you'd like to give it a try, this is the place. Its hire katsu teishoku is good value at ¥1500 and there is a selection of other classic Japanese dishes. Those on a tighter budget might want to opt for cheaper versions of the same at **Shūtarō**, on Takeshita-dōri – good, but not as good.

Momonoki House is a new-agey Japanese health-food restaurant where vegetarians will have plenty to choose from. Count on about ¥1400 for lunch, double that for a really interesting dinner. It's closed on Sunday.

For a quick nibble as you make your way down Omote-sandō, drop in to **Genroku** for good kaiten-zushi. Plates start at ¥120 and there's a lot to choose from.

International Harajuku and Aoyama have more bistros, cafes and trattorias than most small European cities. The heart of it all is the famous promenade of Tokyo's young and beautiful: Omote-sandō. The street is lined with outdoor cafes, most of which are slavish reproductions of French ones. **Cafe**

de Rope and *Stage Y2* are two typical Omote-sandō cafes worth a try. Better still is the fabulously popular *Ferbecco,* on the ground floor of the Vivre building. All the standard coffee drinks can be had here for around ¥350 as well as good sandwiches (from ¥300) and pizza (from ¥500).

Apetito is a popular little shop that sells sandwiches far superior to the limp versions you find in convenience stores. It also sells a variety of coffee-shop drinks – and there's a patio. With lunch or dinner in the ¥700 range (including a drink), this is about the best budget option in these parts.

In a similar vein, but more expensive, *News Deli* serves a lot of the things you might find in a New York deli, including several options for vegetarians. You'll have to spend around ¥1200 to get full here, perhaps more.

Vegetarians will find more to their liking in the Crayon House building, which houses two organic restaurants. The first, *Hiroba,* does an excellent organic lunch buffet for ¥1260. The second, *Organic Restaurant Home,* is more of a sit-down-and-order kind of place, where set lunches start at ¥1800. Both Japanese and Western-style dishes are on offer here. There's also a small organic food store.

A good place to combine drinks and dinner is *Tacos del Amigo,* a Mexican restaurant near Harajuku station with a pleasant indoor-outdoor atmosphere. The food is average and the prices a bit steep, but it's fun all the same. Across the street, *Zest* serves Mexican food of similar quality for similar prices.

Bamboo Cafe is yet another outdoor cafe-style restaurant, where you can have sandwiches made on three different types of bread, and salads to go with them. Expect to drop around ¥1000 for a light lunch with a drink.

Son of Dragon ('Ryunoko' in Japanese) serves pretty good Sichuan cuisine in a smoky basement off Meiji-dōri. Try the *banbanji* (cold chicken and sesame sauce) and any of the noodle dishes. You can fill up here for around ¥2500 per head.

Quit your diet? Try *Tony Roma's* on Aoyama-dōri for some American-style ribs and onion rings. There are also passable salads for the nonravenous.

For a look at expat life in pleasant, expansive surroundings, check out *Las Chicas.* This is where cool and wannabe-cool expats come to pose and peer. The yuppie-style food is pretty good too – from pizzas to salads to sandwiches – and the wine list is solid. There's also a bar to repair to after dinner.

Lastly, for that special splurge, try the French offerings at *Le Papillon de Paris,* a chic spot in the Hanae Mori building. Lunch courses start at ¥1800 and dinner courses at a hefty ¥8000.

Shibuya

Japanese Take the briefest of looks around Shibuya, and it will probably occur to you that there must be a lot of restaurants lurking in all those department stores. There are. Try the 7th floor of Parco Part 1 or the 8th floor of the One-Oh-Nine Building.

Jūnikagetsu Restaurant Building (Jūnikagetsu means '12 months' for all you language students) is a collection of good restaurants all under one roof. Here, you can choose from yaki-niku, shabu-shabu, seafood *teppanyaki* (high-class steak dinner) and, perhaps best of all, sushi served by *Hina Sushi.* Its ¥4000 all-you-can-eat special is good value.

The adventurous (you will some some Japanese) should show their support to *Tamakyū,* the creaking little pile of timber that refused to be budged by the 109 Building; it's about the only non-shiny thing left in Shibuya. Inside is a lively little izakaya, not one of Tokyo's best, but not bad. Expect to pay ¥2000 to ¥2500 with drinks.

A good choice for yakitori is *Akiyoshi,* an approachable place with a large picture menu. Dinner here should cost about ¥3000.

Kushinobo is the place to sample that great Japanese treat, kushi-katsu. It's on the 5th floor of the J & R Building, across from Wendy's. Plan on ¥3000 for dinner. Lunch courses start at ¥1000.

Lastly, for excellent udon, try *Myōkō,* where a pot of delicious noodles in a hearty broth costs ¥980 to ¥1200, depending on what extras you order.

International There's no shortage of international cuisine here. The best places to look are the small streets around the station and the built-up shopping areas around the giant department stores.

One of our favourite stops for lunch is *New York Kitchen,* where you can get proper bagel sandwiches with a variety of fillings for only ¥280. There's also a good deli-bar where you can choose from six or seven different salads etc for ¥580. There's cheap coffee and espresso as well.

In a similar vein, *Segufredo Zanetti* is a popular discount cafe where the espresso is ¥200 and *panini* sandwiches are ¥280. Likewise, *Natural Station,* on the ground floor of the 109 Building, does simple sandwiches, and fresh fruit and vegetable juices from ¥280 for a small cup.

Samrat serves the usual Indian curries and curry sets for less than ¥1000. There's usually a tout outside beckoning people in.

Tainan Taami is a great choice for good Taiwanese fare in raucous, if slightly smoky, surroundings. Plan on around ¥3000 per person. For similar Taiwanese fare and surroundings, check out *Reikyō,* where prices are in the same range. It's in a triangular redbrick building. There's mainland-Chinese cuisine at *Ryūnohige,* where standard noodle and rice dishes start at ¥1000.

Bougainvillea, across from Bunkamura, serves Vietnamese food. It's no great shakes, but if you've got a hankering for South-East Asian, this will probably do the trick. You should be able to fill up on ¥3000 at dinner.

Kantipur is a Nepali restaurant that seems to borrow a lot from India (perhaps *dal bhat* is a limited menu for a restaurant). This place is a little bit back from the street and can be tough to spot. Prices are similar to the aforementioned restaurants.

Lastly, for a minor splurge, try *Siam Thai,* where dinner courses of good Thai food start at ¥3000.

Ebisu & Daikanyama

Japanese Try the 6th floor of the Atre building, over Ebisu station, for all the standard Japanese favourites, including tasty tonkatsu served at *Saboten.* Down on street level,

you'll get even tastier tonkatsu at *Tentsu Tonkatsu,* where the hire katsu teishoku goes for ¥1150. Nearby, *Fujii* is a good place to sample fresh, handmade udon. We recommend the tempura udon for ¥1500. There is no English sign, but you'll see food models in the window, just up the street from KFC.

An An is an offbeat izakaya where the master turns out modern versions of traditional favourites, with a generous sprinkling of international choices thrown in. Seating is communal, so if you don't speak Japanese, just point at whatever looks good from among your neighbours' plates. Look for the very plain wooden front and the portable sign on the sidewalk. Count on spending about ¥4000 per person.

Nanaki Soba is an izakaya with standard-issue food, a picture menu and a good selection of sake. It's only open in the evening.

For a cheap bowl of noodles, try *Ippūdō Rāmen* over on the other side of the station. This place serves Kyūshū-style rāmen into which you can grate garlic cloves laid out specially for the purpose.

For a really special Japanese meal, try *Shunsenbō,* which specialises in tōfu dishes and shabu-shabu. Lunch courses start at ¥1000 and dinner courses from ¥3800 – a real bargain considering the quality of the food and the elegant surroundings. Best of all, there's an English menu. It's in the Ebisu Prime Square Plaza complex, on the ground floor.

You'll find Japanese restaurants few and far between in Daikanyama, as the area has its gaze fixed firmly on the West (see the following International section).

International Daikanyama rivals Harajuku and Aoyama as the centre of Tokyo cafe society and it's a good place to grab a cappuccino and do some people watching. You'll also find plenty of trendy foreign restaurants, some of which are good and some of which are merely fashionable.

Caffe Michelangelo is Tokyo's best impersonation of Paris and it's a good place to watch the beautiful people on a weekend afternoon. You'll pay for the pleasure, though – coffee starts at ¥600.

A more reasonable option is *Café Artifagose*, which has great outdoor seating, good breads and cheeses and a fine selection of drinks. In the same vein but cheaper still is *Gazebo Café*, halfway between Ebisu and Daikanyama. The sandwiches are pretty good here but the view leaves something to be desired.

For pasta, sandwiches (¥700) and similar light fare, try *Café Juliet*, which has a pleasant outdoor eating area. The coffee here, though good, is inexplicably expensive. Downstairs you'll find the chic *KM Fils*, where decent but overpriced French fare starts at ¥2500 for lunch and about twice that for dinner.

In terms of atmosphere, the pick of the bunch in Daikanyama is the interesting *Bombay Bazar*, a restaurant that *claims* to serve organic food (we doubt it). It makes decent curries and has an varied drink selection. Count on spending around ¥1200 for a drink and a meal.

Another good choice out on Kyūyamatedōri is *Monsoon Cafe*, about 300m past the Danish Embassy on the left side of the street. The multilevel affair of outdoor terraces and spacious dining rooms is a great place for a meal and drink on a warm summer evening. The food, though none too special, is an interesting mix of South-East Asian classics like Vietnamese spring rolls and Malaysian satay. Expect to drop about ¥2500 for dinner with a drink.

Akasaka

Japanese Akasaka is packed with excellent Japanese restaurants, though bear in mind that bargains are few and far between. For starters, take a stroll in the streets running off and parallel to Sotobori-dōri. In this neighbourhood there are branches of expensive restaurant chains such as *Tenichi*, where a set dinner-course of tempura in refined surroundings starts at ¥6500; and *Sushi-sei*, a branch of the famous sushi chain, where costs of around ¥4000 per head are the norm (although delicious lunch sets are significantly cheaper).

For an inexpensive lunch try *Kushinobo*, a *kushiage* (skewers of deep-fried meat,

seafood and vegetables) and kushi-katsu specialist on the 3rd floor of the Akasaka Tōkyu Hotel. Dinner courses start at ¥2500. A good tempura place with similar prices is *Tsunahachi*, on the 8th floor of the Belle Vie building.

If the idea of a tōfu restaurant is a new one to you, you'll be surprised at just how many of them there are in Tokyo. *Tōfu-ya* is the perfect introduction to a cuisine that many visitors miss out on – some Japanese-language ability will be helpful here.

For standard izakaya dining, *Yakitori Luis*, close to Akasaka subway station, is a popular yakitori place where prices start at ¥200 per snack.

Finally, for a great bowl of rāmen, try *Jangara Rāmen*, near the entrance to Hiejinja. You can get the standard item here for ¥580, but why not live a little and order the zenbu-iri rāmen for ¥1000.

International Along with nearby Roppongi, Akasaka is one of Tokyo's most cosmopolitan neighbourhoods. While most of the action is in the mid-range bracket, a stroll through the narrow streets just west of Akasaka-mitsuke subway station will turn up a number of good lunch deals.

There are two branches of *Moti*, perhaps Tokyo's best Indian chain, in this neighbourhood, with lunch specials starting at ¥800 and dinners at about ¥2000. Nearby, *The Taj* is a slightly upmarket institution starting to show its age. Nonetheless, the ¥1200 lunch buffet is usually quite well done; dinners run closer to ¥4000 per person.

Trattoria Marumo is a pizzeria that serves a range of Italian fare for reasonable prices. The atmosphere is pleasant and the food is pretty good. There are loads of food models in the window. Count on about ¥1500 for lunch and ¥3000 for dinner. There's a more formal Marumo out on Akasaka-dōri.

Mugyodon is a popular Korean place open for dinner only. This is your chance to sample the real thing, not the usual Japanese version. A good feed will run to about ¥3000. It's upstairs from Uskudar Turkish restaurant.

Down past the TBS complex is *Aozai*, a decent Vietnamese place that serves lunches for around ¥1200 and dinners starting at ¥2500.

Roppongi

Japanese Roppongi's Japanese restaurants tend to be expensive and very accessible to foreigners. This makes it the perfect area for that long-awaited splurge on a special Japanese meal. That said, there are some cheap spots around if you just fancy a quick bite before hitting the bars.

Starting with the cheap stuff, a long-time favourite for Roppongi revellers is *Bikkuri Sushi*, a late-night kaiten-zushi place that's seen it all. For ¥1000 you can make a good dent in your hunger.

For more serious sushi, try the ¥4300 all-you-can-eat special at *Hina Sushi* – a good deal considering the quality of the fare. It's on the B1 floor of the Roppongi Denki building.

Kushimura is a cheapish yakitori spot near some of Roppongi's most notorious bars. You can fill up on yakitori for around ¥2000 a head with a beer to wash it down.

For more serious yakitori, head to *Namban-tei*, something of a Roppongi institution, for excellent yakitori in pleasant surroundings. It won't be cheap – figure on about ¥6000 per head – but it will be delicious.

Kisso (☎ 3582-4191), on the B1 floor of the Axis building, is a good place to sample Japan's gourmet cuisine, *kaiseki ryōri* (beautifully presented multicourse meals). This is without a doubt the most accessible kaiseki in all of Tokyo. Dinner costs about ¥10,000 per person; it's best to order a course and leave everything up to the chef.

Fukuzushi (☎ 3402-4116) serves some of the best sushi in town, in an atmosphere that is decidedly more relaxed than at some of the more traditional places in Ginza and Tsukiji. The fish here is fresh, the portions are large and there's even a cocktail bar. Expect to pay around ¥10,000 each.

Seryna (☎ 3402-1051) is a long-time expat favourite for entertaining important guests from abroad. There are actually three restaurants under the Seryna roof: Seryna Honten (shabu-shabu and sukiyaki), Mon Cher Ton Ton (Kōbe-beef steaks), and Kani Seryna (crab dishes). Dinners cost between ¥10,000 and ¥15,000 per person without drinks. Some lunch specials go for as little as ¥5200 (for shabu-shabu).

Inakaya (☎ 3405-9866), at the Nogizaka end of Gaien-higashi-dōri in Roppongi, has achieved fame as a top-end *robatayaki* (rustic bar-restaurant serving food grilled over charcoal). It does raucous, bustling, don't-stand-on-ceremony robatayaki with gusto. It's possible to spend lots of money (about ¥10,000 a head) *and* have fun. There is also a branch in Akasaka (☎ 3586-3054). It is open daily from 5 to 11 pm.

International It only makes sense that in Roppongi, Tokyo's foreign nightlife playground, there would be a lot of international restaurants. These range from cheap hamburger joints to expensive imports like Wolfgang Puck's Spago. Whatever it is you fancy, you'll find it here – and the bars and clubs of Roppongi are only a step away.

One of the best places to start a Roppongi evening is at the casual *Havana Café*. In addition to great happy-hour drink specials, it serves reliable stuff like burritos and sandwiches for less than ¥1000. The place opens onto a quiet backstreet, and as you sip that first drink, it's difficult to imagine that Roppongi lurks just round the corner.

Hamburger Inn is a Roppongi institution that stays open all night and serves forgettable burgers for around ¥400. Down the hill in Azabu-Jūban, you'll find much better burgers at *Homework's*, the expat burger-joint of preference. Most burgers here run close to ¥1000.

For decent Italian food and excellent streetside people-watching, try *Bellini's Pizza Kitchen*. It has a wide selection of Italian favourites, and lots of drink choices, including cappuccino and espresso. Lunch here is around ¥1500 and dinner ¥3000.

Another fun spot is *Tainam Taami*, an excellent Taiwanese place. Bring a few friends, order lots of dishes and don't be afraid to pick something unusual from the large picture menu. Plan on about ¥2500 per head with a drink.

Moti, right above the subway station, serves up some of Tokyo's best Indian food. Lunch sets cost around ¥1000 and dinners average ¥3000.

For a taste of the south seas, head to the Indonesian *Bengawan Solo*, out on Roppongi-dōri. It's been around for ages, and the food never disappoints. The ¥700 *gado gado* (salad with peanut sauce) lunch is a bargain, and the ¥1100 beef in coconut-cream is delicious. Look for the food models displayed outside.

Another good South-East Asian favourite is *Maenam*, a tackily-decorated but competent Thai place down towards Nishi-Azabu. You can fill up here and down a few festive tropical drinks for about ¥3500 per head.

Next to the Aoyama Reien, *Monsoon Café* serves decent South-East Asian fare in a semi-outdoor cafe-style place. This is a good option for tropical drinks and just hanging out. Again, you're looking at around ¥3500 for a good feed with drinks.

Hard Rock Café and *Tony Roma's* are in the same building. We figure you know what to expect from the former – loud music, oversized portions of passable American food and plenty of reasonably priced drinks. Tony Roma's is another American joint that serves barbecued spare ribs with all the fixings. At either place, a good dinner is in the ¥3000 range, with Tony Roma's the more expensive of the two.

Cheaper Western options include *Salty Box Grill*, a Canadian place that serves a popular brunch for ¥1500; and *Little Tribeca*, a deli that serves coffee starting at ¥180 and bagel sandwiches at ¥350.

Those who fancy a splurge on Western cuisine might want to try the Tokyo branch of *Spago* (☎ 3423-4025), where you can get a fairly reasonable lunch for around ¥3000. Dinners are comfortably double that with a few drinks.

Perhaps a better spot for that splurge would be *Bourbon Street* (☎ 3478-8473), an excellent Cajun place where you can plan on about ¥4500 for dinner with drinks. Whatever the chef is doing with prawns, try them. And the spicy gumbo is a winner too (one order will feed two).

You may fancy a dessert after all this good food. The place to go for this is *Hobson's*, an ice cream parlour right on the Nishi-Azabu crossing.

Odaiba

Japanese There are a few Japanese-style restaurants on this trendy island in the bay. On Restaurant Row you can try *Hina Sushi*, which serves a good all-you-can-eat sushi special for ¥4300. Or, in the Decks Tokyo Beach complex you might try the tonkatsu at *Wakō*, where standard teishoku starts at ¥1000.

International Odaiba is a pleasant place to sample some reasonable international fare, as most of the restaurants have good views of the bay or the beach. On Restaurant Row, *Café Coyote*, a Mexican place, serves passable lunches starting at ¥1200 and dinners at ¥2500. Nearby, *Sam Choy's* serves whopping portions of decent Hawaiian-Asian seafood for similar prices. Up on the 5th floor of the Decks Tokyo Beach complex, the Indian restaurant *Khazana* serves a good ¥1000 all-you-can-eat buffet lunch. You'll have to come early to get one of the coveted tables out on the deck.

ENTERTAINMENT

Tokyo is very much the centre of the Japanese world, and has the best of everything. On the nightlife front, there are those who maintain that Osaka is more cutting edge, but then Osaka offers nowhere near the diversity of entertainment options available in Tokyo – traditional entertainment such as kabuki, avant-garde theatre, countless cinemas, live houses, pubs and bars. See the special colour section 'Performing Arts' for more information on Japanese theatre.

Kabuki

The simplest way to see kabuki in Tokyo is at the *Kabuki-za Theatre* (☎ 5565-6000) in Ginza. Performances and times vary from month to month, so you'll need to check with the TIC or with the theatre directly for program information. Earphone guides providing 'comments and explanations' in

English are available for ¥650 plus ¥1000 deposit. Prices for tickets vary from ¥2400 to ¥16,000, depending on how keen you are to see the stage.

Kabuki performances can be quite a marathon, lasting from 4½ to five hours. If you're not up to it, you can get tickets for the 4th floor from ¥600 to ¥1000 and watch only part of the show (ask for *hitomakumi*) but earphone guides are not available in these seats. Fourth-floor tickets can be bought on the day of the performance. There are generally two performances daily, starting at around 11 am and 4 pm.

Japan's national theatre, *Kokuritsu Gekijō* (π 3265-7411), also has kabuki performances, with seat prices ranging from ¥1500 to ¥9200. Again, earphone guides are available. It's near Nagata-chō station on the Yūraku-chō subway line. Check with the TIC or the theatre for performance times.

Nō

Nō (classical Japanese dance-drama) performances are held at various locations around Tokyo. Tickets cost between ¥2100 and ¥15,000, and it's best to get them at the theatre itself. Check with the TIC or the appropriate theatre for times.

The *Kanze Nō-gakudō* (π 3469-5241) is about a 10- to 15-minute walk from Shibuya station. The *Kokuritsu Nō-gakudō* (π 3423-1331) – the National Nō Theatre – is in Sendagaya. Exit Sendagaya station in the direction of Shinjuku on the left and follow the road that hugs the railway tracks; the theatre is on the left.

Bunraku

Osaka is the home of *bunraku* (classical puppet theatre), but performances do take place in Tokyo several times a year at the *Kokuritsu Gekijō Theatre* (π 3265-7411) in Hayabusa-chō, near Nagata-chō station on the Yūraku-chō subway line. Check with the TIC or the theatre for information.

Tea Ceremonies

A few hotels in Tokyo hold tea ceremonies that you can see and occasionally partici-

pate in for a fee of ¥1000 to ¥1500. *Hotel New Otani* (π 3265-1111) has ceremonies on its 7th floor on Thursday, Friday and Saturday at 11 am and 1 pm. Ring before you go to make sure the day's sitting hasn't been booked out. *Hotel Ōkura* (π 3582-0111) and the *Imperial Hotel* (π 3504-1111) also hold daily tea ceremonies.

Bars & Clubs

Bars and clubs change with the weather in Tokyo, which makes the job of coming up with specific recommendations rather difficult. The following is a run-down on bars and clubs popular at the time of writing. For up-to-the-minute information, check the bars and clubs sections of the Web sites listed in the Internet Resources section earlier.

Ueno & Asakusa This is definitely not the place for a night out in Tokyo. However, if you do find yourself up in old Shitamachi at night, try the *Warrior Celt* pub in Ueno, where drinks are only ¥500 from 5 to 7 pm. It's a friendly place and has a good selection of English and Irish brews. In Asakusa, try the beer halls in the *Asahi Flamme D'Or* complex. Otherwise, check the entry for Kameya, under Asakusa in the Places to Eat section earlier.

Ikebukuro There are lots of izakaya on both sides of the station (see Japanese in the Ikebukuro entry under Places to Eat). If you'd prefer something Western-style, try *The Dubliners*, a faux-Irish pub offering Kilkenny and Guinness draught for ¥850, and fish and chips for ¥750. The only bummer here is that it shuts down at 11 pm. In a similar vein but open much later is *The Black Sheep*, behind Bic Personal Computer Store. The place is often packed on weekend nights when it features live bands.

Another late-night option is *Bobby's Bar*, on the 3rd floor of the Milano building on the western side of the station. There's table soccer, darts and good music and it's open until 3 am on weekends. Early birds will enjoy the happy hour, from 7 to 9 pm from Monday to Thursday, when all drinks are only ¥400.

Shinjuku Gaudy Shinjuku is awash with nightspots of every shape and size. Of course, a lot of these fall into the sleazy category and don't cater to foreigners. That said, there's still plenty to do here by night if you have the energy to face the madness of an evening on the streets of Shinjuku.

Clubhouse is a welcome arrival on the Shinjuku scene. Officially it's a sports bar, but in reality it's just a good, friendly place for a drink, with a selection of imported and domestic brews (including a few of its own custom brews). It also serves a variety of pub food for dinner and a ¥1000 all-you-can-eat international buffet at lunch.

Dubliners is a recent arrival; look for it on the 2nd floor above the Lion Beer Hall. It's a good spot for an early evening get-together, with live Irish folk music and Guinness on tap (although pints are steep at ¥900). At lunch, Irish stews and the like are available at teishoku prices.

Kirin City is a standard-issue Japanese brew-hall on the edge of Kabuki-chō. There's nothing special about this place, but if you fancy a big mug of brew in decent surroundings, this should do the trick. Other bars in the vicinity include *Rock Bar Mother*, a tiny basement bar with an extensive CD collection and a friendly crowd; and *Rockin' Chair*, a rather more sedate spot for a drink.

Out towards Ni-chōme, *Rolling Stone* is a grubby, low-life place that's been around since the dawn of time and still manages to pull in the crowds on Friday and Saturday nights; there's a ¥1000 cover.

Garam is a club that feels like a bar. It's a small, friendly place, where the master plays a range of hip-hop, reggae etc. Entry is ¥1000. Bigger clubs include *Asa*, a reggae club where a dark suntan seems to be de rigeur; and *Liquid Room* (see the Live Music entry later), which has occasional events – look out for notices in *Tokyo Journal* and in the big CD stores around town.

Lastly, the adventurous traveller will want to try *Golden Gai*, one of the city's most interesting night zones. Even if you don't feel like a drink, take a night stroll through this warren of tightly packed establishments, just to feel the atmosphere – the whole place seems lost in a boozy, rundown time warp. Being so thoroughly Japanese, it's understandable that some of these places are a little leery of foreigners. One sure-fire spot is *Bon's*. There's usually a ¥900 cover, and drinks start at ¥700. Look for it next to the police box.

Once you leave the security of Bon's, you're on your own, but that's part of the fun. Before long, an *'Irasshai!'* will be directed at you. Most places charge about ¥900 to enter and ¥1000 per beer – it's overpriced, but you're paying for an institution.

Harajuku & Aoyama These adjoining areas are a good option when the Roppongi crush is too much to bear.

Oh God has been going for years; miraculously, it is still going. The format seems a little tired, but if your needs run to pool tables and movie screenings, it's just the ticket. Practically next door is *Zest*, another popular pub, which also serves food.

Near the Omote-sandō crossing, there's the tiny, hole-in-the-wall *Mix*. You can usually count on this club, even when others in the neighbourhood are flat. It's small, smoky, crowded and always friendly. Music ranges from reggae to hip-hop. Cover charges vary and drinks start at ¥700. It's rather hard to find; look for the stairs heading down to the basement.

Out towards Shibuya, *Las Chicas* restaurant has a bar and a members' club, both of which are good spots for a drink.

Lastly, don't forget that Harajuku and Aoyama are all about cafes, and you can spend an evening drinking beer and wine in them just as you might in Paris.

Shibuya Youth-oriented Shibuya is not the best place for a night out in Tokyo, especially for elderly travellers (in Shibuya that's anyone over 25). That said, the cavernous new *Bar, Isn't It?* is a cheap choice for those who aren't too picky about where they drink. The deal here is that everything costs ¥500, including the food.

A more atmospheric option is *Sugar High*, a stylish but casual club run by two expat Americans. Music runs from lounge to techno and there is a cover of ¥1000 for special events.

If you want to see what the kids are up to, try the massive *Club Asia*, a techno/soul club where events usually cost ¥2500. It also has a restaurant that serves a variety of South-East Asian food.

On the 2nd and 3rd floor of Dr Jeekhan's building, *Harlem* is the gathering place of Tokyo's B-boy and B-girl wannabees. The music is soul and hip-hop and the cover of ¥2000 includes two drinks. On the 4th to 6th floors of the same building, *Pylon* is another youth-oriented dance club, which plays anything from soul to techno. The cover of ¥2500 includes two drinks.

Ebisu & Daikanyama Ebisu and Daikanyama are excellent choices for a night out in Tokyo, striking the perfect balance between hip and casual. They're especially good if you just can't face the mayhem of Roppongi or Shinjuku.

We like *What the Dickens*, a good British pub with the usual beers on tap, some decent pub-grub and the occasional good live music.

Nearby, *Enjoy House* is one of Tokyo's better clubs/lounges, where you can kick back and listen to a variety of music, from rock to house, in an opium-den atmosphere. Best of all, there's no cover charge. Just around the corner, *Guest* is a casual bar where you may feel like you're chilling out in your friend's flat. The place is presided over by two dogs, and draft beer costs ¥550.

Technophiles and house-lovers will want to check out *Lust*, a big club over on the eastern side of Ebisu station. The cover here is ¥1500 on weekdays and ¥2500 on weekends.

See International under Ebisu & Daikanyama in the Places to Eat section, earlier, for information on the *Monsoon Café*, a hip place for a drink on the outskirts of Daikanyama.

Akasaka Akasaka is an expensive and staid place to drink. The best spots are probably the plush bars in the upper reaches of

the area's luxury hotels. Try *Top of Akasaka*, on the 40th floor of the Akasaka Prince Hotel. Drinks start at ¥1300. *The Bar*, on the 40th floor of the New Otani tower, is a similar spot. Down on street level, you can try *Goose Bar* for a drink in a slightly less formal atmosphere; otherwise, just walk the 20 minutes to Roppongi and take your pick.

Roppongi Roppongi is not part of Japan – it's multinational twilight zone where gaijin get together with adventurous locals to drink until the first trains at dawn. Because of this, many long-termers avoid it like the plague, leaving it for punters fresh off the plane and gormless riff-raff out trolling for local talent. That said, Roppongi is still the heart of Tokyo's nightlife scene, particularly for foreigners, and you'll probably want to check it out at least once.

Starting with the bars, right on the famous Roppongi crossing, you'll find *Geronimo*, a shot bar that gets packed out with all sorts of off-work expats and a few of their Japanese associates. It has good happy-hour specials from 6 to 8 pm and beer is ¥800 no matter what time you go.

On the southern side of Roppongi-dōri, you'll find two good choices next to one another. *Mogambo* is the sister-club of Geronimo, with a similar crowd and prices. Next door, *Castillo* is a small club/bar that plays disco and soul classics. You can dance or just kick back and relax here, but you can't enter unless you're wearing 'smart casual clothes' (that's what the sign says).

Across the street is another zone thick with drinking places. On the first street in from the corner, *Motown House* plays standard rock 'n' roll, and has a long bar and drinks that start at ¥800.

Farther down the same road, on the 3rd floor of the MT building you'll find *Bar, Isn't It?*, an offshoot of a successful Osaka bar-chain. The formula here is simple: a big space, so-so bar food and all drinks for ¥500. All together, it works pretty well, and it's a good place to meet people.

Charleston Club is just a few streets farther south. This used to be an institution of sleaze; now it's just a decent, small bar, where you can put away a pizza while you drink.

Above Bikkuri Sushi you'll find *Propaganda*, an inexpensive shot bar with good happy-hour specials. It's now one of Roppongi's more popular pick-up joints, if that does anything for you.

One of Roppongi's rowdier cul-de-sacs is formed by what used to be one big gaijin-bar, *Gas Panic Bar*, which has split into three bars. Along with the original there's *Club 99 Gas Panic* and *Gas Panic Café*. All three are cheap places to drink, particularly during happy hour. On the down side, these places tend to get packed out with all sorts of yahoos, and fights are not unknown. On the same bad-karma cul-de-sac, you'll find *Déjà Vu*, a much smaller place that draws off some of the Gas Panic crowd.

Paddy Foley's is a decent Irish-style pub, popular with the expat business community. If you want a good pint (about ¥900), convivial surroundings and some space to breathe, join the after-work crowd here.

Sports fans might want to pop into *Pints Sportscafé* to catch the big match on one of its many TVs. It has a variety of drink specials to heighten your viewing pleasure.

On the club front, *Velfarre* is Roppongi's disco Hilton. Dance clubs don't get much bigger, flashier or better behaved than this place. There's a ¥4000/5000 cover for women/men, with three drinks. *Lexington Queen* was one of Roppongi's first discos and is still the place that every visiting celebrity ends up in. The cover here is around ¥5000 unless you're a celebrity or model.

For electronica, you're better off heading to *Yellow*, an interesting, inky space that plays host to some of Tokyo's better club events (cover ¥2000 to ¥3500). Nearby, the new *BuL-Let's* is a mellow basement space that plays worldwide trance and ambient sounds. Cover is ¥1000; it's free before 11 pm.

Techno Events Electronica has caught on in Tokyo in a big way. The city attracts some of the world's best DJs and live acts and boasts an impressive line-up of superb

local talent. Some of the better events take place in Nishi-Azabu's *Yellow*, Shibuya's *Club Asia* (see Shibuya under Bars & Clubs, earlier) and Shinjuku's *Liquid Room* (see the Live Music section). Check *Tokyo Classified* to see what's on while you're in town or stop by Cisco or Tower Records in Shibuya to pick up some flyers.

Gay & Lesbian Venues Tokyo's gay and lesbian enclave is Shinjuku-ni-chōme (see the Shinjuku map). There are lots of little bars here, but some can be rather daunting to enter. *Arty Farty* is one gay venue where anyone can comfortably walk into, but women are admitted only on Sunday. Drinks start at ¥800 and there's a ¥500 table charge. Meeting people is easy here, and it's a good place to learn about the area's other possibilities.

For lesbian offerings and some more gay bars and clubs, check out the *Tokyo Journal's* Cityscope section, which sometimes has a special section called 'Tokyo Out'.

Music
Tokyo is the only city in Asia where you may have the luxury of seeing up-and-coming performers playing in intimate venues. Check the latest issue of *Tokyo Classified* or *Tokyo Journal* or pick up some flyers at Cisco, Manhattan or Tower Records in Shibuya to see who's playing around town. Ticket prices generally range from ¥5000 to ¥8000, depending on the performer and the venue.

Live Music Tokyo's home-grown live-music scene is disappointing given how vibrant the city is in other quarters.

Overseas and local acts perform regularly at *Club Quattro* (☎ 3477-8750) and *On Air West* (☎ 5458-4646) in Shibuya, and at *Liquid Room* (☎ 3200-6811) in Shinjuku. These are places you book tickets for, however, not places you just turn up at in the hope of catching a good live act.

In Harajuku, *Crocodile* (☎ 3499-5205) has live music seven nights a week. There's usually a ¥2000 cover with one drink. It's a spacious place with room for dancing if the music allows it.

TOKYO

Trends

Japan is the land of trends. Nowhere else do trends arise, spread and die with such speed. The reasons for this are simple: affluent youth, merciless advertising, high population density and an insatiable appetite for 'the new'. The birthplace of many Japanese fads is Shibuya, Tokyo's youth-oriented shopping mecca. Here are a few of the trends that have swept Japan in recent years.

Bihaku Until the summer of 1999 parasols were the preserve of older women, but that summer the *bihaku* (white beauty) look took off for the fashionable Japanese girl over 20. Face whiteners and parasols have done a roaring trade with girls trying to stay out of the sun as much as possible.

Puri-kura (Print Clubs) Taking advantage of the Japanese fondness for memorialising any and all events with a photo, *puri-kura* are instant-photo booths that produce sticker-sheets of photos with cutesy borders and messages. Japanese high-school girls collect puri-kura pictures in special scrapbooks, and it's not unusual for a collection to run into the hundreds or thousands of pictures. (A common slang term at the moment is *puri-free*. The 'puri' being print-club photo sticker machines and the 'free' meaning 'not there'. In other words there are no print-club machines in the vicinity – quite a disaster for a young girl.) Puri-kura are readily identifiable – look for the Day-Glo machines with the curtained fronts. If you've got a few hundred yen to spare, you can step into the puri-kura and produce some distinctly Japanese souvenirs.

Ganguro (Dark suntans – literally, 'black face') In Japan, a dark suntan is more than just a souvenir of a day at the beach. It's a social statement, part of a whole uniform that includes outrageous make-up, dyed blonde hair and towering platform shoes. Women who sport this look are known as *yamanba*, a word for mythical witches believed to inhabit the mountains of Japan. These days, yamanba are the source of much outrage among conservative older Japanese, one of whom recently remarked in a magazine article, 'Nothing about them is pretty, elegant or stylish; the main effect, I would say, is to frighten.'

Keitai Denwa (Mobile Phones) These are more than a trend in Japan – they're a way of life. With over 40 million in use, there's almost one keitai denwa for every three Japanese. When you're riding a busy train in Japan, you may feel like half of those 40 million keitai denwa are in use around you. When they're not talking on their keitai, it seems that young Japanese are busy programming their automatic dial features or downloading wireless email messages.

Outrageous Make-up For yamanba, a dark tan isn't complete without heavy, outrageous make-up. More often than not, this includes bright pink lipstick, sparkling glitter and thick circles of eye shadow around the eyes. Against the backdrop of a dark tan, the effect is sometimes raccoon-like – disarming to say the least.

High Heels Towering, thick-soled boots, some with soles up to 20cm thick, are currently all the rage in Japan, especially among yamanba, who want to look taller. Needless to say, walking in 20cm platforms can be hazardous, and it's common to see young Japanese women tottering around holding onto friends and signposts for support. Indeed, the shoes are so high and unstable that they've been the cause of scores of injuries and two known fatalities.

Ruusu Sokusu (Loose Socks) 1998 was the year of loose socks in Japan. In an effort to make their legs look slimmer and more attractive, Japanese high-school girls started wearing outrageously loose socks that draped down over their shoes and even dragged on the ground. Before long, giant purpose-made loose socks were available, along with a special glue to affix them to the calf (without which they would simply fall off). Of course, the trend was over almost as fast as it began, and by the time loose socks arrived in Hokkaidō, they were hopelessly passé in Shibuya.

MICK WELDON

Loft (☎ 3365-0698) in Shinjuku is a Tokyo institution. Had they been Japanese, the Rolling Stones would have played here long before they cut their first single. It's smoky, loud and lots of fun on a good night.

Down in Ebisu, beneath What the Dickens (see Ebisu & Daikanyama under Pubs & Bars earlier), is *Milk* (☎ 5458-2826), which has live music on Thursday and Friday nights. Check out the kitchen – there's no food but it's a great place to chat and sip on a gin and tonic between sets.

Roppongi is the place for 'oldies-but-goodies'. *Cavern Club* (☎ 3405-5207) hosts flawless I-wanna-hold-your-hand covers by four Japanese mop-heads; the cover is ¥1300. *Kento's* (☎ 3401-5755) features 50s standards; the live-music cover is ¥1300.

Forget the 50s, forget the Beatles, *Bauhaus* (☎ 3403-0092) is the place for 70s and 80s rock covers; the cover is ¥1800 with one drink. Bauhaus is on the 6th floor of the Wada building.

Jazz Jazz has a serious following in Tokyo. For listings of performances, check the latest issue of *Tokyo Journal* or *Tokyo Classified*.

Tokyo's big-name jazz venue is *Blue Note Tokyo* (☎ 3407-5781) in Aoyama; a cover charge of between ¥6000 and ¥10,000 keeps the riff-raff away and aficionados within spitting distance of the greats of jazz.

A competitor to the Blue Note is *Sweet Basil 139* (☎ 5474-0139) in Roppongi, a big, new space that draws similarly big-name acts. Entry ranges from ¥3000 to ¥7000. Also in Roppongi, the *Roppongi Pit Inn* (☎ 3585-1063) is another spot to check for live jazz.

Cinemas

Shibuya and Shinjuku are Tokyo's cinema meccas, but you'll find cinemas near any major train station. Check the *Japan Times*, *Tokyo Classified* or the *Tokyo Journal* to see what's showing while you're in town. All three of these have theatre maps and phone numbers.

If you can plan ahead, tickets can be bought at certain outlets at discounted prices. Typically, a ¥1700 ticket will cost ¥1300 or less this way. There are ticket out-

lets in the basement of the Tokyo Kōtsū Kaikan building in Ginza, Shinjuku's Studio Alta building (5th floor), Harajuku's Laforet building (1st floor) and Shibuya's 109 Building (2nd floor).

SPECTATOR SPORTS
Sumō

Sumō tournaments at Tokyo's Ryōgoku Kokugikan Stadium (☎ 3866-8700) in Ryōgoku take place in January, May and September and last for 15 days. The best seats are all bought up by those with the right connections, but balcony seats are usually available from ¥6200 and bench seats at the back for about ¥2100. If you don't mind standing, you can get in for around ¥1000. Tickets can be bought up to a month prior to the tournament, or simply turn up on the day (you'll have to arrive very early, say 6 am, to be assured of seats during the last days of a tournament). The stadium is adjacent to Ryōgoku station (Sōbu line), on the northern side of the railway tracks. If you can't go in person, NHK televises sumō from 3.30 pm daily during each tournament.

Baseball

Although soccer has made some headway in recent years, baseball remains Japan's most popular team sport. There are two professional leagues, the Central and the Pacific. The baseball season runs from April until the end of October. Check the *Japan Times* to see who's playing while you're in town. The cheapest unreserved outfield seats start at ¥1500. The two main places to see baseball in Tokyo are the Tokyo Dome (the Big Egg; ☎ 3811-2111), next to Kōraku-en Amusement Park; and Jingū Kyūjo (☎ 3404-8999), close to JR Shitanomachi station.

SHOPPING

Although Tokyo is a notoriously expensive city, the determined shopper can still come up with a few bargains. Naturally, the best one-stop shopping options are the department stores, which stock virtually everything, including souvenirs. Unless a major sale is on, however, department stores are expensive places to shop.

Flea Markets

Flea markets sound like promising places to shop for interesting antiques and souvenirs, but bear in mind that this is Tokyo and there are unlikely to be any real bargains. At the very least, take a look at somewhere like the Oriental Bazaar (see the Antiques & Souvenirs section, following) and make a note of prices before embarking on a flea-market shopping spree. Tokyo's main flea markets are as follows:

Tōgō-jinja 4 am to 4 pm on the first and fourth Sunday of each month; JR Harajuku station

Nogi-jinja Dawn to dusk on the second Sunday of each month; from Nogi-zaka subway station on the Chiyoda line – the shrine is on Gaien-higashi-dōri

Hanazono-jinja 7 am to 5 pm every Sunday; close to Isetan department store on the eastern side of Shinjuku station

Antiques & Souvenirs

One of the best places to look for antiques and interesting souvenirs is in the basement of the Hanae Mori building, in Harajuku, which has more than 30 antique shops. Not far from here, the Oriental Bazaar is open every day and is an interesting place to rummage through. It has a wide range of good souvenirs – fans, folding screens, pottery etc – some at very affordable prices.

Another great selection of souvenirs can be found in Ueno at the Tokyo National Museum's gift shop. In addition to art books, postcards and the like, it has woodblock prints and *komono* (small arts and crafts).

Japanese Dolls Edo-dōri, next to JR Asakusabashi station, is the place to go if you're interested in Japanese dolls. Both sides of the road have large numbers of shops specialising in traditional as well as contemporary Japanese dolls.

Other Japanese Goods *Washi* (handmade paper) is one of the cheaper and more interesting souvenir possibilities. One place that stocks a good selection is Haibara in Nihombashi. All the major department stores have a section devoted to washi.

Kamawanu, in Daikanyama, is a little shop specialising in *tenugui*, those ubiquitous Japanese hand-towels that you find in sento and onsen. It's also got a limited selection of other craft goods.

The Tokyo National Museum is a good spot to pick up a variety of tasteful Japanese goods at reasonable prices.

Photographic Equipment

Check the Shinjuku section for information on the big camera stores there. Ginza's Harumi-dōri is another place for photographic equipment – there are several good second-hand photographic shops where Japanese gear can often be bought at reasonable prices.

Computer Equipment

Akihabara is the place to go for computer equipment, although the vast majority of the offerings are aimed at computers with Japanese operating systems. T-Zone computers is the one store that stocks a small selection of computers with English operating systems, English-language software and related peripherals. It's on the eastern side of Chūō-dōri, 500m north-west of Akihabara.

Clothes

For general off-the-rack wear, Shinjuku and Shibuya are good areas to shop around and compare prices. The department stores are good places to look. Seibu, Isetan, Marui and Parco have a good mix of youth and mature casual-wear at reasonable (by Tokyo standards) prices. Stores such as Takashimaya, Matsuzakaya and Mitsukoshi are more conservative. In Shibuya, in particular, try the three Parco stores and Seed, a Seibu spin-off that brings a host of boutiques together under one roof.

Areas like Harajuku, Aoyama and Nishi-Azabu are the best places for specialised boutiques.

Finally, if you want to see where the Tokyo girls buy those towering high-heel boots, look no further than Shibuya's Frontier shoe shop – last time we checked it had the mother of all high-heel boots on display outside.

Music

Given the number of massive CD emporia in Tokyo, it's worth a quick run-down. Tower Records, Virgin and HMV all have several branches in Tokyo. The best of the lot is the massive new Tower Records store in Shibuya – even if you're not a music lover, the 7th-floor bookshop is worth a look. Imported CDs are *cheaper* than local pressings. Prices range from ¥1500 to ¥2300.

For LP wax, try the record stores in Shibuya, most notably Cisco for electronica, and Manhattan for hip-hop (the latter is worth a trip just to glimpse all the B-Boy poseurs).

Kids' Stuff

Japanese are particularly creative when it comes to finding things to keep their kids occupied, and Tokyo has some great toy shops. Places to take check are Loft in Shibuya and Kiddyland in Harajuku. The latter has five floors of stuff that your kids would probably be better off not knowing about. Hakuhinkan Toy Park in Ginza is a big toy shop that even has a child-oriented theatre and restaurants on its upper floors.

GETTING THERE & AWAY

Air

With the exception of China Airlines, all international airlines use Narita airport rather than the more conveniently located Haneda airport. Because the construction of the airport met with severe protests from the farmers it displaced, security procedures there are strict; be prepared to show your passport when entering the airport.

Arrival Immigration and customs procedures are usually straightforward, but they can be time consuming for non-Japanese. Note that Japanese customs officials are probably the most scrupulous in Asia; backpackers arriving from anywhere remotely third-worldish (the Philippines, Thailand etc) can expect some questions and perhaps a thorough search. Don't carry anything you shouldn't be carrying and try to dress neatly. You can change money in the customs hall after having cleared customs, and

in the arrival hall. The rates are the same as those offered in town.

Narita has two terminals, No 1 and No 2. This doesn't complicate things too much as both have train stations that are connected to JR and Keisei lines. The one you arrive at will depend on the airline you are flying with. Both terminals have clear English signposting for train and limousine bus services. The main information counter for foreign travellers is the TIC (☎ 0476-34-6251), on the 1st floor of Terminal 2. There's another information counter, in Terminal 1, that can handle most questions.

Departure Be sure to check which terminal your flight leaves from, and give yourself plenty of time to get out to Narita. There is a ¥2040 departure tax at Narita but this is included in the purchase price of most tickets (check with your airline if you're unsure).

Airline Offices Following is a list of the major airline offices in Tokyo.

Aeroflot (☎ 3434-9671) No 2 Matsuda Bldg, 3-4-8 Toranomon, Minato-ku
Air China (☎ 5251-0711) AOI Bldg, 3-2-7 Akasaka, Minato-ku
Air India (☎ 3214-1981) Hibiya Park Bldg, 1-8-1 Yūraku-chō, Chiyoda-ku
Air Lanka (☎ 3573-4261) Dowa Bldg, 7-2-22 Ginza, Chūō-ku
Air New Zealand (☎ 3287-1641) Shin-Kokusai Bldg, 3-4-1 Marunouchi, Chiyoda-ku
Alitalia (☎ 3580-2242) Tokyo Club Bldg, 3 2 6 Kasumigaseki, Chiyoda-ku
All Nippon Airways (ANA; ☎ 3272-1212, international toll free ☎ 0120-029-333, domestic toll free ☎ 3552-8800) Kasumigaseki Bldg, 3-2-5 Kasumigaseki, Chiyoda-ku
American Airlines (☎ 3214-2111) Nichirei Higashi-Ginza Bldg, 6-19-20 Tsukiji, Chūō-ku
Asiana Airlines (☎ 3582-6600) Ryuen Bldg, 1-3-1 Shiba-kōen, Minato-ku
Austrian Airlines (☎ 3597-6100) Kokusai Shin-Akasaka Bldg, East Tower, 2-14-7 Akasaka, Minato-ku
Biman Bangladesh Airlines (☎ 3593-1252) Kasumigaseki Bldg, 3-2-5 Kasumigaseki, Chiyoda-ku
British Airways (☎ 3593-8811) Sanshin Bldg, 1-4-1 Yūraku-chō, Chiyoda-ku

TOKYO

Canadian Airlines International (☎ 3281-7426) Hibiya Park Bldg, 1-8-1 Yūraku-chō, Chiyoda-ku

Cathay Pacific Airways (☎ 3504-1531) Tōhō Twin Tower Bldg, 1-5-2 Yūraku-chō, Chiyoda-ku

China Airlines (☎ 3436-1661) Sumitomo Bldg, 1-12-16 Shiba-Daimon, Minato-ku

China Eastern Airlines (☎ 3506-1166) AO1 Bldg, 3-2-7 Akasaka, Minato-ku

Continental Micronesia (☎ 3508-6411) Kokusai Bldg, 3-1-1 Marunouchi, Chiyoda-ku

Delta Air Lines (☎ 5275-7000) Kiochō Bldg, 3-12 Kiochō, Chiyoda-ku

Egypt Air (☎ 3211-4521) Palace Bldg, 1-1-1 Marunouchi, Chiyoda-ku

Finnair (☎ 3222-6801) NK Bldg, 2-14-2 Kōjimachi, Chiyoda-ku

Garuda Indonesia (☎ 3593-1181) Kanzan Kaikan Bldg, 3-2-4 Kasumigaseki, Chiyoda-ku

Iberia (☎ 3578-3555) Ark Mori Bldg, 1-12-32 Akasaka, Minato-ku

Japan Airlines (JAL; ☎ 5489-1111, international toll free ☎ 0120-255-931, domestic toll free ☎ 3456-2111) Dai-ni Tekko Bldg, 1-8-2 Marunouchi, Chiyoda-ku

Japan Air Systems (JAS; ☎ 045-212-2111) 4-47 Ōtemachi, Naka-ku, Yokohama

Japan Asia Airways (☎ 5489-5411) Yūrakuchō Denki Bldg, 1-7-1 Yūraku-chō, Chiyoda-ku

KLM-Royal Dutch Airlines (☎ 3216-0771) Yūrakuchō Denki Bldg, 1-7-1 Yūraku-chō, Chiyoda-ku

Korean Air (☎ 5443-3311) Tokyo KAL Bldg, 3-4-15 Shiba, Minato-ku

Lufthansa Airlines (☎ 3578-6700) 3-2-6 Kasumigaseki, Chiyoda-ku

Malaysia Airlines (☎ 3503-5961) Hankyū International Express Bldg, 3-3 Shimbashi, Minato-ku

Northwest Airlines (☎ 3533-6000) Forefront Tower, 3-12-1 Kachidoki, Chūō-ku

Olympic Airways (☎ 3201-0611) Yūrakuchō Denki Bldg, 1-7-1 Yūraku-chō, Chiyoda-ku

Pakistan International Airlines (PIA; ☎ 3216-6511) Hibiya Park Bldg, 1-8-1 Yūraku-chō, Chiyoda-ku

Philippine Airlines (☎ 3593-2421) Hibiya Mitsui Bldg, 1-1-2 Yūraku-chō, Chiyoda-ku

Qantas Airways (☎ 3593-7000) Tokyo Chamber of Commerce Bldg, 3-2-2 Marunouchi, Chiyoda-ku

Sabena (☎ 3585-6151) Address Bldg, 2-2-19 Akasaka, Minato-ku

Scandinavian Airlines (SAS; ☎ 3503-8101) Tōhō Twin Tower Bldg, 1-5-2 Yūraku-chō, Chiyoda-ku

Singapore Airlines (SIA; ☎ 3213-3431) Yūrakuchō Bldg 709, 1-10-1 Yūraku-chō, Chiyoda-ku

Swissair (☎ 3212-1016) Hibiya Park Bldg, 1-8-1 Yūraku-chō, Chiyoda-ku

Thai Airways International (THAI; ☎ 3503-3311) Asahi Seimei Hibiya Bldg, 1-5-1 Yūraku-chō, Chiyoda-ku

United Airlines (☎ 3817-4411) Kokusai Bldg, 3-1-1 Marunouchi, Chiyoda-ku

Virgin Atlantic (☎ 3499-8811) 3-13 Yotsuya, Shinjuku-ku

Train

All major JR lines radiate from Tokyo station; northbound trains stop at Ueno station, which, like Tokyo station is conveniently on the JR Yamanote line. Private lines – which are often cheaper and quicker for making day trips out of Tokyo – start from various stations around Tokyo. With the exception of the Tōbu Nikkō line, which starts in Asakusa, all private lines originate somewhere on the Yamanote line.

Shinkansen There are three *shinkansen* (bullet train) lines that connect Tokyo with the rest of Japan: the Tōkaidō line, which passes through Central Honshū, changing its name along the way to the San-yō line before terminating at Hakata in Northern Kyūshū; the Tōhoku line, which runs northeast via Utsunomiya and Sendai as far as Morioka, with the Yamagata branch heading from Fukushima to Yamagata and the Akita branch heading from Morioka to Akita; and the Jōetsu line, which runs north to Niigata, with the Nagano branch heading from Takazaki to Nagano-shi. Of these lines, the one most likely to be used by visitors to Japan is the Tōkaidō line, as it passes through Kyoto and Osaka in the Kansai region. All three shinkansen lines start at Tokyo station, though the Tōhoku and Jōetsu lines make a stop at Ueno station.

Other JR Lines The regular Tōkaidō line serves the stations that the Tōkaidō shinkansen line zips through without stopping. Trains start at Tokyo station and pass through Shimbashi and Shinagawa stations on the way out of town. There are *kyūkyō* (express) services to Yokohama and to

Izu-hantō via Atami, and from there trains continue to Nagoya, Kyoto and Osaka (you'll have to change several times to go all the way to Osaka or Kyoto).

Northbound trains start in Ueno. The Takasaki line goes to Kumagaya and, of course, Takasaki, with onward connections from Takasaki to Niigata. The Tōhoku line follows the Takasaki line as far north as Ōmiya, from where it heads to the far north of Honshū via Sendai and Aomori. Getting to Sendai without paying any express surcharges will involve changes at Utsunomiya and Fukushima. For those intent on saving the expense of a night's accommodation, there are also overnight services.

Private Lines The private lines generally service Tokyo's sprawling suburbia and very few of them go anywhere that visitors to Japan would care to visit. Still, those that do pass through tourist areas are usually a cheaper option than the JR lines. Particularly good bargains are the Tōkyū Tōyoko line, running between Shibuya station and Yokohama; the Odakyū line, running from Shinjuku to Odawara and the Hakone region; the Tōbu Nikkō line, running from Asakusa to Nikkō; and the Seibu Shinjuku line from Ikebukuro to Kawagoe.

Bus
Long-distance buses are generally little or no cheaper than trains, but are sometimes a good alternative for long-distance trips to areas serviced by expressways. The buses often run direct, so you can relax instead of watching for your stop as you would have to do on an ordinary train service.

There are a number of express buses running between Tokyo, Kyoto and Osaka. Overnight buses leave at 10 pm from the Yaesu side of Tokyo station and arrive at Kyoto and Osaka between 6 and 7 am the following day. They cost from ¥8000 to ¥8500 (if you're coming back, you'll save money by buying a return ticket). The buses are a JR service and can be booked at one of the Green Windows in a JR station.

Buses also run from Tokyo station to Nara, Kōbe, Hiroshima, Fukui, Shimoda,

Nagano, Yamagata, Takamatsu, Sendai, Morioka and Aomori. From Shinjuku station there are buses running to the Fuji and Hakone regions, including, for Mt Fuji climbers, direct services to the 5th station (see Climbing Mt Fuji in the Around Tokyo chapter). The Shinjuku long-distance bus station is across from the west exit of Shinjuku station (see the Shinjuku map).

Ferry
A ferry journey can be a great way to get from Tokyo to other parts of the country. Fares are not too expensive (by Japanese standards anyway) and there is the advantage that you save the expense of a night or two's accommodation. Prices given here are for 2nd-class travel.

From Tokyo, there are long-distance ferry services to Kushiro (☎ 3528-0950) and Tomakomai (☎ 3578-1127) in Hokkaidō (¥14,700 and ¥6000, respectively); to Kōchi (☎ 3578-1127) and Tokushima (☎ 3567-0971) in Shikoku (¥10,600 and ¥8610, respectively); to Kitakyūshū (☎ 3501-0889) in Northern Kyūshū (¥12,600); and to Naha (☎ 5643-6170) on Okinawa (¥20,050).

Departures may not always be frequent (usually once every two or three days for long distance services) and ferries are sometimes fully booked well in advance, so it pays to make inquiries early. The phone numbers given earlier for ferry companies will require some Japanese-language skills or the assistance of a Japanese speaker. If you have problems, contact the TIC.

GETTING AROUND
Tokyo has an excellent public transport system. Everything of note is conveniently close to a subway or JR station. Bus services are difficult to use if you don't read *kanji* (character-script), but the average visitor to Tokyo won't need the buses anyway.

To/From Narita Airport
Narita airport is 66km from central Tokyo, and is used by almost all the international airlines but by only a small number of domestic operators. Travel to or from Tokyo takes from 50 minutes to 1½ hours or more,

depending on your mode of transport and destination in town.

Depending on where you're going, it is generally cheaper and faster to travel into Tokyo by train than by limousine bus. Rail users will probably need to change trains somewhere, and this can be confusing on a jetlagged first visit. For this reason, some visitors choose to travel on limousine buses that provide a hassle-free direct route to a number of Tokyo's top hotels (you don't have to be staying at the hotels to use these buses).

Train There are three rail services between Tokyo and both terminals at Narita airport: the private Keisei line; the JR Narita Express (N'EX); and the JR 'Airport Narita' service. The Keisei service runs into Nippori and Ueno, from either of which you can change to the Yamanote line for access to Ikebukuro, Shinjuku and other destinations. N'EX and the 'Airport Narita' service run into Tokyo station (from where you can change to almost any line). N'EX also runs to Shinjuku, Ikebukuro and Yokohama.

The Keisei line has two services: the Keisei Skyliner, which does the trip between Narita and Ueno (¥1920, one hour), and the Keisei *tokkyū* (limited express; ¥1000, one hour and 11 minutes). Times and fares to and from Nippori are marginally less. Tokkyū services are much more frequent than the Skyliner, and what's another 11 minutes?

The N'EX services are fast, extremely comfortable and include amenities like drink-dispensing machines and telephones. To or from Tokyo station costs ¥2940 and takes 55 minutes; to Shinjuku station it costs ¥3110 and takes 1½ hours; to or from Ikebukuro station costs ¥3110 and takes one hour and 40 minutes; and to or from Yokohama station costs ¥4180 and takes 1½ hours. N'EX services run approximately half-hourly between 7 am and 10 pm, but Ikebukuro services are very infrequent; in most cases you will be better off heading to Shinjuku and taking the Yamanote line from there. Seats are reserved only, but can be bought immediately before departure if they are available.

'Airport Narita' trains cost ¥1280 and take 1½ hours to or from Tokyo. Trains only run approximately once an hour.

The Keikyū rail line runs between Narita and Haneda airports (¥1560, 1¾ hours), with several direct trains a day. If no direct trains are available, you'll have to switch at Shimbashi or Shinagawa. Ask at the airport information desk for the most convenient route and time.

Limousine Bus Limousine bus ticket offices are clearly marked with the sign 'Limousine' at Narita. Don't be misled by the name; they're just ordinary buses and take 1½ to two hours (depending on the traffic) to travel between Narita airport and a number of major hotels around Tokyo. Check departure times before buying your ticket, as services are not all that frequent. The fare to or from hotels around Asakusa is ¥2700, while to or from Ikebukuro, Akasaka, Ginza, Shiba, Shinagawa, Shinjuku or Haneda airport it is ¥3000. There is also a direct service between the airport and Yokohama (¥3500, two hours).

To/From Haneda Airport
Most domestic flights and China Airlines to/from Taiwan use the convenient Haneda airport.

Transport to or from Haneda airport is a simple matter, as a monorail runs between the airport and Hamamatsu-chō station on the JR Yamanote line (¥270, 20 minutes); trains leave every 10 minutes. The monorail runs from 5.15 am to 11.15 pm in both directions.

Taxis from the airport to places around central Tokyo cost around ¥6000. Limousine buses connect Haneda with TCAT (¥900), Tokyo station (¥900), Ikebukuro and Shinjuku (¥1200) and several other destinations in Tokyo. Ask at any of the airport information desks for the bus most convenient to your destination.

The Keikyū rail line runs between Haneda and Narita airport, with several direct trains a day (¥1560, 1¾ hours). If no direct trains are available, you'll have to switch at Shimbashi or Shinagawa.

There is a direct bus service between Haneda and Narita (¥3000), which can take up to two hours depending on the traffic.

To/From TCAT

Leaving Tokyo, you can get your boarding pass, check your luggage and even clear immigration at TCAT (Tokyo City Air Terminal) before taking the bus out to the airport. This service is available to passengers flying most major airlines; call your airline to check. TCAT is next to Suitengu-mae subway station on the Hanzōmon line, in Nihombashi.

From 5.45 am to 8.50 pm limousine buses run every 15 minutes between Narita and TCAT (¥2900). The journey takes about an hour but you may want to leave extra time in case of traffic. There is a frequent shuttle-bus service between TCAT and Tokyo station (¥200), which departs from the Yaesu side of Tokyo station.

Train

Tokyo has a crowded but otherwise awesome rail network. Between the JR and private above-ground and subway lines, you can get to almost anywhere in town quickly and cheaply. Unfortunately it all shuts down somewhere between midnight and 1 am and doesn't start up again until 5 or 6 am the next day, leaving late-night revellers with no choice but to stay out until dawn or fork over a huge wad of cash for a taxi ride home.

Avoiding Tokyo's rush hour is not often possible. Things tend to quieten down between 10 am and 4 pm, when travelling around Tokyo can actually be quite pleasant, but before 9.30 am and from about 4.30 pm onwards there are likely to be cheek-to-jowl crowds on all the major train lines. Note that after 10 pm some passengers may be drunk and this can make things somewhat unpleasant.

JR Lines Undoubtedly, the most useful line in Tokyo is the JR Yamanote line, which does a 35km loop around the city, taking in most of the important areas. You can do the whole circuit in an hour for the ¥130 minimum charge – a great introduction to the city. Another useful above-ground JR route is the Chūō line, which cuts across the centre of town between Shinjuku and Akihabara. Tickets are transferable on all JR lines.

The major JR stations (Tokyo, Shibuya, Shinjuku, Ikebukuro and Ueno) are massive places with thronging crowds and never enough English signposting. Just working out how to buy a ticket can drive a newcomer to the edge of madness. If it's a JR train you're taking, look for the JR sign (usually green) and the rows of vending machines. If you don't know the fare, put in ¥130 and punch the top left-hand button (the one with no price on it). When you get to your destination you can pay the balance at the ticket gate. English signposting points the way to the railway platforms.

If you're going to be doing a lot of travelling on JR lines (even just the Yamanote line) we strongly suggest buying a JR 'Io' card. These are like train passes that you can insert directly into automated ticket wickets (the correct fare will be deducted automatically). Io cards come in denominations of ¥1000, ¥3000 and ¥5000 and can be purchased from special blue-fronted ticket machines or from ticket windows. Buy one and you'll never go back to waiting in ticket lines and fumbling for change.

For English-language train information, you can call the JR English Information line (☎ 3423-0111), 10 am to 6 pm weekdays.

Subway Lines There are 12 subway lines in Tokyo (13 if you include the Yūraku-chō New Line), of which eight are TRTA lines and four are TOEI lines. This is not particularly important to remember, as the subway services are essentially the same, have good connections from one to another and can be used with the same subway pass or special transfer tickets (see later). Train lines are colour-coded on the excellent maps that are available free at subway stations and tourist information counters around town.

Ticket prices start at ¥160 for short hops, but if your trip involves a change of train you can be sure it will cost ¥190. As with the JR system, if you are in doubt at all (there are still subway stations in Tokyo where the only pricing maps are in Japanese), buy a ticket for ¥160 and upgrade if necessary at your destination.

Unless you purchase a special ticket (and this would require Japanese-reading ability), you'll have to buy a separate ticket when you switch from TRTA and TOEI subway lines.

The subway equivalent of the JR Io card is the SF Metro card. It comes in denominations of ¥1000, ¥3000 and ¥5000 and can be used directly in the automatic ticket gates. Best of all, it's good for travel on both subway systems and saves you time when switching between the two systems.

Discount Tickets & Train Passes There are no massively discounted tickets available for travel around Tokyo, but if you're moving around a lot you can save some yen. Probably the best deal is the Tokyo Combination Ticket, which allows travel on any subway, tram, TOEI bus or JR train in the metropolitan area until the last train of the day. It costs ¥1580 and is available from subway and JR stations and even post offices.

Bus
Many Tokyo residents and visitors spend a considerable amount of time in the city without ever using the bus network. This is partly because the train services are so good and partly because the buses are much more difficult to use. In addition, buses are at the mercy of Tokyo's sluggish traffic flow. Services also tend to finish fairly early in the evening, making them a pretty poor alternative all round.

Pick up a copy of the free *TOEI Bus Route Guide* from the TIC if you are planning to use the bus network. When using a bus, have the name of your destination written in Japanese so that you can either show the driver or match up the kanji with the route map yourself (there's not much in the way of English signposting on buses or at bus stops). Fares are paid as you enter the bus, and it's a flat ¥200 for city destinations.

Taxi
Taxis are so expensive that you should only use them when there is no alternative. Rates start at ¥630, which gives you 2km (1.5km after 11 pm), after which the meter starts to clock an additional ¥80 for every 347m; you also click up ¥80 for every two minutes you sit idly gazing at the scenery in a typical Tokyo traffic jam.

Tram
Tokyo's only remaining tram (streetcar) service, the Toden Arakawa line, runs from opposite Ōtsuka station on the JR Yamanote line. It passes the Sunshine City building in Ikebukuro, heads on to Zoshigaya and then terminates in Waseda, not far from Waseda University. The line is perhaps worth using for a visit to Zoshigaya, an old residential area under threat from Tokyo's rapacious property developers. There are a number of small temples in the area, as well as Zoshigaya-reien, the final resting place of outstanding writers Lafcadio Hearn and Natsume Sōseki.

Car & Motorcycle
Driving yourself around Tokyo is by no means impossible, but is likely to bring unnecessary frustrations. Parking space is limited and expensive, the traffic moves very slowly, traffic lights are posted on virtually every street corner (every 50m or so) and unless you are very familiar with the city, getting lost will be a common occurrence. Overall, you are much better off using public transport. See the Facts for the Visitor chapter for more details.

Car Rental For those who enjoy a challenge, there are car rental agencies in Tokyo that will hire you one of their vehicles upon presentation of an international licence. Three that usually have English-speakers on hand are Dollar Rent-a-Car (☎ 3567-2818), Hertz (☎ 0120-489-882) and Toyota Rent-a-Lease (☎ 3264-0100). Typical rates for small cars are ¥8000 or ¥9000 for the first day, and ¥5500 to ¥7000 each day thereafter. On top of this there is a ¥1000-per-day insurance fee. Mileage is usually unlimited.

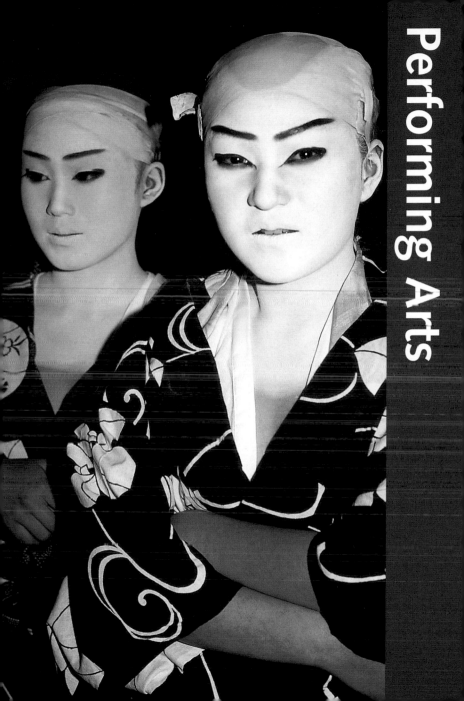

Performing Arts

PERFORMING ARTS

MASON FLORENCE

MASON FLORENCE

Title Page: Kabuki performers (photograph by Frank Carter).

Top & Bottom: Masked nō characters.

THE JAPANESE STAGE

You don't have to venture far to see Japan's remarkable balance of centuries-old tradition and global citizenship in action. Watch a *kimono*-clad woman stand in line for a hamburger. Take a stroll through city streets and marvel at the well-tended old shrines sitting serenely in the shadows of skyscrapers. Better yet, go to the theatre.

Japan's theatre scene is a vital interplay of tradition and innovation, a reflection of the country's breathtaking cultural heritage and of the international influences that shape its society. Japan's stages, it seems, have room for almost everything. Its classical theatre forms are among the oldest in the world still performed, but far from being obscure museum-pieces, they renew themselves with each generation. Contemporary theatre enjoys an international reputation for its avant-garde nature and high artistic standards. Added to the mix are streams of visiting international companies and individual performers.

For foreign visitors, the best sources of information on performances are Tourist Information Centers (TICs), and the excellent Tokyo Q Web site has up-to-date theatre listings and reviews (www.tokyoq.com). English-language publications such as *Tokyo Journal*, *Kyoto Visitor's Guide* and *Kansai Time Out* are also good, though they tend not to cover small scale productions or those performed in Japanese only (unless they are Western works in translation or there are English programs or earphone guides available). If you have a reasonable grasp of Japanese, the entertainment weekly *Pia* contains up-to-date information, as do *Tokyo Walker*, *Yokohama Walker* and *Kansai Walker*.

Right: Minami-za Theatre in Gion, Kyoto, is the oldest kabuki theatre in Japan.

FRANK CARTER

Classical Theatre

There are four principal forms of classical Japanese theatre, ranging from dance-drama to comedy and puppetry. Don't be intimidated by the 'classical' label. While some prior study will help you to understand the nitty-gritty, as with all good theatre this has elements that transcend language – just as well, really, considering that archaic Japanese (used particularly in *kabuki* and *nō*) is as difficult for modern Japanese to understand as Shakespeare is for modern English-speakers. Fortunately the introduction of surtitles, programs and headphone guides in modern Japanese and English have made it easier for people to follow the proceedings on stage. And if you *are* interested in the nitty-gritty of the aesthetic elements, there's a wealth of information available.

Nō

Quite possibly, people will tell you that nō is boring. But if shōgun Ashikaga Yoshimitsu (1358–1408) were around, he'd probably ask you to make up your own mind. He was so impressed by the actor and playwright Kan'ami (1333–1384) that he extended shogunal patronage to him. Kan'ami went on to wow courtly audiences with an amalgamation of elements of popular song-and-dance forms, Shinto sacred dances and Zen Buddhist ideals. Kan'ami's son, Zeami (1363–1444) was responsible for the art's development into its current form, and is commonly considered the greatest of all nō dramatists. Nō was still going strong in the Edo period (1600–1867), when the Tokugawa shogunate endorsed five schools of nō for the entertainment of the *samurai* class.

Nō is an hypnotic dance-drama that reflects the minimalist aesthetics of Zen. The movement is gloriously powerful, the chorus and music sonorous, and the expression subtle. A sparsely furnished cedar stage directs full attention to the performers, who include a chorus, drummers and a flautist. The two principal characters are the *shite*, who is sometimes a living person but more often a demon, or a ghost whose soul cannot rest; and the *waki*, who leads the main character towards the play's climactic moment. Each of the nō schools has its own repertoire, and the art form continues to evolve and develop. One of the

Left: Masked nō character.

many new plays performed over the last 30 years is *Takahime*, based on William Butler Yates' *At The Hawk's Well*.

Although nō is traditionally a family affair, unlike kabuki it accepts performers from outside, on a more-or-less equal basis. Among the actors and musicians who have undertaken the years of training required to master technique are many amateur nō groups and practitioners, and even some Westerner practitioners. While often considered to be a pastime of the elite, nō continues to attract large audiences. The main theatres for nō are the National Theatre, Kanze Nōgaku-dō and the Tessenkai Nōgaku Kenshūjō in Tokyo; the Kongo Nōgaku-dō and Kanze Nōgaku-dō Kaikan in Kyoto; and the Ōsaka Nō Kaikan.

Kabuki

The first performances of kabuki were staged early in the 17th century by a female troupe led by Ōkuni, a dancer consecrated to the shrine, Izumo Taisha, who created and performed short plays interspersed with dances. The performances were erotic, and attracted great support from the merchant classes. In true bureaucratic fashion, Tokugawa officials feared for the people's morality and banned women from the stage in 1629. Since that time, kabuki has been performed exclusively by men, giving rise to the institution of *onnagata*, or *ōyama*, male actors who specialise in female roles.

Over the course of several centuries, kabuki developed a repertoire drawing on popular themes, such as famous historical accounts and stories of love-suicide, while also borrowing copiously from nō, *kyōgen* and *bunraku*. Most kabuki plays border on melodrama, although they vary in mood.

Formalised beauty and stylisation are the central aesthetic principles of kabuki; the acting is a combination of dancing and speaking in conventionalised intonation patterns, and each actor prepares for a role by studying and emulating the style perfected by his predecessors. Kabuki actors are born to the art form, and training begins in childhood – the

Right: Musicians at a kabuki performance.

MASON FLORENCE

leading families of modern kabuki go back generations. Actors today enjoy great social prestige, and their activities on and off the stage attract as much interest as those of popular film and television stars.

Some actors have recently pushed the traditional boundaries of kabuki. Ichikawa Ennosuke's Super Kabuki are high-tech, larger-than-life kabuki spectaculars that use modern language. Although purists have accused him of debasing the art, Ichikawa has attracted thousands of spectators since his first Super Kabuki, in 1986.

Regular kabuki performances are held year-round at Kabuki-za and the National Theatre in Tokyo, the Minami-za in Kyoto and the Shin-Kabuki-za in Ōsaka. Super Kabuki is performed at Shimbashi Embūjō in Tokyo, usually in April and May.

Kyōgen

The humorous aspect of *sarugaku* (monkey music), one of the song-and-dance forms from which nō was developed, evolved into what eventually came to be called kyōgen. These comic vignettes are highly physical; the characters are ordinary people – bumbling samurai, lecherous priests, unfaithful women and lazy servants – and the plays are performed in the vernacular. Performers are not masked, and a chorus often accompanies the action. Kyōgen was originally performed as light relief between nō plays, but today major nō theatres also present kyōgen-only programs.

In addition to giving over hundreds of kyōgen performances a year, leading actors also appear in contemporary plays, movies, television dramas, and advertisements. These performers have sparked a new kyōgen craze and are drawing a whole new group of fans.

BY PERMISSION OF THE JAPANESE CONSULATE, MELBOURNE, AUSTRALIA

Bunraku

Japan's traditional puppet theatre developed at the same time as kabuki, when the *shamisen* (a three-stringed lute), imported from Okinawa, was combined with traditional puppetry techniques and *joruri* (narrative chanting). Bunraku, as it came to be known in the 19th century, addresses many of the same themes as kabuki, and in fact many of the most famous plays in the kabuki repertoire were originally written for the puppet theatre. Bunraku involves large puppets – nearly two-thirds life-size – manipulated

Left: A bunraku performance.

by up to three black-robed puppeteers. The puppeteers do not speak; a seated narrator tells the story and provides the voices of the characters, expressing their feelings with smiles, weeping and starts of surprise and fear. The best places to see bunraku are the National Theatre in Tokyo and the National Bunraku Theatre in Ōsaka.

Yose

Yose entertainment encompasses *rakugo* and *manzai*, and is comparable to stand-up comedy, as well as storytelling, juggling and paper-cutting and other types of vaudeville-like entertainment. Rakugo and manzai, the two most popular of the yose arts still performed, are frequently seen on television and are currently enjoying a revival, particularly among younger audiences.

Rakugo

A traditional Japanese style of comic monologue, rakugo (literally, 'dropped word') dates back to the Edo period. The performer, usually in kimono, sits on a square cushion on a stage. Props are limited to a fan and hand towel. The monologue begins with a *makura* (prologue) followed by the story itself and, finally, the *ochi* (punch line, or 'drop', which is another pronunciation of the Chinese character for *raku* in rakugo). Many of the monologues in the traditional rakugo repertoire date back to the Edo and Meiji (1868–1912) periods, and while well-known, reflect a social milieu unknown to modern listeners. Accordingly, many practitioners today also write new monologues addressing issues relevant to contemporary life.

Manzai

Manzai, a comic dialogue with origins in the song and dance and comedy routines traditionally performed by itinerant entertainers during Shōgatsu (New Year's celebrations), is a highly fluid art that continues to draw large audiences to hear snappy duos exchange clever witticisms on up-to-the-minute themes from everyday life. Although popular everywhere, manzai is identified particularly with the Kansai region, where it traditionally outranks rakugo as the most popular variety of yose entertainment.

Contemporary Theatre

The emergence of a distinct consumer culture during the late Taishō (1912–1926) and Shōwa (1926–1989) periods brought major challenges to popular entertainment. The evolution of new forms of popular theatre and music, and the adjustment of traditional forms – more than mere reflections of the times – they appear to have contributed to the transformation of Japanese society.

Most of Japan's major cities have large commercial theatres, although Tokyo remains the undisputed centre of contemporary

Top: Minami-za Theatre, Gion, Kyoto (Photograph by Frank Carter)

Bottom: A glitzy musical (photograph by permission of the Japanese Consulate, Melbourne, Australia)

theatre in Japan. Venues include venerable institutions such as the Imperial Theatre and the Tokyo Takarazuka Theatre, as well as newer facilities such as New National Theatre, Tokyo Panasonic Globe Theatre and the Ginza Saison Theatre in Tokyo; and the Kintetsu Theatre in Ōsaka. Small, privately owned theatres also abound, including such Tokyo icons as The Suzunari, Theatre Tops, Ekimae Gekijō and Agora Gekijō.

Commercial Theatre

Commercial theatre in Japan today encompasses classical and contemporary dramas and musicals, both home-grown and imported, staged by large entertainment companies and starring well-known actors, singers and other celebrities. So if, when you're in Japan, you happen to be struck by a sudden hankering for a Royal Shakespeare Company production of Richard III, or a Japanese-language performance of *Phantom of the Opera,* you might just be in luck.

Tōhō Musical and the OSK Japan Revue and Gekidan Shiki are known for their splashy, long-running productions of leading musicals from London and New York. Each has its own theatre, and all three troupes tour extensively throughout the country.

The all-female Takarazuka troupe offers a musical experience unlike any other. Founded in 1913, partially as an inversion of the all-male kabuki theatre, Takarazuka combines Japanese traditional elements with Western music in a format aimed at audiences of all ages, every social status, and both sexes. But truth be told, its most devoted admirers by far are young women who, in a state of truly super-human suspension-of-disbelief, swoon with romantic abandon over the troupe's beautiful 'men'. Takarazuka adopted its present revue format in the late 1920s, and with the exception of the years of WWII – during which the troupe proved an ideal propaganda tool – has continued to perform musicals and revues set in exotic locations. You too can ogle the performers in the Takarazuka Theatre near Kōbe, or at the Tokyo Takarazuka Theatre.

Noncommercial Theatre

Contemporary theatre productions not backed by the major entertainment companies have rather limited commercial viability. There is little public-sector support for the theatre in Japan, and although this has begun to change in recent years, very few performing-arts organisations receive financial assistance. It's generally impossible for actors and directors to earn a living from the stage.

Shingeki (New Theatre) began late in the Meiji period (1868–1912), with the establishment of theatre troupes performing Western works in translation, an entirely new concept at the time. Tsukiji Shōgekijo, formed by the writer and director Osanai Kaoru in 1924, played an outstanding role in the development of this movement. Seinenza, established in 1954, started out by performing original productions, dramatising novels by authors such as Mishima Yukio, and presenting

I'm Not Japanese, But My Play Is...

Visitors from multicultural countries can find Japan's apparently watertight sense of national identity a little disconcerting. You can learn the language, navigate your way faultlessly through a maze of social mores, live in the country for years and form close friendships. You can even teach a Japanese friend how to tie an obi, but unless generation upon generation of your forebears called Japan home, you will remain forever foreign. Japan's involvement in the world community has done little to widen the definition of who is Japanese, but it has certainly expanded the traditional, cultural and geographic definition of 'Japanese' experience.

While the country has a long and continuing culture of uniquely Japanese theatrical forms, collaborations between international and Japanese practitioners have produced theatre that is certainly, but not exclusively, Japanese. Projects created and shaped by contributors from vastly different cultural and dramatic backgrounds can make for very potent theatre. And professional theatre companies aren't the only ones revelling in this fluid approach to theatrical convention.

Kee Company (email keecompany@yahoo.ca) sprang to life one afternoon after a conversation in a Tokyo subway. On a mission to explore the mother-daughter relationship from as many perspectives as possible, two Japanese, a Japanese American, a Canadian and an Australian formed the Haha Collective and the task of creating Kee Company's first project, *Haha* (Japanese: mother; English: the sound of laughter), began.

Small theatre companies face terrifying financial challenges at the best of times, but in a city like Tokyo, where space is at a premium and money has a nasty habit of running out, it makes extra sense to aim small. The collective met once a week for rehearsals and impassioned (sometimes even argumentative) exchanges of ideas – and aimed small.

What emerged almost a year later was a fusion of Japanese and Western theatre styles, folk-stories-with-a-twist, original dance, comedy, music, tragedy and song – some of it in English and some in Japanese. With the benefit of extreme audacity, some amazing luck, hard work and the enthusiasm and support of a very talented co-producer, Kee Company's little project played to sell-out houses in its first Tokyo season. Its appeal extended to Japanese- and English-speakers alike; *Haha* went on to be performed at the Toronto Fringe Festival in Canada and, with the support of the Japan Foundation, at the National Multicultural Festival in Canberra, Australia.

Tokyo-based Kee Company has undertaken several projects since *Haha*, and continues its dedication to intercultural theatre. Some stories belong to everyone.

Jane Thompson

works by young Japanese playwrights. It later expanded its focus to include musicals and Western works in translation.

Theatre the world over spent the 1960s redefining itself, and it was no different in Japan. The *shōgekijo* (Little Theatre) movement, also called *angura* (underground), has given Japan many of its leading playwrights, directors and actors. It arose as a reaction to the realism and structure of shingeki and featured surrealistic plays that explored the relationship between human beings and the world. Like their counterparts in the West, these productions took place in any space available – in small theatres, tents, building basements, open spaces and on street corners. The first generation of shōgekijo artists included directors Terayama Shūji, Ninagawa Yukio, Satō Makoto, Kara Jūro and Suzuki Tadashi, and troupes such as Black Tent Theatre (directed by Satō), Red Tent (Kara), Waseda Shōgekijo (Suzuki) and Ninagawa Company (Ninagawa). In the 1970s the movement was dominated by director Tsuka Kōhei, leader of the Tsuka Kōhei Office, who added a comic element. But it was in the 1980s that shōgekijo took off, led by playwrights such as Noda Hideki, Kokami Shōji and Kawamura Tadashi, who took movement in two key directions – speedy comedy using wordplay and images from popular culture to highlight the lunacy of modern life, and mind-game fantasy about nuclear war and its aftermath.

The past decade has brought a shift in the focus of shōgekijo to more realistic and contemporary themes, such as modern Japanese history, war, environmental degradation and social oppression. Changing cultural perceptions have propelled the movement in new directions, notably towards socially and politically critical dramas, such as those by Kaneshita Tatsuo and Sakate Yōji; psychological dramas (Iwamatsu Ryō, Suzue Toshirō and Hirata Oriza); and satirical portrayals of modern society (Nagai Ai and Makino Nozomi). Recent works are attracting considerable attention from overseas: a successful production of Sakate's *Epitaph for Whales* (1993) was held in London in 1998, while Hirata's *Tokyo Notes* was staged in four locations in France in early 2000. Shōgekijo troupes that gained prominence in the 1990s include The Gazira (led by Kaneshita), Rinkō-gun (Sakate), Seinendan (Hirata) and M.O.P (Makino).

A number of developments in the 1990s have begun to blur Japan's modern theatrical boundaries. Shingeki troupes are increasingly producing original plays by Japanese playwrights, and no longer exist in parallel to shōgekijo. New theatrical troupes sit comfortably in neither category, and one-off projects have emerged that combine elements of previously separate genres, like Noda Hideki's NODA MAP productions featuring the leaders and principal actors from other troupes.

Around Tokyo

Tokyo itself may seem like an endless sea of concrete, but there are some surprisingly beautiful oases of green only an hour or so away by train. Apart from the Izu-shotō (also known as the Izu-nana-tō, or Izu Seven Islands) and the islands, Ogasawara-shotō, all the attractions in this chapter can be visited on day trips from Tokyo, although in some cases it would be worth staying away overnight.

The information in this chapter begins with destinations to the north of Tokyo and works anticlockwise to those in the east. The Izu-shotō and Ogasawara-shotō are treated separately at the end of the chapter.

Suggested Itineraries

Foremost among the cultural attractions around Tokyo are Nikkō and Kamakura, both of which rate highly among Japan's must-sees. Of these, Nikkō should be given priority, since nowhere else in Japan can compete with it for sheer visual impact. Kamakura, attractive though it is, can be missed *if* you plan a visit to Kyoto, which offers similar attractions on a much grander scale.

Nature lovers will enjoy the hikes in nearby Chichibu-Tama National Park or the ones in the more distant Oze region. And those hankering for a view of Mt Fuji will get an eyeful, providing the weather cooperates, in the lovely Fuji Go-ko (Fuji Five Lakes) region or the popular Hakone area (we suggest the former unless you enjoy a full tourist circus).

If *onsen* (mineral hot-spring spas) are your thing, you can do an *onsen meguri* (hot-spring tour) of the peninsula, Izu-hantō, which also boasts pleasant mountain scenery and a rugged coastline. In the warmer months, you can swim in the Pacific off some of the peninsula's beaches.

Yokohama, south of Tokyo, is a cosmopolitan port city with a fascinating Chinatown. However, the city ranks fairly low as a destination for travellers coming from

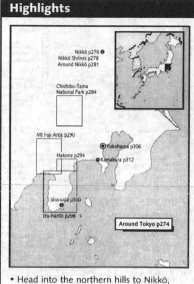

Highlights

- Head into the northern hills to Nikkō, a fabulous complex of gilded shrines and temples quite unlike anything else in Japan.

- Spend a day exploring the Buddhist temples of Kamakura, many of them tucked away in quiet, wooded groves.

- Hike the rugged hills of Chichibu-Tama National Park.

- Take an *onsen* tour of Izu-hantō, a lovely peninsula south-west of Tokyo.

- Journey to the beautiful Fuji Go-ko region for spectacular views of Mt Fuji; better still, in season, climb the mountain itself.

Tokyo, as most of its attractions merely echo those of the capital (Chinatown being the exception).

Other destinations around Tokyo include Narita, a pleasant temple-town near the New Tokyo International Airport; Kawagoe, a

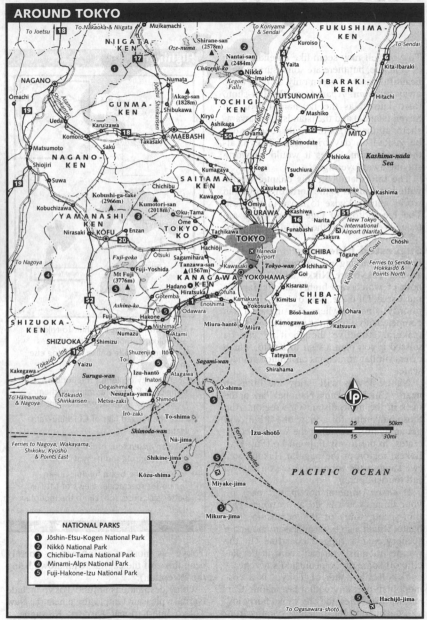

AROUND TOKYO

NATIONAL PARKS
1 Jōshin-Etsu-Kogen National Park
2 Nikkō National Park
3 Chichibu-Tama National Park
4 Minami-Alps National Park
5 Fuji-Hakone-Izu National Park

good place to see traditional Japanese buildings; Mashiko, a rural pottery centre; Kawasaki, home of Nihon Minka-en, an open-air museum of traditional Japanese houses; and Mito, home to one of Japan's three most famous gardens.

Lastly, the semitropical Izu-shotō or the more distant Ogasawara-shotō might lure the adventurous traveller with their good beaches and warm climate.

North of Tokyo

North of Tokyo are the prefectures Saitama-ken and Tochigi-ken, which include numerous places of interest, such as the old town of Kawagoe, Chichibu-Tama National Park and the temple- and shrine-centre of Nikkō.

NIKKŌ 日光
☎ 0288

Nikkō is one of Japan's major tourist attractions, due to its splendid shrines and temples, and it's worth trying to slot Nikkō into even the most whirlwind tour of Japan. Note, however, that Nikkō can get extremely crowded, so it's best to visit early on a weekday to avoid the hordes (most of the attractions are open from 8 am to 5 pm, or until 4 pm from November to March).

History
Nikkō's history as a sacred site stretches back to the middle of the 8th century, when the Buddhist priest Shōdō (735–817) established a hermitage there. For many years it was a famous training centre for Buddhist monks, before declining into obscurity. That is, until it was chosen as the site for the mausoleum of Tokugawa Ieyasu, the warlord who took control of all Japan and established the shogunate that ruled for 250 years until the Meiji Restoration ended the feudal era.

Tokugawa Ieyasu was laid to rest among Nikkō's towering cedars in 1617, but it was his grandson Tokugawa Iemitsu who, in 1634, commenced work on the shrine that can be seen today. The original shrine, Tōshō-gū, was completely rebuilt using an army of some 15,000 artisans from all over Japan. The work on the shrine and mausoleum took two years to complete, and the results continue to receive mixed reviews.

Tōshō-gū was constructed as a memorial to a warlord who devoted his life to conquering Japan. Tokugawa Ieyasu was a man of considerable determination and was not above sacrificing a few scruples in order to achieve his aims. He is attributed with having had his wife and eldest son executed because, at a certain point, it was politically expedient for him to do so. More than anything else, the grandeur of Nikkō is intended to inspire awe; it is a display of wealth and power by a family that for nearly three centuries was the supreme arbiter of power in Japan.

Information
First stop in Nikkō should be the Kyōdo Centre tourist information office (☎ 53-3795). The office (8.30 am to 5 pm) has a wealth of useful pamphlets and maps. There is another tourist information office (☎ 53-4511), in Tōbu Nikkō station, where you can pick up a map of Nikkō.

It's a 30-minute walk uphill from the Japan Railways (JR) and Tōbu stations to the shrine area. Bus Nos 1 and 2 go to the Shin-kyō bus stop for ¥190.

Hikers should pick up a copy of *Yumoto-Chūzenji Area Hiking Guide*. It costs a pittance, is available from some of the pensions in the area as well as at the information counters in Nikkō, and has maps and information on local flora and fauna.

Tickets Although you can buy separate tickets to Nikkō's attractions, it makes sense to buy a 'combination ticket' for ¥900. This covers entry to the temple, Rinnō-ji, and the shrines, Tōshō-gū and Futarasan-jinja, but not to the Nemuri-Neko (Sleeping Cat) in Tōshō-gū, a sight that will set you back ¥500. Even if you do include a visit to the Nemuri-Neko, buying a combination ticket is still much cheaper than buying each of the tickets separately.

Shin-kyō 神橋
The story behind this bridge goes that the Buddhist monk Shōdō Shōnin, who first

AROUND TOKYO

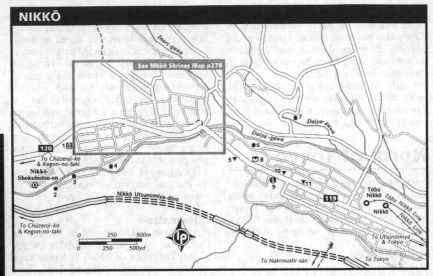

NIKKŌ

See Nikkō Shrines Map p278

Inari-gawa

Daiya-gawa

Daiya-gawa

120   1

To Chūzenji-ko
& Kegon-no-taki

Nikkō-
Shokubutsu-en

4

3

2

Nikkō Utsunomiya-dōro

To Chūzenji-ko
& Kegon-no-taki

0   250   500m
0   250   500yd

7

6

5   8

10
9   11

119

Tōbu
Nikkō

Nikkō

Tōbu Nikkō Line
Nikkō Line

To Utsunomiya
& Tokyo

To Nakimushi-san

To Tokyo

established a hermitage in Nikkō in 782, was carried across the river at this point on the backs of two huge serpents. Today's bridge, a reconstruction of the 17th-century original, is currently being refinished and will not open until 2002 at the earliest.

Rinnō-ji 輪王寺

The original Tendai-sect Rinnō-ji was founded 1200 years ago by Shōdō Shōnin. Sambutsu-dō (Three Buddha Hall) has huge gold-lacquered images, the most impressive of which is of Kannon, the goddess of mercy and compassion. The central image of the *senjū* (1000-armed Kannon) is Amida Nyorai, flanked by *batō* (a horse-headed Kannon), whose special domain is the animal kingdom.

Hōmotsu-den (Treasure Hall), also in the temple grounds, has a collection of treasures associated with the temple, but admission (¥300) is not included in the combination ticket (see Tickets in the earlier information section).

Tōshō-gū 東照宮

A huge stone *torii* (Shintō shrine entrance gate) marks the entrance to this shrine,

while to the left is a five-storey pagoda, originally dating from 1650 but reconstructed in 1818. The pagoda has no foundations and is said to contain a long suspended pole that swings like a pendulum, restoring equilibrium in the event of an earthquake.

The true entrance to the shrine is through the torii at the gate, Omote-mon, protected on either side by Deva kings. Directly through the entrance are the **Sanjinko** (Three Sacred Storehouses). On the upper storey of the last storehouse are imaginative relief carvings of elephants by an artist who famously had never seen the real thing. To the left of the entrance is **Shinkyūsha** (Sacred Stable), a suitably plain building housing a carved white horse. The stable's only adornment is an allegorical series of **relief carvings** depicting the life cycle of the monkey. They include the famous 'hear no evil, see no evil, speak no evil' threesome who have become emblematic of Nikkō.

Just beyond the stable is a granite font at which, in accordance with Shintō practice, worshippers cleanse themselves by washing their hands and rinsing their mouths. Next to the gate is a **sacred library** containing

NIKKŌ

PLACES TO STAY

3 Annex Turtle Hotori-An
　アネックスタートル
　ほとり庵
4 Turtle Inn Nikkō
　タートルイン日光
6 Nikkō Daiyagawa
　Youth Hostel
　日光大谷川ユース
　ホステル
7 Nikkō Youth Hostel
　日光ユースホステル

PLACES TO EAT

5 Eddoko
　江戸っ子
10 Hi No Kuruma
　ひの車
11 Yōrō-No-Taki
　養老の滝

OTHER

1 Nikkō Museum
　日光博物館
2 Ganman-Ga-Fuchi Abyss
　含満ヶ淵
8 Nikkō Post Office
　日光郵便局
9 Kyōdo Center
　Tourist Office
　日光郷土センター

7000 Buddhist scrolls and books; it is not open to the public.

Pass through another torii, climb another flight of stairs, and on the left and right are a drum tower and a belfry. To the left of the drum tower is **Honji-dō**. The hall has a huge ceiling-painting of a dragon in flight known as the Roaring Dragon. A monk in attendance will bang two wooden sticks together to demonstrate the strange acoustic properties of the hall; the echo is said to sound like the roar of a dragon – something of a stretch of the imagination.

Next comes **Yōmei-mon**, which, in contrast with the minimalism that is generally considered the essence of Japanese art, is crowded with detail. Animals, mythical and otherwise, jostle for your attention from among the glimmering gold leaf and red lacquerwork. The walls are decorated with intricate patterning, coloured relief carvings and paintings of, among other things, flowers, dancing girls, mythical beasts and Chinese sages. The overall effect is more Chinese than Japanese, and it's a grand spectacle, no matter what the critics say. Worrying that its perfection might arouse envy in the gods, those responsible for its construction had the final supporting pillar on the left-hand side placed upside down as a deliberate error.

Through the Yōmei-mon and to the right is Nemuri-Neko. While the sleeping cat is famous throughout Japan for its lifelike appearance, you may feel let down by this tiny wooden feline. **Sakashita-mon** here opens onto a path that climbs up through towering cedars to **Ieyasu's tomb**, a relatively simple affair. If you are using the combination ticket, you will have to pay an extra ¥500 to see the cat and the tomb.

To the left of Yōmei-mon is the **Jin-yōsha**, a storage depot for Nikkō's *mikoshi* (portable shrines), which come into action during the May and October festivals. The **Honden** (Main Hall) and **Haiden** (Hall of Worship) can also be seen in the enclosure.

Futarasan-jinja 二荒山神社

Shōdō Shōnin founded this shrine. It's dedicated to the mountain Nantai, the mountain's consort, Nyotai, and their mountainous progeny Tarō. It's essentially a repeat performance of Tōshō-gū on a smaller scale, but worth a visit all the same.

Taiyūin-byō 大院廟

Taiyūin-byō enshrines Ieyasu's grandson Iemitsu (1604–51) and is very much a smaller version of the shrine, Tōshō-gū. The smaller size gives it a less extravagant air and it has been suggested that it is more aesthetically worthy than its larger neighbour. Many of the features to be seen in the Tōshō-gū are replicated on a smaller scale: the storehouses, drum tower and Chinese gate, for example. The shrine also has a wonderful setting in a quiet grove of cryptomeria. Entry is included in the combination ticket (see Tickets under Information earlier).

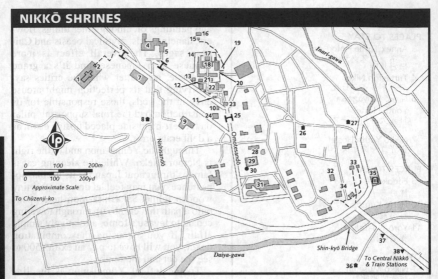

NIKKŌ SHRINES

To Chūzenji-ko

Approximate Scale

Daiya-gawa

Shin-kyō Bridge

To Central Nikkō
& Train Stations

Kosugi Hōan Museum of Art
小杉放庵美術館

Not far from Nikkō's shrines and temples is the Kosugi Hōan Museum of Art (¥700, 9.30 am to 5 pm, closed Monday). This modern museum holds a collection of landscape paintings by local artist Kosugi Hōan (1920–64). This is a good rainy-day option in Nikkō.

Gamman-Ga-Fuchi Abyss
含満ヶ淵

If the crowds of Nikkō have left you yearning for a little quiet, take the 20-minute walk over to Gamman-Ga-Fuchi Abyss, a collection of statues of Jizō, the patron saint of the souls of departed children, set along a wooded path. One of the statues midway along is known as the Bake-jizō, who mocks travellers foolish enough to try to count all the Jizō (they're said to be uncountable).

Nikkō Museum 日光美術館

The Nikkō Museum (¥400, 8 am to 4.30 pm, closed Tuesday) has been recently rebuilt and the new building was opened in July 2000.

Special Events

On 16 and 17 April, Yayoi Matsuri – a festival procession of portable shrines – is held at Futarasan-jinja.

Tōshō-gū Grand Festival, on 17 and 18 May, is Nikkō's most important annual festival. It features horseback archery (on the first day) and a 1000-strong costumed reenactment of the delivery of Ieyasu's remains to Nikkō (on the second day).

Tōshō-gū Autumn Festival is held on 17 October and needs only the equestrian archery to be an autumnal repeat of the performance in May.

Places to Stay

Nikkō has lots of good-value lodgings and most places are used to foreign guests. Thus, it's a good place for a quick night out of Tokyo, and staying the night makes sense if you want to combine a visit to Nikkō with the sights of the lake, Chūzenji-ko, and Yumoto Onsen.

Places to Stay – Budget

Nikkō Daiyagawa Youth Hostel (☎ 54-1974) is a friendly, comfortable place with beds for ¥2730 per person. Breakfast/dinner

NIKKŌ SHRINES

PLACES TO STAY
8 Nikkō Pension Green
  Age Inn
  日光ペンション
  グリーンエイジイン
26 Hotel Seikōen
  ホテル清晃苑
27 Nikkō Tōkan-sō Ryokan
  日光東観荘
36 Nikkō Kanaya Hotel
  日光金谷ホテル

PLACES TO EAT
37 Sawamoto
  澤本
38 Hippari Dako
  ひっぱり凧

OTHER
1 Taiyūin-byō
  大猷院廟
2 Yasha-mon
  夜叉門
3 Niten-mon
  二天門
4 Futara-san-jinja
  二荒山神社
5 Kara-mon
  唐門

6 Bronze Torii
  銅鳥居
7 Hokke-dō
  法華堂
9 Treasury
  宝物殿
10 Ticket Office
  きっぷ売り場
11 Sacred Stable
  神厩舎
12 Drum Tower
  鼓楼
13 Honji-dō
  本地堂
14 Tōshō-gū
  東照宮
15 Tomb of Ieyasu
  奥社
  (徳川家康の墓)
16 Honden
  木殿
17 Honden
  本殿
18 Haiden
  拝殿
19 Sakashita-mon
  坂下門
20 Nemuri-Neko
  眠猫

21 Yōmei-mon
  陽明門
22 Sanjinko
  三神庫
23 Omote-mon
  表門
24 Pagoda
  (5 stories)
  五重塔
25 Granite Torii
  一の鳥居
28 Gohōten-dō
  護法天堂
29 Sambutsu-dō
  三仏堂
30 Ticket Office
  きっぷ売り場
31 Rinnō-ji
  輪王寺
32 Nanshō-in
  南照院
33 Shihonryū-ji
  四本竜寺
34 Hongū
  本宮
35 Kosugi Hōan
  Museum of
  Art
  小杉放庵

AROUND TOKYO

costs ¥420/840. It's behind the post office opposite the Shyakusho-mae bus stop, and is closed from 25 December to 1 January. A 10-minute walk away, on the other side of the river, the Daiya-gawa, *Nikkō Youth Hostel* (☎ 54-1013) was being rebuilt at the time of writing. When reopened, its rates should be similar to the Daiyagawa hostel.

Places to Stay – Mid-Range & Top End

One of the more popular pensions in Nikkō is *Turtle Inn Nikkō* (☎ 53-3168), with rooms for ¥5000/4200 per person with/without bath (prices vary seasonally). Breakfast/dinner costs ¥1000/2000. From the station, take a bus to the Sōgō-kaikan-mae bus stop, backtrack around 50m to the fork in the road and follow the river for around

five minutes. Farther west, over the river but on the same road, is the clean, new *Annex Turtle Hotori-An* (☎ 53-3663), where Japanese and Western-style rooms are ¥5800 (again there's seasonal variation). Breakfast is available for ¥1000; dinners are served at its main building, the Turtle Inn, for ¥2000.

The pleasant *Nikkō Pension Green Age Inn* (☎ 53-3636), which looks like a Tudor mansion, charges ¥9800 per person with two meals (¥5800 without). The clean, spacious *Nikkō Tōkan-sō Ryokan* (☎ 54-0611) might be a good spot for your *ryokan* (traditional Japanese inn) experience (if it's not fully booked by bus tours). Per-person rates start at ¥10,000 with two meals. Single occupancy is impossible at both these places.

The clean *Hotel Seikōen* (☎ 53-5555) has per-person rates starting at ¥13,000 with two meals. Both Western- and Japanese-style rooms are available.

Not far from the bridge, Shin-kyō, is *Nikkō Kanaya Hotel (☎ 54-0001),* Nikkō's oldest and classiest hotel. Twins cost from ¥8000 to ¥35,000, doubles from ¥10,000 to ¥40,000 (prices are for the room).

Places to Eat

Many travellers staying in Nikkō prefer to eat at their lodgings, but there are also a number of places on the main road between the stations and the shrine area. *Yōrō-no-Taki* is a decent *izakaya* (pub) with cheap beer and a good selection of meals. *Hippari Dako* is something of a Nikkō institution among foreign travellers, judging from all the testimonials and business cards affixed to the walls. There's an English menu with filling sets of *yakitori* (chicken on skewers) and rice for ¥800 and *yaki-udon* (fried noodles) for the same price. This place closes at around 7 pm.

Other options include *Edokko,* which does *tempura soba* (noodle soup with lightly battered seafood and vegetables) for ¥850; *Hi No Kuruma,* an inexpensive *okonomiyaki* (meat, seafood and vegetables in a cabbage-and-vegetable batter) place; and *Sawamoto,* a good *unagi* (eel) specialist that serves tasty unagi sets for ¥1700.

Getting There & Away

The best way to visit Nikkō is via the Tōbu-Nikkō line from Asakusa station in Tokyo. The station is in the basement of the Tōbu department store (it's well signposted from the subway). All seats are reserved on *tokkyū* (limited express) trains (¥2740, one hour and 50 minutes), but you can usually get tickets just before setting out. Trains run every 30 minutes or so from 7.30 to 10 am; after 10 am they run hourly. *Kaisoku* (express) trains (¥1320, two hours and 10 minutes, hourly from 6.20 am to 4.30 pm) require no reservation. For trains other than the tokkyū, you *may* have to change at Imaichi.

Travelling by JR is costly and time consuming – it's really only of interest to those with a Japan Rail Pass. The quickest way is to take the *shinkansen* (bullet train) from Tokyo to Utsunomiya (¥4510, 50 minutes)

and change there for an ordinary train to Nikkō (¥740, 45 minutes).

Nikkō-Kinugawa Free Pass This pass may save you money on a multiday trip around Nikkō. It's valid for four days, costs ¥5740 and is available from Tōbu railways in Asakusa. It includes transport from Asakusa to Nikkō (but not the express surcharge) and all bus costs between Nikkō and Chūzenji, Yumoto Onsen, Kinugawa, the plateau of Kirifuri-kōgen, and Ikari-ko as well as cable-car fares around Chūzenji-ko (see the Around Nikkō section for information on Chūzenji and Yumoto).

AROUND NIKKŌ 日光周辺
☎ 0288
Nikkō is part of the Nikkō National Park, which covers 1402 sq km, sprawling over Fukushima, Tochigi, Gunma and Niigata Prefectures. It is a mountainous area, complete with extinct volcanoes, and lakes, waterfalls and marshlands. There are good hiking opportunities in the area and some remote hot-springs resorts.

Yashio-no-yu Onsen
やしおの湯温泉
A short bus ride from Nikkō, this modern onsen (¥500, 10 am to 5 pm, closed Thursday) is a good place to relax after a day of traipsing around shrines and temples. It has several different baths, including a *rotemburo* (outdoor spa bath). Take a Chūzenji-bound bus from Nikkō and get off at the Kiyomizu Itchōme stop. The onsen is across the river from the bus stop; walk back toward Nikkō, under the Route 120 bypass and across the bridge.

Chūzenji-ko 中禅寺湖
The lake, Chūzenji-ko, is chiefly a scenic attraction, and it's probably not worth cutting short your visit to Nikkō in order to see it. If you have plenty of time, however, then the lake and the 97m-high falls, **Kegon-no-taki,** are definitely worth visiting. The waterfall features an elevator (¥530 return) down to a platform where you can observe the full force of the plunging water. Also

A hut on the snow-covered slopes of Mt Fuji – the perfect spot for rest and *rāmen* on the climb up.

MARTIN MOOS

CRAIG McLACHLAN

At 3376m, Mt Fuji, or Fuji-san as it's known, is Japan's highest mountain and most venerated volcano.

Chōzuya (water basin) at a Kamakura shrine.

The Chūzenji-ko area of Nikkō.

Kamakura's most famous sight – the Daibutsu.

Early morning sunlight over Fuji-Yoshida – the closest town to the now dormant volcano.

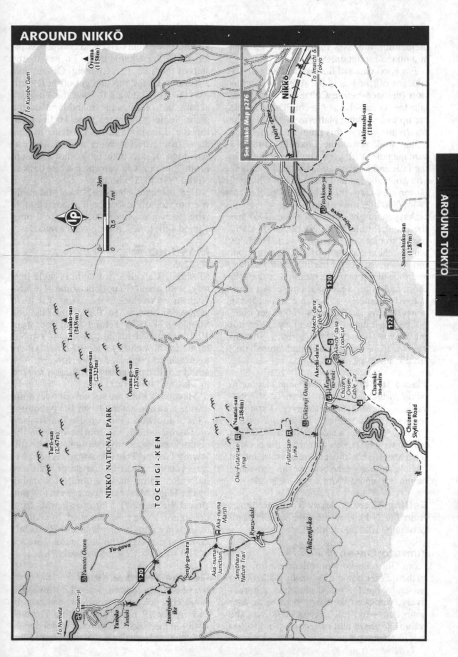

AROUND NIKKŌ

AROUND TOKYO

worth a visit is a third Futarasan-jinja, complementing the ones in the Tōshō-gū area and on the mountain, Nantai-san.

For good views of the lake and Kegon-no-taki, get off the bus at the Akechi-daira bus stop (the stop before Chūzenji Onsen) and take the Akechi-daira (Akechi Plateau) cable car up to a viewing platform (¥390/710 one way/return). From this point, it's a pleasant 1.5km walk across the **Chanoki-daira** to a vantage point with great views over the lake, the falls and Nantai-san (2484m). From here you can walk down to the lake and Chūzenji Onsen or take the Chūzenji cable car (¥440/840 one way/return).

As you might expect, Chūzenji-ko has the usual flotilla of cruise boats all clamouring to part you from your yen. The lake, which reaches a depth of 161m, is a fabulous shade of deep blue in good weather, and this, along with the mountainous backdrop, makes for a pleasant cruise. An alternative to a cruise is to hire one of the rowing boats that are available for ¥1000 per hour.

See the Yumoto Onsen entry, later, for information on the Senjōgahara Shizen-kenkyu-rō (Senjōgahara Plain Nature Trail) from Chūzenji-ko to Yumoto.

Places to Stay We recommend staying in Nikkō, which has a greater variety of good-value accommodation. However, if you prefer to stay in Chūzenji, try *Chūzenji Pension* (☎ 55-0888), which charges from ¥9500 per person with two meals. To get to the pension from the Nikkō-Chūzenji road, turn left at the lakeside, cross the bridge. The pension is on the left, about 100m down the road.

Getting There & Away There are buses from the Nikkō station area to Chūzenji Onsen (¥1100, 50 minutes).

Yumoto Onsen 湯元温泉
From Chūzenji-ko, you might continue on to the quieter hot-springs resort of Yumoto Onsen by bus (¥840, 30 minutes). Alternatively, you can hike there in three or four hours from the falls, Ryūzu-daki, on the central northern part of Chūzenji-ko (or do this in reverse).

The Chūzenji-ko–Yumoto hike takes around three hours and is known as **Senjōgahara Shizen-kenkyu-rō**. To get to the start of the hike from Chūzenji Onsen, take a Yumoto-bound bus and get off at Ryūzu-daki (¥410). The walk follows the Yu-gawa across the picturesque marshland of the plain, **Senjō-ga-hara**, to **Yuno-ko** (look out for the 75m-high falls, **Yu-daki**, in this area), from where it wends around the western edge of the lake to Yumoto Onsen. From Yumoto, you can catch a bus back to Nikkō (¥1650, 1½ hours).

Before heading back to Nikkō, you might want to stop off at **Onsen-ji**, a small temple with its own onsen (¥500, 10 am to 2 pm), a good spot to rest hiking-weary muscles.

MASHIKO 益子
☎ 0285
Mashiko is a centre for country-style pottery, with about 50 potters, some of whom you can see working at their kilns. The town achieved fame when the potter Hamada Shōji (1894–1978) settled there and, from 1930, produced his Mashiko pottery. His influence brought a legion of other potters to Mashiko, many of them foreign. The noted English potter Bernard Leach worked in Mashiko for several years.

Mashiko's kilns are spread out over quite a wide area and getting to see them requires a lot of footwork. Pick up the *Tourist Map of Mashiko* from the tourist information counter at Utsunomiya station (see the following Getting There & Away section) before you go. Even if you don't visit any individual kilns, make a point of stopping by the **Tōgei Messe** complex (9 am to 4 pm, closed Wednesday), a 20-minute walk from the station along the main road. In addition to viewing pottery displays and Hamada's kiln, you can take a pottery lesson here for ¥1200 – call ☎ 72-7555 to book.

Getting There & Away
It's possible to combine Mashiko with a visit to Nikkō if you set off from Tokyo very early and use the JR route. See Getting There & Away in the Nikkō section for travel details to Utsunomiya. From Utsunomiya Tōbu

station, buses run regularly during the day to Mashiko (¥1150, one hour). Ask at the tourist information counter outside Utsunomiya station for bus times and instructions on getting to the bus stop. This office also has tourist maps of Mashiko.

OZE-GA-HARA & LAKE OZE-NUMA 尾瀬沼と尾瀬沼湖

Oze-ga-hara, the 1400m-high marshlands around Lake Oze-numa, are the largest of their kind in Japan, covering an area of around eight sq km. The area is noted for its birdlife and wildflowers, in particular the *mizubashō* (skunk cabbage). Even when the wildflowers aren't in bloom, the hiking is lovely, as much of it is over wooden planks laid across the marshes.

Because Oze is one of the premier hiking destinations around Tokyo, it can be packed on summer weekends. For this reason, we strongly suggest that you go on a weekday during the summer months. Another way to escape the crowds is to ascend the mountain, Hiuchi-ga-take, from which there's a great view over the marshes.

During the hiking season (28 May to 10 October) direct overnight buses run from Tokyo and Shinjuku stations to three of the area's trailheads. There is a slight discount for return travel, but basic one-way rates with Oze Chokutsu Bus (☎ 03-3862-0819) are: ¥4500 to Ōshimizu, ¥5300 to Hatomachi-tōge, and ¥6500 to Numayama-tōge. Make sure you book both ways if you want to use this service.

Otherwise, the best bet for getting into the Oze region is to start from Numata in Gunma-ken. From Ueno station, take a Jōetsu-line *kaisoku* (rapid) train to Takasaki (1½ hours) and then take a *futsū* (local) to Numata (45 minutes). The whole journey costs ¥2520. From Numata station there are regular buses to the Ōshimizu trailhead (¥2200, two hours).

KAWAGOE 川越
● pop 304,000

The principal attraction in Kawagoe is its *dozōzukuri* (merchant warehouses), many of which have been designated National Treasures. The clay-walled buildings were built to be fireproof – by sealing them completely and leaving a candle burning inside, the buildings were starved of oxygen, leaving fires nothing to breathe. Most of them were built after a disastrous fire swept the town in 1893 and several now operate as museums.

Also in the area is **Kita-in**, a temple that was once a major headquarters of the Tendai sect and is still an impressive sight. The Kawagoe Matsuri is held on the second Saturday and Sunday in October; it's a boisterous affair with clashing floats, and activities that go on well into the night.

Getting There & Away
The Seibu Shinjuku line from Tokyo's Seibu Shinjuku station operates to the conveniently located Hon-Kawagoe station (¥470, 55 minutes). Take the middle of the three roads that radiate north from the station – most of the old buildings are along this road or on side streets off it.

CHICHIBU-TAMA NATIONAL PARK 秩父多摩国立公園
While the hikes in Chichibu-Tama National Park cannot compete with those farther afield, they do make a pleasant escape from the concrete jungles of Tokyo. The park is divided into the Chichibu and Oku-Tama regions. These two regions are connected by a two-day hiking trail that runs over the top of Kumotori-san (2018m), the highest point in the Tokyo metropolitan area. For those with less time, a trip to the mountaintop shrine complex of Mitake-jinja in the Oku-Tama region, perhaps paired with a hike to the summit of nearby Ōtake-san (1266m), makes a great day trip from the city.

Chichibu Region 秩父周辺
☎ 0494

Before heading on to other destinations, have a look round the small town of Chichibu. There are several interesting old Japanese and Western buildings on the road that leads to **Chichibu-jinja** from Ohanabatake station. The shrine itself is pleasant, although most of the buildings are modern reconstructions.

AROUND TOKYO

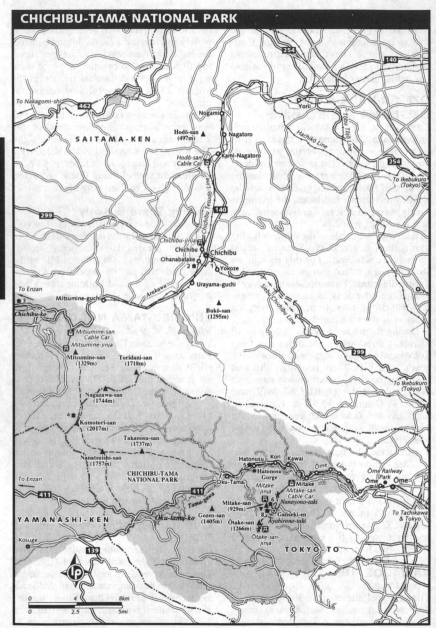

CHICHIBU-TAMA NATIONAL PARK

West of the town, just near the top of Mitsumine-san (1329m), **Mitsumine-jinja** is the starting point for the two-day walk that connects Chichibu with Oku-Tama. The shrine was founded some 2000 years ago and has long been favoured as a mountain retreat by members of the Tendai Buddhist sect. Set in a grove of towering cryptomeria trees, the shrine is worth a visit even if you don't intend to do the hike. Although it's possible to walk up to the shrine in two hours, most people take the Mitsumine-san cable car (¥830/1650 one-way/return).

To get to the cable car, take the Chichibu Tetsudō line from Ohanabatake station to Mitsumine-guchi station (¥460, 15 minutes) then switch to a Chichibu-ko bound bus and get off at Ōwa (¥300, 15 minutes). The cable-car station is a 15-minute walk uphill across the river from the bus stop.

Nagatoro 長瀞
From mid-March to mid-November, boats leave from Oyahana-bashi, 700m from Kami-Nagatoro station, to shoot the **Arakawa River rapids**. The trip costs ¥3550 and lasts 50 minutes. You can also take the **Hodō-san cable car** (¥420/720 one way/return) to the top of Hodō-san (497m), although it isn't as good as the trip up Mitsumine-san (see earlier in this section). The cable car is a 15-minute walk from Nagatoro station.

Places to Stay & Eat A bus trip from Mitsumine-san-guchi to the last stop, Chichibu-ko then a 15 minute walk, *Oku-Chichibu Lake View Youth Hostel* (☎ 55-0056) costs ¥3200. Check-in is from 3 to 10 pm. The business hotel *New Chichibu* (☎ 24-4444), a five-minute walk west of Chichibu station, is the best option in Chichibu itself. Singles/twins cost ¥5500/9800.

The Chichibu region's speciality is *teuchi soba* (handmade buckwheat noodles). A good place to try it is at *Soba Fuku*, across the street from Seibu Chichibu station; we recommend the tempura soba (¥900).

Getting There & Away The cheapest and quickest way of getting to the Chichibu area is via the Seibu Ikebukuro line from Seibu

Chateau Chichibu

That Japan has a long and glorious architectural history is by no means news. But the discovery in early 2000 of shallow post holes on a hillside in Chichibu indicates that this history may be longer than anyone had suspected. It appears that some 500,000 years ago, a group of *Homo erectus* built two huts on the site and scattered 30 or so stone tools around for good measure. If the find is confirmed, it means that hominids were building shelters up to 300,000 years earlier than previously thought – which casts the concept of 'architectural history' in an entirely different light.
Jane Thompson

Ikebukuro station (futsū, ¥750, 1¾ hours with changes en route; tokkyū *Red Arrow,* ¥1370, 1½ hours direct). Alternatively, JR trains run from Ueno station to Kumagaya station on the Takasaki line (¥1090, one hour and 10 minutes), where you will have to change to the Chichibu Tetsudō line to continue to Chichibu station (¥720, 45 minutes). All things considered, unless you're travelling on a Japan Rail Pass, it's cheaper to set off from Ikebukuro even if you're based in Ueno.

Oku-Tama Region 奥多摩周辺
☎ 0428
Like the Chichibu region, Oku-Tama has some splendid mountain scenery and a few good hiking trails. If you're only coming up for a day trip from Tokyo, this is a better and cheaper choice than the Chichibu region. The highlight of the area is the mountaintop shrine complex of Mitake-jinja and the quaint village surrounding it.

Ōme Railway Park There are several steam locomotives and an old shinkansen car on display at this mostly outdoor railway museum (¥100, 9.30 am to 4.30 pm, closed Monday). It's a 15-minute walk from Ōme station: exit the station, walk back along the tracks toward Tokyo for 150m, turn left over the tracks and follow the road up the hill; the park is at the top of the hill.

Kumotori-san Track

Kumotori-san (literally, 'Taker of Clouds Mountain'; 2017m), in Chichibu-Tama National Park, strad-dles the prefectural borders of Yamanashi, Saitama and Tokyo. The hike from the Chichibu region to the Oku-Tama region, over the summit of Kumotori-san, is made easier by the Mitsumine-san cable car (see Chichibu Region in this section), at the Chichibu end, which cuts about 730 vertical metres out of your hike in eight minutes. If you object to having the big climb taken out of your hike, you can always walk up (or do this hike the other way around!).

This hike is a two-day trip, leaving Tokyo on the morning of day one and returning in the evening of day two. There's no real reason to stay in Chichibu or Oku-Tama – one night is spent on the mountain in a mountain hut, camping or in the emergency hut.

This hike is best from April to December (spring to early winter). The main hut on the track, Kumo-tori Sansō, is open year round, but if you go in winter, consider weather conditions with common sense.

Day One: Top of Mitsumine Cable Car to Kumotori Sansō; three to five hours

The Mitsumine cable car should have just whipped you up to 1090m. The first 2km of the hike are virtually flat, so you can warm up as you amble through the shrine complex, Mitsumine-jinja. Pass through the complex and head onto the track to start the climb.

The first target is Kirimo-ga-mine (1523m), which you should reach in one to 1½ hours from the cable car. Stay on the main ridge and descend briefly before making the long climb to Mae-shiraiwa-san (1776m), where you can rest on some benches. Another short descent and climb brings you to *Shiraiwa-goya*, 1½ hours or so from Kirimo-ga-mine. This hut is open daily from 20 July to 31 Au-gust, and on Saturday throughout the rest of the year.

After another 20- to 30-minute climb, you reach Shiraiwa-san (1921m). This is followed by a 30- to 45-minute descent. *Kumotori Sansō* (☎ 0494-23-3338) is a mountain hut that is open year round. It charges ¥6000/3500 with/without meals, and ¥300 for camp sites nearby. It's a short climb from the low point (about three to five hours from the top of the cable car). If you are adequately pre-pared and can invest an extra 20 to 30 minutes in climbing, you can stay for free in the *emergency hut* at the summit of Kumotori-san. There are no facilities there: you'll need a sleeping bag and food.

Day Two: Kumotori Sansō to Oku-Tama; five to seven hours

If you stay at the hut or camp, you'll start day two by climbing to the peak. Views of the surrounding mountains from the bald, rocky top are stunning. This is the highest point in Tokyo! Descend from the peak to the south, keep right at all trail junctions, and after 45 minutes you'll come to *Kumo-tori Oku-tama-goya,* a hut open year round. Camping here is OK, and there's water available.

The track continues along the ridge to Nanatsuishi-yama (Seven Stone Mountain; 1757m), then carries on along the right side of the main ridge to the *emergency hut* on Takanosu-san (Hawk's Nest Mountain; 1737m). At the intersection thereafter, you can either climb the peak, by going left, or avoid it, by going right. The tracks meet up again on the other side, and descend to a spot just to the north of Mutsuishi-yama (Six Stone Mountain; 1479m). You have to take a short side trip south if you want to climb the Takanosu-san peak. The none-too-steep descent from Kumotori-san should have taken three to 4½ hours to this point.

This is where things steepen. It's a 1½- to two-hour drop to the small village of Oku-Tama, where there is a visitors centre, countless places to eat, and a train to take you back to Tokyo. See Oku-Tama in this chapter for details.

Mitake-san Buses run from Mitake station to the Mitake-san cable-car terminus (¥270, 10 minutes), from where the **Mitake-san** **cable car** takes you close to the summit (¥570/1090 one way/return, ¥50 less each way with an Okutama Furii Kippu (Okutama

Free Pass). See Getting There & Away later for details. About 20 minutes on foot from the top of the cable car is **Mitake-jinja**, said to date back some 1200 years. The area around the shrine has great views of the surrounding mountains and the Kantō Plain.

If you plan to hike around Mitake-san (926m), pick up the excellent *Okutama Nature Map* from the Mitake Visitors Center (☎ 78-9363), which is 250m beyond the top of the cable car, near the start of the village (10 am to 4 pm, closed Monday).

Ōtake-san Hike If you've got the time, the three-hour hike from Mitake-jinja to the summit of Ōtake-san (1266m) and back is highly recommended. Although there's some climbing involved, it's a fairly easy hike and the views from the summit are excellent – Fuji-san is visible to the south on clear days. On the way, take the detour down to **Nanoyono-taki**, **Ganseki-en** (a rocky ravine) and **Ayahirono-taki** – all that greenery and silence may come as a shock after a few days cooped up in Tokyo.

Places to Stay & Eat Up on Mitake-san, the very comfortable *Mitake Youth Hostel* (☎ 78-8774) charges ¥2750. It's midway between the top of the cable car and Mitake-jinja. Farther on, just below the shrine, the *minshuku* (Japanese-style B&B) *Komadori San-sō* (☎ 78-8472) is a friendly place at ease with foreigners. It charges ¥4500 to ¥5000 per person (meals are extra). The Mitake Visitors Centre (☎ 78-9363) has a map to both places (see the earlier Mitake-san section).

Down in the valley, the clean *Kokuminshukusha Hatonosu-sō* (☎ 85-2340) charges ¥4500 per person, or around ¥7000 with two meals. It's a short walk from Hatonosu station. Exit the station, walk down to and cross the main road, take the road that bears off left just before the tunnel, and you'll see it down on your left.

We highly recommend lunch on Mitakesan. Try *Momiji-ya*, a soba shop on the main walkway to the shrine. The *kamo-nanban* (duck) soba for ¥1100 is a very good choice.

Getting There & Away You can get to Oku-Tama by taking the JR Chūō line from Shinjuku station to Tachikawa station (¥430, 40 minutes), and changing there to the JR Ōme line to Oku-Tama station (¥590, one hour and 10 minutes). Unless you've got a Japan Rail Pass, we highly recommend the Okutama Free Pass (¥1470), available at JR ticket windows, which covers return travel between Okutama and Tokyo and unlimited use of JR trains in the Okutama region.

MITO 水戸
☎ 0292 • pop 234,000

The capital of Ibaraki-ken, Mito was once a castle town. Today its only notable attraction is **Kairaku-en**, one of Japan's three most celebrated landscape gardens (the other two are Kenroku-en in Kanazawa and Kōraku-en in Okayama). The 18-acre gardens date back to 1842 and are popular for their *ume* (plum blossoms) which bloom in late February or early March.

Entry to the garden is free, though there's a ¥180 entry charge for the pavilion, **Kobuntei**, a tasteful reproduction of a Mito clanlord's villa. To get to the garden take a bus from Mito station to Kairakuen-mae bus stop (20 minutes). From Ueno station take the JR Jōban line to Mito (tokkyū, one hour and 20 minutes). Ordinary services from Ueno take just under two hours and stop at Kairaku-en station (one stop before Mito).

West of Tokyo

Many of the destinations most popular with Tokyo residents lie to the west of the city, including the scenic Fuji Go-ko region, Mt Fuji itself, the tourist mecca of Hakone and the onsen and beach resorts of the Izu-hantō.

MT FUJI AREA 富士山周辺
☎ 0555

Mt Fuji, Japan's most familiar symbol, dominates the region south-west of Tokyo. Although Hakone is probably the most famous spot for Fuji-viewing, those with an aversion to crowds will prefer the scenic Fuji Go-ko region.

Mt Fuji 富士山

Japan's highest mountain stands 3776m high. When it's capped with snow in late autumn, winter and spring, it's a picture-postcard perfect volcanic cone. Fuji-san, as it's known in Japanese (*san* is the Chinese reading of the *kanji*, or character, for 'mountain'), last blew its top in 1707, covering the streets of Tokyo with volcanic ash. On an exceptionally clear day, you can see Mt Fuji from Tokyo, 100km away, but for much of the year you'd be hard pressed to see it from 100m away. Your best chance of seeing the notoriously shy mountain is in the late autumn, winter and early spring when the air is fairly clear. Even during these times, the mountain may only be visible in the morning before it retreats behind a curtain of haze or clouds.

Information *Climbing Mt Fuji*, *Mt Fuji Climber's Guidebook* and *Mt Fuji & Fuji Five Lakes* brochures are available from the Tourist Information Center in Tokyo (TIC, ☎ 03-3201-3331), and provide exhaustive detail on transport to the mountain and how to climb it, complete with climbing schedules worked out to the minute.

During the climbing season, there is a 24-hour taped English climbing information line on ☎ 23-3000. Alternatively, contact the Kawaguchi-ko tourist information centre (☎ 72-6700).

Mt Fuji Views You can get a classic view of Mt Fuji from the shinkansen as it passes the city of Fuji (sit on the northern side of the train). There are also good views from the Hakone area, Nagao-tōge Pass on the road from Hakone to Gotemba, and the northwest coast of the Izu-hantō. But the best and closest views are from the Fuji Go-ko region where, on a clear day, the hulking presence of the mountain seems to fill the sky.

Climbing Mt Fuji Officially, the climbing season on Fuji-san is from 1 July to 31 August, and the Japanese, who love to do things 'right', pack in during those busy months. Actually, you can climb Mt Fuji at any time of year, and it may be preferable to do so just outside the official season to avoid the crowds, but keep in mind that transport services may be less frequent and some of the huts may be closed. Of course, any time there's snow on the mountain you'll need the proper equipment and experience to climb Mt Fuji, and a midwinter ascent is strictly for expert mountaineers.

Although children and grandparents regularly make it to the summit, this is a serious mountain and not to be trifled with. It's high enough for altitude sickness, and as on any mountain, the weather on Mt Fuji can be viciously changeable. On the summit it can go from sunny and warm to wet, windy and cold in remarkably little time. Even if conditions are fine, you can count on it being close to freezing on mornings in season, and much colder out of season. Whatever you do, *don't climb Mt Fuji without clothing appropriate for cold and wet weather*.

The mountain is divided into 10 'stations', from base to summit, but these days most climbers start from one of the four 5th stations, which you can reach by road. From the end of the road, it takes about 4½ hours to climb the mountain and about 2½ hours to descend. Once you're on top, it takes about an hour to make a circuit of the crater. The Mt Fuji Weather Station, on the southwestern edge of the crater, is on the actual summit of the mountain.

You want to reach the top at dawn – both to see *goraiko* (sunrise) and because early morning is the time when the mountain is

A 19th century illustration of Fuji-san, from 'Unbeaten Tracks in Japan' by JF Bishop.

A Wise Man's Climb

I'd started out on a hot August night; at 10 pm the temperature had been around 27°C (80°F). But by 4 am it was below freezing and the wind was whistling past at what felt like hurricane speed. With a surprising number of other *gaijin* (foreigners) and a huge number of Japanese, I'd reached the top of Mt Fuji.

Climbing Fuji-san is definitely not heroic: in the two-month 'season' as many as 180,000 people get to the top – 3000-odd every night. Nor is it that much fun – it's a bit of a dusty slog and when you get to the top it's so cold and windy that your main thought is about heading down again. But the climb and the views aren't really what you do it for. To Japanese Fuji-climbers, it's something of a pilgrimage; to gaijin, it's another opportunity to grapple with something uniquely Japanese.

Like many other climbers, I made my Fuji climb overnight. At 9.30 pm I got off the bus at the Kawaguchi-ko 5th Station, which is where the road ends and you have to start walking. Surprisingly, about half the passengers on my bus were gaijin, most of them a group of Americans planning to convert the Japanese to Mormonism! I'd bought a litre of the isotonic drink Pocari Sweat and a packet of biscuits at a 7-Eleven in the town of Kawaguchi-ko, and wearing a shirt and a coat, I was all set. The night was clear, but dark, and I was glad I'd got some new batteries for my torch before I'd left Tokyo.

My experience of climbing holy mountains is that you always get to the top too early – you work up a real sweat on the climb and then you freeze waiting for dawn. So I hung around for a while before starting out.

Despite the hordes climbing the mountain, I managed to lose the path occasionally. By the time I reached 2390m I'd already stopped to unzip the lining from my coat. By 11 pm I was past 2700m and thinking it was time to slow down if I wanted to avoid arriving too early. By midnight it was getting much cooler, and I zipped the jacket lining back in place and added more clothes to my ensemble. I was approaching 3000m – virtually halfway – and at this rate I was going to be at the top by 2.30 am, in line with the four hours and 35 minutes the tourist-office leaflet said it was supposed to take! In Japan, even mountain climbing is scheduled to the minute.

Although I'd started on my own, some of the faces I met at rest stops were becoming familiar by this point and I'd fallen in with two Canadians and a Frenchman.

Huts are scattered up the mountainside; some stations have a number of huts, and others have none. The proprietors are very jealous of their facilities, and prominent signs, in English and Japanese, announce that even if it is pouring with rain, you can stay outside if you aren't willing to fork over the overnight fee. Fortunately, at 1.30 am we were virtually swept into one hut, probably in anticipation of the numerous bowls of *rāmen* (noodles in soup) we would order. We hung out in this comfortable 3400m-high hideaway until after 3 am, when we calculated a final hour and a bit of a push would get us to the top just before the 4.30 am sunrise.

We made it, and looking back from the top, we saw hordes of climbers heading up towards us. It was no great surprise to find a souvenir shop (there is absolutely no place in Japan where tourists won't find a souvenir shop waiting for them). The sun took an interminable time to rise, but eventually it poked its head through the clouds, after which most climbers headed straight back down. I spent an hour walking around the crater rim, but I wasn't sorry to wave Fuji-san goodbye. The Japanese say you're wise to climb Fuji, but a fool to climb it twice. I've no intention of being a fool.

Tony Wheeler

least likely to be shrouded in cloud. Sometimes it takes an hour or two to burn the morning mist off, however. To time your arrival for dawn you can either start up in the afternoon, stay overnight in a mountain hut and continue early in the morning, or climb the whole way at night. You do not want to arrive on the top too long before dawn, as

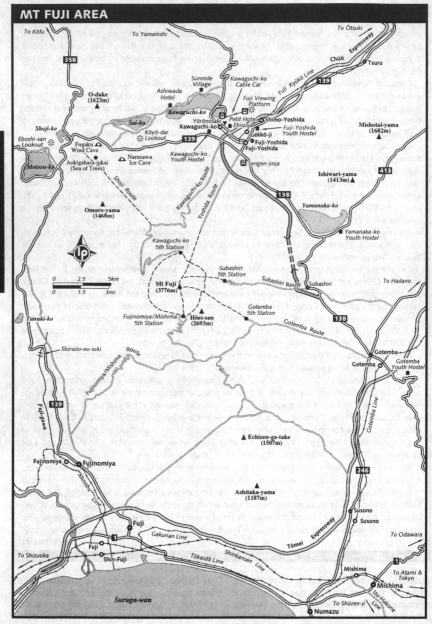

MT FUJI AREA

AROUND TOKYO

To Kōfu

To Yamanishi

To Ōtsuki

358

Chūō Expressway

Tsuru

Fuji Kyūkō Line

139

O-dake
(1623m)

Ashiwada
Hotel

Sunnide
Village

Kawaguchi-ko
Cable Car

Fuji Viewing
Platform

Shimo-Yoshida

Mishotai-yama
(1682m)

Shoji-ko

Sai-ko

Kawaguchi-ko

Yōrōnotaki
Kawaguchi-ko

Kōyō-dai
Lookout

Petit Hotel
Ebisuya

Gekkō-ji

Fuji-Yoshida
Youth Hostel

Eboshi-san
Lookout

Fugaku
Wind Cave

139

Fuji-Yoshida
Fuji-Yoshida

Motosu-ko

Aokigahara-jukai
(Sea of Trees)

Narusawa
Ice Cave

Kawaguchi-ko
Youth Hostel

Sengen-jinja

Ishiwari-yama
(1413m)

413

Omuro-yama
(1468m)

Shoji Route

Kawaguchi-ko Route

Yoshida Route

138

Yamanaka-ko

Kawaguchi-ko
5th Station

0   2.5   5km
0   1.5   3mi

Subashiri
5th Station

Subashiri Route

Subashiri

To Hadano

Yamanaka-ko
Youth Hostel

Mt Fuji
(3776m)

Tanuki-ko

Fujinomiya/Mishima
5th Station

Hōei-san
(2693m)

Gotemba
5th Station

Gotemba Route

138

Gotemba

Shiraito-no-taki

Fujinomiya/Mishima
Route

Gotemba
Youth Hostel

Fuji-gawa

139

Gotemba Line

Echizen-ga-take
(1507m)

Fujinomiya

Fujinomiya

Minobu Line

Ashitaka-yama
(1187m)

246

Susono

Susono

Fuji

Fuji

Gakunan Line

Shinkansen Line

Tōmei Expressway

To Odawara

Shin-Fuji

Tōkaidō Line

Mishima

1

To Atami &
Tokyo

To Shizuoka

Mishima

Izu-Hakone
Line

Suruga-wan

To Shūzen-ji

Numazu

it's likely to be very cold and windy, and if you've worked up a sweat during the climb, you'll be very uncomfortable.

Although nearly all climbers start from the 5th stations, it is possible to climb all the way up from a lower level. The low-level trails are now mainly used as short hiking routes around the base of the mountain, but gluttons for punishment can climb all the way on the Yoshida Route from Fuji-Yoshida, or on the Shoji Route from near Shoji-ko. There are alternative sand trails on the Kawaguchi-ko, Subashiri and Gotemba Routes, which you can descend very rapidly by running and *sunabashiri* (sliding), pausing from time to time to get the sand out of your shoes.

5th Stations There are four 5th stations around Mt Fuji and it's quite feasible to climb from one and descend to another. On the northern side of Fuji is the **Kawaguchi-ko 5th Station** (2305m), which is reached from the town of Kawaguchi-ko. This station is particularly popular with climbers starting from Tokyo. The Yoshida Route (which starts much lower down, close to the town of Fuji-Yoshida) is the same as the Kawaguchi-ko Route for much of the way.

The route from the **Subashiri 5th Station** (1980m) meets the Yoshida Route just after the 8th station. The **Gotemba 5th Station** is reached from the town of Gotemba and, at 1440m, is much lower than the other 5th stations. From Gotemba station it takes seven to eight hours to reach the top of Mt Fuji, as opposed to 4½ to five hours on the other routes. The **Fujinomiya (Mishima) 5th Station** (2380m) is convenient for climbers coming from Nagoya, Kyoto, Osaka and western Japan. It meets the Gotemba Route right at the top.

Equipment Make sure you have plenty of clothing suitable for cold and wet weather, including a hat and gloves. Bring drinking water and some snack food. If you're going to climb at night, bring a torch (flashlight) or headlamp, and spare batteries.

Mountain Huts There are 'lodges' dotted up the mountainside, but they're expensive

– ¥4000 to ¥4500 for a mattress on the floor squeezed between countless other climbers – and you don't get much opportunity to sleep anyway, as you have to be up well before dawn to start the final slog to the top. The huts also prepare simple meals for their guests and for passing climbers, and you're welcome to rest inside so long as you order something. If you don't feel like eating, a one-hour rest costs ¥500. Camping on the mountain is not permitted.

Getting There & Away See the Fuji Go-ko section, following, for details on transport to Kawaguchi-ko, the most popular arrival point for Tokyo Fuji-climbers. Travellers intending to head west from the Fuji area towards Nagoya, Osaka and Kyoto can take a bus from Kawaguchi-ko or Gotemba to Mishima station on the shinkansen line.

From Kawaguchi-ko, there are bus services up to Kawaguchi-ko 5th Station (¥1700, 55 minutes) from April to mid-November. The schedule varies considerably during that period – call Fuji Kyūkō bus on ☎ 72-2911 for details. At the height of the climbing season, there are buses until quite late in the evening – ideal for climbers intending to make an overnight ascent.

Taxis operate from the train station to the 5th Station for around ¥8000, plus tolls, which is not much more than the bus fare when divided among four people.

There are also direct buses (¥2600, 2½ hours) from the Shinjuku bus terminal to the Kawaguchi-ko 5th Station. This is by far the fastest and cheapest way of getting from Tokyo to the 5th Station. If you take two trains and a bus, the same trip can cost nearly ¥6000.

From Subashiri, buses to the Subashiri 5th Station cost ¥1220 and take 55 minutes. From Gotemba station they cost ¥1500.

From Gotemba, buses to the Gotemba 5th Station (¥1080, 45 minutes) operate four to six times daily, but only during the climbing season.

The southern route up the mountain is most popular with climbers from western Japan approaching the mountain by shinkansen. Bus services run from Shin-Fuji

(¥2400) and Mishima train stations (¥2390) to Fujinomiya (Mishima) 5th Station in just over two hours.

Fuji Go-ko 富士五湖

The Fuji Go-ko (Fuji Five Lakes), scattered around the northern side of Mt Fuji, are the perfect reflecting pools for the mountain's majesty. Particularly pleasant during the autumn *kōyō* (maple) season, the lakes make a good overnight trip out of Tokyo. Most folks spend their time in the region doing little more than strolling around and enjoying the views, but those with energy can do some hiking in the mountains above the lakes. Hiking maps are available from the information centres in Kawaguchi-ko and Fuji-Yoshida.

Things to See & Do The town of **Kawaguchi-ko**, on the lake of the same name, is the best place from which to explore the Fuji Go-ko area. It's also a popular departure point for climbing Mt Fuji. Start your explorations with a stop at the Kawaguchi-ko Tourist Information Centre (☎ 72-6700), which is right outside Kawaguchi-ko station and is open from 9 am to 4.30 pm. Around 600m north of the station, on the lower eastern edge of the lake, is the **Kawaguchi-ko cable car** (¥400/700 one way/return) to the **Fuji Viewing Platform** (1104m). You can walk to the cable car from Kawaguchi-ko station; ask at the information centre for a map.

At Fuji-Yoshida, five minutes south of Kawaguchi-ko by train, is the atmospheric **Sengen-jinja**, which dates from 1615 (although this area is thought to have been the site of a shrine as early as AD 788). In the days when climbing Mt Fuji was a pilgrimage and not an annual tourist event, a visit to this shrine was a necessary preliminary to the ascent. The entrance street to the shrine still has some Edo-era pilgrims' inns. From Fuji-Yoshida station, you can take a bus to Sengen-jinja-mae (¥150, five minutes), or walk there in about 15 minutes following a map from the Fuji-Yoshida Tourist Information Centre (☎ 22-7000), next to Fuji-Yoshida station. The centre is open from 9 am to 5.30 pm.

Yamanaka-ko is the largest of the lakes, but it doesn't offer much in the way of attractions – unless you count an enormous swan-shaped hovercraft that does 35-minute circuits of the lake for ¥900.

The area around the smaller **Sai-ko** is less developed than the areas around the larger lakes. There are good views of Mt Fuji from the western end of the lake and from the **Kōyō-dai lookout**, near the main road. Close to the road are the **Narusawa Ice Cave** and the **Fugaku Wind Cave**, both formed by lava flows from a prehistoric eruption of Mt Fuji. There's a bus stop at each of the caves, or you can walk from one to the other in about 20 minutes.

The views of Mt Fuji from farther west are not so impressive, but tiny **Shoji-ko** is said to be the prettiest of the Fuji Go-ko. Continue to Eboshi-san, a one- to 1½-hour climb from the road, to a lookout over the **Aokigahara-jukai** (Sea of Trees) to Mt Fuji. The last lake along is **Motosu-ko**, the deepest and least visited of the lakes.

Special Events On 26 and 27 August, the annual Yoshida no Hi Matsuri (Fire Festival) is held to mark the end of the climbing season and to offer thanks for the safety of the year's climbers. The first day involves a mikoshi procession and the lighting of bonfires on the town's main street. On the second day, festivals are held at the town's Sengen-jinja.

Places to Stay There are two youth hostels in the Fuji area. The cosy *Fuji-Yoshida* (☎ 22-0533) costs ¥2700. It's around 600m south of Shimo-Yoshida station; exit the station, walk down the main street through three sets of lights, and turn down the alley on the right, before Lawson convenience store. The rather regimented *Kawaguchi-ko Youth Hostel* (☎ 72-1431) costs ¥2900. It's about 500m south-west of Kawaguchi station; turn left as you come out of the tourist information centre, left again after the 7-Eleven, right after the post office and, finally, left in front of the power station.

There are many hotels, minshuku and pensions around the Fuji Go-ko, particularly in Kawaguchi-ko. The tourist information office (☎ 72-6700) at Kawaguchi-ko station can make reservations. The best of the bunch is *Sunnide Village* (☎ 76-6004, fax 76-7706), which commands a magnificent view over Kawaguchi-ko towards Mt Fuji (you can enjoy this view from its outdoor bath). Rooms with bath normally cost ¥6000 per person. If you go through the Kawaguchi-ko tourist information centre you can qualify for its ¥4000-per-person 'backpacker plan'. Note that no advance reservations are accepted for this rate; you just have to turn up and hope for the best. There's also a free pick-up service from the station (ask the folks at the information centre to call for you).

The Japanese Inn Group is represented in the area by *Ashiwada Hotel* (☎ 82-2587), at the western end of Kawaguchi-ko (take the No 6 bus from Kawaguchi-ko to the Nagahama stop, ¥270), and *Petit Hotel Ebisuya* (☎ 72-0165), which is just outside Kawaguchi-ko station. Rooms at the Ashiwada cost ¥6000/12,000 for singles/doubles with attached bathroom, while per-person rates at the Ebisuya are ¥5000/6000 with/without bathroom.

Places to Eat Most people eat where they're staying but there are other options. In Kawaguchi-ko, try the *Yoronouki* izakaya, opposite the station. In Fuji-Yoshida, the 6th floor of the station building is a *restaurant floor*. Otherwise, the Fuji-Yoshida tourist information centre (☎ 22-7000) can make arrangements for you to sample homemade *udon* (thick, white wheat noodles) at private homes for around ¥500.

Getting There & Away Kawaguchi-ko and Fuji-Yoshida are the two main travel centres in the Fuji Go-ko area. Buses (¥1700, 1¾ hours) operate directly to Kawaguchi-ko from the Shinjuku long-distance bus station, outside the western exit of Shinjuku station in Tokyo. There are departures up to 16 times daily at the height of the Fuji climbing season. Some buses continue on to Yamanaka-ko and Motosu-ko. In Tokyo, call Keiō Kōsoku bus (☎ 03-

5376-2222) for reservations and schedule information.

You can also get to the lakes by train, although it takes longer and costs more. JR Chūō-line trains go from Shinjuku to Ōtsuki (tokkyū, ¥2890, one hour; futsū, ¥1260, one hour and 50 minutes). At Ōtsuki, cross the platform to the Fuji Kyūkō line, which runs to Kawaguchi-ko (futsū only, ¥1510, one hour). The train actually goes to Fuji-Yoshida first (¥1390, 50 minutes), then reverses out for the final short distance to Kawaguchi-ko. On Sunday and holidays from March to November there is a direct local train from Shinjuku and Tokyo stations (¥2370 from Shinjuku, ¥2530 from Tokyo, two to 2½ hours).

From Fuji-Yoshida and Kawaguchi-ko, buses run north to Kōfu, from where you can continue north west to Matsumoto.

Getting Around There's a comprehensive bus network in the area, including regular buses from Fuji-Yoshida station that pass by the four smaller lakes and around the mountain to Fujinomiya (¥2150, 1½ hours) on the south-western side. From Kawaguchi-ko, there are nine to 11 buses daily to Mishima (¥2130, two hours) on the shinkansen line.

HAKONE 箱根
☎ 0460

Hakone is the Japanese tourist mecca *par excellence*. If the weather cooperates and Mt Fuji is clearly visible, the Hakone region can make a fun day trip from Tokyo. You can enjoy cable-car rides, visit an open-air museum, poke around smelly volcanic hot springs and cruise Ashino-ko. If it's rainy or cloudy, however, you may simply feel that you're riding a conveyor belt whose sole purpose is to strip you of your cash.

An interesting loop through the region takes you from Tokyo by train and toy train to Gōra; then by funicular and cable car up the 1153m-high mountain, Sōun-zan, and down to Ashino-ko; by boat around the lake to Moto-Hakone, where you can walk a short stretch of the Edo-era Tōkaidō highway; and from there by bus back to Odawara, where you catch the train to

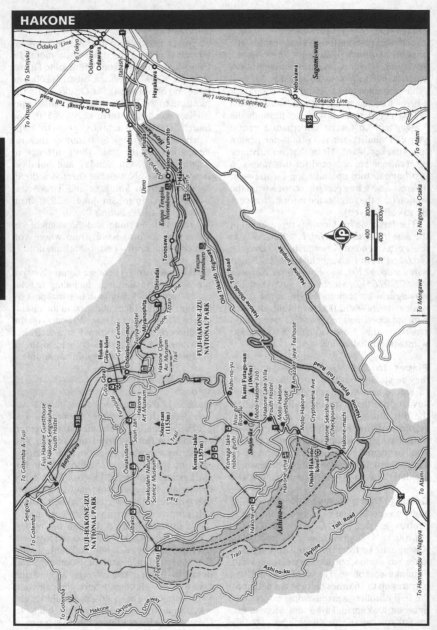

Tokyo. (If you're feeling energetic, you can spend 3½ hours walking the old highway back to Hakone-Yumoto, from where you can catch a train back to Tokyo.)

Odawara 小田原

Odawara is famous for its castle (¥250, 9 am to 4.30 pm), which is an uninspired reconstruction of the original. It's perhaps only worth visiting during the cherry-blossom season – there are some 1000 *sakura* (cherry) trees planted on the grounds. The castle and surrounding park area is a 10-minute walk south-east of Odawara station. There is very little else of interest in the town, which is principally a transit point for Hakone.

Hakone-Yumoto Onsen
箱根湯元温泉

Yumoto is Hakone's most popular hot springs resort. It's possible to stop off between Odawara and Gōra, and you might want to spend the day soaking in the baths here if the weather looks dodgy in Hakone. You might also consider approaching the town on foot from Moto-Hakone via the old Tōkaidō hiking course (see the Moto-Hakone entry later in this section).

Of course, onsen are the main attraction of Hakone-Yumoto. **Kappa Tengoku Notemburo** (¥700, 10 am to 10 pm), behind the station, is a popular outdoor bath ('*no*' means field), worth a dip if the crowds aren't too bad. For something more upmarket, try **Ten-zan Notemburo** (¥900, 9 am to 10.30 pm), which has a larger selection of indoor and outdoor baths. To get there, take the free shuttle bus from the bridge outside the station.

Hakone Open-Air Art Museum
彫刻の森美術館

The Hakone Open-Air Art Museum (¥1600, from 9 am to 5 pm, until 4.30 pm from December to March) is next to Chōkoku-no-Mori station, a stop before Gōra station. The focus is on Western and Japanese 19th- and 20th-century sculpture. The Hakone Free Pass (see Getting Around later in this section for details) does *not* gain you free admission, though it will earn you a discount.

Gōra 強羅

Gōra is the terminus of the Hakone-Tōzan line and the starting point for the funicular and cable-car trip to Tōgendai on Ashinoko. The town also has a couple of its own attractions that may be of minor interest to travellers. If you're in this area between 11.30 am and 2.30 pm, check out *Gyōza Center*, a famous shop with nine kinds of *gyōza* (dumplings). Basic sets with rice and *miso* (soya-bean paste) soup start at ¥900.

Hakone Gōra-kōen Just a short walk beside the funicular tracks up Sōun-zan is the park, Hakone Gōra-kōen (¥900, 9 am to 5 pm, closes slightly later in summer). It has a French rock garden, seasonal flowers, and alpine and tropical plants.

Hakone Art Museum Farther up the hill, 10 minutes from Gōra station, the Hakone Art Museum (¥900, 9 am to 4 pm, closed Thursday) has a moss garden and a decent collection of ceramics from Japan and China.

Sōun-zan & Ōwadakuni
早雲山と大桶谷

From Gōra, continue to the 1153m-high summit of Sōun-zan by funicular ('cable car' in Japanese; ¥410, 10 minutes). If you don't have a Hakone Free Pass (see Getting Around later in this section), tickets are sold at the booth to the right of the platform exit.

Sōun-zan is the starting point for what the Japanese refer to as a ropeway, a 30-minute, 4km cable-car ride to Tōgendai (¥1330/2360 one way/return). On the way, the gondolas pass through Ōwakudani. Get out here and take a look around the volcanic hot springs – the gondolas pass by every 52 seconds, so you can continue your journey whenever you like. In fine weather Mt Fuji looks fabulous from here.

Ōwakudani is a volcanic cauldron of steam, bubbling mud and mysterious smells. The black boiled eggs on sale here are cooked in the boiling mud. Next to the cable-car stop, there's a building with restaurants and souvenir shops.

Ōwakudani Natural Science Museum (¥400, 9 am to 4.30 pm) has displays relating to the geography and natural history of Hakone.

Ashino-ko 芦ノ湖

Ashino-ko is touted as the primary attraction of the Hakone region, but it's Mt Fuji, with its snow-clad slopes glimmering in reflection on the water, that lends the lake its poetry. And unfortunately the venerable mountain is frequently hidden behind a dirty-grey bank of clouds. If this is the case when you visit, you have the consolation of a ferry trip across the lake; you can always buy a postcard of the view. See Getting Around later in this section for details about transport across the lake.

Komaga-take 駒ヶ岳

The mountain, Komaga-take (1357m), is a good place from which to get a view of the lake and Mt Fuji. From Tōgendai, boats run to Hakone-en, from where a cable car (¥620/1050 one way/return) goes to the top. You can leave the mountain by the same route or by a five-minute funicular descent (¥370/630) to Komaga-take-nobori-guchi. Buses run from here to Hakone-machi (¥300), Hakone-Yumoto (¥820) and to Odawara (¥1050).

Rock Carvings Not far from Komaga-take-nobori-guchi is Moto-Hakone Jizō, a group of Buddhas and other figures carved in relief on rocks that lay between Komaga-take and Kami Futago-san (1065m). Although they date from the Kamakura era (1192–1333), most are still fairly well preserved. To get there from the funicular, turn right and follow the road down until you reach a T-junction. Turn left here and then left again; the carvings are around 400m up the road.

Moto-Hakone 元箱根

Moto-Hakone is a pleasant spot with a few places where you can eat or get an overpriced cup of coffee. There are a couple of interesting sights within easy walking distance of the jetty.

Hakone-jinja It's impossible to miss Hakone-jinja (¥300, 9.30 am to 4 pm), with its red torii rising from the lake. Walk around the lake towards the torii; huge cedars line the path to the shrine, which is in a wooded grove. There is a treasure hall in the grounds.

Cryptomeria Avenue Known as Suginamiki, the avenue is a 2km path between Moto-Hakone and Hakone-machi, which is lined with cryptomeria trees that were planted more than 360 years ago. The path runs behind the lakeside road used by buses and other traffic.

Old Tōkaidō Highway Up the hill from the lakeside Moto-Hakone bus stop is the old Tōkaidō highway, the road that once linked the ancient capital, Kyoto, with Edo (now known as Tokyo). It is possible to take a 3½-hour walk along the old road to Hakone-Yumoto station, passing the **Amazake-jaya Teahouse** and **Sōun-ji** along the way.

Hakone-machi 箱根町

Hakone-machi lies farther around the lake, beyond Moto-Hakone. The town's main attraction is the Hakone Sekisho-ato (Hakone Checkpoint), which was operated by the Tokugawa shogunate from 1619 to 1869 as a customs post between Edo and the rest of Japan. The present-day checkpoint is a recent reproduction of the original. Farther back towards Moto-Hakone is the **Hakone History Museum** (¥200, 9 am to 4.30 pm), which displays a small selection of *samurai* artefacts.

Special Events

Ashino-ko Kosui Matsuri, held on 31 July at Hakone-jinja near Moto-Hakone, features fireworks displays over Ashino-ko. On 16 August, in the Hakone Daimonji-yaki Matsuri, torches are lit on Myojoga-take so that they form the shape of the Chinese character for 'big' or 'great'. The Hakone Daimyō Gyoretsu parade on 3 November is a re-enactment by 400 costumed locals of a feudal lord's procession.

An example of prized *nishijin-ori* weaving, found in temples.

Nishi Hongan-ji temple, Kyoto

An ice-encrusted *hishaku* (bamboo ladle) – used to cleanse the hands before entering a shrine.

Handcrafted *kyō-ningyō* doll

A delicate and meticulously crafted *kyō-sensu* fan.

FRANK CARTER

ERIC L WHEATER

A Japanese maple in autumn.

A Kyoto temple, Kiyomizu-dera, during autumn.

FRANK CARTER

Autumn leaves drift by...

FRANK CARTER

Bamboo grove, Sagano, Kyoto

FRANK CARTER

Springtime in Japan is best spent under a cherry tree drinking sake.

Places to Stay

Hakone's local popularity is reflected in the high price of most accommodation in the area. With the exception of two youth hostels and a couple of Welcome Inns, there's little in the way of alternatives.

To get to both *Hakone Sengokuhara Youth Hostel* (☎ 4-8966) and *Fuji Hakone Guest House* (☎ 4-6577) – they're in the same place – take a No 4 bus from Odawara station to Senkyōrō-mae bus stop (50 minutes). There's an English sign close by. Beds at the hostel cost ¥2900 and check-in is from 4 to 6 pm. The guesthouse has singles/doubles from ¥5500/11,000. A natural hot spa is available for bathing.

Moto Hakone Guesthouse (☎ 3-7880) is conveniently located in Moto-Hakone and has rates of ¥5000 per person. From Odawara station, take a bus from the No 3 stand and get off at the Ashino-ko-en-mae stop (55 minutes).

Fujiya Hotel (☎ 2-2211) is one of Japan's earliest Western-style hotels and is highly rated on all fronts; room rates start at ¥20,000. There's also a weekday special for foreign travellers of US$120 for double rooms (you can pay the equivalent sum in yen). The hotel is around 250m west of Miyanoshita station on the Hakone-Tōzan line.

Getting There & Away

There are three ways of getting to the Hakone region from Tokyo: by the Odakyū express bus service, which leaves from the western side of Shinjuku station; by JR from Tokyo station; and by the private Odakyū line from Shinjuku station.

Train JR trains run on the Tōkaidō line between Tokyo station and Odawara (futsū, 1450, 1½ hours; tokkyū, ¥2880, 70 minutes; kodama shinkansen, ¥3640, 40 minutes).

The private Odakyū line runs into Hakone from Shinjuku station. Quickest and most comfortable is the *Romance Car* to Odawara (¥1720, 1¼ hours) or to Hakone-Yumoto (¥2020, one hour and 25 minutes). There's also a *kyūkō* (regular express) service (¥1150, 1½ hours) to Hakone-Yumoto.

At Odawara, it's possible to change to the narrow gauge, or toy train, Hakone-Tōzan line, which takes you to Gōra (¥650). Alternatively, if you are already on the Odakyū line, you can continue on to Hakone-Yumoto and change to the Hakone-Tōzan line (¥390 to Gōra) by walking across the platform.

Bus The Odakyū express bus service has the advantage of running directly into the Hakone region, to Ashino-ko and to Hakone-machi (¥1950, two hours). The disadvantage is that the bus trip is much less interesting than the combination of *Romance Car*, toy train (Hakone-Tōzan line), funicular, cable car (ropeway) and ferry. Buses run from the western exit of Shinjuku station 11 times daily.

Getting Around

Train The Odakyū line offers a Hakone *Furii Pasu* (Free Pass), which costs ¥5500 in Shinjuku or ¥4130 in Odawara (the place to buy it if you are travelling on a Japan Rail Pass) and allows you to use any mode of transport within the Hakone region for four days. The fare between Shinjuku and Hakone-Yumoto is also included in the pass (there's a ¥850 surcharge for the *Romance Car*). This is a good deal for a Hakone circuit, as the pass will save you at least ¥1000 even on a one-day visit to the region.

Bus The Hakone-Tōzan and Izu Hakone bus companies service the Hakone area and between them they manage to link up most of the sights. If you finish up in Hakone-machi, Hakone-Tōzan buses run between here and Odawara for ¥1150. Hakone-en to Odawara costs ¥1270. Buses run from Moto-Hakone to Yumoto for ¥900 every 30 minutes from 10 am to 3 pm.

Boat Ferry services crisscross Ashino-ko, running between Tōgendai, Hakone-machi and Moto-Hakone every 30 minutes. From Tōgendai, the fare is ¥970 to Moto-Hakone or Hakone-machi; between Moto-Hakone and Hakone-machi it's ¥250. The 'Pirate Ship' has to be seen to be believed – tourist kitsch at its worst, but fun all the same.

AROUND TOKYO

IZU-HANTŌ 伊豆半島

Eighty kilometres south-west of Tokyo, the peninsula, Izu-hantō, with its abundant onsen and rugged coastline, is one of Japan's most popular resort destinations. This means that things can get pretty crowded on the peninsula on weekends and holidays, particularly in summer. Luckily, once you get past the touristy resort of Atami, the crowds usually thin out. And over on the west coast, where transport is by bus only, things are always a lot quieter.

A suggested two- or three-day itinerary for the peninsula involves heading straight down the east coast to Shimoda. After exploring the town, neighbouring Rendai-ji Onsen and perhaps the rugged headlands of the cape, Irō-zaki, catch a bus for the scenic ride across the peninsula to Dōgashima on the west coast. Here, you can bathe in a cliff-side onsen, swim in the Pacific in warmer months and enjoy stunning views up and down the coast. From Dōgashima, you can catch another bus to the onsen village of Shuzen-ji. After sampling the excellent baths there, you can take the Izu-Hakone Tetsudō line to Mishima and from there switch to the JR Tōkaidō line for the trip back to Tokyo.

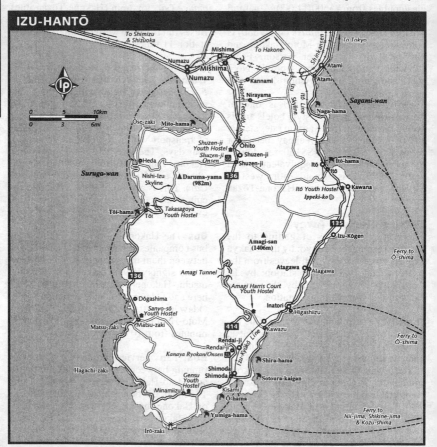

Atami 熱海
☎ 0557

Atami is an overdeveloped hot-springs resort with little to detain foreign travellers. The town's biggest attraction is the overpriced **MOA Art Museum** (¥1600, 9.30 am to 4.30 pm, closed Thursday). Its collection of Japanese and Chinese art includes a few 'national treasures' and a good number of Important Cultural Properties. Take a bus from outside Atami station to the last stop, MOA bijitsukan (¥160, 10 minutes).

Because of Atami's popularity with domestic tourists, rooms are very expensive; head down to Itō or Shimoda to find more reasonable lodgings.

Getting There & Away JR trains run from Tokyo station to Atami on the Tōkaidō line (regular train, ¥1890, two hours; Kodama shinkansen, ¥3570, 55 minutes; limited express *Odoriko*, ¥3770, one hour and 20 minutes). It's also possible to approach Atami via Shinjuku by taking the Odakyū line to Odawara (¥850, one hour and 10 minutes), and then connecting with the Tōkaidō line to Atami (¥390, 20 minutes).

Itō 伊東
☎ 0557

Itō is another hot-springs resort and is famous as the place where Anjin-san (William Adams), the hero of James Clavell's book *Shogun*, built a ship for the Tokugawa shōgunate. Itō station has a tourist information centre (☎ 37-6105) at the beachfront, close to where the bay cruises leave from.

Places to Stay One of the cheapest deals in town is *Business Hotel Itō* (☎ 36-1515). Singles/twins are ¥5250/9450. It's a four-storey building around 300m east of the train station, close to the waterfront.

Getting There & Away Itō is connected to Atami by the JR Itō line (¥320, 25 minutes). The JR limited express *Odoriko* service also runs from Tokyo station to Itō (¥4090, 45 minutes).

Shimoda 下田
☎ 0558

If you only have time for one town on the peninsula, make it Shimoda, the most pleasant of the peninsula's onsen towns. Shimoda is famous as the residence of the American Townsend Harris, the first Western diplomat to live in Japan. The Treaty of Kanagawa, which resulted from Commodore Perry's visit (see History in the Facts about Japan chapter), ended Japan's centuries of self-imposed isolation by opening the ports of Shimoda and Hakodate to US ships and establishing a consulate in Shimoda in 1856.

The southern end of town, around **Perry Road**, is perfect for strolling and has a few temples scattered about.

There is a small information centre (☎ 22-1531, 9 am to 5 pm) near the station, where the staff will help you book accommodation.

Ryōsen-ji & Chōraku-ji About a 25-minute walk south of Shimoda station is the temple, Ryōsen-ji, famous as the site of another treaty, supplementary to the Treaty of Kanagawa, signed by Commodore Perry and representatives of the Tokugawa shōgunate.

Next to the temple is a small **museum** (¥500, 8.30 am to 5 pm), with exhibits relating to the arrival of Westerners in Japan. These include a series of pictures depicting the tragic life of Okichi-san, a courtesan who was forced to give up the man she loved in order to attend to the needs of the barbarian Harris. When Harris left Japan five years later, Okichi was stigmatised for having had a relationship with a foreigner and was eventually driven to drink and suicide. Downstairs, there's an interesting collection of erotic knick-knacks – pickled turnips with suggestive shapes, and stones with vagina-like orifices in them.

Next door to Ryōsen-ji is Chōraku-ji, another pleasant little temple that's worth a quick look.

Hōfuku-ji In the centre of town is Hōfuku-ji, which has a museum (¥300, 8 am to 5 pm) that memorialises the life of Okichi-san and includes scenes from the various movie adaptations of her life.

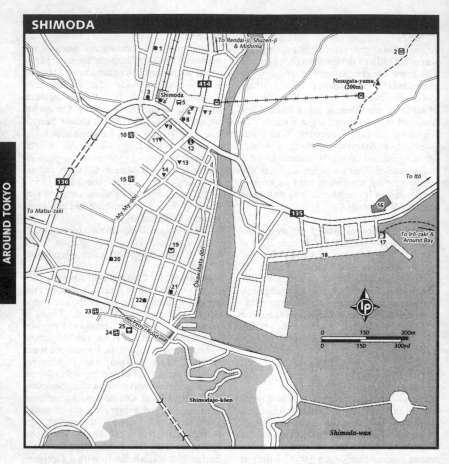

SHIMODA

Nesugata-yama Directly in front of Shimoda station is Nesugata-yama (Mt Nesugata; 200m). Every 10 minutes, cable cars run up to a park (9 am to 5 pm) that has a photography museum, a small temple, good views of Shimoda and the bay, Shimoda-wan, and a reasonably priced restaurant. A return cable-car trip, including admission to the park, costs ¥1200.

Beaches There are some good beaches around Shimoda, particularly around Kisami, south of town. Take an Irō-zaki bound bus; ask to be dropped at Ō-hama

Iriguchi and walk 10 minutes toward the coast. Farther south you can try the more developed beaches of **Yumiga-hama**, which is on the same bus route. Be warned that these places can be packed in late July and August; otherwise, they're relatively quiet.

Bay Cruises Several cruises depart from the Shimoda harbour area. Most popular with Japanese tourists is a 'Black Ship' cruise around the bay (¥920, 20 minutes), which departs every 30 minutes (approximately) from 9.10 am to 3.30 pm.

SHIMODA

PLACES TO STAY
1 Kokumin-shukusha New Shimoda
   国民宿舎ニュー下田
3 Station Hotel Shimoda
   ステーションホテル下田
16 Hotel Kurofune
   黒船ホテル
20 Shimoda-ya (Minshuku)
   下田屋
21 Matsumoto Ryokan
   松本旅館
22 Uraga Hotel
   ウラガホテル

PLACES TO EAT
6 McDonald's
7 Izutarō
   伊豆太郎

9 Matsu Sushi
   松寿し
11 Musashi
   むさし
13 Gorosaya
   ごろさや
14 Isoka-tei
   磯華亭

OTHER
2 Photography Museum
   写真記念館
4 Replica of Admiral Perry's Ship the Susquehanna
   サスケハナ丸の模型
5 Bus Stop
   バス停
8 Convenience Store
   コンビニエンスストア

10 Tōden-ji
   稲田寺
12 Tourist Information
   観光案内所
15 Hōfuku-ji
   宝福寺
17 Bay Cruises
   遊覧船
18 Morning Fish Market
   海の朝市
19 Shimoda Post Office
   下田郵便局
23 Ryōsen-ji
   了仙寺
24 Chōraku-ji
   長楽寺
25 Jah Jah
   ジャジャ

AROUND TOKYO

Three boats a day (9.40 and 11.20 am, and 2 pm) leave on an Irō-zaki course. You can leave the boat at Irō-zaki (¥1530, 40 minutes) and travel on by bus, or stay on the boat to return to Shimoda.

Special Events On the third Friday, Saturday and Sunday in May, the Kuro-fune (Black Ship) Matsuri is held in Shimoda. It commemorates the first landing of Commodore Perry with parades by the US Navy marching band and fireworks displays. It's most interesting to see how the Japanese have made a virtue out of this potentially bitter historical event.

Places to Stay There are two youth hostels in the Shimoda area. *Gensu Youth Hostel* (☎ 62-0035) has beds for ¥2900. It's 25 minutes from town by bus No 3; get off at the Yakuba-mae stop (¥630). Check-in is from 4 to 8 pm. Even farther from town is *Amagi Harris Court Youth Hostel* (☎ 35-7253), which is around 5km inland from Kawazu station, between Itō and Shimoda. It has beds for ¥3200 and check-in is from 3 to 6 pm. Take a Shuzen-ji-bound bus from the No 3 platform outside Kawazu station and get off at the Jige-in-mae stop.

If you prefer to be in town, you'll have to spend a little more. There are lots of minshuku around and the tourist office (☎ 22-1531) can help with reservations. You might try *Shimoda-ya* (☎ 22-0446), which has beds for ¥8500 with two meals, ¥5500 without. The ageing but interesting *Matsu moto Ryokan* (☎ 22-0023) has beds for ¥5000; it doesn't serve meals. *Kokumin-shukusha New Shimoda* (☎ 23-0???) is a decent place that charges ¥7000 per person, with two meals.

Right next to the station, *Station Hotel Shimoda* (☎ 22-8885) is a business hotel with clean singles/doubles for ¥5800/9800. Another good business hotel is *Uraga Hotel* (☎ 23-6000), which has clean new singles/doubles for ¥7000/9800. The upmarket *Hotel Kurofune* (☎ 22-1234) charges ¥22,000 per person, with two meals.

Places to Eat & Drink Seafood is the speciality in Shimoda and there are lots of good places around to try it. The best of the bunch is the friendly *Isoka-tei*, which does hearty seafood sets for lunch and dinner for around ¥1500. There's a picture menu to make ordering easier. *Izutarō* is a standard *kaiten-zushi* (conveyor-belt) spot, where ¥1500 should you buy enough to fill you up. For better sushi, try **Matsu Sushi**, which has sushi sets from ¥1000. **Musashi** does most Japanese *shokudō* (cafeteria) favourites, including tempura soba for ¥850. More up-market is **Gorosaya**, which does good seafood sets starting at ¥1500.

After dinner, you might hit the bar **Jah Jah** to kick back with some good tunes and friendly people. Beers start at ¥600.

Getting There & Away Shimoda is as far as you can go by train on the Izu-hantō. You can take the limited express *Odoriko* from Tokyo station (¥5550, 2¾ hours), or an Izu Kyūkō line train from Itō station (¥1440, one hour). Trains also run from Atami (¥1890, 1½ hours).

Bus platform No 5 in front of the station is for buses going to Dōgashima (¥1360, one hour), while platform No 7 is for those bound for Shuzen-ji (¥2180, two hours).

Rendai-ji & Kanaya Onsen 蓮台寺と金屋温泉

A stop north of Shimoda on the Izu Kyūkō line is Rendai-ji (¥160, five minutes), home to one of the best onsen on the peninsula, Kanaya Onsen (¥700/1000 weekdays/weekends and holidays, 9 am to 9 pm). Housed in atmospheric **Kanaya Ryokan** (☎ 0558-22-0325), this traditional bath is well worth a side trip from Shimoda. The highlight is the enormous bath on the men's side, inside a weathered wooden hall. Women who want to check out this bath are welcome, but bathing suits are not permitted (towels are). The women's bath is nothing to sneeze at, and both sides have private outdoor baths.

Once you see the lovely ryokan, you may be tempted to stay the night; per-person rates start at ¥15,000 with two meals, ¥7000 without meals.

From Rendai-ji station, go straight across the river and main road to the T-junction and turn left; the onsen is 50m on the right.

Irō-zaki 石廊崎

Irō-zaki, the southernmost point of the peninsula, is noted for its cliffs and lighthouse. It also has a jungle park, a tropical garden and some fairly good beaches. You can get to the cape from Shimoda by boat (see Bay Cruises in the Shimoda section earlier) or by bus (¥930, 45 minutes) from the No 4 bus platform.

Matsu-zaki 松崎
☎ 0558

The attraction of Matsu-zaki is its collection of around 200 **traditional houses** with *namako-kabe* walls – diamond-shaped tiles set in plaster. They're concentrated in the south of town, on the far side of the river.

Places to Stay Several kilometres to the east of town, **Sanyo-sō Youth Hostel** (☎ 42-0408) has beds for ¥2850. From Shimoda take a bus from the No 5 platform and get off at the Yūsu-hosteru-mae bus stop. Check-in is from 4 to 6.30 pm.

Getting There & Away Buses from Shimoda to Dōgashima pass through Matsu-zaki. The fare from Shimoda is ¥1170; from Dōgashima ¥490. High-speed ferries also travel from Matsu-zaki to Dōgashima (¥450), Toi (¥1660), Heda (¥2090) and Numazu (¥3400).

Dōgashima 堂ヶ島

From Shimoda, it's a picturesque bus journey to Dōgashima, on the other side of the peninsula. There are no breathtaking views, but the hilly countryside and the narrow road that winds its way past fields and through small rural townships make for an interesting trip.

The main attractions at Dōgashima are the dramatic **rock formations** that line the seashore. The park just across the street from the bus stop has some of the best views. It's also possible to take a boat trip (¥900, 20 minutes) from the nearby jetty to visit the town's famous shoreline **cave**. The cave has a natural window in the roof that allows light to pour in. You can look down into the cave from paths in the aforementioned park.

South of the bus stop, you'll find the stunning **Sawada-kōen Rotemburo** onsen (male/female separate, ¥500, 7 am to 7 pm, closed Tuesday) perched high on a cliff overlooking the Pacific. Go early in the day if possible; around sunset it's standing room only. Nearby, there's a lighthouse high on a cliff, with magnificent views down the coast. To get there, walk to the beach from the bus stop, cut through the small fishing village and turn towards the ocean.

Getting There & Away Buses to Dō-gashima (¥1360, one hour) leave from platform No 5 in front of Shimoda station. From Dōgashima you can catch a bus onward to Shuzen-ji (¥1970, 1½ hours), a journey that affords fantastic views over Suruga-wan north to Mt Fuji. Indeed, when the air is clear and the mountain is blanketed by snow, it's worth the bus fare for the view alone – you'll swear you're looking at a Hokusai print. The best views are to be had a few kilometres south of Toi.

There are high-speed ferries between Dō-gashima and Numazu (¥330, 1¼ hours), which is connected with Tokyo by the Tōkaidō line; there are six departures a day between 10 am and 4.45 pm.

Shuzen-ji Onsen 修善寺
☎ 0558
Shuzen-ji is one of the peninsula's better onsen towns. It's connected to the Tōkaidō line by the Izu-Hakone Tetsudō line, making it, along with Atami, one of the two main entry points to the peninsula. Everything of interest to travellers is in Shuzen-ji Onsen, a bus ride (¥210, 10 minutes) west of Shuzen-ji station.

Things to See & Do In the middle of Shuzen-ji Onsen, you'll find **Shuzen-ji**, an attractive and tranquil temple that dates back to AD 807. It's said to have been founded by Kōbō Daishi, who established the Shingon sect (see Buddhism under Religion in the Facts about Japan chapter). The present structure dates from 1489. Near the temple, you'll find a small **treasure house** (¥300, 8.30 am to 4.30 pm), which has displays on the history of the village.

Of course, the real reason to visit Shuzen-ji is to take a dip in one of its famous onsen. Right in the middle of the village you'll find

the mineral hot-spring, **Tokko-no-yu** (mixed bathing, free, open 24 hours), on a rocky promontory over the Katsura-gawa. Given the bath's central location and lack of proper walls, it's hardly surprising that naked foreigners become instant tourist attractions.

For a little privacy, head to the wonderful baths at **Kikuya Ryokan**, opposite the bus stop. Nonguests are welcome from 11 am to 2.30 pm. Baths here cost ¥1000 and this is one of the few places in Japan where the women's baths are better than the men's.

If the baths at Kikuya are out of your price range, try the nameless local *sentō* (public bath), which uses hot-spring water. It's opposite Kikuya, past the bus stop, 50m up a narrow lane on the left. There's no-one on duty here – just put your ¥300 in the box and watch the locals' jaws drop when you enter.

Places to Stay & Eat *Shuzen-ji Youth Hostel* (☎ 72-1222) is a 15-minute bus ride from Shuzen-ji station. Take a bus from the No 6 platform at Shuzen-ji station to the New Town-guchi stop. It's a five-minute walk from the bus stop. The hostel is closed from 18 to 22 January and from 30 May to 3 June. Beds are ¥2800 and check-in is from 3 to 9 pm.

The aforementioned *Kikuya Ryokan* (☎ 72-2000) is an elegant place, with per-person rates of ¥10,000, including two meals. A cheaper option is the pleasant minshuku *Sakae-sō* (☎ 72-3434). Rates here are ¥5800 (double occupancy) per person, including breakfast.

The shokudō next to the bus stop is the cheapest option in town, with all the standards for around ¥800. A more elegant choice is *Washoku-dokoro Mizu*, about 100m east of the bus stop on the main street. Try the tempura-zen set for ¥1500. Across the street, you'll find *Zen-dera*, a rustic soba place where you can get various soba dishes for around ¥1000.

Getting There & Away From Tokyo, access to Shuzen-ji is via Mishima on the Tōkaidō line (see the Mishima entry following). Izu-Hakone Tetsudō trains between Mishima and Shuzen-ji (¥500) take around

30 minutes. Buses run between Shuzen-ji and Shimoda (¥2180, two hours) and Shuzen-ji and Dōgashima (¥1970, 1½ hours).

Mishima 三島
☎ 0559

Mishima, on the Tōkaidō line, was once an important post-town on the old Tōkaidō highway. You might pause here before heading into the Izu-hantō or back to Tokyo. The town's main highlight is **Rakuju-en** (¥300, 9 am to 5.30 pm, closed Monday), a Meiji-era stroll garden three minutes' walk south of the station. Nearby is **Mishima-taisha**, the most important shrine on the Izu-hantō. It's set in pleasantly wooded environs and has a small treasure hall (¥300) with Kamakura-era exhibits on display. The shrine is a five-minute walk from the south-eastern gate of Rakuju-en.

Getting There & Away You can take a Tōkaidō-line shinkansen to Mishima from Tokyo (¥3890, one hour and five minutes); futsū trains take twice as long and cost ¥2160.

It's only 10 minutes by train from Mishima to Numazu, from where it is possible to continue into the Izu-hantō by boat or by bus (see the Dōgashima section earlier for details).

South of Tokyo

South-west of Tokyo are the cities of Kawasaki and Yokohama, which have virtually merged with the capital to create one immense urban corridor. Beyond these cities is the fascinating old capital of Kamakura.

KAWASAKI 川崎
• pop 1.17 million

Kawasaki is a sprawling industrial port city, partly built on land reclaimed from Tokyo-wan. Its main attractions are the temple, Kawasaki Daishi, and Nihon Minka-en, an excellent museum of traditional Japanese houses.

Kawasaki Daishi 川崎大師
Formerly known as Heigen-ji, the temple, Kawasaki Daish, has a long pedigree (leg-

end has it the temple was founded in 1127) and is Kawasaki's answer to Sensō-ji in Asakusa, Tokyo. Like Sensō-ji, Kawasaki Daishi houses an image that was fished from the water – this time the sea. The image is that of Kōbō Daishi, the founder of the Shingon sect (see Buddhism under Religion in the Facts about Japan chapter), with which the temple is affiliated.

The temple is well worth a visit, as there are interesting shops nearby, an impressive five-storey pagoda and very few foreign tourists about. Entry is free.

Nihon Minka-en 日本民家園
Those with an interest in old Japan shouldn't miss the Nihon Minka-en (¥300, 9.30 am to 4 pm, closed Monday), an open-air museum comprised of 24 traditional Japanese buildings brought from all over the country and reassembled on one site. Most of the structures are farmhouses, although there is also a Shintō shrine and a kabuki stage. The oldest of the buildings dates back to 1688.

Special Events
Kawasaki hosts the famous Jibeta Matsuri, in which processions of costumed locals parade wooden phalluses to celebrate the vanquishing of a sharp-toothed demon. The demon had taken up residence in a fair maiden and had already emasculated two bridegrooms before a local blacksmith came up with the ingenious idea of deflowering the maiden with an iron phallus. History doesn't record the maiden's feelings about this solution, but defeat of the demon gave rise to much celebration and an annual re-enactment of the forging of the metal phallus. Freudians are welcome.

The festival takes place in the late afternoon of 15 April, starting with a procession, followed by a re-enactment of the forging, and rounded off with a banquet. The action takes place close to Kawasaki Daishi station.

Getting There & Away
For the Nihon Minka-en, take an Odakyū line train from Shinjuku station to Mukōgaoka-yuen station (¥240, 20 minutes). Then it's a

15-minute walk from the station's southern exit. For Kawasaki Daishi, take the JR Tōkaidō line from Tokyo station to Kawasaki station (¥290, 18 minutes). Walk from there to Keikyū Kawasaki station and take a Keikyū Daishi-line train to Kawasaki Daishi station, just three stops away (¥130). From Yokohama it takes just 20 minutes to get to Kawasaki (¥210) on the JR Tōkaidō line.

YOKOHAMA 横浜

☎ 045 • pop 3.38 million

The site of present-day Yokohama was little more than mud flats 150 years ago. Today it's Japan's second-largest city. Yokohama's fortunes are very much those of modern Japan. It was opened to foreign trade in 1858; in 1872 Japan's first railway line was laid, connecting the city with Tokyo; by the early 20th century the city had embarked on a course of industrialisation. Nowadays its port facilities are complemented by massive steel-making, automobile, oil-refining and chemical industries.

Effectively, Yokohama forms a vast conurbation with Tokyo and in many ways it's simply a far-flung satellite of the capital city. For the Japanese, however, Yokohama's proximity to the sea and its international associations as a trading port have bestowed upon it a certain cosmopolitan sheen and made it a popular sightseeing destination.

Yokohama's main attractions are its harbour, a lively Chinatown, the greenery of Sankei en and the new seaside developments in the Minato Mirai 21 complex.

Orientation

Arriving in Yokohama can be slightly confusing. Most of the sights are quite a way from Yokohama station and it makes more sense to go to Sakuragi-chō or Kannai stations. From Sakuragi-chō station, the Minato Mirai 21 complex is five minutes away by moving walkway. From the Minato Mirai 21 complex it's possible to walk across Shinko Pier to the park, Yamashita-kōen, in around 25 minutes. From Yamashita-kōen you can walk on to Chinatown, the Silk Museum, the Foreigners' Cemetery and Harbour View Park.

Information

There's a tourist information centre (☎ 211-0111) directly outside the northern exit of Sakuragi-chō station. The office has English speakers on hand and is open from 9 am to 6 pm. Be sure to pick up a copy of its free *Yokohama City Guide,* which has detailed maps of Yokohama's most important neighbourhoods.

There's a Citibank with a 24-hour international automated teller machine (ATM) outside the western exit of Yokohama station on the 2nd floor of the First Building; look for it on the south-western side of the Yokohama Bay Sheraton.

Yokohama Station Area
横浜駅周辺

The Yokohama station area is given over unrelentingly to shopping. Its only real attraction is the **Hiraki Ukiyoe Museum** (¥500, 10 am to 5.30 pm, closed some Tuesdays), on the 6th floor of the Sogō department store — yes, the largest department store in the world. The museum has a collection of over 8000 wood-block prints, both old and new. Sogō is close to the eastern exit of Yokohama station.

Minato Mirai 21
みなとみらい21

This new development (the '21' stands for '21st century') just north of Sakuragi-chō station is another of those Japanese excursions into the metropolis-of-the-future theme. One of the highlights is the new **Landmark Tower**, which not only is the tallest building in Japan, but also has the world's fastest lift (45kph). The **Landmark Tower Sky Garden** (¥1000, 10 am to 9 pm, to 10 pm in July and August) observatory is on the 69th floor.

Across from Landmark Tower you'll find the interesting **Yokohama Maritime Museum** and the *Nippon Maru* sailing ship (entry to both ¥600, 10 am to 5 pm, slightly later in summer, closed Monday). Beyond the Maritime Museum is **Cosmo World** amusement park (price varies according to ride, 1 to 9 pm weekdays, 11 am to 10 pm weekends). The best part of Cosmo World is the **Cosmo Clock** Ferris wheel (¥600,

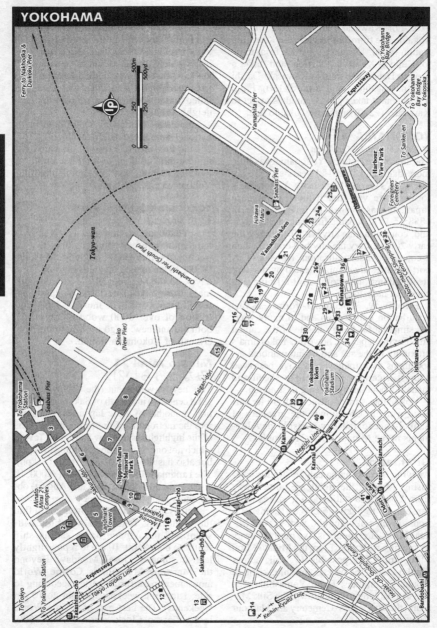

YOKOHAMA

AROUND TOKYO

YOKOHAMA

PLACES TO STAY

5 Yokohama Royal Park
Hotel Nikkō
横浜ロイヤルパーク
ホテルニッコー

12 Kanagawa
Youth Hostel
神奈川ユースホステル

21 Hotel Yokohama
ホテル横浜

22 Hotel New Grand
ホテルニューグランド

23 Star Hotel Yokohama
スター ホテル横浜

27 Holiday Inn Yokohama
ホリデイイン横浜

41 Yokohama Isezakichō
Washington Hotel
横浜伊勢佐木町
ワシントンホテル

PLACES TO EAT

16 Suginoki;
Scandia Garden
杉の木；
スカンジアガーデン

19 Parkside Gourmet Plaza
パークサイド
グルメプラザ

26 Peking Daihanten
北京大飯店

28 Heichinrō
へい珍楼

29 Manchinrō
籬珍楼

37 Garlic Jo's
ガーリックジョーズ

38 Columbo
コロンボ

OTHER

1 Mitsubishi Minato Mirai
Industrial Museum
三菱みなとみらい技術館

2 Yokohama
Museum of Art
横浜美術館

3 Pacifico Yokohama;
National Convention
Hall of Yokohama;
Yokohama Grand
Intercontinental Hotel
パシフィコ横浜；
国立横浜国際会議場；
横浜グランドインター
コンチネンタルホテル

4 Queen's Square
Yokohama;
Pan Pacific Hotel
Yokohama
クイーンズ
スクエア横浜；
パンパシフィック
ホテル横浜

6 Nippon Maru
日本丸

7 Yokohama
Cosmo World
横浜コスモワールド

8 Yokohama
World Porters
横浜ワールド

9 Cosmo Clock
コスモクロック

10 Yokohama Maritime
Museum
横浜マリタイム
ミュージアム

11 Sakuragi-chō Tourist
Information Center
桜木町観光案内所

13 Iseyama-jinja
伊勢山皇大神社

14 Zoo; Nogeyama-kōen
動物園；野毛山公園

15 Yokohama Customs
House
横浜税関

17 Yokohama Archives
of History
横浜開港資料館

18 Silk Museum
シルク博物館

20 Ken-min Hall
県民ホール

24 Marine Tower
マリンタワー

25 Yokohama Doll Museum
横浜人形の家

30 The Missions to Seamen
ミッショントゥシーマン

31 Kita-mon
北門

32 The Tavern
ザタバーン

33 Zenrin-mon
善隣門

34 Windjammer
ウィンドジャマー

35 Kantei-byō
関帝廟

36 Tenchō-mon
天長門

39 Cape Cod
ケープコッド

40 City Hall
市役所

same hours as the park), the world's highest at 105m. Near Cosmo World, **Yokohama World Porters** is a huge shopping complex with lots of restaurants on the ground floor.

North-east of Landmark Tower is the **Queen's Square Yokohama**, yet another shopping and dining complex. Check out the street performers doing their thing outside the main entrance. Next along from Queen's Square is the dramatic, sail-shaped **Pacifico Yokohama** complex, housing the National Convention Hall of Yokohama and the Yokohama Grand Intercontinental Hotel.

Behind Landmark Tower, you'll find the **Yokohama Museum of Art** (¥500, 10 am to 5 pm, closed Thursday), which has a decent collection of modern art. Perhaps more exciting than the art on display is the Tange Kenzō-designed building, particularly the dramatic main hall. Nearby, the **Mitsubishi Minato Mirai Industrial Museum** (¥600/200 adults/children, 10 am to 5.30 pm, closed Monday) is one of Japan's better science and technology museums, with a wildly enjoyable helicopter simulator, along with lots of other good hands-on exhibits.

Yamashita-kōen Area
山下公園周辺

This area, north-east of Kannai station, is traditionally Yokohama's sightseeing district. At the heart of it all is the seafront Yamashita-kōen. Moored alongside the park you'll find the *Hikawa Maru* (¥800/400 adults/children, 9.30 am to 8 pm, to 7 pm in winter), a retired passenger liner that's a lot of fun for the kids.

Across the street is the **Silk Museum** (¥300, 9 am to 4.30 pm, closed Monday), which covers all aspects of silk and silk pro-duction and has some lovely *kimono* and *obi* (sashes) on display. Nearby, the **Yokohama Archives of History** (¥200, 9.30 am to 5 pm, closed Monday) has a fascinating collection of items related to the history of Yokohama port. Across the street, **Yokohama Customs House** (free, 10 am to 4 pm, closed weekends) has a somewhat less interesting collection of exhibits related to customs and trade.

Back in the other direction, you'll find **Marine Tower** (¥700, 10 am to 9.30 pm), a relic from the early days of Japanese

---

Japan and Korea: Football's Uneasy Alliance

If you're visiting Japan in June 2002, don't be surprised to find locals and tourists more interested in Batistuta and Beckham than hot-spring spas and cherry blossoms. The reason is that Japan is co-hosting the month-long football World Cup.

Yes, *co*-hosting. Back in 1996 the Federation Internationale de Football Association (FIFA) made a most controversial decision: rival bidders Japan and South Korea were to share the 2002 World Cup. Following a precedent set by the Union of European Football Associations (UEFA), which awarded the 2000 European Championships to Holland and Belgium, FIFA thought this would diffuse escalating feuding between the two nations.

Each country declared the other was incapable of playing host to Asia's first World Cup. Japan argued that it had begun work on its bid before Korea and its infrastructure was more advanced. Korea cited a superior football record: World Cup participation by the two countries currently stands at Korea 5, Japan 1. Each nation accused the other of underhanded tactics and bribery. Neither country was happy at being told to share: 'It's going to be terrible…but we have to think positive,' J-League coach Okudera Yasuhiko said at the time.

Under FIFA's supervision, the spoils have been evenly split: the opening game will take place in Seoul, Korea, on 31 May and the final will be held at Yokohama, Japan, on 30 June. The preliminary draw (to decide the zonal qualification groups) took place in Japan in December 1999; the final draw (to determine the groups for the first round of the tournament itself) will take place in Korea in December 2001.

The World Cup's initial round-robin event will see four groups of four teams playing in each country. In the second round, the four teams that have played in Japan will play in Korea and vice versa. The same principle will apply to the quarter-finals, with two teams switching countries. Each country will stage a total of 32 matches each in 10 purpose-built stadia.

Japan and Korea automatically qualify for the World Cup (updated score: Korea 6, Japan 2) as does defending champion France. The other 29 nations will qualify from European, South American, North American, African and Asian zones. This will be the 17th World Cup; the first was held in 1930 in Uruguay. Like that other great sporting event, the Olympic Games, the World Cup was the brainchild of a Frenchman: the winning team is presented with the (surprisingly tiny) Jules Rimet Trophy. The most successful side to date is Brazil, with victories in 1958, 1962, 1970 and 1994.

With less than two years before kick-off, Japan and Korea are well on target as far as facilities are concerned. Three of Japan's World Cup venues were completed at the time of writing: Yokohama (with 70,000 seats), Osaka (45,000) and Miyagi (49,000). Stadia in Niigata (41,000), Shizuoka (50,000) and Oita (43,000) are scheduled to be finished in the early months of 2001, with the re-

tourism, offering a diminutive (106m) view over the harbour. Other attractions relatively nearby include **Harbour View Park** and the **Foreigners' Cemetery**, the final resting place of 4000 foreign residents and visitors to Yokohama – a look at some of the headstones reveals some fascinating inscriptions.

Chinatown 中華街

Not far from the harbour area is Chinatown (known as 'Chūkagai' in Japanese). This is one of Yokohama's greatest tourist attrac-

tions and the tiny streets are often packed with visitors who come to ogle the over-the-top Chinese facades of the neighbourhood's stores and restaurants. Needless to say, food is the main attraction here, but be warned that prices are high and you may be disappointed – the cuisine is no match for Hong Kong or New York. Apart from the food, the only other attractions worthy of exploration are **Kantei-byō**, a Chinese temple in the heart of the district; and the gaily coloured Chinese gates scattered around the area.

Japan and Korea: Football's Uneasy Alliance

mainder – Sapporo (43,000), Ibaraki (43,000), Saitama (63,000) and Kobe (42,000) – scheduled to be completed by late 2001. All of Korea's venues – Seoul (63,000), Irichon (51,000), Suwon (43,000), Taejan (41,000), Chonju (42,000), Taegu (70,000), Ulsan (42,000), Kwangju (42,000), Pusan (52,000) and Sogwipo (42,000) – are scheduled for completion in 2001.

Japanese and Korean football have long had an uneasy alliance. The sport was introduced to Japan by English sailors in 1873, and the Japanese football association was formed in 1921. A year later the country staged its first national football tournament, made up of university clubs. Its professional league, the J-League, was formed in 1993, and the country qualified for the World Cup finals for the first time in 1998. Japan is currently ranked 50th on the FIFA world rankings.

The first official records of football in Korea appear after the country was annexed by Japan. The first known team was formed in 1920. College sides followed, and inter-city matches became popular – as did internationals against Japan! The South Korean football association was established in 1928, but was disbanded by Japan 10 years later. From 1936, South Korean players were eligible for the Japanese squad, but liberation in 1945 saw the South Korean football association re-established. Korea is currently the top-ranked Asian nation in the FIFA world rankings, coming in at 43rd.

At the World Cup, both countries will want to better each other in terms of smooth organisation and on-field success. Each team's goal will be to at least equal North Korea's record of being the only Asian side to reach the World Cup quarter-finals (in England in 1966). The possible involvement of North Korea (now ranked a lowly 141st) in the staging of the World Cup was on the table for discussion between Japan, Korea and FIFA at the time of going to press, though there was no question of a third host-team being given automatic qualification.

Tickets are priced in US dollars and range from $60 for a 'category 3' seat at a first-round match to $750 for a 'category 1' seat at the final. For tickets sold in Japan and Korea in the local currency, prices will be fixed based on the US exchange rate. Tickets go on sale in October 2000.

FIFA plans a reservation system by which overseas fans can order tickets for their team's matches and then cancel them should the team fail to qualify. This should be up-and-running by April 2001.

Football fans interested in attending the World Cup should keep an eye on the following Web sites for updated ticketing and scheduling information: FIFA (www.fifa2.com/), Japan Organising Committee (www.jawoc.or.jp/index_e.htm), Korea Organising Committee (www.2002worldcupkorea.org) and the online ticket agency TicketCity.com (http://www.ticketcity.com).

Individual country football associations will also have details. In Japan, there's a telephone inquiry line (☎ 03-3287-1199).

Liz Filleul

Sankei-en 三渓園

Sankei-en (9 am to 4.30 pm, closed from 29 to 31 January) was established in 1906 by a Yokohama silk merchant. The beautifully landscaped gardens feature a 500-year-old three-storey pagoda. There are separate ¥300 admission charges to the outer and inner gardens. The inner one is a fine example of traditional Japanese garden landscaping. Take the No 8 bus from Yokohama or Sakuragi-chō stations to Honmoku Sankei-en-mae bus stop. Alternatively, take a JR Negishi-line train from Sakuragi-chō to Negishi station and change to a city bus bound for Sakuragi-chō (No 54, 58, 99, 101 or 108). Get off at the Honmoku stop, from which it's an easy five-minute walk to the southern entrance of the park.

Places to Stay

Kanagawa Youth Hostel (☎ 241-6503) gets poor reviews from readers as being unfriendly and regimented. It costs ¥2600 (¥2800 in summer).

The cheapest hotel option is the decent *Yokohama Isezakichō Washington Hotel* (☎ 243-7111) which has singles/doubles/twins from ¥8000/14,200/16,200.

There are a number of hotels along the harbourfront facing Yamashita-kōen. *Star Hotel Yokohama* (☎ 651-3111) is the cheapest of these, with singles/doubles for ¥9000/15,000. *Hotel Yokohama* (☎ 662-1321) is an upmarket option with singles/doubles from ¥17,000/24,000. *Hotel New Grand* (☎ 681-1841) has singles/twins from ¥10,000/28,000. Not far away, in Chinatown, *Holiday Inn Yokohama* (☎ 681-3311) is overpriced, with singles/twins from ¥15,000/17,000.

The city's top hotels can be found in the Minato Mirai 21 area. *Yokohama Royal Park Hotel Nikkō* (☎ 221-1111) has the best location, on the upper floors of Landmark Tower. Singles start at ¥25,000 and twins/doubles start from ¥29,000. *Pan Pacific Hotel Yokohama* (☎ 682-2222), in the Queen's Square Yokohama complex, is a stylish new place with twins from ¥35,000. *Yokohama Grand Intercontinental Hotel* (☎ 223-2222), in the Pacifico Yokohama

complex, is another stunningly located hotel. Singles/doubles cost from ¥28,000/34,000.

Places to Eat

In Yokohama, the done thing is to have a bang-up dinner in Chinatown. Plan on spending about ¥5000 per head for a good dinner and perhaps half that for lunch. Most places offer set courses.

Manchinrō is one of the area's more popular spots for Guangdong cuisine, with dinner courses from ¥4000. *Heichinrō* is an elegant Cantonese specialist with *dim sum* sets from ¥2500 and a large picture menu. *Peking Daihanten* is a huge place with an English menu and reasonably priced lunch specials.

On the outskirts of Chinatown you'll find *Garlic Jo's* a great place to eat if you don't have a job interview the next day. Most of the garlic-laden dishes cost around ¥1000. Nearby, *Columbo* is a good Sri Lankan place where you can fill up for about ¥1000 at lunch and double that for dinner.

Back near Yamashita-kōen you'll find *Scandia Garden*, one of Japan's only Danish restaurants, and *Suginoki* which serves various Western dishes. It's worth stopping by Suginoki just to check out the antique plastic food models in the window – they look like they were set out to tempt Admiral Perry and his crew. Dinner at both places costs around ¥2500.

Apart from these streetside restaurants, there are a lot of eating places in Yokohama's giant shopping complexes, like *Queen's Square Yokohama* and *Yokohama World Porters*. You'll find just about anything you want in these places, Western or Japanese, and almost all the restaurants have food models out front so you know what you're getting into. Another, less interesting, bunch of restaurants can be found in *Parkside Gourmet Plaza,* around the corner from the Silk Museum.

Entertainment

There is plenty to do in Yokohama in the evening. Many of the city's bars are on the outskirts of Chinatown. *The Tavern* is a

British-style pub with the usual beers on tap and a good selection of pub food. The bar-restaurant *Windjammer* is another good spot for a few drinks and the occasional live jazz (for which you pay a ¥300 'music charge'). A far rowdier spot is *The Missions to Seamen*, which has cheap beer and billiards. As you might imagine, this place draws an interesting crowd (and you don't have to be a sailor to get in). A similar spot that also attracts a lot of foreigners is *Cape Cod*, in the middle of town.

For drinks with a view, head to the *Sirius* bar on the 70th floor of Landmark Tower, an elegant cocktail lounge in the Yokohama Royal Park Hotel Nikkō. It's open nightly from 5 pm to 1 am and drinks start at ¥1000.

Getting There & Away

Train There are numerous trains from Tokyo – the cheapest being the Tōkyū Tōyoko line from Shibuya station to Sakuragi-chō station (futsū/kyūkō ¥290, 44/37 minutes). Trains stop at Yokohama station on the way to Sakuragi-chō station.

The Keihin Tōhoku line goes through Yokohama station (¥450, 38 minutes) to Kannai station (¥540, 47 minutes) from Tokyo and Shinagawa stations. The Tōkaidō line from Tokyo or Shinagawa stations also runs to Yokohama station (¥450, 25 minutes).

To Kamakura, take the Yokosuka line from Yokohama station (¥380, 27 minutes). The Tōkaidō shinkansen stops at Shin-Yokohama station, a fair way to the northwest of town, on its way between Tokyo and the Kansai region. Shin-Yokohama station is connected to Yokohama, Sakuragi-chō and Kannai stations by the Yokohama line and by a less convenient subway line.

Getting Around

To/From the Airport Both trains and buses connect Narita to Yokohama; take the train to be sure of arriving at a particular time. Trains run from Yokohama station. You can choose Narita Express (N'EX) services (¥4180, 1½ hours) or JR Airport Narita services (¥1890, two hours). Limou-sine buses travel frequently between the Yokohama City Air Terminal (YCAT, in the Sky Building east of Yokohama station, next to Sogō department store) and Narita (¥3500, two hours depending on traffic).

Bus Although trains are more convenient for getting around town, Yokohama does have an extensive bus network. To travel within the city, you pay a flat fee of ¥210.

Boat The *Sea Bass* ferry connects Yokohama station, the Minato Mirai 21 complex and Yamashita-kōen. Boats run between 10 am and 7 pm. The full fare from Yokohama station to Yamashita-kōen is ¥600; the trip takes 20 minutes.

KAMAKURA 鎌倉
☎ 0467

The capital of Japan from 1185 to 1333, Kamakura rivals Nikkō as the most culturally rewarding day trip from Tokyo. There are a huge number of Buddhist temples and the occasional shrine dotted around the surrounding countryside, as well as some very pleasant walks. Although Kamakura – like any other major attraction in Japan – gets packed on weekends and in holiday periods, midweek can be very peaceful in the outlying temples.

History

In the 10th century, the power of the emperor in Kyoto was largely ceremonial; real power had for some time rested in the hands of the Fujiwara clan. As the power of the Fujiwara declined, the Taira clan led by Taira Kiyomori, and the Minamoto clan led by Minamoto Yoshitomo, began an all-out struggle for supreme power. In 1159 the Taira routed the Minamoto forces.

Although many executions followed, by chance Yoshitomo's third son's life was spared and the boy was sent to spend his days in an Izu-hantō temple. As soon as the boy, Minamoto Yoritomo, was old enough, he began to gather support for a counter-attack on his clan's old rivals. In 1180 he set up his base at Kamakura, an area far away from the debilitating influences of Kyoto

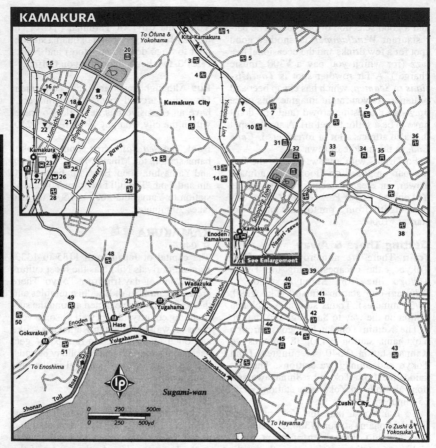

court life, close to other clans loyal to the Minamoto and, being enclosed by the sea on one side and by densely wooded hills on the others, easy to defend.

With a series of victories over the Taira behind him, Minamoto Yoritomo was appointed shōgun in 1192; he governed Japan from Kamakura. When he died without an heir, however, power passed to the Hōjo, the family of Yoritomo's wife.

The Hōjo clan ruled Japan from Kamakura for more than a century until, in 1333, weakened by the cost of maintaining defences against threats of attack from

Kublai Khan in China, the Hōjo clan was defeated by Emperor Go-Daigo. Kyoto once again became capital.

Orientation

Kamakura's main attractions can be seen in a day of walking augmented by the occasional bus ride. Temples are usually well signposted in both English and Japanese. You can either start at Kamakura station and work your way around the area in a circle, or start north of Kamakura at Kita-Kamakura station and visit the temples between there and Kamakura on foot. The

KAMAKURA

PLACES TO STAY
18 City Pension Shangri La
   シティペンション
   シャングリラ鶴岡
19 Ajisai
   あじさい
21 Tsurugaoka
   Kaikan Hotel
   ホテル鶴が丘会館
24 Hotel Kamakura Mori
   ホテル鎌倉Mori
52 Kamakura Kagetsuen
   Youth Hostel/Hotel
   鎌倉花月園ユース
   ホステル/ホテル

PLACES TO EAT
 2 Shōkita no Kamakura
   庄北の鎌倉
 6 Chaya Kado
   茶屋かど
15 Fudō Chaya
   不動茶屋
16 Kushinbō
   Kushin坊
17 Shinmeichō
   神明丁
22 Milk Hall
   ミルクホール

OTHER
 1 Engaku-ji
   円覚寺
 3 Tōkei-ji
   東慶寺
 4 Jōchi-ji
   浄智寺
 5 Meigetsu-In
   明月院

 7 Kenchō-ji
   建長寺
 8 Raigō-ji
   来迎寺
 9 Kakuon-ji
   覚園寺
10 Ennō-ji
   円応寺
11 Kaizō-ji
   海蔵寺
12 Zeniarai-benten
   銭洗弁天
13 Eishō-ji
   英勝寺
14 Jufuku-ji
   寿福寺
20 National Treasure
   Museum
   鎌倉国宝館
23 Bus Station
   バス停
25 Daigyō-ji
   大巧寺
26 Post Office
   郵便局
27 Bicycle Rental
   レンタサイクル
28 Hongaku-ji
   本覚寺
29 Myōhon-ji
   妙本寺
30 Hōkai-ji
   宝戒寺
31 The Museum of
   Modern Art Kamakura
   神奈川県立近代美術館
32 Tsurugaoka
   Hachiman-gū
   鶴岡八幡宮

33 Tomb of Minamoto
   Yoritomo
   源頼朝の墓
34 Egara Ten-jin
   荏柄天神
35 Kamakura-gū
   鎌倉宮
36 Zuisen-ji
   瑞泉寺
37 Sugimoto-dera
   杉本寺
38 Hōkoku-ji
   報国寺
39 Daihō-ji
   大宝寺
40 Anyō-in
   安養院
41 Myōhō-ji
   妙法寺
42 Ankokuron-ji
   安国論寺
43 Hosshō-ji
   法性寺
44 Chōshō-ji
   長勝寺
45 Gosho-jinja
   五所神社
46 Myōchō-ji
   妙長寺
47 Kuhon-ji
   九品寺
48 Daibutsu
   (Great Buddha)
   大仏
49 Hase-dera
   長谷寺
50 Gokurakuji
   極楽寺
51 Jōjuin
   成就院

itinerary in this section follows the latter route.

Information
The Kamakura Tourist Information Centre (☎ 22-3350) is just outside Kamakura station. Maps and brochures are available here and the office should also be able to help you find accommodation.

Engaku-ji 円覚寺
Engaku-ji (¥200, 8 am to 5 pm from April to September, until 4 pm other months) is on the left as you exit Kita-Kamakura station.

It is one of the five main Rinzai Zen temples in Kamakura. Engaku-ji was founded in 1282, allegedly as a place where Zen monks might pray for soldiers who had lost their lives defending Japan against the second of Kublai Khan's invasion attempts. Today the only real reminder of the temple's former magnificence and antiquity is **San-mon**, a 1780 reconstruction. At the top of the long flight of stairs through the gate is the **Engaku-ji bell**, which was cast in 1301 and is the largest bell in Kamakura. The Hondō (Main Hall) inside San-mon is quite a recent reconstruction, dating from the mid-1960s.

Tōkei-ji 東慶寺

Tōkei-ji (¥100, 8.30 am to 5 pm, until 4 pm from November to February), across the railway tracks from Engaku-ji, is notable for its grounds as much as for the temple itself. On weekdays, when visitors are few, it can be a pleasantly relaxing place. Walk up to the cemetery and wander around.

Historically, the temple is famed as having served as a women's refuge. A woman could be officially recognised as divorced after three years as a nun in the temple precincts. Today there are no nuns; the grave of the last abbess can be found in the cemetery.

Jōchi-ji 浄智寺

A couple of minutes farther on from Tōkei-ji is Jōchi-ji (¥100, 9 am to 4.30 pm), another temple with pleasant grounds. Founded in 1283, this is considered one of Kamakura's five great Zen temples.

Kenchō-ji 建長寺

Kenchō-ji (¥300, 8.30 am to 4.30 pm) is Kamakura's most important Zen temple. The grounds and the buildings are well maintained and still in use. The first of the main buildings you come to, the Buddha Hall, was moved to its present site and reassembled in 1647. The second building, the Hall of Law, is used for *zazen* (sitting) meditation. Farther back is the Dragon King Hall, a Chinese-style building with a garden to its rear. The temple bell, the second largest in Kamakura, has been designated a National Treasure.

Ennō-ji 円応寺

Across the road from Kenchō-ji is Ennō-ji (¥300, 9 am to 4 pm, until 3.30 pm in winter), distinguished primarily by its collection of statues depicting the judges of hell. Presiding over them is Emma, an ancient Hindu deity known in Sanskrit as Yama. The ideas of hell and judgement became important Buddhist concepts with the rise of the Jōdo (Pure Land) school (see Buddhism under Religion in the Facts about Japan chapter).

Tsurugaoka Hachiman-gū 八幡宮

Farther down the road, where it turns toward Kamakura station, is Tsurugaoka Hachiman-gū, the main shrine of Kamakura. It was founded by Minamoto Yoriyoshi, of the same Minamoto clan that ruled Japan from Kamakura (see History earlier in this section). There is some debate as to whether Hachiman, the deity to which the shrine is dedicated, has always been regarded as the god of war; the construction of this shrine may simply be a reflection of the fact that Hachiman is also the guardian deity of the Minamoto clan. Whatever the case, this Shintō shrine presents the visitor with an atmosphere drastically different to the repose of the Zen temples clustered around Kita-Kamakura station.

If you enter the shrine from the direction of Kita-Kamakura station, you are actually entering from the rear and not by the proper entrance gates. This is not a problem; after taking a look at the shrine, follow the stairs down to the square below. To the right is a gingko tree, beneath which it is said a famous political assassination was carried out in 1219, making the tree very old indeed.

At the foot of the stairs there is a *nō* (classical dance-drama) stage and the main avenue, which runs to the shrine's entrance. At the entrance on the left is an **arched bridge**, which in times past was designated for the passage of the shōgun and no-one else. The bridge is so steep that every crossing must have been quite a test of shōgunal athletic prowess.

Kamakura National Treasure Museum

To the left of the dancing platform (assuming you're continuing to walk away from the shrine) is the Kamakura Kokuhō-kan, or the Kamakura National Treasure Museum (¥150, 9 am to 4 pm, closed Monday). This museum is recommended, as it provides your only opportunity to see Kamakura art, most of which is hidden away in the temples.

Daibutsu 大仏

The Kamakura Daibutsu (Great Buddha; ¥200, 7 am to 6 pm, until 5.30 pm in winter) was completed in 1252 and is Kamakura's most famous sight. Once housed in a huge hall, the statue today sits in the open, its home having been washed away by a *tsunami* (tidal wave) in 1495. Cast in bronze and weighing close to 850 tonnes, the statue is 11.4m tall. Its construction is said to have been inspired by Yoritomo's visit to Nara (where there is another, even bigger, *daibutsu*) after the Minamoto clan's victory over the rival Taira clan. Even though Kamakura's Daibutsu doesn't quite match Nara's in stature, it is commonly agreed that it is artistically superior.

The Buddha itself is the Amida Buddha ('*amitābha*' in Sanskrit), worshipped by the followers of the Jōdo school as a figure of salvation.

To get to the Daibutsu, take a bus from the No 2, 7 or 10 bus stop in front of Kamakura station and get off at the Daibutsu-mae stop. Alternatively, take the Enoden Enoshima line to Hase station and walk north for 10 minutes.

Hase-dera 長谷寺

Not far from the Daibutsu-mae bus stop is the temple, Hase-dera (¥300, 8 am to 4.30 pm from October to February, to 5 pm other months), also known as Hase Kannon-ji. The grounds have a garden and an interesting collection of statues of Jizō, the patron saint of the souls of departed children. Ranked like a small army of urchins, the statues are clothed, to keep them warm, by women who have lost children by abortion or miscarriage. The main point of interest in the grounds, however, is the Kannon statue.

Kannon ('*avalokiteshvara*' in Sanskrit), the goddess of mercy, is the Bodhisattva of infinite compassion and, along with Jizō, is one of Japan's most popular Buddhist deities. The 9m-high carved wooden **jūichi-men** (11-faced Kannon) here is believed to be very ancient, dating from the 8th century. The 11 faces are actually one primary face and 10 secondary faces, the latter representing the 10 stages of enlightenment. It is commonly believed that the 11 faces allow Kannon, ever vigilant for those in need of her assistance, to cast an eye in every direction.

Other Shrines & Temples

If you're still in the mood for temple tramping, there are plenty more in and around Kamakura, which has somewhere in the vicinity of 70 temples and shrines.

From the Daibutsu it is best to return to Kamakura station by bus and take another bus out to the temples in the eastern part of town. These have the advantage of being even less popular with tourists than the temples in Kita-Kamakura; they may lack the grandeur of some of Kamakura's more famous temples, but they more than make up for this with their charm. There is also a delightfully restful village-like atmosphere in the town's outer fringes.

Egara Ten-jin This shrine would not be particularly noteworthy if it were not so closely associated with academic success. Students write their academic aspirations on *ema* (small wooden plaques), which are then hung to the right of the shrine. In the grounds there's an gingko tree said to be around 900 years old. Buses from stop No 6 in front of Kamakura station run out to Egara Ten-jin Shrine; get off at the Tenjin-mae bus stop.

Zuisen-ji The grounds of this secluded Zen temple (¥100, 9 am to 5 pm) make for a pleasant stroll and include Zen gardens laid out by Kokushi Musō, the temple's founder. It is possible to get there from the Egara Ten-jin shrine on foot in about 10 to 15 minutes, turn right where the bus turns left in front of the ohrino, take the next left and keep following the road.

Sugimoto-dera This interesting little temple (¥200, 8.30 am to 4.30 pm), founded in AD 734, is reputed to be the oldest in Kamakura. Ferocious temple guardians are poised on either side of the entrance, while the temple grounds and the thatch-roofed temple itself are littered with banners boldly announcing '*jūichimen Sugimoto Kannon*' ('11-faced Kannon of Sugimoto') in Chinese characters. The temple houses three Kannon statues, though they are not in the same league as the famous statue at Hase-dera (see that entry earlier in this section).

To get to the temple, take a bus from the No 5 stop in front of Kamakura station and get off at the Sugimoto Kannon bus stop.

Hōkoku-ji Down the road (away from Kamakura station) from Sugimoto-dera, on the right-hand side, is Hōkoku-ji (9 am to 4 pm). This is a Rinzai Zen temple with quiet, landscaped gardens where you can relax under a red parasol with a cup of Japanese tea. This is also one of the more active Zen temples in Kamakura, regularly holding zazen classes for beginners. Entry to most of the temple is free; entry to the hall, Takebayashi-dō is ¥200.

Special Events
The Kamakura Matsuri is a week of celebrations held from the second Sunday to the third Sunday in April. It includes a wide range of activities, most of which are centred on Tsurugaoka Hachiman-gū.

During the Bonbori Matsuri, held from 7 to 9 August, hundreds of lanterns are strung up around Tsurugaoka Hachiman-gū.

The Hachiman-gū Matsuri is held from 14 to 16 September. Festivities include a procession of mikoshi and, on the last day, a display of horseback archery.

Places to Stay
Kamakura Kagetsuen Youth Hostel (☎ 25-1238), right on the beach and with good ocean views, has beds at ¥3150. From Kamakura station take an Enoden Enoshima train to Hase station. From there, walk down to the seafront road and walk west for about 10 minutes. The hostel is inside the Kagetsuen Hotel.

Back in town, the cheapest option is comfortable *Ajisai* (☎ 22-3492) with per-person rates from ¥6500. *City Pension Shangri La* (☎ 25-6363) is nearby and has singles/twins for ¥8000/13,000. Just a few doors down is the expensive *Tsurugaoka Kaikan Hotel* (☎ 24-1111), where per-person costs start at ¥14,000 with two meals. A similar hotel is the clean new *Hotel Kamakura Mori* (☎ 22-5868), where singles/doubles cost ¥13,500/27,000 without meals.

Places to Eat
The station area is cluttered with the inevitable fast-food joints and coffee shops. For more palatable fare, head up into the Komachi-dōri shopping street or the main road to Tsurugaoka Hachiman-gū, both of which run north-east from the station.

On Komachi-dōri, try *Shinmeichō* for good sets of tempura and soba. We recommend the *tempura gozen* (tempura set), for ¥1380. Look for the English sign reading 'Soba House'. Not far away, you'll find *Kushinbō,* a popular izakaya that's only open in the evening. On a narrow street to the west of Tsurugaoka Hachiman-gū, *Fudō Chaya* serves noodle dishes from ¥600. It's worth a look just for the odd cave/shrine out the back of the restaurant. If you just fancy a cup of coffee, try *Milk Hall,* a pleasant little place with an English-speaking owner. Be warned, though, that prices are high – ¥550 per cup.

Up in Kita-Kamakura, *Shōkita no Kamakura* is a fine *tōfu* (soya-bean curd) and soba specialist that serves such things as *zaru soba* (cold soba) with tempura for ¥1900. Look for the food models out front. Down the hill, you'll find *Chaya Kado,* another soba shop, which does sets like tempura gozen for ¥1600 and *oden gozen* (a set of various morsels simmered in a rich broth) for ¥1350.

Getting There & Away
Yokosuka line trains run to Kamakura from Tokyo (¥890, 55 minutes), Shimbashi and Shinagawa stations. It's also possible to catch a train from Yokohama (¥380, 27 minutes) on the Yokosuka line. If you're planning to get off at Kita-Kamakura station, it's the stop after Ōfuna.

It's possible to continue on to Enoshima from Kamakura, either via the Enoden Enoshima line from Kamakura station (¥250, 25 minutes) or by bus from stop No 9 in front of Kamakura station (¥300, 35 minutes).

JR Kamakura-Enoshima Free Pass
This pass is valid for two days, covers the trip to and from Tokyo, and allows unlimited use of JR trains around Kamakura, the Shōnan monorail between Ōfuna and Enoshima, and the Enoden Enoshima line between Fujisawa and Enoshima. From Tokyo station the pass costs ¥1970; from Yokohama station ¥1130.

Getting Around

You can walk to most temples from Kamakura or Kita-Kamakura stations. Sites in the west, like the Daibutsu, can be reached via the Enoden Enoshima line from Kamakura station. Alternatively, you can take buses from Kamakura station. Bus trips around the area cost either ¥170 or ¥190. Another good option is to rent a bicycle; there's a rental shop just outside the eastern exit of Kamakura station that charges ¥500/1500 per hour/day.

ENOSHIMA 江ノ島

Seven kilometres west of Kamakura, the tiny island of Enoshima is a good side-trip from Kamakura if you've got some time left after seeing all those temples. The island is connected to the mainland by a 600m causeway. After crossing the causeway on foot, you have the choice of hiking to Enoshima-jinja or taking the 'outdoor escalator' (¥300). The shrine houses a *hadaka-ben-zaiten* – a nude statue of the Indian goddess of beauty (¥150 to enter the hall housing the statue). After visiting the shrine, there's little to do but wander the island's network of trails, pausing here and there to admire the views. If the weather's clear, you might get views of Mt Fuji to the north-west.

Getting There & Away

Buses and trains run frequently between Kamakura and Enoshima (see Getting There & Away under Kamakura earlier). To return to Tokyo, you can either retrace your steps to Kamakura or take the Odakyū line back to Shinjuku from Katase Enoshima station (kyūkō/tokkyū ¥610/1220, two/1¼ hours). To get to the station from the island, walk back across the causeway, turn left over the river and look for the faux-Chinese station building.

East of Tokyo

Much of Chiba-ken, to the east and southeast of Tokyo, is suburbia. There are few compelling reasons to visit the area. However, a large majority of visitors to Japan will arrive or depart from Narita airport and, if you have a few hours to kill at the airport, there are some points of interest in the town of Narita.

NARITA 成田
☎ 0476

Narita is a pleasant temple town that makes a perfect trip for those stuck on a long layover at Narita airport. It's also ideal for your first or last night in Japan.

Information

Pick up a copy of the map pamphlet *Narita* at the Narita Tourist Information Centre (☎ 24-3198), just outside the eastern exit of JR Narita station. The office is open from 8.30 am to 5.15 pm. You might also stop by the Narita Tourist Pavilion (☎ 24-3232) on Omotesandō to see its exhibits on Narita's history (10 am to 5 pm, closed Monday).

Things to See & Do

The town is centred on the impressive **Narita-san Shinshō-ji** and its attractive grounds, **Narita-san-kōen**. While the temple was founded some 1000 years ago, the main hall is a 1968 reconstruction. The temple itself remains an important centre of the Shingon sect of Buddhism and attracts as many as 10 million visitors a year.

In Narita-san-kōen, you'll find the **Narita-san Calligraphy Museum** (¥500, 9 am to 4 pm, closed Monday), which has a good collection of *shodō* (calligraphy) for real aficionados. The **Reikōkan Historical Material Museum** (¥300, 9 am to 4 pm), under the temple's upper pagoda, and its nearby annex house a collection of artefacts from 18th-century Japanese life and various temple treasures – again, probably of interest only to real aficionados. Even if you skip both of these attractions, be sure to stroll along the ponds at the eastern edge of the park. The town's Omotesandō street is also an interesting walk.

Special Events

The main festivals centred on Narita-san Shinshō-ji are Setsubun (last day of winter in the Japanese lunar calendar), which is on

AROUND TOKYO

3 or 4 February, and Hatsumōde (First Shrine Visit), which is on 1 January. Things get very hectic at the temple on both these occasions, and a high level of tolerance of crowds is a must.

Places to Stay

Narita is a pleasant place to stay and a good choice for those with early flights. The Japanese Inn Group is represented here by *Ohgiya Ryokan (☎ 22-1161)*, a Japanese-style inn charging ¥7000/6000 per person for rooms with/without bathroom. It's a 10-minute walk from JR Narita or Keisei Narita stations. Another good choice is *Kirinoya Ryokan (☎ 22-0724)*, near Narita-san-kōen. The owners are friendly and maintain the place as a 'ryokan museum' – it's filled with all sorts of interesting historical bric-a-brac. Singles/doubles here are ¥5000/9500. Meals are also served. Both places are on the *Narita* map pamphlet given out at the tourist information centre.

Being so close to the airport, Narita has a representative selection of upmarket hotels. Singles/doubles start at ¥14,000/21,000 at *ANA Hotel Narita (☎ 33-1311)*, and at ¥12,000/19,000 at *Holiday Inn Tōbu Narita (☎ 32-1234)*. *Hotel Narita Tokyū (☎ 33-0109)* has singles from ¥11,800 and twins/doubles from ¥19,200. If you don't mind paying a little more, the ANA is the pick of the bunch.

All three hotels operate regular shuttle buses to and from the airport; ask at the hotel reservation counter in the arrivals hall for the correct boarding stand. Coming from Tokyo, it's best to go to the airport and then take the shuttle bus to your hotel.

Places to Eat

Omotesandō is packed with good places to eat. The best is *Kikuya*, which serves lunch sets of typical Japanese fare for ¥1000. Look for the English sign reading 'Chrysanthemum Housu' [sic] across from the Tourist Pavilion. It's closed Tuesday. Vegetarians will like the Japanese veggie fare at *Sosuian*, five minutes north of the JR station on Omotesandō. Lunch sets here go for ¥1600. Lastly, if you hanker for some English-pub fare or a pint or two, try *The Barge Inn*, also on Omotesandō.

Getting There & Away

From Narita airport you can take either the Keisei line (futsū or kyūkō but not the Sky-liner, ¥250, five minutes) or JR (futsū or kyūkō – N'EX usually doesn't stop – ¥190/230 from Terminal 2/1, five minutes). From Tokyo, the easiest way to get to Narita is via the Keisei line from Ueno (kyūkō, ¥810, 1¼ hours) or the JR Airport Narita from Tokyo station (¥1280, one hour and 20 minutes). For information on using these services, see the Getting Around section in the Tokyo chapter.

Izu-shotō

The semitropical Izu-shotō, known in English as the Izu Seven Islands, are peaks of a submerged volcanic chain that projects far down into the Pacific from the Izu-hantō. Until the beginning of the 20th century, the island chain was a place of exile; now it's a popular holiday destination for Tokyo residents. Activities on the islands include swimming, snorkelling, diving, fishing, dolphin watching, bicycling, hiking and relaxing in outdoor onsen.

Although it's relatively expensive to reach the islands, free camp sites are available on most of them and you can take your food over on the ferry. To escape the crowds, avoid holiday periods and head for the more remote islands, such as the fascinating Hachijō-jima, the hands-down pick of the bunch.

Getting There & Away

Ferries to the islands leave from Tokyo's Takeshiba Pier (10 minutes from Hama-matsu-chō station). Most ferries from Tokyo depart at 10 pm and arrive at the islands early the next morning. Some of the islands are also serviced by ferries from Atami and Itō. Call Tōkai Kisen ferry service (☎ 03-5472-9009) for departure times and reservations (in Japanese). The islands, Ō-shima, Miyake-jima and Hachijō-jima have airports and can be reached by plane from Tokyo's Haneda airport.

Getting Around
Island hopping is possible but requires some serious planning, as services vary seasonally and departures can be quite infrequent. If you do intend to island-hop, consult with the Tokyo TIC (☎ 03-3201-3331) to choose the best route and schedule. If you have money to burn, you can also travel from island to island by helicopter. Rates average ¥10,000 per flight and there is usually one flight per day to and from each island. Call Tokyo Island Shuttle at ☎ 04496-2-5222 for details.

Ō-SHIMA 大島
☎ 04992
Due to its proximity to the mainland, Ō-shima is the most popular island in the group. It's also the largest, at 91 sq km. Be warned that Ō-shima is overrun with young Tokyoites on weekends and holidays. Unless you really love crowds, avoid the island during these times, or head to the more southerly islands.

Information
Pick up the TIC's informative *Oshima Island* pamphlet or call the Izu Seven Islands Tourist Federation (☎ 03-3436-6955) in Tokyo for more information before setting out. Once on the island, stop by the helpful Ōshima Tourist Association (☎ 2-2177). It's right at the pier, visible as soon as you get off the ferry. While you're there, pick up some half-price onsen tickets.

Things to See & Do
The main attraction of Ō-shima is the active volcano **Mihara-yama**, which last erupted in November 1986 forcing the evacuation of island residents to Tokyo. Buses run to the summit from Motomachi port (¥680, 25 minutes).

Onsen are the island's other main attraction. **Hama-no-yu** (¥400, 1 pm to 7 pm), 10 minutes' walk north of the port, has good ocean views but gets packed out on weekends. It's mixed bathing but swimsuits are

permitted. A quieter place is **Ōshima Onsen Hotel Onsen** (¥800, 1 to 9 pm), an outdoor onsen with a good view of Mihara-yama. Take a bus from Motomachi port and get off at Mihara-yama onsen stop.

Places to Stay & Eat
Umi-no-Furusatsu-mura (☎ 4-1137) camping ground is the cheapest place to stay, with pre-pitched tents at ¥4000 for six people, plus an extra ¥300 per person. It's on the opposite side of the island and not serviced by any bus – try hitching. Not far from the pier, the institutional *Izu Oshima Kokumin-shukusha* (☎ 2-1285) costs ¥8700 per person, including two meals. A more interesting choice is *Tachibana-sō* (☎ 2-2075), a typical old minshuku that charges ¥4200 per bed, or ¥6300 with two meals. It's conveniently located on the main road, five minutes' walk straight in from the pier.

For good Japanese seafood, try *Kāchan*, a cosy izakaya on the seaside road less than five minutes north of the pier. We recommend the *isodon* (¥1400), a rice bowl topped with a variety of *sashimi*, which comes with miso soup. It's closed Wednesday. Look for the wooden front decorated with glass net-floats.

Getting There & Away
There are three flights a day from Tokyo (Haneda) to Ō-shima with Air Nippon Koku (ANK; ¥8850, 40 minutes).

Ferry services run daily to Ō-shima from Tokyo (2nd class, ¥3810, 7½ hours). From Atami there are two regular ferries a day (2nd class, ¥2750, one hour and 50 minutes) and two express ferries (2nd class, ¥5530, one hour). There's also a daily ferry from Itō (2nd class, ¥2390, 1½ hours).

TO-SHIMA 利島
☎ 04992
To-shima, 27km south-west of Ō-shima, is the smallest island in the Izu-shotō, with a circumference of only 8km. The island is mountainous, although its volcano is now dormant, and there are no swimming beaches. Much of the island is used for the cultivation of camellias, which makes it a picturesque place to

AROUND TOKYO

visit between December and February, when
the flowers are in bloom.

Places to Stay
The island has six minshuku with prices of
¥6000 to ¥6800 with two meals. For information contact the Izu Seven Islands
Tourist Federation (☎ 03-3436-6955).

Getting There & Away
There's a daily ferry from Tokyo to To-
shima (2nd class, ¥4240, 9½ hours).

NII-JIMA 新島
☎ 04992
Nii-jima has an area of 23 sq km and its
beaches have made it so popular that there
are now over 200 minshuku on the island.
Even with this abundance of accommodation, it's a good idea to ring the Niijima
Tourist Association (☎ 5-0048) for help
with reservations if you're visiting during a
holiday period.
  There's a daily ferry from Tokyo to Nii-
jima (2nd class, ¥5120, 10 hours).

SHIKINE-JIMA 式根島
☎ 04992
Six kilometres south of Nii-jima is tiny
Shikine-jima, with an area of only 3.8 sq
km. The island has swimming beaches,
onsen and plenty of accommodation.
  Ferries to Shikine-jima depart Tokyo
once daily (2nd class, ¥5120, 10 hours). Six
ferries a week leave from Shimoda on the
Izu-hantō (2nd class, ¥3600, 3½ hours).

KOZU-SHIMA 神津島
☎ 04992
Kozu-shima (18 sq km) is dominated by an
extinct volcano, Tenjo-san. The island also
has good beaches, Tokyo-ji, and a cemetery for former exiles, including 57 feudal
warriors.

Places to Stay
There are around 180 minshuku on the island, with costs of around ¥8000 with two
meals; bookings can be made in Japanese
through the Kozushima Tourist Association
(☎ 8-0321).

Getting There & Away
There is one daily ferry from Tokyo (2nd
class, ¥5890, 11 hours and 20 minutes).
There are six services weekly from Shimoda
(2nd class, ¥3100, two to three hours).

MIYAKE-JIMA 三宅島
☎ 04994
Known as Bird Island due to its 200 species
of birds, Miyake-jima is 180km south of
Tokyo. It is the third-largest island in the Izu
group, with a circumference of 36km. The island's volcano Osu-yama is said to erupt
every 20 years and last did so in 1983, destroying one of the island's main tourist attractions, the pond, Shinmyō-ike. Miyake-
jima's attractions include some good beaches
as well as three onsen, the best of which is
Furusato-no-yu (¥500, 11 am to 7.30 pm,
closed Wednesday). It's in the Ago area;
walk from Ago bus stop towards the ocean
for about 10 minutes. The best place to see
the island's birds is Tairō-ike on the south
coast. As with the other islands in the chain,
Miyake-jima gets packed on weekends.

Places to Stay
For information (in Japanese) on reasonably priced minshuku, contact the Miyake-
jima Tourist Association on ☎ 6-1144.
Many of the minshuku have very thin walls,
so you really must emphasise that you want
a quiet, private place. There are free camping grounds at Sagiga-hama, Okubo-hama
and Miike-hama; you'll need your own
equipment, however. All have toilets, cooking facilities and cold showers. Book
through the tourist association.

Getting There & Away
Daily ferries depart Tokyo at 10.30 pm (2nd
class, ¥5730, 6½ hours). There are also
daily boats to and from Hachijō-jima (2nd
class, ¥1860, 4½ hours). From Tokyo
(Haneda) there are two flights a day with
Air Nippon (¥11,050, 50 minutes) – you
can call ☎ 0120-029-222 toll free.

Getting Around
Chō-ei buses make clockwise and anticlockwise circuits (¥860) of the island

several times a day. Bicycle rentals are available for ¥1000/1500 a half/full day, or ¥400 per hour. Motorcycle rentals are also available, from ¥2000 for three hours.

MIKURA-JIMA 御蔵島
☎ 04994

Mikura-jima is only 20km from Miyake-jima but is not of great interest. Accommodation is limited, camping is not allowed and transport connections are infrequent. If you're around from April to December, however, you may be able to see some of the dolphins that live in nearby waters. Island diving and snorkelling operators offer dolphin-viewing trips. For more information (in Japanese) call the Mikura-jima Tourist Office (☎ 8-2121). There is a daily ferry from Miyake-jima (¥1510, one hour and 20 minutes). Be aware that the ferry only stops for 20 minutes, so you'll have to stay on the island overnight if you intend to explore – make minshuku reservations through the tourist office before setting out.

HACHIJŌ-JIMA 八丈島
☎ 04996

Hachijō-jima (68 sq km) is 290km south of Tokyo. It is the southernmost and second-largest island in the Izu-shotō. Its distance from Tokyo keeps it relatively free of the crowds that descend on the more northerly islands of the Izu group.

Information

Before leaving Tokyo, pick up the TIC's informative *Hachijojima & Aogashima Islands* pamphlet. The Hachijō-jima Tourist Organisation (☎ 2-1377) can answer questions in Japanese. After arrival, you can get information at the Tourist Information Office (☎ 2-1121) in the town hall, in the centre of the island on the main road.

Things to See & Do

The island is dominated by two dormant volcanoes, **Hachijō-Fuji** and **Mihara-yama**, whose slopes are covered with lush semitropical vegetation.

Hachijō-jima's highlights include good beaches, a botanical garden, and two historical sights, **Tametomo-jinja** and **Sofuku-ji**. There are also some great onsen in which to soak after a day of sightseeing.

Urami-ga-taki Onsen (mixed bathing, bathing suits permitted, free, 10 am to 9 pm) is not to be missed. It's tucked into a thick forest overlooking a waterfall. Take a Sueyoshi-bound bus from the port (you may have to change at Kashitate Onsen Mae) to Nakata-Shōten Mae and walk for 20 minutes towards the ocean. Another good choice is **Sueyoshi Onsen Miharashi-no-yu** (separate bathing for men and women, ¥500, 10.30 am to 9.30 pm, closed Tuesday), which has a great view over the Pacific – try going at sunset. Take the same bus that goes to Urami-ga-taki Onsen and get off at Sueyoshi.

History buffs will be interested in the **Tama-ishi-gaki walls** that the exiled population on the island built to prevent landslides and to protect themselves from typhoons. The walls are made from the uncannily round volcanic rocks that the exiles carried by hand up from the shoreline. These can be seen in the Ōsato-chiku area on the south-west coast of the island.

Places to Stay

Ashitaba-sō (☎ 7-0434) is a good minshuku that charges ¥6500 with two meals. The owner is a friendly, chatty fellow who serves heaped portions of locally caught seafood. Reservations (in Japanese) are required. Next to the Sokodo port is the free *Sokodo Camp-jō* camping area, with toilets, cold showers and cooking facilities. You must reserve (in Japanese only) a spot at the ward office (☎ 2-1121).

Places to eat are a little thin on the ground here. Generally, however, your lodging will provide meals. If you intend to camp it's best to bring food with you.

Getting There & Away

In the summer season, ferries depart Tokyo daily at 10.30 pm and travel via Miyake-jima (2nd class, ¥7180, 11 hours). Departures are less frequent outside the summer (June to August) season. Alternatively, there is a more frequent air service (five flights a day) between Haneda airport and the island with Air Nippon (¥13,400 if booked a day in advance, one hour) Air Nippon's toll-free information line is ☎ 0120-029-222.

Getting Around

You can negotiate most of the island by bicycle and there are rental places along the main street. Otherwise, the Chō-ei bus covers the island's most important destinations.

Ogasawara-shotō

Although technically part of the prefecture, Tokyo-to, these islands are far to the south of the Izu-shotō. They have a climate similar to that of the Nansei-shotō (South-West Islands, often referred to as Okinawa) and, like those islands, remained

occupied by US forces until 1968, long after the occupation of the mainland islands had ended.

The main group of islands includes **Chichi-jima** (Father Island), **Haha-jima** (Mother Island) and **Ani-jima**, on which you will find a number of minshuku and where **scuba diving** is popular. Farther south are the Kazan-shotō (Volcano Islands), which include **Iwo-jima**, one of the most famous battle sites of WWII. The island is still off limits to visitors because of the live ammunition there.

Boats to Chichi-jima leave approximately once a week from Tokyo (2nd class, ¥22,5700, 25 to 30 hours). For more information, call Ogasawara Kaiun (☎ 03-3451-5171). Boats between Chichi-jima and Haha-jima leave daily (2nd class, ¥3780, two hours).

Central Honshū

Central Japan, known in Japanese as Chūbu, extends across the area sandwiched between Tokyo and Kyoto. This chapter covers the prefectures at the heart of the Chūbu region: Aichi-ken, Gifu-ken, Nagano-ken, Toyama-ken, Fukui-ken and Ishikawa-ken. Niigata-ken and the island of Sado-ga-shima have been included in the Northern Honshū chapter.

Chūbu divides into three geographical areas with marked differences in topography, climate and scenery. To the north, the coastal area along the Sea of Japan features rugged seascapes. The central area inland encompasses the spectacular mountain ranges and highlands of the Japan Alps, while the southern Pacific coast area is heavily industrialised, urbanised and densely populated, so it may not be of much interest to travellers.

Transport in the southern area is excellent, with Nagoya functioning as the major transport centre and southern gateway to the region. The mountainous inland area is served by the JR (Japan Railways) Takayama line and JR Chūō line, which run roughly parallel from north to south. The main transport hubs and gateways for this area are Takayama to the west and Matsumoto to the east.

Other useful rail connections are provided by the JR Hokuriku Shinkansen and the JR Shin-etsu line, which link Tokyo with Nagano. Transport in the northern area centres around the JR Hokuriku line, which follows the coast along the Sea of Japan, providing an extremely efficient link between the main transport centres of Kanazawa and Toyama.

Bear in mind that transport outside the main cities in Chūbu, especially around the Japan Alps, is severely restricted between the months of November and May. Access to ski resorts is an exception. Bus fares also tend to be ridiculously expensive, so it is worth investing in the discount bus passes available only in Matsumoto and Takayama.

Highlights

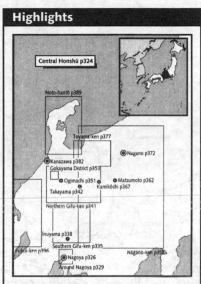

Central Honshū p324
Noto-hantō p389
Toyama-ken p377
Nagano p372
Kanazawa p382
Gokayama District p353
Ogimachi p351
Matsumoto p362
Kamikōchi p367
Takayama p342
Northern Gifu-ken p341
Inuyama p338
Fukui-ken p396
Southern Gifu-ken p335
Nagano-ken p355
Nagoya p326
Around Nagoya p329

- Visit Takayama, a small, beautiful city known for its traditional architecture and skilled woodworkers.

- See Shōkawa Valley, a remote agricultural region where traditional customs and farmhouses remain largely intact.

- Relax at Bessho Onsen, an ancient mineral hot spring and rural temple retreat, easily accessible from Tokyo.

- Follow the superb mountain scenery and hiking trails of Nagano-ken's Kamikōchi and Hakuba.

- Enjoy the cultural and artistic centre of Kanazawa.

- Discover the peninsula Noto-hantō's lovely coastal scenery and fine seafood.

If there are several of you interested in a day trip, renting a car may be the most affordable option.

The attractions of Chūbu lie in the central and northern areas, each of which can be

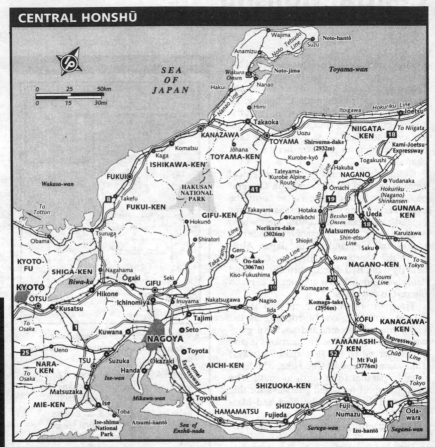

CENTRAL HONSHŪ

skimmed in five days, but preferably give yourself two weeks for both if you really want to enjoy all the region has to offer.

For a lightning trip, make sure you visit at least Takayama and Kanazawa. With three or four days, you should add either Nagano or Matsumoto, the Unesco World Heritage site at Shirakawa-gō, the Kiso post road, or take a jaunt up the peninsula, Noto-hantō, to Wajima. A week will allow you to cover all this, and/or explore the hot springs at Bessho, Fukuchi and Hirayu, or the hiking trails of Kamikōchi and Hakuba. However, a slow, unhurried wander through the

countryside is the best way to enjoy this part of Honshū.

Nagoya 名古屋

☎ 052 ● pop 2,156,000

Nagoya is Japan's fourth-largest city and is mainly a commercial and industrial centre, not a top travel destination. The city, however, has made a push to accommodate foreign visitors, and English-language signs make it easy to get to Nagoya's major sights, including the castle, **Nagoya-jō**, the

Atsuta-jingū shrine, the **IdcN Design Museum**, and the **Nagoya/Boston Museum of Fine Arts**. There are some lesser attractions, many excellent restaurants, and the city itself is fairly pleasant; it's similar to a scaled-down, far more relaxed version of Tokyo. Nagoya is also a convenient transport hub for trips to Gifu and Inuyama or longer excursions into the Japan Alps.

HISTORY

Nagoya rose to power as a castle town during the feudal age. All three of Japan's great historical heroes, Oda Nobunaga, Toyotomi Hideyoshi and Tokugawa Ieyasu, were born in the town or nearby. Tokugawa Ieyasu built the castle, Nagoya-jō, for one of his sons from 1610–14. Not much of the past remains, however. During WWII, the city was flattened by US aerial bombing, which also claimed most of Nagoya-jō.

Nagoya-ites are famed for their displays of wealth, outrageously lavish weddings, and love of *pachinko* (Japanese pinball).

There are just a few significant sights in Nagoya, which can be knocked off in a day or so. Inuyama, Gifu and Seki are within easy reach by train. Ise-jingū (see the Shima-hantō section in the Kansai Region chapter) and Takayama (see the Northern Gifu-ken section later in this chapter) are both feasible as day trips if you make an early start; though, if you have the time it would be better to stay overnight in Takayama at the very least.

ORIENTATION

The city was completely rebuilt after WWII on a grid system with expansive avenues and side streets connecting in straight lines. This makes it easy to find one's way around the central part of the city.

From the east exit of Nagoya station, Sakura-dōri runs directly eastwards to the TV tower, a useful landmark on Hisaya-ōdōri. The area either side of Hisaya-ōdōri, south of the TV tower, is the Sakae entertainment district. The castle, Nagoya-jō, is just north of the TV tower.

Nagoya station, known by its nickname *meieki*, is a city in itself. The *shinkansen* (bullet train) platforms are on the west side of the station. The Meitetsu and Kintetsu lines are on the east side of the station, which is also handy for connections with the subway system, the Meitetsu bus station and the city centre.

Maps *Goodwill Guide* is probably the most comprehensive colour map of the city and surrounding areas. It includes lists of shops, restaurants and hotels where staff speak English. *Live Map Nagoya* is a slightly dated and less-detailed map of the city, with hotels and sights accurately sited. At some subway stations you can also pick up the *Nagoya City Bus and Subway System* map in English, which has just about all the information one needs on the local transit network.

INFORMATION

Tourist Offices There is a Nagoya city tourist information office (☎ 541-4301), open from 9 am to 7 pm, inside Nagoya station – take the central exit and look out for it in the middle of the hall. There are smaller offices at the north exit of Kanayama subway station (☎ 323-0161), open from 9 am to 7 pm, and in the Chunichi Building in Sakae (☎ 262-2918), open from 9 am to 5.45 pm, closed weekends. All have English-language maps of the city, information on sights and accommodation, and at least one English speaker behind the counter.

Better still is Nagoya International Centre (☎ 581-0100), which is located on the 3rd floor of the International Centre (Kokusai Centre) – a 10-minute walk east from the station, along Sakura-dōri (9 am to 8.30 pm Tuesday to Saturday, 8 am to 5 pm Sunday and holidays, closed Monday). Staff here speak English (some also speak Chinese, French, Spanish or Portuguese) and have a wealth of information on both Nagoya and other destinations in Central Honshū. The centre has extensive lists of restaurants, bars, hotels and *ryokan* (traditional Japanese inns), though they're not allowed to make recommendations. Staff can also help arrange home visits with a

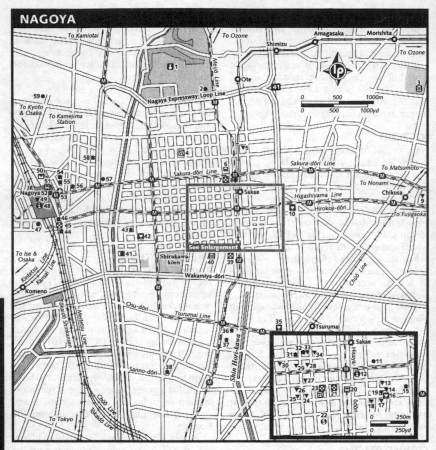

NAGOYA

Japanese family. There's also a library, TV newscasts from the USA and a bulletin board.

Money Citibank has 24-hour Cirrus ATM access at its branch on the 8th floor of the Sugi building three minutes' walk southwest from exit 7 of Sakae station, near Nadya Park (not a park, but a museum/shopping complex resembling the bad guys' spaceship in the movie *Men in Black*).

There is also a Citibank ATM (5 am to 11.30 pm) on the 1st floor of the arrival lobby at Nagoya airport.

Post The main post office is a couple of minutes' walk north of Nagoya station. There is also a smaller office in the station itself, on the west side.

Email & Internet Access The deal with Net cafes is that the majority only allow Web-based mail access. Otherwise they are set up for Japanese mail systems.

Joy Place (☎ 211-3811), on the west side of Honmachi-dōri 100m north of Sakura-dōri, is a friendly cyber-*kissaten*, or cyber-cafe, where you can surf the Web over your breakfast (¥100 for 10 minutes, 7.30 am to

NAGOYA

PLACES TO STAY

15 Nagoya Tōkyū Hotel
  名古屋東急ホテル
31 Nagoya Dai-Ni
  Washington Hotel
  名古屋第二
  ワシントンホテル
32 Sun Hotel Nagoya
  サンホテル名古屋
36 Ryokan Meiryū
  旅館名龍
37 Yamazen Ryokan
  山善旅館
38 Marutame Ryokan
  まるため旅館
41 Aichi-ken Seinen-kaikan
  Youth Hostel
  愛知県青年会館
43 Nagoya Hilton
  名古屋ヒルトン
44 Nagoya Flower Hotel 1
  名古屋フラワーホテル
46 Meitetsu Grand Hotel
  名鉄グランドホテル
47 City Hotel Nagoya
  シティホテル名古屋
52 Hotel Associa Nagoya
  Terminal
  アソシア名古屋
  ターミナルホテル
54 Hotel Sun Plaza
  サンプラザホテル
55 Nagoya Dai-Ichi Hotel
  名古屋第一ホテル
56 Fitness Hotel 330 Nagoya
  フィットネスホテル
  330名古屋
58 Kimiya Ryokan
  きみや旅館

PLACES TO EAT

 5 Carina Pizza
 9 Izakaya Bun
  居酒屋文

13 Cafe de Crie
14 Suien
  翠園中国料理
17 Yagiya China
  やぎやチャイナ
18 Tsubohachi
  つぼ八
19 Hua Lien
  蓮花
24 Mr Donut
25 McDonald's
26 Kentucky Fried Chicken
27 Okonomishokudō-gai
  お好み食堂街
28 Fujiko
  富士子
29 Tsubohachi
  つぼ八
30 Ebisuya
  えびすや
33 Irohanihoheto
  いろはにほへと
34 Torigin Honten
  鳥銀本店
49 Sumiyoshi
  すみよし

OTHER

 1 Nagoya-jō
  名古屋城
 2 Aichi Prefectural
  Gymnasium
  愛知県立体育館
 3 Tokugawa
  Art Museum
  徳川美術館
 4 Joy Place
 5 Airport Bus stop
 7 Tokyu Hands
  Department Store
  東急ハンズ
 8 Nagoya TV Tower
  テレビ塔
10 J-Connection

11 Aichi Arts Center
  愛知芸術文化センター
12 Tourist Information
  (Chunichi Building)
16 Lush – Underground;
  Club Atlantic
20 Sakae Bus Station
  栄バスターミナル
21 Mitsukoshi
  Department Store
  三越デパート
22 Citibank ATM
23 Skyle Building; Marui
  Department Store;
  Media Wave
  丸井デパート
35 Radix
39 Matsuzakaya Department
  Store
  松坂屋デパート
40 International Design
  Centre Nagoya;
  Nadya Park
  国際デザインセンター
42 Across the Border (Bar)
45 Meitetsu & Kintetsu
  Department Stores;
  Meitetsu Shin-Nagoya
  Station
  名鉄デパート；
  近鉄デパート
48 Tourist Information
50 Nagoya Main Post Office
  中央郵便局
51 City Bus Station
  市バスターミナル
53 Dai-Nagoya Building;
  Tachino Clinic
57 Kokusai Centre – Nagoya
  International Centre;
  Daikoku Denki Virtual Zone
  国際センタービル
59 Noritake
  Craft Centre

CENTRAL HONSHŪ

5 pm weekdays, 11 am to 3 pm Sunday, closed Saturday).

Media Wave (☎ 264-6550) on the 9th floor of the Maruei Skyle building in Sakae has 10 PCs and two Macintosh computers (¥1050 per hour, 10 am to 9 pm, closed two Wednesdays a month).

Thirty minutes' free Internet access is available in the 6th floor library of the International Design Centre Nagoya (9 am to 8 pm).

Books Useful local publications with restaurant, entertainment and festival listings include *Alien*, *Eyes* and *Nagoya Avenues*.

Emergency Nagoya International Centre (☎ 581-0100) can provide all the emergency advice you need. The Kyukyuiryō Jōhō Sentā (☎ 263-1133) can advise (in Japanese only) where to receive weekend and holiday emergency treatment. The Tachino Clinic (☎ 541-9130) has staff who speak English, French, German and Spanish. It's in the Dai-Nagoya building, opposite the east exit of Nagoya station.

THINGS TO SEE & DO
Nagoya-jō

Tokugawa Ieyasu built **Nagoya-jō** (¥500, 9 am to 4.30 pm) on the site of an older castle from 1610–14, for his ninth son. It was destroyed in WWII and replaced in 1959 with a ferroconcrete replica. Look out for the 3m-long replicas of the famous *shachihoko*, dolphin-like sea creatures that stand at either end of the roof (and inside every souvenir shop). The interior houses a museum with armour and family treasures that escaped the bombing. The castle also boasts an elevator to save you climbing stairs. The garden, Ninomaru-en, has a teahouse in an attractive setting in the castle grounds. The castle is a five-minute walk from Shiyakusho station on the Meijō subway line.

Atsuta-jingū

This shrine, one of the most important in Japan, dates from the 3rd century and is said to house the *kusanagi-no-tsurugi* (the sacred sword – literally, the 'grass-cutting sword'), one of the three imperial regalia (the others being the curved jewels and the sacred mirror) of the imperial family. The imperial regalia was, according to mythology, handed down to the imperial family by the goddess Amaterasu Ōmikami. Visitors aren't allowed to view the sword or any of the other imperial regalia, but don't feel too bad: no-one but the emperor and a few selected Shintō priests ever get to see them

either. There is a small museum (¥300, ¥500 for special exhibits, 9 am to 4.30 pm, closed the last Wednesday and Thursday of every month) that houses various Shintō and Tokugawa-era artefacts. The shrine grounds are open 24 hours a day.

Just across the river, the Hori-kawa, is **Shirotori-teien** (☎ 681-8929), a beautiful traditional 'stroll garden' designed in the shape of a swan flying down to rest its wings (¥200, 9 am to 4.30 pm, closed Monday). Rooms in its exquisite teahouse may be rented for the day.

From Shiyakusho subway station (close to Nagoya-jō), take the Meijō line south to Jingū-nishi station (seven stops). To reach the shrine from Nagoya station, take the Meitetsu Nagoya Honsen (main) line to Jingū-mae (four stops) and then walk west for five minutes.

Tokugawa Art Museum

The collection here (¥1200, 10 am to 5 pm, closed Monday) includes prints, calligraphy, painted scrolls, lacquerware and ceramics that previously belonged to the Tokugawa family. The priceless 12th-century scroll depicting the *Tale of the Genji* is locked away, so visitors must remain content with a video. Look out, however, for the magnificently horned warrior helmet in Room 1.

The easiest way to reach the museum is to take bus No 16 from Shiyakusho subway station (near Nagoya-jō) and get off at the Shindeki stop.

IdcN International Design Centre and Design Museum

Housed in Nadya Park, the 4th-floor **Design Museum** (¥300, 11 am to 7.30 pm) traces the history of design from the Art Deco years of the 1930s until the present day.

This secular shrine to the deities of conceptualisation, form and function could have benefited from more Japanese exhibits, but it is still a fascinating place to spend a few hours, as are the Loft department store and Kinokuniya bookshop next door. The 6th floor library offers limited free Internet access.

The temple, Zenkō-ji, is Nagano's main attraction.

Matsumoto-jō, otherwise known as Crow Castle.

Red *bangasa* (oiled rice paper umbrellas), Gifu

Farm fresh produce on sale, Wajima

A Shaka, or Historical Buddha, at Katsuyama.

A view of Haku-san from the Murodō plateau.

霊峰

白山頂上

A marker at the peak of Haku-san (2702m).

Traditional thatched *gasshō-zukuri* (hands in prayer) buildings at an open-air museum in Ogimachi.

AROUND NAGOYA

To Gifu
To Gifu & Inuyama
To Minokamo
To Tajimi
To Matsumoto
To Kyoto & Matsumoto
Meitetsu Komaki Line
Nagoya Airport
Chūō Line
19
Tōmei Expressway
Aichi-kanjō Line
To Gifu
Meitetsu Inuyama Line
41
Higashi-Meihan Expressway
To Gifu
22
Tōkaidō Honsen Line
Yada-gawa
Kami-Otai
Shonai Ryōkuchi Kōen
Shin-Moriyama
Asahi Beer Factory
Meitetsu Seto Line
Fujigaoka
To Kyoto
Tōkaidō Shinkansen Line
Kami-Iida
Ozone
Hongo
Nagoya Interchange
Meitetsu Tsushima Line
Nagoya-jō
Higashiyama Line
302
To Hamamatsu & Tokyo
Higashiyama
Nagoya Youth Hostel
Higashiyama-kōen
Nagoya
See Nagoya Map p.316
Meitetsu Toyota Line
To Matsusaka
S. Ōsu-dōri Line
Akaike
Takabata
Atsuta-jingū
To Osaka
Kansai Honsen Line
Kintetsu Nagoya Line
Jingū-nishi
Jingū-mae
Nonami
Aratama-bashi
Meitetsu Nagoya Honsen Line
To Kuwana
Shōnai-gawa
Nikkō-gawa
23
Nagoya-kō
Nagoya Ferry Port
To Okazaki
1
To Tokyo
0   2.5   5km
0   1.5   3mi
LP

CENTRAL HONSHŪ

Nadya Park is five minutes' walk north-west of Yabacho station on the Meijyō line, or eight minutes' walk south-west of Sakae station on the Higashiyama and Meijyō lines.

Nagoya/Boston Museum of Fine Arts

This excellent museum (¥1200 for regular and long-term exhibitions, ¥400 for long-term exhibitions only, 10 am to 4.30 pm, until 9 pm Friday, closed Monday) is a collaborative effort between Japanese backers and the Museum of Fine Arts (MFA), Boston. It showcases both masterpieces of Western art and 'returnee' items of Japanese artwork on long-term loan from the MFA's Asiatic Collection.

The museum is in front of the south-east exit of Kanayama station on the Meijyō subway line.

Nagoya Port Area

Redeveloped to attract tourists, the cargo port now boasts several mildly interesting attractions. These include the hi-tech **Port of Nagoya Public Aquarium** (one of Japan's largest), the **Port Tower**, with good views of the harbour, the **Maritime Museum** on the

3rd floor of the Port Tower and the **Fuji Antarctic Exploration Ship**. All of them can be visited with a combination ticket for ¥2000, provided you roll up before 1 pm. Just visiting the Port Tower and Maritime Museum will only set you back ¥300. Take the Meijō subway line to Nagoya-kō subway station. The attractions are signposted in English.

Pachinko Exhibitions

Love or hate it, pachinko has gripped Japan's postwar imagination like nothing else, and nowhere more so than in Nagoya. The quaint **Pachinko Museum** (☎ 531-3638) traces the game's history, and is dedicated to Takeichi Masamura, founder of the modern pinball machine (free, 11 am to 4 pm weekdays). The collection is on the 3rd floor of the Masamura building, 100m south from exit 2 of Joshin station on the Tsurumai subway line.

The Daikoku Denki Virtual Zone (☎ 581-4817), handily located on the 2nd floor of the Nagoya International Centre, showcases the company's hi-tech computerised slot machines (free, 10 am to 5 pm weekdays). This is a great place to try your hand at the game without exposing yourself to unholy levels of noise and tobacco pollution, but reservations in advance are required.

Factory Tours

Nagoya is an industrial town, and has several good tours of local factories for the commercially curious.

Noritake Craft Centre (☎ 561-7114) offers a look at the production line of Japan's most well-known maker of porcelain tableware. The craft centre (reservations necessary, closed weekends) can be reached by taking the Higashiyama subway line to the Kamejima station and walking 10 minutes north-east.

The automobile giant **Toyota Motor Corporation** (☎ 0565-23-3922) is an hour east of Nagoya, and tours of its main plant in Toyota City can be made by reservation (☎ 0565-29-3355). To get there, take the Meitetsu Toyota line, a continuation of the Tsurumai subway line. Next take the bus from Toyota station bound for Hirayama and get off at the Toyota bus stop.

Lager lovers might think about touring **Asahi Beer's Nagoya factory** (☎ 792-8966). The free tours are held weekdays from 9.30 am to 3 pm, though it would be wise to call ahead just to make sure. To get there, take the JR Chūō line to Shin-Moriyama station. From there it's about a 15-minute walk east.

SPECIAL EVENTS

The festival, Atsuta Matsuri, held on 5 June at the shrine, Atsuta-jingū, features displays of martial arts, sumō matches and fireworks. Street vendors peddle their wares by the light of thousands of lanterns.

On the first Saturday and Sunday of June, the Tennō Matsuri takes place in Dekimachi. Large *karakuri*, or mechanical puppets, are paraded on floats in the precincts of the shrine, Susano-o-jinja.

The Nagoya Basho sumō tournament takes place at the Aichi Prefectural Gymnasium (☎ 962-9300) from the first to the third Sunday of July. Non-reserved seats (from ¥2800) are available from the box office on the day of the bout from 8.30 am. Arrive early in the afternoon and you can walk unchallenged to the very front of the arena to watch the lower-ranked wrestlers up close. It's also a great photo opportunity. The gymnasium is in the grounds of Nagoya-jō, three minutes' walk north-east of Shiyakusho station on the Meijō line.

The Minato Matsuri, held around 20 July at Nagoya port, features a street parade with more than 1500 dancers, and a waterlogging contest that dates back to the Edo period (1600–1867).

Nagoya Matsuri, held in mid-October in Hisaya-ōdōri-kōen, is the big event of the year. It includes costume parades, processions of floats with karakuri, folk dancing, music and a parade of decorated cars.

The shrine, Ohsu Kannon-jinja, hosts a colourful antique market on the 18th and 28th of each month.

PLACES TO STAY

Accommodation in Nagoya is clustered largely around Nagoya station and the

Sakae commercial and entertainment district. Nagoya's excellent subway system means that basing yourself in the station area is no impediment to taking an evening trip into Sakae.

Places to Stay – Budget

Hostels *Aichi-ken Seinen-kaikan Youth Hostel* (☎ 221-6001) is in a good location, not too far from Nagoya station. As a result, it's the first budget place to be booked out – reserve in advance if you want to be sure of a bed. The hostel charges ¥2800 per night. Japanese-style family rooms and guest rooms are available from around ¥4095 per night. From Nagoya station (east exit), the hostel is a 20-minute walk southeast. Alternatively, you can take bus No 20 from the stop in front of the Toyota building and get off at the Nayabashi stop. From there, it's three minutes south on foot. Look out for the blue sign with tiny English writing out front. The hostel is closed from 28 December to 5 January. Check-in is between 3 and 8 pm.

Nagoya Youth Hostel (☎ 781-9845) is farther out to the east of town near Higashiyama-kōen. Beds are ¥2200 per night, and the hostel is closed from 29 December to 3 January. From Nagoya station, take the Higashiyama subway line to Higashiyama-kōen station. From exit 2, turn left and follow the main road, Higashiyama-dōri, to the next main intersection, where you'll see signs for the hostel. Check-in is until 9 pm.

Hotels Most of the business hotels in the station area are fairly pricey, and the cheaper ones tend to be around the rather inconvenient west exit. The best deal is the *Nagoya Flower Hotel Part II* (☎ 451-2200), which has singles/doubles for ¥4980/8500.

Places to Stay – Mid-Range

Ryokan *Ryokan Meiryu* (☎ 331-8686) is a member of the Japanese Inn Group and charges ¥5250/8240 for singles/doubles, all with air-con and TV. It's centrally located, three minutes on foot from Kamimaezu subway station on the Meijō line. Just a few blocks away, *Yamazen Ryokan* (☎ 321-1792) has fairly large rooms for between ¥4800 and ¥5400 per person. The owners don't speak much English, but do welcome foreign guests.

Two other options with per person costs around ¥4000 are *Kimiya Ryokan* (☎ 551-0498), which is north of the Nagoya International Centre building, and the plain but clean *Marutame Ryokan* (☎ 321-7130), which is three blocks west of Higashi Betsuin subway station on the Meijō line. English is spoken at Kimiya, but not at Marutame.

The friendly couple who run *Petit Ryokan Ichifuji* (☎ 914-2867), a member of the Japanese Inn Group, provide clean, comfortable Japanese-style rooms for ¥5000/8000. The communal *hinokiburo* (cedarwood bath) is great. Take the Meijō subway line to Heiandori station, turn right out of exit 2, and walk south for three minutes. The ryokan is signposted in English.

Hotels *Nagoya Flower Hotel I* (☎ 451-2222), directly in front of Nagoya station, has rooms from ¥7200/9800.

City Hotel Nagoya (☎ 452-6223) has singles/twins for ¥6000/9000.

Around the east exit of Nagoya station, *Hotel Sun Plaza* (☎ 563-0691) has singles from ¥6590 and doubles from ¥12,560. A few minutes' walk west is the *Fitness Hotel 330 Nagoya* (☎ 562-0330), where singles range from ¥8500, twins from ¥13,860 and doubles from ¥12,705.

The Sakae area is a more lively part of town in terms of eating out and nightlife. One of the cheapest options around is the would-be-glitzy *Nagoya Dai-Ni Washington Hotel* (☎ 962-7111), which has singles from ¥6000 and twins and doubles from ¥13,000. Just across the road, *Sun Hotel Nagoya* (☎ 971-2781) has singles for ¥6200 and twins for ¥9900.

Places to Stay – Top End

Most of hotels near the east exit of the station range from around ¥9000 upwards. *Hotel Associa Nagoya Terminal* (☎ 561-3751) has singles from ¥9500, twins from

¥17,000 and doubles from ¥16,500. Offering similar rates are the enormous **Meitetsu Grand Hotel** (☎ 582-2211), which allows two people to share a single room for ¥15,000, and the **Nagoya Dai-Ichi Hotel** (☎ 581-4411) close to the east exit.

The Sakae area also has a number of upmarket hotels. Probably the best is **Nagoya Tōkyū Hotel** (☎ 251-2411), which has singles for ¥15,000, twins for ¥27,000 and doubles for ¥23,000. If money is no object, **Nagoya Hilton** (☎ 212-1111) has singles/doubles from ¥22,000/30,000.

PLACES TO EAT

The most famous of Nagoya's regional dishes is *kishimen* (flat, handmade noodles, served either cold or in a hot broth). Its other culinary star is the Nagoya Cochin chicken. Nagoya also has a good range of traditional Japanese dining options as well as some very good Chinese and international dining.

Locals say the best 'secret' spot for kishimen is the humble, stand-up noodle bar **Sumiyoshi** (6 am to 9.40 pm) on the southbound shinkansen platform of Nagoya station. The identical northbound version apparently pales in comparison. The *sansai soba* (buckwheat noodles with mountain vegetables), at ¥400, is especially good. The Sakae main branch of **Ebisuya** (☎ 961-3412) is the city's best-known noodle restaurant (11.30 am to 11 pm), and has kishimen from ¥650.

Competing with Ebisuya in the fame stakes is Sakae's Cochin chicken restaurant **Torigin Honten** (☎ 973-3000), open from 5 pm to midnight. *Teishoku*, or set menus, begin at ¥2900. Be sure to order *kushiyaki* (any skewered food) or *kochin kara'age* (deep-fried chicken pieces) unless you want your chicken raw.

Those just passing through Nagoya (changing trains perhaps) can take the station's central exit and look out for the basement **Gourmet One** dining arcade. It's a fairly relaxed little place with a number of Japanese-style restaurants, and prices are reasonable. The basement of the Sakaemachi building has **Okonomishokudo-gai**, a 'street' of cheap restaurants that are popular with students and other young people. One other place to look out for, close to Sakae subway station, is **Fujiko**, a somewhat dusty-looking corner stall doing a brisk business in *yakitori* – squeeze into one of the three tiny tables around the back or buy to take away.

For lively eating and drinking, look out for one of the branches of the *izakaya* (pub-style eatery) chains, **Tsubohachi** or **Irohaniheto** – expect to pay ¥2000 for dinner and drinks. One of Nagoya's finest *robata*, restaurants specialising in char-grilled fish and other foods, is the trendy but relaxed **Izakaya Bun** (☎ 733-4066), set in an old-style Japanese house near Chikusa station on the Higashiyama subway line (6 pm to midnight, closed Sunday). Take exit 3, turn left at the clock tower, and walk north above the JR train tracks for 2 minutes. The *dote aka wain fu mi* (beef in red wine; ¥500) is recommended. Expect to pay around ¥2500 per head. Some English is spoken.

For good Taiwanese food (an excellent, little-known cuisine), try **Hua Lien** (☎ 262-4550), south-east of Sakae subway station. It has an illustrated menu and a good selection of authentic Taiwanese street-stall snacks (5 pm to 3 am). An evening meal costs from ¥2000 to ¥2500 per head with a drink. Just around the corner is **Suien**, another authentic Chinese restaurant (this time Shanghainese) with a limited illustrated menu. Opposite Hua Lien is **Yagya China** (☎ 241-7022). Its lavish decor belies its prices; most dishes are less than ¥800. There is an extensive English menu (6 pm to midnight).

For decent Italian pizza and pasta, check out **Carina Pizza**, north of the TV tower. There is also a branch on the 9th floor of the Marui Skyle building, part of the Marui department store in Sakae. If running around Sakae has you in need of a jump start, the **Cafe de Crie** coffee shop can provide you with a decent cup of coffee for ¥230.

ENTERTAINMENT

Nagoya's nightlife might not match Tokyo or Osaka's, but what it lacks in scale it makes up for in ebullience. Among the more popular spots are **Lush – the Underground** and **Club Atlantic** (Friday to Sunday only), which are on the 3rd and 4th floors of the same building, respectively. The Underground is basically a dance space with good soul sounds and a cover charge of ¥1000 to ¥2000 on some nights of the week, while Club Atlantic is more of a date spot – both get packed on Friday and Saturday nights. Both places also have a strict dress code – no shorts or sandals.

Radix (☎ 332-0073) beneath JR Tsuramai station is currently Nagoya's hottest dance spot (8 pm to 3 am, until 5 am Friday and Saturday). Unless there is a special event taking place, entrance is just ¥500, including one free drink.

Another drinking option is *Across the Border* (☎ 201-4300), a popular *gaijin* (foreigner) hang-out, not far from the Nagoya Hilton.

Nagoya's gay and lesbian community meet at *The Metro Club* (☎ 531-8405), a dance party held the first Saturday of each month at *J-Connection* (☎ 936-1270), on Hirokōji-dōri opposite the CBC TV building (¥1500, 10 pm to 5 am).

Nagoya also offers a good sampling of live jazz, rock and classical music, including some well-known Japanese and international artists. Check the *Alien* and *Eyes* to see who's playing where and when.

SHOPPING

Nagoya and the surrounding area are known for various arts and crafts such as *arimatsunarumi shibori* (elegant tie-dying), cloisonne (enamelling on silver and copper), ceramics and Seki blades (swords, knives, scissors, etc). For information on the Noritake porcelain factory, see the Factory Tours entry earlier in this section. Nagoya International Centre can provide details of tours of specific factories or museums as well as general shopping information.

The major shopping centres are in Sakae and around Nagoya station. For souvenir items (such as handmade paper, pottery and tie-dyed fabric) you can browse in Sakae in the giant department stores such as Matsuzakaya, Marui and Mitsukoshi, or try Meitetsu, an equally vast department store next to Nagoya station.

GETTING THERE & AWAY

Air Nagoya airport (☎ 0568-29-0765), otherwise known as Komaki airport, is linked by air with most of Japan's major cities by All Nippon Airways (ANA), Japan Airlines (JAL) and Japan Air System (JAS). If you're coming from Tokyo, however, the shinkansen is much quicker, as the bus from Nagoya station to the airport takes 30 to 40 minutes.

An increasing number of international carriers are using Komaki airport, which does not suffer from the chronic congestion of Tokyo's Narita airport. Direct flights are available to Nagoya from Bangkok, Beijing, Cairns, Hong Kong, Los Angeles, London, Manila, Seoul, Singapore, Sydney, Taipei and Vancouver.

Bus JR (☎ 563-0489) and Meitetsu (☎ 561-6381) highway buses share services between Nagoya and Kanazawa (¥4060, four hours, 10 daily), Kyoto (¥4350, 2½ hours, 19 daily), Osaka (¥5050, three hours, 6 daily), and Tokyo (¥11,410, 5½ hours, 13 daily). They also run overnight buses to Hiroshima (¥8400, nine hours), Kōchi (¥9070, 10 hours), Fukuoka (¥10,500, 11 hours) and Nagasaki (¥12,230, 12 hours).

Train The JR shinkansen is the fastest rail service to Nagoya. Fares cost: from Tokyo (Hikari shinkansen, ¥10,070, two hours), Osaka (¥5670, one hour), Kyoto (¥5340, 44 minutes) and Hiroshima (¥12,920, 3 hours).

Ise shima National Park is connected with Nagoya on the Kintetsu line, which runs via Ise-shi station and Toba to Kashikojima. A trip from Nagoya to Ise costs ¥1280 and takes 80 minutes. If you want to use JR, it will take at least two hours (¥1890); take the JR Kansai Honsen to Kameyama, then the Kisei line to Taki and then the Sangū line for Ise.

Nara is connected with Nagoya on the Kintetsu line (¥3750, 2½ hours); change at Yamatoyagi and Saidaiji Nara stations.

For the Japan Alps and related side trips, you can take the JR Chūō line to Nagano (Wide-view Shinano, ¥6620, three hours) via Matsumoto (¥5360, two hours). To reach Takayama from Nagoya, take the JR Hida limited express (Hida *tokkyū*, ¥5870, 2½ hours). If you want to stop at Inuyama en route, the Meitetsu Inuyama line connects with the JR Takayama line at Shin-Unuma station, across the river from Inuyama.

Inuyama is connected with Nagoya station on the Meitetsu Inuyama line (Mu *tokkyū*, ¥890, 23 minutes).

Gifu connects with Nagoya station on the JR Tōkaidō Honsen line as well as the Meitetsu Nagoya line. Either way, the trip takes about 30 minutes.

Hitching To hitch east from Nagoya to Tokyo, or west to Kyoto or Osaka, your best bet is the Nagoya Interchange on the Tomei Expressway. Take the subway on the Higashiyama line from Nagoya station to Hongo station (13 stops) – one stop before the terminus at Fujigaoka. The interchange is a short walk east of the station.

Boat The Taiheiyo ferry (☎ 203-0227) runs between Nagoya and Tomakomai (Hokkaidō) via Sendai. Ferries depart from Nagoya-futō pier, which is 40 minutes by bus from the Meitetsu bus station. Alternatively, take the Meijō subway south to its terminus at Nagoya-kō station.

The 2nd-class passenger fare from Nagoya to Sendai is ¥6300 and the trip takes 21 hours. There are evening departures every second day. The fare from Nagoya to Tomakomai is ¥10,200 and the full one-way trip takes about 40 hours.

GETTING AROUND
To/From the Airport Express bus services run between the airport and the Meitetsu Melsa building, 3rd floor, gate No 5 (¥870, 30 minutes, every seven minutes). Buses also leave from in front of Meitetsu Grand Hotel, across from the west exit of Nagoya station, and from the north-west exit of Hisaya-ōdōri subway station. Taxis also take around 30 minutes and cost about ¥5000.

Bus There is an extensive bus system but the subway is easier to handle for those with a limited grasp of Japanese. The main bus centre is the Meitetsu bus station, which is on the 3rd floor of the Meitetsu department store on the south side of Nagoya station.

Subway Nagoya has an excellent subway system with four lines, all clearly signposted in English and Japanese. The most useful lines for visitors are the Meijō line (purple), Higashiyama line (yellow) and the Sakura-dōri line (red). The last two run via Nagoya station. Fares range from ¥200 to ¥320 on all lines. If you plan to do a lot of travel by bus and subway, you can save money with a one-day pass (¥850), available at subway stations.

Southern Gifu-ken

The prefecture, Gifu-ken, consists almost entirely of mountains, with the exception of the plain around the city of Gifu, the prefectural capital. The two cities of interest to travellers to the south are Gifu and Inuyama, which are famed for *ukai*, or cormorant fishing, and easily visited as side trips from Nagoya.

SEKI 関
☎ 0575 • pop 68,000
Seki is renowned as an ancient swordsmithing centre. It still produces a few *katana* (Japanese swords), however, there isn't a lot of growth in the sword market so the emphasis of production has been switched to more mundane razor blades.

Swordsmithing demonstrations take place on 2 January, the first Sunday of each month from March to September, the second weekend in October and the first Sunday in November. For the latest information, contact the Seki Tourism Association (☎ 22-3131). There are several *minshuku* (family-run lodges) and ryokan around Seki and some visitors combine a stay with dinner on a boat while watching ukai (11 May to 15 October).

The Seki Festival is held on the fourth Sunday in March, and centres around a parade of elaborate floats that winds through the town.

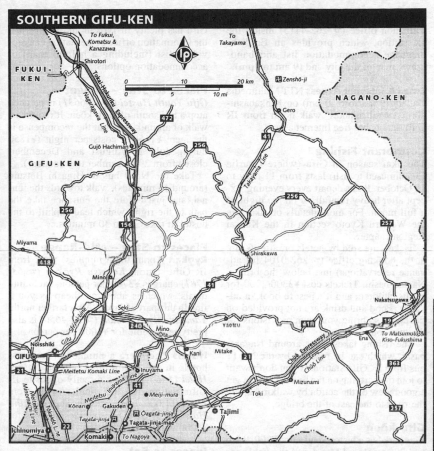

SOUTHERN GIFU-KEN

To Fukui,
Komatsu &
Kanazawa

To Takayama

FUKUI-
KEN

Shirotori

Zenshō-ji

NAGANO-KEN

Gero

GIFU-KEN

Gujō Hachiman

Miyama

Shirakawa

Mino

Nakatsugawa

Seki

Yaotsu

Mino-Ota

To Matsumoto &
Kiso-Fukushima

Noisshiki

Kani

Mitake

Ena

GIFU

Inuyama

Mizunami

CENTRAL HONSHŪ

Meiji-mura

Kōnan

Gakuden

Ōagata-jinja

Toki

Tajimi

Ichinomiya

Tagata-jinja

Tagata-jinja-mae

Komaki

To Nagoya

From Gifu, trains run on the Meitetsu
Minomachi line to Seki in 50 minutes.
Trains leave from the Eki-mae Shin-Gifu
station, which is directly across from the
main exit of the Meitetsu Shin-Gifu station.
There are also buses from Gifu to Seki that
take about 30 minutes.

GIFU 岐阜
☎ 058 ● pop 410,000
Gifu was hit by a colossal earthquake in
1891 and later given a thorough drubbing
in WWII. The city is overlooked by the
mountain, Kinka-zan, which is topped by a

postwar reconstruction of Gifu-jō. A cable
car runs from Gifu-kōen to the top of the
mountain.

Gifu is not wildly attractive from an architectural view and most tourists go there
for ukai and handicrafts.

Orientation & Information
The Meitetsu and JR stations are close to
each other in the southern part of the city.
From the main exit of the Meitetsu Shin-
Gifu station walk straight out to the main
road, turn left and follow the road as it
curves right: ahead and on your left you

will see the JR station. There's a tourist information office (☎ 262-4415) inside the JR station, which provides an English-language accommodation list and hand-drawn map of the city and (9 am to 7pm).

Email & Internet Access NTT Multimedia Gallery (9 am to 6.30 pm) on Kinkabashi-dōri, several minutes' walk north from JR Gifu station, has free Internet access.

Cormorant Fishing
The ukai season in Gifu (where Charlie Chaplin used to fish) lasts from 11 May to 15 October. Boats depart every evening, except after heavy rainfall, or on the night of a full moon. For more details on ukai see the Western Kyoto section in the Kansai Region chapter.

Tickets are sold by hotels or, after 6 pm, at the booking office (☎ 262-0104 for advance reservations) just below the bridge, Nagara-bashi. Tickets cost ¥3300/2900 for adults/children, and it's best to book in advance. Food and drink are not provided on the boats, so bring your own provisions for the two-hour boat ride.

The fishing takes place around Nagara-bashi, which can be reached by the No 11 bus from JR Gifu station. If you don't want to join the partying on the boats, you can get a good view of the action by walking along the river to the east of the bridge.

Gifu-kōen
This park has a history museum (¥300, 9 am to 4.30 pm, closed Monday) and a cable car up to the summit of Kinka-zan (¥1050 return, 9 am to 5 pm). From here you can check out Gifu-jō (¥200, 9 am to 5 pm), a small but picturesque modern reconstruction of the original castle.

Shōhō-ji
The main attraction of this orange-and-white temple is the papier-mache *daibutsu* (Great Buddha), which is nearly 14m tall and was created from about a tonne of paper sutras. Completed in 1747, the Buddha took 38 years to make. The temple is a short walk south-west of Gifu-kōen.

Places to Stay
Gifu has plenty of ryokan and hotels, and the information office at the station can provide a list (including a helpful map) of accommodation options.

Places to Stay – Budget
Gifu Youth Hostel (☎ 63-6631) is perched atop a hill south of Gifu-kōen. It requires a walk of around 2km, but the recompense is the mere ¥1650 it costs per night (¥1850 during July to August and December, closed from 29 December to 3 January).

Take the No 9 bus to Higashi Betsuin (around 15 minutes), walk towards the tunnel, and just before the entrance take the path to the right, which leads uphill to the hostel. It takes 20 to 30 minutes.

Places to Stay – Mid-Range
Ryokan About three minutes' walk from JR Gifu station, *Kogetsu Ryokan* (☎ 63-1781) charges ¥3700 per person, excluding meals, which is about as cheap as you'll find in this part of Japan. A bit farther north, *Yamaguchiya Honkan* (☎ 62-4650) is also pretty reasonable for ¥4000 per person.

Hotels There are a number of business hotels in the station area. *Grand Palace Hotel* (☎ 65-4111) is directly opposite JR Gifu station and has singles/twins from ¥6200/11,000. Just east of the station, *Miho Hotel* (☎ 64-3241) has singles/doubles for ¥5200/9000.

Places to Eat
Gifu boasts one of Central Honshū's finest soba restaurants, though it takes a little searching out. To get to *Kochōan* (☎ 232-6776), take the tram (streetcar) from in front of Shin-Gifu station bound for Ibi or Kurono, and get off at Chūsetsu. Exit through the Meitetsu department store, turn right and walk as far as Lawson's then turn right again. Kochōan (11 am to 7 pm, closed Monday) is the wooden walled building on your right. Especially recommended is the *tenzaru* – cold soba with *tempura* (¥1960), and the Niigata Koizumi *junmaishū* sake (¥800). No children allowed.

CENTRAL HONSHŪ

Shopping

Gifu is famous for its *kasa* (oiled paper parasols) and *chōchin* (paper lanterns), which are stocked in all the souvenir shops.

If you want to see a shop that not only sells but also makes kasa, you should visit Sakaida Honten (☎ 72-3865). It is open from 7 am to 5 pm but often shuts down at lunch time (closed Sunday). It's a 12-minute walk south-east of JR Gifu station.

Ozeki Shōten (☎ 63-0111) is a chōchin factory. Visitors are not permitted into the workshop, but there's a display that explains the processes of frame building, pasting and painting (9 am to 5 pm, except Sunday and holidays). Lanterns are also on sale here. Take the No 11 bus to the Meiji-kōen stop and from there it's a short walk east down the main road.

Getting There & Away

From Shin-Nagoya station, underneath the Meitetsu department store, take the Meitetsu Nagoya line (¥540, 30 minutes) to Shin-Gifu. The JR Tōkaidō line will also get you there.

INUYAMA 犬山

☎ 0568 • pop 69,000

The highlights of Inuyama are its castle and activities such as ukai and river running. The riverside setting of the castle is quite attractive, and inspired a turn-of-the-century Japanese geologist to christen the area the 'Japan Rhine'. Nearby the beautiful garden, Uraku-en, is also worth visiting for its tranquil beauty and 370-year-old teahouse. Other attractions in the area include the Western architecture of the Meiji-mura Museum and boat trips down the Kiso-gawa.

Inuyama is a pleasant enough stop-off on the way up to Takayama and the Alps, but unless you plan a late night ukai party, it can easily be a day trip from Nagoya.

Orientation & Information

The castle and the ukai area are within easy walking distance of Inuyama-yuen station, which is one stop north of the main Inuyama station. Most of the town's restaurants and shops are closer to Inuyama station. The Inuyama Sightseeing Information Centre (☎ 61-1800), on the 2nd floor of Inuyama station, has English-language pamphlets and maps, and can book accommodation.

Inuyama-jō

Dating from 1440, this is Japan's oldest castle (¥400, 9 am to 4.30 pm) and is preserved in its original state – a rarity in Japan. It is also the only privately owned castle in the country, having been in the hands of the Narusune family since 1618. From the top storey of the castle, there's a fine view across the river, the Kiso-gawa.

The castle is a 15-minute walk west of Inuyama-yuen station.

Uraku-en & Jo-an Teahouse

Uraku-en (¥1000, 9 am to 5 pm, until 4 pm from December to February) is 300m east of Inuyama-jō in a corner of the grounds of the Meitetsu Inuyama Hotel. Its Jo-an Teahouse is rated as one of the finest in Japan. It was constructed in 1618 in Kyoto by Oda Urakusai, a younger brother of Oda Nobunaga. Urakusai was a renowned tea master who founded his own tea ceremony school.

Remember to swap your shoes for the sandals provided next to the ticket window before traipsing through the garden.

Cormorant Fishing

Ukai takes place close to Inuyama-yuen station at Inuyama-bashi. The boat dock and booking office are just east of the bridge. Tickets cost ¥2800 during July and August; ¥300 less during June and September. Book your ticket in Inuyama in the morning or call ahead and reserve tickets at the dock office (☎ 61-0057) if your Japanese is up to it.

Sailings are generally at 7 pm nightly except after heavy rainfall or on the night of a full moon. The fishing season lasts from 1 June to 30 September. For details on ukai see the Western Kyoto section of the Kansai Region chapter.

Kiso-gawa Rapids Trip

Flat-bottomed wooden boats shoot the rapids on a 13km section of the Kiso-gawa.

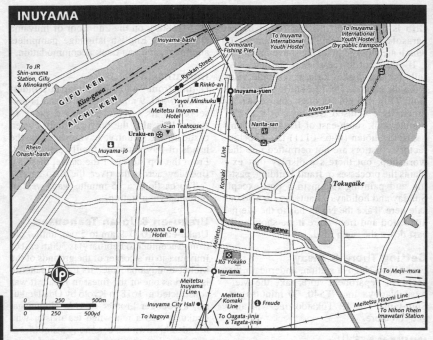

INUYAMA

The ride takes about an hour and costs ¥3400/1700 for adults/children; it entails little risk, except of a soaking. Contact Nihon Rhein Kankō (☎ 0574-28-2727).

From Inuyama station take the Meitetsu Hiromi line for the Nihon Rhein Imawatari station (¥730). From there it's a five-minute bus ride to the boat dock.

Special Events
On the Saturday and Sunday closest to 7 and 8 April, the Inuyama Matsuri takes place at the Haritsuna-jinja. This festival dates back to 1650 and features a parade of 13 three-tiered floats decked out with lanterns. Mechanical puppets perform to music on top of the floats.

Places to Stay
The cheapest option in Inuyama is *Inuyama International Youth Hostel* (☎ 61-1111), a 30-minute walk east of Inuyama-yuen station. There is no dorm accommodation, but

a comfortable single room with your own sink and toilet is only ¥3600. Western-style twin rooms are ¥6200, *tatami* rooms (rooms with tightly woven floor matting) are ¥5600. Advance booking is recommended. The hostel is closed from 28 December to 3 January. From Inuyama-yuen station, follow the river north from Inuyama-bashi to the first intersection (about 20 minutes) and turn right up the steps.

Immediately in front of Inuyama-yuen station, the friendly *Yayoi Minshuku*, also know as *Minshuku Yayoi* (☎ 61-0751), has 32 comfy tatami rooms for ¥6000 or ¥7000 per person, with two meals, and prides itself on its home cooking.

Overlooking the river, *Rinkō-an* (☎ 61-0977) is a cheery hot-spring hotel, popular with the cormorant fishing crowd. It's a little run down, though its *rotemburo* (open-air mineral spa), jacuzzi baths and local cuisine make it worth the ¥10,000 per night per person.

Getting There & Away

Inuyama is connected with Nagoya station via the Meitetsu Inuyama line (Mu tokkyū, ¥890, 23 minutes). At Shin-Unuma station, just across the river, you can connect with the JR Takayama line at the adjacent JR Unuma station. There are frequent trains to Gifu (¥320, 30 minutes) where you can connect with the Tōkaidō line.

AROUND INUYAMA
Meiji-mura Museum

In Meiji-mura (☎ 67-0314), 20 minutes by bus from Inuyama, you can see more than 60 Meiji-era buildings brought together from all over Japan (¥1600, 9.30 am to 5 pm, until 4 pm November to February). The clash of architectural styles on display, both Western and Japanese, provides a sense of that period's cultural schizophrenia. Few Meiji buildings have survived war, earthquake or rabid development; this open-air museum provides a rare chance to see what's left.

Even if you chug around on the free village locomotive or tram, you'll still need at least half a day to enjoy the place at an easy pace.

A bus departs every 20 minutes from Inuyama station for the 20-minute trip (¥380) to Meiji-mura. You can also take a one-hour bus ride from the Meitetsu bus station in Nagoya (¥1190 round trip, one hour, every 30 minutes) direct to Meiji-mura.

Ōagata-jinja 大縣神社

This shrine is dedicated to Izanami, the female Shintō deity, and draws women devotees seeking marriage or the birth of children. The precincts of the shrine contain rocks and other items resembling female genitals.

Ōagata-jinja is a 30-minute walk southeast of Gakuden station on the Meitetsu Komaki line.

The hugely popular Hime-no-Miya Grand Festival takes place on the first Sunday in March at Ōagata-jinja. Locals pray for good harvests and prosperity by parading through the streets bearing a portable shrine with replicas of female genitals.

Tagata-jinja 田県神社

This shrine is dedicated to Izanagi, the male counterpart of Izanami. The main hall of the shrine has a side building containing a collection of phalluses of all dimensions, left as offerings by grateful worshippers.

Tagata-jinja faces Route 41, five minutes' walk west of Tagata-jinja-mae station, one stop farther south of Gakuden station on the Meitetsu Komaki line.

The Tagata Hōnen Sai festival takes place on 15 March at the Tagata-jinja when the highly photogenic, 2m-long, 60kg 'sacred object' is paraded, amid much mirth, around the neighbourhood. Arrive well before the procession starts at 2 pm.

Tajimi

☎ 0572 • pop 94,000

Tajimi has a long history as a pottery centre and is famed for its *Mino-yaki* (Mino ware). It remains one of the largest porcelain-producing centres in Japan. There are two major ceramics festivals held here each year, where local producers gather to display their latest creations, and bargains are to be found. The Tajimi Tōki Festival is held on the second weekend of April, while the Tajimi Minoyaki Danchi Festival is held in late September or early October (the exact date changes each year).

Close to Tajimi station (just over 1km to the east) is the **Prefectural Porcelain Museum** (¥200, 9 am to 4.30 pm, closed Monday). The Gifu Togei Shiryōkan (☎ 23-1191), three minutes' walk from Higashimachi bus stop, allows you to create your own ceramic masterpiece for ¥1300. Reservations are needed, and your finished item can be shipped abroad.

Tajimi is not far to the east of Meiji-mura, but unless you have your own transport it is most easily reached from Nagoya on the JR Chūō line (¥740, 40 minutes).

GUJŌ HACHIMAN 郡上八幡

☎ 0575 • pop 21,024

The main claim to fame of this town is its Gujō Odori Folk Dance Matsuri, held from early July to early September when the townsfolk continue nearly four centuries of tradition and let their hair down for some frenzied dancing. During the four main days of the festival (from 13 to 16 August) the dancing goes on through the night.

The town's other main attraction is Gujō Hachiman-jō (¥300, 9 am to 4.30 pm, 8 am to 6 pm from June to August), built some 400 years ago. However, the castle's historical integrity has been somewhat compromised by the relatively late addition (in 1933) of the donjon. Apparently locals felt their neighbourhood fortress needed the multistorey parapet in order to compete with the likes of Inuyama and Nagoya castles. From the train station, take a bus to the Honchō bus station. The castle lies another 25 minutes by foot to the north-east.

If you decide to stay overnight in Gujō Hachiman, your cheapest choice is probably *Hachiman Cycling Terminal* (☎ 62-2139), a municipal minshuku that doubles as a bicycle rental outlet. A room and two meals costs ¥5800. The only drawback is that it's around 5km out of town. From the train station, catch a bus to the Honchō bus station, and then get on the Meihō bus to the Chuō-bashi. From there it's a three-minute walk. If you want to stay in town, *Bizenya Ryokan* (☎ 65-2068) is 10 minutes' walk from the train station along the main road (¥10,000, with two meals).

From Gifu, take a train to Mino Ōta (JR Takayama line, then the private Nagaragawa line, ¥1680, 90 minutes).

GERO 下呂
☎ 0576 • 15,178

Gero is favoured by Japanese tourists for its *onsen* (mineral hot-spring spa), despite the fact that its name in Japanese is unfortunately a homonym for 'vomit'. The town's sprawl of concrete buildings dampens its appeal, but the waters, reputedly beneficial for rheumatism, athletic injuries and the complexion, are excellent. The town is fairly compact, making it easy to walk around and go hot-spring hopping.

Apart from its numerous spas, including several communal open-air ones, Gero boasts its own hot-spring temple – Onsen-ji – overlooking the town. Some travellers rave about the Takehara Bunraku performances held at Gero Gasshō Village Folklore Museum (¥800, 8.15 am to 5 pm). The puppets are operated by one man, and one or two performances are held daily four to five days a week. Other minor attractions include the Mine-ichigo Relics Park and Zenshō-ji, which is next to the station of the same name, one stop north of Gero.

The Gero Onsen Matsuri (Gero Hot Spring Festival) from 1 to 3 August is a lively one. On 1 August, men clad in *fundoshi* (loincloth) and toting fireworks perform a dance to Ryūjin, the Dragon God. The following day sees a parade of *geisha*, and Gero Odori dancing.

Places to Stay
There are numerous ryokan and minshuku in this resort town. For more options (there are dozens) check with the Gero tourist information office (☎ 0120-310-561), at the west exit of the train station. One of the cheapest spots is *Katsuragawa Minshuku* (☎ 25-2615). Unfortunately there are only six rooms, so it's best to call ahead (singles/twins ¥4500/7000). Katsuragawa is across the river and several blocks north of the train station. On the train side of the river, 15 minutes' walk north-west of the station, *Miyanoya Minshuku* (☎ 25-2399) offers rooms, with two meals (singles ¥6500). Both hotels have baths with onsen water piped directly in. If you're looking for a more upscale place to stay, *Ogawaya Ryokan* (☎ 25-3121) has both an outside onsen bath and a 25m indoor bathing pool! All rooms face out onto the river (¥17,000 per person, with two meals).

Getting There & Away
To get to Gero, take a JR Takayama line train from Gifu station (Hida tokkyū, ¥3280, 67 minutes) or from Nagoya (Hida tokkyū, ¥4500, 1½ hours).

Northern Gifu-ken

The major attractions of the mountainous Gifu-ken region lie to the north in the Hida District, which is part of the Japan Alps.

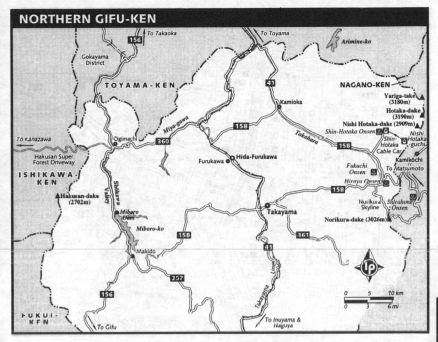

NORTHERN GIFU-KEN

Takayama, the administrative centre of Hida, retains much of its original architecture and small-scale charm. From Takayama, you can make side trips to the spectacular mountain regions around Kamikōchi to the east (where there are numerous hot-spring resorts and excellent scope for short walks or long hikes) or you can visit the Shōkawa Valley for a look at rural life and architecture in remote farming villages to the west. If you go east from Takayama you can cross the Japan Alps to Matsumoto and Nagano, and if you head west, you can continue to Kanazawa.

Access to the remoter parts of Hida is restricted by severe weather conditions that often last from November to mid-May. If you plan to visit during winter, it's best to first check conditions with Japan Travel-Phone (☎ 0120-44-4800 toll free) or the Takayama tourist information office.

More details about the Japan Alps region can be found in the Nagano-ken section later in this chapter.

TAKAYAMA 高山
☎ 0577 • pop 66,000

Takayama lies in the ancient Hida District tucked away between the mountains of the Japan Alps, and should be a high priority on any visit to Central Honshu and the Japan Alps. Give yourself two days to enjoy the place and add a few more if you plan to use it as a base to visit the mountains.

Takayama, with its traditional inns, shops and *sake* breweries, is a rarity – a Japanese city (admittedly a small one) that has managed to retain something of its traditional charm. It's a small place, easily tackled on foot or by bicycle, and a good town to take a break from the more urgent rhythms of larger urban centres.

Historically, the inhabitants of Takayama have been known for their woodworking skills: Hida *takumi* carpenters were drafted to construct imperial palaces and temples in the Kyoto and Nara regions. The woodworking tradition continues to

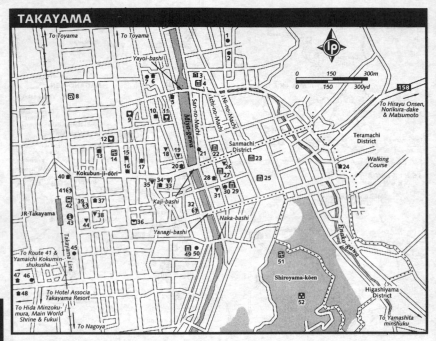

TAKAYAMA

this day with the production of furniture and woodcarvings.

Takayama entered history proper in the late 16th century, when it was established as the castle town of the Kanamori family. The present layout of the town dates from this period.

The Takayama festival (Sannō Matsuri) held in April (see Special Events in this section), is rated as one of the three great festivals in Japan and attracts over half a million spectators. If you plan to go to the festival and want to stay in Takayama, book your accommodation well in advance, or plan to travel in from a nearby town such as Gero. A smaller version (Hachiman Matsuri) is held in October.

Takayama makes a good base for trips into the mountains (Kamikōchi, Hirayu Onsen, Shin-Hotaka or Norikura) or to Shōkawa Valley with its traditional farmhouses.

Sights in town include more than a dozen museums, galleries, collections and

exhibitions. Collections range from wild birds, toys and lion masks to folkcraft and archaeology.

Orientation

All the main sights, except Hida Minzoku-mura (Hida Folk Village), are in the centre of town, a short walk from the station. The streets are arranged in a grid pattern, similar to Kyoto or Nara, and this makes it easy to find your way around. From the centre, you can continue east for 10 minutes along Kokubun-ji-dōri, which is the main street, until you reach Teramachi, the temple district, and Shiroyama-kōen in the Higashiyama (Eastern Mountain) District.

Hida Minzoku-mura is a 10-minute bus ride west of the station.

Information

The Hida tourist information office (☎ 32-5328), directly in front of JR Takayama station, has English-language maps and

CENTRAL HONSHŪ

TAKAYAMA

PLACES TO STAY

5 Sumiyoshi Ryokan
   寿美よし旅館
6 Murasaki Ryokan
   むらさき旅館
10 Takayama City Hotel
   Four Seasons
   高山シティホテル
   フォーシーズン
13 Takayama Central Hotel
   高山セントラルホテル
15 Minshuku Kuwataniya
   民宿桑谷屋
17 Rickshaw Inn
   力車イン
20 Hotel Alpha One
   ホテルアルファワン
24 Hida Takayama
   Tenshō-ji
   Youth Hostel
   飛騨高山天照寺
   ユースホステル
28 Ryokan Gōto
   旅館河渡
34 Ryokan Seiryū
   旅館青龍
37 Best Western Hotel
   ベストウェスタンホテル
40 New Alps Hotel
   ニューアルプスホテル
47 Sōsuke
   惣助
48 Takayama Green Hotel
   高山グリーンホテル

PLACES TO EAT

18 Tom's Bellgins Bell
19 Rengaya
   れんが屋

26 Ebisu
   恵比寿本店
31 Noguchiya Tofu
   Restaurant
   豆腐料理のぐちや
33 Murasaki
   村さ来
35 Suzuya
   すずや
38 Yamamotoya
   やまもとや生そば
44 Myōgaya
   みょうがや

OTHER

1 Festival Floats
   Exhibition Hall
   (Takayama Yatai Kaikan)
   高山屋台会館
2 Lion Mask Exhibition Hall
   獅子会館
3 Yoshijima-ke
   吉島家住宅
4 Kusakabe Folk Art
   Museum
   日下部民芸館
7 Lacquerware Exhibition
   Hall
   春慶会館
8 Takayama Municipal
   Office
   高山市役所
9 Red Hill Pub
11 Tonio Pub
12 Bagus
14 Hida Kokubun-ji
   飛騨国分寺
16 Hara Cycle
   ハラサイクル

21 Miya-gawa Market
   宮川朝市
22 Hachiga Art Gallery
   八賀民俗美術館
23 Oita Wild Bird
   Museum
   老田野鳥館
25 Takayama Museum
   of Local History
   高山市郷土館
27 Fujii Folkcraft
   Art Gallery
   藤井美術民芸館
29 Hirata Folk Art Museum
   平田記念館
30 Matsuoka
   まつおか
32 Hokuriku Bank
   北陸銀行
36 Takayama Post Office
   高山郵便局
39 Jūroku Bank
   十六銀行
41 Gifu Bank (Shunkei
   Kaikan)
   岐阜銀行
42 Takayama Bus Station
   高山バスターミナル
43 Tourist Information Office
   観光案内所
45 Eki Rent-a-Car System
46 Nippon Rent-a-Car
49 Takayama-jinya
   高山陣屋
50 Jinya-mae Market
   陣屋前朝市
51 Shōren-ji
   照蓮寺
52 Takayama-jō Ruins
   高山城跡

information on sights and accommodation (8.30 am to 5 pm, until 6 pm 1 April to 31 October). Also very helpful is the Japan National Tourist Organization (JNTO) pamphlet *Takayama and Shirakawago*, though the office doesn't always have it in stock. The office has English-language bus schedules for services between Takayama and Hirayu Onsen, Shin-Hotaka Onsen, Kamikōchi and Shōkawa Valley.

Those interested in Takayama festivals should ask for the booklets, *Background of Takayama Festival* and *Hida Festival Guide*, which cover local festivals.

If you want to arrange a home visit or home stay, or would like to arrange for a volunteer interpreter for non-Japanese languages (or even sign language), contact the International Affairs Office (☎ 32-3333, ext 2407) one month in advance.

Money There are no international card ATMs in Takayama. The Jūroku, Gifu and Hokuriku banks will advance money on US-issued credit cards only.

Email & Internet Access The Internet is available free of charge at Takayama Municipal Office (9 am to 5 pm weekdays), five minutes' walk north of the station. You can also get on line at Kokumin-shukusha Yamaichi (see Places to Stay later in this section) for ¥500 per hour.

Walking Tour
From the station, you can complete a circular walking tour of the main sights in an hour. A walking tour of the Higashiyama

District that passes through Teramachi and Shiroyama-kōen is also highly recommended. This walk takes about two hours, and includes nearly a dozen temples and shrines. It is particularly enjoyable in the early morning or late afternoon.

Takayama-jinya
Originally built in 1615 as the administrative centre for the Kanamori clan, Takayama-jinya (Historical Government House) is worth visiting to see how the authorities governed at that time (¥420, 8.45 am to 4.30 pm, until 5 pm April to October). The present buildings are reconstructions dating from 1816.

As well as government offices, a rice granary and a garden, there's a torture chamber with explanatory detail. Guided tours in English take place every 45 minutes.

Sanmachi Suji
This area is the centre of the old town, and consists of three streets (Ichi-no-Machi, Ni-no-Machi and San-no-Machi) lined with traditional shops, breweries, restaurants, museums and some private homes. The sake breweries are easily recognised by the round baskets of cedar fronds hanging above the entrances. The best plan is to stroll around without trying to see everything and thus avoid risking an overdose of museums.

Fujii Folkcraft Art Gallery This gallery (¥400, 9 am to 5 pm) is close to the archaeology museum and displays folkcraft from Japan, China and Korea. It's in an old merchant's house.

Hirata Folk Art Museum Hirata Folk Art Museum (¥300, 9 am to 5 pm) is a merchant's house dating from the turn of the century. The displays include items from everyday rural Japanese life. It's worth a look.

Takayama Museum of Local History
This museum (¥300, 8.30 am to 5 pm, closed on Monday except during summer) is devoted to the crafts and traditions of the region. Pride of place is allotted to images carved by

---

Hida's Gasshō-Zukuri

Winter in the Hida region can get quite fierce, and inhabitants faced snow and cold long before the advent of propane heaters and 4WD vehicles. One of the most visible symbols of that adaptability is *gasshō-zukuri* architecture, seen in the steeply slanted straw-roofed homes that still dot the landscape around Takayama and the Shōkawa Valley.

The sharply angled roofs were designed to prevent heavy snow accumulation, a serious concern in a region where nearly all mountain roads close from December to April. The name *gasshō* comes from the Japanese word for 'praying', because the shape of the roofs was thought to resemble two hands clasped in prayer. Gasshō buildings often featured pillars crafted from stout cedar trees to lend extra support.

The gasshō-zukuri building has become an endangered species, with most examples having been gathered together and preserved in folk villages. This sometimes means that two homes that are now neighbours were once separated by several days or weeks of travel on foot or sled. But local authorities have worked hard to recreate their natural surroundings, making it possible to imagine what life in the Hida hills might have looked like hundreds of years ago.

Enshū, a woodcarving priest who wandered around the region in the 17th century.

Kusakabe Mingeikan

This folk-art museum (¥500, 8.30 am to 5 pm), to the north of Sanmachi Suji, is a fine example of a wealthy merchant's home, with the living quarters in one section and the warehouse in another. It is fitted out as it would have been if you'd walked in to talk business in the late 1890s.

Yoshijima-ke

This merchant's house (¥500, 9 am to 5 pm) is on the same street as the Kusakabe Folk Art Museum (Kusakabe Mingeikan). It has more refined architectural details than the latter, such as lattice windows that provide a lighter atmosphere.

Lacquerware Exhibition Hall

The Lacquerware Exhibition Hall (Shunkei Kaikan; ☎ 32-3373) is north-east of the station, a couple of blocks before Yayoi-bashi (¥300, 8 am to 5.30 pm). It features more than 1000 lacquerware items are on display, with an exhibit showing production techniques.

Festival Floats Exhibition Hall

Four *yatai*, or festival floats, are displayed at the Takayama Yatai Kaikan (Festival Floats Exhibition Hall). The hall (¥800, including a glossy leaflet, 8 am to 5 pm) is owned by the neighbouring shrine, Sakurayama Hachiman-gū, and is far more respectful of the religious significance of the festival than the much-publicised tourist trap Hida Takayama Matsuri no Mori, which is nothing more than a sterile, flashy theme park.

The yatai, some of which date from the 17th century, are spectacular creations with flamboyant carvings, metalwork and lacquerwork. A famous feature of the floats is the marionettes, manipulated by eight accomplished puppeteers using 36 strings, which perform amazing tricks and acrobatics.

Lion Mask Exhibition Hall

Just below the Yatai Kaikan is the Lion Mask Exhibition Hall (Shishi Kaikan). It has a display of over 800 lion masks and musical instruments connected with the lion dances that are commonly performed at festivals in central and northern Japan. There are also twice-hourly displays of ancient mechanical puppets – a good chance for a close-up view of these marvellous gadgets in action (¥600, including the mechanical puppet show, 8.30 am to 5.30 pm).

Hida Kokubun-ji

The original temple (¥300, 9 am to 4 pm) was built in the 8th century, but the oldest of the present buildings at this site dates from the 16th century. The old gingko tree beside the three-storey pagoda is impressively gnarled and in remarkably good shape, considering it's believed to be 1200 years old.

Teramachi & Shiroyama-kōen

The best way to link these two areas in the east side of town is to follow the walking trail. Teramachi has over a dozen temples (the youth hostel is in Tenshō-ji) and shrines that you can wander around at your leisure before continuing to the lush greenery of the park. Various trails lead through the park and up the mountainside to the ruins of Takayama-jō. As you descend, you can take a look at the temple, Shōren-ji (¥200), which was transferred to this site from the Shōkawa Valley when a dam was built there in 1960.

From the temple it's a 10-minute walk back to the centre of town.

Hida Minzoku-mura

This folk village (¥700, 8.30 am to 5 pm) is a large open-air museum with dozens of traditional houses that once belonged to craftspeople and farmers in the Takayama region. The houses were dismantled at their original sites and rebuilt here. You should definitely include this museum in your visit.

The eastern and western sections of the village are connected part of the way by a pleasant walk through fields. Allow at least three hours if you want to explore the village on foot at a leisurely pace. On a fine day, there are good views across the town to the peaks of the Japan Alps.

CENTRAL HONSHŪ

The western section, called Hida-no-Sato, has a village of 12 traditional, old houses and a complex of five traditional buildings with artisans demonstrating folk arts and crafts. It takes about two hours, at a leisurely pace, to follow the circular route. The displays are well presented and offer an excellent chance to see what rural life was like in previous centuries.

The eastern section of the village is centred around the Hida Minzokukan (Hida Folklore Museum) at the Minzokukan-mae bus stop. There are four buildings in the museum complex: Wakayama House, Nokubi House, Go-kura Storehouse (used for storage of rice as payment of taxes) and the Museum of Mountain Life.

To walk from the western to the eastern section, take the road downhill and keep an eye out for the wooden sign directing you onto the path to the Minzokukan. The path winds past several fields and ends up at the Museum of Mountain Life.

Hida Minzoku-mura is a 30-minute walk from Takayama station, but the route through the urban sprawl is not enjoyable. Either hire a bicycle in town, or take the Hida-no-Sato bus (¥250, 10 minutes) from gate 2 at the bus station. A discount ticket 'Hida-no-Sato setto ken' is available, combining both the round-trip fare and admission to the park for ¥900, a saving of ¥300. The last bus back from the park leaves the Minzokukan-mae stop at 3.26 pm.

Hida Takayama Teddy Bear Eco-Village

Travellers with children will want to stop off at this quirky museum (¥600, children ¥400, young children free, 10 am to 8 pm, except for irregular holidays in January and February), which uses the furry exhibits to introduce its environmentalist message. Adults too may be impressed by the artwork, especially German artist Dagmar Strunk's garbage dragon. The eco-village is in front of the Hida-no-Sato-shita bus stop.

Main World Shrine

Dominating Takayama's western skyline is the golden roof of Mahikari-kyō's Main

World Shrine. Opinion is divided on whether the New Religion believers are harmless loop-the-loops or anti-Semitic doomsday cultists. A guided tour around the Main World Shrine might allow you to decide for yourself. Try to pick up some of its literature en route – one book contains passionate testimonies from foreign believers, including one letter from a believer in Darwin, Australia whose faith in the energy/light enables him to cure power cuts.

Shopping

Markets The *asa-ichi* (morning markets) take place every morning from 7 to 11 am, starting an hour earlier from April to October. The Jinya-mae Market is a small one in front of Takayama-jinya; the Miya-gawa Market is larger, strung out along the east bank of the Miya-gawa, between Kaji-bashi and Yayoi-bashi. Those in need of an early morning coffee can stop for a steaming cup (¥200) at a stand-up stall in the middle of this market. The markets provide a pleasant way to start the day, with a stroll past gnarled farmers at their vegetable stands and stalls selling herbs, pickles and souvenirs.

Special Events

Sannō Matsuri takes place on 14 and 15 April. The starting point for the festival parade is Hie-jinja. A dozen yatai, decorated with carvings, dolls, colourful curtains and blinds, are drawn through the town. In the evening the floats are decked out with lanterns and the procession is accompanied by sacred music.

Hachiman Matsuri, which takes place on 9 and 10 October, is a slightly smaller version of Sannō Matsuri and starts off at the Sakurayama Hachiman-gū. If you plan to stay in Takayama for either of these festivals, you must book months in advance and expect to pay up to 20% more for accommodation than you would at any other time. Alternatively, you could stay elsewhere in the region and commute to Takayama for the festivals.

Places to Stay

The tourist information office outside Takayama station can help with reservations either in Takayama or elsewhere in the region, and has lists of places to suit all budgets.

Places to Stay – Budget

Hostels *Hida Takayama Tenshō-ji Youth Hostel (☎ 32-6345)* is a temple in the pleasant surroundings of Teramachi, but hostellers should be prepared to stick to a rigid routine. At 10 pm precisely you are lulled to sleep by music and at 7 am you are awakened by the recorded twittering of birds. Dorm beds cost ¥3000, and the hostel is a 25-minute walk across town from the train station. To shave 20 minutes off the walk, board the bus for Shin Hotaka and get off at the Betsuin-mae stop. The youth hostel is a five-minute walk east.

Minshuku On the outskirts of town, with free pick-up (or a 50% contribution to the taxi fare from the station), is *Kokumin-shukusha* (government-run minshuku) *Ya-maichi (☎ 34-6201)*. Room-only rates start at ¥3800. The building is old, but the owners are friendly and Internet access is available.

Places to Stay – Mid-Range

Ryokan Up in the north-east section of town, next to the Lacquerware Exhibition Hall, is the flower-festooned *Murasaki Ryokan (☎ 32-1724)*, which has rooms for ¥4000 per person, without meals. Take a moment to admire the dazzling wall of flowers (200 pots' worth) along the front of the building, the product of 15 years' work.

Minshuku Without doubt one of the most pleasant places to stay is *Rickshaw Inn (☎ 32-2890)*, a modern-style minshuku with almost a South-East-Asian look to it. The owners speak English and are very friendly, and the room rates are good value for money. A bed in one of the comfortable three- or four-bed dorm rooms costs ¥3200, while Japanese-style rooms with attached bath are ¥4900 per person. Singles are available for ¥4200, ¥6000 with attached bath. The inn also has excellent English-language information.

Close to the train station is *Minshuku Kuwataniya (☎ 32-5021)*, by far Takayama's

longest-running minshuku (70 years). Per-person costs are from ¥7000, which includes two meals, with dinner always featuring the famed Hida beef.

Hachibei (☎ 33-0573) is a pleasantly faded, rambling place close to Hida-no-Sato village. Take a bus to the Hida-no-Sato bus stop; from there it's an eight-minute walk north. Prices start at ¥7000 per person and include two meals. Also on the western side of town, closer to the train station, is *Sosuke (☎ 32-0818)*, where you can get a room for ¥4500 per person. The owners are friendly and the building is pleasantly traditional, though it is next to a busy main road.

If you don't mind the outskirts of town, *Yamashita (☎ 33-0686)* is a farmhouse-style minshuku in Enakomachi, about 10 minutes by car south of the city centre. Rooms are ¥7000 per person, including breakfast and a wonderful evening meal around the traditional *irori*, or fireplace. The owner will pick you up from the station.

Hotels *New Alps Hotel (☎ 32-2888)* is just a minute's walk from the station. Singles/doubles start at ¥5000/10,000, which is good value. The recently built, American-owned, *Best Western Hotel (☎ 37-2000)* is equally convenient, and its comfortable rooms start at ¥6500.

Over by the river, *Hotel Alpha One (☎ 32-2211;* the Greek character for 'alpha' and the numeral '1' are on the sign outside) is another reasonably inexpensive place, with singles from ¥5100 and twins/doubles for ¥11,800/10800. Just a 10-minute walk from the station, *Takayama Central Hotel (☎ 35-1881)* has singles for ¥5500 and twins from ¥11,000.

Takayama City Hotel Four Seasons (☎ 36-0088) has singles/twins from ¥6800/13,052, and *Takayama Green Hotel (☎ 33-5500)* has twins and doubles from ¥18,000.

Places to Stay – Top End

Ryokan Most of Takayama's ryokan cost between ¥8000 and ¥15,000 per person including two meals, and in some cases you may need some Japanese before the proprietors will take you.

Sumiyoshi Ryokan (☎ 32-0228), a delightfully traditional place, has rooms from ¥8000 to ¥13,000. Straight ahead (east) from the station and just over the river is the *Ryokan Gōto* (☎ 33-0870), another traditional inn, with rates from ¥10,500. The architecturally modern *Ryokan Seiryu* (☎ 32-0448) is close to the town centre. Prices start at ¥10,000 per person including two meals.

Hotels Several kilometres south of town lies the luxurious *Hotel Associa Takayama Resort* (☎ 36-0001). All rooms here boast views of the Japan Alps, and the hotel has both indoor and outdoor hot-spring baths and a tennis court. Rates start at ¥15,000 per person and climb quickly from there. A free shuttle bus runs hourly between Takayama station and the hotel.

Places to Eat
Takayama is known for several culinary treats. These include *hida-soba* (buckwheat noodles with broth and vegetables), *hoba-miso* (miso paste cooked on a *hoba* leaf, often served with beef or vegetables) and *sansai* (mountain vegetables). You might also want to try *mitarashi-dango* (skewers of grilled rice balls seasoned with soy sauce) or *shio-sembei* (salty rice crackers). Hida beef, though relatively new on the culinary scene, is considered to be among the finest grades of meat in Japan.

Close to Takayama station is a *Yamamo-toya*, one of many little soba places along the street where you can try Hida soba. The restaurant also serves tempura and *katsudon* (fried pork chops over rice) sets from around ¥800.

Most restaurants, especially in the Sanmachi Suji, close quite early, between 7 and 9 pm. If you can't manage an earlier dinner, your best bet is to try the restaurants and izakaya closer to the train station.

Suzuya (☎ 32-2484) is a well-known restaurant with rustic decor in the centre of town, on the station side of the river (11 am to 7.30 pm, closed Tuesday). It serves all the local specialities and its teishoku lunches are good value – prices start from

around ¥1000. To help you order, there's also an English menu.

For a bite of history, try *Ebisu*, a little soba restaurant in the Sanmachi Suji that has been in business for 370 years. There is no English menu. The sansai soba is particularly good. Tofu fans will appreciate nearby *Noguchiya Tofu Restaurant*. Set lunches range from ¥700 to ¥1500, featuring numerous tasty varieties of hot and cold tofu dishes, and there's a picture menu to help with the ordering ordeal. The restaurant closes at 5 pm.

Murasaki, part of an izakaya chain, has a great atmosphere, reasonable food and drink prices and an illustrated menu for easy ordering. There's no English sign: look out for the large red sign hanging on the right side of the street.

Rengaya (☎ 36-1339) next to Hotel Alpha One, is a Western-style izakaya seemingly staffed by off-duty schoolgirls (5.30 pm to 11 pm). It has some good local beer, or *ji-bīru*, on tap, and the English menu boasts the enticing 'vorious simmered delicacies'.

One block east of the station, *Myōgaya* (☎ 32-0426) is a restaurant specialising in organic and vegetarian dishes. There is an English menu (11.30 am to 2 pm, 5 pm to 7.30 pm).

Takayama's finest bagels are to be found at the pleasantly relaxing *Little Bear Cafe* (☎ 37-2525). It is open from 10 am to 8 pm and is alongside the Teddy Bear Eco-Village.

For a complete change, you could try *Tom's Bellgins Bell* (☎ 33-6507), a couple of blocks north-west of Kaji-bashi. Its amiable Swiss owner, Tom Steinmann, fulfils all those cravings for fondue and sausages. His pizzas are excellent, and prices start at around ¥1500.

Entertainment
Pubs & Bars If you're looking for a friendly place to knock back a few cold beers, *Red Hill Pub* (☎ 33-8139) has an excellent selection of domestic and imported brews (7 pm to 12 am, closed Monday). It's a pretty popular spot with locals, and tends

to get crowded after 11 pm, so go a bit earlier if you want a seat. **Tonio Pub** is an English-style place closer to the river with Guinness on tap and reasonable prices – as far as Japanese bars go, that is.

Bagus (☎ 36-4341) is a friendly, youthful reggae bar between the station and Takayama Municipal Office. Its managers, Tsubo and Chako, are excellent sources of local information (7 pm to 2 am, closed Sunday).

Bunched around the old part of town are eight sake breweries with pedigrees dating back to the Edo period. Formerly, the production processes for this *jizake* (local sake) were closed to visitors, but the breweries have recently started to arrange tours and tastings from early January to the end of February only. The information office at the station can arrange for prospective foreign imbibers to join these tours.

Shopping

Takayama is renowned for several crafts. *Ichii ittobori* (woodcarvings) are fashioned from yew and can be seen as intricate components of the yatai floats or for sale as figurine souvenirs. The craft of Shunkei lacquerware was introduced from Kyoto several centuries ago and is used to produce boxes, trays and flower containers. Pottery is produced in three styles ranging from the rustic Yamada-yaki to the decorative ceramics of Shibukusa-yaki. If your house feels empty, local makers of traditional furniture can help you fill it.

The Sanmachi Suji area has many shops selling handicraft items, or you can browse in handicraft shops along the section of Kokubun-ji-dōri between the river and the station.

At Matsuoka (☎ 32-3293), Itae Matsuoka paints beautiful *ema* (horse paintings) that bring good fortune, in her small shop-cum-gallery. The shop is open from 9.30 am to 5 pm (irregular holidays).

The Lacquerware Exhibition Hall (see earlier in this section), which is run by the city, has two adjacent shops with outstanding lacquerware and porcelain, and prices are generally lower than those you'll find in private shops.

Like Takayama's restaurants, many of the shops close in the early evening, usually around 7 to 8 pm.

Getting There & Away

Bus Many roads in this region close in the winter, which means that bus schedules usually only start from early May and finish in late October. For exact dates either phone Japan Travel-Phone (☎ 0120-44-4800 toll free) or check with the tourist offices.

Although Takayama is well situated for day trips to the Shōkawa Valley region and northern Alps resorts such as Hirayu and Shin-Hotaka, only an hour or two away, bus fares are surprisingly expensive. For example, a journey up to Shin-Hotaka and back costs more than ¥4000. Thus the Furī Jōshaken (Free Pass; ¥3800) that allows you unlimited travel for two days on local buses is a good buy. If there are three or four of you, it may be cheaper to hire a car for a day or two (see the Car entry in the following Getting Around section).

A bus service connects Takayama with Hirayu Onsen (¥1530, one hour) and takes another hour (and another ¥1530) to reach Kamikōchi. Direct buses run from Takayama via Hirayu Onsen to Shin-Hotaka Onsen (¥2070) and the nearby cable car (or 'ropeway'). A direct bus runs between Fukuchi Onsen and Takayama (¥1760, one hour and 20 minutes).

Another bus route runs on the spectacular Norikura Skyline Road connecting Norikura with Takayama in 1¾ hours.

A bus/train combination runs from Takayama via Kamikōchi to Matsumoto. Take a bus from Takayama to Kamikōchi then change to another bus bound for Shin-Shimashima station on the Matsumoto Dentetsu line and continue by rail to Matsumoto. For more details see the Kamikōchi section later in this chapter.

Keiō Highway Buses (☎ 32-1688) connects Takayama and Shinjuku (¥6500, 5½ hours, twice daily, reservations needed).

Train Takayama is connected with Nagoya on the JR Takayama line (Hida tokkyū, ¥5870, 2½ hours, 10 daily).

CENTRAL HONSHŪ

Express trains run from Osaka (five hours) and Kyoto (4½ hours) via Gifu or Nagoya and continue on the JR Takayama line to Takayama. If you are travelling on a rail pass, the best course of action would be to take a shinkansen to Nagoya and change there to the Takayama line.

Toyama is connected with Takayama on the JR Takayama line (tokkyū, ¥3280, around 1½ hours, six daily).

Getting Around

With the exception of Hida Folk Village, the sights in Takayama can be covered easily on foot. You can amble from the station across to Higashiyama in 25 minutes.

Bus The bus station is on your left as you exit the station. Although the main sights in town are best seen on foot or by bicycle, the walk to Hida Folk Village is tedious and unattractive. It's preferable to use the bus service (¥250, 10 minutes, half-hourly).

Car Eki Rent-a-Car System, run by JR, has an office at Takayama station (☎ 33-3522), and there's a branch of Nippon Rent-a-Car (☎ 34-5121), west of the train station, near the Takayama Green Hotel and Sosuke minshuku.

Cycling Takayama is a good place to explore by bicycle. Hara Cycle (☎ 32-1657) on Kokubunji-dōri has the best bikes, for ¥300 per hour, ¥1300 for all day (8.30 am to 7.30 pm). The outlets near the station have similar rates, but the cheapest is the youth hostel with rental for ¥80 per hour or ¥600 per day, for hostel guests only.

FURUKAWA 古川
☎ 0577 • pop 16,507

Furukawa, on the route between Takayama and Toyama, was originally a castle town. It's a pleasant place to visit, particularly if you like strolling around areas with white *kura* (mud-walled storehouses), old residences and shops. The main draw for Furukawa are two festivals. If you want to attend, you should stay in Furukawa and reserve your accommodation well in advance.

Information

Information can be obtained at the station, but you may find it easier to use the tourist information office in Takayama, which can also provide maps and leaflets and arrange reservations.

Special Events

The Furukawa Matsuri, on 19 and 20 April, attracts large crowds. Its highlight is the Okoshi Daiko when squads of boisterous young men, dressed in loincloths parade through town at midnight, competing to place small drums atop a stage bearing a giant drum. The event is also called the Hadaka Matsuri (Naked Festival). There are also processions with large yatai similar to those used in the Takayama festivals.

The unusual Kitsune Hi Matsuri (Fox Fire Festival) on 16 October is a more low-key event. Locals make up as foxes, parade through the town by lantern-light, and enact a wedding ceremony at the shrine, Okura Inari-jinja. The ceremony is deemed to bring good fortune, and climaxes with a bonfire at the shrine.

Places to Stay

Hida Furukawa Youth Hostel (☎ 75-2979) is about 3km west of Hida Furukawa station (40 minutes on foot), or 1.2km (15 minutes' walk) west of Hida Hosoe station (two stops north of Hida-Furukawa). Ask for Shinrin-kōen, which is a park next to the hostel. Members are charged members ¥4600 (with two meals), nonmembers pay an extra ¥1000, and the 22-bed hostel is closed from 30 March to 10 April. Bicycles are available for hire.

Ryokan Tanbo-no-Yu (☎ 73-2014) is a straightforward ryokan. Expect to pay ¥7000 per person, with two meals. No English is spoken. Turn right from the station, then take the third left, the first right and look out for the nondescript tan-coloured building with a sign outside on the corner as the road turns to the right.

Shopping

Furukawa is famous for handmade candles. In the centre of town, you can visit

Mishima-ya, a shop that has specialised in traditional candle-making techniques for over two centuries.

Getting There & Away

Hida-Furukawa station is three stops north of Takayama on the JR Takayama line. The trip from Takayama takes 15 minutes. There are also hourly buses from Takayama station to Hida-Furukawa station (30 minutes).

Getting Around

Furukawa is small enough to stroll around, but if you want to see the surrounding countryside (or if you want a quick trip to the youth hostel) you can rent bicycles at the train station for ¥500 for four hours or ¥1000 for the whole day.

SHŌKAWA VALLEY REGION 庄川

This is highly recommended as a side trip from Takayama or as a short stopover en route between Takayama and Kanazawa. Although much of what you see here has been specially preserved for, and supported by, tourism, it still presents a view of rural life found in few other parts of Japan. If you don't like large contingents of tourists, avoid the peak times of May, August and October. Expect snow, and lots of it, between late December and late March.

In the 12th century, the remoteness and inaccessibility of this area is claimed to have attracted a few stragglers from the Taira clan. They sought hideaways here and on Kyūshū after they were virtually wiped out by the Genji clan in a brutal battle at Shimonoseki in 1185.

In the 20th century, construction of the gigantic Miboro Dam in the 1960s submerged many of the villages. The attention this attracted to the region also drew tourists interested in the unusual A-frame architecture of the remaining villages and their remote mountain surroundings. Shirakawa-gō and Gokayama are two districts with dozens of specially preserved houses and are the most commonly visited by travellers. In 1995, Unesco declared three of them, Ogimachi, Suganuma and Ainokura, World Heritage sites.

Bus services to and around Shōkawa Valley are infrequent, so it's important to check the schedule before heading out from Takayama. Exact times change from season to season, but there are generally only two buses daily to Ogimachi. Buses from there to Gokayama are similarly limited. Bus fares are also quite expensive, so if there are several of you interested in a day trip, you may want to consider renting a car. See under Takayama Getting Around earlier in this section for details.

Shirakawa-gō District & Ogimachi 白川郷・荻町
☎ 05769

The Shirakawa-gō District consists of several clusters of houses in villages stretching for several kilometres. Ogimachi, the central cluster, is the most convenient place for bus connections, tourist information and orientation. When arriving by bus, get off at the Gasshō-shuraku bus stop.

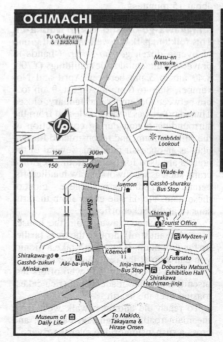

OGIMACHI

CENTRAL HONSHŪ

Information The tourist information office (☎ 6-1013) is next to the Gasshō-shuraku bus stop in the centre of Ogimachi (8.30 am to 5 pm, closed Wednesday). The office has a Japanese map of the whole region, including a detailed map of Ogimachi itself. An English leaflet is also available. The office can help book accommodation, but the staff don't speak English, so you may want to arrange this from Takayama.

Tenbōdai Lookout To get your bearings, climb to the Tenbōdai lookout; from here, you'll obtain the view seen on most tourist brochures. From the Gasshō-shuraku bus stop, walk north along the main road for about 10 minutes and on your right you will see a wooded hill beside the road with a side street leading around the foot of the hill. You can either follow the side street to the top of the hill or, after walking about 10m down the side street, take the steep path on your right that gets you to the top in about 15 minutes.

Shirakawa-gō Gasshō-zukuri Minka-en This folklore park is a well-presented group of over a dozen *gasshō-zukuri* ('hands in prayer' architectural style) buildings (¥700, 8.40 am to 5 pm between April and November, 8 am to 6 pm in August, 9 am to 4 pm between December and January, closed Thursday). It was largely collected from the surrounding region during construction of the Miboro Dam, and reconstructed for display as an open-air museum. Several of the houses are used for demonstrating regional crafts such as woodwork, straw handicrafts, ceramics and painting in Chinese – most of these items are on sale either from the artisans or at the ticket office.

You can wander away from the houses for a pleasant stroll through the trees farther up the mountain. If you don't take a picnic, you can stop at the resthouse near the exit that is run by a chatty lady who offers tea, biscuits and home-made *mochi* (rice cakes) toasted over the hearth.

To reach the entrance, walk west from the main road, through Aki-ba-jinja, and cross a suspension bridge over the river.

Myōzen-ji This temple in the centre of Ogimachi has an interesting museum (¥300, 8.30 am to 5 pm) displaying the traditional paraphernalia of daily rural life.

Wada-ke This house-museum (☎ 6-1958) dates back to 1573, and is a fine example of gasshō-zukuri architecture (¥300, 9 am to 5 pm).

Doburoku Matsuri Exhibition Hall This exhibition hall (Doburoku Matsuri-no-Yakata) is very close to the Shirakawa Hachiman-jinja. The hall (¥300, 9 am to 4 pm, closed from December to April) contains displays devoted to the Doburoku Matsuri, an event clearly not lacking in liquid refreshment (*doburoku* is a type of unrefined sake). The festival is held in mid-October at the shrine, and features, not surprisingly, *niwaka* (improvised buffoonery).

Museum of Daily Life If you walk for about 15 minutes from the centre of Ogimachi back along the road towards Takayama, you'll reach the Museum of Daily Life (Seikatsu Shiryōkan; ¥300, 8 am to 6 pm April to November, 9 am to 6 pm December, closed from January to March), just beyond the second bridge. On display are agricultural tools, rural crafts, equipment for the cultivation of silkworms and various household items from the past.

Onsen Hirase Onsen, 10km south on route 156, has a cosy *kyōdō yokujō* (public bathhouse; ¥300, 10 am to 10 pm April to November, 12 pm to 9 pm February and March, closed Thursday). Kurhaus Shirakawago (☎ 5-2314) boasts a rotemburo (¥800, closed Wednesday).

Places to Stay Some of the gasshō-zukuri buildings function as minshuku and are a popular accommodation option in this region. If you don't speak Japanese, it would be a good idea to enlist the support of the tourist information office in booking one. Ryokan prices start around ¥9000 per person including two meals; minshuku prices for the same deals start at around ¥7000. Two rustic possibilities are ***Kōemon*** (*☎ 6-1446*) and ***Furusato*** (*☎ 6-1033*), with a rate of ¥7700 per person. ***Juemon*** (*☎ 6-1053*) has received favourable comments from foreign visitors, and charges ¥8000.

The cheapest option in the area is the ***Etchū Gokayama Youth Hostel*** (*☎ 0763-67-3331*), near Gokayama. It is a remote but charming gasshō-zukuri house (about 2km on foot from the main road). See the Gokayama District Places to Stay entry later in this section for costs and directions to the hostel.

Places to Eat Breakfast and dinner are usually included in the price of your ryokan or minshuku. The main street in Ogimachi has several restaurants, including the atmospheric ***Shiraogi***, which has dishes from around ¥800. For a real treat, however, try the teishoku, which at ¥2200 gives you a good sampling of the local cuisine. ***Masuen Bunsuke,*** 20 minutes on foot from the bus station at the top end of the village, specialises in trout cuisine. Its teishoku at ¥1500 is good value.

Getting There & Away If you plan to travel in this region during winter, you should check first on the current road conditions by phoning Japan Travel-Phone (*☎ 0120-44-4800* toll free) or the tourist office in Takayama.

Nagoya There is a direct JR bus between Nagoya and Ogimachi, (¥4760, four hours, once daily, mid-April to 30 November only). Advance bookings are recommended.

Another bus service is operated by Nagoya Tetsudō (¥4760, five hours 50 minutes, once a day, between 19 July and 13 November). It continues from Ogimachi to Kanazawa.

Takayama There are three daily bus connections with Ogimachi, made in two stages. The first stage is a bus service operated by Nohi bus company between Takayama and Makido (¥1930, one hour). The second stage is a connecting bus service operated by JR between Makido and Ogimachi (¥1430,

one hour). Departures from Takayama are at 8 am, 1.20 pm and 5 pm.

Kanazawa The Nagoya Tetsudō *futsū* (local) bus runs between Ogimachi and Kanazawa. (¥2680, three hours and 20 minutes). Alternatively take the train from Kanazawa on the JR Hokuriku line to Takaoka (tokkyū, ¥1470, 25 minutes), then from Takaoka station, take a bus to Ogimachi via Gokayama (¥2350, 2½ hours).

Another option is to take the train on the private Jōhana line from Takaoka to Jōhana. From Jōhana there's a bus service to Ogimachi.

Getting Around Ogimachi is easily covered on foot. If you want to visit Gokayama, you will have to wait for infrequent buses.

Gokayama District

Gokayama is just inside the boundaries of Toyama-ken, only a short distance north of Ogimachi. Prior to the Edo period, the feudal lords of Kanazawa used the isolation of Gokayama as a centre for the secretive production of gunpowder. Many of the houses open to the public in this region

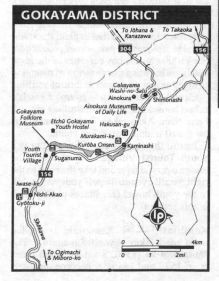

CENTRAL HONSHŪ

have displays of equipment used for making gunpowder. The construction of a road to Gokayama and the provision of electricity didn't occur until 1925.

In the Gokayama area, gasshō-zukuri houses are scattered in small groups along the valley. The following is a brief description of the towns and sights you'll come across as you travel north from Shirakawa-gō District and Ogimachi. There are bus stops at each group of houses.

Nishi-Akao Nishi-Akao is about 20 minutes by bus from Ogimachi. The two attractions here are **Gyōtoku-ji** (¥200, 9 am to 5 pm), which has an excellent collection of work by masters of the *mingei* (folk-art) movement, including Kawai Kanjirō, Bernard Leach and the eccentric genius potter-painter, Munakata Shikō, and the house, **Iwase-ke** (¥300, 8 am to 5 pm), which was once the local centre for the production of gunpowder.

Suganuma Suganuma is 2km beyond Nishi-Akao and lies just below the main road. The **Folklore Museum** consists of two houses (combined admission charge ¥300, 9 am to 4 pm between May and November). The Minzoku-kan displays items from traditional life; the Enshō-kan, across the path, is devoted to exhibits that explain the traditional techniques for gunpowder production. For ¥1000 you can buy cassettes of the local music – a haunting combination of twanging stringed instruments and mournful wailing.

Close by is an attractive group of gasshō-zukuri houses that are worth strolling around. From Nishi-Akao, take a Takaoka-bound bus for the 10-minute ride to Suganuma.

Just to the south-west of Suganuma is a **Youth Tourist Village**. If you cross the bridge over the river and take the road to the right, you'll eventually puff your way uphill to the youth hostel (see Places to Stay later in this section).

Kaminashi 上梨 Kaminashi is on the main road, 4km beyond Suganuma. The **Murakami-ke** (¥300, 8 am to 5 pm) dates from 1578 and has now become an inter-

esting museum. It is well maintained by the proud and enthusiastic owner who conducts visitors on a tour of the exhibits and then sits them down around the irori and sings local folk songs. A detailed leaflet is provided in English.

Also close by and worthy of a look is **Hakusan-gū**. The shrine's main hall dates from 1502 and has been designated an Important Cultural Property. Its Kokiriko Festival on 25 and 26 September features a unique rattle dance. A kilometre farther west, **Kūroba Onsen** (☎ 67-3741) is a good, if simple, place for a hot dip (¥550, 11 am to 9 pm, closed Tuesday).

Takaoka-bound buses from Nishi-Akao take around 15 minutes to reach Kaminashi.

Shimonashi & Ainokura 下梨・相倉
☎ 0763
Shimonashi is on the main road, 4km beyond Kaminashi. Just beyond the bus stop, there's a road on the left leading up a steep hill towards Ainokura. About 100m up this road, you reach **Gokayama Washi-no-Sato** (¥300, 8.30 am to 5 pm April to November) on your left. The production of *washi* (Japanese hand-made paper) has been a speciality of the region for several centuries and you can see the production process here. For ¥550, you can even have a go at it yourself and keep your work of art.

From here it takes another 25 minutes on foot, winding up the hill, to reach the side street leading off to the left to Ainokura. This is the most impressive of the World Heritage gasshō-zukuri villages with fine views across the valley. **Ainokura Museum of Daily Life** (¥200, 8.30 am to 5 pm) displays local crafts and paper.

Places to Stay Several gasshō-zukuri houses in the Gokayama area function as minshuku. Expect to pay around ¥7400 per person for a bed and two meals. The youth hostel near Suganuma offers the most inexpensive way to stay in a gasshō-zukuri building.

The helpful tourist information offices in Takayama and Ogimachi can assist with reservations and there is an information office in the centre of Ainokura. Advance reservations are highly recommended, particularly during the peak seasons of May, August and October.

Etchū Gokayama Youth Hostel (☎ 67-3331) is a fine old gasshō-zukuri farmhouse and a great place to stay; it's only a few kilometres off the main road (¥4500, with two meals, nonmembers ¥1000 extra). The fine dinner often includes grilled trout and sansai.

The hostel is not easy to find. The closest bus stop is at Suganuma, which is only 12 minutes by bus from Kaminashi bus stop or 25 minutes by bus from Ogimachi.

From the Suganuma bus stop on the main road, walk down the side street through the cluster of houses by the river and cross the large bridge. At the other end of the bridge, turn right and wind your way for about 2km uphill. Call ahead in winter to check the roads are open.

Ainokura is a great place for a gasshō-zukuri farmhouse stay, as you can enjoy the atmosphere once the tour-bus crowds have departed. Try *Yomoshiro* (☎ 66-2377), *Sangoro* (☎ 66-2709), *Goyomon* (☎ 66-2154) or *Chōyomon* (☎ 66-2755). All cost around ¥7400 per person, including two meals.

In Kaminashi, *Kokuminshukusha Gokayama-sō* (☎ 66-2316) is a bit of an architectural monstrosity, so if it's charm you're after, look elsewhere (¥7360, with two meals).

If you want to stay in Nishi-Akao, *Nakaya* (☎ 67-3252) is a friendly little ryokan (¥6800, with two meals).

Getting There & Away Gokayama is about 20 minutes from Ogimachi by infrequent bus. Hitching is a good way to avoid long waits for buses. Gokayama is also served by the buses running between Kanazawa and Nagoya via Ogimachi, but only from July to November. About four buses make their way through the various towns between approximately 9 am and 5 pm. For details, refer to the Shirakawa-gō District & Ogimachi Getting There & Away entry earlier in this chapter. Remember that many roads in this region are closed during the winter.

HIRAYU ONSEN 平湯温泉
☎ 0578

This hot-spring resort in the Japan Alps is of primary interest to visitors as a hub for bus transport in the region, though it does have one excellent modern hot-spring complex. The information office (☎ 9-3030) opposite the bus station has leaflets and information on hot-spring ryokan as well as a small nature trail in the area.

Hirayu-no-mori (☎ 9-3338) near the bus station boasts one indoor and six outdoor baths (¥500, 10 am to 8 pm). It's great either for a quick dip between buses, or as part of a day excursion from Takayama.

Compared with other towns in the area, like Shin-Hotaka and Kamikōchi, this is not a very attractive place to stay, though there are a few nice ryokan around. *Ryosō Tsuyukusa* (☎ 9-2620) has a pleasant, though tiny, outdoor onsen bath (¥7000, with two meals). *Eitarō* (☎ 9-2540) is a bit fancier (¥10,000, with two meals). Both are about five minutes' walk from the bus station, along the road leading to Shin-Hotaka. There is also *Hirayu Camping Ground* (☎ 9-2610), about 700m from the bus station in the direction of Takayama (¥600 per person, ¥1500 for parking).

Getting There & Away
Buses from Takayama to Norikura, Kamikōchi and Shin-Hotaka Onsen all run via Hirayu Onsen (¥1800, 40 minutes).

There are frequent bus connections between Hirayu Onsen and Kamikōchi, but only from late April to late October (¥1050, 35 minutes), running via Nakanoyu. The Kamikōchi Getting There & Away entry later in this section has more details regarding combined bus-rail connections with Matsumoto.

There are bus services approximately three times a day between Norikura (Tatami-daira) and Hirayu Onsen, and as many as eight times daily during the peak season of late July to late August (¥2700, 40 minutes). The Norikura Skyline Road is only open from 15 May to 31 October. There are frequent bus connections between Hirayu Onsen and Shin-Hotaka Onsen (¥870, 35 minutes).

FUKUCHI ONSEN 福地温泉
☎ 0578

This relatively untouristed hot spring, a short bus ride from Hirayu Onsen, is worth a visit, for its rural charm, its summer folk dances and morning market, and two outstanding baths.

Yumoto Chōza (☎ 9-2146, fax 9-2010) is one of Central Honshū's finest onsen ryokan (from ¥18,000, with two meals). Its combination of excellent mountain cuisine served at irori hearths, elegant traditional architecture, and five indoor and two outdoor pools make it well worth splashing out on. Reservations are essential. Nonresidents can take a bath for ¥500 after 2 pm, by appointment.

Mukashibanashi no sato (☎ 9-2793), which translates to the overly cutesy Fairy Tale Village, is a restaurant-cum-hot-spring in a traditional farmhouse (bath ¥500, 8 am to 4.30 pm). The sansai-soba teishoku (¥800) is good value. Its small indoor and outdoor baths are excellent, and are free on the 26th of each month.

An *asa-ichi* (morning market) takes place in summer from 6 am to 10 am, in front of Mukashibanashi no sato, and in the early evenings there are theatrical *henbedori* (snake and lion dances).

Getting There & Away
Direct buses run between Takayama and Fukuchi Onsen (¥1760, one hour and 20 minutes, several times daily). There are also buses to and from Hirayu Onsen (¥410, 10 minutes, every two hours). Get off at Fukuchi-onsen-ue bus stop for Mukashibanashi no sato, Fukuchi-onsen-shita for Yumoto Chōza.

SHIN-HOTAKA ONSEN
新穂高温泉
☎ 0578

This is a hot-spring resort with the added attraction of the Shin-Hotaka cable car, reportedly the longest of its kind in Asia, which whisks you up close to the peak of **Nishi Hotaka-dake** (2909m) for a superb mountain panorama. The cable car consists of two sections and a combined ticket costs ¥1500 one

way (¥2800 round trip) and an extra ¥300 if you take your backpack. The cable car is near the Shin-Hotaka Onsen bus station.

If you are fit, properly equipped and give yourself ample time, there are a variety of hiking options from Nishi Hotaka-guchi (the top cable car station). One option that takes a little under three hours would be to hike over to **Kamikōchi**. Near the Shin-Hotaka Onsen bus station is a counter entitled 'Mountaineering Service Centre', which has some maps of the area's hiking trails. Unfortunately, despite the English-language sign, none of the information is in English.

Also near the bus station, adjacent to the car park, is a rather spartan public onsen. During the summer it tends to be crowded with tourists, but in the off-season your only company is likely to be a few weary shift workers from the electric plant across the river.

Places to Stay
This far up into the mountains, low-cost accommodation options are hard to find. Most of the minshuku and ryokan are clustered around the Shin-Hotaka Onsen-guchi bus stop, which is a few kilometres before the Shin-Hotaka Onsen bus station. One of the cheapest spots is the functional *Yamanoyado* minshuku (☎ 9-2733), which charges ¥8000, with two meals. Right next door, *Komagusakan* ryokan (☎ 9-2408) is slightly more upmarket (¥10,000 with two meals). Most of the other options in the area charge between ¥12,000 and ¥16,000 per person.

There are a few more minshuku in the Naka-O Onsen area, two bus stops past Shin-Hotaka Onsen guchi. Of these, your best bet is *Mahoroba* (☎ 9-2382), a friendly place with a very nice outdoor onsen bath (¥8000 with two meals). If you can get a Japanese speaker to book your room for you, they can arrange to have the owner pick you up at the Naka-O-guchi bus stop. Otherwise you'll have to walk a bit. Across from the bus stop is a small road leading uphill. Take it for about 1km: Mahoroba is on the left side of the road, just past the (infrequently served) Naka-o Kōminkan-mae bus stop.

Up near the Shin-Hotaka Onsen bus station, *Shin-Hotaka Campground* (☎ 9-2513) open July and August only) has camp sites for ¥600. If you don't have a tent, they'll rent you one for the princely sum of ¥2500.

Getting There & Away
There are frequent bus connections with Hirayu Onsen (¥870, 40 minutes) and Takayama (¥2100, one hour and 35 minutes). There are several buses daily to Toyama (¥2380, 3½ hours), however, you'll need to change buses at Kamioka and possibly also at Tochio Onsen. There is one direct bus around noon, but this only runs from mid-July to late August. There is also a direct bus to Nagoya (¥5400, six hours) during this period.

Nagano-ken

Most of Nagano-ken consists of the northern, central and southern ranges of the Japan Alps – hence its claim to being the 'Roof of Japan'.

Nagano-ken is one of the most enjoyable regions to visit in Japan, not only for the beauty of its mountainous terrain, but also for the traditional architecture and culture that linger in many parts of the prefecture and which have been spared the industrial zoning often seen elsewhere in Japan. Agriculture is still a major source of income here, but the lack of pollution has also attracted growing numbers of companies from the electronics and precision manufacturing industries (in search of a dust-free environment).

Included in this prefecture are several national parks and quasi-national parks that attract large numbers of campers, hikers, mountaineers and hot-spring aficionados. Skiers can choose from dozens of resorts during the ski season, which lasts from late December to late March.

Getting Around
Travel in the prefecture relies mainly on the JR lines that run parallel to the Japan Alps from south to north, and most travellers follow the north-south route. There are two scenic routes that traverse the Japan Alps: one runs from Matsumoto via Kamikōchi to Takayama (Gifu-ken) and the other runs from Shinano-ōmachi via the Kurobe Dam to Tateyama (Toyama-ken). When making travel plans for the mountains, bear in mind that many roads are closed and bus services are stopped due to heavy snowfall from mid-October to early May. If possible try to avoid major sights and trails during peak tourist seasons (early May, July and August) when they become clogged with visitors.

JNTO publishes *Japan Nagano Prefecture*, a brochure that provides concise details and mapping.

TENRYŪ-KYŌ & KOMAGA-TAKE
天竜峡・駒ヶ岳
☎ 0265
Both the gorge, Tenryū-kyō, and the peak, Komaga-take, lie east of the Kiso Valley and are easily reached via the JR Iida line, which runs roughly parallel to the Chūō line.

The main sightseeing approach for Tenryū-kyō is a one-hour boat trip down the Tenryū-gawa and through the gorge (¥3150). Boats leave from the dock close to close Tenryū-kyō station.

Above Tenryū kyō is **Oku-Tenryū-kyō Fu-dō Onsen** and its single, newly built, luxurious ryokan *Sawaya* (☎ 59-2122). If you want to experience a traditional inn, complete with indoor, outdoor and cave onsen baths, and the full ryokan cuisine, this is good value (¥18,000, with two meals). The owners don't speak English but will pick you up from the station if a Japanese speaker calls.

Komaga-take (2956m) is a popular hiking destination. From Komagane station, a bus ride (¥1000, 35 minutes) takes you up to the base station of the cable car at Shirabi-daira. The cable car ride (¥1130) whisks you up to Senjōjiki. From there, the hike to the peak takes about 2½ hours.

There are numerous pensions, minshuku and ryokan around Komagane, and several mountain huts along the trails. If you want to stay at *Komagane Youth Hostel* (☎ 83-3856), from the Komagane station, take a bus bound for Suganodae for 15 minutes to

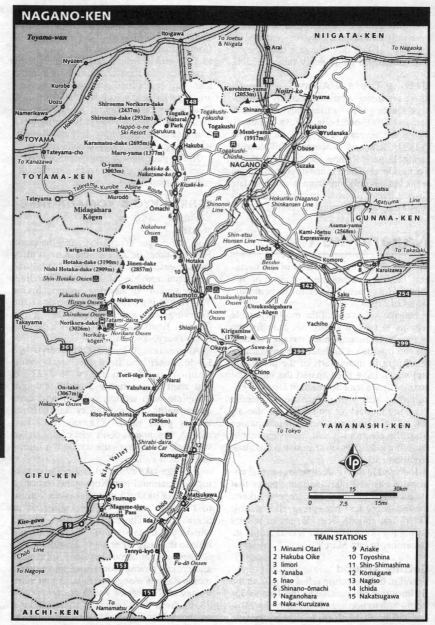

NAGANO-KEN

Toyama-wan

Itoigawa

To Joetsu
& Niigata

NIIGATA-KEN

To Nagaoka

Nyūzen

Arai

Kurobe

Kurohime-yama
(2053m)

Nojiri-ko

Iiyama

Uozu

Shinano

Nakano

Yudanaka

Namerikawa

Shirouma Norikura-dake
(2437m)

Togakushi-
rokusha

Togakushi

Menō-yama
(1917m)

Obuse

TOYAMA

Shirouma-dake (2932m)

Tsugaike
Natural
Park

Suzaka

Happō-o-ne
Ski Resort

Sarukura

Hakuba

Togakushi-
Chūsha

NAGANO

Karamatsu-dake (2695m)

Maru-yama (1377m)

Tateyama-cho

To Kanazawa

TOYAMA-KEN

O-yama
(3003m)

Aoki-ko &
Nakazuna-ko

Kizaki-ko

Kusatsu

Tateyama

Tateyama-Kurobe Alpine
Route

Murodō

JR
Shinonoi
Line

Hokuriku (Nagano)
Shinkansen Line

Agatsuma   Line

GUNMA-KEN

Midagahara
Kōgen

Ōmachi

Nakabusa
Onsen

Shin-etsu
Honsen Line

Kami-Jōetsu
Expressway

Asama-yama
(2568m)

Yariga-take (3180m)

Ueda

To Takasaki

Hotaka-dake (3190m)

Jōnen-dake
(2857m)

Hotaka

Bessho
Onsen

Komoro

Karuizawa

Nishi Hotaka-dake (2909m)

Shin-Hotaka Onsen

Kamikōchi

Matsumoto

Utsukushigahara
Onsen

Saku

Koumi
Line

Fukuchi Onsen
Hirayu Onsen

Nakanoyu

Utsukushigahara
-kōgen

Yachiho

Shirahone Onsen

Asama
Onsen

Takayama

Norikura-dake
(3026m)

Tatami-daira

Shiojiri

Kirigamine
(1798m)

Norikura-
kōgen

Norikura Onsen

Okaya

Suwa-ko

Suwa

Chino

On-take
(3067m)

Torii-tōge Pass

Narai

Nakanoyu Onsen

Yabuhara

To Tokyo

YAMANASHI-KEN

Kiso-Fukushima

Komaga-take
(2956m)

Ina

Kiso Valley

Shirabi-daira
Cable Car

Komagane

GIFU-KEN

Tsumago

Matsukawa

Magome-tōge
Pass

Magome

Iida

Kiso-gawa

Tenryū-kyō

To Nagoya

Fu-dō Onsen

To
Hamamatsu

AICHI-KEN

| 0 | | 15 | 30km |
| 0 | 7.5 | 15mi | |

TRAIN STATIONS

1 Minami Otari	9 Ariake
2 Hakuba Oike	10 Toyoshina
3 Iimori	11 Shin-Shimashima
4 Yanaba	12 Komagane
5 Inao	13 Nagiso
6 Shinano-ōmachi	14 Ichida
7 Naganohara	15 Nakatsugawa
8 Naka-Kuruizawa	

the Grand Hotel-mae bus stop. From there it's a 10-minute walk. Expect to pay ¥2350 per person (¥2650 in winter).

BESSHO ONSEN 別所温泉
☎ 0268

If you only have time to visit one Central Honshū hot-spring town, Bessho would be a good choice, as it is conveniently accessible from Tokyo and retains much old-world charm.

Bessho flourished as an administrative centre during the Kamakura period (1185–1333), which saw the construction of several temples that are still standing today, most notably the beautiful temples **Anraku-ji** (renowned for its octagonal pagoda), **Chūzen-ji** and **Zenzan-ji**.

Anraku-ji is 10 minutes on foot from Bessho Onsen station. Chūzen-ji and Zenzan-ji are a very enjoyable 5km hike away.

Bessho's historical attractions might not have been enough to maintain its popularity, but its excellent waters, reputed to cure diabetes and constipation, and beautify your complexion at the same, have ensured its lasting fame. Heian-era poetess Sei Shonagon is perhaps its best-known visitor. Today there are tourists aplenty, but fortunately Bessho remains undeveloped.

There are three public baths (¥100, 6 am to 10 pm), all located centrally. Ōyu has a small rotemburo, Ishiyu is famed for its stone bath, and Taishi-no-yu, most frequented by the locals, is known for being relatively cool.

The comfortable *Ueda Mahoroba Youth Hostel* (☎ 38-5229) is eight minutes' walk from the station (members ¥4500, with two meals, nonmembers ¥5500).

Ryokan Katsura-sō (☎ 38-2047) serves excellent sansai cuisine. Expect to pay ¥10,000, with two meals. The newly built *Nanakusa no yu* (☎ 38-2323) serves lavish meals including pickled carp in miso (rooms cost ¥14,000, with two meals). It can even provide geisha entertainment (¥9000 for two hours).

Bessho Onsen Ryokan Association (☎ 88-2020, fax 38-8887) can provide information and help with hotel bookings.

To reach Bessho Onsen, take the JR Nagano shinkansen line to Ueda (Asama from Tokyo, ¥6490, one hour; from Nagano, ¥1410, 13 minutes) then change to the Ueda line for the ride to Bessho Onsen (¥570, 27 minutes, every 20 minutes).

KISO VALLEY REGION 木曽
☎ 0264

A visit to this region is highly recommended if you want to see several small towns that have carefully preserved architecture from the Edo period. As a bonus, there's the opportunity to combine your visit to Magome and Tsumago with an easy walk. JNTO publishes a leaflet entitled *Kiso Valley*, which has details and maps for the region.

The thickly forested Kiso Valley lies in the south-west of Nagano-ken and is surrounded by the Japan Alps. It was traversed by the Nakasen-dō Highway, an old post road that connected Edo (present-day Tokyo) with Kyoto and provided business for the post towns en route. With the introduction of new roads and commercial centres to the north, and the later construction of the Chūō train line, the region was effectively bypassed and the once-prosperous towns went into decline. During the '60s, there was a move to preserve the original architecture of the post towns, and tourism has become a major source of income.

Magome was the birthplace of a famous Japanese literary figure, Shimazaki Tōson (1872–1943). His masterpiece, *Ie* (published in English in 1976 and entitled *The Family*), records the decline of two provincial families in the Kiso region.

On 23 November, the Fuzoku Emaki Parade is held along the old post road in Tsumago and features a procession by the townsfolk who dress in costume from the Edo period.

Magome to Tsumago Walk
Magome Magome is a small post town with rows of traditional houses and post inns (and souvenir shops, of course) lining a steep street. The town's tourist information office (☎ 59-2336) is a short way up, on the right-hand side of the street (8.30 am

to 5 pm). It dispenses tourist literature as well as reserving accommodation. Close by is a museum devoted to the life and times of Shimazaki Tōson (¥300, 8.30 am to 4.45 pm, shorter hours in winter), which is a little impenetrable for non-Japanese speakers.

To walk from Magome to Tsumago, continue toiling up the street until the houses eventually give way to a forest path that winds down to the road leading up a steep hill to Magome-tōge Pass. This initial walk from Magome to the pass takes about 45 minutes and is not particularly appealing because you spend most of your time on the road. You can cut out this first section by taking the bus between Magome and Tsumago and getting off at the pass after about 12 minutes.

There's a small shop-cum-teahouse at the top of the pass. From here where the trail leaves the road and takes you down to the right along a pleasant route through the forest. It takes just under two hours to walk from the teahouse to Tsumago.

Tsumago Tsumago is so well preserved that it feels like an open-air museum. Designated by the government as a protected area for the preservation of traditional buildings, no modern developments such as TV aerials or telephone poles are allowed to mar the scene. The tourist information office (☎ 57-3123) is halfway down the main street (9 am to 5 pm, closed Wednesday). The excellent *Short Guide to Tsumago* (in English) is available and the staff are happy to reserve accommodation.

About 50m beyond the post office, on the same side of the street, is the **Okuya Kyō-dokan Folk Museum** (¥600, 9 am to 4.45 pm), which is part of a magnificent house built like a castle. During the Edo period, felling of trees in the Kiso region was strictly controlled. In 1877, following the relaxation of these controls, the owner decided to rebuild using *hinoki* (cypress wood).

If you continue from this house up the main street, the bus station can be reached by taking any of the side streets on your left.

Baggage Forwarding As a special service for walkers on the trail between Magome and Tsumago, the tourist offices in both villages offer a baggage-forwarding service during peak visiting seasons (¥500 per piece of luggage). The deadline for the morning delivery is 8.30 am and for the afternoon delivery, it's 11.30 am. The service operates daily from late July to 31 August (but there's no service from Tsumago on Wednesday), however it is restricted to Saturday, Sunday and national holidays between late March and late July and September through November.

Places to Stay & Eat
Both tourist information offices can help book accommodation at the numerous ryokan and minshuku in the area. Prices for a room and two meals at ryokan start at around ¥9000 while minshuku prices for a similar deal start at around ¥7000. ***Min-shuku Daikichi*** (☎ 57-2595) is a friendly newer place just four minutes on foot from the Tsumago bus station (¥7500 per person, ¥8000 if just one). ***Tsutamuraya*** (☎ 57-3235) is another welcoming inn, in a traditional building with its own irori (¥6500).

Magome and Tsumago have several restaurants on their main streets. The local specialities include *gohei-mochi* (a rice dumpling on a stick coated with nut sauce) and sansai, which can be ordered as a sansai teishoku for about ¥1500. *Yoshimuraya* (☎ 57-3265) in Tsumago is inexpensive (10 am to 5pm, closed Thursday).

Getting There & Away
Nakatsugawa and Nagiso stations on the JR Chūō line provide access to Magome and Tsumago respectively. Some services do not stop at these stations, which are about 12 minutes apart by limited express. Nakatsugawa is connected with Nagoya (Shinano tokkyū, ¥2980, 47 minutes) and Matsumoto (Shinano tokkyū, ¥4180, 85 minutes). Local trains take nearly twice as long, but cost about half as much. From Tokyo, take the JR Chūō line to Shiojiri, and change to Nakatsugawa (Azusa/Shinano tokkyū, ¥9990, about four hours).

Highway buses operate between Nagoya Meitetsu Bus Centre, next to the Nagoya station, and Magome (¥1810, one hour and 40 minutes).

Buses leave hourly from outside the Nakatsugawa station for Magome (¥530, 30 minutes). There's also an infrequent bus service between Magome and Tsumago (¥640, 30 minutes). If you decide to start your walk from the Magome-tōge Pass, take this bus and get off at the bus stop at the top of the pass.

From Tsumago, you can either catch the bus to Nagiso station (¥280, 10 minutes), or if you're still in the mood to hike, walk there in 40 minutes.

Kiso-Fukushima & On-take
木曽福島・御岳
☎ 0264

Kiso-Fukushima was an important barrier gate and checkpoint on the old post road. From the station, it takes about 20 minutes on foot to reach several old residences, museums and temples.

On 22 and 23 July, the astonishing Mikoshi Makuri takes place. On the first day of the festival, the locals parade a newly built, highly expensive portable shrine around the town. The following evening they smash the 400kg sacred object to smithereens by cartwheeling it around the town square. Arrive by 8 pm to ensure a good view of the mayhem. The remaining pieces are then hauled up to Suimu shrine in the early hours of the morning.

On-take (3067m) is an active volcano – entry to the crater area is prohibited. For centuries the mountain has been considered sacred and is an important destination for pilgrims.

There are several trails to the summit. One popular trailhead is at **Nakanoyu Onsen**, 80 minutes by bus from Kiso-Fukushima station. From the trailhead, it takes about 3½ hours to hike to the summit. Another trailhead is at **Tanohara Natural Park** (¥2110, 1½ hours by bus from Kiso-Fukushima station); from here the hike to the summit takes about three hours. Be careful to check the bus schedules before setting out: there are only two to three buses daily to each destination.

Places to Stay An inexpensive and very comfortable place to stay is *Kiso Ryōjōan Youth Hostel* (☎ 23-7716), a short bus ride bus ride (¥510, 25 minutes) from Kiso-Fukushima station. Members can expect to pay ¥2900, nonmembers ¥3900. Get off at Obara-ue bus stop and the hostel is three minutes' walk away. It has excellent baths, air-con rooms, and the manager cooks *nabe* (hotpot meals) each evening for just ¥1000 extra. There are numerous minshuku and ryokan in Kiso-Fukushima itself, including several near the train station. Minshuku prices start at around ¥8000 and ryokan at ¥11,000.

Places to Eat Kiso-Fukushima also boasts a nationally-renowned soba shop, *Kurumaya Honten* (☎ 22-2200). Try the *zaru-soba* (cold soba topped with nori strips), but be warned, the dipping sauce is unusually sweet (10 am to 5 pm, closed Wednesday).

Getting There & Away Kiso-Fukushima is connected with Nagoya (tokkyū, ¥4580, 1½ hours) and Matsumoto (tokkyū, ¥2610, 40 minutes).

Narai 奈良井
☎ 0264

Narai is the least touristed town on the old post road, with a high proportion of traditional buildings from the Edo period, including one highly recommended minshuku. Its single main street extends for about 1km to your left as you exit the train station.

Unlike Magome and Tsumago, Narai allows cars down its main street, but rather than disturbing the village, this adds to its authenticity as a working rural community, not simply a living museum.

Things to See
At intervals along the street there are five old wells that were used by thirsty travellers during the Edo period. The sake brewery is easily recognised by its basket of fronds hanging from the roof above the entrance. Side streets on the right-hand side lead to tranquil temples.

Many of the houses lining the main street originally functioned as inns during the heyday of the old post road; most have been turned into museums, shops or coffee shops, though some still operate as ryokan. Nakamura-tei was once a shop specialising in lacquerware and is now a museum (¥200) run by a friendly proprietor.

If you feel like following the old post road, continue uphill for 4km (about 1¾ hours) to **Torii-tōge Pass**. From there, it's another 4km (1¾ hours) to the station at **Yabuhara**.

Shopping

At Hananoya you can find hand-crafted lacquerware lunchboxes, usually called *bento-bako*, but here called *men-pa*. The town's other famous product is *hyaku-sō-gan* (100 herb balls), a mysterious herbal medicine that is reputedly good for the digestion.

Places to Stay & Eat

Iseya (☎ *34-3051*) is a marvellous minshuku housed in a 170-year-old traditional wooden building (¥7500, including two excellent meals). Ask for one of the old-style rooms at the front. It's 10 minutes' walk south of the train station on the main street. *Echigoya Shokudo* (☎ *34-3048*) serves inexpensive soba (9 am to 6 pm). *Tsuchiya* (☎ *34-3102*) is a coffee shop in an old house with an open rear garden (10 am to 5 pm).

Getting There & Away

Narai is 45 minutes from Matsumoto by futsū (local train, ¥560) on the Chūō line. Express trains do not stop at Narai.

MATSUMOTO 松本
☎ 0263 • pop 200,000
Matsumoto has a superb castle, and is a convenient base for exploration of the Japan Alps.

The city has been around since at least the 8th century, and was the castle town of the Ogasawara clan during the 14th and 15th centuries. It continued to prosper and grow in size during the Edo period, though somewhere along the way things seem to

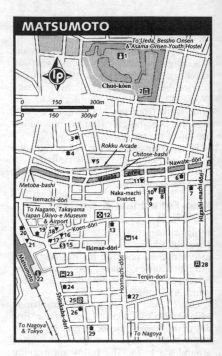

have slowed down. The city has a pleasant lazy *inaka*, or rural, feel to it, and the restored city-centre streets of Naka-machi boast fine galleries and some inexpensive accommodation. An overnight stay here is recommended.

Information

Matsumoto city tourist information office (☎ 32-2814) is on your right at the bottom of the steps leading from Matsumoto station's eastern exit (9.30 am to 6 pm, until 5.30 pm in winter). The English-speaking staff can provide maps and leaflets, help with accommodation and give plenty of other travel information.

JNTO publishes two colour brochures: *Japan Matsumoto*, which has good maps and *Japan Matsumoto & the Japan Alps*, which provides wider regional coverage and a concise leaflet entitled *Matsumoto & Kamikōchi*. The first two are available at the Matsumoto tourist information office.

MATSUMOTO

PLACES TO STAY

4 Nishiya
  にしや旅館
6 Marumo
  まるも旅館
7 Nunoya
  ぬのや旅館
13 Ichiyama
  いちやま
19 Hotel Iidiya
  ホテル飯田屋
20 Hotel New Station
  ホテルニュー
  ステーション
24 Matsumoto
  Tōkyū Inn
  松本東急イン
27 Matsumoto
  Tourist Hotel
  松本観光ホテル

29 Hotel Buena Vista
  ホテルブエナビスタ

PLACES TO EAT

5 Trattoria Graspa
9 Nomugi
  野麦
10 Kissa-kan
  喫茶館
11 Delhi
16 Mr Donut
17 McDonald's
18 Yōrōnotaki
  養老の滝
21 Sushi Snack Restaurant
  寿司スナック

OTHER

1 Matsumoto-jō
  松本城

2 Japan Folklore
  Museum
  日本民俗資料館
3 Coin Laundry
8 Naka-machi
  Chic-Kan
  中町蔵シック館
12 Parco Department Store
  パルコ
14 Main Post Office
  中央郵便局
15 VISA card ATM
22 Tourist information
23 Matsumoto
  Bus Station
  松本バスターミナル
25 People's
26 Ace One Supermarket
28 Fukashi-jinja
  深志神社

Money There is a VISA card ATM (6 am to midnight) on the north side of Ekimae-dōri in front of Matsumoto station.

Email & Internet Access The friendly cyber bar and cafe People's (☎ 37-5011) is on the second floor of the Takazawa building, 10 minutes' walk south of Matsumoto station, opposite Ace One supermarket. Internet access is free when you buy a beer or a meal (6 pm to 2 am).

Matsumoto-jō

Even if you only spend a couple of hours in Matsumoto, make sure you see this splendid castle (¥500, including Folklore Museum admission, 8.30 am to 4.30 pm). It is known as Karasu-jō (Crow Castle) for its dark, corvine facade.

The main attraction in the castle grounds is the original three-turreted castle donjon, built circa 1595, in contrasting black and white. Steep steps and ladders lead you up through six storeys. On the lower floors there are displays of guns, bombs and gadgets with which to storm castles – complete with technicolour graphics, which are useful for those who can't read the Japanese

descriptions. There's even a *tsukimi yagura* (moon-viewing pavilion), which was used as a dainty retreat for those lighter moments when the castle was not under attack.

The castle is 15 minutes on foot from the station; if you take a bus, hop off at the Shiyakusho-mae stop (¥190).

Japan Folklore Museum

To the right of the entrance to the castle grounds is the Nihon Minzoku Shiryōkan (see the earlier entrance fee for Matsumoto-jō), which has exhibits on several floors relating to the archaeology, history and folklore of Matsumoto and the surrounding region. There is an important collection of Tanabata dolls, while another floor displays an extensive Honda clock and watch collection. Look out for the banjo and Rolls Royce timepieces.

In summer the museum loans out bicycles free of charge, though you'll need to show identification.

Naka-machi

This former merchant's district is an excellent place to stroll, as most of its storehouses have been transformed into galleries, coffee shops and restaurants. Naka-machi Chic-Kan features revolving exhibits of locally produced arts and crafts, and the neighbouring cafe *Kissa-kan*, a women's cooperative sponsored by the city, is a very pleasant place for a break from sightseeing.

Japan Ukiyo-e Museum

This is a must for *ukiyo-e* (woodblock print) lovers. Several generations of the Sakai family have collected over 100,000 prints, paintings, screens and old books – the largest private collection of its kind in the world. English labelling is minimal, but an explanatory leaflet in English is provided (¥900, 10 am to 4.30 pm, closed Tuesday).

Access to the museum is a real pain unless you take the 3km taxi ride (¥2000) from Matsumoto station. Otherwise, take the Matsumoto Dentetsu line to the fourth stop, Ōniwa (¥170, 6 minutes). Turn left out of the tiny station, walk about 50m up the street to a main road, bear left again, and continue for about 300m. Pass under an overpass, and turn right at the road mirror. At the traffic lights, continue straight across for another 100m. The museum is on your left. The walk from Ōniwa station takes about 20 minutes.

Utsukushigahara-kōgen

From April to mid-November, this alpine plateau is a popular excursion from Matsumoto. Buses stop at Sanjiro Bokujo (Sanjiro Ranch) and there are pleasant walks and the opportunity to see cows in pasture (a constant source of Japanese fascination) and the open-air **Utsukushigahara-kōgen Art Gallery** (Utsukushigahara-kōgen Bijutsukan). It has a bizarre series of 120 sculptures, including *Venus of Milo in the Castle of Venus* and *Affection Plaza*, but there are likely to be few travellers who would find the exhibits worthy of the hefty admission charge (¥1400). On a clear day there are fine views of the Japan Alps from here. There is also a two-day hiking trail to Kirigamine (1798m).

Matsumoto Dentetsu buses run up to the plateau from the Matsumoto bus station gate No 1 (¥1900, one hour and 20 minutes).

Special Events

During the Heso Matsuri (Navel Festival), held from 6 to 7 June, revellers demonstrate that Matsumoto is the centre of Japan by prancing through the streets wearing costumes that appropriately reveal their navels. On 24 and 25 July, the Tenjin Matsuri at Fukashi-jinja features elaborately decorated *dashi* (floats), and a firework display. The second day is liveliest.

During August, the atmospheric Takigi Nō Matsuri features *nō* (classical Japanese dance-drama) by torch light, which is performed outdoors on a stage in the park below the castle.

Phallic merriment is to be had at the Dōsojin Matsuri, held in honour of *dōsojin* (roadside guardians), on 23 September at Utsukushigahara Onsen. On 3 and 4 October, Asama Onsen celebrates the Asama Hi-Matsuri, a spectacular fire festival with torch-lit parades that are accompanied by drumming. At the beginning of November, the Oshiro Matsuri (Castle Festival) is held – a cultural jamboree including costume parades, puppet displays and flower shows. On 19 and 20 November, Ebisu Matsuri is a thriving merchants' festival with street stalls.

Places to Stay

The tourist information office at the station has lists of accommodation and can help with reservations. If your main objective is to use Matsumoto as a staging point to visit the Japan Alps, there's no compulsion to stay in the town itself, though there are some comfortable lodgings.

Places to Stay – Budget

Hostels A bit regimented and drab, *Asama Onsen Youth Hostel* (☎ 46-1335) does have the advantage of a few nice onsen baths in the neighbourhood (¥3200, doors close 9 pm). The hostel is closed from 28 December to 3 January.

To reach Asama Onsen by bus from the Matsumoto bus station, there are two options: either take bus No 6 to Shita-Asama (¥240) or bus No 7 to Dai-Ichi Koko-mae (¥280). The bus ride takes 20 minutes, and the hostel is then five minutes on foot.

Ryokan A very reasonably priced ryokan close to the station is *Nishiya* (☎ 33-4332). Some English is spoken and the owners are friendly. The place is actually more a min-shuku in terms of standards, but at these prices, who's complaining (¥3600, without meals)? To find it, turn left out of the station's main exit, walk for five minutes until you cross the Metoba-gawa. Nishiya is down the third street on your right.

Places to Stay – Mid-Range

Ryokan *Marumo* (☎ 32-0115) is a delight-ful place with its own bamboo garden and coffee shop in Naka-machi near Metoba-gawa. It's popular with Japanese tourists, so you might want to book ahead (¥6000, with breakfast). Around the corner is the quaint *Nunoya* (☎/fax 32-0545). A traditional wooden building, it has good quality tatami rooms, and Mediterranean cuisine.

If you feel like staying outside of town, *Enjyoh Bekkan* (☎ 33-7233) at Utsukushi-gahara Onsen is a member of the Japanese Inn Group. Rooms cost from ¥5300 to ¥6300 for singles, or ¥9800 for doubles. The hot-spring facilities are available day and night. A Western-style breakfast is available for ¥800. From Matsumoto, take the bus to Utsukushigahara Onsen (20 minutes). From the station it's 300m to the ryokan.

Hotels There are few bargains to be had in this category. One of the cheapest business hotels around is *Matsumoto Tourist Hotel* (☎ 33-9000). Expect to pay at least ¥5800 for singles, and ¥12,000 for doubles. It's about a 10-minute walk from the station.

Hotel Iidaya (☎ 32-0027) is standard business hotel fare (singles from ¥6500, doubles from ¥12,000). Just across the road is the reasonable-value *Hotel New Station* (☎ 35-3850), with singles from ¥6800 and twins from ¥13,600.

Places to Stay – Top End

The recently-built *Ichiyama* (☎ 32-0122) is designed like a kura and has good-quality Western- and Japanese-style rooms with air-con, TV and private bath (¥10,000/16,000

for singles/doubles). It faces the Parco department store.

The upmarket Western-style *Hotel Buena Vista* (☎ 37-0111), with singles from ¥13,090 and twins from ¥17,000, and the dull but efficient *Matsumoto Tōkyū Inn* (☎ 36-0109), with singles for ¥9000 and twins and doubles for ¥17,000, are both close to the station.

Places to Eat

Like Nagano, Matsumoto is renowned for its *shinshū-soba*, a variation on the soba theme that is eaten either hot or cold (zaru-soba) with *wasabi* (Japanese horseradish) and soy sauce. Other specialities more peculiar to the region include raw horsemeat, bee larvae, pond snails and *zazamushi* (crickets).

On the 2nd floor of the station there is an arcade with various restaurants offering inexpensive teishoku. Alternatively, the basement of the bus station also has cheap eateries. You can obtain also *oyaki* (little wheat buns filled with pickles, squash, radish, red bean paste and the like) around here.

In Naka-machi, *Nomugi* (☎ 36-3753) is one of Central Japan's finest soba shops. Its owner used to run a Kyōbashi (Tokyo) French restaurant before returning to his home town to try his hand at the local speciality. The menu is simple soba, served cold in a hand-crafted wicker basket for ¥1000 (closed Tuesday and Wednesday).

Curry fans may want to try out the nearby *Delhi* restaurant, housed incongruously in a kura that is blacker than Matsumoto-jō. There's neither an English sign nor menu. Try asking for the mild 'Indo curry' or the spicier 'Karakuchi curry'. *Trattoria Graspa* (☎ 37-1188) is a trendy bistro in the Rokku arcade west of Nawate-dōri. The friendly owner speaks English. Expect to pay around ¥3000 per person (6 pm to 11 pm, closed Sunday).

Getting There & Away

Air Matsumoto airport has flights to Fukuoka, Hiroshima, Osaka and Sapporo.

Bus The Alpico/Matsumoto Dentetsu company (☎ 35-7400) runs buses between Matsumoto and Shinjuku in Tokyo (¥3400, 3¼

CENTRAL HONSHŪ

hours, 14 daily), Osaka (¥5710, 5½ hours, two daily) and Nagoya (¥3460, 3½ hours, four daily). All departures are from the Matsumoto bus station (reservations advised).

Train Matsumoto is connected with Tokyo and Shinjuku stations (*Super Azusa*, *Azusa*, ¥6200, around three hours, hourly), and Nagoya (Shinano *tokkyū*, ¥5360, two hours) on the JR Chūō Honsen line. The JR Shinonoi line connects Matsumoto with Nagano (*kyūkō* (ordinary express), ¥2770, one hour, futsū, ¥1110, 85 minutes). Matsumoto to Hakuba on the JR Ōito line takes about 1½ hours.

Train and bus travel have to be combined for the connection between Matsumoto and Kamikōchi. For more details about this see Kamikōchi Getting There & Away later in this section.

Getting Around
The castle and the city centre are easily covered on foot.

To/From the Airport An airport shuttle bus connects Matsumoto airport with the city centre (¥540, 25 minutes). Bus departures are timed according to flight schedules. A taxi costs around ¥4500.

Bus Matsumoto bus station is diagonally across the main street to the right as you leave the east exit of the train station. The bus station set-up is a mess: it's part of a large department store, which means you have to negotiate your way down to the basement and make your way through various food counters to find the door to your gate, and then climb the steps to the bus stop up at ground level. Good luck.

SHIRAHONE ONSEN 白骨温泉
☎ 0263
This classic hot-spring resort, literally translating as White Bone Onsen, has retained some traditional inns with open-air hot-spring baths in a mountain setting. Budget travellers, however, will wish to dip and move on as accommodation is pricey. Accessible from Shin-Shimashima station,

it could easily be visited as part of a trip to Kamikōchi or nearby Norikura.

It is said that bathing here for three days ensures three years without a cold, and the milky-blue hydrogen sulphide waters have a wonderful silky feel. The *kōshū rotemburo* (riverside public bath; ¥500, 9.30 am to 5pm) is diagonally opposite the tourist information centre. The inns *Awanoyu* (¥700, 10.30 am to 1.30 pm), *Baikō-an* (¥800, 9 am to 4.30 pm) and *Ebisuya* (¥600, 12 pm to 2 pm) open their baths to the public. *Awanoyu*, farthest up the hill, is the only one to allow *konyoku* (mixed bathing).

The pleasant *Ryokan Tsuruya* (☎ 93-2101) is, believe it or not, the cheapest option (¥16,000, with two meals).

Getting There & Away
From Matsumoto, you first travel by rail on the Matsumoto Dentetsu line to Shin-Shimashima station (¥680, 35 minutes), then take a Matsumoto Dentetsu bus (¥1400, 1½ hours, 7.55 am, 2.10 pm and 3.10 pm) to Shirahone Onsen. Buses to Norikura-kōgen summit and to Norikura-kōgen *kyūka-mura* (vacation village) also pass through Shirahone Onsen (late April to mid-November only).

KAMIKŌCHI 上高地
☎ 0263
Kamikōchi lies in the centre of the northern Japan Alps and has some of the most spectacular scenery in Japan. In the late 19th century, foreigners 'discovered' this mountainous region and coined the term 'Japan Alps'. A British missionary, Reverend Walter Weston, toiled from peak to peak and sparked Japanese interest in mountaineering as a sport. He is now honoured with his own annual festival (see Special Events later in this section) and Kamikōchi has become a base for strollers, hikers and climbers. Kamikōchi is closed from November to May, and in the peak summer season it is busier than Shinjuku station.

If you want to avoid immense crowds, don't plan to visit between late July and late August, or during the first three weeks in

October. Between June and mid-July is the rainy season, which makes outdoor pursuits depressingly soggy.

It's perfectly feasible to visit Kamikōchi from Matsumoto or Takayama in a day, but you'll miss out on the pleasures of staying in the mountains and the opportunity to take early morning or late evening walks before the crowds appear. At the same time, accommodation is expensive: budget travellers beware.

Orientation

On a fine day, the final stages of the approach to Kamikōchi on the road from Nakanoyu provide a superb mountain panorama: there is the pond, Taishō-ike, on your left, and a series of high peaks ranged in the background. There's a pleasant and clearly sign-posted 3km hike uphill, from the Taishō-ike bus stop; or the road continues a short distance to the bus station, which is the farthest point to which vehicles are officially allowed in this valley. A short distance on foot beyond the bus station, the Azusa-gawa is spanned by Kappa-bashi from where a variety of trails snake into the mountains.

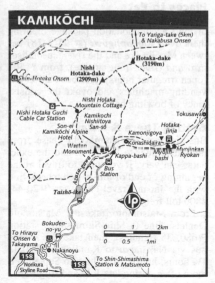

Maps JNTO publishes a leaflet called *Matsumoto & Kamikōchi*, which has brief details and a map of Kamikōchi. The tourist offices also have several large maps (covering Kamikōchi, Shirahone Onsen and the plateau, Norikura-kōgen) that show mountain trails, average hiking times, mountain huts and lists of tourist facilities. However, they are all written in Japanese.

Information

Tourist Office There is an information office (☎ 95-2405) at the bus station (9 am to 5 pm, late April to mid-November only). It has leaflets and maps but is geared mostly to booking accommodation. It's preferable to make prior use of the tourist information offices in Takayama or Matsumoto, which have English-speaking staff.

Day Walks

If you want to do level walking for short distances, stick to the river valley. For a typical three-hour walk (round trip) of this kind you should go east from Kappa-bashi along the right-hand side of the river to Myōjin-bashi (45 minutes) and then continue to Tokusawa (45 minutes) before returning. For variety, you could cross to the other side of the river at Myōjin-bashi.

West of Kappa-bashi, you can amble along the right-hand side of the river to Weston Monument (15 minutes) or keep to the left-hand side of the river and walk to the pond, Taishō-ike (20 minutes).

Hiking

There are dozens of long-distance options for hikers and climbers, varying in duration from a couple of days to a week. *Hiking in Japan* by Paul Hunt, Mason Florence et al provides practical advice. The large Japanese maps of the area show routes and average hiking times between huts, major peaks and landmarks – but you've have to read Japanese. Favourite trails and climbs (which can mean human traffic jams on trails during peak seasons) include Yariga-take (3180m) and Hotaka-dake (3190m) – also known as Oku-Hotaka-dake. Other more distant popular destinations include

Nakabusa Onsen and Murodō, which is on the Tateyama-Kurobe Alpine Route.

If you want to hike between Kamikōchi and Shin-Hotaka Onsen (see Shin-Hotaka Onsen under the Northern Gifu-ken earlier in this chapter), there's a steep trail that crosses the ridge below Nishi Hotaka-dake (2909m) at Nishi Hotaka San-sō (Nishi Hotaka Mountain Cottage) and continues to Nishi Hotaka-guchi, the top station of the cable car for Shin-Hotaka Onsen. The hike takes nearly four hours (because of a steep ascent). Softies might prefer to save an hour of sweat and do the hike in the opposite direction.

Those heading off on long hikes or climbs should be properly prepared. Even in summer, temperatures can plummet, or the whole area can be covered in sleeting rain or blinding fog.

Onsen

Kamikōchi Onsen Hotel (¥600, 6.30 am to 9 am, 12.30 pm to 4.30 pm) and Son-ei Kamikōchi Alpine Hotel (¥500, 7 am to 11.30 am) open their baths to the public. The latter is an artificially heated *reisen* (cold mineral spring).

The area's best-kept secret is at Naka-noyu, just before the bus-only tunnel branches up to Kamikōchi proper. Go in the small store next to the Nakanoyu bus stop, pay ¥500, get the key, and cross the road bridge where you'll find a door set in the mountainside. Open this and inside is Bokuden-no-yu, a tiny gem of a hot-spring cave bath, dripping with minerals. It is yours privately until you return the key.

Special Events

On the first weekend in June, the climbing season opens with the Weston Festival, which honours Walter Weston, the British missionary and alpinist.

Places to Stay

This is Kamikōchi's downside. Accommodation is expensive, advance reservations are essential during the peak season and the whole place shuts down from November to May. You'd be well advised to book a room

before arriving in Kamikōchi; the tourist information offices at Takayama and Matsumoto are convenient because they have English-speaking staff.

There is a handful of hotels, mostly around Kappa-bashi. *Kamikōchi Nishiitoya San-sō* (☎ 95-2206) is relatively expensive (¥13,000, with two meals) but its bunk beds (¥7600) are Kamikōchi's cheapest. Ask for a *ni-dan-beddo* (bunk bed). Up along the river, near Myojin pond, is *Myojinkan Ryokan* (☎ 95-2036). The per-person rate is ¥13,000, with two meals. *Son-ei Kamikōchi Alpine Hotel* (☎ 95-2231) is viciously expensive but has some dorm 'skiers beds' for ¥8500, with one meal. *Kamikōchi Konashidaira Kyampu-jō* (☎ 95-2321), across the river from the bus station, has camp sites for ¥400, rental tents for ¥2000, and a few 'bungalows' for ¥6000. Farther up the river, about 3km north-east of Kappa-bashi, *Tokusawa Kyampu-jō* has similar rates for camp sites and rentals.

Dotted along the trails and around the mountains are dozens of *san-sō* (mountain cottages) or *yama-goya* (mountain huts), which provide two meals and a bed for an average cost of around ¥7000 per person.

Places to Eat

Most visitors either have their meals as part of their accommodation package or bring their own. *Kamonjigoya* (☎ 95-2418) between Myojin-ike and the river, specialises in *iwana* (river trout cuisine), from ¥1500 (open irregular hours). The bus station has vending machines and oyaki the consistency of bowling balls.

Getting There & Away

Bus services for Kamikōchi cease from mid-November to late April and the exact dates can vary. If you plan to travel at the beginning or end of this period, check first with the Japan Travel-Phone (☎ 0120-44-4800 toll free).

From Matsumoto, take the Matsumoto Dentetsu line to Shin-Shimashima station (¥680, 35 minutes), then take the Alpico bus via Nakanoyu to Kamikōchi (¥2050, 1¼ hours, hourly from June to September, more often during late July and August).

From Kamikōchi you can continue by bus via Hirayu Onsen to Fukuchi Onsen or Takayama. Between Takayama and Kamikōchi from April to October only there are frequent bus connections (¥3050, two hours, between 7 am and around 2.30 pm), via Nakanoyu, changing at Hirayu Onsen.

Between Norikura Tatami-daira (near the summit of Norikura-dake) and Kamikōchi, buses run via Hirayu Onsen (two hours, three times daily, more in July and August). The Norikura Skyline Road is only open from 15 May to 31 October (¥2950, two hours). There are buses between Kamikōchi and the town, Norikura-kōgen (¥1800, one daily, two from late July to late August), and between Kamikōchi and Shirahone Onsen (¥1500, 45 minutes, one or two daily).

The road between Nakanoyu and Kamikōchi is closed to private cars – only buses and taxis are permitted, so rent a car to come here.

NORIKURA-KŌGEN & NORIKURA ONSEN
乗鞍高原・乗鞍温泉
☎ 0263

This alpine plateau below Norikura-dake (3026m) is blissfully free of the Kamikōchi crowds, and offers cycling, hiking and skiing possibilities. It is also famous for the Norikura Skyline Road (closed from November to May), a scenic bus route that leads to the Tatami-daira bus stop at the foot of the mountain. From there, a trail leads to the peak in about 40 minutes. You might glimpse a raichō (ptarmigan), the prefectural symbol, or if you're really fortunate, the magnificent inuwashi (dog eagle).

Norikura Onsen is a collection of hot-spring accommodations on the plateau. It has well-marked trails (in English to boot), one of the best being the 40-minute woodland walk from the Suzuran bus stop to the beautiful waterfall, Zengoro-no-taki.

There's also a kubiwa kōmori (collared bat) study centre.

During the last weekend in August, Norikura hosts a national mountain-bike race.

Places to Stay

There is a wide choice of ryokan and min-shuku accommodation, mostly near the Suzuran bus stop. Cheapest, however, is *Norikura Kōgen Youth Hostel* (☎ 93-2748) with shared tatami rooms for ¥3200, a 10-minute trek from the Ski-jō mae bus stop. It has excellent wooden onsen baths and the manager is a great source of local information. On the way to the youth hostel you might want to look out for the unassuming *Ryokan Mitake-sō* (☎ 93-2016), which charges from ¥8000 to ¥10,000, with two meals. *Pension Chimunii* (☎ 93-2902), charging ¥7500, with two meals, is a cosy place right next to the Ski-jō mae bus stop, one past the Suzuran stop.

Tatami-daira, near the summit of Norikura-dake, is not an ideal place to spend the night; it's basically a big car park with a few well-worn trails snaking off from it to the nearby peaks. But if you get stuck up here (quite possible, given the inconvenient bus schedules), there are two ryokan with per person rates of ¥8000 to ¥10,000, including two meals. They are next to each other at the far end of the car park.

Getting There & Away

The bus between Norikura Tatami-daira and Takayama operates along the Norikura Skyline Road between 15 May to 31 October and usually runs via Hirayu Onsen (¥2650, 1½ hours, five or six times daily between 7.30 am and 12.20 pm).

From July to mid-October there are five to six buses a day between Norikura-kōgen and Shin-Shimashima station, where you can catch trains to Matsumoto. The trip takes about an hour and costs ¥1300 (to Suzuran). Services are suspended on Sunday and holidays.

There are also one or two buses a day between Norikura-kōgen, Shirahone Onsen and Kamikōchi. The fare from Suzuran to Kamikōchi is ¥1800.

If you are driving your own vehicle, be aware that the one-way toll for driving on the Norikura Skyline is a hefty ¥1540, and unless you plan to take the toll road onward

CENTRAL HONSHŪ

to Matsumoto (or stay up at Tatami-daira until your next reincarnation), you'll have to buy a round-trip pass for ¥3080.

HOTAKA 穂高
☎ 0263 • pop 32,049

Hotaka is a small town with a couple of interesting sights, but it's especially popular with hikers and mountaineers, who use it as a base to head into the mountains. Both the station and bicycle rental place (to your right as you exit on the east side of the station) have basic maps of the town. You can either walk around the area or rent a bicycle for ¥200 per hour. If you're staying at the youth hostel you can also rent a bicycle there.

Rokuzan Art Museum

Rokuzan Art Museum (Rokuzan Bijutsukan; ¥500, 9 am to 5 pm between April and October, until 4 pm November to March, closed on Monday) is 10 minutes on foot from the station and is worth a visit. On display are sculptures by Rokuzan Ogiwara, a master sculptor whom the Japanese have claimed as the 'Rodin of the Orient'.

Wasabi Farms

Even if you're not a great fan of wasabi (Japanese horseradish), a visit to the Dai-ō Wasabi Farm is a good excuse to cycle or walk through fields crisscrossed with canals. The farm is the largest of its kind in Japan, and is a couple of kilometres directly east of Hotaka station. The basic map provided at the station or at the adjacent bicycle rental office is sufficient for orientation.

Nakabusa Onsen

These remote hot springs are reached by bus from Ariake station (¥1610, 70 minutes), one stop north of Hotaka. Buses, however, only run from mid-July to mid-August and are irregular. A taxi to the onsen costs ¥7000. From here, there are several trails for extended mountain hikes. There is also accommodation if you're in the mood to get away from it all and soak for a few days (see the following Places to Stay entry).

Jōnen-dake

From Toyoshina station, two stops south of Hotaka, it takes 10 minutes by taxi to reach Kitakaidō, which is the start of a trail for experienced hikers to climb Jonen-dake (2857m) – the ascent takes about eight hours. There are many options for mountain hikes extending over several days in the region, but you must be properly prepared. Hiking maps and information are available at the Hotaka, Matsumoto and Nagano tourist offices, although the more detailed maps are in Japanese.

Places to Stay

Azumino Youth Hostel (☎ 83-6170) is 4km west of Hotaka station (a one-hour walk). Bicycles are available for hire. The hostel is closed from 17 January to 7 February (¥3100).

Not far from Hotaka station are numerous pensions and ryokan. *Shioya Ryokan (☎ 82-2012)* is just to the east of the station (from ¥6500, with two meals).

Nestled up near Nakabusa Onsen are two places where you can take a break from the road and soak up the nourishing minerals of the local hot springs. *Ariake-so Kokuminshukusha (☎ 35-9701)* is by far the less expensive of the two (¥8500, including two meals). More luxurious is *Nakabusa Onsen* hotel (☎ 35-9704), where you'll pay ¥8500, including two meals. During peak periods you may have to share your room with other guests: pretty steep prices for a dorm bed. To get there, take a bus from Ariake station (one stop north of Hotaka): Nakabusa Onsen is the last stop.

Getting There & Away

Hotaka is about 30 minutes (¥310) from Matsumoto on the JR Ōito line.

NAGANO 長野
☎ 0262 • pop 347,000

Nagano, capital of the prefecture, has been around since the Kamakura period, when it was a temple town centred around Zenkō-ji. The temple is still Nagano's main attraction, drawing more than four million visitors every year.

After a brief flirtation with international fame hosting the 1998 Winter Olympics, Nagano has reverted to its friendly small-town self, albeit with a few new buildings, improved transportation, and a rather more cosmopolitan touch.

The city is also an important transport hub, providing access to the superb recreational facilities in the surrounding region. As a destination, it shouldn't be a high priority, but it's worth staying overnight here to visit Zenkō-ji and stroll around town.

Orientation & Information

JR Nagano station is at an angle to Chūō-dōri, the main road running north to Zenko-ji, 30 minutes' walk away.

The staff of Nagano city tourist information centre (☎ 26-5626) in the JR Nagano station are extraordinarily helpful (9.30 am to 6 pm). They will ply you with good English-language colour maps and guides to both Nagano and the surrounding areas: the *Guide to Nagano City and Northern Shinano* has a wealth of useful facts and maps.

The International Relations section of Nagano City Hall (☎ 24-5121) has both English and Chinese speakers on hand (8.30 am to 5.15 pm weekdays). The Association of Nagano Prefecture for Promoting International Exchange (☎ 35-7186) can also help visitors, in English (8.30 am to 5.15 pm weekdays). ANPIE, the International Exchange Lounge (8.30 am to 5 pm), 1km west of the station, outside the prefectural office, also has detailed information in English.

Money Nagano's only ATM to accept internationally issued cards (VISA, Cirrus or MasterCard) is on the 1st floor of the West Plaza Nagano (8 am to 10 pm) opposite the station, below the huge TV screen.

Email & Internet Access *Neo Wave Internet Cafe* (☎ 91-6211) has all-day access for ¥1000 (10 am to 7 pm, closed Monday). It's on the 2nd floor of the Beanie Baby boutique on the street that runs diagonally behind the Hotel Annex Kinenkan, five minutes' walk from the station.

Zenkō-ji

Zenkō-ji (¥500, 5 am to 4 pm) is believed to have been founded in the 7th century, and was the home of the Ikkō Sanzon, allegedly the first Buddhist image to arrive in Japan (in 552). There have since been several different stories concerning the image, which was, at times, the subject of disputes, and was lost, rediscovered and finally installed again.

Although the temple buildings have been destroyed several times by fire, donations for reconstruction have always been provided by believers throughout Japan. The immense popularity of this temple stems from its liberal acceptance of believers, including women, from all Buddhist sects (an adroit political move, one might guess). There are some 200 other Zenkō-ji temples scattered throughout Japan. Despite its name it has nothing to do with Zen.

The centre of the temple complex is the Hondō (Main Hall), a reconstruction dating from 1707 and a national treasure.

Once you've entered the inner sanctum of the Hondō, you'll see a small ticket window on your left where English-language pamphlets are available. After you've bought your ticket, take off your shoes (and place them in the bag provided), then proceed through the ticket collector's entrance. At the back of the hall, you descend a flight of steps into complete darkness – the absence of light is intentional and mandatory. Keep groping your way along the right-hand side of the tunnel until you feel something heavy, moveable and metallic – the key to salvation! This is especially enlightening if you share the space with several hundred schoolchildren.

It's worth getting to the temple by 5.30 am to witness the morning service and the *ojuzu chodai*, the blessing of Buddhist holy beads.

The temple is about 1.5km from JR Nagano station, at the northern end of Chūō-dōri. A bus to the Dai-mon (¥200, 10 minutes, every 10 minutes) leaves from gate No 1 in front of the station. A taxi costs ¥900.

Courses

Travellers interested in Japanese cultural pursuits such as martial arts, traditional music and even Zen can check with any of the information centres to arrange one-day study courses. Staff will make arrangements for you or give you a phone number where you can speak with someone in English.

Special Events

Gokaichō Matsuri is held at Zenkō-ji once every seven years from 10 April to 20 May. Millions of pilgrims attend this extravaganza, when a sacred image of Buddha, given to the emperor by a Korean king in 552, is put on display – the next festival is in 2003.

Places to Stay

Shukubō (temple lodgings) are available around Zenkō-ji. If you are interested, the Nagano City Hall International Relations section or the Association of Nagano Prefecture for Promoting International Exchange may be able to help. Per-person rates with two meals generally cost between ¥7000 and ¥10,000.

Places to Stay – Budget

Zenkō-ji Kyōju-in Youth Hostel (☎ 32-2768) is a temple on Nakamise-dōri, a couple of minutes on foot south-east of Zenkō-ji (¥2800). Matronly guidance from the manager ensures an amicable, but strict, regime. Keep things amicable by making an advance reservation.

Places to Stay – Mid-Range

Ryokan *Shimizuya Ryokan* (☎ 32-2672) is a cosy little place not too far from the Daimon of Zenkō-ji (from ¥8000, with two meals). There isn't an English sign, but keep a sharp eye out for a small sign posted above a cold-drink vending machine that says 'Boy Scouts of Japan Office'.

Hotels The station area has a number of standard business hotels. *Nagano Dai-Ichi Hotel* (☎ 28-1211) is just to the east of the station (singles from ¥6000, twins for ¥12,000). Also close to the station is *Hotel New Nagano* (☎ 27-7200), with singles for ¥6500 and twins from ¥12,500. Almost directly opposite the station, *Hotel Ikemon* (☎ 27-2122) has singles for ¥6000, twins

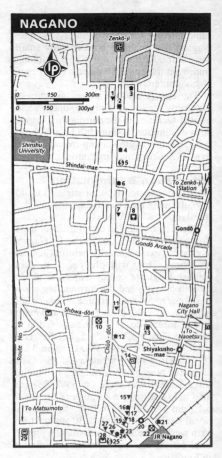

for ¥10,500 and very reasonably priced doubles for ¥8000.

One option worth considering is *Mitsui Garden Hotel Nagano* (☎ 25-1131), which gives you an upmarket stay for standard business hotel rates (singles ¥7500, twins and doubles ¥13,500, semi-doubles – a single room with a small double bed crammed in it – ¥11,000). Other more upmarket options include *Nagano Washington Hotel* (☎ 28-5111), with singles/twins from ¥6000/13,700, and *Hotel Sunroute Nagano* (☎ 28-2222), with singles from ¥7854 and twins and doubles from ¥13,860.

NAGANO

PLACES TO STAY
3 Zenkō-ji Kyōju-in
Youth Hostel
善光寺教授院
ユースホステル
4 Gohonjin Fujiya
御本陣藤屋
6 Shimizuya
Ryokan
旅館清水屋
12 Mitsui Garden Hotel
Nagano
三井ガーデンホテル長野
13 Nagano Washington
Hotel
長野ワシントンホテル
16 Hotel New Nagano
ホテルニューナガノ
21 Nagano Dai-Ichi
Hotel
長野第一ホテル

23 Hotel Sunroute Nagano
ホテルサンルート長野
24 Hotel Ikemon
ホテル池門

PLACES TO EAT
1 Marusei
丸清
7 Ōtaya
太田屋そば
11 Nan Naan
ナンナーン
15 KFC
17 Doutor
18 McDonald's
19 Kinryū Hanten
金龍本店
26 Yōrōnotaki
養老の滝
27 Tsubohachi
つぼ八

OTHER
2 Nakamise-dōri
仲見世通り
5 Eighty-Two Bank
八十二銀行
8 Club Soda
9 Central Post Office
中央郵便局
10 Daiei Department Store
ダイエーデパート
14 Neo Wave Internet Cafe
20 Nagano Train Station
長野駅
22 Midori Department Store
みどりデパート
25 ATM (West Plaza Nagano)
ウエストプラザ長野
28 Post Office
郵便局
29 Bus Station
バスターミナル

Places to Stay – Top End

Ryokan Nagano's most famous hotel is the venerable *Gohonjin Fujiya* (☎ 32-1241), which looks out over Chūō-dōri and the Dai-mon (¥9000 per person, with two meals). The first hostel on the site opened its doors in the late 18th century and the same family has run the business ever since. The current building, which dates from 1923, is rather Western-looking in design but still functions as a traditional Japanese inn.

Places to Eat & Drink

Midori, a department store immediately on your right as you exit the station, has a cluster of inexpensive restaurants on the 5th floor (11 am to 9 pm, closed some Tuesdays), a good place for a quick bite to eat. Prices generally range from ¥800 to ¥1200 for teishoku.

On the local speciality front, Nagano is famed for its buckwheat noodles, and there are many soba restaurants around Zenkō-ji. Local knowledge favours *Marusei* (☎ 232-5776), just below the temple entrance (11 am to 6 pm, closed Wednesday). It also serves *tonkatsu* (pork cutlets).

If you walk downhill from Dai-mon along the left hand side of Chūō-dōri, after about 300m you'll see a shop window with a mill grinding flour. This is *Ōtaya*, a restaurant that specialises in home-made soba. Prices for a soba teishoku lunch start at around ¥680.

Another local speciality is oyaki. There's a little stand right in front of the train station that serves up several tasty varieties for around ¥130 a piece.

Nan Naan (☎ 237-7576) serves Indian curries and has a great lunch buffet deal for ¥800 (11.30 am to 2pm, 5.30 pm to 11 pm, closed Sunday, English menu available). It's on the 2nd floor of the Taiheidō building at the junction of Chūō-dōri and Shōwa-dōri.

The Australian-owned live-house-cum-gaijin-bar *Club Soda* (☎ 235-5667) is a good place to meet the locals. It's one street east of Ōtaya (from 6pm).

The izakaya chains *Yōrōnotaki* and *Tsubohachi* have branches near the station. *Winds East* (☎ 225-6464) is a good izakaya serving inexpensive Italian cuisine (11 am to 11.50 pm). It's on the third floor of the Stella Building A, opposite the east exit of Nagano station.

CENTRAL HONSHŪ

Getting There & Away

Nagano shinkansen trains run regularly from Tokyo station (Asama, ¥7980, one hour and 50 minutes, twice-hourly). The JR Shinonoi line connects Nagano with Matsumoto (kyūkō, ¥2770, one hour; futsū, ¥1110, 85 minutes). To Nagoya it takes three hours and costs ¥3260, plus a ¥2610 limited express surcharge.

Getting Around

Nagano is small enough to comfortably navigate on foot. Any city bus from in front of the station goes to Zenkō-ji.

TOGAKUSHI 戸隠
☎ 0262 • pop 5214

Togakushi, famed for soba, lies north-west of Nagano and is a popular destination for hikers, particularly in late spring and during autumn. In the winter, skiers favour the slopes around Menō-yama and Kurohime-yama. The one-hour hike from Okusha bus stop includes a pleasant section along a tree-lined approach. The Nagano tourist information centre has maps for hiking in the area.

Togakushi is reached by taking a bus from Nagano to the Chūsha bus stop. An inexpensive place to stay is *Togakushi Kōgen Yokokura Youth Hostel* (☎ 54-2030), a couple of minutes from Chūsha bus stop and next to a ski slope (¥4750, with two meals). There are also quite a few ryokan in the area: prices generally start at around ¥8000 to ¥10,000 per person.

There are buses from Nagano bus station to Chūsha (¥1160, one hour), which run via the scenic **Togakushi Birdline Highway**. Buses to Chūsha leave Nagano approximately once an hour between 6.50 am and 6.40 pm, and in summer continue to Okusha bus stop (¥1360).

OBUSE 小布施
☎ 0262

If you are interested in ukiyo-e, then you should make the short trip to Obuse, northeast of Nagano, and visit the **Hokusai-kan Museum**. (☎ 47-5206). This museum displays 30 paintings of wood-block prints by the master, Hokusai, and two festival floats

(¥500, 9 am to 4.30 pm). The museum shop also stocks some hilarious reproductions of his lesser-known, scurrilous illustrations.

To reach Obuse, take the Nagano Dentetsu line from Nagano (¥650, 30 minutes). The museum is eight minutes on foot from the station. Exit the station and walk straight ahead until you reach the main road. Turn right, walk past two sets of traffic lights, and after 50m take the side street to your left, which leads to the museum.

Obuse also boasts the nearest rotemburo to Nagano, Obuse Onsen (☎ 47-2525), which costs ¥500 (bring a towel), a bonsai museum and Ganshō-in Temple.

YUDANAKA 湯田中
☎ 0269

This town is famous for its hot springs, particularly those known as **Jigokudani Onsen** (Hell Valley Hot Springs), which attract monkeys keen to escape the winter chill with a hot soak.

Uotoshi Ryokan (☎ 33-1215) is a member of the Japanese Inn Group (¥8000, with two meals). The owner may demonstrate *kyūdō* (Japanese archery) on request. You can arrange to be picked up at the station, or walk from there to the ryokan (seven minutes).

If you want to commune with the monkeys, try a night at *Kōraku-kan* (☎ 33-4376), which is perched up a small valley next to Jigokudani Onsen (¥12,000 per person, with two meals). Accommodation is fairly basic for the money, as is the food, but the onsen baths are pleasant, and available 24 hours. Getting there is a bit of a trek. From Yudanaka station, take the bus to Kanbayashi Onsen (¥220, 15 minutes) and get off at the last stop. From here walk uphill along the road about 400m until it curves 180°, where you come to a large sign over a trailhead. Follow that trail for a pleasant, tree-lined 1.6km to get to the ryokan. If you arrive during the morning carrying bags of food, keep a sharp eye out for any marauding monkeys: some of the nasty beasts may try to snatch your goodies from you.

From Nagano, take the Nagano Dentetsu line to Yudanaka (kyūkō, ¥1230, hourly;

futsū, ¥1130). Make sure when boarding at Nagano that your train goes all the way to the Yudanaka station, as some trains stop at Nakano.

HAKUBA & AROUND 白馬
☎ 0261

The town of Hakuba, north-west of Nagano, is used as an access point for outdoor activities in the nearby mountains. Skiing in the winter and hiking or mountaineering in the summer attract large numbers of visitors. The hiking trails tend to be less clogged during September and October. Even if you plan to ascend the highest peaks in mid-summer you should be prepared for hiking over snow-covered terrain.

Shirouma-dake 白馬岳
The ascent of this mountain (2932m) is a popular hike, but you should be properly prepared. There are several mountain huts that provide meals and basic accommodation along the trails.

From Hakuba station there are buses (¥960, 30 minutes, 30 May to 30 September) to Sarukura, where the trailhead is located. From here, you can hike west to the peak in about six hours; note that there are two *huts* on this route. A more leisurely option is to follow the trail for about 1¾ hours to Daisekkei (Great Snowy Gorge).

The trail south-west of Sarukura leads uphill for three hours to Yari Onsen, and its open-air hot spring with breathtaking mountain views. There's also a mountain hut if you feel compelled to stay.

Tsugaike Shizen-en 栂池自然園
Tsugaike Natural Park lies below Shirouma Norikura dake in an alpine marsh land (¥300). A three-hour hiking trail takes in most of the park, which is renowned for its alpine flora. Admission to the park is ¥300.

From Hakuba Oike station, two stops north of Hakuba station, it takes an hour by bus to reach the park. During summer there are one to two buses an hour. Between June and late October there's also a bus from Hakuba station that takes about 1½ hours.

Happō-o-ne Ski Resort 八方尾根スキーリゾート
This is a busy ski resort in the winter and a popular hiking area in the summer. From Hakuba station, a five-minute bus ride takes you to Happō; from here it's an eight-minute walk to the cable car base station. From the top station of the cable car you can use two more chairlifts, and then hike along a trail for an hour or so to Happō-ike on a ridge below Karamatsu-dake. From this pond you can follow a trail for an hour up to Maru-yama, continue for 1½ hours to the Karamatsu-dake San-sō (mountain hut) and then climb to the peak of Karamatsu-dake (2695m) in about 30 minutes. The total round-trip fare for the 'gondola' and two chair lifts is ¥2270. The main 'gondola' runs between 8 am and 5 pm, while the chairlifts close at 4.30 pm.

Nishina San-ko 仁科三湖
While travelling south from Hakuba, there is Nishina San-ko (Nishina Three Lakes), which provides scope for some short walks. Nakazuna-ko and Aoki-ko are close to Yanaba station, and Kizaki-ko is next to Inao station.

Shio-no-Michi 塩の道
In the past, Hakuba lay on the route of the Shio-no-Michi (Salt Road), which was used to carry salt on oxen from the Sea of Japan to Matsumoto. Parts of this road still exist and there's a popular three-hour hike along one section that starts at Otari Folklore Museum (Otari Kyodokan) – three minutes' on foot from Minami Otari station – and continues via Chikuni Suwa shrine before finishing at Matsuzawa-guchi. From there, it's a further 15 minute bus ride to Hakuba Oike station.

If you are thirsting for more background on salt, you could take the train farther down the line to Shinano-ōmachi station and visit the Salt Museum.

Places to Stay
Not far from the cable car base station at Happō-o-ne is *Wada Ryokan* (☎ 72-5552), a kokumin-shukusha that caters to hikers

and skiers (¥7500, with two meals). This place fills up quickly, so it would be wise to book ahead, for which you will probably need the help of a Japanese speaker. To get there, take the bus to Happō-o-ne ski resort from Hakuba station.

Across the road is *Lodge Hakuba* (☎ 72-3095), another hiker/skier place with similar prices to Wada Ryokan.

Hajimeno Ippo (☎ 75-3527) is a minshuku and is a member of the Toho network (dorm rooms ¥3800, with two meals, ¥4800 between December and May). You'll probably need to know some Japanese and it's a small place, so advance reservations are a necessity. The minshuku is 12 minutes on foot from Iimori station (one stop south of Hakuba) and is usually closed in June and November.

Getting There & Away

Hakuba is connected with Matsumoto by the JR Ōito line (futsū, ¥1110, 1¾ hours; tokkyū, ¥2770, one hour). From Shinano-ōmachi station allow 35 minutes to reach Hakuba.

Continuing north, the Ōito line eventually connects with the JR Hokuriku Honsen line at Itoigawa, which offers the options of heading north-east towards Niigata or south-west to Toyama and Kanazawa. However, at the time of writing, the service between Hakuba and Itoigawa had been suspended for one year due to massive river flooding and landslides that had buried a section of the line north of Minami Otari. JR has not yet announced a date for reopening the section, which means it may be closed for an extended period of time. Limited bus services are available to cover the gap, but they're scheduled mainly for local use. If the line is still out, it would be best to approach Hakuba from the south.

ŌMACHI 大町
☎ 0261

The city of Ōmachi has several stations, but the one to use is called Shinano-ōmachi, which has tourist information facilities. The main reason for visiting Ōmachi is to start or finish the **Tateyama-Kurobe Alpine**

Route, which is an expensive but impressive jaunt by various means of transport across the peaks between Nagano-ken and Toyama-ken. See the Toyama-ken section later in this chapter for details. If you have time in Ōmachi while waiting for connections, the **Salt Museum** (Shio-no-Michi Haku-butsukan; ¥500, 9 am to 4.30 pm, closed Wednesday from November to April) is five minutes' walk from the station.

Places to Stay

An inexpensive place to stay is *Kizaki-ko Youth Hostel* (☎ 22-1820), 15 minutes on foot from Shinanosazaki station (just south of Kizaki-ko), two stops north of Shinano-ōmachi station (¥3150). From the station, walk north in the direction of the lake; at the south end of the lake, turn left and look for the hostel on the right. Close to the hostel, clustered around the southern end of the lake, are numerous hotels, pensions and minshuku. If you need to stay overnight near Shinano-ōmachi station, *Omachi Station Hotel* (☎ 22-7111) is opposite the train station (singles from ¥5900, twins/doubles from ¥10,900/10,700).

Getting There & Away

Local trains on the JR Ōito line connect Ōmachi with Matsumoto (¥620, one hour). For connections with Hakuba on the same line, allow 35 minutes waiting time. The main approach or departure is via the Tateyama-Kurobe Alpine Route – see the following Toyama-ken section for more details.

Toyama-ken 富山県

TOYAMA
☎ 0764 • pop 321,000

Toyama is a heavily industrialised city with few tourist attractions. But it does provide a convenient access point for a visit to the northern Japan Alps, and the Japan Sea coast.

If you've got time to kill here, it's worth a visit to Chokei-ji and its 500 statues of *rakan* (Buddha's disciples), or the nearby

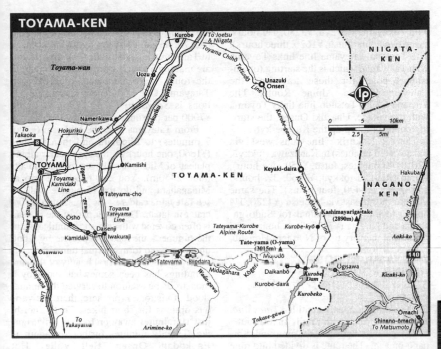

TOYAMA-KEN

Toyama Municipal Folkcraft Village (¥620, 9 am to 4.30 pm, closed Monday), a collection of museums displaying local crafts. You might also try to find *yakuzen-ryōri*, the area's traditional medicinal cuisine.

Information
The information office in front of Toyama station (☎ 32-9751) has the useful *Toyama City Guide* and pamphlets on the Tateyama-Kurobe Alpine Route, Unazuki Onsen and Gokayama (8 am to 8 pm, English spoken). JNTO issues a leaflet entitled *Tateyama, Kurobe & Toyama*, which has details on transport links and accommodation.

Money The Hokuriku and Sumitomo banks will advance money on credit cards, with a passport, from 9 am to 3 pm weekdays.

Email & Internet Access Internet cafe *Captain* (☎ 31-7419) is on the 2nd floor of the Urban Place building, on the north side

of Toyama station (10 am to 9 pm, closed 2nd and 4th Monday of every month). Between 11 am and 2 pm, Net access is free with lunch (¥850).

Places to Stay
If you have to stay in Toyama, there are plenty of business hotels just a few minutes on foot from the station. Best value is the *Business Hotel Sado* (☎ 33-4311), which has rooms with bath at ¥5500. *Marui Ryokan* (☎ 32-1698) has good Japanese-style rooms, and is five minutes' walk south-west of the station.

Toyama Youth Hostel (☎ 37-9010) lies inconveniently north-east of the city, 45 minutes by bus from the station (Nos 7 and 8). Beds cost from ¥2200 to ¥2350, depending on the season.

Getting There & Away
Air Daily flights operate between Toyama and Tokyo.

Train The JR Takayama line links Toyama with Takayama (tokkyū, ¥3280, 1½ hours, every two hours; futsū, ¥1620, three hours). The Toyama Tateyama line links Toyama with Tateyama, which is the starting (or finishing) point for those travelling the Tateyama-Kurobe Alpine Route. The Toyama Chihō Tetsudō line links Toyama with the village, Unazuki Onsen, the starting point for a trip up the Kurobe-kyō.

The JR Hokuriku line runs west via Takaoka (15 minutes) to Kanazawa (tokkyū, ¥2610, 40 minutes; futsū, ¥950, one hour), Kyoto (Rai-chō tokkyū, ¥7660, 3½ hours) and Osaka (¥8490, four hours). The same line runs north-east via Naoetsu (¥4280, 1¼ hours) to the ferry terminal for Sado-ga-shima and Niigata (¥7130, three hours) and Aomori at the very tip of Northern Honshū.

TATEYAMA-KUROBE ALPINE ROUTE
立山 – 黒部アルペンルート
☎ 0764

JNTO publishes a leaflet entitled *Tateyama, Kurobe & Toyama* with details on this route, which extends between Toyama and Shinano-ōmachi. The route is divided into nine sections using various modes of transport. The best place to take a break, if only to escape the Mickey Mouse commentaries and enjoy the tremendous scenery, is Murodō. Transport buffs will want to do the lot, but some visitors find that a trip from Toyama as far as Murodō is sufficient, therefore skipping the expense of the rest. Transport costs for the 90km trip from Toyama to Shinano-ōmachi add up to ¥10,320 for adults.

Peak season is between August and late October and transport and accommodation reservations are strongly advised for travel in these months. Better yet, avoid this period.

The route is closed from late November to late April. For the precise dates, which vary each year, check with a tourist office or call Japan Travel-Phone (☎ 0120-44-4800 toll free).

The Route
This route will take you from Toyama to Shinano-ōmachi, but travel is possible in either direction. From Toyama station, take the chug-a-lug Toyama Tateyama line (¥1170, 45 minutes) through rural scenery to Tateyama (at an altitude of 454m). If you are making an early start or a late finish on the route, there are plenty of ryokan in Tateyama. One of the more reasonable options is *Senzanso* (☎ 82-1726), charging ¥7000 per person, including two meals.

From Tateyama, take the cable car (¥700, 7 minutes) to **Bijodaira** and then the bus (¥1660, one hour) via the spectacular alpine plateau of Midagahara-kōgen to **Murodō** altitude 2450m). You can break the trip at Midagahara and do the 15-minute walk to see **Tateyama caldera** – the largest non-active crater in Japan. The upper part of the plateau is often covered with deep snow until late into the summer – the road is kept clear by piling up the snow to form a virtual tunnel.

At Murodō, the natural beauty of the surroundings has been somewhat spoilt by a monstrous bus station to service the annual flood of visitors. From here, there are various options for short hikes. To the north, just 10 minutes away on foot, is **Mikuriga-ike**. Twenty minutes further on again is **Jigokudani Onsen** (Hell Valley Hot Springs): no bathing here, unless you don't mind boiling bath water. To the east, you can hike for about two hours – including a very steep final section – to the peak of **O-yama** (3003m) for an astounding panorama. For the keen long-distance hiker who has several days or even a week to spare, there are fine routes south to Kamikōchi or north to Keyaki-daira in the Kurobe-kyō.

Continuing on the route from Murodō, there's a bus ride (¥2100, 10 minutes) to Daikanbō, via a tunnel dug through Tateyama. By our calculations this is roughly 3½ times the per-minute cost of a Tokyo to Kyoto shinkansen.

At **Daikanbō** you can pause to admire the view before taking the cable car for the (¥1260, seven minutes) to Kurobe-daira, where another cable car whisks you down (¥840, five minutes) to Kurobeko beside the vast **Kurobe Dam**.

There's a 20-minute walk from Kurobeko to the dam, where you can descend to the water for a cruise, or climb up to a lookout point, before taking the trolley bus to **Ogisawa** (¥1260, 16 minutes). From here, a bus ride (¥1330, 40 minutes) takes you down to Shinano-ōmachi station – at an altitude of 712m. From here there are frequent trains to Matsumoto (one hour), from where you can connect with trains for Tokyo, Nagoya and Nagano.

There's no denying that it's a unique way to travel but not everyone will agree it's worth the cost.

KUROBE-KYŌ & UNAZUKI ONSEN
黒部峡・宇奈月温泉
☎ 0765
From Unazuki Onsen, the Kurobe Kyokoku tram line provides a superbly scenic alpine run past hot-spring lodges, and continues up the Kurobe-kyō to Keyakidaira. Here you can hike to an observation point for a panorama of the northern Japan Alps. Keyaki-daira is also linked with Hakuba and Murodō by trails that are suitable for seasoned hikers who are properly prepared and have several days to spare.

Places to Stay
There's no shortage of luxury accommodation in this area, but there are a few reasonably priced places as well. In Unazuki, the NTT-owned *Etsuzan-so* (☎ 62-1016) is one of the best deals (around ¥8000 per person, with two generous meals). Also in Unazuki is *Kurobe-so* (☎ 62-1149), with its own rotemburo (¥8200). In Kuronagi, farther up the gorge on the Kurobe Kyokoku line (¥470, 25 minutes), *Kuronagi Onsen Ryokan* (☎ 62-1820) also has private hot-spring baths. Expect to pay ¥9000 per person, with two meals. Reservations are recommended, as these cheaper spots fill up quickly. Unless you speak Japanese, you'll probably need to enlist the help of a tourist office to book a room by phone.

Getting There & Away
Take the train on the Toyama Chihō Tetsudō line from the separate terminus (next to Toyama station) to Unazuki Onsen (¥1790, 1½ hours, once an hour). If you're arriving on the JR Hokuriku line from the north,

change to the Toyama Chihō Tetsudō line either at Kurobe (the stations are separate) or at Uozu (the stations are together).

When you arrive at the train station at Unazuki Onsen, you then have to walk for five minutes to the station for the Kurobe Kyōkoku Tetsudō (tram line). The tram line only operates from early May to late November and open carriages are used on most runs. The fare from Unazuki Onsen to Keyaki-daira is ¥1440 and the trip takes one hour and 20 minutes. A surcharge is payable for travel on the daily run with enclosed carriages.

GOKAYAMA
This remote region, famous for its gasshō-zukuri architecture, is in the south-western corner of Toyama-ken, near the border with Gifu-ken. See Gokayama under Shōkawa Valley Region in the Northern Gifu-ken section earlier in this chapter.

Getting There & Away
To visit Gokayama, you can either take a Kaetsuno bus from Takaoka station (¥1700, two hours to Suganuma) or you can take a Jōhana line train from Toyama to Jōhana (¥560, 50 minutes) and continue from there by bus (one hour to Suganuma). Several buses run further, linking Gokayama with Ogi-machi and Shirakawa-gō. From Ogi-machi you can take buses to Takayama. Buses are not that frequent, so build some extra time into your itinerary.

Ishikawa-ken
石川県

This prefecture offers visitors a nice blend of cultural and historical sights, and natural beauty. Kanazawa, longtime power base of the Maeda clan, boasts several excellent museums, traditional architecture and one of Japan's most famous gardens. To the north, the peninsula, Noto-hantō, has beautiful seascapes, rolling hills and quiet fishing villages. Hakusan National Park, near the southern tip of Ishikawa, offers the chance for some great hiking.

CENTRAL HONSHŪ

KANAZAWA 金沢

☎ 076 • pop 442,000

During the 15th century, Kanazawa came under the control of an autonomous Buddhist government, but this was ousted in 1583 by Maeda Toshiie, head of the powerful Maeda clan that continued to rule for another three centuries. The wealth acquired from rice production allowed the Maeda to patronise cultural and artistic pursuits – Kanazawa is still one of the key cultural centres in Japan.

During WWII, the absence of military targets in Kanazawa spared the city from destruction and thus several historical and cultural sites were preserved. As the capital of Ishikawa-ken, Kanazawa has its fair share of functional urban architecture. However, it has retained some attractive features from the old city, including the famous Kenroku-en.

The main sights can be seen in a day or so and side trips to Noto-hantō and Eihei-ji in Fukui-ken are highly recommended.

Orientation

Kanazawa is a sprawling city, and the central city area is a bus ride (¥200, 15 minutes, stops 7, 8 and 9) to the south-east of JR Kanazawa station. Fortunately the city has an excellent bus service, making it easy to get to the main sightseeing districts, which can then be covered on foot. The Katamachi District is the commercial and business hub of Kanazawa. From here it's a short walk east to Kenroku-en and its surrounding attractions. The *samurai* (warrior class) houses in the Nagamachi District are a short walk west from the Kohrinbo 109 department store, a useful orientation point in the centre of Katamachi. Just south of Katamachi, across the river, is the temple district of Teramachi.

On the eastern side of Kanazawa, the hills rising behind the Higashiyama District are popular for walks and views across the city.

Information

Tourist Offices Inside Kanazawa station, by the Chūō-guchi exit, is the Kanazawa tourist information office (☎ 232-6200). The staff provide maps and can help with hotel bookings. English is spoken (9 am to 7 pm).

An essential port of call for anyone planning an extended stay in Kanazawa is the Ishikawa Foundation for International Exchange (☎ 262-5931), which has reams of information, foreign newspapers and satellite TV news (9 am to 6 pm, until 5 pm Sunday). It's on the 3rd floor of the Rifare Building, a few minutes' south-east of the station on foot.

The city government produces an excellent bilingual map *(Kanazawa)* that contains information on sights, places to stay, shopping areas and attractions around the prefecture. JNTO's similarly titled pamphlet has similar, but less detailed information.

Post The most convenient post office (9 am to 6 pm weekdays) is in Katamachi, close to Kohrinbo 109 department store. There's also a branch inside Kanazawa station.

Money There are ATMs that accept internationally issued cards in the Daiwa department store (7th floor, 10 am to 6 pm, closed Wednesday) and Labro department store (1st floor, 10 am to 6 pm, closed Wednesday). The Hokuriku bank will advance money on credit cards, with a passport, 9 am to 3 pm weekdays.

Email & Internet Access The Ishikawa Foundation For International Exchange (☎ 262-5931) offers free access (limited to 30 minutes) from 9 am to 6 pm, until 5 pm Sunday.

Bookshops Shinshindo in the Rifare building has the region's largest selection of English-language titles. Maruzen and Utsunomiya bookshops are both near the Kohrinbo 109 department store.

Courses

Japanese-language classes are offered at the International Culture Exchange Centre (☎ 2-23-9575) in the Shakyo Centre, next to Kenroku-en. The Ishikawa Interhuman Network (☎ 221-9901) offers classes in calligraphy, *chanoyu* (tea ceremony), *ikebana* (flower arrangement) and other cultural pursuits.

Nagamachi Samurai Houses

The Nagamachi District, once inhabited by samurai, has retained a few of its winding streets and tile-roofed mud walls. **Nomura Samurai House** (¥500, 8.30 am to 4.30 pm), though partly transplanted from outside Kanazawa, is worth a visit for its decorative garden.

Close by is **Yūzen Silk Centre** (Saihitsu-an), where you can see the silk-dyeing process (¥500, including an English leaflet, tea and a sweet, 9 am to noon, 1 to 4.30 pm, closed Thursday).

Kenroku-en

Usually billed as the star attraction of Kanazawa, Kenroku-en (¥300, 7 am to 6 pm, from 16 October to 1 March, 8 am to 4.30 pm) is ranked by Japanese as one of their three top gardens – the other two are Kairaku-en in Mito and Kōraku-en in Okayama.

The name of the garden (*kenroku* translates as 'combined six') refers to a renowned Chinese garden from the Sung dynasty that required six attributes for perfection, including seclusion, spaciousness, artificiality, antiquity, abundant water and broad views. In its original form, Kenroku-en formed the outer garden of Kanazawa-jō, but from the 17th century onwards it was enlarged until it reached completion in the early 19th century. The garden was opened to the public in 1871.

Kenroku-en is certainly attractive, but its fame has attracted enormous crowds, which, by sheer weight of numbers, make severe inroads into the intimacy and enjoyment of the garden. Visit at 7 am and you'll have the place to yourself. By 8 am, the tour buses have descended.

Seison-kaku Villa

This retirement villa, on the south-eastern edge of Kenroku-en, was built in 1863 by a Maeda lord for his mother. It's worth making a visit to this stylish residence with its elegant chambers and furnishings. A detailed English-language pamphlet is provided. Admission is ¥600 (8.30 am to 4.30 pm, closed Wednesday).

Ishikawa Prefectural Museum for Traditional Products and Crafts

Next to Seison-kaku Villa, this contemporary craft museum (¥250, closed every third Thursday and every Thursday from December to March) is well worth visiting to see modern Kanazawa artistry at its finest. It is beside the east gate of Kenroku-en.

Ishikawa-mon

Just outside Kenroku-en, this elegant gate with its lead tiles (useful if ammunition ran short) is all that's left of Kanazawa-jō, which burnt down so many times that the locals obviously got sick of rebuilding the thing.

Ishikawa Prefectural Art Museum

This museum (¥350, more for special exhibitions, 9.30 am to 5 pm), specialises in antique exhibits of traditional arts, with special emphasis on *kutani-yaki* (colourful ceramics), Japanese painting and *kaga yūzen* (silk-dyed) fabrics and costumes.

Nakamura Memorial Museum

The Nakamura Memorial Museum (¥300, including green tea, 9.30 am to 4.30 pm, closed Tuesday) is reached via a narrow flight of steps below the Ishikawa Prefectural Art Museum. The museum displays the collection of a wealthy sake brewer, Nakamura Eishun. Exhibits are changed throughout the year, but usually include chanoyu utensils, calligraphy and traditional crafts.

Honda Museum

Members of the Honda family were chief retainers to the Maeda clan and this museum (¥500, 9 am to 5 pm, closed Thursday between November and February) exhibits the family collection of armour, household utensils and works of art. The bulletproof coat and the family vase are particularly interesting. One good reason to visit this museum is the detailed, descriptive catalogue written in English.

Gyokusen-en

If you want to visit a delightful garden with more intimacy and fewer crowds than at

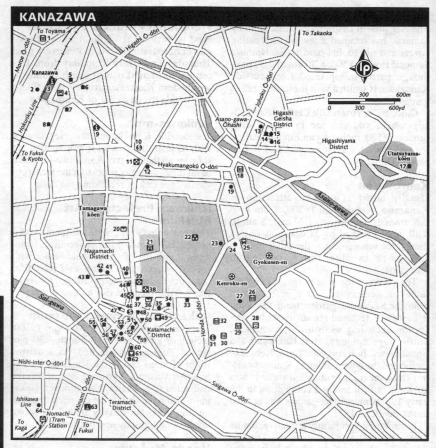

KANAZAWA

Kenroku-en, Gyokusen-en is definitely rec-ommended. The garden (¥500, including detailed English leaflet, 9 am to 4 pm, closed from early December to early March) dates from the Edo period and con-sists of several gardens rising on two levels up a steep slope. You can take tea here for an additional ¥400.

Ōhi Pottery Museum
This museum (¥500, 9 am to 5 pm) was es-tablished by Nagazaemon, who developed Ōhi pottery, a special type of slow-fired, amber-glazed ceramic specifically for use

in the chanoyu. The exhibit includes exam-ples of Nagazaemon's work.

Terashima Samurai House
This residence (¥300, including a detailed pamphlet in English, 9 am to 4 pm, closed Thursday) of a middle-class retainer of the Maeda clan was built in 1770. There's a peaceful garden, and tea is available for ¥300 in the chanoyu room.

Higashi Geisha District
If you follow the main road north from Tera-shima Samurai House and cross Asano-

KANAZAWA

PLACES TO STAY

5 Holiday Inn Kanazawa
ホリデーイン金沢
6 Kanazawa Station Hotel
金沢ステーションホテル
7 Garden Hotel Kanazawa
ガーデンホテル金沢
8 Kanazawa ANA Hotel
金沢全日空ホテル
14 Yōgetsu Minshuku
民宿陽月
17 Kanazawa
Youth Hostel
金沢ユースホステル
33 Ryokan Kikunoya
34 Kanazawa Dai-Ichi
Hotel
金沢第一ホテル
43 Yamadaya
山田家
44 Kanazawa Tōkyū Hotel
金沢東急ホテル
52 Matsui Youth Hostel
松井ユースホステル
54 Murataya Ryokan
村田屋旅館
60 Kanazawa Prince Hotel
金沢プリンスホテル
62 Kanazawa Washington
Hotel
金沢ワシントンホテル

PLACES TO EAT

37 Mr Donut
47 Sayur
48 McDonald's
50 Doutor
51 Suisei Club
彗星倶楽部
53 Tsubohachi
つぼ八
55 Legian; Polé Polé Bar
56 Tamazushi
57 Irohanihoheto
いろはにほへと
59 Kopkunka

OTHER

1 Yasue Gold Leaf Museum
2 JR Rent-a-Cycle
JRレンタサイクル
3 Tourist Information
4 Hokutetsu Kankō Bus
Company
北鉄観光バスターミナル
9 Ishikawa Foundation for
International Exchange;
Rifare Building;
Shinshindo Bookshop
国際交流センター；
リファーレ
10 Hokuriku Bank
北陸銀行
11 Meitetsu Marukoshi
Department Store
名鉄丸越スカイプラザ
12 Ōmichō Market
13 Sakuda Gold Leaf & Silver
作出金箔
15 Shima Geisha House
志摩
16 Kaikarō
懐花楼
18 Ōhi Pottery Museum
大樋美術館
19 Terashima Samurai House
寺島応養邸
20 Post Office
郵便局
21 Oyama-jinja
尾山神社
22 Kanazawa-jō Ruins
金沢城跡
23 Ishikawa-mon
石川門
24 Ishikawa Local Products
Shop
石川観光物産館
25 Kenroku-en-shita Bus Stop
兼六園下バス停
26 Ishikawa Prefectural
Museum for Traditional
Products & Crafts
石川県立伝統産業工芸館

27 Seison-kaku Villa
成巽閣
28 Ishikawa Prefectural
Nō Theatre
石川県立能楽堂
29 Honda Museum
本多蔵品館
30 Nakamura Memorial
Museum
中村記念美術館
31 Shakyo Centre;
International Culture
Exchange Centre
32 Ishikawa Prefectural
Art Museum
石川県立美術館
35 Utsunomiya Bookshop
うつのみや書店
36 Post Office
郵便局
38 Atrio Shopping Plaza
39 Daiwa Department
Store
ダイワ
40 Maruzen Bookshop
丸善
41 Yūzen Silk Centre
彩筆庵
42 Nomura Samurai House
野村家跡
45 Kohrinbo 109
Department Store
香林坊
46 Labro ATM
ラブロ
49 Sapporo Lion
Beer Hall
58 Katamachi Intersection
片町交差点
61 I no Ichiban
いの一番
63 Ninja-dera
忍者寺
64 Kutani Kosen
Gama Kiln
久谷光仙窯

CENTRAL HONSHŪ

gawa, you reach the Higashi Geisha District, which was established early in the 19th century as a centre for geisha to entertain wealthy patrons. There are several streets still preserved with the slatted, wooden facades of the geisha houses.

Kanazawa Walking Tour

This tour will take a half to full day, depending on what you choose to visit.

- Nagamachi samurai houses
- Katamachi shopping and entertainment district
- Kenroku-en
- Ishikawa Prefectural Art Museum
- Honda Museum
- Ishikawa Prefectural Museum for Traditional Products and Crafts
- Higashi Geisha district
- Ōmichō Market

If your legs are itching for exercise and your mind is ready for a healthy dose of culture, you can try tackling Kanazawa's sights in one fell swoop. Start with a 10-minute bus ride (for example, bus No 20, 21 or 22) from the station to the Kohrinbo bus stop. From there it's a 10-minute walk to the **samurai houses** in **Nagamachi**.

You can then return to **Kohrinbo** and walk east for 15 minutes to Kenroku-en and **Seison-kaku Villa**. There are plenty of relaxing spots to sit down and enjoy the scenery here and it's a good spot to take a breather.

Next door to the Seison-kaku Villa is the **Ishikawa Prefectural Museum for Traditional Products and Crafts**. A five-minute walk south will then bring you to the **Ishikawa Prefectural Art Museum**, which is also close to the **Honda Museum**.

If, at this point, you've had your fill of sightseeing, you can catch bus No 11 or 12 back to the station, or walk back to **Katamachi**, if that's where you're staying.

Otherwise, head north from the park to the **Asano-gawa Ōhashi** (Asano River Bridge), cross the river, and head into the **Higashi Geisha district**. Keen walkers can even head past this area and up into the wooded hills of **Higashiyama** – there is a walking course with posted signs in English that takes you to some temples and nice views of the city.

Heading back across the bridge, a 15-minute stroll along **Hyakumangoku ō-dōri** will bring you to **Ōmichō Market**, where you can wind up your day with an excellent seafood meal at one of the many little restaurants there, as long as you arrive before 8 pm, when most places close.

There are numerous variations on the above route. For example, after hitting Kenroku-en, you could head back through Katamachi and then turn south to cross the river into the **Teramachi temple district**. And if you don't feel like walking for six to eight hours, the **Kanazawa Historical Trail** bus does a loop through the city that runs near almost all the major sights. See the Getting Around entry later in this section for details.

A former geisha house that is open to the public is **Shima** (¥400, 9 am to 6 pm, closed Monday). Across the street is **Kaikarō** (9 am to 5 pm), a 180-year-old home that has been refurbished and had a tearoom added to it. Admission is a bit steep at ¥700, and the tea isn't cheap either, but it's a beautiful setting. Yōgetsu is another former geisha house in this district that now functions as a minshuku – see Places to Stay later in this section.

The Sakuda Gold Leaf and Silver Shop (☎ 251-6777) is a good place to pick up inexpensive souvenirs. You'll also be offered a free cup of tea containing *kinpaku* (gold leaf) – a tiny gold leaf in your tea is meant to be good for rheumatism.

Teramachi District

Teramachi stretches beside Sai-gawa, just south of the city centre. This old neighbourhood was established as a first line of defence, and still contains dozens of temples and narrow backstreets – a good place for a peaceful stroll. The temple, **Ninja-dera**, also known as Myōryū-ji, is about five minutes on foot from the river. Completed in 1643, it resembles a labyrinthine fortress with dozens of stairways, corridors, secret chambers, concealed tunnels and trick doors. The popular name of Ninja-dera refers to the temple's connection with *ninjutsu* (the art of stealth) and the *ninja* (practitioners of ninjutsu). Although the gadgetry is mildly interesting, the tour (conducted in Japanese) can make the visit unduly time-consuming.

Admission is by reservation (☎ 241-2877). Expect to pay ¥700 (9 am to 12.30 am, 1 pm to 4.30 pm, closes 30 minutes earlier between December and February). For more information on the activities of the elusive ninja, see the Iga-Ueno section of the Kansai Region chapter.

Those interested in the production of kutani-yaki might like to visit the nearby **Kutani Kosen Gama Kiln** (free, 8.30 am to noon and from 1 to 5 pm), which is open to the public. The kiln is in an area of the city that was known as the Nishi Geisha District, a precinct that had similar functions to its counterpart in the eastern part of the city.

Special Events

Some of the major festivals celebrated here are:

Kagatobi Dezomeshiki 6 January. Scantily clad firemen brave the cold, imbibe sake and demonstrate ancient firefighting skills on ladders.
Dekumawashi (Puppet Theatre Festival) 10 to 16 February. Displays of *jōruri*, a traditional form of puppet theatre, are held in the evening at the village of Oguchi.
Asano-gawa Enyūkai Early April. Performances of traditional Japanese dance and music are held on the banks of Asano-gawa.
Hyakumangoku Matsuri 13 to 15 June. This is the main annual festival in Kanazawa, commemorating the first time the region's rice production hit 1,000,000 *goku* (around 150,000 tonnes), under the leadership of the first Lord Maeda. The highlight is a huge parade of townsfolk dressed in costumes from

the 16th century. Other events include *takigi nō* (torch-lit performances of nō drama), *tōrō nagashi* (lanterns floated down the river at dusk) and a special chanoyu at Kenroku-en.
Bon Odori (Folk-Dancing Festival) Mid-August. Folk-dancing festivals are held in several places including the Futamata area, and the village of Hatta where the festival is called Sakata Odori.

Places to Stay

The tourist information office in the station can help with accommodation reservations. The Kohrinbo and Katamachi areas are more convenient for sightseeing than the station vicinity, and the Higashiyama district retains a traditional atmosphere.

Places to Stay – Budget

Hostels *Matsui Youth Hostel* (☎ 221-0275) is small and relaxed, but closes at 10 pm (members ¥3250). The hostel is closed from 31 December to 2 January. From the station, take a bus from terminal No 7, 8 or 9 for the 14-minute ride to the city and get off at the Katamachi bus stop. Walk a few metres back up the street to a large intersection. Turn right here, then take the second side street on your right. The hostel is halfway down this street.

Kanazawa Youth Hostel (☎ 252-3414) is way up in the hills to the east of the city and commands a superb position (dorm bed ¥2900 for members, private rooms ¥3900) Unfortunately, this also means that access to the hostel is mighty inconvenient, unless you have your own transport – bus services are infrequent.

The reception is only open from 4 pm to 10 pm, and loudspeakers marshal the slumbering troops for breakfast. During peak season, the hostel may take members only. Bicycle rental is available.

To reach the hostel from the station, take bus No 90 for Utatsuyama-kōen and get off after about 25 minutes at the Suizokukan-mae bus stop, which is virtually opposite the hostel.

Places to Stay – Mid-Range

Ryokan *Murataya Ryokan* (☎ 263-0455) is a member of the Japanese Inn Group (¥4500

CENTRAL HONSHŪ

without meals). There are English signs everywhere, though not too many English speakers to accompany them. Follow the directions for Matsui Youth Hostel, then having turned right at the large intersection, take the first side street on your left and continue about 20m until you see the ryokan sign on your left. There is a midnight curfew.

Tucked away up a little lane near the Utsunomiya bookshop is **Ryokan Kikunoya** (☎ 231-3547), a modest-looking place (¥5000 without meals). Over near the Nagamachi samurai houses is **Yamadaya** (☎ 261-0065). Expect to pay ¥5300, including breakfast. Dinner costs an additional ¥2500.

Minshuku The pleasant **Yōgetsu Minshuku** (☎ 252-0497) is a geisha house dating from the 19th century (¥4500 without meals). This minshuku is on the same street as the Shima geisha house, about 20 minutes on foot from the station or 10 minutes by bus No 11 or 12: get off at Hashiba-chō, walk across the bridge, take the third right and walk for two or three minutes.

Hotels Directly in front of the station is the very convenient **Garden Hotel Kanazawa** (☎ 263-3333), with singles from ¥6300 and twins/doubles from ¥12,000/¥11,000. Close by is **Kanazawa Station Hotel** (☎ 223-2600), with singles from ¥6600 to ¥8000, twins from ¥12,000 to ¥15,000 and doubles from ¥10,000 to ¥15,000.

Most of the central Kanazawa hotel accommodation is fairly expensive. One of the cheaper places around is **Kanazawa Dai-Ichi Hotel** (☎ 222-2011), which is just east of the Kohrinbo 109 department store, close to Kenroku-en (singles/doubles ¥5500/9000). Not far from the Katamachi intersection is **Kanazawa Prince Hotel** (☎ 223-2131), a decent mid-range place (singles from ¥6500, twins and doubles from ¥10,500).

Places to Stay – Top End

The most upmarket choice in the area is **Kanazawa Tōkyū Hotel** (☎ 231-2411), with singles and twins from ¥12,000, doubles from ¥21,000.

Places to Eat

Kanazawa's speciality is seafood, and it pops up everywhere – even the humble *obentō* (box lunches) at the train station nearly all feature some type of fish. *Oshizushi*, a thin layer of pressed fish laid atop vinegared rice and cut into pieces, is said by some to be the precursor to modern *sushi*. *Jibuni*, duck or chicken coated with flour and boiled with shiitake mushrooms and green vegetables, is another favourite.

The station area is not particularly exciting on the dining front. The area around the Katamachi intersection in central Kanazawa offers much more variety. For quality set lunches (from around ¥800), the 4th floor of Kohrinbo 109 department store has a variety of inexpensive places to eat.

For delicious and relatively cheap sushi, try one of the tiny restaurants that line the walkways of Ōmichō Market. There are not many English menus to be found, but if you grab a seat at the counter you should be able to get your order across. A lot of places here also serve seafood *donburi* – seafood served on top of a deep bowl of rice. Donburi teishoku, which include pickles and miso soup, are around ¥800 to ¥1200. The restaurants here close around 7 to 8 pm, so it is best to come here for lunch or early supper.

Down near Sai-gawa in Katamachi, **Tamazushi** (☎ 221-2644) has earned a reputation as one of Kanazawa's best sushi restaurants (5 pm to 2.30 am, closed Sunday). Prices, while not cheap, won't blow your budget either. Sushi teishoku range from ¥1000 to ¥2500, and a lot of individual sushi items are priced from ¥100 to ¥200 (though there are a few ¥800 picks in there, too). There isn't an English menu, but the various sushi sets are displayed in the front window, giving you an idea of what's on offer.

The Katamachi District also has a surprising number of international restaurants. **Legian** (☎ 262-6510) is a popular Indonesian restaurant down by the river (noon to 1 am). The food is good and authentic. The Patio building on the first parallel street to the east of Katamachi-dōri has an excellent Thai restaurant, **Kopkunka**. It's not exactly cheap (Thai restaurants never are in Japan), and you should figure on around ¥3000 per head with drinks.

One place definitely worth trying is *Sayur*, a tiny place that serves organic food and drinks. Dishes are a mix of Japanese and South-East Asian cuisine, and are delicious. It also has a small but interesting selection of microbrew beer and organic sake. You are likely to spend around ¥2500 per person, including drinks.

Just around the corner from Murataya Ryokan, *Suisei Club* (☎ 264-0088) serves good, inexpensive home cooking, and the friendly owner speaks English and French (8.30 am to 6 pm, closed Sunday).

Entertainment

Nō theatre is alive and well is Kanazawa, and performances are held fairly often (once a week during summer) at Ishikawa Prefectural Nō Theatre (☎ 264-2598). It is also possible to attend rehearsals free of charge. Inquire at the Kanazawa tourist information office (☎ 232-6200).

Although Kanazawa is not a huge city, it has an incredible number of bars and clubs. Most are of the hole-in-the-wall variety, jam-packed into high rises in Katamachi. One place that seems to draw a good mix of gaijin and locals is *Polé Polé*. It's grungy and dark, the floor is littered with peanut shells and the music (reggae) is loud. The truly adventurous might want to order the house cocktail speciality called Elephant Wank. If not, then there's the old stand by, the Screaming Orgasm. It's in the same building as the Legian Indonesian restaurant (owned by the same people) – walk to Legian along the river and then walk through the building to find Polé Polé.

On the same street as Murataya Ryokan, *I no Ichiban* (6 pm to 3 am, until midnight Sunday) is a modern, hip-hop-playing izakaya, with a bar beside the open-fronted kitchen and a neat indoor bamboo grove.

Shopping

Kanazawa is a centre for traditional crafts such as kaga yūzen, kutani-yaki, *kaga maki-e* (lacquerware with gold, silver or

pearl overlay), woodcarving using *kiri* (paulownia) and kinpaku.

For a quick view or purchase of these crafts, you can visit Kankō Bussankan (Ishikawa Local Products Shop). The tourist information office can set up visits to workshops or direct you to museums of specific interest such as the Yasue Gold Leaf Museum (Yasue Kinpaku Kōgeikan), right by the station.

Markets Ōmichō Market lies on the main bus route between the station and the Kohrinbo area in the centre of the city. The most convenient bus stop for the market is Musashi-ga-tsuji. The market is a warren of several hundred shops, many of which specialise in seafood. Take a break from sightseeing and just wander around here to watch market life.

Getting There & Away

Air Komatsu airport) has air connections with Tokyo, Sendai, Fukuoka and Sapporo. There's also an international connection with Seoul (Korea).

Bus There are regular expressway bus services from the Hokutetsu bus station in front of Kanazawa station's Chūō-guchi (central exit) to Tokyo (Ikebukuro, ¥7840, 7½ hours), Yokohama (¥8250, 7½ hours), Kyoto (¥4060, four hours) and Nagoya (¥4060, four hours). Buses to Wajima (¥2200, two hours) also leave from the Kenrokuen-shita bus stop.

Train Kanazawa is linked to south-western destinations by the JR Hokuriku line: Fukui (tokkyū, ¥2950, one hour), Kyoto (tokkyū, ¥6710, 2½ hours) and Osaka (tokkyū, ¥7440, three hours). The same line runs north-east to Takaoka (tokkyū, ¥1980, 45 minutes), Toyama (tokkyū, ¥2610, one hour) and farther north up the coast. To travel to Takayama (tokkyū, ¥5890, 2½ hours), you need to change to the JR Takayama line at Toyama. The quickest way to travel between Tokyo and Kanazawa is by taking the Jōetsu shinkansen from Tokyo station to Nagaoka (one hour and 40 minutes) and then travelling onwards by limited express to Kanazawa (three hours). The whole trip costs ¥13,510. There are two daily departures of the limited express Hakusan service from Ueno to Kanazawa. The journey takes just over six hours and costs ¥10,690.

The JR Nanao line (together with the privately run Noto Tetsudo line) connects Kanazawa with Wajima (Noto-hantō) in 2¼ hours.

Getting Around

To/From the Airport A good bus service connects Komatsu airport with Kanazawa station (¥1100, 40 minutes, one to two departures hourly from 7 am to 6 pm). Buses leave from the No 4 gate of the Hokutetsu bus station.

Bus The bus network is extensive and fares start at ¥200. From the station, bus Nos 10 and 11 will take you to the Kenroku-enshita bus stop, a useful point if you just want to visit the main sights around Kenroku-en. To ride from the station to the centre of the city you can take bus Nos 20, 21 or 30, and get off at the Kohrinbo bus stop. The bus company also operates the 'Kanazawa Historical Trail' bus, which makes a 45-minute loop through the city and passes by all the major tourist attractions. There are two to three buses per hour from 9 am to 4 pm, and you can get on them at any of the tourist attractions.

The office of the Hokutetsu Kankō bus company just outside the station sells a Kanazawa Shūyū Jōshaken (Kanazawa Sightseeing Pass) for ¥900 that allows unlimited travel on local buses for one day. These passes can also be bought on buses.

Bicycle Rental is available (¥1000 for the day or ¥600 for four hours) at the station, but be prepared for some hill climbing. JR Rent-a-Cycle is to the left of the station's Nishi-guchi (west exit).

Kanazawa Youth Hostel also has bicycles for rent (cheaper prices), for guests only, but it's quite a puff returning up the hill to the hostel.

NOTO-HANTŌ 能登半島
☎ 0768

For an enjoyable combination of rugged seascapes, traditional rural life and a light diet of cultural sights, this peninsula is highly recommended. Noto-hantō is easily accessible from Kanazawa, Takaoka or Toyama. The wild, unsheltered western side of this peninsula is probably of more interest: the indented coastline of the eastern side has been heavily developed to cater to tourists and has lost quite a bit of its charm.

It's not really possible to do justice to the peninsula with a day trip in which you tick off all the sights in hurried procession; this leaves little time to savour the pace of rural life. A better idea might be to spend at least two nights and three days gradually working your way around the coastline, which has plenty of youth hostels, minshuku and ryokan. The rather erratic bus schedules will make rushing around the peninsula fairly difficult in any case, so you may as well just do like the locals and take it slowly.

Information

Kanazawa tourist information office (☎ 232-6200) in JR Kanazawa station can help reserve accommodation and deal with most other queries regarding Noto-hantō. The office has copies of *Easy Living Map*, which has good detail on Ishikawa-ken, including the peninsula. Also available are copies of the *Guide to Northern Noto*, a colourful English-language pamphlet with background on the various sights around the northern section of the peninsula.

JNTO's leaflet *Noto Peninsula* has concise information on sights, maps, timetables and lists of places to stay for Noto-hantō.

There are also information offices at Wajima and Nanao stations; Nanao also has its own Society to Introduce Nanao to the World (☎ 0767-53-1111), which arranges home visits.

Special Events

Noto-hantō has dozens of festivals throughout the year. Seihaku-sai Matsuri, held in Nanao from 13 to 15 May, includes

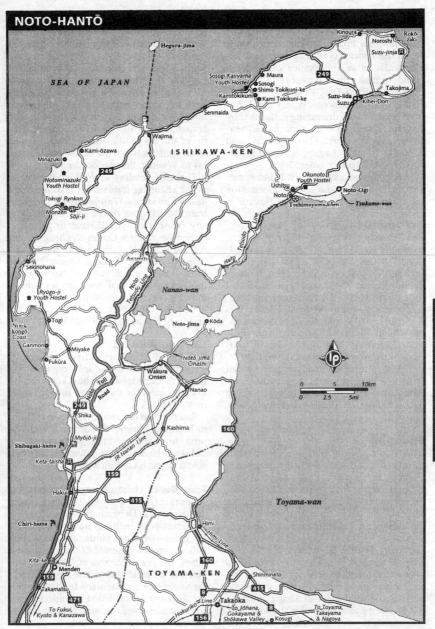

NOTO-HANTŌ

SEA OF JAPAN

Hegura-jima

Kinoura
Noroshi
Rokō-zaki
Suzu-jinja
Maura
Sosogi Kajiyama
Youth Hostel
Sosogi
Shimo Tokikuni-ke
Kamitokikuni
Kami Tokikuni-ke
Suzu-Iida
Takojima
Suzu
Kihei-Don
Senmaida

Wajima
ISHIKAWA-KEN

Kami-ōzawa
Minazuki
249
Notominazuki
Youth Hostel
Tokugi Rynkan
Okunoto
Youth Hostel
Ushitsu
Noto-Ugi
Monzen
Sōji-ji
Noto
Toshimayama-kōen
Tsukumo-wan

Anamizu
Noto Tetsudo Line
Noto Tetsudo Line

Sekinohana
Nanao-wan

Ryūgo-ji
Youth Hostel
Noto-jima
Kōda

Togi

Nishi
kongō
Coast
Ganmon
Miyake
Notō jima
Ōhashi

Fukūra
Wakura
Onsen
Nanao

Noto Toll Road
249
Shika
Kashima
160

Myōjō-ji
JR Nanao Line
Toyama-wan

Shibagaki-hama
159

Keta-taisha

Hakui
415

Chiri-hama
Himi
Himi Line

Kita-ke
160
Menden
159
Shinminato
Takamatsu
471
TOYAMA-KEN
415
Hokuriku Line
To Fukui,
Kyoto & Kanazawa
Takaoka
8
To Jōhana,
Gokayama &
Shōkawa Valley
Kosugi
To Toyama,
Takayama
& Nagoya
156

0   5   10km
0   2.5   5mi

CENTRAL HONSHŪ

a spectacular procession of festival floats. On 31 July, the small community of Kōda on Noto-jima hosts a spectacular, almost pagan fire festival (you'll need to book accommodation well in advance, camp on the island, or make the trip over from Wakura Onsen). Gojinjō Daikō Nabune Matsuri, held in Wajima between 31 July and 1 August, features wild drumming performed by drummers wearing demon masks and seaweed headgear. Ishizaki Hoto Matsuri, held in Nanao in early August, is famed for its parade of tall lantern poles.

Full details on annual festivals and events are available from the tourist information offices in Kanazawa, Wajima or Nanao.

Accommodation

The peninsula has plenty of youth hostels, minshuku and ryokan. Reservations are advisable during the peak season months of July and August and can be made through the Kanazawa, Wajima or Nanao tourist information offices. If you have the money, it's worth spending at least one or two nights in one of the minshuku or ryokan, especially if you're a seafood lover: most places serve up healthy portions of delicious *sashimi*, grilled fish and shellfish.

There are also camping grounds tucked away in a few pockets of the peninsula, although most are difficult to reach using public transport. Call ahead to reserve sites, especially in summer.

Shopping

You won't have to look too far on your travels around the peninsula before you see shops groaning with the main regional craft – lacquerware. A large proportion of Wajima's townsfolk are engaged in producing *Wajima-nuri*, lacquerware renowned for its durability and rich colours.

Getting There & Away

Bus Hokutetsu Kankō bus company's Okunoto express bus service runs direct between Kanazawa and Wajima, and some buses go on to Sosogi and Maura. Services run between Kanazawa and Wajima (¥2200, 55 minutes) and Kanazawa and Suzu

(¥2600, 2¾ hours). There are around eight or nine buses daily between Kanazawa and Wajima, and around two daily to Suzu.

Train This is less convenient than taking the bus. The JR Nanao line runs from Kanazawa to Wakura Onsen. Here you will usually have to change to the private Noto Tetsudo line, which runs up to Wajima and also branches off to Suzu and Takojima, near the tip of the peninsula. Beware that the train often splits in two – the first carriage heads off to Wajima, the rear one to Suzu.

If you're heading to Wajima, the way to avoid changing trains is to take the once-daily Kanazawa-Wajima limited express train, which goes direct (2¼ hours). With any other train, you'll have to get off at Nanao or Wakura Onsen to change to the Noto Tetsudo line. From here most trains from Nanao or Wakura Onsen head to Suzu-Iida, so you'll have to change trains, this time at Anamizu, and wait seven to 20 minutes for a train to Wajima.

The fare from Nanao to Wajima is ¥990 and from Nanao to Suzu, ¥1550.

Getting Around

Bus Local buses are infrequent and it's sometimes worth the added expense to use one of the scheduled tour buses (see the following entry) for short hops to reach more remote places.

Useful local bus services include: Wajima to Monzen, Monzen to Anamizu, and Wajima to Ushitsu via Sosogi and Kami Tokikuni-ke. Local bus timetables are available at some tourist information offices.

Tour Buses There are regular sightseeing buses that follow a variety of routes around the peninsula. Depending on the itinerary, the ticket price includes transport, lunch, a Japanese-speaking guide and admission fees for sights. In terms of transport, these buses are very convenient. However, the lunch is no great shakes and any pauses in the rapid-fire commentary from the guide are filled with recorded sounds ranging from jungle noises to songs and breaking waves. Ear plugs are advised.

There are many permutations, but most of the itineraries use Kanazawa or Wajima as a starting or finishing point. Some tours operate throughout the year, others only operate between March and November. Tickets for a full-day tour start at ¥7200.

Train The train lines stay mainly inland on the peninsula, so they're not really useful for getting around the more interesting western and northern coastal areas. If you are using trains, Nanao, Wajima and Suzu are all possible staging points to start or finish your tour.

Bicycle The peninsula should appeal to cyclists as its coastal terrain is flat, and inland there's only an occasional gradient. The camping grounds and youth hostels are spread out at convenient intervals. The tourist information offices (Kanazawa, Wajima and Nanao) have a very good map (in Japanese) called *Noto Hantō Rōdo Mappu*, which covers the area on a scale of 1:160,000.

Kita-ke
This is the former residence of the Kita family (¥700, including a detailed leaflet in English, 8.30 am to 5 pm), which once administered over 100 villages in the region. It is on the coast, about 30 minutes by bus north of Kanazawa. Kita-ke is built in local farmhouse style, and inside there are displays of weapons, ceramics, farming tools, folk art and documents. There is also a fine garden.

To get there by train, take the JR Nanao line to Menden station, then walk north for 20 minutes.

Chiri-hama & Hakui
千里浜・羽咋
This long beach near Hakui station on the west coast has become an attraction for motorists, and at times it resembles a sandy motorway with droves of buses, motorcycles and cars roaring past the breakers. Hakui is famed as Japan's UFO-viewing capital, with flying-saucer-shaped *sembei* (rice crackers) on sale everywhere to prove it.

Keta-taisha 気多大社
This shrine (¥100, 8.30 am to 4.30 pm), set in a wooded grove close to the sea, is believed to have been founded in the 8th century, but the architectural style of the present building dates from the 17th century. The shrine is just 10 minutes via the Togi-bound bus from Hakui station (approximately 10 buses run daily). Get off at the Ichinomiya bus stop.

Myōjō-ji
Myōjō-ji (¥350, including an excellent English leaflet with map, 8 am to 5 pm) was founded in 1294 by Nichijō, a disciple of Nichiren, as the main temple of the Myojō-ji school of Nichiren Buddhism. The temple complex is composed of several buildings including the strikingly elegant **Gojū-no-tō** (Five-Storeyed Pagoda). To reach the temple from Hakui station, take the Togi bus and get off at Takiya-guchi (¥370, 18 minutes), then walk for 15 minutes.

From the temple, it takes about 25 minutes on foot to reach **Shibagaki-hama** with its small fishing community.

Noto-kongō Coast
能登金剛海岸
The stretch of rocky shoreline known as Noto-kongō extends for about 16km between Fukūra and Sekinohana and includes a variety of rock formations such as Ganmon, which resembles a large gate. Buses go from Hakui station to Fukūra (¥920, 70 minutes), and often you'll have to change buses at Miyake. There are around 10 buses daily to Miyake/Togi. The ride offers pleasant sea views as the road winds along the coast, passing fishing villages with their protective concrete breakwaters.

Close to Monzen there's the famous **Sōji-ji** (¥400, 8 am to 5 pm), which was established in 1321 as the head temple of the Sōtō school of Zen. After a fire severely damaged the buildings in 1898, the temple was restored, but it now functions as a branch temple; the main temple has been transferred to Yokohama. To reach the temple from Anamizu station, take a 40-minute bus ride to the Sōji-ji-mae bus stop. There are buses to Monzen (¥640) every one to two hours.

CENTRAL HONSHŪ

Places to Stay The snotty *Notominazuki Youth Hostel* (☎ 46-2022) is at Minazuki, 35 minutes by bus from Monzen (¥2600). There's a coastal hiking trail (about 2½ hours) between Minazuki and Kami-ōzawa. The hostel is closed from 29 December to 7 January, and from 1 October to 31 March it only operates from Thursday to Sunday.

If you're looking for a more upscale stay in Monzen, *Tokugi Ryokan* (☎ 42-0010) has rooms for ¥7000 per person, including two meals.

Minazuki Seishōnen Ryokōmura Campsite (☎ 46-2103) is perched on the coast in Minazuki, not too far from Notominazuki Youth Hostel.

Wajima 輪島

Wajima is a small town but has long been renowned as a centre for the production of lacquerware. It has now become a significant, if understated, centre for tourism. There's a reasonably pleasant beach nearby, and the morning market is fun. The town is also the best base for exploring the surrounding area.

The tourist information office at Wajima station provides English leaflets and maps and the staff can help you book accommodation. NTT, located in front of the shrine, Jūzō-jinja, 15 minutes' walk east from the town centre has free Internet access from 9 am to 5 pm weekdays.

Wajima Shitsugei Bijutsukan/Shiki Kaikan The Lacquerware Hall and museum (¥200, 8 am to 5.30 pm) is in the centre of town next to the Shin-bashi. The 2nd floor has a display of lacquerware production techniques, as well as some impressively aged pieces: there are a few bowls that were being swilled out of when Hideyoshi was struggling to unify Japan 500 years ago. There's a shop downstairs where you can purchase some contemporary examples. None are cheap, but they are undeniably beautiful.

Wajima Urushi Art Museum This museum (¥600, 9 am to 4.30 pm) has a significantly larger collection of lacquerware –

enough to fill galleries on two floors. Pieces from around Asia as well as from Japan are on display. It's about 15 minutes' walk west of the train station.

Kiriko Kaikan This hall (¥500, 8 am to 5 pm) houses the huge lacquered floats used in regional festivals. From the station, it is 20 minutes on foot or you can take the six-minute bus ride from the station and get off at the Tsukada bus stop – if you're lucky enough to catch one of the infrequent buses.

Hegura-jima Those interested in a day trip and boat ride can take the ferry to Hegura-jima, which boasts a lighthouse, several shrines and no traffic. Bird watchers flock to the island in spring and autumn. If you want to extend your island isolation by staying overnight, there are plenty of minshuku. Reservations (in Japanese only) can be made at the booking office (☎ 22-4961).

From early April to late October, the ferry (¥3040 return) departs Wajima at 9 am and reaches the island at 10.30 am. The return ferry leaves at 3 pm (to 2 pm during winter). Weather conditions sometimes cause sailings to be cancelled.

Shopping The asa-ichi (morning market; 8 am to noon, closed on the 10th and 25th of each month), though undeniably touristed, is highly entertaining. The fishwives ply their wares, everything from raw abalone to load-of-baloney, with plenty of sass and humour. If you can bring along a Japanese speaker the experience is even better, but the rough humour cuts across the language barrier. To find the market, walk north along the river from the Wajima Lacquerware Hall and turn right just before Iroha-bashi.

The *yu-ichi* (evening market) is altogether more low key, and takes place from 3.30 pm until dusk in the grounds of Sumiyoshi-jinja. Most tourists depart once the market is over, but for entertainment of a different kind, cross the Iroha bridge, turn north and after 100m you'll come to the spot where the vendors throw unsold raw squid into the estuary, whereupon the other customers arrive – the *tombi* (Siberian black kites). The birds of prey wheel and dive and grab the discarded fish by the score. Even nonornithological types will find it a dramatic sight.

Places to Stay & Eat The tourist information office at Wajima station can help you find accommodation. Wajima has dozens of minshuku with prices starting at around ¥7000 per person, and these include two meals (copious and delicious seafood). Worth a try is *Asunaro* minshuku (☎ 22-0652), about 15 minutes on foot from the station on the other side of Shin-bashi from the Wajima Lacquerware Hall. Rates are ¥6500 per person, with two meals included. Across the Kawarada-gawa, *Heguri* (☎ 22-1018), with similar rates to Asunaro, is a very pleasant place to stay. It is usually filled with local anglers, and some rooms overlook a garden.

About 10 minutes by bus to the west of town is *Sodeguhamu Campground* (☎ 22-2211). Sites cost ¥600 and the grounds are open from 4 pm to 9 am. Take one of the Monzen-bound buses to Sodega-hama or hike for 20 minutes.

Most visitors to Wajima eat in their minshuku, but for a quick bowl of noodles, *Sarashina* (☎ 22-1192), on the main street north of the station, is an unpretentious and quality soba shop.

Getting There & Away For details on getting to Wajima from Kanazawa, see Getting There & Away at the beginning of Noto-hantō earlier in this section.

Wajima is the main transport hub for the northern section of the peninsula. The bus station is opposite the train station. From here you can take buses along the northern coast to Sosogi, where you can change for buses to Kinoura and Rokō-zaki. Bus services also link Wajima with Ushitsu on the inland coast, from where you can catch a train or bus to Tsukumo-wan and Suzu. There are also buses to Monzen, on the western shore.

There are buses from Wajima to Ushitsu (¥1250, one hour and 20 minutes, eight daily), which pass by Sosogi (¥740, 40 minutes). Buses to Monzen (¥740, 1½ hours) leave every one to two hours.

Sosogi 曽々木

The village of Sosogi, about 10 minutes by bus from Senmaida, with its attractive *dan-dan-batake* (rice terraces), has a couple of things to see. After the Taira were defeated in 1185, one of the few survivors, Taira Tokitada, was exiled to this region. The Tokikuni family, which claims descent from this survivor, eventually divided into two parts and established separate family residences here.

Shimo Tokikuni-ke (Lower Tokikuni Residence; ¥500, including an English leaflet, 8.30 am to 5 pm, 9 am to 4.30 pm from December to March) built in 1590, is a smaller version of its counterpart Kami Tokikuni-ke, but it has an attractive garden.

Just a few minutes walk away, **Kami Tokikuni-ke** (Upper Tokikuni Residence; ¥420, including an English leaflet, 8.30 am to 6 pm, until 5 pm from December to March), with its impressive thatched roof and elegant interior, was constructed early in the 19th century. From Wajima station, the bus ride to Kami Tokikuni-ke takes about 40 minutes.

Places to Stay Sosogi is a pleasant, quiet spot, and not a bad choice for an overnight stay. *Sosogi Kajiyama Youth Hostel* (☎ 32-1145) is seven minutes on foot from the Sosogi-guchi bus stop, and costs ¥2800 a night. The hostel is a convenient base for walking along the nearby coastal hiking trail.

There is a string of minshuku along the road east of the Sosogi-guchi bus stop. *Yokoiwaya* (☎ 32-0603) is about 150m down the road from the bus stop (walk around the large cliff face on the inland side of the road). For ¥7000 you get a comfortable room and an outstanding seafood dinner – in most Japanese cities the dinner alone would easily cost this price. If Yokoiwaya is full, don't worry: there are plenty of other choices in the area.

Rokō-zaki

The road north-east from Sosogi passes the cape, and winds round the tip of the peninsula to the less dramatic scenery on its eastern coast. At the cape, you can amble up to Noroshi lighthouse where a nearby signpost marks the distances to Vladivostok, Tokyo,

CENTRAL HONSHŪ

and Shanghai. A coastal hiking trail runs west along the cape. The scenery is nice, and during the week when the tourist buses run less frequently, the town of Noroshi reverts to its true role as a sleepy, remote fishing village. There are some beaches in the area, but they're nothing special, being fairly rocky and somewhat polluted. But Noroshi is a good place to laze around for a few days, hike along the coast and soak up the beauty of Noto-hantō.

Places to Stay There are several camping grounds in the area, including *Yamabushi-yama Campground* (☎ 88-2737), perched on a hilltop east of Noroshi, and *Kinoura Campsite* (☎ 86-2204), near the little town of Kinoura, about 8km west of Noroshi.

One of Noroshi's more unique accommodation options is *Garō Minshuku Terai* (☎ 86-2038). The name of the place means 'Terai's Art Gallery Minshuku', and artwork adorns the walls and shelves of the inn. Expect to pay ¥6500, including two meals.

Nearby, *Rokō-zaki Lighthouse Pension* (☎ 86-2030) is a nicely appointed European-style inn (¥10,000, with two meals).

Getting There & Away Rokō-zaki is one of the more inconvenient places to access on the peninsula. The easiest way to get there is from Suzu, which is on the Noto Tetsudo line. From the Suzu station there are five to six daily JR buses to Noroshi (¥730, 6.30 am to 6.30 pm). There are five buses a day back to Suzu from Noroshi between 8 am and 5.30 pm.

If you're coming from Wajima, you'll first have to get a bus to Sosogi-guchi, where you then change for buses to Kinoura. There are only three of these a day (¥770, 12.30, 3.45 and 5.45 pm), and only the *first two* get you there in time to link up with a JR bus, which will then take you from Kinoura to Noroshi (¥290). On Sunday, there is only one JR bus from Kinoura to Noroshi (4.30 pm). Services back from Noroshi to Kinoura are similarly sparse, though they are better timed to allow you to catch the onward Kinoura-Sosogi bus. The above times are subject to change: check

the schedule at one of the tourist information offices or at the bus station.

To avoid this logistical tap dance, you might try catching a ride with one of the tour buses run by Hokutetsu Kankō bus company, which usually leave Wajima around 8 am. Drivers may not take you, especially if the tour is full or close to it, but if you do get on, expect to pay around ¥1200 for the ride to Noroshi.

Tsukumo-wan

Tsukumo-wan, heavily indented and dotted with islands, is a mildly scenic bay, but it's not really worth spending ¥750 on the boat tour despite the boat's glass bottom. From the bay, it's five minutes on foot to Noto-Ogi station, which has train connections via Ushitsu to Kanazawa. If you want an inexpensive place to stay right next to the water, *Tsukumo-Wan Youth Hostel* (☎ 74-0150) is only 15 minutes on foot from the station (¥3100). There are also plenty of ryokan and minshuku around.

Ushitsu うしつ

The limited attractions of Ushitsu are around Toshimayama-kōen, which has good views out to sea. The town itself is not all that interesting, and its main function for travellers is likely to be as a transportation link. From here there are six to seven buses daily to Wajima (¥1190), which pass by Sosogi-guchi (¥800).

HAKUSAN NATIONAL PARK 白山
☎ 0761

Travellers with a thirst for exercise (and time on their hands) may want to venture down to this national park, which is in the south-east corner of Ishikawa-ken and spills over into neighbouring Fukui, Toyama and Gifu prefectures. The park has several peaks reaching above 2500m, with the highest being Hakusan (2702m). In the summer, hiking and scrambling uphill to catch mountain sunrises are the main activities, while in winter, skiing and onsen bathing take over.

The alpine section of the park is crisscrossed with trails, offering hikes of up to 25km. For hikers who are well equipped and in no hurry, there is a 26km trek from the park over to Ogimachi in Shōkawa Valley, Gifu. However, camping is prohibited in the park except at designated camping grounds, which means you'll have to either hike very fast or break the rules.

Those looking to hike on and around the peaks are required to stay overnight at either Murodō Centre or Nanryu Sansō Mountain Lodge (see the following Places to Stay entry). Getting to either of these requires a minimum of 3½ to five hours on foot. That doesn't stop the park from swarming with visitors, however. In the peak season of July–August, visitors are required to make reservations a week in advance if they plan to stay up here.

The area surrounding the alpine section of the park is dotted with little villages offering onsen baths, minshuku and ryokan accommodation and camping grounds.

Public transport to Hakusan consists mainly of infrequent buses between April and November, and shuts down altogether during the winter months. Check at tourist information office in Kanazawa before setting out.

Places to Stay

In the alpine area of the park your two choices are *Murodō Center* (☎ 9-31001) and *Nanryu Sansō Mountain Lodge* (☎ 9-82022). Murodo can hold up to 750 people in its four lodges, and per-person rates are ¥6400, including two meals. It is open from 1 May to 15 October, weather permitting. Nanryu is smaller (holding 150 people), and has similar rates, but is only open in summer. There is also a camping ground at Nanryu, which is the only place in the alpine area where camping is permitted. There is an overnight fee of ¥300; renting a tent will cost you another ¥2200. During the peak season of July–August, reservations must be made at least one week in advance for both Murodō and Nanryu.

There are several ways to hike up to both places but the closest access point is Bettōde-ai. From here it's 6km to Murodō (about 4½ hours' walk) and 5km to Nanryu (3½ hours). You can also access the lodges from trail-

heads at Ichirino and Chūgū Onsen, but these involve hikes of around 20km. See the following Getting There & Away section for details on transport to the trailheads.

Ichirino, Chūgū Onsen, Shiramine and Ichinose all have minshuku and ryokan. Per person rates with two meals start at ¥7000 and ¥9000 respectively.

There are several camping grounds in the area. *Ichinose Yaeijō* (☎ 9-82121) has 20 camp sites near Ichinose, which is in turn close to the trailhead at Bettōde-ai. *Midori no Mura Campground* (☎ 9-82716), near Shiramine, has tents and bungalows for rent. There is also a camping ground near Chūgū Onsen. Most of the camping grounds are only open from June to October, with the exception of the one at Nanryu Sansō Mountain Lodge, which operates year-round.

Unless you speak Japanese, you'll probably need to go through the tourist information office at Kanazawa or another major city to book accommodation. You can also try the Shiramine Town Hall (☎ 9-82011), which reportedly has one or two staff who can handle basic inquiries in English.

Getting There & Away

This is not easily done, even during the peak summer period. The main mode of transport to the Hakusan area is the Hokutetsu Kankō bus from Kanazawa station. Between 27 April and 6 May there is one bus daily to Bettōde-ai (¥2000, two hours), leaving around 6.30 am. Frequency increases to between two and four buses a day from mid-July to mid-August, and then reverts back to one bus daily in late August. From September to mid-October, bus services are scaled back to weekends and holidays, weather permitting.

Hokuriku Tetsudo also has several daily departures for Ichirino and Chūgū Onsen. Check with the Kanazawa tourist information office or the Hokutetsu Kankō bus company office at Kanazawa station for the latest schedule.

If you're coming from Fukui, you can take the Echizen Honsen line for the one-hour ride out to Katsuyama, where you can change to a Hokuriku Tetsudo bus to Shiramine. At the time of writing, bus departures from Katsuyama to Shiramine were at 8.20 am and 7.55 pm. From Shiramine you'll have to either wait for an infrequent bus, take a taxi or hitch a ride.

Fukui-ken

FUKUI 福井
☎ 0776 • pop 252,000

Fukui is the prefectural capital. It was given quite a drubbing in 1945 during the Allied bombing, and what was left largely suc-cumbed to a massive earthquake in 1948. It was totally rebuilt, and is now known as a major textile centre. There's no real reason to linger here, but Fukui is useful as a staging point to visit sights in the prefecture. Between 19 and 21 May, Fukui celebrates the Mikuni Matsuri with a parade of giant warrior dolls.

Fukui City Sightseeing Information (8.30 am to 5 pm, no English spoken) is next to the central exit inside Fukui station, and can provide maps and pamphlets in English. Fukui International Activities Plaza (☎ 28-8800), 10 minutes on foot north of the station, has

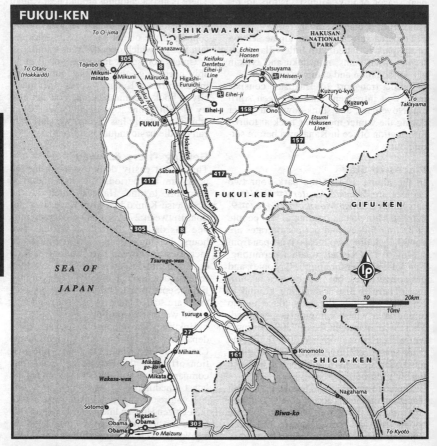

FUKUI-KEN

CENTRAL HONSHŪ

To O-jima
To Kanazawa
ISHIKAWA-KEN
HAKUSAN NATIONAL PARK
To Otaru (Hokkaidō)
Tōjinbō
Mikuni-minato
Mikuni
Maruoka
Keifuku Dentetsu Eihei-ji Line
Echizen Honsen Line
Katsuyama
Heisen-ji
Higashi-Furuichi
Keifuku Mikuni Awara Line
Eihei-ji
Eihei-ji
158
Ōno
Kuzuryū-kyo
Kuzuryū
To Takayama
FUKUI
Hokuriku
Etsumi Hokusen Line
157
Sabae
417
Hokuriku Line
FUKUI-KEN
GIFU-KEN
Takefu
Expressway
305
8
SEA OF JAPAN
Tsuruga-wan
Tsuruga
27
Mihama
161
Kinomoto
SHIGA-KEN
Mikata go-ko
Mikata
Wakasa-wan
Sotomo
Higashi-Obama
Obama
303
To Maizuru
Nagahama
Biwa-ko
To Kyoto

0   10   20km
0   5   10mi

lots of English information and offers free Internet access (9 am to 6 pm, until 8 pm Tuesday and Thursday, closed Monday).

If you need to stay in Fukui, there's the rather drab *Fujin Seinen Kaikan Youth Hostel* (☎ 22-5625), around 500m northwest of the station next to Chūō-kōen (dorm rooms ¥3100). Close to the east exit of Fukui station (the main exit is the west exit) is *City Hotel Fukui* (☎ 23-5300). Expect to pay ¥5500 to ¥6300 for singles, from ¥10,000 for twins, and ¥8600 for doubles. A more upscale option is *Hotel Akebono Bekkan* (☎ 22-0506). From the station, walk straight ahead and take the second street on the left that crosses over the river (singles/doubles for ¥6800/13,200). There are no traditional-style accommodations within the city.

Fukui is connected by the JR Hokuriku Honsen with Kanazawa (55 minutes) and Tsuruga (40 minutes, which provides convenient access to Nagoya, Kyoto and Osaka).

EIHEI-JI 永平寺

Founded in 1244 by Dōgen, Eihei-ji is now one of the two head temples of the Sōtō sect of Zen Buddhism and is ranked among the most influential centres of Zen in the world. It is a palpably spiritual place, despite the constant onslaught of tour buses, and serious students of Zen should consider a retreat here.

The temple (¥400, 5 am to 5 pm) is geared to huge numbers of visitors who come either as sightseers or for the rigorous Zen training. The complex has about 70 buildings, set within the beautiful cedar forests. The standard circuit usually concentrates on the seven major buildings: *tosu* (toilet), San-mon, *yokushitsu* (bath), *daikuin* (kitchen), Butsuden (Buddha Hall), Hattō (Dharma Hall) and the Sō-dō (Priests' Hall).

Look for the wooden block with the huge hole in the centre: this is where the disciples bang their foreheads to reawaken themselves to the moment – try it yourself, and you'll realise how many hundreds of thousands of blows it must have taken to reach this point.

The temple is frequently closed for periods varying from a week to 10 days – before you visit, check with a tourist information office or use Japan Travel-Phone (☎ 0120-44-4800 toll free).

You can attend the temple's three-day, four-night *sanrōsha* (religious trainee program), which follows the monks' training schedule, complete with 3 am prayers, cleaning, *zazen* (sitting meditation), and ritual meals in which not a grain of rice may be left behind. It costs ¥9000, and reservations must be made at least a fortnight in advance (☎ 63-3631, fax 63-3640). Japanese ability is not necessary, but you must be able to sit in the half-lotus position. Everyone who has completed this course agrees it is a remarkable experience. A single night's stay is also possible for ¥8000.

Places to Stay

If you prefer a less spartan experience, the youth hostel *Eihei-ji Monzen Yamaguchi-sō* (☎ 63-3123) is five minutes on foot from Eihei-ji station (¥2900). Near the front gate to Eihei-ji is *Green Lodge* (☎ 63-3126), a two-storey wooden inn (¥7300 per person, with two meals).

Getting There & Away

From Fukui, take the Keifuku Dentetsu Eihei-ji line to Eihei-ji station (¥710, 35 minutes). If you don't catch a direct train, you'll need to change trains at Higashi-Furuichi. Trains run once to twice an hour between 6.30 am and 10.30 pm.

The temple is about 10 minutes from Eihei-ji station. Turn right as you exit the station and plod uphill past the souvenir shops.

TOJINBO 東尋坊

About 25km north-east of Fukui are the towering rock columns and cliffs at Tōjinbō, which is a popular tourist destination. One little fact that you may not find in the tourist brochures is that Tōjinbō's cliffs have long been a popular spot for suicides. But don't worry, fewer people have been taking the plunge lately and the chances are extremely remote that you'll happen upon any unpleasantness. Perhaps one of the reasons Tōjinbō attracted depressed types was its history. It was named after an evil priest from Katsuyama's Heisen-ji, who was finally cast off the cliff by angry villagers in 1182. Legend has it that the sea surged for 49 days thereafter, a demonstration of the priest's fury from beyond his watery grave.

Visitors can take a boat trip to view the rock formations (¥1010, 30 minutes) or travel farther up the coast to **O-jima**, a small island with a shrine that is joined to the mainland by a bridge.

The Keifuku Mikuni Awara line connects Fukui with Mikuni-minato station (45 minutes). From there, it's a few minutes by bus to Tōjinbō.

TSURUGA 敦賀

The city of Tsuruga, south of Fukui and just north of Biwa-ko, is a thriving port and major train junction. The Shin Nihonkai ferry company (☎ 0770-23-2222) operates four sailings a week between Tsuruga and Otaru (Hokkaidō) (¥6710 2nd class, one way, 30 hours). Tsuruga-kō port is 20 minutes by bus from Tsuruga station. If you don't mind walking, it's around 2km to the north of Tsuruga station.

The Wakasa-wan region, south-west of Tsuruga, has fine seascapes and coastal scenery. Close to Mikata station are the **Mikata-go-ko** (Mikata Five Lakes). See the Wakasa-wan section in the Western Honshū chapter for details.

Kansai Region

The region described as Kansai in this chapter encompasses the prefectures of Kyoto, Nara, Osaka, Mie, Wakayama, Hyōgo and Shiga.

Kansai means 'west of the barrier', an allusion to the historical barrier stations or checkpoints that separated Kansai from Kantō, the area 'east of the barrier'. The barriers were located in different places at different times in Japanese history, finally ending up in Hakone during the period in which the Tokugawa shogunate ruled from Edo (contemporary Tokyo) in Kantō.

Following the opening of Kansai international airport in 1994, Kansai is now a convenient first port of call in Japan. This is a good option for those who are more interested in Japan's traditional culture than its modern one. Indeed, nowhere else in the country can you find so much of historical interest in such a compact area.

Kansai's major drawcards are, of course, Kyoto and Nara. Kyoto, with its hundreds of temples and gardens, was the imperial capital between 794 and 1868, and is still considered by most Japanese to be the cultural heart of Japan. Nara predates Kyoto as an imperial capital and also has an impressive array of temples, burial mounds and relics. Both cities should feature prominently in even the busiest travel itinerary.

Osaka, like Tokyo, is a great place to sample Japanese city life in all its busy, mind-boggling intensity, while Kōbe, now almost completely recovered from the disastrous earthquake of 1995, is one of Japan's most cosmopolitan and attractive cities. Himeji, just east of Kōbe, has what is probably the best of Japan's many feudal castles.

The main attractions of the prefecture, Mie-ken, are Ise-jingū, Japan's most sacred Shintō shrine, and the seascapes around the peninsula, Shima-hantō. Wakayama-ken offers *onsen* (mineral hot-spring spas), a rugged coast and the temple complex of Kōya-san, one of Japan's most important Buddhist centres.

Highlights

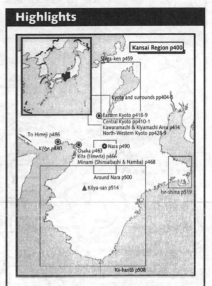

Kansai Region p400
Shiga-ken p459
Kyoto and surrounds pp404-5
Eastern Kyoto p418-9
Central Kyoto pp410-1
Kawaramachi & Kiyamachi Area p414
North-Western Kyoto pp428-9
To Himeji p486
Kōbe p480
Nara p490
Osaka p463
Kita (Umeda) p466
Minami (Shinsaibashi & Namba) p468
Around Nara p500
Kōya-san p514
Ise-shima p519
Kii-hantō p508

- Visit Kyoto, Japan's cultural capital, with more than 2000 temples and shrines.

- Sample the bustling nightlife of Osaka, Japan's most down-to-earth city.

- Stroll through cosmopolitan Kōbe, a lovely, picturesque city by the bay.

- Uncover the roots of Japanese culture in Nara, the country's ancient capital.

- Soak in open-air hot springs in mountainous Wakayama-ken.

- Spend a quiet night in atmospheric temple lodgings atop sacred Kōya-san.

- Hike from the mossy peak of Ōdai-gahara down into the stunning Ōsug-dani gorge.

Suggested Itineraries

Kyoto should be given the highest priority in any Kansai travel itinerary. Not only does the city have an almost endless list of things to see and do, it also has cheap lodgings,

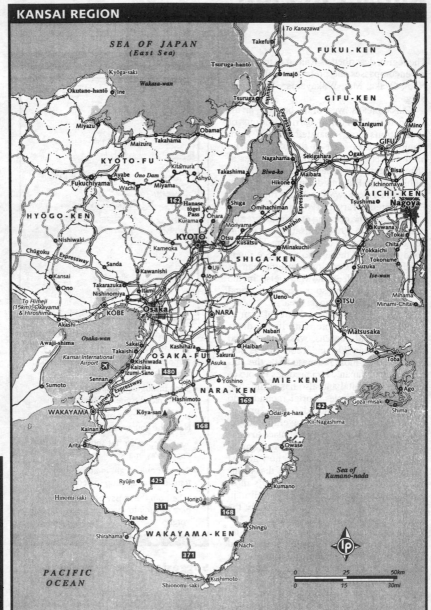

KANSAI REGION

SEA OF JAPAN
(East Sea)

To Kanazawa
Takefu
FUKUI-KEN

Kyōga-saki
Okutano-hantō • Ine
Wakasa-wan
Tsuruga-hantō
Imajō
GIFU-KEN

Miyazu
Maizuru Takahama
Obama
Tsuruga
Tanigumi
Mino

KYOTO-FU
Ayabe Ōno Dam
Kitamura
Takashima
Nagahama
Sekigahara
Ōgaki
GIFU
Bisai

Fukuchiyama
Wachi
Miyama
Ashyū
Biwa-ko
Maibara
Ichinomiya
AICHI-KEN

162
Hanase
tōgei
Pass
Shiga
Hikone
Tsushima
Nagoya

HYŌGO-KEN
Nishiwaki
Kameoka
Kurama
Ohara
KYOTO
Otsu
Ōmihachiman
Meishin
Kuwana
Tokai

Chūgoku
Sanda
Kawanishi
Uji
Kusatsu
SHIGA-KEN
Minakuchi
Yokkaichi
Chita
Tokoname
Suzuka

Kansai
Ono
Takarazuka
Nishinomiya
Itami
Jōyō
Ueno
TSU
Ise-wan
Mihama
Minami-Chita

To Himeji
(15km), Okayama
& Hiroshima
Akashi
KŌBE
Osaka
NARA
Nabari
Matsusaka

Awaji-shima
Osaka-wan
Sakai
Kashihara
Haibari
Ise
Toba

Kansai International
Airport
Takaishi
Kishiwada
Kaizuka
Izumi-Sano
OSAKA-FU
Sakurai
Asuka
MIE-KEN

Sumoto
Sennan
480
Gojō
Yoshino
Ago
Goza-misaki
Shima

Hanwa Expressway
Hashimoto
NARA-KEN
169
Ōdai-ga-hara
42
Kii-Nagashima

WAKAYAMA
Kōya-san
168
Owase

Kainan
Arita

Ryūjin
425
Sea of
Kumano-nada

Hinomi-saki
Hongū
Kumano

311
168
Shingū
Tanabe

Shirahama
WAKAYAMA-KEN
Nachi

371

PACIFIC
OCEAN
Kushimoto
Shionomi-saki

0   25   50km
0   15   30mi

great food, wonderful shops and pleasant hikes in its surrounding hills.

If you only have a week or less in Kansai, base yourself in Kyoto and take day trips to Nara and Osaka and perhaps an overnight trip to the mountaintop temple complex of Kōya-san. If you're keen on Japanese castles, you might also like to take a day trip out to Himeji to see the castle, Himeji-jō, visiting Kōbe on the way there or back.

If you have two weeks, you can travel to some of Kansai's more distant sights. In addition to following the Kyoto-based itinerary listed earlier, you could head down to Mie-ken's Ise-jingū, and perhaps hit some of the attractions in southern Nara. Alternatively, if you're a nature lover, you might consider doing the beautiful Ōdai-ga-hara hike in southern Nara, after which you could easily visit Ise-jingū on your return.

In three weeks you can include destinations that are even more remote, such as the onsen in Wakayama-ken's Hongū region and the seaside spa town of Shirahama.

Kyoto 京都

☎ 075 • pop 1.4 million

If there are two cities in Japan that *have* to be included in anyone's Japan itinerary, they are Tokyo and Kyoto. Some of what you've seen in Tokyo you'll see again in Kyoto: the glare of neon by night and the large-scale urban ugliness. But Kyoto, more than any other city in the country, offers what all Westerners long for from Japan: raked pebble gardens, the sensuous contours of a temple roof, the tripping step of a latter-day geisha in pursuit of a taxi.

Despite this, first impressions are likely to be something of an anticlimax. The beauty of Kyoto doesn't force itself upon the visitor. If you do take the time to seek it out, however, you will be impressed by how much there is to see: more than 2000 temples and shrines, a trio of palaces and dozens of gardens and museums. Months, or even years, could be spent exploring Kyoto and turning up still more surprises.

The city's one major drawback is that its fame attracts huge numbers of visitors (nearly 40 million annually), particularly during holidays and festivals. The spring and autumn periods, when Kyoto is at its most beautiful, are also very busy. Making an early start to the day can help you avoid the crushes, but sooner or later you will collide with tour groups. If this annoys you, don't spend all your time on the major attractions. Often just a short walk from the big-name sights are lesser attractions that are nearly deserted because they don't figure in the standard tour-group itinerary.

HISTORY

The Kyoto basin was first settled in the 7th century, and by 794 it had become Heian-kyō, the capital of Japan. Like Nara, a previous capital, the city was laid out in a grid pattern modelled on the Chinese Tang dynasty capital, Chang'an (contemporary Xi'an). Although the city was to serve as home to the Japanese imperial family from 794 to 1868 (when the Meiji Restoration took the imperial family to the new capital, Tokyo), the city was not always the focus of Japanese political power. During the Kamakura period (1185–1333), Kamakura served as the national capital, and during the Edo period (1600–1867) the Tokugawa shogunate ruled Japan from Edo (now Tokyo).

The problem was that from the 9th century the imperial family was increasingly isolated from the mechanics of political power, and the country was ruled primarily by military families, or shogunates. While Kyoto still remained capital in name and was the cultural focus of the nation, imperial power was for the most part symbolic, and the business of running state affairs was often carried out elsewhere.

Just as imperial fortunes have waxed and waned, the fortunes of the city itself have fluctuated dramatically. During the Ōnin War (1466–67), which marked the close of the Muromachi period, the Kyoto Gosho (Imperial Palace) and most of the city was destroyed. Much of what can be seen in Kyoto today dates from the Edo period

KANSAI REGION

(1600–1867). Although political power resided in Edo, Kyoto was rebuilt and flourished as a cultural, religious and economic centre. Fortunately, Kyoto was spared the aerial bombing that razed other Japanese urban centres in the closing months of WWII.

Today, even though it has seen rapid industrialisation, Kyoto remains an important cultural and educational centre. It has some 20% of Japan's National Treasures and 15% of Japan's Important Cultural Properties. Perhaps more impressive, Kyoto is home to a total of 17 Unesco World Heritage Sites (see the 'Unesco World Heritage Sites in Kyoto' boxed text). In addition, there are 24 museums and 37 universities and colleges scattered throughout the city. And even if the city centre looks remarkably like the centre of a dozen other large Japanese cities, a little exploration will turn up countless reminders of Kyoto's long history.

SUGGESTED ITINERARY

Kyoto is worth considering as a base for travel in Japan, especially as it is within easy reach of Osaka Itami and Kansai international airports. Kyoto is by far the best choice as a base for travel in Kansai because it has a wealth of accommodation and is close to Nara, Osaka, Kōbe, Mie-ken and Wakayama-ken.

It is difficult to suggest a minimum itinerary for Kyoto – you should certainly consider it a city you must see while you are in Japan and allocate it as much time as possible. Be selective about which sights you visit while you are there, however, and take your time: there's no point in spoiling your stay by overloading your senses or spending more than you can afford on admission fees.

The absolute minimum amount of time you should spend in Kyoto is two days, during which you could just about scratch the surface by visiting the Higashiyama area in eastern Kyoto. Five days would give you time to include Arashiyama, western Kyoto and central Kyoto. Ten days would allow you to cover these areas and also northern, southern and south-eastern Kyoto, while leaving a day or so for places farther afield or for in-depth exploration of museums, shops and culture.

Kyoto is also an excellent place to indulge specific cultural interests, whether they be in the arts, Buddhism or crafts. The best place to find information on these subjects is the Tourist Information Center (TIC – see the later Information section), which is used to dealing with both ordinary and extraordinary requests.

A final word of advice is that it's easy to overdose on temples in Kyoto. If you don't find temples to your liking, don't visit them. Instead, go for a hike in the mountains (see the various hikes covered in boxed text in this chapter), browse in the shops around Shijō-dōri (see Shopping later in this chapter), do some people-watching on Kiyamachi-dōri or, best of all, find a good restaurant and sample some of the finest food in all of Japan (see Places to Eat later in this chapter).

PLANNING
When to Go

Kyoto is a city that has attractions at any time of the year, with the possible exception of the muggy height of summer. It is probably best to visit Kyoto in spring or autumn, but as these are also the seasons most popular with

---

Unesco World Heritage Sites

In 1994, 13 of Kyoto's Buddhist temples, three Shintō shrines and one castle met the criteria to be designated World Heritage Sites by the United Nations. Each of the 17 sites has buildings or gardens of immeasurable historical value and all are open for public viewing.

Castle
Nijō-jō

Shrines
Kamigamo-jinja, Shimogamo-jinja, Ujigami-jinja

Temples
Byōdō-in, Daigo-ji, Enryaku-ji, Ginkaku-ji, Kinkaku-ji, Kiyomizu-dera, Kōzan-ji, Ninna-ji, Nishi Hongan-ji, Ryōan-ji, Saihō-ji, Tenryū-ji, Tō-ji

---

Japanese tour groups, the city can be very crowded at such times. Winter in Kyoto is quiet and not unbearably cold – a viable option for those with an aversion to crowds.

During the ephemeral cherry-blossom season, which usually starts in early April and lasts about a week, the Japanese succumb to 'cherry blossom mania' and descend on their favourite spots in hordes. The top spots for *hanami* (cherry-blossom viewing) include Tetsugaku no-michi (the Path of Philosophy); the park, Maruyama-kōen; the shrine, Heian-jingū; and Arashiyama and Kyoto-gyōen (Imperial Palace Park). A good place to see the cherry blossoms without the crowds is along the river, the Kamo-gawa, north of Demachiyanagi station.

Autumn colours are similarly spectacular and attract huge numbers of leaf-gazers. Popular viewing spots include Ōhara, Kurama Rikyu (Kurama Imperial Village), Shūgaku-in Rikyu (Shūgaku Imperial Village) and the temple, Daigo-ji. Perhaps the best place to enjoy the foliage away from the crowds is in the Takao region (see the 'Kiyotaki River Hike' boxed text later in this chapter).

ORIENTATION

Kyoto is a fairly easy city to find your way around. Japan Railways (JR) Kyoto station is in the south, and from there Karasuma-dōri runs north past Higashi Hongan-ji, the commercial centre of town and Kyoto Gosho. The commercial and nightlife centres are between Shijō-dōri and Sanjō-dōri (to the south and north, respectively) and between Kawaramachi-dōri and Karasuma-dōri (to the east and west, respectively).

Although some of Kyoto's major sights are in the city centre, most of Kyoto's best sightseeing is on the outskirts of the city, in the eastern and western parts of town. These areas are most conveniently reached by bus or bicycle. Outside the city itself, the mountain villages of Ōhara, Kurama and Takao make wonderful day trips and are easily accessible by public transport.

Kyoto has retained a grid system based on the classical Chinese concept. This system of numbered streets running east to west and avenues running north to south makes it relatively easy to move around with the help of a map from the TIC. Addresses are indicated with the name of the closest intersection and the location *agaru* or *sagaru* (literally 'up' or 'down' respectively, and in this instance meaning 'north' or 'south') of that intersection.

Efficient bus services crisscross the city. There's a simplified bus map on the reverse of the TIC Kyoto map. The quickest way to move between the north and south of the city is to take the subway. The TIC has a leaflet called *Walking Tour Courses in Kyoto* that has detailed walking maps for major sightseeing areas (Higashiyama, Arashiyama, North-Western Kyoto and Ōhara) in and around Kyoto.

Finally, a general note: as a rule in Kyoto, the closer you get to the mountains, the better the scenery. Kyoto's most beautiful areas lie right at the base of the mountains that surround the city to the north, east and west. So if you find yourself in need of relief from the concrete maze of downtown, do as the locals do and head for the hills.

Maps

Available at the TIC, the *Tourist Map of Kyoto, Nara* fulfils most map needs and includes a simplified map of the subway and bus systems. *Walking Tour Courses in Kyoto* details ways to see the sights in Kyoto on foot. You might also want to pick up a copy of the Japanese city bus map at any major bus stop; even if you don't read Japanese, the detailed route maps are useful. The best map of Kyoto, intended for long-term foreign residents, is the *Guide to Kyoto*, available at the Kyoto International Community House (KICH; see the later Useful Organisations section for details).

INFORMATION
Tourist Offices

The best source of information on Kyoto, the Kansai region and Japan in general is the Japan National Tourist Organization's TIC (☎ 371-5649). It's a one-minute walk north of JR Kyoto station, just past Kyoto Tower on the western side of Karasuma-dōri (9 am

KYOTO & SURROUNDS

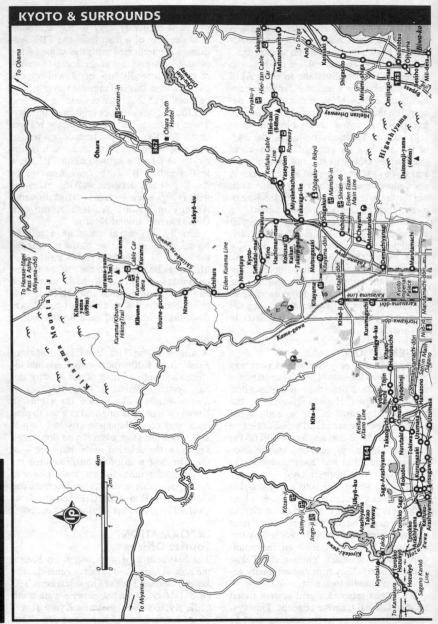

KYOTO & SURROUNDS

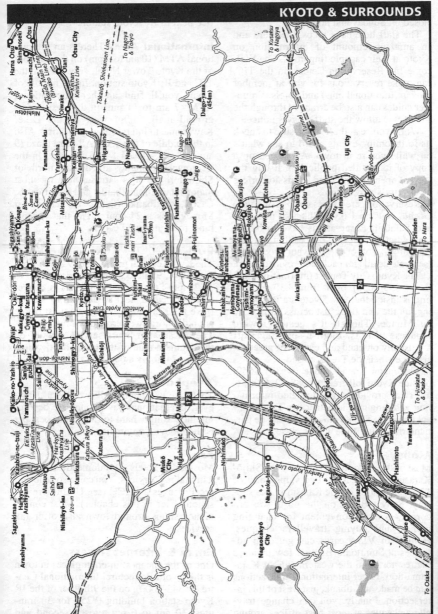

to 5 pm weekdays, 9 am to noon Saturday, closed on Sunday and holidays).

The staff here have maps, literature and an amazing amount of information on Kyoto at their capable fingertips. The Welcome Inn Reservation Centre, in the TIC, can make reservations for you at member *ryokan* (traditional inns) and hotels. Volunteer guides can also be arranged through the TIC if you allow the staff a day's notice.

While you're at the TIC, be sure to check its forthcoming-events board to see what's on while you're in town. Also, pick up a copy of its untitled publication listing the current opening hours and admission prices of the city's major sights.

Reservations are necessary to visit Kyoto Gosho, Katsura Rikyu, Shūgaku-in Rikyu and Saihō-ji. Reservations have to be organised at the relevant offices, but the TIC can inform you of the relevant procedures (separate details for each are provided later).

The Kyoto City Tourist Information Centre (☎ 343-6656), open from 8.30 am to 7 pm, is inside the new Kyoto station building, on the 2nd floor just across from Café du Monde. Though it's geared toward Japanese visitors, English-speaking staff are usually on hand and can be of great assistance when the TIC is closed.

The Japan Travel-Phone (☎ 371-5649; outside Kyoto toll-free ☎ 0088-22-4800) is a service providing travel-related information and language assistance in English (9 am to 5 pm). The Kyoto number can be particularly useful if the TIC is closed.

Money
Most of the major banks are near the Shijō-Karasuma intersection, two stops north of JR Kyoto station on the Karasuma line subway. Sanwa Bank, on the north-western corner, is most convenient for changing money and buying travellers cheques. Holders of VISA cards can get cash advances at Sumitomo Bank, a few hundred metres north, on the western side of Karasuma-dōri. Other international transactions can be made at Citibank, just west of this intersection. Finally, you can change travellers cheques at most post offices around

town, including the Kyoto central post office next to JR Kyoto station.

International ATMs There's an international ATM (10 am to 9 pm) on the B1 floor of the Kyoto Tower Hotel, very close to the TIC and JR Kyoto station. In the middle of town, you'll find another international ATM (7 am to 11 pm) in the Zest underground mall, 200m west of the Oike-Kawaramachi intersection, near exit 7. Also in the middle of town, the All Card Plaza (9 am to 8 pm, closed 1 to 3 January) in the Teramachi shopping arcade just north of Shijō-dōri provides card services for most major international banks and credit cards. Lastly, Citibank (listed earlier under Money) has a 24-hour ATM that accepts most foreign-issued cards.

Post
The Kyoto central post office (9 am to 7 pm weekdays, 9 am to 5 pm Saturday, 9 am to 12.30 pm Sunday and holidays) is conveniently located next to JR Kyoto station (take the Karasuma exit, as the post office is on the north-western side of the station). There's an after-hours service counter on the southern side of the post office, which is open 24 hours a day, 365 days a year.

Telephone
There are pay phones all over town. However, international pay phones are becoming increasingly hard to find. Your best bet is the lobby of any major hotel.

Fax
Most larger hotels offer domestic and international fax services. You can also send and receive faxes at KICH (see Useful Organisations later in this chapter). Most convenience shops around town also offer fax services.

Email & Internet Access
One of the cheapest Internet places in town is the Kyoto Prefectural International Centre (☎ 342-5000), on the 9th floor of the JR Kyoto station building (¥250 for 30 minutes, 10 am to 6 pm, closed second and

fourth Tuesday each month). English support is available here.

Aspirin Internet cafe (☎ 251-2351) is in the Teramachi shopping arcade, on the 3rd floor of the A-Break building, next to a *pachinko* (vertical pinball) parlour. It charges ¥500 an hour and is open from 10 am to 9 pm; it's closed over the New Year period.

MEIX Internet cafe (☎ 213-1201) is on Karasuma-dōri, a one-minute walk south of Kyoto Gosho (¥700 for two hours, noon to 7 pm, closed Sunday). Note that you must pay a ¥3000 deposit here, ¥2500 of which will be returned to you when you close your account.

Buttercups (☎ 751-9537), a cafe in eastern Kyoto, has one terminal available for surfing (¥250 for 30 minutes, 10 am to 11 pm, closed Tuesday). You can send email for ¥50 per batch (typing time is free) and also use the cafe's in-box (email bttrcps@ dd.iij4u.or.jp) to receive email (your own mail box is created free of charge).

There are several places in Kyoto offering reasonable (or free) access to the Internet without the benefit of email. NTT has a few demonstration showrooms about town where it's possible to surf free of charge; the most accessible of these is on the 7th floor of Takashimaya department store at the Shijō-Kawaramachi intersection.

KICH (see Useful Organisations later) also offers cheap Internet access.

Internet Resources
For travel information and general tidbits on Kyoto, there are a myriad of Web sites worth visiting. The following sites are good places to begin, and will lead to many other links:

Japan National Tourism Organization
www.jnto.go.jp
Kansai Time Out
www.kto.co.jp
Kyoto Prefecture Covers the greater Kyoto area
www.pref.kyoto.jp/index_e.html

Travel Agencies
Kyoto has several good central travel agents who can arrange discount air tickets, visas, car rental, accommodation and other services. We recommend A'cross Travellers'

Bureau (☎ 255-3559) and No 1 Travel (☎ 251-6970), both in the Kawaramachi and Kiyamachi area.

Books & Bookshops
The best bookshop in Kyoto is Maruzen (☎ 241-2161), on Kawaramachi-dōri between Sanjō-dōri and Shijō-dōri (10 am to 8 pm, closed third Wednesday of each month). It has a large selection of English-language books, magazines and maps as well as a limited number of French-, German- and Spanish-language books. Of special interest is its excellent selection of English-language books on Kyoto and Japan.

Exploring Kyoto, by long-term Kyoto resident Judith Clancy, is an excellent guide to exploring Kyoto on foot. It documents more than 25 walks and hikes through the city.

Perhaps the most detailed guide to Kyoto's cultural attractions is *Kyoto – A Cultural Guide to Japan's Ancient Imperial City* by John & Phyllis Martin.

Old Kyoto: A Guide to Traditional Shops, Restaurants & Inns by Diane Durston, is a must for those in search of specific Kyoto handicrafts. It also has information on atmospheric old ryokan and restaurants.

Also by Diane Durston, *Kyoto, Seven Paths to the Heart of the City* is somewhat similar to *Exploring Kyoto*. It details seven walks through some of the city's most atmospheric old neighbourhoods.

For those anticipating a long stay in Kansai, John Ashburne's *The Best of Kansai* is a great introduction to the region's best restaurants, shops, bars and attractions.

Also intended for residents is *Easy Living in Kyoto* (Kyoto City International Foundation), available at KICH (see Useful Organisations for details).

Newspapers & Magazines
The free *Kyoto Visitor's Guide* is the best source of information about forthcoming events in Kyoto. In addition to listings of events, it has restaurant reviews, day hikes, detailed maps of the city, useful information sections and feature articles about various aspects of the city. Try to pick up a copy as soon as you arrive in Kyoto. It's

available at the TIC, Maruzen bookshop, KICH and most major hotels.

Another excellent source of information about Kyoto and the rest of the Kansai area is *Kansai Time Out*, a monthly English-language listings magazine. Apart from lively articles, it has a large section of ads for employment, travel agencies, meetings, lonely hearts etc. It's available at Maruzen bookshop, at the TIC, or by calling ☎ 078-232-4516.

Kansai Flea Market is a free monthly publication aimed at foreign residents. It has work and housing listings, as well as entertaining personal advertisements. It's also available at Maruzen bookshop.

Those with a literary bent might want to look out for the nonprofit *Kyoto Journal*, which publishes high-quality articles and artwork by Kyoto residents and others. It's also available at Maruzen bookshop or by calling ☎ 761-1433.

Useful Organisations

KICH (☎ 752-3010) is an essential stop for those planning a long-term stay in Kyoto, but it can also be quite useful for short-term visitors (9 am to 9 pm, closed Monday, or the following Tuesday if Monday is a national holiday).

Here you can rent typewriters, and send and receive faxes. It has a library with maps, books, newspapers and magazines from around the world and a notice board displaying messages regarding work, accommodation, rummage sales etc. It's also just introduced an Internet service (¥200 for 30 minutes).

While you're there you can pick up a copy of its excellent *Guide to Kyoto* map and *Easy Living in Kyoto* book (please note that both of these are intended for residents). You can also chill out in the lobby and watch CNN news or have a cup of coffee in the cafe.

You can also make arrangements through KICH to meet a Japanese family at home. Let staff know at least one day – preferably two days – in advance.

Lastly, see the Kyoto Activities section later for information on cultural demonstrations held at KICH.

KICH is in eastern Kyoto, about 500m west of Nanzen-ji. You can walk from Keihan Sanjō station in about 20 minutes. Alternatively, take the Tōzai line subway from central Kyoto and get off at Keage station, from which it's a five-minute walk downhill to KICH.

Medical Services

Kyoto Holiday Emergency Clinic (☎ 811-5072) is actually spread over three different hospitals according to the complaint. If you require urgent attention, contact the clinic and they will direct you to the appropriate hospital.

Sakabe International Clinic (☎ 231-1624) also provides a 24-hour emergency service. Its normal opening hours are 9.20 am to 12:30 pm from Monday to Saturday, and 6.30 pm to 8.30 pm on week nights except Thursday, closed on Sundays and public holidays. It's five minutes' walk from Shiyakusho-mae station on the Tōzai line.

The Kyoto Holiday Emergency Dental Clinic (☎ 441-7173) provides an emergency dental service (10 am to 4 pm, Sunday and public holidays). It's a 10-minute walk from Kitaō-ji station.

For nonurgent medical attention, try the Japan Baptist Hospital (☎ 781-5191), which usually has some English-speaking doctors on its staff. You can visit without an appointment from 8.30 to 11 am and 1 to 3.45 pm Monday to Friday. It's in north-eastern Kyoto; to get there take bus No 3 from the intersection of Shijō and Kawaramachi streets, and get off at the Baptist Byōin-Mae stop. It's a short walk up the hill.

The TIC has listings of additional hospitals and clinics with English-speaking doctors and can help you find one to meet your needs.

Emergency

The national toll-free emergency number for the police is ☎ 110; to call for an ambulance or report a fire, dial ☎ 119. The person answering the phone may not always be able to speak English, but if you speak slowly and have your address in hand, you should be able to get your point across.

If you need to use English and want help finding the closest suitable service, try the Japan Travel-Phone (☎ 371-5649) or Japan Helpline (☎ 0120-461-997).

Dangers & Annoyances

The western bank of Kamo-gawa between Sanjō-dōri and Shijō-dōri can be a little rough on hot summer nights, as can some of the streets around Kiyamachi-dōri. Keep your wits about you and try to avoid walking alone at night in these areas.

CENTRAL KYOTO 京都中央

Central Kyoto looks much like any other Japanese city, but there are a few major sights in the area, such as Kyoto Gosho, Nijō-jō and several museums.

The area around JR Kyoto station (just below the city centre) is a fairly dull part of town; the main sights are Nishi Hongan-ji and Tō-ji.

Kyoto Gosho 京都御所

The original imperial palace was built in 794 and was replaced numerous times after destruction by fire. The present building, on a different site and smaller than the original, was constructed in 1855. Enthronement of a new emperor and other state ceremonies are still held there.

Foreigners are privileged to be given preferential access – Japanese visitors have to wait longer for permission to visit – but Kyoto Gosho does not rate highly in comparison with other attractions in Kyoto.

If you do visit, you will be given a guided tour of the palace that includes the Shishinden Hall, Ko Gosho (Small Palace), Tsune Gosho (Regular Palace) and Oike-niwa (Pond Garden).

To reach Kyoto Gosho, take the Karasuma line subway to Imadegawa or a bus to the Karasuma-Imadegawa stop and walk south-east.

Reservation & Admission This is organised by Kunaichō, the Imperial Household Agency (☎ 211-1215), which is inside the walled park surrounding the palace, a short walk from Imadegawa subway station on the Karasuma line (8.45 am to noon and 1 to 4 weekdays, closed national holidays and 28 December to 4 January). You have to fill out an application form and show your passport. Children can visit if accompanied by adults over 20 years of age (but are forbidden entry to the other three imperial properties of Katsura Rikyu, Sentō Gosho and Shūgaku-in Rikyu). Permission to tour the palace is usually granted the same day (try to arrive at the office at least 30 minutes before the start of the tour you'd like to join). Guided tours, usually in English, are given at 10 am and 2 pm from Monday to Friday. The tour lasts about 50 minutes.

The Imperial Household Agency is also the place to make advance reservations to see Sentō Gosho, Katsura Rikyu and Shūgaku-in Rikyu. Application forms are also available from JNTO offices outside the country and JNTO-run TICs inside Japan.

Sentō Gosho 仙洞御所

This is a few hundred metres south-east of Kyoto Gosho. Visitors must obtain advance permission from the Imperial Household Agency and be over 20 years old (see the Kyoto Gosho section for details). Tours (in Japanese) start at 11 am and 1.30 pm. The gardens, which were laid out in 1630 by Kobori Enshū, are the main attraction.

Kyoto-gyōen 京都御苑

Kyoto Gosho is surrounded by the spacious park, Kyoto-gyōen, which is planted with a huge variety of flowering trees and open fields. It's perfect for picnics, strolls and just about any sport you can think of. Best of all, it's free. Take some time to visit the pond at the park's southern end, which contains gorgeous carp. The park is most beautiful in the plum- and cherry-blossom seasons (March and April respectively). It is between Teramachi-dōri and Karasuma-dōri (to the east and west) and Imadegawa-dōri and Marutamachi-dōri (to the north and south).

Nijō-jō 二条城

The castle, Nijō-jō, was built in 1603 as the official Kyoto residence of the first Tokugawa shōgun, Ieyasu. The ostentatious style

CENTRAL KYOTO

Kamo-gawa

See Eastern Kyoto map p418-9

Kyoto Gosho

Sentō Gosho

Kyōtō-gyoen

Nijō-jō

KANSAI REGION

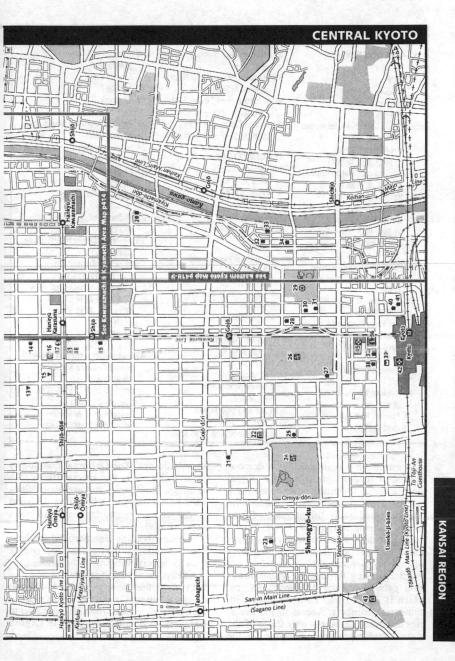

CENTRAL KYOTO

CENTRAL KYOTO

PLACES TO STAY
1 Takaya
鷹屋
3 YWCA
5 Uno House
宇野ハウス
7 International Hotel Kyoto
国際ホテル京都
8 ANA Hotel Kyoto
全日空ホテル京都
19 Karasuma Kyoto Hotel
からすま京都ホテル
20 Ryokan Hinomoto
旅館ひのもと
21 Kyoto Tōkyū Hotel
京都東急ホテル
23 Guest Inn Kyoto
ゲストイン京都
27 Pension Station Kyoto
ペンションステーション京都
28 Matsubaya Ryokan
松葉屋旅館
30 Ryokan Murakamiya
旅館村上家
31 Ryokan Kyōka
旅館京花
32 Riverside Takase
リバーサイド高瀬
33 Ryokan Hiraiwa
旅館平岩
34 Yuhara Ryokan
ゆはら旅館

37 Hokke Club Kyoto
法華クラブ
38 Hotel New Hankyū Kyoto
ホテル新阪急
40 Kyoto Dai-ni Tower Hotel
京都第二タワーホテル
41 Kyoto Century Hotel
京都センチュリーホテル

PLACES TO EAT
9 Obanzai
おばんざい
13 Mukade-ya
百足屋
15 Bistrot de Paris
パリの食堂

OTHER
2 Imperial Household Agency
宮内庁
4 MEIX (Internet Cafe)
メイックス
6 Ippo-dō
一保堂
10 Japan Air Lines (JAL)
日本航空
11 Nijō Jinya
二条陣屋
12 Sumitomo Bank
住友銀行
14 Japan Foundation Kyoto Office
国際交流基金京都支部

16 Kongō Nō Stage
金剛能樂堂
17 Sanwa Bank
三和銀行
18 Citibank
シティバンク
22 Period Costume Museum
風俗博物館
24 Nishi Hongan-ji
西本願寺
25 Kunkgyoku-dō
薫玉堂
26 Higashi Hongan-ji
東本願寺
29 Shōsei-en
渉成園
35 Kintetsu Department Store
近鉄百貨店
36 Tourist Information Center (TIC); Kyoto Tower; International ATM
国際観光振興会京都案内所；京都タワー；国際ATM
39 Kyoto Central Post Office
京都中央郵便局
42 Isetan Department Store; Hotel Granvia Kyoto
伊勢丹；ホテルグランビア京都
43 Umekōji Steam Locomotive Museum
梅小路蒸気機関車館

KANSAI REGION

of construction was intended as a demonstration of Ieyasu's prestige and to signal the demise of the emperor's power. As a safeguard against treachery, Ieyasu had the interior fitted with 'nightingale' floors (floors that sing and squeak at every move, making it difficult for intruders to move about quietly) and concealed chambers where bodyguards could keep watch.

After passing through the grand Karamon gate, you enter **Ninomaru Palace**, which is divided into five buildings with numerous chambers. Access to the buildings depended on rank – only those of the highest rank were permitted to enter the inner buildings. The Ohiroma Yon-no-Ma (Fourth Chamber) has spectacular screen paintings. Don't miss the excellent **Ninomaru Palace Garden**, which was designed by the tea master and landscape architect Kobori Enshū.

The neighbouring **Honmaru Palace** dates from the middle of last century and is only open for special viewing in the autumn.

Admission to Ninomaru Palace and garden is ¥600; they're open from 8.45 am, and the last admission is at 4 pm (gates close at 5 pm). They're closed from 26 December to 4 January. A detailed fact sheet in English is provided.

While you're in the neighbourhood, you might want to take a look at the garden, Shinsen-en, just south of the castle (it's outside the walls and therefore free). This forlorn garden, with its small shrines and pond, is all that remains of the original imperial palace, abandoned in 1227.

To reach the castle, take bus No 9 from JR Kyoto station to the Nijō-jō-mae stop. Alternatively, take the Tōzai line subway to the Nijō-jō-mae station.

Nijō Jinya
A few minutes' walk south of Nijō-jō is Nijō Jinya (Nijō Fortified House) one of Kyoto's hidden gems. Seldom seen by short-term visitors, it was built as a merchant's home in the mid-1600s and served as an inn for provincial feudal lords visiting the capital. What appears to be an average Edo-period mansion, however, is no ordinary dwelling.

The house contains fire-resistant earthen walls and a warren of 24 rooms that were ingeniously designed to protect the *daimyō* (domain lords) against possible surprise attacks. Here you'll find hidden staircases, secret passageways and an array of counter-espionage devices. The ceiling skylight of the main room is fitted with a trap door through which *samurai* could pounce on intruders, and sliding doors feature alternating panels of translucent paper to expose the shadows of eavesdroppers.

One-hour tours are conducted several times a day in Japanese and advance reservations must be made (also in Japanese – ring ☎ 841-0972). Those who don't speak Japanese are asked to bring a Japanese-speaking guide; consider arranging a volunteer guide through the TIC. Admission is ¥1000.

Pontochō 先斗町
Pontochō-dōri, a traditional centre for night entertainment, is a narrow alley running between Sanjō-dōri and Shijō-dōri just west of Kamo-gawa. It's best visited in the evening, when the traditional wooden buildings and hanging lanterns create a wonderful atmosphere of old Japan. Many of the restaurants, teahouses and bars here prefer Japanese customers (and are hideously expensive to boot), but there are some casual places that welcome foreigners (see the Kyoto Places to Eat section). This is also a good place to spot *geisha* (see the boxed text 'The Living Art of the Geisha' in this chapter) and *maiko* (apprentice geisha) on their way to or from appointments. On weekend evenings, you will probably notice one or two if you stand for a few minutes at the Shi-jō end of the alley.

Nishiki-kōji Market
If you're interested in seeing all the weird and wonderful foods required for cooking in Kyoto, wander through Nishiki-kōji market, Kyoto's best full-time market. It's in the centre of town, one block north of (and parallel to) Shijō-dōri. This is a great place to visit on a rainy day or as a break from temple hopping. The variety of different foods on display is staggering, and the frequent cries of *'Irasshiamase!'* (Welcome!) are heart warming.

KYOTO STATION AREA
京都駅周辺
Although most of Kyoto's attractions are farther north, there are a few attractions within walking distance of the station. And, of course, now that it's been redone, the station itself is something of an attraction.

Kyoto Station
Kyoto's new station building is a striking steel and glass structure – a futuristic cathedral for the transportation age. Unveiled in September 1997, the building met with some decidedly mixed reviews. Some critics assailed the building as entirely out of keeping with the traditional architecture of Kyoto; others loved its wide-open spaces and dramatic lines.

Whatever the critics' views, we're sure that you'll be impressed by the huge atrium that soars over the main concourse. Take some time to explore the many levels of the station, all the way up to the 15th-floor observation level. And if you don't suffer from fear of heights, try riding the escalator from the 7th floor on the eastern side of the

KANSAI REGION

KAWARAMACHI & KIYAMACHI

building up to the 11th-floor aerial skywalk high over the main concourse.

In the station building you'll find several food courts (see the Kyoto Places to Eat section), the Kyoto Prefectural International Centre, a Joypolis game centre, a performance space and Isetan department store.

Nishi Hongan-ji 西本願寺

In 1591, Hideyoshi Toyotomi built this temple (free, 6 am to 5 pm, slightly longer hours in spring and summer), known as Hongan-ji, as a new headquarters for the Jōdo Shin-shū (True Pure Land) school of Buddhism,

which had accumulated immense power. Later, Tokugawa Ieyasu saw this power as a threat and sought to weaken it by encouraging a breakaway faction of this school to found Higashi Hongan-ji (higashi means 'east') in 1602. The original Hongan-ji then became known as Nishi Hongan-ji (nishi means 'west'). It now functions as the headquarters of the Hongan-ji branch of the Jōdo Shin-shū school, with over 10,000 temples and 12 million followers worldwide.

The temple contains five buildings, featuring some of the finest examples of architecture and artistic achievement from the

KAWARAMACHI & KIYAMACHI

PLACES TO STAY

3 Hotel Fujita Kyoto
ホテルフジタ京都
6 Kyoto Hotel
京都ホテル
9 Hotel Gimmond
ホテルギンモンド
11 Hiiragiya Ryokan
柊屋旅館
12 Tawaraya Ryokan
俵屋旅館
38 Sun Hotel Kyoto
サンホテル京都
70 Kinmata Ryokan
近又旅館

PLACES TO EAT

1 Shin-shin-tei
新進亭
4 Ōiwa
大岩
5 Ganko Nijō-en
がんこ二条苑
10 Yoshikawa
吉川
15 Kerala
ケララ
16 Tōsui-rō
豆水楼
18 Morita-ya
モリタ屋
19 Ganko Sushi
がんこ寿司
23 Musashi Sushi
むさし寿司
24 Misoka-an Kawamichi-ya
晦庵河道屋
25 Kōsendō-sumi
光泉洞寿み
28 Biotei
びお亭
30 Sarasa
サラサ
31 Mishima-tei
三嶋亭
32 Capricciosa
カプリチョーザ
37 Kane-yo
かねよ

39 Koharu
小はる
40 Kuishinbo
くいしんぼ
44 Tenka-ippin
天下一品
46 Zu Zu
ずず
47 Uzuki
うずき
51 Kappa-zushi
かっぱ寿司
52 Fujino-ya
藤の家
53 Yamatomi
山とみ
54 A-Bar
アバー
55 Shirukō
志る幸
56 Kobeya Dining
コウベヤダイニング
58 Sancho
サンチョ
61 Tomi-zushi
とみ寿司
62 Takasebune
高瀬舟
66 Ashoka
アショカ
67 Mr Young Mens
ミスタ ヤングメンズ
72 Doutor Coffee
ドトールコーヒー
73 Starbuck's
スターバックス
74 Fūkei
風景
75 Daniel's
ダニエルズ

OTHER

2 Lab Tribe
ラブトライブ
7 Kyoto City Hall
京都市役所
8 Lodge Outdoor
Sports
ロッジ

13 ANA
全日空
14 Zest Underground
Shopping Mall
17 Teddy's
テディーズ
20 Backgammon
バックゲモン
21 Asahi Cinema
朝日シネマ
22 Medic
メディック
26 Museum of Kyoto
京都博物館
27 Nakagyō Post Office
中京郵便局
29 A'cross Travellers
Bureau
アクロストラベル
ビューロー
33 Rub-a-Dub
ラバダブ
34 Pontochō Kaburen-jō
Theatre
先斗町歌舞練場
35 Bar, Isn't It?
バーイズントイット
36 Sukara-za Theatre
スカラ座
41 Sama Sama
サマサマ
42 Virgin Records
ヴァージンレコード
43 Step Rampo Bar
45 Ing
イング
48 Maruzen Bookshop
丸善書店
49 Vivre Department Store;
Tower Records
ビブレ
50 Zappa
ザッパ
57 OPA Shopping Centre
オーパ
59 Shizuka
静
60 No 1 Travel
ナンバーワントラベル

KAWARAMACHI & KIYAMACHI

63 Hankyū
   Department Store
   阪急百貨店
64 Takashimaya
   Department
   Store
   高島屋百貨店

65 Fujii Daimaru
   Department Store
   藤井大丸百貨店
68 All Card Plaza
   オールカードプラザ
69 Aspirin Internet Cafe
   アスピリン

71 Aritsugu
   有次
76 Daimaru Department
   Store
   大丸デパート
77 House of Kajinoha
   森田和紙

Azuchi-Momoyama period (1568–1600). Unfortunately, the Goe-dō (Main Hall) is presently being restored and will be 'under wraps' until 2010. Nonetheless, it's worth a visit to see the Daisho-in Hall, which has sumptuous paintings, carvings and metal ornamentation. A small garden and two *nō* (classical Japanese dance-drama) stages are connected with the hall. The dazzling Kara-mon has intricate ornamental carvings. Both the Daisho-in Hall and the Kara-mon were transported here from Fushimi-jō.

If you'd like a guided tour of the temple (in Japanese only), reservations (preferably several days in advance) can be made either at the temple office (☎ 371-5181) or through the TIC. The temple is a 12-minute walk north-west of JR Kyoto station.

Higashi Hongan-ji 東本願寺
When Tokugawa Ieyasu engineered the rift in the Jōdo Shin-shū school of Buddhism, he founded this temple (free, 6.20 am to 4.30 pm, slightly longer hours in spring and summer) as competition for Nishi Hongan-ji. Rebuilt in 1895 after a fire, it's certainly monumental in its proportions, but it's less impressive artistically than its counterpart. A curious item on display is a length of rope made from hair donated by female believers, which was used to haul the timber for the re-construction. The temple, which is a five-minute walk north of JR Kyoto station, is now the headquarters of the Ōtani branch of the Jōdo Shin-shū school of Buddhism.

Tō-ji 東寺
This temple was established in 794 by imperial decree to protect the city. In 818, the emperor handed over the temple to Kūkai,

the founder of the Shingon school of Buddhism. Many of the temple buildings were destroyed by fire or fighting during the 15th century; most of those that remain date from the 17th century.

The Kōdō (Lecture Hall) contains 21 images representing a Mikkyō (Esoteric Buddhism) mandala. The Kondō (Main Hall) contains statues depicting the Yakushi (Healing Buddha) trinity. In the southern part of the garden stands the five-storey pagoda, which burnt down five times, was rebuilt in 1643 and is now the highest pagoda in Japan, standing 57m high.

Kōbō-san market fair is held here on the 21st of each month. The fairs held in December and January are particularly lively.

Admission to the temple grounds is free; admission to the Kondō and the Hōmotsu-kan (Treasure Hall) is ¥500 (9 am to 4.30 pm). Tō-ji is a 15-minute walk south-west of JR Kyoto station.

Umekōji Steam Locomotive Museum
A hit with steam-train buffs and kids, this museum features 18 vintage steam locomotives (dating from 1914 to 1948) and related displays. It's in the former Nijō station building, which was recently relocated here and carefully reconstructed. Entry is ¥400 (¥100 for children); for another ¥200 (¥100 for children) you can take a 10-minute ride on one of the fabulous old trains (departures at 11 am and 1.30 and 3.30 pm). It's open from 9.30 am to 5 pm (closed Monday). From JR Kyoto station, take bus No 33, 205 or 208 to the Umekō-ji Kōen-mae stop (make sure you take a west-bound bus).

EASTERN KYOTO 京都東部

The eastern part of Kyoto, notably the Higashiyama (Eastern Mountains) district, merits top priority for its fine temples, peaceful walks and traditional night entertainment in Gion.

Allocate at least a full day to cover the sights in the southern section, and another full day for the northern section. JNTO publishes a leaflet, *Walking Tour Courses in Kyoto*, which covers the whole of eastern Kyoto.

Sanjūsangen-dō 三十三間堂

The original temple, Sanjūsangen-dō (¥600, 8 am to 5 pm from 1 April to 15 November, 9 am to 4 pm from 16 November to 31 March), was built in 1164 at the request of the retired emperor Go-shirakawa. It burnt to the ground in 1249 but a faithful copy was constructed in 1266.

The temple's name refers to the 33 *sanjūsan* (bays) between the pillars of this long, narrow building housing 1001 statues of the 1000-armed Kannon (the Buddhist goddess of mercy). The largest Kannon is flanked on either side by 500 smaller Kannon images, neatly lined up in rows.

There are an awful lot of arms, but if you're picky and think the 1000-armed statues don't have the required number of limbs, then you should remember to calculate according to the nifty Buddhist mathematical formula that holds that 40 arms are the equivalent of 1000 arms, because each saves 25 worlds. Visitors also seem keen to spot resemblances between friends or family members and any of the hundreds of images.

At the back of the hall are 28 guardian statues in a great variety of expressive poses. The gallery on the western side of the hall is famous for the annual **Tōshi-ya Matsuri**, held on 15 January, during which archers shoot arrows the length of the hall. The ceremony dates back to the Edo period, when an annual contest was held to see how many arrows could be shot from the southern end to the northern end in 24 hours. The all-time record was set in 1686, when an archer successfully landed over 8000 arrows at the northern end.

The temple is a 20-minute walk east of JR Kyoto station; alternatively, take bus No 206 or 208 and get off at the Sanjūsangen-dō-mae stop. It's also very close to Keihan Shichijō station. From the station, walk east along Shichijō-dōri; the temple is on the right.

Kyoto National Museum 京都国立博物館

The Kyoto National Museum (¥420, 9 am to 4.30 pm, closed Monday) is housed in two buildings opposite Sanjūsangen-dō. There are excellent displays of fine arts, historical artefacts and handicrafts. The fine arts collection is especially highly regarded, containing some 230 items that have been classified as National Treasures or Important Cultural Properties.

There's an additional charge for special exhibitions.

Kawai Kanjirō Memorial Hall 河井寛次郎博物館

This museum (¥900, 10 am to 5 pm, closed Monday and from 10 to 20 August and 24 December to 7 January) was once the home and workshop of one of Japan's most famous potters, Kawai Kanjirō. The house is built in rural style and contains examples of his work, his collection of folk art and ceramics, and his kiln.

The hall is a 10-minute walk north of the Kyoto National Museum. Alternatively, take bus No 206 or 207 from JR Kyoto station and get off at the Umamachi stop.

Kiyomizu-dera 清水寺

This temple (main hall ¥300, other areas free, 6 am to 6 pm) was first built in 798, but the present buildings are reconstructions dating from 1633. As an affiliate of the Hossō school of Buddhism, which originated in Nara, it has successfully survived the many intrigues of local Kyoto schools of Buddhism through the centuries and is now one of the most famous landmarks of the city. This, unfortunately, makes it a prime target for busloads of Japanese tourists, particularly during cherry-blossom season. Some travellers are also put off by the rather

EASTERN KYOTO

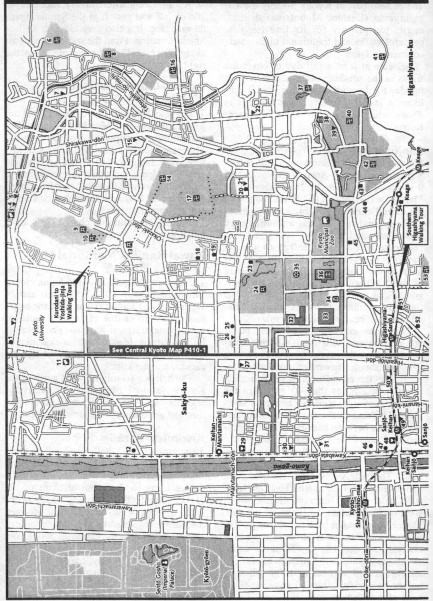

Higashiyama-ku

Sakyō-ku

Kyoto University

Kurodani to Yoshida-jinja Walking Tour

See Central Kyoto Map P410-1

Southern Higashiyama Walking Tour

Kyoto Municipal Zoo

Shirakawa-dōri

Tetsugaku-no-michi

Okazaki-dōri

Marutamachi-dōri

Kawabata-dōri

Kawaramachi-dōri

Nijō-dōri

Higashiōji-dōri

Sanjō-dōri

Oike-dōri

Kamo-gawa

Keihan Marutamachi

Keihan Sanjō

Sanjō Keihan

Higashiyama-Sanjō

Keage

Keage

Sanjō

Sentō Gosho (Imperial Palace)

Kyoto-gyoen

Kyoto Shiyakusho-mae

KANSAI REGION

EASTERN KYOTO

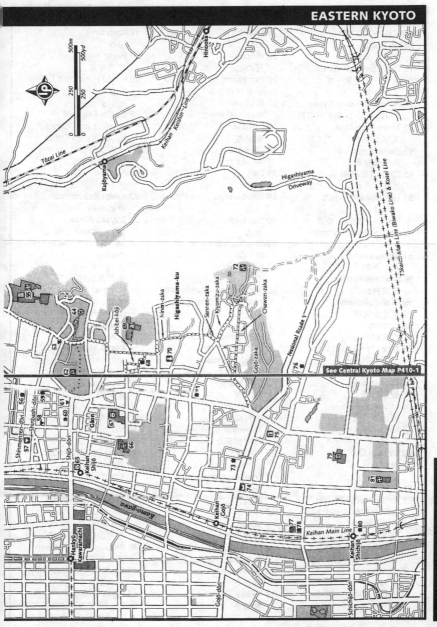

Hinooka

Higashiyama
Driveway

Keihan Keishin Line

Tōzai Line

Kujōyama

Tōkaidō Main Line (Biwako Line & Kosei Line)

National Route 1

Higashiyama-ku

72

Ninen-zaka

Sanren-zaka

Kiyomizu-zaka

Chawan-zaka

Ish-hei-kōji

Gojō-zaka

70

68

64

63

62

See Central Kyoto Map P410-1

76

Shinbash-dōri
Shinmonten-dōri

57
58
59
60
61

Gion

56

67

79

75

Keihan
Shijō
65
66

73

74

81

Kamo-gawa

Keihan
Gojō

Keihan Main Line

77
78
80

Keihan
Shichijō

Hankyū
Kawaramachi

Gojō-dōri

Shichijō-dōri

EASTERN KYOTO

PLACES TO STAY
18 ISE Dorm
アイエスイードーム
19 Three Sisters Annex
スリーシスターズ
アネックス
20 Hotel Sunflower Kyoto
ホテルサンフラワー京都
23 Three Sisters Inn
スリーシスターズイン
43 Yachiyo Ryokan
八千代旅館
45 Kyoto Traveller's Inn
京都トラベラーズイン
51 Higashiyama Youth
Hostel
東山ユースホステル
52 Pension Higashiyama
ペンション東山
54 Miyako Hotel
都ホテル
56 Iwanami Ryokan
岩波旅館
59 Gion Fukuzumi
ギオン福住
68 Uemura
うえむら
71 Amenity Capsule Hotel
アメニティ
カプセルホテル
73 Ryokan Seiki
旅館晴輝
76 Mishima-jinja
宿坊みしま
78 Kyoto Park Hotel
京都パークホテル
80 Ryokan Ōtō
旅館鴨東

PLACES TO EAT
2 Eating House Hi-Lite
和洋食堂ハイライト
4 Tenka-ippin
天下一品
5 Kuishinbō-no-mise
くいしん坊の店
7 Omen
おめん
15 Buttercups
バターカップス

21 Okariba
お狩り場
22 Hinode
日の出
26 Zac Baran
ザックバラン
27 El Latino
エルラティーニョ
30 Mikōan
彌光庵
31 Chabana
ちゃばな
39 Okutan
奥丹
49 Ichi-ban
一番
50 Dai-kitchi
大吉
58 Sen-mon-ten
泉門天
61 Gion Koishi
祇園小石
63 Imobō Hiranoya Honten
いもぼう平野屋本店

OTHER
1 Hyakumanben Crossing
百万遍交差点
3 British Council
英国文化センター
6 Ginkaku-ji
銀閣寺
8 Hōnen-in
法然院
9 Takenaka-Inari-sha
竹中稲荷社
10 Yoshida-jinja
吉田神社
11 Institut
Franco-Japonais
du Kansai
関西日仏学館
12 Goethe Institut
Kyoto
関西ドイツ文化センター
13 Muretada-jinja
宗忠神社
14 Shinnyo-dō
真如堂
16 Reikan-ji
霊鑑寺

17 Kurodani
黒谷
24 Heian-jingū
平安神宮
25 Kyoto Handicraft Center
京都ハンディクラフト
センター
28 Osaka Regional
Immigration Bureau
Kyoto Branch Office
大阪入国管理局
京都出張所
29 Metro
メトロ
32 Kyoto Kaikan Hall
京都会館
33 Miyako Messe;
Fureai-Kan Kyoto
Museum of Traditional
Crafts
みやこめっせ；
ふれあい館
34 National Museum of
Modern Art
国立近代美術館
35 Okazaki-kōen
岡崎公園
36 Kyoto Municipal
Museum of Art
京都市立美術館
37 Eikan-dō
永観堂
38 Nomura Museum
野村美術館
40 Nanzen-ji
南禅寺
41 Nanzen-ji Oku-no-in
南禅寺奥の院
42 Konchi-in
金地院
44 Kyoto International
Community House
(KICH)
京都国際交流会館
46 Kitazawa Bicycle Shop
キタザワサイクル
47 Rental Cycle Yasumoto
レンタサイクルやすもと
48 Pig & Whistle
ビッグアンドホィッスル

EASTERN KYOTO

53 Shōren-in 青蓮院	66 Kennin-ji 建仁寺	74 Higashiyama Post Office 東山郵便局
55 Chion-in 智恩院	67 Gion Corner; Gion Kōbu Kaburen-jō Theater 祇園コーナー； 祇園甲部歌舞練場	75 Kawai Kanjirō Memorial Hall 河井寛次郎博物館
57 Malt's Club モルツクラブ		
60 Kyoto Craft Centre 京都クラフトセンター		77 Shomen-yu 正面湯
62 Yasaka-jinja 八坂神社	69 Kōdai-ji 高台寺	79 Kyoto National Museum 京都国立博物館
64 Maruyama-kōen 円山公園	70 Yasaka-no-tō 八坂の塔	
65 Minami-za Theatre 南座	72 Kiyomizu-dera 清水寺	81 Sanjūsangen-dō 三十三間堂

mercantile air of the temple – stalls sell good-luck charms, fortunes, and all manner of souvenirs. If this would bother you, head to some of the quieter temples farther north.

The main hall has a huge veranda that is supported by hundreds of pillars and juts out over the hillside. Just below this hall is the waterfall, Otawa-no-taki, where visitors drink sacred waters believed to have therapeutic properties. Dotted around the precincts are other halls and shrines. At the shrine, Jishu-jinja, visitors try to ensure success in love by closing their eyes and walking about 18m between a pair of stones – if you miss the stone, your desire for love won't be fulfilled!

The steep approach to the temple is known as Chawan-zaka (Teapot Lane) and is lined with shops selling Kyoto handicrafts, local snacks and souvenirs.

To get there from JR Kyoto station take bus No 206 or 207, get off at either the Kiyōmizu-michi or Gojō-zaka stop and plod up the hill for 10 minutes.

Kōdai-ji

Kōdai-ji (¥500, 9 am to 5 pm) was founded in 1605 by Kita-no-Mandokoro in memory of her late husband, Toyotomi Hideyoshi. The extensive grounds include gardens designed by the famed landscape architect Kobori Enshū, and teahouses designed by the renowned master of the tea ceremony Sen-no-Rikyū.

The temple is a 10-minute walk north of Kiyomizu-dera (see that section earlier in this chapter). Check at the TIC for the scheduling of summer night-time illuminations of the temple (when the gardens are lit by multicoloured spotlights).

Maruyama-kōen 円山公園

This park is a favourite with locals and visitors alike, a great place to escape the bustle of the city centre and amble around gardens, ponds, souvenir shops and restaurants. Peaceful paths meander through the trees and carp glide through the waters of a small pond in the centre of the park.

For two weeks in April, when the park's ample cherry trees come into bloom, the calm atmosphere of the park is shattered by hordes of revellers (some drunken, some not) enjoying hanami. The centrepiece of it all is a massive *shidarezakura*, a weeping cherry tree – truly one of the most beautiful sights in Kyoto, particularly when lit from below at night. For those who don't mind crowds, this is a good place to observe the Japanese at their most uninhibited. It is best to arrive early and claim a good spot high on the eastern side of the park, from which point you can safely peer down on the mayhem below.

The park is a five-minute walk east of the Shijō-Higashiōji intersection. To get there from JR Kyoto station, take bus No 206 or 207 and get off at the Gion stop.

KANSAI REGION

Southern Higashiyama Walking Tour

Time half a day to a full day
Distance about 5km
Major Sights Kiyomizu-dera, Kōdai-ji, Yasaka-jinja

One of the most enjoyable strolls around the back streets and temples of Kyoto follows a winding route between Kiyomizu-dera and Maruyama-kōen (see the Eastern Kyoto map in this chapter or, for more details, the TIC's *Walking Tour Courses in Kyoto*).

The walk begins near the Gojō-zaka slope. Start your walk after a look at the pottery shops on the slope near the north-western corner of the intersection of Gojō-dōri and Higashiōji-dōri. Cross Higashiōji and head east (uphill) until you reach the first fork in the road; bear right and continue up to **Kiyomizu-dera**. When you reach the top, the temple entrance will be on your left. Take a short detour uphill to the right for an amazing view of the neighbouring cemetery before heading towards the temple.

After touring Kiyomizu-dera, exit down the **Kiyomizu-zaka slope**, the steep approach to the temple also known as Chawan-zaka (Teapot Lane). It is lined with shops selling Kyoto handicrafts (notably Kiyomizu-yaki pottery), local snacks and souvenirs. After walking about 200m, you'll see a small street on your right down a flight of steps. This is **Sannen-zaka**, lined with old wooden houses and traditional shops and restaurants. There are also pleasant teahouses with gardens. It's a good place to relax over a bowl of steaming noodles.

Halfway down Sannen-zaka, the road bears sharp left. Follow it a short distance, then turn right and walk down a flight of steps into **Ninen-zaka**, another street lined with historic houses, shops and teahouses. At the end of Ninen-zaka zigzag left then right and continue north for five minutes to reach the entrance of **Kōdai-ji**, on the right up a long flight of stairs. Just before this entrance you can detour into **Ishibei-kōji** on your left – perhaps the most beautiful street in Kyoto, though it's actually a cobbled alley which is lined on both sides with elegant, traditional Japanese inns and restaurants.

Exit Kōdai-ji the way you came and walk to the 'T' in the road; turn right here and zigzag right and left into **Maruyama-kōen**, a pleasant spot to take a rest. From the park, head west into the grounds of **Yasaka-jinja**. From here you can exit west to Shijō-dōri, or head back through the park and north toward **Chion-in** and **Shōren-in**. From either temple, it's about a 10-minute walk back to the bright lights of Shijō-dōri.

Yasaka-jinja 八坂神社

This colourful shrine is just down the hill from Maruyama-kōen. It's considered the guardian shrine of neighbouring Gion and is sometimes endearingly referred to as 'Gion-san'. This shrine is particularly popular as a spot for *hatsu-mōde* (the first shrine visit of the new year). If you don't mind a stampede, come here around midnight on New Year's Eve or over the next few days. Surviving the crush is proof that you're blessed by the gods! Yasaka-jinja also sponsors Kyoto's biggest festival, Gion Matsuri (for details, see the Special Events section later in this chapter).

Gion 祇園周辺

Gion is a famous entertainment and geisha district on the eastern bank of Kamo-gawa. Modern architecture, congested traffic and contemporary nightlife establishments rob the area of some of its historical beauty, but there are still some lovely places left for a stroll.

Hanami-kōji is a street running north to south that bisects Shijō-dōri. The southern section is lined with 17th-century traditional restaurants and teahouses, many of which are exclusive establishments for geisha entertainment. If you wander around here in the late afternoon or early evening, you can often glimpse geisha or maiko on their way to or from appointments.

If you walk north from Shijō-dōri along Hanami-kōji, the fourth intersection you will come to is Shinmonzen-dōri. Wander in either direction along this street, which is packed with old houses, art galleries and shops specialising in antiques. Don't expect flea-market prices.

For more historic buildings in a waterside setting, wander down **Shirakawa Minami-dōri**, which is parallel with, and a block south of, the western section of Shinmonzen-dōri. This is one of Kyoto's most beautiful streets, especially in the evening.

Chion-in 知恩院

Chion-in was built in 1234 on the site where a famous priest by the name of Hōnen had taught and eventually fasted to death. Today it is still the headquarters of the Jōdo school of Buddhism, which was founded by Hōnen, and a hive of religious activity. For visitors with a taste for the grand and glorious, this temple is sure to satisfy (main hall ¥400, other areas free, 9 am to 5.40 pm from March to November, until 4.30 pm from December to February).

The oldest of the present buildings date back to the 17th century. The two-storey **San-mon**, a Buddhist temple gate at the main entrance, is the largest temple gate in Japan and prepares you for the massive scale of the temple. The immense main hall contains an image of Hōnen. It's connected to another hall, the Dai Hōjō, by a 'nightin gale' floor. The massive scale of the buildings reflects the popularity of the Jōdo school, which holds that earnest faith in the Buddha is all you need to achieve salvation.

After visiting the main hall, with its fantastic gold altar, you can walk around the back of the same building to see the temple's gardens. On the way, you pass a darkened hall with a small statue of Amida Buddha on display, glowing eerily in the darkness. It makes a nice contrast to the splendour of the main hall.

The giant bell, cast in 1633 and weighing 74 tonnes, is the largest in Japan. The combined muscle-power of 17 monks is needed to make the bell budge for the famous ceremony that rings in the new year.

The temple is close to the north-eastern corner of Maruyama-kōen. From JR Kyoto station take bus No 206 and get off at the Chion-in-mae stop or walk up (east) from the Keihan Sanjō or Shijō station.

Shōren-in 青蓮院

Shōren-in (¥400, 9 am to 5 pm) is hard to miss, with its giant camphor trees growing just outside its walls. This temple was originally the residence of the chief abbot of the Tendai school of Buddhism. The present building dates from 1895, but the main hall has sliding screens with paintings from the 16th and 17th centuries. Often overlooked by the crowds that descend on other Higashiyama temples, this is a pleasant place to sit and think while gazing out over the beautiful gardens.

The temple is a five-minute walk north of Chion-in (see the Chion-in section for transport details).

National Museum of Modern Art 国立近代美術館

This museum (¥420, more for special exhibits, 9.30 am to 5 pm, closed Monday) is renowned for its collection of contemporary Japanese ceramics and paintings. Exhibits are changed on a regular basis (check with the TIC or *Kansai Time Out* for details).

Fureai-Kan Kyoto Museum of Traditional Crafts 伝統産業会館

While you're in the Heian-jingū area (see the Heian-jingū entry later), you might want to stop by this new underground museum (free, 10 am to 6 pm, closed Monday and the day after national holidays) to check out some of its interesting displays of traditional Kyoto crafts. Exhibits include woodblock prints, lacquerware, bamboo goods and gold-leaf work.

Heian-jingū 平安神宮

Heian-jingū (shrine precincts free, garden ¥600, 8.30 am to 5.30 pm from 15 March to 31 August, closing slightly earlier during the rest of the year) was built in 1895 to

The Living Art of the Geisha

Behind the closed doors of the exclusive teahouses and restaurants that are dotting the back streets of Kyoto, women of exquisite grace and refinement entertain gentlemen of considerable means. Patrons may pay more than $3000 to spend an evening in the company of two or three geisha – kimono-clad women versed in an array of visual and performing arts, including playing the three-stringed shamisen, singing old teahouse ballads and dancing.

An evening in a Gion teahouse begins with an exquisite kaiseki dinner – a dinner presented in accordance with strict rules of etiquette that apply to every detail of the meal and the diner's surroundings. While their customers eat, the geisha or maiko (apprentice geisha) enter the room and introduce themselves in Kyoto dialect.

A shamisen performance, followed by a traditional fan dance, is often given, and all the while the geisha and maiko pour drinks, light cigarettes and engage in charming banter.

It is virtually impossible to enter a Gion teahouse and witness a geisha performance without the introduction of an established patron. With the exception of public performances at annual festivals or dance presentations, they perform only for select customers. While geisha are not prostitutes, those who decide to open their own teahouses once they retire at 50 or so may receive financial backing from well-to-do clients with whom they may or may not be intimately involved.

Knowledgeable sources estimate that there are perhaps 80 maiko and just over 100 geisha in Kyoto. Although their numbers are ever-decreasing, geisha (geiko in the Kyoto dialect) and maiko can still be seen in some parts of Kyoto, especially after dusk in the back streets between Kamo-gawa and Yasaka-jinja and along the narrow Pontochō alley. Geisha and maiko can also be found in other parts of the country, most notably Tokyo. However, it is thought that there are less than 1000 geisha and maiko remaining in all Japan.

commemorate the 1100th anniversary of the founding of Kyoto. The buildings are gaudy replicas, reduced to two-thirds of the size of the Kyoto Gosho of the Heian period.

The spacious garden, with its large pond and Chinese-inspired bridge, is also meant to represent the kind of garden that was popular in the Heian period. About 500m in front of the shrine there is a massive steel *torii* (Shintō shrine entrance gate). Although it appears to be entirely separate from the shrine, this is actually considered the main entrance to the shrine itself.

Two major events are held here: Jidai Matsuri (Festival of the Ages), on 22 October, and Takigi Nō, from 1 to 2 June. Jidai Matsuri is described later in the Special Events section, while details for Takigi Nō are under Traditional Dance & Theatre in the later Entertainment section.

Take bus No 5 from JR Kyoto station or Keihan Sanjō station and get off at the Kyoto Kaikan Bijutsu-kan-mae stop, or walk up from Keihan Sanjō station (15 minutes).

Nanzen-ji 南禅寺

This is one of the most pleasant temples in all Kyoto, with its expansive grounds and numerous subtemples. It began as a retirement villa for Emperor Kameyama but was dedicated as a Zen temple on his death in 1291. Civil war in the 15th century destroyed most of the temple; the present buildings date from the 17th century. It operates now as headquarters for the Rinzai school of Zen.

At its entrance stands the massive **Sanmon**. Steps lead up to the 2nd storey, which has a fine view over the city. Beyond the gate is the **Hōjō**, a hall with impressive screens painted with a vivid depiction of tigers.

Within the precincts of the same building, the **Leaping Tiger Garden** is a classic Zen garden well worth a look. While you're in the Hōjō, you can enjoy a cup of tea while sitting on *tatami* (tightly woven matting) gazing at a small waterfall (¥400, ask at the reception desk of the Hōjō). It's an inexpensive way to sample the tea ceremony in pleasant surroundings.

FRANK CARTER

SIMON ROWE

Squeezing in a few more passengers – morning rush hour in Kyoto.   A *maiko* (geisha in training)

FRANK CARTER

Sumō is pure ritual – a commencement ceremony takes place before any wrestling begins, Osaka.

MARTIN MOOS

SIMON ROWE

A fetching look, Kyoto   Shintō priests at Kyoto's annual Jidai Matsuri.

ERIC L WHEATER

Umbrellas – Nara

FRANK CARTER

Wood-block impression of Kyoto by the foreign artist, Karhu.

FRANK CARTER

Japan has a medley of folk gods including the gods of luck.

SIMON ROWE

Japanese cartoon, Kyoto.

MARTIN MOOS

Sumō banners

Perhaps the best part of Nanzen-ji is overlooked by most visitors: **Oku-no-in**, a small shrine/temple hidden in a forested hollow behind the main precinct. To get there, walk up to the red brick aqueduct in front of the subtemple of Nanzen-in. Follow the road that runs parallel to the aqueduct up into the hills, past several brightly coloured torii until you reach a waterfall in a beautiful mountain glen. Here, pilgrims pray while standing under the waterfall, sometimes in the dead of winter. Hiking trails lead off in all directions from this point; by heading due north, you'll eventually arrive at the top of Daimon-ji-yama (two hours), and by going east you'll eventually get to Yamashina (also about two hours).

Most of the grounds can be explored free of charge. Admission to the Hōjō is ¥400 and to the San-mon, ¥300; both are open from 8.40 am to 5 pm. From JR Kyoto or Keihan Sanjō station take bus No 5 and get off at the Nanzen-ji Eikan-dō-michi stop. You can also take the Tōzai line subway from downtown to Keage and walk for five minutes downhill to Nanzen-ji.

Dotted around the grounds of Nanzen-ji are several subtemples that are often skipped by the crowds and consequently easier to enjoy.

Nanzen-in This subtemple is on your right if you are facing the Hōjō – follow the path under the aqueduct. It has an attractive garden designed around a heart-shaped pond.

Kurodani to Yoshida-jinja Walk

Time two to three hours
Distance about 4km
Major Sights Kurodani temple, Shinnyo-dō temple, Yoshida-jinja

This fine walk (see the Eastern Kyoto map) is a good way to escape the crowds that flock to the northern Higashiyama area's better known sights. You might try doing it in the late afternoon or evening, but time it so that you don't get stuck here after dark, as the cemeteries around here can be distinctly spooky once the sun goes down.

The walk starts at an alley a few metres west of the Hotel Sunflower Kyoto (look for the small shrine next to the hotel). Walk up the alley, climb the steps and continue straight on for 75m to the base of the Kurodani cemetery. Climb to the pagoda at the top of the steps for a good view over Kyoto.

Return to the bottom of the steps, cross the stone bridge, turn right and walk up the steps to the main precinct of **Kurodani temple**. If you look south from the wide-open plaza in front of the main hall of the temple, you will see the impressive *san-mon*, or main gate, of the temple.

Facing the main hall, turn left and then quickly right and walk out of the grounds of Kurodani, passing a statue of the seated Buddha. Farther along, you pass another cemetery on the right, and several subtemples. Continue straight ahead for about 200m, go through a wooden gate and continue on for another 100m to the entrance to **Shinnyo-dō** on your right. After exploring this temple, retrace your steps and walk west to a stone *torii* (Shintō shrine entrance gate) at the base of a hill. Climb the steps here to Muretada-jinja. Next, walk straight ahead through another stone torii and ascend through a procession of orange torii to Takenaka-Inari-sha, a small shrine near the top of Yoshida-yama.

From here, take the steps that lead west over the crest of the hill. Descend through a small park down to the left. Take the first trail down the hill on the right, bearing west (downhill). A few zigzags down the fall line bring you to the back of **Yoshida-jinja**. After exploring the shrine, you can descend its main stone steps to the west and walk out to Higashioji-dōri, where you can catch buses to all parts of Kyoto.

This garden is best in the morning or around noon, when sunlight shines directly into the pond, illuminating the colourful carp. Admission is ¥350.

Tenju-an The temple, Tenju-an, stands at the side of the San-mon, a four-minute walk west of Nanzen-in. Constructed in 1337, the temple has a splendid garden and a great collection of carp in its pond. Admission is ¥300.

Konchi-in When leaving Tenju-an, turn left and continue for 100m – Konchi-in (¥400, 8.30 am to 5 pm from March to November, closing 30 minutes earlier the rest of the year) is down a small side street on the left. The stylish gardens fashioned by the master landscape designer Kobori Enshū are the main attraction.

Nomura Museum 野村美術館
The Nomura Museum (¥600, 10 am to 4.30 pm, closed Monday) is a 10-minute walk north of Nanzen-ji. Exhibits include scrolls, paintings, tea-ceremony implements and ceramics that were bequeathed by the very wealthy business magnate Tokushiki Nomura.

Eikan-dō 永観堂
Eikan-dō (¥500, 9 am to 4 pm), also known as Zenrin-ji, is made interesting by its varied architecture, gardens and works of art. It was founded in 855 by the priest Shinshō, but the name was changed to Eikan-dō in the 11th century to honour the philanthropic priest Eikan.

The best way to appreciate this temple is to follow the arrows and wander slowly along the covered walkways connecting the halls and gardens.

In the Amida-dō Hall, at the southern end of the complex, is the famous statue of Mikaeri Amida (Buddha Glancing Backwards). On the right of this statue is an image of a bald priest with a superb expression of intense concentration.

From the Amida-dō Hall, head north to the end of the covered walkway. Change into the sandals provided, then climb the steep steps up the mountainside to the Tahotō (Taho Pagoda), where there's a fine view across the city.

Tetsugaku-no-michi 哲学の道
Tetsugaku-no-michi (the Path of Philosophy) has long been a favourite with contemplative strollers who follow the traffic-free route beside a canal lined with cherry trees that are spectacular when in bloom. It only takes 30 minutes to complete the walk, which starts just north of Eikan-dō and ends at Ginkaku-ji. During the day, be prepared for crowds of tourists; a night stroll will definitely be quieter. A map of the walk is part of the *Walking Tour Courses in Kyoto* leaflet, available at the TIC.

Hōnen-in 法然院
This temple (grounds free, main hall ¥500, 7 am to 4 pm) was established in 1680 to honour Hōnen, the charismatic founder of the Jōdo school. This is a lovely, secluded temple with carefully raked gardens set back in the woods. Be sure to visit in early April for the cherry blossoms and early November for the maple leaves, when the main hall is opened for a special viewing.

The temple is a 12-minute walk from Ginkaku-ji (see the following section), on a side street that is just east of Tetsugaku-no-michi. Cross the bridge over the canal and follow the road uphill through the bamboo groves.

Ginkaku-ji 銀閣寺
Ginkaku-ji (¥500, 8.30 am to 5 pm from 15 March to 30 November, 9 am to 4.30 pm the rest of the year) is definitely worth seeing, but be warned that bus loads of visitors often jam the narrow pathways.

In 1482, Shōgun Ashikaga Yoshimasa constructed a villa here as a genteel retreat from the turmoil of civil war. The villa's name translates as 'Silver Pavilion', but the shōgun's ambition to cover the building with silver was never realised. After Yoshimasa's death, the villa was converted into a temple.

You approach the main gate between tall hedges, before turning sharply into the

Daimonji-yama Climb

Time two hours
Distance 5km
Major Sights Ginkaku-ji, Daimonji Yaki site

Located directly behind Ginkaku-ji, Daimonji-yama is the main site of the Daimonji Yaki fire festival (also known as the Daimonji Gozan Okuribi). From almost anywhere in town the Chinese character for *dai* (great) is visible in the middle of a bare patch on the face of this mountain. On 16 August, this character is set ablaze to guide the spirits of the dead on their journey home. The view of Kyoto from the top is unparalleled.

Take bus No 5 to the Ginkaku-ji Michi stop and walk up to Ginkaku-ji. Here, you have the option of visiting the temple or starting the hike immediately. To find the trailhead, turn left in front of the temple and head north for about 50m toward a stone *torii* (shrine gate). Just before the torii, turn right up the hill.

The trail proper starts just after a small car park on the right. It's a broad avenue through the trees. A few minutes of walking brings you to a red banner hanging over the trail (warning of forest fires). Soon after this you must cross a bridge to the right then continue up a smaller, switchback trail. When the trail reaches a saddle not far from the top, go to the left. You climb a long flight of steps before coming out at the top of the bald patch. The sunset from here is great, but bring a torch.

extensive grounds. Walkways lead through the gardens, which include meticulously raked cones of white sand (probably symbolic of a mountain and a lake), tall pines and a pond in front of the temple. A path also leads up the mountainside through the trees.

From JR Kyoto or Keihan Sanjō station, take bus No 5 and get off at the Ginkaku-ji-michi stop. From Demachiyanagi station or Shijō station, take bus No 203 to the same stop.

NORTH-WESTERN KYOTO
京都北西部

The north-western part of Kyoto is predominantly residential, but there are a number of superb temples with tranquil gardens in secluded precincts. For Zen fans, a visit to Daitoku-ji and Ryōan-ji is recommended. Kinkaku-ji is another major attraction. JNTO's *Walking Tour Courses in Kyoto* leaflet also covers this area, but most of the walk is along unremarkable city streets.

Those who have the time and inclination to escape the tourist trail might consider a visit to the Takao District.

Daitoku-ji 大徳寺

The precincts of this temple, which belongs to the Rinzai school of Zen, contain an extensive complex of 24 subtemples, of which two are mentioned in following sections; eight are open to the public. If you want to examine Zen culture intensively, this is the place to visit. Be prepared, however, for temples that are thriving business enterprises and often choked with visitors.

Daitoku-ji itself is on the eastern side of the grounds. It was founded in 1319, burnt down in the next century and rebuilt in the 16th century. The San-mon contains an image of the famous tea master, Sen-no-Rikyū, on the 2nd storey.

According to some historical sources, Toyotomi Hideyoshi was so enraged when he discovered he had been demeaning himself by walking *under* Rikyū that he forced the master to commit *seppuku* (ritual suicide) in 1591.

Two subtemples particularly worth a visit are **Daisen-in**, for its two famous (if small) gardens and **Kōtō-in** for its lovely maples in autumn.

Admission charges to the various subtemples vary but are usually around ¥350. Those temples that accept visitors are usually open from 9 am to 5 pm. The temple bus stop is Daitoku-ji-mae. Convenient buses from JR Kyoto station are Nos 205 and 206. Daitoku-ji is also not a long walk west of Kitaō-ji subway station on the Karasuma line.

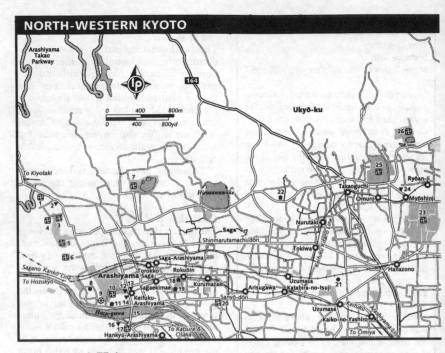

NORTH-WESTERN KYOTO

Kinkaku-ji 金閣寺

Kinkaku-ji, the famed Golden Temple, is one of Japan's best-known sights (¥400, 9 am to 5 pm). The original building was constructed in 1397 as a retirement villa for Shōgun Ashikaga Yoshimitsu. His son converted it into a temple. In 1950, a young monk consummated his obsession with the temple by burning it to the ground. The monk's story was fictionalised in Mishima Yukio's *The Golden Pavilion*.

In 1955, a full reconstruction was completed that exactly followed the original design, but the gold-foil covering was extended to the lower floors. The temple may not be to everyone's taste, and the tremendous crowds just about obscure the view anyway.

To get to the temple from JR Kyoto station, take bus No 205 and get off at the Kinkaku-ji-michi stop. From Keihan Sanjō, take bus No 59 and get off at the Kinkaku-ji-mae stop.

Ritsumeikan University Kyoto Museum for World Peace

While you're in north-western Kyoto, you might want to drop by this excellent little museum (9.30 am to 4 pm, closed Monday, the day after national holidays and from 28 December to 6 January), which has exhibits covering Japan's actions leading up to WWII, the events of WWII and the conventional and atomic bombing of Japan by Allied forces at the end of the war. Unlike many similar museums in Japan, this one does not downplay the atrocities committed by Japanese forces in favour of highlighting the suffering of Japan in the closing stages of the war. As such, it's a very educational, if a little sobering, way to spend an hour or two in Kyoto. It's a 15-minute walk east of Ryōan-ji.

Ryōan-ji 龍安寺

This temple (¥400, 8 am to 5 pm, 8.30 am to 4.30 pm from December to March) belongs to the Rinzai school of Zen and was founded

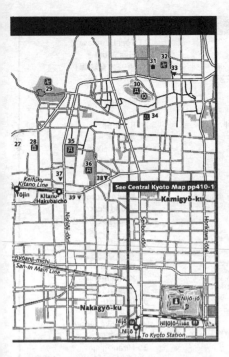

The extensive grounds are full of cherry trees that bloom in early April.

Admission to most of the grounds is free, but separate admission fees are charged for some of the temple's buildings, many of which are closed most of the year. To get there, take bus No 59 from Keihan Sanjō station and get off at the Omuro Ninna-ji stop. From JR Kyoto station take bus No 26.

Myōshin-ji 妙心寺

Myōshin-ji (¥400, 9 am to 5 pm), a vast temple complex dating back to the 14th century, belongs to the Rinzai school of Zen. There are over 40 temples, but only four are open to the public.

From the northern gate, follow the broad stone avenue flanked by rows of temples to the southern part of the complex.

The real highlight here is the wonderful garden of Taizō-in, a temple in the south-western corner of the grounds.

The northern gate of Myōshin-ji is an easy 10-minute walk south of Ninna-ji; alternatively, take bus No 10 from Keihan Sanjō station to the Myōshin-ji Kita-mon-mae stop.

Kitano-Tenman-gū 北野天満宮

This shrine (free, 5.30 am to 5.30 pm) is of moderate interest. However, if you're in town on the 25th of any month, be sure to catch the Tenjin-san market fair held here. This is one of Kyoto's two biggest markets and is a great place to pick up some interesting souvenirs. The markets held in December and January are particularly colourful.

From JR Kyoto station, take bus No 50 and get off at the Kitano-Tenmangū-mae stop. From Keihan Sanjō station, take bus No 10 to the same stop.

Kōryū-ji 広隆寺

Kōryū-ji (¥600, 9 am to 5 pm, until 4.30 pm from December to end of February), one of the oldest temples in Japan, was founded in 622 to honour Prince Shōtoku, who was an enthusiastic promoter of Buddhism.

The Hattō (Lecture Hall), to the right of the main gate, houses a magnificent trio of 9th-century statues: Buddha flanked by manifestations of Kannon.

in 1450. The main attraction is the garden arranged in the *kare-sansui* (dry landscape) style. An austere collection of 15 rocks, apparently adrift in a sea of sand, is enclosed by an earthen wall. The designer, who remains unknown, provided no explanation.

The viewing platform for the garden can become packed solid but the other parts of the temple grounds are also interesting and less of a target for the crowds. Among these, Kyoyo-chi pond is perhaps the most beautiful, particularly in autumn. Probably the best advice at Ryōan-ji is to come as early in the day as possible.

From Keihan Sanjō station, take bus No 59 to the Ryōan-ji-mae stop.

Ninna-ji 仁和寺

Ninna-ji (9 am to 4.30 pm) was built in 842 and is the head temple of the Omura branch of the Shingon school of Buddhism. The present temple buildings, including a five-storey pagoda, are from the 17th century.

KANSAI REGION

NORTH-WESTERN KYOTO

PLACES TO STAY
11 Arashiyama Benkei
   Ryokan
   嵐山慶旅館
18 Rokuō-in
19 Minshuku
   Arashiyama
   民宿嵐山
22 Utano Youth Hostel
   宇多野ユースホステル
31 Tani House
   谷ハウス

PLACES TO EAT
 2 Bokuseki
   木石
12 Seizansō-dō
   西山堂
13 Gyātei
   ぎゃあてい
14 Nakamura-ya
   中村屋
16 Togetsu-tei
   渡月亭
24 Okara House
   おからはうす
33 Daitoku-ji Ikkyū
   大徳寺一休
37 A Ri Shan
   阿里山

38 Taco Tora
   蛸虎
39 Toyouke-jaya
   とようけ茶屋

OTHER
 1 Adashino
   Nembutsu-ji
   化野念仏寺
 3 Danrin-ji
   檀林寺
 4 Giō-ji
   祇王寺
 5 Nison-in
   二尊院
 6 Jōjakkō-ji
   常寂光寺
 7 Daikaku-ji
   大覚寺
 8 Ōkōchi-sansō
   大河内山荘
 9 Kameyama-kōen
   亀山公園
10 Tenryū-ji
   天竜寺
15 Togetsu-kyō
   渡月橋
17 Hōrin-ji
   法輪寺
20 Kōryū-ji

21 Tōei Uzumasa
   Eiga Mura
   東映太秦映画村
23 Myōshin-ji
   妙心寺
25 Ninna-ji
   仁和寺
26 Ryōan-ji
   龍安寺
27 Ritsumeikan
   University
   立命館大学
28 Ritsumeikan University
   Kyoto Museum for
   World Peace
   立命館大学国際平和
   ミュージアム
29 Kinkaku-ji
   金閣寺
30 Funaoka-yama-kōen;
   Kenkun-jinja
   船岡山公園；建勲神社
32 Daitoku-ji
   大徳寺
34 Funaoka Onsen
   船岡温泉
35 Hirano-jinja
   平野神社
36 Kitano-Tenman-gū
   北野天満宮

The Reihōkan (Treasure House) contains numerous fine Buddhist statues, including the Naki Miroku (Crying Miroku) and the world-renowned Miroku Bosatsu, which is extraordinarily expressive. A national upset occurred in 1960 when an enraptured student clasped the statue and snapped off its little finger.

Take bus No 11 from Keihan Sanjō station, get off at the Ukyō-ku Sogo-choshamae stop and walk north.

Takao District 高雄周辺

This is a secluded district tucked far away in the north-western part of Kyoto. It is famed for autumn foliage and the temples of **Jingo-ji**, **Saimyō-ji** and **Kōzan-ji**.

Jingo-ji (¥400, 9 am to 5 pm) is the best of the three temples in the Takao District.

This mountain temple sits at the top of a long flight of stairs that stretch up from Kiyotaki-gawa to the temple's main gate. The Kondō (Gold Hall) is the most impressive of the temple's structures; it's roughly in the middle of the grounds, at the top of another flight of stairs.

After visiting the Kondō, head in the opposite direction along a wooded path to an open area overlooking the valley. Don't be surprised if you see hordes of people tossing small disks over the railing into the chasm below. These are *kawarakenage* – light clay disks that people throw to rid themselves of their bad karma. Be careful: it's addictive, and at ¥100 for two, it can become expensive. You can buy the disks at a nearby stall. The trick is to flick the disks very gently, convex side up, like a Frisbee.

When you get it right, they sail all the way down the valley, taking all that bad karma away with them.

The other two temples are within easy walking distance of Jingo-ji; Saimyō-ji (free, 9 am to 5 pm) is the better of the two. It's about five minutes' walk north of the base of the steps that lead up to Jingo-ji (follow the river upstream). To get to

---

Kiyotaki-gawa Hike

Time about two hours
Distance 5km
Major Sights Jingo-ji, Kiyotaki-gawa and Hozu-gawa

This is one of the better hikes in the Kyoto area, especially in autumn, when the maples set the hillsides ablaze with colour. Start from **Jingo-ji** (see the Jingo-ji section of this chapter for transport details). The trail begins at the bottom of the steps leading up to the temple and follows Kiyotaki-gawa south (downstream).

After one hour of riverside walking, you come to the small hamlet of **Kiyotaki**, with its quaint riverside inns and restaurants. Just before the town there's a trail junction that can be confusing: the trail leaves the riverside for a while and comes to a junction on a hillside. At this spot, head uphill back towards the river, not farther into the woods. After passing through the town, cross a bridge and continue downstream. The trail hugs the river and passes some excellent crystal-clear swimming holes – great on a hot summer day.

After another 30 minutes or so you come to a road. Turn right, walk through the tunnel and continue along this road for another 30 minutes to reach Hozukyō station. The riverside below the bridge here is a popular summer picnic and swimming spot – bring a bathing suit and picnic basket and join the fun (but be warned that currents can be treacherous – parents take note). From Hozukyō station you can catch a futsū back to Kyoto (¥230, 20 minutes).

Kōzan-ji (¥600, 8.30 am to 5 pm) you must walk back up to the main road and follow it north for about 10 minutes.

There are two options for bus services to Takao: an hourly JR bus that takes about an hour to reach the Takao stop from JR Kyoto station; and Kyoto city bus No 8 from Shijō-Karasuma. To get to Jingo-ji from the Takao bus stop, walk down to the river then look for the steps on the other side.

Hozu-gawa Trip 保津川下り

This ride is a great way to enjoy the beauty of Kyoto's western mountains without any strain on the legs. The river winds through steep, forested mountain canyons before it arrives at its destination, Arashiyama. Between 10 March and 30 November, there are seven trips (from 9 am to 3.30 pm) a day down Hozu-gawa. During the winter, the number of trips is reduced to four a day and the boats are heated. There are no boat trips from 29 December to 4 January.

The ride lasts two hours and covers 16km between Kameoka and Arashiyama through occasional sections of white water – a scenic jaunt with minimal danger.

The price is ¥3900 a person. The boats depart from a dock that is eight minutes on foot from Kameoka station. Kameoka is accessible by rail from JR Kyoto station or Ni-jō station on the JR San-in (Sagano) main line. The Kyoto TIC provides a leaflet in English and a photocopied timetable sheet for rail connections. The train fare from Kyoto to Kameoka is ¥400 one way by regular train (don't spend the extra for the express as it makes little difference in time).

WESTERN KYOTO 京都西部

Arashiyama and Sagano are two districts worth a visit in this area if you feel like strolling in pleasant natural surroundings and visiting temples tucked into bamboo groves. The JNTO leaflet *Walking Tour Courses in Kyoto* has a good map of the area, and you should make an effort to pick up a copy before heading out. Note that Arashiyama is wildly popular with Japanese tourists and can be packed, particularly

KANSAI REGION

in the cherry-blossom and maple-leaf seasons. To avoid the crowds, go early on a weekday or head to some of the more off-beat spots.

Bus No 28 links JR Kyoto station with Arashiyama. Bus No 11 connects Keihan Sanjō station with Arashiyama. The most convenient rail connection is the ride from Shijō-Omiya station on the Keifuku-Arashiyama line to Arashiyama station (20-minute). You can also take the JR San-in line from JR Kyoto station or Nijō station and get off at Saga Arashiyama station (be careful to take only the local train, as the express does not stop in Arashiyama).

Togetsu-kyō 渡月橋

The bridge, Togetsu-kyō, is the main landmark in Arashiyama, a couple of minutes on foot from the station. Upon arrival here, you may wonder why the Japanese make such a fuss about this place; it's not very beautiful, particularly with all the tacky shops and vending machines nearby. The best advice is to head north immediately to the quieter regions of Sagano.

The area around the bridge, however, is a good spot to watch *ukai* (cormorant fishing) on summer evenings. If you want to get close to the action, you can pay ¥1300 to join a passenger boat. The TIC can provide a leaflet and further details.

Kameyama-kōen

Just upstream from Togetsu-kyō behind Tenryū-ji, this park is a nice place to escape the crowds of Arashiyama. It's laced with trails, the best of which leads to a lookout over Katsura-gawa and up into the Arashiyama mountains.

Tenryū-ji 天竜寺

Tenryū-ji (¥500, 8.30 am to 5.30 pm from April to October, until 5 pm the rest of the year) is one of the major temples of the Rinzai school of Zen. It was built in 1339 on the former site of Emperor Go-Daigo's villa after a priest had dreamt of a dragon rising from the nearby river. The dream was interpreted as a sign that the emperor's spirit was uneasy and the temple was constructed as appeasement – hence the name *tenryū* (heavenly dragon). The present buildings date from 1900, but the main attraction is the 14th-century Zen garden.

Ōkōchi Sansō 大河内山荘

This villa is the lavish home of Ōkōchi Denjiro, a famous actor in samurai films. The extensive gardens allow fine views over the city and are open to visitors. Admission is a hefty ¥900 (including tea and a cake). The villa is a 10-minute walk through bamboo groves north of Tenryū-ji.

Temples North of Ōkōchi Sansō

If you continue north of Ōkōchi Sansō, the narrow road soon passes stone steps on your left leading up to the pleasant grounds of **Jōjakkō-ji**. If you walk for another 10 minutes, you will come to **Nison-in**, which is in an attractive setting up the wooded hillside.

If you have time for a detour, there are several small temples west of Nison-in you might like to visit. **Adashino Nembutsu-ji** is a rather unusual temple where the abandoned bones of paupers and destitutes without next of kin were gathered. Thousands of stone images are crammed into the temple grounds, and these abandoned souls are remembered each year with candles here in the **Sentō Kuyō** ceremony held on the evenings of 23 and 24 August. Admission is ¥500.

Daikaku-ji 大覚寺

Daikaku-ji (¥500, 9 am to 4.30 pm) is a 25-minute walk north-east of Nison-in. It was built in the 9th century as a palace for Emperor Saga, who converted it into a temple. The present buildings date from the 16th century but are still palatial in style, with some impressive paintings. The large pond, Osawa-no-Ike, was once used by the emperor for boating.

Close to the temple entrance, there are separate terminals for Kyoto city buses (bus No 28 connects with JR Kyoto station) and Kyoto buses (No 71 connects with JR Kyoto station and No 61 with Keihan Sanjō station).

SOUTH-WESTERN KYOTO
京都南西部
Katsura Rikyū 桂離宮

Katsura Rikyū (Katsura Detached Palace) is considered to be one of the finest examples of Japanese architecture. It was built in 1624 for the emperor's brother, Prince Toshihito. Every conceivable detail of the villa, the teahouses, the large pond with islets and the surrounding garden has been given meticulous attention.

Tours, in Japanese, start at 10 and 11 am, and 2 and 3 pm and last about 40 minutes. You should be there 20 minutes beforehand. An explanatory video is shown in the waiting room and a leaflet is provided in English. Admission is free, but you *must* make reservations in advance through the Imperial Household Agency (see earlier details for Kyoto Gosho). Visitors must be over 20 years of age.

To get to the villa from JR Kyoto station take bus No 33 and get off at the Katsura Rikyū-mae stop, which is a five-minute walk from the villa. The easiest access from the city centre is to take a Hankyū line train from Hankyū Kawaramachi station to Hankyū Katsura station, which is a 15-minute walk from the villa.

Saihō-ji 西芳寺 (苔寺)

The main attraction at this temple is the heart-shaped garden, designed in 1339 by Musō Kokushi. The garden is famous for its luxuriant mossy growth – hence the temple's other name, Koke-dera (Moss Temple). Visiting the temple is recommended only if you have the time and patience to follow the reservation rules. If you don't, visit nearby Jizo-in (see that section later in this chapter) to get a sense of the atmosphere of Saihō-ji without the expense or fuss.

Reservations Reservations are required to visit Saihō-ji. Send a postcard at least one week before the date you wish to visit and include details of your name, number of visitors, address in Japan, occupation, age (you must be over 18) and desired date (choice of alternative dates preferred). The address is

Saihō-ji, 56 Kamigaya-chō, Matsuo, Nishikyō-ku, Kyoto. Enclose a stamped self-addressed postcard for a reply to your Japanese address. You might find it convenient to buy an *ōfuki-hagaki* (send and return postcard set) at a Japanese post office.

You should arrive at the time and on the date indicated by the temple office. After paying your ¥3000 'donation', you must spend up to 90 minutes copying or chanting *sutras* (collection of dialogues and discourses) or doing Zen meditation before finally being guided around the garden for 90 minutes.

Take bus No 28 from JR Kyoto station to the Koke-dera-michi stop and walk southwest.

Jizo-in 地蔵院

This delightful little temple (¥400, 9 am to 5 pm) could be called the 'poor man's Saihō-ji'. It's only a few minutes' walk south of Saihō-ji, in the same atmospheric bamboo groves. While the temple does not boast any spectacular buildings or treasures, it has a nice moss garden and is almost completely ignored by tourists, making it a great place to sit and think. For directions, see the Saihō-ji section.

SOUTH & SOUTH-EASTERN KYOTO
京都南部と南東部

The district to the south of Kyoto is mostly devoted to industry (also famed for *sake* breweries), but Tōfuku-ji and Fushimi-Inari Taisha (Fushimi-Inari Shrine) are worth a visit.

To the south-east, Daigo-ji is in rural surroundings and offers scope for a gentle hike to complement the architectural splendours. The city of Uji isn't exactly part of Kyoto, but it's easy to reach on a day trip or as a convenient stop when travelling between Kyoto and Nara.

Tōfuku-ji 東福寺

Founded in 1236 by the priest Enni, Tōfuku-ji (¥400 for each hall, grounds free, 9 am to 4 pm) now belongs to the Rinzai sect of Zen Buddhism. Since this temple was intended to compare with Tōdai-ji and Kōfuku-ji in Nara, it was given a name combining characters from the names of each of these temples.

Despite the destruction of many of the buildings by fire, this is still considered one of the five main Zen temples in Kyoto. The huge San-mon is the oldest Zen main gate in Japan. The *tōsu* (lavatory) and *yokushitsu* (bathroom) date from the 14th century. The present temple complex includes 24 sub-temples; at one time there were 53.

The Hōjō was reconstructed in 1890. The gardens, laid out in 1938, are worth a visit. As you approach the northern gardens, you cross a stream over Tsūten-kyō (Bridge to Heaven), which is a pleasant leafy spot – the foliage is renowned for its autumn colour. The northern garden has stones and moss neatly arranged in a chequerboard pattern.

The nearby **Reiun-in** subtemple receives few visitors to its attractive garden.

Tōfuku-ji is a 20-minute walk south-east of JR Kyoto station. You can also take a local train on the JR Nara line and get off at Tōfukuji station, from which it's a 10-minute walk south-east.

Fushimi-Inari Taisha 伏見稲荷大社

This intriguing shrine was dedicated to the gods of rice and sake by the Hata family in the 8th century. As the role of agriculture diminished, deities were enrolled to ensure prosperity in business. Nowadays, the shrine is one of Japan's most popular, and is the head shrine for some 30,000 Inari shrines scattered the length and breadth of Japan.

The entire complex, consisting of five shrines, sprawls across the wooded slopes of Inari-yama. A pathway wanders 4km up the mountain and is lined with hundreds of red torii. There are also dozens of stone foxes. The fox is considered the messenger of Inari, the god of cereal grains. The Japanese traditionally see the fox as a sacred, somewhat mysterious figure capable of 'possessing' humans – the favoured point of entry is under the fingernails. The key often seen in the fox's mouth is for the rice granary.

The walk around the upper precincts of the shrine is a pleasant day hike. It also makes for a very eerie stroll in the late afternoon and early evening, when the various graveyards and miniature shrines along the path take on a mysterious air.

Local delicacies sold on the approach streets include barbecued sparrow and Inari-sushi, which is fried *tōfu* wrapped around sweetened *sushi* – commonly believed to be the favourite food of the fox.

To get to the shrine from JR Kyoto station, take the JR Nara line train to Inari station. From Keihan Sanjō station take the Keihan line to Fushimi-Inari station. There is no admission charge for the shrine. The shrine is just east of both of these stations.

Daigo-ji 醍醐寺

Daigo-ji was founded in 874 by the priest Shobo, who gave it the name of Daigo. This refers to the five periods of Buddha's teaching, which were often compared to the five forms of milk prepared in India, the highest form of which is called *daigo* (ultimate essence of milk).

The temple was expanded into a vast complex of buildings on two levels – Shimo Daigo (Lower Daigo) and Kami Daigo (Upper Daigo). During the 15th century, the buildings on the lower level were destroyed, with the sole exception of the five-storey pagoda. Built in 951, this pagoda still stands and is lovingly pointed out as the oldest of its kind in Japan and the oldest existing building in Kyoto.

In the late 16th century, Hideyoshi took a fancy to Daigo-ji and ordered extensive rebuilding. It is now one of the main temples of the Shingon school of Buddhism. To explore Daigo-ji thoroughly and leisurely, mixing hiking with temple viewing, you will need at least half a day.

To get to the Daigo-ji, take the Tōzai line subway from central Kyoto to the last stop, Daigo, and walk east (toward the mountains) for about 10 minutes. Make sure that the train you board is bound for Daigo, as some head to Hama-Ōtsu instead.

Hōkō Hanami Gyōretsu On the second Sunday in April, a procession called Hōkō Hanami Gyōretsu takes place in the temple precincts. This re-enacts in full period costume the cherry-blossom party that Hideyoshi held in 1598. As a result of this party, the temple's abbot was able to secure Hideyoshi's support for restoration of the dilapidated temple complex.

Sampō-in This was founded as a subtemple in 1115, but received a total revamp under Hideyoshi's orders in 1598. It is now a fine example of the amazing opulence of that period (¥500, 9 am to 5 pm from March to October, until 4 pm the rest of the year). The Kanō paintings and the garden are special features.

The garden is jam-packed with about 800 stones. The most famous one here is Fujito-no-ishi, which is linked with deception, death and a fabulous price that was spurned; it's even the subject of a nō play, *Fujito*.

Hōju-in Treasure House This museum, close to Sampō-in, is only open to the public from 1 April to 25 May and from 1 October to 25 November. Despite the massive admission fee of ¥700, it really should not be missed if you happen to be there at the right time. The display of sculptures, scrolls, screens, miniature shrines and calligraphy is superb.

Climb to Kami Daigo From Sampō-in in Shimo Daigo (Lower Daigo), walk up the large avenue of cherry trees, through the Niō mon and past the pagoda. From there you can continue for a pleasant climb through Kami Daigo (Upper Daigo), browsing through temples and shrines on the way. Allow yourself 50 minutes to reach the top.

Mampuku-ji 万福寺

Mampuku-ji (¥500, 9 am to 4.30 pm) was established as a Zen temple in 1661 by the Chinese priest Ingen. It is a rare example in Japan of a Zen temple built in the pure Chinese style of the Ming dynasty. The temple follows the Ōbaku school of Zen, which is linked to mainstream Rinzai Zen but incorporates a wide range of Esoteric Buddhist practices.

The temple is a short walk from the two railway stations (JR Nara line and Keihan Uji line) at Ōbaku – about 30 minutes by rail from Kyoto.

Uji 宇治

Uji is a small city to the south of Kyoto. Its main claims to fame are the Byōdō-in, tea cultivation and ukai. The stone bridge at Uji – the oldest of its kind in Japan – has been the scene of many bitter clashes in previous centuries – traffic jams seem to dominate nowadays.

Uji can be reached by rail in about 40 minutes from Kyoto on the Keihan Uji line or JR Nara line.

Byōdō-in This temple (¥500, 9 am to 4.30 pm from March to November, until 4 pm the rest of the year) was converted from a Fujiwara villa into a Buddhist temple in 1052. The Hōō-dō (Phoenix Hall), more properly known as the Amida-dō, was built in 1053 and is the only original remaining building. The phoenix was a popular mythical bird in China and was revered by the Japanese as a protector of Buddha. The architecture of the building resembles the shape of the bird, and there are two bronze phoenixes perched opposite each other on the roof. The building was originally intended to represent Amida's heavenly palace in the Pure Land. This building is one of the few extant examples of Heian-period architecture, and its graceful lines make one wish that far more had survived the wars and fires of Kyoto's past.

Inside the hall is the famous statue of Amida and 52 Bosatsu (Bodhisattvas) dating from the 11th century and attributed to the priest sculptor, Jōchō.

The temple, complete with its reflection in a pond, is one of Japan's top attractions and draws huge crowds. For a preview without the masses, take a look at the ¥10 coin.

Between 17 June and 31 August, ukai trips are organised in the evening around 7 pm on the river near the temple. Prices start at ¥1500 a person. The TIC has a leaflet with up-to-date information about how to book.

KANSAI REGION

NORTHERN KYOTO 京都北部

The area north of Kyoto provides scope for exploration of rural valleys and mountainous areas. The twin valleys of Kurama and Kibune are perhaps the most pleasant day trip in the Kyoto area, giving one the feeling of being deep in the country without the necessity of long travel. Ōhara also makes another pleasant day trip, perhaps combined with an excursion to Hiei-zan and Enryaku-ji or Shūgaku-in Rikyū.

Shūgaku-in Rikyū 修学院利休

This imperial villa, or detached palace, was begun in the 1650s by the abdicated emperor Go-Mizunoo, and work was continued after his death in 1680 by his daughter Akenomiya. Designed as an imperial retreat, the villa grounds are divided into three large garden areas on a hillside: lower, middle and upper. The gardens' reputation rests on their ponds, pathways and impressive use of 'borrowed scenery' in the form of the surrounding hills; the view from the Rinun-tei Teahouse in the upper garden is particularly impressive.

Tours, in Japanese, start at 9, 10 and 11 am and 1.30 and 3 pm (50 minutes). Get there early. Admission is free, but you must make advance reservations through the Imperial Household Agency (see the earlier Kyoto Gosho section for details).

From JR Kyoto station, take bus No 5 and get off at the Shūgaku-in Rikyū-michi stop. The trip takes about an hour. From the bus stop it's a 15-minute walk to the villa. You can also take the Eiden Eizan line from Demachiyanagi station to the Shūgaku-in stop and walk east about 25 minutes toward the mountains.

Shisen-dō & Manshū-in 詩仙堂と曼殊院

Both these temples are in the vicinity of Shūgaku-in Rikyū. Due to their somewhat inconvenient location, they are less popular with tourists than the main Higashiyama temples farther south.

Shisen-dō (¥500, 9 am to 5 pm) was built in 1641 by Jōzan, a scholar of Chinese classics and a landscape architect, who wanted

a place to retire to at the end of his life. The garden is a fine place to relax, with only the rhythmic 'thwack' of a bamboo *sōzu* (animal scarer) to interrupt your snooze.

The temple is a five-minute walk from the Ichijōji-sagarimatsu-mae bus stop on the No 5 route.

Manshū-in (¥500, 9 am to 4.30 pm) was originally founded by Saichō on Hiei-zan, but was relocated here at the beginning of the Edo period. The architecture, works of art and garden are impressive.

The temple is a 10-minute walk from Shūgaku-in Rikyū.

Hiei-zan & Enryaku-ji 比叡山と延暦寺

Poised high on the shoulders of 848m Hiei-zan, Enryaku-ji is a sprawling complex of temples and subtemples that makes for a good afternoon of lazy strolling and poking about. In addition to the temple, you'll find a small ski field, an observation tower and a tiny amusement park. We strongly recommend avoiding these second-rate tourist attractions in favour of Enryaku-ji.

Enryaku-ji was founded in 788 by Saichō, the priest who established the Tenzai school of Buddhism. The Tenzai school did not receive imperial recognition until 1823, after Saichō's death. But from this time the temple continued to grow in power; at its height it possessed some 3000 temple buildings and an army of thousands of *sōhei*, or warrior monks. In 1581, Oda Nobunaga saw the temple's power as a threat to his aims to unify the nation. He destroyed most of the temple buildings along with the monks inside.

As it now stands, the temple area is divided into three sections – Tōdō, Saitō and Yokawa (of minimal interest). The Tōdō (Eastern Section) contains the Kompon Chū-dō (Primary Central Hall), which dates from 1642 (¥500, 8.30 am to 4.30 pm April to November, 9 am to 4 pm the rest of the year).

The Saitō (Western Section) contains the Shaka-dō Hall, dating from the Kamakura period. The Saitō, with its stone paths winding through forests of tall trees, temples shrouded in mist and the sound of distant gongs, is the most atmospheric part of the temple.

Getting There & Away You can reach Hiei-zan and Enryaku-ji by either train or bus. The most interesting way is to take the train/cable-car/ropeway route described at the end of this section. If you're in a hurry or would like to save money, take a direct bus from JR Kyoto or Keihan Sanjō station.

If you are travelling by train, take the Keihan main line north to the last stop, Demachiyanagi, and change to the Yase-yūen/Hiei-bound Eiden Eizan line train (be careful not to board the Kurama-bound train, which sometimes leaves from the same platform). At the last stop, Yase-yūen (¥260), board the cable car (¥530, nine minutes) and then the ropeway (¥310, three minutes) to the peak, from where you can walk down to the temples.

If you are travelling by bus, take Kyoto bus (not Kyoto city bus) No 17 or 18 from JR Kyoto station to the Yaseyūen stop (¥390, about 50 minutes). From there it's a short walk to the cable-car station described earlier.

Alternatively, you can save money by avoiding the cable car and ropeway and taking direct buses from JR Kyoto and Keihan Sanjō stations to Enryaku-ji (both cost ¥800, 70 and 50 minutes respectively).

Enryaku-ji is also accessible from Sakamoto on the Biwa-ko side of the mountain (see the Shiga-ken Sakamoto section for transport details). A cable car up the mountain from Sakamoto costs ¥840.

Ōhara 大原

Ōhara, a quiet farming town about 10km north of Kyoto, provides a glimpse of old rural Japan along with picturesque Sanzen-in and Jakkō-in Convent. It's most popular in autumn, when the maple leaves change colour and the mountain views are spectacular. From late October to mid-November avoid this area on weekends, as it will be packed.

From JR Kyoto station, Kyoto bus Nos 17 and 18 run to Ōhara (¥580, one hour). From Keihan Sanjō, take Kyoto bus No 16 or 17 (¥490, 45 minutes). Be careful to board a tan Kyoto bus, not a green Kyoto city bus of the same number. Allow half a day for a visit, possibly twinned with an excursion to Hiei-zan and the Enryaku-ji. JNTO includes a basic walking map for the area in its leaflet *Walking Tour Courses in Kyoto*.

Sanzen-in Founded in 784 by the priest Saicho, Sanzen-in (¥600, 8.30 am to 5.30 pm from March to November, until 5 pm the rest of the year) belongs to the Tendai sect of Buddhism. Saicho, considered one of the great patriarchs of Buddhism in Japan, also founded Enraku-ji on nearby Hiei-zan. The temple's Yusei-en is one of the most oft-photographed gardens in Japan, and rightly so. Take some time to sit on the steps of the Shin-den Hall and admire its beauty. Then head off to the Ojo-gokuraku Hall (Temple of Rebirth in Paradise) to see the impressive Amitabha trinity, a large Amida image flanked by attendants Kannon and Seishi, gods of mercy and wisdom, respectively. After this, walk up to the hydrangea garden at the back of the temple, where, in late spring and summer, you can walk among hectares of blooming hydrangeas.

If you feel like a short hike after leaving the temple, head up the hill around the right side of the temple to the **Soundless Waterfall** (you'll note that it sounds pretty much like any other waterfall). The sound of this waterfall is said to have inspired Shomyo Buddhist chanting.

If you have time, **Shorin-In**, just 100m to the left of the entrance to Sanzen-in, is worth a look, if only through its admission gate, to admire its unique thatched roof.

To get to Sanzen-in, follow the signs from Ōhara's main bus stop up the hill past a long arcade of souvenir stalls. The entrance is on your left as you crest the hill.

Jakkō-in Convent This convent (¥500, 9 am to 5 pm) lies to the west of Ōhara. Walk out of the bus station up the road to the traffic lights, then follow the small road to the left; the temple is at the top of a steep flight of stone steps.

The history of Jakkō-in Convent is exceedingly tragic – bring a supply of hankies. The actual founding date of the convent is subject to some debate (somewhere between the 6th and 11th centuries), but it acquired fame as the nunnery that harboured Kenrei Mon'in, a lady of the Taira clan. In 1185, the Taira were soundly defeated in a sea battle with the Minamoto clan. With every other member of the Taira clan slaughtered or drowned, Kenrei Mon'in threw herself into the waves with her son, the infant emperor; she was fished out – the only member of the clan to survive.

She was returned to Kyoto, where she became a nun living in a bare hut until it collapsed during an earthquake. Kenrei Mon'in was accepted into Jakkō-in temple and stayed there, immersed in prayer and sorrowful memories, until her death 27 years later.

The convent itself is quite plain, its real beauty coming from the wooded glade in which it is set. Unfortunately, like many Japanese temples, the tranquillity of the place is shattered by periodic announcements, in this case a version of Kenrei Mon'in's tragic tale read in a melodramatic voice.

Perhaps it's best to climb to the entrance gate and look from there, as the admission price is quite steep considering the small size of the convent.

Kurama & Kibune 鞍馬と貴船

Only 30 minutes north of Kyoto on the Eiden Eizan main line, Kurama and Kibune are a pair of tranquil valleys long favoured by Kyoto-ites as places to escape the crowds and stresses of the city below. Kurama's main attractions are its mountain temple and onsen. Kibune, over the ridge, is a cluster of ryokan overlooking a mountain stream. Kibune is best enjoyed in the summer, when the ryokan serve dinner on platforms built over the rushing waters of Kibune-gawa, providing welcome relief from the summer heat.

The two valleys lend themselves to being explored together. In the winter, one can start from Kibune, walk for 30 minutes over the ridge, visit Kurama-dera and then soak in the onsen before heading back to Kyoto.

In the summer, the reverse is best; start from Kurama, walk up to the temple, then down the other side to Kibune to enjoy a meal suspended above the cool river. If you happen to be in Kyoto on the night of 22 October, be sure not to miss the Kurama-no-hi Matsuri (Kurama Fire Festival), one of the most exciting festivals in the Kyoto area (see the Kyoto Special Events section for details).

To get to Kurama and Kibune, take the Eiden Eizan main line from Kyoto's Demachiyanagi station. To get to Kibune, get off at the second-to-last stop, Kibune Guchi, turn right out of the station and walk for about 20 minutes up the hill. To find Kurama, go to the last stop, Kurama, and walk straight out of the station. The fare to both destinations is ¥410 and it takes about 30 minutes to reach either.

Kyoto bus No 32 also leaves from the Demachiyanagi station to both destinations but is much slower than the train.

While you're at Demachiyanagi, be sure to pick up a copy of the *Kitayama Hiking Map* at the Kyoto bus office around the corner from the Eiden Eizan station (just past the fast food restaurant).

Kurama-dera In 770 the monk Gantei left Nara's Tōshōdai-ji in search of a wilderness sanctuary in which to meditate. Wandering in the hills north of Kyoto, he came across a white horse that led him to the valley known today as Kurama (¥200, 9 am to 4.30 pm). After seeing a vision of the deity Bishamonten, guardian of the northern quarter of the Buddhist heaven, he established Kurama-dera in its present location, just below the peak of Kurama-yama. Originally belonging to the Tendai sect, Kurama has been independent since 1949, describing its own brand of Buddhism as Kurama Kyō.

The entrance to the temple is just up the hill from the Eiden Eizan main line's Kurama station. A tram goes to the top for ¥100; alternatively, hike up by following the main path past the tram station. The trail is worth taking if it's not too hot, as it winds through a forest of towering old-growth cryptomeria trees. At the top, there is a courtyard dominated by the Honden (Main

Hall). Behind the Honden a trail leads off to the mountain's peak.

At the top, those who want to continue to Kibune can take the descending trail down the other side. It's a 30-minute hike from the Honden of Kurama-dera to the valley floor of Kibune. On the way down there are two pleasant mountain shrines.

Kurama Onsen Kurama Onsen, one of the few onsen within easy reach of Kyoto, is a great place to relax after a hike. The outdoor bath, with a fine view of Kurama-yama, costs ¥1000. The inside bath costs ¥2300, but even with the use of sauna and locker thrown in, it's difficult to imagine why one would opt for the indoor bath. For both baths, buy a ticket from the machine outside the door of the main building (instructions are in Japanese and English). The onsen is open from 10 am to 9 pm.

To get to Kurama Onsen, walk straight out of Kurama station, turn left up the main road and follow it for about 10 minutes. You'll see the baths down on your right. There's also a free shuttle bus that runs between the station and the onsen, leaving approximately every 30 minutes.

Kibune Kibune's main attractions are its dining platforms above the river, which are open from 1 June to the end of September. In addition to these, all the ryokan in the valley are open year round and serve as romantic escapes for travellers willing to pay mid-level ryokan prices. **Kibune-jinja**, halfway up the valley, is worth a quick look, particularly if you can ignore the plastic horse statue at its entrance. Admission is free.

From Kibune you can hike over the mountain to Kurama-dera, along a trail that starts halfway up the valley on the eastern side (or vice versa – see the earlier Kurama-dera section).

Miyama-chō
- pop 5000

Nestled in the northern Kitayama mountains between Kyoto and the Sea of Japan is Miyama-chō, a delightful place in which to explore a charming piece of rural Japan.

The 'town' is composed of several village clusters spread over a vast area. These picturesque hamlets are home to an abundance of traditional *kayabuki-ya* (thatched-roof) farmhouses with a thick roof of long *susuki* (pampas grass) reeds. The Japanese countryside was once covered with such homes, though in recent years a frightful number of the magnificent structures have been abandoned and razed, in favour of modern conveniences.

Miyama-chō has become a popular home for artists, and is also gaining attention from outdoor enthusiasts for its excellent hiking, camping and kayaking on Yura-gawa. If you travel by car, you can visit Miyama-chō as a day trip from Kyoto, although it makes a much nicer overnight trip.

Kitamura Miyama-chō's star attraction is Kitamura, a small hamlet boasting a cluster of some 50 thatched-roof farmhouses. In 1994 the village was designated a National Preservation Site, and the local government has been generously subsidising the exorbitant cost of rethatching the roofs. The average cost? More than US$40,000!

Stop in at the **Minzoku Shiryō-kan**, a history and folk museum in one of the village's farmhouses (¥200, 9 am to 4 pm). Across the road, *Kitamura* serves good noodles and light food from 10 am to 5 pm every day except Wednesday.

Ashyū The quiet village of Ashyū sits on the far eastern edge of Miyama-chō and is the access point to 4200 hectares of virgin forest safeguarded under the administration of Kyoto University's Department of Agriculture.

Serious hikers should pick up a copy of Shōbunsha's *Kitayama 2* map (Japanese only, ¥700) in Kyoto, with detailed trails and topography of the area. Before setting out on any hike, you must fill out a short form and drop it in a box at the trailhead (include your name, address and how long you expect to be out).

Getting There & Away Miyama-chō is about 50km due north of Kyoto over a series of mountain passes. As there are no train lines passing through Miyama, it is best reached by road. There is an infrequent bus service taking about three hours (¥2280); check with the TIC for routes and times. You are far better off arranging private transport (about 1½ hours by car).

A good choice if you are planning to hike in the Ashyū area is to take Kyoto bus No 32 from Demachiyanagi to the last stop, Hirogawara (¥1050, two hours) and hike over the next ridge north into Ashyū. To do this, you'd need the map mentioned in the earlier Ashyū section.

As for getting around: if you are without private transport, you must depend on very infrequent buses or hitch, as the distances between areas are far too long to cover on foot.

BATHS

After a day spent marching from temple to temple, nothing feels better than a good hot bath. Kyoto is full of *sento* (public baths), ranging from small neighbourhood baths with one or two tubs to massive complexes offering saunas, mineral baths and even electric baths. The following baths are worth a visit and could even double as an evening's entertainment. Of course, if you don't feel like making the trek to one of these places, there's probably a sento within a few minutes' walk of where you're staying (just ask the proprietor of your lodgings or at any police box).

Funaoka Onsen

This old bath on Kuramaguchi-dōri is the best in all Kyoto (¥340, 3 pm to 1 am, closed Tuesday). It boasts an outdoor bath, a sauna, a cypress-wood tub, an electric bath, a herbal bath and a few more for good measure. Be sure to check out the museum-quality *ranma* (woodcarvings) in the changing room. Carved during Japan's invasion of Manchuria, they offer insight into the prevailing mindset of that era (frankly, we're surprised that they haven't been taken down). To find it, head west about 400m on Kuramaguchi-dōri from the Kuramaguchi/ Horiikawa intersection. It's on the left not far past Lawson convenience store. Look for the large rocks out the front.

Shomen-yu

This ageing concrete structure might be called the mother of all sentos (¥340, 2 pm to 1 am, open 9 am Sunday, closed Tuesday). Three storeys high, with an outdoor bath on the roof, this onsen's your chance to try riding an elevator naked (if you haven't already had the pleasure). Everything is on a grand scale here, including the sauna, which boasts a TV and has room for 20.

The Japanese Bath

The *o-furo* (Japanese bath) is another ritual that has to be learnt at an early stage and, like so many other things in Japan, is initially confusing but quickly becomes second nature. The all-important rule for using a Japanese bath is that you wash *outside* the bath and use the bath itself purely for soaking. Getting into a bath unwashed or, equally dreadful, without rinsing all the soap off your body, would be a major error.

People bathe in the evening, before dinner; a pre-breakfast bath is thought of as distinctly strange. In a ryokan there's no possibility of missing bath time: You will be told clearly when to bathe lest you not be washed in time for dinner. In a ryokan or in a *sento* (public bath), the bathing facilities will either be communal (but sex segregated) or there will be smaller family bathing facilities for families and couples.

Take off your *yukata* (light cotton kimono) or clothes in the ante-room to the bath and place them in the baskets provided. The bathroom has taps, plastic bowls (wooden ones in very traditional places) and stools along the wall. Draw a stool up to a set of taps and fill the bowl from the taps or use the bowl to scoop some water out of the bath itself. Sit on the stool and soap yourself. Rinse thoroughly so there's no soap or shampoo left on you, then climb into the bath. Soak as long as you can stand the heat, then leave the bath, rinse yourself off again, dry off and don your yukata.

Men, don't be surprised if you spot some *yakuza* (Japanese mafia) among the bathers (instantly recognisable by their tattoos). Shomen-yu is south of Gojō-dōri about 300m east of Kamo-gawa. Look for the sign in English and Japanese.

ACTIVITIES
There are loads of things to do in Kyoto besides visiting temples. In addition to shopping, people-watching and hiking, the following activities are all good ways to spend a day here.

KICH Cultural Demonstrations
KICH offers the following introductory courses in Japanese culture: The Way of Tea (tea ceremony), Tuesday from 2 to 4 pm; An Introduction to Sencha (another kind of tea ceremony), Thursday from 2 to 4 pm; The Koto (a Japanese string instrument), Wednesday from 2 to 4 pm; and Introduction to Nō, Thursday from 10 am to noon. To join any of these classes for a full three-month term costs ¥5000. However, you can sit in on a class for a fee of ¥1000 (call ☎ 752-3512 a day in advance to make a booking). See the KICH entry in the Useful Organisations section earlier in this chapter for more details and directions.

The Miyako Hotel (☎ 771-7111) in the Higashiyama area offers demonstrations of the tea ceremony from 10 am to 7 pm for ¥1155. No reservation is necessary, as demonstrations are performed upon request.

ORGANISED TOURS
Some visitors on a tight schedule find it convenient to join an organised tour of the city that will allow them to see more sights than they would be able to visit on their own.

JTB Sunrise Tours (☎ 341-1413) offers morning, afternoon and all-day tours. Morning and afternoon tours cost ¥5300, while all-day tours with buffet lunch thrown in are ¥11,200. All tours have English-speaking guides and the company offers free pick-up from most of Kyoto's larger hotels (call for details).

A more intimate tour is offered by a private English-speaking tour guide named Hajime Hirooka, who calls himself Johnny Hillwalker. He takes small groups of travellers on walking tours of the city starting from JR Kyoto station and covering some of the sights in central and eastern Kyoto. Readers who have gone on this tour highly recommend it (adults ¥2000, children aged 13 to 15 ¥1000, younger children free, admission prices for museums and temples extra). Four-hour tours are given on Monday, Wednesday and Friday from 1 March to the end of November (no tours on national holidays). Meet at 10 am in the sunken concrete area 100 paces north of JR Kyoto station, on the way to Kyoto Tower. No reservations are necessary. Call ☎ 622-6803 or ☎ 090-189-000-96 for more details.

SPECIAL EVENTS
There are hundreds of festivals in Kyoto throughout the year. Listings can be found on the TIC's forthcoming-events board or in *Kyoto Visitor's Guide*, *Kansai Time Out* or the weekend editions of the English-language newspapers available in Japan. The following are some of the major or most spectacular festivals. These attract hordes of spectators from out of town, so you need to book accommodation well in advance.

February
Setsubun Matsuri at Yoshida-jinja 3 or 4 February (check with the TIC) – This festival is held on the day of setsubun, which marks the last day of winter in the Japanese lunar calendar. In this festival, people climb up to Yoshida-jinja in the northern Higashiyama area to watch a huge bonfire. It's one of Kyoto's more dramatic festivals. The action starts at dusk.

May
Aoi Matsuri (Hollyhock Festival) 15 May – This festival dates back to the 6th century and commemorates the successful prayers of the people for the gods to stop calamitous weather. Today, the procession involves imperial messengers in ox carts and a retinue of 600 people dressed in traditional costume; hollyhock leaves are carried or used as decoration. The procession leaves at around 10 am from the Kyosho Gosho and heads for Shimogamo-jinja, where ceremonies take place. It sets out from here again at 2 pm and arrives at Kamigamo-jinja at 3.30 pm.

July
Gion Matsuri 17 July – Perhaps the most renowned of all Japanese festivals, this one reaches a climax on the 17th with a parade of over 30 floats depicting ancient themes and decked out in incredible finery. On the three evenings preceding the main day, people gather on Shijō-dōri, many dressed in beautiful *yukata* (light summer *kimono*), to look at the floats and carouse from one street stall to the next.

August
Daimon-ji Gozan Okuribi 16 August – This festival, commonly known as Daimon-ji Yaki, is performed to bid farewell to the souls of ancestors. Enormous fires are lit on five mountains in the form of Chinese characters or other shapes. The fires are lit at 8 pm and it is best to watch from the banks of Kamo-gawa or pay for a rooftop view from a hotel. Better yet, head up to Hirosawano-ike in north-western Kyoto, rent a rowing boat and watch *torii-gata* (the character for 'gate') burn over the pond. Here, in addition to the burning figure, people float hundreds of lanterns with burning candles inside them on the surface of the pond – the effect is magical.

October
Kurama-no-hi Matsuri (Kurama Fire Festival) 22 October – Perhaps Kyoto's most dramatic festival; portable shrines are carried through the streets and accompanied by youths with flaming torches. The festival climaxes around 10 pm at Yuki-jinja in the village of Kurama, which is 30 minutes by train from JR Kyoto station on the Eiden Eizan Line. The train leaves from Demachiyanagi station.
Jidai Matsuri (Festival of the Ages) 22 October – This festival is of recent origin, only dating back to 1895. More than 2000 people, dressed in costumes ranging from the 8th century to the 19th century, parade from Kyoto Gosho to Heian-jingū.

PLACES TO STAY
Kyoto has the widest range of foreigner-friendly accommodation in all Japan, with a variety of options in every budget range. Choices range from the country's finest and most expensive ryokan to youth hostels and funky old guesthouses. You can save time spent traversing the city if you organise your accommodation around the areas of interest to you. To help with planning, the following accommodation listings have been sorted according to location and price range. In addition to these listings, the TIC can offer advice and help with finding suitable lodgings.

Places to Stay – Budget
Budget accommodation in Kyoto consists of youth hostels and guesthouses. The former tend to be clean and well run but regimented (with early curfews) while the latter can be cramped and run down but easygoing about the hours you keep. When making your choice, think hard about these factors and about where you want to be based.

Central Kyoto A longtime fixture of Kyoto guesthouse scene is *Uno House* (☎ 231-7763), which has a convenient central location and casual atmosphere. Sure, it's a little noisy and run down, but you can't beat the price. Dorm beds start at ¥1650, and private rooms (which hold from two to four people) range from ¥2250 to ¥5200 (for the room). Take the Karasuma line subway from JR Kyoto station, get off at the Marutamachi stop (seven minutes) and walk east for 10 minutes.

Guest Inn Kyoto (☎ 341-1344) is another inexpensive choice, with decent singles/doubles starting at ¥3500/6800, including private bath. It's just west of Nishi Hongan-ji. Take bus No 6 or 206 from JR Kyoto station (stand B4, 10 minutes) to the Shimabara-guchi stop and walk west for 150m. There's no curfew.

Near Kyoto Gosho is *Takaya* (☎ 431-5213), which provides private rooms at ¥4000 a day or starting at ¥50,000 for one month. Be sure to call in advance, though, as it's often fully occupied by long-term clients. Take the Karasuma line subway from JR Kyoto station to Imadegawa station (10 minutes) and walk south-west for five minutes.

The location of the *Tani Guest House* (☎ 681-7437) is not the best, but it may be a reasonable option for those intending to stay long term. Dorm beds are ¥1900 and single/double rooms are ¥2300/4600. Monthly rates are from ¥35,000 to ¥55,000. To get there, take the JR *futsū* (local) train from JR Kyoto station one stop to Nishiōji station and call for a pick-up (or call before departing JR Kyoto station).

Not far away, the *Tōji-An Guesthouse* (☎ 691-7017) has dorm accommodation at ¥2000 and private rooms from ¥2300. There's no curfew, but it's rather cramped and inconveniently located. Call from JR Kyoto station to get precise directions.

A short distance from Pension Station Kyoto (see the Places to Stay – Mid-Range entry), and close to Nishi-Hongan-ji, *Tour Club* (☎ 353-6968, fax 353-6978, email tour club@kyotojp.com) is a newly opened 'B&B'. Dorms cost ¥2300, and add on another ¥290 for a simple breakfast. Some single rooms are also available from ¥4900. From Pension Station Kyoto (see the Mid-Range entry), walk three blocks and turn right. The fifth house on the left is Tour Club.

Eastern Kyoto An excellent base very close to the sights of Higashiyama is the spiffy *Higashiyama Youth Hostel* (☎ 761-8135). Rates are ¥2700 a person. It's very regimented, but if you're the kind of person who likes being in bed by 9.30 pm, this might be just your ticket. To get to it, take bus No 5 from JR Kyoto station (stand A1, 30 minutes) to the Higashiyama-Sanjō stop. If you're in the Keihan Sanjō station area, you can walk to the hostel in 15 minutes.

ISE Dorm (☎ 771-0566) provides basic accommodation (42 rooms) at rates of ¥2800 a day. Monthly rates start at ¥45,000. Facilities on offer include phone, fridge, air-con, shower and washing machine. On the negative side, the place can be noisy and some of the rooms are a little run down. However, there is usually a room available, and arrangements for a stay can be made very quickly. Take bus No 206 from JR Kyoto station (stand B4, 30 minutes) to the Kumano-jinja-mae stop.

North-Western Kyoto The best youth hostel in Kyoto is the friendly, well-organised *Utano Youth Hostel* (☎ 462-2288). Bear in mind, though, that while it's conveniently located for touring sights in the north-west of the city, it's something of a hike to those downtown. Rates are ¥2650 most of the year, and ¥2800 from December to March and July and August. Take bus No 26 from JR Kyoto station (stand B2, 50 minutes) to the Yūsu Hosuteru-mae stop. Alternatively, from Keihan Sanjō station, take bus No 10 or 59 (stands 5 and 3, respectively, 50 minutes) to the same stop. The hostel is a one-minute walk up the hill from the stop.

Northern Kyoto An old favourite for short-term and long-term visitors on a tight budget is *Tani House* (☎ 492-5489). There is a certain charm to this fine old house, with its warren of rooms and quiet location next to Daitoku-ji. Costs per night are ¥1700 for a space on the floor in a tatami room and from ¥4200 to ¥4600 for a private double room. There's no curfew, and free tea and coffee are provided. Take bus No 206 from JR Kyoto station (stand B4, 45 minutes), get off at the Kenkun-jinja-mae stop then ask at the police box on the south-eastern side of the temple for directions.

Kitayama Youth Hostel (☎ 492-5345) charges ¥2800 for a dorm bed. Take bus No 6 from JR Kyoto station (stand B4, 35 minutes) to the Genkoan-mae stop. Walk west past a school, turn right and continue up the hill to the hostel (five minutes on foot). This hostel is an excellent base from which to visit the rural area of Takagamine, which has some fine, secluded temples such as Kōetsu-ji, Jōshō-ji and Shoden-ji.

Places to Stay – Mid-Range

Kyoto is a good place in which to sample the ryokan experience, and there are dozens of inexpensive ryokan in the city that specialise in serving foreign guests. Keep in mind, though, that staying in a ryokan can be like staying at the home of a relative; if you want real freedom you might consider staying in a business hotel instead.

Central Kyoto & Kyoto Station Area
Our three favourite ryokan are in this area.

Ryokan There are several foreigner-friendly ryokan in central Kyoto, all of which are members of the Japanese Inn Group. While there is little to distinguish them, our three favourites are listed first here (but keep in mind that the others in this section are all good choices). At all these places, there are common baths, and breakfast is available for an additional fee.

Ryokan Hinomoto (☎ *351-4563*) is most convenient to the city's nightlife action and has a nice wooden bathtub. Singles are priced from ¥4000 to ¥5500, doubles from ¥7500 to ¥8000. Take bus No 17 or 205 from JR Kyoto station (stand A2, 15 minutes) and get off at the Kawaramachi-matsubara stop.

Ryokan Hiraiwa (☎ *351-6748*) is a friendly place conveniently close to central and eastern Kyoto. Singles/doubles start at ¥4000/8000 and facilities include bilingual TV, air-con and coin-operated laundry facilities. To get there from JR Kyoto station you can either walk (15 minutes) or take bus No 17 or 205 from JR Kyoto station (stand A2, 10 minutes) and get off at the Kawaramachi Shomen stop, from which it's a five-minute walk.

Matsubaya Ryokan (☎ *351-4268*) is a welcoming place with singles/doubles starting at ¥4500/9000; triples cost ¥12,600. It's a 10-minute walk north of JR Kyoto station.

Just around the corner, *Ryokan Murakamiya* (☎ *371-1260*) is a cosy place with rooms starting at ¥4000/8000.

Riverside Takase (☎ *351-7925*) has five comfortable rooms. Singles/doubles start at ¥3300/6400, while triples start at ¥9600. Follow the directions for Ryokan Hiraiwa, mentioned earlier in this section.

Yuhara Ryokan (☎ *371-9583*) has a family atmosphere and a riverside location popular with foreigners. Prices are ¥4000/8000. Follow the directions for the Ryokan Hiraiwa, mentioned earlier.

Ryokan Kyōka (☎ *371-2709*) has 10 spacious rooms starting at ¥4000/8000. It's a 10-minute walk north of JR Kyoto station.

Hotels & Pensions Directly opposite the northern side of JR Kyoto station, *Hokke Club Kyoto* (☎ *361-1251*) has singles and twins starting at ¥8500 and ¥15,000, respectively, with bath, and ¥7000 and ¥12,000 without.

One minute's walk east of JR Kyoto station, the *Kyoto Dai-ni Tower Hotel* (☎ *361-3261*) has clean singles/doubles with bath starting at ¥6000/15,000 and clean twins with bath starting at ¥12,000.

Farther north, on Karasuma-dōri, the *Karasuma Kyoto Hotel* (☎ *371-0111*) has clean, new singles/doubles starting at ¥8800/20,000 and clean, new twins starting at ¥16,000. It's a five-minute walk from Shijō station on the Karasuma subway line.

Our favourite business hotel in Kyoto is *Sun Hotel Kyoto* (☎ *241-3351*). Small but clean singles/doubles are ¥7000/12,200, while clean twins are ¥12,200. It's right on Kawaramachi-dōri, in the heart of Kyoto's nightlife district. From JR Kyoto station take bus No 5 (stand A1, 20 minutes) to the Kawaramachi-Sanjō stop and backtrack for 100m.

Lastly, *Pension Station Kyoto* (☎ *882-6200*) is a quiet place with decent rooms only 10 minutes' walk north of JR Kyoto station. Singles are ¥4400 on weekdays and ¥5400 on weekends. Twins go for ¥8800. For a room with a bath you must pay an additional ¥1600.

Eastern Kyoto There are a few economical hotels in this area.

Ryokan Beside the river is *Ryokan Ōtō* (☎ *541-7803*), which charges ¥4000/7600. You can get there via bus No 206 or 208 from JR Kyoto station (stand D2, five minutes) to Shichijō Keihan-mae bus stop. Or, you can walk there in about 15 minutes.

Not far from Kiyomizu-dera, the *Ryokan Sieki* (☎ *682-0311*) is another good choice, with singles/double starting at ¥3600/7500 and triples starting at ¥11,000. Take bus No 206 from JR Kyoto station (stand D2, 10 minutes) to the Gojō-zaka stop, walk down Gojō-dōri for five minutes and turn right down the small street just after the pedestrian crossing.

A step up in price and comfort is the excellent *Three Sisters Inn* (☎ *761-6336*). It is perfectly situated in Okazaki for exploration of the Higashiyama area. Here, spacious singles/doubles start at ¥8900/13,000, while triples start at ¥19,500. Take bus No 5 from JR Kyoto station (stand A1, 30 minutes), get off at Dōbutsuen-mae stop and walk for five minutes. *Three Sisters Annex* (☎ 761-6333), close by, is run by the same management and has singles/doubles without bath for ¥5635/11,270 and single/doubles with bath for ¥10,810/18,170. Triples with bath are ¥23,805. Both places have been highly recommended.

Iwanami Ryokan (☎ 561-7135) is a pleasant, old-fashioned ryokan with a faithful following of foreign guests. It's right in the heart of Gion, on a quiet side street. Book well in advance. Prices start at ¥9500 a person including breakfast. Take bus No 206 from JR Kyoto station (stand D2, 30 minutes) to the Chio-in-mae stop and walk for five minutes.

Nearby, *Gion Fukuzumi* (☎ 541-5181) is a big new ryokan in a modern, Western-style building with rooms starting at ¥8000/12,000. Follow the directions for Iwanami, mentioned earlier in this section.

Uemura (☎/fax 561-0377) is a beautiful little ryokan at ease with foreign guests. It's on Ishibei-kōji, a quaint cobblestone alley, just down the hill from Kōdai-ji. Per-person prices are ¥9000 with breakfast, and there is a 10 pm curfew. You'll have to book well in advance, as there are only three rooms. Note that the manager prefers bookings by fax and asks that cancellations also be made by fax (with so few rooms, it can be costly for management when bookings are broken without notice). Take bus No 206 from JR Kyoto station (stand D2, 30 minutes) and get off at Yasui bus stop, then walk in the direction of Kōdai-ji.

Mishima-jinja (☎ 551-0033) is an interesting option in the southern Higashiyama area. It's a shrine that runs its own *shukubō* (temple accommodation). Singles/doubles cost ¥4000/7000, triples cost ¥10,500, and there is no curfew. Take bus No 206 from JR Kyoto station (stand D2, 15 minutes), get off at the Umamachi stop and walk uphill for about 10 minutes.

Hotels & Pensions An economical business hotel is *Kyoto Traveller's Inn* (☎ 771-0225),

which is very close to the Heian-jingū and offers both Western- and Japanese-style rooms with bath. Prices for Western-style singles and twins start at ¥5500 and ¥10,000 respectively. Japanese-style rooms start at ¥5000 a person. There's no curfew, and the *Green Box* restaurant on the 1st floor is open until 10 pm. Take bus No 5 from JR Kyoto station (stand A1, 30 minutes) to the Bijutsu-kan-mae stop and walk north for one minute.

Pension Higashiyama (☎ 882-1181) is a modern building alongside Shira-kawa and is a convenient base from which to visit the sights in Higashiyama. Rooms are ¥4400/8800. Meals are served on the premises, but since you're so close to downtown, it's probably better to eat out. To get there, take bus No 206 from JR Kyoto station (bus stand D2, 30 minutes), get off at Higashiyama-Sanjō and walk east for five minutes.

If you fancy the freedom of a hotel but can't afford the prices, try the *Amenity Capsule Hotel* (☎ 525-3900), where you can get your own little capsule for ¥3600. From JR Kyoto station take bus No 206 (stand D2, 20 minutes) to the Kiyomizu-michi stop, from which it's less than a minute's walk.

Northern Kyoto One good choice is *Ryokan Rakucho* (☎ 721-2174), which has rooms for ¥4500/8000. The quickest way to get there is to take the subway from Kyoto station to Kitaōji station, walk east across the river and then turn north at the post office. To get there by bus, take bus No 205 from JR Kyoto station (bus stand B3) and get off at the Furitsu-daigaku-mae stop, from which it's a one-minute walk.

Western Kyoto The quaint *Minshuku Arashiyama* (☎ 861-4398) is within walking distance of most of Arashiyama's main sights (a *minshuku* is a Japanese B&B). Here, per-person rates are ¥7000 with two meals, or ¥5000 without meals. It might be best to have a Japanese speaker make your reservation here. You can walk there in 10 minutes from Saga-Arashiyama station on JR San-in line.

Pension Arashiyama (☎ 881-2294) has clean, Western-style singles/doubles starting at ¥4200/8400 and triples starting at ¥12,000. To get there, take the 30-minute ride on Kyoto bus Nos 71, 72 or 73 and get off at the Arisugawa-mae stop.

Places to Stay – Top End

Central Kyoto Detailed directions are not provided for places in this price range, as you will probably be travelling to them from the station by taxi (refer to maps for locations).

Ryokan Top-end ryokan accommodation in Kyoto is, as you might expect, very expensive. Listed here are some of the ryokan that occasionally have foreign guests.

Kinmata Ryokan (☎ 221-1039) commenced operations early in the last century and this is reflected in the original decor, interior gardens, antiques and *hinoki* (cypress) bathroom. Per-person rates with two meals are ¥25,000, ¥30,000 and ¥35,000, depending on the type of *kaiseki* (Japanese cuisine prepared and served according to strict rules of etiquette) meal you are served for dinner. It's in the centre of town, very close to the Nishiki-kōji market.

Hiiragiya Ryokan (☎ 221-1136) is another elegant ryokan favoured by celebrities from around the world. For a room and two meals, per-person costs range from ¥30,000 to ¥100,000. Close by, the *Hiiragiya Annexe* (☎ 231-0151) also offers top-notch ryokan service and surroundings but at slightly more affordable rates. Per-person costs start at ¥15,000 with two meals. Hiiragiya Annex is located in Gokō-machi. Gokō-machi is one street west of Teramachi-dōri. Catch the Tōzai line and get off at Shiyakusho-mae.

Tawaraya Ryokan (☎ 211-5566) has been operating for over three centuries and is classed as one of the finest places to stay in the world. Guests at this ryokan have included the imperial family and royalty from overseas. It is a classic in every sense. Per-person costs range from ¥35,000 to ¥75,000.

Hotels The upmarket ryokan experience is not for everyone. There are a number of high-class hotels in the central district.

The cheapest hotel in this class, and just a shade above business-hotel level, is the centrally located and clean *Hotel Gimmond* (☎ 221-4111), where singles/doubles/twins start at ¥8300/14,000/14,500.

In the middle of town, convenient to the nightlife areas and many sightseeing spots, is *Hotel Fujita Kyoto* (☎ 222-1511), which has good rooms starting at ¥9800/23,000/16,000.

Up in the north of town, near Takano, *Holiday Inn Kyoto* (☎ 721-3131) has good facilities and a free shuttle bus to/from JR Kyoto station. Rooms here start at ¥10,000/14,000/18,000.

Right next to JR Kyoto station, the *Kyoto Century Hotel* (☎ 351-0111) is a convenient choice, with relatively spacious and clean rooms starting at ¥14,000/18,000/20,000.

Across the street from JR Kyoto station, the *Hotel New Hankyū Kyoto* (☎ 343-5300) has clean but rather drab rooms starting at ¥12,000/22,000/17,000.

Built into the station building right over JR Kyoto station, the gleaming new *Hotel Granvia Kyoto* (☎ 344-8888) takes the prize in terms of convenient location and has an extensive variety of restaurants and bars on its premises. Spacious and modern singles/doubles/twins here start at ¥14,000/25,000/20,000.

Within walking distance of JR Kyoto station, the *Kyoto Tōkyū Hotel* (☎ 341-2411) is a big, modern hotel with extensive on-site facilities. Rooms here start at ¥12,000/24,000/20,000.

A good choice in terms of on-site facilities (pool, restaurants, shopping) is the *ANA Hotel Kyoto* (☎ 231-1155). Rooms here start at 11,000/19,000/16,000. It's just opposite Nijō-jō.

Right next door is the *International Hotel Kyoto* (☎ 222-1111), a slightly less appealing choice, with rooms starting at ¥9000/23,000/14,000.

Lastly, the enormous new *Kyoto Hotel* (☎ 211-5111) is right in the centre of town at the Oike-Kawaramachi intersection and commands an impressive view of the Higashiyama mountains. Spacious rooms here start at ¥16,000/31,000/25,000.

Eastern Kyoto This area includes the very well situated Western-style Miyako Hotel.

Ryokan An elegant ryokan close to Nanzen-ji is *Yachiyo* (☎ 771-4148), where per-person prices start at ¥20,000 without bath, ¥25,000 with bath. Meals are extra.

Hotels Perched on the hills and a classic choice for visiting foreign dignitaries is *Miyako Hotel* (☎ 771-7111), a graceful, Western-style hotel. The hotel surroundings stretch over 6.4 hectares of wooded hillside and landscaped gardens. Western-style singles/doubles/twins start at ¥15,000/19,000/19,000. Japanese-style rooms start at ¥28,000. Prices are higher on weekends.

Down near Sanjūsangen-dō, *Kyoto Park Hotel* (☎ 525-3111) is a pleasant, airy place with well appointed rooms starting at ¥9500/21,000/16,500. Call ahead and ask about discounts, as it frequently runs special deals.

Conveniently close to the sights of the northern Higashiyama area, *Hotel Sunflower Kyoto* (☎ 761-9111) has clean, plain rooms starting at ¥9000/16,000/16,000.

North-Western Kyoto If you fancy a little luxury in the Arashiyama area, try the *Arashiyama Benkei Ryokan* (☎ 872-3355), where per-person rates are ¥20,000 including two excellent Japanese meals (kaiseki at dinner). It's right on Katsura-gawa, just upstream of Togetsu kyō.

Other Accommodation

Shukubō The shukubō listed here have English speakers on hand. For more information and a list of the shukubō in Kyoto, check with the TIC, where you can also pick up a copy of its free pamphlet entitled *Shukubos in Kyoto*.

The relaxed and friendly temple lodging, *Myōren-ji* (☎ 451-3527) charges ¥3500 a person (no meals are served and there's an 11 pm curfew). Take bus No 9 from JR Kyoto station (stand B1, 25 minutes) to the Horikawa-Teranouchi stop.

Hiden-in (☎ 561-8781) charges ¥4500 with breakfast. From JR Kyoto station, take bus No 208 (stand A2, 10 minutes) to the Sennyuji-michi stop.

Women-Only Accommodation Temple lodgings for women only can be found at *Rokuō-in* (☎ 861-1645) – it's in western Kyoto, close to Rokuō-in station on the Keifuku Arashiyama line. The per-person price is ¥4500, including breakfast.

For long-term accommodation (minimum three months) the *YWCA* (☎ 431-0351) offers monthly rates from ¥27,000 (room only) to ¥35,000 (with kitchen and bathroom). It is a short walk west of Kyoto-gyōen.

The TIC can give additional details about women-only accommodation.

PLACES TO EAT

Kyoto is famed for *kyō-ryōri*, a local variation on kaiseki cuisine. A kyō-ryōri course might cost ¥6000 a person, a full spread ¥15,000, and then there are exclusive establishments where you can shell out ¥50,000 (if you are deemed fit to make a reservation). For lesser mortals with punier budgets, some restaurants do a kaiseki *bentō* (boxed lunch) at lunch time from around ¥2500.

Luckily, there's a lot more to the Kyoto restaurant scene than elite restaurants serving rarefied food. Kyoto has great restaurants in every price bracket and it's one of the best places in Japan to make a thorough exploration of Japanese cuisine. In addition to Japanese restaurants, Kyoto has lots of good international restaurants.

For an extended exploration of Kyoto's culinary delights, you might supplement the information in this section with the *Kyoto Visitor's Guide* and Diane Durston's book *Old Kyoto: A Guide to Traditional Shops, Restaurants & Inns*. Both have listings of kaiseki and kyō-ryōri restaurants for those who feel like splashing out.

Note that in this section, we list phone numbers only for those restaurants where reservations are suggested. Some of these restaurants can be entered without a reservation, particularly at lunch time. All places are open daily for lunch and dinner unless otherwise noted.

Kyoto Station

The new Kyoto station building is chock-a-block with restaurants and just about every type of Japanese and foreign food is represented. For a quick cuppa while waiting for a train, try *Café du Monde* on the 2nd floor overlooking the central atrium. Up on the 7th floor on the eastern side, *Musica La La* cafe has an even more commanding location in an open courtyard with a view over the upper reaches of the station.

For more substantial meals, there are several food courts scattered around. On the 10th floor on the western side of the building the *Cootocco* food court (who thinks of these names?) has a variety of fast-food restaurants. You can sit down to a meal in either *The Cube* food court or Isetan department store's *Eat Paradise* food court on the 11th floor on the western side of the building (the latter is better for Japanese food).

For bentō to take with you on the train, try the shopping mall on the B1 floor of the station or the stores inside the turnstiles on the way to the platforms.

Kawaramachi & Kiyamachi Area

Japanese At lunch time, *Kane-yo* (11.30 am to 3 pm) is a good place to try that great Japanese favourite, grilled eel. You can sit downstairs with a nice view of the waterfall or upstairs on the tatami mats. The excellent ¥850 *kane-yo donburi* (meat and rice) set meal is about the cheapest you'll find anywhere.

Another good lunch spot is *Fūkei*, at the end of the Nishiki-kōji market. It has the best *teishoku* (set meals) in town; try the *ebi-furai teishoku* (fried shrimp set meal) for ¥900. While you're there, check out the decorations – the owner has dedicated the restaurant to John Lennon. It's on the corner, on the 2nd floor.

Kōsendō-sumi (11.30 am to 2 pm, closed Sunday and holidays) serves a daily set lunch in a classic old Japanese house for ¥800.

For inexpensive *tempura* (battered and fried seafood and vegetables) try *Takase-bune* (closed Monday), which serves fine tempura set meals for lunch or dinner in a classic old Japanese house behind Hankyū department store for ¥800/1500/2000. The *sashimi* is also good and there's a simple English menu.

If you're low on cash, *Koharu* serves Kyoto's cheapest *okonomiyaki* (Japanese-style egg-based savoury pancakes): its mixed okonomiyaki is only ¥400. This place is run-down, funky and a lot of fun. You'll be given a bowl with the ingredients of your order; mix it well and pour it onto the griddle and let it cook. Don't worry if you don't know what you're doing – the old ladies who run the place will keep a close eye on you.

If you prefer someone to make your okonomiyaki for you, try *Mr Young Mens*, where the Mr Young Mens Lunch costs ¥790 and includes okonomiyaki, *yakisoba* (Chinese-style buckwheat noodles), rice and *miso* (fermented soya-bean paste) soup.

If you've never tried automatic sushi, don't miss *Musashi Sushi*, at the junction of Sanjō-dōri and Kawaramachi-dōri. Sure, it's not the best sushi in the world, but the price is right (about ¥1500 a head).

For proper sushi in lively surroundings, head to *Tomi-zushi* (5 pm to midnight, closed Thursday), near the Shinkyōgoku shopping arcade. One person can fill up here for about ¥4000 with a beer or some sake. Go early or wait in line.

For vegetarian fare, try *Biotei* (closed Sunday and Monday), where a lunch-time set meal of Japanese vegetarian/whole food is ¥850 (the occasional bit of meat is offered as an option, but you'll be asked your preference).

Near the bridge, Sanjō-Ōhashi, *Gankō Sushi* is a good place for sushi or just about anything else. It serves elegant set lunches starting at ¥1000 and set dinners starting at about ¥3000 a person (there's a picture menu to make ordering easier).

A few streets north, you'll find *Gankō Nijō-en* (☎ 223-3456), the sister restaurant of Gankō Sushi. This is a much more elegant affair, with a fantastic Japanese garden to stroll in before or after your meal. There's a picture menu with a variety of kaiseki set meals, but you'd do better to order a la carte. Try some of the *age mono* (fried dishes) and sushi assortments. Plan on spending about ¥3000 a head (double that for any of the kaiseki set meals).

North of Oike-dōri, there are some more interesting choices. For *rāmen* (Chinese egg noodles in a broth), try **Shin-shin-tei** (10.30 am to 5 pm, closed Sunday), famous for its *shiro miso rāmen* (white miso rāmen) for ¥600.

For excellent *kushi-katsu* (skewered pork cutlet) try **Ōiwa** (5 to 10 pm, closed Wednesday), just south of the Hotel Fujita. Ordering is easy – just ask for the course (30 skewers) and say 'stop' when you're full (you'll only be charged for what you've eaten; the whole course is ¥5000).

For good sashimi, *age mono* (fried morsels) and sake, try **Kuishinbo** (open evenings only, closed Monday) in the Kiyamachi area. There's no English menu; we suggest the sashimi (¥850), tempura (¥1000) and *sake hito masu* (sake in a wooden cup, ¥650).

For dinner, you might want to head to atmospheric Pontochō-dōri (you may see some geisha along the way). About midway along, **Kappa Zushi** (open evenings only) is a popular sushi bar with fair prices and an English menu. Prices are about ¥3000 a head.

Also on Pontochō-dōri, the *izakaya* (pub-style eatery) **Zu Zu** is a fun place to eat and drink, and has an English menu. The fare is sort of *nouveau* Japanese – things like shrimp and tōfu or chicken and plum sauce. Count on about ¥3000 a person (open evenings only).

Yamatomi is another jewel on Pontochō-dōri, where you can try your hand at the house special, *teppin-age*, involves frying up tasty tempura on skewers in a cast-iron pot (¥2800 a person). It's closed on Monday.

Also on Pontochō-dōri is **Fujino-ya**, which has tatami rooms overlooking Kamo-gawa. Here you can feast on tempura, okonomiyaki, yakisoba and kushi-katsu. Prices are reasonable at around ¥2000 a head. It's open from 5 to 10 pm (closed Wednesday).

One final Pontochō spot is **Uzuki** (☎ 221-2358), where you can splash out on the

wonderful kaiseki cuisine. It's an elegant place with a great platform for riverside dining in the summer. Set kaiseki courses start at ¥5000. You should have a Japanese speaker call for you and decide on the evening's fare. It's open from 5 to 11 pm (closed Wednesday).

For a taste of some of Kyoto's best soba in traditional surroundings, head for **Misoka-an Kawamichi-ya** (☎ 221-2525), north of Sanjō-dōri on Fuyachō-dōri. A simple bowl of *nishin soba* (buckwheat noodles topped with fish) costs ¥1000, and more elaborate *nabe* (rapidly cooked stew) dishes start at around ¥3800 a person. It's closed on Thursday.

For a light meal, **Shiruko** has been serving simple Kyoto *obanzai-ryōri* (homestyle cooking) since 1932. The restaurant features more than 10 varieties of miso soup, and the *rikyū* bentō for ¥2600 is a bona fide work of art. The restaurant is closed on Wednesday.

For a special dinner **Morita-ya** (☎ 231-5118) serves excellent sukiyaki and *shabu-shabu* (sliced beef cooked in boiling water) in traditional tatami rooms, some overlooking Kamo-gawa. Set meals start at ¥3800 a person. Look for the narrow alley leading towards the river.

Another great sukiyaki spot with similar fare, decor and prices is **Mishima-tei** (☎ 221-0003), in the Teramachi covered arcade (closed Wednesday). There's an English tourist menu here with reduced prices; set meals start at ¥4400.

Tōsui-rō is a few alleys down from Morita-ya, mentioned earlier. Here, you'll find superb tōfu set meals and pleasant tatami rooms overlooking Kamo-gawa. Expect to spend about ¥3000 a head. Look for the alley leading to the river; it's at the very end, on the left.

For superb tempura, head for **Yoshikawa** (☎ 221-5544). It offers fancy table seating with lunch starting at ¥6000 and dinner starting at ¥12,000, but it's much more interesting to sit around the small counter and observe the chefs at work. Special counter-only lunches start at ¥2000, while dinners start at ¥6000. It's closed on Sunday.

KANSAI REGION

For a great late-night snack after hitting the bars of Kiyamachi, try *Tenka-ippin*. The rāmen here is damn good and averages ¥700 a bowl. Our favourite is *ninniku-iri wantan-men kotteri-de* (thick-soup rāmen with wantons and garlic).

Lastly, for a truly raucous Kyoto izakaya, see *A-Bar* in the Entertainment section.

International For a light lunch, a snack or just a cuppa, try the airy cafe *Kobeya Dining* across from Hankyū department store. The place is modelled on a New York cafe and serves a range of sandwiches, light meals and drinks (expect to pay about ¥1000 for lunch).

A much more down-to-earth cafe is the woodsy *Saracca* (closed Wednesday). This is a peaceful spot in which to relax with a book; it has a variety of interesting dishes to snack on, including lots of vegetarian choices. Coffee drinks average ¥450 here.

Cafe David is named after the art connoisseur David Kidd. It was opened as a tribute to Kidd by his lifelong partner Morimoto Yasuyoshi, who has turned the cafe into a stylish gallery of traditional Asian art. It serves plunger coffee (¥500), tea, freshly baked cakes and light sandwiches. The cafe is on Sanjō-dōri, across from the Museum of Kyoto (noon to 9.30 pm, closed Wednesday).

Kerala is a competent Indian restaurant on Kawaramachi-dōri at which you can get vegetarian and nonvegetarian set lunches for around ¥900 (dinners will easily be double that).

For more elegant Indian, try *Ashoka* in the Shinkyōgoku arcade (on the 3rd floor at the corner). Here, the excellent lunch special runs to ¥1500 (including tax) and dinners are about double that.

For heaped portions of cheap Italian food, try *Capricciosa*. The food here is no great shakes, but you can't beat the price (plan to spend about ¥900 a head for lunch and double that for dinner).

Behind Daimaru department store, *Daniel's* serves much more authentic Italian food and makes its own pasta. It has a daily lunch special for ¥750 that includes salad.

For ¥1000, the same special includes coffee and dessert. Note that portions are small.

Finally, in a country where 'salad' usually means a tiny helping of shredded cabbage, *Sancho* is a blessing. It serves up grilled chicken, meats and delicious salads on the side, or you can order a salad a la carte. Count on spending around ¥1500 a head.

Central Kyoto

A little out of the way, but good value, is *Obanzai*, which serves an all-you-can-eat vegetarian lunch for ¥840 and dinner for ¥2100 (slightly more on weekends). Most of the ingredients are organically grown – a rarity in this country.

Mukade-ya (☎ 256-7039), or centipede house (closed Wednesday), is in an exquisite *kyō-machiya* (Kyoto town house). For lunch, try the special bentō – two rounds (five small dishes each) of delectable obanzai-style fare for ¥3000. Kaiseki courses start at ¥5000.

Bistrot de Paris is a competent little French restaurant that serves a lunch special (main and coffee) for ¥850 (bigger set meals cost ¥1200 and ¥1600, and you have to pay more for some choices). Dinner courses start at ¥2500.

Eastern Kyoto

Japanese Budget travellers take heart: there are some real bargains to be had in Eastern Kyoto! Kyoto University is there, and the surrounding streets are packed with cheap eateries. The cheapest of these is the *Eating House Hi-Lite*, where you can get filling teishoku for as little as ¥500. Try the *cheezu chicken katsu teishoku* (deep-fried chicken cutlet with cheese) for ¥540; it's a little oily, but how can you complain at these prices? Up the street, *Kuishinbō-no-mise* serves higher-quality versions of the same fare for about ¥750 a set meal, or try the daily specials, which average ¥550. Almost next door, *Tenka-ippin* serves filling rāmen set meals with rice for around ¥700. Again, it's oily but good stuff.

For more salubrious fare, try the great noodle shop *Omen* (closed Thursday), five minutes' walk from Ginkaku-ji. Just say 'omen' and you'll be given your choice of hot or cold noodles, a bowl of soup to dip them in and a plate of vegetables (you put these into the soup along with some sesame seeds). The standard dish here is ¥900, the salads are good, and there's an English menu listing other dishes.

Near Nanzen-ji and Tetsugaku-no-michi is *Hinode*, which serves filling noodle and rice dishes in a pleasant little shop with an English menu. Plain *udon* (thick wheat noodles) is only ¥400 here, but we recommend the *nabeyaki udon* (pot-baked udon in broth) for ¥750. It's closed on Sunday.

Vegetarians should head to *Mikōan*, where there's a daily set lunch of mostly organic Japanese vegetarian fare for ¥800. At dinner a similar set meal goes for ¥1000.

On Sanjō-dōri there are two good yakitori restaurants. *Ichi-ban* (5 pm to midnight, closed Sunday) has an English menu and a friendly young owner to help with ordering. Farther up the street, on the left side just before Higashiyama-dōri, look for the red lanterns outside *Dai-kitchi* (5 pm to 1 am). At both places, expect to pay about ¥3000 a person with beer or sake.

In the Higashiyama area, tucked inside the northern gate of Maruyama-kōen, there's a traditional restaurant called *Imobō Hiranoya Honten* (☎ 561-1603) that specialises in the kind of food that was typical in landlocked Kyoto before the advent of refrigeration. It's called *imobō*, and consists of a type of sweet potato and dried fish. All meals are served in restful, private tatami rooms. An English menu is available and prices for a set meal start at ¥2400.

Next to Nanzen-ji, you'll find *Okutan* (☎ 771-8709), a restaurant inside the luxurious garden of Chōshō-in (10.30 am to 6 pm, closed Thursday). This is a popular place that has specialised in vegetarian temple food for hundreds of years. A course of *yudōfu* (tōfu cooked in a pot) together with vegetable side dishes costs ¥3000.

For an experience you won't soon forget, try *Okariba* (5 to 11 pm, closed Sunday), a restaurant specialising in wild game and good sake. The *inoshishi* (wild boar) barbecue is a good start, and those who prefer not to eat meat can try the fresh *ayu* (sweet river fish). Also, be sure to try the *hoba miso* – thick miso cooked on a giant leaf over a *hibachi* (brazier) into which you dip assorted vegetables. More daring options include bear meat, venison, and even horsemeat sashimi (animal lovers look elsewhere). Expect to spend about ¥3000 a person.

At the bottom of Nijō-dōri, on the eastern side of Kamo-gawa, *Chabana* (5 pm to 4 am), is the classic okonomiyaki joint. If you don't have a favourite, just ask for the mixed okonomiyaki (¥750). It's good for a late-night snack; look for the rotating light outside.

Lastly, if it's a hot summer day and you need a cooling break, try *Gion Koishi* for some typical Japanese summer treats. The speciality here is *Uji kintoki* (¥700), a mountain of shaved ice flavoured with green tea, sweetened milk and sweat beans (it tastes a lot better than it sounds, trust us). Note that this is only available in the summer months.

International A favourite of the local expat community is *Buttercups* (closed Tuesday), a great place for lunch, dinner or a cup of coffee. It serves a wide range of international dishes that average around ¥650. For dessert, try the home-made cakes, pies and cookies. There's also a good selection of books and magazines to read and a computer with Internet access.

On Marutamachi-dōri, near the Kyoto Handicraft Centre, *Zac Baran* is another spot popular with Kyoto ex-pats. It's good for a meal or just a cup of coffee, particularly if you like jazz, which is always playing (sometimes a little too loudly). It serves a variety of spaghetti dishes and has a good daily lunch special. It's open from noon to 4 am.

El Latino is a fun little Mexican joint that serves good tacos, *taquitos* (tortilla wrapped around meat or chicken), guacamole and chips and tasty frozen margaritas. Plan on spending ¥2000 a head here. It's only open in the evening.

Lastly, for the best *gyōza* (Chinese dumplings) in all Japan, try *Sen-mon-ten* (evenings only, closed Sunday) in Gion.

KANSAI REGION

Gyōza and beer are just about the only things on the menu and that seems to suit most folks just fine. Order your gyōza in multiples of 10 (¥460 for 10). Make a dipping sauce from the soy sauce, hot pepper oil and vinegar on the counter.

North-Western Kyoto

Just beside Keifuku Arashiyama station, *Gyātei* offers a ¥1500 all-you-can-eat lunch buffet of healthy obanzai-ryōri (over 30 dishes) from 11 am to 2.30 pm. From 5 to 10.30 pm, Gyātei turns into an izakaya, with a la carte choices from ¥500. It's closed on Monday.

For a light snack, *Nakamura-ya* is a stall that sells skewers of deep-fried pork (¥110) and crispy potato puffs (¥70). They're oily and delicious and are easy to tote with you as you explore. It's diagonally across from Keifuku Arashiyama station.

For a sample of the area's acclaimed tōfu, *Seizansō-dō* (11.30 am to 5 pm, closed Wednesday) serves a great yudōfu set meal for ¥3000.

On the southern side of Togetsu-kyō, *Togetsu-tei* has great riverside views. Try the delightful *take-kago* (bamboo basket) bentō, with locally grown bamboo shoots (¥2700), or tōfu courses starting at ¥3500.

In the Sagano area, on the road up to Adashino Nembutsu-ji, *Bokuseki* (10 am to 5 pm, closed Wednesday) serves a wholesome, all-organic lunch set meal (¥1800).

Back east a bit, in the vicinity of Ninna-ji, *Okara House* (10 am to 4 pm, closed Sunday) serves an organic veggie set lunch for ¥850 and has a good selection of herbal teas.

Across from Kitano-Tenman-gū, *Toyouke-jaya* (10 am to 6.30 pm, closed Thursday) serves a daily yudōfu set lunch for only ¥1000. It's a popular place, so be prepared to wait in line.

Down the street, *Taco Tora* (5 pm to 2 am, closed Monday) is the best place in town to try that great Japanese delight *takoyaki* (round, battered octopus pieces). An order of nine costs ¥600.

Lastly, *A Ri Shan* (5 to 10 pm) is a fun Taiwanese izakaya where you can feast on a wide variety of dim-sum and related fare.

ENTERTAINMENT

Most of Kyoto's cultural entertainment is of an occasional nature, and you'll need to check with the TIC or a magazine like *Kansai Time Out* to find out whether anything interesting coincides with your visit. Regular cultural events are generally geared at the tourist market and tend to be expensive and, naturally, somewhat touristy.

In addition to cultural entertainment, Kyoto has a great variety of bars, clubs and discos, all of which are good places to meet young Japanese.

Traditional Dance & Theatre

Gion Corner (☎ 561-1119) presents shows every evening at 7.40 and 8.40 pm between 1 March and 29 November; it's closed on 16 August. You should think carefully about whether tourist-oriented events of this kind are your scene before forking out the ¥2800 entry charge. While you get a chance to see snippets of the tea ceremony, *koto* (13-stringed instrument played flat on the floor) music, flower arrangement, *gagaku* (court music), *kyōgen* (ancient comic plays), *kyōmai* (Kyoto-style dance) and *bunraku* (puppet play), you will be doing so with a couple of camera- and video-toting tour groups, and the presentation is a little on the tacky side. On top of this, 50 minutes of entertainment for ¥2800 is a bit steep by anyone's standards.

Dance The Miyako Odori (Cherry Blossom Dance) takes place four times a day throughout April at the *Gion Kōbu Kaburen-jō Theatre* (☎ 561-1115). Maiko dress elaborately to perform a sequence of traditional dances in praise of the seasons. The performances start at 12.30, 2, 3.30 and 4.50 pm. The cheapest ticket is ¥1650 (nonreserved on the tatami mat); the ¥4300 ticket includes participation in a tea ceremony.

A similar series of dances, Kamogawa Odori, takes place from 1 to 24 May and from 15 October to 7 November at *Pontochō Kaburen-jō Theatre* (☎ 221-2025). Ticket prices start at ¥1650 (for a nonreserved seat on the 2nd floor). The ¥4300 ticket also includes participation in a tea ceremony.

Performances of *bugaku* (court music and dance) are often held in Kyoto shrines during festival periods. The TIC can provide information on performances.

Kabuki The *Minami-za Theatre* (☎ 561-0160) in Gion is the oldest *kabuki* theatre in Japan. (Kabuki is a form of Japanese theatre based on popular legends and is characterised by elaborate costumes, stylised acting and the use of male actors for all roles.)

The major event of the year is the **Kaomise Festival** (1 to 26 December), which features Japan's finest kabuki actors. Other performances take place infrequently and on an irregular basis. Ticket prices vary widely and those interested in seeing a performance should check with the TIC. The most likely months for performances are May, June and September.

Nō For performances of nō, the main theatres are *Kanze Kaikan Nō Theatre* (☎ 771-6114), *Kongō Nō Stage* (☎ 221-3049) and *Kawamura Nō Stage* (☎ 451-4513). Takigi-Nō is an especially picturesque form of nō performed with lighting from blazing fires. In Kyoto, this takes place in the evenings of 1 and 2 June at Heian-jingū – tickets cost ¥2000 if you pay in advance (ask at the TIC for the location of ticket agencies) or pay ¥3300 at the entrance gate.

Musical Performances Musical performances featuring the *koto*, *shamisen* (three-stringed instrument resembling a banjo with an extended neck) and *shakuhachi* (wind instrument imported from China) are held in Kyoto on an irregular basis. The same is true of gagaku. Check with the TIC to see if any performances are scheduled to be held while you're in town.

Bars
Perhaps the best place to start a Kyoto evening is at *A-Bar*, a raucous student izakaya with a log-cabin interior. There's a big menu to choose from and everything's cheap. When they add up the bill, you'll swear they've undercharged you by half. It's a little tough to find – look for the small

black-and-white sign at the top of a flight of concrete steps above a place called Reims.

Another place we highly recommend is *Sama Sama*, a great little bar/restaurant built with an interior that looks like a cave (but brighter than that image suggests). The Indonesian-born owner turns out great Indonesian food and is happy to chat in English, Japanese or Bahasa Indonesia. Drinks here might be a touch more expensive than at some other spots around town, but it's worth it for the great atmosphere.

Kyoto's most popular gaijin bar is the *Pig & Whistle*, a British-style pub with darts, pint glasses and, of course, fish and chips. The pub's two main drawcards are Guinness on tap and its friendly bilingual manager, Ginzo. This is an excellent place to meet local ex-pats and Japanese, and is also highly recommended.

For a more intimate venue, you can't beat *Zappa* (closed Sunday), a cosy little place that once played host to David Bowie (he's said to have discovered the place by chance and decided to drop in for a drink). The friendly owner, Hiroko-san, serves up savoury South-East Asian fare and a few Japanese tidbits for good measure. Prices are reasonable and the music is groovy (but no Frank Zappa?). It's down a narrow alley; turn south at the wooden torii.

Ing is another one of our favourite spots. This little joint is a good place for cheap bar snacks and drinks, good music and friendly company. It's on the 2nd floor of the Royal building; you'll know you're getting close when you see all the hostesses out trawling for customers on the streets nearby.

If you'd like to try a real old Kyoto izakaya, head to *Shizuka*. Tucked down a tiny little alley near the Shinkyōgoku shopping arcade, this place has a classic old Japanese atmosphere and cheap beer and sake. There's no English menu and that's just as well – the food is truly dreadful (eat before you come).

If you fancy something a little more upscale, try *Malt's Club* in the Gion area. Located in a converted *machi-ya* (Kyoto-style house), this is actually three bars under one roof, each with a different atmosphere.

Simple food is served and both food and drink prices reflect the fancy address.

In addition to these spots, there are lots of other options in the Kiyamachi area. *Rub-a-Dub* is a funky little reggae bar downstairs from the popular Nagahama Rāmen shop. *Bar, Isn't It?* is a large bar popular with young Japanese and foreign men desperately searching for soul mates. Everything on the menu here, drinks and food, is just ¥500. *Teddy's* is part club and part bar. It really gets going late in the evening when the tables are cleared away and the dancing starts (usually to dancehall reggae). On weekend nights there's a cover charge of ¥500. It's on the 7th floor of the Empire building.

On a little alley north of Sanjō-dōri, *Backgammon* is a Kyoto late-night institution. Small, dark and loud, it's a place for serious drinking. Check out the crow's nest drinking area at the top of the ladder – if you don't want to climb down for the next round, staff will send it up to you with a special drink elevator.

Another late-night spot to check out is *Step-Rampo*, a 7th-floor bar overlooking Kawaramachi-dōri. This place doesn't really get going until around 2 am, and it's been known to stay open until way past dawn. It's on Kawaramachi-dōri, one building north of the Hagen Daaz building.

Lastly, if you happen to be in Kyoto in the summer, many hotels and department stores operate rooftop beer gardens with all-you-can-eat and drink deals and good views of the city. The best of these is the *Sunflower Hotel Beer Garden* (☎ 761-9111), at the very eastern end of Marutamachi-dōri. Admission is ¥4000 and includes an all-you-can-eat barbecue and all the beer you can drink. It's a little expensive, but the view from the roof is the best in town.

Clubs

One of the most popular clubs in town is *Metro* (☎ 752-4765). It's part disco, part live house and even hosts the occasional art exhibition. Every night is a different theme (pick up a schedule in Rub-a-Dub – see the earlier Bars section) or check the *Kansai Time Out* for forthcoming events. Some of the best parties are Latin Night, Diamond Night Transvestite Cabaret and Non-hetero-At-The-Metro Night. On weekends there's usually an admission charge of between ¥1500 and ¥2000 (with one drink), while Wednesday and Thursday are usually free. It's inside the exit 2 of the Keihan Marutamachi station.

Lab Tribe is another spot for techno/electronica events. Cover charges vary according to the event. Again, check the *Kansai Time Out* to see if anything's on while you're in town. If nothing special is happening here don't bother going by – it's often quite dead.

Lastly, check out *Teddy's*, listed under Bars, for one more dance spot.

SHOPPING

There are several crafts that are specific to Kyoto. *Kyō-ningyō* are display dolls, *kyō-shikki* is lacquerware with designs formed using gold or silver dust, *kyō-sensu* are ritual fans made from bamboo and Japanese paper, *kyō-yaki* are ceramics with elegant decorations, *zogan* is a damascene technique laying pure gold and silver onto figures engraved on brass, *nishijin-ori* is a special technique of silk textile weaving and *kyō-yūzen* is a form of silk dyeing.

The TIC provides shopping maps and can help you track down specialist shops. *Old Kyoto: A Guide to Traditional Shops, Restaurants & Inns* by Diane Durston is useful for finding unusual traditional items sold (and often produced) by elegant shops with vintage character.

The heart of Kyoto's shopping district is around the intersection of Shijō-dōri and Kawaramachi-dōri. The blocks running north and west of here are packed with all sorts of stores selling both traditional and modern goods. Kyoto's largest department stores (Hankyū, Takashimaya, Daimaru and Fujii Daimaru) are grouped together in this area. The 6th floor of Takashimaya is a good place for deals on pottery and kitchenware.

Japanese Arts & Crafts

Not far from Shijō-dōri, the House of Kajinoha (☎ 341-1419) sells a fabulous variety of handmade *washi* (Japanese paper) for reasonable prices.

In the Teramachi shopping arcade, Nishiharu (☎ 211-2849) is a venerable dealer in wood-block prints. All of the prints are accompanied by English explanations and the owner is happy to take the time to find something you really like. It's on the corner of Sanjō-dōri and Teramachi-dōri.

North of city hall, the area around Teramachi-dōri has a number of classic old Kyoto shops and is pleasant for strolling around and window shopping. Three shops well worth a look are: Ippō-dō (☎ 211-4321), an old-fashioned teashop selling all sorts of tea; Kakimoto (☎ 211-3481), a shop dealing in exquisite washi; and Unsodo (☎ 231-3613), a shop specialising in woodblock prints, open from 9 am to 5.30 pm and closed on Thursday.

In eastern Kyoto, the paved streets of Ninnen-zaka and Sannen-zaka (close to Kiyomizu-dera) are renowned for their crafts and antiques. You'll also find a lot of pottery shops on Gojō-dōri, between Kawabata-dōri and Higashiōji-dōri.

Across from the main gate of Higashi Hongan-ji, Kungyoku-dō (☎ 371-0162) is a shop that has dealt in incense, herbs, spices and fine aromatic wood (which is burnt like incense) for four centuries. It's a haven for the olfactory senses and a great place to shop for unique souvenirs. It's closed on the first and third Sunday of each month.

If you want to do all your shopping under one roof, the following places offer a wide selection of Kyoto handicrafts. *Kyoto Craft Centre* (☎ 561-9660), near Maruyama-kōen, exhibits and sells handicrafts and is open from 10 am to 6 pm daily except Wednesday. The *Kyoto Handicraft Centre* (☎ 761-5080), just north of the Heian-jingū, is a huge cooperative that sells, demonstrates and exhibits crafts and is open from 9.30 am to 6 pm (wood-block prints are a good buy here).

Food & Kitchen Utensils
Nishiki-kōji, in the centre of town, is Kyoto's most fascinating food market. See the entry in the Central Kyoto section for

details on this market. If you do choose to visit, be sure to stop into the knife shop Aritsugu (☎ 221-1091) near the eastern end of the market. Here, you can find some of the best kitchen knives available in the world, as well as a variety of other kitchenware.

For an even more impressive display of foodstuffs, check out the basements of any of the big department stores on Shijō-dōri (perhaps Daimaru has the largest selection). It's difficult to believe the variety of food on display, as well as some of the prices (check out the ¥10,000 melons or the Kōbe beef, for example). In these basement food emporiums, you really get a sense of the wealth of modern Japan.

Antiques
The place to look for antiques in Kyoto is Shinmonzen-dōri, in Gion. The street is lined with great old shops, many of them specialising in one thing or another (furniture, pottery, scrolls, prints etc). You can easily spend an afternoon strolling from shop to shop here, but be warned: if something strikes your fancy you're going to have to break out the credit card – prices here are steep!

For antiques with an explanation in English, try Golden Years (☎ 721-8178), an antique shop north of Ginkaku-ji on Mikake-dōri, owned and operated by a Kiwi-expat Paul Rivers (noon to 7 pm). There's an interesting range of furniture, pottery and bric-a-brac to choose from, and prices are reasonable. From the corner of Kita Shirakawa-dōri and Mikake-dōri, head uphill east to the first traffic light: It's on the north-eastern corner, next to a barber shop.

Markets
If you're in town when one of the following markets is on, by all means go! Markets are the best places to find antiques and bric-a-brac at reasonable prices and are the only places in Japan where you can actually bargain for a better price. What's more, they're a lot of fun.

On the 21st of each month, Kōbō-san is held at Tō-ji to commemorate the death of Kōbō Taishi (Kūkai), who in 823 was appointed abbot of the temple.

Another major market, Tenjin-san, is held on the 25th of each month at Kitano Tenman-gū, marking the day of the birth (and, coincidentally, the death) of the Heian-era statesman Sugawara Michizane (845–903).

For each of these huge markets, the January (Hatsu-Kōbō and Hatsu-Tenjin) and December (Shimai-Kōbō and Shimai-Tenjin) gatherings are by far the biggest and most lively.

If you aren't in Kyoto on the 21st, there's also a regular antiques fair at Tō-ji on the first Sunday of each month and a major annual fair there from 1 to 4 January.

GETTING THERE & AWAY
Air

Kyoto is served by Osaka Itami airport, which handles mostly domestic traffic, and the new Kansai international airport (KIX), which handles most international flights. There are frequent flights between Tokyo and Osaka – flight time is about 70 minutes – but unless you're very lucky with airport connections you'd probably find it as quick and more convenient to take the *shinkansen* (bullet trains). There are ample connections to and from both airports, though the trip to Kansai international airport can be both expensive and time consuming.

Train

Shinkansen All prices listed are one way unless otherwise indicated. Kyoto is on the Tōkaidō/San-yō shinkansen line (to/from Tokyo – Hikari shinkansen, ¥13,220, two hours 50 minutes; to/from Nagoya – Hikari shinkansen, ¥5440, 44 minutes; to/from Osaka – Hikari shinkansen, ¥1380, 15 minutes; to/from Hakata – Hikari shinkansen, ¥15,210, three hours 40 minutes). Other stops on this line include Hiroshima, Okayama Kōbe and Yokohama.

Osaka The fastest train other than shinkansen (see the earlier section) between JR Kyoto station and Osaka is the JR *shinkaisoku* (special rapid train), which takes 29 minutes (¥540). In Osaka, the train stops at both Shin-Osaka and Osaka stations.

There is also the cheaper private Hankyū line, which runs between Hankyū Kawaramachi, Karasuma and Ōmiya stations in Kyoto and Hankyū Umeda station in Osaka (between Umeda and Kawaramachi – *tokkyū*, or limited express, ¥390, 40 minutes).

Alternatively, you can take the Keihan main line between Sanjō, Shijō or Shichijō stations in Kyoto and Keihan Yodoyabashi station in Osaka (to/from Sanjō – tokkyū, ¥400, 45 minutes). Yodoyabashi is on the Midō-suji subway line.

Nara Unless you have a Japan Rail Pass, the best option is the Kintetsu line (sometimes written in English as the Kinki Nippon railway) linking Kyoto (Kintetsu Kyoto station, in the main Kyoto station building) and Nara (Kintetsu Nara station). There are direct limited express trains (¥1110, 35 minutes) and ordinary express trains, which may require a change at Saidai-ji (¥610, 45 minutes).

The JR Nara line connects JR Kyoto station with JR Nara station (shinkaisoku, ¥690, 46 minutes) but departures are often few and far between.

Tokyo The shinkansen line has the fastest and most frequent rail links (see the earlier Shinkansen section). The journey can also be done by a series of regular express trains, but keep in mind that it takes around eight hours and involves at least two (often three or four) changes along the way. The fare is ¥7980. Get the staff at the ticket counter to write down the exact details of each transfer for you when you buy your ticket.

Bus

The overnight bus (JR Dream Kyoto Go) runs between Tokyo station (Yaesu-guchi long-distance bus stop) and JR Kyoto station (the long-distance bus stop is adjacent to the city bus terminal).

The trip takes about eight hours and there are usually two departures in either direction, at 10 and 11 pm. The fare is ¥8180/14,480 one-way/return. You should be able to grab some sleep in the reclining seats. If you find sleep a bit of a struggle, you can console yourself with the thought that you

The famed Golden Temple, Kinkaku-ji, has had a tumultuous history since it was first built in 1597.

FRANK CARTER

Dragon fountain at Kiyomizu-dera, Kyoto

MARTIN MOOS

FRANK CARTER

A Buddhist priest, Kyoto

Daitoku-ji, the centre of all things Zen, Kyoto.

FRANK CARTER

Ryōan-ji, Kyoto

Kyoto's Nijō-jō was built in 1603 by Tokugawa Ieyasu.

A traditional leisure boat at Arashiyama, an area that is wildly popular with local tourists.

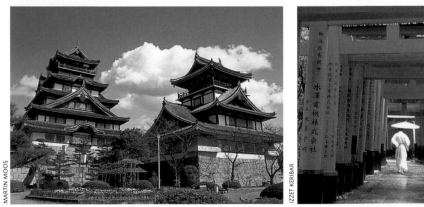

The castle, Fushimi-Momoyama-jō in southern Kyoto.

Fushimi-Imari shrine, Kansai

are saving on accommodation and will be arriving at the crack of dawn to make good use of the day. There is a similar service to/from Shinjuku station's Shin-minami-guchi in Tokyo.

Other JR bus possibilities include (fares are given as one-way/return) Kanazawa (¥4060/7310), Tottori (¥3870/6970), Hiroshima (¥6620/11,720), Nagasaki (¥11,310/20,380) and Kumamoto (¥10,800/19,440).

Hitching

Although we never recommend it, for long-distance hitching, head for the Kyoto-Minami Interchange of the Meishin Expressway, about 4km south of JR Kyoto station. Take the No 19 bus from JR Kyoto station and get off when you reach the Meishin Expressway signs. From here you can hitch east towards Tokyo or west to southern Japan.

GETTING AROUND
To/From the Airport

Osaka Itami Airport There are frequent limousine buses between Osaka Itami airport and JR Kyoto station (the Kyoto station airport bus stop is opposite the southern side of the station, in front of Avanti department store). Buses also run between the airport and various hotels around town, but on a less regular basis (check with your hotel). The journey should take around 55 minutes and the cost is ¥1370. Be sure to allow extra time in case of traffic.

Kansai International Airport (KIX) The fastest, most convenient way to travel between KIX and Kyoto is on the special Haruka airport express, which makes the trip in about 75 minutes. Most seats are reserved (¥3490) but there are usually two cars on each train with unreserved seats (¥2980). Open seats are almost always available, so you don't have to purchase tickets in advance. First and last departures from Kyoto to KIX are 5.45 am and 8.16 pm; first and last departures from KIX to Kyoto are 6.29 am and 10.18 pm.

If you have time to spare, you can save some money by taking the *kanku kaisoku* (Kansai airport express) between the airport

and Osaka station and taking a regular shinkaisoku to/from Kyoto. The total journey by this method takes about 90 minutes with good connections and costs ¥1700, making it the cheapest option.

It's also possible to go by limousine bus between Kyoto and KIX (¥2300, about two hours). In Kyoto, the bus departs from the same spot as the Itami-bound bus (see Osaka Itami opposite).

Remember that there is a departure tax at KIX of ¥2650, which must be paid in yen. It's a good way to get rid of that last loose change (and also a good way to get stuck if you're not prepared for it).

Bus

Kyoto has an intricate bus network that is an efficient way to get around at moderate cost. Many of the bus routes used by foreign visitors have announcements in English. The core timetable for buses is between 7 am and 9 pm, though a few run earlier or later.

The bus terminal at JR Kyoto station is on the northern side of the station and has three main departure bays (departure points are indicated by the letter of the bay and number of the bus stand within that bay).

The TIC's *Kyoto Transportation Guide* is a good map of the city's main bus lines, with a detailed explanation of the routes and a Japanese/English communication guide on the reverse side.

Bus stops throughout the city usually display a map of bus stops in the vicinity on the top section. On the bottom section there's a timetable for the buses serving that stop. Unfortunately, most of this information is written in Japanese, and those who don't speak the language will simply have to ask locals waiting at the stop for help.

Entry to the bus is usually through the back door and exit is via the front door. Innercity buses charge a flat fare (¥220), which you drop into the clear plastic receptacle on top of the machine next to the driver. The machine gives change for ¥100 and ¥500 coins or ¥1000 notes, or you can ask the driver.

On buses serving the outer areas, you take a *seiri-ken* (numbered ticket) when entering. When you leave, an electronic board

KANSAI REGION

above the driver displays the fare corresponding to your ticket number.

To save time and money, you can buy a *kaisū-ken* (book of five tickets) for ¥1000 at bus centres or from the driver.

An *ichinichi jōsha-ken* is a one-day pass valid for unlimited travel on city buses and available for ¥700 at bus centres and subway stations. A similar ticket that also allows for unlimited use of the subways costs ¥1200. A *futsuka jōshā-ken* (two-day pass) is also available and costs ¥2000. The passes can be picked up in subway stations and the bus ticket centre in front of the northern side of JR Kyoto station.

When heading for locations outside the city centre, be careful which bus you board. Kyoto city buses are green, Kyoto buses are tan and Keihan buses are red and white.

Subway

The quickest way to travel between the north and the south of the city is to take the Karasuma subway line, which operates from 5.30 am to 11.30 pm. The minimum fare is ¥200.

There's also the new Tōzai subway line, which runs east/west across the city, from Daigo station in the east to Nijō station in the west, stopping at Sanjō-Keihan en route.

Taxi

Kyoto is well-endowed with taxis. Fares start at ¥630 for the first 2km. The exception is MK Taxis (☎ 0721-2237), which start at ¥580. If you have a choice, always take an MK Taxi – in addition to being cheaper, this company's cars are driven by scrupulously polite drivers who can often speak a bit of English.

MK Taxi also provides tours of the city with English-speaking drivers. For a group of up to four people, prices start at ¥12,620 for a three-hour tour. Another company offering a similar service is Kyōren Taxi Service (☎ 672-5111).

Cycling

Kyoto is a great city to explore on a bicycle; with the exception of outlying areas, it's mostly flat and there is a new bike path running the length of Kamo-gawa.

Near Keihan Sanjō station, Kitazawa Bicycle Shop (☎ 771-2272) rents bicycles for ¥200 per hour and ¥1000 per day, with discounts for rentals for periods of more than three days. A passport is necessary for rental, though one will suffice for a group. It's open from 8 am to 5 pm. Nearby, Rental Cycle Yasumoto (☎ 751-0595) has similar rates. Both places are a short walk north of Keihan Sanjō on the eastern side of Kawabata-dōri.

Nippon Rent-a-Cycle is near Nishiōji station, one stop from JR Kyoto station. Ask for a map to the store at the TIC. Expect rental rates of around ¥1100 a day, but different rates apply depending on the kind of bicycle you choose. Both Higashiyama and Utano youth hostels rent bicycles.

Shiga-ken 滋賀県

Just across the Higashiyama mountains from Kyoto is Shiga-ken, a small prefecture dominated by Biwa-ko, Japan's largest freshwater lake. The prefecture has a variety of attractions that are easily visited as day trips from Kyoto. Ōtsu and Hikone are the major sightseeing centres. Hiei-zan and Enryaku-ji are covered under Northern Kyoto in the earlier Kyoto section of this chapter.

JNTO publishes a leaflet entitled *Lake Biwa, Ōtsu & Hikone*, which has useful maps and concise information. The Kyoto TIC has more detailed information on transport, sights and events in this region.

ŌTSU 大津
☎ 077 • pop 286,000

Ōtsu has developed from a 7th-century imperial residence (the city was capital of Japan for just five years) into a lake port and major post station on the Tōkaidō highway between eastern and western Japan. It is now the capital of Shiga-ken.

The information office (☎ 522-3830) at JR Ōtsu station is open from 8.45 am to 5.25 pm. Some English is spoken here, and it has an excellent free map of the area entitled *Biwako Otsu Guide Map*.

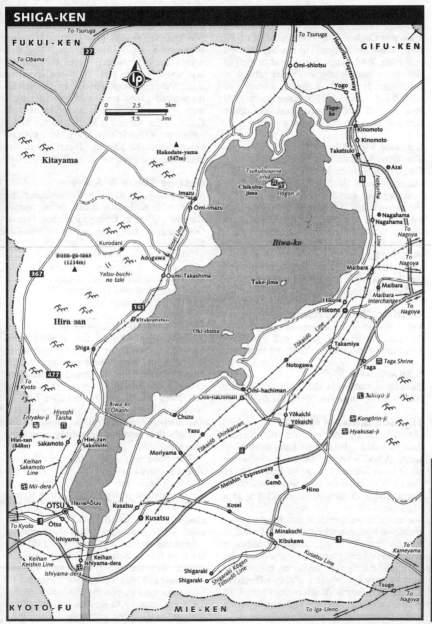

SHIGA-KEN

FUKUI-KEN

To Tsuruga

To Obama

27

GIFU-KEN

To Tsuruga

Hokuriku Expressway

Ōmi-shiotsu

Yogo

Yogo-ko

Kinomoto
Kinomoto

Takatsuki

Hakodate-yama
(547m)

Kitayama

Azai

Tsukubusuma-jinja

Chikubu-jima

Hōgon-ji

Imazu

Ōmi-imazu

Nagahama
Nagahama
To Nagoya

Biwa-ko

Kurodani

Kosei Line

Buna-ga-take
(1214m)

Adngawa

Yatsu-buchi-no taki

To Nagoya

367

Ōumi-Takashima

Take-jima

Maibara

Maibara

Maibara interchange
To Nagoya

161

Hikone
Hikone

Hira-san

Kitakomatsu

Oki-shima

Shiga

Tōkaidō Line

Takamiya

To Kyoto

477

Notogawa

Taga Taga Shrine

Biwa-ko Ōhashi

Ōmi-hachiman Ōmi-hachiman

Saimyō-ji

Chuzu

Kongōrin-ji

Eiryaku-ji

Hiyoshi Taisha

Hiei-zan Sakamoto

Yōkaichi
Yōkaichi

Hyakusai-ji

Hiei-zan
(848m)

Sakamoto

Yasu

Tōkaidō Shinkansen

Keihan Sakamoto Line

Mii-dera

Moriyama

Meishin Expressway

Gamō

Hino

8

ŌTSU

Hama-Ōtsu

Kusatsu

Kosei

To Kyoto

1

Ōtsu

Kusatsu

Ishiyama

Minakuchi

Kibukawa

To Kameyama

Keihan Keishin Line

Keihan Ishiyama-dera

Ishiyama-dera

Kusatsu Line

1

Shigaraki

Shigaraki

Shigaraki Kōgen Tetsudō Line

Tsuge

To Nagoya

KYOTO-FU

MIE-KEN

To Iga-Ueno

0   2.5   5km
0   1.5   3mi

Mii-dera 三井寺

Mii-dera (¥450, 8 am to 5 pm), formally known as Onjō-ji, is a short walk from Keihan Hama-Ōtsu station. The temple, founded in the late 7th century, is the head branch of the Jimon branch of the Tendai school of Buddhism. It started its days as a branch of Enryaku-ji on Hiei-zan, but later the two fell into conflict, and Mii-dera was repeatedly razed by Enryaku-ji's warrior monks.

Special Events

The Ōtsu Matsuri takes place on 7 and 8 October at Tenson-jinja, close to JR Ōtsu station. Ornate floats are displayed on the first day and paraded around the town on the second day. If you're in town on 8 August, be sure to catch the Ōtsu Dai Hanabi Taikai (Ōtsu Grand Fireworks Festival), which starts at dusk. The best spots to watch are along the waterfront near Keihan Hama-Ōtsu station. But be forewarned: trains to and from Kyoto are packed for hours before and after the event.

Getting There & Away

From Kyoto you can either take the JR Tōkaidō line from JR Kyoto station to Keihan Hama-Ōtsu station (¥190, 10 minutes).

SAKAMOTO 坂本

Sakamoto station is the main station for access from Shiga-ken to Enryaku-ji.

Hiyoshi-taisha 日吉大社

If you fancy a detour on your visit to Hiei-zan, Hiyoshi-taisha, also known as Hie-taisha (¥300, 9 am to 5 pm), is a 15-minute walk from Sakamoto station. Dedicated to the deity of Hiei-zan, the shrine is closely connected with Enryaku-ji. Displayed in a separate hall are the *mikoshi* (portable shrines) that were carried into Kyoto by the monks of Hiei-zan whenever they wished to make demands of the emperor. Since it would have been gross sacrilege to harm the sacred shrines, this tactic of taking the shrines hostage proved highly effective. During the Sannō Matsuri on 13 and 14 April, there are mikoshi fighting festivals and a procession of mikoshi on boats.

Places to Eat

For lunch in Sakamoto, try *Tsuruki Soba*, which serves *tennan soba* (shrimp tempura soba) for ¥930. To find it, head west (towards the mountains) out of the station, take the first left, and you'll see it on the right. Alternatively, for a cup of *matcha* (powdered green tea) in lovely surroundings, try the teahouse in Kyū-Chikurin-in. Entry to the garden is ¥310 and tea and a sweet are ¥350. It's on the main road just before Hiyoshi Taisha (described in the preceding section).

Getting There & Away

Sakamoto is best reached by taking the Kyoto Tōzai line subway from Sanjō-Keihan station in Kyoto to Keihan Hama-Ōtsu station; change there to a Keihan-line Sakamoto-bound futsū. The total fare is ¥590, and with good connections the trip takes about 40 minutes. You can also take the JR line to the Hiei-zan Sakamoto station – be careful to take the Kosei (West Lake) line (¥320, 20 minutes).

ISHIYAMA-DERA 石山寺

This temple (¥400, 8 am to 4.45 pm), founded in the 8th century, now belongs to the Shingon sect. The room next to the Hondō (Main Hall) is famed as the place where Lady Murasaki wrote *The Tale of the Genji*. Local tourist literature masterfully hedges its bets with the statement that *The Tale of the Genji* is 'perhaps the world's first novel and certainly one of the longest'.

The temple is a 10-minute walk from Keihan Ishiyama-dera station. Take the Kyoto Tōzai line subway from Sanjō-Keihan station in Kyoto to Keihan Hama-Ōtsu and change there to a Keihan line Ishiyama-dera-bound futsū (the whole trip costs ¥520 and takes about 37 minutes). Alternatively, take the JR Tōkaidō line from JR Kyoto station to JR Ishiyama-dera station. *Kaisoku* (rapid) and futsū trains run this route (¥230, 10 minutes). Switch at JR Ishiyama-dera station to the Keihan line for the short journey to Keihan Ishiyama-dera station (¥160, three minutes).

KANSAI REGION

HIKONE 彦根
☎ 0749 • pop 106,000
Hikone is the second-largest city in the prefecture and of special interest to visitors for its castle, which dominates the town.

Orientation & Information
There is a good tourist information office (☎ 22-2954), on your left as you leave the station, with helpful maps and literature. The *Street Map & Guide to Hikone* has a map on one side and a suggested one-day bicycle tour of Hikone's sights on the back.

The castle is straight up the street from the station – about a 10-minute walk away. There's another tourist office (Hikone Sightseeing Association Office) just before the entrance to the castle grounds.

Hikone-jō 彦根城
This castle (¥500, 8.30 am to 5 pm) was completed in 1622 by the Ii family, who ruled as *daimyō* (feudal lords) over Hikone. It is rightly considered one of the finest remaining castles in Japan. Much of it is original, and you can get a great view across the lake from the upper storeys. The castle is surrounded by more than 1000 cherry trees, making it a popular spot for spring-time hanami activities.

After visiting the castle, don't miss nearby Genkyū-en, a lovely Chinese influenced garden that was completed in 1677. Buy yourself a bag of fish food for ¥20 at the gate to feed the bloated ornamental carp in the garden's pond. Entry to this garden is included in the admission ticket for the castle (opening hours here are the same as for the castle). There's a teahouse in the garden where ¥500 gets you a cup of matcha and a sweet to enjoy as you gaze over the scenery.

Admission to the castle includes entry to Genkyū-en. Remember to hang onto your ticket if you plan to visit the garden. English-language guided tours of the castle are available for groups of five or more – call ☎ 22-2742 a week in advance to book.

Next to the main gate of the castle is Hikone-jō Museum (¥500, 9 am to 5 pm). Items on display belonged to the Ii family and include armour, nō costumes, pottery and calligraphy.

Other Attractions
If you have more time in Hikone, you can follow the cycling route in the *Street Map & Guide to Hikone*. The route passes through the old town to the west of the castle, then south-west via Ichiba (Market Street) to Kawaramachi. There you can take a look at a candlemaker's shop (this is also the bar and nightlife district of Hikone). The route then crosses to the other side of Seri-gawa.

From there, you can cross the town and visit a couple of Zen temples in the southeast. The most interesting is Ryōtan-ji (¥300, 9 am to 5 pm), which has a fine Zen garden.

Special Events
Hikone-jō Matsuri takes place at the castle during the first three days in November. Children dress up in the costume of feudal lords and parade around the area.

Getting There & Away
Hikone is less than an hour (shinkaisoku, ¥1110) from Kyoto on the JR Tōkaidō line. If you take the shinkansen, it is best to ride from Kyoto to Maibara (25 minutes) and then backtrack from there on the JR Tōkaidō line to Hikone (¥180, five minutes). Maibara is a major rail junction, the meeting place of the JR Tōkaidō, Hokuriku and Tōkaidō shinkansen lines. By shinkaisoku (special rapid train), Maibara is 52 minutes from Kyoto on the JR Tōkaidō line (¥1110).

NAGAHAMA 長浜
☎ 0749
Nagahama is interesting for its old machiya and *kura* (storehouses), which are built in a distinctly different style than those of Kyoto. Most of these can be found in the streets 10 minutes' walk north-west of the station. Some of the old buildings have been converted into atmospheric shops and restaurants and are worth popping into as your explore the area. However, you'll want to avoid the overly gentrified main street of the area, Hokkoku-kaidō.

If you're in the area from 14 to 16 April, check out the Nagahama Hikiyama Matsuri, in which costumed children perform

Hikiyama kyōgen (comic drama) on top of a dozen festival floats decked out with elaborate ornamentation.

Places to Stay & Eat
The *Kokumin-shukusha Hōkō-sō (☎ 62-0144)* has per-person rates of ¥4200. It's five minutes' walk west of the station in Hōkōen Park (*kokumin-shukusha* are people's lodges – cheap accommodation.) The old-style *shokudō* (dining room) *Tora-ya* is the best place for cheap eats in town, with such things as *kitsune donburi* (rice with pieces of fried tōfu) for only ¥350. It is a three-minute walk east of the station on the right side of Eki-mae-dōri. It's closed on Thursday.

Getting There & Away
Nagahama is a 10-minute ride north of Maibara on the JR Hokuriku line (shinkaisoku, ¥190 from Maibara, 10 minutes). See the Hikone Getting There & Away section for transport details to Maibara.

Osaka 大阪

☎ 06 • pop 2.48 million
Osaka is the working heart of Kansai. Famous for its down-to-earth citizens and hearty cuisine, Osaka combines a few historical and cultural attractions with all the delights of a modern Japanese city. Indeed, Osaka is surpassed only by Tokyo as a showcase of the Japanese urban phenomenon.

This isn't to say that Osaka is an attractive city; almost bombed flat in WWII, it appears an endless expanse of concrete boxes punctuated by pachinko parlours and elevated highways. But the city somehow manages to rise above this and exert a peculiar charm. And by night, the city really comes into its own. This is when all those drab streets and alleys come alive with flashing neon, beckoning residents and travellers alike with promises of tasty food and good times.

Osaka's highlights include Osaka-jō and its surrounding park, Osaka Aquarium with its two resident whale sharks, and the *Blade Runner* nightscapes of the Dōtombori area.

But Osaka has more to offer than its specific sights; like Tokyo, Osaka is a city to be experienced in its totality, and casual strolls are likely to be just as rewarding as structured sightseeing tours.

HISTORY
Osaka has been a major port and mercantile centre from the beginning of Japan's recorded history. It was also briefly the first capital of Japan (before the establishment of a permanent capital at Nara). During its early days, Osaka was Japan's centre for trade with Korea and China, a role which it shares today with Kōbe and Yokohama.

In the late 16th century, Osaka rose to prominence when Toyotomi Hideyoshi, having unified all of Japan, chose Osaka as the site for his castle. Merchants set up around the castle and the city quickly grew into a busy economic centre. This development was further encouraged by the Tokugawa shogunate, which adopted a hands-off approach to the city, allowing merchants to prosper unmolested by government interference.

In the modern period, Tokyo has usurped Osaka's position as economic centre of Japan, and most of the companies formerly headquartered in Osaka have moved east. Nonetheless, Osaka remains an economic powerhouse, and the prefecture has recorded a GDP bigger than the individual GDPs of all but eight countries in the world in the past several years. However, the city has been hard hit by Japan's ongoing recession, and homeless people are becoming increasingly visible, particularly in Osaka-jō-kōen and around Tennō-ji station.

ORIENTATION
Osaka is usually divided into two areas: Kita and Minami. Kita (Japanese for 'north') is the city's main business and administrative centre and contains two of its biggest train stations, JR Osaka and Hankyū Umeda.

Minami (Japanese for 'south') is the city's entertainment district and contains the bustling shopping and nightlife zones of Namba and Shinsaibashi. It's also home to two major train stations, JR Namba and Nankai Namba stations.

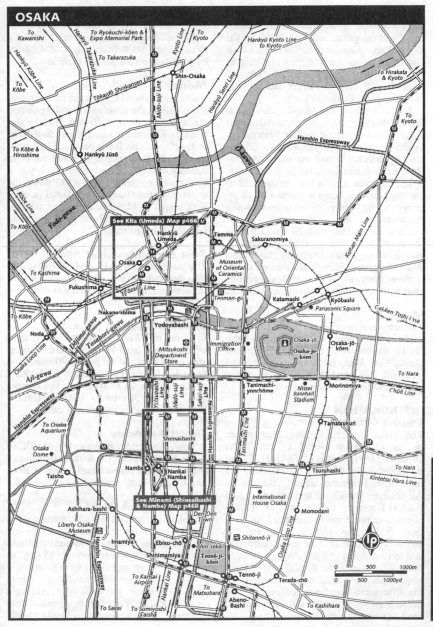

OSAKA

To Kawanishi
To Ryokuchi-kōen &
Expo Memorial Park
To Kyoto
Hankyū Kyoto Line
to Kyoto
Hankyū Takarazuka Line
Kyoto Line
To Takarazuka
Tōkaidō Shinkansen Line
Hankyū Senri Line
Shin-Osaka
To Hirakata
& Kyoto
Hankyū Kōbe Line
To Kōbe
Mido-suji Line
To Kyoto
Hanshin Expressway
To Kōbe &
Hiroshima
Hankyū Jūsō
Kōsei Line
To Kōbe
Yodo-gawa
Ōkawa
See Kita (Umeda) Map p466
To Kashima
Hankyū Umeda
Temma
Sakuranomiya
Osaka
Museum of Oriental Ceramics
Keihan Main Line
To Kōbe
Fukushima
Tōzai Line
Tenman-gū
Katamachi
Kyōbashi
Gakken Toshi Line
Nakano-shima
Panasonic Square
Dōjima-gawa
Tosabori-gawa
Yodoyabashi
Noda
Osaka Loop Line
Mitsukoshi Department Store
Immigration Office
Osaka-jō
Osaka-jō-kōen
Ajī-gawa
Tanimachi-yonchōme
Nissei Baseball Stadium
Morinomiya
To Nara
Chūō Line
Hanshin Expressway
Yotsubashi Line
Mido-suji Line
Sakai-suji Line
Tamatsukuri
To Osaka Aquarium
Hanshin Expressway
Shinsaibashi
Tanimachi Line
To Nara
Osaka Dome
Namba
Nankai Namba
Tsuruhashi
Kintetsu Nara Line
Taisho
International House Osaka
Ashihara-bashi
See Minami (Shinsaibashi & Namba) Map p468
Den-Den Town
Momodani
Liberty Osaka Museum
Imamiya
Ebisu-chō
Shitennō-ji
Shin-sekai
Osaka Loop Line
Shinimamiya
Tennō-ji-kōen
Nankai Line
To Kansai Airport
Tennō-ji
Terada-chō
To Matsubara
Abeno-Bashi
To Sakai
To Sumiyoshi Taisha
To Kashihara

0   500   1000m
0   500   1000yd

KANSAI REGION

The dividing line between Kita and Minami is formed by two rivers, Dōjima-gawa and Tosabori-gawa, between which you'll find Nakano-shima, a peaceful green island that is home to the Museum of Oriental Ceramics. About 1km east of Nakano-shima you'll find Osaka-jō and its surrounding park, Osaka-jō-kōen.

To the south of the Minami area you'll find another group of sights clustered around Tennō-ji station. These include Shitennō-ji, Tennō-ji-kōen, Den-Den Town (the electronics neighbourhood) and the seriously low-rent entertainment district of Shin-Sekai.

The bay area, Osaka-wan, to the west of the city centre, is home to another set of attractions, including the excellent Osaka Aquarium.

Keep in mind that while JR Osaka station is centrally located in the Kita area, if you're coming from Tokyo by shinkansen you will arrive at Shin-Osaka station, which is three stops (about 10 minutes) north of Osaka station on the Midō-suji subway line.

Maps
The information offices (see the following section) have two excellent maps of the Osaka region, *Your Guide to Osaka* and *Osaka City Map*. Both have subway and transport maps and detailed insets of the city's most important areas.

INFORMATION
Tourist Offices
The Osaka Tourist Association has offices in Shin-Osaka (☎ 6305-3311), in Osaka (☎ 6345-2189), Namba (☎ 6643-2125) and in Tennō-ji (☎ 6774-3077) stations, the main office being the one in Osaka station. All are open from 8 am to 8 pm and closed from 31 December to 3 January. Many travellers have problems finding the tourist office in Osaka station. It's in the south-eastern corner of the station complex, and to find it you should take the Midōsuji (east) exit. Osaka and Kansai international airports also have information counters. All the offices can help book accommodation, but to avail yourself of this service you will have to visit the office in person.

Immigration Office
The Osaka immigration office (☎ 6941-0771) is the main one for the Kansai region and is a three-minute walk from exit 3 of Temma-bashi station on the Keihan main line.

Money
There are several banks in the underground malls and on the streets surrounding Osaka, Hankyū Umeda and Nankai Namba stations. In Kita, there's an international ATM in the Sumitomo Bank on the B1 floor of Hankyū Umeda station (it's not far from subway exit 1). Up on street level, you'll find another international ATM down the street from the Osaka Hilton Hotel (see the Kita map). In Minami, there's an international ATM at the Citibank in Shinsaibashi (see the Minami map).

Post & Communications
The main post office (☎ 6347-8034) is outside the southern side of Osaka station. For fax services, try the front desks of major hotels or almost any convenience store.

Email & Internet Access
In Kita, try Web House (☎ 6367-9555), which is open from 11 am to 9 pm; membership is ¥500, while the fee for 30 minutes is ¥600. In Minami, try Kinko's (☎ 6245-1922), which is open 24 hours a day and charges ¥500 for every 30 minutes. The tourist offices have lists of additional Internet cafes.

Travel Agencies
A'cross Travellers Bureau (☎ 6345-0150) in the Kita area (see the Kita map) is one of the best and cheapest travel agents in town and English speakers are always on hand.

Books & Bookshops
Kinokuniya, inside Hankyū Umeda station, has the best selection of foreign books and magazines in Osaka. In Minami, Athens bookshop has a decent selection of English books and magazines on its 4th floor.

For up-to-date information on events happening while you're in town, pick up a copy of *Kansai Time Out* magazine. Those planning to set up house in Osaka should also pick up a copy of the *Kansai Flea Market*, a small monthly publication that has information on accommodation, employment and nightlife. Both are available at the bookshops listed in this section. Also worth picking up at the information offices is *Meet Osaka*, a pocket-sized reference guide to forthcoming events and festivals.

CENTRAL OSAKA
Osaka-jō 大阪城
This is Osaka's most popular attraction (¥500, 9 am to 5 pm) but unfortunately it is merely a 1931 concrete reconstruction of the original, which was completed in 1583. It was built as a display of power by Toyotomi Hideyoshi after he achieved his goal of unifying Japan. One hundred thousand workers toiled for three years to construct an 'impregnable' granite castle. However, it was destroyed just 32 years later, in 1615, by the armies of Tokugawa Ieyasu.

Within 10 years the castle had been rebuilt by the Tokugawa forces, but it was to suffer a further calamity when another generation of Tokugawas razed it to the ground rather than let it fall to the forces of the Meiji Restoration in 1868.

Refurbished at great cost in 1997, today's castle has a decidedly modern look (to see a more authentic castle, head west to Himeji-jō). The interior of the castle houses a museum of Toyotomi Hideyoshi memorabilia as well as displays relating the history of the castle. While these are of marginal interest, the 8th floor does provide a good view over Osaka.

On Sundays, check out the live music scene along the road leading from Osaka-jō-kōen station (on the JR Osaka Loop line) to Osaka-jō Hall. Here, local bands perform for their adoring teenage fans and bemused older folks who happen to wander by. It's noisy, and most of the music is pretty bad, but for people-watching, it can't be beaten. The entertainment usually starts at noon and ends at 6 pm.

The Ōte-mon, the gate that serves as the main entrance to the park, is a 10-minute walk north-east of Tanimachi-yonchōme station on the Chūō and Tanimachi subway lines. You can also take the Osaka Loop line, get off at Osaka-jō-kōen station and enter through the back of the castle.

Nakano-Shima 中之島
Sandwiched between Dōjima-gawa and Tosabori-gawa, this island is a pleasant oasis of green in the midst of Osaka's unrelenting grey. It's also home to Osaka City Hall, the Museum of Oriental Ceramics (see that section) and Nakano-shima-kōen. The latter, on the eastern end of the island, is a good place for an afternoon stroll or picnic lunch.

Museum of Oriental Ceramics 東洋陶磁美術館
With more than 1300 exhibits, this museum (¥500, 9.30 am to 5 pm, closed Monday) has one of the finest collections of Chinese and Korean ceramics in the world.

To get to the museum, go to Yodoyabashi station on either the Midō-suji line or the Keihan line (different stations). Walk north to the river and cross to Nakano-shima. Turn right, pass the city hall on your left, bear left with the road, and the museum is on the left.

KITA AREA キタ
By day, Osaka's centre of gravity is the Kita area. While Kita doesn't have any great attractions to detain the traveller, it does have a few good department stores, lots of places to eat and the Umeda Sky building.

Umeda Sky Building 梅田スカイビル
Just north-west of Osaka station, the Umeda Sky building is Osaka's most dramatic piece of modern architecture. The twin-tower complex looks like a space-age version of Paris' Arc De Triomphe. Residents of Osaka are sharply divided about its appearance: some love its futuristic look while others find it an eyesore. What is certain is that the view from the top on a clear day or evening is impressive.

There are two observation galleries, an outdoor one on the roof and an indoor one on the floor below. Getting to the top is half the fun as you take a glassed-in escalator for the

KANSAI REGION

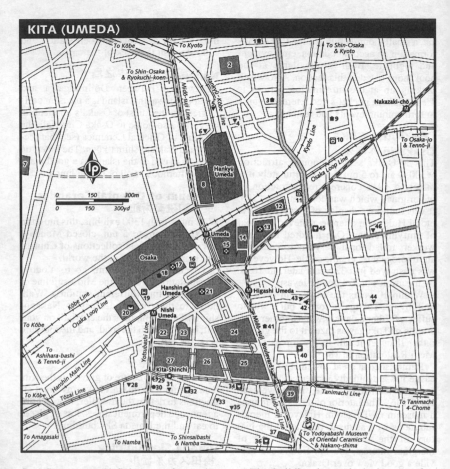

KITA (UMEDA)

final five storeys (definitely not for vertigo sufferers). The observation decks are open year round from 10 am to 10 pm and admission (including the white-knuckled escalator ride) is ¥700. Tickets for the observation decks can be purchased on the 3rd floor of the east tower.

On the 39th floor there is a Chinese restaurant and a bar that can be reached free of charge via a conventional elevator in the eastern tower. Below the towers, you'll find **Takimi-koji Alley**, a re-creation of a Showa-era market street crammed with restaurants and izakaya.

The building is reached via an underground passage that starts just north of Osaka or Umeda stations (see the Kita map).

Umeda Chika Centre
梅田地下商店街

Below Osaka and Hankyū Umeda stations is a labyrinthine underground shopping arcade so complex that even long-term residents have trouble finding their way around – you half expect to meet the Minataur blundering around down there, lost somewhere between all the stores and restaurants. If you find yourself getting confused

KITA (UMEDA)

PLACES TO STAY
1 Hotel Sunroute Umeda
  ホテルサンルート梅田
2 Hotel Hankyū International
  ホテル阪急インター
  ナショナル
3 Osaka Tōkyū Hotel
  大阪東急ホテル
8 Hotel New Hankyū
  新阪急ホテル
9 Hotel Green Plaza Osaka
  ホ皿ルグリーン
  ブラザ大阪
18 Granvia Osaka
  グランヴィアホテル大阪
22 Osaka Hilton Hotel; The
  In Place; Victoria Station;
  Windows on the World
  人阪ヒルトンホテル；
  ザ・インプレス；
  ビクトリアステーション
  ；ウインドーズ
  オンザワルド
23 Osaka Dai-ichi Hotel;
  Osaka Maru Building
  大阪第1ホテル；
  大阪マルビル
41 Umeda OS Hotel
  梅田OSホテル

PLACES TO EAT
4 Hatago
  旅篭
5 Kappa Yokochō Arcade;
  Pina Khana; Gataro
  かっぱ横丁；
  ピーナカナ；がたろ
6 Isaribi
  漁火

28 Shabu-zen;
  Blue Note Osaka
  しゃぶ禅；ブルーノート
  大阪
31 Court Lodge
  コートロッジ
33 Maguro-tei
  まぐろ亭
35 Kani Dōraku
  かに道楽
42 Nawasushi
  縄寿司
43 Kamesushi
  亀寿司
44 Machapuchare
  マチャプチャレ
46 Herradura
  ヘラドラ

OTHER
7 Umeda Sky Building
  梅田スカイビル
10 Osaka Nō Theatre
  大阪文楽劇場
11 Web House
  ウェブハウス
12 Hankyū Hep
  Five Complex;
  Ferris Wheel
  阪急ファイブ；大観覧車
13 Hankyū Navio Store
  阪急ナビオ
14 Hankyū Grand Building
  阪急グランドビル
15 Hankyū Department
  Store
  阪急百貨店
16 City Bus Terminal
  市バスターミナル

17 Daimaru Department
  Store
  大丸百貨店
19 JR Highway Bus Terminal
  JR高速バスターミナル
20 Osaka Central Post Office
  大阪中央郵便局
21 Hanshin Department
  Store
  阪神百貨店
24 Ekimae Daiyon Building
  駅前第四ビル
25 Ekimae Daisan Building
  駅前第三ビル
26 Ekimae Daini Building
  駅前第二ビル
27 Ekimae Daiichi Building
  駅前第一ビル
29 International ATM
  国際ATM
30 A'cross Travellers Bureau
  アクロストラベラーズ
  ビューロー
32 Karma Bar
  カルマ
34 Canopy Bar
  キャノピー
36 Bar, Isn't It?
  バーイズントイット
37 Discount Ticket Shop
  格安チケット売り場
38 American Consulate
  アメリカ領事館
39 Dōwa Kasai Building
  同和火災ビル
40 Pig & Whistle Bar
  ビッグアンドホイッスル
45 Bar, Isn't It?
  バーイズントイット

after a few hours of urban spelunking, do the smart thing and head up to street level to get your bearings.

MINAMI AREA ミナミ
A few stops south of Kita on the Midō-suji subway line (get off at either Shinsaibashi or Namba stations), the Minami area is the place to spend the evening in Osaka. It's highlights include the Dōtombori Arcade,

the National Bunraku Theatre, Dōgusuji-ya Arcade and Amerika-mura.

Dōtombori 道頓堀
Dōtombori is Osaka's liveliest nightlife area. It's centred around **Dōtombori Canal** and **Dōtombori Arcade**, a strip of restaurants and theatres where a peculiar type of Darwinism is the rule for both people and shops: survival of the flashiest. In the

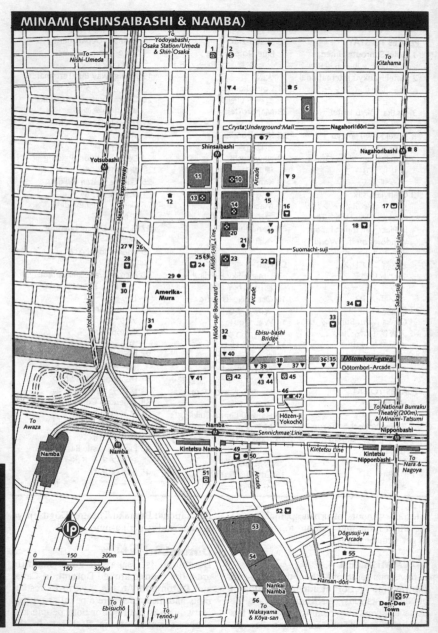

MINAMI (SHINSAIBASHI & NAMBA)

MINAMI (SHINSAIBASHI & NAMBA)

PLACES TO STAY

5 Hotel Do Sports Plaza
ホテルドゥスポーツ
クラブ

8 Ark Hotel Osaka
アークホテル大阪

11 Hotel Nikkō Osaka
ホテル日航大阪

12 Hotel California
ホテルカリフォルニア

30 Asahi Plaza Hotel
Amenity Shinsaibashi
朝日プラザホテル
アメニティー心斎橋

32 Holiday Inn Nankai
Osaka
ホリデーイン南海大阪

54 Nankai South Tower
Hotel; Namba City
南海サウスタワ
ホテル；なんばシティ

55 Business Hotel Nissei
ビジネスホテルニッセイ

PLACES TO EAT

3 Namaste
ナマステ

4 Field of Farms
フィールド・オブ・
ファームス

9 Nishiya
にし家

19 Capricciosa
カプリチョーザ

27 McDonald's

35 Chibō
丁房

36 Sawasdee
サワディ

37 Kani Dōraku
かに道楽

38 Zuboraya
づぼらや

39 Kani Dōraku Main Store
かに道楽本店

40 Shabu-zen; Gin Sen
しゃぶ禅；銀扇

41 Santana
サンタナ

43 Ganko Sushi
がんこ寿司

44 Kuidaore
くいだおれ

46 Tempura Maki
天ぷら牧

48 Akiyoshi
秋吉

56 Hard Rock Cafe
ハードロックカフェ

OTHER

1 Kinko's
キンコース

2 Sumitomo Bank
住友銀行

6 Tōkyū Hands
Department Store
東急ハンズ

7 Sony Tower
ソニータワー

10 Sogo Department Store
そごう百貨店

13 OPA Shopping Centre
オーバ

14 Daimaru Department
Store
大丸百貨店

15 Naniwa Camera
カメラのナニワ

16 Diva
ディーバ

17 Post Office
郵便局

18 Murphy's
マフィーズ

20 Daimaru Department
Store Annex
大丸百貨店別館

21 Athens Bookshop
アテネ書店

22 Pig & Whistle
ピッグアンドホィッスル

23 Vivre 21 Department
Store
ビブレ21

24 Uncle Steven's
アンクルスティーブンス

25 Citibank
シティバンク

26 Amerika Mura
Triangle Park
アメリカ村三角公園

28 Someplace Else
サムプレイスエルス

29 Mitsugu-jinja
御津八幡神社

31 Tower Records
タワーレコード

33 Bar's Bar
バ ズバ

34 Nell's
ネルズ

42 Shōchikuza Theatre
松竹座

45 Nakaza Theatre
中座

47 Hōzen-ji
法善寺

49 Southside Blues & Co
サウスサイド
ブルース＆Co

50 Discount Ticket Shop
格安チケット売り場

51 Shin Kabukiza Theatre
新歌舞伎座

52 Karapara
カラパラ

53 Takashimaya
Department
Store
高島屋百貨店

57 Takashimaya
Department Store
East Building
高島屋百貨店東館

evening, head to the bridge, **Ebisu-bashi**, to sample the glittering nightscape, which brings to mind a scene from the science-fiction movie *Blade Runner*.

Only a short walk south of Dōtombori Arcade, you'll find **Hōzen-ji**, a tiny temple hidden down a narrow alley. The temple is built around a moss-covered **Fudō-myōō** statue.

This statue is a favourite of people employed in the so-called *mizu shobai* (water trade). Before heading off to work at the area's myriad hostess bars, massage parlours and strip clubs, many young women and mama-sans (as well as heaps of regular folk) stop by to throw some water on the statue. This is thought to ensure a lucky evening (and it does wonders for the statue's luxuriant coat of moss). Nearby, you'll find the atmospheric **Hōzen-ji Yokochō**, a tiny alley filled with traditional restaurants and bars.

To the south of Dōtombori in the direction of Nankai Namba station you'll find a maze of colourful arcades with more restaurants, pachinko parlours, strip clubs, cinemas and who knows what else. To the north of Dōtombori, between Midō-suji and Sakai-suji, the narrow streets are crowded with hostess bars, discos and pubs.

Dōgusuji-ya Arcade 道具筋屋

If you desperately need a *tako-yaki* (octopus ball) fryer, a red lantern to hang outside your shop or plastic food-models to lure the customers in, this shopping arcade is the place to go. You'll also find endless knives, pots, pans and just about anything else that's even remotely related to the preparation and consumption of food. Hint: you'll find the plastic-food-model stores in the alleys just west of the main arcade.

Sony Tower ソニータワー

If it's a rainy day or you've got kids in tow, you can easily spend an hour or two here poking through the displays of Sony's latest electronic products. There's a cafe on the roof where parents can relax while their kids amuse themselves on the floors below. The tower is open from 11 am to 7 pm. When you're finished here, you might want to head down to the basement exit, which leads out to the Crysta Underground Mall. This isn't an attraction you must see, but the water sculptures are worth a look.

National Bunraku Theatre 国立文楽劇場

Although bunraku, or puppet theatre, did not originate in Osaka, the art form was popularised here. The most famous bunraku playwright, Chikametsu Monzaemon (1653–1724), wrote plays set in Osaka concerning the classes that traditionally had no place in Japanese art: merchants and the denizens of the pleasure quarters. Not surprisingly, bunraku found an appreciative audience among these people, and a theatre was established to put on the plays of Chikametsu in Dōtombori. Today's theatre is an attempt to revive the fortunes of bunraku.

Performances are only held at certain times of the year: check with the tourist information offices. Tickets normally start at around ¥2300, and program guides in English and earphones are available.

Amerika-Mura アメリカ村

Amerika-mura (which means 'America Village') is a compact enclave of trendy shops and restaurants, with a few discreet love hotels thrown in for good measure. The best reason to come is to check out the hordes of colourful Japanese teens living out the myth of *Amerika*.

In the middle of it all is Amerika-mura Triangle Park, an all-concrete park with benches where you can sit and watch the parade of fashion victims. Amerika-mura is one or two blocks west of Midō-suji, bounded on the north by Suomachi-suji and the south by the Dōtombori Canal.

TENNŌ-JI & AROUND 天王寺と周辺
Shitennō-ji 四天王寺

Shitennō-ji founded in 593, has the distinction of being one of the oldest Buddhist temples in Japan. However, none of the present buildings are originals; most are the usual concrete reproductions, with the exception of the big stone torii. The torii dates back to 1294, making it the oldest of its kind in Japan. Apart from the torii, there is little of real historical significance, and the absence of greenery in the raked-gravel grounds makes for a rather desolate atmosphere. The adjoining museum (¥200) is of limited interest.

The temple (free, 9 am to 5 pm) is most easily reached from Shitennōji-mae station on the Tanimachi subway line. Take the southern exit, cross to the left side of the road and take the small road that goes off at an angle away from the subway station. The entrance to the temple is on the left.

Tennō-ji-kōen 天王寺公園
A visit to this park can easily be combined with a visit to Shitennō-ji and Shin-Sekai (see that section).

The park has a botanical garden, a zoo and a circular garden known as Keitaku-en (¥150, 9.30 am to 5 pm, closed Monday). However, the best reason to visit the park is for the Sunday karaoke songfests held on the road that runs through the middle of the park. Here, enterprising members of Tennō-ji's sizeable homeless population rig up generators and karaoke machines and charge passers by ¥50 or ¥100 to belt out classic *enka* (something akin to a Japanese version of country and western) numbers. If you've really got guts, you can step up to the mike yourself, but don't expect any English songs.

The park is above Tennō-ji station, which is on the Midō-suji subway line and the Osaka Loop line.

Shin-Sekai 新世界
For something completely different, take a walk through this retro entertainment district just west of Tennō-ji-kōen. At the heart of it all you'll find crusty old Tsūten-kaku tower, a 103m-high structure that dates back to 1912 (the present tower was rebuilt in 1969). When the tower first went up it symbolised everything new and exciting about this once-happening neighbourhood (*shin-sekai* is Japanese for 'New World').

Now, Shin-Sekai is a world that time forgot. You'll find ancient pachinko parlours, run-down theatres, dirt-cheap restaurants and all manner of raffish and suspicious characters. Keep your wits about you, especially in some of the smaller side streets, as this is about the only neighbourhood in Japan that might actually merit the term 'dangerous'.

Sumiyoshi Taisha 住吉大社
This shrine (free, 6 am to 6 pm) is dedicated to Shintō deities associated with the sea and

sea travel, in commemoration of a safe passage to Korea by a 3rd-century empress.

Having survived the bombing in WWII, Sumiyoshi Taisha actually has a couple of buildings that date back to 1810. The shrine was founded in the early 3rd century and the buildings that can be seen today are faithful replicas of the originals. They offer a rare opportunity to see a Shintō shrine that predates the influence of Chinese Buddhist architectural styles.

The main buildings are roofed with a kind of thatch rather than the tiles used on most later shrines. Other interesting features are a collection of more than 700 stone lanterns donated by seafarers and business people, a stone stage for performances of bugaku and court dancing and the attractive Taiko-bashi, an arched bridge set in a park.

It's next to both Sumiyoshi station on the Nankai line and Sumiyoshi-tori-mae station on the Hankai line (the tram line that leaves from Tennō-ji station).

OTHER ATTRACTIONS
Tempōzan Area 天保山エリア
The Osaka Aquarium is the highlight of this area.

Osaka Aquarium This is one aquarium (and Japan has a glut) that is worth a visit. It's centred around the world's largest aquarium tank, which is home to the aquarium's star attractions – two enormous whale sharks – and a variety of smaller sharks, rays and other fish (adults ¥2000, children junior high school age and under ¥900, 10 am to 8 pm).

A walkway winds its way around the main tank and past displays of life found on eight different ocean levels. The giant spider crabs in the Japan Ocean Deeps section look like alien invaders from another planet. Presentations have both Japanese and English captions and an environmentally friendly slant to them.

Take the Chūō subway line to the last stop (Osaka-kō), from which it's about a five-minute walk to the aquarium. Get there for opening time if you want to beat the crowds – on weekends and holidays long queues are the norm.

Suntory Museum On the southern side of Osaka Aquarium is the Suntory Museum complex (¥1000, 10.30 am to 7.30 pm), which holds an IMAX 3-D theatre and an art gallery with a collection of modern art posters and glass artwork. The building itself, designed by Andō Tadao, is at least as impressive as any of the displays. The IMAX theatre has screenings on the hour (¥1000, 11 am to 8 pm, closed Monday).

Osaka Human Rights Museum/Liberty Osaka
大阪人権博物館／リバティ大阪

This museum (¥250, 10 am to 5 pm, closed Monday), which goes by two names, is dedicated to the suffering of Japan's Burakumin people and other oppressed groups, including Koreans, the handicapped, the Ainu and women. The most fascinating exhibits deal with the Burakumin, who were the outcasts in Japan's four-tiered caste system that was officially outlawed in 1879 under the Emancipation Edict issued by the Meiji government.

An English-language leaflet is available, and you can borrow a tape recorder and English tape for free. Take the JR Osaka Loop line to Ashihara-bashi station, exit via the southern exit, walk south down the main street for five minutes and the museum is on the right of the pedestrian crossing.

Open Air Museum of Old Japanese Farmhouses
日本民家集落博物館

In Ryokuchi-kōen is a museum (¥500, 10 am to 5 pm April to October, until 4 pm from November to March) comprising 11 *gasshō-zukuri* (thatched-roof) farmhouses brought from different parts of the country. Each of the farmhouses represents a different regional building style used in preindustrial Japan. An English-language pamphlet is available.

Take the Midō-suji subway line to Ryokuchi-kōen and walk north-west into the park.

SPECIAL EVENTS
The major festivals held in Osaka include the following:

January
Toka Ebisu 9 to 11 January. Huge crowds of more than a million people flock to the Imamiya Ebisu Shrine to receive bamboo branches hung with auspicious tokens. The shrine is near Imamiya Ebisu station on the Nankai line.
Doya Doya 14 January. Billed as a 'huge naked festival', this event involves a competition between young men, clad in little more than headbands and loincloths, to obtain the 'amulet of the cow god'. This talisman is said to bring a good harvest to farmers. The festival takes place from 2 pm at Shitennō-ji.

April
Shōryō-e 22 April. Shitennō-ji holds afternoon performances of bunraku. Performances are usually held from 1 pm to 5 pm.

June
Otaue Shinji 14 June. Women and girls dressed in traditional costume commemorate the establishment of the imperial rice fields. The festival is held at Sumiyoshi Taisha.

July
Tenjin Matsuri 24 to 25 July. This is one of Japan's three biggest festivals. Try to make the second day, when processions of portable shrines and people in traditional attire start at Temman-gū and end up in O-kawa (in boats). As night falls, the festival is marked with a huge fireworks display.

September
Kishiwada Danjiri Matsuri 14 to 15 September. Osaka's wildest festival, a kind of running of the bulls except with *danjiri* (festival floats), many weighing over 3000kg. The danjiri are hauled through the streets by hundreds of people using ropes, and in all the excitement there have been a couple of deaths – take care and stand back. Most of the action takes place on the second day. The best place to see it is west of Kishiwada station on the Nankai Honsen line (from Nankai station).

PLACES TO STAY
The best place to stay when visiting Osaka is Kyoto. It can be reached in about 30 minutes by a variety of train lines, there's a far better choice of accommodation (particularly in the budget bracket) and it has a much more restful atmosphere. However, if

KANSAI REGION

you prefer to stay in Osaka, there are lots of business hotels and regular hotels in both Kita and Minami.

Places to Stay – Budget

The nearest youth hostel to downtown Osaka is *Osaka Shiritsu Nagai Youth Hostel* (☎ *6699-5631*). A bed in the dorm room is ¥2950 or ¥2700, depending upon the season, while a private room is ¥3000 a person, and a family room for up to four people is ¥3500 a person. Take the Midō-suji subway line south from the centre of town to Nagai station, go out exit No 1 and walk for 10 minutes toward the stadium. The hostel is at the back of the new stadium.

About 15 minutes from Kita or 30 minutes from Minami is the *Osaka-fu Hattori Ryokuchi Youth Hostel* (☎ *6862-0600*), where beds are ¥2300 (no membership necessary). Take the Midō-suji line to Ryokuchikōen station, take the western exit, enter the park and follow the path past a fountain and around to the right alongside the pond.

Places to Stay – Mid-Range

Kita Area There are a few business hotels scattered around Hankyū Umeda and Osaka stations. Perhaps the best value is the *Hotel Sunroute Umeda* (☎ *6373-1111*), a reasonable business hotel just north of Hankyū Umeda, where singles/doubles/twins start at ¥7640/12,600/13,600. Not far away, the drab but economical *Hotel Green Plaza Osaka* (☎ *6374-1515*) has rooms that start at ¥6500/9000/13,500. About five minutes south of Osaka station, the clean, modern *Umeda OS Hotel* (☎ *6312-1271*) is a step up, with rooms from ¥8300/14,800/11,800.

Minami Area Considering the wealth of dining and entertainment options in the area, the Minami area is probably the best place in Osaka to be based.

The cheapest hotel in the area is the *Business Hotel Nissei* (☎ *6632-8111*), which has small but clean singles/doubles/twins starting at ¥6300/10,000/11,000. Almost as cheap, but less convenient, the *Ark Hotel Osaka* (☎ *6252-5166*) has somewhat drab rooms from ¥7500/12,000/13,000.

Worth a special mention is the wonderfully kitsch *Hotel California* (☎ *6243-0333*). The bar downstairs is a very Japanese interpretation of California style, complete with garish wooden marlin, parrots and vertical ducks hanging on the walls. The hotel is starting to show its age, but it's still an interesting choice. Rooms start at ¥7000/11,000/10,000.

South-west of the Hotel California is the *Asahi Plaza Hotel Amenity Shinsaibashi* (☎ *6212-5111*), where decent rooms start at ¥7800/14,500/14,500.

Lastly, the oddly named *Hotel Do Sports Plaza* (☎ *6245-3311*) has basic rooms priced at ¥9700/12,000/13,000 (for the latter, ask for an 'economy twin').

Itami Airport The best deal near Itami is *Hotel Crevette* (☎ *6843-7201*), which has singles/doubles/twins starting at ¥6500/15,000/12,000. Prices are discounted if you make reservations at the main tourist information counter at the airport. The folks at the information counter can also arrange for the hotel's shuttle bus to pick you up.

Places to Stay – Top End

Kita Area This area is brimming with top-end accommodation. The most conveniently located is the *Granvia Osaka* (☎ *6344-1235*) in the building directly over Osaka station. Clean new singles/doubles/twins start at ¥13,500/28,000/24,000.

The *Osaka Tōkyū Hotel* (☎ *6373-2411*), north-east of Hankyu Umeda station, has the cheapest rooms in this bracket, with rooms starting at ¥10,000/16,000/18,000.

The *Hotel New Hankyū* (☎ *6372-5101*), next to Hankyū Umeda station, is another reasonable choice with decent rooms starting at ¥12,000/24,000/19,000.

The *Osaka Hilton Hotel* (☎ *6347-7117*), just outside Osaka station, is one of the city's more luxurious hotels, with rooms starting at ¥26,000/32,000/32,000. Nearby, the *Osaka Dai-ichi Hotel* (☎ *6341-3411*) is less appealing but cheaper, with rooms starting at 12,500/24,500/21,000.

The most luxurious hotel in town is the *Hotel Hankyū International* (☎ *6377-2100*),

KANSAI REGION

just north of Hankyū Umeda station. Rooms here start at ¥27,000/40,000/42,000.

Minami Area While most of Osaka's luxury hotels are in Kita, you'll find a few top-end choices in Minami as well. The most reasonable is the *Holiday Inn Nankai Osaka* (☎ 6213-8281), which is about mid-way between Shinsaibashi and Namba subway stations. Clean, reasonably spacious singles/doubles/twins start at ¥12,000/20,000/19,000.

Up in Shinsaibashi, the *Hotel Nikkō Osaka* (☎ 6244-1111) is a slightly more elegant choice, with rooms starting at ¥17,000/26,5000/27,000.

Lastly, the most impressive hotel in the area is *Nankai South Tower Hotel* (☎ 6646-1119), directly above Nankai Namba station. Clean, well-appointed rooms start at ¥17,000/28,000/28,000. The views from the rooms are great and the on-site facilities are excellent.

Kansai International Airport The only hotel at the airport is the expensive *Hotel Nikkō Kansai Airport* (☎ 0724-55-1111), which has clean, new singles/doubles/twins starting at ¥18,000/28,000/28,000. You should definitely ask for a discount or promotional rate outside peak travel times.

PLACES TO EAT

What Osaka offers is a chance to enjoy what ordinary Japanese enjoy – good food and drink in a rowdy atmosphere. The Osakans call it *kuidaore*, which means 'eat until you drop'. Osaka presents ample opportunities to do just that, with thousands of restaurants lining its cramped streets.

Kita

Japanese A great place to eat in the Kita area is the *Kappa Yokochō Arcade*, just north of Hankyū Umeda station. Here, you'll find heaps of good, cheap restaurants, all vying for your attention with plastic food-models on display outside. For dinner in this area, we recommend the izakaya *Gataro*, which does creative twists on standard izakaya themes. Expect to pay

¥3000 a person. Look for the glass front on the left as you head north.

Nearby, you'll find two fun *robatayaki* (similar to an izakaya but specialising in char-grilled dishes). *Isaribi* is downstairs at the north-western end of the station. Count on spending ¥2500 a person for dinner here. On the other side of the station, just down a little side street, *Hatago* is a better choice, with its warm, rustic interior. The set menus start at ¥2500 but it's more fun to order a la carte by pointing at what you want. It also serves one of the cheapest lunches in town, for around ¥500. Look for the low doorway and the wooden facade.

A short walk east of Hanshin department store brings you to a neighbourhood that must have the highest concentration of sushi restaurants on the planet. *Nawasushi* offers good value (three pieces of sushi per order, usually around ¥400) in a pleasant atmosphere. Just down the street, *Kamesushi* offers similar fare in slightly more spacious digs.

In one of the narrow streets just south of the Osaka Ekimae Dai-San building, *Kani Dōraku* serves anything to do with crab, with lunch set meals from ¥1600 and dinners from about ¥3000. Look for the giant crab out the front.

The nearby *Maguro-tei* is a modern, noisy, automatic sushi place that does an all-you-can-eat sushi and cake special (that's right, sushi and cake) for ¥1000 for women and ¥1500 for men.

Lastly, for delicious shabu-shabu in a pleasant setting, try *Shabu-zen* (☎ 6343-0250), on the 10th floor of the AX building, not far from the Osaka Hilton. It serves full shabu set meals starting at ¥3300.

International There are several cafes in Osaka station itself, the best of which is the *Kitchen Deli Bakery*. Otherwise, you might try the offerings in the nearby Osaka Hilton. On the 1st floor of the Hilton, *The In Place* serves a curry buffet with a choice of six curries starting at ¥1700 including salad and dessert daily from 11.30 am to 2.30 pm. Downstairs, on level B2 of the Hilton Plaza, *Victoria Station* has about the best salad bar in town and a reasonable steak menu. At lunch time, the salad bar with bread or rice costs ¥1380; at dinner time it's ¥1480. If none of these strike your fancy, you'll also find dim-sum, Italian and Japanese places in the Hilton Plaza.

Around the corner, *Court Lodge* serves delicious and filling Sri Lankan food in a tiny keyhole of a restaurant. Set lunches here start at ¥800. Look for the beer signs in the window. Another good spot for curries is *Pina Khana* Indian restaurant in the Kappa Yokochō, just north of Hankyū Umeda station. Set lunches here start at around ¥900.

Herradura is a good Mexican restaurant just off a shopping arcade to the east of Hankyū Umeda station. It serves all the usual Mexican favourites, including taco platters and frozen margaritas. Expect to pay around ¥2500 a head for dinner.

Not far away, *Machapuchare* serves filling set meals of Nepalese food. Set lunches, which usually include two kinds of curry and chai, cost ¥850. It's closed on Sunday.

Minami

Japanese The place to eat in Minami is restaurant-packed Dōtombori Arcade. The restaurants in this area win no points for their refined atmosphere, but the prices are low and the portions are huge.

Kuidaore is easy to spot, with a lively drum-beating mechanical clown posted outside its doors. The restaurant has eight floors serving almost every kind of Japanese food. There are lunch and dinner set meals available for as little as ¥1000.

Not far from the drum-pounding clown is a restaurant that sports a huge mechanical crab helplessly waving its pincers around. This is *Kani Dōraku*, a crab specialist that does all kinds of imaginative things to the unfortunate crustaceans. Lunch set meals here start at ¥1500 and dinners at around ¥3000. If the main store is full, there's an annex just down the road.

Zuboraya is the place to go when you've worked up the nerve to try *fugu* (Japanese puffer fish). You won't find cheaper fugu anywhere in Japan – a plate of fugu sashimi here is only ¥1800 (note that in Osaka fugu is called *techiri*). For a full dinner, plan to

spend around ¥3000 a person. Look for the giant fugu hanging out the front.

Two other places worth a try in the Dōtombori Arcade are *Ganko Sushi*, a big sushi restaurant with set lunches starting at around ¥1000, and *Chibō*, a good spot to sample one of Osaka's most popular dishes, okonomiyaki. Chibō's *modan yaki* (a kind of okonomiyaki) is a good bet at ¥950.

If you leave Dōtombori and head north, you'll pass the Gurukas building just across the Dōtombori Canal. On the 6th floor of this building, *Shabu-zen* (☎ 213-2935) serves excellent shabu in an elegant setting. Courses start at ¥3000. On the 2nd floor of the same building, *Gin Sen* serves an all-you-can-eat kushi-katsu special at lunch time for ¥1980 and at dinner time for ¥2980.

In the neighbourhood behind Sogo department store, you'll find *Nishiya*, which serves Osaka udon noodles and a variety of hearty nabe dishes for reasonable prices, including a tempura udon set meal for ¥1200.

Across Nagahori-dōri, *Field of Farms* is a good choice for vegetarians. It serves a buffet style lunch for ¥900 and has an extensive, bilingual menu for dinner. It's in a basement, but there's a sign on street level.

For a real treat try *Tempura Maki* in the atmospheric Hōzen-ji Yokochō. Delicious tempura courses here start at ¥3900 and credit cards are accepted. Nearby, *Akiyoshi* is a good spot for yakitori, with a picture menu and a casual atmosphere. Expect to spend ¥2500 a person for dinner with a beer or two.

International Dōtombori also has a wide range of international restaurants, including *Sawasdee*, a small Thai restaurant with friendly staff and good food. Look for the English sign at ground level, the restaurant is upstairs.

In the neighbourhood north of Dōtombori, *Capricciosa* serves heaped portions of so-so pasta for reasonable prices. Lunch here runs about ¥900 a person and dinners just about double that.

One of our favourite places for Indian food in Minami is the friendly *Santana*, which serves filling set lunches starting at ¥1000 and set dinners starting at ¥2000. It has lots of vegetarian choices, an English menu and English-speaking staff. For a tasty snack, be sure to try its vegetable samosa. It's closed on Monday.

Another good Indian place is *Namaste*, up in the Shinsaibashi area. Set lunches here start at ¥750, and you can expect to pay about ¥2000 a person at dinner time.

Finally, Osaka has its own branch of the *Hard Rock Café* (also an entertainment option), serving drinks and American-style eats. It's south of Nankai Namba station, in front of the remains of Osaka baseball stadium.

ENTERTAINMENT
Traditional Japanese Entertainment

You can visit the *National Bunraku Theatre* (☎ 6212-1122) described earlier if you'd like to watch bunraku. *Osaka Nō Hall* (☎ 6373-1726), a five-minute walk east of Osaka Station, holds nō shows about four times a month, some of which are free. There are also five *manzai* (comic dialogue) theatres around the city, which means there's a performance being given somewhere most nights. It should also be possible, if your timing is right, for you to take in one of the *rakugo* (comic monologue) performances held in small theatres in Osaka.

Unfortunately, none of these places has regularly scheduled shows. The best way to discover what's on while you're in town is to check with the tourist information offices, check the listings in the *Meet Osaka* guide or look in *Kansai Time Out*.

Bars & Clubs

Osaka has a very lively nightlife scene, with lots of bars and clubs catering to a mixed foreign and Japanese clientele. For up-to-date listings of forthcoming club events, check *Kansai Time Out*.

Kita Area Check out *Karma*, a popular spot with Japanese and foreigners alike. On weekends, it usually hosts techno, for which there is a cover charge of around ¥2500. A short walk east on the same street brings you to *Canopy*, a popular spot with expats

for after-work snacks and drinks (it's open until the wee hours).

Walking north toward the station again, you'll find the *Pig & Whistle*, a British-style pub that serves good fish and chips and imported beer. A few minutes' walk east of Hankyū department store brings you to *Bar, Isn't It?*, a large bar popular with the young, after-work crowd. It's on the 5th floor of the Kakusha building. There's another branch in Kita-Shinchi (near the river).

For something more elegant, head up to the *Windows on the World* bar on the 35th floor of the Osaka Hilton. The view over the city here is unparalleled, but you really have to pay for it: there's a ¥2500 per-person table charge and drinks average ¥1000.

Minami In Minami, there are lots of bars and clubs in the back streets of Shinsaibashi, Namba and Amerika-mura. You won't believe the number of people who flock here on a weekend night – simply looking at them is half the fun.

The beer hall *Karapara* is a good place to start your pub crawl, as you should be relatively sober to appreciate the zany, futuristic look of the place (¥2.3 billion spent on decor) – the effect is something like *Flintstones* meets *Star Wars*.

North of Dÿtombori Canal is an enclave thick with bars and restaurants. *Murphy's* is an Irish pub that's very popular with local expats and Japanese alike. On the same street, *Diva* is a karaoke place specialising in English songs (look for the English sign at street level, then take the elevator to the 6th floor). Not far away, *The Pig & Whistle* is an English-style pub with Guinness on tap and decent fish and chips.

In the same neighbourhood as these bars is *Nell's*, a good spot for a late-night drink. It draws a fairly alternative crowd. A few streets back toward the river, *Bar's Bar* is a classic hole-in-the-wall hidden down a small alley. This is where the serious drinkers wind up when lesser mortals have gone home.

When you're in the mood for something a little more trendy, head across Midosujidōri to Amerika-mura. Here, you'll find

KANSAI REGION

Uncle Steven's, a Tex-Mex bar good for spicy food, music and beer. *Someplace Else*, in a basement just across from the Triangle Park in Amerika-mura, is also very popular with ex-pats. It can become pretty wild late at night when a lot of the hostesses and bartenders from other clubs knock off and drop in for a drink.

Lastly, for something a little swank, head up to the *Arc en Ciel* bar, on the 36th floor of the Nankai South Tower Hotel. The view is fantastic, and there are prices to match: a table charge of ¥1500 a person and drinks priced at around ¥1200.

Live Music
If you are interested in live blues and jazz, check *Kansai Time Out* to see who's scheduled to play at the *Blue Note Osaka*, which is a short walk from the Osaka Hilton. It draws some fairly big-name acts; the price of tickets to shows averages ¥7000.

At the opposite end of the spectrum *Southside Blues & Co.* is a good place to enjoy blues and blues-influenced music in a mellow atmosphere (see the Minami map). Forthcoming shows will be listed in *Kansai Time Out*, but you can always simply drop by if you're in the neighbourhood.

SHOPPING
Osaka has almost as many shops as it has restaurants. Look for department stores in the area around JR Osaka and Umeda stations. Most of the major department stores are represented here.

Osaka's speciality is electronics, and Den Den Town is Osaka's version of Tokyo's Akihabara. Taking its name from the Japanese word for electricity, '*denki*', Den Den Town is an area of shops almost exclusively devoted to electronic goods. To avoid sales tax, check if the store has a 'Tax Free' sign outside and bring your passport. Most stores are closed on Wednesday. Take the Sakaisuji subway line to Ebisu-cho station and exit at No 1 or No 2 exit. Alternatively, it's a 15-minute walk south of Nankai Namba station.

For anything related to cooking and eating, head to the Dōgusiji-ya Arcade (for more on this, see the entry in the Minami section). Also in Minami, you'll find Naniwa Camera, which has the lowest prices on cameras, equipment and film in town. For used camera equipment, try the many shops on the ground floors of the Ekimae Dai-San buildings (there are four of them) south of Osaka station.

GETTING THERE & AWAY
Air
Osaka is served by two airports: the old Itami airport, which now handles only domestic traffic, and the new Kansai international airport (KIX), which handles all international and some domestic flights. Built on an artificial island south of Osaka city, KIX is something of a technological marvel and makes an impressive introduction to Kansai.

Train
Shinkansen Osaka is on the Tōkaidō/San-yō shinkansen line that runs between Tokyo and Hakata in Kyūshū (to/from Tokyo – Hikari shinkansen, ¥13,750, two hours 55 minutes; to Hakata – Hikari shinkansen, ¥14,590, three hours 20 minutes). Other cities on this line include Hiroshima, Kyoto, Kōbe and Okayama.

Kyoto The fastest way other than shinkansen to travel by train between Kyoto and Osaka is to take the JR shinkaisoku (¥540, 29 minutes).

There is also the cheaper private Hankyū line that runs between Hankyū Umeda station in Osaka and Hankyū Kawaramachi, Karasuma and Ōmiya stations in Kyoto (to Kawaramachi – tokkyū, ¥390, 40 minutes).

Alternatively, you can take the Keihan main line between Sanjō, Shijō or Shichijō stations in Kyoto and Keihan Yodoyabashi station in Osaka (to Sanjō – tokkyū, 400, 45 minutes). Yodoyabashi is on the Midō-suji subway line.

Nara The JR Kansai line links Osaka (Namba and Tennō-ji stations) and Nara (JR Nara station) via Hōryū-ji (kaisoku, ¥540, 35 minutes).

The private Kintetsu Nara line also connects Osaka (Kintetsu Namba station) with

Nara (Kintetsu Nara station). Kyūkō and futsū services take about 35 minutes and cost ¥540. Tokkyū trains do the journey in five minutes less time but at almost double the cost, making them a poor option.

Kōbe The fastest way between Kōbe and Osaka is the JR shinkaisoku that runs between Osaka station and Kōbe's Sannomiya and Kōbe stations (¥390, 21 minutes).

There is also the private Hankyū line, which takes a little more time but is cheaper. It runs from Osaka's Hankyū Umeda station to Kōbe's Sannomiya station (tokkyū, ¥300, 30 minutes).

Bus
There is long-distance highway bus service between Osaka and cities all across Honshū, Shikoku and some cities in Kyushū. Destinations include Tokyo (¥8610, eight hours), Nagasaki (¥11,000, 10 hours) and Kagoshima (¥12,000, 12 hours). Buses usually depart from Osaka, Hankyū Umeda or Namba stations; check with the tourist information offices for more details.

Boat
Ferries to Shanghai in China depart Osaka twice a month (2nd class, ¥20,000). The ferries leave from the Osaka Nankō international ferry terminal, which can be reached by taking the New Tram service from Suminoe-kōen station to Nankoguchi station. You can ring the Nitchū Kokusai ferry company (☎ 6536-6541, in Japanese) for details, but Osaka tourist information offices are a better source of information on schedules and bookings.

Ferries also depart from Nankō ferry terminal and Kanome-futō and Benten-futō piers for various destinations around Honshū, Kyūshū and Shikoku. Kyūshū destinations include Beppu (¥7030) and Miyazaki (¥8380). Other possibilities in Kyūshū are Shinmoji in the north of the island near Shimonoseki and Shibushi in the south of the island. Possibilities in Shikoku are Kōchi (¥4610), Matsuyama (¥5000), Takamatsu (¥6100, hydrofoil) and Tokushima (¥4620, hydrofoil). Note that

prices listed here are for a 2nd-class ticket, which, on overnight ferries, usually means a place on a tatami-mat floor in a large, open room.

For detailed information about sailing schedules and bookings contact the tourist information offices.

GETTING AROUND
To/From the Airport
Itami Airport There are frequent limousine buses running between the airport and various parts of Osaka. Buses run to/from Shin-Osaka station every 15 minutes from about 6.30 am to 7.30 pm and cost ¥490. The trip takes around 25 minutes. Buses run at about the same frequency to/from Osaka and Namba stations (¥620, 30 minutes). At Itami, buy your tickets from the machine outside the arrivals hall.

There are also direct airport buses to/from Kyoto and Kōbe.

Kansai International Airport There are a variety of routes between KIX and Osaka. Limousine buses travel to/from Shin-Osaka, Osaka Umeda, Kyobashi, Tenmabashi, Osaka City Air Terminal (OCAT) Namba, Uehonmachi, Tennō-ji and Nanko (Cosmo Square) stations. The fare is ¥1300 for most routes and the journeys take an average of 50 minutes, depending on traffic conditions. OCAT, in JR Namba station, allows passengers on Japanese and some other airlines to check in and deposit baggage before boarding trains to the airport. Check with your airline for details.

The fastest way by train to and from the airport is the private Nankai express Rapit, which departs from Nankai Namba station on the Midō-suji subway line (¥1400, 30 minutes). The JR Haruka limited airport express operates between the airport and Tennō-ji station (35 minutes, ¥1760) and Shin-Osaka (45 minutes, ¥2470).

Regular JR expresses called kanku kaisoku also operate between the airport and Osaka station (¥1160, 66 minutes), Kyōbashi station (¥1160, 70 minutes), Tennō-ji station (¥1030, 50 minutes) and JR Namba station (¥1030, 61 minutes).

Train

Osaka has a good subway network and, like Tokyo, a JR loop line (known in Japanese as the JR *kanjō-sen*) that circles the city area. In fact, there should be no need to use any other form of transport while you are in Osaka unless you stay out late and miss the last train.

There are seven subway lines, but the one that most short-term visitors are likely to find most useful is the Midō-suji line, which runs north to south stopping at Shin-Osaka, Umeda (next to Osaka station), Shinsaibashi, Namba and Tennō-ji stations.

If you're going to be using the rail system a lot on any day, it might be worth considering a 'one-day free ticket'. For ¥850 (¥650 on Fridays and the 20th of every month) you get unlimited travel on any subway, the New Tram line and all city buses (but not the JR line). Note that you'd really have to be moving around a lot to save any money with this ticket. These tickets are available at the staffed ticket windows in most subway stations.

Bus

Osaka has a bus system, but it is nowhere near as easy to use as the rail network. Japanese-language bus maps are available from the tourist offices.

Kōbe 神戸

☎ 078 • pop 1.42 million

Perched on a hillside overlooking Osaka-wan, Kōbe is one of Japan's most attractive cities. It's also one of the country's most famous, largely as a result of the tragic earthquake of 17 January 1995, which levelled whole neighbourhoods and killed more than 6000 people. Fortunately, the city has risen, Phoenix-like, from the ashes and is now more vibrant than ever.

One of Kōbe's best features is its relatively small size – most of the sights can be reached on foot from the main train stations. Of course, it must be noted that none of these sights are attractions you really must see: Kōbe is likely to appeal more to residents than to travellers. However, it

does have some great restaurants, hip bars and happening clubs and is a good place for a night out in Kansai if you just can't face the mayhem of Osaka.

ORIENTATION

Kōbe's two main entry points are Sannomiya and Shin-Kōbe stations. Shin-Kōbe station, in the north-east of town, is where the shinkansen pauses. A subway runs from here to the busier Sannomiya station, which has frequent rail connections with Osaka and Kyoto. It's possible to walk between the two stations in around 15 minutes. Sannomiya (not Kōbe) station marks the city centre, although a spate of development in Kōbe Harbor Land is starting to swing the city's centre of gravity to the south-west. Before starting your exploration of Kōbe, pick up a copy of the *Kōbe Town Map*, at one of the two information offices (see the following Information section).

INFORMATION

The city's main tourist information office is outside Sannomiya station (☎ 322-0220) and is open from 9 am to 7 pm. Staff speak English, and a variety of English-language publications are available. There's a smaller information counter on the 2nd floor of Shin-Kōbe station.

There's an international ATM in the shopping arcade just south of Phoenix Plaza. Behind Kōbe city hall there's a Citibank with machines that also accept a variety of cards.

Email & Internet Access

For Internet access try The Real Thing cafe (free access with a drink or meal, noon to 4 pm, 6 pm to 2 am, closed Monday and national holidays). It's near the YMCA. Further up the hill on the same street you'll find Nailey's cafe (free access with a drink or meal, 11 am to midnight). Both are good places to hang out.

Bookshops

There's a branch of Maruzen near Nankin-machi (Chinatown). For second-hand books, try Wantage Books (☎ 232-4517), up near Shin-Kōbe station. It has a great

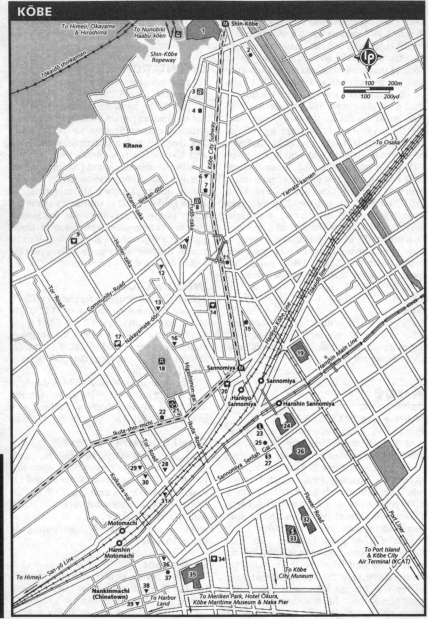

KŌBE

KŌBE

PLACES TO STAY
4 Green Hill
  Hotel Kōbe
  グリーンヒルホテル神戸
5 Kōbe YMCA
  神戸YMCAホテル
7 Green Hill
  Hotel Urban
  グリーンヒルホテル
  アーバン
15 Tomoe
  ともえ
22 Kōbe Washington
  Hotel Plaza
  神戸ワシントン
  ホテルプラザ

PLACES TO EAT
6 Mikami
  みかみ
10 Marrakech
  マラケッシュ
12 Court Lodge
  コートロッジ
13 Gaylord
  ゲイロード
16 Daruma
  達磨
28 Chai Pasal
  チャイパサル
29 Modernark Pharm
  モダンアークファーム

30 Tuto Benne; Tooth Tooth
  トゥートベーネ；
  トゥーストゥース
31 Omoni
  おもに
36 Kintoki
  金時
38 Minsei
  民性
39 Motomachi Gyōza-en
  元町ぎょうざ苑

OTHER
1 OPA Shopping Centre;
  Shin-Kōbe Oriental Hotel
  オーパ；新神戸オリエン
  タルホテル
2 Wantage Books;
  Kansai Time
  Out Office
  ワンタージ書店；
  関西タイムアウト事務所
3 Nailey's
  ネイリーズ
8 The Real Thing
  ザリアルスィング
9 Sunflower; Seed
  サンフラワー；スィード
11 Troop Cafe
  トゥループカフェ
14 Oto-ya
  音屋

17 South Korea Consulate
  韓国領事館
18 Ikuta-jinja
  生田神社
19 Daiei Department Store
  ダイエー
20 Ryan's
  ライアンズ
21 Tōkyū Hands
  Department Store
  東急ハンズ
23 Tourist Information Office
  観光案内所
24 Sogō Department Store
  そごう百貨店
25 Phoenix Plaza
  フェニックスプラザ
26 Kōbe Kokusai Kaikan
  神戸国際会館
27 International ATM
  国際ATM
32 Kōbe City Hall
  神戸市役所
33 Citibank
  シティバンク
34 Dubliners
  ダブリナーズ
35 Daimaru Department
  Store
  大丸百貨店
37 Maruzen Books
  丸善書店

selection, and low prices, and all proceeds go to charity. In the same building is the office of *Kansai Time Out*, Kansai's best 'what's on' magazine.

KITANO 北野
Twenty minutes' walk north of Sannomiya is the pleasant hillside neighbourhood of Kitano, where local tourists come to enjoy the feeling of foreign travel without leaving Japanese soil. The European/American atmosphere is created by the winding streets and *ijinkan* (literally 'foreigners' houses') that housed some of Kōbe's early Western residents. Admission to some is free, to others ¥300 to ¥700, and most are open from 9

am to 5 pm. Although these brick and clap board dwellings may not hold the same fascination for Western travellers that they hold for local tourists, the area itself is pleasant to stroll around and is dotted with good cafes and restaurants.

SHIN-KŌBE CABLE CAR & NUNOBIKI HABU-KŌEN
新神戸ロープウェイと布引ハーブ園
The Shin-Kōbe cable car ('ropeway' in Japanese) leaves from behind the OPA shopping centre near Shin-Kōbe station and ascends to a mountain ridge 400m above the city. The views from the top over Kōbe and the bay are particularly pretty after sunset.

KANSAI REGION

There's a complex of gardens, restaurants and shops below the top station known as the Nunobiki Habu-kōen (Nunobiki Herb Garden). The cable car operates from 9.30 am to 5 pm in winter, until 8 pm in spring and autumn and until 9 pm in summer. Fares are ¥550/1000 one-way/return and admission to the Herb Garden is ¥200. Note that you can easily walk down to the bottom station from the Herb Garden in about 30 minutes.

PHOENIX PLAZA
フェニックスプラザ
Phoenix Plaza (free, 10 am to 7 pm) is both an earthquake museum and a clearing house of information for Kōbe citizens affected by the quake. There are videos, dioramas, photos and explanations of the quake and its aftermath. Most of the information is in Japanese. It's just south of the main tourist information office at Sannomiya station.

KŌBE CITY MUSEUM
神戸市立博物館
Kōbe City Museum (¥200, 10 am to 4.30 pm, closed Monday) has a collection of so-called Namban (literally 'southern barbarian') art and occasional special exhibits. Namban art is a school of painting that developed under the influence of early Jesuit missionaries in Japan, many of whom taught Western painting techniques to Japanese students.

NANKINMACHI (CHINATOWN)
南京町
Nankinmachi, Kōbe's Chinatown, is not on a par with Chinatowns elsewhere in the world, but it is a good place for a stroll and a bite to eat. It's particularly attractive in the evening, when the lights of the area illuminate the gaudily painted facades of the shops. See the Places to Eat section for details on some of the area's restaurants.

KŌBE HARBOR LAND & MERIKEN PARK
神戸ハーバーランドとメリケンパーク
Five minutes' walk south-east of Kōbe station, Kōbe Harbor Land is awash with new mega-mall shopping and dining developments. This may not appeal to foreign

travellers the way it does to the local youth, but it's still a nice place for a stroll in the afternoon. For a good view of the area, take the free glass elevator to the 18th floor of the **Ecoll Marine building**.

On the way from Kōbe station to Harbor Land, take a look at the **Kōbe Crystal building** next to the elevated highway, just east of Kōbe station. It's a high-rise office building in the style of a Gothic cathedral! It is, to be frank, a monstrosity.

A five-minute walk to the east of Harbor Land. you'll find Meriken Park, on a spit of reclaimed land jutting out into the bay. The main attraction here is the **Kōbe Maritime Museum** (¥500, 10 am to 5 pm, closed Monday). The museum has a good collection of ship models and displays, with some English explanations. Nearby, the **Port Tower** looks like a relic from an earlier age of tourism. It's not worth paying the ¥500 to ascend to the viewing platform of the tower when you can ride the elevator at the Ecoll Marine building for free.

PORT ISLAND ポートアイランド
Many of the city's foreign residents live on this artificial island, but it has little to attract the visitor. A monorail (the Port Liner) circuits the island from Sannomiya station and stops at the sights along the way for ¥240.

ROKKO ISLAND
六甲アイランド
Another artificial island, the main attraction here is the **Kōbe Fashion Museum** (¥700, 11 am to 6 pm, until 8 on Friday, closed Wednesday). The museum's collection of mostly foreign fashion is not quite up to the dramatic building in which it's housed but it may be worth a look, depending on your interests. To reach the museum, take the Rokko Liner monorail (¥240) from JR Sumiyoshi (four stops east of Sannomiya) and get off at the Island Centre stop.

SPECIAL EVENTS
The **Luminarie**, Kōbe's biggest yearly event, is held every evening from 13 to 26 December to celebrate the city's miraculous recovery from the 1995 earthquake

(check with the Kōbe Tourist Information Office to be sure of the dates as they change slightly every year). The streets south-west of Kōbe City Hall are decorated with countless illuminated metal archways, which when viewed from within look like the interior of some otherworldly cathedral. Be warned though that this event draws huge throngs from all over Kansai and the streets can be completely jammed.

PLACES TO STAY
Places to Stay – Budget
The *Kōbe Tarumi Youth Hostel* (☎ 707-2133) has dormitory beds for ¥2800, single rooms for ¥4000 and twins for ¥3500 a person. Check-in is from 5 to 9 pm. To get there, take a futsū on the JR San-yō line west from Kōbe station and get off after six stops at Tarumi station. The hostel is an eight-minute walk west along the road that runs parallel to the southern side of the railway tracks.

A much more central option is the *Kōbe YMCA* (☎ 241-7205), which has reasonable singles/twins/triples starting at ¥5700/10,000/15,000. Check-in is from 4 to 10 pm. It's less than 10 minutes' walk from Shin-Kōbe station.

Places to Stay – Mid-Range
The *Green Hill Hotel Urban* (☎ 222-1221) is good value, with singles/doubles/twins starting at ¥6500/11,500/11,500. Nearby is the *Green Hill Hotel Kōbe* (☎ 222-0909), which has slightly larger singles/twins from ¥7500/11,000.

Close to Sannomiya station, the *Kōbe Washington Hotel Plaza* (☎ 331-6111) has small but clean singles/doubles/twins starting at ¥7900/15,000/15,000.

Tomoe (☎ 221-1227) is a ryokan/hotel with per-person rates starting at ¥6600 for Japanese- and Western-style rooms. It's not as appealing as the choices listed above but it's very close to Sannomiya station.

Places to Stay – Top End
Towering above Shin-Kōbe station, the *Shin-Kōbe Oriental Hotel* (☎ 291-1121) claims the best views of any hotel in town. Singles/doubles start at ¥13,000/23,000.

On the waterfront behind Meriken Park, the *Hotel Ōkura Kōbe* (☎ 333-0111) is the most elegant hotel in town, with fine rooms from ¥16,000/19,000.

PLACES TO EAT
Japanese
Although Kōbe is mainly famous for its international cuisine, there are plenty of good Japanese restaurants to be found here. *Mikami* is a friendly spot for good-value lunch and dinner set meals of standard Japanese fare. It has an English menu with noodle dishes starting at ¥400 and teishoku set meals starting at ¥600. It's closed on Sunday.

For a taste of what Japan was like before it got rich, try *Kintoki*, an atmospheric old shokudō that serves the cheapest food in the city. You can order standard noodle and rice dishes from the menu (plain soba noodles are ¥250 and a small rice is ¥160) or choose from a variety of dishes laid out on the counter.

Daruma is an izakaya that specialises in the cuisine of the Hida Takayama region of Gifu-ken. We recommend the *hoba yaki* (miso and vegetables cooked on a big leaf over a hibachi at your table). Expect to spend ¥2500 a person for dinner (it's not open for lunch).

Vegetarians might be interested in the offerings at *Modernark Pharm*, a trendy new spot that does Japanese-style veggie set lunches starting at ¥950.

Lastly, for Kōbe beef try *Sazanka*, on the 1st floor of Hotel Ōkura. As always with this delicacy, you really have to pay for the pleasure – plan on ¥10,000 a person at dinner time.

International
Kōbe is also famous for its Indian food, and there are lots of places to choose from. *Chai Pasal* is a favourite of the locals; it has set lunches starting at ¥900 and dinners starting at about ¥2000 a person. For more elegant Indian food, try *Gaylord*, where massive set dinners start at ¥3500.

If you're in the Kitano area, try the Sri Lankan restaurant *Court Lodge*, which serves a variety of set lunches for ¥1000 (dinners will be more than double that). Another Kitano highlight is *Marrakech*, where you can sample tasty, if expensive, Moroccan food. Set dinners start at ¥3500.

For authentic Korean cuisine, try *Omoni*, under the tracks between Sannomiya and Motomachi stations. There's an annex a few shops down if the main store is full. Count on ¥2000 per head for dinner.

Tuto Benne, near Motomachi station, is a fashionable Italian cafe/restaurant that serves all the standard Italian favourites for around ¥2000 a person at dinner. Around the corner, the teahouse *Tooth Tooth* serves a variety of cafe drinks and mouth-watering pastries.

For Chinese food, the natural choice is Nankinmachi, just south of Motomachi station. Unfortunately, most of the food is overpriced and doctored to suit local tastes. One bright spot is *Motomachi Gyōza-en*, a Chinese dumpling specialist where you can sample six wonderful *yaki gyōza* (fried dumplings) at lunch or dinner for ¥340. In the evening they also make *sui gyōza* (steamed gyōza), which cost ¥340 for six. Use the vinegar, soy sauce and *miso* (fermented soya-bean paste) on the table to make a dipping sauce. The sign is in Japanese only (it's red) so you may have to ask someone to point out the store.

For a more complete meal, try *Minsei*, a popular Cantonese place where a la carte dinners cost about ¥2500 a head. Look for the English writing on the yellow sign.

If you don't fancy a sit-down meal, there's plenty of takeaway food on offer for reasonable prices; try the gyōza, *butaman* (pork buns) or *shumai* (another sort of dumpling).

ENTERTAINMENT

Kōbe has a relatively large foreign community and a number of bars that see mixed Japanese and foreign crowds. Local expats like *Ryan's*, an authentic Irish pub with all the trimmings. *Dubliners* is another Irish pub that doesn't quite measure up to Ryan's, perhaps because it's part of a national chain.

Up in Kitano, the *Sunflower* is a good, casual bar with English-speaking staff and

a wide selection of drinks. Upstairs, the club *Seed* is a chic spot with a wide bar, big dance floor and lounges to relax in. It often hosts special events on weekends.

Back down towards Sannomiya, *Troop Cafe* is a modern, minimalist cafe/bar that stays open until the wee hours and attracts a bunch of hip young Japanese and tuned-in foreigners.

Oto-ya is a live house that attracts some good local bands. Check *Kansai Time Out* to see what's happening at Seed, Troop Cafe and Oto-ya while you're in town.

For Japanese-style drinking establishments, try the izakaya in the neighbourhoods lying between the JR tracks and Ikuta-jinja.

GETTING THERE & AWAY
Train
JR Sannomiya station is on the JR Tōkaidō line as well as the private Hankyū and Hanshin lines (both of which run to/from Osaka and some other areas). The fastest way between Kōbe and Kyoto or Osaka is the JR shinkaisoku (to/from Kyoto – ¥1030, 50 minutes; to/from Osaka station – ¥390, 21 minutes).

The Hankyū line is the more convenient of the two private lines (to/from Osaka's Hankyū Umeda station – limited express, ¥300, 30 minutes; to/from Kyoto – change at Osaka's Jūsō station – tokkyū, ¥590, one hour).

Shin-Kōbe station is on the Tōkaidō/San-yō shinkansen line (to/from Fukuoka – Hikari shinkansen, ¥14,080, three hours 10 minutes; to/from Tokyo – Hikari shinkansen, ¥13,760, three hours 15 minutes).

Boat
There are regular ferries between Kōbe and Shikoku (Imabari and Matsuyama) and Kyūshū (Ōita). Most ferries depart from Rokko Island and are operated by Diamond Ferry Company (☎ 857-9525, in Japanese). The cheapest rates are as follows: Imabari ¥4170, Matsuyama ¥4980, and Ōita ¥7020.

Osaka-Shanghai ferries also stop in Kōbe. For more information, see the Osaka Boat section.

GETTING AROUND
To/From the Airport
Itami Osaka Airport It's possible to take a bus directly to/from Osaka's Itami airport (¥1020, 40 minutes). In Kōbe, the buses stop on the south-western side of Sannomiya station.

Kansai International Airport There are a number of routes between Kōbe and KIX. By train, the fastest way is the JR shinkaisoku to/from Osaka station, and the JR kanku kaisoku between Osaka station and the airport (total cost ¥1660, total time 90 minutes with good connections). There is also a direct limousine bus to/from the airport (¥1800, 70 minutes). The Kōbe airport bus stop is on the south-western side of Sannomiya station.

There are also jet shuttle boats that make the trip between KIX and the Kōbe City Air Terminal (KCAT) on Kōbe's Port Island in 27 minutes for ¥2400 one way, including the bus fare between KCAT and Shin-Kōbe or Sannomiya stations.

Public Transport
Kōbe is small enough to travel around on foot. JR, Hankyū and Hanshin railway lines run east to west across Kōbe, providing access to most of Kōbe's more distant sights. A subway line also connects Shin-Kōbe station with Sannomiya station (¥200). There is also a city loop bus service which makes a grand circle tour of most of the city's sightseeing spots (¥250 per ride, ¥650 for an all-day pass). The bus stops at both Sannomiya and Shin-Kōbe stations.

Himeji 姫路

☎ 0792

If you see no other castles in Japan you should at least make an effort to visit Himeji-jō, unanimously acclaimed as the most splendid Japanese castle still standing. It's also known as Shirasagi, the 'White Egret', a title that derives from the castle's stately white form. The surrounding town itself is pretty drab, but the nearby Hyōgo

Prefectural Museum of History and Kōko-en are worth a visit.

Himeji can easily be visited as a day trip from Kyoto, Osaka or Kōbe. On the way to Himeji, take a look out the train window at the new Akashi Kaikyō Suspension Bridge. Its 3910m span links the island of Honshū with Awaji-shima, making it the longest suspension bridge in the world. It comes into view on the southern side of the train about 10km west of Kōbe.

ORIENTATION & INFORMATION
There's a tourist information counter at the station (☎ 85-3792); it's on the ground floor to the right as you come off the escalator). Between 10 am and 3 pm, English-speaking staff are on duty and can help with hotel/ryokan reservations etc. The castle is a 15-minute walk straight up the main road from the north exit of the station. If you don't feel like walking, free rental cycles are available; inquire at the information counter.

HIMEJI-JŌ 姫路城
Himeji-jō is the most magnificent of the handful of Japanese castles that survive in their original (nonconcrete) form. Although there have been fortifications in Himeji since 1333, today's castle was built in 1580 by Toyotomi Hideyoshi and enlarged some 30 years later by Ikeda Terumasa. Ikeda was awarded the castle by Tokugawa Ieyasu when the latter's forces defeated the Toyotomi armies. In the following centuries the castle was home to 48 successive lords.

The castle has a five-storey main donjon and three smaller donjons, the entire structure being surrounded by moats and defensive walls punctuated with rectangular, circular and triangular openings for firing guns and shooting arrows at attackers. The walls of the donjon also feature *ishiotoshi* – openings that allowed defenders to pour boiling water or oil on to anyone who made it past the defensive slits and was thinking of scaling the walls. All things considered, visitors are recommended to pay the ¥500 admission charge and enter the castle by legitimate means.

If at all possible, take a tour of the castle with one of the volunteer English-speaking guides who wait at the castle ticket office. Appointments are not accepted, so you just have to show up and hope for the best (there are more guides present on weekends). The people at the information office can call the castle to check if any guides are available that day. Alternatively, call the castle yourself on ☎ 85-1146 (Japanese only).

It takes about 1½ hours to follow the arrow-marked route around the castle. The castle is open from 9 am to 5 pm (last entry 4 pm) most of the year, but until 6 pm (last entry 5 pm) in June, July and August. It's closed the last three days of the year.

HYŌGO PREFECTURAL MUSEUM OF HISTORY
兵庫県立博物館

This museum (¥200, 10 am to 5 pm, closed Monday and the day after national holidays) is well laid out and has good displays on Himeji-jō and other castles around Japan (and, indeed, around the whole world). At 10.30 am and 1.30 and 3.30 pm you can try on a suit of samurai armour or a kimono. In the event of competition for this singular honour, the museum staff resolve the conflict by the drawing of lots. Tell the staff at the main reception desk that you'd like to participate and they'll take care of the details.

The museum is a five-minute walk north of the castle.

KŌKO-EN 好古園

Just across the moat on the western side of Himeji-jō, you'll find Kōko-en (¥300, 9 am to 5 pm, until 6 pm in summer), a reconstruction of the former samurai quarters of the castle. There are nine separate Edo-style gardens, two ponds, a stream, a tea arbor (¥500 for matcha) and the restaurant *Kassui-ken*, where you can enjoy lunch while gazing over the gardens. It's open daily.

ENGYŌ-JI 円教寺

Around 8km north-east of Himeji station, this mountaintop temple complex (¥300, 9 am to 5 pm) is well worth a visit if you've got time left after visiting the castle. The temple and surrounding area is most beautiful in the April cherry-blossom season or

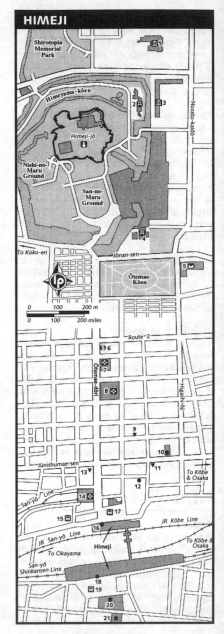

HIMEJI

HIMEJI

PLACES TO STAY

10 Himeji Washington
   Hotel Plaza
   姫路ワシントン
   ホテルプラザ
20 Hotel Sun Garden
   Himeji
   ホテルサンガーデン姫路
21 Hotel Himeji Plaza
   ホテル姫路プラザ

PLACES TO EAT

9 Fukutei
   福亭
11 Conservo
   コンサーボ
13 Salaryman Stand
   サラリーマンスタンド

OTHER

1 Hyōgo Prefectural
   Museum of History
   兵庫県立歴史博物館
2 Himeji-jinja
   姫路神社
3 Himeji City
   Museum of Art
   姫路市立美術館
4 Gokoku-jinja
   護国神社
5 Himeji Post Office
   姫路郵便局
6 Sumitomo Bank
   住友銀行
7 Daiei Department
   Store
   ダイエー

8 Yamatoyashiki
   Department Store
   ヤマトヤシキ
12 Discount Ticket Shop
   格安チケット売り場
14 San-yō Department
   Store; San-yō Himeji
   山陽百貨店；山陽姫路
15 Shinki Bus Centre
   神姫バスターミナル
16 North Exit
   北口
17 City Bus Terminal
   市バスターミナル
18 South Exit
   南口
19 City Bus Terminal South
   市バス南ターミナル

November *momiji* (maple leaf) season. Eight of the temple buildings and seven Buddha images have been designated Important Cultural Properties. Take your time to explore the temple grounds, which continue quite a way up the mountain (Shosha-zan) from the cable-car stop.

To get there, take bus No 6 or 8 from Himeji station (¥260, 25 minutes). Get off at Shosha, and board the cable car (¥500 one way, ¥900 return).

SPECIAL EVENTS

The **Mega-Kenka Matsuri**, held on 14 and 15 October, involves a conflict between three mikoshi (portable shrines) that are battered against each other until one smashes. Try to go on the second day, when the festival reaches its peak. The festival is held about a five-minute walk from Shirahamanomiya station (10 minutes from Himeji station on the San-yō line); just follow the crowds.

PLACES TO STAY

Himeji is best visited as a day trip from other parts of Kansai. If you'd like to stay, however, there are plenty of choices. The cheapest is the drab *Seinen-no-Ie Youth Hostel* (☎ 93-2716), which has per-person rates of ¥1000 for a Japanese-style dorm room, or

¥700 for a Western-style dorm room. There's also a ¥200 per-night sheet fee. Cooking and laundry facilities are available. Take bus No 3 bound for Himeji-ko and get off at the Chūo Kōen Guchi bus stop. The hostel is about 600m west of the stop past a Japanese garden. The tourist information office in Himeji station has a map.

In Himeji itself, the best hotel option is the *Himeji Washington Hotel Plaza* (☎ 25-0111), which has clean singles/doubles starting at ¥6750/13,508. On the other side of the station, *Hotel Himeji Plaza* (☎ 81-9000) is a similar choice with rooms starting at ¥5900/12,300. For those who want something fancier, the *Hotel Sun Garden Himeji* (☎ 22-2231) has clean new rooms starting at ¥9000/17,500.

PLACES TO EAT

There's a food court in the underground mall at JR Himeji station with all the usual Western and Japanese dishes. It's just to the right as you exit the northern ticket gate of JR Himeji station. One of the stands here serves *Akashi-yaki*, a type of tako-yaki popular in this region.

On the way to the castle, you might stop for coffee and sandwiches at the *Conservo* bakery. It also has also a good selection of

KANSAI REGION

things to take away if you'd prefer a picnic in the castle grounds. For something much more elegant, try *Fukutei*, which serves kaiseki cuisine at comparatively reasonable prices. From 11 am to 2 pm, its mini-kaiseki course is ¥1400. Kaiseki dinners, served from 6 to 9.30 pm, start at ¥5000. It's closed on Thursday.

For dinner, you might try the oddly named *Salaryman Stand*, an izakaya that serves a variety of teishoku meals in the ¥1000 range. In the winter, it specialises in Hiroshima oyster dishes.

GETTING THERE & AWAY

The best way to Himeji from Kyoto, Osaka or Kōbe is a shinkaisoku on the JR Tōkaidō line (to/from Kyoto – ¥2210, one hour and 20 minutes; to/from Osaka – ¥1450 one hour; to/from Kōbe – ¥950, 40 minutes). From Okayama, to the west, a tokkyū JR train on the San-yō line takes 1½ hours and costs ¥1450. You can also reach Himeji from these cities via the Tōkaidō/San-yō shinkansen line, and this is a good option for Japan Rail Pass holders.

Nara 奈良

☎ 0742 • pop 363,000

Japan's first real capital, Nara, is the number-two tourist attraction in Kansai after Kyoto. Like Kyoto, Nara is uninspiring at first glance, but careful inspection will reveal the rich history and hidden beauty of the city. Indeed, with eight Unesco World Heritage Sites, Nara is second only to Kyoto as a repository of Japan's cultural legacy. Whatever you do, try to go to Nara on a fine day, as visiting the sites requires a lot of walking, and it's no fun at all in bad weather.

Suggested Itinerary

Nara is so small that it's quite possible to pack the most worthwhile sights into one full day. It's preferable, of course, to spend at least two days here, but this will depend on how much time you have for the Kansai region. Those with time to spare should

allow a day for Nara-kōen and another day for the sights in western and south-western Nara. If you only have one day in Nara, spend it tramping around Nara-kōen; you would only exhaust yourself if you tried to fit in some of the more distant sights as well.

HISTORY

Nara is at the northern end of the Yamato plain, a fertile valley where members of the Yamato clan rose to power as the original emperors of Japan. The remains of these early emperors are contained in *kofun* (burial mounds), some of which date back to the 3rd century AD.

Until the 7th century, however, Japan had no permanent capital, as native Shintō taboos concerning death stipulated that the capital be moved with the passing of each emperor. This practice died out under the influence of Buddhism, and with the Taika reforms of 646, when the entire country came under imperial control.

At this time it was decreed that a permanent capital be built. Two locations were tried before a permanent capital was finally established at Nara (which was then known as Heijōkyō) in 710. Permanent status, however, lasted a mere 75 years. When a priest by the name of Dōkyō managed to seduce an empress and nearly usurp the throne, it was decided to move the court to

Unesco World Heritage Sites

In 1998, eight sites in Nara met the criteria to be designated World Heritage Sites by the United Nations. They are the Buddhist temples of Tōdai-ji, Kōfuku-ji, Gango-ji, Yakushi-ji and Tōshōdai-ji; the shrine, Kasuga Taisha; Kasuga-yama Primeval Forest; and the remains of Heijō-kyō Palace.

Each of these sites is considered to be of immeasurable historical value. All are open for public viewing. Five are covered in detail in the text; of the remaining three, Kasuga-yama Primeval Forest is directly behind Kasuage Taisha, Gango-ji is in Naramachi, and the Heijō-kyō Palace Ruins are 10 minutes' walk east of Saidai-ji station on the Kintetsu line.

a new location, out of reach of Nara's increasingly powerful clergy. This led to the new capital being established at Kyoto, where it remained until 1868.

Although brief, the Nara period was extraordinarily vigorous in its absorption of influences from China, a process that laid the foundations of Japanese culture and civilisation. The adoption of Buddhism as a national religion made a lasting impact on government, arts, literature and architecture. With the exception of an assault on the area by the Taira clan in the 12th century, Nara was subsequently spared the periodic bouts of destruction wreaked upon Kyoto, and a number of magnificent buildings have survived.

ORIENTATION

Nara retains the grid pattern of streets laid out in Chinese style during the 8th century. The two main train stations, JR Nara station and Kintetsu Nara station, are roughly in the middle of the city and Nara-kōen, which contains most of the important sights, is on the eastern side, against the bare flank of Wakakusa yama. Most of the other sights are south-west of the city and are best reached by buses that leave from both train stations (or by train in the case of Hōryū-ji). It's easy to cover the city centre and the major attractions in nearby Nara-kōen on foot, though some may prefer to rent a bicycle (see the Getting Around section).

Maps

Nara tourist information offices have two very useful maps: the *Strolling Around Nara* map, which is best for sightseeing within the city limits, and the *Japan, Nara Prefecture* map, which is best for outlying areas.

INFORMATION

If you're heading to Nara from Kyoto, the TIC in Kyoto has good information on the city. In Nara, the best source of information is the Nara City Tourist Centre (☎ 22-3900), which is open from 9 am to 9 pm. It's a short walk from JR Nara or Kintetsu Nara station.

It can put you in touch with volunteer guides who speak English and other foreign languages, but you must book in advance.

Two of these services are the YMCA Goodwill Guides (☎ 45-5920) and Nara Student Guides (☎ 26-1991). These services are a pleasant way to meet the Japanese – the guides are often students keen to practise their foreign languages. Remember that the guides are volunteers, so you should offer to cover their day's expenses; however, most temple and museum admission fees are waived for registered guides, so you needn't worry about those.

There are three more tourist information offices in Nara that stock maps and have staff who can answer basic questions in English: the JR Nara station office (☎ 22-9821), the Kintetsu Nara station office (☎ 24-4858) and the Sarusawa information office (☎ 26-1991). All three are open from 9 am to 5 pm. The JR Nara station office may be able to help with ryokan and minshuku reservations.

There is an ATM that accepts international cards on the ground floor of the building opposite Kintetsu Nara station. In the same building you can purchase tickets for highway buses (to Tokyo etc), airport buses (to Kansai airport) and tour buses (around Nara and surrounding areas).

Outside NTT Telecom Square on Sanjō-dōri there is a bank of international phones. You may be able to log onto the Internet in this building (it was under construction at the time of writing). Otherwise, the closest place for Internet services is the Digital Cats Internet cafe (☎ 0120-816-280) in Saidai-ji, one stop west of Nara on the Kintetsu Nara line. It's on the 2nd floor of the Kokusai-Shoken building, across from the northern exit of the station.

The Nara City Tourist Centre office also has comprehensive listings of places to stay, information on bus tours, hiking maps and the like. For a more academic look at Nara's sights, pick up a copy of *Historical Nara* by Herbert Plutschow.

NARA-KŌEN AREA 奈良公園

The park was created from wasteland in 1880 and covers a large area at the foot of Wakakusa-yama. The JNTO's leaflet entitled *Walking Tour Courses in Nara* includes a map for this area. Although walking time

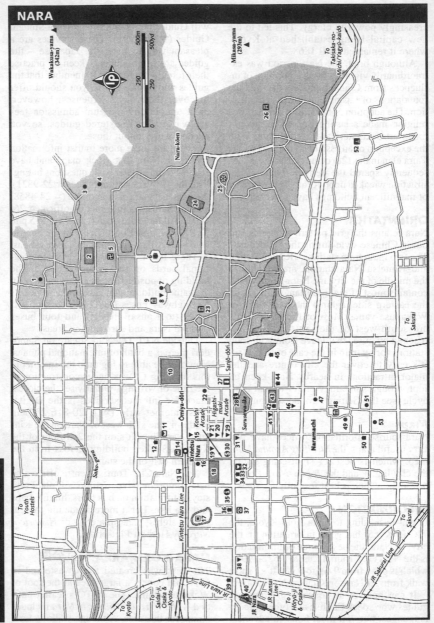

NARA

Waikakusa-yama
(342m)

Mikasa-yama
(293m)

To
Takisaka-no-
Michi/Yagyū-kaidō

500m
500yd

Nara-kōen

26

52

3
4

24
25

2
5

1

6

9
8
7

23

To
Sakurai

45

10

27

44

Sanjō-dōri

22

28

43

47

Higashi-
muki
Arcade

46

48

Konishi
Arcade

15
21
29

Sarusawa-ike

51

11

Omiya-dōri

42

41

49
53

12
14

Kintetsu
Nara

19
20

31

50

Naramachi

16
30

18

34 33 32

13

Saho-gawa

To
Youth
Hostels

35

36

37

17

To
Sakurai

38

39

Kintetsu Nara Line

To
Kyoto

To
Saidai-ji,
Osaka &
Kyoto

40

JR Nara

JR Nara
Line

JR Kansai
Line

To
Hōryū-ji &
Osaka

JR Sakurai Line

To
Sakurai

NARA

PLACES TO STAY

12 Green Hotel Ashibi
グリーンホテルあしび

33 Ryokan Hakuhō
旅館白鳳

36 Hotel Fujita Nara
ホテルフジタ奈良

39 Nara Kokusai Hotel
奈良国際ホテル

42 Ryokan Matsumae
奈良ホテル

44 Hotel Sunroute Nara
ホテルサンルート奈良

45 Nara Hotel
奈良ホテル

50 Ryokan Seikan-sō
旅館静観荘

PLACES TO EAT

8 Sanshū
三秀

15 Tsukihi-tei
月日亭

19 Shanti
シャンティー

20 Okaro
おかろ

21 Za Don
ザ・どん蔵

29 Beni-e
べに江

31 Miyono
三好野

34 Toku Toku
得々

38 Maguro-tei
まぐろ亭

41 Hirasō
平宗

46 Tempura Asuka
天ぷら飛鳥

OTHER

1 Shōso-in Treasure
Repository
正倉院

2 Tōdai-ji Daibutsu-den
Hall
東大寺大仏殿

3 Nigatsu-dō Hall
二月堂

4 Sangatsu-dō Hall
三月堂

5 Tōdai-ji Chū-mon
東大寺中門

6 Tōdai-ji Nandai-mon
東大寺南大門

7 Isui-en
依水園

9 Neiraku Art Museum
寧楽美術館

10 Nara Prefectural
Office
奈良県庁

11 Post Office
郵便局

13 Local Bus Stop
市バス停

14 Tour Bus Tickets;
Highway Bus Tickets;
Airport Bus Tickets;
International ATM
観光バス切符売り場；
高速バス切符売り場，
エアポートリムジンバス
切符売り場；国際ATM

16 Kintetsu Sunflower
Rent-a-Cycle
近鉄サンフラワー
レンタサイクル

17 Emperor Kaika's
Tomb
開化天皇陵

18 Vivre Department
Store
ビブレ

22 Kōfuku-ji National
Treasure Hall
(Kokuhō-kan)
興福寺国宝館

23 Nara National Museum
奈良国立博物館

24 Nara Prefectural
Public Hall
奈良県民ホール

25 Kasuga Taisha
Garden
春日大社庭園

26 Kasuga Taisha
春日大社

27 Kōfuku-ji Five-Storeyed
Pagoda
興福寺五重塔

28 Sarusawa Information
Office
猿沢観光案内所

30 Sumitomo Bank
住友銀行

32 Rumours (Bar)
ルーマーズ

35 Nara City Tourist
Center (main
Tourist Information
office)
奈良市観光センター

37 NTT Telecom Square;
International Phones
テレコムスクウェアー；
国際電話

40 JR Nara Station Tourist
Information Office
JR奈良駅観光案内所

43 Naramachi Center
ならまちセンター

47 Gangō-ji
元興寺

48 Naramachi
Shiryō kan
Museum
奈良町資料館

49 Nara Orient Kan
奈良オリエント館

51 Naramachi Koshi-no-Ie
ならまち格子の家

52 Shin-Yakushi-ji
新薬師寺

53 Hanazono Shin-Onsen
花園新温泉

KANSAI REGION

is estimated at two hours, you'll need at least half a day to see a selection of the sights and a full day to see them all.

The park is home to about 1200 deer, which in pre-Buddhist times were considered messengers of the gods and today enjoy the status of National Treasures. They roam the park and surrounding areas in search of hand-outs from tourists, often descending on petrified children who have the misfortune to be carrying food. You can buy *shika-sembei* (special biscuits) from vendors for ¥150 to feed to the deer (don't eat the biscuits yourself, as we saw one misguided foreign tourist doing).

Kōfuku-ji 興福寺

This temple was transferred here from Kyoto in 710 as the main temple for the Fujiwara family. Although the original temple complex had 175 buildings, fires and destruction as a result of power struggles have left only a dozen still standing. There are two pagodas – a three-storey one and a five-storey one – dating from 1143 and 1426 respectively. The taller of the two pagodas is the second tallest in Japan, outclassed by the one at Kyoto's Tō-ji by only a few centimetres.

The Kokuhō-kan (National Treasure Hall) contains a variety of statues and art objects salvaged from previous structures (¥500, 9 am to 4.30 pm). A descriptive leaflet in English is provided.

Nara National Museum 奈良国立博物館

The Nara National Museum (Nara Kokuritsu Hakubutsukan) is devoted to Buddhist art and is divided into two wings. The western gallery exhibits archaeological finds, while the eastern gallery displays sculptures, paintings and calligraphy. The galleries are linked by an underground passage.

A special exhibition featuring the treasures of the Shōsō-in Hall, which holds the treasures of Tōdai-ji, are displayed here in May, as well as from 21 October to 8 November (call the Nara City Tourist Centre to check, as these dates vary slightly each year). The exhibits include priceless items from the cultures along the Silk Road. If you are in Nara during these periods, you should make a point of visiting the museum. The museum is open from 9 am to 4.30 pm (¥420, special exhibitions ¥830).

Isui-en & Neiraku Art Museum 依水園と寧楽美術館

This garden, dating from the Meiji era, is beautifully laid out and features abundant greenery and a pond filled with ornamental carp (museum and garden ¥600, 10 am to 4.30 pm, closed Tuesday and 18 December to 6 January). It's without a doubt the best garden in the city and well worth a visit. For ¥450 you can enjoy a cup of tea on tatami mats overlooking the garden or have lunch in nearby *Sanshū* restaurant, which also shares the view.

The adjoining art museum (Neiraku Bijutsukan), which displays Chinese and Korean ceramics and bronzes, is something of an anticlimax after the garden.

TŌDAI-JI 東大寺

This temple, with its vast Daibutsu-den Hall and enormous bronze Buddha image, is Nara's star attraction. For this reason, it is often packed with groups of school children being herded around by microphone-wielding tour guides. Nonetheless, it is an awe-inspiring sight and should be high on any sightseeing itinerary.

On your way to the temple you'll pass through Nandai-mon, an enormous gate containing two fierce looking Niō guardians. These recently restored wooden images, carved in the 13th century by the sculptor Unkei, are some of the finest wooden statues in all of Japan, if not the world. They are truly dramatic works of art and seem ready to spring to life at any moment.

Daibutsu-den Hall 大仏殿

Tōdai-ji's Daibutsu-den (Hall of the Great Buddha) is the largest wooden building in the world. Unbelievably, the present structure, rebuilt in 1709, is a mere two-thirds of the size of the original! The Daibutsu (Great Buddha) contained within is one of the largest bronze figures in the world and was originally cast in 746. The present statue, recast in the Edo period, stands just over 16m high and consists of 437 tonnes of bronze and 130kg of gold.

The Daibutsu is an image of the Dainichi Buddha, the cosmic Buddha believed to give rise to all worlds and their respective historical Buddhas. Historians believe that Emperor Shōmu ordered the building of the Buddha as a charm against smallpox, which had ravaged Japan in preceding years. Over the centuries the statue took quite a beating from earthquakes and fires, losing its head a couple of times in the process (note the slight difference in colour between the head and the body).

As you circle the statue towards the back, you'll see a wooden column with a hole through its base. Popular belief maintains that those who can squeeze through the hole, which is exactly the same size as one of the Great Buddha's nostrils, are ensured of enlightenment. It's great fun to watch the kids wiggle through nimbly and the adults get wedged in like champagne corks – you wonder how often they have to call the fire department to extricate trapped visitors. A hint for determined adults: it's a lot easier to go through with both arms held above your head.

Admission to the Daibutsu-den is ¥400, and your ticket has a convenient list of the Daibutsu's vital statistics. Opening hours are as follows: from 8 am to 4.30 pm from November to February; from 8 am to 5 pm in March; from 7.30 am to 5.30 pm from April to September; and from 7.30 am to 5 pm in October.

Shōsō-in Treasure Repository 正倉院

The Shōsō-in Treasure Repository is a short walk north of Daibutsu-den. If you discount the slight curve to the roof, the structure is reminiscent of a log cabin from North America. The building was used to house fabulous imperial treasures and its wooden construction allowed precise regulation of humidity through natural expansion and contraction. The treasures have been removed and are shown twice a year, in spring and autumn, at the Nara National Museum. The Shōsō-in building is open to the public at the same time.

Kaidan-in Hall 戒壇院

This hall a short walk west of the entrance gate to the Daibutsu-den was used for ordination ceremonies and is famous for its clay images of the Shi Tennō (Four Heavenly Guardians). The hall's opening hours are the same as those of the Daibutsu-den and admission is ¥400.

Nigatsu-dō & Sangatsu-dō Halls 二月堂と三月堂

Walk east from the entrance to the Daibutsu-den, climb up a flight of stone steps, and continue to your left to reach these two halls.

Nigatsu-dō Hall is famed for its **Omizutori Matsuri** (see the later section on Nara Special Events for details) and a splendid view across Nara, which makes the climb up the hill worthwhile – particularly at dusk. Opening hours here are the same as those of the Daibutsu-den and admission is free.

A short walk south of Nigatsu-dō is Sangatsu-dō Hall, which is the oldest building in the Tōdai-ji complex. This hall contains a small collection of fine statues from the Nara period. Admission is ¥400 and it's open the same hours as the Daibutsu-den.

Kasuga Taisha 春日大社

This shrine was founded in the 8th century by the Fujiwara family and completely rebuilt every 20 years according to Shintō tradition, until the end of the 19th century. It lies at the foot of the hill in a pleasant, wooded setting with herds of sacred deer awaiting hand-outs.

The approaches to the shrine are lined with hundreds of lanterns and there are many hundreds more in the shrine itself. The **lantern festivals** held twice a year at the shrine are a major attraction. For details about these and other festivals held at the nearby Wakamiya-jinja, see the later section on Nara Special Events.

The Hōmotsu-den (Treasure Hall) is just north of the entrance torii for the shrine. The hall (¥420, 9 am to 4 pm) displays Shintō ceremonial regalia and equipment used in bugaku, nō and gagaku performances.

Shin-Yakushi-ji 新薬師寺

This temple (¥500, 9 am to 5 pm) a pleasant 15-minute walk from Kasuga Taisha was founded by Empress Kōmyō in 747 in thanks for her husband's recovery from an eye disease. Most of the buildings were destroyed or have been reconstructed, but the present main hall dates from the 8th century. The hall contains sculptures of Yakushi Nyorai (Healing Buddha) and a set of 12 divine generals.

NARAMACHI ならまち

South of Sanjō-dōri and Sarusawa-ike pondx you will find the pleasant little neighbourhood of Naramachi, with many well-preserved machiya and *kura* (traditional storehouses). It's a nice place for a stroll before or after hitting the big sights of Nara-kōen, and there are several good restaurants in the area to entice hungry travellers (see the Places to Eat & Drink section later).

Highlights of Naramachi include the **Naramachi Shiryō-kan Museum** (free, 10 am to 4 pm, closed Monday), which has a decent collection of bric-a-brac from the area, including a display of old Japanese coins and bills. Perhaps more interesting is the off-beat **Nara Orient Kan** (¥300, 10 am to 5 pm, closed Monday), which makes the most of Nara's old Silk Road connections, displaying various arts and crafts from mainland Asia. More than the displays, however, it's worth a visit simply to enjoy the wonderful old building that houses the collection. Another place you can go to see a traditional Japanese house is the **Naramachi Koshi-no-Ie** (free, 9 am to 5 pm, closed Monday). Unfortunately, this place has been a little too thoroughly restored – you'll almost certainly prefer the Nara Orient Kan.

TEMPLES SOUTH-WEST OF NARA

There are several important temples southwest of Nara, the most important of which are Hōryū-ji, Yakushi-ji and Tōshōdai-ji. These three can be visited in one afternoon. The best way to do this is to head straight to Hōryū-ji (the most distant from downtown Nara) and then continue by bus No 52, 97 or 98 (¥560, 30 minutes) up to Yakushi-ji and Tōshōdai-ji, which are a 10-minute walk apart.

Hōryū-ji 法隆寺

This temple (8 am to 4.30 pm, until 5 pm from 11 March to 19 November) was founded in 607 by Prince Shōtoku, considered by many to be the patron saint of Japanese Buddhism. Legend has it that Shōtoku, moments after birth, stood up and started praying. A statue in the treasure museum depicts this auspicious event. Hōryū-ji is renowned not only as the oldest temple in Japan but also as a repository for some of the country's rarest treasures. Several of the temple's wooden buildings have survived earthquakes and fires to become the oldest of their kind in the world. The temple is divided into two parts, Sai-in (West Temple) and Tō-in (East Temple).

The entrance ticket costs ¥1000 and allows admission to Sai-in, Tō-in and the Great Treasure Hall. A detailed map is provided and a guidebook is available in English and several other languages. The JNTO leaflet called *Walking Tour Courses in Nara* includes a basic map for the area around Hōryū-ji.

The main approach to the temple proceeds from the south along a tree-lined avenue and continues through Nandai-mon and Chū-mon before entering the **Sai-in precinct**. As you enter this precinct, you'll see the **Kondō** (Main Hall) on your right and a pagoda on your left.

The Kondō houses several treasures, including the triad of the Buddha Sākyamuni, with two attendant Bodhisattvas. Though it is one of Japan's great Buddhist treasures, it is dimly lit and barely visible (you may want to bring a flashlight). Likewise, the pagoda contains clay images depicting scenes from the life of Buddha that are barely visible without a flashlight.

On the eastern side of Sai-in are the two concrete buildings of the **Daihōzō-den** (Great Treasure Hall), containing numerous treasures from Hōryū-ji's long history. Renowned Buddhist artefacts in this hall include the Kudara Kannon and two miniature shrines: the Tamamushi Shrine and the Shrine of Lady Tachibana.

The **Tamamushi Shrine** is named for the insect *tamamushi*, or jewel beetle, whose wings were used to decorate it. The colour in the original has faded, but an example of fresh tamamushi wings is on display and one can only imagine how the shrine must have looked when it was entirely covered with shimmering blue-green wings.

If you leave this hall and continue east through Tōdai-mon you reach **Tō-in**. The Yumedono (Hall of Dreams) in this temple is where Prince Shōtoku is believed to have meditated and been given help with problem sutras by a kindly, golden apparition.

At the rear of the Tō-in compound is the entrance to **Chūgū-ji Nunnery**, which is drab in appearance, but contains two famous art treasures: the serene statue of the Bodhisattva Miroku and a portion of the embroidered Tenjukoku (Land of Heavenly Longevity) mandala, which is believed to date from the 7th century and is the oldest remaining example of this art in Japan. Admission to this temple is ¥400 and it's open from 9 am to 4.30 pm.

Getting There & Away To get to the Hōryū-ji, take the JR Kansai line from JR Nara station to Horyu-ji station (¥210, 10 minutes). From there, a bus shuttles the short distance between the station and Hōryū-ji (No 73, ¥170, five minutes), or you can walk it in 20 minutes. Alternatively, take bus No 52, 60, 97 or 98 from either JR Nara station or Kintetsu Nara station and get off at the Hōryū-ji Mae stop (¥760, 50 minutes).

Yakushi-ji 薬師寺

Yakushi-ji (¥500, 8.30 am to 5 pm) was established by Emperor Temmu in 680. With the exception of the **East Pagoda**, the present buildings either date from the 13th century or are very recent reconstructions.

The main hall was rebuilt in 1976 and houses several images, including the famous Yakushi Triad (the Buddha Yakushi flanked by the Bodhisattvas of the sun and moon), dating from the 8th century. Originally gold, a fire in the 16th century turned the images an appealingly mellow black.

The East Pagoda is a unique structure because it appears to have six storeys, but three

of them are *mokoshi* (lean-to additions), which give a pleasing balance to its appearance. It is the only structure to have survived the ravages of time, and dates from 730.

Behind the East Pagoda is **Tōin-dō** (East Hall), which houses the famous Shō-Kannon image, built in the 7th century and showing obvious influences of Indian sculptural styles.

An English-language leaflet about the temple is provided.

Getting There & Away To get to Yakushi-ji, take bus No 52, 63, 70, 97 or 98 from either JR Nara station or Kintetsu Nara station and get off at the Yakushi-ji Higashiguchi stop (¥240, 18 minutes).

Tōshōdai-ji 唐招提寺

This temple (¥600, 8.30 am to 4.30 pm) was established in 759 by the Chinese priest Ganjin (Jian Zhen), who had been recruited by Emperor Shōmu to reform Buddhism in Japan. Ganjin didn't have much luck with his travel arrangements from China to Japan: five attempts were thwarted by shipwreck, storms and bureaucracy. Despite being blinded by eye disease, he finally made it on the sixth attempt and spread his teachings to Japan. The lacquer sculpture in the Miei-dō Hall is a moving tribute to Ganjin: blind and rock steady. It is shown only once a year, on 6 June – the anniversary of Ganjin's death.

If you're not lucky enough to be in Nara on that day, it's still well worth visiting this temple to see the fantastic trinity of Buddhas in the **Kon-dō** hall of the temple. The centrepiece is a seated image of Rushana Buddha, which is flanked by two standing Buddha images, Yakushi-nyorai and Senjū-Kannon.

The Shin Hōzō (Treasure Hall) has some fine sculptures and images. Admission is ¥100, and it's open during the same hours as the temple, but only from late March to late May, and from mid-September to early November.

A detailed leaflet is provided in English, including a precise map of the extensive temple grounds.

Tōshōdai-ji is a 10-minute walk north of Yakushi-ji's northern gate; see that section for transport details from Nara.

ORGANISED TOURS

Nara Kōtsū (☎ 22-5263) runs daily bus tours on a variety of routes, two of which include Nara city sights only and two of which include more distant sights like Hōryū-ji and the burial mounds around Asuka. An explanation tape in English is available for all but the Asuka route. Prices for the all-day trips average ¥7000 for adults (which includes all temple fees and tape-recorder rental). Lunch at a Japanese restaurant on the route is optional (reserve when buying your ticket). Nara Kōtsū has offices in JR Nara station and across the street from Kintetsu Nara station.

SPECIAL EVENTS

Nara has plenty of festivals throughout the year. The following is a brief list of the more interesting ones. More extensive information is readily available from Nara tourist offices or from the TIC in Kyoto.

January
Yamayaki (Grass Burning Festival) 15 January. To commemorate a feud many centuries ago between the monks of Tōdai-ji and Kōfuku-ji, Wakakusa-yama is set alight at 6 pm, with an accompanying display of fireworks. Arrive earlier to bag a good viewing position in Nara-kōen.

February
Mantōrō (Lantern Festival) 2 to 4 February. Held at Kasuga Taisha at 6 pm, this is a festival renowned for its illumination, with 3000 stone and bronze lanterns; a bugaku dance also takes place in the Apple Garden on the last day.

March
Omizutori (Water-Drawing Ceremony) 1 to 14 March. The monks of Tōdai-ji enter a special period of initiation during these days. On the evening of 12 March, they parade huge flaming torches around the balcony of Nigatsu-dō (in the temple grounds) and rain down embers on the spectators to purify them. The water-drawing ceremony is performed after midnight.
Kasuga Matsuri 13 March. This ancient spring festival features a sacred horse, classical dancing (Yamato-mai) and elaborate costume.

May
Takigi Nō 11 to 12 May. Open-air performances of nō held after dark by the light of blazing torches at Kōfuku-ji and Kasuga Taisha.

August
Mantōrō (Lantern Festival) 14 to 15 August. The same as the festival held in February.

October
Shika-no-Tsunokiri (Deer Antler Cutting) Sundays & national holidays in October. Those pesky deer in Nara-kōen are pursued in a type of elegant rodeo into the Roku-en (deer enclosure) close to Kasuga Taisha. They are then wrestled to the ground and their antlers sawn off. Tourist brochures hint that this is to avoid personal harm, though it's not clear whether they are referring to the deer fighting each other or the deer mugging the tourists.

December
On Matsuri 15 to 18 December. This festival, dating back to the Heian period, is held to ensure a bountiful harvest and to ward off disease. It takes place at Wakamiya-jinja (close to Kasuga Taisha) and features a procession of people dressed in ancient costume (on 17 December), classical dances, wrestling and performances of nō.

PLACES TO STAY

Although Nara is favoured as a day trip from Kyoto, accommodation can still be packed out for festivals and holidays and at weekends, so make reservations in advance if you plan to visit at these times. The Nara City Tourist Centre has extensive lists of hotels, minshuku, pensions and ryokan. The JR Nara station tourist office may be able to help with minshuku and ryokan reservations.

Places to Stay – Budget

The *Nara-ken Seishōnen Kaikan Youth Hostel (☎ 22-5540)* is a nondescript, concrete place with friendly staff. Dorm rooms are ¥2650 per person. It also has private double rooms for ¥3350 a person and triples for ¥3050 a person. Check-in is until 8 pm. It's a 30-minute uphill walk from the centre of town to the hostel. From JR Nara station or Kintetsu Nara station you can also take bus No 12, 13, 131 or 140 and get off at the Ikuei-gakuen bus stop, from which it's a five-minute walk.

The *Nara Youth Hostel* (☎ 22-1334) is close to Kōno-ike, a short walk from the other youth hostel. This is a ritzier hostel that charges ¥2300 a person. Check-in is from 3 pm to 9.30 pm. It is often booked out and swarming with school children on excursions. From either JR or Kintetsu Nara station, take bus No 108, 109, 111, 115 or 130 and get off at the Shieikyū-jō-mae bus stop, from which it's a one-minute walk.

Places to Stay – Mid-Range

The best ryokan value in Nara is *Ryokan Seikan-sō* (☎ 22-2670), a friendly place with wooden architecture and a pleasant garden. It's a 15-minute walk south of Kintetsu Nara station. Prices for a Japanese-style room without bath start at ¥4000 a person.

The *Ryokan Matsumae* (☎ 22-3686) is close to Nara-kōen. Prices for a Japanese-style room without bath start at ¥4500 a person. It lacks the atmosphere of the Seikan-sō but it's in a very convenient location.

The *Ryokan Hakuhō* (☎ 26-7891) is in the centre of town, just a five-minute walk from JR Nara station. It's starting to show its age and has less atmosphere than the Seikan-sō. Prices for a Japanese-style room without bath start at ¥6500 a person.

The city centre has a few business hotels. The *Green Hotel Ashibi* (☎ 26-7815) is a small place with singles/doubles/twins starting at ¥6400/11,000/12,000. It's close to Kintetsu Nara station.

Places to Stay – Top End

Hotel Fujita Nara (☎ 23-8111) is a clean, new hotel with singles/doubles/twins from ¥8000/13,000/15,000. During off-peak times, you might be able to negotiate a reduced rate if you reserve through the Kintetsu Nara tourist information office.

Close to the south-western corner of Nara-kōen, the *Hotel Sunroute Nara* (☎ 22-5151) has singles from ¥8000 and doubles/twins from ¥15,000.

The *Nara Kokusai Hotel* (☎ 26-6001) is close to JR Nara station and works on the ryokan plan, meaning that rooms come with meals (¥12,000 a person with two meals).

Not far from the Hotel Sunroute Nara, the atmospheric old *Hotel Nara* (☎ 26-3300) was built near the turn of the century and still ranks as Nara's premier hotel. Singles/doubles/twins start at ¥14,000/23,000/22,000. Rooms in the old wing have much more character than those in the new wing.

PLACES TO EAT

Nara is full of good restaurants, most of which are in the central area near the two main train stations and the tourist offices. If you need help finding a place, the main tourist information office has lists of restaurants by category (Japanese, Chinese, Western etc) and can help with reservations and recommendations.

Japanese Cuisine

Just outside Kintetsu Nara station, the Higashi-muki shopping arcade is a good place to hunt for reasonable restaurants. *Za Don* ('Don' being short for 'donburi', or rice bowl) takes the honours in the cheapest eats category, with donburi starting at ¥390. It's healthy Japanese fast food and there's a picture menu to make ordering easier. Just a few doors down, *Okaro* serves good okonomiyaki starting at ¥680 – look for the food models in the window.

In the same arcade, close to the northern end on the 2nd floor, is *Tsukihi-tei*, which serves simple kaiseki dishes at reasonable prices. The *tenshin* bento is a good bet at ¥1500. It includes sashimi, rice, vegetables and *chawan-mushi*, a savoury custard. At the opposite end of the arcade, *Beni-e* serves good tempura set meals starting from ¥1500. It's a little back from the street, behind a shoe store.

If you leave the arcade and walk out onto Sanjō-dōri, you run right into *Miyono*, which serves good-value set lunches of typical Japanese fare starting at ¥650. Stop by and check the daily lunch specials on display outside. Down the same street, in the direction of JR Nara, is *Toku Toku*, an udon specialist that should satisfy even the biggest appetites. When you order, you can ask for double or triple the normal amount of noodles for the same price! Expect to pay around ¥750 for most dishes. Just down the street, big eaters will also be tempted by *Maguro-tei*, a *kaiten* (conveyor-belt) sushi place that offers an all-you-can eat sushi binge at the unbelievably low prices of ¥1575 for men and ¥1050 for women.

Nara is also a good place to sample some of Japan's more elegant culinary offerings. Naramachi's *Hirasō* serves elegant kaiseki set meals starting at ¥4500 and set lunches starting at ¥2100. It's closed on Monday. Also in Naramachi is *Tempura Asuka*, which serves elegant set meals of tempura, sashimi and other delightful little accompaniments. At lunch time, try its nicely presented *yumei-dono bentō*, a full set lunch including tempura for ¥1500. Set dinners start at ¥2000. It's closed on Wednesday.

Lastly, perhaps the most interesting place for lunch in all of Nara is *Sanshū*, next to the beautiful Isui-en near Nara-kōen. It serves a traditional Japanese dish called *tororo* which is made from grated yam, barley and rice. Guests sit on tatami mats enjoying the food while gazing out over the splendour of one of Nara's best gardens. Ordering is simple: you can have either the *mugitoro gozen* (without eel) for ¥1200 or the *unatoro gozen* (with eel) for ¥2500. Lunch is served every day except Tuesday from 11.30 am to 2 pm.

International Cuisine
If you need a break from Japanese food, there are all the usual fast-food favourites in Nara. For something a little more salubrious, try the Indian restaurant *Shanti*, which serves decent set meals with rice, curry, naan, salad and *chai* for around ¥900. It's in a small enclave of shops of the alley between Higashi-muki and Konishi shopping arcades.

ENTERTAINMENT
For Japanese-style drinking, you can choose any of the izakaya around town, although if you want to mingle, head to the English-style pub *Rumours* on Sanjō-dōri. You'll meet a crowd of friendly locals and resident expats.

GETTING THERE & AWAY
Train
Kyoto Unless you have a Japan Rail Pass, the best option is the Kintetsu line (sometimes written in English as the Kinki Nippon railway) linking Kyoto (Kintetsu Kyoto station) and Nara (Kintetsu Nara station). There are direct tokkyū trains (¥1110, 35 minutes) and kyūkō trains that may require a change at Saidai-ji (¥610, 45 minutes).

The JR Nara line connects JR Kyoto station with JR Nara station (kaisoku, ¥690, 46 minutes) but departures are often few and far between.

Osaka The Kintetsu Nara line connects Osaka (Kintetsu Namba station) with Nara (Kintetsu Nara station). Kaisoku and futsū services take about 35 minutes and cost ¥540. Tokkyū services do the journey in five minutes less but cost almost double, making them a poor option.

The JR Kansai line links Osaka (Namba and Tennō-ji stations) and Nara (JR Nara station) via Hōryū-ji (kaisoku, ¥540, 45 minutes).

Bus
There is an overnight bus service between Tokyo's Shinjuku (highway bus terminal) and Nara that costs ¥8400 one way or ¥15,120 return. The bus leaves Nara at 10.30 pm and reaches Tokyo the next day at 6.15 am. The bus from Tokyo leaves at 11.15 pm and arrives in Nara the next day at 6.50 am. In Nara, call ☎ 22-5110 or check with the Nara City Tourist Centre for more details. In Tokyo, ask at the TIC.

GETTING AROUND
To/From The Airport
Nara is served by Kansai international airport. There is a limousine service between Nara and the airport with departures roughly every hour in both directions (¥1800, 1½ hours). At Kansai international airport ask at the information counter, and in Nara go to the bus stop in front of Kintetsu Nara station (the same bus platform as is used for the daily bus tours). Reservations are a good idea and can be made on ☎ 22-5110. There

are no trains directly to the airport so take the JR line in either direction and change at Tennō-ji station in Osaka (see the Osaka Getting Around section for details).

Bus

Most of the area around Nara-kōen is covered by two circular bus routes. Bus No 1 runs counter-clockwise and bus No 2 runs clockwise. There's a ¥180 flat fare. You can easily see the main sights in the park on foot and use the bus as an option if you are pushed for time or get tired of walking.

The most useful buses for western and south-western Nara (Tōshōdai-ji, Yakushi-ji and Hōryū-ji) are Nos 52, 97 and 98, which link all three destinations with the Kintetsu and JR stations. Buses run about every 30 minutes between 8 am and 5 pm, but are much less frequent outside these times.

Taxi

Taxis are plentiful but expensive. A taxi ride from JR Nara station to either of the youth hostels costs about ¥1000.

Cycling

Nara is a convenient size for getting around on a bicycle. Kintetsu Sunflower Rent-a-Cycle (☎ 24-3528) is close to the Nara City Tourist Centre. Weekday rates are ¥300 per hour and ¥900 per day on weekdays and ¥350 and ¥1000 on weekends. It's just off Konishi Arcade, down a small street opposite a supermarket.

Around Nara 奈良周辺

Southern Nara-ken was the birthplace of imperial rule and is rich in historical sites that are easily accessible as day trips from Osaka, Kyoto or Nara provided that you make an early start. Of particular historical interest are the kofun that mark the graves of Japan's first emperors; these are concentrated around Asuka and Sakurai (see the 'Kofun Burial Mounds' boxed text in this chapter). There are also several isolated temples where you can escape the crowds that plague Nara's city centre. Farther

afield, the mountaintop town of Yoshino is one of Japan's cherry-blossom meccas.

Easily reached by rail, Sakurai and Yamato-Yagi serve as useful transport hubs for the region. Keep in mind that the Kintetsu line is far more convenient than JR for most of the destinations in this section.

If you're starting from Nara, you may want to pick up a copy of the detailed *Japan: Nara Prefecture* map at any of the tourist information offices in Nara city before starting out.

AROUND SAKURAI 桜井周辺

There are a few interesting places to visit close to the town of Sakurai that can be reached directly from Nara on the JR Sakurai line (futsū, ¥320, 30 minutes). To reach Sakurai via Yamato-Yagi (when coming from Kyoto or Osaka), take the Kintetsu Osaka line (futsū, ¥200, five minutes)

Ōmiwa-jinja 大神神社

This shrine is near Miwa station, one stop north of Sakurai on the JR Sakurai line (futsū, ¥140, two minutes). Since there are few departures on this line, it might be more convenient to take bus No 60 or 62 from Sakurai station to the shrine (¥170, six minutes). Alternatively, you could walk, which would take about 40 minutes. Ōmiwa-jinja boasts the highest torii in Japan (32.2m) and is one of Japan's oldest Shintō shrines. The mountain behind the shrine, Miwa-yama, is considered sacred because it is the abode of the shrine's *kami* (spirit gods); there is a trail for pilgrims to hike up the wooded slopes.

Tanzan-jinja 談山神社

Tanzan jinja lies south of Sakurai and can be reached by bus No 14 from stand No 1 outside the southern exit of Sakurai station (¥440, 25 minutes). It's tucked away in the forests of Tōnomine-san, famous for their autumn colours. Enshrined here is Nakatomi no Kamatari, patriarch of the Fujiwara line, which effectively ruled Japan for nearly 500 years. Legend has it that Nakatomi met here secretly with prince Naka no Ōe over games of kickball to

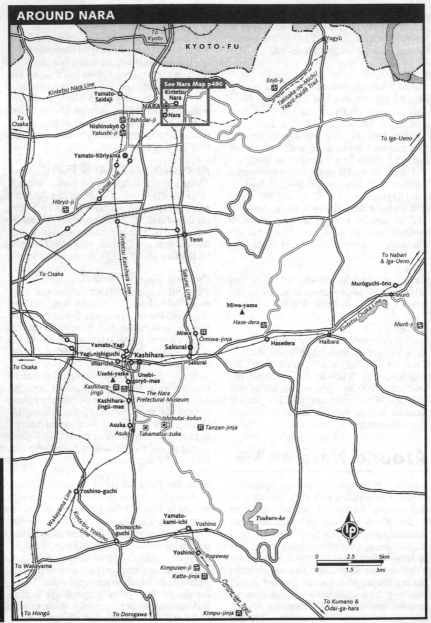

AROUND NARA

KYOTO-FU

To Kyoto

Yagyū

Enjō-ji

Takisaka-no-Michi
Yagyū-Kaidō Trail

See Nara Map p490

Kintetsu Nara Line

Yamato-
Saidaji

Kintetsu
Nara

NARA

Nara

To Iga-Ueno

Tōshōdai-ji

To Osaka

Nishinokyō
Yakushi-ji

Yamato-Kōriyama

Hōryū-ji

Tenri

To Nabari
& Iga-Ueno

Murōguchi-ōno

Murō

Miwa-yama

Kintetsu Ōsaka Line

Murō-ji

To Osaka

Hase-dera

Yamato-Yagi

Yagi-nishiguchi

Miwa

Ōmiwa-jinja

Sakurai

Hasedera

Haibara

Kashihara

Imai-chō

Sakurai

Unebi-yama

Kashihara-
jingū

Unebi-
goryō-mae

To Osaka

The Nara
Prefectural Museum

Kashihara-
jingū-mae

Ishibutai-kofun

Asuka

Takamatsu-zuka

Tanzan-jinja

Yoshino-guchi

Tsuburo-ko

Shimoichi-
guchi

Yamato-
kami-ichi

Yoshino

Yoshino

Ropeway

To Wakayama

Kimpusen-ji

Katte-jinja

To Hongū

To Dorogawa

Kimpu-jinja

To Kumano &
Ōdai-ga-hara

Ōmine-san Trail

0   2.5   5km

0   1.5   3mi

KANSAI REGION

discuss the overthrow of the ruling Soga clan. This event is commemorated on the second Sunday in November by priests playing a game of kickball – call it divine hackey sack.

The central structure of the shrine is an attractive 13-storey pagoda best viewed against a backdrop of maple trees ablaze with autumn colours.

Hase-dera 長谷寺

Two stops east of Sakurai on the Kintetsu Osaka line is Hasedera station. From the station, it's a 20-minute walk to lovely Hase-dera (¥500, 8.30 am to 5 pm). After a long climb up seemingly endless steps, you enter the main hall and are rewarded with a splendid view from the gallery, which juts out on stilts over the mountainside. Inside the top hall, the huge Kannon image is well worth a look. The best times to visit this temple are in the spring, when the way is lined with blooming peonies, and in autumn, when the temple's maple trees turn a vivid red. From the station, walk down through the archway, cross the river and turn right onto the main street that leads to the temple.

Murō-ji 室生寺

This temple was founded in the 9th century and has strong connections with Esoteric Buddhism (the Shingon sect). Women were never excluded from Murō-ji as they were from other Shingon temples, and it is for this reason that it came to be known as 'the Woman's Koya'. Unfortunately, the temple's lovely five-storey pagoda, which dates from the 8th or 9th century, was severely damaged in a typhoon in the summer of 1999. Repairs should be finished by the summer of 2000, but it's likely that the pagoda will have lost some of its rustic charm. Nonetheless, Murō-ji is a peaceful, secluded place in thick forest and is well worth a visit (¥400, 8 am to 4.30 pm).

Murōguchi-ōno station on the Kintetsu Osaka line is two stops east of Hasedera station. It's a 15-minute bus ride from Murōguchi-Ōno station to Murō-ji on bus No 43, 44, 45 or 46 (¥400).

AROUND YAMATO-YAGI 大和八木周辺

Easily reached on the Kintetsu line from Osaka, Kyoto or Nara, Yamato-Yagi is the most convenient transport hub for sights in southern Nara-ken. From Kyoto take the Kintetsu Nara/Kashihara line direct (kyūkō, ¥860, one hour). From Nara take the Kintetsu Nara line to Saidaiji and change to the Kintetsu Kashihara line (kyūkō, ¥430, 30 minutes). From Osaka's Uehonmachi station, take the Kintetsu Osaka line direct (kyūkō, ¥540, 35 minutes).

Imai-chō 今井町

South-west of Yamato-Yagi is Imai-chō, a neighbourhood with several classic machiya preserved virtually intact from the Edo period. (Unfortunately, some have been a little over-restored, robbing them of their charm). It's a pleasant place to walk around and seven of the buildings are open to the public (¥170, 10 am to noon, 1 to 5 pm). To get there, take a train one stop south from Yamato-Yagi to Yagi-Nishiguchi (¥150, two minutes). The town is a 10-minute walk south-west of the station; take the western exit out of the station, go left across the bridge and walk under the JR tracks.

Kashihara 橿原

Three stops south of Yamato-Yagi, on the Kintetsu Kashihara line, is Kashihara-jingū-mae station (¥200 from Yamato-Yagi, five minutes). There are a couple of interesting sights within easy walking distance of this station.

Kashihara-jingū This shrine, at the foot of Unebi-yama, dates back to 1889, when many of the buildings were moved here from Kyoto Gosho. The shrine buildings are built in the same style as those of Ise-Jingū's Grand Shrine (Japan's most sacred shrine) and are a good example of classical Shintō architecture. The shrine is dedicated to Japan's mythical first emperor, Jimmu, and an annual festival is held here on 11 February, the legendary date of Jimmu's enthronement. The vast, park-like grounds are pleasant to stroll around. The shrine is five minutes' walk from

KANSAI REGION

Kashihara-jingū-mae station; take the central exit out of the station and follow the main street in the direction of the mountain.

Nara Prefectural Museum This museum (¥400, 9 am to 5 pm, closed Monday) is highly recommended for those with an interest in the history of the Japanese people. The objects on display come from various archaeological sites in the area, including several kofun. Although most of the explanations are in Japanese, there's enough English to give you an idea of what's going on.

To get there from Kashihara-jingū, walk out the northern gate of the shrine (to your left when you stand with your back to the main hall), follow the wooded avenue for five minutes, cross the main road and continue on in the same direction for 100m before turning left. It's on the left soon after this turn.

ASUKA 飛鳥
☎ 0744

Five stops south of Yamato-Yagi (change at Kashihara-jingū-mae) and two stops south of Kashihara-jingū-mae on the Kintetsu Yoshino line is Asuka station (¥220 from Yamato-Yagi, 20 minutes). There's a tourist information office at the station (☎ 54-3624) where you can get maps of the area's temples, palace remains, tombs and strange stones. It's open from 8.30 am to 4.45 pm.

The best way to explore the area is by bicycle, and bicycles are available for rent at Manyō Rent-a-Cycle (☎ 54-3500) for ¥300 an hour or ¥1000 a day. You can drop bikes off at Kashihara or Asuka-dera if you've taken one of these longer tours. Manyō Rent-a-Cycle is across the street from the station – it's the second shop on your right.

Two tombs worth seeing are **Takamatsu-zuka** and **Ishibutai-kofun**. The former (excavated in 1972) is closed to the public but has a museum (¥210, 9 am to 5 pm, closed Monday) displaying a copy of the frescoes. History buffs will note that the entire tomb was built in the Chinese style of the time (T'ang), indicating the degree to which early Japanese civilisation was influenced by continental culture. The Ishibutai-kofun (¥250, 9 am to 5 pm) is open to the public

but has no frescoes. It is said to have housed the remains of Soga no Umako but is now completely empty.

The best museum in the area is **Asuka Historical Museum** (9 am to 4 pm), which has exhibits from regional digs. It's across the street (you take the underpass) from Takamatsu-zuka.

Lastly, if you have time left after visiting the earlier sights, take a look at **Asuka-dera**, which dates from 596 and is considered the first true temple in all of Japan. Housed within is the oldest remaining image of Buddha in Japan – after more than 1300 years of venerable existence, you'll have to excuse its decidedly tatty appearance. Admission is ¥300, though you can just glimpse the Buddha image through the open doorway (and that's about all there is to do at the temple).

YOSHINO 吉野
☎ 07463

Yoshino is Japan's top cherry-blossom destination, and for a few weeks in early to mid-April, the blossoms of thousands of cherry trees form a floral carpet gradually ascending the mountainsides. It's definitely a sight worth seeing, but the narrow streets of the village become jammed tight with thousands of visitors at this time, and you'll have to be content with a day trip unless you've booked accommodation long in advance. Outside cherry-blossom season, Yoshino is not a particularly worthwhile destination. However, it is a good starting point for hikes on Ōmine-san and Ōdai-ga-hara (see the 'Ōdai-ga-hara to Ōsugi-dani Track' boxed text in this chapter).

History

In early times the remote, mountainous regions around Yoshino were considered the mysterious abode of the kami and later became a centre for Shugendō, a Buddhist school that incorporated ancient Shamanistic rites, Shintō beliefs and ascetic Buddhist traditions. The school has its origin in the banding together of Buddhist hermits who practised their faith deep in the mountains, though the legendary En-no-Gyōja, to whom powers of exorcism and magic are

Kofun Burial Mounds

The origins of the Japanese imperial line and the Japanese people in general are shrouded in mystery. Much of what we do know comes from large, earthen burial mounds scattered around the islands of Honshū, Kyūshū and Shikoku. These burial mounds, called *kofun*, served as tombs for members of Japan's early nobility, primarily members of the imperial household. The practice of building these mounds started quite suddenly in the 3rd century and died out gradually, finally ending in the 7th century. It was during this period that the forerunners of the present imperial family, the Yamato clan, were consolidating their power as rulers over Japan's warring factions.

The practice of kofun burial started in the region known today as Kinai, which encompasses Kyoto, Osaka and Nara. Early burial mounds were built on hilltops overlooking fertile land, usually in a round or keyhole shape. Along with the imperial corpse, a variety of both military and ceremonial objects were buried, many of which were Chinese in origin, testifying to the extent to which early Japanese civilisation was influenced by continental culture. This influence was the result of frequent contact between Japan and Korean and Chinese cultures present on the Korean peninsula.

In the 4th century the practice of kofun burial spread along the inland sea to western Honshū, Shikoku and Kyūshū, and finally to regions in the east near present-day Tokyo. Mounds of this period contain, along with the body, vast amounts of funerary objects, most of them continental in origin and military in nature. One mound, the Ōjin mausoleum in Ariyama, was found to contain about 3000 swords buried in a separate treasure mound. The richness of these tombs gives some indication of the absolute power held by these early emperors over the labour and resources of their societies.

Some of the largest mounds were built in the 5th century, including the tomb believed to house the remains of Emperor Nintoku, in southern Osaka. This keyhole-shaped mound is 28m high, 486m in length and covers an area of 32 hectares. The volume of material in this mound is said to be greater than that of the Great Pyramid of Cheops. The use of moats to surround and protect the central chamber also appeared during this period.

Under the influence of Buddhism, which favoured cremation over burial, the practice of kofun burial gradually died out and disappeared by the end of the 7th century.

Some of the best-preserved mounds are in Nara-ken, concentrated around the village of Asuka. Most interesting is the stone Ishibutai-kofun, said to house the remains of Soga no Umako, a 7th-century noble. Its exposed stone burial chamber looks over the Nara plain and speaks of a time in Japanese history when the emperor held power over his subjects, not unlike the power wielded by some of history's other great tomb builders, the Pharaohs of ancient Egypt.

---

ascribed, is frequently referred to as the founder of the school.

Yoshino came to historical prominence in the years following Emperor Go-Daigo's efforts to wrest imperial rule from the Kamakura shogunate. In 1333, Emperor Go-Daigo successfully toppled the Kamakura shogunate with the help of disgruntled generals. The return to imperial rule, known as the Kemmu Restoration, only lasted three years, however. Go-Daigo failed to reward his supporters adequately and was ousted in a revolt by one of his generals, Ashikaga Takauji, who set up a rival empire.

Go-Daigo beat a hasty retreat to the remote safety of Yoshino, where he set up a competing court. This period of rivalry between the two courts (known as Nanbokuchō – the Northern and Southern Courts period) continued for about 60 years, ending only when Ashikaga made a promise (which was not kept) that the imperial lines would alternate.

Orientation & Information

The village's main tourist information office (☎ 2-8014) is about 400m up the main street from the top cable-car station, on your right just after Kimpusen-ji. It's open from

9 am to 4 pm, and closed Monday and Tuesday. The staff don't speak much English but are quite helpful and have a specially prepared English-Japanese phrasebook to help foreign travellers. They can help with minshuku bookings if necessary.

Things to See

As you walk up the main street, you pass through two torii before coming to the stone steps leading to the Ni-ō-mon of **Kimpusen-ji** (8 am to 5 pm). Check out the fearsome *Kongo Rikishi* (guardian figure statues) in the gate and then continue on to the massive **Zaō-dō Hall** (¥300) of the temple. Said to be the second-largest wooden building in Japan, the hall is most interesting for its unfinished wooden columns. For many centuries Kimpusen-ji has been one of the major centres for Shugendō, and pilgrims have often stopped here to pray for good fortune on the journey to Ōmine-san.

About 500m farther up the street is **Katte-jinja**, where the road forks. Take the left fork and then the next right up the hill. You soon pass **Zenkō-in** on your left and **Chikurin-in** on your right (see Places to Stay & Eat). A few minutes' walk farther on there is another fork, where you'll find some steps leading up to a wooden torii. Take the left fork and the next right up the hill for the 3km hike to **Kimpu-jinja**, a small shrine in a pleasantly wooded mountain setting. If you don't fancy this somewhat strenuous uphill hike, there are plenty of smaller shrines and temples on the streets and alleys off Yoshino's main street.

Ōmine-san Pilgrimage Trail
大嶺山巡礼コース

From Kimpu-jinja in Yoshino, there's a Shugendō pilgrimage trail running all the way across the ranges of sacred Ōmine-san to coastal Kumano. During the Heian period, the pilgrimage became immensely popular, with pilgrims and *yamabushi* (Shugendō priests) trekking from as far as Kyoto and undergoing austere rites en route. Pilgrims who contravened the rules or lacked sufficient faith were given a gentle lesson by being hung over a precipice by

their heels. Between May and September many pilgrims still hike this route.

Women were barred from the entire route until as recently as the 1960s. Today, there are still points at either end of the route beyond which women definitely may not pass; any who defy this tradition are met with fierce resistance. The most popular part of the route is the climb up Ōmine-san, which can be done either by walking all the way from Kimpu-jinja outside Yoshino (about 30km) or by taking a train and bus to the village of Dorogawa and starting from there.

Places to Stay & Eat

The cheapest option, at ¥2800 a person, is *Yoshino-yama Kizō-in* (☎ 2-3014), a temple that doubles as the local youth hostel. It's a pleasant place to stay, and several of the hostel's rooms look out across the valley. See the earlier Things to See section for directions to the temple.

Not far past Kizō-in, on the opposite side of the street, is *Chikurin-in* (☎ 2-8081), an exquisite temple that now operates primarily as a ryokan. Both present and previous emperors have stayed here, and a look at the view afforded by some of the rooms explains why. Per-person prices start at ¥15,000, including two meals. Reservations are essential for the cherry-blossom season, a good idea at all other times. Even if you don't plan to stay at the temple, you should at least visit its splendid garden, said to have been designed by the famous tea master Sen no Rikyū. Admission to the garden is ¥300, but this fee is sometimes waived.

There are several minshuku in the village. Ask at the main information office if you would like assistance with booking a room.

The speciality of Yoshino is *kaki-no-ha sushi* (mackerel sushi wrapped in persimmon leaves). Almost every store and restaurant in town sells it and you can buy two pieces to take away for ¥250. If you fancy something more substantial, try *Yatsuko*, opposite the tourist information office, which has the usual shokudō favourites. Closer to the top cable-car station, *Hatsu-on* restaurant, in an atmospheric old wooden building, serves tempura donburi for ¥1300.

Getting There & Away

The village of Yoshino is on a shoulder of Yoshino-yama, at the bottom of which is Yoshino station. From Yoshino station, you can take the cable car to the village (¥350/600 one-way/return) or walk up in 15 minutes on the path that leaves from beside the cable-car station.

To get to Yoshino station from Kyoto or Nara, take the Kintetsu Nara/Kashihara line (it changes name halfway) to Kashihara-jingū-mae (kyūkō, ¥860 from Kyoto, one hour 10 minutes; kyūkō, ¥480 from Nara, 40 minutes) and change to the Kintetsu Yoshino line (kyūkō, ¥460, 40 minutes).

You can take a direct train on the Kintetsu Minami-Osaka/Yoshino lines from Osaka (Abenobashi station, close to Tennō-ji station) to Yoshino (kyūkō, ¥950, 1½ hours).

The closest JR station to Yoshino is Yoshino-guchi, where you can transfer to trains to/from Nara, Osaka and Wakayama.

ŌDAI-GA-HARA & ŌSUGI-DANI 大台ケ原と大杉谷

One of Japan's rainiest spots, the high alpine plateau of Ōdai-ga-hara, in south-eastern Nara-ken, is famous for its mossy forests and abundant wildlife. On all sides of the plateau, mountain walls drop away into deep gorges. One of the most beautiful of these gorges is Ōsugi-dani, which is accessible via a hiking course from Ōdai-ga-hara (see the boxed text 'Ōdai-ga-hara to Ōsugi-dani Track' later in this chapter for details). Much of the hiking in the gorge is along precipitous cliff walls, many of which have been fitted with chains to protect hikers. Highlights of the trip down the gorge are eight waterfalls and the clear waters of Ōsugi-dani-gawa. All in all, this two-day hike may be the finest in Kansai and is well worth a trip if you are an outdoor enthusiast.

IGA-UENO 伊賀上野

This rather drab town, about an hour west of Nara by train, is famous for having been a major training centre for ninja (practitioners of ninjutsu, the 'art of stealth'). The town also derives considerable literary and tourist clout from being the birthplace of Bashō, Japan's most celebrated writer of haiku (17-syllable poems). There's an information office with maps and English leaflets just outside Ueno-shi station.

Most of the town's sights are contained in Ueno-kōen, a 12-minute walk north of Ueno-shi station; walk under the tracks and you'll soon see the park on your left. First on your right as you enter the park is the **Bashō Memorial Museum** (¥300, 8.30 am to 5 pm, closed Monday, the day after national holidays and 29 December to 1 January). This small museum displays some of the poet's original works, but since everything on display is in Japanese and there are no English explanations, there is little to interest the casual visitor.

Next along is the **Ninja Yashiki House** (¥700, 9 am to 5 pm, closed 29 December to 1 January), a hokey attempt to cash in on the town's ninja history. 'Highlights' include shows of ninja skills by pink-suited young ladies and a smattering of displays relating to ninja. Overlooking both these attractions is **Ueno-jō** (¥400, 9 am to 5 pm, closed 29 December to 1 January), a castle built in 1608 by the lord of Iga and Ise, Todo Takatora. The present concrete structure is a reconstruction dating from 1935.

The **Ueno Tenjin Matsuri** takes place at Sugiwara-jinja between 23 and 25 October. Dating from the 16th century, the festival features a parade of mikoshi on ornate floats that are accompanied by fearsomely attired demons.

Getting There & Away

Iga-Ueno is on the JR Kansai line. From Nara, the journey costs ¥1110 and takes 50 minutes with changes at Kizu and Kamo. From Osaka, the journey costs ¥1450 and takes one hour and 40 minutes with changes at Kamo. After arriving at Iga-Ueno station, it's necessary to switch to a Kintetsu futsū for the eight-minute, ¥220 ride down to Ueno-shi station, a short walk from the town's major sights. If you're coming from the south-west (Sakurai, Kashihara etc), it's possible to take the Kintetsu Osaka line directly to Ueno-shi station.

KANSAI REGION

Ōdai-ga-hara to Ōsugi-dani Track

Time 2 to 3 days
Distance 29.1km
Standard Medium-Hard
Start Ōdai-ga-hara bus stop
Finish Ōsugi-dani bus stop
Nearest Towns Nara, Yoshino
Public Transport Access Yes

This is a stunning hike that starts on a moss-covered mountaintop and works its way down through a deep gorge and past a procession of waterfalls.

The hike from the peak of Ōdai-ga-hara down through Ōsugi-dani is generally done in two days. The night is spent at the Momonoki-yama-no-ie hut halfway along the gorge. To undertake the hike described here, you must take a bus to the top of Ōdai-ga-hara and walk down.

The Ōdai-ga-hara hiking season extends from 25 April to 23 November. During this time, buses run to the top of Ōdai-ga-hara and all the mountain huts are open. If you can handle the crowds, this hike is most beautiful when the trees have their autumn foliage (late September to late October).

The best map for this hike is Shobunsha's 1:50,000 Ōdai-ga-hara, No 58, in its Yama to Kōgen Chizu series (available at bigger Japanese bookshops).

The Walk

Day 1: Ōsugi-dani bus stop to Momonoki-yama-no-ie hut, 12.9km, six to eight hours Fill water bottles at the Ōdai-so hut before setting out. Take the wide trail that leaves from the end of the Ōdai-ga-hara car park and walk past the sign reading 'Nature Trail Ōdai-ga-hara' in English. After you have walked about 50m, take the first fork to the right and work your way slowly downhill. From here it's an easy 25-minute walk through sparse forest to the Owase-tsuji (Owase Trail Junction). At Owase-tsuji, turn right and walk for about 30 minutes to the turn-off to Daijagura. From this turn-off it's a 10-minute descent down a rocky ridge to the final rocky outcrop of Daijagura, with a stunning view down into the **Higashi-no-kawa gorge**.

From Daijagura retrace your steps to Owase-tsuji and turn right up the trail to the 1694m summit of Hide-ga-take, the ascent of which takes about 40 minutes. On clear days the view from the summit lookout platform is excellent, and is dominated by the Ōmine-san range to the north-west.

From the summit of Hide-ga-take it's a three- to four-hour, 7.9km walk down to **Momonoki-yama-no-ie**, starting with a continuous 90 minute descent along a ridge toward the Dōkura-sonan-goya hut. From the Dōkura-sonan-goya hut, turn right on the mountain road; the trail branches off on the left just before the first bend in the road. From this point it's an unrelenting 50-minute descent to the beginning of the **Ōsugi-dani gorge**.

Just past the end of the descent, the trail passes the lovely 20m **Dōkura-daki falls** on the right. From these falls, it's a challenging 3.2km hike to Momonoki-yama-no-ie. The falls mark the beginning of the Ōsugi-dani gorge proper, and from here the walk can be difficult and dangerous – watch your footing at all times, even over apparently dry rock. On the way to the hut you pass a series of lovely waterfalls, including the stunning 80m **Nanatsugama-daki**.

Immediately past these falls is a rockslide. An old, impassable trail continues down along the river here; ignore it and climb up the rockslide to the left (follow the red arrow). From here on you encounter a few chained sections of track as the trail gently rises and falls before finally arriving at Momonoki-yama-no-ie (☎ 05973-2 2052). It's open from 25 April to 25 November, and charges ¥7300 a night with two meals or ¥4200 without meals.

Ōdai-ga-hara to Ōsugi-dani Track

Day 2: Momonoki-yama-no-ie to Ōsugi bus stop, 16.2km, six to eight hours If you intend to walk all the way down to the Ōsugi bus stop, you will need to get an early start to make the 12.02 pm bus to Misedani. Otherwise, you can take your time and shoot for the 2.10 pm bus. Alternatively, if you don't fancy walking the last 10km on the road, you can catch the tourist boat from one of the docks along the Miyagawa-chosuichi reservoir. The staff at the Momonoki-yama-no-ie have the details of departures times and locations.

The first part of the walk from the Momonoki-yama-no-ie is along the narrow walls of the gorge and takes in several lovely waterfalls, including the 135m **Senpiro-daki**, which appear to fall directly out of the sky down to the river below. Just past these falls, the trail flattens out and broadens as you exit the narrow gorge. Just after exiting the gorge you come to an elbow bend in the river with a pleasant gravel beach where you can take a dip on hotter days. From this point it takes about half an hour to walk to the trailhead and the beginning of the paved road, from which it's an easy 10km walk to the Ōsugi bus stop.

Getting There & Away

With a very early start, this hike can be done from Kyoto, Osaka or Nara if you take the Kintetsu line. However, it's probably better to spend the night in Yoshino before setting out (see the Yoshino section for transport and lodging details). The following morning, backtrack two stops on a local Kintetsu line train to nearby Yamato-kami-ich-eki, from where buses leave to Ōdai-ga-hara.

From Yamato-kami-ichi-eki, take a Nara Kōtsu bus (☎ 0747-52 4101) to Ōdai-ga-hara (¥2130, about two hours). Bus times vary but on most days there's a departure at 9.30 am and additional departures on weekends and holidays. However, there are no buses from 24 November to the last Friday in April.

On your return, take a Miyagawa Sonei bus (☎ 05987 6 1111) from Ōsugi to Misedani (¥1000, about one hour) and then switch to a Mei Kōtsu bus (☎ 0598-51 5240) to Matsuzaka (¥1090, one hour). Convenient buses depart Ōsugi at 12.02 pm and 2.10 pm and Misedani almost hourly. From Matsuzaka-eki, take a *kyūkō* (ordinary express) on the Kintetsu Osaka line west to Osaka's Abenobashi station (¥1640, 2½ hours). For Kyoto or Nara, switch at Yagi (¥750, 2½ hours to Kyoto).

Wakayama-ken

和歌山県

This remote and mountainous prefecture on the western side of Kii-hantō is best known for the mountaintop temple complex of Kōya-san, one of Japan's most important Buddhist centres. The prefecture's onsen are also worth a visit – particularly those clustered around the remote village of Hongū. Among other attractions are the beachside town of Shirahama and the rugged coastline near Kushimoto. If you're planning a trip to the area, keep in mind that transport connections can be slow and infrequent, whether you are chugging along the coastline by train or taking a bus through the remote, mountainous interior.

JNTO publishes a leaflet called *Shirahama & Wakayama Prefecture* that provides concise details about sights and transport in the area. Also, the International Exchange section (☎ 0734-32-4111) of Wakayama Prefectural government publishes *Welcome to Wakayama Prefecture*, which has detailed maps and information. You'll need to be able to speak Japanese.

SHINGŪ 新宮

☎ 0735

This town is nothing exceptional to look at but functions as a useful transport hub for access to the three major Shintō shrines of the area, known as the Kumano Sanzan

KANSAI REGION

KII-HANTŌ

(Kumano Hayatama Taisha, Kumano Hongū Taisha and Nachi Taisha). There's a helpful information office (☎ 22-2840) at the station.

If you're killing time between trains or buses, you could visit the colourful **Kumano Hayatama Taisha**, a 15-minute walk northwest of Shingū station. The shrine's **Boat Race Festival** takes place on 16 October. Another shrine worth looking at is **Kamikura-jinja**, which is famous for its **Otō Matsuri** (6 February), during which more than 1000 people carrying torches ascend the slope to the shrine. The shrine is a 15-minute walk west of the station.

Shingū Hayatama Youth Hostel (☎ 22-2309) has beds for ¥2700. It's a 15-minute walk from the station, just before Kumano Hayatama Taisha. Slightly more upmarket is *Hase Ryokan* (☎ 22-2185), a two-minute walk north of the station (call from the station and someone from the ryokan will meet you). Rooms with shared bath are ¥7000 a person with two meals, ¥5000 without. The tourist information office has a map to both places.

There are several places to eat around the station. For a good yakitori dinner, try *Daikichi*, directly across from the station. For other Japanese rice and noodle standards, try the little shokudō *Marusan*, just past the pachinko parlour north of the station. Expect to spend ¥900 for lunch or dinner. Look for the food models in the window.

Getting There & Away
The JR Kisei line connects Shingū with Nagoya station (tokkyū, ¥6680, three hours) and Osaka's Tennō-ji station (tokkyū, ¥6500, four hours). Futsū are cheaper but take significantly longer.

There are buses between Shingū and Hongū, all of which make a loop of the three surrounding onsen (Watarase, Yunomine and Kawa-yu). The trip takes about two hours and costs ¥1500. Some of these buses start/finish in Kii Tanabe or Gojō.

DORO-KYŌ 瀞峡
Glass-roofed boats leave from Shikō for a dramatic two-hour trip (¥3340) on Kitayama-gawa through Doro-kyō, one of Japan's finest gorges. Boats generally operate from 9.30 am to 2.10 pm (slightly longer in summer). Buses connect Shikō with Shingū station (42 minutes). There are special bus/boat tickets available from Shingū for ¥5200 (ask at the ticket office by the station).

HONGŪ 本宮
Hongū itself isn't particularly interesting but it makes a good starting point for the onsen villages nearby. Hongū is also home to **Kumano Hongū Taisha**, one of the three famous shrines of the Kumano Sanzan (see the 'Kumano Kodō' boxed text in this chapter). The shrine is close to the Ōmiya Taisha-mae bus stop (the buses listed in this section stop here). While you're in Hongū you might want to try the local speciality, *mehari sushi* (rice wrapped in edible leaves). Look for the sushi stands outside many of the town's restaurants.

Nara Kōtsū and JR buses leave for Hongū from Gojō in the north (¥3900, five hours), Kii-Tanabe in the west (¥2100, two hours) and Shingū in the south-east (¥1500, two hours). Shingū is the most convenient of these three access points (departures are most frequent from there). Buses in both directions make stops at the three onsen listed below.

YUNOMINE, WATARASE & KAWA-YU ONSEN
湯の峰、渡瀬、川湯温泉
☎ 07354
These three onsen are among the best in all of Kansai. Because each has its own distinct character, it's worth doing a circuit of all three. There are several ryokan and minshuku in the area, but if you are on a tight budget, you might prefer to camp on the riverbanks above and below Kumano Hongū Taisha. See the Hongū section earlier for transport details.

Yunomine Onsen 湯峰温泉
The town of Yunomine is nestled around a narrow river in a wooded valley. Most of the town's onsen are contained inside ryokan or minshuku but charming little **Tsubo-yu Onsen** (¥260, 7 am to 9.30 pm) is open to all. It's right in the middle of town, inside a tiny wooden shack built on an island in the river. Buy a ticket at the sento next to **Toko-ji**, the town's main temple. Admission is granted to only one group at a time, so if someone is already there, just sit on the bench outside and wait your turn. The water in the onsen is reputed to change colour seven times a day – you'll certainly change colour waiting for it to do so.

While you're there, try your hand at cooking some *onsen tamago* – eggs boiled in the hot water of an onsen. There is a pool of hot-spring water just downstream from Tsubo-yu for cooking. The shop across from the temple sells bags of five eggs for ¥200. Put them in the water before you enter the bath and they should be cooked by the time you get out.

Yunomine has plenty of minshuku and ryokan for you to choose from. At the upper end of the village, *Yunotanisō* (☎ 2-1620) has pleasant tatami rooms for ¥7500 a person with two meals, ¥4000 without. There's also an excellent *rotemburo* (open-air bath) on the premises. At the lower end of the village, *Minshuku Azumayasō* (☎ 2-0238) has rooms for ¥8000 a person with two meals. They've also got a built-in onsen.

Kawa-yu Onsen 川湯温泉
Kawa-yu Onsen is in a flatter, less attractive valley than Yunomine Onsen. It is rather

interesting, though, because the hot-spring water bubbles out of the riverbed itself. You can make your own private bath here by digging out some of the stones on the riverbank and letting the hole fill with hot water; you can then spend the rest of the day jumping back and forth between the bath and the cool waters of the river. Admission is free. In the winter, from 1 December to 28 February, bulldozers are used to turn the river into a giant 1000-person rotemburo.

If you don't fancy splashing about in the river, try the **Kawa-yu Koshū Yokujō** (¥150, 7 am to 9 pm, closed the first and third Wednesday of each month), a public bath that uses natural hot-spring water. It's near the town's footbridge. Across the footbridge there's a free outdoor bath for use by guests of the town's ryokan. Since there's usually no-one around to check, you can probably take a dip even if you're not staying at a ryokan – the sign is written in Japanese so...

Places to Stay The cheapest place in Kawa-yu is the drab *Kajika-sō* (☎ 2-0518), a combination youth hostel/minshuku. Rates for the youth hostel are ¥3195 a night (plus a ¥100 onsen tax – only applies at this youth hostel). At ¥8000 a person, the minshuku is overpriced.

Hotels in Kawa-yu, as in other Japanese onsen towns, tend to be expensive. *Pension Ashita-no-Mori* (☎ 2-1525) is a pleasant wooden building where per-person rates are ¥10,000 with two meals. Next door is *Fujiya* (☎ 2-0007), a more upmarket ryokan where a tasteful room will set you back ¥18,000 or more with two meals.

Watarase Onsen 渡瀬温泉

Watarase Onsen (¥700, 6 am to 10 pm) is built around a bend in the river directly between Yunomine Onsen and Kawa-yu Onsen. It's not as interesting as its neighbours, but it does boast the largest rotemburo in Kansai.

NACHI & KII-KATSUURA 那智と紀伊勝浦

The Nachi and Kii-Katsuura area has several sights grouped around the sacred **Nachi-no-**taki, Japan's highest waterfall (133m). **Nachi Taisha**, near the waterfall, was built in homage to the waterfall's kami. Although it is one of the three great shrines of Kii-hantō, it is gaudy and a long climb from the waterfall car park. If you do decide to visit this shrine, you can take a trail from there to two hidden waterfalls above the main falls: these are seldom visited by tourists and are worth seeing. You can also pay ¥200 at the base of the falls to hike up to a lookout that affords a better view of the falls.

The **Nachi-no-Hi Matsuri** (Fire Festival) takes place at the falls on 14 July. During this lively event mikoshi are brought down from the mountain and met by groups bearing flaming torches.

Buses from Nachi station to the waterfall take 20 minutes and cost ¥470. From Kii-Katsuura station buses take about 30 minutes and cost ¥600.

Getting There & Away

Kii-Katsura can be reached by JR Kisei line trains from Osaka's Tennō-ji station (tokkyū, ¥6190, four hours) and from Nagoya station (tokkyū, ¥7000, 3½ hours). Futsū are significantly cheaper but take almost twice as long.

A leisurely way of reaching Kii-hantō from Tokyo is to take the ferry between Tokyo Ferry Terminal (Ariake Pier in Toyocho) and Kii-Katsuura. There's one sailing every second day (from ¥8800, 12 hours). There is a connecting bus (¥300, six minutes) between the port and Kii-Katsuura station (¥300, six minutes).

The same ferry runs between Ukui-kō port and Kōchi on Shikoku in about eight hours. Fares start at ¥5300 for this section of the trip.

KUSHIMOTO & SHIONOMI-SAKI 串本と潮岬

☎ 07356

Shionomi-saki was an island off the southern tip of the Kii-hantō until a sandbar formed connecting it to the mainland. Now the sandbar is buried underneath the city of Kushimoto. The city itself is rather drab, but the rugged, rocky coastline is worth seeing. It's a short ferry ride from Kushimoto to the

KANSAI REGION

island of **Kii-Ō-shima** (¥170, 10 minutes), which has a beautiful coastline and is a pleasant place to explore on foot. The ferry pier is a 300m walk east of the train station.

Kushimoto is renowned for the **Hashi-kui-iwa**, a line of pillar-like rocks that have been imaginatively compared to a line of hooded monks heading towards Kii-Ō-shima. To see the rocks, take a Shingū-bound bus from Kushimoto station, and get off five minutes later at the Hashi-kui-iwa stop (¥130). For more local information contact the Kushimoto Tourist Association (☎ 2-3171).

The best place to stay in the area is *Misaki Lodge Youth Hostel* (☎ 2-1474), which charges ¥4550 a person. It's in a good position, on the southern side of the cape overlooking the Pacific. It's also a minshuku, offering large rooms for ¥7000 a person including two meals. Take a Shiono-misaki bound bus from Kushimoto station (20 minutes) and get off at the last stop, Sugu-mae.

Kushimoto is one hour from Shirahama by JR tokkyū, and three hours (¥5770) from Tennō-ji in Osaka. Futsū services are significantly cheaper but take almost twice as long

SHIRAHAMA 白浜
☎ 0739

Shirahama is Kansai's leading beach/onsen resort and has all the trappings of a major Japanese tourist attraction. However, if you can look beyond the tourist schlock, you may well have a good time on the town's white-sand beach and in its excellent hot-springs baths. Indeed, as long as you visit out of season, which is anytime other than July and August, you'll probably be quite taken with the town's laid-back atmosphere.

There's a tourist information office (☎ 42-2240, 9.15 am to 5 pm) in the station. Since the station is a fair distance from the main sights, you'll need to take a bus (¥330, 20 minutes) or rent a bicycle if you arrive by rail. The bicycle rental outlet at the station charges ¥300 for two hours or ¥1000 a day (there's a discount if you can produce your JR ticket, so make sure you hang on to it). Mountain bikes are available for ¥1000 for four hours or ¥2000 a day (again, a discount applies if you can produce your JR ticket).

Shirara-hama
The town's main beach is famous for its white sand. If it reminds you of Australia don't be surprised – the town had to import sand from down under after the original stuff washed away. This place is packed during July and August. In the off-peak season, it can actually be quite pleasant. The beach is hard to miss, as it dominates the western side of town. You may discover quieter spots if you explore the town's other beaches to the north and west of this beach.

Onsen
Onsen are the other main attraction of Shirahama. The free **Sakino-yu Onsen** is sensational (8 am to 6.30 pm in summer, until 5 pm the rest of the year, closed Wednesday). It's built on a rocky point with great views of the Pacific Ocean. Come early in the day to beat the crowds. It's 1km south of the main beach; walk along the seafront road and look for the point below the big Hotel Seymor. The baths are segregated by sex.

Other baths include **Shirara-yu** (¥300, 7 am to 10.30 pm, from noon on Tuesday), a pleasant bath right on Shirara-hama, and **Murono-yu** (¥300, 7 am to 11 pm, from noon on Thursday), a simple onsen not far from Sakino-yu, in front of Shirahama post office.

Isogi-kōen
This park, on a point just south of town overlooking the ocean, is a great place for a picnic away from the crowds of Shirahama. Bushwhack through the woods from the car park to the sea and you'll be rewarded with a great view of the Pacific and the rocky coast south of Shirahama. It's spectacular when big waves are rolling in. To get to the park, take a bus from the station to Sandan (¥460, 25 minutes) and walk south for 20 minutes or walk from the main beach, which takes about 30 minutes.

Places to Stay & Eat
If you don't mind staying outside the town of Shirahama, the cheapest option is the friendly, comfortable *Ohgigahama Youth Hostel* (☎ 22-3433). The hostel is 10 minutes

on foot from Kii-Tanabe station, which is three stops north of Shirahama station on the JR Kisei line. Per-person rates are ¥2300 and meals are not served.

In Shirahama itself, there are several Kokumin-shukusha and minshuku. The best of these is the central *Katsuya* (☎ 42-3814), which is only two minutes' walk from the main beach. It's built around a Japanese garden and has a small natural hot-springs bath and a friendly owner. It's also cheap, at ¥5000 a person, or ¥8000 with two meals (rates are ¥1000 lower outside summer). If Katsuya is full, try the *Kokumin-shukusha Hotel Shirahama* (☎ 42-3039), which offers similar rates. The tourist information office at the station has maps to both places.

Kiraku serves standard teishoku in the ¥800 range. *Ginchiro* is more upmarket, serving tempura and *unagi* (eel) set meals for around ¥1500 (there's a picture menu). The tourist information office at the station can provide a map to both places. Alternatively, ask directions at your accommodation venue.

Getting There & Away

Shirahama is on the JR Kisei line. A tokkyū train from Tennō-ji station in Osaka takes two hours and costs ¥4620. The same line also connects Shirahama to other cities on Kii-hantō such as Kushimoto, Nachi, Shingū and Wakayama city.

WAKAYAMA 和歌山
☎ 0734

Wakayama, the prefectural capital, is a pleasant little city useful as a transport hub for travellers heading for other parts of the prefecture. The city's main attraction is Wakayama-jō (grounds free, castle's keep ¥350, 9 am to 4.30 pm), a 20-minute walk from JR Wakayama station. The original castle was built in 1585 by Toyotomi Hideyoshi and destroyed by bombing in WWII. The present structure is a passable post-war reconstruction. If you're in Wakayama on the three days around the full moon in September, check out the full-moon festival held here – best described as the Japanese Woodstock.

Places to Stay & Eat

The most relaxing place to stay in Wakayama is the Shinwaka Ura area, a pleasant collection of minshuku and ryokan on a point south-west of the city. The most reasonable place is *Kokumin-shukusha Shinwaka Ura Lodge* (☎ 44-9000). Per-person rates are ¥4500, or ¥6500 with two meals. Take bus No 7 from JR Wakayama station to the last stop, Shinwaka Ura (¥380, 40 minutes), continue on in the same direction along the main road, go through the tunnel and look for it on your left.

Overlooking the beach, *Bagus Café* (☎ 44-2559) is one of the most unusual places in Kansai. It's built in what looks like a cave and has a distinctly South Seas feeling. It's open from 1 July to 28 August. It serves curry for ¥700 and a variety of drinks. It's just past the earlier Kokumin-shukusha, down the steps to the beach. Look for the driftwood-framed entrance.

Nearby, in a beautiful old Japanese house, the Indonesian restaurant *Bulan Bintang* (☎ 47-3958) serves *nasi goreng* (fried rice) for ¥750 and a brown rice set meal for ¥950 including coffee (11 am to 8 pm, closed Wednesday). It's up the hill across the road from the Kokumin-shukusha.

In the arcade on the basement floor beneath JR Wakayama station, *Mendori-tei* serves excellent *kushi-age* (deep-fried seafood on skewers) and kushi-katsu dishes. Try its kushi-age teishoku for ¥750. Look for the red curtains. Close to JR Wakayama station is the restaurant *Ide* (5 pm to midnight, closed Thursday), a must for rāmen lovers. Here, you can try the local speciality, *shoyū rāmen* (soy sauce rāmen) for ¥450. Be careful: the rāmen here is called *chuka soba* (Chinese noodles), and you should call it this too, or risk being laughed out of the joint. It's two blocks south and one block west of JR Wakayama station.

Getting There & Away

Wakayama is on the JR Hanwa line, which operates from Osaka's Tennō-ji station (futsū, ¥830, one hour). Some trains on this line start/finish at Shin-Osaka station. From

Osaka's Namba station you can also take the private Nankai line to Wakayama-shi station (kyūkō, ¥1400, one hour), which is linked to JR Wakayama station by the JR Kisei main line (futsū, ¥180, six minutes).

Wakayama is a convenient starting point for the trip to Kōya-san (see that section for transport details).

From Wakayama-kō port, there's a ferry service to Tokushima on Shikoku (☎ 31-4431); a 2nd-class ticket is ¥1730. From Fuke-kō port, just north of Wakayama, there are ferries to Sumoto on Awaji-shima (☎ 0724-69-3821); the trip takes 30 minutes and a 2nd-class ticket is ¥1980. Ask at the tourist office in JR Wakayama station for details on getting to the respective piers.

KŌYA-SAN 高野山
☎ 0736 • pop 7000

Kōya-san is a raised tableland in northern Wakayama-ken covered with thick forests and surrounded by eight peaks. The major attraction on this tableland is the monastic complex, also known as Kōya-san, which is the headquarters of the Shingon school of Esoteric Buddhism. Though not quite the Shangri-la it's occasionally described as, it is one of the most rewarding places to visit in Kansai, not just for the natural setting of the area but also as an opportunity to stay in temples and get a glimpse of long-held traditions of Japanese religious life.

More than a million visitors come here annually so you should be prepared for congestion during peak holiday periods and festivals. Summer is a popular time to visit and escape from the lowland heat. You can miss large crowds by getting up really early for a stroll around the area before returning to take part in the morning religious service usually held around 6 am. Late-night strolls are peaceful and quiet, and spring and autumn foliage are especially attractive. Some hardy visitors even enjoy wandering round Kōya-san in the snow.

Although you could visit Kōya-san as a day trip from Nara, Kyoto or Osaka, it's much better to reduce the travel stress and stay overnight in one of the town's excellent shukubō.

History

The founder of the Shingon school of Esoteric Buddhism, Kūkai (known after his death as Kōbō Daishi), established a religious community here in 816. Kōbō Daishi travelled as a young priest to China and returned after two years to found the school. He is one of Japan's most famous religious figures and is revered as a Boddhisattva, scholar, inventor of the Japanese kana syllabary and as a calligrapher. He is believed to be simply resting in his tomb, not dead but meditating, awaiting the arrival of Miroku (Maitreya – Buddha of the Future).

Over the centuries, the temple complex grew in size and attracted many followers of the Jōdo (Pure Land) school of Buddhism. During the 11th century, it became popular with both nobles and commoners to leave hair or ashes from deceased relatives close to Kōbō Daishi's tomb, handy for his reawakening. This practice continues to be very popular today and accounts for the thousands of tombs around Okuno-in.

In the 16th century, Oda Nobunaga asserted his power by slaughtering large numbers of monks at Kōya-san. The community subsequently suffered confiscation of lands and narrowly escaped invasion by Toyotomi Hideyoshi. At one stage, Kōya-san numbered about 1500 monasteries and many thousands of monks. The members of the community were divided into *gakuryō* (clergy), *gyōnin* (lay priests) and *hijiri* (followers of Pure Land Buddhism).

In the 17th century, the Tokugawa shogunate smashed the economic power of the lay priests, who managed considerable estates in the region. Their temples were destroyed, their leaders banished and the followers of Pure Land Buddhism were bluntly pressed into the Shingon school. During the Edo period, the government favoured the practice of Shintō and confiscated the lands that supported Kōya-san's monastic community. Women were barred from entry to Kōya-san until 1872.

Kōya-san is a thriving centre for Japanese Buddhism, with more than 110 temples remaining and a population of 7000. As the headquarters of the Shingon school, it

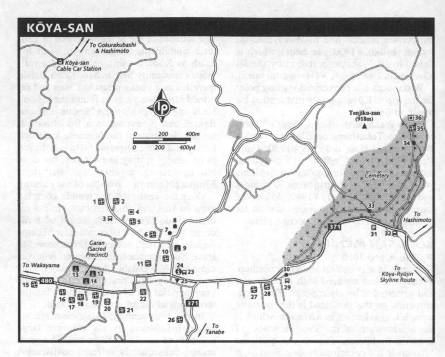

KŌYA-SAN

To Gokurakubashi
& Hashimoto

Kōya-san
Cable Car Station

Tenjiku-zan
(918m)

Cemetery

To
Hashimoto

Garan
(Sacred
Precinct)

To Wakayama

To
Kōya-Ryūjin
Skyline Route

To
Tanabe

0   200   400m
0   200   400yd

KANSAI REGION

numbers 10 million members and presides over nearly 4000 temples all over Japan.

Orientation & Information

There's a small information office at the top cable-car station. However, the main office of the Kōya-san Tourist Association (☎ 56-2616, fax 56-2889) is in the centre of town in front of the Senjūin-bashi-mae bus stop (8.30 am to 4.30 pm, until 5.30 pm in summer). Staff speak some English, and brochures and maps are available.

The precincts of Kōya-san are divided into the Garan (Sacred Precinct) in the west and Okuno-in, with its vast cemetery, in the east.

Okuno-in 奥の院

Any Buddhist worth their salt in Japan has had their remains, or just a lock or two of hair, interred at this temple to ensure pole position when the Buddha of the Future and Kūkai return to the world.

The best way to approach Okuno-in is to walk or take the bus east to Ichi-no-hashi-mae bus stop. From here you cross the bridge, Ichi-no-hashi, and enter the cemetery grounds along a winding, cobbled path lined by tall cypress trees and thousands of tombs. As the trees close in and the mist swirls, the atmosphere can be quite ghostly, especially as night falls. Fortunately, the stone lanterns are lit at night.

The Tōrō-dō (Lantern Hall), the main building of the complex, is at the northern-most end of the graveyard. It houses hundreds of lamps, including two believed to have been burning for more than 900 years. Behind the hall you can see the closed doors of the Gobyō, Kūkai's mausoleum.

On the way to the Lantern Hall is Mimyo-no-hashi. Worshippers ladle water from the river and pour it over the nearby Jizō statues as an offering for the dead. The inscribed wooden plaques in the river are in memory of aborted babies and those who

KŌYA-SAN

PLACES TO STAY & EAT
8 Kōya Youth Hostel
　高野ユースホステル
25 Nankai-shokudō
　南海食堂

OTHER
1 Haryō-in
　巴陵院
2 Rengejō-in
　蓮華定院
3 Isshi-guchi-mae Bus Stop
　一心口バス停
4 Tokugawa Mausoleum
　徳川家霊台
5 Nan-in
　南院
6 Fukuchi-in
　福智院
7 Kōya Town Office
　高野町役場
9 Muryōkō-in
　無量光院
10 Ichijō-in
　一乗院
11 Kongobu-ji
　金剛峯寺

12 Dai-tō
　大塔
13 Sai-to
　西塔
14 Kondō (Main Hall)
　金堂
15 Sainan-in
　西南院
16 Hōon-in
　報恩院
17 Hōki-in
　宝亀院
18 Yōchi-in
　桜池院
19 Henjōson-in
　遍照尊院
20 Treasure Museum
　霊宝館
21 Jōju-in
　成就院
22 Tentoku-in
　天徳院
23 Senjūin-bashi-mae
　Bus Stop
　千手院橋前バス停
24 Kōya-san Tourist
　Association Office
　高野山観光協会

26 Kongōsanmai-in
　金剛三昧院
27 Karukaya-do
　苅萱堂
28 Eikō-in
　恵光院
29 Ichi-no-hashi-mae
　Bus Stop
　一の橋前バス停
30 Ichi-no-hashi
　一の橋
31 Naka-no-hashi
　Parking
　中の橋駐車場
32 Okuno-in-mae
　Bus Stop
　奥の院前バス停
33 Naka-no-hashi
　中の橋
34 Mimyo-no-hashi
　御廟橋
35 Okuno-in &
　Tōrō-do
　奥の院、灯ろう堂
36 Kūkai
　Mausoleum
　空海の墓

died by drowning. Just below the Jizō statues there's a hall with a kitchen at the back where you can join tired, bedraggled pilgrims and brew your own tea.

Buses return to the centre of town from the terminus just across from the concrete shopping complex.

Kongōbu-ji 金剛峯寺

This is the headquarters of the Shingon school and the residence of Kōya-san's abbot. The present structure dates from the 19th century and is definitely worth a visit.

The main hall's Ohiro-ma room has ornate screens painted by Kanō Tanyu in the 16th century. The Yanagi-no-ma (Willow Room) has equally pretty screen paintings of willows but the rather grisly distinction of being the place where Toyotomi Hidetsugu committed *seppuku* (ritual suicide by disembowelment).

The rock garden is interesting for the sheer number of rocks used in its composition, giving the effect of a throng of petrified worshippers eagerly listening to a monk's sermon. The nearby moss garden has seen better days – its moss is very dry.

Admission is ¥350 and includes tea and rice cakes served beside the stone garden. It's open daily from 8.30 am to 4.30 pm.

Danjōgaran 壇上伽藍

This is a temple complex of several halls and pagodas (¥100 to each building, 8.30 am to 4.30 pm). The most important buildings are the Dai-tō (Great Pagoda) and Kondō (Main Hall). The Dai-tō, rebuilt in 1934 after a fire, has recently been repainted and many find it a little gaudy. This pagoda is said to be the centre of the lotus flower mandala formed by the eight mountains around Kōya-san. The nearby Sai-tō (Western Pagoda) was most

KANSAI REGION

recently rebuilt in 1834 and is more subdued. It's worth going into the Dai-tō to see the Dainichi-nyōrai (Cosmic Buddha) and his four attendant Buddhas.

Treasure Museum 霊宝館

The Treasure Museum (Reihōkan) has a compact display of Buddhist works of art, all collected in Kōya-san. There are some very fine statues, painted scrolls and mandalas. Admission is ¥500 and it's open from 8.30 am to 4.30 pm.

Tokugawa Mausoleum 徳川家霊台

Admission to the Tokugawa-ke Reidai (Tokugawa Mausoleum) is ¥100 and your view is from behind densely barred doors. It's not worth a detour.

Special Events

The **Aoba Matsuri** is a festival held on 15 June to celebrate the birth of Kōbō Daishi. Various traditional ceremonies are performed at the temples around town.

A more interesting festival is the **Rōsoku Matsuri** (Candle Festival), which is held on 13 August. In remembrance of dead relatives, thousands of mourners light candles along the approaches to Okuno-in.

Places to Stay

There are more than 50 temples in Kōya-san offering shukubō. It is well worth staying the night at a temple here, especially to sample *shōjin-ryōri* (vegetarian food – no meat, fish, onions or garlic). Because shukubō is intended for religious pilgrims, in the morning you'll be asked to participate in *o-inori* (Buddhist prayer services) or *o-tsutome* (work). While participation is not mandatory, taking part in these practices would enable you to appreciate the daily workings of a Japanese temple.

Kōya-san's temples have recently formed a group to fix prices and now almost all lodgings start at ¥9000 a person including two meals. One exception to this is the **Haryō-in** (☎ 56-2702), which functions as a Kokumin-shukusha and has per-person rates of ¥6500 including two meals.

During the high season and holidays you should make advance reservations by fax through the Kōya-san Tourist Association or directly with the temples. If you arrive in Kōya-san after hours or you want to do things yourself, the following shukubō have English-speaking staff and are at the lower to middle end of the price spectrum.

Eikō-in (☎ 56-2514) is one of the nicer temples in town. It's run by a friendly bunch of young monks and the rooms look out on beautiful gardens. It's easy to think you're staying at a good ryokan here, at least until you're woken at 6.30 am for morning prayers! Per-person rates are ¥10,000 (an exception to the ¥9000 set price at most other temples). This is also one of the two temples in town (the other is Kongōbu-ji) where you can study *zazen* (sitting Zen meditation). Call ahead to make arrangements.

Henjōson-in (☎ 56-2434) is another good choice. Here you get a pleasant room with a garden view, tatami furnishings, an excellent vegetarian dinner served in your room and the use of terrific wooden bathtubs. There's even a temple bar!

Other good choices include elegant **Rengejō-in** (☎ 56-2233) and down-to-earth **Muryōkō-in** (☎ 56-2233).

If the prices at the temples are out of your range, try the friendly and comfortable **Kōya Youth Hostel** (☎ 56-3889), which has per-person rates of ¥3200. It's closed for parts of December and January. Call ahead for reservations.

Places to Eat

The culinary speciality of Kōya-san is *shōjin ryōri* (vegetarian), which you can sample at your temple lodgings. Two tasty tōfu specialities are *goma-tōfu* (sesame tōfu) and *kōya-tōfu* (local tōfu). If you're just in town for the day, you can try shōjin ryōri at any of the temples that offer shukubō. Ask at the Kōya-san Tourist Association office and staff will call ahead to make reservations. Prices are fixed at ¥2500/3500/5000, depending upon how many courses you have.

There are various coffee shops dotted around town where you can have breakfast; a convenient one is at the main crossroads close to the tourist office. For lunch you can try the *Nankai-shokudō*, where all the standard lunch items are represented by plastic food-models in the window. *Katsu-donburi* (pork cutlet over rice) is ¥800 and noodle dishes start at ¥520. It's diagonally across from the main tourist office.

Getting There & Away

All rail connections to and from Kōya-san run via Gokurakubashi, which is at the base of the mountain. A cable car runs frequently from the base to the top of the mountain (five minutes, price included in most train tickets). From the cable-car station, you must take a bus into the centre of town, as walking is prohibited on the connecting road (see the Getting Around section for details).

From Osaka (Namba station) you can travel directly by kyūkō on the Nankai-Dentetsu line to Gokurakubashi station (¥1230 including cable-car ticket, 1½ hours). For the slightly faster tokkyū service with reserved seats you pay a supplement of ¥760.

From Wakayama you can go by rail on the JR Wakayama line to Hashimoto (¥820, one hour 20 minutes) and then continue on the Nankai-Dentetsu line to Gokurakubashi station (¥810 including cable-car ticket, 40 minutes).

From Kyoto it's probably best to go via Osaka (see earlier in this section). From Nara, you can take the JR line to Hashimoto, changing at Sakurai and Takadate en route.

Getting Around

Buses run on three routes from the top cable-car station via the centre of town to Ichi-no-hashi and Okuno-in. The fare to the tourist office in the centre of town at Senjūin-bashi is ¥280. The fare to the final stop, Okuno-in, is ¥400. An all-day bus pass is available for ¥800 but once you get into the centre of town you can reach most destinations quite easily on foot (including Okuno-in, which takes about 30 minutes).

If you don't feel like walking, bicycles can be rented for ¥400 an hour or ¥1200 for the day at the Kōya-san Tourist Association Office.

Shima-hantō 志摩半島

The Ise-Shima region, on Mie-ken's Shima-hantō, is most famous for Ise-jingū, Japan's most sacred Shintō shrine. It also encompasses the tourist mecca of Toba and some fine beaches around Kashikojima. Most of the region is within the boundaries of Iseshima National Park, but this is little more than a legal designation and tourist development continues unchecked across the area. Ise-Shima is easily reached from Nagoya, Kyoto or Osaka and makes a good two-day trip.

JNTO publishes *Ise-Shima*, a leaflet providing basic mapping and concise travel information for the area. Information is also available at the tourist information office across the street from Ise-jingū's Gekū shrine.

ISE 伊勢

Although the town of Ise is rather drab, it's worth making the trip here to visit the spectacular Ise-jingū. This is arguably Japan's most impressive shrine; its only rival to this claim is Nikkō's Tōshō-gū, which is as gaudy as Ise-jingū is austere.

Ise-Jingū 伊勢神宮

Dating back to the 3rd century, Ise-jingū is the most venerated Shintō shrine in Japan. Shintō tradition has dictated for centuries that the shrine buildings (about 200 of them) be replaced every 20 years with exact imitations built on adjacent sites according to ancient techniques – no nails, only wooden dowels and interlocking joints. Upon completion of the new buildings, the god of the shrine is ritually transferred to its new home in the Sengū No Gi ceremony, first witnessed by Western eyes in 1953. The wood from the old shrine is then used to reconstruct the torii at the shrine's entrance or is sent to shrines around Japan for use in rebuilding their structures. The present buildings were rebuilt in 1993 (for the 61st time) at a cost exceeding ¥5 billion.

The reason for this expensive periodic rebuilding is not clear. The official version

KANSAI REGION

holds that rebuilding the shrine every 20 years keeps alive traditional carpentry techniques. Perhaps the real reason goes back to pre-Buddhist Japanese taboos concerning death. Before the establishment of a permanent capital at Nara it was thought that the emperor's residence was defiled by death. This meant that the entire capital had to be razed and rebuilt with the passing of each emperor. This thinking may have carried over to the dwellings of Shintō gods resulting in the periodic reconstruction of the shrines, which continues to this day.

Visitors to the shrine are often shocked to discover that the main shrine buildings are almost completely hidden from view. Only members of the imperial family and certain shrine priests are allowed to enter the sacred inner sanctum. This is unfortunate, as the buildings are stunning examples of pre-Buddhist Japanese architecture. Don't despair, though, as determined neck craning over fences allows a decent view of the upper parts of the buildings. You can also get a good idea of the shrine's architecture by looking at any of the lesser shrines nearby which are exact replicas built on a smaller scale. The structure of the shrine is thought to derive from rice storehouses used in pre-Buddhist Japan. That the structure of these granaries would come to be used in shrine buildings says something about the importance of rice in Japanese culture.

There are two parts to the shrine, Gekū (Outer Shrine) and Naikū (Inner Shrine). The former is an easy 12-minute walk from Ise-shi station; the latter is accessible by bus from the station or from outside Gekū (see below for details). If you only have time to visit one of the shrines, Naikū is by far the more impressive of the two.

No admission is charged and the shrines are open from sunrise to sunset. There are restrictions on photography and smoking.

Gekū The Outer Shrine dates from the 5th century and enshrines the god of food, clothing and housing, Toyouke-no-Ōkami.

A stall at the entrance to the shrine provides a leaflet in English with a map. The main hall is approached along an avenue of tall trees and surrounded by closely fitted wooden fences that hide most of the buildings from sight.

Take some time to pause in front of the main sanctuary to observe an interesting Shintō ritual. While most pilgrims are content to pray outside the four walls surrounding the shrine, those with particularly urgent wishes can pay a fee and enter the outermost of four enclosures round the shrine. After consulting a priest, the pilgrim is ritually purified with salt and then led into the enclosure. As the priest waits patiently by, the pilgrim goes through a long series of bows and prayers. The seriousness with which this is done gives some insight into the reverence the Japanese have for this shrine. While you're watching, take a look at the priest's footwear – perhaps the mother of all clogs.

From Ise-shi station or Uji-Yamada station it's a 12-minute walk down the main street to the shrine entrance.

Naikū The Inner Shrine is thought to date from the 3rd century and enshrines the sun goddess, Amaterasu-Ōmikami, who is considered the ancestral goddess of the imperial family and the guardian deity of the Japanese nation. Naikū is held in even higher reverence than Gekū because it houses the sacred mirror of the emperor, one of the three imperial regalia (the other two are the sacred beads and the sacred sword).

Since being enshrined here in the 3rd century, this mirror has not been seen by human eyes. Members of the imperial family technically have the right to see it, but apparently no-one has ever tried to do so. It stands on a wooden pedestal wrapped in a brocade bag. As each bag wears thin, the bag with the mirror inside is simply placed inside another bag. This ensures that the mirror is never sullied by the gaze of a human and has resulted in what one writer has suggested must be the world's best collection of Japanese brocade weaving.

Speculation abounds as to what is inscribed on the back of the mirror. Some have even suggested that it bears ancient

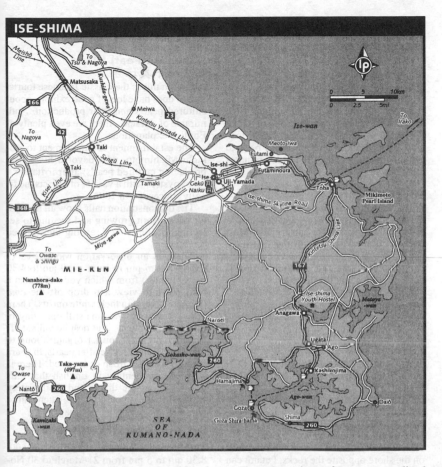

ISE-SHIMA

Hebrew inscriptions. Unless a member of the imperial family can be convinced to sneak a peak, it is doubtful that this mystery will be solved any time soon.

A stall just before the entrance to the shrine provides the same English leaflet given out at Gekū. Next to this stall is the Uji-bashi, which leads over the crystal-clear Isuzu-gawa into the shrine. One path leads to the right and passes Mitarashi, a place for pilgrims to purify themselves in the river before entering the shrine. This isn't easy, as the river is teeming with colourful carp awaiting hand-outs.

The path continues along an avenue lined with towering cryptomeria trees to the main hall. Photos are only allowed from the foot of the stone steps. Here too, you can only catch a glimpse of the structure, as four rows of wooden fences obstruct the view. If you're tempted to jump the fence when nobody's around, think again – they're watching you on closed-circuit TV cameras not so cleverly disguised as trees!

A better view of the shrine can be had by walking along its front (western) side towards the separate Aramatsurinomiya shrine. Here, you can see a large section of the shrine, and on sunny days the cypress wood of the shrine gleams almost as brightly as the gold tips of its roof beams.

On your return to the bridge, take the path to your right and visit the sacred white horse that seems a little bored with its easy life.

To get to Naiku, take bus No 52 or 55 from the stop outside Ise-shi station or the stop on the main road in front of Gekū (¥410, 15 minutes). Get off at Naikū-mae stop. From Naikū there are buses back to Ise-shi station via Gekū (¥410, 15 minutes from bus stop No 1).

Special Events

Since Ise-jingu is Japan's most sacred shrine, it's not surprising that it's also a favourite destination for hatsu-mōde. Most of the action takes place in the first three days of the year, when millions of worshippers pack the area and accommodation is booked out for months in advance.

The Kagurai-sai Matsuri, celebrated on 5 and 6 April, is a good chance to see performances of *kagura* (sacred dance), bugaku, nō and Shintō music.

FUTAMI 二見

The big attractions here are Futami Okitama-jinja and the Meoto-iwa (Wedded Rocks). These two rocks are considered to be male and female and have been joined in matrimony by *shimenawa* (sacred ropes), which are renewed each year in a special festival on 5 January. The rocks are a 20-minute walk from the station. The shrine is on the shore opposite the rocks. Futami can be reached from Ise by JR (¥200, 10 minutes). Get off at Futaminoura station.

TOBA 鳥羽

Unless you have a strong interest in pearls or enjoy a real tourist circus, you can safely give this place a miss. The JR line runs from Ise-shi station via Futami to Toba and then on to Kashikojima. There are ferry connections from Toba-ko port to Irako on Atsumi-hantō in Aichi-ken (¥1050, one hour). Boats leave from Ise-wan ferry terminal, two minutes' walk south of Mikimoto Pearl Island. Toba can be reached from Ise in 20 minutes

by both the Kintetsu line (kyukō, ¥320) or the JR line (futsū, ¥230).

Mikimoto Pearl Island ミキモト真珠島

Although this is the classic Japanese tourist trap, it does have lots of good exhibits about cultured pearls and their production. And, miracle of miracles, there are even plenty of English explanations.

The establishment is a monument to Kokichi Michimoto, who devoted his life to producing cultured pearls: after irritating a lot of oysters with a variety of objects, he finally succeeded in 1893.

The demonstration halls show all the oyster tricks from growing and seeding to selecting, drilling and threading the finished product.

There is an observation room (¥1500, 8.30 am to 5 pm in summer, 9 am to 4.30 pm in winter) from which you can watch a boat put into view and drop off the *ama* (women divers) in their white outfits. There are several thousand ama still operating in these coastal areas – but despite valiant efforts by regional tourist organisations to make you think they're after pearls, they are actually after shellfish or seaweed. There is a taped commentary in English that tells you all about the divers and their watery ways. Just ask if you'd like the attendant to put in a tape in another language.

Toba Aquarium 鳥羽水族館

This rather expensive aquarium (¥2400, 8.30 am to 5 pm from 21 March to 30 November, 9 am to 5 pm the rest of the year) does have some interesting fish and marine mammals on display, but their small number does not justify the admission price. That said, this would make a good destination on a rainy day.

AGO-WAN & KASHIKOJIMA 英虞湾と賢島

Ago-wan is a pleasant stretch of coastline, with sheltered inlets and small islands. Kashikojima, an island in the bay, is the terminus of the Kintetsu line, only 40 minutes from Ise (see the Getting There &

SIMON ROWE

Himeji-jō, also known as Shirasagi or 'White Egret' because of its stately white form, is a masterwork of impregnability and grace. Built in 1580 by Toyotomi Hideyoshi, it was later enlarged by Ikeda Terumasa.

Detail of Inari-Taisha roof, Kyoto

ERIC L WHEATER

MARTIN MOOS

Replica of the Imperial Palace, Heian-jingū, Kyoto

MARTIN MOOS

Statue's head inside Daibutsu-den, Tōdai-ji.

Traditional Japanese decorations

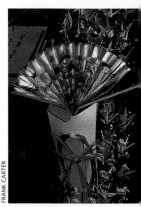

New Year good luck charms

Strike a pose – a geisha adds to the beauty of a Japanese garden.

Samurai armour breast plate

San-mon, the Buddhist temple gate of Chion-in, Kyoto.

Away section for details), and a good base for exploration of Ago-wan. The island itself is probably of little interest to foreign travellers as it is dominated by large resort hotels. Those in search of peace and quiet might want to take a ferry to **Goza** on the other side of the bay. From the station, it's a three-minute walk down to the pier. A ferry runs between Kashikojima and Goza. The 25-minute, ¥600 ride spins you past oyster rafts along the coast.

Goza is a sleepy fishing community where the main attractions are the fish market, the occasional *ama* shell-divers, and Goza Shirahama, a long white-sand beach on the southern side of town. The beach is mobbed in late July and early August but is quite nice at other times. After the beginning of August, there may be some *kurage* (jellyfish) in the water, so ask the locals about conditions.

Shirahama camping ground is on a beach close to Goza, but like most camping grounds in Japan, it is a dismal affair. Unofficial camping is possible in some of the more sheltered bays for those willing to hike.

If you'd like to continue exploring the beaches, you can take a ferry from the pier at Goza to Hamajima (¥300, 15 minutes). **Hamajima** is a point on the other side of the bay with several beaches within walking distance of the pier. The best of these is just before Minami Hari-kōen. All of the beaches here are likely to be less crowded than the beach at Goza.

SOUTH OF KASHIKOJIMA
賢島以南

If you want to continue down Kii-hantō but avoid the tortuous coastal road, backtrack to Ise and then take a train on the JR Kisei main line. This line crosses from Mie-ken into Wakayama-ken and continues down to Shingū on its way round Kii-hantō, finally ending up in Osaka's Tennō-ji station.

PLACES TO STAY

There are plenty of places to stay in Ise itself, but you'll also find lots of minshuku in Futami, Kashikojima or Goza. Be aware that prices for all ryokan and minshuku go up on weekends and holidays.

There are two youth hostels in the Ise-shima region. One, *Youth Hostel Taikōji* (☎ 0596-43-2283), is an atmospheric temple hostel in Futami. Unfortunately, it looked on the verge of closing when we stopped by. Call before heading out there to see if it's still operating. If it's open, per-person rates are ¥2000. It's a little tricky to locate; ask for directions when you call.

A safer choice is the excellent *Ise-Shima Youth Hostel* (☎ 05995-5-0226), built on a hill overlooking an attractive bay. It's close to Anagawa station on the Kintetsu line (only futsū trains stop). Walk east out of the station along the waterfront road; it's uphill on the right. Per-person rates are ¥2800.

In Ise itself, *Hoshide Ryokan* (☎ 0596-28-2377) is a quaint wooden ryokan with some nice traditional touches, seven minutes' walk north of Ise-shi station. It's a member of the Japanese Inn Group and the friendly owners offer vegetarian and macrobiotic food. Per-person rates are ¥4500, or ¥6000 with two meals. Ask for a *suikinkutsu* (Japanese water zither) demonstration while you're there. To get there from the station, ask for directions to Kōyōdai Kōkō (the high school). It's on the right just past the high school.

Another one is *Yamada-kan* (☎ 0596-28-2532), an atmospheric old ryokan about 500m south of Ise-shi station. Per-person rates start at ¥10,000 with two meals. Look for the pink framing.

Down past Kashikojima in the beach village of Goza, you'll find plenty of minshuku that provide cosy seaside lodging. It's very crowded here during July and August but almost deserted the rest of the year. *Shiojisō* (☎ 05998-8-3232), just off the beach, is one of the better minshuku. Per-person prices are ¥7000 with two meals.

PLACES TO EAT

There are lots of places to eat around Ise-shi station. One of the more interesting spots is homely little *Nanakoshi*, which serves the local speciality, *Ise-udon* (thick noodles in a rich sauce), for ¥250. For dessert, you simply must order a *kaki-gōri* (snow cone) for ¥200. They come in a variety of flavours and it's worth the money for the visual impact alone – a giant white snow afro is the best description we can think of. It's 200m west of the station, on the opposite side of the street from the train tracks.

Near Naikū, try the shopping arcade just outside the shrine compound. *Nikōdōshiten* is a good place to try some of the local specialities in a rough, roadhouse atmosphere. A light lunch of Ise-udon is ¥400. *Ōasari* (large steamed clams) are also tasty and cost ¥480. The restaurant is about 100m north of the entrance to the arcade. About 200m farther on you can follow your nose to *Akafuku Honten*. Here, *akafuku mochi*, a kind of Japanese sweet, is served with tea for ¥340. Look for the large, steaming cauldrons and the queue out the front.

GETTING THERE & AWAY

Ise is well endowed with direct rail connections for Nagoya, Osaka and Kyoto. For those without a Japan Rail Pass, the Kintetsu line is by far the most convenient way

to go. Note that there are two stations in Ise – Ise-shi station and Uji-Yamada station – which are only a few hundred metres apart; most trains stop at both.

From Nagoya, the tokkyū service on the Kintetsu line takes one hour and 20 minutes to reach Ise-shi station (¥2690) and another 30 minutes to reach its terminus at Kashikojima (¥3480). A JR kaisoku from Nagoya takes up to two hours (¥1940).

From Osaka (Uehonmachi or Namba stations), the Kintetsu limited express takes about two hours to Ise-shi station and costs ¥3030. The same train continues on to Kashikojima (¥3810, 30 minutes).

From Kyoto, the Kintetsu tokkyū takes two hours and 10 minutes to Ise-shi station (¥3520) and continues for another 30 minutes to its terminus in Kashikojima (¥4320).

If you're taking JR from Kyoto or Osaka you'll have to change up to four times and pay ¥2210 from Kyoto and ¥3260 from Osaka. Inquire at the station office for transfer details.

Western Honshū

Western Honshū is known in Japanese as Chūgoku or, literally, the 'Middle Lands' – and it is written in Japanese, incidentally, using the same characters that the Chinese use to refer to China. Over time, much of the artistic and cultural influences from China and Korea that were to shape Japanese society entered through this region. There are three main routes from the Kansai region through the western end of Honshū to the island of Kyūshū. Most visitors choose the southern route through the San-yō region. This is a heavily industrialised and densely populated area with a number of important and interesting cities, including Kurashiki and Hiroshima. The island-dotted waters of the Inland Sea, sandwiched between Honshū and Shikoku, are also reached from ports on the San-yō coast. An additional reason for choosing this route is that the Tokyo-Kyoto-Osaka-Hakata *shinkansen* (bullet train) rail route runs along the San-yō coast.

The usual alternative to this route is the San-in coast in the north. By Japanese standards, the north coast is comparatively uncrowded and rural. Although there are not as many large cities on the northern route as on the southern, the north-coast route takes you to the historically interesting town of Hagi. Matsue, Izumo and Tsuwano are also worth visiting. Despite the lower population density in the north, travel along the San-in coast is likely to be slower, as the train services are less frequent and not as fast as those in the south. Road travel may also be slower in the north than it is in the south, as there are not the long stretches of expressway in the north that are found along the southern coast. Still, as the traffic is lighter in the north than in the south, the San-in coast is an excellent part of Japan to visit if you have your own transport.

Finally, there is the central route, which is a fast road-route between Kyoto or Osaka and Shimonoseki at the western end of Honshū. The Chūgoku Expressway runs the full length of Western Honshū, more or

Highlights

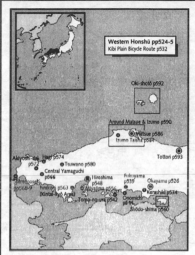

Western Honshū pp524-5
Kibi Plain Bicycle Route p532

Oki-shotō p592

Around Matsue & Izumo p590
Matsue p586
Izumo Taisha p584

Tottori p593

Akiyoshi-dai   Hagi p574
p572   Tsuwano p580
Central Yamaguchi
p566   Hiroshima   Fukiyama
                 p548   p539   Okayama p526
Shimonoseki   Hirakubi p563   Miyajima p556   Kurashiki p534
pp568-9   (Kintai-kyō Area)   Tomo-no-Ura p542
                          Onomichi
                          Shōdo-shima p560

- Experience the quiet of the Japanese countryside at one of Okayama-ken's International Villas.

- Potter through the well-preserved warehouses and wonderful museums along the canal in Kurashiki.

- Visit the sombre, affecting Hiroshima Peace Museum and A-bomb dome, then walk out into the city's vibrant, party-filled streets.

- Seek out the hideaway rural 'health spa' of Tawarayama Onsen, and its curious phallic shrine dedicated to the Goddess of Mercy.

- Enjoy a half-day trip to the charming fishing village of Tomo-no-Ura in Hiroshima-ken.

- See the floating *torii* (Shintō shrine gates) and the shrine, Itsukushima-jinja, on the island of Miyajima.

less equidistant from the north and south coasts. Attractions along this route are comparatively limited and can usually be

WESTERN HONSHŪ

visited as side trips from the north- or south-coast routes. Some of these central excursions – particularly one to the mountain town of Takahashi – are well worth the trip.

Suggested Itineraries

Those on a tight schedule should at least visit Hiroshima and Kurashiki, which are both easily accessible on the Tōkaidō shinkansen route. With several days to spare, also make a trip out to the rural Okayama international villas, hike around Miyajima, or search out the countrified hot springs at Tawarayama Onsen. A longer trip could include Hagi, Tsuwano, Matsue and Kinosaki, but remember that train journeys along the Japan sea coast are time consuming. For a short trip, stick to the Tōkaidō shinkansen route along the south coast.

ACCOMMODATION

In a brave attempt to attract foreign visitors to the less frequently visited areas of the region, the Okayama Prefectural Government has established six **International Villas** scattered around the prefecture. Rates are ¥3500/6000 for single/doubles, and ¥500 less per person for students and subsequent stays. The accommodation is well equipped, with cooking facilities, instructions in English on where to shop locally or where to find local restaurants, and bicycles for visitors' use. There's not always a lot to do once you get there – it's good to do the Japanese thing: go in a group.

There are villas in the mountain villages of Fukiya, Koshihata and Hattoji (where the villas are restored thatched-roof farm cottages), Ushimado, overlooking the Inland Sea, on Shiraishi-jima, and Takebe, to the north of Okayama city. For reservations or more information contact the *Okayama International Villa Group* (☎ 086-256-2535, fax 256-2576) at Okayama International Exchange Centre. Members of the staff speak English.

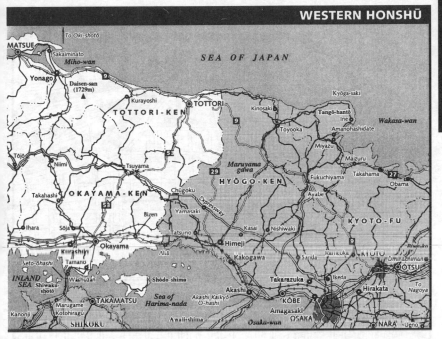

GETTING THERE & AWAY

Although there are flights to a number of cities in the region and ferry connections between the major ports and surrounding islands, shinkansen is the main means of getting to and through Western Honshū (travelling from one end of the region to the other takes a little less than three hours).

Okayama-ken

The prefecture of Okayama-ken includes the cities of Okayama and Kurashiki along with numerous other interesting towns and tourist attractions. The Seto-ōhashi forms the main road and rail link from Honshū to Shikoku.

OKAYAMA 岡山

☎ 086 • pop 593,000

Okayama is so close to the smaller, but more attractive town of Kurashiki that it's very easy to stay in one town and day-trip to the other. Although Okayama is not as interesting as Kurashiki, there are a number of important places to visit, including one of Japan's 'big three' gardens.

Orientation & Information

The town's main street, Momotarō-dōri, leads directly from the station to the castle, Okayama-jō, and the garden, Kōraku-en. Tram lines run down the middle of the street.

JR Okayama station has a tourist information counter (☎ 222-2912). The staff are helpful and can provide excellent English advice about Okayama and Kurashiki (9 am to 6 pm). The Okayama International Exchange Centre (☎ 256-2000), five minutes' walk east of the station, is also a good information source (9 am to 9 pm, closed Monday).

The Kinokuniya and Maruzen bookshops both have reasonable English-language sections.

WESTERN HONSHŪ

OKAYAMA

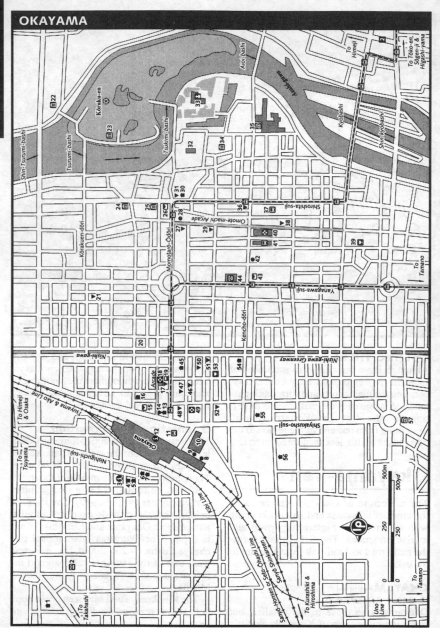

OKAYAMA

PLACES TO STAY
1 Okayama Seinen-kaikan
  Youth Hostel
  岡山青年会館
4 Saiwai-sō
  ビジネスホテル幸荘
5 New Station Hotel
  ニューステーション
  ホテル
6 Dai Ichi Inn
  第一イン
7 Okayama Tower Hotel
  岡山タワーホテル
10 Granvia Hotel
  グランビアホテル
13 Hotel New Okayama
  ホテルニュー岡山
16 Eki Mae Business Hotel
  駅前ビジネスホテル
30 Chisan Hotel
  チサンホテル
45 Washington Hotel Plaza
  ワシントンホテル
54 Hotel Maira
  ホテルマイラ
55 Castle Hotel
  キャッスルホテル
56 Makibi Kaikan
  まきび会館

PLACES TO EAT
14 Sushi Land-Marine
  Polis
17 Mister Donut
21 Itako Sanuki Udon
  いたこさぬきうどん
27 Itchō; Pizza Patio
  一丁
29 Kirin City

31 Jolly Fox
36 Pizza Patio
38 Bukkake-tei
  ぶっかけ亭
46 Murasaki
  村さ来
47 Pizza & Salad St Moritz
48 McDonald's
50 Zen
51 Eikokuryō-Honkoku
  英国領本国
52 Pizza Patio

OTHER
2 NTT
3 Okayama International
  Exchange Centre
  岡山国際交流センタ
8 JR Rentacycle
  JRレンタサイクル
9 Eki Rent-a-Car
  Ekiレンタカー
11 Chū-tetsu Bus Centre
  中鉄バスターミナル
12 Tourist Information
  Office
  旅行案内所
15 Post Office
  郵便局
18 Dai-ei Department Store
19 Night Bus Stop
  夜行バス停
20 Okabiru Market
  岡ビル
22 Yumeji Art Museum
  夢二郷土美術館
23 Okayama Prefectural
  Museum
  県立博物館

24 Okayama Prefectural
  Museum of Art
  県立美術館
25 Okayama Orient Museum
  市立オリエント美術館
26 Post Office
  郵便局
28 Maruzen Bookshop
  丸善書店
32 NHK
33 Okayama-jō
  岡山城
34 Hayashibara Museum of
  Art
  林原美術館
35 Okayama Prefectural
  Office (Kenchō)
  岡山県庁
37 Uno Bus Station
  宇野バス本社
39 Desperado
40 Tenmaya Department
  Store
  天満屋百貨店
41 Tenmaya Bus Station
  天満屋バスセンター
42 Kinokuniya Bookshop
  紀伊国屋書店
43 Main Post Office
  中央郵便局
44 NTT
49 Takashimaya
  Department Store;
  ATM
  高島屋
53 Hunters
57 Okayama City Office
  (Shiyakusho)
  岡山市役所

Money There's an ATM that accepts VISA and MasterCard on the 8th floor of the Takashimaya department store (10 am to 7 pm), to the east of Okayama station.

Post The Okayama main post office faces Okayama station, on the east side.

Email & Internet Access The Okayama Prefectural Office (Kenchō) and City Office (Shiyakusho) both have free Internet access (Monday to Friday, 9 am to 4 pm). The Prefectural Office has five terminals and the City Office has one.

Kōraku-en

Kōraku-en means 'the garden for taking pleasure later', taken from the Chinese proverb that 'the lord must bear sorrow before the people and take pleasure after

Momotarō – the Peach Boy

Okayama-ken and neighbouring Kagawa-ken on the island of Shikoku are linked with the legend of Momotarō, the tiny 'Peach Boy' who emerged from the stone of a peach and, backed up by a monkey, a pheasant and a dog, defeated a three-eyed, three-toed, people-eating demon. There are statues of Momotarō at JR Okayama station, and the main road of Okayama is named after him. Another statue of the boy stands at the end of the Kōraku-en island in Okayama. Megashima, off Takamatsu in Shikoku, is said to be the site of the clash with the demon.

Momotarō may actually have been a Yamato prince who was deified as Kibitsuhiko. His shrine, the Kibitsu-jinja, is visited on the Kibi Plain bicycle ride (see the boxed text 'Kibi Plain Bicycle Route').

them'. The Japanese penchant for rating and numbering things is apparent once again at this garden, which is said to be one of the three finest in Japan. The other official members of the big three are the Kairaku-en in Mito (Northern Honshū) and Kenroku-en in Kanazawa (Central Honshū).

Constructed between 1687 and 1700, Kōraku-en (¥350, 7.30 am to 6 pm spring and summer, 8 am to 5 pm autumn and winter) is a stroll garden. Part of its attraction in crowded Japan is its expanse of flat lawn but there are also attractive ponds, a hill in the centre, a curious, tiny tea plantation and rice paddy, and a neatly placed piece of 'borrowed scenery' in the shape of Okayama-jō. Look for the nō stage, the pretty little Ryuten Building where poetry composing contests were once held, and the nearby Yatsu-hashi zigzag bridge.

There's a reduction in price if you buy a 'combined ticket' for Okayama-jō, and an excellent English-language brochure describes the garden's attractions.

From the station take the Higashi-yama tram to the Shiroshita stop (¥140). Alternatively, take an Okaden bus from stand No 5 at the station to Kōrakuen-mae (¥150).

Okayama-jō

Known to locals as U-jō (¥300, 9 am to 5 pm), the 'Crow Castle' was built in 1597; and it's said that its very striking black colour was a *daimyō's* (domain lord) jest at Himeji's pristine 'White Egret Castle'. Like many other great castles in Japan, U-jō was destroyed in WWII; only the small *tsukima-yagura* (moon-viewing turret) survived. It was rebuilt in 1966, a modern reinforced concrete construction like most of the postwar reconstructions. Nevertheless, there is an interesting display inside and much of it is labelled in English.

Combined tickets are available to include Okayama Orient Museum (¥440); Kōraku-en (¥520); or the castle, garden and the Hayashibara Museum (¥670).

Museums

Close to the castle's back entrance, quite near the corner of the moat, the **Hayashibara Museum of Art** (¥300, 9 am to 4.30 pm) houses a private collection of Japanese and Chinese artefacts. Beside the main entrance to Kōraku-en is the worthwhile **Okayama Prefectural Museum** (¥300, 9 am to 5 pm, closed Monday), which has displays about local history. Just north of Kōraku-en is the **Yumeji Art Museum**, displaying work by famed artist Yumeji Takehisa (¥600, 9 am to 5 pm, closed Monday).

Just north of the end of Momotarō-dōri, where the tram line turns south, is the excellent **Okayama Orient Museum** (¥300, closed Monday). The small collection of Middle Eastern art is beautifully displayed. Behind this museum is the **Okayama Prefectural Museum of Art** (¥300, 9 am to 4.30 pm, closed Monday).

Other Attractions

Only a block east of the station, the canal-like **Nishi-gawa**, flanked by its gardens and sculptures, makes for a pleasant short stroll.

South-east of central Okayama is **Tōko-en** (¥400, 9 am to 5 pm), which is easy to overlook in a town with one of the 'big three' gardens. It's worth taking the bus (Stand 9, bound for Saidai-ji) to visit this small, attractive early 17th-century garden just beyond Asahi-gawa. The garden circles a large pond, and it actually predates Kōraku-en by 70 years. Beyond Tōko-en is the temple, **Sōgen-ji** (6 am to 6 pm), which also has a noted Zen garden.

Special Events

The **Saidai-ji Eyō** (Naked Festival) takes place from midnight on the third Saturday in February at the temple, Kannon-in, in the Saidai-ji area. A large crowd of near-naked men fight for two sacred wooden sticks (*shingi*) while seasonally freezing water is poured over them. For such a masochistic purification ritual everyone seems to have a good time.

To reach Kannon-in from Okayama bus station, in front of Okayama station, take the Saidai-ji bound bus (from stand No. 12) to the Ryobi bus terminal (about 45 minutes); from where it's a seven-minute walk.

Places to Stay – Budget

Okayama Seinen-kaikan Youth Hostel (☎ 252-0651) is 10 minutes' walk west of the train station. Dorm beds cost ¥2900 per night. Perhaps the cheapest option in hotels is the *Eki Mae Business Hotel* (☎ 222-0073) with rooms starting at ¥4500.

Places to Stay – Mid-Range

One of the cheaper places around is the *Makibi Kaikan* (☎ 232-05110), just south of the station. It's on the 5th floor of an educational institute and only has 24 rooms, so it may be booked out. Singles/twins cost ¥6200/9900. Another less expensive business hotel not far from the station is the *Hotel Maira* (☎ 222-5601), with singles/twins for ¥6700/13,000. The nearby *Chisan Hotel* (☎ 225-1212) has adequate singles starting at ¥6600. The *Okayama Castle Hotel* (☎ 234-5678), south-east of the station, has singles/doubles for ¥6200/17,000. Further down Momotarō-dōri is the decent-value *Washington Hotel Plaza* (☎ 231-9111), with singles at ¥7600.

In the quieter area west of the station, there are more hotels only a few minutes' walk from the centre of things. The *Okayama Tower Hotel* has clean singles/

doubles starting at ¥6680/12,700. The *New Station Hotel* (☎ 253-6655) charges ¥5200/9000 for singles/doubles and the *Dai Ichi Inn* (☎ 253-5311) has singles/twins starting at ¥7090/12,900.

Unfortunately, Okayama has no centrally located traditional accommodation. *Saiwai-sō* (☎ 254-0020), near the station's west exit, is at least a business hotel with *tatami* (woven floor matting) rooms. Singles start at ¥7090, including two meals.

Places to Stay – Top End

The *Granvia Hotel* (☎ 233-3131) has rooms starting at ¥9500 and is rather plush. The conveniently-placed *Hotel New Okayama* (☎ 223-8211) has comfortable singles/twins from ¥9000/14,000.

Places to Eat & Drink

The small street parallel to, and immediately south of, Momotarō-dōri has a varied collection of places to eat, including the popular *robatayaki* (restaurant specialising in char-grilled fish), *Murasaki*, which has a fully illustrated menu; and *Pizza & Salad St Moritz* (☎ 223-6956), on the 2nd floor of the Communication Building (10.30 am to 11 pm, closed Wednesday).

Curiously, Okayama is brimming with Italian restaurants. There are two branches of the *Pizza Patio* in town, one close to the station and one by Ōte-machi arcade. Both have an excellent selection of pizzas and pasta dishes for ¥700. The popular, woodsy (and delightfully nonsmoking) *Jolly Fox* (☎ 221-2621), just north of the Chisan Hotel, has pastas, pizza and praiseworthy salads. Lunch specials are ¥950 and set dinners are ¥2000 (12 pm to 3 pm, 6 pm to 10 pm, closed Monday).

Zen (☎ 224-3677) is a good value 'Beer and Herb' restaurant. Alas, by herb it probably means parsley or dill. All dishes are ¥500, there's an English-language menu and, despite the title, this is more microbeer than macrobiotic (6 pm to 3 am). It's two blocks east of Takashimaya. Nearby, *Eikokuryō-Honkoku* (☎ 234-0429) is a trendy, graffiti-daubed *izakaya* (pub-style eatery). It's open from 5 pm to midnight.

Itako Sanuki Udon (☎ 223-4056), is famed not only for its *al dente*-style *udon* (thick wheat noodles) but also its perennially unsmiling chef. In addition to the noodles, rice balls and vegetable tempura are recommended (¥500). It's just west of Yanagawa-dōri (11.20 am to 2.40 pm, 5.30 pm to 9 pm, closed Saturday evening and Sunday).

For sushi, it's worth heading over to the Omote-machi arcade, where you'll find *Itcho* (☎ 223-1648), a good sushi bar with affordable prices (9.30 am to 8 pm, closed Tuesday); and the renowned noodle shop *Bukkake-tei* (☎ 223-3023), open from 11 am to 7.30 pm and closed Tuesday. In the arcade behind the New Okayama Hotel is *Sushi Land – Marine Polis*, a revolving sushi restaurant.

Popular bars with the local foreign community include *Hunter* (☎ 225-9228), open from 6 pm to 3 am, and *Desperado* (☎ 225-9228), open from 7 pm to 3 am and closed Monday. Both feature occasional live music.

Getting There & Away

All Nippon Airways (ANA) flies to Okayama from Tokyo several times daily. There are also international flights to Seoul (five times weekly) and Shanghai (twice weekly). A bus runs to the airport (¥680, 40 minutes) from the Chūtetsu Bus Centre.

Okayama is connected by the Sanyō Hikari shinkansen to Kyoto (¥7330, one hour) and Tokyo (Hikari, ¥16,380, 3¼ hours).

See the Kurashiki section for details on travelling between Okayama and Kurashiki. When travelling west, it's quicker to transfer from the shinkansen at Okayama than at Shin-Kurashiki. You also change trains at Okayama if you're heading to Shikoku across the Seto-ōhashi.

Buses run from in front of the station, from the Tenmaya bus station in the Tenmaya department store, from the nearby Uno bus station, and in front of Dai-ei department store.

Getting Around

Getting around Okayama is a breeze since the Higashi-yama tram route (on your right as you leave the station) will take you to all the main attractions. Trams charge a standard ¥140 to anywhere in town.

JR Rentacycle (7.30 am to 7.30 pm, last rental 5.30 pm) offers bike hire for ¥350/600 half-day/all day. It's at the south-east end of the station building. Next-door is the office of Eki Rent-a-Car (☎ 224-1037).

AROUND OKAYAMA

There are a number of places of interest in the Okayama-Kurashiki area including the pottery centre of Bizen, the Inland Sea, the Seto-ōhashi lookout at Washūzan and the enjoyable Kibi Plain bicycle route.

For those with time to venture out into the northern parts of the prefecture, there are several *onsen* (mineral hot-spring spa) resort areas worth seeking out including Okutsu Onsen, Yunogō Onsen, and Yubara Onsen where there is a mixed, 24-hour, free *rotemburo* (outdoor mineral hot spring) on the banks of the Asahi-gawa. Staff at the Okayama tourist information counter can provide more information.

Kibi Plain Bicycle Route

An excellent way to spend half a day seeing a less-visited part of Japan is to follow the Kibi Plain bicycle route. The route follows bicycle paths for most of its length and visits a number of temples, shrines and other sites. You can rent a bicycle *(renta saikaru)* at any JR station along the route and leave it at another (see the boxed text 'Kibi Plain Bicycle Route').

Takamatsu-jō & Ashimori

Places of interest on the Kibi Plain, but not on the bicycle route, include the site of Takamatsu-jō where Toyotomi Hideyoshi defeated Shimizu. Toyotomi hastened the siege by flooding the castle, and the remains of the great dykes can still be seen.

North-west of the Takamatsu-jō site is Ashimori, with its well-preserved samurai residence and the lovely **Omizu-en**, which is another stroll garden in the Enshū style.

The castle is around 15 minutes on foot north-east of Bitchū Takamatsu station on the JR Kibi line, but the samurai residence and the garden are some distance north of Ashimori station. The best way to get to Omizu-en is to take a bus to Ashimori-machi from outside Okayama station. It takes approximately 40 minutes and the fare is ¥600.

Although there is little to be seen at the site of Takamatsu-jō, it played a crucial part in the finale to the chaotic 'Country at War' century. In 1582, Hideyoshi besieged the castle on behalf of the ruthless Oda Nobunaga and agreed to allow the castle's defenders to surrender on condition that their commander, Lord Shimizu, committed suicide. On the very eve of this event, word came from Kyoto that Oda Nobunaga had been assassinated. Hideyoshi contrived to keep this news from the castle garrison and in the morning his unfortunate opponent killed himself. Hideyoshi then sprinted back to Kyoto and soon assumed command himself.

Bizen
☎ 0869 • pop 29,424

East of Okayama on the JR Akō line is the 700-year-old pottery region of Bizen, which is renowned for its unglazed Bizen-yaki pottery. Much prized by tea ceremony connoisseurs, Bizen ceramics are earthy, dramatic and, more often than not, rather expensive. At Imbe station, the drop-off point to explore the area, there is a tourist information counter (☎ 64-1100), which has a useful English-language pamphlet on the history of Bizen-yaki, though foreign language assistance is limited at best.

On the 2nd floor of the station is the Bizen Ceramic Crafts Museum (free, 9.30 am to 5.30 pm, closed Tuesday) and on the north side of the station are the Okayama Prefectural Bizen Ceramics Art Museum (¥500, 9.30 am to 4.30 pm, closed Monday) and the Bizen Ceramics Center (☎ 64-2453), with free admission (10 am to 4.30 pm, closed Monday), all of which display the pottery of the area. Of all the galleries in Bizen's main street, Kibi-dō (☎ 64-4467) is the oldest and most interesting (10 am to 6 pm).

There are several kilns in the area that, for around ¥3000, offer a chance to try your

hand at making Bizen-yaki (reservations necessary). Try Bishū Gama (☎ 64-1160), where some English is spoken. In about two hours you can sculpt a masterpiece (you'll need to arrange to have your creation shipped to you after it's been fired). Another option is the Bizen-yaki Traditional Pottery Centre (☎ 64-1001) on the 3rd floor of Imbe station, where there are workshops (¥3000) held on weekends and holidays from April to November.

Seto-ōhashi Area 瀬戸大橋
☎ 0864

From the peninsula south of Kurashiki and Okayama, the Seto ōhashi connects Honshū (Japan's biggest island) with Shikoku (its fourth largest). The 12km-long bridge (or more correctly bridges, since there are six of them stepping from island to island across the strait) was opened in 1988 and has considerably shortened travel time to Shikoku. The long span at the Honshū end is the world's longest double-level suspension bridge carrying both road and rail traffic.

Washū-zan near the end of the peninsula, was long renowned as a lookout point over the Inland Sea. Now it looks out over the bridge as well. The best views are from the No 2 viewing platform at an elevation of 133m. Shitaden buses from Kurashiki run direct to the platform (¥900, 70 minutes).

If you are particularly interested in taking a look at the bridge, the best way to do so is via a boat tour around it from Kojima. During the summer months (March to November), boats depart approximately hourly between 9 am and 4 pm (¥1550, one hour). The cruise boats leave just a couple of hundred metres to the south-east of Kojima station.

Places to Stay

There are a good number of hotels, pensions and ryokan in the Kojima/Washūzan area, but particularly well located is the *Washūzan Youth Hostel* (☎ 79-9280), at the foot of the hill right at the end of the peninsula. Dorm beds cost ¥2100, or ¥3570 with two meals. Buses run to it from in front of Kojima station; ask the driver for the '*yūsu-hosuteru-mae basu-tei*'. Those

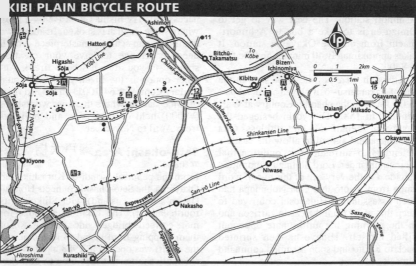

Kibi Plain Bicycle Route

To access this excellent cycling course, take a local JR Kibi line train from Okayama three stops to Bizen Ichinomiya, ride the 15km route to Sōja, drop off your bike and take a JR Hakubi/San-yō line train back through Kurashiki to Okayama. Bicycles cost ¥200 per hour or ¥1000 for the day.

From **JR Bizen Ichinomiya** station turn right, then right again to cross the railway line and in just 300m you reach the shrine, **Kibitsuhiko-jinja**, which fronts a large pond. From here you soon pick up the bicycle path following a canal through the fields until it rejoins the road just before the temple, Fudenkai-ji. Just 200m further is the **Kibitsu-jinja**, where a wide flight of steps leads up to its attractive hilltop setting. Have your fortune told (in English) for ¥100 by the serve-yourself oracle in the courtyard. The shrine, built in 1425, is unusual in having both the oratory and main sanctum topped by a single roof. The legendary peach boy, Momotarō, is connected with the shrine.

Pedalling on, you pass **Koikui-jinja**, which is also connected with the legendary figure Kibitsuhiko, and reach the huge 5th-century **Tsukuriyama-kofun Burial Mound**, rising like a rounded hill from the surrounding plain. You really need to be in a hot-air balloon or a helicopter to appreciate that it's really a 350m-long keyhole-shaped mound, not a natural hill. Just north of here is the birthplace of famous artist **Sesshū** (1420–1506). He was once a novice monk at **Hōfuku-ji**, which is 3km north-west of JR Sōja station.

Finally, there are the foundation stones of the **Bitchū Kokubun-niji Convent**, the nearby **Kibiji Archaeological Museum** (closed Monday), the excavated **Kōmorizuka Burial Mound** and **Bitchū Kokobun-ji**, with its picturesque five-storey pagoda. From here it's a few more kilometres into Sōja.

There are countless drink-vending machines along the way, and occasionally the bicycle path passes close enough to a main road to divert for food. If you start early you can arrive in Sōja in time for lunch, or buy a sandwich from the **Little Mermaid** bakery near the station and eat on the train on your way back. If this bicycle ride appeals to you, you can easily plot others on the network of tracks that cover the area. A walking path also runs very near the bicycle route.

KIBI PLAIN BICYCLE ROUTE

1 Hōfuku-ji
   宝福寺
2 Sōja
   総社宮
3 Anyō-ji
   安養寺
4 Sumotoriyama Burial Mound
   すもとり山古墳
5 Bitchū Kokubun-ji
   備中国分寺
6 Kōmorizuka Burial Mound
   こうもり塚古墳
7 Kibiji Archaelogical Museum
   吉備路郷土館
8 Bitchū Kokubun-niji Convent
   備中国分尼寺跡
9 Tsukuriyama-kofun Burial Mound
   造山古墳
10 Sesshū's Birthplace
   雪舟誕生の地
11 Takamatsu-jo Site
   高松城跡
12 Koikui-jinja
   鯉喰神社
13 Kibitsu-jinja
   吉備津神社
14 Kibitsuhiko-jinja
   吉備津彦神社
15 Ikeda Zoo
   池田動物園

looking for upmarket digs should ask at the Kojima station tourist information counter (☎ 72-1289).

Getting There & Away

Buses run to Kojima from Kurashiki and Okayama, and the JR Seto-ōhashi line from Okayama to Shikoku runs through Kojima station before crossing the bridge. Buses run from Kojima station to Washūzan (¥270, 20 minutes), but are not all that frequent. There's also the Shimotsui Narrow Gauge Railway, which runs from Kojima (near the Seto-ōhashi Memorial Bridge Museum) at one end, via Washūzan station to Shimotsui station at the other. Shimotsui is an interesting little fishing port and ferries cross from here to Marugame on Shikoku.

KURASHIKI 倉敷

pop 435,379

Kurashiki's claim to fame is a small quarter of picturesque buildings around a stretch of moat. There are a number of old black-tiled warehouses that have been converted into an eclectic collection of museums. Bridges arch over, willows dip into the water and the whole effect is quite delightful – it's hardly surprising that the town is a favourite with tourists, or that *kurashiki* means 'warehouse village'.

In the feudal era, the warehouses were used to store rice brought by boat from the surrounding rich farmlands. As this phase of Kurashiki's history faded, the town's importance as a textile centre increased and the Kurabō Textile Company expanded. Ōhara Keisaburō, the owner of the company, gathered together a significant collection of European art and, in the 1920s, opened the Ōhara Museum. It was the first of a series of museums that have become the town's principal attraction and is still its finest.

Beware that many of Kurashiki's prime attractions, and most of the eateries, close on Monday.

Orientation & Information

It's about 1km from the station to the old canal area and, if you walk, the typical urban Japanese scenery makes you wonder whether you are in the right town. But when you turn into the canal area, everything changes; Ivy Square is just beyond the canal. A number of shops along the main street, Kurashiki Chūō-dōri, sell Bizen-yaki.

The staff at the station's information counter (☎ 426-8681) will make accommodation bookings (9 am to 5 pm), and there is also a helpful tourist information office near the bend in the canal.

Don't be surprised if you have the fortune of running into Sato-san, an eccentric white-haired gentleman (and retired English teacher) who frequents the canal area daily and has managed to stir up the local volunteer guide association with his unlicensed befriending of foreign visitors and his resounding tongue. Despite his persistence and vigour, he expects nothing in return for

WESTERN HONSHŪ

his guide services, except that you loan him an ear (or two).

Museums

Ōhara Museum of Art This is undoubtedly Kurashiki's number one museum (¥1000, 9 am to 5 pm, closed Monday) housing the predominantly European art collection of the textile magnate Ōhara Keisaburō (1880–1943). Rodin, Matisse, Picasso, Pissarro, Monet, Cézanne, Renoir, El Greco, Toulouse-Lautrec, Gauguin, Degas and Munch are all represented here. The museum's neo-classical facade is Kurashiki's best known landmark.

Your ticket also takes you to the museum's folk art and Chinese art collections and to the contemporary art collection, housed in a new building behind the main one. You have to exit the old building and walk down the street to enter the new gallery, where you will find works by Pollock, Rothko, de Kooning, Henry Moore and others.

Kurashiki Museum of Folkcraft The folkcraft museum's impressive collection is mainly Japanese, but also includes furniture and other items from many other countries. The collection is housed in a rustic, attractive complex of linked *kura* (warehouses). Admission is ¥700; the museum is open from 9 am to 4.15 pm (December to February) or until 5 pm (March to November) and is closed Monday.

Japan Rural Toy Museum This interesting little museum displays folkcraft toys from Japan and around the world. Japanese rural toys are also on sale (¥500, 8 am to 5 pm, daily).

Other Museums If you've not had your fill of museums there's also the **Museum of Natural History** (¥100) and the **Kurashiki City Art Museum** (¥200). Both museums are open from 9 am to 5 pm, closed Monday. The recently-restored **Ōhashi-ke** (Ōhashi House; ¥500, closed Monday) is a reasonable example of a late 18th-century merchant's house. It's a shame however that the spacious tatami rooms aren't furnished.

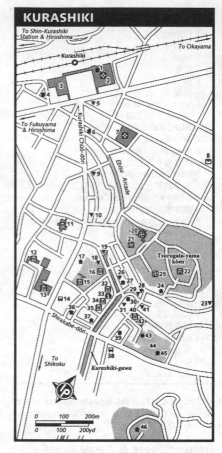

Ivy Square

The Kurabō textile factories have moved on to more modern premises and the fine old Meiji-era factory buildings (dating from 1889 and remodelled in 1974) now house a hotel, restaurants, shops and yet more museums. Ivy Square, with its ivy-covered walls and open-air cafe, is the centre of the complex.

The **Torajirō Kojima Museum** (¥350, 9 am to 5 pm, closed Monday) displays work by the local artist who helped Ōhara establish his European collection, along with some fine pieces from the Middle East in the associated Orient Museum.

KURASHIKI

PLACES TO STAY
1 Hotel Kurashiki
3 Kurashiki
　Terminal Hotel
　倉敷ターミナルホテル
4 Young Inn Kurashiki
　ヤングイン
6 Kurashiki Station Hotel
　倉敷ステーションホテル
17 Kurashiki Kokusai Hotel
　倉敷国際ホテル
24 Kamoi Minshuku
　カモ井民宿
27 Ryokan Tsurugata;
　Restaurant & Cafe
　鶴形イン
30 Ryokan Kurashiki
　旅館くらしき
36 El Paso Inn
　エルパソイン
37 Kawakami Minshuku
　かわかみ民宿
39 Tokusan Kan
　特産館民宿
45 Kurashiki Ivy Square Hotel
　倉敷アイビースクエア
46 Kurashiki Youth Hostel
　倉敷ユースホステル

PLACES TO EAT
5 McDonald's
9 Domino

10 Rentenchi Due Rentenchi
　煉天地
18 El Greco
19 Kiyū-tei
　亀遊亭ステーキハウス
23 Kanadean
26 Kamoi Restaurant
　カモ井
28 Tsuneya
29 Mamakari-Tei
　ままかり亭
31 Coffee-Kan
　献琥館
41 Kana Izumi
　かないずみ

OTHER
2 Mitsukoshi Department Store
　三越百貨店
7 Tenmaya Department Store
　天満屋百貨店
8 Post Office
　郵便局
11 Ōhashi-ke
　大橋家
12 Museum of Natural History
　自然史博物館
13 Kurashiki City Art Museum
　市立美術館
14 Mizushima Washūzan
　Bus Stop
　水島鷲羽山バス停

15 Ōhara Museum Annexe
　大原美術館分館
16 Ōhara Museum of Art
　大原美術館
20 Kanryū-ji
　観竜寺
21 Seigan-ji
　誓願寺
22 Achi-jinja
　阿智神社
25 Honei-ji
　本栄寺
32 Ninagawa Museum
　倉敷蜷川博物館
33 Tourist Information;
　Traveller's Rest Area
　観光案内所
34 Museum of Folkcraft
　倉敷民芸館
35 Japan Rural Toy Museum
　日本郷土玩具館
38 Kojima Washūzan Bus Stop
　小島鷲羽山バス停
40 Torajirō Kojima Museum;
　Orient Museum
　児島虎次郎記念館
42 Kurabō Memorial Hall
　倉紡記念館
43 Ivy Academic Hall
　アイビー館
44 Ivy Square
　アイビースクエア

The museum in the **Kurabō Memorial Hall** outlines Kurashiki's growth as a textile centre, and the curious **Ivy Academic Hall** (combined entry ticket ¥350, 9 am to 5 pm), traces the development of Western art through reproductions of notable paintings.

Shrines & Temples
Achi-jinja shrine tops Tsurugata-yama-kōen, which overlooks the old area of town. The Honei-ji, Kanryū-ji and the Seigan-ji temples are also found in the park.

Places to Stay
Kurashiki is a great town for staying in a traditional Japanese inn, with an ample selection of minshuku and ryokan.

Places to Stay – Budget
Youth Hostels *Kurashiki Youth Hostel* (☎ 422-7355), is south of the canal area. Dorm beds cost ¥2800, or ¥3800 for non-members. It's a long climb to its hilltop location, but the view is great and the staff are very friendly. From the station you can take a bus to the Shimin Kaikan stop. The fare is ¥150. The hostel is a 15-minute walk uphill.

Hotels The *Young Inn* (☎ 425-3411), behind the Kurashiki Terminal Hotel, is quite a bargain; singles/twins without bath cost ¥4000/7000. There are also slightly more expensive rooms with bathrooms in this vaguely hostel-like hotel.

Places to Stay – Mid Range

Minshuku & Ryokan There are several good-value minshuku conveniently close to the canal. The *Tokusan Kan* (☎ 425-3056), is near Ivy Square. Rooms start at ¥7000 with two meals. Right by the canal near the toy museum, the simple *Kawakami Minshuku* (☎ 424-1221) has rooms for only ¥4500, or ¥6000 with two meals.

The *Kamoi Minshuku* (☎ 422-4898) is easy to find (at the bottom of the steps to the Achi-jinja) and is also conveniently close to the canal area. Although this minshuku is new, it looks very traditional – an atmosphere enhanced by the antiques throughout the building. Rooms cost ¥6000 with two meals. The Kamoi also has a popular *restaurant* by the canal.

Hotels The best place to look for hotels is around the popular canal area, or near the train station. Part of the Ivy Square complex, *Kurashiki Ivy Square Hotel* (☎ 422-0011) has singles for ¥7000, or ¥11,000 with bath, doubles and twins range from ¥11,500 to ¥12,800 without bath, or ¥27,000 with bath. Rooms without a bath or shower have a toilet and sink only – there are large communal baths and showers.

JR-operated *Hotel Kurashiki* (☎ 426-6111), in the station building, has singles/twins starting at ¥8500/16,000. The *Kurashiki Terminal Hotel* (☎ 426-1111), has singles at ¥6800, and doubles/twins at ¥11,500/13,000. It's immediately to the right as you leave the station and the entrance is on the 9th floor.

The *Kurashiki Station Hotel* (☎ 425-2525) is a short distance along Kurashiki Chūō-dōri towards the canal. The entrance is around the side of the building, with reception on the 5th floor. The rooms in this older, but cheaper, business hotel are tiny and utterly straightforward; singles/doubles start at ¥6000/10,000.

Places to Stay – Top End

Ryokan The canal-side *Ryokan Tsurugata* (☎ 424-1635) dates from 1744. The ryokan's *restaurant* serves nonguests, mainly at lunch time, and there is also a *cafe*. Rooms cost from ¥15,000 to ¥35,000 per person. Also by the canal, *Ryokan Kurashiki* (☎ 422-0730) is old, elegant and expensive. Rooms cost ¥20,000 per person with two meals. Either of these ryokan would make a good introduction to staying at a traditional inn.

Hotels Backing onto the Ōhara Museum is the expensive *Kurashiki Kokusai Hotel* (☎ 422-5141), with singles/doubles starting at ¥9900/18,700. There are also more expensive Japanese-style rooms in this popular and attractive hotel. Also close to the canal is the stylish *El Paso Inn* (☎ 421-8282), with doubles/twins starting at ¥9900/11,000.

Places to Eat

Don't leave eating out too late. Many of the restaurants you may notice at lunch time will be closed by early evening. The hordes of day-trippers will have disappeared by then and many of the visitors staying in Kurashiki will be eating in their ryokan or minshuku.

Beside the canal is the *Kamoi Restaurant* (☎ 422-0606), which is run by the same people as the popular Kamoi Minshuku (9 am to 5.30 pm, closed Monday). Not far from the Ryokan Kurashiki is *Mamakari-tei* (☎ 427-7112), a cosy, traditional spot named and famed for the local sardine-like fish it dishes out daily (served both raw and cooked). If you're not a sardine lover, try the *tōfu manjū* (fried tofu patties). It has lunch sets from ¥1500 (11 am to 2 pm, 4 pm to 10 pm, closed Monday). Nearby is *Tsuneya* (☎ 427-7111), a welcoming place frequented more by locals than tourists, which specialises in charcoal-grilled dishes *(sumibiyaki)*. It's open from 11 am to 2 pm and 5 pm to 10 pm, but is closed Wednesday. At the northern end of the canal is *Kiyū-tei* (☎ 422-5140), a steakhouse in an old traditional Japanese house. It has good set lunch meals for under ¥1000 and a fixed evening meal of soup, salad, steak, bread and coffee costs ¥2500 (11 am to 9 pm, closed Monday).

Just back from the canal is *Kana Izumi* (☎ 421-7254), a pleasant, modern restaurant with plastic meals displayed in the window and a fully illustrated menu. You can get good tempura and noodles for ¥1650 (10.30 am to 8 pm, closed Monday).

There's a *snack bar* in Ivy Square and several *restaurants* in and near the square. South-east of Tsurugata-yama-kōen, *Kanadean (☎ 421-7160)* a small place specialising in 'Asian' cuisine (11 am to 6 pm, closed Monday). It has milk tea and 15 kinds of spicy curries, with set meals starting at ¥1000. Look out for the blue latticework windows and the blue sign.

There are also a number of places to eat along Kurashiki Chūō-dōri. A neat little place, *Domino (☎ 425-0868)* serves a good *teishoku* (set meal) lunch for under ¥800 (9 am to 9 pm, closed Monday). Not far away, Italian restaurant, *Due Rentenchi (☎ 426-0355)*, has coffee for ¥300 and pasta dishes starting at ¥700 (10 am to 8 pm, closed every 3rd Wednesday).

El Greco (☎ 422-0297), by the canal near the Ōhara Museum (you can't miss its ivy-clad walls), is a fashionable place for coffee and cakes (10 am to 5 pm, closed Monday). It has an English-language menu. Another great spot for coffee – and coffee only – is the cavernous tavern *Coffee-Kan (☎ 426-9190)*, just beside the Ryokan Kurashiki. It offers an amazing selection of home-roasted java (24 hours, daily).

Getting There & Away

Kurashiki, only 16km from Okayama, is not on the shinkansen line. Travelling westwards, it's usually faster to disembark at Okayama and take a San-yō line *futsū* (local train) to Kurashiki (¥320, 15 minutes). If you're eastbound, get off at the Shin-Kurashiki station, two stops on the San-yō line from Kurashiki.

To get to Washūzan and Shikoku from Kurashiki, you can either travel by train to Okayama and change trains there for Washūzan, or take a bus (¥860, 1¼ hours) direct to Kojima or Washūzan from outside the station or the canal area.

Getting Around

Walking is the way to go – it's only 15 minutes on foot from the station to the canal area, where almost everything is within a few minutes' stroll.

TAKAHASHI 高橋
☎ 0866

Built along the banks of a river, the Takahashi-gawa, this pleasant small town, midway between Kurashiki and the central Chūgoku Expressway, gets few Western visitors even though it has a temple with a very beautiful Zen garden and is overlooked by an atmospheric, even spooky, old castle.

Orientation & Information

While the town is Takahashi, the train station is known as Bitchū-Takahashi, which is a bit confusing. The tourist information counter in the bus terminal beside the train station (☎ 21-0229) has some information in English as well as maps in Japanese (7.15 am to 6.40 pm). The temple, Raikyū-ji, is about 1km to the north of the station, on the east side of the tracks, though to get there you'll need to walk north on the west side and then cross over. Bitchū-Matsuyama-jō is about 5km north of the station, up a steep hillside. If you are not up to the hefty walk or cycle up there, a taxi should run you up for about ¥1800. There are bicycles for hire at the station for ¥200 per hour.

Raikyū-ji

The classic Zen garden (¥300, 9 am to 5 pm) in this small temple is the work of the master designer Kobori Enshū and dates from 1604. A peaceful place to sit on the veranda and contemplate, it contains all the traditional elements of this style of garden, including stones in the form of turtle and crane islands, a series of topiary hedges to represent waves on the sea, and it even incorporates the mountain, Atago-san, in the background as 'borrowed scenery'.

Bitchū-Matsuyama-jō

High above Takahashi stands the highest castle in Japan (430m), a relic of an earlier period of castle construction when fortresses were designed to be hidden and inaccessible, unlike the later, much larger constructions designed to protect the surrounding lands. The road winds up the hill to a car park, from where you have a steep climb to the castle itself. On a dark and overcast day you can almost feel the inspiration for a film like Kurosawa's *Throne of Blood*.

The castle (¥300, 9 am to 4 pm) was originally established in 1240 and in the following centuries was enlarged until it finally covered the whole mountain top. It fell into disrepair after the Meiji Restoration, but the townspeople took over its maintenance from 1929. It was finally completely restored in the 1950s and has recently undergone further repairs and additions.

Other Attractions

Takahashi has some picturesque old samurai streets with traditional walls and gates, mainly in the area around Raikyū-ji. Around 500m to the north of Raikyū-ji is the **Takahashi Bukeyashiki-kan** (¥300, 9 am to 5 pm), a well-preserved samurai residence dating from the 1830s. If you walk up to Raikyū-ji, you'll pass the **Local History Museum** (Kyōdō shiryō-kan; ¥300, 9 am to 5 pm), which is a fine wooden Meiji structure dating from 1904. It has displays of items associated with the area's mercantile and agricultural past. The temple, **Shōren-ji**, directly east of the station, has unique terraced stone walls (9 am to 5 pm).

Places to Stay

Takahashi Youth Hostel (☎ 22-3149) is about 1km north of the station, just south of Raikyū-ji. It charges ¥2600 per night. *Business Hotel Takahashi* (☎ 22-6766), just west of the station is par for the course; singles/twins cost ¥5000/9000. The *Takahashi-shi Cycling Terminal* (☎ 22-0135) is a 20-minute bus trip from the JR station at the Wonderland amusement park. It costs ¥5000 with two meals. You can rent bicycles from the terminal for ¥400 for four hours, but think twice before setting out to ride up to the castle!

There are also several ryokan and minshuku in town that are worth a look. Just west of the station is the very attractive *Midori Ryokan* (☎ 22-2537). Per-person rates are ¥4200, or ¥8000 with two meals. The elegant *Aburaya Ryokan* (☎ 22-3072) is on the main road facing the river. Rooms cost ¥13,000 with two meals.

Places to Eat

Savoury Shikoku-style udon can be found at *Sanukiya* (☎ 22-1481), beside the canal, west of Raikyū-ji. Though there's no English-language menu, the choices are pretty straightforward and the staff can help you order (11 am to 9 pm, closed Wednesday afternoon). The speciality of the house is a hearty udon stew with duck meat called *kamo nabe udon*.

There is good *rāmen* (Chinese egg noodles in broth) at *Ajiya* (☎ 22-2568), just north along the same street (11 am to 1.30 am, closed Tuesday).

Also close by, on the main road facing the river, is *Nishimura*, a unique little cafe housed in an old *sake* warehouse, which offers tea or coffee and delicious sweet jellies flavoured with *yuzu* (citron fruit). These delectable little sweets can be purchased as souvenirs nearby at *Enshūdō* (☎ 22-2427), a local candy manufacturer in production since the Edo period! It's open from 8 am to 7 pm, but is closed Sunday.

Getting There & Away

Although Takahashi is not on any of the regular tourist routes through Western Honshū, it would not take a great effort to include it in an itinerary. The town is about 50km north of Okayama or 60km from Fukuyama. It's on the JR Hakubi line (from Okayama, futsū, ¥820, 50 minutes) so a stop could be made when travelling between Okayama on the south coast and Yonago (near Matsue) on the north coast.

FUKIYA 吹屋

The beautifully situated village of Fukiya, north-west of Takahashi, was once a rich copper mining centre and has many attractive buildings from the latter years of the Edo period and the first years after the Meiji Restoration. One of the prefecture's International Villas is in the village. To get to Fukiya, take a JR limited express *(tokkyū)* from Okayama to Bitchū-Takahashi station; from there it's about an hour by bus.

Hiroshima-ken

In addition to the primary attractions in Hiroshima city related to the horrific bombing in 1945, the prefecture has a number of other noteworthy places of interest including nearby Miyajima, with the famed Itsukushima-jinja, the quaint fishing village at Tomo-no-Ura and a marathon temple walk (supplemented by rāmen of some renown) in Onomichi.

FUKUYAMA 福山
☎ 0849 ● pop 370,000
Fukuyama is a modern industrial town of little interest to the tourist, but its convenient location on the Osaka-Hakata shinkansen route makes it a good jumping-off point for the pretty fishing port of Tomo-no-Ura; or for Onomichi, which in turn is a jumping-off point for Inland Sea cruises. If you do have a few hours to spend

in Fukuyama, you can visit the art gallery and museum, and the reconstructed castle.

Orientation & Information
Most of the places of interest, as well as the hotels and restaurants, are close to the station. Route 2 runs parallel to the railway line, about half a kilometre south. There is a tourist information and accommodation booking counter (☎ 22-2869) in the busy, modern train station (8.30 am to 5 pm).

FUKUYAMA

PLACES TO STAY
2 Fukuyama Grand Hotel
福山グランドホテル
6 Fukuyama Castle Hotel
福山キャッスルホテル
7 Fukuyama Kokusai Hotel;
Fukuyama Station Inn
福山国際ホテル；
福山ステーションイン
8 Fukuyama New Kokusai Hotel
福山ニュー国際ホテル
9 New Castle Hotel
ニューキャッスルホテル
10 Fukuyama Tōbu Hotel
福山東武ホテル

PLACES TO EAT
12 Studebaker
13 McDonald's
14 Zuccheroe Sale
16 Fujimoto Garden Chō-ji
フジモトガーデン

OTHER
1 Gokoku-jinja
護国神社
3 Fukuyama Museum of Art
福山美術館
4 Hiroshima Prefectural
History Museum
広島県立歴史博物館
5 Fukuyama-jō
福山城
11 NTT
15 Tenmaya Department Store
天満屋
17 Main Post Office
中央郵便局

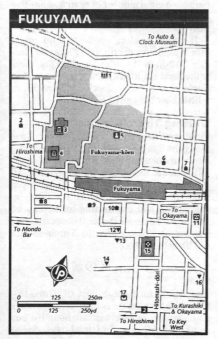

FUKUYAMA

Fukuyama-jō

Fukuyama-jō (¥200, 9 am to 4 pm, closed Monday) was built in 1619, torn down during the 'one realm, one castle' period, and reconstructed in 1966. It overlooks the train station, which is only a couple of minutes' walk away. As well as the imposing donjon of the castle itself, there are turrets, the fine Sujigane-Go-mon, a bathhouse, and a mildly interesting set of medieval bits and pieces.

Museums

Immediately to the west of the castle hill are Fukuyama's **Museum of Art** (¥300, 9.30 am to 5 pm, closed Monday) and the Hiroshima **Prefectural History Museum** (¥290, 9 am to 4.30 pm, closed Monday).

The Fukuyama **Auto & Clock Museum**, north of the town centre, charges an exorbitant ¥900 entry fee, but the strange little collection makes an interesting change from the usual feudal artefacts. Anything old is a little strange in modern Japan, so the 1950 Mazda motorcycle taxi looks particularly curious. The 1961 Datsun Fairlady sports car would have been no competition at all for a British sports car of that period – 40 years on how things have changed! The museum also houses waxwork figures of US presidents Abraham Lincoln and George Washington, James Dean, Elvis Presley, General Douglas MacArthur and a very dissolute-looking Commodore Matthew Perry.

Places to Stay

There are lots of business hotels close to the train station. Two of the cheaper ones are the well-equipped *Fukuyama Kokusai Hotel* (☎ 24-2411), behind the station, which charges ¥6000/10,200 for singles/twins; and in front of the station, the *Fukuyama New Kokusai Hotel* (☎ 24-7000), with singles for ¥5600. The *Fukuyama Station Inn* (☎ 25-3337) is another cheapie, with singles starting at ¥5300 and a few twins/doubles for ¥8400/7500.

Immediately in front of the station is the *Fukuyama Tōbu Hotel* (☎ 25-3181), with singles/twins starting at ¥6500/11,000.

Nearby is the uninspiring *New Castle Hotel* (☎ 22-2121), with rooms starting at ¥9000/18,000.

The *Fukuyama Castle Hotel* (☎ 25-2111) is directly behind the station; rooms start at ¥7000/12,000. The *Fukuyama Grand Hotel* (☎ 21-5511) has singles starting at ¥8200 and twins/doubles at ¥16,000/15,000.

Places to Eat

The full complement of fast-food places can be found immediately south of the train station. *Studebaker* (☎ 26-1144) is open from 11 am to 10 pm and is a Japanese-Italian restaurant curiously named after a US car manufacturer that went belly up in the early 1960s. The menu features a selection of spaghetti, though for more authentic (and pricey) Italian food head for *Zuccheroe Sale* (☎ 28-3543), which is open from 11.30 am to 2.30 pm and 5.30 pm to 11 pm, but is closed Monday.

The alleys either side of McDonald's harbour a good number of *rāmen shops* that do a busy lunch-time trade with the salaryman set.

If you're heading out for a drink and a bite at night, try the tropical *Fujimoto Garden Chō-ji*; or if you're just drinking, there is the local gaijin hang-out, the *Mondo Bar*. For a bit more style check out *Bar 333*, or a little shot bar called *Key West*.

Getting There & Away

Fukuyama is on the main railway lines along the San-yō coast. If you are travelling between Fukuyama and Kurashiki, it's usually quicker to stick to the San-yō line all the way rather than travelling from Fukuyama to Shin-Kurashiki station by shinkansen and transferring to the San-yō line there. There are frequent buses from the Fukuyama station area to Tomo-no-Ura (¥530, 40 minutes).

TOMO-NO-URA 鞆の浦
☎ 0849
The delightful fishing port of Tomo-no-Ura, with its numerous interesting temples and shrines, is just half an hour by bus south of Fukuyama. In feudal days, due to

Tomo-no-Ura Bicycle Tour

An excellent way to explore the narrow streets of Tomo-no-Ura and take in its temples and sights is by bicycle. Bicycles (renta-saikaru) are available near the ferry building and cost just ¥5100 for two hours. The map shows an interesting circuit of the main attractions.

Right across the road from the ferry landing is the **Muronoki Song Monument** with a sad poem composed by a Korean emissary whose wife had died en route to Tomo-no-Ura. Climb the headland to the ruins of the castle, **Taigashima-jō**, where you will also find the temple, **Empuku-ji**, and a monument to the haiku poet Bashō.

Cross the headland to the harbour and continue until you reach the steps leading to the **Museum of History** (¥5150, 9 am to 4.30 pm). This interesting and well-presented museum features a great model of the Tai-ami Matsuri (Sea Bream Fishing Festival). Back on the road, have a look in the nautical equipment shop on the corner and then head down towards the harbour to the **Shichikyō-ochi Ruins**. This one-time sake shop isn't a ruin at all but played a small part in the Meiji Restoration when a fleeing anti-shogunate group paused here long enough for one member of the group to compose a waka (31-syllable poem) extolling the virtues of the shop's sake.

Continue towards **Iou-ji** – although it's easier to park your bicycle at the bottom of the steep hill and walk up. From the temple, steep steps lead to a fine view over the town from Taishiden Hill. Back on your bicycle, continue to **Hōsen-ji**, originally founded in 1358. Just beyond the temple, the **Sasayaki-bashi** (Whispering Bridge) commemorates an illicit romance which, according to a local tourist brochure, resulted in the lovers being 'drowned into the sea'. Beside the bridge is the **Yamanaka Shikanosuke Monument**, where, after a failed vendetta, the hapless Shikanosuke had his 'head severed for inspection'.

The **Nunakuma-jinja** has a portable nō (stylised dance-drama) stage used by Toyotomi Hideyoshi to enjoy performances during sieges. It has been designated as an Important National Treasure. The shrine itself is picturesquely sited, with a gentle flight of stairs leading up to it. **Ankoku-ji** (¥5100) dates from 1270 and houses two wooden statues that are national treasures. It has a slightly tatty kare-sansui (waterless-stream garden), which was relaid in 1599.

From here you head back towards your starting point, pausing to take in 'eastern Japan's most scenic beauty' on the way. Whether it deserves the appellation or not you can decide for yourself, but that is how it seemed to a visiting Korean dignitary in 1711. The **Taichō-rō Guest House**, built in 1690 for visitors from Korea, is in the Fukuzen-ji compound and the cheerful priest will usher you in and let you sit to admire the view of Kōgo, Benten and Sensui Islands.

its central location on the Inland Sea, the port played an important role as host to fishing boats that would wait in the harbour to determine the next shift in the tides and winds before heading back out to sea.

Although foreign visitors to Tomo-no-Ura are infrequent, an English-language map and brochure is available and explanatory signs are dotted around town. If you set aside a day to travel from Kurashiki to Hiroshima you can spend a pleasant morning exploring Tomo-no-Ura, get back to Fukuyama for lunch, and visit Onomichi in the afternoon before heading to Hiroshima.

Four kilometres beyond Tomo-no-Ura is the temple, Abuto Kannon-ji, with superb Inland Sea views.

Cruises

Ferries run on a regular basis to Sensui-jima from the harbour area (¥240 return, 5 minutes). There are some quiet walking trails on the island.

If you can rustle up five interested parties, you can putter around the bay and Sensui-jima in a small boat for ¥6000. As well, boats will also take you south to Abuto Kannon-ji, which is at the foot of the peninsula, Numakuma-hantō, a trip that will set a party of five back about ¥9000. You'll need at least some Japanese-language skills, but try to track down Miyake-san (☎ 82-2278), a local fisherman who often takes people out touring and fishing, particularly during *tai* (sea bream) season in May and November.

Special Events

The Tai-ami Matsuri (Sea Bream Fishing Festival) takes place throughout May.

Places to Stay

A night in Tomo-no-Ura, an altogether more picturesque location, would be a more pleasant experience than staying in Fukuyama. Right by the water, not far from the harbour, is the friendly *Taizan-kan (☎ 83-5045)*. It charges ¥16,000 with two meals. The *Tomo Seaside Hotel (☎ 83-5111)*, charging from ¥12,000 to ¥35,000, is near the bus terminal. Prices depend on how extravagantly you want to be fed.

Over on Sensui-jima there are a couple of options. The *New Kinsui Kokusai Hotel (☎ 82-2111)* charges ¥18,000 with two meals, although it has pushy kimono-clad waitresses who spoil the great seafood. A cheaper, more relaxed alternative is the *Kokuminshukusha*, which costs around ¥6000 per person with two meals.

Getting There & Away

It's only 14km from Fukuyama to Tomo-no-Ura; frequent buses run from stand No 2 outside JR Fukuyama station (¥530, 40 minutes).

ONOMICHI 尾道
☎ 0848 • pop 94,350

At first glance, Onomichi is an undistinguished-looking industrial town, hemmed in against the sea by a backdrop of hills. Yet along the base of this backdrop is a fascinating temple walk. It's well signposted in English, and English-language brochures are available at the station inquiry desk. The walk itself is pleasant, although you'd have to want to be obsessed to want to visit all of the 30-odd temples and shrines (see the boxed text 'Onomichi Temple Walk'). Of late Onomichi has achieved nationwide fame for its rāmen.

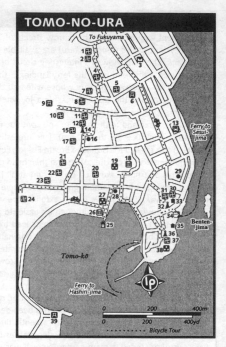

TOMO-NO-URA

Places to Stay and Eat

A lot of the nicer accommodation in Onomichi is very expensive, though there are a few business hotels with reasonable rates, including the *Sunroute Onomichi (☎ 25-3161)*, with singles/twins for ¥7500/12,500, and the *Onomichi Dai-Ichi Hotel (☎ 23-4567)*, with rooms for ¥5000/10,500. The newly built *Greenhill Hotel (☎ 24-0100)*, in front of JR Onomichi station, is the plushest budget choice, with rooms starting at ¥7500/16,000.

The old-style and rather elegant *Nishi-yama Honkan (☎ 37-2480)* has rooms from ¥15,000 with two meals. The topnotch *Nishiyama Bekkan (☎ 37-3145)* is set in exquisite grounds; rooms cost from ¥24,000.

Riding high on the tidal-wave of Onomichi rāmen popularity, *Shūka-en (☎ 37-2077)* is currently so famous that even midweek you'll have to queue for half an hour or more to get in (11 am to 8 pm,

TOMO-NO-URA

PLACES TO STAY
33 Tomo Seaside Hotel
　鞆シーサイドホテル
35 Taizan-kan Ryokan
　対山館

OTHER
1 Ankoku-ji
　安国寺
2 Shōbō-ji
　正法寺
3 Post Office
　郵便局
4 Jitoku-in
　慈徳院
5 Zengyō-ji
　善行寺
6 Kogarasu-jinja
　小烏神社
7 Hongan ji
　本願寺
8 Daikan-ji
　大観寺
9 Nunakuma-jinja
　沼名前神社
10 Komatsudera
　小松寺
11 Kensjō-ji
　顕政寺

12 Myōren-ji
　妙蓮寺
13 Bus Terminal
　バスターミナル
14 Yamanaka
　Shikanosuke
　Monument
　山中鹿乃助
15 Jōkan-ji
　静観寺
16 Sasayaki
　ささやき橋
17 Hōsen-ji
　法宣寺
18 Tomo-no-Ura
　Museum of History
　鞆の浦歴史民俗資料館
19 Tomo-jō Ruins
　鞆城跡
20 Jizōin
　地蔵院
21 Nanzenbō-ji
　南禅坊寺
22 Amida-ji
　阿弥陀寺
23 Myōen-ji
　妙円寺
24 Iou-ji
　医干寺

25 Old Lighthouse
　常夜燈
26 Iroha-maru Museum
　いろは丸展示館
27 Shichikyō-ochi Ruins
　七卿落遺跡
28 Nautical Equipment
　Shop
　船具店
29 Taisensuirō
　対仙楼
30 Jōsen-ji
　浄泉寺
31 Fukuzen-ji
　福善寺
32 Muronoki Song
　Monument
　むろの木歌碑
34 Ferry Landing
　渡船場
36 Bashō Monument
　芭蕉の句碑
37 Empuku-ji
　円福寺
38 Taigashima-jō
　Ruins
　大可島城跡
39 Yodohime-jinja
　淀姫神社

Onomichi Temple Walk

Several of Onomichi's many temples were locations in films by the famed, local-born movie director Ōbayashi Nobuhiko. The director's admirers often spend a whole day seeking them out on an extended temple walk; but it is also possible to do a shorter version. Take a bus from outside the station and continue for three stops to the Nagaeguchi bus stop, near the cable car station. From there, you can follow the walk all the way to the temple, **Jōdo-ji**, almost at the end of the route, then take a bus back to the station from the Jōdoji-shita bus stop. A cable car ascends to the top of **Senkō-ji Hill**, where there is a museum and fine views over the town. You can look down on **Senkō-ji**, founded In AD 806, then walk to it along the **Path of Literature**, where poets and authors have their works immortalised in stones beside the path. From the temple, continue downhill past the three-storey **Tennei-ji**, which was originally built with five storeys in 1388, but rebuilt with three in 1692.

The walk continues past **Fukuzen-ji**, dating from 1573, with its impressive gates carved with cranes and a dragon. **Saikoku-ji** is entered through the **Niō-mon** (Two Deva Kings Gate), which is hung with gigantic 2m-long straw sandals. From there, a steep flight of steps leads up to the temple, overlooked by a red three-storey pagoda. **Jōdo-ji** has an unusual two-storey temple in its compound and a fine garden and teahouse moved here from Fushimi-jō. The temple houses a number of important art works including a painting damaged by the fire that destroyed the temple in 1325.

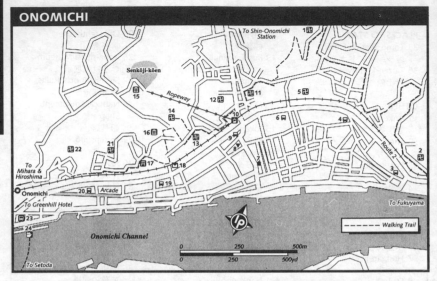

ONOMICHI

closed Thursday). It's just south of the cable-car station bus stop.

Getting There & Away

The Shin-Onomichi shinkansen station is 3km north of the JR San-yō line station. Buses connect the two stations and also run straight to the cable-car station (¥170), but it's easier to reach Onomichi on the JR San-yō line and change to the shinkansen line either at Fukuyama (to the east) or Mihara (to the west). Regular trains run frequently to Hiroshima (local train, ¥1450, 1½ hours).

Ferries run from Onomichi to Setoda, the starting and finishing point for the popular Setoda-Hiroshima-Miyajima cruises (see the Inland Sea section). Car ferries (¥890, one hour, five daily) also operate from Onomichi to Imabari and Matsuyama, which are both on Shikoku.

ONOMICHI TO HIROSHIMA

Mihara 三原

Mihara is on the San-yō shinkansen line and is a convenient departure or arrival point for Setoda on Ikuchi-jima, for other islands of the Inland Sea and for Shikoku. The harbour is directly south of the station, 200m behind the Tenmaya department store. There is a tourist information centre (☎ 67-6074) in the modern JR station, which can provide a useful English-language brochure and map of the area (10 am to 6 pm, closed weekends).

Next to the north exit of the station are the ruins of the castle, **Mihara-jō**. Slightly more interesting is the **furu-machi** (old town), which is a short walk to the right of the north exit. There is a considerable number of photogenic wooden houses, and if you continue further on and bear left, there is a string of small temples of minor interest.

Just to the south of town, **Hitsuei-zan**, at 330m, provides good views of the area and is reportedly particularly beautiful in cherry blossom season. Kure line buses run from Mihara station to the hill (¥180, 5 minutes).

Takehara 竹原

Takehara is on the coastal JR San-yō line or can be reached by boat from Omi-shima. There is also a convenient bus service from Mihara (¥940, one hour). Takehara was an important centre for salt production in the Edo period and still retains some interesting **Edo-period houses**.

ONOMICHI

PLACES TO STAY & EAT
7 Nishiyama Honkan
  西山本館
8 Shūka-en
  朱華園

OTHER
1 Saikoku-ji
  西国寺
2 Jōdo-ji
  浄土寺
3 Jōdoji-shita Bus Stop
  浄土寺下バス停
4 Bōjiguchi Bus Stop
  防地口バス停
5 Jōsen-ji
  浄泉寺
6 Rakutenjiguchi Bus Stop
  楽天寺口バス停

9 Nagae-guchi Bus Stop
  長江口バス停
10 Ropeway Station
  ロープウエイ山麓駅
11 Fukuzen-ji
  福善寺
12 Jikan-ji
  慈観寺
13 Tennei-ji
  天寧寺
14 Senkō-ji
  千光寺
15 City Museum of Art;
  Senkō-ji Hill Lookout
  市立美術館；
  千光寺山展望台
16 Memorial Hall of Literature
  文学記念館

17 Kibitsuhiko-jinja
  吉備津彦神社
18 Post Office
  郵便局
19 Watashibadōri
  Bus Stop
  渡し場通りバス停
20 Tsuchidōshōshita
  Bus Stop
  土堂小下バス停
21 Kōmyō-ji
  光明寺
22 Jikō-ji
  持光寺
23 Bus Terminal
  バスターミナル
24 Onomichi Pier
  尾道駅前桟橋

The old part of town is north of the station area. Follow the tree-lined avenue in front of the station, turn right into the main avenue about 200m up the road and follow it until you cross a river. A left turn here will take you up an attractive area with traditional-style homes, some of which are open to the public. The temple, **Shōren-ji**, is slightly north of this area and has an impressive 'bell gate', but little else to recommend it.

South of Takehara, **Ōkuno-jima** has the dubious distinction of harbouring the largest resort in Western Honshū. Boats run out to it from Takehara harbour (¥1640, 30 minutes), five minutes' walk south of the station.

This is also the site of the **Museum of Poisonous Gas of Ōkuno-jima** (☎ 08462-6-3036), which gives a little known footnote to the country's WWII history. The Japanese Imperial Army forced conscripted workers to produce poison gasses on the island, which was later used as a secret storage site. How many died from exposure to the fumes is unknown. Admission is ¥150 (9am to 4.30pm, closed Tuesday).

Okunojima Kokumin Kyūka Mura (☎ 08 462-6-0321) has rooms with two meals for ¥8000/9000 on weekdays/weekends.

Kure 呉
☎ 0823

The giant battleship, *Yamato*, which sank off the Nagasaki coastline on a suicide mission to Okinawa during WWII, was just one of the many naval vessels built in Kure. The town, virtually a suburb of Hiroshima, is still an important shipbuilding centre, and there is a naval museum on the nearby island of **Eta-jima** – although it takes a while to get there. The information booth in JR Kure station (☎ 23-7845) has city maps, but only in Japanese. The gorge, **Nikyu-kyō**, is 15km north-east of Kure.

NORTHERN HIROSHIMA-KEN
Taishaku-kyō 帝釈峡

North of Onomichi, very close to the central Chūgoku Expressway, this 15km limestone gorge presents a real chance to get off the beaten track. There are natural rock bridges, limestone caves and, for Japanese tourists, a major attraction is the lake, **Shinryū-ko**, which has cruise boats.

Transport connections to the area are not as convenient as for most other attractions in this part of Japan, but this will be part of the fun for some. Probably the best means of transport is to take a direct bus from the

Hiroshima bus centre (¥1880, two hours). Alternatively there are buses running to the area from both Bingo-Shōbara and Tōjō stations on the JR Geibi line. Tōjō station is closest (25 minutes by bus), but it is also a lot further from Hiroshima and not particularly convenient to anywhere else.

Sandan-kyō 三段峡

The gorge, Sandan-kyō, about 70km north-west of Hiroshima, is another area that you could get lost in for a few days. The gorge itself isn't as interesting as the one at Taishaku, but at least this area isn't overrun by tourists.

Buses run from Hiroshima station and the Hiroshima bus centre to Sandan-kyō station (¥1400, two hours), at the southern end of the 16km-long gorge. Ordinary trains go to JR Sandan-kyō station (¥1100, 2½ hours), which is the terminus of the Kabe line.

A **walking trail** winds through the gorge.

HIROSHIMA 広島

☎ 082 • pop 1,090,000

A busy, prosperous and attractive city, Hiroshima will forever be remembered for that terrible instant on 6 August 1945 when it became the world's first atomic bomb target. Hiroshima's Peace Memorial Park is a constant reminder of that tragic day and attracts a steady stream of visitors from all over the world. Yet Hiroshima is far from a depressing place; on the contrary, its citizens have recovered from nuclear holocaust to build a thriving, livable and internationally minded community.

The city's history dates back to 1589, when the feudal lord Mōri Terumoto named the city and established a castle.

Orientation & Information

Hiroshima ('broad island') is a city built on a series of sandy islands on the delta of the Ōta-gawa. JR Hiroshima station is east of the city centre and, although there are a number of hotels around the station, the central area with its very lively entertainment district is much more interesting.

Peace Memorial Park and most of the atomic bomb reminders are at the northern end of an island immediately west of the city centre.

Hiroshima's main east-west avenue is Heiwa-Ō-dōri (Peace Boulevard), but the busiest road (with the main tram lines from the station) is Aioi-dōri, which runs parallel to Heiwa-Ō-dōri. Just south of Aioi-dōri, and again parallel to it, is the busy Hon-dōri shopping arcade.

An excellent source of information is the widely available *The Outsider*, a locally produced magazine, with news on clubs, movies, restaurants and so on. A living mine of information is Peter Berg who runs the centrally located Book Nook (see the Bookshops entry in this section).

Tourist Offices There are two information offices (☎ 261-1877) in JR Hiroshima station (one at the north exit, the other at the south), where the English-speaking staff can make accommodation bookings (9 am to 5 pm). For the benefit of those arriving by sea, Hiroshima's port, Ujina, also has an information counter. The most comprehensive information about the city and the island of Miyajima, can be found at the Hiroshima Rest House (☎ 247-6738) in the Peace Park, next to Motoyasu-bashi (9.30 am to 6 pm, April to September, 8.30 am to 5 pm for the rest of the year). Finally, the International Conference Centre Hiroshima (☎ 247-9715) also in the Peace Park, has English-language information, satellite TV and English-language newspapers (10 am to 6 pm). Try to pick up the free bilingual map, *Guide of Hiroshima City*.

Money There's an International ATM in front of the Sumitomo bank, near the corner of Rijō-dōri and Aioi-dōri. It accepts MasterCard, VISA and Cirrus (6 am to midnight).

Post The main post office is near the Shiyakusho-mae tram stop (9 am to 7 pm weekdays, until 5 pm Saturday and until 12.30 pm Sunday). The Higashi post office (9 am to 7 pm weekdays, until noon Saturday), near the south exit of the station, is more convenient. The Naka post office is next to the Sogō department store and is also handily located.

Email & Internet Access Free net access is available on the 5th floor of Deo-Deo Com City electronics store (10 am to 7.30 pm) in the Hondōri Arcade. Best Denki, 15 minutes' walk east of the station, also has free access at its 5th floor coffee shop (10 am to 9 pm).

Bookshops The Book Nook (☎ 244-8145) has lots of second-hand English-language book bargains, a handy notice board and back copies of *The Outsider*. You're welcome to sit and read, or have a quick game of *shōgi* (Japanese chess) with the friendly bibliophile owner (10 am to 9 pm weekdays, until 6 pm Saturday, 1 pm to 6 pm Sunday). It's in Kamiya-chō, one block west of the Hiroshima Kokusai Hotel.

English language books can also be found in the Kinokuniya bookshop on the 6th floor of the Sogō department store; or nearby in the Maruzen bookshop, opposite Andersen's bakery and restaurant in the shopping arcade.

John Hersey's *Hiroshima* (1946) is still the classic reporter's account of the bomb and its aftermath. In 1985 a new edition, available in paperback, followed up the original protagonists. Eleanor Coerr's children's book *Sadako & the Thousand Paper Cranes* tells the sad but inspiring story of a 12-year-old girl's death from leukaemia, contracted due to exposure to the bomb's radiation.

The A-Bomb Dome
The symbol of the destruction visited upon Hiroshima is the A-Bomb Dome (Gembaku Dōmu) just across the river from Peace Memorial Park. Amid some controversy, it was declared a **UNESCO World Heritage** site in December 1996. The building was previously the Industrial Promotion Hall until the bomb exploded almost directly above it and effectively put a stop to any further promotional activities. Its propped-up ruins, floodlit at night, have been left as an eternal reminder of the tragedy. The dome is fronted with piles of the colourful origami cranes that have become a symbol

of Hiroshima's plea that nuclear weapons never be used again. The actual hypocentre of the explosion was just south of the dome.

The A-Bomb Dome is the only blast survivor left in ruins, although some of the damaged buildings were repaired and still stand. On Rijō-dōri, just 380m south-east of the hypocentre, the former Bank of Japan building looks rock solid; however, although the shell survived intact, the interior was totally destroyed and all 42 people in the bank at the time were killed. It was back in limited business only two days later.

Peace Memorial Park
From the A-Bomb Dome, cross the T-shaped bridge, Aioi-bashi, to Peace Memorial Park (Heiwa-kōen). It is thought that the T-shape may have been the actual target used by the bombardier. If so, his aim was accurate. The park is dotted with memorials including the **cenotaph** that contains the names of all the known victims of the bomb (less the Korean victims) and frames the A-Bomb Dome across the river. The flame burning beneath the arched cenotaph is not designed to be eternal – when the last nuclear weapon on earth has been destroyed it will be extinguished.

Nearby is what for many is the most poignant memorial in the park – the **Children's Peace Memorial**, inspired by leukaemia victim Sadako. When she developed leukaemia at 10 years of age she decided to fold 1000 paper cranes, the symbol of longevity and happiness in Japan, and was convinced that if she could achieve that target she would recover. She died having completed her 644th crane, but children from her school folded another 356, with which she was buried. Her story inspired a nationwide bout of paper crane folding, which continues to this day. Around the memorial are heaped not thousands but millions of cranes, regularly delivered by the box-load from schools all over Japan.

Just across the river from the park is a memorial to the bomb's Korean victims. Great numbers of Koreans were shipped from their homeland to work as slave labourers in Japanese factories during WWII, and

HIROSHIMA

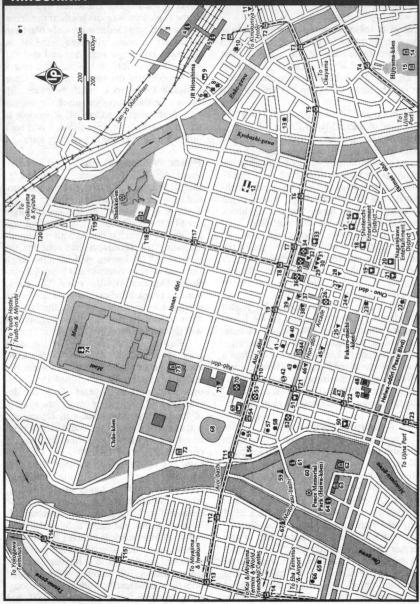

HIROSHIMA

PLACES TO STAY
3 Hiroshima Granvia
  広島グランビア
6 Hiroshima Ekimae
  Green Hotel
  広島駅前グリーンホテル
7 Hotel Sun Palace
  ホテルサンパレス
8 Hotel Yamato
  ホテルやまと
10 Hotel Kawashima
  ホテルかわしま
13 Mikawa Ryokan
  三河旅館
22 Hiroshima Tōkyū Inn
  広島東急イン
23 Sera Bekkan Ryokan
  世羅別館
40 Hiroshima Kokusai Hotel
  広島国際ホテル
48 Hokke Club Hotel
  法華クラブ広島
49 ANA Hotel Hiroshima
  広島全日空ホテル
58 Hiroshima Green Hotel
  広島グリーンホテル
65 Minshuku Ikedaya
  民宿池田屋

PLACES TO EAT
11 Tsukemen-tei
  つけ麺亭
24 Okonomi-mura
  お好み村
25 Pizza Mario Expresso
27 Chikara Soba
  ちから
28 Michan
  みっちゃん
29 Capriciossa & Namiki
  Junction
  カプリチョーザ；
  並木ジャンクション
30 McDonald's
31 Tonkatsu Tokugawa
  とんかつ徳川
32 Tokugawa
  徳川
37 Rally's Steakhouse
38 Spaghetteria San
  Mario1

39 Yōrō-no-Taki
  養老の滝
45 Namche Bazaar
46 Andersen's
71 Tandoor; Pacela

OTHER
1 Pagoda of Peace
  平和塔
2 Hiroshima Prefectural
  Art Museum
  県立美術館
4 Tourist Information
  観光案内所
5 Tourist Information
  観光案内所
9 Higashi Post Office
  東郵便局
12 World Peace Memorial
  Cathedral
  世界平和記念堂
14 Hiroshima City
  Manga Library
  広島まんが図書館
15 Hiroshima City
  Museum of
  Contemporary Art
  広島現代美術館
16 Jacara
17 Snappers
18 Jammin'
19 Mac
20 Ultra
21 Twisters Cafe
26 Parco
33 Harry's Bar
34 Mitsukoshi Department
  Store
  三越百貨店
35 Tenmaya Department
  Store
  天満屋百貨店
36 Fukuya Department Store
  福屋百貨店
41 Book Nook
42 Sumitomo Bank
  ATM;
  住友銀行
43 Maruzen Bookshop
  丸善

44 Deo-Deo Com City
  デオデオコムシティ
47 Former Bank of Japan
  Building
  旧日本銀行
50 Kemby's
51 Bar 13
52 Sogō Sports-kan;
  Spaghetteria San Mario
53 Deo Deo Honten
  デオデオ本店
54 KDD (International
  Telephone)
55 ANA
  全日空
56 A-Bomb Dome
  (Gembaku Dōmu)
  原爆ドーム
57 Atomic Bomb Hypocentre
  爆心地
59 Children's Peace Memorial
  原爆の子の像
60 Cenotaph; Flame of Peace
  原爆慰霊碑；平和の灯
61 Hiroshima Rest House
  (Information)
  広島市レストハウス
62 Peace Memorial Hall
  平和記念館
63 Peace Memorial
  Museum
  平和記念資料館
64 International Conference
  Centre Hiroshima
66 Laundrette
  コインランドリー
67 Korean A-Bomb
  Memorial
  韓国人原爆犠牲者慰霊碑
68 Hiroshima Carp's
  Baseball Stadium
  広島市民球場
69 Naka Post Office
  中郵便局
70 Sogō Department Store;
  Sogō Bus Terminal;
  Kinokuniya Bookshop
  そごう百貨店；
  そごうバスターミナル；
  紀伊国屋書店

HIROSHIMA

72 Science & Culture Museum
for Children
こども文化科学館
73 Hiroshima Museum of Art
広島美術館
74 Hiroshima-jō
広島城

TRAM STOPS

T1 Hiroshima-ekimae
広島駅前
T2 Enkōbashi
猿こう橋
T3 Matoba-chō
的場町
T4 Danbara Ōhata-chō
段原大畑町
T5 Inarimachi
稲荷町

T6 Kanayama-chō
銀山町
T7 Ebisu-chō
胡町
T8 Hatchōbori
八丁堀
T9 Tatemachi
立町
T10 Kamiya-chō
紙屋町
T11 Genbaku Dōmu-mae
(A-Bomb Dome)
原爆ドーム前
T12 Honkawa-chō
本川町
T13 Tōkaichimachi
十日市町
T14 Dobashi
土橋

T15 Teramachi
寺町
T16 Betsuin-mae
別院前
T17 Jogakuin-mae
女学院前
T18 Shukkeien-mae
縮景院前
T19 Katei Saibansho-mae
家庭裁判所前
T20 Hakushima
Line Terminus
白島
T21 Hon-dōri
本通
T22 Fukuro-machi
袋町
T23 Chūden-mae
中電前

more than one in 10 of those killed by the bomb was a Korean. The **Korean memorial**, erected long after the war in 1970, carries a bitter reminder that no prayers were said for the Korean victims, and that despite the plethora of A-bomb monuments, not one had been erected in their memory.

Peace Memorial Museum

The A-bomb museum, as the Peace Memorial Museum is commonly known, expresses a simple message, driven home with sledgehammer force. The exhibits tell the story of the bomb and the destruction it wrought on Hiroshima and its people. A model showing the town after the blast highlights the extent of the damage – seeing this, you might ponder the frightening destructive potential of modern atomic weapons. Admission is ¥50 (9 am to 5.30 pm, May to November, until 4.30 pm December to April).

Hiroshima-jō

Also known as Ri-jō, or 'Carp Castle', Hiroshima-jō (¥300, 9 am to 4.30 pm October to March, until 5.30 pm April to September) was originally constructed in 1589; however, much of it was dismantled fol-

lowing the Meiji Restoration, leaving only the donjon, main gates and turrets. The remainder was totally destroyed by the bomb and rebuilt in modern ferro-concrete in 1958. There are some interesting displays, including an informative and amusing video with some three-dimensional laser embellishments about the castle's construction.

Shukkei-en

Modelled after Xi Hu (West Lake) in Hangzhou, China, Shukkei-en dates from 1620 but was badly damaged by the bomb. The garden's name literally means 'shrunk' or 'contracted view', and it attempts to recreate grand vistas in miniature. It may not be one of Japan's celebrated classic gardens, but it makes a pleasant stroll (¥250, 9 am to 5.30 pm, until 4.30 pm from October to March). A ticket including entry to Hiroshima Prefectural Art Museum is ¥600; enter the garden through the museum.

Other Attractions

Hijiyama-kōen, directly south of JR Hiroshima station, is noted for its cherry blossoms in spring, and hosts two visit-worthy attractions. The **Hiroshima City Museum of Contemporary Art** (¥320, special exhibits

¥910, 11 am to 4.30 pm) has excellent displays by Japanese and foreign modern artists. Check out the spooky clanging, banging heartbeat machine near the entrance. The **Hiroshima City Manga Library** (free, 10 am to 5 pm, closed Monday) is a small Comic Museum. Interestingly, its main customers are women in their early twenties. To get to Hijiyama-kōen, take a No 5 tram from the station towards Ujina (Hiroshima's port) and get off at the Hijiyama-shita stop.

The splendid **Hiroshima Prefectural Art Museum** (¥500, ¥600 including Shukkeien, closed Monday) features Dali's 'Dream of Venus' and the staggering artwork of Hirayama Ikuo, who was in the city during the bombing.

The **Hiroshima Museum of Art** (¥1000, 9 am to 4.30 pm) and the **Science & Culture Museum for Children** (free, except for the planetarium) are both in Chūō-kōen (Central Park), just south-west of the castle.

Fudō-in, a temple directly north of the station and about half a kilometre beyond the youth hostel, is one of the few old structures in Hiroshima that survived the bomb blast.

Mitaki-ji (Three Waterfalls Temple), just 15 minutes by bus north-west of the town centre, is the perfect escape from the city bustle, especially in summer. The temple is nestled in a cleft in the surrounding ravine and is served by three waterfalls, hence its name. It's beautiful, unvisited and pleasantly cool, and if you walk up to the lookout there's a great view over the city. Take a No 25 bus from outside Pacela on Rijō-dōri.

Special Events
On the 6 August anniversary of the bombing, paper lanterns are floated down the Ōta-gawa towards the sea from in front of the A-bomb Dome. It's an odd occasion, with ropey singers blasting out dire pop songs. There seems little sense of the importance of what is being commemorated.

Places to Stay
Hiroshima has places to stay for a range of budgets, both around JR Hiroshima station and within walking distance of Peace Memorial Park.

An American in Hiroshima

A ride in a Japanese taxi can prove to be a cultural experience. From white-gloved cabbies and auto-open/close doors to complimentary breath mints for the ride. Then there's Hiroshima, where perhaps Japan's only *gaijin* taxi driver has been cruising the streets since the summer of 1995.

After discovering his job as a long-distance delivery driver was keeping him away from his family, American Stephen Outlaw-Spruell took a friend's advice and began driving a cab for Hiroshima's Tsubame Kōtsū. His meter soon became a hit with locals and visitors and these days his unique charter tours around the city are in high demand with Japanese and fellow gaijin alike.

Beside the appeal of being foreign, and speaking English, he takes a different approach to his fares. Unlike standard Japanese taxi tours, where the drivers simply drop customers in front of attractions to fend for themselves, Outlaw-Spruell stays by his clients' side, providing sight-by-sight historical tidbits and unique insight (he says he has been contacted on several occasions by A-Bomb survivors who wish him to pass on their stories to others).

Outlaw-Spruell offers a three-hour tour taking in the city's main attractions, and also a six- to eight-hour route including nearby Miyajima and other less-travelled areas. Though the price is not cheap (around ¥5500/hour), split between up to five people it can be a worthwhile and enlightening way to discover Hiroshima. Outlaw-Spruell can be reached at Tsubame Kōtsū (☎ 082-222-8180, or ☎/fax 082-228-5200). He is also listed with JTB (Japan Travel Bureau) offices around the world.

Places to Stay – Budget
Youth Hostels *Hiroshima Youth Hostel* (☎ 221-5343) charges ¥1940. It's in a rather inconvenient location, about 2km north of the city centre. Take a bus from platform 22 in front of the JR station or from platform 29 behind it. The hostel is very clearly marked.

Minshuku & Ryokan The *Minshuku Ikedaya* (☎ *231-3329*) is modern, bright and cheerful. Rooms cost ¥4200 per person. The helpful manager speaks English well, and there's a laundrette on the corner of the road. It's on the other side of Peace Memorial Park in a quiet area, but an easy walk via the park from the town centre. Take tram No 6 or a Miyajima tram from the station to Dobashi.

The *Mikawa Ryokan* (☎ *261-2719*), a short stroll from JR Hiroshima station, has singles/doubles for ¥3500/6000. Although the ryokan is convenient for train travellers and the staff are friendly, the rooms are very cramped and gloomy.

The comfortable *World Friendship Center* (☎ *503-3191*) is an anti-nuclear non-profit organisation. Its small tatami rooms cost ¥3500 and this includes a Western-style breakfast. The American retiree couple who run it are very well connected with Hiroshima's large peace-activist community, and they can arrange for you to meet A-bomb victims or take a Peace Park tour in English. Take either the No 2 or Miyajima tram to Koami-chō. Cross the Tenmagawa and turn left heading south, along the river bank. Cross Heiwa Ō-dōri and turn right at the third small street on your right. The centre is signposted, tucked in behind the fifth house on your right.

Places to Stay – Mid-Range
Station Area Bang in front of Hiroshima station, *Hotel Kawashima* (☎ *263-3535*), boasts a 100-year history, but today it's a comfortable if unremarkable family-run hotel. It is extremely handy if you've just staggered off a train. Singles/doubles cost ¥6750/11,000.

A five-minute walk south-east from the station, the *Kinokuniya Hotel* (☎ *264-2200*) is a popular and cosy option. Rooms cost ¥6000/11,000. Walk past the Yamaguchi bank and it's four blocks east, on the north side of the street.

The *Hotel Yamato* (☎ *263-6222*) overlooks the Enkō-gawa. Rooms cost ¥6000/12,300. Next to it is the *Hotel Sun Palace* (☎ *264-6111*), with rooms for ¥6000/10,000. Also near the station is the decent

Hiroshima Ekimae Green Hotel (☎ *264-3939*), with rooms for ¥6300/10,000.

Central Hiroshima The *Hiroshima Kokusai Hotel* (☎ *248-2323*), with singles/doubles for ¥7000/12,500, is right in the city centre. The down-at-heel *Hiroshima Green Hotel* (☎ *248-3939*) is redeemed by its proximity to the riverside and Peace Memorial Park. It has rooms for ¥6200/9200.

The *Hokke Club Hotel* (☎ *248-3371*) has tiny rooms, but the noon check-in/checkout is a good deal. Rooms cost ¥6500/10,500.

Places to Stay – Top End
Ryokan Hiroshima does have traditional Japanese ryokan but most are in modern, anonymous buildings. The *Sera Bekkan* (☎ *248-2251*) is centrally located, near Fukurō-machi-kōen. It has rooms from ¥12,000, including two meals.

Hotels *Hotel Granvia Hiroshima* (☎ *262-1111*), directly behind the station, is the best-value upmarket option near the station. Singles/doubles start at ¥9800/15,500.

In Central Hiroshima, directly behind the Hokke Club Hotel, the luxurious *ANA Hotel Hiroshima* (☎ *241-1111*), on Heiwa-Ō-dōri, has singles starting at ¥11,000 and twins/doubles at ¥20,000. At the north-west corner of Heiwa-Ō-dōri and Chūō-dōri, the *Hiroshima Tōkyū Inn* (☎ *244-0109*) costs ¥8700/16,000 and is a cheaper mid-range option.

Places to Eat
Hiroshima is noted for its seafood, particularly oysters, and also *hiroshima-yaki*, a local version of *okonomiyaki* (egg-based savoury pancakes) made with *soba* (thin buckwheat noodles) and fried egg. Check out *Okonomi-mura* (11 am to 2 am), which is an amazing grouping of some 30 mini-restaurants on the 2nd, 3rd and 4th floors of the Shintenchi Plaza Building behind the Parco department store. All specialise in this tasty dish (most under ¥1000) and the boisterous atmosphere alone is worth the visit. A few have English on their menus and display

Kyoto's Maruyama-kōen comes to life during *hanami* when this majestic weeping cherry tree blooms.

The propped up ruins of the A-bomb Dome – a reminder of the tragedy unleashed upon Hiroshima.

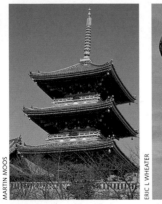

Kiyomizu-dera, Yasugi

A memorial: figure of a mother with children, Hiroshima.

photos of the choices. Other popular spots to taste hiroshima-yaki include the 20-year-old *Michan* (☎ 221-5438), nearby on Chūō-dōri (11 am to 3.30 pm and 4.30 pm to 9 pm, closed Monday), and *Tokugawa* (☎ 241-7100), behind the Mitsukoshi department store; it's open from 11 am to 11 pm. There is good pasta at *Capriciossa* (☎ 241-2368), which is open from 11 am to 10 pm. It's next to McDonald's.

Tsukemen-tei (☎ 247-6000) is an excellent, inexpensive noodle shop (11 am to 7 pm, closed Thursday) in front of Exit 3 of the station underground shopping mall. The *sanuki-udon* set is especially good value.

The popular Mario Italian restaurants serve pastas and pizza and are a great bet for an inexpensive lunch or dinner. Across from Fukurō-machi-kōen is the local favourite *Pizza Mario Expresso* (☎ 241-4956). Just off Hon-dōri arcade there is a *Spaghetteria San Mario* (☎ 225-2342), which is open from 10.30 am to 9.30 pm. There is another branch on the 2nd floor of the Sogo Sports-kan at the Peace Park end of Hon-dōri arcade.

Andersen's (☎ 2472403), on Hon-dōri, is a popular restaurant complex (10 am to 8 pm, closed Wednesday), with an excellent bakery section. It's a good place for an economical breakfast, watching the world pass by from the tables in the front window.

On the 7th floor of the Pacela department store, *Tandoor* (☎ 502-337) is a popular Indian restaurant (11 am to 3 pm, 5 pm to 10 pm), with good lunch time specials.

Namche Bazaar (☎ 246-1355), on the 2nd floor of the K Building in Fukurō-machi, is a hugely popular place serving a variety of Vietnamese, Indonesian and other Asian dishes (5 pm to midnight). Reservations are recommended.

Just north of the Hon-dōri arcade, near the Kokusai Hotel, *Yōrō-no-Taki* (☎ 227-1355) is an excellent, boisterous robatayaki, with cheap draught beer. Across the road is *Rally's* (☎ 248-2941), a steakhouse (11 am to 10 pm). This whole area is great for seeking out good Japanese restaurants, and probably the best advice is to wander around the arcades looking at the window displays of

restaurants until you find one you like. Look out for *Chikara Soba* (☎ 292-5822), which is an interesting soba eatery (10 am to 8.30 pm, closed Sunday), with very economical prices. *Tonkatsu Tokugawa* (☎ 243-4566) is a snazzy place (11 am to 10.30 pm, closed 3rd Thursday), with a good selection of breaded-pork cutlet dishes.

Entertainment

Hiroshima has its fair share of boozing establishments – somewhere in the vicinity of 4000. Shintenchi and Nagarekawa are the entertainment districts. If you're male (even if you have dreadlocks, a pierced nose, and tattoos) and you want to go clubbing, you may have to carry ID to prove you're not from the US base in Iwakuni.

Much loved by resident gaijin is wonderful *Mac* (☎ 243-0343) a hole-in-the-wall, party-till-you-drop place (6 pm to 4 am, Friday and Saturday to 6 am) to the rear of the Rakutenchi Building, next to the Hiroshima central car park in Nagarekawa; it's on the 2nd floor. It has an astoundingly wide selection of CDs and LPs, and the cheerful owners, Mac and Yuri, will regale you with 'pick a song, any song' – and they've probably got it.

Snappers (☎ 541-4485), run by Mitch, a Harley-riding Tasmanian, is pleasantly scrungy, with beers from ¥500 and cocktails from ¥600 (8 pm to early morning). *Jammin'* (☎ 246-7068), on the 3rd floor of the Morita Building in Nagarekawa, occasionally has visiting DJs from the UK, though generally it's a quiet, relaxed place (7pm to 5am, until 6 am Friday and Saturday).

Ultra (☎ 247-8667) is an art-bedecked, small club, which features different DJs each month playing every genre except metal. There's no charge, drinks start at ¥500, and English is spoken. It hots up after midnight (7 pm to the early hours). *Twisters Cafe* (☎ 243-0466) is a wild scene (8pm to 4 am weekdays, Friday and Saturday until 5 am, closed Sunday). Midweek it's full of testosterone-crazed GIs on the loose from Iwakuni, and party-hard young Japanese girls. At weekends it has a more varied crowd, and after midnight it transforms into a hip-hop club. There's a ¥1500 charge for men, and ¥1000 for women; the entry charge includes one free drink. Originally it was going to be called Nipple-Twisters, until its eminently sensible Filipina manageress, Jing, objected.

Jacara (☎ 248-4000) is Hiroshima's most popular dance club (7 pm to 1 am weekdays, until 3 am Friday and Saturday, closed Sunday). Try to get there on a Thursday night when the hot funk-revival outfit take to the stage. The emphasis is on dance music (The Village People score big) and there's a ¥1000 charge, which includes one drink.

The American-style beer and burger place *Kemby's* (☎ 249-6201) is popular despite being off the party track in Ōtemachi (6 pm to 1 am weekdays, until 2 am Friday and Saturday). There are three pool tables, you can design your own burger, and the staff are bilingual. Draft beers are ¥500.

Another option is the up-market *Harry's Bar* (☎ 541-1051), in the basement of the Apple 2 building (6 pm to 2 am). As the sign outside notifies prospective customers, it's '15% off drink prices for foreigners'; reverse discrimination, of course, but then a cheap beer is a cheap beer.

Shopping
The city's main department stores are open from 10 am to 7 pm and include Sogō (closed Tuesday), Mitsukoshi (closed Monday), Fukuya (closed Wednesday) and Tenmaya (closed Thursday). The city's newest shopping mall, Pacela (closed first and third Tuesday), is a sightseeing attraction in itself, and comes complete with external escalators. Opposite Sogō, the huge Deo Deo Honten (10 am to 8 pm, sometimes closed Tuesday) is a good place to pick up discount electrical goods. There's a native-English speaker on the staff.

Getting There & Away
Air There are frequent flights between Hiroshima and Tokyo (Haneda) (¥22,000 one way, ¥39,500 return); Sapporo (¥33,700 one way, two hours); and Okinawa (¥22,800, 1¾ hours).

Train Hiroshima has long been an important railway junction, one of the factors that led to it being the A-bomb target. Today it is an important stop on the Tokyo-Osaka-Hakata shinkansen route. It's connected with Tokyo (Hikari, ¥18,050, 4½ to five hours), Kyoto (Hikari, ¥10,790, 1½ to two hours) and Hakata (Hikari, ¥8700, one hour 25 minutes).

The JR San-yō line passes through Hiroshima onwards down to Shimonoseki, hugging the coastline much of the way. The ordinary local services move along fairly quickly and are the best way to visit the nearby attractions of Miyajima and Iwakuni.

If you're on a tight budget, you can take the slow train all the way to Shimonoseki (¥3570, four hours).

Bus Long-distance buses run from the shinkansen exit of Hiroshima station, and the bus terminal on the 3rd floor of Sogo/Pacela department store. Buses connect Hiroshima with: Tokyo station's JR bus terminal (¥12,060, 10 hours); Nagoya (¥8400, 8¾ hours); Kyoto (¥6620, 7¾ hours); and Nagasaki (¥6620, 8½ hours).

Boat Hiroshima is an important port with a variety of Inland Sea cruises as well as connections to other cities. The Hiroshima to Matsuyama ferry and hydrofoil services are a popular way of getting to or from Shikoku. (See the Matsuyama section in the Shikoku chapter.) Ferries also operate to Imabari on Shikoku (¥4450, two hours, five daily). For information (Japanese-only) ring Hiroshima-Imabari Kōsoku-sen (☎ 254-7555).

Getting Around
To/From the Airport Hiroshima's airport is conveniently close to the south-west of town, and is best reached by tram (¥200, 30 minutes).

Bus Buses are more difficult to use than the trams as they are not numbered and place names are in *kanji* only, but the stands outside the station are clearly numbered. Take a bus from stand No 1 to the airport, and from No 2 to the port.

Tram When much of the rest of Japan decided to scrap its trams in favour of diesel-belching buses, Hiroshima went on a second-hand buying spree. Thus today Hiroshima has an extensive, easy-to-use, and rather fun street-car service. It will get you pretty well anywhere you want to go (sometimes in exquisite, wood-outfitted ex-Kyoto streetcars) for a flat fare of ¥130 (¥90 on the short No 9 route). There is even a tram that runs all the way to Miyajima port (¥250). Note that the tram colours have no connection with the routes, a result of them being snapped up from all around the country. If you have to change trams to get to your destination, you should ask for a *norikaeken* (transfer ticket; ¥150, plus a further ¥50 if you need to change twice).

Onose-no-Taki 小野瀬の滝
This secluded, 30m-high waterfall is a great day trip from Hiroshima. In summer you can swim in the pool below the falls. It's a perfect picnic spot and there's a beautiful **shrine complex** on the Slower stream. Nearby is **Me-taki**, the falls' female counterpart, a 50m-waterfall cascading down a sheer cliff. Take the JR Sanyō line to Onoura (¥480, 31 minutes), turn right out of the station and walk for 15 minutes to the intersection with a petrol station. Turn left, and the shrine is at the top of a short rise. From the station it's about a 25-minute walk.

MIYAJIMA 宮島
☎ 0829 • pop 22,203
Correctly known as Itsuku-shima, Miyajima is easily reached from Hiroshima. The famous 'floating' *torii* (Shintō shrine gate) of the shrine, Itsukushima-jinja, is one of the most photographed tourist attractions in Japan and, with the island's Misen-san as a backdrop, it is classified as one of Japan's 'three best views'. The other two are the sandspit at Amanohashidate (northern coast of Western Honshū) and the islands of Matsushima-wan (near Sendai, Northern Honshū). Apart from the shrine, the island has some other interesting temples, some good walks, and remarkably tame deer that

even wander the streets of the small town. Look out for signs warning of the dangers of fraternising with the horned varieties.

Orientation & Information
There's an information counter (☎ 944-2011) in the ferry building (9 am to 6 pm). Turn right as you emerge from the building and follow the waterfront to get to the shrine and the centre of the island's small town. The shopping street, packed with souvenir outlets and restaurants, is a block back from the waterfront.

Itsukushima-jinja 厳島
The shrine (¥300, 6.30 am to sunset, daily), which gives the island its real name, dates from the 6th century, and in its present form from 1168. Its pier-like construction is a result of the island's holy status. Commoners were not allowed to set foot on the island and had to approach the shrine by boat, entering through the **floating torii** out in the bay. Much of the time, however, the shrine and torii are surrounded by water but by mud. The view of the torii, which is immortalised in thousands of travel brochures, requires a high tide.

On one side of the floating shrine is a **floating nō stage** built by a Mōri lord. The orange torii, dating from 1875 in its present form, is often floodlit at night. A **'son et lumière'** is sometimes performed, particularly in summer (6 pm to 11pm). You can hear it on headphones in English (¥300).

The **Treasure House** (¥300, 8 am to 5 pm) is west of the shrine. The collection of painted sutra scrolls dating from the 12th century is only rarely on display and the exhibits are not of great interest except, perhaps, to the scholarly

Temples & Historical Buildings
Topping the hill immediately north of Itsukushima-jinja is **Senjō-kaku** (Pavillion of 1000 Mats), built in 1587 by Toyotomi Hideyoshi. This huge and atmospheric hall is constructed with equally massive timber pillars and beams, and the ceiling is hung with paintings. It looks out on a colourful five-storey pagoda dating from 1407. Senjō-kaku

should have been painted to match but was left unfinished when Toyotomi died.

Miyajima has numerous other temples including **Daigan-ji** just south of the shrine, which is dedicated to the god of music and dates from 1201. The colourful and glossy **Daishō-in**, just behind the town, can be visited on the way down Misen-san. This is a temple with everything – statues, gates, pools, carp, you name it. The rituals performed at the main Itsukushima-jinja are also administered by Daigan-ji. South of Itsukushima-jinja is the picturesque pagoda, **Tahō-tō**.

Miyajima History & Folklore Museum

This interesting museum (☎ 44-2019), set in a fine garden, combines a 19th-century merchant's home with exhibits on trade in the Edo period, as well as displays connected with the island. An excellent brochure in English is available. Admission is ¥260 (8.30 am to 5 pm).

Misen-san & Other Walks

The ascent of Misen-san (530m) is the island's finest walk, although the uphill part of the round trip can be avoided by taking the two-stage **cable car** (¥900/1500 one way/return). The cable car leaves you about a 15-minute walk from the top. Around the cable-car station there are monkeys as well as deer. On the way to the top look for the **giant pot** said to have been used by the Buddhist saint, Kōbō Daishi (774–835), and kept simmering ever since! It's in the smaller building beside the main temple hall, also said to have been used by the founder of the Shingon sect.

There are superb views from the **summit** and a variety of routes leading back down. The descent takes a good hour and walking paths also lead to other elevated points on the island; or you can just follow the gentle stroll through **Momiji-dani** (Maple Valley), which leads to the cable-car station.

Other Attractions

Miyajima also has an **aquarium**, a popular **beach**, a **seaside park** and, across from the

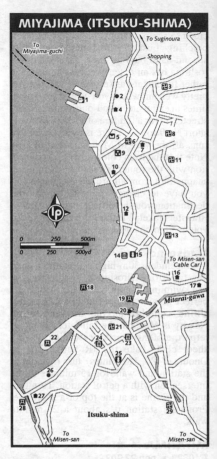

MIYAJIMA (ITSUKU-SHIMA)

ferry landing, a display of **local crafts** in the Hall of Industrial Traditions.

Special Events

Festivals on the island include **fire-walking rites** by the island's monks on 15 April and 15 November, a **fireworks** display on 14 August and the **Kangensai Boat Festival** on 16 June.

Places to Stay

There is no inexpensive accommodation on Miyajima, although the nearby *Miyajima-guchi Youth Hostel* (☎ 56-1444) charges

MIYAJIMA (ITSUKU-SHIMA)

PLACES TO STAY
4 Miyajima
 Royal Hotel
 宮島ロイヤルホテル
7 Pension
 Miyajima
 ペンション宮島
10 Kamefuku Hotel
 ホテルかめ福
12 Kinsuikan Hotel
 錦水館
16 Miyajima
 Grand Hotel
 宮島グランドホテル
17 Iwasō Ryokan
 岩惣
27 Kokuminshukusha
 Miyajima Lodge
 国民宿舎宮島ロッジ

OTHER
1 Ferry Terminal
 宮島港

2 Hall of Industrial
 Traditions
 (Handicraft
 Display)
 伝統産業会館
3 Tokuju-ji
 徳寿寺
5 Post Office
 郵便局
6 Zonkō-ji
 存光寺
8 Shinkō-ji
 真光寺
9 Castle Ruins
 城跡
11 Konju-in
 金寿院
13 Kōmyō-in
 光明院
14 Senjō-kaku
 千畳閣
15 Gō-jū-noto
 五重塔

18 Floating Torii
 大鳥居
19 Itsukushima-jinja
 厳島神社
20 Nō Stage
 能舞台
21 Daigan-ji
 大願寺
22 Kiyomori-jinja
 清盛神社
23 Treasure House
 宝物館
24 Miyajima History &
 Folklore Museum
 歴史民俗資料館
25 Tahō-tō Pagoda
 多宝塔
26 Aquarium
 水族館
28 Omoto-jinja
 大元神社
29 Daishō-in
 大聖院

members/nonmembers ¥2730/3730, plus ¥430 for breakfast. It's on the mainland near the ferry terminal and JR Miyajimaguchi station.

If you can afford to stay on the island, it's well worth it – you'll be able to enjoy the island in the evening, minus the daytripping hordes. The *Kokuminshukusha Miyajima Lodge* (☎ 44-0430), south-west of the shrine, charges from ¥7800, including two meals. A moderately priced place is the friendly and very pleasant *Pension Miyajima* (☎ 44-0039), which is just back from the ferry landing. It charges ¥10,000 for rooms with bathroom, and includes two meals.

At the large and pleasant *Iwasō Ryokan* (☎ 44-2233), or at the *Miyajima Grand Hotel* (☎ 44-2411), you can count on at least ¥20,000 per person with meals. There are a number of fairly expensive hotels and ryokan along the waterfront, including the *Kamefuku Hotel* (☎ 44-2111), the *Kinsuikan Hotel* (☎ 44-2133) and the *Miyajima Royal Hotel* (☎ 44-2191).

Although there are many restaurants and cafes on Miyajima, most cater to day trippers and close early.

Getting There & Away
The mainland ferry terminal for Miyajima is near Miyajima-guchi station on the JR San-yō line between Hiroshima and Iwakuni. Miyajima trams from Hiroshima terminate at the Hiroden-Miyajima stop by the ferry terminal. The tram (¥270, 70 minutes) takes longer than the train (futsū, ¥400, 25 minutes), but runs more frequently and can be boarded in central Hiroshima. On some trams you may have to transfer at the Hiroden-Hiroshima stop.

From the terminal, ferries shuttle across to Miyajima (¥170, 10 minutes). One of the ferries is operated by JR so JR pass holders should make sure they use this one. Ferry services also operate to Miyajima direct from Hiroshima. High-speed ferries (¥1460, 20 minutes, eight times daily) from Hiroshima's Ujina Port. The SKK (Seto Naikai-kisen) Inland Sea cruise on the

Ginga starts and finishes at Miyajima; the Miyajima to Hiroshima leg (¥1280, once daily) departs Miyajima at 12.50 pm.

Getting Around

Bicycles can be rented from the ferry building or you can walk around quite easily. A free bus operates from in front of the Iwasō Ryokan to the Misen-san cable-car station.

The Inland Sea

The Inland Sea is bounded by the major islands of Honshū, Kyūshū and Shikoku. Four narrow channels connect the Inland Sea with the ocean. To the north the straits, the Kanmon-kaikyō, separate Honshū from Kyūshū and lead to the Sea of Japan; to the south, leading to the Pacific, the Hoya-kaikyō separate Kyūshū from Shikoku; at the other end of Shikoku, the Naruto-kaikyō and Kitan-kaikyō straits flow each side of Awaji-shima, which is connected with Honshū by the bridge, Akashi-Kaikyō-ōhashi.

The most interesting area of the Inland Sea is the island-crowded stretch from Hiroshima east to Takamatsu (Shikoku) and Okayama. There are said to be more than 3000 islands, depending on what you define as an island! There are a number of ways of seeing the Inland Sea. One is to simply travel through it as there are numerous ferry services crisscrossing the sea or even running its full length, such as the service from Osaka on Honshū to Oita, near Beppu, on Kyūshū. Alternatively, but more expensively, there are Inland Sea cruises ranging from short day trips to longer overnight cruises. Also, you can visit single islands in the Inland Sea for a first-hand experience of a part of Japan which, though rapidly changing, is still quite different from the fast-moving metropolitan centres.

Information

Brochures, maps and general tourist information are readily available but Donald Richie's *The Inland Sea*, originally published in 1971 and now available in paperback, makes an excellent introduction to the region. Although much of the Inland Sea's slow-moving and easygoing atmosphere has disappeared since his book was published (and indeed he emphasised its rapidly changing nature even at that time), it still provides some fascinating insights.

Getting Around

Miyajima to Setoda The popular SKK (☎ 321-5111) cruises, between Miyajima and Setoda on Ikuchi-jima or on to Onomichi, offer the easiest (though rather touristy) way of seeing one of the finest stretches of the Inland Sea. Day cruises offered by SKK are seasonal (most halt services in the winter months) and typically offer routes between Onomichi, Setoda, Ōmi-shima, Kure and Miyajima. Prices vary between ¥7000 and ¥12,000, and also depend on whether you take lunch on board or not.

SKK has numerous other ships operating, including day cruises from Hiroshima to Eta-jima, Miyajima and Eno-shima.

The Japan Travel Bureau (JTB) and other tour operators also have a variety of overnight cruises from Osaka. Check with local tourist offices for details on times and current prices.

ŌMI-SHIMA 大三島

This hilly rather than mountainous island boasts the mountain god's treasure house, **Ōyamatsumi-jinja**, which once commanded much respect from the Inland Sea's pirates. In fact, the pirates were more like a local navy than real pirates but, until Toyotomi Hideyoshi brought them to heel, they wielded real power in these parts. Along the way, an **armour collection** was built up in the shrine's treasure house, including more than half the armour in Japan; 80% of the armour and helmets designated as National Treasures are held here, but despite the importance of the collection, saturation soon sets in and it's probably of more interest to those with a specific interest in Japanese military accoutrements than to the average visitor (¥1000, 8.30 am to 4.30 pm, daily).

In an adjacent building is a boat used by Emperor Hirohito in his marine science investigations, together with a somewhat tatty natural history exhibit. The shrine's history is actually one of the most ancient in Japan, ranking with the shrines at Ise and Izumo.

Miyaura port is a 15-minute walk from the shrine. The *Omi-shima Suigun* restaurant is near the shrine.

Getting There & Away
The *Akinada* cruise from Hiroshima visits Ōmi-shima but you can also get there by ferry service from Onomichi, Mihara or Setoda on the neighbouring island of Ikuchi-jima; and also from Takehara, further west on the Honshū coast.

IKUCHI-JIMA 生口島
☎ 08452
At Setoda, the main town on the island, Ikuchi-jima is actually linked to neighbouring **Takane-jima** by a bridge. The town is noted for the temple, **Kōsan-ji**, a wonderful exercise in kitsch. Local steel tube magnate Kanemoto Kōzō devoted a large slab of his considerable fortune from 1935 on to recreating numerous important temples and shrines all in this one spot and all in grateful homage to his mother. If you haven't got time to visit the originals, this is an interesting substitute.

Entry is ¥1000, which includes the **1000 Buddhas Cave**, the **art museum** and the **treasure house**. It costs another ¥300 to visit Kanemoto Kōzō's mother's quarters. The extraordinary 1000 Buddhas Cave includes an introductory 'hell', which is very much like the dilapidated religious theme park, Tiger Balm Garden in Singapore, with its tableaux of the damned being mangled, chopped, fried and generally hard done by. From there you follow winding tunnels and spiral stairs lined with 1000 Buddhas. One sour note at this temple is the poor Australian emu penned up in far too small an enclosure by the main entrance.

To get to the temple, turn right as you leave the boat landing then left up the shop-lined 600m-long street. The **Setoda History & Folklore Museum** is at the start of this street and entry is free. Halfway up the same street you can turn left towards a temple on the hillside; around the back of this temple and much further up the hill is **Kōjō-ji**, dating from 1403, with a three-storey pagoda and fine views over the island. You can also get there by turning left from the pier (towards the bridge) and heading straight up the hill.

Places to Stay
The *Ikuchi-jima Tasrumi Youth Hostel* (☎ 7-3137) charges members/nonmembers ¥2500/3500 per night, or ¥4000/5000 with two meals. The *Setoda Youth Hostel* (☎ 7-0224) is a short walk from the dock and offers similar prices.

Getting There & Away
You can get to Ikuchi-jima by the regular cruise from Hiroshima or by ferries from Mihara or Onomichi on Honshū. Mihara has the widest range of services, some continuing on to Ōmi-shima and Imabari on Shikoku. It pays to shop around at the harbour area. Fares range from ¥300 to ¥1400, depending on the speed and luxury of the ferry. No matter how you want to travel, you shouldn't have to wait more than an hour.

INNO-SHIMA 因島
Famed for its flowers and abundance of fruit, Inno-shima is connected by bridge to Mukai-shima and on to Onomichi. The island has a moderately interesting **pirate castle** (¥310, 8.30 am to 5 pm) and, atop Shirataki-yama, there are 500 *rakan* statues, the disciples of Buddha. On the first Saturday and Sunday in September, there's the lively **Suigun Furusato Matsuri** with boat races and *jindaiko* drumming.

SHIWAKU-SHOTŌ 塩飽諸島
North of Marugame on Shikoku are the scattered Shiwaku-shotō, literally the 'tired of salt' islands, once the haunt of daring pirates and seafarers. Hon-jima is a larger island just west of the Seto-ōhashi with some fine old buildings and interesting sites. From Marugame port, the island can be reached by ferry (¥530, 35 minutes).

SHŌDO-SHIMA 小豆島
☎ 0879 • pop 36,483

Famed for its vast olive groves and the location for the Japanese film classic *Twenty-Four Eyes*, Shōdo-shima translates literally as 'island of small beans'. It offers a number of interesting places to visit and makes an enjoyable short escape from big-city Japan. The second largest island in the Inland Sea, Shōdo-shima even has a miniature version of neighbouring Shikoku's 88 Temple Circuit. Though Shōdo-shima can't muster 88 temples, the itinerary is padded out with a number of other notable sites.

Orientation & Information

Tonoshō, at the western end of the island, is the usual arrival point from Takamatsu, Uno or Okayama and makes a good base from which to explore the island. Fukuda in the north-east and Sakate in the south-east are other busy ports. If you arrive on Shōdo-shima from Takamatsu (the most popular jumping-off point) you'll find an information office (☎ 62-5300) just inside the ferry building.

Coastal Area

The island's olive-growing activities are commemorated at **Olive Park** on the south coast. Nearby is the **Shōdo-shima Folk Museum** (¥310, 9 am to 5 pm, closed Monday). The end of the peninsula to the south of Ikeda is marked by the **Jizōzaki Lighthouse** and the area offers fine views over the Inland Sea. Just north of Sakate is the turn-off to the small village of **Tanoura**, the site of the village school in the novel *Twenty-Four Eyes* and the later film of the same name. There's a distinct feeling that this was Shōdo-shima's sole brush with fame; the real school and its movie set version are both open for inspection (¥630 combined ticket). A **statue** of the teacher and her pupils (the film version) stands outside the Tonoshō ferry terminal.

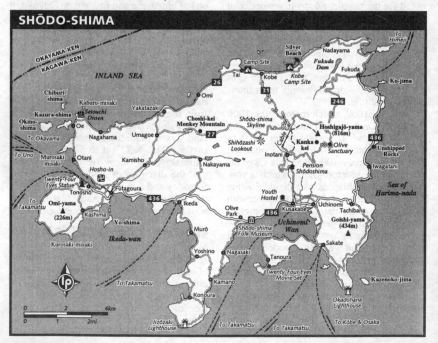

SHŌDO-SHIMA

South of Fukuda, on the eastern side of the island, huge rocks cut for Osaka-jō now lie jumbled down a cliffside at **Iwagatani**. The unused rocks are classified as *zanseki* (rocks left over) or *zannen ishi* (rocks that were sorry not to be in time for shipment) and each bears the seal of the general responsible for their quarrying and dispatch. The north-eastern corner of the island is still one big quarry to this day. More unshipped castle rocks can be seen on the northern coast at **Omi**, along with the site of a shipyard used by Toyotomi Hideyoshi.

Central Mountains
The **Kanka-kei cable car** is the main attraction in the central mountains, making a spectacular trip up through the gorge, Kanka-kei, in the shadow of Hoshigajō-yama (¥700/1250 one way/return). There's a walking track if you really want to walk one way. Around the eastern side of the mountain the island's tenuous connection with Greece (they both grow olives) is celebrated in the **Olive Sanctuary** where there's even a fake mini-Parthenon.

As you descend towards Tonoshō you pass **Choshi-kei monkey mountain** (¥370, 8 am to 5 pm) where wild monkeys come for a daily feed. Beside the car park is a restaurant offering *somen nagashi*, a curious dish where a bowl of soba is dropped into a sort of water racetrack that swirls around a circular channel in the middle of the table. You intercept them with your chopsticks as they come by! You'll pay ¥600 for the experience!

Between Tonoshō and Otani is the temple, **Hosho-in**, which is famed for its huge and ancient juniper tree.

Special Events
The village, Shikoku-mura, at Yashima, just outside Takamatsu on Shikoku, has a village kabuki theatre that was originally from Shōdo-shima. **Farmers' kabuki performances** are still held on the island on 3 May at Tonoshō and on 10 October at Ikeda.

Places to Stay & Eat
There are two camping grounds on the island. The eastern-most of the two sites is

Kobe Camp (☎ 67-3040). **Shōdo-shima Olive Youth Hostel** (☎ 82-6161) charges members/nonmembers ¥3100/4100, plus ¥1600 with two meals. It's on the south coast, just beyond Olive Park and the folk museum, heading towards Kusakabe and Sakate. The **Uchinomi-chō Cycling Terminal** (☎ 82-1099) in Sakate charges ¥2835 or ¥5250 with two meals. It rents bikes (¥525, four hours, ¥50 each extra hour). In Ikeda there is the reasonable **Kokuminshukusha Shōdo-shima** (☎ 75-1115), which costs ¥4000, or ¥6600 with two meals.

Tonoshō has a variety of hotels, ryokan and minshuku, particularly along the road running straight back from the waterfront. The neat and tidy **Maruse Minshuku** (☎ 62-2385) has room for only ¥4000, or ¥6000 with two meals. It's next to the post office.

North of the youth hostel, on the road to Inotani, are a couple of pensions. The friendly **Pension Shōdo-shima** (☎ 82-0181) has rooms for only ¥3700/4800 without/with bath, or ¥8000 with two meals and bath.

Getting There & Away
There is a variety of ferry services from Honshū and Shikoku to various ports on the island. Popular jumping-off points include Uno on Honshū (trains go to Uno from Okayama) and Takamatsu on Shikoku. There are high-speed ferries (¥1000, 35 minutes) and regular ferries (¥500, around an hour) from Takamatsu to Tonoshō.

Getting Around
There are plenty of bus services around the island and a host of bus tours (¥3000 to ¥5000) that seem to set off with every ferry arrival at Tonoshō. Alternatively, you can rent a car from a couple of agencies by the Tonoshō ferry terminal. With adequate time, touring by bicycle presents a great way to see the island and there are several places that have bikes for rent.

AWAJI-SHIMA 淡路島
Awaji-shima, the Inland Sea's largest island, forms the region's eastern boundary and connects with Honshū via the Akashi Kaikyo-ōhashi. At the Shikoku end, the

Naruto-ōhashi spans the Naruto-kaikyō (Naruto Channel) across the well-known **Naruto Whirlpools** to connect Shikoku with Awaji-shima. (See the Around Tokushima section of the Shikoku chapter.) The northern part of the island will be long remembered as the epicentre of the massive January 1995 earthquake which claimed over 6000 lives, mostly in and around the Kōbe area.

The island is densely populated, relatively flat and has some good beaches. It was the original home of *ningyō jōruri* puppet theatre, which preceded the development of bunraku theatre. Short performances are given several times daily in the small puppet theatre in Fukura. Near the Kōshien ferry terminal, at **Onokoro Ai-rando-kōen** (¥1200, 9.30 am to 5.30 pm, closed Tuesday), there is a bizarre grouping of **miniature replica** world-sightseeing attractions (constructed one twenty-fifth their original size). They include the Taj Mahal, the Parthenon, Pisa's leaning tower and other international favourites.

Yamaguchi-ken 山口県

This prefecture, marking the western end of Honshū, straddles both the southern San-yō coast and the northern San-in coast. Southern highlights of the prefecture include Iwakuni, with the great bridge, Kintai-kyō, and the shrine and floating torii on Miyajima (see the Hiroshima section), while Shimonoseki acts as the gateway to Kyūshū and Korea. The northern stretch includes the historically important town of Hagi and, in the central mountains, the vast cave at Akiyoshi-dai.

IWAKUNI 岩国
☎ 0827 • pop 109,124

The five-arched bridge Kintai-kyō is Iwakuni's major attraction, although the town also has a US military base (an 'unattraction' perhaps?) and a number of points of interest in the Kikko-kōen area.

Orientation & Information

Iwakuni has three widely separated areas, which at first can be somewhat confusing for

---

IWAKUNI (KINTAI-KYŌ AREA)
1 Iwakuni-jō   岩国城
2 Fukkō-ji
3 Iwakuni Historical Museum   岩国歴史美術館
4 Cable Car Station   ケーブルカー駅
5 Kinun-kaku   金雲閣
6 Chōkokan Library   徴古館
7 Mekata House   目加田家旧宅
8 White Snake Viewing Facility   白蛇観覧所
9 Youth Hostel   ユースホステル
10 Nagaya-mon   長屋門
11 Iwakuni Kokusai Kankō Hotel   岩国国際観光ホテル
12 Bus Stop   バス停
13 Shiratame Ryokan   白為旅館
14 Iwakuni Kankō Centre   岩国観光センター
15 Hangetsu-an   半月庵

---

visitors. To the far west of the town centre is the Shin-Iwakuni shinkansen station, totally separate from the rest of town. Its tourist information office (☎ 46-0656), open from 10.30 am to 4.30 pm, is very helpful. In the central area is the old part of town with the bridge, the samurai quarter, the castle and all the other tourist attractions. To the east, in the modern part of town, the JR Iwakuni station has a helpful information centre (☎ 21-6050), as well as hotels, restaurants, bars and other conveniences. There is also a tourist information centre, Iwakuni Kankō Centre, just downriver from the bridge.

Kintai-kyō

Kintai-kyō (Brocade Sash Bridge) was built in 1673 and washed away by a flood in 1950. It was authentically rebuilt in 1953, albeit with some cunningly concealed steel

IWAKUNI (KINTAI-KYŌ AREA)

reinforcements. The bridge is immediately recognisable by the five extremely steep arches. In the feudal era only samurai could use the bridge, which connected their side of the river with the rest of the town; commoners had to cross the river by boat. Today visitors have to pay a ¥220 toll to walk across and back. The ticket office at the entrance to the bridge also sells an all-inclusive ticket *(setto-ken)* for ¥840 that covers the bridge (¥220), the return cable car or ropeway trip (¥540), and entry to Iwakuni-jō (¥260), which is a saving of ¥180 if you plan to visit all three attractions.

The bridge and castle are also brightly flood-lit nightly until 10 pm, making an interesting photo opportunity (bring a tripod, and wide and long lenses).

Samurai Quarter
Some traces remain of the old samurai quarter by the bridge. The area is overlooked by Iwakuni-jō and, beside the castle cable car, is the **Iwakuni Historical Museum** (¥500, 9 am to 5 pm), with its extensive collection of **samurai armour** and equipment. It's said to be one of the best collections in Japan, but only a small part of it is displayed at one

time (and very little is labelled in English); and it is unlikely to impress those already suffering from feudal artefact overload.

The old samurai quarter is now part of **Kikko-kōen** and includes some picturesque moats and remnants of the feudal buildings such as **Kagaya-ke-mon**, a fine old samurai gateway. Beside the moat, close to the cable-car station, is the pavilion, **Kinun-kaku**. Look for the **swan houses** in the moat. Also beside the cable-car car park is **Mekata House**, a fine old samurai home. The **Chōkokan Library** houses documents from the samurai period.

Iwakuni-jō

The original castle was built between 1603 and 1608, but stood for only seven years before the daimyō was forced to dismantle it and move down to the riverside. It was rebuilt in 1960 during Japan's great castle reconstruction movement; but modern Japanese castles were built for tourism, not warfare, so it now stands photogenically on the edge of the hillside, a short distance in front of its former hidden location. The well beside the path indicates where it was originally built.

You can get to the castle by cable car (¥320 one way, ¥540 return) or by the road (walking only) from beside the youth hostel. See the Kintai-kyō entry for the all-inclusive ticket.

Imazu White Snake Viewing Facility

Iwakuni is famed for its albino snakes, said to embody the spirit of the goddess of good fortune, Benzaiten. Visitors come to pray here for good luck in business. The Imazu White Snake Viewing Facility (☎ 43-4888) has four of the strange-looking creatures. It's just in front of Kikko-kōen. Admission is free (9 am to 5 pm).

Special Events

On April 29 each year, the photogenic **Kin-tai-kyō Matsuri** takes place with a re-enactment of a *yakko-san* (the colloquial term for geisha) parade across the bridge. For the huge **Nishiki-gawa Hanabi Taikai** (Nishiki River Fireworks Festival) on the first Satur-

day in August, make sure to get a good viewpoint from the west bank of the river.

Ukai (cormorant fishing) takes place at Kintai-kyō every night from June to August, except when rain makes the water muddy or on full-moon nights. For about ¥3500 you can catch your own dinner. Sightseeing boats operate on the Nishiki-gawa during these months.

Places to Stay – Budget

Youth Hostel The 106-bed *Iwakuni Youth Hostel* (☎ 43-1092) charges members ¥2580, or ¥4160 with two meals (non-members add ¥1000). It is close to most of the attractions on the samurai-quarter side of the bridge.

Places to Stay – Mid-Range

Around JR Iwakuni station, there's a choice of business hotels. The *Iwakuni Kinsui Hotel* (☎ 22-2311), right beside the station, costs ¥7500/13,200 for singles/twins. Only two minutes' walk from the station, *City Hotel Andoh* (☎ 22-0110) has rooms starting at ¥4900/10,500. The *A-1 Hotel* (☎ 21-2244) is not much further away and has clean, tidy, well-equipped rooms for ¥5830/12,460.

The *Ōgiya Station Hotel* (☎ 46-0050), at Shin-Iwakuni shinkansen station is OK if you've just flopped off a train, but its miles from the attractions. Rooms cost ¥5500/12,000.

The '70s-kitsch *Iwakuni Kokusai Kankō Hotel* (☎ 43-1111) has seen better days but it's right at the centre of the action. Singles/twins cost from ¥8500/18,000.

Places to Stay – Top End

The only real incentive to stay in Iwakuni is the traditional ryokan near Kintai-kyō. One of the cheaper of these is the central *Hangetsu-an* (☎ 41-0021), which charges ¥9000 per person, with two meals. The nearby *Shiratame Ryokan* (☎ 41-0074) is a little more luxurious, with rooms for ¥18,000, including two meals. Both ryokan offer local specialities, such as *ayu* (sweetfish), and the unusual nine-hole *renkon* (lotus-root).

Places to Eat
There are several small restaurants and cafes around the bridge and a wide variety of restaurants, bars and fast-food outlets around the station area.

Getting There & Away
Iwakuni is only 44km from Hiroshima, and is connected by shinkansen to Shin-Iwakuni station (Hikari, ¥1520, 17 minutes); or regular JR San-yō line trains (futsū, ¥740, 44 minutes) to the central JR Iwakuni station.

Getting Around
Kintai-kyō is almost equidistant from the two main stations; it is about 5km from either. Buses shuttle back and forth between JR Iwakuni station and the bridge (¥240) and Shin-Iwakuni station and the bridge (¥280).

YAMAGUCHI
☎ 083 • pop 129,000
During the Sengoku-jigai, or Warring States period (1467–1573), Yamaguchi prospered as an alternative capital to chaotic Kyoto. In 1550 the Jesuit missionary Francis Xavier paused for two months in Yamaguchi on his way to the imperial capital, but quickly returned to the safety of this provincial centre when he was unable even to find the emperor in Kyoto! In the following centuries, Yamaguchi took turns with Hagi as the provincial capital and, like Hagi, Yamaguchi played an important part in the Meiji Restoration. Today it's a pleasantly peaceful town with a number of interesting attractions.

Orientation & Information
Ekimae-dōri is the main shopping street, running straight up from the station and crossing the main shopping arcade before it reaches Route 9. There's a very helpful information office (☎ 933-0090) on the 2nd floor of the train station, with some useful English-language brochures. It's open from 9 am to 6 pm.

Email & Internet Access Opposite McDonalds in the arcade west of Ekimae-dōri, Internet Jōhō-kan (9 am to 5.20 pm) offers online access for ¥200 for 30 minutes.

Xavier Memorial Chapel
The chapel overlooks the town centre from a hilltop in Kameyama-kōen this church was built in 1952 to commemorate the 400th anniversary of Francis Xavier's visit to the city. It recently burned down under mysterious circumstances, and was rebuilt at a cost of ¥3,000,000,000.

Art Gallery & Museums
At the foot of the hill stands the **Yamaguchi Prefectural Art Museum** (¥190, 9 am to 4.30 pm, closed Monday), where frequent special exhibitions are held. Just north is the **Yamaguchi Prefectural Museum**, which has the same opening hours and costs ¥130. The **Yamaguchi History Museum** (¥100, 9 am to 5 pm, closed Monday) is just off Route 9.

Kōzan-kōen & Ruriko-ji
Further north again from the town centre is Kōzan-kōen, where the **five-storey pagoda** of Rurikō-ji, dating from 1404, is picturesquely sited beside a small lake. A small **museum** (¥200, 9 am to 5 pm) has photos and details of all 40 Japanese five-storey pagodas, plus a map indicating where they're located. From mid-July to October it's illuminated at night. Rurikō-ji, with which the pagoda is associated, is also in the park and was moved here from a small village.

The park's **teahouse** was also moved here – the Yamaguchi daimyō held secret talks in the house under the pretext of holding a tea ceremony. The park is also the site of the temple, **Tōshun-ji**, and the graves of the Mōri lords.

Jōei-ji
Jōei-ji, 3km north-east of the JR station, was originally built as a house and is notable for its beautiful **Zen garden** (¥300, 8 am to 5 pm) designed by the painter Sesshū. Visitors bring bentō (boxed lunches) and sit on the veranda to eat while admiring the garden.

Other Attractions
North of Route 9, the river, **Ichinosaka-kawa**, has a particularly pretty stretch that is lined with cherry trees. Naturally they're at their best during the blossoming time in spring, but

they're also lovely on summer evenings when large fireflies flit through the trees.

During the festival, Gion Matsuri, held on July 20, the **Sagi-mai** (Egret Dance) is held at **Yasaka-jinja**. On August 6 and 7, during the **Chōchin Tanabata Matsuri**, 10,000 decorated lanterns illuminate the city.

Ten minutes' west of the city on Route 204 is the hot-spring resort of **Yuda Onsen**. It's rather developed and concrete-clad, but you can use the baths at *Ryokan Kamefuku* (¥600), *Kokuminshukusha Koteru* (¥300) and, for a taste of luxury, at the traditional ryokan *Umenoya* (¥800). Buses run regularly from Yamaguchi station (10 minutes).

Places to Stay

Yamaguchi Youth Hostel (☎ 928-0057), is about 4km from Miyano station (two stops east of Yamaguchi), and has 30 beds at ¥2600/3200 for members/nonmembers. From Miyano station you can catch a bus (¥220, every 30 minutes) to Miyano Onsen and get off at the last stop; the hostel is a five-minute walk to the north. A JR bus also stops at Oku-yuda bus stop, which is a 15-minute walk to the hostel. You can rent bicycles there and a bicycle tour map is available.

There's the usual assortment of modern business hotels around the station area including the *Sun Route Kokusai Hotel Yamaguchi (☎ 923-3610)*, with singles/twins for ¥6000/7900; English is spoken. A short distance from the station, down Ekimae-dōri, the *Yamaguchi Kankō Hotel (☎ 922-0356)* and the *Taiyō-dō Ryokan (☎ 922-0897)* both have rooms from ¥6000 to ¥7000 (with two meals).

The *Fukuya Ryokan (☎ 922-0531)*, a 10-minute walk up Ekimae-dōri from the station, is a wonderful establishment. Its effervescent owner, when she's not reminiscing about her misspent hippie youth, or gently reciting a bit of Shakespeare, is a mine of local information. The traditional building is comfy – and there's even the definitive *Kodansha Encyclopedia of Japan* (in English) to browse through. Best of all, room rates are 'somewhat negotiable' if you're feeling poor. This is one of those rare places you could stay, and stay, and

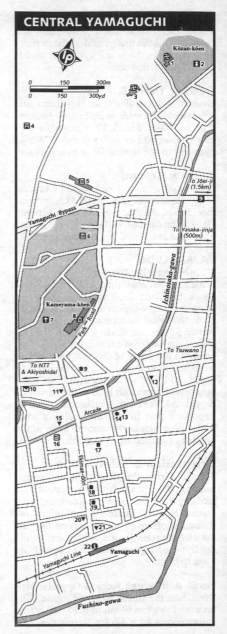

CENTRAL YAMAGUCHI

CENTRAL YAMAGUCHI

PLACES TO STAY
9 Sun Route
  Kokusai Hotel
  Yamaguchi
  サンルート国際ホテル山権
17 Fukuya Ryokan
  福屋旅館
18 Taiyō-dō Ryokan
  太陽堂旅館
19 Yamaguchi Kankō Hotel
  山口観光ホテル

PLACES TO EAT
11 Green Park Restaurant
12 Yamabuki
  そば処やまぶき
13 Lotteria

15 McDonald's
20 Ikoi
  いこい
21 Shiva

OTHER
1 Rurikō-ji
  瑠璃光寺
2 Five-Storeyed Pagoda
  五重塔
3 Tōshun-ji
  洞春寺
4 Yamaguchi Dai-jingū
  山口大神宮
5 Yamaguchi History
  Museum
  山口市歴史民俗資料館

6 Yamaguchi
  Prefectural
  Museum
  山口県立美術館
7 Xavier Memorial
  Chapel
  ザビエル記念聖堂
8 Yamaguchi
  Prefectural Art
  Museum
10 Post Office
  郵便局
14 JTB
16 Internet Jōhō-kan
  インターネット情報館
22 Tourist Information
  観光案内所

stay, just for the place itself. Rooms cost ¥6000, with two meals.

Yuda Onsen, 10 minutes from the station by bus, has a number of traditional ryokan including the expensive but historically interesting *Matsudaya Hotel* (☎ 922-0125), with rooms from ¥22,000 to ¥39,000.

Places to Eat
The arcade off Ekimae-dōri has lots of restaurants, coffee bars and fast-food places. Just a couple of streets north-east from the arcade and Ekimae-dōri is *Yamabuki* (☎ 22-0243), a pleasant old soba shop, where you can eat well for ¥500; closed Sunday.

There are a number of good places along Ekimae-dōri. *Shiva* (☎ 932-4800), an excellent Indian eatery, has lunch specials from ¥800. It's open from 11 am to 3 pm and 5 pm to 9 pm; it has a fully illustrated menu. Across the street is *Ikoi*, with a plastic display of Japanese fare to choose from. At the top of the road, the *Green Park* restaurant is worth a try.

Getting There & Away
The Yamaguchi line connects the city with Ogōri (futsū, ¥230, 15 minutes), which is on the main Tokaidō shinkansen line. JR and Bōchō Kōtsu buses run between Yamaguchi and Hagi (¥1680, 70 minutes),

Akiyoshi-dai (¥1130, one hour) and Hiroshima (¥2450, 2½ hours).

Getting Around
Bicycles can be rented from the train station and since the town's attractions are somewhat scattered (it's 8km just to Jōei-ji and back) and the traffic is not too chaotic, this is a good idea. The first two hours cost ¥310, or it's ¥820 for a day.

AROUND YAMAGUCHI
Ogōri 小郡
Ogōri, only 10km south-west of Yamaguchi, is of no particular interest except as a place to change trains. It's at the junction of the San-yō Osaka-Hakata shinkansen line and the JR Yamaguchi line, which continues to Tsuwano and Masuda on the San-in coast.

Hōfu 豊府
The shrine, **Hōfu Tenman-gū** (¥200, 9 am to 4.30 pm), about a 10-minute walk north of Hōfu station, originally dates from AD 904 and is rated highly along with Dazaifu's Tenman-gū (near Fukuoka on Kyūshū). Close by is the temple, **Suōkokubun-ji**, a structure that is said to date back to AD 741.

Not far east of Hōfu Tenman-gū, the **Mōri Hontei Villa** (¥700, 9 am to 4.30 pm,

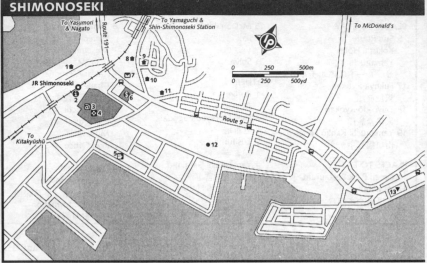

SHIMONOSEKI

closed Sunday) dates from the Meiji era and has a famous painting by the artist, Sesshū, on display. The extensive villa gardens (3300 sq metres) are very picturesque.

Three kilometres north of the station is **Tsuki-no-Katsura-no-tei** (¥300, 9.30 am to 4.30 pm, weekends and holidays only), a beautiful if diminutive Zen rock garden. The scattered rocks include one in the shape of a crescent moon (the *'tsuki'* of the garden's name means 'moon').

Hōfu is connected with Ogōri on the San-yō line (futsū, ¥310, 16 minutes).

SHIMONOSEKI 下関
☎ 0832 • pop 256,000

Shimonoseki is a plain, modern city, but for travellers it's also an important crossroads. At the extreme western tip of Honshū only a narrow strait separates Shimonoseki from the island of Kyūshū. The expressway crosses the strait, Kanmon-kaikyō, by the bridge, Kanmon-bashi; while another road, the shinkansen railway line and the JR railway line all tunnel underneath. The town is also an important connection to South Korea, with a daily ferry service to and from Pusan. Shimonoseki has a number of points of minor interest, and some excellent, if potentially deadly, cuisine.

Information
There's a tourist information office in both the JR Shimonoseki station (☎ 32-8383, 9 am to 7 pm) and the Shin-shimonoseki shinkansen station (☎ 56-3422, 9 am to 5 pm). Beside the station is the large Sea Mall Shimonoseki shopping centre and just east is the new Kaikyō Yume Tower (it looks like a midget skyscraper topped by a futuristic billiard ball). A ¥600 ticket to the tower gets you to the observatory on the 30th floor, where you can take in an impressive 360° view of the surrounding scenery.

Money If you're arriving from Korea, note that there is no bureau-de-change in the ferry terminal, and you can only change money at the Yamaguchi bank (9 am to 3 pm, weekdays); however, you cannot change Korean currency (the nearest place to do that is Osaka!). Nor is there a Korean consulate in the city.

Email & Internet Access At the rear of the second floor of the large Sea Mall

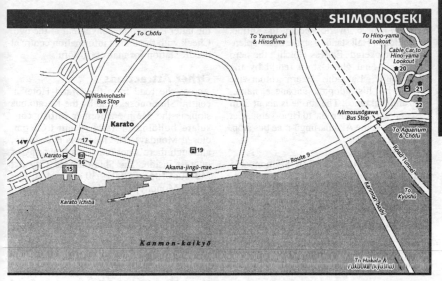

SHIMONOSEKI

shopping centre, *Tips* (open from 10 am to 7 pm, with irregular Wednesday closing) allows you to get on-line (30 minutes costs ¥525).

Akama-jingū

The bright vermilion shrine, Akama-jingū, is dedicated to the child-emperor Antoku who died in 1185 in the naval battle of Dan-no-

SHIMONOSEKI

PLACES TO STAY
1 Shimonoseki
  Tōkyū Inn;
  Shimonoseki
  Eki Nishi
  Washington Hotel
  下関東急イン;
  下関西ワシントンホテル
8 Kirishima
  ビジネス霧島
9 Shimonoseki Station Hotel
  下関ステーションホテル
10 Hotel Thirty Eight
  ホテル38
11 Shimonoseki Green Hotel
  下関グリーンホテル
15 Shimonoseki Grand Hotel
  下関グランドホテル
20 Genpei-sō
  源平荘

21 Kaikan-sō
  海関荘
22 Hinoyama
  Youth Hostel
  下関火の山
  ユースホステル

PLACES TO EAT
13 Sunday's Sun;
  Jolly Pasta
14 Kitagawa
  喜多川
17 Rosan-tei
  魯山亭
18 Nakao
  なかお

OTHER
2 Tourist Information
  観光案内所

3 Tips
  チップス
4 Sea Mall Shimonoseki
  Shopping Centre
  シーモール下関
5 Ferry Terminal;
  Kampu Ferry Service
  フェリーターミナル;
  関釜フェリー
6 Yamaguchi Bank
  山口銀行
7 Post Office
  郵便局
12 Kaikyō Yume Tower
  海峡ゆめタワー
16 Former British Consulate
  (Museum)
  旧英国領事館
19 Akama-jingū
  赤間神宮

Ura. The battle took place in the straits of the Kanmon-kaikyō, overlooked by the shrine. In the **Hōichi Hall** stands a statue of the splendidly monickered 'Earless Hōichi', the hero of a traditional ghost story retold by the Japanophile, Lafcadio Hearn (otherwise known by his adopted Japanese name, Koizumi Yakumo). The shrine is about 3km east of the station, en route to Hino-yama. Get off the bus at the Akama-jingū-mae bus stop.

Hino-yama

About 5km north-east of JR Shimonoseki station there are superb views over the Kanmon-kaikyō from the top of Hino-yama (268m). You can walk, drive or travel by cable car to the top (¥200/400 one way/return). Take a Ropeway-mae bus to the Mimosusōgawa bus stop near the cable-car station or a Kokuminshukusha-mae bus right to the top; these depart hourly from stand No 1 at the station.

Sumiyoshi-jinja

The Sumiyoshi-jinja (9 am to 4 pm, closed from 8 to 15 December), dating from 1370, is north of Hino-yama, near Shin-Shimonoseki station.

Chōfu 長府

If you have any time in Shimonoseki, a trip up to Chōfu to stroll around the streets is the best way of utilising it. It is the old castle town area (jōka-machi) and, while little remains of the old coastal castle itself, there are old earth walls and samurai gates in Chōfu, along with a museum and some important temples and shrines. **Kōzan-ji** has a Zen-style hall dating from 1327 and **Chōfu Museum** (¥200, 9 am to 5 pm, closed Monday) is also in the temple grounds. Other interesting temples and shrines include **Kakuon-ji**, **Iminomiya-jinja** and **Nogi-jinja**.

The elegant garden **Mōri-tei** (¥200, 9 am to 5 pm, until 8 pm April to May and September to October) dates back to the Taishō period, and has several tea-ceremony houses surrounding an ornamental pond.

Buses run fairly frequently up Route 9 from Shimonoseki station to Chōfu (¥350). Two bus stops service the area: Matsubara to the south and Jōka-machi to the north – the latter is the more convenient of the two. Check with the tourist information centre at the JR station for maps of Chōfu.

Other Attractions

Across the road from the Grand Hotel in central Shimonoseki and by the Karato bus stop, is the Meiji-era former **British consulate building** of 1906 (9 am to 5 pm, closed Monday). The facade is interesting, although there's not much that's worthy of interest inside. The **Shimonoseki City Art Museum Hino** (¥200, 9.30 am to 4.30 pm, closed Monday) in Chōfu features contemporary Japanese artists. Perhaps most fun though is people-watching at the fish market, **Karato Ichiba**, down by the seafront (4 am to noon).

Places to Stay – Budget

Youth Hostels The 52-bed *Hinoyama Youth Hostel* (☎ 22-3753) is at the base of Hino-yama, only 100m from the lower cable-car station. Beds cost ¥2575 per night. Take a Hino-yama bus from the station; you can't miss the huge 'YH' sign on top of the building.

Minshuku The cheapest of the lot is *Isaribi* (☎ 24-0881) at ¥3000 a room. It's a spartan but friendly place mainly used by fishermen. It's a 10-minute walk from the station. Head west along route 191, and turn left in front of the Pachinko Cisco.

Hotels Next to the post-office *Kirishima* (☎ 22-2706), with singles for ¥3500, is unassuming and convenient.

Places to Stay – Mid-Range

Minshuku & Ryokan Over in the Chōfu area is the *Chōfu Ryokan* (☎ 45-0404), a rustic-looking little place with rooms for ¥6300, with two meals. Farther out of town still, in the Hino-yama area, is the *kokuminshukusha* (people's lodge) *Kaikan-sō* (☎ 23-0108), which costs ¥6300, with two meals. *Genpei-sō* (☎ 32-5900) is a government sponsored ryokan that charges ¥7600, with two meals.

The nearest hot-spring is **Yutani Onsen**, where the minshuku *Yutani-sō* (☎ *84-0221*) specialises in *sansai* (mountain-vegetable cuisine), and has its own radium onsen bath. As with most radium hot springs, the water is not so hot, but the radioactive element really warms you up. It costs ¥7600, with two meals. Take the JR line to Ozuki (20 minutes) and then bus (13 minutes) to Yutani.

Hotels A number of business hotels can be found close to the station, including *Hotel Thirty Eight* (☎ *23-1138*), with singles/twins starting at ¥4500/8500. It's only two minutes' walk from the station. Close by is the pricier *Shimonoseki Station Hotel* (☎ *32-3511*), with rooms starting at ¥5500/8800.

Cross the road from the station and turn right to reach the *Shimonoseki Green Hotel* (☎ *31-1007*), with rooms starting at ¥5500/8800. Right next to the station is the *Shimonoseki Tōkyū Inn* (☎ *33-0109*), with rooms starting at ¥6700/12,200.

Places to Stay – Top End
Just by the station, the new and rather plush *Shimonoseki Eki Nishi Washington Hotel* (☎ *31-5000*) has singles/twins for ¥8800/14,000.

Places to Eat
There are lots of fast-food places and restaurants with plastic meal displays around the station area and in the Sea Mall shopping centre. On the road that leads up past the Shimonoseki Station Hotel, the popular *Yasumori* (☎ *22-6542*) is a *yakiniku* (Korean-style barbecued beef) place. It's strictly for carnivores, but Shimo's proximity to Korea means the dishes are particularly authentic (noon to midnight, closed Thursday).

Shimonoseki's famed dish is *fugu* (blowfish). Giant plastic fugu even adorn the phone boxes around the station. Those wanting to play this gourmet game of Russian roulette (though not in the summer months – fugu is primarily a winter dish) might try downtown *Rosan-tei* (☎ *0120-633-163*), which is open from 11 am to 2 pm and 5 pm to 11 pm; or *Kitagawa* (☎ *32-3211*), which is open from 11 am to 8.30 pm. Karato's excellent *Nakao* (☎ *31-4129*) is a pricier place to try fugu – plan to spend around ¥7000 per person for dinner (noon to 8 pm, closed Sunday). Nakao's set-lunches are ¥1200 and are good value.

Getting There & Away
Train Shinkansen trains stop at the Shin-Shimonoseki station, two stops from JR Shimonoseki station in the town centre. There are frequent trains and buses between the two. The shinkansen connects Shimonoseki with Hakata (Hikari, ¥3640, 30 minutes), Hiroshima (Hikari, ¥7330, two hours) and Osaka (Hikari, ¥13,430, 4½ hours). The easiest way to cross over to Kyūshū is to take a train from Shin-Shimonoseki station to Mojiko and Kitakyūshū.

Car From Shimonoseki, the bridge and tunnel connect roads in Honshū with Kyūshū. Eastbound travellers can take Route 191 along the northern San-in coast, Route 2 along the southern San-yō coast or the Chugoku Expressway through Central Honshū.

Bus Sanden night buses run between Shimonoseki station and Tokyo station's Yaesu south exit (¥13,950, 13 to 14 hours, twice daily). Reservations are necessary (☎ 34-2929).

Ferry within Japan Ferries run regularly from early morning to late at night from the Karato area of Shimonoseki to Moji-ko in Kyūshū (¥270). From Shin-moji in Kitakyūshū there are ferries to Kōbe, Osaka and Tokyo in Honshū and to Matsuyama in Shikoku.

Ferry to Korea The Kampu Ferry Service (☎ 24-3000) operates the Shimonoseki-Pusan ferry service from the Shimonoseki International Ferry Terminal (Shimonoseki-kō Kokusai Taaminaru) a few minutes' walk from the station. Head up to the 2nd floor of this enormous desolate building for bookings (8.30 to noon and 1 pm to 6 pm, Friday until 7 pm). There are daily departures of the *Hamayū* or the *Pukwan* at 6 pm from Shimonoseki and Pusan, arriving at the other end at 8.30 am the following morning. You must board by 2.30 pm, and it's imperative to arrive early to clear customs and immigration. (The same applies should you return from Pusan.) Immigration and customs officials clock off several hours before the ferry actually sets sail, so even if you turn up an hour before departure, you won't be allowed on board. One-way fares start from ¥6800 for students and continue up to ¥8500 for an open tatami area, ¥10,500 (six-berth cabin), ¥12,000 (four-berth cabin) and ¥14,000 (two-berth cabin). There's a 10% discount on return fares.

This route is used by many long-term Western residents in Japan (especially English-language teachers), as such expect to have your passport rigorously inspected.

Hitching If you're hitching out of Shimonoseki, you'll need to get on the expressway. There's a complicated mass of junctions north of the youth hostel and Hino-yama. Roads diverge in a variety of directions – to Kyūshū by the tunnel or bridge, to Hiroshima by the Chūgoku Expressway and to Yamaguchi by Routes 2 and 9.

SHIMONOSEKI TO HAGI

There's some good coastal scenery, small fishing villages and interesting countryside along the coast road between Shimonoseki and Hagi, which is at the western extremity of Honshū.

Ōmi-shima, with its scenic, rocky coast, is immediately north of **Nagato** (population 28,000) and connected to the mainland by a bridge. The island is part of the Kita Nagato Coastal Park, which extends eastwards beyond Hagi.

AKIYOSHI-DAI 秋吉台
☎ 0837

The rolling Akiyoshi-dai tablelands are about halfway between Yamaguchi on the southern San-yō coast and Hagi on the northern San-in coast. The green fields are dotted with curious rock spires, and beneath this picturesque plateau are hundreds of limestone caverns, the largest of which,

Akiyoshi-dō (¥1240, 8.30 am to 4.30 pm) is open to the public.

Akiyoshi-dō is of interest principally for its size; the stalagmites and stalactites are not particularly noteworthy. In all, the cave extends about 10km, a river flows through it and a pathway runs through for about a kilometre. At the midpoint of the cave trail you can take an elevator up to the surface where there is a lookout over the surrounding country. There are entrances to the cave at both ends of the pathway as well as at the elevator. Buses run between the two ends if you do not want to retrace your steps.

Places to Stay

The 120-bed *Akiyoshi-dai Youth Hostel* (☎ 62-0341) is close to the cave entrance. It charges members ¥2600, or ¥4000 with two meals (nonmembers add ¥1000). There is a variety of accommodation around the cave area, from the good value *Kokumin-shukusha Wakatake Sansō* (☎ 62-0126),

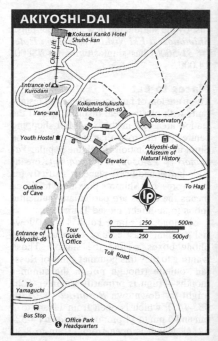

AKIYOSHI-DAI

Kokusai Kankō Hotel
Shuhō-kan

Chair Lift

Entrance of
Kurodani

Yano-ana

Kokuminshukusha
Wakatake San-só

Observatory

Youth Hostel

Akiyoshi-dai
Museum of
Natural History

Elevator

Outline
of Cave

To Hagi

Entrance of
Akiyoshi-dō

Tour
Guide
Office

0   250   500m
0   250   500yd

Toll Road

To
Yamaguchi

Bus Stop

Office Park
Headquarters

which costs ¥4200 with two meals, to the pricey **Kokusai Kankō Hotel Shu-hōkan** (☎ 62-0311), which charges from ¥15,000 per person.

Getting There & Away

It takes a little over an hour by bus from Yamaguchi or Hagi to the cave. Buses also run to the cave from Ogōri, Shimonoseki and other centres.

Tawarayama Onsen 俵山温泉
☎ 0837

This is a gem of an onsen, a fascinating backwater (literally) given over to curative bathing (toji). It's well off the beaten track, and very serious about its purpose – there are no karaoke bars, no pachinko (vertical pinball) halls, no neon, no restaurants; bathers come here for their health, staying for weeks at a time in the 40-odd ryokan, but bathing mainly in the two public baths, **Machi-no-yu** and **Kawa-no-yu**. The latter, overlooking the river, is the most pleasant. Ryokan in the area are inexpensive – try **Hachimandō** (☎ 9-0600), which charges ¥6000, with two meals.

Two kilometres east of the village is the remarkable shrine, **Mara Kannon-jinja**. 'Kannon' is the Japanese deity, usually female, of compassion (in Sanskrit, Avalokitesvara). 'Mara' is, well, the most graphic word imaginable for the male procreative organ, somewhere off the vulgar scale beyond 'knob-end'. Put the two together and you have this astonishing little shrine. It looks more like a garden shed than a place of worship, and it's festooned in **phallic statuary**. According to the English-language explanation, it was founded to commemorate a local dignitary slain by ne'er-do-well bandits. Where the goddess of compassion and the willies come into the picture is anybody's guess. On May 1, it's the scene of a highly photographic fertility rite, the **Mara Kannon Matsuri**.

Take the Mine line from Asa (futsū, ¥740, 51 minutes) or Nagato-shi (futsū, ¥180, 7 minutes) to Nagato-Yumoto. Buses run from there up to Tawarayama (¥200, 30 minutes). The last bus is in the early evening.

HAGI 萩
☎ 0838 • pop 50,000

If there is a single reason for travelling along the northern coast of Western Honshū it is Hagi, with its interesting combination of temples and shrines, a fascinating old samurai quarter, some picturesque castle ruins and fine coastal views. Hagi also has important historical connections with the events of the Meiji Restoration. It is ironic that the town's claim to fame is its role in propelling Japan directly from the feudal to the modern era, while its attractions are principally its feudal past. Hagi is also noted for its fine ceramics.

History

Hagi in Honshū and Kagoshima in Kyūshū were the two centres of unrest that played the major part in the events leading up to the Meiji Restoration. Japan's long period of isolation from the outside world under the Tokugawa rule had, by about the mid-19th century, created tensions approaching breaking point. The rigid stratification of society had resulted in an oppressed peasantry, while the progressive elements of the nobility realised Japan had slipped far behind the rapidly industrialising European nations and the USA. The arrival of Commodore Perry brought matters to a humiliating head as the 'barbarians' simply dictated their terms to the helpless Japanese.

Japan could not stand up against the West if it did not adopt Western technology, and this essential modernisation could not take place under the feudal shogunate. Restoring the emperor to power, even if only as a figurehead, was the route the progressive samurai chose and Shōin Yoshida of Hagi was one of the leaders in this movement. On the surface, he was also a complete failure. In 1854, in order to study the ways of the West first-hand, he attempted to leave Japan on Perry's ship, only to be handed over to the authorities and imprisoned in Edo (Tokyo).

When he returned to Hagi he hatched a plot to kill a shogunate official, but talked about it so much that word leaked out to his enemies. He was arrested again and, in

WESTERN HONSHŪ

HAGI

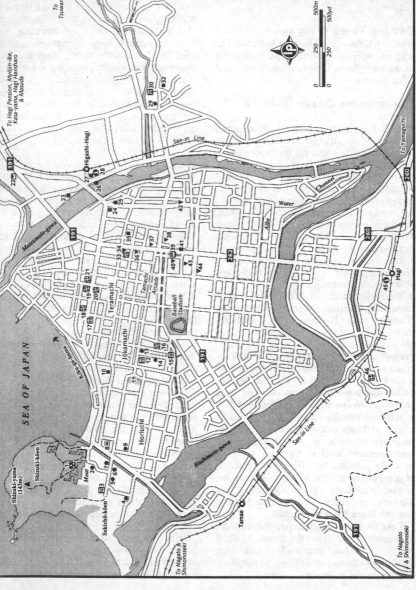

HAGI

PLACES TO STAY
6 Hagi Youth Hostel;
   Bicycle Rental
   萩ユースホステル
7 Kokuminshukusha Jō-en;
   Shogetsu Kiln
   国民宿舎城苑
23 Minshuku Higashi Hagi
   民宿東萩
24 Hagi Travel Inn
   萩トラベルイン
25 Hotel Orange
   ホテルオレンジ
26 Riverside Hotel
   萩リバーサイドホテル
27 Hagi Royal Hotel
   萩ロイヤルホテル
35 Nakamura Ryokan
   中村旅館
41 Urban Hotel Hasegawa
   アーバンホテル長谷川

PLACES TO EAT
34 Shizuki
36 Restaurant &
   Tea Room Shizuki
   シズキ
37 Beer City Hagi
   ビアシティー萩
38 Tsubohan
   つぼ半
40 Restaurant &
   Tea Room Takadai
   レストラン高大

42 Akashi
   明石
43 Hagi-kō
   萩っ子
44 Nagasaki
   Chanmen
   長崎ちゃんめん

OTHER
1 Hagi-jō Ruins
   萩城跡
2 Hagi-jō Kiln
   萩城窯
3 Hagi-yaki Museum
   萩焼陶芸会館
4 Christian Cemetery
   キリシタン墓地
5 Mōri House
   旧毛利家萩屋敷長屋
8 Tomb of Tenjuin
   毛利天樹院墓所
9 Fukuhara-ke Yashiki-mon
   福原門
10 Masuda House
   益田家矢倉長屋
11 Sosui-en
   そすい園
12 Gallery Saitō-an
   彩陶庵
13 Kikuya House
   菊屋家住宅
14 Takasugi Shinsaku
   House
   高杉晋作旧宅

15 Ishii Chawan Museum
   石井茶碗美術館
16 Ensei-ji
   円政寺
17 Kumaya Art Museum
   熊谷美術館
18 Baizō-in
   梅蔵院
19 Kyōtoku-ji
   亨徳寺
20 Kaichō-ji
   海潮寺
21 Hōfuku-ji
   保福寺
22 Post Office
   郵便局
28 Tourist Information
   観光案内所
29 Shōkasonjuku School
   松下村塾
30 Shōin-jinja
   松陰神社
31 Tōkō-ji
   東光寺
32 Itō Hirobumi House
   伊東博文旧宅
33 Jōnen-ji
   常念寺
39 Bus Station
   バス停
45 Tourist Office
   観光案内所
46 Daisho-in
   大照院

1859 at the age of 29, he was executed. Fortunately, while Shōin was a failure when it came to action he was a complete success when it came to inspiration and in 1865 his followers led a militia of peasants and samurai that overturned the Chōshū government of Hagi. The Western powers supported the new blood in Hagi and Kagoshima, and when the shogunate army moved against the new government in Hagi, it was defeated. That the downfall of the shogunate had come at the hands of an army, not just of samurai but of peasants as well, was further proof of the changes taking place.

In late 1867, the forces of Kagoshima and Hagi routed the shogunate, the emperor was restored to nominal power and in early 1868, the capital was shifted from Kyoto to Tokyo, as Edo soon became known. To this day, Hagi remains an important site for visitors interested in the history of modern Japan and Shōin Yoshida 'lives on' at the Shōin-jinja.

Orientation & Information

Hagi consists of three parts. Western and central Hagi are effectively an island created by the rivers, the Hashimoto-gawa and

Matsumoto-gawa; while eastern Hagi (with the major JR station, Higashi-Hagi) lies on the eastern bank of the Matsumoto-gawa.

The main road through central Hagi starts from JR Hagi station and runs north, past the bus station in the centre of town. There's a wide variety of shops along Tamachi arcade, close to the bus station. West of this central area is the old samurai quarter of Jōkamachi, with its picturesque streets and interesting old buildings. More interesting old buildings can be found in Horiuchi to the north-west and Teramachi to the north-east of Jōkamachi.

Hagi's tourist information office (☎ 25-1750) is just beside Higashi-Hagi station. It's open from 9 am to 5 pm. Try to pick up the concise but informative *Hagi Sightseeing Guide*.

Hagi Pottery & Kilns

Connoisseurs of Japanese pottery rank *hagi-yaki*, the pottery of Hagi, second only to Kyoto's *raku-yaki*. As in other pottery centres in Japan, the craft came from Korea when Korean potters were brought back after Toyotomi Hideyoshi's unsuccessful invasion in the late 1500s. There are a number of shops and kilns where you can see the pottery being made and browse through the finished products. Hagi-yaki is noted for its fine glazes and delicate pastel colours. The small notch in the base of each piece is also a reminder of the pottery's long history. In the feudal era only samurai were permitted to use the pottery, but by cutting a tiny notch in some pieces, the potters 'spoilt' their work and it could then be used by common folk.

The **Hagi-jo Kiln** in Horiuchi has particularly fine pieces. The western end of Hagi has several interesting **pottery kilns** near the park, Shizuki-kōen. Hagi-yaki pottery can also be inspected in the **Hagi-yaki Museum** (Hagi-yaki Togei Kaikan) near the park; there's a big souvenir area downstairs.

Long-time foreign resident **Bertil Persson** (☎ 25-2693) has his own kiln, near Nanmyo-ji and is happy to meet anyone seriously interested in ceramics.

During the first week of May, the **Hagi-yaki Matsuri** takes place at the city gymna-

sium, with works on sale from 51 local kilns. It's a good opportunity to pick up ceramic bargains, and for ¥2100 you can throw your own masterpiece. Free buses run from city hall to the gym during the festival.

Gallery Saitō-an (9.30 am to 6 pm, closed third Monday) is the best place to buy contemporary artwork.

Hagi-jō Ruins & Shizuki-kōen

There's not much of the old Hagi-jō to see, apart from the typically imposing outer walls and its surrounding moat. The castle (¥210 including Mōri House, 8 am to 4.30 pm) was built in 1604. It was dismantled in 1874 during the Meiji Restoration – since Hagi played a leading part in the end of the feudal era and the downfall of the shogunate, it was appropriate that the town also led the way in the removal of feudal symbols.

Now the grounds are a pleasant park with the **Shizukiyama-jinja**, **Hanano-e Teahouse** (Hanano-e Satei) and other buildings. From the castle ruins you can climb the hillside to the peak of Shizuki-yama (143m). Also in the park is the small **Hagi Museum** (¥350, 9 am to 4.30 pm).

Sekichō-kōen

About five minutes' walk to the west of Shizuki-kōen is the new park Sekichō-kōen (Sculpture Park), with its collection of sculptural works from around the world. It's open daily and entry is free.

Mōri House

South of the park is Mōri House, a row (terrace) house where samurai soldiers were once barracked. It's open daily and the same ticket covers entry to the castle ruins. There's an interesting Christian cemetery to the south of the samurai house.

Jōkamachi, Horiuchi & Teramachi Areas

Between the modern town centre and the moat that separates western Hagi from central Hagi is the old samurai residential area, with many streets lined by whitewashed walls. This area is fascinating to wander around and there are a number of interesting houses and temples, particularly in the area known as Jōkamachi. Teramachi is noted particularly for its many fine old temples.

Kikuya House The Kikuya family were merchants rather than samurai but their wealth and special connections allowed them to build a house well above their station. The house (¥500, 9 am to 5 pm) dates from 1604 and has a fine gate, attractive gardens and there are numerous examples of construction details and materials that would normally have been forbidden to the merchant class. Tea-bowl enthusiasts may also find the **Ishii Chawan Museum** interesting (¥500, 9 am to 5 pm, closed Tuesday).

Kumaya Art Museum This art museum (¥700, 9 am to 5 pm) in Jōkamachi has a small collection, which includes tea bowls, screens and other items displayed in a series of small warehouses dating from 1768. The Kumaya family handled the trading and commercial operations of Hagi's ruling Mōri family.

Other Buildings The Horiuchi and Teramachi areas are dotted with temples and shrines. The gate, **Fukuhara-ke Yashiki-mon**, is one of the finest of the samurai gates in Horiuchi. Nearby is the **Tomb of Tenjuin**, dedicated to Mōri Terumoto, the founder of the Mōri dynasty. There are numerous old temples in the Teramachi area including the two-storey **Kaicho-ji**; **Hōfuku-ji**, with its Jizō statues (the Buddha for travellers and the souls of departed children); **Jonen-ji**, with its gate carvings; and **Baizo-in**, with its Buddha statues. Large **Kyotoku-ji** has a fine garden.

Tōkō-ji
East of the river stands this pretty temple (¥200, 8.30 am to 5 pm), with the tombs of five Mōri lords. The odd-numbered lords (apart from number one) were buried here; the even-numbered ones were buried at the temple, Daishō-in. The stone walkways on the hillside behind the temple are flanked by almost 500 stone lanterns erected by the lords' servants.

Shōin-jinja
This Meiji-era shrine is dedicated to Shōin Yoshida. His life is illustrated in the nearby **Shōin Yoshida Rekishikan** (Shōin Yoshida History Hall; ¥650, 9 am to 5 pm). South of the shrine, **Itō Hirobumi House**, is the early home of the four-term prime minister who was a follower of Shōin Yoshida, and who later drafted the Meiji Constitution. Shōin Yoshida's tomb is near Toko-ji.

Daishō-in
South of the centre, near JR Hagi station, this funerary temple (¥200, 8 am to 5 pm) was the resting place for the first two Mōri generations and after that, all even numbered generations of the Mōri lords. Like the better known and more visited Tōkō-ji, it has pathways lined by stone lanterns erected by the Mōri lords' faithful retainers. The original Mōri lord's grave is accompanied by the graves of seven of his principal retainers, all of whom committed *seppuku* (ritual suicide) after their lord died. An eighth grave is that of a retainer to one of the retainers who also joined in the festivities. The shogunate quickly banned similar excessive displays of samurai loyalty.

Myōjin-ike & Kasa-yama
A couple of kilometres east of the town, the pond, Myōjin-ike, is actually connected to the sea and shelters a variety of saltwater fish. The road beside this small lagoon continues to the top of Kasa-yama, a small extinct volcano cone, from where there are fine views along the coast. Buses run from Hagi to Kasa-yama (¥240, 15 minutes).

Other Attractions
At the south-eastern end of Hagi 'island', carp can be seen swimming in the roadside **Aiba water channel**. East of the town and close to the main road to Masuda, is the **Hagi Hansharo**, an old reverberating furnace dating from 1858, which was used to make gun and ship parts.

Places to Stay
The 120-bed *Hagi Youth Hostel* (☎ 22-0733) is south of the castle at the western

end of the town. It charges members/non-members ¥2800/3100. The hostel is closed from mid-January to mid-February. Tamae is the nearest JR station.

There are ryokan and minshuku in town with affordable prices. *Minshuku Higashi Hagi* (☎ 22-7884), near Higashi Hagi station, is a friendly family-run place; English is spoken, and there's free morning coffee. It charges ¥4000, ¥5000 with breakfast, or ¥7000 with two meals. Close to Shizuka-kōen is *Kokuminshukusha Jō-en* (☎ 22-3939), with room for only ¥5500, or ¥8000 with two meals.

Over the river from Higashi-Hagi station is the slightly up-market *Nakamura Ryokan*

(☎ 22-0303), with rooms starting at ¥10,000, with two meals.

The *Hagi Royal Hotel* (☎ 25-9595) is right by Higashi-Hagi station. Rooms cost ¥7000. Cheaper hotels in the same area include the *Riverside Hotel* (☎ 22-1195), with good singles/doubles for ¥5000/15,000, and the *Hagi Travel Inn* (☎ 25-2640), just across the river from the Higashi-Hagi station, which costs ¥5000/10,000.

Just across the road from the Hagi Travel Inn is *Hotel Orange* (☎ 25-5880), where the receptionist speaks English. It charges ¥4500/8000 for singles/twins. The best bet comfort-wise is the newly refurbished *Urban Hotel Hasegawa* (☎ 22-0450), across from the bus station, which costs ¥5500.

Pension Hagi (☎ 28-0071) is a pleasant, modern pension, 10km east of town in the fishing port of Nagato-Ohi (pronounced 'oy'). JR Nagato-Ohi station is two stops from Higashi-Hagi and the pension's owner, Yukio Yamazaki, who learnt his excellent English in Papua New Guinea, will meet you at the station. Rooms cost only ¥5500.

Places to Eat

Hagi prides itself on *uni* (sea-urchin). The most economical place to try this gourmet delicacy is *Tsubohan* (☎ 22-1684), near the bus station. Try it served on rice *(unikama setto)* for ¥1980.

A couple of places worth looking out for, both in the east of town, are *Shizuki* (☎ 22-0660), which is open from 11 am to 9 pm, and *Takadai* (☎ 22-0065). The former, in a Tudor-fronted building, has French cuisine and although a lot of it is pretty expensive, there are some good set lunches and dinners. The latter is well known for its Hagi cuisine and has a pricey but excellent special lunch for ¥2000. *Akashi* is east of the centre, on the main through route, and has good *teishoku* (set meals).

There are some fast-food specialists, including one of the *Nagasaki Chanmen* noodle restaurants.

Getting There & Away

The JR San-in line runs along the north coast through Tottori, Matsue, Masuda and

---

Can You Eat Natto?

Sooner or later, should you spend any length of time eating with Japanese acquaintances, you'll see your hitherto gracious hosts – amid much winking and elbow nudging – suddenly perform a culinary Jekyll and Hyde, in the game of 'Let's Gross Out the Gaijin'.

The rules, unstated but recognised intuitively by all, are simple: produce the weirdest food you can, and present it to the foreign guest in a situation so laced with *giri* (social obligation) that they are forced to eat it. Watch as they turn the same colour as freshly salted squid intestines. Suggested weapons in this game of gastronomic sabotage are *natto* (fermented soy beans, best topped off with a raw quail's egg); *inago* (locusts), hmmm, good and crunchy whole; and *uni* (sea urchin), orangey-yellow and the consistency and shape of wet brains.

If that fails to work, bring out the heavy guns: *odori-dako*, (octopus, chopped up, but very much alive, wriggling and adhering itself to the roof of one's mouth) should do the trick, but if all else fails there's one infallible weapon: *shira-ko* (raw cod sperm).

However, *gaijin* visitors are not without their own culinary arsenal. If you want to be on equal terms, stuff your backpack with liquorice bootlaces, steak & kidney pie, Vegemite, or, that horror of horrors, rice pudding.

Hagi to Shimonoseki. The faster expresses take four hours to Matsue (tokkyū, ¥6710).

JR buses connect Hagi with Ogōri (¥1900, 1½ hours, every 70 minutes), which is south of Hagi on the Tokyo-Osaka-Hakata shinkansen line. The buses go via Akiyoshi-dai. There are also buses from Yamaguchi, and buses also go to Tsuwano (a little under two hours).

Getting Around

Hagi is a good place to explore by bicycle and there are plenty of rental places, including one at the youth hostel and several around the castle and JR Higashi-Hagi station.

Shimane-ken 島根県

Along the northern San-in coastline of the Sea of Japan, Shimane-ken has several important places worth getting to, as well as a slew of less travelled areas including the spectacular islands of the Oki-shotō. Tsuwano, one of Japan's many 'little Kyotos'; Matsue, where the writer and Japanophile Lafcadio Hearn lived and produced some of his best known works; and the great shrine at Izumo. All of which should not be missed by those in this part of the country.

TSUWANO 津和野
☎ 0856

In the far western reaches of Shimane-ken, about 40km east of Hagi, is Tsuwano, a pleasant and relaxing mountain town with some fine castle ruins, interesting old buildings and a wonderful collection of carp swimming in the roadside water channels (the 65,000 or so of these colourful fish outnumber the local population by tenfold!). The town is noted as a place to get to by the superb old steam-train service from Ogōri and as a place to explore by bicycle, of which there are quite a phenomenal number for rent.

Orientation & Information

Tsuwano is a long, narrow town wedged into a deep north-south valley. The Tsuwano-kawa, JR Yamaguchi line and main road all run down the middle of the valley. The staff at the tourist information office (☎ 72-1144), by the train station, are very helpful and have excellent English information on hand (9 am to 5 pm). Try to pick up the excellent, bilingual booklet *Yū ni shin sai Tsuwano*, which translates to 'make yourself at home' in the local dialect.

Tsuwano-jō

The ruins of Tsuwano-jō seem to brood over the valley, with the broken stone walls draping along the ridge. The castle was originally constructed in 1325 and remained in use until the Meiji Restoration. A short chair lift takes you up the hillside for ¥450 (return trip), from where there's a further 15-minute walk to the castle ruins. At the top there is a splendid view over the town and surrounding mountains. If you've got the energy and time, it is possible to follow a trail on foot all the way up from Taikodani-Inari-jinja.

Taikodani-Inari-jinja

Just below the castle chair-lift station, this brightly painted shrine is one of the largest Inari shrines in Japan. You can walk up to it from the main road through a 'tunnel' created by over 1100 red torii. Festivals are held here on 15 May and 15 November every year. The annual **Sagi Mai Matsuri** (Heron Dance Festival) is performed on 20 and 27 July at Yasaka-jinja, near the start of the torii tunnel.

Tonomachi District

Only the walls and some fine old gates remain from the former **samurai quarter** of Tonomachi. 'Ditches' (the word used in the local tourist brochure) is too plain a word to apply to the water channels that run alongside this picturesque road: the crystal-clear water in the **channels** is home to tens of thousands of large and healthy carp. It's said that these fish were bred to provide a potential source of food should the town ever be besieged. The feared attack never came and the fish have thrived.

At the northern end of the street is the **Catholic church**, a reminder that Nagasaki Christians were once exiled here. At the other end of Tonomachi, just north of the river, is the **Yōrō-kan**. This was a school for young samurai in the late Edo period, a relatively innovative idea at that time. The building now houses the **Minzoku Museum** (¥200, 8.30 am to 5 pm), an interesting little folk art museum, with all sorts of farming and cooking equipment.

Down near the post office, is the **Katsushika Hokusai Museum** (¥500, 9.30 am to 5 pm), featuring a collection by the master Edo-period painter Hokusai and his disciples.

Some Hokusai humour, from a collection of his doodles 'Hokusai manga', published 1878.

Chapel of St Mary

The tiny Maria-Seido Chapel dates from 1948 when a German priest built it as a memorial to the exiled Catholics who died in the final period of Christian persecution, before the anti-Christian laws were repealed in 1872. Tsuwano's own **Via Dolorosa** leads along the side of the valley from the chapel with markers for the Stations of the Cross. At the end of this winding pathway through the forest, a road leads down by **Yōmei-ji** (¥300, 8.30 am to 5 pm), a Zen temple, which dates from 1420. The tomb of Mori Ōgai (see the Other Attractions entry) is at this temple.

Other Attractions

The beautiful former residences of Nishi Amane, who played an important part in

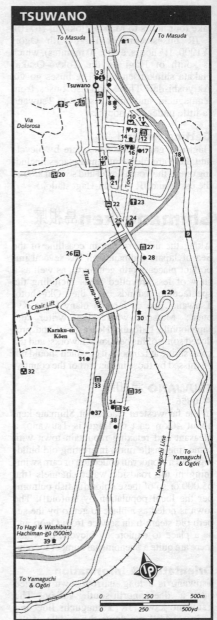

TSUWANO

TSUWANO

PLACES TO STAY
1 Hotel Sun Route
ホテルサンルート
9 Hoshi Ryokan
星旅館
14 Hiroshimaya Minshuku
広島屋
16 Meigetsu Ryokan
明月
18 Tsuwano Grand Hotel
津和野グランドホテル
21 Tsuwano Kankō Hotel
津和野観光ホテル
29 Kokuminshukusha
Aonesanso
国民宿舎青根山荘
30 Wakasagi-no-Yado
Minshuku
民宿わかさぎの宿
39 Tsuwano Youth Hostel
津和野ユースホステル

PLACES TO EAT
8 Shō-kyōto
小京都
11 Furusato
ふるさと
13 Roku-roku
六六

15 Sekishin-tei
石心亭
19 Waraji-ya
わらじ屋
25 Azemichi
あぜみち

OTHER
2 Eki Rent-a-Cycle
3 Tourist Information Centre
観光案内所
4 Kamai Shōten
5 Chapel of St Mary
マリア聖堂
6 Kōmyō-ji
光明寺
7 Tsuwano Documentary
Photography Gallery
産業資料館
10 Post Office
郵便局
12 Katsushika Hokusai Museum
葛飾北斎美術館
17 Hashimoto Sake Brewery
橋本酒店
20 Yōmei-ji
永明寺
22 Bus Station
バスターミナル

23 Catholic Church
津和野カトリック教会
24 Yōrōkan; Minzoku
Museum
養老館
26 Taikodani-Inari-jinja
太鼓谷稲成神社
27 Musée de Morijuku
杜塾美術館
28 Kusakari Jitensha
31 Dentō Kōgeisha
津和野伝統工芸舎
32 Tsuwano-jō Ruins
津和野城跡
33 Jingasa Museum
津和野陣笠民芸館
34 Itahashi Antique
Doll Museum
板橋アンティック
ドール美術館
35 Sekishukan (Washi Kaikan
Museum)
和紙会館
36 Mori Ōgai House;
Memorial Museum
森鴎外記念館
37 Nishi Amane House
西周旧宅
38 Tachibana Cycle

the Meiji Restoration government, and Mori Ōgai, a highly regarded novelist, are in the south of the town and definitely worth checking out. At the rear of the latter is the **Mori Ōgai Memorial Museum** (¥500, 9 am to 4.45 pm, closed Monday), a striking modern building that houses many of the writer's personal effects. Entry to the grounds of his residence only (which is far more interesting than the museum) is ¥100. Nearby is the **Sekishu-kan**, also known as the Washi Kaikan, a museum dedicated to *washi* (handmade paper), where you can watch the process and pick up some fine souvenirs. Entry is free.

The **Itahashi Antique Doll Museum** houses an astounding collection of fine European antique dolls, though the ¥800 entry fee keeps most without a penchant for such

away. Perhaps more interesting (and still with a bit of European flavour) is the **Musée de Morijuku** (foreigners pay a discounted ¥300 entry fee, 9 am to 5 pm). Housed in an old farmhouse, there is a room of Goya etchings and paintings by local artists. Make sure to see the pinhole camera feature on the 2nd floor (the proprietor will gladly show you).

The **Dentō Kōgeisha** centre (¥200, 9 am to 5 pm) also has paper-making displays. Across the road from it is the **Jingasa Museum**, with its collection of old items and costumes used in the annual Sagi Mai Matsuri.

The **Tsuwano Documentary Photography Gallery** (¥200, 9 am to 4.45 pm) is a small but excellent collection dedicated to contemporary photojournalism. The standing collection features work by Tsuwano-born Kuwabara Shisei, mostly shot in Vietnam, South Korea and Minamata.

There are a number of sake breweries in town, some of which you can stop in for tastings. Try **Hashimoto**, midway between the Catholic church and the Katsushika Hokusai Museum. Toba-san, one of the resident staff, can answer your questions in English while you sample the local brew.

South of the town is the shrine, **Washibara Hachiman-gū**, about 4km from the station. Archery contests on horseback are held here on 2 April.

Special Events

The **Sagi Mai Matsuri**, in which the participants dress like the ubiquitous river birds, is a major annual festival held in July. Lighted lanterns are floated down the river in August.

Places to Stay

The information counter outside the train station will help with bookings for the town's many minshuku and ryokan.

Places to Stay – Budget

The 28-bed *Tsuwano Youth Hostel* (☎ 72-0373) charges ¥2900/3900 for members/nonmembers. Breakfast is available for ¥600. The hostel is a couple of kilometres south of the station, beside a small temple.

Places to Stay – Mid-Range

Minshuku & Ryokan The *Wakasagi-no-Yado Minshuku* (☎ 72-1146) is not in the town centre but it's a pleasant, friendly and frequently recommended place. The staff will even pick you up at the station. Rooms cost ¥7000, with two meals.

Other similarly priced minshuku and ryokan include the *Hoshi Ryokan* (☎ 72-0136) and *Hiroshimaya Minshuku* (☎ 72-0204). Both are centrally located and charge ¥6000, which also includes two meals.

Across the river, away from the centre is the government-run *Kokuminshukusha Aonosansō* (☎ 72-0436), which costs ¥6800, with two meals.

Hotels Hotels in town include the *Hotel Sun Route* (☎ 72-3232), with singles/twins starting at ¥6800/10,600. It's a bland, modern hotel overlooking the town from the eastern slope of the valley.

Places to Stay – Top End

Ryokan The *Meigetsu Ryokan* (☎ 72-0685) is a traditional and more expensive ryokan, with rooms from ¥10,000 to ¥20,000. This is a place where by request you may get to try Tsuwano's famine food – carp!

Hotels The *Tsuwano Kankō Hotel* is right in the centre of town, while the *Tsuwano Grand Hotel* (☎ 72-0888) is on the eastern valley side by Route 9; both are expensive at around ¥12,000 per person, with two meals.

Places to Eat

Most visitors to Tsuwano eat in their minshuku or ryokan, so dining possibilities are limited. For lunch, *Furusato* (☎ 72-0403) in Gion-chō across from the post office, serves the local speciality *uzume-meshi* (rice served in a soup with tofu, mushrooms and mountain vegetables) for about ¥1200. It's open from 11 am to 3 pm.

In front of the station, *Shō-kyoto* has run-of-the-mill, but cheap, curries, *katsudon* (pork cutlet served over rice) and coffee. In the evening by far the best bet is the inexpensive izakaya *Roku-roku* (☎ 72-0443), a short walk south-west of the post office. It is inexpensive, friendly, and a good place to meet partying locals (7 pm to 2 am, closed Sunday). The *kabuto-ebi shio-yaki*, a kind of mini-lobster, grilled and salted, at ¥500 is highly recommended.

The rustic *Waraji-ya* (☎ 72-3221), serves noodles in a traditional shop (11.45 am to 2 pm, closed Tuesday), with an *irori* (open fireplace). *Azemichi* (☎ 72-1884) boasts *chōgekikara ramen*, 'hellish spicy hot' Chinese noodles. It's open from 9.30 am to 5 pm.

Getting There & Away

The JR Yamaguchi line runs from Ogōri on the south coast through Yamaguchi to Tsuwano and on to Masuda on the north coast. Tsuwano is connected with Ogōri

(1¼ hours) and Masuda (30 minutes). A bus runs from Tsuwano to Hagi (two hours) and, overnight, to Osaka (¥9000, 8¾ hours, one daily) and Tokyo (¥13,100, 14 hours, one daily).

During the late April to early May Golden Week holiday, and from 20 July to 31 August, as well as sometimes on Sunday and national holidays, a popular steam locomotive service operates between Ogōri and Tsuwano. It takes two hours each way and you should book well ahead (☎ 082-264-5725).

Getting Around
Tsuwano is packed with bicycle rental places and rates start at ¥400 for two hours, with a maximum of ¥800 for a day.

MASUDA 益田
Masuda is a modern industrial town with two temples, **Mampuku-ji** and **Iko-ji**. Both have notable gardens said to have been designed by the famed-painter **Sesshū**. The temples are about 10 minutes by bus from the JR station.

Masuda is the junction for the JR Yamaguchi line, which runs between Ogōri, Yamaguchi, Tsuwano and Masuda, and the JR San-in line, which runs from Shimonoseki, through Hagi and Masuda. Trains run from Masuda to Tsuwano (¥570, 40 minutes), Higashi-Hagi (¥950, one hour 20 minutes) and Izumo (¥2520, three hours).

IZUMO
☎ 0853 • pop 87,591
Only 33km west of Matsue and just north of Izumo itself, the small town of Izumo has one major attraction – the great Izumo Taisha.

Orientation & Information
Izumo Taisha is actually several kilometres north-west of the central area of Izumo. There's no real reason to visit central Izumo, since the shrine area, basically one main street running straight up to the shrine, has two train stations and a range of (generally expensive) accommodation and restaurants. There's a very poorly stocked tourist information office (☎ 53-2298),

which is open from 9 am to 5 pm, near the shrine entrance.

Izumo Taisha 出雲大社
This is the oldest Shintō shrine in Japan and is second in importance only to the shrines of Ise. Although it is only a shadow of its former self – the buildings once towered to a colossal 96m, whereas today they are a more modest 24m – this is still an enormously significant structure, both architecturally and spiritually.

A shrine has existed on the site for the last 1500 years. The current main shrine was last rebuilt in 1744, its 25th reincarnation, whereas the surrounding buildings date back to 1874. All are constructed in the Taisha-zukuri style, considered Japan's oldest form of shrine architecture. The wooded grounds are pleasant to wander through and the shrine itself enjoys the 'borrowed scenery' of Yakumo Hill as a backdrop.

Okuninushi, to whom the shrine is dedicated, is the *kami* (Shintō spirit god) of among other things, marriage. Hence, visitors to the shrine summon the deity by clapping four times rather than the normal two – twice for themselves and twice for their partner or partners to be.

The **Haiden** (Hall of Worship) is the first building inside the entrance torii and huge *shimenawa* (twisted straw ropes) hang over the entry. The main building is the largest shrine in Japan but the **Honden** (Main Hall) cannot be entered. The shrine compound is flanked by *jūku-sha*, long shelters where Japan's eight million Shintō spirit gods stay when they turn up for their annual shindig.

On the south-eastern side of the compound is the **Shinko-den** (Treasure House; ¥150, 8 am to 4.30 pm), which has a collection of shrine paraphernalia. Behind the main shrine building in the north-western corner is the former **Shōkōkan** (Treasure Hall), with a large collection of images of Okuninushi in the form of Daikoku, a cheerful chubby character standing on two or three rice bales with a sack over his shoulder and a mallet in his hand. Usually his equally happy son Ebisu stands beside him with a fish tucked under his arm.

WESTERN HONSHŪ

Hino-misaki

It's less than 10km from Izumo Taisha to the cape, Hino-misaki, where you'll find a picturesque lighthouse, some fine views and an ancient shrine. On the way, you pass the pleasant **Inasano-hama**, a good swimming beach, just 2km from Ichihata Izumo Taisha station. Buses run regularly from the station out to the cape, via the beach (¥490, 35 minutes).

Hinomisaki-jinja is near the cape bus terminus. From the cable-car park, coastal paths lead north and south offering fine views, particularly from the top of the lighthouse. The shrine is open from 9 am to 4.30 pm and from 8.30 am to 4 pm between April and September (¥150). Beyond the cape is **Owashi-hama** and then **Uryū**, two picturesque fishing villages.

Special Events

The lunar calendar month corresponding to October is known throughout Japan as Kan-nazuki (Month without Gods). In Izumo, however, it is known as **Kan-arizuki** (Month with Gods) for this is the month when all the Shintō gods congregate for an annual get-together at Izumo Taisha.

In accordance with the ancient calendar, an important **festival** takes place here from 11 to 17 October. The month of October is also a popular time for weddings at the shrine.

Places to Stay & Eat

There's no imperative reason to stay overnight in Izumo Taisha since it's easy to day trip there from Matsue or to simply pause there while travelling along the coast. If you do want to stop, there are a host of places along the main street of Izumo Taisha, which runs down from the shrine to the two train stations.

The *Ebisuya Youth Hostel* (☎ 53-2157) is just off the main street. Rates are ¥2800/3800 for members/nonmembers. Breakfast and dinner cost ¥600 and ¥1000 respectively.

Places along the main street include *Matsuya Ryokan* (☎ 72-2327), with rooms for ¥6200; *Inabaya Ryokan* (☎ 53-3180)

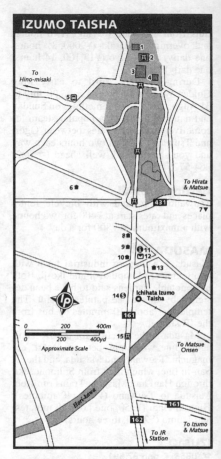

IZUMO TAISHA

which has rooms from ¥10,000 to ¥28,000 with two meals; the classy *Takenoya Ryokan* (☎ 53-3131), which has rooms from ¥12,000 to ¥35,000 with two meals; and *Fujiwara Ryokan* (☎ 53-2009), with rooms starting at ¥12,000.

Izumo's soba gets high praise, particularly for the dish known as *warigo*, where a broth is poured over soba. There are a number of noodle shops along the main street. One local favourite is *Yashiroya* (☎ 53-2596), to the right of the lower entrance to the shrine. It's open from 10 am to 7 pm, closed Tuesday.

IZUMO TAISHA

1 Shōkokan (Treasure Hall)
彰古館
2 Honden (Inner Hall)
本殿
3 Haiden (Hall of Worship)
拝殿
4 Shinko-den
(Treasure House)
神祐殿
5 Ichihata Bus Terminal
一畑バス停
6 Inabaya Ryokan
いなばや旅館
7 Yashiroya
やしろや
8 Takenoya Ryokan
竹野屋旅館
9 Fujiwara Ryokan
藤原旅館
10 Hotel Matsuya
ホテル松屋
11 Tourist Information
観光案内所
12 Post Office
郵便局
13 Ebisuya Youth Hostel
えびすやユースホステル
14 Shimane Bank
島根銀行
15 Otorii
大鳥居

Getting There & Away

The private Ichihata line starts from Matsue-onsen station in Matsue and runs on the northern side of Shinji-ko to Izumo Taisha station (¥790, 55 minutes). The JR line runs from JR Matsue station to JR Izumo station (¥740, one hour), where you transfer to an Izumo Taisha train. The private-line service is more frequent (more than 20 services a day) and takes you closer to the shrine.

The one-day L&R 'Free Kippu' ticket (¥1000) allows unlimited travel on Ichihata trains and Shinji-ko Lakeside buses, and is definitely worthwhile if you plan to visit Matsue.

Izumo has an airport with JAS flights to and from Tokyo.

MATSUE 松江

☎ 0852 • pop 143,000

Matsue straddles the river, Ōhashi-gawa, which connects Shinji-ko to Nakaoumi-ko and then the sea. A compact area in the north of the town includes almost all of Matsue's important sites: an original castle, a fine example of a samurai residence, the former home of writer Lafcadio Hearn (otherwise known by his adopted Japanese name, Koizumi Yakumo) and a delightful teahouse and garden.

Information

The tourist information office (☎ 21-4034) at the JR station (on the left as you leave the station, just past Mister Donut) has a surprising amount of information in English, and the English-speaking staff are extremely helpful. They will help with finding and reserving accommodation, and can arrange free Goodwill Guide English-language tours if you call a few days in advance, or call Sasaki Kazuko (☎ 21-4034).

Money The Gōdō Bank directly in front of the station will advance money on credit cards with passport proof of ID (9 am to 3 pm, weekdays).

Email & Internet Access Free Internet access is available at NTT (9 am to 4 pm, weekdays), but is limited to 30 minutes.

Matsue-jō

Matsue's castle (¥500, 8.30 am to 5 pm, until 6.30 pm in summer) is not huge or imposing, but it is original, dating from 1611. Modern Japan has so many rebuilt castles, externally authentic-looking but internally totally modern, that it can almost be a shock to step inside one where the construction is wood not concrete. With a 'Universal Pass' (¥800), which combines entry to the castle, Buke Yashiki Samurai Residence and the Koizumi Yakumo (Lafcadio Hearn) Memorial Museum, you can save ¥200.

The regional museum **Matsue Cultural Museum** (free, 8.30 am to 4.30 pm) is within the castle precincts. The road alongside the moat on the north-eastern side of

MATSUE

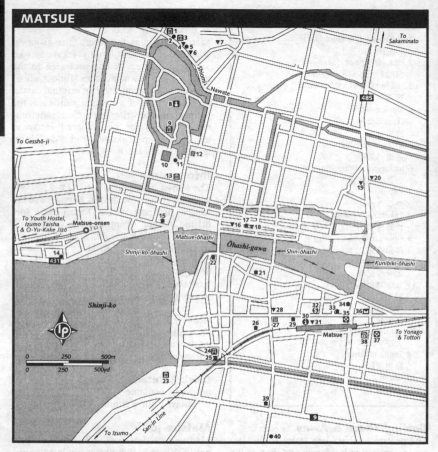

the castle is known as **Shiomi Nawate**, and was, at one time, a narrow lane through the old samurai quarter. The high tile-topped walls still remain from that era and there are a number of places of interest. Take bus No 1 or 2 bus from the JR station to Kenchō-mae.

From March to November, there's a fun open-top boat tour (¥1200, 9 am to 5 pm, until 6 pm in July/August), which circum-navigates the castle moat and then zips you around some of the city's canals. The boat tour company's office is near the Prefectural Hall.

Koizumi Yakumo (Lafcadio Hearn) Residence

Hearn was a British writer (although he was born in Greece in 1850, educated in France and the UK and lived in the USA from 1869) who came to Japan in 1890 and was to remain there for the rest of his life. Hearn's adopted Japanese name was Koizumi Yakumo. His first book on Japan, *Glimpses of Unfamiliar Japan*, is a classic, providing an insight into the country at that time. The Japanese have a great interest in the outsider's view of their country so Hearn's pretty little house is an important

MATSUE

PLACES TO STAY
15 New Urban Hotel
　ニューアーバンホテル
17 Matsue Washington
　Hotel
　松江ワシントンホテル
21 Daiei Business Hotel
　ダイエービジネスホテル
22 Young Inn Matsue
　ヤングイン松江
25 Terazuya
　旅館寺津屋
26 Business Ishida Hotel
　ビジネス石田ホテル
29 Green Hotel Matsue
　グリーンホテル松江
33 Matsue Tōkyū Inn
　松江東急イン
34 Matsue Urban Hotel
　松江アーバンホテル
39 Business Hotel
　Lake Inn
　ホテルレーク イン

PLACES TO EAT
4 Yakumo-an
　八雲庵
6 Yakumo-an Bekkan
　八雲庵別館

7 Meimei-an
　明々庵
16 Kawa-kyō
　かわきょう
18 Benkei Robatayaki
　弁慶
19 KFC
20 McDonald's
28 Ippon-yari
　一本槍
31 Mister Donut

OTHER
1 Koizumi Yakumo (Lafcadio
　Hearn) Memorial Museum
　小泉八雲記念館
2 Koizumi Yakumo (Lafcadio
　Hearn) Residence
　小泉八雲旧宅
3 Tanabe Art Museum
　田部美術館
5 Buke Yashiki Samurai
　Residence
　武家屋敷
8 Matsue-jō
　松江城
9 Matsue Cultural
　Museum
　松江郷土館

10 Prefecture Hall
　県庁
11 Moat Tours
　乗船場
12 Matsue Prefectural Product
　& Craft Centre
　物産観光館
13 Shimane Prefectural Museum
　島根県立博物館
14 Matsue Folk Art Centre
23 Shimane Prefectural
　Art Museum
　島根県立美術館
24 Matsue Tenmangū
　松江天満宮
27 JTB
30 Tourist Information
　観光案内所
32 Gōdō Bank
　島根合同銀行
35 Ichihata Department Store
　一畑百貨店
36 Post Office
　郵便局
37 SATY
　サティ
38 NTT
40 Laundrette
　コインランドリー

attraction, despite the fact that he only lived in Matsue for just over a year. While you're admiring the garden you can read his essay *In a Japanese Garden*, which describes how it looked a century ago. There's no mention, however, that he died embittered and disillusioned with the country.

Hearn's former residence (¥200, 9 am to 4.30 pm) is at the northern end of Shiomi Nawate, and next to it is the Koizumi Yakumo Memorial Museum.

Koizumi Yakumo (Lafcadio Hearn) Memorial Museum
Next to Lafcadio Hearn's home is a museum, the Koizumi Yakumo Memorial Museum, with displays about his life, his writing and his residence in Matsue. There are a stack of Japanese newspapers on which Hearn had

written simple words and phrases to teach his son English. There is an English-language brochure and map showing points of interest around the town mentioned in his writings. Entry is ¥250 (8.30 am to 4.30 pm).

Tanabe Art Museum
This museum (¥500, 9 am to 4.30 pm, closed Monday) principally displays family items from the many generations of the region's Tanabe clan, particularly tea bowls and other **tea ceremony** paraphernalia.

Buke Yashiki Samurai Residence
The Buke Yashiki (¥250, 8.30 am to 5 pm) is a well-preserved middle Edo-period samurai residence built in 1730. There's a useful English-language leaflet that describes the various rooms and their uses in this large but

somewhat spartan residence. This was not the home of a wealthy samurai.

Meimei-an Teahouse

A little further south is the turn-off to the delightful Meimei-an teahouse (¥200, 9 am to 5 pm) with its well-kept gardens and fine views to Matsue-jō. The teahouse was built in 1779 and was moved to its present site in 1966. Look for the steep steps up from the road to the thatched-roof building. You can sample some tea with sweets for ¥350.

Shimane Prefectural Art Museum

This brand spanking new, futuristic-looking museum displays work by Monet, Rodin and current Japanese artists (¥300, 10 am to 6 pm, closed Monday). It's in a fabulous location overlooking the lake, and on a sunny day it's fun to wander around the outdoor sculptures. Look out for the quirky sculpture, *Kaiwa* (Conversation). It's a 15-minute walk west of the station.

Other Attractions

About a kilometre west of the castle is Gesshō-ji, which was converted from an ordinary temple to a family temple for Matsue's Matsudaira clan in 1664, but was dismantled during the Meiji Restoration. The graves of nine generations of the clan remain and family effects are displayed in the treasure house.

Matsue has its own onsen area, just north of the lake near Matsue-onsen station on the Ichihata-Dentetsu line. There are a number of hotels and ryokan in the area and a popular 'hell' or *jigoku* (very hot springs that are definitely not for bathing in), known as O-Yu-Kake Jizō. The sunset views over the lake, Shinji-ko, are fine and best appreciated from the bridge, Matsue-ōhashi. The Matsue Folk Art Centre (Matsue Meisan Sentaa) in the onsen area by the lake, displays regional crafts, as does the Matsue Prefectural Product & Craft Centre just south-east of the castle in the town centre.

Places to Stay – Budget

Youth Hostels The 50-bed *Matsue Youth Hostel* (☎ 36-8620) is about 5km from the

centre of town in Kososhimachi, on the northern side of the lake at the first station you come to along the Ichihata line from Matsue-onsen station. It charges ¥2800/3800 for members/nonmembers Breakfast (¥600) and dinner (¥1000) are available.

Hotels As usual, there are a lot of business hotels around the station including the unbusiness-like *Business Ishida Hotel* (☎ 21-5931), in Teramachi, which doesn't have a sign in English. It's a simple Japanese-style hotel with tatami rooms and shared bathrooms. It's good value at ¥4000 and is conveniently close to the station. Just continue walking past the tourist information office through the bicycle and car parks and it's right beside the elevated railway lines.

Other possibilities, all with shared bathrooms, include the *Daiei Business Hotel* (☎ 24-1515), down by the river, with per-person rates starting at ¥3800; the *Business Hotel Lake Inn* (☎ 21-2424), behind the station on the corner of Route 9, with singles/twins for ¥4500/8000. Not far from the Daiei Business Hotel is the small, bargain priced *Young Inn Matsue* (☎ 22-2000), with twins for ¥3090.

Places to Stay – Mid-Range

Minshuku & Ryokan *Pension Tobita* (☎ 36-6933), in Hamasada-machi, is in the same direction as the youth hostel and has Japanese and Western-style rooms. It costs ¥6000, with breakfast.

Near the shrine, Matsue Tenmangū, *Terazuya* (☎ 21-3484) is a clean, friendly minshuku. Rooms cost ¥4000, or ¥7000 with two meals. Expect to be woken early by drumming from the shrine.

Hotels More expensive hotels include the *Matsue Tōkyū Inn* (☎ 27-0109), with singles starting at ¥7000 and doubles/twins at ¥15,200. It's just across the road from the station. Also in front of the station, the *Green Hotel Matsue* (☎ 27-3000) has singles/twins starting at ¥6200/11,200). The *Matsue Urban Hotel* is a cheaper place behind the Tōkyū Inn, with rooms starting at ¥5500/9500.

The *Matsue Washington Hotel* (☎ 22-4111) is across the river from the JR station but is still convenient to the town centre. Rooms cost ¥6900/14,400.

An interesting option is the new *New Urban Hotel* (☎ 22-0002) and its neighbouring annex, towards Matsue Onsen station. The top floor of the complex boasts a huge hot-spring bath. Singles cost ¥6000.

Places to Eat

If you're wandering Shiomi Nawate, the old samurai street, in the shadow of the castle, pause for lunch at *Yakumo-an* (☎ 22-2400), next to the samurai house. It's a delightfully genteel noodle house (9 am to 4.30 pm), with a pond full of very healthy-looking carp. Dishes range from ¥500 to ¥750 for *niku udon* or *niku soba*. The local speciality, *warigo*-style noodles cost ¥600. There is also a pleasant teahouse annex, *Yakamo-an Bekkan*, just on the other side of Buke Yashiki, with a tea-and-sweets set for ¥550.

Kawa-kyo (☎ 22-1312), near the Washington Hotel north of the river, offers the seven local specialities (see the boxed text 'Exotic Dishes from the Lake' later) on an English-language menu with prices from ¥250 for *shijimi* to ¥1500 for *hōsho yaki*. It's open from 6 pm to 10.30 pm, closed Sunday.

Just north-west of the station, on the edge of the Ise-miya entertainment district, *Ippon-yari* (☎ 27-6437) is a raucous, friendly izakaya (6 pm to 1.30 am). The secret of its success seems to be that it ignores its own prohibition 'No-one Under Twenty' and is packed with partying teenagers. The *niku-jagga* (beef stew) and spare ribs (tasty but miniature) are recommended. Most of the customers seem to lean at the same off-kilter angle as the fridge.

The tourist office at the station can also recommend restaurants.

Getting There & Away

Matsue is on the JR San-in line, which runs along the north coast. You can head down to Okayama on the south coast (tokkyū, ¥5610, around four hours) via Yonago. See the Izumo section earlier for information on the two railway lines running west from Matsue.

Exotic Dishes from the Lake

Matsue's *kyodo ryōri*, or regional cuisine, includes 'seven exotic dishes from Shinji-ko'. They are:

suzuki or *hōsho yaki* – steam-baked paper-wrapped bass
shirauo – whitebait tempura or sashimi
amasagi – sweet tempura or teriyaki
shijimi – tiny shellfish in miso shiro
moroge ebi – steamed shrimp
koi – baked carp
unagi – broiled freshwater eel

Matsue is also a jumping-off point for the Oki-shotō (see the Oki-shotō section later).

Yonago is the airport for Matsue. There are ANA flights to Tokyo and JAS flights to the Oki-shotō.

Getting Around

Airport buses run between Matsue-onsen station and the airport (¥920, 40 minutes). Tour buses leave from stand No 8 in front of JR Matsue station. Other bus routes include Matsue-onsen (No 1), Kaga (No 4), Izumo (No 6) and Yonago (No 7). You pick up a ticket on entering the bus and the relevant fare for your starting point is displayed as you leave.

If you're planning to visit Izumo Taisha, make sure you invest in the one-day L&R 'Free Kippu' ticket (¥1000), which allows unlimited travel on Ichihata trains and Shinji-ko lakeside buses.

Matsue is a good place to explore by bicycle: these can be hired at the Matsue and Matsue-onsen stations for ¥600 for two hours, ¥100 per additional hour or ¥1000 per day.

AROUND MATSUE & IZUMO

There are a number of places of interest in the vicinity of Matsue and neighbouring Izumo.

Shinji-ko 宍道湖

Sunset over the Yomega-shima islet in Shinji-ko is a photographer's favourite and the lake also provides the region's seven

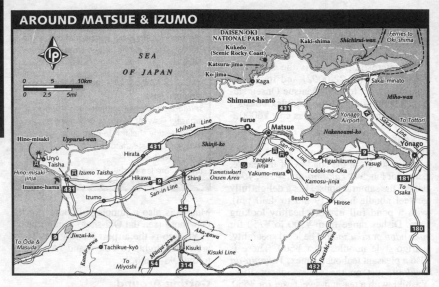

AROUND MATSUE & IZUMO

favourite local delicacies (see the boxed text earlier 'Exotic Dishes from the Lake'). At the western end of the lake, the garden in Gakuen-ji in Hirata is noted for its autumn colours.

At the south-western corner of the lake, the town of Shinji has one of the **finest ryokan in Japan**, *Yakumo Honjin* (☎ 66-0136). Parts of the inn are 250 years old; but if you stay here ask for the old wing or you'll end up in the modern air-conditioned one. Per-person rates start at ¥15,000; casual visitors can have a look around for ¥300.

Shimane-hantō 島根半島

North of Matsue, the coastline of the peninsula, Shimane-hantō, has some spectacular scenery, particularly around Kaga – Kagano-Kukedo is a cave you can enter by boat.

Fūdoki-no-Oka & Shrines

Five kilometres south of Matsue, around the village of Yakumo-mura, there are interesting shrines and important archaeological finds. The hill, Fūdoki-no-Oka, is a 1st century AD archaeological site, with finds displayed in the **Fūdoki-no-Oka Archaeological Museum** (¥300, 9 am to 5 pm,

closed Monday). Nearby is the **Okadayama Tumuli**, an ancient burial mound. Haniwa pottery figures were found here, similar to those of Miyazaki on Kyūshū.

West of Fūdoki-no-Oka is the ancient shrine, **Kamosu-jinja**, dedicated to Izanami, the mother of the Japanese archipelago. The shrine's Honden (Main Hall) dates from 1346. A little further west is **Yaegaki-jinja**, which is dedicated to the gods of marriage and commemorates a princess's rescue from an eight-headed serpent. The events are illustrated in fine 12th-century **wall paintings**, and the shrine sells **erotic amulets** to ensure fruitful marriages! There's a pretty little wood with shrines and ponds close by.

Fūdoki-no-Oka is best visited on the way back from Bessho. Get off at the Fūdoki-no-Oka Iriguchi bus stop, walk to the archaeological museum and on to the two shrines, then take another bus to Matsue from the Yaegaki-danchi Iriguchi bus stop, north of Yaegaki-jinja.

Bessho 別所

About 15 minutes' south of Fūdoki-no-Oka is Bessho, which features the **Abe Eishiro**

Museum (9 am to 4.30 pm). It is dedicated to the craftsman credited with revitalising the making of paper by hand. You can also visit paper-making workshops in the village. A bus from stand No 3 at the JR Matsue station will get you to Bessho; it stops at Fūdoki-no-Oka on the way back.

Yasugi 安来

East of Matsue on Nakanoumi-ko is Yasugi. The temple, **Kiyomizu-dera**, has a beautiful three-storey pagoda and an important 11-faced statue of Kannon, the goddess of mercy. However, the real reason to trek out here is the **Adachi Art Museum** (¥2300, ¥1100 for foreigners, 9 am to 5 pm). It is set in exquisite extensive gardens (all 43,000 sq metres of 'em), and features wonderful artworks by the likes of painter Yokoyama Taikan, *mingei* (folk-craft) potter Kawai Kanjiro and, best of all, firebrand ceramicist Kitaoji Rosanjin. It is worth getting out here early in the day just to slowly lap up the art. There's a beautifully illustrated English-language pamphlet. You may need to show your passport to get the discount.

Tachikue-kyō 立久恵峡

Immediately south of Izumo is this 1km-long, steep-sided gorge. It takes 30 minutes by bus to the Tachikue-kyō station from Izumo.

Sanbē-san

Sanbē-san is inland from Ōda and reaches 1126m; its four separate peaks are known as the Father, the Mother, the Child and the Grandchild. It's part of the Daisen-Oki National Park and is a popular skiing centre during the winter. Buses leave for Ōda from Izumo.

It takes about an hour to climb Sanbē-san from Sanbē Onsen. Buses regularly make the 20km run from Ōda to Sanbē Onsen. The lake, Ukinuno-no-ike, is near the hot springs.

If you follow the Go-gawa south-west from Sanbē-san, the gorge, Dangyo-kei, is 6km south of Inbara and there's a 4km-long walking track along the ravine.

OKI-SHOTŌ 隠岐諸島
☎ 08512

Directly north of Matsue, the Oki-shotō, with their spectacular scenery and steep cliffs, are strictly for those who want to get away from it all. At one time, they were used to exile political prisoners and daimyō (and on one occasion an emperor) who came out on the losing side of political squabbles. The islands consist of the larger Dōgo island and the three smaller Dōzen islands, plus associated smaller islands. The 7km-long cliffs of the Oki Kuniga coast of **Nishino-shima**, at times falling 250m sheer into the sea, are particularly noteworthy. **Kokobun-ji** on Dōgo dates from the 8th century. **Bullfights** are an attraction on Dōgo during the summer months – not man-versus-bull, but bull-versus-bull.

There's a tourist information office (☎ 2-0787), though no-one speaks English. It's open from 8 am to 6 pm.

Places to Stay

The islands have numerous minshuku and other forms of accommodation. On Dōgo, *Okino-shima Youth Hostel* (☎ 7-4321) is the best budget option. Rates are ¥2260, or ¥3840 with two meals (nonmembers add ¥700). The *Oki Plaza Hotel* (☎ 2-0111) has pricey Japanese-style rooms for ¥13,000, with two meals.

On Chiburi-jima, the minshuku *Kamishima* (☎ 08514-8-2355) and the *Hashine Ryokan* (☎ 08514-8-2351) both have reasonable rooms at ¥7000, with two meals. On Nishino-shima there is the *Seaside Hotel Tsurumaru* (☎ 08514-6-1111), which has Japanese-style rooms for ¥12,000; and on Nakano-shima the *Marine Port Hotel* (☎ 08514-2-0033) has rooms starting at ¥9000, with two meals.

Getting There & Away

There are ferry services to the Oki-shotō from Shichirui or Sakaiminato. For Dōgoshima, from Matsue bus terminal (Stand No 4) take the 7.55 am bus to Shichirui (¥990, one hour) then the 9.20 am ferry (¥2530, 2½ hours). JAS flights operate to the islands from Yonago, Izumo and Osaka.

OKI-SHOTŌ

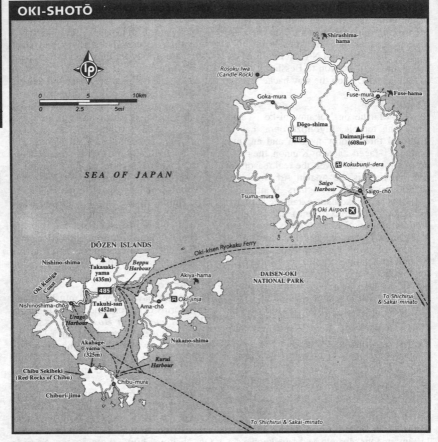

SEA OF JAPAN

DAISEN-OKI
NATIONAL PARK

DŌZEN ISLANDS

YONAGO 米子

Yonago is an important railway junction connecting the north and south coasts and, as such, is a place to pass through rather than visit. From Yonago airport, there are flights to and from Osaka and Tokyo and on to the Oki-shotō.

Daisen-san 大山

Although not one of Japan's highest mountains, at 1729m, Daisen-san looks very impressive because it rises straight from sea level – its summit is only about 10km from the coast. The popular climb up the volcano cone is a six- to seven-hour round trip from the ancient **Daisen-ji**. Bring plenty of water and take care on the final, narrow ridge to the summit. From the top there are fine views over the coast and, in perfect conditions, all the way to the Oki-shotō.

Buses run to the temple from Yonago (50 minutes). The information centre in Yonago (☎ 0859-22-6317) can provide details on making the climb; it's open from 9 am to 6 pm. The mountain snags the north-west monsoon winds in the winter, bringing deep snow and difficult conditions for winter climbers.

Tottori-ken 鳥取県

Though perhaps the least enticing prefecture in western Japan, Tottori has a couple of attractions worth checking out if you are travelling along the San-in coast of the Sea of Japan. The Tottori sand dunes are the most commonly associated landmark in the region and the steep slopes of beautiful Daisen-san are popular with hikers.

TOTTORI

☎ 087 • pop 142,000

Tottori is a large, busy town some distance back from the coast. The main coast road passes through Tottori's northern fringe in a blizzard of car dealers, pachinko parlours and fast-food outlets. The town's main attraction is its famous sand dunes. There's a helpful tourist information booth (☎ 22-3318) inside the station, with English-language pamphlets and maps. It's open from 6 am to 7 pm.

The Dunes 鳥取砂丘

Used as the film location for Teshigahara Hiroshi's classic 1964 film *Woman in the Dunes*, the Tottori sand dunes are on the coast a couple of kilometres from the city. There's a viewing point on a hillside overlooking the

TOTTORI

1 Tottori Prefectural Museum
  鳥取県立博物館
2 Tottori-jō Ruins
  鳥取城跡
3 Jinpū-kaku Villa & Museum
  仁風閣
4 Kannon-in
  観音院
5 Flags
6 Tottori Green Hotel Morris
  鳥取ホテルグリーンモリス
7 Folkcraft Museum
  民芸美術館
8 Hotel Taihei
  ホテル太平
9 Tottori Washington Hotel
  鳥取ワシントンホテル

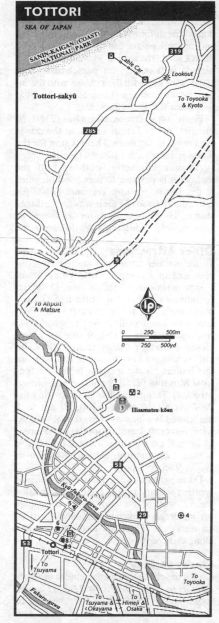

dunes, along with a huge car park and the usual assortment of tourist amenities. The dunes stretch for over 10km along the coast and, at some points, can be a couple of kilometres wide. The section where the dunes are highest is popular with parachutists who stand at the edge, fill their chutes with the incoming sea breezes and leap off the dune top to sail down towards the sea.

From Tottori station, take a bus (¥360, 20 minutes) out to Tottori-sakyū, as the dunes are known in Japanese. The bus stop for the dunes is *sakyū-sentā* (Dunes Centre).

About a kilometre south-west of the lookout it is possible to rent good bicycles at the Tottori Cycling Terminal (¥300 for four hours). Buses on their way to the dunes stop at the terminal – ask for *'kodomo-no-kuni iriguchi'* (Children's World entrance).

Other Attractions

Tottori's other attractions are mainly concentrated in a compact little group about 1.5km north-east of the station. Only the foundations remain of **Tottori-jō**, which overlooked the town from the hillside. Below the castle walls is the European-style **Jinpū-kaku Villa** (¥150, 9 am to 5 pm, closed Monday) dating from 1906. The villa is now used as a museum. Across from this building is the modern **Tottori Prefectural Museum** (¥180, 9 am to 5 pm, closed Monday). Tottori also has an interesting little **Folkcraft Museum** (¥500, 10 am to 5 pm, closed Wednesday) near the JR station, with folkcraft items from Japan, Korea, China and even Europe. East of the station is the 17th-century garden, **Kannon-in** (¥600, 9 am to 5 pm).

Dune-parachuting is not the only seaside sporting activity around Tottori. A few kilometres' west of the town there's a popular surfing break, packed with Japanese surfies on weekends. There are also other breaks along this coast.

Places to Stay & Eat

One of the cheaper places around is the *Tottori Green Hotel Morris* (☎ 22-2331), with rooms from ¥5000 to ¥13,100; the sign in English outside says 'Hotel Morris'. The

Hotel Taihei (☎ 29-1111) has singles/twins starting at ¥5300/¥9500. The *Tottori Washington Hotel* (☎ 27-8111) has singles/doubles or twins starting at ¥6700/13,500). It's next to the train station.

There are plenty of places to eat (with the usual plastic food displays) around the station, including a *Mister Donut*. A few streets north from the station on the left is a good little pizzeria, *Flags* (☎ 29-8857) (11 am to 10 pm). There is also a coffee shop next door run under the same name (7.30 am to 10 pm). A wide selection of fast-food joints also operate along Route 9, the main road through town.

Getting There & Away

The coastal JR San-in line runs through Tottori from Toyo'ōka (¥1450, 1½ hours). The JR Inbi line connects with Tsuyama (¥1280, two hours) and on to Okayama (¥2230, 3½ hours) on the south coast.

Tottori has an airport and ANA has flights from Osaka and Tokyo.

Wakasa-wan Area

The area around the bay, Wakasa-wan, at the eastern end of the San-in coast, takes in parts of the three prefectures Fukui, Kyoto and Hyōgo. From Amanohashidate, which has the distinction of being one of Japan's 'three great views', to the pleasant fishing hamlet of Ine and the onsen town of Kinosaki, the area makes a worthwhile side trip from Kyoto, or an interesting stop if you're travelling along the San-in coast of the Sea of Japan.

WAKASA-WAN 若狭湾

At the eastern end of the bay, the **Mikatago-ko** (Mikata Five Lakes) are joined to the sea. **Obama** is a port town with the ruins of the castle, **Obama-jō**, and a number of interesting old temples including **Myōtsū-ji**, **Mantoku-ji** and **Jingū-ji**. Tour buses operate from JR Obama station and there are also boat trips around the picturesque **Sotomo coastline** with its inlets, arches and caves, just north of Obama.

Continuing around the bay, more interesting coastal scenery can be reached by boat trips from Wakasa-Takahama. From Maizuru there are regular ferry services to Otaru in Hokkaidō. Ferries also run to Otaru from Tsuruga, at the other end of Wakasa-wan (see the Fukui-ken section of the Central Honshū chapter).

AMANOHASHIDATE 天橋立
☎ 0772

Amanohashidate (Bridge to Heaven) is rated as one of Japan's 'three great views', along with Miyajima (near Hiroshima) and the islands of Matsushima-wan (near Sendai). The 'bridge' is really a 'pier', a tree-covered sandspit 3.5km long, with just a couple of narrow channels preventing it from cutting off the top of the bay, Miyazuwan, as a separate lake.

The town of Amanohashidate consists of two separate parts, one at each end of the spit. At the southern end there are a number of hotels, ryokan, restaurants, a popular temple and JR Amanohashidate station. There's an information counter (☎ 22-8030), open from 10 am to 6 pm, at the train station.

At the other end, a funicular railway (¥640 return) and a chair lift run up the hillside to the Kasamatsu-kōen vantage point from where the view is reputed to be most pleasing. From here, incidentally, you're supposed to view the sandspit by turning your back to it, bending over and observing it framed between your legs!

A bridge and swing bridge cross the two channels at the southern end of the spit and cycling along the spit is a popular activity.

Places to Stay
The modern *Amanohashidate Youth Hostel* (☎ 27-0121) is at Ichinomiya, close to the funicular railway lookout point. Rates are ¥2700, or ¥4000 with two meals. To get there take a Tankai bus from JR Amanohashidate station and get off at the Jinjamae bus stop, from where it's a 10-minute walk. The *Amanohashidate Kankōkaikan Youth Hostel* (☎ 27-0046) is also near the park, Kasamatsu-kōen, and has similar rates to the Amanohashidate Youth Hostel.

There are a number of ryokan and hotels, though they're generally fairly expensive, near the station at the other end of the 'bridge'. The *Toriki Ryokan* (☎ 22-0010) charges ¥12,000, with two meals, as does the similarly priced *Shoehino Ryokan*. Other places include the *Hotel Taikyo* and the *Hotel Monju-sō*.

Getting There & Away
The Kita-kinki Tango Tetsudō runs via Nishi-Maizuru (¥620, 40 minutes) to Fukuchiyama (¥750, one hour), where you can change to the JR lines for Kyoto or Osaka. There are several direct trains from Kyoto daily, but JR pass holders will have to fork out for the Kita-kinki Tango Tetsudō part of the route.

A bus runs from Kyoto's Shijo-Kawaramachi to Amanohashidate (¥2700/5000 one way/return, 3½ hours).

Getting Around
You can cross the 'bridge to heaven' on foot, bicycle or on a motorcycle of less than 125cc capacity. Bicycles can be hired at a number of places for ¥400 for two hours or ¥1600 a day. Tour boats also operate across Miyazu-wan.

TANGO-HANTŌ 丹後半島
☎ 0772

Travelling westward, Amanohashidate marks the start of the Tango-hantō, jutting north into the Sea of Japan. A coast road runs around the peninsula, passing a number of small scenic fishing ports. The village of Ine, on a perfect little bay, is particularly interesting, with *funaya* houses that are built right out over the water, under which boats are drawn in, as if in a car port.

From the hilltop Funaya-no-Sato-kōen, where the tourist information office (☎ 32-0277) has Japanese maps and brochures (open from 9 am to 6 pm, closed Tuesday), there's a fine view over the harbour. Below the park, Ine-wan Meguri tour boats putter around the bay (¥650, 30 minutes). There are no services in January and February.

There are several fine minshuku in the town including *Yoza-sō* (☎ 32-0278), which

WESTERN HONSHŪ

charges ¥8000, with two meals. Buses reach Ine in half an hour from Amanohashidate. The fare is ¥1100.

At the end of the peninsula, a large car park and restaurant mark the start of the one-hour round-trip walk to the **Kyōga-saki Lighthouse**.

KINOSAKI 城崎
☎ 0796

In the north part of Hyōgo-ken, the little onsen town of Kinosaki makes a pleasant overnight excursion from Kyoto, Osaka or Kōbe. It is a laid-back place to roam around and soak in hot springs. **Gokuraku-ji** in the town centre has a good miniature rock landscape garden.

Kinosaki's biggest attraction is its hot-spring bathhouses, of which there are six open to the public (¥300). Guests staying in town stroll the canal from bath to bath donning *yukata* (summer kimono) and *geta* (wooden sandals). Most of the ryokan and hotels in town also have their own *uchi-yu* (private baths), but also provide their guests with free tickets to the ones outside *(soto-yu)*.

Savoury crab from the Sea of Japan is a speciality in Kinosaki during the winter months. On October 14 and 15 the **Danjiri Matsuri** sees teams of *mikoshi*-bearers clashing for pole position to get to the local shrine, jostling each other with the huge portable shrines. It sometimes turns bloody!

Information
There is a tourist information centre (☎ 32-3663), open from 9 am to 5 pm, closed Wednesday, in the JR Kinosaki station; and also a ryokan reservation centre (☎ 32-4141), which can provide accommodation help and also make bookings (8 am to 6 pm). Japanese only is spoken.

Places to Stay
There is a slew of mostly expensive accommodation in town, though if you don't mind paying a bit of money, Kinosaki is a great place to experience a night in a traditional Japanese inn. The ultimate of inns here is the classic *Nishimura Honkan Ryokan* (☎ 32-2211), with per person rates starting at ¥28,000.

Other more affordable options, where some English is spoken, are *Tsutaya* (☎ 32-2511) along the canal, as well as *Mikuniya* (☎ 32-2414), in front of the JR Kinosaki station. Both have per person rates with two meals starting at ¥15,000. A touch more expensive, *Yutōya* (☎ 32-2121) charges ¥16,000.

Getting There & Away
Trains run to Kinosaki from Kyoto (¥4710, two hours 40 minutes). From Amanohashidate, change trains at Toyo'oka (on the JR Miyazu line) to the San-in line to go to Kinosaki or the caves, Gembu-dō.

Northern Honshū (Tōhoku)

As we turn the corners of the narrow road to the deep north, we may soar with exhilaration, or we may fall flat on our faces...

Bashō, 1644–94

The northern part of Honshū, known in Japanese as Tōhoku, comprises the prefectures of Fukushima-ken, Miyagi-ken, Iwate-ken, Aomori-ken, Akita-ken and Yamagata-ken. This chapter begins with Fukushima-ken, then moves north along the eastern side of Tōhoku, continues round the northern tip, and finally travels down the western side covering Niigata-ken and the island, Sado-ga-shima.

At the turn of the 19th century, a popular saying in Edo (Tokyo) joked that in Tōhoku, 'you can buy a mountain for a penny'. While the budget traveller will certainly regret this isn't the case now, for those who want to see traditional rural life and enjoy vast areas of unspoilt natural scenery, the relative 'backwardness' of this mostly mountainous region provides a strong incentive to visit.

The few major cities generally merit no more than a cursory stop before heading off into the back country, which offers hikes along spectacular rocky coastlines or in volcanic regions, where scores of hot springs are tucked away in the mountains. Several excellent ski resorts benefit from the long and severe winters and heavy snowfalls. Tōhoku is also studded with cultural sights – temples, *samurai* villas, traditional farmhouses and vibrant festivals.

The region was originally inhabited by a people known in previous centuries as the Ezo. The Ezo are believed to have been related to the Ainu, who now live in Hokkaidō. Although the Ezo were conquered and pushed back during the Kamakura period, it wasn't until the 17th century that the area came under complete government control.

During the Meiji era, the region suffered from years of neglect. This trend was only

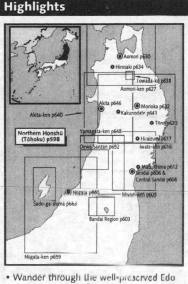

Highlights

- Wander through the well-preserved Edo era post town of Ōuchijuku.
- Experience the peaceful beauty of Miyagi-ken's Kinkazan Island.
- Visit the historic town of Hiraizumi, home to some of Tōhoku's finest temples.
- Stroll around the scenic tree-lined streets of Kakunodate's historic samurai district.
- View Dewa Sanzan, a trio of sacred peaks that have attracted Buddhist pilgrims for more than 1400 years.
- Enjoy the beautiful island seascapes, sleepy fishing villages, rural temples and colourful festivals on the island of Sado-ga-shima.

reversed after WWII, with a drive for development based heavily on industrial growth. Despite this, the region still relies heavily on agriculture and many Japanese consider it a place in the back of beyond – an economic laggard compared to the rest of Japan.

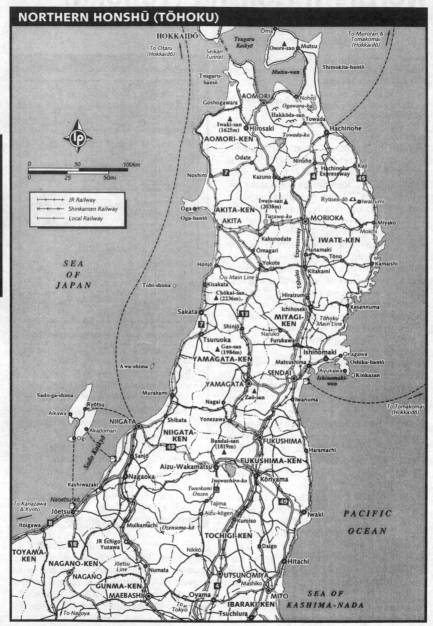

NORTHERN HONSHŪ (TŌHOKU)

Suggested Itineraries

In addition to straight coastal or central routes, the following are interesting, yet practical, east-west tours:

In Bashō's footsteps (two weeks) Matsu-shima–Kinkazan–Hiraizumi–Naruko Onsen-Kisakata–Sakata/Tsuruoka–Dewa Sanzan–Yamadera
Festive Far North (one week) Aomori Nebuta Matsuri–Hirosaki Neputa Matsuri–Tazawa-ko & Nyūtō Onsen–Kakunodate–Akita Kantō Matsuri.

Both itineraries are best in summer, but remember to book accommodation well in advance if you plan to travel during festival times.

Information

As Tōhoku is less travelled by foreigners, and sources of tourist information about it are less common outside major cities, your queries may be answered more easily by phoning the Japan Travel-Phone toll free on ☎ 0088-22-4800 (see the Facts for the Visitor chapter).

Exploring Tōhoku by Jan Brown is a detailed guide to the region that provides comprehensive background information on sights, including useful indexes with place names in *kanji* (Chinese script used for writing Japanese). The Tōhoku Tourism Promotion Council publishes *Japan Tōhoku*, a glossy brochure that includes an English map and details of sights, festivals and transport.

For some literary refreshment en route you could dip into any of the many translations of *Oku-no-Hosomichi (The Narrow Road to the Deep North)*, which contains classic *haiku* penned by Bashō, perhaps the most famous Japanese poet, on his travels through central and southern Tōhoku in 1689. If you'd like to bring yourself up to date, read *The Narrow Road to the Deep North: Journey into Lost Japan*, by Lesley Downer, which is an account of a walk that retraced Bashō's celebrated trip.

Getting Around

Transport in the region focuses on three major railway lines: two of these run north-south down the east and west coasts and the third snakes down between them in the centre, closely following the Japan Railways (JR) Tōhoku *shinkansen* (bullet train) line, which links Tokyo with Morioka in the lightning time of 2¼ hours. Transport in the region has accelerated with the opening of the 1997 Akita shinkansen line running west from Morioka to Akita and the recent extension of the Yamagata shinkansen north to Shinjō.

Exploration of the more remote parts of Tōhoku, particularly if you're zigzagging from east to west, requires a greater amount of time chugging patiently along local railway lines or winding up mountains on local bus services.

Fukushima-ken

AIZU-WAKAMATSU 会津若松
☎ 0242

During feudal times, this castle town developed into a stronghold for the Matsudaira clan. The clan later remained loyal to the Tokugawa shogunate during the Edo period then briefly defied imperial forces in the Boshin Civil War (at the start of the Meiji era). The resistance was crushed and the town went up in flames – the heroic 'last stand of the samurai'.

The tourist information office (☎ 32-0688) is inside Aizu-Wakamatsu station (10 am to 6 pm, until 5 pm Sunday). Detailed English-language maps of the area that are excellent for orientation are available. The tourist information office at the castle, Tsuruga-jō, also has English-language material on hand.

The Japan National Tourist Organization (JNTO) leaflet *Aizu-Wakamatsu and Bandai* has good transport maps and details of sights and accommodation in the area.

Iimori-yama 飯盛山

The mountain, Iimori-yama, is renowned as the spot where teenage members of the Byakkotai (White Tigers Band) retreated from imperial forces and committed ritual suicide in 1868. The standard account of this tragedy maintains that the boys killed themselves after they looked down from the

NORTHERN HONSHŪ

hilltop and thought they saw the town and its castle go up in flames; in reality, only the town was alight – the Meiji government did not get around to razing the castle until 1874 – and it would be weeks until the town was finally defeated by food shortages.

The graves of 19 Byakkotai members are lined up on the hill. The event has received attention not only from Japanese admirers of loyalty but also from foreigners with similar sentiments. Close to the graves are two monuments, one from a German military attache and another from Italian fascists. Some of the inscriptions were erased by the US military occupation force after WWII but were later restored.

Apart from the **Byakkotai Kinenkan** (Byakkotai Memorial Hall; ¥400), there's also **Sazae-dō**, an 18th-century hexagonal hall with an intricate set of double spiral staircases arranged around 33 Kannon (a Buddhist goddess of mercy) images, representing the famous pilgrimage of Kansai (¥300, 8.15 am to sunset, 9.30 am to 4.30 pm in winter).

The hill is a 15-minute bus ride from the train station and can be climbed on foot; alternatively, use the hillside escalator (¥250). Bus No 15 from the station stops at Iimoriyama (¥220) before continuing to Tsuruga-jō, stopping first at Aizu Bukeyashiki, but only between 10 am and 3 pm.

Tsuruga-jō 鶴ヶ城

Tsuruga-jō is nicknamed Crane Castle, and the present building is a 20th-century reconstruction containing an historical museum (¥400, 8.30 am to 4.30 pm). Also on the castle grounds is **Rinkaku**, a 400-year-old teahouse that was rescued from the castle's destruction by a local family and returned here in 1990 (¥200, combined ticket with castle entry ¥500, 10 am to 3 pm).

Take bus No 14 from the train station and get off at Tsuruga-jō-kitaguchi (¥210). The bus then continues to Iimori-yama, stopping first at Aizu Bukeyashiki, but only between 10.30 am and 3.30 pm.

Oyaku-en 御薬園

Oyaku-en is a splendid garden complete with a tea arbour, a large central carp pond

and a section devoted to the cultivation of medicinal herbs, as encouraged by former Aizu lords (¥310, 8.30 am to 5 pm). In the souvenir shop you can sample herbal tea and purchase packets of *daimyō* (domain lords) herbal brew.

From the train station, take bus No 3 bound for Higashiyama Onsen and get off at the Oyaku-en Iriguchi stop (¥250, 10 minutes). Later, you can continue via the same bus to Aizu Bukeyashiki.

Aizu Bukeyashiki 会津武家屋敷

This is an interesting large-scale reconstruction of an opulent samurai villa from the Edo period (¥850). An English leaflet and map are provided to guide yourself around dozens of rooms, from the kitchen to the principal residence (8.30 am to 5 pm, 9 am to 4.30 pm from December to March). Take bus No 3 from the station bound for Higashiyama Onsen and get off at the Bukeyashiki-mae stop (¥290, 15 minutes).

Other Attractions

Two blocks north of Tsuruga-jō, **Aizu Sake History Museum** is housed in an historic brewery where local *sake* is still produced and mannequins demonstrate the Edo-period production processes (¥300, 9 am to 4.30 pm). Behind a distinctive Western-style facade, **Shirokiya** produces the city's most distinguished lacquerware and exhibits it in an attached museum (free, 9 am to 5.30 pm). The store is two blocks west of the post office, a 10-minute ride south of Aizu-Wakamatsu station (¥160).

Special Events

The Aizu Aki Matsuri (Aizu Fall Festival), held from 22 to 24 September, features a parade on the 23rd with large wheeled shrines and participants dressed as daimyō and their retainers.

Places to Stay

The tourist information office can provide an English-language map detailing budget and mid-range accommodation options.

Aizu-no-Sato Youth Hostel (☎ 0241-27-2054) is a 10-minute walk from Shiokawa station, which is 10km from Aizu-Waka-matsu and a little closer to Kitakata. This extremely basic hostel charges ¥2200 per person and is part of a liquor store. Although inconveniently located, *Aizuno Youth Hostel (☎ 55-1020)* makes for a more pleasant stay and charges ¥3200. This hostel is a 20-minute walk from Aizu-Takada station, 20 minutes from Aizu-Wakamatsu (¥230) on the scenic JR Tadami line. Trains along this line are extremely infrequent except in the late afternoon.

A *minshuku* (family-run budget accommodation) option is *Minshuku Takizawa (☎ 25-3183)*, which costs ¥5500 per person with two meals. Walk straight out from the station for about 10 minutes and turn left at the intersection with a McDonald's on one corner; the minshuku is up a side street on the right past the police station. The lovely *Minshuku Takaku (☎ 26-6299)* charges only slightly higher rates for better-quality accommodation. It's a five-minute walk east of Aizu Bukeyashiki.

Just south of Aizu-Wakamatsu station is the *Eki-mae Fuji Grand Hotel (☎ 24-1111)*, with singles from ¥4800 and not too-cramped twins and doubles from ¥9800.

Places to Eat
The main eating and drinking area is around Nanokamachi-dōri, a 20-minute walk south of the train station along Chūō-dōri. The best value for lunch is at *Hyōtan-zushi*, where ¥500 buys you unbelievably delicious *ten-don* (lightly battered seafood and vegetables, over rice). The restaurant is two blocks south of the Ichi-no-machi bus stop. On the same side-street is *Takino*, a famous traditional-style restaurant serving *wappa-meishi* (seasonal meat and vegetables served over rice in a steamer). Very close to Shirokiya lacquerware shop, the equally renowned *Matsutaya* serves mouth-watering *dengaku*, which are snacks grilled in sweet *miso* (soya-bean paste).

Getting There & Away
From Tokyo, take the JR Tōhoku shinkansen to Kōriyama then change to a *kaisoku* (a

rapid service stopping at limited stations) train on the JR Banetsu-sai line for Aizu-Wakamatsu (¥9330, three hours). There is only one daily kaisoku train between Aizu-Wakamatsu and Niigata (¥2210, 2½ hours), but express buses from the Aizu-Wakamatsu station run to Niigata four times daily (¥2000, 1¾ hours).

If you're heading to Nikkō (¥3380, 3½ hours) or Asakusa (¥4540, 5¼ hours), you can take a combination of private train lines from JR Aizu-Wakamatsu station via Yunokami Onsen and Aizu-Kōgen station, eventually transferring to a train bound for Asakusa via Shimo-imaichi (where you can connect with trains to Tōbu-Nikkō station). All trains run frequently and connections are usually good, except at Shimo-imaichi.

Getting Around
From Aizu-Wakamatsu station, two bus lines conveniently circle the main sights – No 15 runs clockwise and No 14 anticlockwise. Bus No 3 passes Oyaku-en and Aizu Bukeyashiki on the way to Higashiyama Onsen. All buses run frequently; a one-day pass costs ¥920.

ŌUCHIJUKU 大内宿
An important post town on the Aizu Nishi-kaidō route, as well as a battle site during the Boshin Civil War, Ōuchijuku was forgotten after the construction of a new highway farther east. Now designated as a special preservation area for historic buildings, the town's main street is lined with an impressive number of traditional inns, farmhouses, restaurants and shops, all earning their livelihood from travellers much as they did during the Edo era. The Ōuchijuku Cultural Museum (Ōuchijuku Machinami Tenjikan) is a reconstruction of an inn that was originally used by travelling feudal lords (¥250, 9 am to 4.30 pm).

After meandering through town, turn off at the *torii* (Shintō shrine entrance gate) and follow a dirt road out into the fields to the shrine, Takakura-jinja, dedicated to Prince Mochihito Takakura, the second son of Emperor Goshirakawa, who allegedly fled here after being defeated by the Heike clan. On 2 July, the festival, **Hange Matsuri**, commemorates his flight with a feudal procession through town.

Ōuchijuku is best visited as a day trip from Aizu-Wakamatsu, but there are also a dozen or so minshuku that can put you up for the night for around ¥6500 per person, including two meals.

From JR Aizu-Wakamatsu station, take the private Aizu Tetsudō line to Yunokami Onsen (¥1000, 40 minutes), from where you could later continue to Tokyo (Asakusa) or Nikkō (see the Aizu-Wakamatsu Getting There & Away section earlier). There is no bus service to Ōuchijuku from Yunokami Onsen, but you can walk or hitch the 6km along Route 329 in about an hour (a taxi costs ¥5000). Ask the staff at the train station for an English-language pamphlet on Ōuchijuku and a sketch map before you head out.

KITAKATA 喜多方
☎ 0241

Just 20 minutes by train (¥320) from Aizu-Wakamatsu, Kitakata is famed for its thousands of coloured *kura* (mud-walled storehouses), which come in all sorts of colour schemes and now function as living quarters, stores and workshops. Some are still used as sake breweries, and a few of these will let you in to peer at the production process.

The tourist information office (☎ 24-2633) outside Kitakata station can provide an English-language map for self-guided wandering – allow three hours at an easy pace. Bicycle rental is also available near the station, and a horse-drawn tourist carriage (a sort of double-decker 'kuramobile') does the rounds in 1½ hours (¥1300); the commentary is in Japanese only.

Brick-built, Western-style kura can be seen at the tiny town of **Mitsuya**, 6km north of Kitakata on Route 121. Take a bus bound for Hirasawa via Negoya and get off at the Mitsuya stop (¥380, 15 minutes, six per day between 6.50 am and 5.40 pm).

The community of **Sugiyama**, 3km farther north from Mitsuya on the same bus line, is almost solid with kura, all of which

---

Targeting Tourists' Tastebuds

As it stood, Kitakata was already an attractive little town, with its well-preserved traditional inns, *sake* breweries and *kura* (storehouses). But as Japan soared toward the peak of its mid-1980s economic boom, locals felt the town needed something more to attract tourist dollars. Enter the now-renowned Kitakata *rāmen* (Chinese egg noodles in a soup).

This was not exactly a new trick – you can't swing a dead cat in Japan without hitting some place touting its 'famous' variety of the ubiquitous soup noodle dish. The Kitakata version got its start at the Genraiken restaurant, and its inventive twist was special wavy noodles designed to 'catch' as much clear pork broth as possible.

Not the stuff of culinary fantasy perhaps. But the recipe seems to have struck a chord with Japanese tourists and Kitakata is now home to a staggering 66 rāmen shops. If you want to try the original, Genraiken is a 10-minute walk from the station (closed Tuesday). Staff at the Kitakata tourist information office will gladly show you how to get there with their *Kitakata Rāmen Daisuki* (I love Kitakata Rāmen) map.

---

are still in private hands. The appropriate bus stop is Jirikyoku-mae (¥470).

Seven kilometres south-west of Kitakata station is **Kumano-jinja**, a shrine renowned for its Nagatoko-dō (Nagatoko Hall), which was built more than 900 years ago and has neither walls nor doors – more than 40 massive columns support the roof. From the station, take a bus to Shingū (¥470, 25 minutes, six per day).

Places to Stay
Although Kitakata is an easy day trip from Aizu-Wakamatsu, die-hard kura fans could stay at the friendly *Kura Inn Sasaya Ryokan* (☎ 22-0008), 1km north of the train station. Rates are ¥8500 per person, including two meals. (A *ryokan* is a traditional Japanese inn.)

INAWASHIRO-KO
猪苗代湖
☎ 0242

Although it's the fourth-largest lake in Japan, Inawashiro-ko is really nothing special, and the town of Inawashiro is mostly a stop en route to the more scenic area around the mountain, Bandai-san. The tourist information office (☎ 62-2048) outside JR Inawashiro station has maps and useful information on the lake and Bandai-kōgen. It's open from 8.30 am to 5.15 pm. Ten minutes by bus from Inawashiro station is **Aizu Minzokukan** (¥500), a folk museum with two Edo-period farmhouses, a mill and a candle-making shop (8 am to 5 pm, 8.30 am to 4.30 pm from mid-November to March, closed Thursday).

The JR Banetsu-sai line connects Aizu-Wakamatsu with Inawashiro station (kaisoku, ¥480, 35 minutes). Hourly buses between Aizu-Wakamatsu station and Inawashiro station (¥1140, 45 minutes) run along the lake shore past the folk museum. From Inawashiro station you can catch fairly frequent buses up to Bandai-kōgen.

BANDAI-SAN & BANDAI-KŌGEN
磐梯山・磐梯高原
☎ 0241

Bandai-san erupted on 15 July 1888 and destroyed dozens of villages and their inhabitants. At the same time it completely rearranged the landscape, creating the plateau, Bandai-kōgen, and damming local rivers, which then formed numerous lakes and ponds. Now a national park, the whole area offers spectacular scenery, and there's ample scope for walks or long hikes, plus skiing in winter.

The most popular walk, sometimes jammed with hikers from one end to the other, takes about an hour and follows a trail around Goshiki-numa (Five-Coloured Lakes). The trailheads for the Goshiki-numa walk are at Goshiki-numa Iriguchi

NORTHERN HONSHŪ

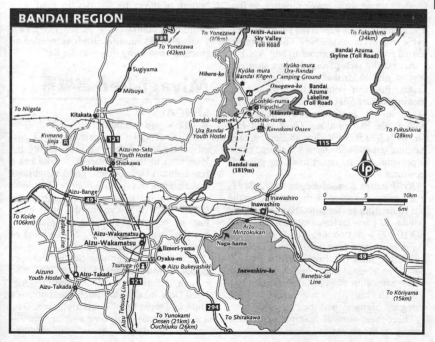

and Bandai-Kōgen-eki, the main transport hub on the edge of Hibara-ko. Along with pleasure-boat rides there are various walking trails on the eastern shore of Hibara-ko, and on the shores of nearby **Onogawa-ko** and **Akimoto-ko**.

The visitors centre (8.30 am to 4 pm, closed Wednesday), near the Goshiki-numa Iriguchi trailhead, and the Ura-Bandai Youth Hostel (see Places to Stay) both have maps in Japanese outlining routes and approximate times for hikes in the area. The most popular hiking destination is **Bandai-san** (1819m), which can be climbed in a day if you start as early as possible. A popular route for this hike starts from Bandai-Kōgen-eki and climbs up through the skiing ground to the summit.

Places to Stay

Ura Bandai Youth Hostel (☎ 32-2811) is a little the worse for wear, but it's in a quiet spot next to one of the trailheads for the Goshiki-numa walk, seven minutes on foot from the Goshiki-numa Iriguchi bus stop. The hostel charges ¥2850 per person and bicycle rental is available. The hostel is closed from late November to late April.

Across the street from the bus stop is a row of minshuku that cater to hikers and skiers. First on your right, the modern-looking *Resort Shiki* (☎ 32-2155) has nice Japanese-style rooms for ¥7000 per person with meals. Farther along, *Goshiki-no-Hotori* (☎ 32-2356/2671) has an English sign hanging outside and charges the same rates. It provides free transport to skiing grounds in winter.

Kyūkamura Bandai-Kōgen (☎ 32-2421) is in a remote location, at the last stop on the bus route from Inawashiro, 10 minutes past Bandai-Kōgen-eki. Rates range from ¥8500 to ¥10,000 with two meals.

For more upmarket accommodation look no farther than the *Fraser Hotel* (☎ 32-3470), an elegant European-style pension where rates start at ¥12,000, including two meals. The hotel is a few minutes' walk along the highway past the bus stop.

There are several camping grounds nearby on the shores of Hibara-ko.

Getting There & Away

There is one direct bus per day from Aizu-Wakamatsu to Bandai-Kōgen-eki (¥1670, 1½ hours); otherwise, a change of bus is required at Inawashiro station. Frequent buses leave from Inawashiro before 6 pm and pass by the Goshiki-numa Iriguchi stop (¥750, 25 minutes) and Bandai-Kōgen-eki (¥870, 30 minutes) before continuing to the terminus at Kyūkamura Bandai-Kōgen.

Between Bandai-Kōgen-eki and Fukushima there is a bus service along two scenic toll roads – Bandai Azuma Lakeline and Bandai Azuma Skyline (¥2870, three hours). There are two to three buses daily from late April to early November. The trip provides great views of the mountains and is highly recommended if you are a fan of volcanic panoramas. The bus makes a 30-minute stop at Jōdodaira, a superb lookout, where you can climb to the top of Azumakofuji (1707m) in 10 minutes and, if you still feel energetic, scramble down to the bottom of the crater. Across the road is Issaikyō-yama (1949m), which belches steam, in dramatic contrast to its passive neighbour; a steepish 45-minute climb is needed to reach the sweeping views at the top.

Miyagi-ken 宮城県

SENDAI 仙台
☎ 022 • pop 100,000

Sendai is Tōhoku's largest and most cosmopolitan city. If you've been hiking the long road to the deep north, Sendai has a few cultural sights, some good restaurants and a couple of nightlife options (but don't get too excited). Those coming from the bright lights of Tokyo, on the other hand, may be better off skipping the place and heading straight to nearby Matsushima or the coastal towns farther north.

The dominant figure in Sendai's history is Date Masamune (1567–1636), who earned the nickname Dokuganryū (One-Eyed Dragon) after he caught smallpox as a child and went blind in his right eye. Date adopted Sendai as his base and, in a combination of military might and administrative

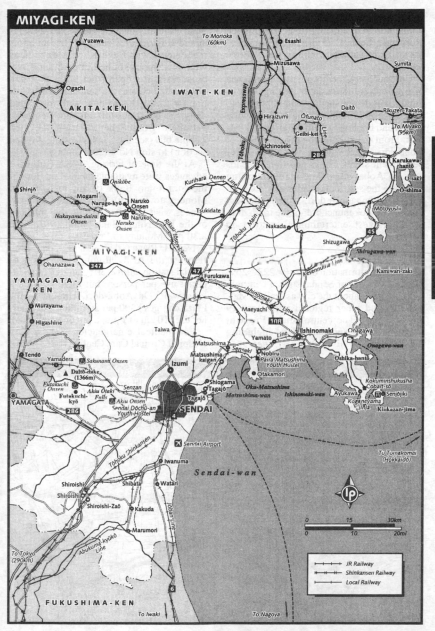

skills, became one of the most powerful feudal lords in Japan. An accomplished artist and scholar, Date also raised Sendai to the status of cultural centre of the Tōhoku region.

Unfortunately, there's not much evidence of high culture these days. During WWII, Sendai was demolished by Allied bombing, and the city was later rebuilt with wide streets and boulevards laid out in a grid pattern. From the station, the broad sweep of Aoba-dōri, lined with many of the major department stores, banks and hotels, leads west to Aoba-yama. The main shopping areas are the series of arcades along Chūō-dōri and Ichibanchō-dōri, which intersect just east of Kokubunchō-dōri, the main drag of the largest entertainment district in Tōhoku.

Information

The tourist information office (☎ 222-3269) on the 2nd floor of Sendai station can help with inquiries about the city as well as Matsushima and other regional attractions (9 am to 8 pm). The centre stocks English-language maps and pamphlets, including the detailed *Sendai: How to Get There*.

Near the Sendai City Museum, the Sendai International Centre (☎ 265-2471) is aimed at foreign residents but has an information desk with English-speaking staff, as well as a library, bulletin board and CNN broadcasts. It's open from 9 am to 8 pm. The centre operates the Sendai English Hotline (☎ 224-1919) to help with travel and daily-life questions (10 am and 8 pm). To get there from Sendai station take the Loople bus (see the Sendai Getting Around section) to stop No 5 (20 minutes).

At the time of writing, VISA card cash advances were available on the 2nd floor of the Sumitomo Bank (9 am to 5.20 pm, Monday to Friday). For MasterCard advances, visit UC Card Co, on the 3rd floor of the Kita-Nihon Bank building (9 am to 5.30 pm, Monday to Friday).

Netto U Plaza (10 am to 8 pm), on the 5th floor of the AER building, just north of Sendai station, allows 30 minutes of free Internet use per person, but there is often a long wait. On Aoba-dōri, Hitachi's HIT Plaza charges ¥300 per 30 minutes of Internet use (10 am to 7 pm, 6 pm on weekends).

For medical emergencies, Sendai City Hospital Critical Care Centre (☎ 263-9900)

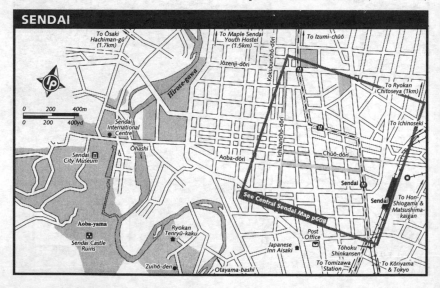

SENDAI

at 3-1 Shimizu Kōji, Wakabayashi-ku, and Sendai Open Hospital Critical Care Centre (☎ 252-0100) at 5-22-1 Tsurugoya, Miyogine-ku, are open 24 hours.

Zuihō-den 瑞鳳殿

Zuihō-den, the mausoleum of Date Masamune, was originally built in 1637 but was later destroyed by bombing in WWII. The present building is an exact replica of the original, faithful to the ornate and sumptuous style of the Momoyama period (¥550, 9 am to 4.30 pm, until 4 pm from November to March). From Sendai station, take the Loople bus to stop No 4 (15 minutes).

Sendai City Museum 仙台市博物館

Interesting exhibitions of art and samurai armour, as well as a scale model of Sendai-jō, make this museum a worthwhile stop (¥400, 9 am to 4.15 pm, closed Monday). From Sendai station, take the Loople bus to stop No 5 (20 minutes).

Sendai-jō Ruins 仙台城跡

Sendai-jō was built on Aoba-yama in 1602 by Date Masamune. It was nicknamed Aoba-jō (Green Leaves Castle) for a nearby spring that flowed even during times of drought. The castle's partial destruction during the Meiji era was completed by bombing in WWII. The castle ruins – a restored *sumiyagura* (turret) and that's about it – are presided over by a statue of Date on horseback. At the **Aoba Castle Exhibition Hall**, a CAD (computer-aided design) film depicts the castle's former glory – English-language headsets are available (¥700, 9 am to 4.30 pm, closing earlier in winter). From Sendai station, take the Loople bus to stop No 6 (22 minutes).

Ōsaki Hachiman-gū 大崎八幡神社

The shrine, Ōsaki Hachiman-gū, has peaceful grounds that date from the 12th century. The main hall, a National Treasure dating from 1607, is a luxurious, black-lacquered edifice with eye-catching carved designs. Entry is free and the shrine closes at sunset. From Sendai station, take a bus from stop No 10 and get off at Hachimangū-mae (¥220, 15 minutes).

Special Events

The **Tanabata Matsuri** (Star Festival), held from 6 to 8 August, is the big tourist event in Sendai. According to Chinese legend, a princess and a peasant shepherd were in love but forbidden to meet. The only time of year when the star-crossed lovers could sneak a tryst was when the stars Vega and Altair met in the Milky Way on 7 July. Sendai seems to have stretched the dates a bit, but celebrates in grand style by decorating the main streets and holding afternoon parades along Jōzenji-dōri. Several million visitors ensure that accommodation is booked solid at this time.

On the second Sunday in September, up to 250 busker bands from across Japan perform during the **Jōzenji Street Jazz Festival**.

If you're in Sendai on the evening of 14 January, Ōsaki Hachiman-gū is the main host for **Donto-sai**, a festival in which men brave subzero weather conditions to hop around almost naked in a show of collective madness.

Places to Stay – Budget

The closest youth hostel to the city centre is the cosy *Ryokan Chitoseya* (☎ 222-6329), a 20-minute walk from the western exit of Sendai station. If you want to give your feet a rest, take any bus going via Miyamachi from stop No 17 at Sendai station, and get off at Miyamachi ni-chōme. The hostel is tucked down a small side street three blocks east of the bus stop and charges ¥3000 per person.

Sendai Dōchu-an Youth Hostel (☎ 247-0511), about 5km south of Sendai in an old farmhouse, has a high reputation for hospitality to foreigners. The discounted nightly rate for foreigners is ¥2950 and bicycle rental is available. From Sendai station, take the subway to Tomizawa then walk for 10 minutes to the hostel. Alternatively, you can walk to the hostel in 20 minutes from JR Nagamachi station, one stop south of Sendai.

The bland *Maple Sendai Youth Hostel* (☎ 234-3922) is inconveniently located in

NORTHERN HONSHŪ

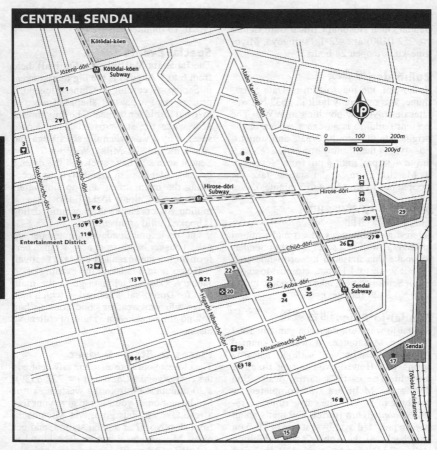

CENTRAL SENDAI

the northern part of the city and charges ¥2800. From stop No 24 in front of the Sendai Hotel, take a bus going via Shihei-chō to the Tōhokukai Byōin-mae stop (¥180, 15 minutes). The hostel is on the northern side of the hospital, hidden in an alley. Ask the tourist information office to mark the location on a map before heading out.

Places to Stay – Mid-Range
Ryokan There are a few ryokan to choose from. Next to Hirose-dōri subway station, the stylish *Takenaka Ryokan* (☎ 225-6771) charges ¥4500 per person without meals.

Five minutes farther from the station, the welcoming *Ryokan Iwai* (☎ 222-7041) charges the same rates.

Japanese Inn Aisaki (☎ 264-0700), a member of the Japanese Inn group, is near the post office, a 15-minute walk from Sendai station. Prices for singles/twins start at ¥4700/8400 without meals.

Just below the entrance to Zuihō-den, *Ryokan Tenryū-kaku* (☎ 222-9957) is in a peaceful setting surrounded by trees and greenery. Rooms with two meals cost ¥6500 per person and guests have free access to hot-springs baths.

CENTRAL SENDAI

PLACES TO STAY
7 Takenaka Ryokan
竹中旅館
8 Ryokan Iwai
旅館いわい
15 Sendai Kokusai Hotel
仙台国際ホテル
16 Hotel Central Sendai
ホテルセントラル仙台
17 Hotel Metropolitan
Sendai
21 Tokyo Dai-Ichi Hotel
Sendai
東京第一ホテル仙台

PLACES TO EAT
1 Häagen Dazs
Ice Cream
2 Hoshiyama
Kōhī-ten
ホシヤマ珈琲店

4 Yoshinoya
吉野家
5 Tonton Rāmen;
Soba-no-Kanda;
Don-tei
とんとんラーメン；
そばの神田；どん亭
6 Asian Kitchen
10 Mister Donut
13 Pronto
22 McDonald's
28 Sari
左利

OTHER
3 Simon's Bar
9 Tower Records
11 HMV
12 Bar Isn't It?
14 Maruzen Bookstore
丸善書店

18 Kita-Nihon Bank
北日本銀行
19 Sendai Orthodox Church
ハリストス正教会
20 Daiei Department Store
ダイエー
23 Sumitomo Bank
住友銀行
24 HIT Plaza
25 Ticket OFF
チケットOFF
26 Vilevan
27 Tokyo Ticket
東京チケット
29 AER Building;
Netto U Plaza
アエル
30 Bus Stop No 40
バス乗り場40番
31 Bus Stop No 41
バス乗り場41番

NORTHERN HONSHŪ

Hotels The city centre is packed with business hotels. One of the cheapest is the new *Hotel Central Sendai* (☎ 711-4111), with singles from ¥6800 to ¥8000 and doubles/twins for ¥12,000/13,500. In the centre of town, the *Tokyo Dai-Ichi Hotel Sendai* (☎ 262-1355) has quality singles/twins starting from ¥7000/14,000.

Places to Stay – Top End
There are many top-end alternatives to these cheaper business hotels. A 10-minute walk from the station, the classy *Sendai Kokusai Hotel* (☎ 268-1112) has singles/doubles for ¥11,500/18,000.

Places to Eat
Steer yourself in the direction of the shopping arcades along Chūō-dōri and Ichibanchō-dōri, where you'll find dozens of restaurants serving everything from fast-food pasta and *sushi* to upmarket Japanese and international cuisine.

Off the eastern end of Chūō-dōri, *Sari* serves up Sendai's speciality, *gyūtan* (grilled beef tongue), for ¥700 or in combi-

nation with different set meals. Along Ichibanchō-dōri arcade, *Asian Kitchen* serves pan-Asian cuisine in the style of an *izakaya* (pub/eatery) from ¥500 per dish.

Some of Sendai's most affordable eating options are found along Hirose-dōri. At *Soba-no-Kanda*, noodle dishes all cost less than ¥400. Upstairs is *Don-tei*, where a generous serving of *ten-don* (tempura over rice) costs ¥680. Next door, *Tonton Rāmen* serves up huge bowls of noodles for under ¥900.

During summer, several rooftop beer gardens open on top of department stores and hotels, charging around ¥2000 for all-you-can-drink (and sometimes eat) specials.

The 'most prestigious coffee in Sendai' can be found at *Hoshiyama Kōhii-ten*, where impeccably mannered staff serve hand-brewed java at ¥800 to ¥1000 per cup. It's an experience.

Entertainment
For a couple of affordable beers with your meal, the best option is *Vilevan*. It was formerly called the Village Vanguard, but

apparently the original New York establishment got wind of this and suggested a name change. This laid-back jazz bar and restaurant is open from 11 am to midnight, with live performances on some weekends. The menu specialises in garlic dishes and has an extensive list of vegetarian options.

In the Ichibanchō-dōri arcades the enormous *Bar Isn't It?* prices all food and drinks at ¥500, with ¥300 drink specials on Thursday and a two-for-one happy hour on most other days.

The northern end of Kokubunchō-dōri makes for an interesting evening stroll but doesn't offer much that the average traveller could afford. One pub that occasionally gets foreign customers is *Simon's Bar*. There's no service charge if you're willing to stand at the bar, and drinks are reasonably priced from ¥450.

Getting There & Away

Discount train and flight tickets are available a short distance from Sendai station at Ticket OFF and Tokyo Ticket.

Air From Sendai airport, 18km south of the city centre, there are international flights to Seoul, Beijing, Guam, Hong Kong, Shanghai and Honolulu. Domestic destinations include Osaka, Kansai, Sapporo, Nagoya, Fukuoka and Okinawa. If you are travelling from Tokyo, the shinkansen is so fast that it's not really sensible to take a plane.

Train From Sendai, the JR Tōhoku shinkansen line runs south to Tokyo in only two hours (¥10,080) and north to Morioka in just over an hour (¥5780). At Morioka, you can transfer to the Akita shinkansen line. The JR Senzan line connects Sendai with Yamagata (kaisoku, ¥1110, one hour). Matsushima-kaigan is linked with Sendai by the JR Senseki line (kaisoku, ¥400, 25 minutes).

Bus Sendai has a huge – and initially confusing – network of bus services and over 40 stops scattered around JR Sendai station. The tourist information office has a bilingual leaflet listing relevant bus numbers and bus destinations, and the names of the appropriate bus stops.

From stop No 42 outside Sendai station's eastern exit, there are a few day buses to Shinjuku (¥6210, 5½ hours) and Niigata (¥4500, four hours).

North of the station, day and night buses to Tokyo depart from stop No 41 (¥6210, 7¼ hours) at noon and 11 pm. From stop No 40 across the street, there is a night bus to Kyoto and Osaka departing at 7.30 pm (¥12,230, 12¼ hours) as well as day buses to Morioka (¥2850, 2¾ hours), Akita (¥4000, 3¾ hours) and Aomori (¥5700, 1¾ hours). Discounted return tickets are available for most routes.

Boat Sendai-kō is a major port with ferries once or twice daily to Tomakomai on Hokkaidō (¥6300 to ¥7600, 15 to 16½ hours). Ferries depart at noon every second day for Nagoya (¥4900, 21 hours).

To get to Sendai-kō, take a *futsū* (local) train on the JR Senseki line to Tagajō station (¥230); it's then a 10-minute taxi ride. There are also five direct buses from stop No 34 at Sendai station, but only until 6 pm (¥490, 30 minutes).

Getting Around

Buses from stop No 15 at Sendai station depart frequently for the airport between 7 am and 5.45 pm (¥910, 40 minutes).

The new tourist Loople bus (actually a trolley) makes a useful loop around the city every 30 minutes from 9 am to 4.30 pm (¥250 per ride). A one-day pass costs ¥600 and comes with an English-language booklet detailing the bus route schedule and generous sightseeing discounts for pass holders at local sights, including Zuihō-den, Sendai City Museum and the Aoba Castle Exhibition Hall at the Sendai-jō Ruins. Passes can be purchased on the bus or from the information office near the Loople bus stop in front of Sendai station.

Sendai's present subway system runs from Izumi-Chūō in the north to Tomizawa in the south. Prices range from ¥200 to ¥290, but it's not very convenient for sightseeing.

AROUND SENDAI

Tōhoku Shinkansen Repair Depot (Tōhoku Shinkansen Nosharyōkichi; ☎ 022-356-5223) is a major inspection facility for Japan's famed shinkansen. Over a thousand technicians work day and night on assembly, testing, repairs and development. Free (but short) bus tours of the 53-hectare depot are scheduled at 10 am, and 1 and 3 pm on weekdays (Japanese commentary only). Advance bookings are necessary, especially for the festivities of the annual **Shinkansen Matsuri** at the end of July.

The depot is a 10-minute walk from JR Rifu station, 20 minutes by train from Sendai (¥230).

AKIU ONSEN 秋保温泉
☎ 022

This *onsen* (mineral hot-spring spa) is a good base for side trips into the mountains to see **Akiu Ōtaki**, a 55m-high waterfall, and the gorge, **Futakuchi-kyō**, with its *banji-iwa* (rock columns). There are hiking trails along the river valley and a trail from Futakuchi Onsen to the summit of **Daitō-dake** (1366m), taking about three hours. Hiking maps are available at the tourist information office (☎ 398-2323) in Akiu Onsen (9 am to 6 pm). At **Akiu Handicrafts Village**, a 25-minute walk from Akiu Onsen, you can observe Edo-era toy making, *tansu* (cabinet) making and cloth dyeing.

Places to Stay

There are numerous hotels, minshuku, and camping grounds scattered throughout the area. *Banjisan-sō* (☎ 399-2775) is at Futakuchi Onsen, fairly close to trailheads for Daitō-dake and Futakuchi-kyō. Rooms with two meals start at ¥8000 per person.

Getting There & Away

Buses leave frequently from stop No 8 outside Sendai station for Akiu Onsen (¥780, 50 minutes), but only a few continue to Akiu Ōtaki (¥1070, 1½ hours). There is one afternoon bus departing from stop No 10 at Sendai station for Futakuchi Onsen via Akiu Ōtaki (¥1110, 80 minutes).

MATSUSHIMA 松島
☎ 022

Matsushima and the islands in the bay, Matsushima-wan, constitute one of the *Nihon Sankei* (Three Great Sights) of Japan – the other two are the floating torii of Miya-jima island and the sandspit at Amanohashidate. Bashō was reportedly so entranced by the surroundings in the 17th century that his flow of words was reduced to simply: '*Matsushima, ah! Matsushima! Matsushima!*'

It's certainly a picturesque place that merits a half-day visit, but there are also impressive and less-touristed seascapes farther east where you can stay overnight. Just to confuse things, there's a Matsushima station on the Tōhoku main line, but the station that's within easy walking distance of the sights and the harbour is Matsushima-Kaigan on the JR Senseki line.

The English-speaking staff at the tourist information office (☎ 354-2263) outside Matsushima-Kaigan station can provide pamphlets and maps (10 am to 5 pm); luggage storage is available next door (¥200 per day).

Zuigan-ji 瑞巌寺

Though founded in 828, the present buildings of Zuigan-ji, were constructed in 1606 by Date Masamune to serve as a family temple. This is one of Tōhoku's finest Zen temples and well worth a visit to see the painted screens and interior carvings of the main hall and the Seiryū-den (Treasure Hall) displaying works of art associated with the Date family (¥700).

Zuigan-ji is open from 8 am to 5 pm from April to September, though for the rest of the year opening hours vary month by month; the core opening hours are 8 am to 3.30 pm. The temple is approached along an avenue lined with tall cedars, to the right of which are small caves sheltering weathered Buddhas, altars and rock carvings.

Godai-dō 五大堂

The interior of this small wooden temple is only open once every 33 years (next viewing in 2006), so you will probably have to be content with the weather-beaten exterior –

NORTHERN HONSHŪ

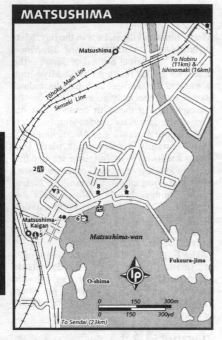

MATSUSHIMA

1 Sakuragawa Ryokan
桜川旅館
2 Zuigan-ji
瑞巌寺
3 Donjiki Chaya
どんじき茶屋
4 Kanran-tei; Matsushima
Hakubutsukan
観らん亭；松島博物館
5 Tourist Information Office
松島観光案内所
6 Cruise Boats
松島観覧船
7 Godai-dō
五大堂
8 Matsushima Kankō Hotel
(Ryokan Matsushima-jō)
松島観光ホテル
9 Matsushima Century Hotel
松島センチュリーホテル

note the 12 animals of the Chinese zodiac carved in the eaves – and the view out to sea.

Kanran-tei 観らん亭
The pavillion, Kanran-tei, was presented to the Date family by Toyotomi Hideyoshi in the late 16th century and served as a genteel venue for tea ceremonies and moon viewing (the names means 'a place to view ripples on the water'). The garden includes the **Matsushima Hakubutsukan**, a small museum housing a collection of relics from the Date family (¥200, 8.30 am to 5 pm, until 4.30 pm from November to March).

Fukuura-jima 福浦島
The island, Fukuura-jima, is connected to the mainland by a 252m-long red wooden bridge. It has been made into a botanical garden, with walking trails that wind around the island in a leisurely half-hour walk. The bridge gate remains open on the return side after hours for stragglers (¥200, 8 am to 5 pm).

Special Events
Seafood lovers will appreciate the **Matsushima Kaki Matsuri** (Matsushima Oyster Festival), which is held on the first Sunday in February. On August 15, Tōrō Nagashi Hanabi Taikai honours the souls of the departed with the O-Bon (Festival of the Dead) ritual of floating lighted lanterns out to sea (see Cultural Events in the Facts for the Visitor chapter).

Places to Stay
Most of the accommodation in Matsushima is very pricey. One of the cheaper places in town is *Sakuragawa Ryokan* (☎ 354-2513), where nicely furnished rooms and two sumptuous meals start at ¥8000 per room. The inn is two minutes on foot from Takagimachi station, one stop past Matsushima-kaigan. From Matsushima-kaigan station it's a 20-minute walk.

Most of the luxury hotels charge at least ¥20,000 per person. One exception is the *Matsushima Century Hotel* (☎ 354-4111), which has singles/twins for ¥5000/12,000. This price buys you a view of the car park rather than the sea, but the interior is quite deluxe, with a pool and sauna. If you want to splash out, a unique choice is the *Matsushima Kankō Hotel* (☎ 354-2121), a ryokan that looks like a castle, hence its other name, Ryokan Matsushima-jō. Costs here range from ¥10,000 to ¥25,000 per person with two meals.

Cheaper options can be found farther east along the coast in the town of Nobiru, in Oku-Matsushima (see the Oku-Matsushima section).

Places to Eat

Donjiki Chaya, a small teahouse near the entrance to Zuigan-ji, serves delicious tricoloured *dango* (dumplings) for ¥450 and iced *matcha* (powdered green tea) as well as more substantial fare. The shady benches make a nice retreat from the crowds. A handwritten English menu hangs out the front.

Getting There & Away

The easy way to get to Matsushima is from Sendai on the JR Senseki line (kaisoku, ¥400, 25 minutes). There are usually only around two trains an hour to Matsushima, though there are usually twice that many as far as Higashi-Shiogama (¥320). Travelling by train to Hon-Shiogama (one stop before Higashi-Shiogama) and then onwards by boat is a popular way of reaching Matsushima, taking in one of Japan's most self-celebrated strips of coastline on the way.

Shiogama itself is not particularly noteworthy, though it's a thriving fishing port and has a port festival on 5 August, with a parade of colourful boats decked out with streamers and banners. The harbour is 10 minutes on foot from Hon-Shiogama station – turn right as you exit. Cruises between Shiogama and Matsushima depart every 30 minutes between 8.30 am and 4 pm from April to November, and hourly the rest of the year (¥1420, 50 minutes). The loudspeakers on the boat are cunningly placed so that there is no escape from the full-blast Japanese commentary – unless you leap overboard.

From Shiogama-kō, there are also boats to Kinkazan island between mid-May and October (¥3300, one hour, daily at 2 pm).

Frequent cruises also set forth from Matsushima itself between 8.30 am and 4.30 pm for ¥1400 for a 45-minute loop through the pine-covered islets. Before shelling out for your ticket, be advised that you will probably share your journey with about 100 seagulls and an equal number of tourists who eagerly feed the birds fried shrimp crackers.

OKU-MATSUSHIMA 奥松島
☎ 0225

On the eastern curve of Matsushima-wan, Oku-Matsushima is less touristed and offers several trails for exploration by bicycle or on foot. Although not the cleanest, the swimming beaches are popular with daytrippers from Sendai.

To reach Oku-Matsushima from Matsushima-kaigan, take the JR Senseki line six stations east (two stops by kaisoku) to Nobiru (¥230). Inside Nobiru station, the tourist information office (☎ 88-2611) has a few bicycles for rent (8.30 am to 5.30 pm). From the station you can cycle the 5km to Otakamori, where a 20-minute climb up the hill provides a fine panorama of the bay.

Places to Stay

Paira Matsushima Youth Hostel (☎ 88-2220) is quite deluxe, but can become packed with noisy groups of school children. Rates are from ¥3000 to ¥3700 per person and bicycle rental is available for ¥800 per day. The hostel can also provide directions for the hiking trails. To get to the hostel from Nobiru station, walk across the bridge and towards the ocean for about 10 minutes until you reach an intersection with a blue youth hostel sign pointing down the road to the right. From there it's about 800m. Staff at the tourist information office can give you a map to the hostel.

The roads running along the beach are overflowing with minshuku. *Minshuku Bōyō-sō* (☎ 88-2159) has clean, spacious rooms from ¥6500 per person, including two seafood meals. It's in a Western-style blue-and-white building near the intersection with the youth hostel sign.

NORTHERN HONSHU

Oshika-hantō 牡鹿半島

AYUKAWA 鮎川
☎ 0225

Ayukawa, on the peninsula, Oshika-hantō, was once a major whaling centre but is now a mostly run-down fishing port. Its main purpose for the visitor is as a jumping off point for exploring Kinkazan island – try not to miss the boat.

If you get stranded, *Kokuminshukusha Cobalt-sō* (☎ 45-2281) is an excellent place to stay. This people's lodge is modern and in a superb position on a forested hilltop opposite Kinkazan island. For ¥6500 you get two seafood meals and a well-maintained room. There is no bus service here, but the staff will pick you up in Ayukawa if you phone ahead.

In Ayukawa itself there are several minshuku, mostly along the road that slopes uphill behind the bus station. All charge ¥6000 per night including two meals. The first you'll come to is *Minami-sō* (☎ 45-2501), which may not be much to look at but is a friendly port in a storm.

Getting There & Away
The main gateway to this beautiful, secluded peninsula is Ishinomaki. Outside JR Ishinomaki station is a useful tourist information office (☎ 93-6448) where you can pick up combined rail, bus and ferry timetables (9.30 am to 5.30 pm). Ishinomaki station is 70 minutes from Sendai (kaisoku, ¥950) via Matsushima-kaigan and Nobiru on the JR Senseki line. Ishinomaki can also be reached via the JR Ishinomaki line from Ichinoseki on the Tōhoku main line.

From Ishinomaki station there are around seven buses a day to Ayukawa between 7 am and 6 pm (¥1460, 1½ hours). On the ride down the peninsula the bus climbs across forested hills before dropping down into bays and inlets where tiny fishing villages are surrounded by mounds of sea shells, and the ocean is full of rafts and poles for oyster and seaweed cultivation.

From Ayukawa you can get a ferry to Kinkazan, arguably the highlight of any visit to Oshika-hantō. Boats leave from the pier opposite the bus station.

KINKAZAN 金華山
☎ 0225

For those in search of peace and quiet, an overnight stay on Kinkazan (Golden Mountain) is highly recommended. The island features a pyramid-shaped mountain (445m), an impressive shrine, a handful of houses around the boat dock, few cars, droves of deer and monkeys and mostly untended trails. Most visitors seem to be day-trippers, which means the island is virtually deserted in the early morning and late afternoon.

The island is considered one of the three holiest places in Tōhoku, and women were banned until the late 19th century. On the first and second Sunday in October, there's a deer-horn cutting ceremony to stop the deer from injuring each other during mating season. On the last weekend in July, the **Ryūjin Matsuri** (Dragon Festival) features giant dragon floats supported by up to 50 dancers.

From the boat dock, it's a steep 15-minute walk uphill to **Koganeyama-jinja**, which was built in AD 794 by Emperor Shōmu as thanks for finding gold here to finish the Great Buddha at Nara's Tōdai-ji. Below the shrine are grassy expanses where tame deer cadge titbits from visitors.

Walking up the steep trail from the shrine to the summit, through thick forests and via wayside shrines, takes about an hour. From the shrine at the summit there are magnificent views out to sea and across to the peninsula. On the eastern shore of the island is **Senjōjiki** (1000 Tatami Mats Rock), a large formation of white, level rock.

A very basic sketch map of the island is provided by the ticket window at the Kinkazan ferry pier. It has neither contour lines nor scale and its only use is to demonstrate that there *are* trails and to provide the kanji for various places on the island (this may be useful when you come across one of the weather-beaten trail markers). Hiking around the island is a great way to find some peace and solitude as some areas are deserted, so be prepared to find a few of the trails almost fully overgrown. Be sure to stock up on food and drink at the dock or at the shop outside the shrine; and be careful – the deer can mug the unwary! If you get lost, head downhill towards the sea – there's a dirt road or trail circling the entire island (24km) along the shore.

Places to Stay

On the tranquil shrine grounds *Koganeyama-jinja* (☎ *45-2264*) offers rooms with two meals for ¥9000 per person. Advance reservations are usually necessary and a minivan picks guests up at the pier. If you get up before 6 am you may be allowed to attend morning prayers.

A five-minute walk south of the pier is the popular *Minshuku Shiokaze* (☎ *45-2244*), which charges ¥6000, including two meals. You must book in advance, as the owners actually live in Ayukawa and only come out to Kinkazan if they have customers. This minshuku can be fully booked on weekends and during summer.

Getting There & Away

From April to early November ferries depart Ayukawa for Kinkazan almost hourly between 8.30 am and 3.40 pm (¥900, 30 minutes); the last return ferry is at 4.20 pm. Service is greatly reduced the rest of the year. There are four daily high-speed catamarans between Kinkazan and Onagawa, the eastern gateway to the peninsula, from April to early November (¥1600, 35 minutes). The last departure from Onagawa is at 2.45 pm. Some of the boats have open-air fantail decks, which make for a pleasant ride.

From mid-May to October there is a daily boat at 12.50 pm going from Kinkazan to Shiogama-kō (see the Matsushima Getting There & Away section earlier).

ONAGAWA 女川

This fishing town is another access point for Kinkazan. Onagawa is also the terminus for the JR Ishinomaki line, 30 minutes from Ishinomaki (¥320), where you can either catch a train south-west towards Sendai or west towards Furukawa on the Tōhoku shinkansen line (a change of train may be necessary, en route, at Kogota).

From Onagawa station, walk straight to the waterfront, turn right and walk about 200m to the pier. The ferry ticket office is down a side street opposite the pier, little more than a hole in the wall on the right-hand side across from 77 Bank.

NARUKO ONSEN 鳴子温泉
☎ 0229

A major hot-spring spa resort in the north-western corner of Miyagi-ken, Naruko is famous for its distinctive style of lacquerware and its *kokeshi* (wooden dolls with brightly painted floral designs).

The entrance to **Narugo-kyō** can be reached in 20 minutes on foot from Naruko station. From the entrance, a pleasant 4km trail leads along the river valley to Nakayama-daira. If you turn right just after the bridge but before reaching the gorge entrance, you'll find the old **Shitomae checkpoint** and the start of a quiet 5km country path along the route Bashō once walked.

The tourist information office (☎ 83-3441) inside JR Naruko Onsen station (8.30 am to 6 pm) has photocopies of a detailed English guide to the entire area with useful maps and extensive background on local attractions, including the town's lovely wooden bathhouse onsen at **Taki-no-yu**.

Places to Stay

There are dozens of ryokan and hotels in the area, most of which are fairly expensive. One of the cheaper options is *Ryokan Sumei-sō* (☎ *83-2114*), where basic rooms cost ¥6000 for up to two people, ¥1000 more for each additional person. The gracious owner doesn't speak English, but meals are available and guests have access to hot-spring baths. To get there, turn left after exiting the station and walk about 10 minutes down the main street. The ryokan is on your left before you cross the tracks.

Ryokan Bentenkaku (☎ *83-2461*), a member of the Japanese Inn group, charges from ¥5000 to ¥6000 per person for Japanese-style accommodation. It's quite a hike across the river from the station, but the staff can usually come to pick you up if you call ahead.

Getting There & Away

On the JR Rikuu-tōsen line, Naruko Onsen is connected with Furukawa on the JR

Tōhoku shinkansen line (kaisoku, ¥650, one hour) and with Shinjō (¥950, one hour) for transfers to the Yamagata shinkansen line or local trains west to Sakata.

Iwate-ken 岩手県

HIRAIZUMI 平泉
☎ 0191

From 1089 to 1189, three generations of the Fujiwara family created a political and cultural centre in Hiraizumi which allegedly approached the grandeur and sophistication of Kyoto. This short century of fame and prosperity was brought to an end when the last Fujiwara leader, Fujiwara Yasuhira, was manipulated by Minamoto Yoritomo, who soon after ordered the annihilation of the Fujiwara clan and the destruction of Hiraizumi.

Only a couple of the original temple buildings now remain; the rest have been restored or added to over the centuries.

Information
Just outside Hiraizumi station, the tourist information office (☎ 46-2111) provides maps and English-language pamphlets (8.30 am to

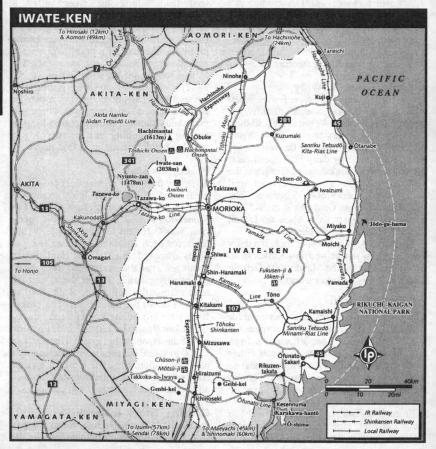

CRAIG MCLACHLAN

Okama, the volcanic crater lake atop Zaō-san – a popular hiking destination in Northern Honshū.

MASON FLORENCE

The summit of Akita Komaga-take (1637m) – hike down to the *rotemburo* at Nyūtō Onsen from here.

View along a hiking trail in Yamagata-ken.

A humble wooden *torii*, Northern Honshū.

Pilgrims of the Shugendō Buddhist sect on the sacred peak of Gas-san, Northern Honshū.

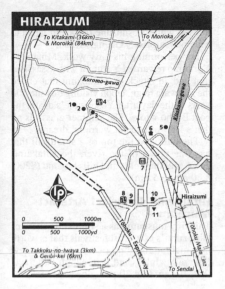

HIRAIZUMI

1	Kyōzō
	経蔵
2	Konjiki-dō
	金色堂
3	Sankōzō
	讃衡蔵
4	Chūson-ji
	中尊寺
5	Takadachi Gikei-dō
	高館義経堂
6	Minshuku Yoshitsune-sō
	民宿義経荘
7	Hiraizumi Historical
	Artefacts Museum
	平泉郷土館
8	Mōtsū-ji
	毛越寺
9	Mōtsū-ji Youth Hostel
	毛越寺ユースホステル
10	Ryokan Komatsushiro
	旅館こまつしろ
11	Seoul Shokudō
	ソウル食堂

5 pm). Email and Internet access is, unbelievably, free. Luggage storage is available outside the station for ¥100 per day.

Some of the sights in outlying areas, such as Geibi-kei, are best reached by buses leaving from Ichinoseki station, not Hiraizumi. frequent buses between Ichinoseki and Hiraizumi means this is not a problem. Inside Ichinoseki station there is another tourist information office (☎ 21-3062) that can answer queries about transport and area sights (10 am to 4.30 pm).

The JNTO leaflet *Sendai, Matsushima and Hiraizumi* has useful details of sights, transport and accommodation.

There is a post office behind Ryokan Komatsushiro, off of the main road from the station leading to Mōtsū-ji.

Chūson-ji 中尊寺

This temple was originally established in 850 by the priest Ennin, the third abbot of the Tendai sect who also established most of Tōhoku's other famous temples. However, it was the first lord of the Fujiwara clan who decided in the early 12th century to expand the site into a complex with more than 40 temples and hundreds of residences

for priests. A massive fire in 1337 destroyed most of the complex; even so, what you can see now is still impressive.

The steep approach to the temple follows a long, tree-lined avenue past the Hon-dō (Main Hall) to an enclosed area with the splendid Konjiki-dō (Golden Hall) and several ancillary buildings.

Sankōzō The temple treasury contains the coffins and funeral finery of the Fujiwara clan, and scrolls, swords and images transferred from halls and temples that no longer exist.

Konjiki-dō A National Treasure, built in 1124, the Konjiki-dō is small but packed with gold ornamentation, black lacquerwork and inlaid mother-of-pearl. The centrepiece of the hall is a statue of Amida with attendants. Beneath the three side altars are the mummified remains of three generations of the Fujiwara family. The fourth and last lord of the family, Fujiwara Yasuhira, was beheaded at the order of Minamoto Yoritomo, who further required the severed head to be sent to Kyoto for inspection before returning it for interment next to the coffin of Yasuhira's father.

Admission costs ¥800 – the ticket is also valid for admission to Kyōzō and Sankōzō. It's open daily from 8 am to 4.30 pm (8.30 am to 4 pm from mid-November to March).

Kyōzō Built in 1108, this sutra treasury is the oldest structure in the temple complex. The original collection of more than 5000 sutras was damaged by fire and the remains of the collection have been transferred to the Sankōzō.

Mōtsū-ji 毛越寺

Also established by the priest Ennin in 850, this temple once rivalled Chūson-ji in size and fame. All that remains now are foundation stones and the attractive Jōdo-en (Paradise Garden) which gives a good impression of the luxurious, sophisticated lifestyle of the Heian period. The temple and gardens attract large numbers of visitors for the **Ayame Matsuri** (Iris Festival), held from late June to mid-July (¥500, 8.30 am to 6 pm, until 5.30 pm from December to March). Entry is free for guests staying at the youth hostel on the temple grounds.

Takadachi Gikei-dō 高館義経堂

This is a small memorial honouring Minamoto Yoshitsune, a member of the powerful Minamoto family. Yoshitsune grew up with and trained under the Fujiwara clan but left Hiraizumi to fight by his brother Yoritomo's side in their battles against the rival Taira family. Unfortunately, the brothers soon had a serious falling out, and Yoshitsune unsuccessfully tried to raise a rebellion against his brother, retreating to Hiraizumi when his plan failed.

The third Fujiwara leader then in power resisted Yoritomo's subsequent decrees to have his brother killed, but the fourth leader, Yasuhira, betrayed Yoshitsune. At Takadachi, Yoshitsune was attacked. Seeing no way out, he set his own castle on fire, killed his family and then himself to avoid the shame of capture and execution. According to local legend, it was actually Yoshitsune's loyal

retainer, the giant Benkei, who sacrificed himself while Yoshitsune fled from Japan to become (surprise!) Ghengis Khan.

For performing his dirty work, Minamoto Yoritomo rewarded Yasuhira with assassination and an attack on Hiraizumi that ended the Fujiwara reign. Upon visiting this site 500 years to the day after Yoshitsune's death, the poet Bashō wrote 'The summer grass / Is all that's left / of ancient warriors' dreams'.

The hall is at the top of a small hill that has fine views of the river, the Kitakamigawa, and the fields and hills beyond (¥200, 8.30 am to 5 pm).

Hiraizumi Historical Artefacts Museum

This tiny museum has a short slide show of Hiraizumi's colourful festivals that is worth the small admission price, as well as a few folkcraft exhibits and 12th-century artefacts (¥100, 9 am to 4.30 pm, closed Monday).

Takkoku-no-Iwaya Bishamon-dō 達谷窟

Five kilometres south-west of Mōtsū-ji, this cave temple is dedicated to Bishamon, the Buddhist guardian deity of warriors. The present structure is a replica of the temple built here in 801 by a famous general after a victorious battle against the Ezo, the original inhabitants of northern Honshū (¥300, 8.30 am to 6 pm, until 5.30 pm from November to March).

You can cycle to the cave along a paved path from Mōtsū-ji in about 25 minutes.

Genbi-kei 巌美渓

Genbi-kei is a small gorge that can be explored on foot, allowing you to see where the river has carved elaborate shapes from the rocks. Frequent buses depart from stop No 9 at Ichinoseki station (¥490, 20 minutes). There are also a few buses from Hiraizumi, but the best way to get there is to cycle 3km along the path from Takkoku-no-Iwaya.

Geibi-kei げい鼻渓谷

This is a much more impressive gorge than Genbi-kei. Flat-bottomed boats with singing boatmen ferry passengers up and down the river between the sheer cliffs (¥1500, 1½ hours). Boats depart hourly from 8.30 am to 4.30 pm (9 am to 3 pm from late November to April).

The best way to reach the gorge is by bus from stop No 7 at Ichinoseki station (¥620, 40 minutes, hourly); or take the train from Ichinoseki to Geibikei station on the JR Ōfunato line (kaisoku, ¥480, 25 minutes).

Special Events
The **Haru-no-Fujiwaru Matsuri** (Spring Fujiwara Festival) held from 1 to 5 May, features a costumed procession, performances of *nō* (classical Japanese dance-drama) at Chūson-ji and traditional *ennen-no-mai* (longevity dances) at Mōtsū-ji, as well as an enormous rice-cake carrying competition in memory of the giant Benkei. A similar **Aki-no-Fujiwaru Matsuri** (Autumn Fujiwara Festival) takes place from 1 to 3 November.

Bonfire nō performances are held at Chūson-ji on 14 August.

On 20 January, Mōtsū-ji hosts **Hatsukayasai** (20th Night Festival), in which near-naked men run around carrying torches, after which priests perform ennen-no-mai.

Places to Stay & Eat
Mōtsū-ji Youth Hostel (☎ 46-2331) is part of the temple and a peaceful, if a bit mouldy, place to stay; rates are ¥2800 per person. The temple is about 10 minutes on foot from the station.

Closer to the station, the well-established *Ryokan Komatsushiro* (☎ 46-3323) has rates of around ¥8000, including two meals.

About 15 minutes north of the station, near Takadachi Gikei-dō, is *Minshuku Yoshitsune-sō* (☎ 46-4355), a quiet little place with rooms for ¥6300 with two meals. From here it's only about five minutes to the entrance of Chūson-ji.

Unlike most restaurants in town, *Seoul Shokudō* is open late and serves good, cheap Korean fare. It's about five minutes on foot from the station on the way to Mōtsū-ji.

Getting There & Away
From Sendai, take a JR Tōhoku shinkansen to Ichinoseki (35 minutes), then a bus via Hiraizumi station to Chūson-ji (¥350, 22 minutes). You can also take a local train on the JR Tōhoku main line from Sendai to Hiraizumi (futsū, ¥1890) but a change of trains is usually necessary at Ichinoseki and the trip takes about two hours.

Ichinoseki is connected to Morioka by the JR Tōhoku shinkansen line (40 minutes) and the JR Tōhoku main line (futsū, ¥1450, 1½ hours).

Getting Around
Frequent buses from Ichinoseki station connect Hiraizumi station with Chūson-ji (¥140, 10 minutes). On foot it's about 20 minutes; take the road east of the railway tracks as it's much quieter.

Bicycle rental is available for ¥1000 per day outside Hiraizumi station (8 am to 5 pm, April to November).

TŌNO 遠野
☎ 0198

Tōno excited attention at the beginning of this century when a collection of regional folk tales were compiled by Yanagida Kunio and published under the title *Tōno Monogatari*. The English translation by Robert Morse, *Legends of Tōno*, is available at the Tōno Municipal Museum. The tales cover a racy collection of topics from supernatural beings and weird occurrences to the strange ways of the rustic folk in traditional Japan.

One legend relates the history of Oshirasama, a fertility goddess who was once just a local girl. Against her father's wishes, she married her horse. The outraged father hung the horse from a mulberry tree and beheaded it, after which the unhappy bride and horse-husband were whisked away to paradise. Oshira-sama dolls are still important ceremonial objects for *itako* mediums (see the Shimokita-hantō entry later in this chapter).

The present city of Tōno was formed by the merger of eight rural villages. The region still has some examples of the local style of L-shaped farmhouse, known as *magariya*, where farmfolk and their prized horses lived under one roof – but definitely in different sections.

NORTHERN HONSHŪ

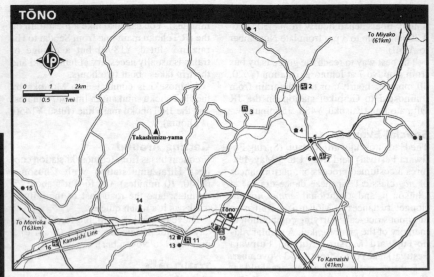

TŌNO

(map with locations labelled)

To Miyako
(61km)

Takashimizu-yama

To Morioka
(163km)

Kamaishi Line

Tōno

To Kamaishi
(41km)

Information

The tourist information office (☎ 62-1333) outside JR Tōno station has an English-language brochure entitled *Come and See Traditional Japan in Tōno* with full details on transport, accommodation and sights (8 am to 6.30 pm). It also includes an accurate scaled map for three different cycling routes. Bicycle rental is available near the station and also at the youth hostel. Cycling is a convenient alternative to the infrequent bus services if you want to visit more remote sights such as the **Water Mill**, which still functions, about 10km north-east of Tōno station. Tono's main post office is a 10-minute walk from the station in the direction of the Tōno Municipal Museum.

Tōno Municipal Museum
遠野市立博物館

On the upper floors of the city library, this museum has exhibits of folklore and traditional life and audiovisual presentations of the legends of Tōno (¥300, 9 am to 4.30 pm, closed last day of the month, from November to March it is also closed Monday). To reach it, walk straight out from the station for about 500m until you cross the river.

Tōno Mukashibanashi-mura
遠野昔話村

Tōno Mukashibanashi-mura is a folktale village that consists of a restored ryokan where Yanagida Kunio once stayed and an exhibition hall for folk art (9 am to 4.30 pm, closed on Monday from December to March). Admission costs ¥300; a combined ticket for the Tōno Municipal Museum costs ¥500.

Fukusen-ji 福泉寺

This temple lies 8.5km north-east of Tōno station, about half an hour by bicycle. Founded in 1912, its major claim to fame is the wooden Fukusen-ji Kannon statue – 17m high – which is supposedly the tallest of its type in Japan (¥300, 9 am to 4 pm). If you're not cycling, take a bus bound for Sakanoshita and get off at Fukusen-ji (¥370, eight per day).

Tōno Furosato-mura

About 3.5km beyond Fukusen-ji, this is the largest folk village in Tōno, comprised of several different farmhouses, a water wheel and a folkcraft gallery. Guides are on hand in most buildings to explain (in Japanese

TŌNO

PLACES TO STAY

4 Tōno Youth Hostel
遠野ユースホステル

12 Minshuku Magariya
民宿曲り屋

OTHER

1 Tōno Furusato-mura
遠野ふるさと村

2 Fukusen-ji
福泉寺

3 Matsuzaki Kannon-dō
松崎観音堂

5 Denshōen
伝承園

6 Kappa-buchi
カッパ淵

7 Jōken-ji
常堅寺

8 Water Mill
水車

9 Tōno Mukashibanashi-mura
遠野昔話村

10 Tōno Municipal Museum
遠野市立博物館

11 Unedori-sama
卯子西様

13 Gohyaku Rakan
五百羅漢

14 Haguroiwa Monuments
羽黒岩

15 Chiba Family Magariya
千葉家の曲り屋

16 Kōmyō-ji
光明寺

only) the relevant history and farming culture, as well as demonstrate crafts (¥500, 9 am to 4 pm). If you are not cycling, buses run once or twice an hour from Tōno station (¥490, 25 minutes).

Jōken-ji & Kappa-buchi
常堅寺・カッパ淵

Jōken-ji is a peaceful temple 2.5km south of Fukusen-ji. Outside the temple is a distinctive lion statue; inside the temple is the famous deity image **Obinzuru-sama**, which some believe will cure their illness if they rub the part on its body that corresponds to the part where their own body ailment is.

Behind the temple is a stream and a small pool, **Kappa-buchi**. *Kappa* are considered to be mischievous, mythical creatures but legend has it that the kappa in this pool once put out a fire in the temple. The lion statue was erected as a gesture of thanks to honour the kappa. See the Folklore & Gods section in the Facts about the Country chapter for more details about kappa.

Also in this vicinity is **Denshōen**, a small folk village with an old magariya farmhouse, a water wheel, a wooden kura, various traditional farming implements and exhibits (¥300, 9 am to 4.30 pm, closed the last day of the month). Two-hour lessons in various folkcrafts cost ¥300 each.

From Tōno station, you can take a direct bus to Denshōen-mae (¥300, 15 minutes) or more frequent buses bound for Sakanoshita to the Nitagai stop (¥300), which is 10 minutes on foot from Denshōen.

Gohyaku Rakan 五百羅漢

On a wooded hillside above Unedori-sama shrine, about 3km south-west of Tōno station, are the Gohyaku Rakan (500 Disciples of Buddha). These rock carvings were fashioned by a priest to console the spirits of those who died in a disastrous famine in 1754.

Chiba Family Magariya
千葉家曲り家農家

Eleven kilometres west of Tōno station, this magariya has been restored to give an impression of the traditional lifestyle of a wealthy farming family of the 18th century (¥350, 8.30 am to 5 pm). Unless you want to fork out several thousand yen for the taxi ride, you'll have to cycle here.

Special Events

The **Tōno Matsuri** takes place on 14 September with *yabusame* (horseback archery), traditional dances and costume parades.

Places to Stay

There are a couple of hotels and ryokan and at least a dozen minshuku in the station area with rates from around ¥6500 per person with two meals. None can be especially recommended, and many seem reluctant to accept foreign guests.

Pleasantly located amid rice fields, *Tōno Youth Hostel* (☎ 62-8736) provides a good base for cycling or walking around the area. Rates are ¥3150 and there is no curfew, but reception closes at 9 pm. Bicycle rental is available for ¥800 per day. From Tōno station, take a bus bound for Sakanoshita to the Nitagai stop (¥300, 12 minutes). From there it's a 10-minute walk to the hostel.

Minshuku Magariya (☎ 62-4564), about 2km south-west of the station, is a popular place where you can stay inside a traditional farmhouse. Prices start at ¥10,500, including two meals. From the station, take a bus to the *basu-sentā* (bus centre), a ride of about 10 minutes. From there it's another 15 minutes on foot to the minshuku. Alternatively, you can take a taxi from Tōno station or walk in around 30 minutes.

Getting There & Away

On the JR Kamaishi line local trains connect Tōno with Shin-Hanamaki on the Tōhoku shinkansen line (¥740, one hour) and Hanamaki on the Tōhoku main line (¥820, 70 minutes).

There are two afternoon buses from Morioka to Kamaishi that stop at Tōno's Topia department store (¥1890, two hours). In the reverse direction, buses to Morioka pass by at around 7 and 10 am.

MORIOKA 盛岡

☎ 019 • pop 285,000

Morioka is the capital of Iwate-ken, and dates back to the early Edo period when it was the castle town of the Nambu clan. Though Morioka's tourist literature still paints it as a 'castle town', the fortress in question was razed during the Meiji Restoration. Genuinely interesting sights are in very short supply, and for most travellers Morioka is just a useful staging point for

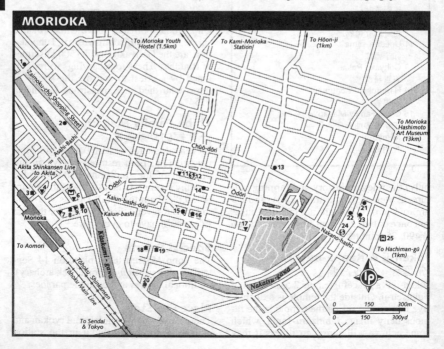

visiting the northern part of Tōhoku. That said, it's a pleasant place with a few nice shops scattered about, so don't panic if you find yourself having to spend the night here.

Orientation & Information

The city centre is east of the station, on the other side of the Kitakami-gawa. Ōdōri, which heads over the Kaiun bridge up to the park, Iwate-kōen, is the main shopping street.

Kita Tōhoku information centre (☎ 625-2090) is on the 2nd floor of Morioka station; it's open from 9 am to 7 pm. There should be at least one English speaker on hand, and there is a good supply of information material on the city as well as many other areas of Tōhoku.

The Iwate International Plaza (☎ 654-8900) is a 15-minute walk south-east of the station and has an information counter with English-speaking staff, though the centre is geared towards long-term residents (weekdays 10 am to 9 pm, weekends and holidays until 5 pm). Free Internet access is available but there are often long queues.

There is an ATM that accepts foreign-issued cards inside Sawaya Bookshop on Ōdōri (9.30 am to 8.30 pm).

Iwate-kōen 岩手公園

Iwate-kōen, in the centre of town, is where Morioka-jō once stood. Today there's nothing left but the moss-clad walls. On the grounds is Sakurayama-jinja and a totem pole presented by Morioka's sister city, Victoria, British Columbia. The totem was the collaborative effort of a Native North American chief and a local woodcarver.

Morioka Hashimoto Art Museum 盛岡橋本美術館

Perched halfway up the slope of Iwate-san, this museum was founded by Hashimoto Yaoji (1903–79), a local artist who built the museum according to his own fancy – there's a magariya farmhouse sitting on the roof. Exhibits include some of his own sculptures and paintings as well as local folk art (¥700, 10 am to 4.30 pm).

From Morioka station, take a bus from stop No 8 to the museum (¥270, six per day from mid-March to November).

Hōon-ji

This quiet Zen temple is in Morioka's *tera-machi* (temple district), where the novelist, Miyazawa Kenji, lived and wrote after being expelled from boarding school. The

NORTHERN HONSHŪ

MORIOKA

PLACES TO STAY
3 Hotel Metropolitan Morioka
　ホテルメトロポリタン盛岡
8 Morioka City Hotel
　盛岡シティーホテル
10 Hotel Rich
　ホテルリッチ盛岡
15 Hotel Carina
　ホテルカリーナ
16 Hotel New Carina
　ホテルニューカリーナ
18 Ryokan Kumagai
　旅館熊ヶ井
19 Taishōkan
　大正館

PLACES TO EAT
4 Gen Plaza
　ゲンプラザ

6 Cappuccino Shiki
　カプチノ詩季
7 Azumaya
　東家
9 Koiwai Regley
　小岩井リグレ
11 Doutor
17 Spanish Reiz
　スパニッシュReiz

OTHER
1 Nambu Antique
　Design Prints
　小野染彩所
2 Kōgensha Craft
　Shop
　光原社
5 Post Office
　郵便局

12 Iwate Bank
　岩手銀行
13 Morioka Court
　of Justice; Rock splitting
　Cherry Tree
14 Sawaya Bookshop
20 Iwate International Plaza
　岩手県立国際交流プラザ
21 Shirozawa Senbei
　Factory
　白沢せんべい
22 Gozaku
　ござ九
23 Workshop Kamasada
24 Iwate Bank
　(Ex-Head Office)
　岩手銀行
25 Morioka Bus Centre
　盛岡バスセンター

temple's impressive San-mon (Main Gate) has a Kannon image, but the real attraction here is the musty **Rakan-dō**, a small hall containing 18th-century statues of the 500 disciples of Buddha, each posed in different comic or serious attitudes (¥300 donation).

To reach the temple, take a bus from stop No 11 in front of Morioka station and get off after about 15 minutes at the Honmachi-dōri Itchōme stop (¥140).

Special Events
The Chagu-Chagu Umakko Matsuri, held on 15 June, celebrates the finish of the rice planting season, and features a parade of brightly decorated horses and children in traditional dress. Starting outside town, the procession passes near Iwate-kōen (best view from Nakano-hashi) around 1 pm and finishes at Hachiman-gū.

Iwate was historically famous for breeding horses, first for battle steeds during the Japanese civil war period and then agricultural workhorses during peacetime. The festival allegedly originated when farmers took their horses to shrines to rest them after harvest and pray for their health. The name 'chagu-chagu' is said to describe the sound of the horses' bells.

During the Hachiman-gū Matsuri from 14 to 16 September, portable shrines and colourful floats are paraded to the rhythm of *taiko* (drums) and chants, with yabusame on the 15th.

Places to Stay
Morioka Youth Hostel (☎ 662-2220) is quite run down and far from the city centre; rates are ¥2900 per person. From stop No 11 at Morioka station, buses depart frequently for Matsuzono bus terminal; get off at the Takamatsu-no-ike-guchi stop (¥210, 20 minutes, last bus 7.30 pm). The Kita Tōhoku information centre can give you an English map with precise directions to the hostel.

Most ryokan near Morioka station appear dilapidated, and most are overpriced. *Ryokan Kumagai* (☎ 651-3020), a member of the Japanese Inn group, is in an attractive building about 15 minutes on foot from the station. Singles/doubles/triples start at

¥4500/8000/10,000. Next door, the well-worn but friendly *Taishōkan* (☎ 622-4436) charges ¥3800 per person without meals.

Morioka has no shortage of business hotels, but everything can get booked out during summer. Affordable options close to the station include the standard *Morioka City Hotel* (☎ 651-3030), which has singles/doubles from ¥6100/7800 and the better-quality *Hotel Rich* (☎ 625-2611), which has singles from ¥6500 and doubles/twins starting at ¥10,000/13,000. The *Hotel Metropolitan Morioka* (☎ 625-1211) is considerably classier with singles/twins from ¥7500/15,500.

In the city centre, the reliable *Hotel Carina* (☎ 624-1111) has singles for ¥5500 and doubles/twins for ¥8000/9000. The *Hotel New Carina* (☎ 625-2228), across the street, has newer rooms at slightly higher rates.

Places to Eat
Wanko soba is an all-you-can-eat feast of noodles dish where you aren't allowed to stop until you manage to put the lid back on your bowl before the staff can fill it up again. This memorable experience usually costs around ¥2000, though *Azumaya* restaurant, in front of Morioka station, may give discounts to youth hostellers. Morioka's other speciality is *reimen*, cold soba noodles with *kim chi*, egg, cucumber and even watermelon! *Seirōkaku* serves large portions of this summer favourite (¥900) on the 2nd floor of Gen Plaza, across from the station.

You can find these dishes, and just about anything else, in the enormous *Fasen* food plaza in the basement of Morioka station. On the ground floor of the station, the local Ginga Kōgen microbrewery has its own bar conveniently located near the northern exit. The beer is quite good (¥480 per glass) and the lunch sets – mostly meat-and-potatoes fare – are also reasonable (¥800).

Also near the station, *Koiwai Regley* bakery/restaurant serves up a two-cup pot of coffee for ¥380. The food is mainly Western-style and uses ingredients from the renowned Koiwai farm outside the city near Iwate-san. The filling lunch sets are good value. Across the street *Cappuccino*

Shiki has good cappuccino (¥480) as well as affordable breakfast sets starting at ¥500 (closed Monday).

On Ōdori and around Iwate-kōen there are a number of Japanese restaurants and noodle shops. Another interesting option is *Spanish Reiz*, where tapas dishes range from ¥450 to ¥1000. The bar stocks a selection of wines.

Shopping

The Morioka region is famous for the production of *nanbu tetsubin* (cast ironware). One of the best places to browse is at Workshop Kamasada, which sells affordable gift items alongside tea kettles that cost as much as a small car. It's located across the Nakatsu-gawa near Gozaku, a traditional merchants area of kura warehouses, coffee shops, craft studios and a *senbei* (rice cracker) factory. To get there, take a bus from stop No 6 at Morioka station to Morioka bus centre. From there it's a three-minute walk to the old Iwate Bank building at the south-western corner of the street leading to Gozaku.

Nearer to the station, attractive Zaimoku-chō district is chock full of quality craft shops. Among these, Kōgensha wins the prize for atmosphere: in addition to tastefully displayed pottery, lacquerware and fabrics, this little complex houses a coffee shop and a garden looking out over the river. For hand-woven and dyed fabrics, check out the impressive selection at Nanbu Antique Design Prints – even the emperor himself came by to do some window shopping. Across the street towards the bridge is a colourful *washi* (Japanese paper) shop.

Getting There & Away

On the JR Tōhoku shinkansen line, the fastest trains from Tokyo (Ueno) reach Morioka in a mere 2¼ hours (¥13,330). From Morioka, the Akita shinkansen line runs west to Akita (¥3990, 1½ hours) via Tazawa-ko and Kakunodate, which can also be reached by infrequent local trains on the JR Tazawa-ko line. From Morioka you can continue north to Aomori on the JR Tōhoku main line; a *tokkyū* (express) train costs ¥5460 (2¼ hours). To reach Miyako, on the eastern coast of Tōhoku, take the JR Yamada line.

To visit the Hachimantai area, north-west of Morioka, you can take the JR Hanawa line to either Hachimantai or Kazuno-Hanawa stations and then continue by bus (late April through October only) to Hachimantai Chōjō in about an hour; however, it is far easier to go by direct bus.

The bus terminal at Morioka station is well organised and has abundant English signs and a directory showing which buses leave from which stops, as well as journey times and fares. Popular destinations include Iwate-san, Miyako, Ryūsen-dō, Hachimantai Chōjō, Towada-ko and Tazawa-ko. See the sections on these places for more details. Fairly frequent long-distance buses also depart for Aomori (¥3160, three hours), Hirosaki (¥2930, 2¼ hours) and Sendai (¥2850, 2¾ hours). There is one night bus to Tokyo leaving at 10.30 pm (¥7850, 7½ hours).

Getting Around

Morioka is small enough to navigate comfortably on foot. Most local and long-distance buses leave from in front of the station, though there are also some departures from the Morioka bus centre, which is close to Iwate-kōen.

Between May and September, the Dendenmushi tourist bus makes a convenient loop around town, departing from stop No 15 in front of Morioka station between 9 am and 6.30 pm. It costs ¥100 per ride, or ¥300 for a one-day pass.

IWATE-SAN 岩手山

The volcanic peak of Iwate-san (2038m) is a dominating landmark north-west of Morioka, and a popular destination for hikers. At the time of writing the mountain was closed due to volcanic activity. Ask at the Kita Tōhoku tourist information office in Morioka about current conditions and hiking practicalities. If you want to stay near Iwate-san, there is no shortage of accommodation at **Amihari Onsen**, which is the start of one of the main trails to the summit. You could also stay at the *SL Hotel* (☎ 692-4316), on the renowned Koiwai farm, which charges from ¥4000 per person without meals. From early May to early November, buses from Morioka bound for Shimahari Onsen (¥1140, one hour) pass by Koiwai farm (¥720, 35 minutes).

MIYAKO 宮古
☎ 0193
Miyako is a small city in the centre of Rikuchū-kaigan National Park, a 180km stretch of interesting rock formations and seascapes along the eastern coastline of Tōhoku, from Kesennuma in the south to Kuji in the north.

The tourist information office (☎ 62-4060) outside the train station can provide transport timetables and an English-language brochure with a useful map and details of area sights (8.30 am to 5.30 pm).

Jōdo-ga-hama 浄土ヶ浜
Jōdo-ga-hama is a very attractive beach with white sand, dividing rock formations and a series of walking trails through forests of pine trees on the steep slopes above.

From Miyako station, frequent buses bound for the beach (¥210, 20 minutes) stop in front of a concrete souvenir centre, from where a path leads down to the excursion boat dock. Apart from tame cruises to a few rock formations, there are also departures every hour or two between 8.30 am and 3.30 pm for Tarō, a fishing village farther north up the coast (¥1420, 40 minutes, late April to October). Afterwards you can return to Miyako by bus or by train on the private Sanriku-Tetsudō line.

You can escape some of the crowds by leaving the tarmac road along the beach and climbing trails into the hills, where there are good views across the beach. One trail leads along the coast for a two-hour hike to the visitors centre at the cape, Ane-ga-misaki, from where you can catch a bus back to Miyako station (30 minutes, last bus 7.30 pm).

Places to Stay & Eat
The well run *Suehiro-kan Youth Hostel* (☎ 62-1555) has elegant Japanese-style shared accommodation for ¥2850 per person. Reception closes at 9 pm, but there is no curfew. From Miyako station, walk straight out and turn right at the intersection with the main street; the hostel is 20m farther down on the right-hand side.

The spotless *Hamadaya Ryokan* (☎ 62-3155) has more upmarket rooms for ¥8000 per person, including two meals. The ryokan and its annex are opposite each other about 1½ blocks down the street immediately to the right as you exit the station.

On the way there you'll pass *Uomoto*, a traditional seafood restaurant with indoor fish pools. The picture menu makes ordering easy: *donburi* (rice dishes) start at ¥700 and the superb tempura *teishoku* (set meal) is ¥1400. The restaurant has white paper lanterns hanging outside the gate.

Getting There & Away
The JR Yamada line links Morioka with Miyako (kaisoku, ¥1890, two hours) then continues south down the coast to Kamaishi (¥1110, 75 minutes) and inland to Tōno (¥1800, two hours).

The private Sanriku-Tetsudō Kita-Rias line runs north from Miyako past Tarō (¥440) along the coastline to Kuji (¥1800, 1½ hours) – the scenery is mostly obscured by tunnels. From Kuji, you can connect with JR trains to Hachinohe (¥1110, two hours).

From stop No 6 in front of Miyako station there are frequent buses to Morioka (¥1970, 2¼ hours) and one night bus to Tokyo departing at 9 pm (¥9170, 9½ hours).

RYŪSEN-DŌ 龍泉洞
Close to Iwaizumi (north-west of Miyako), Ryūsen-dō is one of the three largest stalactite caves in Japan. It contains a huge underground lake, said to be one of the clearest in the world. Admission is ¥1000, which also includes entry to the adjacent Ryūsen Shindō, a cave in which a number of stone tools and earthenware were found (8.30 am to 6 pm, until 5 pm from November to April).

From Morioka there are direct buses to Ryūsen-dō (¥2590, 2½ hours, four to six per day). From Miyako, the most convenient route is to take a train on the private Sanriku-Tetsudō Kita-Rias line to Omoto (¥750, 30 minutes), where you can change to a bus to the cave (¥600, 35 minutes).

Aomori-ken 青森県

As a special incentive for foreign tourists, Aomori-ken has introduced the Aomori Welcome Card, which entitles travellers to discounts on hotels, attractions, restaurants, and transport (an astounding 50% off tickets purchased at major bus company outlets) – well worth the five minutes it takes to get the card. The card is issued on the spot at tourist information centres in Mutsu (Shimokita-hantō), Hachinohe, Aomori, Hirosaki and Towada-ko.

HACHINOHE 八戸
☎ 0178

Travellers to Hokkaidō can take the ferry from Hachinohe-kō to either Tomakomai (¥3970, nine hours, three per day) or Muroran (¥3970, eight hours, twice daily).

Hachinohe-kō is inconveniently located around 15 minutes by taxi or 20 minutes by bus from Hon-Hachinohe station on the JR Hachinohe line, two stops east of Hachinohe station (¥180). Tokkyū trains on the JR Tōhoku main line link Hachinohe station with Morioka (¥3260, 70 minutes) and Aomori (¥2570, 60 minutes). Local trains to

NORTHERN HONSHŪ

Aomori (¥1620, 1¾ hours) go via Noheji where you can transfer to trains to Shimokita-hantō. If you are heading down the coast to Miyako, you can take the JR Hachinohe line as far as Kuji (¥1110, two hours) and then transfer to the private Sanriku-Tetsudō Kita-Rias line to Miyako (¥1800, 1½ hours).

The four-star *Kawayo Green Youth Hostel* (☎ 56-2756) charges ¥3250 per person and is a 10-minute walk from Mukaiyama station, three stops north of Hachinohe (¥320, 15 minutes). The hostel is convenient for visiting the enormous **Komaki Onsen** complex, where for ¥500 you can stroll around a park that contains several traditional farmhouses and a pleasant tea-house and afterwards soak in the enormous baths at the Komaki Dai-ni Grand Hotel. Komaki Onsen is adjacent to Misawa station, one stop north of Mukaiyama.

SHIMOKITA-HANTŌ 下北半島
☎ 0175
Looking like a giant axe poised at the top of Honshū, this peninsula is still fairly isolated, and has long stretches of sparsely inhabited coastline and remote mountain valleys. The main draw is **Osore-zan**, a barren volcanic mountain that has for centuries been considered one of Japan's most sacred places (¥500, 6 am to 6 pm, May to October). The sprawling temple complex of **Bodai-ji** originally consisted of only Entsū-ji, founded here in the 9th century. Osore-zan is a destination for those seeking to commune with the dead, especially parents who have lost their children. Several statues of the guardian deity Jizō overlook hills of craggy, sulphur-strewn rocks and hissing vapour. Visitors help lost souls with their underworld penance by adding stones to the cairns. With the murky **Usuri-ko** and ravens swarming about, it's an appropriate setting for Buddhist purgatory; even the name, Osore, means fear or dread. If you care to bathe on the doorstep of 'hell', there are free hot springs off to the sides as you approach the main hall (sex-segregated options are on the left).

On the western edge of Shimokita-hantō is scenic **Hotokegaura**, a spectacular stretch of coastline dotted with 100m-tall cliffs. Water and wind have carved delicate patterns into the rock faces, which are said to resemble Buddha. There are also several hot-springs resorts and numerous fishing villages dotting the peninsula.

Orientation & Information
The main transport and accommodation hub on Shimokita-hantō is Mutsu. Confusingly, the train station for Mutsu is Tanabu station on the private Shimokita-Kōtsū line.

North of Mutsu is Ōhata, where you can get buses to Yagen Onsen, a hot-springs resort area up in the hills. To the east is the cape, Shiriya-zaki, to the west is Ōma, the northernmost point on Honshū. At the bottom tip of the peninsula is Wakinosawa, which is linked by ferry to Aomori.

The tourist association office (☎ 22-0909) inside Masakari Plaza (to the right as you exit Tanabu station) can provide a few pamphlets and maps (9 am to 6 pm, closed Tuesday from October to March).

The main post office in Mutsu is a five-minute walk north-west of Tanabu station. There is also a post office on Wakinosawa's main street.

Special Events
Osore-zan Taisai, a festival held from 20 to 24 July, attracts huge crowds of visitors keen to consult *itako*. A similar, but smaller, festival is held from 9 to 11 October. Itako are mediums who act on behalf of visitors wishing to contact dead family members. More traditional itako still recite the Buddhist sutras and hold Oshira-sama dolls (see the Tōno section earlier) as they invoke the spirits. Historically, Itako have been blind, middle-aged women but nowadays some of the popular itako are quite young and can clearly see the long lines of patrons camped out in front of their tents, waiting with donations in hand.

Places to Stay & Eat
Wakinosawa Youth Hostel (☎ 44-2341) charges ¥2850 and is well placed for an excursion along Hotokegaura and the ferry connection to Aomori. It's perched on a

hillside about 10 minutes on foot from the Wakinosawa bus stop, 15 minutes from the ferry pier. The manager is helpful, and her husband is an avid photographer and local ranger who sometimes leads hikes in the nearby hills to observe colonies of 'snow monkeys' (Japanese macaque).

If you can make advance reservations in Japanese, *Osore-zan Bodai-ji* (☎ 22-3825) costs ¥5000 per person, including two meals. It makes for an interesting night, as you'll probably sleep in a Japanese-style room jam-packed with friendly pilgrims.

There are plenty of minshuku and ryokan in the drab confines of Mutsu, clustered around the bus terminal and Tanabu station. *Murai Ryokan* (☎ 22-4755) is excellent value at ¥7000 for cheerful Japanese-style rooms, including two meals. The ryokan is next to Masakari Plaza, a two-minute walk from Tanabu station.

Other accommodation is spread out around the peninsula. On the northern coast, between Ōhata and Ōma, is *Minshuku Maruyama* (☎ 36-2217), a pleasant place facing the sea, charging ¥6500 with meals. It's five minutes on foot from the Shimofuro Onsen-mae bus stop.

Top-end accommodation is available at Yagen Onsen. *Hotel New Yagen* (☎ 34-3311) charges ¥15,000 to ¥25,000 per person, including two meals.

Getting There & Away

On the JR Ominato line, there are a few direct kaisoku trains from Aomori via Noheji to the terminus at Ōminato, but be careful to get off one stop before Ōminato at Shimokita station, where you can transfer to the private Shimokita-Kōtsū line to Tanabu station (Mutsu, ¥200). The entire journey costs ¥2090 from Aomori, ¥1310 from Noheji. The Shimokita-Kōtsū line continues north from Tanabu as far as Ōhata (¥410, 30 minutes).

If you find yourself stuck between trains at Shimokita station, there are frequent buses outside the station to the Mutsu bus terminal or Tanabu (¥200, 15 minutes). There are also buses every one to two hours

between Mutsu bus terminal and Aomori (¥2520, 2½ hours) via Noheji (¥1450, 1¼ hours).

Comfortable high-speed ferries link Aomori with Wakinosawa (¥2540, 55 minutes), and most of these then continue up the coast of the peninsula to Sai. Boats to Aomori depart twice daily from Wakinosawa at 8.30 am and 2 pm. From Ōma, there are ferries to Hakodate on Hokkaidō (¥1010, 1¾ hours, two to four per day).

Getting Around

You can catch buses to nearly all destinations on the peninsula from the Mutsu bus terminal. Some buses also pass by Tanabu station before heading out of Mutsu. From April to October buses to Osore-zan leave every hour or so (¥750, 35 minutes). There are also eight buses per day along the northern shore of the peninsula, passing Ōhata, Shimofuro Onsen and Ōma before terminating at Sai (¥2260, two hours). To get to Yagen Onsen, first take a bus or train to Ōhata, from where there are a few buses per day to the hot-springs resort (¥540, 30 minutes).

JR buses operate between Mutsu and Wakinosawa (¥1790, 1½ hours, seven per day), where ferries from Aomori stop twice daily at 10.35 am and 4.15 pm before continuing to Sai via the Hotokegaura coastline (¥2640, 1½ hours). From November to March, only the morning boat continues.

Between late April and early November, round trip sightseeing boats for Hotokegaura depart from both Wakinosawa (¥3800, two hours, once daily) and Sai (¥2170, 1¾ hours, two to three per day).

AOMORI 青森
☎ 0177 • pop 296,000
Aomori is the prefectural capital and an important centre for shipping and fishing. It was bombed heavily during WWII and has since been completely rebuilt. Although the city is showing signs of prosperity, it's still somewhat out of Japan's economic mainstream, and retains a sleepy fishing town quality.

For the traveller, Aomori is a useful transport hub for ferries to Hokkaidō or visits to

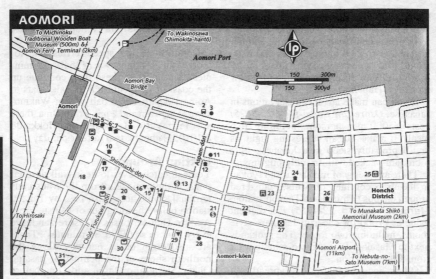

Shimokita-hantō, Towada-ko and the scenic region around Hakkōda-san.

Information

The city tourist information office (☎ 23-4670) is near the southern exit of Aomori station. The staff can provide lists of accommodation, as well as English-language maps and pamphlets (8.30 am to 5 pm).

The prefectural tourist information counter (☎ 34-2500) is on the ground floor of the distinctive pyramid-shaped ASPAM building (9 am to 6 pm). The Network Centre, on the 8th floor, offers free Internet access and great views of Aomori-wan (9 am to noon and 1 to 5 pm, Monday to Friday).

Aomori's main post office is far east of the city centre, but there are two smaller branch post offices within easy reach of the station.

Things to See

The prime reason for a visit to Aomori would be the Nebuta Matsuri (see Special Events later). If you miss the festival, the Nebuta-no-sato Museum can give you a taste of it (¥630, 9 am to 5.30 pm April to November, until 8pm June to September).

Buses to the museum, 9km south of town, leave fairly frequently from Aomori station (¥450, 30 minutes).

The most impressive sight in Aomori is Shōwa Daibutsu, Japan's largest outdoor Buddha, at a height of 21m and weighing 220 tonnes. Seen from the highway, Buddha's head seems to float eerily above the trees. The breezy temple grounds are full of spinning pinwheels left by parents for their children who died young (¥400, 8 am to 5.30 pm). Buses from Aomori station are timed so that you have about an hour to look around before catching the next bus back (¥540, 45 minutes).

The Munakata Shikō Memorial Museum houses a collection of wood-block prints, paintings and calligraphy by Munakata Shikō, an Aomori native whose art and wit won him international fame. The museum displays around 30 paintings and prints at a time. The building itself is azekura-style, with walls of geometric wooden planks fitted together without upright supports (¥300, 9.30 am to 4.30 pm, until 4 pm and closed Monday from December to March). The bus ride from Aomori station to the Munakata Shikō Kinenkan-dōri stop takes 15

AOMORI

PLACES TO STAY
6 Hotel New Murakoshi
　ホテルニュームラコシ
7 Ryokan Nanjō
　旅館南條
8 Ryokan Fukuya
　旅館福家
10 Aomori Grand Hotel
　青森グランドホテル
12 Hotel JAL City Aomori
　ホテルJALシティ青森
17 Hotel New Aomori-kan
　ホテルニュー青森館
20 Aomori Kokusai Hotel
　青森国際ホテル
22 Aomori Plaza Hotel
　青森プラザホテル
24 Takko Ryokan
　田子旅館
26 Hotel Shibata
　ホテルシバタ

PLACES TO EAT
14 Caffeol Coffee
　Shop

15 McDonald's
16 Kakigen
　柿源
18 Fish & Fresh
　Food Market
　市場団地
29 Saigon

OTHER
1 Aomori Port Passenger
　Ferry Terminal
　青森港旅客船
　ターミナル
2 Bus Stand
　バス乗り場
3 ASPAM Building
　(Aomori Prefectural
　Centre for Industry and
　Tourism); Network
　Centre
　アスパム青森
　観光物産館
4 JR Highway Bus Terminal
　JRハイウエイ
　バス乗り場

5 Orix Rent-a-Car
　オリックスレンタカー
9 Aomori City Buses
　青森駅前市営バス停
11 Toyota Rent-a-Car
　トヨタレンタカー
13 Michinoku Bank
　みちのく銀行
19 Post Office
21 Aomori Bank
　青森銀行
23 Shrine
　善知鳥神社
25 Aomori Cultural
　Museum
　青森郷土館
27 Matsukiya
　Department Store
　松木屋デパート
28 Aomon Prefectural
　Office
　青森県庁
30 Post Office
31 Kotobukiya
　ことぶきや

minutes (¥190). An enormous wood-block print by Munakata also hangs in the Aomori Prefectural Office.

Across the Bay Bridge, the **Michinoku Traditional Wooden Boat Museum** (Michinoku Hoppō-gyosen Hakubutsukan) boasts a floating replica of a 19th-century Macau junk and an exhibition hall full of fishing boats from several Asian countries (¥200, 8.30 am to 6.30 pm, closed mid-December to mid-March). There's an hourly free shuttle service to the museum from Aomori station between 9.45 am and 3.45 pm – look for a white van with green lettering on the side.

Those interested in folk crafts could visit the **Aomori Cultural Museum** (¥310) in the city centre. However, more interesting displays can be found at the free **Museum of Historical Folkcraft of the Snow Country** (9 am to 4 pm, closed Thursday). The museum is 25 minutes by bus from Aomori station to the Kami-tamagawa stop (¥290).

Special Events
The Nebuta Matsuri, held from 2 to 7 August, is renowned throughout Japan for its parades of colossal illuminated floats accompanied by thousands of rowdy, chanting dancers. The parades start at sunset and last for hours, except on the final day when the action starts around noon. For further details see the boxed text 'Nebuta or Neputa'.

Places to Stay
Aomori is a popular place to break one's journey between Tokyo and Hokkaidō and can be a difficult place in which to find accommodation even in off-peak periods. If you're planning to see the Nebuta Matsuri you'll need to book a room well in advance (or plan to commute from a nearby town like Hirosaki), as it's not uncommon for *all* accommodation in town to be booked out.

I arrived in Aomori at around 7.30 pm from Hakodate and started ringing around the ryokan…and then the hotels. An hour and a half later I was ringing Hirosaki, then Morioka. Nothing. It seemed as if every hotel in Tōhoku was full. In the end I slept with the tramps on one of the bus stop benches across from the station. Not that I got much sleep. Passing drunks took a great deal of interest in the down-and-out gaijin, with one trying to drag me off to a brothel...I politely declined and whiled away the rest of the night with a delightful hobbit-like old man who regaled me with incomprehensible *rakugo* stories.

Chris Taylor

Nebuta or Neputa?

Even Japanese people may not be able tell you the difference between Aomori's Nebuta and Hirosaki's Neputa festivals, which not only sound confusingly alike but both take place at the beginning of August.

Most Japanese would say that Aomori's Nebuta is the more impressive party, but Hirosaki's Neputa may well be more beautiful, with its delicately painted floats, dignified parades and dramatic drumming. Historical accounts of the origins of either festival do not always agree, but Hirosaki's Neputa Matsuri is generally said to signify ceremonial preparation for battle. The fan-shaped Neputa floats are rotated during festival parades so that the heroic *kagami-e* painting on the front and the tear-jerker *miokuri-e* ('seeing-off picture') on the back can both be viewed.

Aomori's Nebuta Matsuri, on the other hand, celebrates the triumphant return from battle. The most dramatic account of this festival's origins is the tale of Sakanoue Tamuramaro, an 8th-century general who was sent by the imperial palace to quash a rebellion by the native Ezo tribe. The crafty Tamuramaro is said to have used giant lanterns, along with drums and flutes, to lure the unsuspecting Ezo from their redoubts, after which they were swiftly subdued.

Others theorise that Nebuta began as a way to ward off the stupor that comes with late summer heat, and Aomori's boisterous parades with monster floats and hundreds of dancers jangling hand-held bells is certainly enough to wake anyone up.

Places to Stay – Budget
Tucked away down a narrow street near the station are several ryokan of variable quality but charging similar rates of ¥3500 to ¥4000 per person without meals. The better choices are **Ryokan Nanjō** (☎ 22-6540) and **Ryokan Fukuya** (☎ 22-3521). Squeezed in among this group is a small business hotel, **Hotel New Murakoshi** (☎ 22-8095), where singles cost ¥5000 and twins range from ¥7000 to ¥12,000. If all of the above are full, you may have better luck farther from the station at **Takko Ryokan** (☎ 22-4825), where quality rooms cost ¥4500 per person.

Places to Stay – Mid-Range
One of the cheaper hotels within easy striking distance of the station is the sharp-looking **Hotel New Aomori-kan** (☎ 22-2865), which offers singles/twins from ¥6000/ 10,500. More expensive but even classier, the **Aomori Grand Hotel** (☎ 23-1011) sprawls across an entire block and the cheapest singles/twins start at ¥6600/13,200.

A bit farther from the station, but less grandiose, **Hotel Shibata** (☎ 75-1451) has rooms for ¥5600/10,400. The **Aomori Plaza Hotel** (☎ 75-4311) offers comparable rooms starting at ¥5500/10,000.

Probably the nicest place in town is the new **Hotel JAL City Aomori** (☎ 32-2580), where rooms start at ¥8200/14,000. The hotel also has doubles for ¥11,000, very good value for money.

Places to Eat & Drink
Shinmachi-dōri, the main shopping street, runs east from the station and has some good sushi shops, seafood restaurants and a couple of fast-food places. One spot worth visiting is **Kakigen**, which specialises in scallops, an Aomori speciality. You can ask for *hotate furai teishoku* (fried scallop set) or the mouth-watering *hotate batā yaki teishoku* (scallops grilled with butter), both of which cost ¥1300. One block south of the main drag, **Saigon** serves up passable Thai, Vietnamese and Indonesian food. Popular lunch-time set menus start at around ¥800.

Seafood lovers may also want to venture into the fish and fresh food market, just south of the station, where there are good deals to be had on seafood, *rāmen* (Chinese-style egg noodles) and set lunches. The covered alley next to the JR Highway Bus Terminal comes alive at night with a dozen or so small eateries, some of which serve the local specialities: *ke-no-shiru* (winter vegetable miso stew) and *ichigo-ni* (strawberry sea urchin soup, so named because the cooked urchins curl up to resemble wild strawberries).

A 15-minute walk south of Aomori station, *Kotobukiya* offers nightly dinner shows featuring *tsugaru-jamisen*, a kind of Japanese bluegrass music, starting at around 7 pm (¥5000). If you can't afford dinner you could turn up later for discounted admission and a few drinks.

Getting There & Away

Air There are frequent flights from Aomori airport to Tokyo, Nagoya, Osaka, Sapporo and Fukuoka. International destinations include Seoul and Khabarovsk (Russia). Airport buses are timed to flights and depart from in front of the ASPAM building and Aomori station (¥560, 40 minutes)

Train The JR Tsugaru Kaikyo line runs from Aomori via the Seikan Tunnel to Hakodate on Hokkaidō (tokkyū, ¥4830, two hours). Kaisoku trains do the trip in 2½ hours, and on some of these services (¥3150) you take the Seikan Tunnel tour (see the boxed text 'Seikan Tunnel Tour' in the Hokkaidō chapter). The JR Tōhoku main line runs south from Aomori to Morioka (tokkyū, ¥5460, 2¼ hours), from where you can zip back to Tokyo in 2½ hours on the shinkansen. The Ōu main line runs via Hirosaki to Akita.

Bus Between April and mid-November JR runs five to eight buses a day from Aomori to Towada-ko (¥3000, three hours). One hour out of Aomori, the bus reaches Hakkōda ropeway (¥1070), then continues through a string of hot-springs hamlets to the lake. JR also operates buses to Morioka (¥3160, three hours) and Sendai (¥5700, five hours), and a night bus to Tokyo (¥10,190,

9½ hours). Buses depart from the JR Highway Bus Terminal outside Aomori station.

For a visit to Osore-zan (Shimokitahantō), you can take a direct bus from the ASPAM building via Noheji to Mutsu (¥2520, 2¾ hours).

Boat From March to December, highspeed Unicorn ferries operate up to three times daily between Hakodate and Aomori (¥2130, 2¼ hours). Regular ferries make the same trip more frequently year round (¥1420, 3¾ hours). From Aomori, there is one afternoon ferry to Muroran (Hokkaidō); in the opposite direction, it's an overnighter leaving Muroran at 11.25 pm (¥3460, seven hours). The ferry terminal, on the western side of the city, is a 10-minute taxi ride from Aomori station (¥1000). Buses run from the station to the terminal only twice daily (¥260).

Ferries for Wakinosawa on Shimokitahantō leave twice daily at 9.40 am and 3.20 pm from the Aomori port passenger ferry terminal, a 10-minute walk north of the station.

HAKKŌDA-SAN 八甲田山
☎ 0177

Just south of Aomori is the scenic region around Hakkōda-san, a series of peaks that are popular with hikers, hot-spring enthusiasts and skiers.

The Hakkōda ropeway (cable car) whisks you up Tamoyachi-dake to the 1326m summit (¥1150 one way, ¥1800 return, 9 am and 4 pm). From there you can follow a network of hiking trails. One particularly pleasant route scales the three peaks of Akakura-dake (1548m), Ido-dake (1550m) and Ōdake (1584m), and then winds its way down to Sukayu Onsen, which is about 10 minutes by bus beyond the cable car station, in the direction of Towada-ko. The 8km hike can be done in a leisurely four hours. Hakkōda-san can easily be done as a day trip from Aomori. If you make the hike to Sukayu Onsen and want to spend the night, *Sukayu Onsen Ryokan (☎ 38-6400)* is right at the end of the trail with rates starting at ¥11,000 per person, including two meals. Budget-conscious travellers can soak in the ryokan's 1000-person cedar bath for just ¥500. There is a camping ground nearby.

To get to the cable car station, take a JR bus from Aomori station bound for Towada-ko and get off at Hakkōda Ropeway-eki (¥1070, four to eight per day, April to mid-November). In winter, buses to Sukayu Onsen run past the ropeway stop, then continue for another 10 minutes to the Sukayu terminus (¥1240).

HIROSAKI 弘前
☎ 0172 • pop 147,000

Founded in the 17th century, this castle town developed into one of the leading cultural centres in Tōhoku. With the exception of its dreary modern centre, Hirosaki has retained much of its original architecture, including a large portion of its castle area, temple districts and even a few Meiji-era buildings. Hirosaki is recommended for its atmosphere and a collection of sights that can be covered in one day at an easy walking pace.

Orientation & Information

The main train station is JR Hirosaki station. All bus connections for destinations outside Hirosaki are made at the Hirosaki bus terminal adjacent to Itō Yōkadō department store, few minutes' walk west of the station.

Hirosaki is compact and easily covered on foot. To give yourself a quick start – and avoid the drab town centre – take the ¥100 tourist loop bus from in front of the station for the 15-minute ride to Tsugaruhan Neputa-mura, where you can start your circuit of the castle and the other sights.

The Hirosaki City Tourist Bureau (☎ 32-0524) is outside Hirosaki station. Be sure to pick up *Hirosaki City: Castle Town of Cherry Blossoms and Apples* which lists sights, festivals and accommodation and has an excellent map. The bureau is open from 8.45 am to 6 pm, and until 5 pm in winter.

On the south side of Hirosaki-kōen, the Hirosaki Sightseeing Information Centre (☎ 37-5501) is inside the Kankōkan (Tourism Building). In addition to displays of local products and festival floats, the centre stocks information material on Hirosaki and other destinations in Aomori-ken (9 am to 6 pm, until 5 pm during winter and later during festivals). The main post office is a 20-minute walk north-west of the station.

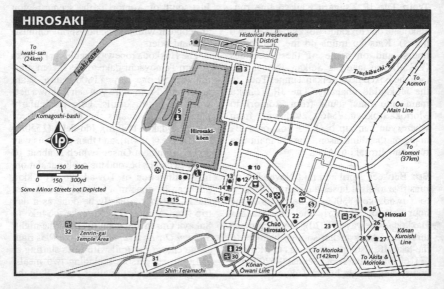

NORTHERN HONSHŪ

Tsugaruhan Neputa-mura

This museum has a fine display of Neputa floats that are paraded during the Neputa Matsuri. Museum staff frequently demonstrate festival drumming techniques (¥500 for a quick hands-on lesson). You can also try making local folk crafts here, such as kokeshi dolls, Neputa lanterns, *Tsugaru-yaki* (Tsugaru pottery) or kite painting. Entry is ¥500 (9 am to 5 pm, until 4 pm from December through March).

Just south of Neputa-mura, Koyama senbei factory sells huge bags of fresh rice crackers. Nearby, Genbē craft shop has fine examples of Tsugaru lacquerware, nicknamed *baka-nurii* ('fool's lacquer') for its more than 40 layers of multicoloured designs.

Historical Preservation District

Just north of Tsugaruhan Neputa-mura, this residential district was once reserved for samurai, although it now contains mostly modern houses, some of which are still in the hands of samurai descendants. The traditional houses of the Umeda and Iwata families, as well as the former clan doctor's home (Itō House), have been restored and are open a few days a week to the public; free entry.

Hirosaki-jō 弘前城

Construction of the castle was completed in 1611, but it was burnt down in 1627 after being struck by lightning. One of the castle's corner towers was rebuilt in 1810 and now houses a small museum of samurai weaponry and garments (¥200, 9 am to 5 pm, April to late November). The castle grounds have been turned into a splendid park that attracts huge crowds for *hanami* (cherry blossom viewing) during late April and early May. The ramparts across from the castle tower offer nice views of Iwaki-san, as

HIROSAKI

PLACES TO STAY
6 Ishiba Ryokan
　石場旅館
10 Hirosaki Grand Hotel
　弘前グランドホテル
14 Ryokan Edogawa
　旅館江戸川
15 Hirosaki Youth Hostel
　弘前ユースホステル
16 Kobori Ryokan
　小堀旅館
26 City Hirosaki Hotel
　シティ弘前ホテル
27 Hotel Shinjuku
　ホテル新宿
31 Minshuku
　Henshō-ji
　民宿遍照寺

PLACES TO EAT
17 Kagi-no-Hana
　かぎのはな
19 Tea & Co. Cafe
23 McDonald's
28 Live House
　Yamauta
　ライブハウス山唄

OTHER
1 Old Umeda House;
　Old Itō House
　旧梅田家；旧伊東家
2 Old Iwata House
　旧岩田家
3 Tsugaruhan
　Neputa-mura
　津軽藩ねぷた村
4 Koyama Senbei Factory;
　Genbē Craft Shop
　小山工場；源兵衛
5 Hirosaki-Jō
　弘前城
7 Fujita Kinen Tei-en
　藤田記念庭園
8 City Hall
　市役所
9 Kankōkan (Hirosaki
　Sightseeing Information
　Centre)
　弘前市観光館
11 Hokusaikan
　北菜館
12 Tanakaya Lacquerware
　Store
　田中屋

13 Aomori Bank
　Memorial Hall
　青森銀行記念館
18 Nakasan Department
　Store
　中三デパート
20 Hirosaki Post Office
　弘前郵便局
21 Michinoku Bank
　みちのく銀行
22 Kinokuniya
　Bookshop
　紀伊國屋書店
24 Itō Yōkadō
　Department Store;
　Hirosaki Bus
　Terminal
　イトーヨーカドー；
　弘前バスターミナル
25 Tokyo Ticket
　東京チケット
29 Gojū-no-tō
　五重塔
30 Saishō-in
　最勝院
32 Chōshō-ji
　長勝院

does **Fujita Kinen Tei-en**, a well-manicured garden outside the south-west corner of the park (¥300, 9 am to 5 pm, closed Monday and from mid-November to mid-April).

Saishō-in 最勝院

About a 15-minute walk south of Hirosaki-jō, the temple, Saishō-in, is worth a visit to see the Gojū-no-tō, a splendid five-storey pagoda constructed in 1667 and recently restored (free, 9 am to 4.30 pm).

Zenrin-gai 禅林街

About 20 minutes on foot west of the pagoda, this temple district is a peaceful place to walk in the early morning or late afternoon. A central avenue – flanked by temples on either side – leads to **Chōshō-ji**. After passing through the impressive temple gate, continue past a large 14th-century bell to the main hall which dates from the 17th century (at the time of writing it was undergoing restoration). On the left side of the courtyard is a smaller building housing several dozen colourful statues of Buddhist disciples, all striking different poses. To the left of the main hall, a path through the trees leads to a row of mausoleums built for the early rulers of the Tsugaru clan, which dominated the region around Hirosaki during the Edo period.

Special Events

From 1 to 7 August, Hirosaki celebrates Neputa Matsuri, a festival famous throughout Japan for its beautifully painted fan-shaped floats which are illuminated from within and paraded on different routes every evening to the accompaniment of flutes and drums. Like its more rowdy counterpart held in Aomori, this festival attracts thousands of visitors – book accommodation well in advance if you plan to attend. See the boxed text 'Nebuta or Neputa?' for further information.

Places to Stay – Budget

Hirosaki Youth Hostel (☎ 33-7066) charges ¥2950 and is in a good location for the sights. There's no curfew at this party hostel, so don't expect much sleep. From Hirosaki station or the bus terminal, take the yellow (¥100) loop bus to the Daigaku-byōin stop. If it's before 10 am or after 6 pm, you can still get a bus from the station (stop No 6) or the bus terminal (stop No 9 or 10) to Daigaku-byōin (¥170, 15 minutes). Walk straight up the street for five minutes, cross the intersection and look for the hostel down an alley on your left.

Places to Stay – Mid-Range

Minshuku For temple lodging, you could try *Minshuku Henshō-ji* (☎ 0172-32-8714) in the Shin-Teramachi district. Rates are ¥6000 with two meals.

Ryokan There are several ryokan not far from Hirosaki-kōen, also convenient for taking in the sights. *Kobori Ryokan* (☎ 32-5111) is in a large traditional-style building, and has rates starting at ¥9000 per person, including two meals. Just around the corner is *Ryokan Edogawa* (☎ 32-4092) in a less appealing three-storey modern structure, but the rooms are comfortable and cost ¥7000 with two meals. A few blocks north, the lovely *Ishiba Ryokan* (☎ 32-9118) is a bit more upmarket, with rates ranging from ¥8,000 to ¥12,000.

Hotel There are also a few business hotels in the station area, although this is not a particularly good part of town to be based in. The petite *Hotel Shinjuku* (☎ 32-8484) couldn't be more welcoming, with singles/doubles for ¥6500/11,000.

More centrally located, the upmarket *Hirosaki Grand Hotel* (☎ 32-1515) is good value with singles/twins for ¥5700/11,000.

Places to Eat & Drink

The three-storey *Hokusaikan* is a food- and drink-fest, with more than 240 brands of local, international and microbrew beer to choose from. Going through the lot would use up the family fortune for several generations, but a few cold ones shouldn't set you back more than ¥2000, including table charge (¥350). The 1st floor is an 'Irish pub', the 2nd floor serves Western food, and the 3rd floor is a Japanese-style izakaya

(11 am to 1 pm). There are excellent views of Neputa parades from the upper floors.

In Kajimachi, the town's diminutive entertainment district, a good place to sample the local cuisine (mountain vegetables, river fish and so on) is *Kagi-no-Hana*, with teishoku from ¥1600. It's hidden on the bottom floor of a black concrete and steel building. Look for the vertical sign that reads, however oddly, 'Eas Buil2'; the entrance is on the left-hand side.

Just in case you were wondering, the neon-coloured building that looks to be sporting a gigantic colander is the Nakasan department store. The 7th floor has several places with decent food, reasonable prices and lots of point-and-choose displays and picture menus. Just across the river is *Tea & Co.*, a tiny cafe that serves good espresso (¥380) and baked goods.

If you want to combine food and entertainment then splurge on a visit to *Live House Yamauta* (☎ 36-1835), in a large plaster and wood building just five minutes on foot from the station. The place is run by a family who serve the drinks and food, then pick up three-stringed, thick-necked musical instruments, known as *tsugaru-jamisen*, and launch into local music. You can hear the same heartbreaking vocals and hard, fast-picking tunes at Kotobukiya in Aomori. If you order a teishoku and a couple of beers, you can expect to pay around ¥2000. Live House Yamauta is open from 5 to 11 pm, and there are usually two sets of music each night. It's closed one night a month, however, so you may want to call ahead (reservations accepted).

Getting There & Away

Hirosaki station is on the JR Ōu main line which runs north to Aomori (futsū, ¥650, 50 minutes) and south to Akita (tokkyū, ¥3870, two hours).

Most local buses stop at the train station as well as the Hirosaki bus terminal, which serves destinations farther afield including Sendai (¥5090, 4½ hours, three per day), Towada-ko (¥2350, 2¼ hours, three per day from early April to late October), and Iwaki-san (see the Iwaki-san section later).

AONI ONSEN 青荷温泉

The bus from Hirosaki to Towada-ko climbs through the mountains via a series of remote hot-spring hamlets. Halfway through the journey it passes by Aoni Onsen (☎ 0172-54-8588), a rustic group of ryokan that prefer oil lamps to electricity and serve wholesome mountain food. Advance reservations are necessary and rates start at ¥6500 per person, including two meals. The nearby camping ground receives good reports from travellers, but charges ¥1000 even if you bring your own tent.

To get to Aoni Onsen you'll have to get off the bus at the Aoni Onsen-iriguchi bus stop and walk six kilometres up the trail. If you call ahead, a pick-up service may be available. When buses between Hirosaki and Towada-kō aren't running, you can take a bus from Hirosaki to Kuroishi-eki (¥570), then transfer to any bus going via Aoni Onsen-iriguchi (¥780).

IWAKI-SAN 岩木山

Soaring above Hirosaki is the sacred volcano of Iwaki-san (1625m) which is a popular peak for both pilgrims and hikers.

From early April to late October, there are three buses before noon from the Hirosaki bus terminal to Dake Onsen (¥900, 50 minutes), where you'll need to change to a shuttle bus to Hachigōme (¥880, 30 minutes), at the foot of the cable car to the summit (Eighth Station). After a seven-minute cable car ride (¥410 one way, ¥750 return), it takes another 45 minutes to climb to the summit. This route is the shortest and easiest, but it is also possible to hike to the top in about four hours starting from Iwaki-jinja. This is the same route used by farmers during their annual mountain pilgrimage, called Oyama Sankei, when they carry huge coloured banners and flags to the inner shrine on the summit. The festival usually takes place in early August, but the date varies; call the tourist information offices in Hirosaki or Aomori for more information.

Near Iwaki-jinja in Hyakuzawa Onsen, *Kokuminshukusha Iwaki-sō* (☎ 0172-83-2215) has rates of ¥6500 including two meals, or ¥7500 on weekends and holidays. To get there, take a bus from Hirosaki bus terminal bound for Iwaki-sō and get off at the last stop (¥660, one hour).

TOWADA-KO 十和田湖
☎ 0176

This large crater lake has some impressive scenery and opportunities for hiking and skiing. Nenoguchi, a small tourist outpost on the eastern shore of the lake, marks the entrance to the 14km **Oirase Valley Nature Trail**, probably the most enjoyable thing to do around the lake. The path winds through thick deciduous forest following the Oirase-gawa, with its mossy boulders, plunging waterfalls and tumbling tracts of white water. Unfortunately, it also runs uncomfortably close to a highway clogged with tour buses that pull right onto the path. On the plus side, if you tire easily, you can catch a bus back to Nenoguchi or Yasumiya just about anywhere along the way. After three hours, the path ends at Yakeyama, from where frequent buses return to Nenoguchi (¥660, 30 minutes) and Yasumiya (¥1100, one hour). Early morning and late afternoon are the best times to do

the hike, particularly if you visit during the peak viewing season in autumn.

The other main tourist spot on the lake, **Yasumiya**, has numerous boat tours of the lake, which are not really worth the time or money. One practical route is the one-hour cruise between Yasumiya and Nenoguchi (¥1320 one way). Boats leave approximately once to twice an hour between 8 am and 4 pm from April to early November. You can find hiking maps (only Japanese-language) at the Towada-ko Visitors Centre near the pier. The hole-in-the-wall tourist information centre (☎ 75-2506), just north of the JR bus station, also stocks a few pamphlets and maps but is really only useful for booking accommodation (8 am to 5 pm).

Places to Stay & Eat
There are three camping grounds around the edge of the lake. The most convenient is *Towada-ko Oide Campground*, about 4km west of Yasumiya (¥300, open late April to early November). JR buses from Yasumiya to Towada-Minami pass by the Oide Kyampu-jo-mae stop (¥220).

Hakubutsukan Youth Hostel (☎ 75-2002) is tucked away inside the Towada-ko Grand Hotel, across from the bus station and a few hundred metres from the pier in Yasumiya. Fairly comfortable two-person dorms are squeezed into the old wing of the hotel; charges are ¥3200 per person, which includes the use of the hot-spring bath.

In Yakeyama, the *Oirase Youth Hostel* (☎ 74-2031) is a laid-back, cheery place with no curfew and rates of ¥2800. Buses running between the lake and Aomori pass by the Yakeyama bus stop, from where it's 200m up a small hill past the Oirase Grand Hotel car park to the hostel.

There are innumerable minshuku in the area, mostly along the road leading out of Yasumiya away from the lake. The last inn you'll come to on the left-hand side is *Min-shuku Towada-ko San-sō* (☎ 75-2710) in a modern grey building with a traditional interior. Rates are ¥4000 without meals. The friendly *Minshuku Hōkosō* (☎ 75-2417) charges ¥6000 for the same deal and is located in Utarube, about 20 minutes by bus

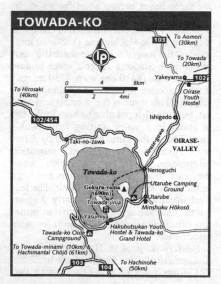

east of Yasumiya. Buses to Aomori pass by the Utarube bus stop, which is a three-minute walk from the minshuku.

In Yasumiya across from the Towada Kankō Hotel, *Yamagoya* serves tasty *yakiniku* (Korean-style barbecued beef) fare. You can pick and choose from the menu, or go with a teishoku set (¥1000). Late at night, this place turns into a karaoke bar, so go early (or late, depending on your inclination).

Getting There & Away

There are two bus centres in Yasumiya, one for JR buses and one for other services. Both are a couple of minutes on foot from the pier.

Between late April and early August, JR buses run frequently to Aomori (¥3000, three hours) – more details are provided in the Aomori Getting There & Away section. There are also a few buses per day between April and early November from Towada-ko to Hirosaki (¥2350, 2¼ hours) and Morioka (¥2420, 2¼ hours). From late April to October, there is one afternoon bus around 2.30 pm to Hachimantai Chōjō, the main point of access for the Hachimantai region (¥2250, 2½ hours). There is also one night bus to Tokyo (Ikebukuro, Tokyo station) departing from Towada-ko at around 9 pm (¥10,090, 9½ hours).

The nearest train station is at Towada-Minami, on the JR Hanawa line with connections to Morioka (kaisoku, ¥1800, 1¾ hours). From April to early November, buses run from Towada-Minami to Yasumiya four times daily (¥1130, one hour). However, you'll probably find it easier to opt for the bus services listed above.

Akita-ken 秋田県

HACHIMANTAI 八幡平

Farther south from Towada-ko is the mountain plateau region of Hachimantai, which is popular with hikers, skiers and hot-spring enthusiasts.

The Aspite Line Hwy, open late April to November, runs east to west across the plateau. Transport connections revolve around Hachimantai Chōjō, the main access

point for the summit. Although the views are nice, the mostly paved walks around the ponds on the summit only take about an hour and are rather tame. Longer hikes are possible over a couple of days from nearby **Tōshichi Onsen**, which is a 2km walk downhill from the Hachimantai Chōjō car park.

West of the summit, the Aspite Line Hwy winds past several hot-spring resorts before joining Route 341, which leads either south to Tazawa-ko or north towards Towada-ko.

There is a small visitors centre next to the car park at Hachimantai Chōjō where you can purchase good contour maps (in Japanese) of the region and consult bilingual hiking sketch maps on the walls. However, the best places to pick up English-language information on Hachimantai are the tourist information offices at Morioka and Tazawa-ko stations. Although outdated, the INTO pamphlet *Towada-Hachimantai National Park* contains good maps and details on the numerous hot-springs resorts.

Places to Stay

Yuki-no-Koya (☎ 0186-31-2118) is a member of the Toho network (see Accommodation in the Facts for the Visitor chapter) and functions as an alternative youth hostel and mountain lodge. It's closed from mid-November until Christmas and from February until late April. The lodge is in a quiet riverside location at Shibari Onsen, which is on Route 341, north of the turn-off for the Aspite Line Hwy to Hachimantai. Rates start at ¥4900 per person for dormitory-style accommodation, including two excellent meals. Infrequent buses from Hachimantai Chōjō pass by Shibari Onsen (¥790, 40 minutes, last bus 3.30 pm) before going to either Towada-ko or Kazuno Hanawa and Hachimantai stations, which are both on the JR Hanawa line, for connections to Morioka (kaisoku, ¥1260, two hours).

Tōshichi Onsen Saiun-sō (☎ 0195-78-3962) has rates starting at ¥11,000, including two meals. It's open from late April to early November. Entry to the hot-spring baths cost ¥500 – be warned that entering the *rotemburo* (open-air mineral spa) entails flashing passing traffic on the highway.

NORTHERN HONSHŪ

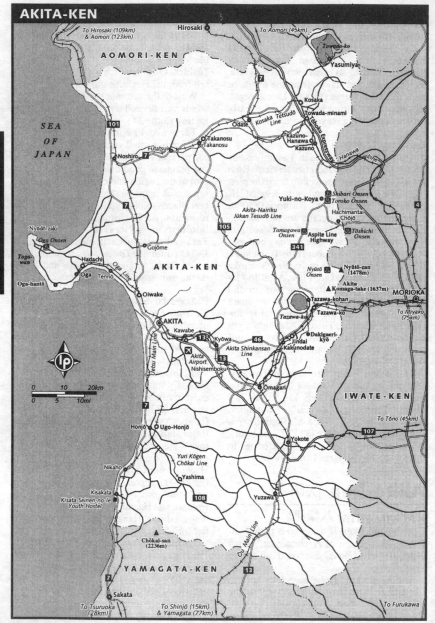

The scenic *Hachimantai Youth Hostel* (☎ 0195-78-2031) is 20 minutes by bus east of the summit; get off at the Hachimantai Kankō Hoteru-mae stop (three to five buses daily, last bus 3.40 pm). Though the hotel costs ¥5000 per night including two meals, travellers give the management and the food good reviews. Guests also have access to nearby hot springs.

Getting There & Away

All bus services to Hachimantai Chōjō only operate between late April and October.

From Morioka station, there are up to eight buses daily to Hachimantai Chōjō (¥1320, two hours, hourly until noon). Kaisoku trains on the JR Hanawa line run from Morioka to Hachimantai and Kazuno-Hanawa stations (¥1260, two hours), where you can change to infrequent buses departing before noon to Hachimantai Chōjō via Shibari Onsen. Two stops farther west on the Hanawa line is Towada-minami station for access to Towada-ko (see the Towada-ko Getting There & Away entry earlier). However, you'll probably find it easier to opt for the direct bus to Towada-ko departing from Hachimantai Chōjō at noon.

There are three buses per day from Hachimantai Chōjō to Tazawa Kohan (¥1880) and Tazawa-ko station (¥1990, 2½ hours). The last bus departs before 3 pm.

TAZAWA-KO 田沢湖
☎ 0187

Tazawa-ko is the deepest lake in Japan and a popular place for watersports and skiing. Foreign travellers may find more enjoyment by using the lake as a base for hikes around Akita Komaga-take and the isolated hot springs scattered around Nyūtō Onsen.

The main access point for the area is JR Tazawa-ko station, which is 15 minutes by bus from the town on the east side of the lake, Tazawa Kohan. Inside Tazawa-ko station, the spacious 'Fo-Lake' (short for Forest-Lake) tourist information centre (☎ 43-2111) has plentiful bilingual maps and leaflets and the staff can help book accommodation (8.30 am to 6.30 pm). If you're planning on doing any hiking in the Tazawa-ko or Hachimantai regions, detailed contour maps in Japanese, as well as sketch maps in English, are available here.

Things to Do

The lake offers boat excursions, swimming beaches and a 20km perimeter road for which you can rent bicycles (¥400 per hour) or scooters (¥1000 per hour) in Tazawa Kohan. About 15 minutes north of the bus station, **Heart Herb** offers herbal saunas (¥500, 11 am to 9 pm, mid-April to mid-November). In winter, there's good skiing at Tazawa-kōgen, about halfway between the lake and Nyūtō Onsen.

Hiking

The easiest approach to **Akita Komaga-take** (1637m) is to take a bus from Tazawa-ko station via the lake to Komaga-take Hachigōme (Eighth Station). From there it's an easy one-hour climb to the summit area where you can choose trails circling several peaks. A popular trail leads across to the peak of Nyūtō-zan (1478m) in about four hours from where you can hike down to Nyūtō Onsen (another 5km). This is an all-day trek, so make sure you are properly prepared. After soaking in a few of Nyūtō Onsen's renowned rotemburo, you can catch a bus back to Tazawa Kohan (¥740, 50 minutes).

Direct buses run to Komaga-take Hachigōme from the bus terminal near JR Tazawa-ko station via Tazawa Kohan five times daily during July and August, less frequently on weekends and holidays from June to late October (¥810, one hour). At other times you can take a bus from Tazawa-ko to Kōgen Onsen, from where more frequent buses run to Komaga-take Hachigōme. If even these buses aren't running, buses from the lake to Nyūtō Onsen stop at Komaga-take Tozan-guchi (¥460), a 7km walk from Komaga-take Hachigōme.

Places to Stay – Budget

Though its ramshackle building has seen better days, the *Tazawa-ko Youth Hostel* (☎ 43-1281) charges ¥2900 and serves up delicious country-style meals at the adjacent people's lodge. If you're arriving by bus from Tazawa-ko station, get off at the Kōen-iriguchi stop which is virtually opposite the hostel's front door. Reception closes at 8 pm, but there is no curfew. Bike rental is available here at more affordable rates than near the bus terminal, which is 10 minutes on foot from the hostel.

Places to Stay – Mid-Range & Top End

There are a few affordable minshuku and some overpriced hotels strung out along the lake shore in Tazawa Kohan. Five minutes on foot from the bus terminal, *Beach House Kosui* (☎ 43-0396) is a family-run minshuku charging a reasonable ¥6400 per person, including two meals in the coffee shop on the ground floor.

If you have a bit more cash to spare, the *café+inn THAT SOUNDS GOOD!* (☎/fax 43-0127, email sanzoku@hana.or.jp) has an excellent atmosphere that justifies, not only the long-winded name, but also rates of ¥8500 to ¥10,000 per person, including two meals. You should book accommodation at least a month in advance during peak seasons. From time to time, the English-speaking owner hosts performances by well-known jazz musicians from Japan and abroad. You can also organise outdoor activities here. If you phone ahead, the owner will pick you up from the bus terminal in Tazawa Kohan.

To really get away from it all, you can stay at one of the rustic hot-spring ryokan around Nyūtō Onsen. *Tsuru-no-yu Onsen Ryokan* (☎ 46-2139), *Kuroyu Onsen Ryokan* (☎ 46-2214), and *Magoroku Onsen Ryokan* (☎ 46-2224) are traditional places with a variety of open-air baths and all are at least 1km from the nearest bus stop. Prices for accommodation and two meals start at ¥8500. Some of the ryokan close from early November until late April, and all are quite popular, so it would be best to call ahead. The tourist information office at Tazawa-ko station can provide you with a sufficient sketch map of the entire area detailing appropriate bus stops and directions for all.

Buses from Tazawa Kohan to Nyūtō Onsen also pass by the front door of the elegant *Tae-no-yu Onsen Ryokan* (☎/fax 46-

2740), which charges ¥10,000 to ¥13,000 per person with two meals. Near the terminus, *Ganiba Onsen Ryokan* (☎ 46-2021) has a large open-air, mixed sex rotemburo for the more adventurous (¥500). There is also a popular camping ground about 10 minutes on foot in the direction of the lake from the Tsurunoyu bus stop (¥400).

Places to Eat

A 15-minute walk north of Tazawa Kohan, *ORAE* (11 am to 9 pm) serves up local microbrews (¥470 a glass) as well as an endless variety of izakaya-style food and snacks – try the pineapple ice (¥600). The restaurant also has an outdoor deck that is a popular gathering place on summer evenings.

Getting There & Away

On the Akita shinkansen line, Tazawa-ko is within easy reach of Morioka (¥1470, one hour), Kakunodate (¥1050, 15 minutes) and Akita (¥2770, one hour). Local trains run infrequently along the JR Tazawa-ko line to Morioka (¥740) and Kakunodate (¥320). For local connections to Akita, a change of train is almost always required at Ōmagari though connections are only good during rush hours. If you're heading west, it's far easier to take the bus from Tazawa Kohan via Tazawa-ko station to Kakunodate (¥850, 45 minutes, five per day); departures before 3 pm continue to Akita (¥1680, two hours). From December to March, service to and from Tazawa Kohan, but not Tazawa-ko station, is suspended.

Between late April and late October, there are three buses per day from Tazawa-ko station via the lake to Hachimantai Chōjō (¥1990, 2½ hours).

KAKUNODATE 角館
☎ 0187

This small town with its well-preserved samurai district dating from 1620 and avenues of cherry trees is well worth a visit. You can cover the main sights in a few hours or devote a lazy day to browsing around town.

The friendly tourist information office (☎ 54-2700) is in a small kura-like building

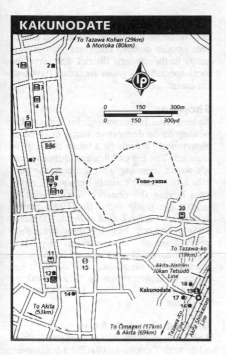

KAKUNODATE

outside the JR Kakunodate station. It can help with reservations and provide a detailed English-language map with lists of sights, restaurants and accommodation.

Bicycle rental is available near the station for ¥300 per hour. If you tire of pedalling around, you can hire a rickshaw outside Denshōkan in the samurai district. The Japanese-speaking driver will obligingly pull you a short way down the street and back while animatedly explaining the local sights (¥1500, 15 minutes).

Samurai Residences

The interior of **Kawarada-ke** can be viewed for free from a path leading through the garden. Next door is **Bukeyashiki Shiryōkan**, a cramped museum with an interesting assortment of samurai martial equipment (¥300, 8.30 am to 5 pm).

Farther north, **Aoyagi-ke** is actually a conglomeration of mini-museums: one focuses on folk art, another exhibits heir-

looms from the Aoyagi family and a 'new-fangled gadget' museum displays all the things that seemed so modern in the Meiji era (¥500, 9 am to 5 pm, closing at 4 pm from December to March).

Next door, **Ishiguro-ke** has a sweeping thatched roof and meticulously laid out gardens (¥300, 9 am to 5pm). Free tours are available in Japanese only.

Denshōkan 伝承館

This museum houses exhibits of armour, calligraphy and *Shiraiwa-yaki* (pottery), as well as tools, products and demonstrations of *kabazaiku* (cherry-bark craft). The museum is open from 9 am to 4.30 pm, closing at 4 pm from December to March. Admission costs ¥300, or ¥510 for a discount ticket that also gives you entry to the nearby **Hirafuku Kibijitsukan**, which displays Japanese and Western modern art, as well as ¥100 off admission to Ishiguro-ke.

Special Events

A **cherry tree tunnel** beside the river and weeping cherry trees (originally brought from Kyoto) in the samurai district attract crowds of visitors in late April.

From 7 to 9 September, Kakunodate celebrates the Hikiyama Matsuri in which participants haul enormous seven-tonne *yama* (wooden carts) around in the evenings, seeking out narrow streets where they can crash into each other.

Places to Stay & Eat

A long-time favourite with foreign visitors is *Minshuku Hyakusui-en* (☎ 55-5715), an old house 15 minutes on foot from the station. Excellent meals are served around an *irori* (open hearth). The owner believes that beer and sake should flow freely and guests are seated next to each other so there's less isolation and more chat. Prices start around ¥9800 with two meals, or ¥7000 without.

If that's a bit beyond your budget, *Sakura-no-Sato* (☎ 55-5652), a minshuku in a traditional two-storey building, is set on a quiet street in the northern part of town. Rooms with two meals start at a reasonable ¥5700, and the tourist office can call ahead to make sure there's room before you start your trek.

Folklore Kakunodate (☎ 53-2070) is next to Kakunodate station in a traditional kura-like building. Twins or family rooms for four people cost ¥12,000/22,000 in the off-season; prices drop as much as ¥4000/8000 for multiple-day stays.

Next to Kawarada-ke is *Sakura-no-Sato*, a cosy teahouse that serves matcha and affordable noodle dishes. There are also several shops in the samurai district that serve the local speciality – *goma* (sesame) flavoured ice cream.

Shopping

Kakunodate is renowned for kabazaiku, household or decorative items covered in cherry bark, a craft first taken up by poor samurai. The tea caddies are attractive and it's worth spending a bit more on the genuine article made entirely from wood, rather than buying the cheaper version with an inner core made from tin. High-quality kabazaiku can be found at Fujiki Denshirō Shōten, which has its own workshop nearby, and the Denshōkan gift shop.

Itaya-zaiku objects woven from maple branches are made and sold on the front porch of **Matsumoto-ke**, a low-ranking samurai residence built just before the Meiji era.

Getting There & Away

The Akita shinkansen line connects Kakunodate with Tazawa-ko (¥1050, 13 minutes), Morioka (¥2260, 50 minutes) and Akita (¥2430, 45 minutes). Extremely infrequent local trains run on the JR Tazawa-ko line from Kakunodate east to Tazawa-ko (¥320, 20 minutes) and Morioka (¥1110, 50 minutes). Connections west to Akita usually require a change of trains at Ōmagari but good connections are rare.

Budget-conscious travellers should instead opt for buses running from Kakunodate to Tazawa Kohan (¥850, 45 minutes) and Tazawa-ko station (¥490, 35 minutes), as well as to Akita (¥1330, 1½ hours). From December to March, these buses do not stop at Tazawa Kohan. The bus station in Kakunodate is 10 minutes on foot north of the train station.

AKITA 秋田

☎ 018 • pop 316,000

Akita, the prefectural capital, is a large commercial and industrial city. It has only a few sights of interest to travellers and is best used as a staging point for visits to Kakunodate or Tazawa-ko.

Information

The tourist information office (☎ 832-7941), on the 2nd floor of Akita station, stocks the oversized *Akita Info Map* which details local bus routes (should you need them). Near Senshū-kōen, the prefectural tourist information office (☎ 836-7835) is located inside the distinctive Atorion building, which also houses displays of local products, an art museum, several restaurants and an observatory.

One block west of the bus stands in front of Akita station, Internet Café Departure charges ¥1000 per hour, including a free drink (open 11 am to 8 pm, closed the first Monday of every month).

Things to See

It's just 10 minutes on foot from the station to Senshū-kōen, which was once the site of Kubota-jō and now contains the castle ruins. At the northern end is Osumi-yagura (¥100), a reconstruction of one of the eight turrets of Kubota-jō, the top of which offers a nice view of the city (9 am to 4.30 pm, until 7 pm from late July to late August, closed late December through March). In the middle of the park near Hachiman Akita-jinja, you can see Omonogashira-obansho guardhouse, the only remaining original castle building. In the south-east corner of the park is the tiny Satake Historical Museum which has rotating exhibitions of Japanese armour and art (¥100, 9 am to 4.30 pm).

The nearby Masakichi Hirano Art Museum is notable for its enormous canvas painting *Events of Akita*, which measures 3.65m by 20.5m and depicts traditional Akita life and festivals throughout the seasons (¥610, 10 am to 4.30 pm, closed Monday).

A 10-minute walk west of the park across the river is the Kanto Festival Centre (Neburi Nagashi-kan). If you haven't arrived during any of the region's many festivals, the two exhibition floors have videos, props and music from all of the prefecture's major events, including Akita's Kantō Matsuri (¥100, 9.30 am to 4.30 pm).

Five minutes farther south past Daiei department store you'll come to **Akarengakan Museum** in a Meiji-era Renaissance-style red brick building. The most interesting displays are towards the back of the complex, including wood-block prints of traditional Akita life by self-taught folk artist Katsuhira Tokushi. (¥200, 9.30 am to 4.30 pm). A combined ticket with the Kantō Festival Centre is available at either place for ¥250.

Special Events

From 4 to 7 August, Akita celebrates the Kantō Matsuri (Pole Lantern Festival), one of the most famous festivals in Tōhoku. Starting in the evening along Kantō Ōdori, more than 160 men balance giant poles, hung with illuminated lanterns, on their heads, chins, hips and shoulders to the beat of taiko drumming groups (which you can see photos of at www.kantou.gr.jp). The poles, up to 10m long and weighing 60kg, often crash into stoplights, telephone wires, even the enthusiastic crowds. During the day, exhibitions of music and pole-balancing are held in Senshū-kōen.

Places to Stay

A member of the Japanese Inn group, *Ryokan Kohama* (☎ 832-5739) is 10 minutes on foot south of Akita station. Prices for singles/doubles start at ¥5000/10,000; triples start at ¥15,000. *Ryokan Chikuba-sō* (☎ 832-6446) is closer to the station in a lively area and charges ¥7000 per person, including two meals.

Stuck in its own time warp, the retro *Hotel Hawaii Eki-mae* (☎ 833-1111) has a lot of singles (more than 300 of them) with/without bath for ¥4100/6000 and twins with/without bath for ¥5500/9000, as well as a few doubles/triples with bath for ¥7000/11,000. You'll need to book ahead for the cheaper rooms. Across town, *Hotel Hawaii Lagoon* (☎ 833-1112) and the newer *Hotel Hawaii Shin Honten* (☎ 833-1110) offer slightly nicer rooms (all with attached bath) for slightly higher prices. The decor at all three hotels is pretty funky, but don't expect any hula skirts.

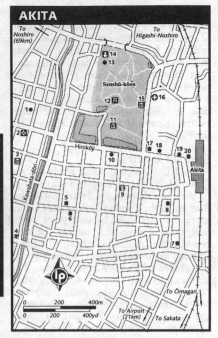

AKITA

To Noshiro (69km)

To Higashi-Noshiro

Senshū-kōen

Hirokōji

Akita

To Omagari

To Airport (21km)

To Sakata

0   200   400m
0   200   400yd

AKITA

PLACES TO STAY & EAT

4 Yama-zushi
山寿司
5 Hotel Hawaii Lagoon
ホテルハワイラングーン
6 Hotel Hawaii
Shin-Honten
ホテルハワイ新本店
7 Ryokan Kohama
小浜旅館
8 Ryokan Chikuba-sō
旅館竹馬荘
17 Hotel Hawaii Eki-mae
ホテルハワイ駅前
20 Hotel Metropolitan Akita
ホテルメトロポリタン
秋田

OTHER

1 Kantō Festival Centre
ねぶし流し館
2 Daiei Department Store
ダイエー
3 Akarengakan Museum
赤れんが郷土館
9 Iwate Bank
岩手銀行
10 Atorion Building; Prefectural
Tourist Information Centre
アトリオン
11 Hirano Masakichi Art Museum;
Prefectural Art Museum
12 Hachiman Akita-jinja
13 Omonogashira-obansho
14 Kubota-jō (Osumi-yagura)
久保田城御隅櫓
15 Satake Historical Museum
佐竹史料館
16 Municipal Emergency Hospital
市立夜間休日応急診療所
18 Tower Records
19 Akita Ticket
秋田チケット

Hotel Metropolitan Akita (☎ *831-2222*), by the station, is one of the better hotels in town; singles/twins cost from ¥8300/16,000.

Places to Eat

Local specialities include two types of hot-pot – *kiritanpo* (chicken with rice cakes) and *shottsuru* (with local fish). You can try these and other delights at *Suginoya*, on the 3rd floor restaurant arcade of Akita station.

A 15-minute walk west of the station is Kawabata-dōri, the main street of Akita's entertainment district. At *Yama-zushi*, a sparkling clean establishment, you can feast on a variety of sushi sets from ¥1000.

Near Akarenga-kan, the 5th floor of Daiei department store also has some restaurants offering great lunch deals with plenty of point-and-choose plastic displays.

Getting There & Away

Discounted air and rail tickets are available at Akita Ticket near Hotel Hawaii Eki-mae.

There are flights from Akita to Fukuoka, Nagoya, Osaka, Sapporo and Tokyo. Akita's airport is well south of the town, 40 minutes by bus from in front of JR Akita station (¥890).

The JR Akita shinkansen line runs via Tazawa-ko and Kakunodate to Morioka (¥3990, 1½ hours), cutting total travel time between Akita and Tokyo to four hours (¥16,300). Painfully infrequent local trains still chug along the JR Tazawa-ko line to Kakunodate (¥1280, 1½ hours) and Tazawa-ko (¥1620, two hours), though a transfer at Ōmagari (difficult except during rush hour) is often necessary. The JR Uetsu line connects Akita with Niigata via Sakata and Tsuruoka (tokkyū, ¥6510, 3¾ hours).

A convenient bus service runs from Akita station via Kakunodate to Tazawa-ko six times per day between 9 am and 4 pm (¥1680, two hours). Direct night buses to Tokyo (Shinjuku) depart from the Nagasakiya bus terminal and stop at Akita station at around 9 and 10 pm (¥9450, nine hours).

Shin Nihonkai morning ferries connect Akita with Niigata (¥2200, 6½ hours, daily except Monday), Tsuruga (¥5450, 21½ hours, Saturday only) and Tomakomai on Hokkaidō (¥3730, 11¼ hours, daily except Monday). Akita's port is 8km north-west of the station, half an hour by bus (¥390).

KISAKATA 象潟
☎ 0184

South of Akita on the Japan Sea coast is Kisakata, a boisterous waterfront town with a popular swimming beach. The local landscape is dominated by **Chōkai-san** (2236m), Tōhoku's second highest peak, which is also known as 'Dewa Fuji' and is an object of veneration by the same *yamabushi* (mountain priests) who worship at Dewa Sanzan in Yamagata-ken.

A small tourist information office (☎ 43-2174) inside JR Kisakata station can provide you with photocopied contour maps for hiking Chōkai-san and the *Kisakata Guide Map* detailing background on local sights, such as **Kanman-ji** (visited by Bashō) just north of the town centre (8.15 am to 5.15 pm).

The most convenient access to Chōkai-san is to take a bus from Kisakata station to Hokodate (5th Station), from where you can climb to the summit in about 4½ hours.

These buses run on weekends and holidays from July to September, but operate daily during mid-July to mid-August. Departures from Kisakata station are at around 6 and 8 am; the last bus back from Hokodate leaves at 4.20 pm.

Places to Stay & Eat
The *Kisakata Seinen-no-Ie Youth Hostel* (☎ 43-3154) is a bit worn and boiling hot in summer, but it's cheap at ¥2500, and the management is quite relaxed. Reception closes at 10 pm, but there's no curfew. From Kisakata station, walk straight out the main street and continue across Route 7 for two more blocks until you reach the intersection with a blue-and-white hostel sign pointing to the left. The hostel is five minutes on foot from there, located behind a supermarket. Next to the hostel is a popular camping ground (¥500 per site, plus ¥400 per person, May to October only).

The best deals for lunch or dinner can be found at *Masaen*, where the gregarious chef dishes up enormous portions of rāmen and various rice dishes. The teishoku are a bargain at ¥800. The restaurant is located at the intersection with the youth hostel sign – look for the Chinese temple facade.

Getting There & Away
Local trains on the JR Uetsu main line connect Kisakata with Sakata (¥650, 40 minutes), where you will probably need to change trains to continue to Tsuruoka (¥1110, 1½ hours). Local trains head north on the same line from Kisakata to Akita (1¼ hours, ¥1280).

Yamagata-ken 山形県

SAKATA 酒田
☎ 0234 • pop 100,000
This large port city has a couple of interesting sights and is a useful starting point for boat trips on the Mogami-gawa or an island hop to Tobi-shima. City maps and bicycle rental are free at the tourist information office (☎ 24-2459) outside JR Sakata station (9 am to 5 pm).

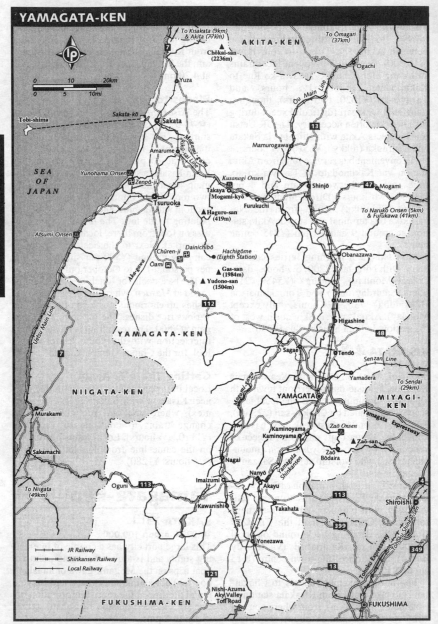

YAMAGATA-KEN

NORTHERN HONSHŪ

To Kisakata (9km)
& Akita (77km)

To Ōmagari
(37km)

AKITA-KEN

Chōkai-san
(2236m)

Ogachi

Yuza

Ōu Main Line

13

Sakata-kō

Tobi-shima

Sakata

Mamurogawa

Amarume

Kusanagi Onsen

Shinjō

47 Mogami

Yunohama Onsen

Zenpō-ji

Takaya
Mogami-kyō

Furukuchi

To Naruko Onsen (5km)
& Furukawa (41km)

SEA
OF
JAPAN

Tsuruoka

Haguro-san
(419m)

Atsumi Onsen

Chūren-ji

Dainichibō

Hachigōme
(Eighth Station)

Obanazawa

Aka-gawa

Ōami

Gas-san
(1984m)

Yudono-san
(1504m)

Murayama

112

Higashine

48

Uetsu Main Line

YAMAGATA-KEN

Sagae

Tendō

Senzan Line

Yamadera

To Sendai
(29km)

NIIGATA-KEN

YAMAGATA

MIYAGI-
KEN

Murakami

Kaminoyama
Kaminoyama

Zaō Onsen

Yamagata Expressway

Sakamachi

Nagai

Zaō
Bōdaira

Zaō-san

Imaizumi

Nanyō

Akayu

Yamagata
Shinkansen

To Niigata
(49km)

Oguni

113

Kawanishi

Takahata

113

Shiroishi

Yonesaka Line

399

Mogami-gawa

Yonezawa

349

121

13

Nishi-Azuma
Aku Valley
Toll Road

FUKUSHIMA-KEN

FUKUSHIMA

Tōhoku Shinkansen

Tōhoku Expressway

0   10   20km

0   5   10mi

- ┼ ┼ ┼ JR Railway
- ┼┼┼┼ Shinkansen Railway
- ┼ ┼ ┼ Local Railway

7

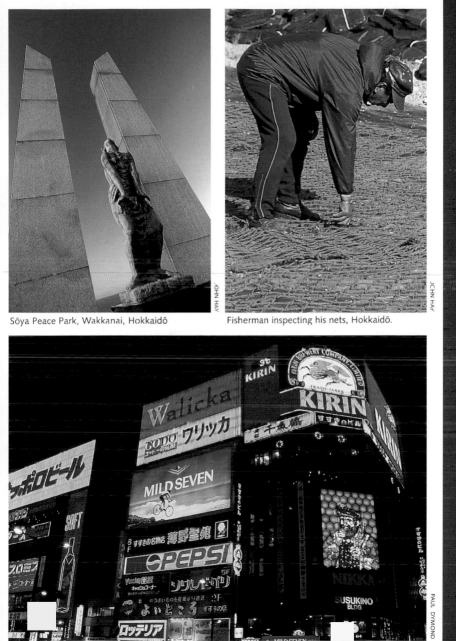

Sōya Peace Park, Wakkanai, Hokkaidō

Fisherman inspecting his nets, Hokkaidō.

Neon by night – the Susukino entertainment quarter of Sapporo is wall-to-wall bars and restaurants.

A performance of an Ainu dance at Poroto Kotan, a reconstructed Ainu village in Shiraoi, Hokkaidō.

Introduced species – Daisetsuzan National Park.

Deer in the wild, Shiretoko National Park

The perpendicular rock colums of the gorge, Sōun-kyō, in the Daisetsuzan National Park.

The **Homma Art Museum** is a couple of minutes on foot north-west of Sakata station – turn right at the main road after you exit the station. In the museum grounds is an impressive former villa of the Homma family and a delightful garden (¥700, 9 am to 4.30 pm, closed Monday from November to February).

In the centre of town, near the intersection of Ōdori and Honmachi-dōri, the nicely preserved **Homma-ke Kyū-hontei** was originally a lodging place for visiting inspectors of the Edo shogunate. Inside are more displays of art from the Homma family collection (¥600, 9.30 am to 4.30 pm, closing at 4 pm from November to February).

Just down the street, the reconstructed **Abumiya House** once belonged to the wealthiest Edo-period rice shipping merchant in Japan (¥310, 9 am to 4.30 pm, closed Monday from December to March). The rice was stored down by the river in eye-catching white kura storehouses (now restored) before being sent as tribute to Edo (Tokyo).

Over the bridge and a few kilometres farther along is the **Ken Domon Memorial Museum** (¥420, 9 am to 4.30 pm, closed Monday from December to March). Domon Ken believed that photography should touch on social issues, and his photographs often provide sensitive insight into the underside of Japanese life in the postwar years. He is also renowned for his photos of Buddhist images in Nara and Kyoto. If you're not cycling, infrequent buses from Sakata station bound for Jūrizuka pass by the Domon Ken Kinenkan-mae stop (¥340, 20 minutes).

Special Events
On the 15 and 17 of February, farmers perform *kabuki* at Hie-jinja in Kumori, 50 minutes by bus from Sakata. If you plan to attend, you must make reservations several months in advance – phone the Sakata tourist information office for more details.

Places to Stay
Miyako Ryokan (☎ 22-0431), next to the enormous Tōkyū Inn, has dingier rooms starting at ¥4500 without meals, but the management is welcoming.

The traditional *Kameya Ryokan* (☎ 22-0585) has airy rooms for ¥5800 per person, including two meals. To get there, walk straight out from the station for 10 minutes and turn left at the first intersection. The ryokan is farther along on the left-hand side of the street.

There's business hotel accommodation in the station area, the most affordable is *Hotel Alpha One Sakata* (☎ 22-6111), which offers standard-issue singles/doubles from ¥5350/11,200.

Getting There & Away
From Sakata station there are buses to Shōnai airport (¥790, 40 minutes) that are timed to coincide with check-in for flights to Tokyo, Kansai and Sapporo.

The JR Uetsu main line runs north from Sakata to Kisakata (futsū, ¥650, 40 minutes) and Akita (¥1890, 1¾ hours). The same line runs south to Tsuruoka (¥650, 35 minutes) and Niigata (tokkyū, ¥4620, 2¼ hours).

There are also occasional buses from Sakata to Sendai (¥2750, 3¾ hours, last bus 5.30 pm) via the Tsuruoka bus terminal (¥820, 50 minutes). There is one night bus to Tokyo (Shibuya, Ikebukuro) departing Sakata at 9.30 pm (¥7870, nine hours).

TOBI-SHIMA 飛島
☎ 0234
Tobi-shima, a mere speck of an island (2½ sq km), the main attractions are rugged cliffs, sea caves, scuba diving, wildflowers, black-tailed gulls and, reportedly, excellent fishing. You can also organise boat trips out to smaller islands.

On the island there are more than two dozen ryokan charging between ¥7000 and ¥10,000 per person, with two meals; and minshuku charging ¥7000, including meals. *Sawaguchi Ryokan* (☎ 95-2246), the island's youth hostel, is seven minutes on foot from the ferry pier. Rates vary seasonally from ¥2200 to ¥2400 and bicycle rental is available.

Ferries run at least once and usually twice daily from Sakata-kō to the island (¥2040, 1½ hours). Advance reservations (☎ 22-3911) are recommended in summer.

To get to Sakata-kō, take a local Sakata city bus to Yamagata-ginkō-mae, then walk for 10 minutes. A taxi from Sakata station to the port costs about ¥850.

MOGAMI-KYŌ 最上峡
Boat tours are operated through this gorge on a section of the Mogami-gawa between Sakata and Shinjō. It's harmless fun complete with a boatman singing a selection of local folk tunes.

From Sakata, trains on the JR Rikuu-saisen line run to Furukuchi station (¥740, 55 minutes), though you may have to change trains en route at Amarume. From Furukuchi station, it's eight minutes on foot to the boat dock. Boats depart up to nine times daily during the main season from April to November (¥1970). The boat trip takes an hour to reach **Kusanagi Onsen** where arriving passengers are met by shuttle buses heading to Takaya station on the JR Rikuu-saisen line.

TSURUOKA 鶴岡
☎ 0235 • pop 101,000
In the middle of the Shōnai plain, Tsuruoka was formerly an important castle town. It has developed into a modern (though rather laid-back) city with a few interesting sights. It's primary interest is as the main access point for the nearby trio of sacred mountains, known collectively as Dewa Sanzan.

Information
Outside JR Tsuruoka station, the tourist information office (☎/fax 25-7678) has an enormous amount of information on Dewa Sanzan, and can help book accommodation both there and in Tsuruoka (9.30 am to 5.30 pm, until 5 pm in winter). If you speak a little Japanese, they can help you arrange classes in e-rōsoku (candle-painting), tea ceremony, calligraphy, flower arrangement, Japanese dance and even zazen (sitting meditation). There is a small post office on the east side of Ekimae-dōri, a five-minute walk straight out from the station.

Chidō Hakubutsukan 致道博物館
This intriguing museum (¥700, 9 am to 4.30 pm) was founded in 1950 by the former

Lord Shōnai in order to develop and preserve local culture. The family residence, with its collection of craft items and large strolling garden, forms the nucleus of the museum which is rounded out by two Meiji-era buildings, a traditional storehouse and kabuto-zukuri ('samurai helmet'-style thatched roof farmhouse).

The museum is just west of Tsuruoka-kōen, a 10-minute bus ride from Tsuruoka station. Frequent buses bound for Yunohama Onsen pass by the Chidō Hakubutsukan-mae stop (¥240, 10 minutes).

Zenpō-ji 善法寺
Seven kilometres west of Tsuruoka, this Sōtō Zen Buddhist temple, with its five-tier pagoda and large gateway, dates from the 10th century when it was dedicated to the Dragon King, guardian of the seas. Most of the remaining buildings were built in the 19th century, and make for interesting and relaxing viewing. Take a minute to check out the imposing wooden fish hanging from the ceilings and paintings depicting fishing scenes, the latter donated by local fishing companies hoping to gain favour from the gods of the seas.

Near the temple is a more contemporary attraction, the famous jinmen-gyo (human-faced fish). When viewed from above, the fish actually do look to have human faces, but picking them out from the dozens of ordinary carp sharing the pond can be tricky.

From the station, take a bus bound for Yunohama Onsen past the Chidō museum and get off at the Zenpō-ji stop (¥580, 30 minutes). If you're in the mood for surf and sand, the beach at **Yunohama Onsen** is 10 minutes farther down the road by bus, or around 4km on foot.

Special Events
Tsuruoka's most well-known festival is the Tenjin Matsuri, also known as the Bake-mono Matsuri (Masked Faces Festival). People used to stroll around in masks and costume for three days, serving sake to passers by and keeping an eye out for friends and acquaintances. The object was to make it through all three days without

anyone recognising you. The festival is now reduced to one masked parade held only on 25 May, and most of the participants are thought to be employed by the local tourist association.

On 1 and 2 February, nō performances are held at night near Tsuruoka in Kurokawa village. You must reserve tickets well in advance – call the Tsuruoka tourist information for more details.

Places to Stay & Eat
On the main street leading out from the station, *Nara Ryokan* (☎ 22-1202) is a modern pension-style inn where Japanese-style rooms cost ¥4600 per person excluding meals. The management is cheerful and the ryokan is just a five-minute walk from the station.

If you feel like staying long enough to take in some of Tsuruoka's sights, definitely head for the *Tsuruoka Hotel* (☎ 22-1135), an atmospheric Japanese inn at the centre of town. Rooms with/without two meals cost ¥8500/5500 per person. To get there, take the Yunohama Onsen-bound bus to the Hitoichi-dōri stop (¥180), then walk back up the street and the hotel is on the right-hand side.

The best value in business hotel accommodation is the *Petit Hotel Tsuruoka* (☎ 25-1011), with singles/twins for ¥6000/11,400 and Japanese-style rooms for two/three people at ¥12,000/16,800. This cute hotel is adjacent to the station and its cosy lobby feels your grandmother's living room. Meals are available, but reservations are necessary for dinner (☎ 25-5804).

Across from Jusco department store, *Chugusa Shokudō* serves up generous bowls of delicious *donburi* and noodle dishes at reasonable prices (¥600 to ¥1000); look for the yellow sign in Japanese. There are plenty of other restaurants, including gourmet and international options, located off of the main shopping street, Ginza-dōri, in the centre of town.

Getting There & Away
Flights from Shōnai airport link Tsuruoka with Tokyo, Kansai and Sapporo. Bus departures from Tsuruoka station are timed to coincide with flights (¥740, 30 minutes).

From Tsuruoka station, the JR Uetsu main line runs north to Akita (tokkyū, ¥3530, 1¾ hours) and south to Niigata (tokkyū, ¥3890, 2¼ hours). Taking the train to Yamagata usually requires three changes, one at the very least. The extension of the Yamagata shinkansen line as far as Shinjō has slightly improved the situation, but it will still be far more convenient to take the bus.

If you have time to spare, you can take a series of scenic local trains along the JR Rikuu-sai and Rikuu-tō lines from Tsuruoka east to Naruko Onsen (Miyagi-ken) in about three hours if you make good connections (¥1890).

Buses are run by the Shōnai Kōtsū Bus Company. The main terminal is a five-minute walk west of the train station. All buses (except those to Sendai) pass by the station, so you only need go to the terminal if you want to assure yourself of a seat for a longer ride. There are up to seven buses a day from Tsuruoka to Sendai (¥2550, three hours).

From late June to early November, regular buses between Tsuruoka and Yamagata (¥2150, 2¼ hours) run via the Yudono-san Hotel (¥1330, 50 minutes), which provides access to Yudono-san. Services are often cut back during the winter months due to snowdrifts. Between late April and early November, there are also up to four direct buses between Tsuruoka and Yudono-san that stop by the hotel on the way up to the Sennin-zawa trailhead (¥1480, 80 minutes). For details on buses to Haguro-san and Gassan, see the Dewa Sanzan Getting There & Away section later.

There is also a night bus to Tokyo (Ikebukuro, Shibuya) which departs from in front of the Tokyo Dai-ichi Hotel in Tsuruoka (¥7540, 8½ to nine hours).

DEWA SANZAN 出羽三山
☎ 0235
Dewa Sanzan is the collective title for three sacred peaks – Haguro-san, Gas-san and Yudono-san – that have been worshipped for centuries by yamabushi and followers of

NORTHERN HONSHŪ

the Shugendō sect (see Religion in the Facts about the Country chapter.) During the pilgrimage seasons you can see white-clad pilgrims (equipped with wooden staff, sandals and straw hat) and the occasional yamabushi (equipped with conch shell, check jacket and voluminous white pantaloons) stomping along mountain trails or sitting under icy waterfalls as part of arduous ascetic exercises intended to train both body and spirit.

Theoretically, if you hiked at a military pace and timed the buses perfectly, you might be able to cover all three peaks in one day. However, this would leave you no time

to enjoy the scenery, and chances of missing a key bus connection are good. If you want to tackle all three mountains it's best to spend at least two days doing it. You can book accommodation and stock up on information and maps at the tourist office in Tsuruoka before starting out.

Haguro-san 羽黒山

Haguro-san (419m) has several attractions and easy access, ensuring a steady flow of visitors. At the base of the mountain is Haguro village, consisting mainly of *shukubō* (pilgrims' lodgings). The **Ideha**

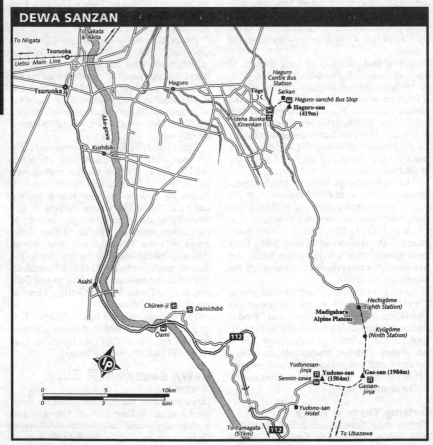

DEWA SANZAN

Bunka Kinenkan is a small museum of Dewa Sanzan history featuring films of yamabushi rites and festivals (¥400, 9 am to 5 pm, closed Tuesday).

The orthodox approach to the shrine on the summit requires the pilgrim to climb 2466 steps but the less tiring approach is to take the bus to the top. However, the climb is well worth the trouble and can be done in a leisurely 50 minutes – take your time and enjoy the woods.

From Haguro centre bus station, walk straight ahead through the torii gate and continue across a bridge into beautiful cryptomeria woods with trees forming a canopy overhead. En route you pass Goju-no-to, a marvellous, weather-beaten five-storey pagoda dating from the 14th century. Then comes a very long slog up hundreds of stone steps arranged in steep sections. Pause halfway at the teahouse for refreshment and breathtaking views. If you detour to the right just past the teahouse, you will come upon the temple ruins of Betsu-in, visited by Bashō during his pilgrimage here.

The scene at the top is a slight anticlimax. There are several shrines, often crowded with visitors except during early mornings or late afternoons, and an uninspiring history museum. From the top you can either walk or catch a bus back down to the bottom. In summer there are two buses in the morning that go on to Gas-san (see the following Getting There & Away section for details).

Gas-san 月山

Gas-san (1984m), the highest of the three sacred peaks, attracts pilgrims to Gassan-jinja, a shrine on the peak itself (¥300, including ritual purification). The peak is usually accessed from the trailhead at Hachigome (Eighth Station). The trail passes through an alpine plateau to the Kyūgōme (Ninth Station) in 1¾ hours and then grinds uphill for 70 minutes to the shrine. The trail between Hachigōme and Gas-san-jinja is only open from 1 July to 10 October.

The steep descent down the other side to Yudono-san-jinja takes another 2½ hours (keep choosing the right fork). After about 45 minutes of this descent, you also have

the choice of taking the trail to Ubazawa, the main ski resort on Gas-san, which has its own cable car. If you continue to Yudono-san, you'll eventually have to descend rusty ladders chained to the cliffside and carefully pick your way down through a slippery streambed at the end of the trail.

Yudono-san 湯殿山

The Sennin-zawa trailhead for Yudono-san (1504m) is approached via a 3km toll road from the Yudono-san Hotel. From there it's a 10-minute hike farther up the mountain to Yudonosan-jinja. This sacred shrine is not a building but a large orange rock continuously lapped by water from a hot spring. Between April and November, ¥300 gains you admission to the inner sanctum where you perform a barefoot circuit of the rock, paddling through the cascading water.

Dainichibō & Chūren-ji

Off Route 112 between Yudono-san and Tsuruoka, these two ordinary country temples house the exotic mummies of former priests who have become 'Buddhas in their own bodies'. Outlawed since the 19th century, the ascetic practice of self-mummification involved coming as close to death as possible through starvation before being buried alive while meditating. The mummy at Dainichibō, pictured in many tourist pamphlets, is dressed in bright orange robes and is quite ghoulish (¥300, 8 am to 6 pm). At Chūren-ji, the mummy is allegedly a reformed murderer who became a powerful Buddhist priest (¥500, 8 am to 5 pm). Both temples are five minutes on foot from the Ōami bus stop, approximately halfway between Tsuruoka (¥950) and Yudono-san (¥910). Buses are spaced about two hours apart, which is more than enough time to look around.

Special Events

The Dewa Sanzan-jinja, on the peak of Haguro-san, is the site of several major festivals. On the night of 31 August, yamabushi perform ancient fire rites to pray for a bountiful harvest. During the Shōrei-sai festival on New Year's Eve, yamabushi perform similar rituals in competition with each other after completing 100-day long austerities.

If just being an observer isn't enough, you too can learn to jump through fire at yamabushi training camp. On selected weekends in July and September, the Ideha Bunka Kinenkan (☎ 62-4727) offers three-day 'beginners' classes (¥26,000) that are not easy: fasting, mountain sprints and 4.30 am wake-up calls are only for the serious. Dewa Sanzan-jinja (☎ 62-2355) runs even more intensive 'real' yamabushi courses, as well as five-day training programs for women during early September (¥40,000). None of this is for the faint of heart.

Places to Stay

There are more than 30 *shukubō* (temple lodgings) in the Tōge district of Haguro village, at the base of Haguro-san. This is a lot, but it's a far cry from the 300 or so that were in business here during the Edo period. Be forewarned that many of the places only take pilgrims or repeat guests. Rates are around ¥7000 to ¥8000 per person, including two meals.

At the top of Haguro-san is *Saikan* (☎ 62-2357), which has temple lodgings open to all visitors. Airy rooms, often with spectacular views, cost ¥7000, including two of the temple's gourmet vegetarian meals. Advance reservations are strongly advised.

The *Yudono-san Hotel* (☎ 54-6231) wins no high marks for style or atmosphere, and the rates (starting at ¥8500 per person including a vegetarian dinner) are not great value. But it is a convenient place to start or finish the Yudono-san to Gas-san hike.

Getting There & Away

Buses to Haguro centre bus station depart Tsuruoka hourly (¥680, 35 minutes), continuing to Haguro-sanchō (Haguro summit) between 8 am and 4 pm (¥990, 55 minutes). From early July to late August, and then on weekends and holidays until late September, there are two buses from Haguro-sanchō at around 10 and 11 am which save the sweat of pilgrims by allowing them to travel towards the peak of Gas-san, as far as Hachigōme (¥1240, 50 minutes). There are

two earlier buses from Tsuruoka to Hachigōme (¥1650, 1½ hours) which only run via Haguro centre bus station.

From late June to early November, there are buses from the Yudono-san Hotel to Yamagata (¥1750, 1½ hours, last bus 4 pm) or to Tsuruoka via Ōami (¥1330, 50 minutes, last bus 4.30 pm). Between late April and early November, there are up to four more buses from the Sennin-zawa trailhead to Tsuruoka (¥1480, 80 minutes) which also pass by the hotel and Ōami.

YAMAGATA 山形
☎ 023 • pop 250,000
Yamagata is the prefectural capital and a thriving industrial city. For the traveller, the city is a useful base for day trips to Yamadera, Tendō and Takahata, as well as a gateway to the sacred mountains of Dewa Sanzan and the skiing and hiking region around Zaō Onsen.

Orientation & Information

Yamagata's layout is pretty straightforward. From the station, Ekimae-dōri runs east past several hotels before intersecting Nanoka-machi-dōri, the main shopping and eating drag. The main post office is also on Nanoka-machi-dōri, although there is a smaller post office just north of Yamagata station.

On the 2nd floor of Yamagata station, the tourist information office (☎ 631-7865) can answer queries and help book accommodation (11 am to 6 pm, until 5 pm on weekends).

In the Coco 21 building on Nanoka-machi-dōri, the international relations association centre (☎ 624-0043) publishes a monthly newsletter detailing local festivals and hidden sightseeing spots (9 am to 5.30 pm, closed Sunday). The nearby prefectural tourism information office (☎ 631-9233) is open from 9 am to 5.30 pm, closed Monday.

Hirashimizu Pottery District

Located along the Hazukashii-kawa (Shy River), these recently revived kilns turn out beautiful spotted-glaze pieces, nicknamed *nashi-seiji* (peach skin), all displayed for sale in attached workshops. The renowned

Shichiemon-gama (☎ 642-7777) offers instruction in pottery-making. To get there, take a bus from Yamagata station bound for Nishi-Zaō or Geikō-dai to the Hirashimizu stop (¥200, 20 minutes).

Special Events
From 6 to 8 August, the Hanagasa Matsuri features large crowds of dancers wearing *hanagasa* (flower-laden straw hats) and singing folk songs. The lyrics are said to be derived from the impromptu, often salacious tunes once improvised by construction workers to keep time to the rhythm of their labour.

Places to Stay & Eat
Yamagata Youth Hostel (☎ 88-3201) has rates of ¥2800 and is small and often booked out. It's located at Kurosawa Onsen, a 25-minute ride from Yamagata station by bus bound for Takamatsu-Hayama Onsen. The hostel is a five-minute walk from the Kurosawa Onsen stop.

Yamashiroya Ryokan (☎ 22-3007) has air-conditioned Japanese-style rooms for ¥4400 per person. This friendly inn is five minutes on foot north of Yamagata station. The best value in business hotels is *Hotel Green Tohoku* (☎ 632-6666), a 15-minute walk north-east of the station. Though not the newest place in town, the prices are hard to beat: Japanese-style rooms for two cost ¥8000 and Western-style singles/doubles start at ¥4500/9000.

Inside Yamagata station, *Skylark* has good value family restaurant fare: huge breakfast sets start at ¥600 and there are free refills on drinks.

Entertainment
Home away from home for many foreign residents, *Night Dew* is a tiny oasis where ¥2500 (foreigners price) buys you unlimited drinks and two karaoke songs. Otherwise, the cover charge is ¥500, which may be worth it considering Internet use is free after 11 pm until the bar closes (as late as 5 am). It's located three blocks east of McDonald's off of Nanokamachi-dori; look for a small English sign on your left.

Getting There & Away
There are flights from Yamagata to Kansai, Nagoya, Sapporo and Tokyo. Buses to the airport run from Yamagata station (¥710, 40 minutes, four per day).

NORTHERN HONSHU

Yamagata International Documentary Film Festival

The innovative Yamagata International Documentary Film Festival (YIDFF) was established in 1989 to mark the 100th anniversary of the municipalisation of the city of Yamagata. The biennial festival was the first of its kind in Asia, and served to put this little-known city, considered to be somewhat *inaka* (outback) to southern Japanese, on the map.

Yamagata takes on an exciting, international flavour during the festival week in October and foreigners are welcome to take part in the fun. The YIDFF is recognised internationally not only for the quality of its films but also for the hospitality of its staff, many of whom are local volunteers. The late night get-together by staff and patrons at the Komian Club (a restored Japanese warehouse) has also become well known in its own right.

YIDFF '99 screened 200 films and videos from 76 countries. The International Competition and Asia Program constitute the bulk of the festival, and additional categories include retrospectives, symposiums and a Japan panorama. Prizes are awarded to outstanding works. All screenings contain both English and Japanese subtitles and most festival publications are bilingual; simultaneous interpreting (via headphones) is available at some symposiums.

For more information contact the YIDFF Organising Committee Office (☎ 023-624-8368, fax 023-624-9618, email kokusai@city.yamagata.yamagata.jp) or check out the Web site at www.city.yamagata.yamagata.jp/yidff/.

Jennifer Swanton

The JR Senzan line connects Yamagata with Yamadera and Sendai (kaisoku, ¥1110, one hour). The JR Ōu main line run south to Yonezawa (futsū, ¥820, 45 minutes) and north along the centre of Tōhoku to Ōmagari for access to the region around Tazawako and Akita (kaisoku, ¥2940, four hours).

The JR Yamagata and Tōhoku shinkansen lines connect Yamagata with Yonezawa (¥1550, 35 minutes), Fukushima (¥2600, 1¼ hours) and Tokyo (¥11,060, 2¾ hours). The extension of the Yamagata shinkansen line north to Shinjō opened in December 1999, but travellers heading to Tsuruoka will still save themselves headaches by taking a direct bus instead.

Buses start at the Yama-kō bus station inside Daiei department store, but most stop at Yamagata station before heading out. There are frequent buses from Yamagata to Zaō Onsen (¥840, 40 minutes) and less to Yamadera (¥580, 40 minutes). Highway buses also run to Sendai (¥1000, every 30 minutes), Niigata (¥3500, 3¾ hours, 8 am and 4 pm) and Yamagata (¥2150, 2¼ hours). Between late June and early November these buses run via the Yudono-san Hotel (see Dewa Sanzan Getting There & Away earlier). There is also a night bus to Tokyo (Asakusa, Ueno) departing the Yama-kō terminal at 9.30 pm (¥6420, eight hours).

TENDŌ 天童
☎ 023
Producing over 90% of Japan's chess pieces annually, Tendō is an interesting half-day excursion from Yamagata. Begun by poor samurai during the Edo period, the making of chess pieces here has become an exquisite art. The Tendō Shōgi Museum is part of JR Tendō station and displays chess sets and chess-related art from Japan and abroad (¥300, 9 am to 5.30 pm, closed Wednesday).

You can see chess pieces being made at the Eishundō museum, a 15-minute walk straight out from the station, just past the Tendō Park Hotel. Across the street is the Hiroshige Art Museum, which displays wood-block prints by famous Edo-period master Hiroshige (¥600, 9.30 am to 6 pm, closed Tuesday).

The tourist information centre (☎ 653-1680), on the 2nd floor of JR Tendō station (9 am to 6 pm), can provide you with maps and directions to other local museums, including the eccentric Tendō Mingeikan, a folkcraft museum housed in a *gasshō-zukuri* farmhouse (¥500, 8 am to 6 pm).

On the last weekend in April at Tendō-kōen you can see the theatrical Ningen Shōgi – chess matches using real people as pieces on a huge outdoor gameboard. The tradition is credited to Toyotomi Hideyoshi who once played a similar match with his son in Kyoto. More details on becoming a human 'piece' are available at www.ic-net.or.jp/home /ikechang/chess/jcmap-e.htm.

Tendō is six stops north of Yamagata by local train (¥230) or 40 minutes by bus from Yamagata station (¥440).

ZAŌ-SAN 蔵王山
☎ 0236
The region around these mountains is very popular with skiers (mainly from December to April) and a destination for hikers in summer. The main ski resorts are around Zaō Onsen and Zaō Bōdaira. In winter, free shuttles connect extensive networks of ropeways and lifts. One-day passes start at ¥4300 (discounted night skiing available).

In summer you can make your way up to Okama, a volcanic crater lake atop Zaō-san, considered by many to be the area's premier sight. The most convenient access is via Katta Chūsha-jo car park, where a chair lift takes you to within spitting distance of the Okama overlook (¥400, 9 am to 4 pm). There are numerous trails around the area, including a one-hour walk out to Jizōsanchō-eki, from where you can hike or catch two chair lifts down through Juhyō-kōgen (Ice Monster Plateau) to Zaō Onsen (¥1350). The 'monsters', best viewed from late February to early March, are really just frozen conifers covered in snow by Siberian winds.

After a long day of hiking or skiing, you can soak at Zaō Onsen Dai-rotemburo, where each outdoor hot-spring pool can hold up to 200 people (¥450, 9 am to sunset). Near Zaō bus terminal, the tourist information office (☎ 94-9328) has maps and can advise on transport and accommodation (9 am to 5.30 pm).

There are plenty of minshuku, pensions and ryokan, but advance reservations are essential if you visit during jam-packed peak seasons or on weekends. At Zaō Onsen, you can try *Lodge Chitoseya* (☎ 94-9145) or *Yūgiri-sō* (☎ 94-9253), both with comfortable rooms from around ¥7000 per person, including two meals. At Zaō Bōdaira, *Pension Alm* (☎ 79-2256) and *Pension Ishii* (☎ 79-2772) charge around ¥8000 for the same deal.

Buses from Yamagata station depart frequently for Zaō Onsen (¥840, 40 minutes). To cope with demand during the winter more than a million visitors to the region – there is a regular bus service direct from Tokyo. Between late April and early November there are two buses at around 9 am and noon connecting Yamagata via Zaō Onsen with Katta Chūsha-jo (¥1630, 1½ hours); buses in the reverse direction leave from Katta at around 12.30 pm and 3.30 pm.

YAMADERA 山寺
☎ 0236

Yamadera's main attraction is **Yama-dera** (also known as Risshaku-ji), a temple which was founded here in 860 with sacred flames brought from Enryaku-ji near Kyoto. On most days the place is a tourist circus, so visit in the early morning or late afternoon if you're hoping for some meditative moments. The temple is actually a cluster of buildings and shrines perched on wooded slopes. Stone steps leading up to the temple area from street-level will bring you to Konponchū-dō, a National Important Cultural Asset. Walking to the left will bring you to Hihōkan, the temple treasury, and, after paying a ¥300 entry fee, you'll start the steep climb up hundreds of steps through the trees to the Niō-mon and the Oku-no-in (Inner Sanctuary) where trails lead off on either side to small shrines and lookout points. The temple area is generally open during daylight hours, but the core opening hours are 8 am to 5.30 pm.

There is a small tourist information office (☎ 695-2816) near the bridge before reaching Yama-dera (9 am to 4 pm). The staff can provide useful English-language pamphlets and accommodation information, but no English is spoken. Ten minutes on foot on the other side of the station, **Bashō Kinenkan** is a quiet museum exhibiting scrolls and calligraphy related to the poet's famous northern journey as well as documentary videos of the places he visited (¥400, 9 am to 4.30 pm, closed Monday).

The spic-and-span *Pension Yamadera* (☎ 95-2240) is just a one-minute walk from the station and has rooms with two meals from around ¥8000 per person.

The JR Senzan line links Yamadera with Yamagata station (kaisoku, ¥230, 15 minutes) and Sendai (¥820, 50 minutes). There are also infrequent buses from Yamagata station to Bashō Kinenkan (¥580, 40 minutes).

TAKAHATA 高畠
☎ 0238

Takahata is a pleasant place to while away an afternoon along the **Mahoroba Cycling Road**, which takes in some excellent rural scenery, a few museums, ancient burial mounds, an historical park and the eye-catching three-storey pagoda of **Atsuku Hachiman-Jinja**. You can cycle the entire 6km path in about three hours return-trip and afterward enter what is probably Japan's only onsen located *inside* a train station (¥200, 7 am to 9.40 pm).

The station itself was built to resemble a fairy castle in honour of local children's author Hamada Hirosuke. A small tourist information desk (☎ 57-3844) rents bicycles and provides maps of the cycling route that include background on many local sights, including the **Takahata Winery**.

Takahata is on the JR Ōu main line, south of Yamagata (futsū, ¥650, 40 minutes) and closer to Yonezawa (¥200, 10 minutes).

YONEZAWA 米沢
☎ 0238

During the 17th century the Uesugi clan built their castle in this town which later developed into a major centre for silk weaving. It's a quiet, unpretentious place, worth a brief stopover if you are passing through.

You can pick up maps and information at the tourist information office (☎ 24-2965) inside the station (8 am to 6 pm). Rental bicycles are available nearby for ¥200 per hour and are a good alternative to the infrequent buses that ply the main street between the station and the sights.

Matsugasaki-kōen contains the castle ruins and Uesugi-jinja. The shrine's treasury, Keishō-den, displays armour and works of art belonging to several generations of the Uesugi family (¥400, 9 am to 4 pm, closed December to March). Just south of the shrine is Uesugi Kinenkan, which is a fine Meiji-era residence with more relics from the Uesugi family (¥300, 9 am to 5 pm, closed Tuesday). To get to the park, take a bus from the station bound for Shirabu Onsen to the Uesugi-jinja-mae stop (¥190, 10 minutes).

The clan mausoleum, Uesugi-ke Gobyōsho, is farther west of the park, about 15 minutes on foot. A dozen generations of the Uesugi clan are entombed here in a gloomy row of individual mausoleums overshadowed by tall trees (¥200, 9 am to 5 pm).

Special Events
The Uesugi Matsuri starts off with folk singing on 29 April and mock ceremonial preparation for battle in Matsugasaki-kōen on the evening of 2 May. The real action takes place on 3 May with a re-enactment of the battle of Kawanakajima featuring over 2000 participants looking, as one tourist brochure notes, like 'feudal-period picture scrolls come to life'.

Places to Stay & Eat
Hotel Otowaya (☎ 22-0124) is in an atmospheric, 100-year-old castle-like building in front of the station. It was the only inn in town not to be destroyed by the Japanese military or US occupying authorities at the end of World War II. Former prime ministers, famous kabuki actors and pop stars have all stayed here. Singles/doubles in the modern addition start at ¥5300/11,000.

Friendly *Yonezawa Station Hotel* (☎ 21-4111) has singles/twins for ¥4600/8000. It's five minutes on foot from the station.

Marbled Yonezawa beef is reknowned, so expect to pay at least ¥2500 for a nice bite of steak anywhere in town. For the more frugal gourmand, delicious *yakiniku teishoku* (grilled beef sets) cost only ¥980 at *Marubun*, a busy place on the right-hand side of the street leading out from the station.

Getting There & Away
The JR Ōu main line runs north from Yonezawa to Yamagata (¥820, 50 minutes) and east to Fukushima (¥740, 45 minutes). The JR Yonesaka and Uetsu main lines link Yonezawa with Niigata (kaisoku, ¥2520, 2¾ hours, twice daily).

Niigata-ken 新潟県

NIIGATA 新潟
☎ 025 • pop 480,000
Niigata, the prefectural capital, is an important industrial centre and major transport hub, as well as an historic port. The city itself has few sights and most foreign visitors use Niigata as a gateway for Sado-ga-shima.

Information
The tourist information centre (☎ 241-7914) is outside the Bandai exit of Niigata station (8.30 am to 5.45 pm). English-speaking staff can load you with maps and pamphlets and assist with accommodation or transport queries relating to Niigata or Sado-ga-shima. The Niigata International Friendship Centre (☎ 225-2777/225-2727) is aimed more at long-term residents but has CNN broadcasts, a small library and helpful staff (10 am to 6 pm, closed Wednesday). Their monthly *Niigata English Journal* lists local events and free Japanese culture classes.

There is a UC Card Co ATM that accepts foreign-issued cards; it's tucked in an alley behind the Niigata Chūō Ginkō ATM in the Furumachi arcade. In the same part of town, Tokyo-Mitsubishi Bank gives VISA cash advances.

Internet access is available at Media 1 Bar, outside Billboard Place shopping centre (¥700 per hour).

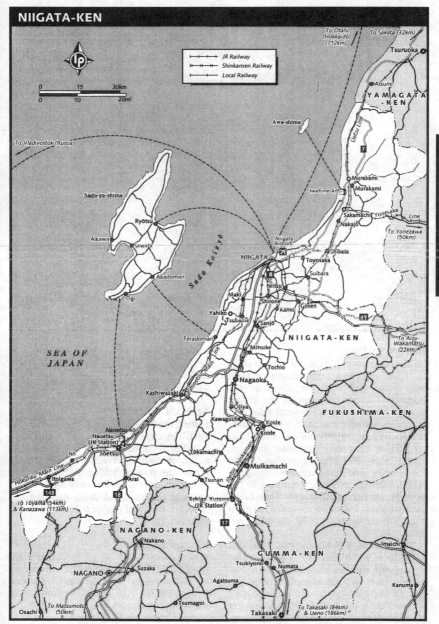

NORTHERN HONSHŪ

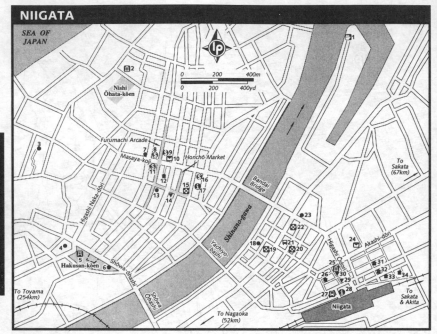

NIIGATA

SEA OF
JAPAN

Things to See
On the outskirts of Niigata the former palatial residence and art collection of a local
land baron has been preserved as the
Northern Culture Museum. In the attractive garden complex are several relocated
farmhouses, traditional earthen warehouses
and individual tea arbours including San-
raku-tei, a diminutive triangular teahouse
dating from 1890 where everything, even
the flooring and furniture, are triangular
(¥700, 8.30 am to 5 pm, 9 am to 4.30 pm
from December to February). Tour buses
run four times daily directly to the museum
from Niigata station (¥1670, including admission).

The grounds of **Hakusan-jinja**, dedicated
to the local god of marriage, contain a fine
lotus pond and the historic **Enkikan** teahouse (9 am to 5 pm, closed the first and
third Monday of the month). From Niigata
station, take a bus from stop No 8 and get
off at Shiyakusho-mae (¥200, 15 minutes).

Near the station, the **Tsurui Museum of
Art** has permanent exhibits of Japanese arts
and local crafts (¥500, 10 am to 5 pm, closed
Monday).

Special Events
During the Niigata Matsuri from 7 to 9 August, the streets are filled with afternoon
parades of colourful floats and shrines. At
night, thousands of folk dancers parade
across the Bandai Bridge. A bumper fireworks display on the final day lights up the
passage of decorated boats carrying the
shrine of the local god of the sea across the
Shinano-gawa.

Places to Stay
Most Japanese-style accommodation is far
from the station and reputedly unwelcoming to foreigners. Near the station, *Ryokan
Takeya* (☎ 244-1050) has basic rooms from
¥4300 per person. Much more stylish accommodation can be found across town at

NIIGATA

PLACES TO STAY

12 Niigata Ōnoya Ryokan
大野屋旅館
26 Niigata Keihin Hotel
新潟京浜ホテル
31 Single Inn Niigata 2;
Single Inn Niigata 2
Shin-kan
シングルイン新潟 2 ；
シングルイン新潟 2
新館
32 Single Inn Niigata 1
シングルイン新潟 1
33 Ryokan Takeya
たけや旅館
34 Single Inn Niigata 3
シングルイン新潟 3

PLACES TO EAT

14 Santei Pub
サンテイパブ
29 Menkomachi
麺小町
30 Enka of Moon
月のえんか

OTHER

1 Sado Kisen Ferry Terminal
佐渡汽船
フェリーターミナル

2 Niigata City Art
Museum
新潟市美術館
3 Nihon-kai Tower
日本海タワー
4 City Hall
市役所
5 Hakusan-jinja; Enkikan
白山神社；燕喜館
6 Prefectural Government
Memorial Hall
新潟県政記念館
7 NEXT 21 Building
8 Tokyo-Mitsubishi Bank
東京三菱銀行
9 UC Card Co. (ATM)
10 Naka Post Office
中郵便局
11 Sumitomo Bank
住友銀行
13 Meidi-ya Grocery Store
明治屋
15 Itō Yōkadō Department
Store
イトーヨーカドー
16 Fuji Bank
富士銀行
17 Niigata International
Friendship Centre
新潟国際友好会館

18 Magic City Niigata
マジックシティ新潟
19 Billboard Place;
Media 1 Bar
ビルボードプレイス
20 Mitsukoshi
Department Store;
Kinokuniya Bookshop;
Sazaby Afternoon
Tea Room
三越デパート；
紀伊国屋書店
21 Rainbow Tower;
Bandai Bus Centre
レインボータワー；
万代バスセンター
22 Daiei Department
Store
ダイエー
23 Korean Airlines (KAL)
Office
24 Central Post Office
中央郵便局
25 Tsurui Museum of Art
敦井美術館
27 Bus Terminal
バスターミナル
28 Tourist Information
Centre
観光案内センター

Niigata Ōnoya Ryokan (☎ 229-2951) where rates, including two meals, range from ¥10,000 to ¥20,000.

The cheapest rooms in a fiercely competitive business hotel market can be found at the *Single Inn Niigata 3* (☎ 243-3900), where thin-walled singles cost ¥4280 on the upper floors or ¥4980 downstairs. If they're full, slightly more expensive singles and a few twins/doubles can be found at *Single Inn Niigata 1* (☎ 241-3003), *Single Inn Niigata 2* (☎ 243-2980) and *Single Inn Niigata 2 Shin-kan* (☎ 246-4980). All of these hotels are within easy walking distance of the station.

The *Niigata Keihin Hotel* (☎ 249-1177) has classier singles/doubles from ¥5800/ 10,000. As an added bonus, the 1st-floor

cafe has an all-you-can-eat breakfast buffet for ¥780 and set lunches from ¥500.

Places to Eat

Near the station, *Menkomachi* is open late and serves generous bowls of rāmen, gyōza (dumpling) in·fruit-flavoured wrappers and fried *fugu* (blowfish) in summer (¥380). Just up the street is *Enka of Moon*, a posh izakaya with plenty of seafood on the menu: scallop and radish salad or sesame shrimp crackers with cream cheese both cost ¥680, and there's fruit-flavoured sherbet for dessert.

On the 1st floor of Mitsukoshi department store, *Sazaby Afternoon Tea Room* has a great selection of baked goods and set lunches (bilingual menu available). In the Honchō street market, the hole-in-the-wall

Santei Pub has an equally small menu – banana sandwich (¥300), Thai curry (¥700) and *chai* (tea) (¥400). The shop keeps odd hours, but is easily recognised by its bright red exterior.

Getting There & Away

North-east of the city, Niigata airport has international flights to Seoul, Shanghai, and Xian. Domestic destinations include Tokyo, Osaka, Nagoya, Hiroshima and Sapporo. Kyokushin Air (☎ 273-0312) light aeroplanes link Niigata with Ryōtsu on Sado-ga-shima (¥7350, 20 minutes). Buses from Niigata station to the airport leave every half hour from 7 am to 7 pm (¥350, 25 minutes).

The JR Jōetsu shinkansen line runs from Niigata to Echigo-Yuzawa (¥4730, 40 minutes) and Tokyo (Ueno) (¥10,070, two hours); get off at Takisaki for transfers to the Nagano shinkansen line. On the JR Uetsu line, there are tokkyū trains north from Niigata to Tsuruoka (¥3890, 2¼ hours) and Akita (¥6510, 3¾ hours). Travelling south-west on the JR Hokuriku line, it takes four hours to Kanazawa, where some direct trains then continue to Kyoto and Osaka.

Originating at the Bandai bus centre across the river, a few long-distance buses link Niigata with Sendai (¥4500, four hours), Yamagata (¥3500, 3¾ hours), Aizu-Wakamatsu (¥2000, 1¾ hours), Kanazawa (¥4580, 4¾ hours) and Nagano (¥3060, 3½ hours). There are also night buses to Tokyo (Ikebukuro) (¥5250, 5¼ hours) and Kyoto/Osaka (¥9450, 9¼ hours). Most buses pass by Niigata station on their way out of town.

Shin-Nihonkai ferries from Niigata to Otaru (Hokkaidō) are excellent value (¥5250, 17¾ hours, daily except Monday). The appropriate port is Niigata-kō: take the bus from Niigata station to Rinko-nichōme and get off at Suehiro-bashi (¥180, 20 minutes).

From the Sado Kisen terminal, there are frequent ferries and hydrofoils to Ryōtsu on Sado-ga-shima (see the Sado-ga-shima Getting There & Away section later). The terminal is 15 minutes by bus from Niigata station or the Bandai bus centre (¥180).

To/From Russia Dalavia Far East Airways (☎ 03-5405-2727) flies from Niigata to Khabarovsk (Russia) for connections with the Trans-Siberian Railway. Vladivostok Airlines (☎ 03-3431-2788) has two flights per week to Vladivostok. Discounted round-trip tickets for either destination can be purchased through Earthdesk Co, Ltd in Tokyo (☎ 03-3586-3380, email airinfo@ mail.erch.or.jp).

There are also ferries from Niigata to Vladivostok (☎ 03-3249-4412) departing a few times per month between June and October (¥27,600, 41½ hours).

You can start the long paper chase for a Russian visa at Niigata's Russian Consulate-General (☎ 244-6015). For more details see the Web site: embassy.kcom.ne.jp/russia /index.htm.

SADO-GA-SHIMA 佐渡島
☎ 0259

In medieval times, this was an island of exile for intellectuals who had fallen out of favour with the government. Among those banished here were Emperor Juntoku, nō drama master Ze-Ami and Nichiren, the founder of one of Japan's most influential Buddhist sects. When gold was discovered near Aikawa in 1601, there was a sudden influx of gold-diggers – often vagrants shipped from the mainland as prisoners and made to work like slaves. Today the island relies on fishing, rice farming and tourism.

The southern and northern mountain ranges of this island are connected by a flat, fertile plain. The best season to visit is between late April and early November – during the winter, the weather can be foul, much of the accommodation is closed and transport is reduced to a minimum.

The real attraction of the island is its unhurried pace of life and natural scenery. A minimum of two days is recommended to visit the rocky coastline and remote fishing villages, or to wander inland to the mountains and their temples.

Information

The tourist information centre (☎ 23-3300) in Ryōtsu is squeezed in between coffee and

SADO-GA-SHIMA

SADO-GA-SHIMA

PLACES TO STAY
1 Sotokaifu Youth Hostel
  外海府ユースホステル
2 Sado Belle Mer Youth Hostel
  佐渡ベールメア
  ユースホステル
5 Sado Hakusan Youth Hostel
  佐渡白山ユースホステル
7 Green Village Youth Hostel
  グリーンVillage ユースホステル
8 Sado Seaside Hotel
  佐渡シーサイドホテル
9 Kazashima-kan Youth Hostel
  風島館ユースホステル
15 Ogi Sakuma-sō Youth Hostel
  小木佐久間荘ユースホステル

OTHER
3 Sado Kinzan Gold Mine
  佐渡金山
4 Dōyū-no-Wareto
  道遊の割戸
6 Myōshō-ji
  妙照寺
10 Konpon-ji
  根本寺
11 Myōsen-ji
  妙宣寺
12 Sado Rekishi Denshōkan; Mano-gū
  佐渡歴史伝承館；真野宮
13 Kokubun-ji
14 Mano Go-ryō
  真野御陵

souvenir shops across the street from the ferry terminal (8.30 am to 7 pm during summer). It has an enormous selection of maps, timetables and pamphlets covering the entire island. The knowledgeable staff can also help find accommodation.

Over in Sawata, the Sado Travel Bureau (☎ 57-2126) provides pamphlets, books and advice in English (9 am to 5.30 pm, until noon on Sunday). The Sado Kisen ferry company has offices at the Niigata and Ryōtsu terminals also stock bus and ferry timetables (Japanese only) and can help book accommodation.

Though outdated, the JNTO leaflet *Niigata and Sado Island* has great details on some sights around the island.

There are small post offices in all of the island's main towns

Ryōtsu 両津
This is the main town and tourist resort and a good place to pick up information before heading to more interesting parts of the island. The central area is a 10-minute walk north of the ferry terminal. From the terminal, there are special buses to **Sado Nōgaku-no-sato**, a hi-tech museum of nō drama (¥1000 return, including entry fees).

Sawata 佐和田

The town of Sawata, 15km south-west of Ryōtsu, is on the main road between Ryōtsu and Aikawa. If you get off the bus 1km east of town at Kaminagaki (¥150), you can walk for about 30 minutes up into the hills to Myōshō-ji. This temple, set in dilapidated grounds, belongs to the Nichiren sect. From the shrine at the top of the steps, a pleasant path leads through the woods to rice paddies.

Near the bus terminal in Sawata, the Silver Village resort holds short traditional puppet performances three times daily in the afternoon from April to November (¥350).

Frequent buses from Ryōtsu to Sawata (¥600, 50 minutes) usually continue to Aikawa.

Aikawa 相川

From a tiny hamlet, Aikawa developed almost overnight into a boom town when gold was discovered nearby in 1601. Private mining continued to the end of the Edo period and the town once numbered 100,000 inhabitants. Now the town's population has dwindled to a few thousand and its main source of income is tourism.

From Aikawa bus terminal, you can either walk for 40 minutes up a steep mountain or take a 10-minute bus ride to Sado Kinzan Gold Mine. There are also five direct buses daily from Ryōtsu to the mine (¥860, 1¼ hours, last departure at 1 pm). Visitors descend into the chilly depths, where mechanical puppets dramatise the tough existence led by miners in the past (¥600, 8 am to 5 pm, until 4 pm from November to March). A farther 300m up the mountain is Dōyū-no-Wareto, the original open-cast mine where you can still see the remains of the workings.

You can return on foot down the mountain road to Aikawa in about half an hour. On the way you'll pass several temples and Aikawa Kyōdo Hakubutsukan, a folk museum with more exhibits from the old mine (¥300, 8.30 am to 5 pm, closed Saturday afternoons and Sunday from December to February). If you reserve in advance (☎ 74-4313) you can try pottery-making or traditional weaving here. Farther downhill, the

Sado Hanga-mura Art Museum displays and sells wood-block prints from artists living and working on Sado-ga-shima (¥300, 9 am to 5 pm, closed November to March).

Both museums are a 20-minute walk from Aikawa's bus terminal, a major transport hub for bus services on the island. There are frequent buses to Ryōtsu (¥780, one hour, every 30 minutes), as well as Ogi (¥810) and Sawata (¥260).

Senkaku-wan 尖閣湾

A 20-minute bus ride north of Aikawa (¥280), this bay features striking rock formations, which can be viewed on 30-minute boat excursions that depart four times daily from April to October (¥700). For ¥850 you can go on a glass-bottom vessel which sails as soon as it fills up.

The scenery along the coast road farther north is more interesting, with fishing villages, racks of drying seaweed, sea mist and calm waters. You can make your own tour up the western coast of an island by taking a local bus from Aikawa to Iwayaguchi (¥1010, 70 minutes). There's a youth hostel at Iwayaguchi – see Places to Stay later.

Mano 真野

Mano was the provincial capital and cultural centre of the island from early times until the 14th century. Buses between Ryōtsu and Mano on the No 2 Minami-sen line stop in front of Konpon-ji. This temple, with its thatched roof and pleasant gardens, stands on the location where Nichiren was first brought when exiled.

There are several other temples in the vicinity of Mano, many of which lie along a peaceful 7km nature trail that begins just west of Konpon-ji near the Danpū-jo bus stop. It's a short walk from there to Myōsen-ji, a temple lying in an attractive forest setting with a five-storey pagoda. The temple was founded by Endo Tamemori, a samurai who became Nichiren's first disciple on Sado-ga-shima.

The trail then passes through rice fields and up old wooden steps set into the hillside to Kokubun-ji, Sado-ga-shima's oldest temple, now sadly neglected but still atmospheric. Another 3km brings you past great lookout points to **Mano Go-ryō**, tomb of Emperor Juntoku. From there, it's a short walk down to **Sado Rekishi Denshōkan**, where robots animate dioramas of Sado's history and festivals (¥700, 8 am to 5.30 pm). Next door is **Mano-gū**, a small shrine dedicated to Emperor Juntoku. It's 15 minutes' walk from here back to the main road. Back in town at Shin-machi-hon-chō bus stop, the Mano tourist information office (☎ 55-3589) rents bicycles and has sketch maps of the trail if you want to hike in the reverse direction (8.30 am to 5.15 pm).

Local bus lines connect Mano with Ryōtsu (¥630, 40 minutes), Sawata (¥260, 15 minutes) and Ogi (¥830, 50 minutes).

Akadomari 赤泊

This port provides an alternative ferry connection to Teradomari (Niigata-ken). Local buses link Akadomari with Ogi (¥570, 30 minutes) and Sawata (¥830, 65 minutes).

Ogi 小木

Ogi is a drowsy port kept in business by the ferry connection with Naoetsu. The big tourist attraction here is a ride in a *taraibune* (tub boat) poled by women in traditional fisherwomen's costumes. The tub boats were once the means to collect seaweed and shellfish but are no longer a common sight. A 10-minute spin in a tub costs ¥450.

Buses run hourly between Ogi and Sawata via Mano (¥910, 65 minutes), but there is no direct bus service between Ogi and Ryōtsu.

Special Events

There seem to be festivals happening almost every week especially during April and the summer season. The island is famed for its *okesa* (folk dances), *ondeko* (demon drum dances) and *tsuburosashi* (a phallic dance with two goddesses).

April
Sado Geinō Matsuri 28 to 29 April. Huge crowds attend this performing arts festival held in Mano; performances include ondeko, folk songs, tsuburosashi and just about anything else.

June–August
Hamochi Matsuri 15 June. Held at Kusukari-jinja in Hamochi town near Ogi, this festival features okesa and tsuburosashi dancers (who are also known to give out sake).

Kōzan Matsuri 25 to 27 July. Held in Aikawa, this is one of Sado's big three festivals and features fireworks, okesa, ondeko, costume and float parades.

Ogi Minato Matsuri (Ogi Port Festival) 28 to 30 August. This festival features lion dances, folk songs, tub-boat races and fireworks.

October
Mano Matsuri 15 to 16 October. Held in Mano, the highlight of this festival is the unusual *jizō-odori* dancers who dance with stone *jizō* (Buddhist statues) that can weigh up to 60kg, on their backs.

Between April and November there are nightly performances of okesa and ondeko dances at Okesa Kaikan in Ryōtsu, at Sado Kaikan (the bus terminal building) in Aikawa, and at Yahata Onsen in Sawata (¥800).

Places to Stay

The island is well furnished with minshuku, ryokan, hotels, *kokumin shukusha* (peoples' lodges) and youth hostels. There are several camping grounds as well. You can get help with booking accommodation from the tourist information offices and the Sado Kisen offices at the ferry terminals. Booking your accommodation in advance (even if it means doing it in Niigata or Naoetsu before boarding) is highly recommended in the hectic summer months.

Places to Stay – Budget

Youth hostels can be found all over the island, making it possible to really see Sado on a budget. Most have only around 20 beds, so it's important to book in advance.

Green Village Youth Hostel (☎ 22-2719) is a cheerful little house in the hills west of Ryōtsu that charges ¥2900 per person. From Ryōtsu take a bus bound for Sawata on the No 2 Minami-sen bus line and get off at the Uryūya stop (¥350, 10 minutes). Be careful not to take buses bound for Aikawa via Sawata because they follow a different

Festive Sado

One of Sado's biggest draws for foreign visitors is the Earth Celebration, a three-day music, dance and arts festival usually held during the third week in August. The focal point of the festival is performances by the world-famous Kodo Drummers, who live in a small village north of Ogi, but are on tour eight months out of the year. The group was formed in the early 1980s to help revive interest in the art of *taiko* (drumming) and all members are required to adhere to strict physical and mental as well as spiritual training regimens.

The main concerts during the Earth Celebration feature original compositions by Kodo group members, often incorporating Buddhist ceremonial flutes and cymbals. Other festival performances range from African dance to Tuvan throat singing to Irish folk music. Workshops are offered throughout the festival by international guest performers and Japanese artists, though the latter usually require participants to have basic Japanese-language ability, at least. There's a competitive sign-up lottery for the workshops and you'll have to submit an application by June to even be considered.

Evening performances usually cost around ¥4000, and there are various package deals available. Travellers, expats living in Japan and Japanese all rave about the festival, and everyone seems to feel it's worth the fairly high ticket prices. Details for each year's festival and workshop availability are provided by the organisers, Kodo (☎ 0259-86-3630), at www.kodo.or.jp. It's highly recommended that you buy tickets and arrange accommodation in advance. Tickets are available at Japan Railways (JR) East reservation centres, Ticket Pia and Lawson convenience stores.

route. Bike rental is available (¥1000 per day) for visiting any of the several pleasant temples and shrines around Mano.

Sado Belle Mer Youth Hostel (☎ 75-2011) is in the tourist area of Senkaku-wan, close to Aikawa and charges ¥3200. From Aikawa, take the Kaifu-sen bus line north to the Minami-Himezu stop (¥310, 20 minutes); from there it's a five-minute walk in the direction of the shore.

Sado Hakusan Youth Hostel (☎ 52-4422) has rates of ¥2700 and is inland in a farming area. Take the bus from Ryōtsu bound for Aikawa, but get off after about 40 minutes at Kubota (about 2km west of Sawata). Then it's a 25-minute walk up the side street opposite the bus stop. If you phone the hostel, they'll pick you up at the bus stop. Guests can use nearby hot springs.

Sotokaifu Youth Hostel (☎ 78-2911), with rates of ¥2300, is in a tiny fishing hamlet in the middle of nowhere run by a friendly family. From late July to mid-August you can get there from Ryōtsu via the Sotokaifu-sen bus line which runs to Ōnogame and continues round the northern tip of the island to deposit you at the Iwayaguchi bus stop – in front of the hostel door (¥1180, 1¾ hours, twice a day). There are more frequent buses to Iwayaguchi from Aikawa on the Kaifu-sen line (¥1010, 1½ hours).

Ogi Sakuma-sō Youth Hostel (☎ 86-2565) is 20 minutes on foot from Ogi, in the far south of the island. It is only open between March and November. Rates are ¥2700 and guests can use nearby hot springs.

Kazashima-kan Youth Hostel (☎ 29-2003), on the south-eastern side of the island in Katanō, charges ¥2750 but a few travellers have given this hostel poor reports.

Places to Stay – Mid-Range
Minshuku There are dozens of minshuku all costing a uniform ¥7000, which includes two meals. Most are clustered along the Nanaura coastline, 15 minutes by bus south of Aikawa on the Nanaura-kaigan-sen line. Next to the Ōura bus stop (¥230), ***Takimoto*** (☎ 74-3103) has, among other amenities, a bath with an ocean view. A few stops father along, the staff at ***Nanaura-sō*** (☎ 76-2735) speak some English, and several of the rooms have balconies overlooking the ocean; get off at the Nagatemisaki-iriguchi stop (¥330). Both minshuku can also be reached by bus from Sawata (25 minutes), which is the southern terminus for the Nanaura-kaigan-sen line. Note that the

Hon-sen line, which also links Sawata and Aikawa, follows an inland road which won't get you to the minshuku along the coast.

One of Sado's most popular minshuku is **Kunimisō** (☎ 22-2316), which is set in an inland valley about 15 minutes by bus from Ryōtsu to Uryūya (same stop as the Green Village Youth Hostel). The minshuku's popularity is said to stem in part from its impressive collection of *bunya* puppets, which the owner often shows to guests. From the bus stop, it's a long walk so you may want to phone ahead and ask to be picked up.

If you're taking the ferry to or from Naoetsu, **Ryosō Sakaya** (☎ 86-2535) is conveniently located a few minutes' walk east of the Ogi ferry terminal. Rooms are pretty basic but clean.

Hotels Most of Sado's hotels are near Ryōtsu, and many charge criminally high rates. One exception is the **Sado Seaside Hotel** (☎ 27-7211), at Sumiyoshi Onsen, about 2km (25 minutes on foot) from Ryōtsu. A free shuttle service is available to and from the port, and for the dance and music performances in Ryōtsu in the evening. Guests have access to hot-spring baths and the seafood dinners are a specialty. Costs with/without meals start at around ¥5500/10,000 per person.

Out at Senkaku-wan, the modern **Familio Sado Aikawa** (☎ 75-1020) resort is 10 minutes by bus north of Aikawa (ask the driver to let you off at the resort entrance near Kami-ogawa). Twin and four-person family rooms are available starting at ¥11,000/18,000 in low season, with discounts of up to 40% for multiple-day stays.

Getting There & Away

Kyokushin Air (☎ 23-5005) flights link Ryōtsu on Sado-ga-shima with Niigata (¥7210, 25 minutes, three to four flights daily). Buses between the airport and Ryōtsu are timed to flights (¥240, 15 minutes).

Sado Kisen passenger ferries and hydrofoils run between Niigata and Ryōtsu. There are up to six regular ferries per day (¥2060, 2¼ hours). As many as 10 'jet foils' per day zip across in merely an hour, but

service is greatly reduced between December and February (¥5960 one way, ¥10,730 return trip).

From Naoetsu-kō, south-west of Niigata, there are ferry and hydrofoil services to Ogi, in the south-west part of Sado-ga-shima. Between April and late November, there are four or more regular ferry departures daily (2½ hours) and two hydrofoils (one hour). During the rest of the year the hydrofoil service is suspended and regular ferries run only twice daily. Fares are the same as for the Niigata-Ryōtsu service. From JR Naoetsu station, it's a 10-minute bus ride (¥160) and then a 15-minute walk to the port.

From Akadomari, on the southern edge of Sado-ga-shima, there are ferries to Teradomari, a short distance south-west of Niigata (¥1410, two hours, one to three per day, suspended during February). However, Teradomari port is only convenient if you have your own transport.

Getting Around

Local buses are fine on the main routes – between Ryōtsu and Aikawa, for example. However, services to other parts of the island are often restricted to two or three a day. If you plan to make extended use of local buses, a vital piece of paper is the *Sado Tōnai Basu Jikokuhyō*, the island's bus timetable (in Japanese), which is available from bus and ferry terminals and tourist information offices. The timetable has a map showing the numbered bus routes for you to match up to the individual timetables. During summer extra bus departures are added to handle the flow of tourists, but in winter services are sharply scaled back.

Teiki kankō (sightseeing buses) have neatly packaged itineraries super convenient, sanitised, hectic and brassy. One itinerary that merits a recommendation is the Panorama Course because it follows the spectacular Ōsado Skyline Hwy from Ryōtsu to Aikawa – there is no local transport alternative for this particular highway (¥3040, 2½ hours).

Renting a car might make sense for a small group since it frees visitors from relying on the bus services. Rates at Sado

Kisen ferry company offices in both Ryōtsu (☎ 27-5195) and Ogi (☎ 86-3010) start at ¥9800 for 24 hours.

Cycling is quite feasible and an enjoyable way to potter around off the beaten track. Bicycle rental is available at Sado Kisen company offices in Ryōtsu, Aikawa and Ogi (¥500 for the first hour, ¥100 for each hour thereafter), as well as some of the tourist offices and hostels. Unfortunately some places charge exorbitant rates, as much as ¥800 for the first hour.

ECHIGO-YUZAWA ONSEN
越後湯沢温泉

☎ 0257

Within easy reach of Tokyo, Echigo-Yuzawa Onsen is a popular winter resort, with almost 20 major skiing grounds. The town was also the setting for Nobel Prize-winning writer Kawabata Yasunari's *Snow Country*, a novel about decadent hot-springs geisha and their patrons. The main ski season lasts from December until as late as May. There are a few opportunities for hiking in summer around **Yuzawa Kōgen**, an alpine plateau accessed via ropeway from the town, and at **Daigenta Canyon**.

The tourist information office (☎ 85-5505) outside Echigo-Yuzawa station can provide some English-language information materials and advise on accommodation (9 am to 5 pm). The narrow streets of the town are packed with minshuku, hotels and ski lodges. Outside of peak ski season, you should have no trouble finding accommodation from around ¥6500 with two meals.

Overlooking the town and its own skiing grounds, the *NASPA New Ōtani Resort* (☎ 80-6111, toll-free 0120-227021) often advertises special deals to lure foreign guests on its Web site at www.naspa.co .jp/english. Luxurious rooms for up to three people start as low as ¥14,000, which is incredibly good value. Free shuttles run between the station and the resort and, in winter, to many of the other major ski areas (up-to-the-minute conditions and reviews of which can be found at www.skijapanguide.com). Hotel guests are given a guidebook with area maps and information on sightseeing in English.

Asahikan (☎ 87-3205, email asahikan@ hotmail.com) is a friendly family-run minshuku located at the base of Yuzawa Park ski area. All rooms are Japanese-style and rates start at ¥5000 on weekdays, including breakfast. The owners speak some English and a free welcome bus from Echigo-Yuzawa station and to certain skiing grounds may be available.

Echigo-Yuzawa station is on the JR Jōetsu shinkansen line between Niigata (¥4730, 40 minutes) and Tokyo (Ueno) (¥5780, 1¼ hours).

Hokkaidō

Hokkaidō is the northernmost and second largest of Japan's islands. Although it accounts for one-fifth of Japan's land area, only 5% of the Japanese population lives here (its population is 5,721,000). However, during peak travel times it can seem as if the rest of the country has come to visit. The real beauty of Hokkaidō lies in its wilderness regions, where there are superb opportunities for outdoor activities such as hiking, camping, skiing, relaxing in hot springs and observing wildlife.

In the Meiji era, Hokkaidō was divided into three administrative districts. This proved an impediment to development so the island was unified as one *dō* (district) divided into 14 *shichō* (subprefectures). Casually speaking, Hokkaidō has four major areas, nicknamed Dō-nan (southern), Dō-ō (central), Dō-hoku (northern) and Dō-tō (eastern). Daisetsuzan National Park spreads across much of the central region, while the fertile plains of Tokachi are to the south.

Suggested Itineraries

Even if you only want to skim the surface of all Hokkaidō has to offer, the absolute minimum duration of your visit should be a week. It is essential that you check the operating dates for transport services, as they vary seasonally.

If you are short of time, stick to the southern and central regions: Hakodate, Tōya-ko, Niseko, Sapporo, Biei and Biratori are all within fairly easy reach of ferry and rail connections with Honshū.

The real treasures of Hokkaidō, however, are its national parks. To visit these, you will need either more time or your own transport. From Abashiri or Sapporo, you can rent a car and really explore the beauty of Shiretoko and Akan National Parks in three or four days. If you're using public transport, allow more time and head for Daisetsuzan National Park, where bus services provide access to rustic hot springs,

Highlights

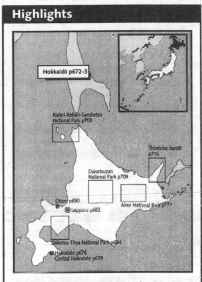

- Glimpse the towering ice sculptures at Sapporo's Yuki Matsuri (Snow Festival).
- Catch a ferry over to Rishiri-tō and Rebun-tō, islands with spectacular hiking and seascapes.
- Encounter Ainu culture in the village of Niputani (Biratori).
- Explore the dramatic mountain scenery and remote hot springs of Daisetsuzan National Park.
- Discover the peninsula, Shiretoko-hantō, one of Japan's most pristine wilderness areas.
- Take in Akan National Park's crystal clear lakes and hike up volcanic peaks.

ski resorts and mountains aplenty for hikers. If time is not a concern, you can't get much farther away from it all than Wakkanai and the scenic islands of Rebun-tō and Rishiri-tō.

Top 10 Sights

1. Mashū-ko on a clear day
2. Winter drift ice in the Sea of Okhotsk (Abashiri)
3. Whales, dolphins and porpoises during summer boat cruises from Muroran
4. Kuril seals basking below the cliffs at the cape, Erimo-misaki
5. The white peaks of Tokachi-dake mountains rising behind the lavender fields of Furano and Biei
6. Tōya-ko's frisky young volcanoes, Shōwa Shin-zan and Usu-zan
7. Boats sailing in and out of Hakodate's harbour
8. Skyline views of Sapporo from Moiwa-yama
9. Sunset over Momo-iwa on Rebun-tō
10. An ocean sunset while soaking in the warm pools of Kamuiwakka-no-taki

History

Until the Edo period, Hokkaidō, or Ezo as it was known prior to the Meiji Restoration, was a backwater in the currents of Japanese history. The island was largely left to its indigenous inhabitants – notably the Ainu, who referred to it as Ainu Moshiri, Ainu meaning 'human' and Moshiri meaning 'island' or 'world'.

During the Muromachi period, settlers began to immigrate from Honshū. In the 16th century, the Matsumae clan arrived in force and established a foothold on the south-western tip of the island, negotiating a trading monopoly with the Ainu, who in turn received a share of the taxes paid on commercial shipping.

The Meiji Restoration of 1868 saw a major shift in Japan's approach to its northernmost island. The Kaitakushi (Colonial Office) was established to encourage vigorous expansion, and the new name Hokkaidō (literally the 'North Sea Road') was formally adopted. At the same time, various Ainu customs were banned, such as women's tattoos and men's earrings. Foreign advisers were called in to help with the aggressive development of the island: Sapporo's grid-like layout was planned by a US architect, and US agricultural experts introduced the farm architecture that has endured as a characteristic of Hokkaidō's landscape.

Hokkaidō's sparsely populated landmass has made it an important agricultural base, and it is Japan's largest food producer. Wheat, potatoes, corn, rice and dairy products make up the bulk of its production. The island is also home to forestry, and pulp and paper industries, as well as fishing and mining.

In the past decade Hokkaidō has become a top destination for Japanese tourists, and ecotourism is on the rise. The business this brings is now a major source of income, particularly for remote communities that would otherwise find it hard to continue to make a living from fishing or agriculture.

Climate

Hokkaidō does not have a rainy season per se, but the beginning of summer can be wet and miserable. From May to October the island attracts hikers and campers, but the biggest crowds arrive in June, July and August. While transport services are more frequent and extensive in the high season, it can also be quite difficult to find accommodation then – a tent is a good idea. It's possible to avoid the crowds by timing your trip to take advantage of the last of the autumn weather from October to early November.

After November, winter sets in, and the next five months are characterised by heavy snowfall and subzero temperatures. During these months, the majority of tourists are skiers, though some visitors come specifically to see the Sapporo Yuki Matsuri (Sapporo Snow Festival) in February. Whatever time of year you visit, don't underestimate the weather – take clothing that will keep you warm and dry.

Information

English-language information is scarce in Hokkaidō, so it's a good idea to stop in Sapporo to pick up information, organise transport, make bookings and change money before heading for more remote parts. Bear in mind that you can always use the Japan Travel-Phone (☎ 371-5649, ☎ 0088-22-4800 toll free) if you're having trouble communicating (see Tourist Offices in the Facts for the Visitor chapter).

The Sapporo tourist information offices have an English-language pamphlet for just about every area on the island. The best of these publications include scaled maps, background information about sights, and seasonal travel information. Among the titles available are *Eastern Hokkaido*, *Tourist Map Hokkaidō Japan* and *English Travel Guide Hokkaidō*. Comprehensive *jikokuhyō* (timetables) for train, bus and air routes are available in Japanese at most bookshops.

Money Outside Sapporo, only a few major banks give credit-card advances on foreign-issued cards. Try Sumitomo Bank for VISA and Mitsubishi Bank for MasterCard. ATMs that accept foreign-issued cards seem to pop up and then disappear again with alarming speed. For more information see Money in the Facts for the Visitor chapter.

Email & Internet Access The idea of Internet cafes is slowly catching on, though only in the bigger cities. If you ask politely, you *may* be able to log on free of charge at tourist information offices, international friendship centres and youth hostels or Toho inns.

Books *Race, Resistance and the Ainu of Japan*, by Richard Siddle, is a contemporary history of the Ainu struggle for self-determination. For a more personal account, try *Our Land Was a Forest: an Ainu Memoir*, written by Kayano Shigeru, the first person of Ainu descent to be elected to the Japanese Diet.

Accommodation If you plan to visit Hokkaidō during the peak summer months or during the Sapporo Yuki Matsuri it's an extremely good idea to book your accommodation well in advance. Hordes of holiday-makers put such a squeeze on accommodation at all levels that even a big city like Sapporo can be totally booked out.

The island has the largest concentration of youth hostels in Japan; many are in superb surroundings and offer excellent food, advice on outdoor pursuits and a surprisingly laid-back atmosphere. As a rule, reception will close at around 8 or 9 pm and there will be a curfew at 10 or 11 pm. You may be able to check in later if you phone ahead to let staff know when you expect to arrive. Although a bit outdated, the *Youth Hostel Hokkaidō Guide* (¥400) has useful transport information and maps. It's available at the Sapporo International Plaza *i*.

There are nearly 90 Toho network inns in Hokkaidō, offering a flexible and reasonably priced alternative to youth hostels. There are also innumerable 'rider houses', which provide extremely basic shared accommodation priced from around ¥1000 a night. If you can read some Japanese, pick up a spiral bound *Touring Mapple Hokkaidō*, available at most bookshops. It indicates all the rider houses and also suggests cheap places to eat along the way. For more details on the Toho network and rider houses, see Accommodation in the Facts for the Visitor chapter.

Getting There & Away

While Sapporo is the hub of Hokkaidō's air traffic, smaller cities also have flights to Tokyo, Osaka and other Honshū destinations. You can save up to 30% by purchasing tickets during summer sales or buying them from discount ticket outlets in major cities.

Two of the fastest rail connections to Hakodate and Sapporo from Tokyo are the Hokutosei Express, which is a direct sleeper, and a combination of the *shinkansen* (bullet train) to Morioka followed by a *tokkyū* (limited express) via Aomori. New Cassiopeia luxury express sleepers follow the same route but the cheapest twin rooms with TV and attached bath cost a whopping ¥30,750 a person – that is if you can even get a ticket for this popular service.

Japan Railways (JR) offers special round-trip deals to Hokkaidō, as well as free passes entitling you to unlimited travel on JR buses and trains (excluding sleeper services) and a few private long-distance buses while you're on the island. A seven-day

HOKKAIDŌ

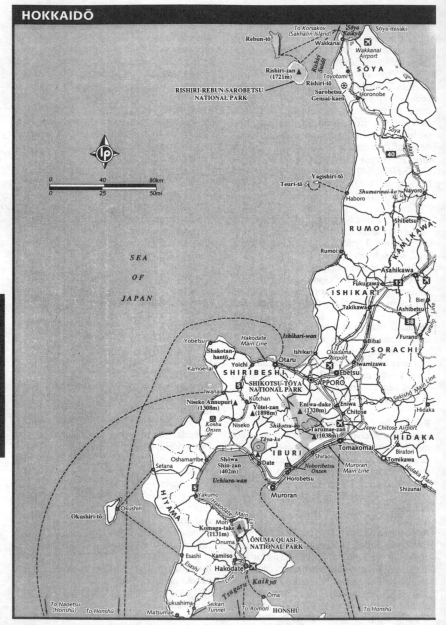

To Korsakov
(Sakhalin Island)

Rebun-tō

Sōya
Kaikyō

Sōya-misaki

Wakkanai

Wakkanai
Airport

SŌYA

Rishiri-zan
(1721m)

Rishiri-tō

Rishiri
Suidō

Toyotomi

RISHIRI-REBUN-SAROBETSU
NATIONAL PARK

Sarobetsu
Gensai-kaen

Horonobe

40

Sōya

Main Line

Yagishiri-tō

Teuri-tō

Shumarinai-ko

Nayoro

Haboro

RUMOI

Shibetsu

KAMIKAWA

SEA

OF

JAPAN

Rumoi

Asahikawa

Fukugawa

12

ISHIKARI

Biei

Takikawa

Ashibetsu

Furano

38

Furano Line

Yobetsu

Hakodate
Main Line

Ishikari-wan

Bibai

SORACHI

Shakotan-
hantō

Ishikari

Okadama
Airport

Iwamizawa

Kamoenai

Yoichi

Otaru

SHIRIBESHI

5

SHIKOTSU-TŌYA
NATIONAL PARK

SAPPORO

Ebetsu

Sekishō Main Line

Iwanai

Kutchan

Niseko Annupuri
(1308m)

Yōtei-zan
(1898m)

Eniwa-dake
(1320m)

Eniwa

Hidaka

Konbu
Onsen

Niseko

Shikotsu-ko

Chitose

New Chitose Airport

HIDAKA

Tōya-ko

Tarumae-zan
(1038m)

Oshamanbe

IBURI

Shiraoi

Tomakomai

Biratori

Setana

Shōwa
Shin-zan
(402m)

Date

Noboribetsu
Onsen

Muroran
Main Line

Tomikawa

Uchiura-wan

Horobetsu

Shizunai

Hidaka Main

HIYAMA

5

Yakumo

Muroran

Okushiri-tō

Okushiri

Hakodate Main Line

Mori

Komaga-take
(1131m)

ŌNUMA QUASI-
NATIONAL PARK

Ōnuma

Esashi

Kamiiso

Hakodate

Esashi

Esashi

Line

Tsugaru Kaikyō

To Naoetsu
(Honshū)

To Honshū

Fukushima

Matsumae

Seikan
Tunnel

Ōma

HONSHŪ

To Aomori

To Honshū

0   40   80km
0   25   50mi

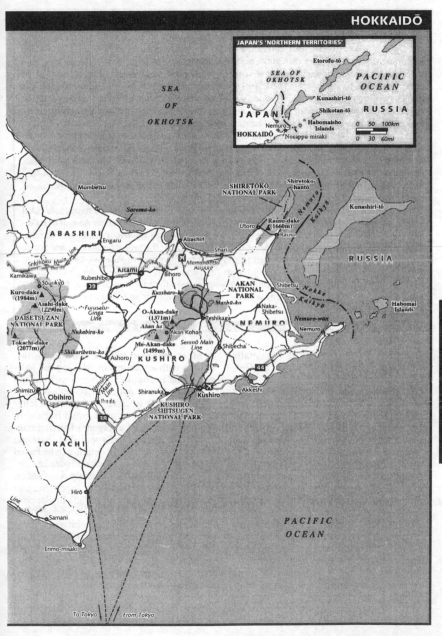

HOKKAIDŌ

JAPAN'S 'NORTHERN TERRITORIES'

SEA OF OKHOTSK

Etorofu-tō

PACIFIC OCEAN

Kunashiri-tō

Shikotan-tō

RUSSIA

JAPAN

Nemuro

Habomaisho Islands

HOKKAIDŌ

Nosappu-misaki

0   50   100km
0   30   60mi

SEA

OF

OKHOTSK

Mombetsu

Saroma-ko

SHIRETOKO NATIONAL PARK

Shiretoko-hantō

Kunashiri-tō

ABASHIRI

Engaru

Abashiri

Shari

Utoro

Raúsu-dake (1660m)

Rausu

RUSSIA

Sekihoku Main Line

Kamikawa

Sōunkyō

Rubeshibe

Kitami

Bihoro

Memanbetsu
Aipiore

Nokke Kaikyō

Kuro-dake (1984m)

39

Kussharo-ko

AKAN NATIONAL PARK

Shibetsu

Habomai Islands

Asahi-dake (2290m)

Furusato-Ginga Line

Mashū-ko

Naka-Shibetsu

DAISETSUZAN NATIONAL PARK

O-Akan-dake (1371m)

Teshikaga

NEMURO

Nukabira-ko

Akan-ko

Nemuro-wan

Tokachi-dake (2077m)

Shikaribetsu-ko

Akan Kohan

Me-Akan-dake (1499m)

Sennō Main Line

Shibecha

Nemuro

Shimizu

Ashoro

KUSHIRO

44

Obihiro

Nemuro Main Line

Shiranuka

Kushiro

Akkeshi

38

KUSHIRO SHITSUGEN NATIONAL PARK

TOKACHI

Line

Hirō

PACIFIC OCEAN

Samani

Erimo-misaki

To Tokyo   From Tokyo

Seikan Tunnel Tour

Fancy spending two hours in a concrete tube at the bottom of the ocean? If the idea appeals, you can try JR's Seikan Tunnel Tour, conducted at the Yoshioka-kaitei (Hokkaidō) and Tappi-kaitei (Honshū) stations, both more than 100m below sea level.

The tour takes you through a maze of service corridors and passageways, quickly showing the immensity of this tunnel, which, at 53.85km, is the world's longest. Staff use bicycles and even cars to make their rounds. Longer tours include some of the tunnel's unique features, such as a 600m-long cable-car link to the shore of Honshū and a narrow passageway between the railway tracks that gives visitors a worm's eye view of trains roaring past.

During the 17 years it took to construct the tunnel, an unusual number of accidents and fatalities occurred. *Feng shui*, the Chinese art of geomancy, has an unique explanation for these events. According to interpretation, Japan is shaped like a powerful dragon, with Hokkaidō as its head, Honshū as the main body and the southern islands forming the tail. Unfortunately, the Seikan Tunnel cuts like a knife across the 'neck' of the dragon at the straits of the Tsugaru-kaikyō, thus severing Japan's lifeblood artery and bringing bad luck, injury and death.

If you are still undeterred from visiting, you must purchase a combined rail and tunnel tour ticket at least one day in advance from travel agencies or JR reservation centres in either Aomori or Hakodate. Only a few trains a day in either direction are actual through-train/tour combinations; other trains return to their station of origin (Aomori or Hakodate) after the tour is finished. In addition to the *kaisoku* (rapid) train fare, you'll need to pay ¥840 for the standard Yoshioka-kaitei or Tappi-kaitei station tour (in Japanese only), which lasts from one to 2½ hours, depending on when the next train comes by to pick you up. For ¥1900, you can take the tour that continues from Tappi-kaitei station via the cable car formerly used by construction workers up to the Seikan Tunnel Museum on dry land.

pass of this kind costs ¥23,750. For details on discount rail tickets, see Train in the Getting Around chapter.

The cheapest way to visit Hokkaidō is by long-distance ferry from Honshū – if you travel overnight, you save the cost of a night's accommodation. Most boats are quite comfortable (some even have saunas or gyms). All ferry prices quoted in this chapter are for the cheapest 2nd-class open sleeping-mat areas. However, these can be jam-packed during peak season, when it may be worth the extra ¥2000 or so for a shared 2nd-class berth. Cruise System (☎ 03-5276-4231) in Tokyo offers Toho Ferry Packs entitling you to discounts on 2nd-class ferry tickets if you book one night of accommodation at a Toho network inn.

Sakhalin Ferry From early May to mid-September ferries run regularly between Wakkanai in Hokkaidō and Korsakov on Russia's Sakhalin Island.

Most Japanese tourists who make this trip go with a tour group. Making the journey alone is possible but requires time and a healthy dose of patience. To get a Russian visa you need to have an invitation letter from a hotel or tourist organisation in Sakhalin and must apply at a Russian consulate (there's one in Sapporo) at *least* one week in advance. More details can be found at embassy.kcom.ne.jp/russia/index.htm.

The Japan-Russia Friendship Association (☎ 011-737-6221) and the Japan Eurasia Association (☎ 011-707-0933) in Sapporo are accustomed to making arrangements for Japanese citizens, but can provide some general information about Sakhalin. For information about tours, try Polar Star Japan (☎ 011-271-2466).

Getting Around

When planning a route around Hokkaidō, it's essential to remember the time (and expense) required by the sheer size of the place.

A network of internal flights radiating from Sapporo makes it possible for those in a hurry to travel the long distances quickly, but air fares are not cheap.

The rail network in Hokkaidō has only a few major lines with fast and frequent services, while the remainder have mainly slow or infrequent trains. JR Hokkaidō offers discounted return tickets on many routes that may reduce the expense somewhat. The S-kippu (S-ticket) is valid on unreserved seats for four to six days from the time you start your outbound trip and offers savings of 20% to 40% of the cost of two one-way tickets. The R-kippu offers similar discounts for reserved seats. *Naito-to-dei kippu* (Nite-&-Day tickets) are usually valid for six days and allow you to take a sleeper train one way and a daytime tokkyū reserved seat on the return leg.

Hokkaidō's bus network is far more extensive than its train network. Inter-city buses are usually almost as quick as the trains, tend to run more often and cost less. However, buses to more remote regions tend to run infrequently, or only during the peak tourist season, and fares are often expensive.

If you can afford it, rent a car, so you can reach remote areas at your own pace. Most cities have car-rental agencies, and rates for smaller cars start at around ¥7000 for 24 hours, including insurance. Bear in mind, however, that you will also have to pay expressway tolls and buy fuel. Rates automatically rise ¥2000 or more during July and August. Toyota Rent-a Car (☎ 011-251-0100) and Orix Rent-a-Car (☎ 011-241-0543) generally offer the best rates; they also do not always charge for excess mileage, which can result in significant savings in Hokkaidō. Mazda Rent-a-Car should give you discounted rates and unlimited mileage if you ask for its Toho Plan. At the time of writing, Mazda was also promoting a limited free-return system that allowed you to start and end your trip at different points within a designated area.

Bicycles and motorcycles are also popular modes of transport in Hokkaidō; many of the roads around the coast have low gradients and stunning scenery. Residents and even passing tourists seem happy to offer rides to hitchhikers, but some single travellers (especially women) have reported being harassed. If you ask around, it's sometimes possible to arrange a ride with other guests at youth hostels – the hostel manager usually knows who's going where.

Dō-nan (Southern Hokkaidō)

HAKODATE 函館
☎ 0138 • pop 291,700

Hakodate, a convenient gateway to Hokkaidō, is a laid-back place with an historical heritage. It was one of the first foreign trading ports to be opened up under the terms of the Kanagawa Treaty of 1854, following which a small foreign community took root here.

Hakodate is fairly spread out. The western area, within easy reach of JR Hakodate station by tram and bus, houses the bulk of the historical sights and lies below the slopes of the mountain, Hakodate-yama. Several kilometres east of the station is the sprawling city centre and the mildly interesting remains of the fort, Goryō-kaku.

The Hakodate tourist information centre (☎ 23-5440) is to the right as you exit the station. It's open from 9 am to 7 pm, except from November to March, when it closes at 5 pm. The office has English-language maps and information, including the useful *Hakodate Guide Map* and *Romantic Hakodate*. There is also a small information desk in the park, Motomachi-kōen. Information about Hakodate's history and sights can be found at www.hakodate.or.jp.

At the time of writing, VISA cash advances could be obtained at Hokkaido Bank (9 am to 2.30 pm weekdays) and the Saison counter on the 6th floor of Seibu department store (10 am to 7 pm).

Hakodate-yama 函館山
Fine views of Hakodate can be enjoyed from the summit of this mountain (334m), preferably on a clear night. A ropeway

(cable car) whisks you up to the top in a few minutes and relieves you of ¥1160 for the return trip (10 am to 10 pm, until 9 pm November to late April). At the summit, there is a monument to Sir Thomas Blakiston, the man who established the strait, the Tsugaru-kaikyō, as a major dividing line for flora and fauna species.

From Hakodate station, take tram No 2 or 5 to the Jūjigai stop (¥200). The cable car station is then a seven-minute walk uphill. From late April to mid-November, you can also take a bus directly from the station to the summit (¥360, 30 minutes).

If you feel fit, there's a trail winding up the mountain, though it's closed from late October to late April.

Motomachi District 元町

This district, at the base of Hakodate-yama, has several 19th-century Western-style buildings and is a pleasant place to stroll around.

The easiest building to recognise is the **Russian Orthodox Church**, an attractive reconstruction dating from 1916. Other sights in Motomachi worth checking out are the **Chinese Memorial Hall** (¥500); and the **Hakodate City Museum of Northern Peoples**, which has displays of traditional tools and ceremonial objects used by the Ainu and other indigenous peoples (¥500, 9 am to 7 pm, until 5 pm November to March). If you continue past the Foreigners' Cemetery on the road heading west alongside the water you'll reach *Penguin's Valley*, a popular watering hole to have a drink while watching boats sail into the harbour.

To reach Motomachi, take tram No 5 from Hakodate station to the Suehiro-chō stop (¥200), then walk uphill for about 10 minutes.

Goryō-kaku 五稜郭

Japan's first Western-style fort was built here in 1864 in the shape of a five-pointed

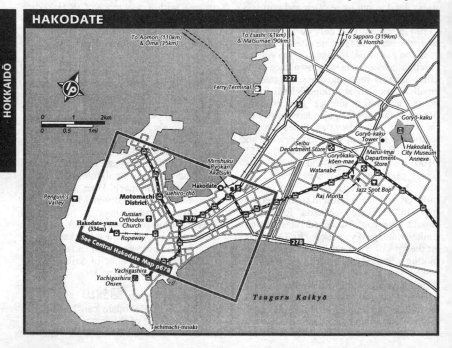

star (goryō-kaku translates literally as 'five-sided fort'), designed to trap attackers in deadly crossfire. Five years later, forces loyal to the Tokugawa shogunate, who had declared their own independent republic recognised by France and Britain only a year earlier, held out for just seven days before surrendering to the troops of the Meiji Restoration. All that remain are the outer walls and the **Hakodate City Museum Annexe**, which displays weaponry and the inevitable blood-stained uniforms (¥100, 9 am to 4.30 pm, until 4 pm November to March).

Close to the park's entrance is **Goryō-kaku Tower**, which provides a bird's-eye view of the ruins and the surrounding area (¥630, 9 am to 6 pm). For a bottom-up perspective, you can rent a rowing boat for the 2km circuit around the moat; be careful not to get your oars caught in the lily pads.

To reach the fort, take tram No 2 or 5 to the Goryōkaku-kōen-mae stop (¥220, 15 minutes). From there, it's a 10-minute walk to the fort.

Other Attractions

The enormous mineral hot spring spa at **Yachigashira Onsen**, accommodating some 600 bathers, is not a major attraction, but it does give you a good opportunity to take a look at Japanese onsen culture (¥630). The spa is open from 6 am to 9.30 pm, except from December to March, when it's open from 7 am to 9.30 pm; it's closed on the second and fourth Friday of every month and over New Year. To get there, take tram No 2 from Hakodate station to Yachigashira, the final stop (¥220).

If you're an early bird, the **Asa-Ichi** (morning market) near Hakodate station is open from 5 am to noon. Try the ika-somen (squid with fine, white noodles) or ika-sumi (squid ink) ice cream. Most of the real action is over by 8 am, after which the activity is aimed primarily at tourists.

Special Events

On the third weekend in May, the festival, **Hakodate Goryōkaku Matsuri**, features a parade of townsfolk dressed in the uniforms of the soldiers who took part in the Meiji Restoration battle of 1868.

From 1 to 5 August, you can see 10,000-person 'squid' dances, parades and fireworks during the **Hakodate Minato Matsuri** (Hakodate Port Festival).

Places to Stay

During the busy summer months, Hakodate is swamped with tourists heading northwards to other parts of Hokkaidō, and accommodation can be hard to find. If you don't have a reservation, it's a good idea to call into the tourist information office next to the station: Staff here will know which ryokan (traditional Japanese inns), minshuku (family-run budget accommodation) and hotels, if any, have vacancies.

Budget Close to the Hōrai-chō tram stop is the **Hakodate Youth Guesthouse** (☎ 26-7892), touted as one of Hokkaido's best youth hostels. Per-person rates in two- or three-person dorms are ¥4000, except from July to September, when they rise to ¥4500. The guesthouse is closed at different times throughout winter, so phone ahead.

Minshuku Ryokan Akatsuki (☎ 22-4978) looks a bit tattered, but the rooms are cheap at ¥3500 a person. The minshuku is a two-minute walk north of the station, behind Mazda Rent-a-Car.

On a side street near the morning market, **Niceday Inn** (☎ 22-5919) charges ¥3000 a person for rather cramped bunk-bed dorms, but the friendly management speaks excellent English. **Minshuku Kumachi** (☎ 22-3437, 27-1580) is in an old house nearby with flowers on the balcony. Basic rooms cost ¥3800 a person.

Mid-Range One of the cheapest hotels close to the station is **Hakodate Plaza Hotel** (☎ 22-0121), where singles and twins cost ¥4300 and ¥8000, respectively.

Top End Highly recommended by some travellers is **Auberge Kokian** (☎ 26-5753). The building, dating from 1897, is typical of Hakodate architecture: Western-style exterior on top, Japanese-style on the ground

HOKKAIDŌ

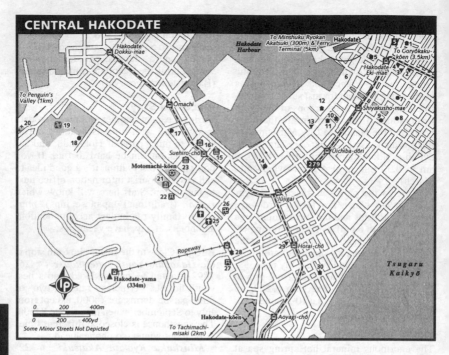

CENTRAL HAKODATE

floor. Hotel-quality rooms cost ¥9800 to ¥12,000 a person, including two meals.

An upmarket option in the station area is *Hakodate Harbourview Hotel* (☎ 22-0111), where prices for singles/doubles vary seasonally, starting at ¥9000/13,000.

Places to Eat

The station area doesn't offer a great deal in the way of restaurants. Near *Mr Donut* and *KFC* is *The Don*, a tiny place specialising in *donburi* (meat or seafood atop a heaped bowl of rice) from ¥400.

At the foot of Hakodate-yama, *Jolly Jellyfish* bar and restaurant has reasonably priced seafood, pizza and Thai dishes. It's open until after midnight and is popular with local expats.

In the Nishi-hatoba (West Wharf) district, there are plenty of trendy eateries in converted Western-style buildings. *Hakodate Beer* is an enormous place with live music on some evenings. The food may be over-

priced, but you can try all three varieties of microbrew produced here for ¥1000.

Near the Goryōkaku-kōen-mae tram stop there are some good spots. *Raj Morita* has lunch-time specials of authentic Indian curry and nan for around ¥1000. *Watanabe* is an affordable *yakitori* shop with out-of-this-world *chiizu-yaki onigiri* (rice triangles grilled with cheese).

Entertainment

Jazz Spot Bop is a small basement pub crowded with antiques – try the hot chocolate (¥500).

Getting There & Away

All Nippon Airlines (ANA) and Japan Airlines (JAL) connect Hakodate airport with Nagoya, Kansai, Sendai, Niigata, Hiroshima, Fukuoka and Tokyo. All Nippon Koku (ANK) has flights from Hakodate to Sapporo's Okadama airport (¥11,800, 45 minutes, five a day).

CENTRAL HAKODATE

PLACES TO STAY
1 Hakodate Plaza Hotel
  函館プラザホテル
5 Hakodate Harborview
  Hotel
  函館ハーバービュー
  ホテル
10 Minshuku Kumachi
  民宿くまち
11 Niceday Inn
  ナイスディイン
12 Hakodate Kokusai Hotel
  函館国際ホテル
14 Auberge Kokian
  ペンション古稀庵
29 Hakodate-yama Hotel
30 Hakodate Youth
  Guesthouse
  函館ユースゲストハウス

PLACES TO EAT
2 KFC

3 Mr Donut
4 The Don
13 Hakodate Beer
  函館ビール
28 Jolly Jellyfish

OTHER
6 Asa-Ichi
  (Morning Market)
  朝市
7 NTT
8 Hakodate Municipal Office
  函館市役所
9 Orix Rent-a-Car
  オリックスレンタカー
15 The Kanemori Museum
  金森美術館
16 Hakodate City Museum
  of Northern Peoples
  函館市北方民族博物館
17 Chinese Memorial Hall
  中華会館

18 Old Russian Consulate
  旧ロシア領事館
19 Kōryū-ji
  高龍寺
20 Foreigners' Cemetery
  外人墓地
21 Old Public Hall of
  Hakodate Ward
  旧函館区公会堂
22 Funadama-jinja
  船魂神社
23 Old British Consulate
  旧イギリス領事館
24 Russian Orthodox Church
  ハリストス正教会
25 Hakodate Episcopal
  Church of Japan
  聖ヨハネ教会
26 Higashi Hongan-ji
  東本願寺
27 Gokoku-jinja
  護国神社

The JR Tsugaru-Kaikyō line runs between Hakodate and Aomori via the Seikan Tunnel (tokkyū, ¥4830, two hours). Cheaper *kaisoku* (rapid) trains make the trip in about 2½ hours (¥3150). Some of these trains also give you the option of taking the Seikan Tunnel Tour (see the 'Seikan Tunnel Tour' boxed text in the main Getting Around section of this chapter).

There is a Hokutosei Express sleeper service to Tokyo's Ueno station (¥21,000, 12 hours) and also a sleeper service to Osaka (¥23,100, 17 hours). Either trip costs ¥9450 with a Japan Rail Pass. A combination of tokkyū and shinkansen (from Morioka) takes about seven hours to Tokyo (¥17,640).

The JR Hakodate main line runs north from Hakodate to Sapporo (tokkyū, ¥6820, 3½ hours) via New Chitose airport and Tomakomai; R-kippu (¥14,160) and Nite-&-Day tickets (¥12,180) are available for this route.

Buses depart from in front of Hakodate station for Sapporo's Chūō bus station and Ōdōri bus centre (¥4680, five hours, five a

day). There are also two night buses leaving around midnight for the same fare. Buses for Esashi leave six times a day (¥1830, two hours).

Between March and December, high-speed 'Unicorn' ferries zip between Hakodate-kō and Aomori (¥2130, 2¼ hours, two or three a day). Ferries depart year round for Aomori (¥1420, 3¾ hours, up to nine a day) and Ōma on the peninsula, Shimokita-hantō (¥1010, 1¾ hours, two to four a day)

Getting Around

Buses to Hakodate airport depart frequently from in front of the Harbourview Hotel near Hakodate station (¥300, 20 minutes).

A taxi from JR Hakodate station to the ferry terminal costs around ¥1500. Between May and September, there are a few direct buses from Hakodate station that coincide fairly closely with some ferry departures (¥230, 15 minutes). City bus No 16 runs much more frequently between the ferry terminal and the Goryōkaku-kōen-mae tram stop, from where you can catch a tram to Hakodate station.

HOKKAIDŌ

One-day (¥1000) and two-day (¥1700) passes offering unlimited travel on city buses and trams are available at the tourist information offices or from the drivers. These passes are not valid for travel on Hakodate Bus Company buses. This is no problem, however, as the city transport services are more than sufficient and even include the bus service to the top of Hakodate-yama.

MATSUMAE 松前

As the farthest-flung outpost of the Tokugawa shogunate, Matsumae was once the stronghold of the Matsumae clan and the centre of political power on Hokkaidō. In the 19th century, the Tokugawa shogunate, followed by the forces of the Meiji Restoration, gradually took over governmental functions and Matsumae's political importance faded. With its rich history, Matsumae is an easy day trip from Hakodate, or a pleasant detour en route from Honshū.

Matsumae-jō, Hokkaidō's only castle and the last one to be built in Japan, was completed in 1854 (the same year as Commodore Perry arrived) as a possible defence against Russian expansion down from Sakhalin. The restored castle houses typical feudal relics and a small collection of Ainu items. There is a small tourist information office (☎ 01394-2-3868) near the castle. Farther uphill is a 17th-century temple district and the burial grounds of the Matsumae clan. Even farther along is **Matsumae Hanyashiki**, an interesting replica of an Edo-period village built using authentic materials and construction techniques. Admission to either the castle or the village costs ¥310 and both are open from 9 am to 4.30 pm from mid-April to mid-December.

To reach Matsumae from Hakodate, take the JR Esashi line to Kikonai (kaisoku, ¥810, 45 minutes), which is also on the JR Tsugaru-Kaikyō line for connections with Honshū. From Kikonai station there are direct buses to Matsumae; get off at the Matsumae-jō stop (¥1220, 85 minutes). Buses then continue to the Matsumae station across town, from where there are buses to Esashi between April and November (¥2480, two hours, four a day).

ESASHI & OKUSHIRI-TŌ 江差・奥尻島
☎ 01397

Esashi is a major fishing town 67km west of Hakodate. The town is renowned for its annual festival, from 9 to 11 August, featuring parades of more than a dozen ornate floats in honour of Ubagami Dai-jingū, Hokkaido's oldest shrine. Among other attractions are **Yokoyama House**, a 19th-century **nishin-goten** (the residence for barons of the herring fishing industry and their employees), and **Nakamura House**, an early Meiji-era shipping merchant's residence.

Okushiri-tō is a sleepy place with small fishing villages, beautiful coastal scenery and a few tourism sights cluttering up the view. Public transport on the island is restricted to infrequent buses. Car, motor scooter and bicycle rental is available near the ferry terminal upon arrival.

Places to Stay

There are plenty of minshuku near the ferry terminal in Okushiri. The popular **Minshuku Honobono-sō** (☎ 2-3395) and **Minshuku Hemmi** (☎ 2-2020) are both about five minutes from the pier and have rooms for ¥6000 a person, including two meals. At the northern end of the island near the cape, Inaho-misaki, **Minshuku Inaho** (☎ 2-2230) has per-person rates ranging from ¥6000 to ¥8000, including two meals. There are several camping grounds scattered around the coast, but they only open from May to September.

Getting There & Away

In summer, Air Hokkaidō (☎ 0138-26-3521) flies up to three times a day between Okushiri-tō and Hakodate (¥13,180, 35 minutes).

On the JR Esashi line, there are infrequent local trains between Hakodate and Esashi (¥1790, 2¾ hours). From Esashi station, it's a 25-minute walk across town to the ferry terminal. Direct buses from Hakodate (¥1830, two hours, six a day) stop across the street from the terminal. From April to November there are buses between Esashi and Matsumae (¥2480, 1¾ hours, four a day).

From Esashi, ferries depart at 6.50 am and 1 pm for Okushiri-tō (¥2100, 2¼ hours). Between January and March only the afternoon ferry is in service. Another ferry service operates from Okushiri-tō to Setana, farther north of Esashi, between late April and October (¥1560, 1¾ hours, up to twice a day). From Setana there are buses to Oshamanbe (¥1380, 1¾ hours) on the JR Hakodate main line.

Sapporo 札幌

☎ 011 • pop 1.8 million

Sapporo is Hokkaidō's administrative hub, its main population centre and a lively, prosperous city. The cosmopolitan flavour of the city, with its sweeping tree-lined boulevards, makes it worth a stopover, especially to pick up information and change money before heading out into the hinterlands. There may not be a wealth of 'sights' here, but Sapporo gives you a peek at modern Japan without the pressing crowds that prevail in cities like Tokyo and Osaka.

Orientation

Sapporo is one of the only cities in Japan where it's almost possible to find places by their addresses. The blocks (not the streets) of its precise grid pattern are named and numbered according to the points of the compass (north, east, south, west). Addresses are also given in terms of blocks: for example, Sapporo's famous *tokei-dai* (clock tower) is in the block of North 1, West 2. The centre point is near the TV tower. The street names reflect this block numbering pattern, with the exception of Ōdōri along Ōdori-kōen, which is the dividing line between north and south.

From Sapporo station, the major artery West 3-4 makes a beeline straight through the administrative, commercial and entertainment areas of the city, crossing the huge Ōdōri on the way. North of the station is the Hokkaidō University area, with its student coffee shops and cheap restaurants, as well as a selection business hotels and ryokan. South of Ōdōri is a shopping district, with a large number of department stores and restaurants. Between South 4 and South 9 is Susukino, the largest entertainment area north of Tokyo.

Information

Sapporo has several tourist offices with helpful English-speaking staff.

The information counters are run by the Sapporo International Communication Plaza Foundation. The Sapporo International Information Corner (☎ 213-5062) is inside the western concourse JR reservation centre. It's open from 9 am to 5 pm during summer and daily except the second and fourth Wednesday of every month during the rest of the year. The staff here have a wide range of maps and information on Sapporo and the rest of Hokkaidō – at the very least pick up the excellent *Traveler's Sapporo* visitors handbook and *Traveler's Map*. Although the staff are not authorised to book accommodation, they can make recommendations according to your budget.

The Sapporo International Plaza *i* (☎ 211-3678) is on the 1st and 3rd floors of the MN building, just opposite the clock tower. The 1st-floor information desk is the place to ask questions before heading off to more remote parts of the island – if the information exists, the staff will find it for you. It is also possible to organise youth hostel membership here. If you plan to spend some time in Sapporo, pick up *What's On in Sapporo* for current events listings, including free Japanese language and culture classes. Those planning a long-term stay in Sapporo should visit the 3rd-floor help desk; there are also notice boards and a selection of foreign newspapers and magazines here. The entire plaza is open from 9 am to 5.30 pm daily, but the 3rd floor is closed on Sunday.

There is an information counter (☎ 232-7712) in the Ōdōri subway station, near exit 14 (10 am to 6 pm weekdays).

Money At the time of writing, only two ATM corners were accepting foreign-issued cards. One was conveniently located in the Paseo shopping centre adjacent to the

HOKKAIDŌ

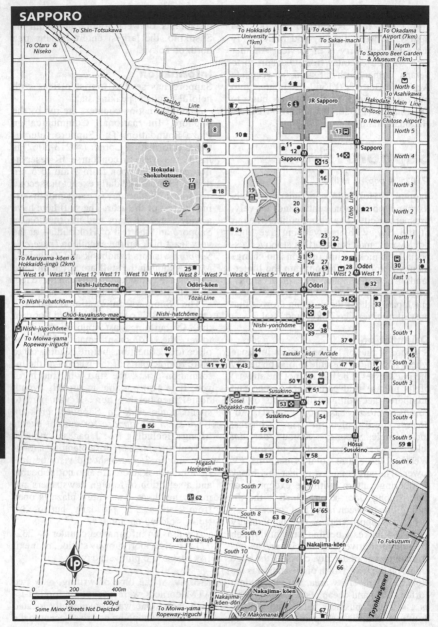

SAPPORO

To Shin-Totsukawa

To Otaru &
Niseko

To Hokkaidō
University
(1km)

■1

To Asabu

To Okadama
Airport (7km)

To Sakae-machi

North 7

To Sapporo Beer Garden
& Museum (1km)

5
North 6

To Asahikawa

Hakodate Main Line

■2

■3

4■

6■

JR Sapporo

Chitose Line

To New Chitose Airport

13■

Sassō Line

■7

Hakodate Main Line

8

10■

North 5

9

■11
12

Sapporo

M

14■

Sapporo

North 4

Hokudai
Shokubutsuen

17

■15

16

North 3

■18

19

20

■21

North 2

■24

23
22

North 1

To Maruyama-kōen &
Hokkaidō-jingū (2km)

West 14 West 13 West 12 West 11 West 10 West 9 West 8 West 7

25■

29■

26 27

28 Ōdōri

West 6 West 5 West 4 West 3 West 2

30

31

M West 1

East 1

Nishi-Juitchōme

M

Ōdōri-kōen

Ōdōri

M

●32

To Nishi-Juhatchōme

Tōzai Line

34■

33

Chūō-kuyakusho-mae

Nishi-hatchōme

35 36

Nishi-jūgochōme

To Moiwa-yama
Ropeway-iriguchi

Nishi-yonchōme

39 38

37●

South 1

40

44

Tanuki kōji Arcade

42
41 43

43

47

45

46

South 2

48
49

South 3

50

51

Susukino

Sōsei
Shōgakkō-mae

53

M

52

Susukino

54

■56

55

Hōsui
Susukino

South 4

59■

South 5

■57

58

South 6

Higashi
Honganji-mae

●61

60

62

South 7

64 65

63■

South 8

Yamahana-kujō

South 9

South 10

Nakajima-kōen

To Fukuzumi

0   200   400m

0   200   400yd
Some Minor Streets Not Depicted

Nakajima-
kōen-dōri

Nakajima- kōen

To Moiwa-yama
Ropeway-iriguchi

To Makomanai

66

67■

Toyohira-gawa

HOKKAIDŌ

SAPPORO

PLACES TO STAY
1 Tōyoko Inn Sapporo
  Hokudai-mae
  東横イン札幌北大前
2 Yūgiri Ryokan
  夕霧旅館
3 Izumiya Bekkan
  泉屋別館
4 Sapporo Station Hotel
  札幌ステーションホテル
7 Sapporo House
  Youth Hostel
  札幌ハウスユースホステル
8 Keiō Plaza Hotel Sapporo
  京王プラザホテル札幌
10 Sapporo Washington Hotel 2
  札幌第2ワシントンホテル
11 Sapporo Washington Hotel 1
  札幌第1ワシントンホテル
18 Nakamuraya Ryokan
  中村屋旅館
21 Hotel New Ōtani Sapporo
  ホテルニューオータニ札幌
24 Hotel Sapporo Garden Palace
  ホテル札幌ガーデンパレス
25 Hotel Center Park
  ホテルセンターパーク
56 Sapporo Inn NADA
  札幌インNADA
57 Sauna Hokuō Club
  サウナ北欧クラブ
59 Tōyoko Inn Sapporo
  Susukino Minami
  東横イン札幌すすきの南
63 Sapporo Oriental Hotel
  札幌オリエンタルホテル
64 Hotel Sunlight
  ホテルサンライト
65 Sapporo Marks Inn
  札幌マークスイン
67 Hotel Paco Sapporo
  ホテルパコ札幌

PLACES TO EAT
40 Warung Hutan
41 Mokkiru de Cuicuilco
  モッキルデキキルコ
42 Restaurant Cam Cam

43 Cafe & Deli Sū'a; Sa Pa
  カフェとデリスーア；
  サパ
45 Ni-jō Ichiba Market
  二条市場
46 Doutor
47 Delhi Restaurant
50 Taj Mahal
51 KFC
52 Mister Donut; Yoshinoya
54 Rāmen Yokochō Alley
  ラーメン横丁
55 Hōran Rāmen
  芳蘭ラーメン
58 Tokei-dai Rāmen
  時計台ラーメン
66 Kirin Beer Garden
  キリンビール園

OTHER
5 Sapporo Central
  Post Office
  札幌中央郵便局
6 Sapporo International
  Information Corner
9 Toyota Rent-a-Car
  トヨタレンタカー
12 ANA; Qantas;
  Cathay Pacific
13 Sapporo Station
  Bus Terminal;
  Sogō Department
  Store
  札幌駅バスターミナル；
  そごうデパート
14 Tōkyū Department
  Store
  東急デパート
15 Seibu Department Store
  西武デパート
16 American Express Office
  アメリカンエキスプレス
17 Hokkaidō University
  Ainu Museum
  北方民族資料館
19 Old Prefectural Office
  旧道庁
20 Citibank

22 Tokei-dai (Clock Tower)
  時計台
23 Sapporo International
  Plaza i
  札幌国際プラザ
26 Daiwa Bank;
  Australian Consulate
27 Tokyo-Mitsubishi Bank
  東京三菱銀行
28 Ōdōri Post Office
  大通り郵便局
29 Sapporo City Hall
  札幌市役所
30 Chūō Bus Terminal
  中央バスターミナル
31 ANT English School
  アント英語スクール
32 TV Tower
  テレビ塔
33 Kinokuniya Books
  紀伊国屋書店
34 Marui Imai Department
  Store
  丸井今井デパート
35 Mitsukoshi Department
  Store
  三越デパート
36 Maruzen Books
  丸善
37 Tower Records
38 Virgin Megastore CD &
  Video
39 Parco Department Store
  パルコデパート
44 Royal Gift Ticket Shop
  ロイヤルギフト
  チケットショップ
48 Jazz Spot Jericho
49 Meidi-ya Grocery Store
  明治屋
53 Robinson's Department
  Store
  ロビンソン札幌
60 Rad Brothers Bar
61 King Xmhu
  キングシェムー
62 Higashi Hongan-ji
  東本願寺

HOKKAIDŌ

eastern concourse of JR Sapporo station, hidden beside Vie de France bakery. Its operating hours were 10 am to 7 pm, except on the 3rd Monday of every month, when it was closed. A few blocks away, Citibank had 24-hour ATMs available every day of the year.

VISA and MasterCard users can get cash advances on the 2nd floor of the Tokyo-Mitsubishi bank near Ōdōri-kōen. American Express client services are available at the AmEx office across from Seibu department store.

Email & Internet Access ANT English school (☎ 232-0209) charges ¥500 for each 30 minutes for Internet access, but you should phone ahead to see whether a computer is available. On the northern side of the city, Internet Cafe System K charges the same rates (9 am to 6 pm). It's at North 15, East 1, a five-minute walk from Kita 13-jō-Higashi station on the Tōhō subway line.

Bookshops Sapporo has branches of both Maruzen and Kinokuniya bookshops in the Chūō shopping district. Kinokuniya has a small selection of foreign books on its 2nd floor. The 4th-floor selection of foreign books in Maruzen, however, is much more extensive and is the best place in Hokkaidō to pick up reading material.

Libraries The Sapporo Library at South 22, West 13 has over 2500 English-language titles on its 2nd floor. It also has copies of English-language newspapers. It has slightly bewildering opening hours. Basically, it's open from 9.15 am to 7 pm Wednesday to Friday, 9.15 am to 5.15 pm on weekends and noon to 7 pm on Tuesday; it's closed on Monday. To get there, take the tram to the Toshokan-mae stop.

Consulates Sapporo has a few consulates:

Australia (☎ 242-4381) Daiwa Bank Bldg, 5th floor, North 1, West 3
China (☎ 563-5563) South 13, West 23
Russia (☎ 561-3171) South 14, West 12
South Korea (☎ 621-0288) North 3, West 21
USA (☎ 641-1115) North 1, West 28

THINGS TO SEE & DO
Hokudai Shokubutsuen
植物園
This botanical garden and museum complex, run by Hokkaidō University, has more than 5000 varieties of Hokkaidō's flora on 14 hectares and is a relaxing spot for an afternoon nap.

Near the main gate is a small **Ainu Museum** with a good collection of Ainu tools, clothing, household utensils and ceremonial objects from the collection of 19th-century Sapporo resident and Ainu researcher Rev John Batchelor. The display cases hold around 200 of the 2000 items that are in the care of Hokkaido University.

Admission to the garden is ¥400. It's open from 9 am to 4 pm daily, but it closes at 3.30 pm and on Monday during October and early November. Between early November and April, only the greenhouse is open to visitors (¥150, 10 am to 3 pm, closed Sunday).

Old Prefectural Office
旧本庁舎
Built in 1888, this distinctive neo-baroque building now houses the **Archives of Hokkaidō** (9 am to 5 pm weekdays), with permanent exhibitions of historical documents, photographs and other items relating to the activities of the Kaitakushi, Hokkaidō's colonial office, during the early Meiji period.

Tokei-dai 時計台
This clock tower was constructed in 1878 and has now become *the* symbol of Sapporo and a useful landmark for visitors. It's not particularly stunning, but you can enter the building and wander around a small museum of local history (¥200, 9 am to 5 pm, closed Monday).

The clock tower reopened in October 1998 after renovations to the building. Ironically, the clock itself did not need repairs, for two generations of the Inoue family have voluntarily maintained it in meticulous working order – allegedly, the clock has never missed tolling the hour in over 120 years.

Sapporo Beer Garden & Museum
サッポロビールビヤガーデン・博物館

The Sapporo Beer Garden and Museum are on the site of the original Sapporo Brewery. Dating back to 1876, it was the first brewery to be established in Japan. Free tours of the museum, lasting on average just over an hour, are given throughout the year from 9 am to 3.40 pm (until 4.40 pm from June to August). Be sure to ask for the English-language audiotape guide from the front desk before setting off with your enthusiastic tour-group leader.

The cavernous beer 'garden' (it's actually three halls plus outdoor seating in summer) offers the opportunity for some serious drinking and pigging out (11.30 am to 9 pm). In the Kessel Hall (with its enormous 1912 brew vat), you can indulge in 'Chengis-Khan Barbecue' – all you can eat and drink in 100 minutes for ¥3400. Prices for other dishes on the menu start at around ¥1000, and a mug of draught beer costs ¥450.

The beer garden and museum are about 10 minutes on foot from the Higashi-Kuyakusho-mae subway station exit 4 on the Tōhō line. You can also get there by taking a Higashi 88 (Factory Line) bus from in front of Seibu department store, close to JR Sapporo station (¥200).

TV Tower テレビ塔

This landmark in Ōdōri-kōen provides good views of Sapporo from its 90m-high viewing platform (¥700, 9 am to 8.50 pm, 9.30 am to 6.20 pm October to April). You can get a view that's almost as good, free of charge, by going up to the observation deck on the 19th floor of the *shiyakusho* (city hall), just across the street from the TV tower (10 am to 4 pm weekdays, closed in winter). There's a little coffee shop here and you can take your food or drink outside to the observation deck. There's also a cheap cafeteria on the 18th floor.

Moiwa-yama Ropeway
藻岩山ロープウエイ

When the weather is clear, the panoramic views from the summit of Moiwa-yama (531m) are breathtaking, especially at night. A ropeway (cable car) and chairlift whisk you to the top in eight minutes (¥1300/round trip). Operating hours vary throughout the year, but it's usually running from 10 am to 5 pm, and until as late as 9 pm during summer. The ropeway is an eight-minute walk uphill from the Moiwa-yama Ropeway-iriguchi tram stop. Discount coupons (¥400 off) are available on the tram – be sure the driver stamps yours.

Hokkaidō Kaitaku-no-Mura

Covering some 54 hectares in the suburbs of Sapporo, Hokkaidō Kaitaku-no-Mura (Historical Village of Hokkaidō; ¥610, 9.30 am to 4 pm, closed Monday) exhibits over 50 buildings from the 'pioneer' period of Japanese expansion into Hokkaidō. A few are replicas, but most are quaint wooden originals rebuilt here in four main areas; town, farm, fishing and mountain village. Horse-drawn trolleys and, in winter, sleighs ply the main street.

Direct JR buses to Kaitaku-no-Mura depart from the Sogo station between 9 and 10.30 am (¥230, 50 minutes). Buses in the opposite direction leave the village between 1.15 and 5.50 pm. You could also take the Tozai subway line to Shin-Sapporo station, changing there to a bus bound for Kaitaku-no-Mura (¥200, 15 minutes).

Special Events

The **Sapporo Yuki Matsuri** (Sapporo Snow Festival) held in early February and centred on Ōdōri-kōen, is probably Hokkaidō's major event. Thousands of visitors arrive to see dozens of large, and in some cases amazingly elaborate, ice and snow sculptures. If you plan to visit at this time, you should book accommodation well in advance or take a course in igloo construction.

The **Hokkaidō-jingū Matsuri** (Hokkaidō Shrine Festival) takes place in Maruyama-kōen from 14 to 16 June. It features portable shrines and costume processions, as well as performances of *nō* (classical Japanese dance-drama) and *kagura* (sacred music and dances).

The **Sapporo Summer Festival** (21 July to 20 August) kicks off with the setting up of

Unusual Hokkaido Events

1. Sapporo's Yuki Matsuri (Snow Festival)
2. The Women's Sumō National Championship (Onna-zumō Senshuken Taikai) in Teshikaga
3. Orochon-no-Hi (Fire Festival) in Abashiri
4. Japan Cup National Dogsled Races in Wakkanai
5. The Kyōkoku Hi Matsuri (Fire Festival) at Sōunkyō Onsen

beer gardens in Ōdōri-kōen and features the Pacific Music Festival, which was started by famous conductor Leonard Bernstein.

Places to Stay – Budget

Accommodation in the budget range comes in a variety of forms.

Youth Hostels Although there are three hostels in Sapporo, only one, *Sapporo House* (☎ 726-4235), has convenient access, being only a 10-minute walk from Sapporo station. It's not a memorable place to stay, however. Reception closes at 8 pm, and there is a curfew at 10 pm. It charges ¥2670 a person.

The *Sapporo Miyaga-oka Youth Hostel* (☎ 611-9016) is close to Maruyama-kōen in the west of Sapporo, but it's only open from July to September; it charges ¥3050. Take the Tōzai subway line to Maruyama-kōen, then city bus No 14 or 15 to Sōgō-gurando-mae, which is a two-minute walk from the hostel. You can check in until 9 pm, and there is a curfew at 10 pm.

Sapporo Lions Youth Hostel (☎ 611-4709) is farther west, close to the Miyanomori Ski Jump, and charges ¥3200. To get there, take the Tōzai subway line to Maruyama-kōen and then change to the No 14 bus bound for Araiyama. Get off after 15 minutes at the Miyanomori-shanze-mae stop and walk for seven minutes. You can check in until 8.30, and there is a curfew at 10 pm.

Toho Network The founding member of the Toho Network, *Sapporo Inn NADA* (☎ 551-5882), is probably the most popular budget place to stay in Sapporo. It's close to the Susukino entertainment area and has no curfew, making it an ideal base for a late-night foray into Hokkaidō's most happening entertainment district. Per-person rates for shared accommodation are ¥3500 (¥3700 in winter). Breakfast is available for ¥600. It's around a 10-minute walk west of Susukino subway station; if you are disoriented when first you come up from underground, follow the tram tracks.

Ryokan & Inns The most popular place with foreigners is the *Yugiri Ryokan* (☎ 716-5482), which has rooms for ¥3900 a person. The management doesn't speak English but tries hard to please. It's a five-minute walk north-west of Sapporo station, close to Hokkaidō University. Nearby, *Izumiya Bekkan* (☎ 736-2501), a ryokan with a very home-like character, charges comparable rates.

Places to Stay – Mid-Range

Most hotels fall into this price range.

Ryokan & Inns Prices at the *Nakamuraya Ryokan* (☎ 241-2111), a member of the Japanese Inn group, are relatively high, at around ¥6000 to ¥7000 a person. The ryokan is a seven-minute walk south-west of the station, on the eastern side of the botanical garden.

Cottage Ichii (☎ 612-1710) charges only ¥4700 a person, including two meals, but it's inconveniently located out near Maruyama-kōen. The friendly owner will pick you up at Maruyama-kōen station on the Tōzai subway line, three stops west of Ōdōri, if you book in advance.

Hotels Despite the fact that Sapporo has more than 100 hotels, during summer *everything* can become booked out early in the day, or even weeks in advance. If you can't find anything, you might try asking staff at the Sapporo International Information Corner to suggest some hotels in one of Sapporo's suburbs or Chitose.

During busy seasons, you may still be able to find a room in the love-hotel area just south of King Xmhu disco in Susukino (see Entertainment later in this section). With names like Hotel XO and Hotel Apple, most places are easily recognised. The neon signs hanging out the front clearly state the rates: to 'stay' all night (as opposed to staying for a two-hour 'rest') costs from ¥3500 for the most basic rooms to as much as ¥10,000 for wacky theme accommodation. The management sometimes tacks on surcharges on Sunday night or before holidays, as well as for same-sex couples or groups. Discounts are sometimes available for check-in after midnight.

If you're targeting Sapporo's nightlife you may be better off staying down in the Susukino district. The area between the station and Ōdōri, however, has convenient access to transportation and more sights.

North of the station, *Toyoko Inn Sapporo Hokudai-mae* (☎ 717-1045) has pleasant singles/doubles for ¥4700/7100. The friendly *Hotel Center Park* (☎ 231-5651) has basic singles and twins for ¥5500 and ¥10,000, respectively, and semi-doubles with attached bath for ¥12,000.

The reliable *Sapporo Washington Hotel 1* (☎ 251-3211) has singles ranging from ¥6300 to ¥9300, and twins and doubles at ¥18,200. Rooms are discounted between October and May. It would be a good idea to book ahead for one of the cheaper singles.

There are dozens upon dozens of hotels in the Susukino area, which is a fun part of town in which to be based. *Sauna Hokuo Club* (☎ 531-2233) is a luxurious capsule hotel with separate floors for women and men. Per-person rates are ¥4900 a night including two meals and use of the hotel's baths, sauna and enormous swimming pool. Slight discounts are given for check-in after 11.30 pm.

The *Toyoko Inn Sapporo Susukino Minami* (☎ 551-1045) is one of the cheapest hotels in the area and has good-quality rooms for ¥4800/6800. *Sapporo Marks Inn* (☎ 512-5001, ☎ 0120-27-2400 toll free) has more standard rooms for ¥7000/8000 (less during the off season). If you purchase a ¥1000 membership card, you're entitled to 15% off regular rates at all Marks Inn ho-

tels across Japan for one year. The *Sapporo Oriental Hotel* (☎ 562-8000) and *Hotel Sunlight* (☎ 562-3111) offer rooms of comparable quality for around ¥6300/8000.

A bit farther south, near Nakajima-kōen, the *Hotel Paco Sapporo* (☎ 562-8585) is newer and has a pleasant rock garden in the entryway. Singles and twins here start at ¥8000 and ¥19,000, respectively.

Places to Stay – Top End

The *Sapporo Station Hotel* (☎ 727-2111) has singles/doubles for ¥8300/13,600, or around ¥3000 less from mid-October to June. The *Sapporo Washington Hotel 2* (☎ 222-3311) has rooms of a quality similar to that of the Sapporo Washington Hotel 1 but charges higher rates. Perhaps better value for money is the *Hotel Sapporo Garden Palace* (☎ 261-5311), where singles start at ¥8500, while twins and doubles start at ¥15,000 and ¥18,000, respectively.

The station area also has some of Sapporo's top-class hotels. Rooms at the opulent *Hotel New Ōtani Sapporo* (☎ 222-1111) start at ¥14,000/25,000.

Places to Eat

Sapporo is a big city and there's a lot to choose from in the dining category. As you'd expect, the fast-food huts are well represented, mainly in Susukino and the shopping district just to the north. *KFC* and *Mr Donut* are quite close to the Susukino subway station.

Hokkaidō is famous for its *rāmen* (Chinese egg noodles), and there are rāmen shops all over the city. You'll usually have your choice of broth: *miso* (fermented soya-bean paste), *shōyu* (soy sauce) or *shio* (salt). Popular with Japanese tourists, *Rāmen Yokochō* is an alleyway crammed with some two dozen shops. Other good places are *Tokei-dai Rāmen* and *Hōran Rāmen*. The latter has autographed photos of famous people who have come to dine here hanging on the walls – try the *kara-kuchi* (hot mouth) or the even spicier *gehikarai rāmen*.

For 'Ghengis-Khan Barbecue' you can try the *Sapporo Beer Garden*, or the *Kirin Beer Garden*, which has a similar setup in its

2nd/3rd floor SpaceCraft dining hall, which seats up to 560 people. For ¥3300 you get all the vegetables and lamb you can grill and all the beer, whisky or soft drinks you can quaff in 100 minutes. For ¥2500 more, you can get all the crab you want, too. It's open from lunch time until 10 pm (11 pm in summer).

Good Indian cuisine is available at the **Delhi Restaurant** and the **Taj Mahal**, both in the Chūō shopping district. The latter is part of a Japanese chain and its best deals are the lunch-time specials (English menu available). Delhi, on the other hand, has authentic dishes and is inexpensive by Japanese standards – curries start at ¥600, plus ¥400 if two people wish to share.

At the western end of Tanuki-kōji arcade is **Warung Hutan**, which serves tasty Indonesian fare, including *gado-gado* (salad with peanut sauce); beware of the ¥350 charge just for sitting down. Just south of the arcade is a string of affordable, international places with a funky, friendly atmosphere. **Restaurant Cam Cam** serves pan-Asian dishes from its English menu starting at ¥500. For Mexican food, try next door at **Mokkiru de Cuicuilco**. One block east, **Sa Pa** specialises in delicious Vietnamese stall foods. All of these restaurants are open only for dinner until around midnight, but **Cafe & Deli Sǔ'a** beneath Sa Pa has good value lunch-time set menus, too.

The **Ni-jō Ichiba** fish market is open from around 7 am to 6 pm. It's around 10 minutes on foot from Ōdōri subway station.

Entertainment

Susukino is wall-to-wall bars, karaoke parlours and kinky soaplands. That said, most of this kind of action is prohibitively expensive and probably of little interest to foreign travellers. This doesn't mean you should shun Susukino altogether – there are loads of great places to eat and quite a few bars that serve as watering holes for local *gaijin* (foreigners).

The best thing to do is ask around for the latest 'in' spot. **Bazoku**, a cosy basement bar and grill near the Tanuki-kōji arcade, is a popular place to hang out now that the ramshackle wooden building that housed

the old **Gaijin Bar** has burned down. **Rad Brothers** stays open from 6 pm to 6 am daily, and by all accounts, the basement dance floor is hopping on weekends. All-you-can-drink specials for ¥1000 after 3 am don't hurt. For those seeking something just a little more low key, **Jazz Spot Jericho** frequently has live performances, and on weekdays there's no cover charge.

One place that has to be mentioned, even if it would probably break the average traveller's budget, is the opulent **King Xmhu** (everyone calls it King Moo's), Sapporo's answer to Juliana's in Tokyo. Cover charges vary but hover around ¥4000 with two drinks, though some evenings there are discounts for those aged 25 and over. Even if you don't venture into the fabulous interior, just wander down and take a look: King Xmhu himself, massively carved in stone, presides wearily bemused over the neon of Susukino.

Getting There & Away

Discount tickets for flights, trains and long-distance buses are available at Royal Gift ticket shop in the Tanuki-kōji shopping arcade (10 am to 7.30 pm, until 5 pm Saturday, closed Sunday).

Air Flights connect Sapporo with most of the major cities on Honshū and even Okinawa. Air Do (☎ 200-7333) has brought almost every major carrier's price down to ¥16,000 for the two-hour flight to Tokyo. Regular flights to Osaka or Kansai cost ¥30,850, but special summer fares start as low as ¥21,000. International destinations include Guam, Seoul and Amsterdam.

Several international airlines have offices in Sapporo: Cathay Pacific (☎ 0120-355-747); Continental Micronesia (☎ 221-4091); Korean Air (☎ 210-3311); Qantas Airways (☎ 242-4151); Thai Airways (☎ 241-6055) and KLM (☎ 232-0775).

The main airport for Sapporo is New Chitose airport (Shin-Chitose Kūkō), which is about 40km south of the city. Sapporo has a subsidiary airport at Okadama, about 10km north of the city. Ask, if you're not certain, which airport is stated on your ticket.

Train Two of the fastest rail connections from Tokyo are the Hokutosei Express, a direct sleeper to Sapporo (¥23,520, or ¥9450 with a Japan Rail Pass, 16 hours, three a day), and a combination of the shinkansen to Morioka followed by a tokkyū via Aomori (¥21,670, 10 hours). There is also a sleeper service to Osaka (¥27,130, or ¥10,960 with a Japan Rail Pass, 22½ hours).

From Sapporo to Hakodate, it takes 3½ hours by tokkyū via New Chitose airport and Tomakomai (¥6820). R-kippu (¥14,160) and Nite-&-Day tickets (¥12,180) are also available on this route.

The JR main Hakodate line runs west to Otaru (kaisoku, ¥620, 30 minutes) and north-east to Asahikawa (tokkyū, ¥3370, 90 minutes). From Sapporo to Wakkanai, there's a sleeper service that leaves Sapporo at around 10 pm and arrives in Wakkanai around 6 am, nicely timed for you to take the early ferry across to Rishiri-tō or Rebun-tō, and three daytime *kyukō* (ordinary express) trains (¥8400, six hours). For the sleeper service, the cheapest berth costs an additional ¥5250. Nite-& Day tickets (¥18,320) are also available for this route.

Bus Sapporo is linked with the rest of Hokkaidō by an extensive network of long-distance bus services. The main bus station is the one next to Sapporo station, adjacent to Sogo department store. Access is via the underground shopping plaza, from where you ascend to the platforms, which are at ground level. Some buses also leave from the Chūō bus station and Ōdōri bus centre near Ōdōri-kōen.

Buses depart from the Sogo station several times a day for destinations including Wakkanai (¥5650, 6¼ hours), Asahikawa (¥2000, two hours), Muroran (¥2000, 2¼ hours), Noboribetsu Onsen (¥1900, 2½ hours), Tōya-ko Onsen (¥2700, 2¾ hours) and Furano (¥2100, 2½ hours).

From the Chūō bus station there are a few departures a day to Kushiro (¥5610, 6½ hours), Obihiro (¥3670, 4¼ hours) and Abashiri (¥6210, six hours) via Kitami and Bihoro. Buses to Hakodate depart from both the Chūō station and Ōdōri bus centre (¥4680, five hours).

Discounted return tickets are available for most routes. There are also night buses to Hakodate, Abashiri, Obihiro and Kushiro that are worth considering if you are backtracking, short on time or wish to save money on accommodation costs. However, you may lose out on some spectacular scenery along the way.

Car Most major car-rental agencies have offices in Sapporo, including Orix Rent-a-Car inside the Sapporo Grand Hotel and Toyota and Mazda on opposite sides of Sapporo station. For more details on car rental, see the Hokkaidō Getting Around section.

Getting Around

To/From the Airport New Chitose airport is accessible from Sapporo by kaisoku train (¥1040, 36 minutes) or bus (¥820, 70 minutes). The airport is also just a few minutes by bus from the city of Chitose, an expanding industrial centre. The airport has its own railway station and bus centre, as well as car rental counters located on the 1st floor. From the airport there are convenient bus services to various destinations on Hokkaidō, including Shikotsu-ko, Tōya-ko Onsen, Noboribetsu Onsen and Niseko.

ATMs are located in the departure hall near the centre plaza. You can ask at any of the information desks for *Chitose Handy Guide Map* or the *Beautify Chitose Guide Map*. These bilingual pamphlets include details of bus services and maps, as well as information on touring Chitose's four major breweries, the Grace winery, and the Kikkoman plant, which is famous for its shōyu.

For Sapporo's Okadama airport, buses leave every 20 minutes or so from in front of the ANA ticket offices, opposite Sapporo station (¥310, 30 minutes).

Bus & Tram The main station for city buses is adjacent to the Sogo department store.

From late April to early November, the Sapporo Lincle tourist bus makes a loop of 22 major sights and attractions around the city from 9 am to 5 pm (until 7 pm during July and August). A one-day pass costs ¥1200.

There is a single tram line that heads west from Ōdōri, turns south and then loops back to Susukino. It's convenient for Moiwa-yama and the fare is a flat ¥170.

Subway This is the most efficient way to get around Sapporo. There are three lines, the two most useful being the Nanboku line, which runs on a north-south axis, and the Tōzai line, which runs on an east-west axis. Fares start at ¥200 and one-day passes cost ¥800; there are also passes for ¥1000 that are valid for Sapporo's buses and trams in addition to the subway.

Dō-ō
(Central Hokkaidō)

OTARU 小樽
☎ 0134 • pop 154,000

The importance of Otaru as a port in the early development of Hokkaidō and the herring industry has left a small legacy of old Western-style buildings and an attrac-

tive canal area. For travellers arriving by ferry from Honshū, it's a good place to spend a leisurely day admiring the architecture and the lingering signs of Russian trading influence.

The tourist information office (☎ 29-1333) is inside JR Otaru station and is open from 9 am to 6 pm. The *Otaru Handy Map* has several maps and details of sights, transport and accommodation. There are also tourist information offices near the Otaru Museum and at Asakusa-bashi in the canal area.

Things to See & Do

Perhaps the best known of Otaru's attractions, at least for Japanese tourists, is the **Otaru Canal**, which runs east to west close to the harbour area. Beside the canal is a granite path with gas lamps – very romantic at dusk. Sections of the canal are lined with photogenic Meiji- and Taishō-era buildings. Rated highly are the Ex-Nippon Yūsen Company building and the Mitsui Bank building. There are also a few glass-blowing workshops, hence Otaru's tenuous and self-promoting comparison with Venice. At **K's Blowing** you can get a 10-minute lesson for ¥1800.

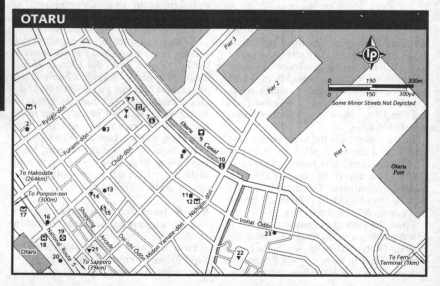

OTARU

The **Otaru Museum** is housed in an old brick warehouse dating from 1893. It now houses a tastefully presented collection of pieces relating to local history, including items from the herring industry and ceramics kilns (¥100, 9.30 am to 5 pm).

The most fascinating sight in Otaru is the well-preserved **nishin-goten**, built in 1897 and relocated to the coast at Shukutsu in 1956. The original owners were barons of the herring fishing industry during the Meiji and Taishō eras and lived in this enormous complex along with seasonal labourers (¥200, 9 am to 5 pm from early April to late November). To get there, take bus No 11 from Otaru station to the last stop at Otaru Suizokukan (Otaru Aquarium; ¥200, 25 minutes). From late April to mid-October you can also get to Shikotsu kō port by sightseeing boat from Otaru's Pier 3 (¥1550, 85 minutes).

Places to Stay – Budget

The tourist information office can give you directions to any of several rider houses around town, all costing from ¥1200 a night. A few are accessible by public transport. *Otaru Tengu-yama Youth Hostel* (☎ 34-1474), which charges ¥2750 a person, is close to the Tengu-yama cable car and ski area, a 20-minute bus ride south-west of Otaru station (¥200, last bus at 8.10 pm). Reception closes at around 8 pm, so phone ahead if you'll be arriving a bit late. In winter, ski rental and discounted lift tickets are available here.

A member of the Toho network, the friendly *Ponpon-sen* (☎ 27-0866) is just 10 minutes on foot uphill behind Otaru station. It is only open during Golden Week (see the National Festivals & Events section in the Facts for the Visitor chapter) and from early June to early November. Dormitory-style accommodation costs ¥3000 (¥3200 in winter), plus ¥500 if you want breakfast.

There are several ryokan scattered around town that, while not particularly interesting, are a pleasant alternative to business hotels. Closest to the station are *Wakaba-sō Ryokan* (☎ 27-3111) and *Satsuki Minshuku* (☎ 32-4984), two cosy inns with rooms for ¥3000 to ¥3500 a person.

Places to Stay – Mid-Range

Quiet a walk from the station, the *Ebiya Ryokan* (☎ 22-2317) is farther from the station than Satsuki Minshuku. It's in a quiet

---

OTARU

PLACES TO STAY		
2 Wakaba-sō Ryokan; Satsuki Minshuku 若葉荘旅館	21 Rāmen Kitaya ラーメン北屋	12 Main Post Office 小樽郵便局
3 Ebiya Ryokan 海老屋旅館	22 Sushiya-dōri 寿司屋通り	13 Charinko Otaru Rent-a-Cycle ちゃりんこおたる レンタサイクル
11 Otaru Grand Hotel Classic 小樽グランドホテル クラシック	**OTHER**	15 Hokkaidō Bank 北海道銀行
16 Otaru Kokusai Hotel 小樽国際ホテル	1 Post Office 郵便局	17 Post Office 郵便局
	6 Otaru Museum 小樽市博物館	18 Bus Station バスターミナル
PLACES TO EAT	7 Unga Plaza Tourist Information Booth 運河プラザ観光案内所	19 Nagasakiya Shopping Centre 長崎屋
4 Uminekoya Coffee Shop 海猫屋	8 Orix Rent-a-Car オリックスレンタカー	20 Kinokuniya Books 紀伊国屋書店
5 Takinami Restaurant マンジャーレTakinami	9 Otaru Beer Pub 小樽ビール	23 K's Blowing
14 KFC	10 Asakusa-bashi Tourist Information Office 浅草橋観光案内所	

HOKKAIDŌ

area close to the canal. Per-person rates with two meals range from ¥6500 to ¥7800.

Places to Stay – Top End
An interesting, and more expensive, option is a night at the *Otaru Grand Hotel Classic* (☎ 22-6500), which occupies one of the renovated Western-style buildings near the canal. This little slice of history will cost you ¥10,000 for a single or ¥16,500 for two in a Japanese-style room.

Places to Eat
The area along the canal has numerous little European-style cafes and restaurants. Just one street back from the canal is *Takinami Restaurant*, a relaxing place with wooden rafters, ceiling fans and excellent pasta and fish set lunches for around ¥900. Housed in an old brick warehouse nearby, *Uminekoya Coffee Shop* has set lunches during the day; at night it doubles as a pub.

Fish aficionados can stroll along *Sushiya-dōri*, where sushi shops serve up the catch of the day. Near the station, *Rāmen Kitaya* has dirt cheap, delicious yakitori takeaways.

One of Otaru's most popular spots is *Otaru Beer Pub* (11 am to 11 pm), one of the new breed of microbreweries found all over Hokkaidō and northern Japan. It's in a large, renovated warehouse along the canal, where you can quaff several varieties of beer (including a banana-flavoured Weiss for ¥750) amid solid wood furnishings and gleaming copper beer vats. The menu (available in English and Russian) has a good selection of seafood dishes from ¥500. The pub has live jazz performances on some evenings.

Getting There & Away
On the JR Hakodate main line, Otaru is 30 minutes from Sapporo (kaisoku, ¥620). Special airport kaisoku trains run via Sapporo to New Chitose airport (¥1420, 75 minutes). There are only a few local trains that run south along the same line to Niseko (¥1410, two hours).

You can catch frequent buses to Sapporo (¥590, one hour) and a few direct buses to Niseko (¥1330, 1¾ hours) from in front of Otaru station.

There are almost daily ferry departures from Otaru to Niigata (¥5250, 19 hours), Tsuruga (¥7420, 21 hours) and Maizuru (¥6710, 31 hours). Most boats depart from Otaru in the morning. To get to the ferry terminal, take bus No 10 from in front of the station (¥200, 10 minutes). The Marine-go tourist-loop bus also stops at the port, but only twice a day.

Getting Around
The main part of town is small enough to tackle on foot. Between April and November, bicycle rental is available near the station at Charinko Otaru for ¥400 an hour, but the shop offers two-for-one 'happy hour' deals from 4 to 9 pm.

Marine-go and Roman-go tourist buses loop through the city taking in most of the sights (¥200 a ride, ¥750 for a one-day pass). Buses leave approximately every 20 minutes from Otaru station between 9 am and 5 or 6 pm.

NISEKO ニセコ
☎ 0136
Lying between Yōtei-zan and Niseko Annupuri, Niseko is one of Hokkaidō's prime ski resorts during winter and a hiking base during summer and autumn. Numerous hot springs in the area are also popular. There are plenty of opportunities for canoeing, kayaking and river rafting in summer, and ice climbing, snowshoeing or even dog sledding in winter. Many of these activities are organised by Niseko Outdoor Centre (☎ 44-1133) near the Annupuri skiing ground and Niseko Adventure Centre (☎ 23-2093) in Hirafu.

The comprehensive magazine *Niseko Information Gallery* provides seasonal information on outdoor pursuits, accommodation and transport. It's available at the Sapporo International Communication Plaza *i* or via the Internet at www.teleweb.or.jp/use1/yr1407.

Places to Stay
Most places to stay in Niseko are hard to reach by public transport, except in winter, when there are frequent direct buses to the area's ski slopes.

Places to Stay – Budget

The four-star *Niseko Annupuri Youth Hostel* (☎ 58-2084) is a mountain lodge near the Annupuri Kokusai (Annupuri International) skiing ground that charges ¥3100 a person. The hospitable owner is an excellent source of information about outdoor activities and can provide hiking and cycling maps of the area. Meals here are highly recommended. From Niseko station, take one of the infrequent buses bound for Konbu Onsen and get off at the Annupuri Kokusai ski-jo stop (¥310, 13 minutes). From there it's about seven minutes on foot to the hostel. If you phone ahead, someone will pick you up at the station.

On Hwy 66 close to the Annupuri Kokusai skiing ground entrance is *Panorama Rider's House* (☎ 58-2200), where accommodation costs ¥1000 for the first night and ¥700 every night thereafter. The rider house organises rafting, mountain biking and evening onsen tours.

Places to Stay – Mid-Range

A popular member of the Toho network is *Niseko Ambishiasu* (☎ 44-3011). The owners will pick you up from the station, which is 10 minutes by car from the inn. Per-person rates are ¥4300, including two meals (¥4600 in winter). Ski rental is also available.

One of the largest concentrations of accommodation in the Niseko area is at Hirafu ski resort (Hirafu station is one stop north of Niseko). *Hirafu Sansō* (☎ 22-0285) is near the Hirafu ski lifts and charges ¥5000 a person, including two meals. Nearby, *Mountain Jam* (☎ 23-2020) is a pension with rates of around ¥7500 for the same deal. In winter there are shuttle buses to the ski resort from Hirafu station, as well as buses running from Kutchan station (one stop north of Hirafu). There is no bus service in summer.

Getting There & Away

Unfortunately, Niseko suffers from poor public transport links in the summer. At that time, there are a few direct kaisoku trains from Sapporo (¥2100, 2¼ hours), otherwise you'll have wait up to 1½ hours when changing trains at Otaru. Alternatively, you could hop on a direct bus to Niseko outside Otaru station (¥1330, 1¾ hours). From June to September, there is a daily bus from New Chitose airport to the Niseko Hotel Nikko Annupuri (¥2300, 2½ hours).

Winter is a different story: there are frequent direct buses to the area's ski resorts from Sapporo (three hours) and New Chitose airport (3¼ hours); either costs ¥2190/3660 one way/return. There are also special ski trains that make the trip more quickly but cost about twice as much. During the ski season, there are shuttle buses between the train stations and major ski areas at Niseko, Hirafu and Kutchan.

TŌYA-KO 洞爺湖
☎ 01427

Part of Shikotsu-Tōya National Park (983 sq km), Tōya-ko is a large and attractive lake. However, most foreign visitors who come here concentrate on seeing the 'upstart' volcanoes near by. Fast and easy access from Sapporo or New Chitose airport makes it a favourite with those who have only a short time to spend in Hokkaidō. The centre of activity for the lake is Tōya-ko Onsen, a resort on the southern shore of the lake.

Shōwa Shin-zan & Usu-zan
昭和新山・有珠山

In 1943, after a series of earthquakes, Shōwa Shin-zan first emerged as an upstart bump in some vegetable fields and then continued to surge upwards for two more years to reach its present height (402m). It is still an awesome sight as it sits there, hissing and issuing steam and keeping the locals guessing about its next move.

From the car park you can see Usu-zan (737m), a frisky volcano that was the force behind the creation of Shōwa Shin-zan. On 31 March 2000, after 23 years of dormancy and a mere few days of rumbling, the volcano shot white, then black smoke 2700m straight up into the air, which then drifted and completely covered the lake, Tōya-ko. This steam was caused by hot magma colliding with water underground, and though no lava flows resulted, massive flying rocks threatened to down the news helicopters

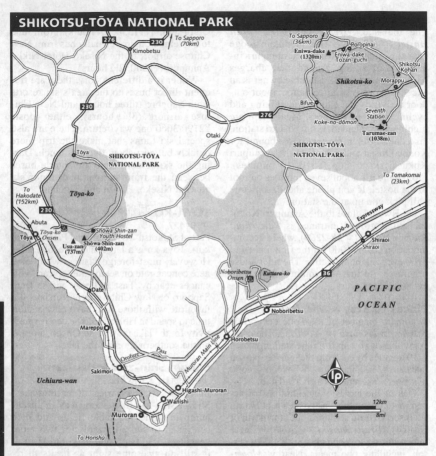

SHIKOTSU-TŌYA NATIONAL PARK

recording the event from above. All local residents were safely evacuated in advance and no deaths were recorded, although farmers lamented lost crops and townsfolk were pessimistic about the future of tourism. In the end, there was far less fall-out this time than when 30cm of ash rained down on Tōya-ko Onsen during the last eruption in 1977.

At the base of the mountain is a large car park with some irritating tourist facilities that will slowly come back into service. At the front end of the car park, hidden behind the souvenir shops, is the **Masao Mimatsu Memorial Museum**. It's an intriguing mu-

seum that displays many items collected by the local postmaster, who purchased the ground that turned into a volcano. For many years he diagrammed the volcano's growth using an ingenious method, now a standard for vulcanologists.

At the time of the initial eruption, the Japanese government was keen to hush it up as it was thought the event might be misinterpreted as a bad omen and thereby hamper the progress of WWII. The postmaster was even requested to find a way to shield the volcanic glare so that the volcano couldn't be used by enemy aircrew for orientation!

Once they are safe enough to visit, the volcanoes will once again be a short bus ride south-east of Tōya-ko Onsen.

Tōya-ko Onsen

If you have time to spare after seeing the volcanoes, the recovering Tōya-ko Onsen is not completely devoid things to do.

Above the bus terminal is the somewhat dusty Volcano Science Museum where you can experience the visual and aural fury of an eruption – the 16-woofer speakers will certainly clean your ears out! Admission costs ¥600 and it's open from 9 am to 5 pm.

During the summer, there are fireworks displays every evening. For ambitious cyclists, there's a 37km cycling course around the lake; bicycle rental is available at extortionate rates near the bus terminal or at more affordable rates at the youth hostel. Tame boat cruises out to Ō-shima, an island in the middle of the lake, depart every 30 minutes (¥1320, 60 minutes, 8.30 am to 4.30 pm).

Places to Stay – Budget

There are five camping grounds around the lake, none of which is very convenient unless you have your own transport. On the eastern edge of the lake, *Naka-tōya Camping Ground* (☎ 0142 66 3131) has its own onsen (¥360) and rents canoes (¥2000/hour). Tent sites cost ¥300 a person and tents can be rented. Only two or three buses a day from Tōya-ko Onsen pass the Naka-tōya stop (¥630).

At the beginning of the steep road leading uphill to Usu-zan and Shōwa Shin-zan is *Shōwa Shin-zan Youth Hostel* (☎ 5-2283), a comfortable converted ryokan charging ¥3000 a day. Bicycles can be rented for ¥1000 a day. To get there take an eight-minute bus ride from Tōya-ko Onsen to the Tozan-guchi stop.

Places to Stay – Mid-Range

Near the bus station is the *KKR Tōya Suimei-sō* (☎ 5-2826), which has large rooms, hot-springs baths, excellent food and friendly English-speaking management. Per-person rates start at ¥7000, in-

cluding two meals. The inn is a five-minute walk uphill from the bus station on the right-hand side of the street.

On the main street beneath the bus station is the spartan *Tōya Green Hotel* (☎ 5-3030), offering rooms starting at ¥4000 a person. Farther down on the opposite side of the street is *Pension Fujiya* (☎ 5-1727), where rooms cost ¥4500 a person; there are also a few triples for ¥9000.

Places to Stay – Top End

Tōya-ko Onsen is overrun with resort hotels along the lakefront, where per-person rates start at around ¥15,000.

Getting There & Away

Buses run every 30 minutes between Tōya-ko Onsen and JR Tōya-ko station (¥320, 15 minutes). From the station you can catch tokkyū trains to Hakodate (¥4830, 1½ hours) or Sapporo (¥5250, 1¾ hours). R-kippu on the Sapporo route cost ¥8060.

There are cheaper direct buses from Tōya-ko Onsen to Sapporo's Sogo station (¥2700, 2¾ hours, hourly), Hakodate (¥2800, 3½ hours, once a day from May to October) and Muroran (¥1170, 1¾ hours, frequent). Between late April and late November, there are also up to four buses a day via the scenic Orofure pass to Noboribetsu Onsen (¥1530, 1¼ hours), some of which continue to New Chitose airport (¥2140, 2½ hours).

MURORAN

☎ 0143 • pop 106,200

Muroran is a huge industrial hub, convenient for its handy ferry links with Honshū.

Between May and August, fascinating whale-watching tours depart once in the morning and again in the early afternoon (¥6000, three hours). Both departures give you equally good chances of observing a variety of whale species as well as dolphins, porpoises and even seals. These tours are often booked out, but you can make reservations through the tourist information office (☎ 23-0102), which is in a large building near the harbour (9 am to 7 pm). You can buy same-day tickets from the boat company office near the departure pier, 20 minutes on foot from JR Muroran station and closer to the tourist information office.

Places to Stay

Muroran Youth Hostel (☎ *44-3357)* is a 15-minute walk from Wanishi station, three stops east of Muroran station (¥200), and charges ¥2800 a person. From Wanishi station, turn left and head down the road along the tracks until you see a youth hostel sign pointing down the street to the right; from there it's about 1km. The hostel is closed a few days a month, so call ahead.

Most of the business hotel accommodation is along Route 36, in front of Muroran station. About 500m south of the station is the *Hotel Bayside* (☎ *24-8090)*, which has a pleasant atmosphere and singles and twins starting at ¥4800 and ¥8600, respectively.

Getting There & Away

Direct tokkyū trains on the JR Muroran main line run south to Hakodate (¥5670, two hours) and north to Sapporo (¥4200, 1¼ hours). Most long-distance trains depart from Higashi-Muroran station, three stops east of Muroran station. Frequent local trains connect Higashi-Muroran with Muroran station (¥270).

From the bus station on Route 36 there are fairly frequent departures for Sapporo's Sogo station (¥2000, 2¼ hours), Noboribetsu Onsen (¥710, 80 minutes) and Tōyako Onsen (¥1170, 1¾ hours).

Ferries from Muroran depart twice a day for Hachinohe (¥3970, eight hours). There are overnight ferries to Aomori (¥3460, seven hours, daily); Oarai, near Tokyo (¥9750, 19 hours, daily except Sunday); and Naoetsu (¥5250, 17 hours, three a week). The ferry terminal is a 10-minute walk from Muroran station.

NOBORIBETSU ONSEN 登別温泉
☎ 0143

Noboribetsu may be the most popular hot-springs resort in Hokkaidō but it's a brutally ugly town. Like Beppu in Kyūshū, it's way overdone as a tourist destination and the tacky resort hotels are often booked out by tour groups, whose buses clog the narrow streets.

A couple of minutes on foot uphill from the main bus station is a small tourist association office where you can pick up a helpful English brochure that includes a map clearly showing accommodation and sights, most of which are accessible on foot from the main street.

The **Dai-Ichi Takimoto-kan** is a luxury hotel boasting one of the largest bath complexes in Japan. Plan to make the most of your admission ticket (¥2000, 9 am to 5 pm) by spending half a day or longer wandering from floor to floor trying out the mineral pools (very hot!), waterfalls, walking pools, cold pools (freezing!), steam room, and swimming pool with waterslide.

A five-minute walk farther uphill is **Jigokudani** (Hell Valley), with its steaming and sulphurous vents and streams of hot water bubbling out of vividly coloured rocks. Bearing left up the valley you come to a lookout over **Ōyu-numa**, where water bubbles violently on the pond's sickly coloured surface. The entire area is crisscrossed by a network of hiking trails.

Places to Stay – Budget

Unfortunately, both of the youth hostels are damp, mouldering and unpleasant. The better choice is *Akashiya-sō Youth Hostel* (☎ *84-2616)*, a couple of minutes' walk downhill from the bus station past the fire station. It charges ¥2900 and is closed from late November to late April.

Places to Stay – Mid-Range

Next to the Hanaya-mae bus stop, downhill and on the opposite side of the street from the youth hostel, is *Ryokan Hanaya* (☎ *84-2521)*, a member of the Japanese Inn group. It's quite a nice spot, with many rooms overlooking the river ranging in price from ¥6000 to ¥7000 a person.

Getting There & Away

Noboribetsu station is on the JR Muroran main line, with local train connections to Higashi-Muroran (¥350, 20 minutes), Shiraoi (¥350, 25 minutes) and Tomakomai

Sunrise view from Kuro-dake of O-Akan-dake and Me-Akan-dake, Daisetsuzan National Park.

Looking out from the Rebun-dake trail across the straits to the scenic island of Rishiri-tō.

A lighthouse on the cliffs of the rugged Ashizuri-misaki coast overlooks the Pacific Ocean, Shikoku.

Yonaha Mae-hama on the south-west coast of Okinawa – said to be the finest beach in Japan.

(¥810, 45 minutes). From Noboribetsu station, it's a 13-minute bus ride to Noboribetsu Onsen (¥330, hourly).

From Noboribetsu Onsen there are direct express buses to Sapporo (Sogo station) as well as buses to Sapporo via Tomakomai (¥1900, 1½ to 2¾ hours). There are also buses to New Chitose airport (¥1330, 65 minutes, one to three times a day) and Muroran (¥710, 80 minutes, hourly). Between late April and late November, there are also up to four buses a day via the scenic Orofure pass to Tōya-ko Onsen (¥1530, 1¼ hours).

The fastest way to get to Shikotsu-ko is to take a bus to New Chitose airport and change there to another bus bound for Shikotsu Kohan (¥920, 50 minutes, four to six a day). You could also take a bus to Tomakomai station (¥1070, one hour), but buses from there to Shikotsu Kohan run only three times a day (¥700, 10 minutes). It's best to get an early start.

SHIRAOI 白老

The big attractions in this small town are **Poroto Kotan**, a reconstructed Ainu village, and the **Ainu Museum** (Ainu Minzoku Hakubutsukan; ¥650, 8 am to 5 pm April to October, 8.30 am to 4.30 pm November to March), an excellent museum of Ainu culture in a modern building past the souvenir shop ghetto. The museum exhibits are labelled in both Japanese and English and a museum guide (¥500) is also available in both languages. The museum maintains an educational Web site at www.asahi-net .or.jp/~kt9m-ysd/english0.html.

The village is a 10-minute walk from JR Shiraoi station – turn left when you walk out of the southern side of the station. Most bus services drop passengers off at the Poroto Kotan bus stop opposite the approach road to the village.

Shiraoi is on the JR Muroran main line between Noboribetsu station (¥350, 30 minutes) and Tomakomai (¥440, 25 minutes). Shiraoi is just over an hour from Sapporo by tokkyū (¥2940), though not all tokkyū trains along this route stop here. There are buses to Shiraoi from Sapporo (¥1600, two hours) and Tomakomai (¥460, 35 minutes).

TOMAKOMAI 苫小牧
☎ 0144

Tomakomai's main point of interest is its port, which is a hub for ferry links with Honshū. Tomakomai is within easy reach of other, more interesting destinations, so unless you have an early morning ferry or arrive late at night, there shouldn't be any need to stay here.

Places to Stay – Budget
The nearest youth hostel is *Utonai-ko Youth Hostel* (☎ 58-2153), which is by the shore of Utonai-ko, a popular spot for bird-watching. It charges from ¥1400 to ¥1600 a day. From Tomakomai station take a bus bound for New Chitose airport or Chitose and get off at the Utonai-ko Yūsu-hosuteru-mae stop (¥390, 25 minutes) – from there it's a 10-minute walk in the direction of the lake.

Places to Stay – Mid-Range
The pleasant *Shiwa Ryokan* (☎ 32-3403, 35-2358) is a few minutes' walk from the bus station, next to Don-Don Jazz coffee shop. Japanese-style rooms cost ¥4500 a person.

Most of the business hotels around the station area seem to be trying hard to attract customers by discounting rates. The *Tomakomai Green Hotel* (☎ 32-1122) has singles/doubles for ¥6100/9500, as well as Japanese-style rooms for two people at ¥8400.

Getting There & Away
On the JR Muroran main line, there is a service from Tomakomai station to Sapporo (*futsū* – local train, ¥1410, 70 minutes). There are also infrequent trains on the JR Hidaka main line to JR Samani (futsū, ¥2730, three hours), where you can connect with buses bound for the cape, Erimo-misaki.

Buses depart from the bus station and from in front of Daie department store; both are a few minutes on foot from the station. Buses run three times a day between Tomakomai and Shikotsu-ko (¥700, 40 minutes). There are more frequent buses to Noboribetsu Onsen (¥1070, 1½ hours) and New Chitose airport (¥600, 50 minutes). Buses to Shiraoi leave only a few times in the morning and again in the afternoon (¥460, 45 minutes). For connections to Niputani, see the Biratori Getting There & Away section.

Ferry services link Tomakomai with Sendai (¥6300 to ¥7600, 14½ to 16½ hours, one or two a day); Nagoya (¥10,200, 38½ hours, every second day); Oarai, north of Tokyo (¥6000, 33 hours, one or two a day); and Hachinohe (¥3970, nine hours, three a day). The main Tomakomai ferry terminal is at Nishi-kō, a 15-minute bus ride east of Tomakomai station (¥240, two to three a day); taking a taxi will cost around ¥1400. Buses from the ferry terminal to Tomakomai usually continue to Sapporo's Sogo station (¥1270, 1¾ hours).

There are also ferries to Akita (¥3730, 12 hours) and Niigata (¥5250, 19¼ hours) departing at around 10 pm every day (except Sunday) from Tomakomai's Higashi-kō Shūbun ferry terminal. A few of these ferries continue directly to Tsuruga (¥6710, 34¼ hours). From Tomakomai station, there is only one bus a day, at 6 pm, making the 30km journey to Higashi-kō (¥700).

BIRATORI 平取

Located in the remote and mountainous Hidaka district, Biratori is actually a conglomeration of three villages: Nioi, Shiunkotsu and Niputani. Well worth the trouble of getting to, Niputani village is arguably the best place in Hokkaidō to learn about Ainu culture (see the boxed text 'Better Late than Never' in this section). At the excellent **Niputani Ainu Culture Museum** you could easily spend half a day watching documentary videos about Ainu folkcrafts, traditional dances, epic songs and

Better Late than Never

US writer Mark Twain once joked that 'reports of my death have been greatly exaggerated', and this could equally be said of the Ainu people in Japan today. Although tourist literature has pronounced Ainu culture already dead, people of Ainu descent are meanwhile dedicated to cultural preservation associations, established to ensure that religious ceremonies, traditional arts and the Ainu language are passed on.

These Ainu cultural associations were, originally, often tied to the political vanguard of the Ainu community, which, in the 1980s, called for the repeal of the Hokkaidō Former Natives Protection Act (1899). In its original form, this law denied Ainu land ownership and gave the governor of Hokkaidō sole discretion over the management of communal Ainu funds, making the Ainu dependent on the welfare of the Japanese state. Although this law had been amended over the years, many Ainu people still objected even to the law's title, which used the word kyūdo-jin ('dirt' or 'earth' people) to describe them.

In 1997, the Japanese government struck down the old law and replaced it with a new law that allocated government funds for Ainu research and the promotion of Ainu language and culture, as well as better education about Ainu traditions in public schools.

However, the new law fell far short of that proposed by the Ainu Association of Hokkaidō, which called for guaranteed seats for Ainu representatives in the Diet, increased agricultural land grants and fishing rights, year-round employment opportunities for seasonal labourers and the transfer of funds from government welfare programs into an independent Ainu-managed fund for self-reliance.

The new law has, despite its other limitations, increased funding for Ainu cultural associations. Foreign travellers to Hokkaidō now have a better chance than ever of enjoying authentic Ainu festivals, cultural performances and exhibitions of traditional arts (such as woodcarving and weaving). You can find out about some of these events by contacting the Foundation for the Research and Promotion of Ainu Culture (☎ 011-271-4171) in Sapporo. The foundation has a Web site at www.frpac.or.jp. Other useful sources of information are the Ainu Culture Centre (☎ 03-3245-9831) in Tokyo and the Ainu Association of Hokkaidō (☎ 011-221-0462), which maintains a few exhibits, a research library and events listings at its Sapporo office.

traditional ceremonies, including the controversial **Iyomante** or Bear Festival. Exhibits are divided into three areas – Ainu (meaning 'people'), Kamui (gods) and Moshiri (earth). Highlights include a loom for weaving traditional tree-bark cloth and a collection of prayer sticks known as *inaw* and *ikupasuy*. The museum is open from 9.30 am to 4.30 pm but is closed Monday from mid-November to mid-April and from 16 December to 15 January. Admission is ¥400.

Across Route 237, the **Kayano Shigeru Ainu Memorial Museum** (¥300, 9 am to 5 pm daily April to November) houses the private art collection of Ainu elder statesman Kayano Shigeru. Since many of his Ainu items were donated to the Niputani Ainu Culture Museum, Kayano's book may be of more interest to travellers than his museum (see Books in the Hokkaidō Information section at the beginning of this chapter). A combined ticket for this museum and Niputani Ainu Culture Museum is ¥700.

Niputani is a good place to buy fine Ainu woodcarving and chat with the local craftspeople at several workshops in the vicinity of the museums. There are also a few minshuku scattered about if you miss the last bus.

Getting There & Away

It's just possible to visit Biratori as a day trip. The main approaches are Sapporo to the north and Tomakomai to the west. Between late April and October, there are one or two direct buses leaving Sapporo at around 9 am for Biratori and passing through Niputani on the way (¥2040, two hours). If you want to return to Sapporo the same day, there is one afternoon bus via Niputani departing Biratori at 3.45 pm. If you're heading to Tomakomai, there are three or four buses after 1 pm from Biratori as far as Tomikawa (¥520, 25 minutes), where you can transfer to local trains on the JR Hidaka main line to Tomakomai (¥900, 45 minutes). If you're starting at Tomakomai (or coming up from Honshū on an overnight train), take a morning train from Tomakomai to Tomikawa, from where you can catch buses for Biratori between 8 am and 9 am (¥520, 25 minutes).

Niputani is 15 minutes by bus north of Biratori towards Sapporo; the appropriate stop for the museums is Hakubutsukan-mae. If you're hitching, take comfort in the fact that you only have to travel 5km.

SHIKOTSU-KO 支こつ湖
☎ 0123

Part of Shikotsu-Tōya National Park (983 sq km), Shikotsu-ko is a caldera lake surrounded by several volcanoes. It's Japan's second-deepest lake after Tazawa-ko in Akita-ken. The main centre for transport and information is **Shikotsu Kohan**, which consists of a bus station, a visitors centre, a pier for boat excursions and assorted souvenir shops, restaurants and places to stay.

The visitors centre information office (☎ 25-2404), open from 9.30 am to 4.30 pm, is just downhill from the bus station and has maps, pamphlets and a slide show of the lake. From the boat pier, there are rather tame sightseeing cruises that stop at a couple of places around the lake (¥930, 30 minutes, April to November).

If you cross the bridge on your far left as you walk down to the lake shore, you can follow a nature trail around the forested slopes for an hour or so to Morappu. There's not much of a bus service around the lake, but you can cycle to various destinations, or even take on the full circuit (50km). The youth hostel rents bicycles for ¥500 an hour or ¥2000 a day (less for hostel members).

Hiking

The mountain hikes are perhaps the most interesting things to do around Shikotsu-ko. The youth hostel or visitors centre can advise on access, routes and timings.

Eniwa-dake (1320m) lies on the northwestern side of the lake. The start of the mountain trail is about 10 minutes on foot from the Eniwa-dake Tozan-guchi bus stop near Poropinai. It takes about 3½ hours to hike to the summit, where there is a fine panorama of the surrounding lakes and peaks. Don't bother with this hike if it rains – some of the steeper sections of the trail become dangerously slippery at such times.

HOKKAIDŌ

Buses from Shikotsu Kohan to Sapporo pass the Eniwa Tozan-guchi stop (¥340).

Tarumae-zan (1038m) lies on the southern side of the lake. Here you can enjoy the rugged delights of wandering around the crater of an active volcano, though at the time of writing hikers were warned against climbing due to increased activity. The crater is an easy 40-minute hike from the seventh station, which can be reached from Shikotsu Kohan in three hours on foot (¥3500 by taxi). There is a bus service as far as the turn-off from the main highway, but it's 12km from there to the seventh station.

From the crater, you can follow a trail north-west down the mountain for 2½ hours to **Koke-no-dōmon**, a spectacular mossy gorge. Between mid-July and mid-September, there are also buses twice a day to and from Koke-no-dōmon from Shikotsu Kohan that allow you about 25 minutes to look around. If you miss the last bus you'll have to walk or hitch the 15km back to Shikotsu Kohan. The gorge is officially open from 9 am to 5 pm from June to October only. You cannot officially enter after 4 pm.

Places to Stay
There are over a dozen minshuku, ryokan and hotels on the edge of the lake at Shikotsu Kohan.

Places to Stay – Budget
Across the car park from the bus station is *Shikotsu-ko Youth Hostel* (☎ 25-2311), a friendly place that has family rooms, as well as the usual dormitory-style accommodation for ¥2900 a person. Bicycle rental and a hot-springs bath are also available. Staff can offer advice on hiking and cycling routes and may be able to help you organise transport to trailheads.

There is a nicely situated camping ground (¥400, open early May to late October) near the Lapland lodge (see the following Mid-Range section).

Places to Stay – Mid-Range
Just behind the bus station is *Shikotsu-sō* (☎ 25-2718), a cheerful little minshuku with per-person rates of ¥5800, including

two meals. Tucked away in the alley behind Shikotsu-sō is *Log Bear* (☎ 25-2738), a log cabin B&B with per-person rates of ¥5000. The owner speaks excellent English.

Out at Morappu is *Lapland* (☎ 25-2239), a great little log cabin with nice views of the lake. It's a member of the Toho network and has dormitory-style accommodation for ¥4900, including two meals; for ¥1000 extra a person you can have your own room. The owners will pick you up and take you back to the bus station, or to mountain trailheads. Buses bound for Koke-no-dōmon from Shikotsu Kohan pass Morappu (¥240, 10 minutes).

Getting There & Away
Between mid-June and mid-October, there are three to four buses a day from Shikotsu Kohan to Sapporo's Sogo station (¥1330, 80 minutes). Other buses run year round to New Chitose airport (¥920, 55 minutes) and Tomakomai (¥700, 40 minutes).

Dō-hoku (Northern Hokkaidō)

WAKKANAI 稚内
☎ 0162 • pop 44,700
This windswept port on the northernmost fringe of Hokkaidō is the access point for the islands of Rishiri-tō and Rebun-tō, as well as Sakhalin Island. While not of compelling interest itself, Wakkanai has plenty of delicious seafood and Russian shops that make it a pleasant enough stopover en route to the islands.

Information
Wakkanai station has a tourist information counter (☎ 22-2384) where you can ask for pamphlets, maps and ferry timetables (10 am to 6 pm June to September). At the ferry terminal you'll find another small information counter (6.30 am to 4 pm June to September).

Things to See & Do
If you find yourself in town with time on your hands, you could head up to **Wakkanai-**

kōen, which sits atop a grassy hill a few blocks west of the railway station. There are a number of walking trails and an observation tower (open late April to November) with fine views of northern Hokkaidō and, on clear days, Sakhalin Island. Also nearby are a number of eclectic monuments, including the **Gate to Ice and Snow**, a memorial to the former Japanese settlements on Sakhalin, and **Monument to the Nine Ladies**, which commemorates postal workers on Sakhalin who committed suicide after Japan's defeat in WWII.

Wakkanai Onsen is just a 15-minute bus ride from the Sōya bus station (¥600, 10 am to 9.30 pm daily).

Twenty-seven kilometres east of Wakkanai is **Sōya-misaki**, the northernmost point of Japan, which is just 43km from Cape Khrion on Sakhalin. There's actually not a great deal to see and you should only make the trip if you like the idea of reaching the very top of the country. One interesting memorial is dedicated to the victims of Korean Airlines flight 007, which was shot down by a Soviet fighter jet off the Sakhalin coast in 1988. Buses run four times a day between Wakkanai's Sōya bus station and Sōya-misaki (¥1350, 50 minutes).

Special Events
The **Japan Cup National Dogsled Races** are held in Wakkanai during the last weekend in February. A similar event, using artificial ice and wheeled carts, takes place in August during the **Wakkanai Minato Matsuri** (Wakkanai Port Festival).

Places to Stay – Budget
A five-minute walk from Wakkanai station or eight minutes on foot from the port is *Wakkanai Moshiripa Youth Hostel (☎ 24-0180)*, which charges ¥3100 a person. Bicycles can be rented for ¥1500 a day. The hostel is also closed at different times during the winter, so phone ahead.

Friendly *Wakkanai Youth Hostel (☎ 23-7162)*, which charges ¥2900 a person, has received good reviews from travellers. Bicycle rental is free for guests. The hostel is a 15-minute walk from Minami-Wakkanai station,

one stop before the terminus at Wakkanai. From Wakkanai station fairly frequent buses bound for Midori-roku-chōme run past the Minami-shōgakkō-mae stop (¥210, 10 minutes). From there it's a 10-minute walk uphill to the hostel. On the way you'll pass *Rider House Midori-yu (☎ 22-4275)*, where spartan shared accommodation costs ¥1000. It's to your left off of the main road, adjacent to a local *sentō* (public baths).

Most motorcyclists seem to camp out at Wakkanai Dome, a 427m-long concrete structure beside the ferry terminal. It can get pretty cold and noisy here, but it's convenient for early-morning ferry departures.

Down the small street just to the right of the station is *Saihate Ryokan (☎ 23-3556)*, a well-maintained little place that has per-person rates starting at ¥4000 without meals. At the end of the block, *Tenno Ryokan (☎ 23-3501)* has comfortable rooms starting at ¥3500 a person, or ¥6000 including two meals. Bicycle and car rental are available.

Places to Stay – Mid-Range
A 10-minute walk from the station is *Ryokan Kanno (☎ 23-3587)*, a traditionally run place that once played host to the visiting Shōwa emperor. Housed in a large concrete block, it doesn't look like much from the outside, but the rooms are spacious and comfortable, the staff friendly and the seafood dinners delicious. Per-person rates with two meals start at ¥8000. To get there, walk straight out from the station for three blocks, turn left at the post office and continue for two more blocks. The ryokan is on the right-hand side of the street.

Places to Eat
Of course, fresh seafood is the answer. One cheap place to get it is *Wakkanai Chūō Renbai*, reputedly the 'kitchen of Wakkanai', which discounts its takeaways late in the day. It's a covered alley market on the right-hand side of the main street leading straight out from the station.

Getting There & Away
Between Wakkanai and Sapporo, there is one flight a day to New Chitose airport (50

HOKKAIDŌ

minutes) and two to Okadama (one hour); both cost ¥16,350. Make sure you know which airport you are going to be using. Wakkanai also has direct flights to Tokyo (¥31,450, 1¾ hours) and during summer to Osaka (¥37,950, 2½ hours). Buses to Wakkanai airport depart from the Sōya bus station, just north of Wakkanai station (¥590, 35 minutes).

There are a few rather slow kyūkō trains between Wakkanai and Asahikawa (¥6510, four hours), almost all of which continue to Sapporo (¥8400, six hours). S-kippu cost ¥11,980 to Sapporo and ¥8800 to Asahikawa. There is also a sleeper service (¥14,700) that leaves Sapporo at 10 pm and arrives via Asahikawa in Wakkanai at 6 am, in time for the early ferry across to Rishiri-tō or Rebun-tō. Nite-&-Day tickets on this route cost ¥18,320.

Buses to Sapporo depart twice a day from the Sōya bus station just north of the station and four times a day from the ferry terminal (¥5750, 6¼ hours). There is also a daily bus from the Sōya station to Asahikawa (¥4350, 4¾ hours). Discounted return tickets are available for either trip.

Rishiri-tō & Rebun-tō Ferries The ferry to Oshidomari, on Rishiri-tō, departs from Wakkanai at least twice a day throughout the year, with four departures a day between May and September (¥1800, 1¾ hours). From Oshidomari there are one or two departures a day to Kafuka on Rebun-tō (¥730, 40 minutes). Between May and September there are also two slightly slower ferries a day between Kutsugata on Rishiri-tō and Kafuka for the same price. Direct ferries from Wakkanai to Kafuka depart two to five times a day (¥2100, two hours).

The port at Wakkanai is 10 minutes on foot from the station – turn right as you exit the station and head towards the water. The ticket offices are inside a large building to the left of the pier.

Sakhalin Ferry Between early May and mid-September Nichiro Ferry (☎ 011-231-4111) sails five to seven times a month between Wakkanai and Korsakov on Sakhalin Island. The cheapest 2nd-class fare is ¥35,000 one way, but 1st-class Japanese-style rooms cost only ¥5000 more. Discounted return tickets are available. For details on Russian visa requirements, see the Hokkaidō Getting There & Away section.

RISHIRI-REBUN-SAROBETSU NATIONAL PARK
利尻礼文サロベツ国立公園
Rishiri-Rebun-Sarobetsu National Park is made up of the two islands of Rishiri-tō and Rebun-tō, but also includes a 27km strip of coast on the mainland of Hokkaidō known as Sarobetsu Gensei-kaen, a vast swampy region famous for its vistas of flowers – mainly rhododendrons, irises and lilies, which bloom in June and July.

Rishiri-tō 利尻島
☎ 01638
This island is dominated by the volcanic peak of Rishiri-zan (1721m), known locally as Rishiri-Fuji, which soars majestically above the sea. A road circles the island and a bus service links the small fishing communities. The main activity for visitors is hiking on the various trails and lakes below the summit of the mountain. Providing you have warm clothes and proper footwear, the hike to the summit can be comfortably completed in a full day.

Oshidomari and Kutsugata are the main ports for the island. Information booths at the ferry terminals (8 am to 5.30 pm May to October) provide maps and information about transport, sights and hiking. The staff can also book accommodation.

Hiking The two most reliable trails to the summit of Rishiri-zan start at Oshidomari and Kutsugata. The Oshidomari route trailhead is 3km from Oshidomari proper, while the Kutsugata route begins about 3km outside Kutsugata town. There is not much in the way of a bus service to the trailheads, but buses to Rishiri-Fuji Onsen will take you part of the way to the Kutsugata trailhead. Otherwise you must either walk (for a little over an hour), hitch or take a taxi.

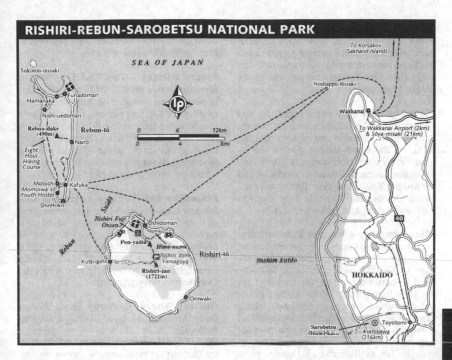

RISHIRI-REBUN-SAROBETSU NATIONAL PARK

You may be able to arrange a ride if you're staying at the youth hostel.

Prepare properly for a mountain hike. Aim for an early start and allow at least 10 hours for the ascent and descent. The best time to hike is from late June to mid-September. Advice and maps with excellent hiking details and contour lines, mostly in Japanese, are available from the information booths at the ports and the youth hostel.

About two hours below the summit, just past the eighth station, is Rishiri-dake Yamagoya, an unstaffed mountain hut, which perches on the edge of a precipice and provides the bare minimum for a roof over your head (no water). If you're coming from Kutsugata, you'll have to head down the mountain for over an hour from where you meet up with the Oshidomari trail to reach the hut. Take your own food (purchase it from shops in the ports) and water. If you stay here, be warned that it's bloody cold at night and the wind contributes generously to the drop in temperature. If you can't sleep, the night views are absolutely amazing, and providing the clarity holds, the views during the day extend as far as Sakhalin Island. There is severe erosion on the sections between the mountain hut and the summit, especially around the ninth station, and rockslides sometimes occur after heavy rain, so hike with care.

If you don't feel like hiking to the summit, there are several enjoyable hikes that are less strenuous. One of these follows the trail from Oshidomari for an hour past the Hokuriku Camping Ground towards the summit, but branches left in thick forest, about 10 minutes after reaching a group of A-frame chalets at the end of a paved road. This trail leads in 1¾ hours to Hime-numa, with the option of a 30-minute side trip to Pon-yama. From Hime-numa, it's 6km to Oshidomari along Route 108.

Rishiri-Fuji Onsen (¥400, 10 am to 8.30 pm) has hot-spring bubble baths, *rotemburo* (open-air baths) and an indoor pool. The onsen is a 30-minute walk from Oshidomari on the way to the camping ground and trailhead for Rishiri-zan. A couple of buses a day from Oshidomari also pass the onsen (¥150, 10 minutes).

Places to Stay Most of the minshuku and ryokan are in Oshidomari and Kutsugata, though there are also one or two in Oniwaki, on the south-eastern side of the island. Prices for mid-range to top end accommodation fluctuate seasonally and are around ¥2000 less than quoted here between October and April. In July and August, everything can be booked out.

Places to Stay – Budget There are five camping grounds widely dispersed around Rishiri-tō; all are open from approximately May to October and are free unless you need to rent a tent. Near the trailhead for the Oshidomari route up to Rishiri-zan is the *Hokuriku Camping Ground*, which can now be recommended as it recently had a facelift and has become quite popular with hikers. There is an infrequent bus service as far as Rishiri-Fuji Onsen, from where you can walk to the camping ground in about an hour. The camping ground at Kutsugata-misaki-kōen has also received good reviews and is less than 1km from the port at Kutsugata.

Rishiri Green Hill Youth Hostel (☎ 2-2507), which charges ¥2900 a person, is a 25-minute walk from Oshidomari-kō port, or a five-minute bus ride to the Gurin Hiru Yuusu-hosuteru-mae stop (¥150). The staff can provide information on hiking Rishiri-zan and bicycles can be rented. The hostel is usually closed from October to February.

Places to Stay – Mid-Range Friendly *Ryokan Narita (☎ 2-2361)* charges ¥7500 a person, including two meals. From the pier, walk out to the main road and turn right. After about five minutes, the ryokan is on the left-hand side, before the road curves. Look for the 'Welcome to Rishiri' sign.

In Kutsugata, about 10 minutes from the ferry pier (near the town's main intersec-

tion), is *Minshuku Kutsugata-sō (☎ 4-2038)*, a fairly basic place with per-person rates of ¥6500 without meals.

Places to Stay – Top End The *Pension Herasan-no-Ie (☎ 2-2361)* has well-maintained rooms (some with nice sea views) costing ¥9000 per person, including two meals. From the pier, walk out to the main road and turn right. After about 10 minutes the road will curve to the left; the pension is straight ahead in a wooden Western-style house on top of a small rise.

Places to Eat If you're looking for seafood, try *Aji-no-Ichiba*, which serves food straight from the local fishing boats to your mouth, sometimes without any cooking in between. The live *uni* (sea urchin) is ¥500. The restaurant is in a small blue building next to the water to the right as you exit the Oshidomari ferry terminal.

Getting There & Away From Rishiri there are one or two flights a day to Wakkanai (¥8340, 20 minutes) and Sapporo (¥17,000, 50 minutes). The island bus runs by the airport only once a day from Oshidomari (¥310, 20 minutes) or Kutsugata-kō port (¥520, 25 minutes). A taxi from the airport to Oshidomari costs ¥1500.

For details of ferry services from Oshidomari and Kutsugata to Kafuka on Rebun-tō and Wakkanai, see the Wakkanai Getting There & Away section.

Getting Around There are two bus lines, one each running clockwise and anticlockwise around the island. There are six buses a day from Kutsugata that complete a clockwise circuit of the island in 1¾ hours (¥2200). Travelling anticlockwise, the trip from Oshidomari to Kutsugata costs ¥730 and takes 30 to 50 minutes, depending on whether or not the bus stops at the onsen and/or the airport.

Cycling is a great way to get around the island and bicycles can be rented at the youth hostel and from shops near the Oshidomari ferry terminal. You can complete a leisurely circuit (56km) of the island in about five to seven hours. There is also a 29km cycling path running from Oshidomari past Kutsugata.

Rebun-tō 礼文島
☎ 01638

In contrast to the conical height of its neighbour, Rebun-tō (82 sq km) is a low, arrow-shaped island that has one major road down its east coast. The main attractions of the island are the hiking trails. Its terrain is more varied than that of Rishiri, making Rebun a better place if you want to spend several days trying different hiking routes and distances. Between late May and early September, the island's alpine flowers – over 300 species – pull out all the stops for a floral extravaganza: a memorable experience. Unfortunately, almost every species of tour group seems to be on the island at this time as well.

Kafuka is the main community and port at the southern end of the island. There is a tourist information counter (☎ 6-2655) at the Kafuka ferry terminal that can provide a few maps and help book accommodation (9 am to 5 pm daily April to October).

Hiking The classic hike down the entire length of the western coast is known as the *hachijikan haikingu kōsu* (eight-hour hiking course). It's a marvellous hike across grassy cliff tops, fields of dwarf bamboo, forests of conifers, deserted, rocky beaches and remote harbours with clusters of fishing shacks and racks of seaweed. There doesn't seem to be much sense in following the example of many Japanese hikers who turn it into an endurance race. If you have the extra day, it may be more enjoyable to break the hike into two four-hour sections (*yonjikan haikingu kōsu*).

The eight-hour hike runs from Sukotonmisaki on the northern tip down to Motochi near the southern tip. The four-hour hiking course starts at Sukoton-misaki, runs down to Nishi-uedomari and then heads up to the bus stop at Hamanaka. Another variation would be to start at Nishi-uedomari and hike down to Motochi. You can follow the trails in either direction, but most people

seem to hike from north to south. Momoiwa-sō Youth Hostel and other places to stay on the island can provide information on hiking and transport to trailheads.

Although the eight-hour hike is not a death-defying feat, it has some tricky stretches, mostly in the southern half, including steep slopes of loose scree and several kilometres of boulder-hopping along beaches, which can become very nasty in the unpredictable weather of these northern regions. Much of the trail is several hours away from human habitation, and for the most part, those who slip off a cliff or twist an ankle will require rescue by boat. There's no need to be paranoid, but this is the reason why group hiking is encouraged. Momoiwa-sō Youth Hostel martials hikers into groups.

You'll need proper footwear, warm clothes and some form of raingear. A Japanese hiking staple is *onigiri* – rice wrapped in dried seaweed with a bit of plum, salmon or pickles stuffed in the middle. Take water or soft drinks with you. Do *not* drink the water from the streams: during the 1930s, foxes were introduced from the Kurile Islands (Russia) and their faeces now contaminate the streams.

Another popular hike is from Nairo, halfway down the east coast, to the top of Rebun-dake. The peak is a tiddler at 490m, but it's a pleasant 3½-hour return hike. If you want to hike to the southern tip of the island, there is a trail starting near Kafuka running by the Momo-iwa (Peach Rock) observation point and down to the lighthouse at Shiretoko-misaki.

Places to Stay There are many minshuku and ryokan, a couple of hotels, a Toho inn and a youth hostel on the island. If you phone ahead, most of the more remote places will arrange for you to be picked up at the port.

Places to Stay – Budget There is a good camping ground in a pretty lakeside setting at Funadomari (¥300). *Momoiwa-sō Youth Hostel* (☎ 6-1421) has a hard-earned reputation as one of Japan's craziest youth hostels: group hiking by day, and skits and camp songs until the mandatory lights-out at

HOKKAIDŌ

10 pm. It's in an unbeatable location close to one of the trailheads for the eight-hour hike, with good views out to sea and of the nearby Momo-iwa. The hostel is open only from June to September, as there's no way the staff could keep up their insanity year round. Crowded Japanese-style dorms for women and much nicer 2nd-floor bunks for men cost ¥2800. The staff always have someone waiting when ferries dock – call ahead for reservations and look out for the enthusiastic guys vigorously waving the Momoiwa-sō banner and screaming, '*okaeri nasai*' ('Welcome home!'). From Kafuka-kō there are also a few buses bound for Motochi that pass the Momoiwa-sō Iriguchi stop after about 15 minutes. From there it's a seven-minute walk to the hostel. (The hostel meals are not recommended – see Places to Eat for an alternative.)

Places to Stay – Mid-Range A member of the Toho network, *Field Inn Seikan-sō* (☎ 7-2818) is a more peaceful alternative to Momoiwa-sō and gets good reviews from travellers. Per-person rates are ¥5500 for dormitory-style accommodation including two meals, ¥1500 more for your own room. The inn is on the northern side of the island next to one of the eight-hour hiking-course trailheads. It's closed from March to mid-April and late October to mid-December. Buses from Kafuka-kō stop right in front of the inn before continuing to Sukoton-misaki, but staff will come and pick you up at the port if you phone ahead.

Minshuku and ryokan are dispersed among Kafuka, Motochi, Shiretoko and Funadomari. Prices fluctuate seasonally; expect to pay about ¥2000 less than the prices quoted here between October and April.

Minshuku Sukoton-misaki (☎ 7-2878) is a rustic spot perched at the very northern tip of the island. Per-person rates are ¥7000, but it's open only from May to September. At the opposite end of Rebun-tō, in the fishing hamlet of Shiretoko, the popular *Kaachan Yado* (☎ 6-1406), meaning 'Mom's Place', receives enthusiastic reports from travellers and charges ¥7500 per person including two meals. *Minshuku*

Shiretoko (☎ 6-1335) is a clean, friendly place charging the same rates; some of the rooms have great views across the water to Rishiri-zan.

Places to Stay – Top End With so many other more scenic options providing better access to hikes, there's little reason to settle for the generally overpriced accommodation found in Kafuka. Formerly Rebun Youth Hostel, *Nature Inn Hanashin* (☎ 6-1648) in Kafuka is still a popular place, about 25 minutes on foot from Kafuka-kō. You could also take a bus bound for Sukoton-misaki or Nishi-uedomari and get off after five minutes at the Yūsu-mae stop. Rooms are not cheap, however, at ¥10,000 a person, including two meals.

Places to Eat If you arrive early enough at Momoiwa-sō Youth Hostel, you can eat next door at *Ben and Joe*, a cafe with flower-power paintings, cheesecake, real coffee, and curry and rice. It's open from 7 am to 5 pm.

Getting There & Away From Wakkanai there are one or two flights a day to Rebun-tō (¥9680, 20 minutes). Between June and August, there is also one flight a day from Sapporo's New Chitose airport (¥17,000, 50 minutes). The closest bus stop to the airport is Kūkō-shita, about a 15-minute walk from the terminal. A taxi to Kafuka costs the exorbitant sum of ¥7500.

For details of the boat service between Wakkanai, Kafuka, Oshidomari and Kutsugata, on Rishiri-tō, see the Wakkanai Getting There & Away section.

Getting Around Most of the time you'll be getting around the island on foot. The youth hostel and other accommodation will usually help with your transport arrangements on arrival or departure. Careful attention to the bus timetables should be enough to get you to the key points for hiking. Some of the minshuku have bicycles to rent. Scooters and cars can be rented near the ferry terminal in Kafuka.

The main bus service follows the island's one major road from Kafuka in the south to

Sukoton-misaki in the north (¥1180, 70 minutes). En route it passes the Kūkō-shita (airport) bus stop (¥830) and Funadomari (¥900). Some buses turn off after Funadomari and head to Nishi-uedomari. Buses run on this route up to six times a day: four go to Sukoton-misaki, two to Nishi-uedomari. There are also three to five buses a day from Kafuka to Shiretoko (¥300, 13 minutes) or Motochi via Momo-iwa Tozan-guchi (¥440, 16 minutes). All services are sharply reduced from November to April. Be sure to pick up a copy of the island's bus timetable from the information counter at the Kafuka ferry terminal.

ASAHIKAWA 旭川
☎ 0166 • pop 361,000
Asahikawa is an unimpressive urban sprawl and the second-largest city on Hokkaidō. Historically, the area was one of the largest Ainu settlements in Hokkaidō. The present city had its origins in the Meiji period as a farmer militia settlement and has since developed into a major industrial centre. For the traveller, its importance is largely as a transport hub: to the north, it's a long haul to Wakkanai; to the south, there are the attractions of Daisetsuzan National Park.

Information
There's an information counter (☎ 22-6704) inside Asahikawa station (9 am to 7 pm, until 5.30 pm Sunday). Though only Japanese is spoken, the staff can supply you with the relevant timetables for Daisetsuzan National Park and a bilingual *Map of Asahikawa*. It's easy to find your way around town because addresses are numbered on a grid. At 3-jō 10-chōme, *Media* computer shop provides Internet access for ¥300 for every 30 minutes (closed Tuesday).

Things to See
The **Hokkaido Folk Arts and Crafts Village** is actually three separate museums. The only one worth the money is the **International Dyeing and Weaving Art Museum**, which has an extensive display of textiles from different regions of Japan, plus embroidered traditional Ainu tree-bark cloth

(¥550, 9 am to 5.30 pm, closed December to March). Between May and October, the museum provides a free hourly shuttle between 10 am and 4 pm from its gallery shop on the southern side of 3-jō 5-chōme, about 10 minutes on foot from the station. Staff at the tourist information counter have photocopies of directions to the shop and alternative city bus routes.

North-west of the city centre, the **Kawamura Kaneto Ainu Memorial Museum** (¥500, 9 am to 5 pm, 8 am to 6 pm July and August) has an interesting, if tiny exhibition hall and a notice board advertising Ainu cultural events and Ainu-owned businesses across Hokkaidō. The ticket office sells Ainu music recordings and an English-language booklet, *Living in the Ainu Moshir*, written by the present curator and founder's son, Kawamura Shinrit Eoripak Ainu. Take bus No 24 from bus stop No 3 in front of Asahikawa station to the Ainu Kinenkan-mae stop (¥170, 15 minutes).

You can sample one of Japan's most historic brands of sake at the **Otokoyama Sake Brewery Museum** (free, 9 am to 5pm daily), where exhibits demonstrate the production process and include a sizeable *ukiyo-e* (woodblock print) collection. Several city buses from bus stop No 18 in front of Marui Imai department store pass Otokoyama – ask the driver where to get off (¥280, 15 minutes).

Special Events
The **Ainu Kotan Matsuri** (Ainu Village Festival) usually takes place in late September at the traditional ceremonial grounds on the banks of Ishikari-gawa, south of the city. According to Ainu legend, a hero once defeated an evil deity here, throwing its severed head and its body into the river and turning them into two large rocks. During the festival you can see traditional dances, music, and *kamui-nomi* and *inau-shiki* prayer ceremonies offered to the deities of fire, river, kotan and mountain.

At the beginning of February, you can see enormous ice sculptures during Asahikawa's own **Yuki Matsuri** (Snow Festival) which is the second-largest such festival in Hokkaidō after Sapporo's.

HOKKAIDŌ

Places to Stay

Asahikawa Youth Hostel (☎ 61-2751), which charges ¥3200 a person, is 15 minutes by bus No 444 or 550 from bus stop No 11 at 1-jō 7-chōme, across from the Asahikawa Prince Hotel; get off at the Yuusu-hosuteru-mae stop (¥200). The hostel is far from the city centre and can be deserted; bicycles are available free of charge to guests.

In an atmospheric building, the historic *Echigoya Ryokan* (☎ 23-5131) is the longest-running inn in Asahikawa. The polite management charges ¥10,000 a person, and this price includes two elaborate meals. For security reasons, the front gate closes at midnight. Next door is the less grandiose, but still inviting, *Tokeiya Ryokan* (☎ 23-2237), where per-person rates are ¥6000 with two meals. Both inns are about 15 minutes on foot from the station on the northern side of a small street running between 2-jō dōri and 1-jō dōri through the 9-chōme block.

Closer to the station, the *Asahikawa Prince Hotel* (☎ 22-5155) has sparkling clean singles/doubles starting at ¥5300/10,500. Competition among the many business hotels in the station area can drive prices even lower. Beware of the cheapest options just in front of the station, which are mostly crash pads for drunk businessmen who have missed the last train.

Getting There & Away

Asahikawa has flights to Fukuoka, Kansai, Nagoya and Tokyo. Buses between the airport and Asahikawa station are timed to connect with flight arrivals and departures (¥570, 35 minutes).

The JR Hakodate main line links Asahikawa with Sapporo (tokkyū, ¥3690, 1½ hours). There are a few afternoon kaisoku trains on the same route (¥2420, 2½ hours). S-kippu cost ¥4940.

The JR Furano line runs from Asahikawa via Biei to Furano (futsū, ¥1040, 70 minutes). The JR Sekihoku main line runs east via Kamikawa and Bihoro to Abashiri (¥7240, 3¾ hours). On the JR Sōya main line kyūkō trains run north to Wakkanai three times a day (¥6510, four hours). For

¥5250 more, you can take the sleeper service from Sapporo to Wakkanai that stops at Asahikawa just after midnight.

Many bus services leave and arrive in front of Asahikawa station, though others depart from bus stops scattered around the nearby department stores. There are several bus services running from Asahikawa into Daisetsuzan National Park. From bus stop No 4 in front of the station, there are two or three buses a day to Tenninkyō Onsen (65 minutes) and Asahidake Onsen (95 minutes). The ride, believe it or not, is free (see the Asahidake Onsen Getting There & Away section for details). From May to October, there are hourly buses to Sōunkyō Onsen via Kamikawa (¥1900, 1¾ hours, last bus at 5.20 pm).

Other bus services include Wakkanai (¥4350, 4¾ hours, one a day), Furano (¥860, 1½ hours, last bus at 5 pm) and Sapporo's Chūō and Sogo bus stations (¥2000, two hours, two or three an hour).

Daisetsuzan National Park
大雪山国立公園

This is Japan's largest national park (2309 sq km), consisting of several mountain groups, volcanoes, hot springs, lakes and forests. It also includes Asahi-dake, which at 2290m is Hokkaidō's highest peak. The park is spectacular hiking and skiing territory but you should bear in mind that a few days are needed to get away from the tourist areas. If you have limited time, Asahidake Onsen is a good spot for a quick look at the park. Tokachidake Onsen is more remote and may be good for those wanting to escape the crowds (a key consideration in summer and early autumn). Only a couple of hikes on the more well-trodden trails have been mentioned here, but there are many more routes leading to more remote regions if you have several days, or even a week, to spare.

Buses run to the interior of the park from Asahikawa and the area around Furano and

Biei in the west, Kamikawa in the north, Kitami in the east and Obihiro in the south. You can pick up English-language maps and information about the park in Sapporo or try the tourist information offices in Asahikawa, Biei, Sōunkyō Onsen and Asahidake Onsen. One of the most useful brochures is *Daisetsuzan National Park Sounkyo*, which has English text, a hiking map and a table showing times for various hikes starting from Sōunkyō Onsen. Stores in Sōunkyō Onsen and Asahidake Onsen also sell *Daisetsuzan Attack* (¥1200), a very detailed map of the park in Japanese.

FURANO 富良野
☎ 0167

At the absolute geographical centre of Hokkaidō, the slopes of Furano house one of Japan's most famous ski resorts, with over a dozen ski lifts and excellent facilities for powder skiing.

Information

Outside Furano station there is a small information hut (☎ 23-3388) that has a few maps, but no English is spoken (9 am to 6 pm). Across the street you can rent bicycles for ¥200 an hour.

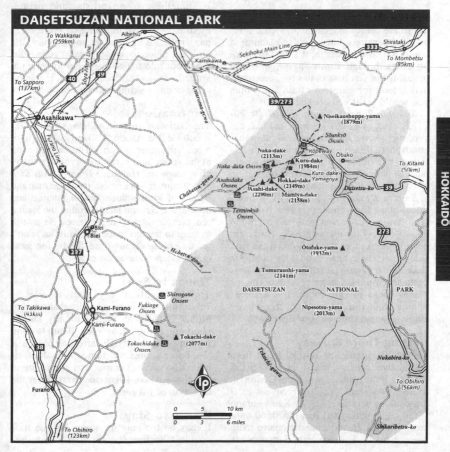

DAISETSUZAN NATIONAL PARK

HOKKAIDŌ

Things to See & Do

In summer, you can cycle to the **Furano Wine Factory** 4km north-west of the station for free tastings and demonstrations of the wine-making process. The eager gourmand could also visit the **Furano Cheese Factory**, **Ice Milk Factory** and **Handicraft Factory**, all 3km south-west of the station. The factories are free and generally open from 9 am to 4.30 pm (closed on weekends from November to April). Between June and September buses run infrequently from the station to most local attractions, including the famous lavender fields at **Farm Toyoda**.

Places to Stay

There are plenty of minshuku, ryokan, hotels and pensions, but if you're planning a winter ski trip to Furano, it's best to make bookings through a travel agent, who will probably get you better rates for accommodation (and sometimes for train fares) than you would get if you booked directly.

Rokugō Furarin Youth Hostel (☎ 29-2172) charges ¥2850 a person and has, according to some travellers, a real 'at home' atmosphere. From Furano station, it's a 35-minute bus ride to the terminus at Rokugō, but free pick-up is available from the station after 4.45 pm if you phone ahead.

Sumire Ryokan (☎ 23-4767) is a traditional place five minutes on foot from Furano station. Per-person rates start at around ¥3500, or ¥6000 with two meals. Turn right outside the station, then left down the first side street; the ryokan is on your right. *Mr Bike Raider House* (small English sign) has basic accommodation for ¥800 in dorms, or ¥2000 for a private room. It's a three-minute walk straight out from the station, above a rāmen shop on your right.

Getting There & Away

On the JR Furano line kaisoku trains from Asahikawa reach Furano in 1¼ hours (¥1100), some continuing as far as Obihiro in another two hours (¥2420). Frequent local trains along this line stop at Kami-Furano (¥350, 20 minutes) and Biei (¥620, 40 minutes). The JR Hakodate and Nemuro main lines connect Furano with Sapporo via Takikawa (tokkyū, ¥3570, two hours). Although these trains usually run only on weekends and holidays, they are more frequent during the peak summer and ski seasons.

Fairly frequent buses connect Furano with Asahikawa (¥860, 1½ hours) and Sapporo (¥2100, 2½ hours). Buses run in the morning, and then again in the afternoon and early evening.

BIEI 美瑛
☎ 0166

With the dramatic Daisetsuzan mountains as a backdrop, the picturesque town of Biei is something of an artists' and nature-lovers' mecca. In late June and early July, thousands of visitors come to see the expansive fields of lavender and poppies. It's an ideal place to spend a day cycling dirt roads out into the countryside, lingering at art galleries and coffee shops, or, in winter, cross-country skiing and snowshoeing.

Information

The tourist information building (☎ 92-4378) is outside Biei station (8.30 am to 7 pm, until 5 pm November to April). The staff here and at the youth hostels can supply you with cycling maps and *Hokkaido Town of Hills Biei*, which contains an English-language map and details of local sights, outdoor pursuits and art classes. Several shops around the station rent bicycles at reasonable prices. Be careful to keep to the dirt roads and paths and don't go trampling through the fields, for local farmers depend upon the crops.

Things to See

The highlight of any visit to Biei is **Takushinkan**, a small museum dedicated to Shinzō Maeda, an internationally known photographer (9 am to 5 pm, 10 am to 4 pm November to April). His arresting photos of the Tokachi area are famous for their vibrant and unusual colour and composition. The museum is a 10km ride from Biei in the direction of Bibaushi.

Places to Stay

It may be too cute for some, but the staff couldn't be friendlier at *Biei Potato-no-*

Oka Youth Hostel (☎ *92-3255*). Nightly rates are ¥3200 for comfortable four-person dorms, or ¥4800 including two excellent meals. Bike rental is available and the gregarious owner presides over nightly 'guidance' sessions for cyclists and hikers. In winter, there are cross-country skiing trips. The hostel is far from Biei station but there is a free pick-up service in the afternoons if you phone ahead.

In the same area, Toho network inn *Seino-Anne* (☎ *92-4993*) comes highly recommended by some travellers. Dormitory-style accommodation is ¥5000 a person, including two meals. The inn is open only from April to November, over the New Year and in February. If you make advance reservations, staff will come to pick you up at the station.

Closer to Takushinkan and charging ¥3200 a person is *Bibaushi Liberty Youth Hostel* (☎ *95-2141*). It's in a white house set among coffee shops and galleries surrounding Bibaushi station, one stop south of Biei. In winter the hostel offers cross-country skiing and snowshoeing

Getting There & Away
Biei is on the JR Furano line between Asahikawa (futsū, ¥520, 35 minutes) and Furano (¥620, 40 minutes). From near Biei station, there are frequent buses to Asahikawa (¥520, 50 minutes) and a few departures a day for Tokachidake Onsen (¥600, one hour).

TOKACHIDAKE & SHIROGANE ONSEN 十勝岳・白金温泉
A short distance north-east of Furano are the remote hot-springs villages of Tokachidake Onsen and Shirogane Onsen, which make good crowd-free bases for hiking and skiing. You can climb Tokachi-dake (2077m) in a day; some trails extend as far as Tenninkyō Onsen or Asahi-dake, though these require three or four days of hiking.

Places to Stay
None of the places to stay in Tokachidake is particularly cheap, and there are only a few to choose from. *Kokuminshukusha Kamihoro-sō* (☎ *0167-45-2970*) has per-person rates starting at ¥8100, including

two meals. Nearby, at Fukiage Onsen, *Hakugin-sō* (☎ *0167-45-4126/45-3251*) has a beautiful rotemburo and charges only ¥2600 for dormitory-style accommodation or ¥300 to enter the baths (10 am to 3 pm).

An inexpensive place to stay at Shirogane Onsen is *Kokuminshukusha Shirakaba-sō* (☎ *0166-94-3344*), which charges ¥2550 a person including access to the hot-springs bath. *Onsen Minshuku Rindō* (☎ *0166-94-3036*) has more comfortable rooms starting at ¥6800 a person. There is also a camping ground 500m from Shirogane Onsen open from June to October (tent rental is ¥350).

Getting There & Away
From Kami-Furano station on the JR Furano line, it's a 45-minute bus ride to Tokachidake Onsen (¥490, up to three a day). Buses to Shirogane Onsen leave from Biei up to five times a day (¥600, one hour). There are also up to four direct buses a day to Shirogane Onsen from Asahikawa (¥1100, 1¼ hours).

ASAHIDAKE ONSEN 旭岳温泉
☎ 0166
This relatively small hot-springs resort consists of some 10 hotels and several houses surrounded by forest at the foot of **Asahidake**. The nearby cable car usually runs in two stages to a point within easy hiking distance of the peak, but it was closed for reconstruction at the time of writing. It was scheduled to reopen as early as July 2000. Though Asahidake Onsen is not yet overdeveloped, it can become quite crowded, especially given the unbeatably low bus fares (see Getting There & Away later in this section).

Hiking
There are dozens of hiking options in this region. Near the base of the Asahi-dake cable car, the Asahidake Visitors Centre (☎ *82-2111*) has great contour maps that the helpful staff will mark with the latest trail conditions (9 am to 5 pm, 10 am to 4 pm and closed Monday November to May). The most popular hike follows trails from the cable car via several peaks to **Sōunkyō Onsen** – allow seven to eight hours, plus 2½ hours if the cable car is not in operation.

HOKKAIDŌ

Take warm clothing, appropriate footwear and sufficient food and drink.

From the top station of the cable car, it takes 1½ hours to climb along a ridge overlooking steaming, volcanic vents to reach the peak of Asahi-dake. From there, it's a one-hour hike to the trail junction at Mamiya-dake for the northern and southern routes leading to Sōunkyō: the southern is more scenic, but the northern is usually recommended, as it has less snow and better trails.

For the northern route, turn left at the junction and hike over Mamiya-dake (2185m) and Naka-dake (2113m, two hours) to where the trail rejoins with the southern route at Kuro-dake Yamagoya (mountain hut). For the southern route, turn right at the original junction and continue via Hokkai-dake (2136m, 45 minutes) and **Kuro-dake Ishimuro** (another hour) until you come to Kuro-dake Yamagoya.

From the mountain hut, it's 30 minutes' walk to the peak of **Kuro-dake** (1984m), and then a steep descent (40 minutes) to the top station of the Sōunkyō Onsen chairlift. The lift takes 15 minutes to connect with a cable car that whisks you down to Sōunkyō Onsen in seven minutes.

There are rotemburo off the northern route at **Naka-dake Onsen**; branch left at Nakadake-bunki just before ascending Naka-dake. Do *not* enter Yudoku Onsen – it's poisonous.

From Asahidake Onsen there's also a 5.5km trail leading through the forest in about two hours to **Tenninkyō Onsen**, a small hot-springs resort with a scenic gorge and the beautiful **Hagoromo-no-taki** (Angels' Robe Waterfall).

Places to Stay

Daisetsuzan Shirakaba-sō (☎ 97-2246), the youth hostel at Asahidake Onsen, charges ¥2700 a person. It's a Canadian-style log cabin with a Japanese-style interior and both indoor and outdoor hot-springs baths (¥150). The hostel can provide advice on hiking, together with a compass and a jingle-bell (to keep the bears away). In winter, there's cross-country skiing. Those coming from Asahikawa by bus should get off at the Kyampu-jō-mae stop before Asahidake Onsen – the hostel is across the road from the camping ground.

Next door, *Lodge Nutapukaushipe* (☎ 97-2150) is another atmospheric place. Per-person rates with two meals cost ¥7000, and the lodge has a rotemburo. The owner speaks English and the meals are reputedly excellent. Both of these places are below the cable-car station on the road to Asahikawa.

Getting There & Away

It's hard to believe, but buses from Asahikawa to Tenninkyō Onsen and Asahidake Onsen are free. If you have a coupon from the place you stayed overnight, the ride back will also be free. This coupon is worth using as the one-way fare otherwise is ¥1320. Buses run twice a day (three times a day from mid-June to October). Buses leave from in front of Asahikawa station and take one hour to Tenninkyō Onsen, plus another 30 minutes to Asahidake Onsen. The last bus from Asahikawa is at 3.10 pm and the last bus leaves Asahidake Onsen at 5 pm.

This free service has its disadvantages. While it makes it cheap and easy for you to get to Asahidake Onsen, it also does so for everyone else. In summer and early autumn (when the leaves change colour) the place can be absolutely packed.

SŌUNKYŌ ONSEN 層雲峡温泉
☎ 01658

Sōunkyō is the tourist hub of the park and consists of the garish hot springs, as well as the gorge, Sōun-kyō. Because Sōunkyō Onsen is a gateway for hikes into the interior of the park, the gorge itself may be of only secondary interest to travellers. Although Sōunkyō Onsen once possessed a degree of charm, it has become an aggressive, overpriced resort and many travellers leave it disappointed; you may be better off starting your hikes at Asahidake Onsen.

The tourist information office (☎ 5-3350) next to the bus station has several maps and English-language pamphlets and can also help book accommodation (10 am to 5.30 pm). The booking service may be useful if you arrive at a time when almost everything

The charming street of Yōkaichi in Uchiko.

Waterwheel, Tsuru-no-yu, Northern Honshū

An outing to Kompira-san, Kotohira.

Recreated Jōmon-era dwellings at Sannai-Maruyama, Aomori-ken, Northern Honshū.

MASON FLORENCE

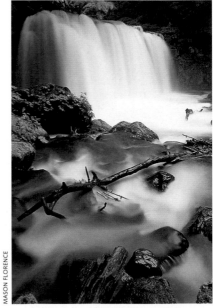

Koinobori flying – Yoshino-gawa gorge, Iya

'Pissing boy' statue – Iya-kei

Harvesting potatoes, Iya Valley

Remote vine bridge, Higashi Iya

Oirase-kyō, Aomori-ken, Northern Honshū

is full. After a hard day of cycling or hiking, **Kurodake-no-yu** offers brand-new hot-springs baths (including rotemburo) for ¥600 (10 am to 9 pm daily, reduced hours between November and April) and is on the town's one main street, at the bottom of the hill and close to the bus station.

Sōun-kyō 層雲峡

This rather tame gorge stretches for about 8km beyond Sōunkyō Onsen and is renowned for its waterfalls – Ryūsei-no-taki (Shooting Stars Falls) and Ginga-no-taki (Milky Way Falls) are the main ones – and for two sections of perpendicular rock columns that give an enclosed feeling – hence their names of Ōbako (Big Box) and Kobako (Little Box).

Since the view from the road is restricted by tunnels, a separate walking/cycling path has been constructed and local entrepreneurs derive a sizeable income from mountain-bike rental (¥2000/day). You could speed things up by taking a bus to Ōbako (¥350, 35 minutes, thrice daily) and walking back in a couple of hours. If you take only a quick look around at Ōbako, you can catch the same bus 30 minutes later on its return trip.

Hiking

The combination of a ropeway (cable car; ¥900/1650 one way/return) and a chairlift (¥400/600 one way/return) provides fast access to Kuro-dake for hikers and sightseers. Hours of operation vary with the season (6 am to 7 pm between June and August, usually closed intermittently in winter).

The most popular hike is the one to Asahi-dake from either Sōunkyō Onsen or Asahidake Onsen – see the section on Asahidake Onsen for details. You can arrange to leave your baggage at either end and pick it up later or simply restrict your baggage to the minimum required for an overnight stay. Better yet, take advantage of the coin lockers inside Asahikawa station before heading into the park. You could also do simple day hikes from the top of the Sōunkyō lift station to nearby peaks.

There is one bus a day from the youth hostel to the trailhead for **Aka-dake** (2078m) at

Ginsen-dai. The bus leaves Sōunkyō Onsen at 8.30 am and returns from Ginsen-dai at 4.30 pm (¥800, 50 minutes), leaving you plenty of time for your ascent and descent.

Special Events

On 24 and 25 July, Sōunkyō celebrates the Kyōkoku Hi Matsuri (Kyōkoku Fire Festival), one of Hokkaidō's big three festivals, to purify the hot springs and appease the mountain and fire deities. There are performances of traditional Ainu owl dances and drumming, the climax of which comes when archers shoot flaming arrows into the gorge.

Places to Stay

About a 10-minute walk uphill from the bus station and dwarfed by the Prince and Taisetsuzan Hotels is *Sōunkyō Youth Hostel* (☎ 5-3418), which charges ¥2800 a person. The hostel has information on trails in the park, organises hikes and rents out gear for braving the elements. It is closed from November to May.

Apart from the youth hostel, most of the accommodation options consist of expensive, ugly hotels. The tiny *Minshuku Midori* (☎ 5-3315) has spic-and-span rooms costing ¥6000 per person, including two meals. It's on the 2nd floor of a building across from the Ginsenkaku Hotel.

More upmarket and quite inviting is *Pension Milky House* (☎ 5-3517), which has per-person rates starting at ¥8500, including two meals. The pension is at the bottom of the hill across from the bus station.

Getting There & Away

Buses from Sōunkyō Onsen run approximately hourly via JR Kamikawa station to Asahikawa (¥1900, two hours). There are also up to four buses a day direct to Kitami (¥2500, two hours), where you can transfer to the JR Sekihoku main line for connections to Bihoro (¥530, 30 minutes) or Abashiri (¥1040, one hour). From May to October, there are up to three buses a day from Bihoro to Kawayu Onsen in Akan National Park (¥2690, two to 2¾ hours).

From Sōunkyō Onsen there are two buses a day to Kushiro (¥4790, five hours) via

Akan Kohan (¥3260, 3¼ hours) in Akan National Park. There are also two buses a day to Obihiro (¥2200, 2¼ hours) that follow a scenic route via Nukabira-ko.

Dō-tō (Eastern Hokkaidō)

ABASHIRI 網走

☎ 0152 • pop 43,000

Abashiri is a good transport hub for access to Shari and the peninsula, Shiretoko-hantō. It is primarily a harbour, though the harbour itself is closed each winter due to ice floes from Russia that arrive in late January or early February and continue to expand, until up to 80% of the sea is ice-clogged in March. During this time, the *Aurora* icebreaker sightseeing boats depart from Abashiri-kō port for cruises into the Sea of Okhotsk (¥3000, one hour, four to six times a day).

Information

The tourist information office (☎ 44-5849) outside Abashiri station is open from 8 am to 5 pm and has maps and discount coupons for local attractions.

Things to See

The Abashiri Prison Museum (¥1050, 8 am to 5 pm, 9 am to 4 pm from November to March) is actually a prison dating from the Meiji era and is best known for its radial five-winged design and for a popular Japanese TV series set there. It has long since been replaced by the maximum security facility nearby, so if it's live prisoners you're after, you're out of luck. It's halfway up Tento-zan, about 5km from the station.

On the top of Tento-zan, there's a lookout point and the Museum of Ice Floes, which you can safely skip. But don't miss the Museum of Northern Peoples, a short walk downhill from the lookout, which has fascinating exhibits and documentary videos on the culture of indigenous tribes of northern Eurasia and North America, including the Ainu and Sakhalin peoples (¥250, 9.30 am to 4.30 pm, closed Monday).

Special Events

On the last Saturday in July is Orochon-no-Hi, a fire festival derived from shamanistic ceremonial rites of the indigenous Gilyak people, who once lived in the Abashiri area.

Places to Stay – Budget

In the middle of a wildflower preserve is *Abashiri Gensei-kaen Youth Hostel* (☎ 46-2630), which charges ¥3050 a person. When the weather is good, it offers great views across the lake to Shari-dake and Shiretoko-hantō. The extra-friendly staff rent bicycles and advise on local outings. The hostel is 1km from Kitahama station, four stops east of Abashiri (¥230). Turn left outside the station, walk past the second stoplight and turn right at the 'Lake Toufutsu' sign, then follow the youth hostel signs. It is closed from mid-November to mid-January and during the last part of April.

Abashiri Ryūhyō-no-Oka Youth Hostel (☎ 43-8558) is in the northern part of the city and charges ¥3100 a person. To get there, take a bus bound for Futatsu-iwa and get off after eight minutes at Meiji-iriguchi; from there it's a 10-minute walk up the signposted dirt path. Bicycles are available for rent.

Places to Stay – Mid-Range

A member of the Toho network, *Minshuku Hokui 44* (☎ 44-4325) offers dormitory-style accommodation that's a bit cramped but costs only ¥4300, including two home-cooked meals and free admission (and a lift) to the nearby luxury onsen hotel. The inn is 20 minutes on foot west of the station, but if you phone ahead, a member of the family will pick you up. No English is spoken.

Opposite Abashiri station is *Hotel Shinbashi* (☎ 43-4307), a classy Japanese-style hotel with singles and twins at ¥6000 and ¥10,000, respectively.

Places to Eat

The snug *Remontai* (literally, 'lemon tea') is a five-minute walk down the main street to the right after you exit The handmade pizza (¥800 to ¥1000) is just OK but the atmosphere is friendly and it's a good place to meet Japanese travellers, as the owners advertise through the Toho network.

Getting There & Away

Memanbetsu airport links Abashiri with Sapporo, Fukuoka, Nagoya, Osaka and Tokyo. Airport buses are approximately timed to flights and run from the bus station via Abashiri station to the airport (¥750, 30 minutes).

Abashiri is the terminus for the JR Sekihoku main line, which runs across the centre of Hokkaidō to Asahikawa (tokkyū, ¥7240, 3¾ hours). Local trains along the same route stop at Bihoro (¥530, 30 minutes) and Kitami (¥1040, one hour). Between May and October, there are up to three buses a day from Bihoro to Kawayu Onsen in Akan National Park (¥2690, two to 2¾ hours). From Kitami you can catch buses to Sōunkyō Onsen in Daisetsuzan National Park (¥2500, two hours).

Abashiri is also the terminus for the JR Senmō main line, which runs east to Shiretoko-Shari station (futsū, ¥810, 45 minutes, infrequent) then turns south to Kushiro. There is one direct bus a day from Abashiri station to Shari (¥1120, 65 minutes), though there are four other buses a day bound for 18-sen that connect well with onward buses to Shari.

Direct buses from Abashiri to Sapporo leave from the bus terminal, a 10-minute bus ride east of Abashiri train station (¥6210, six hours). There is also one night bus to Sapporo departing at around 11 pm for the same price. Between June and mid-October there are three buses from Memanbetsu airport via Abashiri to Utoro Onsen in Shiretoko National Park (¥2800, 2¼ hours).

Renting a car is recommended if you really want to explore Shiretoko and Akan National Parks. Toyota Rent-a-Car is about 500m west of JR Abashiri train station down Route 238. Orix Rent-a-Car has an office at Memanbetsu airport. See the Hokkaidō Getting Around section for more details on car rental.

Getting Around

A convenient tourist loop bus (9 am to 4 pm, hourly) stops at the train station, the bus terminal and all the major sights on Tento-zan, as well as passing close to the Ryūhyō-no-Oka Youth Hostel. The one-day pass may be worth the ¥900, as it entitles you to discounted admission to many of the sights.

Bicycles can be rented at the youth hostels and near Abashiri station.

SHARI 斜里
☎ 01522

Unless you miss the last bus there's no reason to stay in this slightly run-down town, as accommodation in Shiretoko National Park is only an hour's ride away. Staff at the tourist information office (☎ 3-2424) outside Shiretoko-Shari station can provide maps and help book accommodation (10 am to 5 pm).

Places to Stay

Just a five-minute walk from the station is *Shari Youth Hostel* (☎ 3-2220), which charges ¥3000 a person. To find it, walk straight out from the station to the first intersection, turn left, left again at the next road and, after crossing the railway tracks, look for the hostel on the left. It's usually closed from January to April.

Shari Central Hotel (☎ 3-2355, ☎ 0120-801144 toll free) has well-maintained rooms for ¥6300 per person. The hotel is a few minutes down the street immediately to the right of the station. Around the corner, the attractive *Ryokan Tanakaya* (☎ 3-3165) charges ¥7000 per person, including two meals.

Getting There & Away

Infrequent trains on the JR Senmō main line connect Shiretoko-Shari station with Abashiri (futsū, ¥810, 45 minutes) and Kushiro (kaisoku, ¥2730, 2¼ hours). Shari's bus centre is to the left as you exit Shiretoko-Shari station. There are between seven and nine buses a day year round to Utoro (¥1490), but there are only three buses between late April and October that continue as far as Iwaobetsu (¥1770, 70 minutes).

UTORO ウトロ
☎ 01522

Utoro is the only town of any size on the northern side of Shiretoko-hantō and is the

HOKKAIDO

main gateway to Shiretoko National Park. The tourist information office in the front section of the bus centre can provide maps and timetables, as well as point out places to rent bicycles or motorcycles.

Two boat excursions operate from Utoro: one runs once a day out to the soaring cliffs of Shiretoko-misaki (¥6000, 3¾ hours, June to September) and the other runs up to five times a day for a short cruise along the coast as far as Kamuiwakka-no-taki (¥2700, 1½ hours, late April to late October). Short of hiking for several days, the longer boat cruise is the only way to catch a glimpse of the very tip of the peninsula. That said, your money might be better spent on bicycle rental or bus fares to more accessible attractions.

Places to Stay

There are minshuku aplenty along the main road through town. Opposite the bus station is *Minshuku Taiyō* (☎ 4-2939), which charges only ¥4000 a person, with two meals included. The owners say they haven't changed the price since they opened almost 20 years ago. Next door is *Minshuku Peleke* (☎ 4-2236), with more up-market rooms for ¥7500 a person, including two meals. Just down the street, on the same side as the bus station, is *Bon's Home* (☎ 4-2271), a member of the Toho network. Dormitory-style accommodation costs ¥3500 a person and scooters and mountain bikes can be rented. The inn is usually closed from November to January.

Getting There & Away

The Utoro bus station, sometimes referred to as Utoro Onsen, is the transport hub for the park, but services are infrequent. From late April to October buses run three times a day along the northern side of the peninsula, passing Shiretoko Nature Center, Iwaobetsu Youth Hostel, Shiretoko Go-ko (Shiretoko Five Lakes) and Kamuiwakka-no-taki before terminating at Shiretoko-ōhashi (¥1080, 50 minutes). The rest of the year buses run only as far as the nature centre. From mid-June to mid-October there are also buses twice a day to Rausu via the dramatic Shiretoko-Toge pass (¥1310, 55 minutes).

From 1 July to 30 September there are two buses a day between Utoro and Akan Kohan in Akan National Park, running via Shari, Kawayu Onsen, Mashū-ko observation point No 1 and Teshikaga (¥5400, four hours).

SHIRETOKO-HANTŌ
知床国立公園

Shiretoko National Park (386 sq km) covers almost the whole of this remote peninsula, with its range of volcanic peaks leading out to the rugged cliffs around Shiretoko-misaki. The area has seen little development and remains one of the most pristine wilderness areas in Japan. The main season for visitors is from mid-June to mid-September, and most of the peninsula's many hikes are not recommended outside this season. Roads run along each side of the peninsula, but they peter out well before the tip. Another road crosses the peninsula from Utoro to Rausu. Renting a car in Abashiri is a good idea if you really want to explore the

SHIRETOKO-HANTŌ

area, possibly in combination with Akan National Park.

About 5km outside Utoro is **Shiretoko Nature Center** (8 am to 5.40 pm, 9 am to 4 pm mid-October to mid-April), where you can pick up hiking maps and watch a 20-minute slide show about the peninsula (¥500), which may be a worthwhile substitute if the weather outside is foul.

Bus services from Utoro pass the nature centre and Iwaobetsu Youth Hostel before reaching **Shiretoko Go-ko**, where wooden walkways have been laid out for visitors to stroll around the five lakes in an hour or so. The trails are sometimes closed due to bear sightings.

After travelling for another 30 minutes by bus down the dirt road towards the tip of the peninsula, you come to the spectacular rotemburo that form part of **Kamuiwakka-no-taki**. It takes about 30 minutes to climb up through the warm waterfalls to cascades of hot water emptying into a succession of pools. (Rubber-soled sandals or deck shoes are highly recommended for this hike.) Bathers simply strip off (although many bring bathing suits), soak in the pools and enjoy the superb panorama across the ocean. Near the trailhead are a few entrepreneurs who do a brilliant business renting out straw sandals at ¥500 a pop – you'll find it's worth every yen if you haven't brought adequate footwear.

Hiking

There are several hikes on the peninsula, and Iwaobetsu Youth Hostel can provide more detailed advice on routes, trail conditions and organising transport. Proper footwear and warm clothes are essential. Avoid all contact with the peninsula's foxes because they carry the parasite Echinococcosis.

A road almost opposite the youth hostel leads 4km uphill to Iwaobetsu Onsen, which lies at the start of a trail up **Rausu-dake** (1660m). There's only one bus a day, there and back, but the youth hostel may be able to give you a lift to the trailhead; allow four hours from there to reach the top at a comfortable pace. For an alternative approach to the mountain, see Rausu later in this section.

There is also a much shorter hike to Rausu-ko, near **Shiretoko-Toge** pass. The trailhead is several kilometres south of the pass, on the way to Rausu. The hike takes about four hours there and back and takes you through virtually untouched wilderness. Buses between Utoro and Rausu run via the pass, which on clear days offers great views of the mountains and Kunashiri-tō, the closest of Japan's 'northern territories', currently still in Russian hands.

Iwaobetsu 岩尾別
☎ 01522

Iwaobetsu is a hamlet 8km farther up the coast from Utoro, and *Shiretoko Iwaobetsu Youth Hostel* (☎ 4-2311), which charges ¥2900 a person, deserves recommendation as a friendly and convenient base for exploring the peninsula. The hostel runs 'briefing' sessions to outline hikes and rents out mountain bikes, albeit at budget-blowing rates. It is usually closed from late October to April. (It opens in February and March, but only for those who have signed up for special three-day winter hiking tours, costing ¥20,000.) Buses from Utoro to Shiretoko-ōhashi and Rausu both pass the

HOKKAIDŌ

hostel. If you've missed the bus from Utoro, you'll probably have to hitch; it's only 9km.

Nearby, at the trailhead for Rausu-dake, is *Kinoshita-goya* (☎ 4-2824), a cheery mountain hut that offers extremely basic but clean accommodation for ¥1500 a night. It's open only from June to September and it would be best to book ahead.

RAUSU 羅臼
☎ 01538
This is a small fishing village that once grew wealthy on herring fishing, though there's not much reason to come here unless you're planning to hike around the peninsula or take an alternative approach to Rausu-dake. A challenging but well-marked trailhead for Rausu-dake starts a few kilometres outside town towards Shiretoko-Toge, near the camping ground (free) at Kuma-no-yu Onsen.

Only genuinely experienced hikers should consider hiking up the eastern side of the peninsula to Shiretoko-misaki, which will take one to three days. Weather permitting, you could then hire a local fishing boat for a ride back to the start of the trail at *Rider House Kuma-no-yado* at the end of Route 87, 24km outside of Rausu. Be warned: this hike is *extremely* difficult, as the eroded trail sometimes crawls along steep cliffs or over slippery boulders. If you get hurt, there is no one to help until a fishing boat happens by. In some parts, swimming is often a preferable shortcut, but watch out for jellyfish. One traveller wrote:

I ended up walking on my hands and in push-up fashion letting my feet rest on the few inches of trail that were available, sometimes pushing them against the wall when the path disappeared. I suppose I looked somewhat like a crab inching its way along the shore...

Steve Maki

If you go, take plenty of food and water, as well as hiking boots with good ankle support, and keep an eye out for bears.

Places to Stay
Rausu Youth Hostel (☎ 7-2145), which charges ¥2400 a person, only gets a one-star rating from the Japan Youth Hostel Association, so don't expect much. Turn left out of the bus station and walk down the main street for about 10 minutes until you reach the convenience store, then turn right and cross a red bridge. The hostel is about 200m farther along on the left-hand side. Before the hostel is *Takashimaya Ryokan* (☎ 7-2191), which has per-person rates of ¥6500, including two meals.

From mid-June to mid-October, there are two buses a day between Utoro and Rausu via Shiretoko-Toge (¥1310, 55 minutes). From Rausu, buses run four times a day year round to Kushiro (¥4740, 3½ hours).

AKAN NATIONAL PARK 阿寒国立公園
This large park (905 sq km) in eastern Hokkaidō contains several volcanic peaks, some large caldera lakes and extensive forests. The gorgeous scenery attracts some 6.6 million visitors a year, but in late spring and early autumn the crowds really thin out, giving you ample opportunity to actually commune with nature rather than tour groups. There aren't many extended hikes, but there are several interesting day-hike options.

The main gateways on the fringe of the park are Abashiri and Bihoro in the north and Kushiro in the south. The major centres inside the park are the towns of Kawayu Onsen and Akan Kohan. The small town of Teshikaga (Mashū Onsen) lies outside the park proper, but is a useful transport hub.

The only efficient and speedy transport in the park is provided by Akan Bus Company sightseeing buses. The running recorded commentary gets a bit tiresome, but the ride brings you past all the major sights and through beautiful scenery – on clear days there are outstanding views of the park's mountains and lakes. Abashiri would be a convenient place to rent a car, giving you the option of adding a side trip to Shiretoko National Park as well.

KAWAYU ONSEN 川湯温泉
☎ 01548
This pleasant little hot-springs resort is a convenient base for visiting the nearby sights of Kussharo-ko, Iō-zan and Mashū-

ko. The town itself is centred on a small park and bordered on all sides by forest. Even the pint-sized bus station sits amidst a grove of trees.

There's a tourist information office (☎ 3-2670) about 10 minutes on foot down the main street from the bus station past the bubbling pools (9 am to 6.30 pm). Staff have maps of the town and the area around Kussharo-ko and Mashū-ko. They can help book accommodation but sometimes charge a large fee for doing so.

The Kawayu Eco Museum Centre (☎ 3-4100) is a five-minute walk through the park from the bus station. English-language pamphlets with basic information on the park, as well as more detailed hiking and nature guides in Japanese, are available (8 am to 5 pm, 9 am to 4 pm from November to April).

Things to See

Just outside Kawayu Onsen is Iō-zan (512m), which is unmistakable for its distinctive smell and impressive hissing vents, billowing clouds of steam and bright yellow sulphur deposits. A beautiful nature trail leads from behind the bus station for 2.5km through dwarf pines to the mountain in about 50 minutes.

Mashū-ko is about 15km south-east of Kawayu Onsen. The small isle (it's actually a lava hill rising from the lake bottom) in the centre of the lake is known to the Ainu as the Isle of the Gods, and there is certainly an unusual atmosphere to the whole lake, which is surrounded by steep rock walls that reach a height of 300m. If you are fortunate enough to visit when the lake is not wreathed in mist, the clarity of the water and its intense blue colour is quite startling – its transparency depth of over 35m was once a world record. Visitors view the lake from observation point Nos 1 and 3 (No 2 was eliminated during construction of the road now linking points 1 and 3). From observation point No 1 you can hike to Mashū-dake (857m), the craggy volcanic peak that lords over the eastern shore of the lake. Allow two hours or more for the ascent. One traveller reports that the footing is

now good all the way except for the very summit, but walk with care.

About 3km from Kawayu Onsen is Kussharo-ko, the largest inland lake in Hokkaidō and a deservedly popular, yet laid-back, spot for swimming and camping. This gorgeous lake even has its own resident Loch Ness monster, 'Kusshie'. At Suna-yu Onsen, on the eastern shore, a few small hot springs warm the sand on the beach, while at Wakoto Onsen, on the southern shore, there are hot springs bubbling into open-air pools. On the south-eastern side of the lake at Kussharo Kotan you'll find a small Museum of Ainu Folklore in an eccentric-looking concrete building with an Ainu hut sitting outside (¥310, 9 am to 5 pm, mid-April to October).

Next to the bus station, sumō fanatics can stop in at the tiny Koki Taiho Sumō Memorial Hall, dedicated to hometown hero and 48th sumō grand champion Koki Taiho (¥300, 9 am to 5 pm, extended hours during summer).

If you have the time, a bicycle is a good way to see some of the closer sights such as Iō-zan and Kussharo-ko. Mashū-ko observation point No 1 is a 15km ride from Kawayu Onsen, but be forewarned that it's a pretty steep climb. You can rent bicycles at the bus station.

Places to Stay – Budget

There are seven camping grounds in the area, and one of the nicest is Wakoto-hantō Kohan Camping Ground on the southern shore of Kussharo-ko. It's open from May to September and costs ¥300 per person. There are also extremely basic cabins, canoes and kayaks available for rent. Buses between Mashū station and Wakoto-hantō stop here, as do some buses from Bihoro and Kawayu Onsen.

There are two youth hostels in the area, though none in Kawayu Onsen itself. The luxurious four-star Mashū-ko Youth Hostel (☎ 2-3098) charges ¥3000 and is about 5.5km south of Mashū-ko. From Mashū station at Teshikaga, two stops south of Kawayu Onsen, take a bus bound for Bihoro or Kawayu and get off after 10 minutes at

HOKKAIDŌ

the Yūsu-hosuteru-mae stop. If you arrive at Mashū station after 4 pm, ring the hostel for a lift. The hostel organises free night hikes around the lake, as well as providing information on other outdoor pursuits, including canoeing, dairy-farm 'school' and cross-country skiing.

Kussharo-Genya Youth Guesthouse (☎ 4-2609) is a bit fancier than your average hostel, with commensurate rates (from ¥3500 a night). The guesthouse is usually closed for a time during November, December and April. It's located south of Kussharo-ko, off Route 243, and you can rent bicycles to cycle around the lake. Buses between Mashū station and Wakoto-hantō pass the turn-off for the hostel, but the staff will come and pick you up at the station if you phone ahead.

Places to Stay – Mid-Range
If you're arriving on a late train, ***Sanzoku-no-Ie*** (☎ 3-2725) is a member of the Toho network and conveniently located five minutes on foot from Kawayu Onsen station. The inn is open only from April to October, however. Per-person rates are ¥4500, including two meals.

There are numerous hotels and minshuku in Kawayu Onsen itself and rates may vary with the season. One of the cheapest places is ***Minshuku Nire*** (☎ 3-2506), which charges ¥5500 a person, including two meals. From the bus station, turn right and walk for a minute or two until you reach an intersection at the edge of town, just before the road signs for Iō-zan and Mashū-ko. The minshuku is down a driveway to the left, in the shadow of the glaring green-and-white Kozan-sō Hotel.

In Nibushi Onsen, 4km from Kawayu Onsen and on the shore of Kussharo-ko, is ***Onsen Minshuku Nibushi-no-Sato*** (☎ 3-2294), a casual place with a log-cabin feel. The laid-back owner will pick you up at the Kawayu Onsen bus station. You can rent mountain bikes to get around on your own. Per-person rates with two meals start at around ¥7000. There's also a nice indoor hot-springs bath with a view of the lake.

The Trout Inn ('Masuya' in Japanese, ☎ 2-5489) is in a nice wooden building set back from the road off Route 243, outside Teshikaga on the way to Kussharo-ko. The inn is a member of the Toho network, and dormitory-style accommodation here including two meals costs ¥5500 per person. You can go canoeing in summer and snowshoeing and cross-country skiing in winter. If you call ahead, staff will come to pick you up at Mashū station. Buses between Mashū station and Wakoto-hantō also pass nearby; get off at the Sattomonai bus stop.

Places to Eat
Next door to the Museum of Ainu Folklore in Kussharo Kota is ***Marukipune*** restaurant (☎ 4-2644), where delicious *kotan-don* (pork, egg and vegetables over rice) or *howaitu rāmen* (noodles in milk broth) cost ¥1000. Live performances of traditional and contemporary Ainu music are occasionally given in the evenings; tickets cost ¥3600 and reservations are advised.

Next door to the Mashū-ko Youth Hostel, ***The Great Bear*** restaurant serves fresh farm meals that are highly recommended.

Getting There & Away
The JR Senmō main line runs north from Kawayu Onsen station to Shiretoko-Shari (kaisoku, ¥1230, 45 minutes) and south to Kushiro (kaisoku, ¥1410, 1½ hours). The bus station in the town of Kawayu Onsen proper is actually a 10-minute ride from Kawayu Onsen station (¥280, last at 6 pm). Bus departures are timed to meet most trains, but you'll only have a minute or two to transfer.

From Kawayu Onsen bus station there are up to three buses a day to Bihoro (¥2690, two to 2¾ hours) and two buses a day to Kushiro (¥2810, 2½ hours). The Bihoro service runs via scenic Bihoro pass and only operates from May to October; some of these buses continue as far as Memanbestu airport. These buses also pass Nibushi, Sunayu and Wakoto Onsen en route.

Between May and October a sightseeing bus service operates four times a day from Kawayu Onsen bus station via the main sights in the park to Akan Kohan (¥3250, 2¼ hours). The bus makes stops of around 20 minutes each at Iō-zan and Mashū-ko observation point No 1. You can get off the bus at observation point No 3 after about 40 minutes (¥920), but then you'll have to wait for the next bus to continue onward. Between May and September there are also up to three buses before noon to observation point No 1 from Mashū station (¥730, 25 minutes). Both services run past the stop for Mashū-ko Youth Hostel, which is south of the lake on the road to Teshikaga.

If you're heading to Kawayu Onsen from Mashū station, you'll have to change buses at observation point No 1; the total cost is ¥1720. Direct buses between Mashū station and Wakoto-hantō pass the turn-offs for the Trout Inn, Kussharo-Genya Youth Guesthouse and the camping ground at Wakoto-hantō (¥880, 35 minutes).

TESHIKAGA 弟子屈 (MASHŪ ONSEN)

Teshikaga (also known as Mashū Onsen) is the midpoint of the sightseeing bus route between Kawayu Onsen and Akan Kohan. It's also on the JR Senmō main line; the station name is Mashū. There is a small tourist information office (☎ 2-2642) at the station.

Teshikaga lies just outside the park and although it's a convenient transport hub, there's no reason to stay here unless it's the first weekend in September, when the town hosts the **Women's Sumō National Championship** (Onna-zumō Senshuken Taikai). The grand prize is an aeroplane ticket and a horse, for which, according to the rules, contestants must bring their own pick-up truck. In case you're wondering, the contestants do not wear loincloths – white T-shirts and denim shorts are the usual uniform.

You can catch buses from Mashū station to Mashū-ko observation point No 1. This station is also the best place to get off if you're headed to either of the youth hostels, the Trout Inn or Wakoto-hantō (see the Kawayu Onsen Getting There & Away section earlier).

Between Akan-ko and Teshikaga is a particularly scenic stretch on Route 241, with an outstanding lookout at **Sokodai** that overlooks the lakes Penketō and Panketō.

AKAN KOHAN 阿寒湖畔
☎ 0154

Akan Kohan is one of the largest Ainu kotan settlements on Hokkaidō. Unlike Kawayu Onsen, this hot-springs resort on the edge of **Akan-ko** has done little to try and blend in with its surroundings. You can safely skip the boat trips (¥1120) on the lake out to the Marimo Exhibition and Observation Centre. The small **Ainu Seiwa Kinenkan** – basically a hut with a few Ainu items inside – is not worth the price of admission (¥300) if you've already visited Ainu museums elsewhere. However the nearby **Akan Forest & Lake Culture Museum** has better displays of traditional Ainu ways and area wildlife, and the congenial owner is usually on hand to explain the exhibits, run the slide show and offer you a cup of coffee (¥500, 10 am to 5 pm May to October).

On the eastern side of town is the tourism information office (☎ 67-3200), where you can pick up English-language pamphlets about the park, including excellent alpine trail guides with contour maps of O-Akan-dake and Me Akan-dake (9 am to 5 pm).

Farther east, at the edge of town, is the national park's **Akan Kohan Visitors Centre** (☎ 67-2785), which has hiking maps and exhibits on area flora and fauna (9 am to 5 pm, later during summer). The centre also has tanks where you can come face to face with *marimo*, a globe-shaped algae peculiar to the lake. These green fuzzballs can take 200 years to grow to the size of a baseball. Ironically, the algae became endangered only after they were declared a National Treasure because tourists began to steal them as souvenirs. In response, the local Ainu community started the **Marimo Matsuri**, still held on 10 October and led by an Ainu elder who ceremonially returns marimo to the lake, one by one.

Behind the centre is a scenic nature trail through the woods to **Bokke** (a collection of spluttering mud holes beside the lake) and then returns via the lake shore to town.

Hiking
About 6km north of **Akan Kohan** is O-Akan-dake (Male Mountain, 1371m).

Buses to Kushiro pass the Takiguchi trail entrance five minutes out of Akan Kohan. The ascent takes a fairly arduous 3½ hours and the descent about 2½. From the peak there are fine views of the lakes Penketō and Panketō, and in summer the top is covered with alpine wildflowers. On clear days one can see as far as Daisetsuzan National Park.

Me-Akan-dake (Female Mountain, 1499m) is the highest mountain in the park and an active volcano, but was closed to hikers at the time of writing. Ask at the tourist information office in Akan Kohan about current conditions. If you do climb this peak, watch out for the noxious effects of the sulphur fumes from the vents.

For an excellent short hike, try the climb up to the observation platform on Hakutō-zan (650m), where you get fine views of the lake and the surrounding peaks. The trail starts at the Akan Kohan skiing ground, about 2km south of town. The ascent from the ski ground takes about an hour, winding through birch and fir forests and past several groups of bubbling sulphur hot springs.

Places to Stay – Budget

A 12-minute walk from the bus station at Akan Kohan is *Akan Angel Youth Hostel* (☎ 67-2309), which charges ¥2850 a person. The owner can provide advice on area hikes and often takes groups himself. Bicycle rental is also available.

Nonaka Onsen Youth Hostel (☎ 01562-9-7454) charges ¥2850 a person. It's about 20km south-west of Akan-ko, in a beautiful setting, and provides a base for climbing Me-Akan-dake. From July to October, buses from Akan Kohan bound for Lake Onnetō reach Nonaka Onsen in about 25 minutes (¥970, three a day), but from there you'll have to arrange your own transport. The hostel is often fully booked and closes for a time around November, so phone ahead.

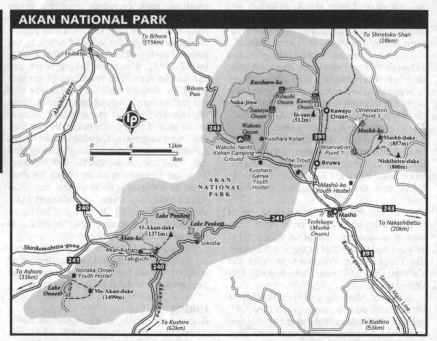

AKAN NATIONAL PARK

Places to Stay – Mid-Range

There are around a dozen minshuku in Akan Kohan. Two of the very best places to stay are on the western side of town. *Minshuku Kiri* (☎ 67-2755) is an attractive place with per-person costs of ¥5500, including two meals. It's opposite the Akan Grand Hotel on the road that runs alongside the lake: look for the woodblock-print style sign. A bit farther down the road, on the opposite side of the street, is *Yamaguchi* (☎ 67-2555), which charges the same rates and has clean rooms, friendly staff and hot-springs baths.

Places to Stay – Top End

Akan Kohan has numerous upmarket resort hotels. Per-person rates with two meals start at ¥10,000 on weekdays in summer, plus ¥2000 more on weekends, but drop to as low as ¥7000 during winter. Among the best choices in this category are the *New Akan Hotel* (☎ 67-2121) and the *Hotel Akanko-sō* (☎ 67-2231).

Getting There & Away

See the Kawayu Onsen Getting There & Away section for details of the park sightseeing bus service. From Akan Kohan bus centre there are several buses a day to Kitami (¥1830, 1½ hours) and a few afternoon departures for Bihoro (¥2160, 70 minutes); both are on the JR Sekihoku main line to Abashiri for access to Shiretoko National Park. From July to September there are also two buses a day to Utoro on Shiretoko-hantō (¥5400, four hours). Buses to Asahikawa run via Sōunkyō Onsen in Daisetsuzan National Park (¥4580, five hours). There are also up to five buses a day to Kushiro (¥2650, 2¼ hours).

KUSHIRO 釧路

☎ 0154 • pop 195,000

Kushiro is the industrial and economic centre of eastern Hokkaidō and one of the main gateways to Akan National Park. It is also a convenient port for ferry connections to Hirō near Erimo-misaki, and Tokyo.

Information

There is a tourist information counter in Kushiro station (☎ 22-8294) that can supply you with information on the national parks and maps detailing the sparse offering of sights in the city itself (9 am to 5.30 pm). An adjacent counter can help book accommodation, though an overnight stay in Kushiro is best avoided.

Things to See

If you have time to spare, you might want to visit **Kushiro Shitsugen National Park** (also referred to as Kushiro Marshlands Park), a swampy area famed for its flora and increasing numbers of protected *tanchō-zuru* (red-crested white cranes), traditional symbols of Japan and longevity. From the Kushiro Marsh Observatory, wooden walkways thread their way for several kilometres through the reeds and your best chance of observing the over 600 resident birds is during winter. Frequent buses from in front of the Akan bus station (next to Kushiro station) run to the observatory in 35 minutes (¥1320 return). Between late April and late October there are also several early morning or late afternoon tour buses that do a circuit of all the park observation stations (¥2340 to ¥2700, 4½ to 6½ hours). During the same period, special 'safariesque' JR trains with large observation windows run two or three times a day into the park as far as Tōro station.

Places to Stay – Budget

Recommended by many travellers is *Kushiro Shitsugen Tōro Youth Hostel* (☎ 01 548-7-2510), which charges ¥3150 a person. It's on the eastern edge of the park, convenient to a few of the observation stations. From Kushiro, take the JR Senmō main line north to Tōro station (futsū, ¥530, 30 minutes), a two minute walk from the hostel.

In Kushiro, *Yasumi-zaka* (☎ 41-5503) is a member of the Toho network and doubles as a curry shop during the day. Nightly rates are ¥3360 for dormitory-style accommodation, ¥500 more for breakfast. From Kushiro station, take city bus No 1 to the Yasumi-zaka stop; the inn is a 10-minute walk uphill in the vicinity of a shrine. Pick-up service from the station may be available if you phone ahead. From MOO bus station, the inn is a 20-minute walk across the bridge and east of the traffic roundabout.

Places to Stay – Mid-Range
Opposite the station, the inviting *Eki-mae Hotel Adachi (☎ 22-3111)* has singles and twins starting at ¥5500 and ¥9500 respectively. The best part of this place is the small coffee shop next door that resembles an old-time movie theatre.

Places to Eat
At the *Eigakan*, next door to the Eki-mae Hotel Adachi, meals after 5 pm are buffet style. A beer and a good helping of various tasty dishes should start at around ¥2000.

If you have the time to wander over to the river, the fisherman's wharf complex (which bears the perplexing moniker of MOO, with an arboretum next door called EGG) is a popular place to get a bite to eat or have a drink. You could drown your sorrows over being stranded in Kushiro in the nearby Suehiro entertainment district, where there are a few international restaurants and gaijin-friendly bars.

Getting There & Away
Flights connect Kushiro with Sapporo's Okadama airport (¥14,250, 55 minutes) and Tokyo (¥28,550, 1¾ hours). Kushiro airport is 50 minutes by bus from Kushiro station (¥910).

The JR Senmō main line runs north from Kushiro through Akan National Park to Shiretoko-Shari station (kaisoku, ¥2730, 2¼ hours). Trains on the JR Nemuro main line head west via Ikeda and Obihiro to Sapporo (tokkyū, ¥8610, 3½ to 4½ hours). Local trains take 2¼ hours to Ikeda (¥2100) and three hours to Obihiro (¥2420).

A sleeper service departs Kushiro at 11 pm, arriving around 6 am in Sapporo; the cheapest berth costs ¥14,910, or ¥8820 with a Japan Rail Pass. Nite-&-Day tickets on this route cost only ¥18,280.

Buses leave from bus stations outside Kushiro train station and at the fisherman's wharf MOO complex. There are a few buses a day to Akan Kohan (¥2640, 2¼ hours), Kawayu Onsen (¥2810, two hours), Obihiro

(¥2240, 2½ hours) and Asahikawa via Sōunkyō Onsen (¥9680, 6¼ hours). Between mid-June and mid-October, there are up to four buses a day to Rausu on Shiretoko-hantō (¥4740, 3½ hours). Buses to Sapporo's Sogo terminal leave three times a day (¥5610, 6¼ hours). In the opposite direction, buses depart Sapporo from the Chūō bus station. There is also a night bus that leaves only from MOO bus station around 11.30 pm, arriving in Sapporo at 6 am.

Kinkai Yūsen ferries depart just about every second day for Tokyo (¥14,700, 41½ hours). Ferries to Tokyo (but not in the opposite direction) also stop at Tokachi-kō in Hirō (¥1500, 3¾ hours), where you can connect with buses to Erimo-misaki.

Getting Around
The 'Kururin' free bus (actually, it's a sprightly trolley) makes a loop around town from the train station to MOO bus station and back every 30 minutes from 10 am to 7 pm.

The ferry terminal is a 15-minute bus ride west of Kushiro station (¥400). Buses run from the Akan bus station to Nishi-kō at around noon on days when there are ferry departures or arrivals. Alternatively, the ferry terminal is just over 500m south of Shin-Fuji station, one stop west of Kushiro station.

Tokachi 十勝

OBIHIRO 帯広
☎ 0155 • pop 174,000
Obihiro is the central city of the Tokachi plain, squeezed between the Hidaka and Daisetsuzan mountain ranges. Although historically an Ainu stronghold, the modern city was founded in 1883 by the Banseisha, a group of 'land reclaimers' (colonial settlers) from Shizuoka. For travellers, Obihiro is the south-eastern back door to Daisetsuzan National Park, but you may also find yourself passing through en route to Ikeda or Erimo-misaki.

Information
There is a small tourist information counter (☎ 23-6403) inside Obihiro station (10 am

to 6 pm). More comprehensive information on Obihiro and the surrounding areas can be found at the Tokachi Plaza Information Centre (☎ 22-8511) behind the station, next to Nagasakiya department store (8.45 am to 8 pm). Be sure to pick up a copy of *What's Happening in Obihiro?*, a monthly newsletter listing local events including not-to-be-missed performances by **Kamuy-to Upopo**, an Ainu cultural preservation association. The group of traditional dancers, officially designated as an Important Intangible Living National Treasure, is led by elder Ainu women who can still chant the Ainu epics from memory.

Places to Stay & Eat

Obihiro has no shortage of reasonably priced accommodation. The *Hotel Musashi* (☎ 25-1181) has special weekend rates for singles and twins of ¥4000 and ¥8000, respectively (slightly more during the week).

Toipirka Youth Hostel (☎ 30-4165) is outside town towards Tokachigawa Onsen and charges ¥3200 a person. Buses from Obihiro station pass the Shimoshihoro-shō-gakkō-mae stop (¥470, 20 minutes, last at 7.30 pm). From there it's a 12-minute walk to the hostel, but if you phone ahead the staff will pick you up at the bus stop.

Obihiro's speciality is *buta-donburi*, delicious barbecued pork on rice. Across the street from the station at *Panchō*, it's the only thing on the menu – the smallest *matsu* (pine) set costs ¥850.

Getting There & Away

Flights connect Obihiro with Tokyo, Fukushima and Nagoya. Buses from in front of Obihiro station are timed to meet flights (¥1000, 40 minutes).

Tokkyū trains on the JR Sekishō main line run west from Obihiro to New Chitose airport (¥5390, 1¾ hours) and Sapporo (¥6510, 2¼ hours). R-Kippu to Sapporo cost ¥11,940. The JR Nemuro main line runs east to Ikeda (kaisoku, ¥440, 30 minutes) and Kushiro (tokkyū, ¥3690, 1½ hours).

From in front of the station, long-distance buses depart a few times a day for Sapporo (¥3670, 4½ hours), Kushiro's MOO bus

station (¥2240, 2½ hours) and Asahikawa (¥3150, 3¾ hours). Buses to Asahikawa run along two different routes through Daisetsuzan National Park, conveniently passing either Furano/Biei or Sōunkyō Onsen. Local buses to Ikeda take about an hour (¥590).

IKEDA 池田
☎ 01557

In the eastern part of the Tokachi plain, Ikeda is a small farming town that became famous when the municipal government began making wine there. It's a pleasant place to spend a lazy afternoon walking the fields and back roads. Town maps are available at the small tourist information desk inside JR Ikeda station. In front of the station are two bizarre works of art: an overflowing wine glass fountain and a huge revolving silver corkscrew.

The **City Winery**, also known as the *wain-jō* (wine castle), is on a hillside overlooking the town. Gala wine festivals take place here on the second Sunday in May and the first Sunday of October. After observing the production process and partaking of free tastings, it's a pleasant walk beside wheat fields and vineyards to **Happiness Dairy** where you can try fresh cheese or home-made gelato. On the way back to town, you could detour to **Moon Face Gallery & Café**, which displays works by local artists, or swing by the wool weaving workshop at **Spinner's Farm** (closed Monday).

If you're looking for accommodation, *Ikeda Kita-no-kotan Youth Hostel* (☎ 2-3666), which charges ¥2900 a person, is also a member of the Toho network and a real treat – friendly management and excellent dinners (¥1000, including wine). Bicycles can be rented. The hostel is five minutes on foot from Toshibetsu station, one stop west of Ikeda.

On the JR Nemuro main line, Ikeda is 30 minutes by local train from Obihiro (¥440). There are also frequent buses between Ikeda and Obihiro (¥590, 55 minutes). On the privately owned Furusato-Ginga line, there are four trains a day to Kitami (¥3100,

HOKKAIDŌ

2¼ to three hours), from where you can catch buses to Sōunkyō Onsen in Daisetsuzan National Park or take the JR Sekihoku main line east to Bihoro and Abashiri.

ERIMO-MISAKI えりも岬
☎ 01466

With its windswept cliffs and dramatic ocean views, Erimo-misaki is worth the trouble of visiting. Fifty years ago the entire cape was severely deforested – it was nicknamed 'Erimo Desert' – but the hills surrounding the area have since been replanted with Japanese black pines.

At the cape there is a lighthouse and a wind museum, Kaze-no-kan, where for ¥500 you can enjoy being blasted by gale-force winds inside a simulated wind tunnel. In the early mornings, a colony of Kuril seals lounges on the rocks below, while local fishing boats harvest kelp. These seals are called *zenigata-azarashi*, meaning 'money-shaped', because of the way the white spots on the seals' black bodies appear like old Japanese coins.

Erimo Misaki Youth Hostel (☎ 3-1144) is a rustic place charging ¥4350, including two home-cooked seafood meals. Buses from Hirō to Erimo-misaki pass the Shōgakkō-mae stop right in front of the hostel. From the hostel you can walk to the cape in 20 minutes, where you'll find *Misaki-sō* (☎ 3-1316), a homely minshuku with per-person rates ranging from ¥6000 to ¥8000, including two meals. There is also a camping ground (open May to November) on the beach at Hyakunin-hama, 8km north-east of the cape; buses to Hirō pass nearby.

From Obihiro, there are fairly frequent buses to Hirō (¥1830, two hours) but only about two a day from Hirō to Erimo-misaki (¥1510, one hour). Ferries from Kushiro stop at Hirō's Tokachi-kō port (¥1490, 3¾ hours) before continuing to Tokyo.

Buses run more frequently from Erimo-misaki to Samani (¥1300, 50 minutes), which is on the JR Hidaka main line. You may have to wait at Samani quite a while, however, for the next local train to Tomakomai (¥2730, three hours).

Shikoku

In Japan's feudal past, the island of Shikoku was divided into four regions ('shi' literally means four, while 'koku' means region) which today exist as four prefectures, or *ken*, (Kagawa, Tokushima, Kōchi and Ehime). Although Shikoku is Japan's fourth largest island, it's predominantly rural and remains well off the standard tourist track. The population stands at 4,200,000.

In addition to the four castles (Kōchi, Marugame, Matsuyama and Uwajima) that managed to survive both the Meiji Restoration and WWII, there are countless attractions, both natural and otherwise, which make Shikoku a worthwhile excursion.

Suggested Itineraries

Most travellers approach Shikoku from Honshū, particularly the Kansai area. One popular route involves arriving in Takamatsu or Tokushima, winding down through the Iya Valley, heading south to Kōchi, then around to the cape, Ashizuri misaki, and up the coast toward Matsuyama. Others prefer to remain on the coast, while some adventurous souls travel as pilgrims along Shikoku's famed 88 Temple Circuit.

For more leads on setting your itinerary, there are links to all four of Shikoku's prefectural home pages on the extensive Japan National Tourist Organization (JNTO) Web site at www.jnto.go.jp.

Getting There & Away

There are three bridges linking Shikoku with Honshū. The Seto-ōhashi connects Okayama to Sakaide, which is west of Takamatsu. The Akashi Kaikyo-ōhashi is west of Kōbe and leads to Tokushima (via Awaji-shima). Finally, the new Kurushima Kaikyo-ōhashi island-hops along the Shimanami Highway (Shimanami-kaido) from Onomichi in Hiroshima-ken to Imabari in Ehime-ken.

Air services connect major cities in Shikoku with Tokyo, Osaka and other centres on Honshū.

- Make the hike up Shikoku's most sacred mountains, Tsurugi-san and Ishizuchi-san.

- Explore the deep gorges, abundant nature and vine suspension bridges in Tokushima-ken's secluded Iya Valley.

- Stroll through Takamatsu's exquisite garden, Ritsurin-kōen, or take in the spectacular views from Yashima plateau.

- Trek up the 800-odd granite steps to pay homage at the sacred shrine Kompira-san in Kotohira.

- Soak your bones in the ancient hot springs at Matsuyama's famed Dōgo Onsen.

- Stroll down the well preserved Edo-era street Yokaichi in picturesque Uchiko.

Numerous ferries ply the waters of the Inland Sea (Seto-nai-kai), linking points on Shikoku with neighbouring islands and ports on the San-yō coast of Honshū.

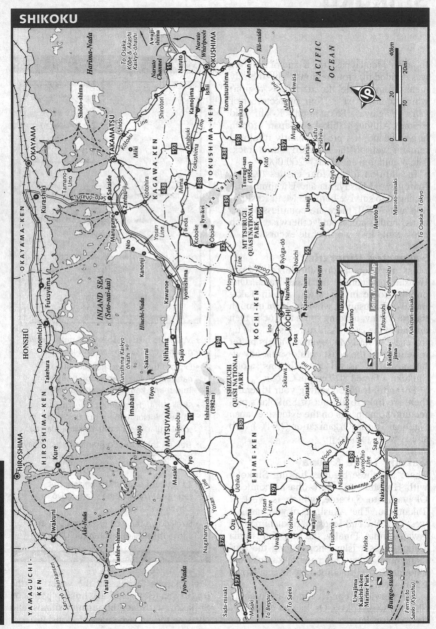

SHIKOKU

ONSEN MANIA!

In his quintessential tome *Things Japanese* (1890), humorist and Japan-expert Basil Hall Chamberlain wryly observed 'Cleanliness is one of the few original items of Japanese civilisation'. Chamberlain was impressed by the Japanese mania for *onsen* (mineral hot-spring spas), not least by the pool in rural Gunma-ken where: 'the bathers stay in the water for a month on end, with a stone on their lap to prevent them from floating in their sleep'.

A century later, onsen addicts may not be weighing themselves down with boulders, but the fascination with hot springs remains as strong as ever, and the activity has developed into a fine art with its own rules of etiquette. Baths are found just about everywhere due to plenty of underground thermal activity – poke a stick in the ground and out comes *o-yu* (literally 'honourable hot water'). Onsen range from pristine mountain retreats to workaday bath-houses and kitsch, overdeveloped spa towns.

Right: Soaking in 'honourable hot water' – an indoor bath at Nyūtō Onsen in Northern Honshū.

MASON FLORENCE

Onsen Mania!

Getting naked with total strangers is not, for most of us, the cultural norm (California readers please forgive me), but shy *gaijin* bathers should know that the Japanese perceive bathing as a great social leveller – company presidents rub naked shoulders with truck drivers, priests with publicans; and all revel in the anonymity that nudity allows. Only the *yakuza*, or Japanese mafia, stand out with their magnificent *irezumi* (tattoos), or in Yakuza parlance, *iremono*. They are often happy if you show an interest.

The baths themselves come in as many different shapes and sizes as the customers. Essentially you will either visit solely for an *o-furo* (literally 'the honourable bath'); or you will stay at an *onsen ryokan* (traditional hot-spring inn) to partake of good food, copious amounts of alcohol, *karaoke* and a soak in the establishment's private baths, either indoors or out. Ryokan will also often allow you to have a soak without booking accommodation (ask for *'ofuro-nomi'*). This is an excellent and affordable way to experience some beautiful, traditional baths. Unfortunately, bathing is also big business and rampant commercialism has marred many once lovely onsen.

While famed commercial resorts, such as Dōgo Onsen in Shikoku or Beppu in Kyūshū, provide a good introduction to onsen, the effort it takes to seek out less touristed springs is worthwhile. If you find a rare, unvisited bath, the effect is scintillating. A few special onsen well-worth visiting include Ibusuki and Kurokawa (Kyūshū); Yunomine (Kansai) and Bessho Onsen (Central Honshū).

There are two excellent books devoted to hot springs *A Guide to Japanese Hot Springs* and *Japan's Hidden Hot Springs* (see Guidebooks under the Books section in Facts for the Visitor). Both are worth seeking out for anyone looking to onsen-hop their way through Japan.

So whether it's being buried up to the neck in a thermally heated sand bath, soaking in a pool in a remote forest, or luxuriating in a glitzy resort, the onsen experience is one of Japan's greatest treasures. And where else can you safely get naked with a mobster?

MASON FLORENCE

Left: Tsuru-no-yu near Beppu (Kyūshū) is tucked away out of the public eye. Locals built and maintain this lovely rotemburo up on the edge of Ogi-yama. During July and August only, a natural stream emerges to form the milky blue bath.

Onsen Etiquette

The Japanese hot-spring o-furo is blissfully free of the rules and regulations that make life a minefield of potential societal gaffes for the average Japanese citizen. No doubt this liberation from the strictures of polite society is what makes it so popular. The first-time-naked foreign bather needn't be intimidated – once the basics have been mastered.

Soap is a commodity kept as far from the bath water as possible. Have a rinse in the adjacent shower. If there's no shower, ladle hot water over your body whilst outside the bath, using one of the available buckets, while squatting on one of the Lilliputian stools provided. Then gracefully ease yourself into the water. Incidentally, stealing someone else's bucket or stool whilst they are soaking is officially infra-dig but, in fact, it seems to be a secretly undeclared national pastime.

One should endeavour to slip into the water with the minimum of disturbance, not unlike a cherry blossom petal delicately slipping into a moonlit Kyoto temple pond. Doing a double-pike with a half-somersault into the ornamental stone bath might impress your travelling companions, but not only will it result in cerebral haemorrhaging as you strike cranium to bath-bottom, it will mean instant social death – blood in the bath-water is a strict no-no.

In the event that the water is hot enough to strip the skin off a rhino, it is perfectly acceptable to do a reverse long jump action, although if you can slowly ease yourself into the superheated water, grimacing is positively encouraged. If you accompany your facial contortions with a long drawn out, anguished 'Achee, AcheEE, AAAcheeeel' ('Hot, Hooo-ot, HOOoo-ot!') you will be considered a professional.

An essential piece of onsen equipment is a 'modesty' towel to delicately cover your most private bits 'n' pieces. Once they are safely

Right: A group of bathers seated on plastic stools having a good scrub before entering a rotemburo.

CRAIG MCLACHLAN

Onsen Mania!

CHRIS ROWTHORN

underwater, this useful item can be dipped in the water, rinsed out (outside the bath) and placed on your head, a la Northern England male beach-goer, circa 1958. This is rumoured to prevent you from passing out (another minor social infringement). In the more rural, single-sex baths, however, no one bothers with a modesty towel – bathers wibble and wobble around, starkers as the day they were born.

It's that simple. And if you do commit a faux pas, most customers are too busy forgetting work and looking forward to a night of *karaoke* to care. And in the event that you inadvertently fart, just try *'Kyo tansan wa kitsui desu ne'* – 'Carbonation's strong today, isn't it?'.

John Ashburne

Onsen Lingo

dansei-no-yu	男性の湯	male bath
otoko-yu	男湯	male bath
josei-no-yu	女性の湯	female bath
onna-yu	女湯	female bath
konyoku	混浴	mixed bath
kazoku-no-yu	家族の湯	family bath
rotenburo	露天風呂	outdoor bath
kawa-no-yu	川の湯	river bath
dōkutsuburo/	洞窟風呂	
anaburo	穴風呂	cave bath
sunaburo	砂風呂	sand bath

Left: Sakino-yu Onsen, in Shirahama (Kyūshū) is sensational. It's a string of rotemburo built on a rocky point with great views of the Pacific Ocean.

The 88 Temple Circuit

Japan's best known pilgrimage is Kōbō Daishi's 88 Temple Circuit of Shikoku. Kūkai (774–835), known as Kōbō Daishi after his death, is the most revered of Japan's saints. He founded the Shingon Buddhist sect in 807, after a visit to China. Shingon, often referred to as Esoteric Buddhism, is related to Tantric Buddhism, with its mystic rituals and multi-armed deities.

Shikoku-born Kōbō Daishi is said to have personally selected the 88 temple route. Today, most pilgrims on the circuit travel by tour bus, but many still walk. Set aside two months and be prepared to hoof it over 1500km if you want to join them. Some temples are only a few hundred metres apart and you can walk to five or six in a day, however, at the other extreme, it can be 100km between other temples.

Individually, none of the temples is exceptionally interesting; it's the whole circuit that counts. The 88 temples represent the same number of evil human passions defined by the Buddhist doctrine, and completing the circuit is said to rid oneself of these. The route begins in Tokushima and is generally made clockwise. The pilgrims, known as o-henro-san, wear white robes (hakui), carry a staff (otsue) and often top the ensemble with a straw hat (kasa). Though rare, some pilgrims stamp their robes (byakue) with the temples' red seals.

About half of the 88 temples have lodging facilities for pilgrims, which cost around ¥4000 a night (including meals). Shikoku tourist information offices can provide more information on making the pilgrimage.

Oliver Statler's classic book Japanese Pilgrimage follows the circuit; other English books on the subject include Craig McLachlan's Tales of a Summer Henro (Yohan) and Japanese Pilgrimages (Weatherhill) by Ed Readicker-Henderson. Echoes of Incense, an 88 temple travelogue by Tokushima resident Don Weiss, can be picked up at Ryōzen-ji, which is temple No 1, or viewed on Weiss's praiseworthy Web site: www.mandala.ne.jp/echoes/index.html.

There are frequent train services from Okayama to Shikoku via the Seto-ōhashi, as well as direct bus services from both Osaka and Tokyo.

Getting Around

Most of Shikoku is well accessed by public transport, though to reach remote mountain areas, private transport is a boon (cars can be rented in Shikoku's major cities and airports).

Kagawa-ken 香川県

Formerly known as Sanuki, Kagawa-ken is the smallest of Shikoku's four island regions and sits on the north-western coast overlooking the Inland Sea. The completion of the Seto-ōhashi in 1986 reinforced Kagawa's importance as a major arrival point on Shikoku.

Highlights in Takamatsu include the beautiful gardens of Ritsurin-kōen and the folk village, Shikoku-mura. The celebrated shrine of Kompira-san at Kotohira is another must-see.

TAKAMATSU 高松

☎ 087 • pop 330,000

Takamatsu was founded during the rule of Toyotomi Hideyoshi (1537–98) as the castle town of the feudal lord of Kagawa. The city was virtually destroyed in WWII, but rapidly rebounded.

Despite its rail link, Takamatsu remains an important port for Inland Sea ferry services, particularly to the popular island, Shōdoshima (see Shōdo-shima under The Inland Sea in the Western Honshū chapter). Outside the city there are numerous excursion possibilities including Isamu Noguchi's extraordinary sculpture garden in Mure-chō; and west of Takamatsu, the castle, Marugame-jō, and the 9th century Buddhist temple, Zentsū-ji.

Orientation & Information

Takamatsu is surprisingly sprawling. It's a 2km walk to Ritsurin-kōen from JR

SHIKOKU

Takamatsu station. There's an information office (☎ 851-2009) outside the station where staff can provide useful leaflets and maps, and another at the east entrance to Ritsurin-kōen. Both can help with booking accommodation. Equidistant from these two, on the north-west corner of Chūō-kōen, is the Kagawa International Exchange Center (I-PAL KAGAWA). This resource centre has a message board, foreign books and magazines, international phone and fax access, satellite TV and Internet access (9 am to 6 pm, closed Monday).

Visitors can pick up the free Kagawa Welcome Card at I-PAL and the tourist information offices (you'll need to show your passport). The card provides minor discounts around town, and comes with a mini-guidebook and fold-out city map.

At the time of writing there was major upheaval going on around JR Takamatsu station as the city makes way for Sunport Takamatsu, a massive reclaimed land project. It will eventually support train stations, offices, leisure facilities and more.

Chūō-dōri, the main street through Takamatsu, extends south from Kotoden Chikkō train station. A busy shopping arcade extends across Chūō-dōri and then runs parallel to it, passing through the entertainment district. The main shopping area is farther south, near Kotoden Kawaramachi train station. The Miyawaki Shoten bookshop has a wide selection of English-language books and magazines on the 5th floor.

Ritsurin-kōen 栗林公園

Although not one of Japan's 'big three' gardens, Ritsurin-kōen could easily be a contender. The garden, dating from the mid-1600s, winds around a series of ponds with lookouts, tearooms, bridges and islands. It took more than a century to complete and was used as a villa garden for more than 200 years prior to the Meiji Restoration. In one direction, Shiun-zan forms a backdrop to the garden, but in the other direction there is some much less impressive 'borrowed scenery' in the form of dull modern buildings. (In Japanese garden design, 'borrowed scenery' refers to a view

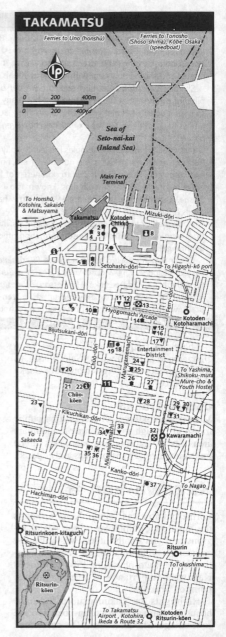

TAKAMATSU

PLACES TO STAY

2 Station Hotel
ステーションホテル

4 Pearl Hotel
高松パールホテル

5 Hotel New
Frontier
ホテルニューフロンティア

6 Takamatsu
Terminal Hotel
高松ターミナルホテル

10 Takamatsu
Tōkyū Inn
高松東急イン

14 Hotel Kawaroku
ホテル川六

25 Business Hotel
Japan
ビジネスホテルジャパン

26 Takamatsu
Washington Hotel
高松ワシントンホテル

27 Royal Park Hotel
ロイヤルパークホテル

PLACES TO EAT

9 Tenkatsu
天勝本店

11 Cafe An
カフェアン

15 Kawa Fuku
川福本店

16 Grill Yama
グリル山

17 Kanaizumi
かな泉

20 Macous Bagel
マーカスベーグル

23 Sakaeda

24 Goemon
五右衛門

28 Fumiya
ふみや

29 Delta Market
デルタマーケット

30 Asian Junkfood
アジアンジャンクフード

31 Sea Dragon
シードラゴン

33 Spice Kingdom
スパイス王蔵

34 Capriciosa;
KFC
カプリチョーザ

35 Milk Doll
ミルクドール

36 La Provence
ラ・プロバンス

OTHER

1 Tourist Information
Center (TIC)
観光案内所

3 ANA
全日空

7 JAL
日航

8 Takamatsu-jō &
Tamamo-kōen
高松城／玉藻公園

12 Post Office
高松郵便局

13 Mitsukoshi Department
Store
三越百貨店

18 Miyawaki Shoten
Bookstore
宮脇書店

19 Takamatsu City
Museum of Art
高松市美術館

21 Kagawa International
Exchange
アイパル香川

22 East Entrance to Park/TIC

32 Sōgō Department Store
そごう百貨店

37 NTT

of distant scenery that is revealed at some place along the path.)

In the garden, the **Sanuki Folkcraft Museum** (free, 8.45 am to 4.30 pm) displays local crafts. The feudal-era **Kikugetsu-tei** teahouse, also known as the Chrysanthemum Moon Pavilion, offers Japanese tea and sweets with the ¥1030 entry fee. There are several other small teahouses inside the park including the lovely thatch-roofed **Higurashi-tei** (¥400). Entrance to the park's zoo costs ¥600.

Entry to Ritsurin-kōen, open from sunrise to sunset, is ¥350. You can get there by Kotoden or JR train, but the easiest way is by bus (¥230) from JR Takamatsu station.

Takamatsu-jō 高松城

There's very little left of Takamatsu-jō, which is a stone's throw from Kotoden Chikkō station. The castle grounds today form a pleasant park, **Tamamo-kōen**, yet are only one-ninth their original size. When the castle was built in 1588, the moat was filled with sea water, with the sea itself forming the fourth side (¥150, 8.30 am to 6 pm, April to September; otherwise it closes at 5 pm).

Yashima 屋島

The 292m-high tabletop plateau of Yashima stands 5km east of the centre of Takamatsu. Today, it's the locale of **Yashima-ji (No 84 on the 88 Temple Circuit),** and offers fine views over the surrounding countryside and the Inland Sea.

In the 12th century it was the site of titanic struggles between the Genji and Heike clans. The temple's Treasure House collection relates to the battle. Just behind the treasure house is the **Pond of Blood,** where victorious warriors washed the blood from their swords, staining the water red.

A funicular railway runs to the top of Yashima from near a smaller shrine at the

SHIKOKU

bottom (¥700/1300 one way/return). At the top you can rent a bicycle to pedal around the attractions (¥300, plus ¥1000 deposit).

The best ways of getting to Yashima are by Kotoden train or bus. From Kotoden Chikkō station it takes around 20 minutes (¥270) to Kotoden Yashima station. From here you can take the cable car to the top, or hike up in about 30 minutes. Kotoden buses run directly to the top from JR Takamatsu station (¥750, 30 minutes).

Shikoku-mura 四国村

At the bottom of Yashima is Shikoku-mura, an excellent village museum with old buildings brought from all over Shikoku and neighbouring islands. There are explanations in English of the many buildings and their history. Highlights include a traditional vine suspension bridge, modelled after the ones that cross the deep gorges in Iya (see the Iya Valley section under Tokushima-ken later in this chapter).

The village's fine *kabuki* stage came from Shōdo-shima, which is famed for its traditional farmers' kabuki performances. Other interesting buildings include a border guardhouse from the Tokugawa era (a time when travel was tightly restricted) and a bark steaming-hut that was used in paper making. There's also a water-powered rice-hulling machine and a fine old stone storehouse.

Shikoku-mura is north of Kotoden Yashima station and takes around seven minutes on foot. Entry is ¥800, although the small museum in the village charges an extra ¥100 (8.30 am to 5 pm, until 4.30 pm from November to March).

Other Attractions
Isamu Noguchi Garden Museum イサム・ノグチ庭園美術館
Consider an excursion out to Mure-chō, east of Takamatsu, to witness the legacy of noted sculptor Isamu Noguchi (1904–88). Born in Los Angeles to a Japanese poet and an American writer, Noguchi set up a studio and residence here in 1970. Today the complex is filled with hundreds of Noguchi's works, and holds its own as an impressive overall art installation. Inspiring sculptures are on display

in the beautifully-restored Japanese buildings and in the surrounding landscape.

Entry is ¥2000 and is decidedly worth it. Hour-long tours are conducted between 10 am and 5 pm on Tuesday, Thursday and Saturday; visitors should fax ahead for reservations – preferably two weeks in advance (☎ 870-1500, fax 845-0505).

Megi-jima 女木島
Just offshore from Yashima is Megi-jima, also known as Oniga-shima or 'Demon Island'. Several homes on the island are surrounded by *ōte* (high stone walls built to protect a house from waves, wind and ocean spray). It was here that Momotarō, the legendary 'Peach Boy' (see the boxed text 'Momotarō – the Peach Boy' in the Western Honshū chapter), met and conquered the horrible demon. You can tour the caves where the demon was said to have hidden (¥500, 8.30 am to 5 pm).

Boats run to Megi-jima from Takamatsu (¥340, 20 minutes). There are *minshuku* and *campsites* on the island.

Places to Stay – Budget
Youth Hostels The *Takamatsu Yashima-sansō Youth Hostel* (☎ 841-2318) is a five-minute walk north-east of Kotoden Yashima station. This notoriously dingy place charges ¥2750 per night; breakfast/dinner costs ¥600/650.

Hotels The *Business Hotel Japan* (☎ 851-8689), south of the station in the shopping and entertainment district, is at the grotty end of the business hotel spectrum, but offers singles/twins for ¥4000/7000.

Places to Stay – Mid-Range
There are several budget business hotels around JR Takamatsu station. The *Pearl Hotel* (☎ 822-3382) is small, clean and quite acceptable with singles/doubles starting from ¥5500/10,000. Nearby is the similar *Station Hotel* (☎ 821-6989), with rooms starting from ¥6300/11,500.

A few minutes' walk from the station, the *Takamatsu Terminal Hotel* (☎ 822-3731) is a small, clean place with singles/doubles/

twins starting from ¥6100/10,000/11,000. Close by, the *Hotel New Frontier* (☎ 851-1088) offers similar standards for ¥6900/11,500 for singles/twins.

The Japanese-style *Hotel Kawaroku* (☎ 821-5666) is south of the shopping arcade, just off Chūō-dōri. Rooms cost from ¥6000/12,000 for singles/twins without meals, and from ¥18,000 per person with meals.

Places to Stay – Top End
The *Takamatsu Tōkyū Inn* (☎ 821-0109) is a popular chain hotel on Chūō-dōri, just beyond the arcade, and has singles/twins/doubles starting at ¥8500/15,600/17,400.

In the entertainment district, the *Royal Park Hotel* (☎ 823-2222) has singles/doubles from ¥12,700/15,000. A few steps away is the *Takamatsu Washington Hotel* (☎ 822-7111), with singles/twins from ¥8400/14,500.

Places to Eat
Kotoden Kawaramachi station (as well as the basement of the attached Sogo department store) is a centre for a variety of cheap eats and drinks. Look for *Sea Dragon*, a tiny bar/restaurant serving home-made soft-shell tacos, nachos and pitchers of cold beer. Across the road is the *izakaya*-style

(pub-style) *Asian Junkfood*, dishing up a variety of inexpensive, Asian-influenced dishes. Just next door on the 2nd floor is the trendy *Delta Market*, with trippy day-glo walls, which is more bar than restaurant.

North-west of the station, the family-run *Fumiya* serves top-notch *okonomiyaki* (combination of meat, seafood and vegetables in a cabbage and vegetable batter) and *yakisoba* (fried noodles), and has an English-language menu.

Milk Doll has reasonable lunch and dinner specials, and the fine French restaurant *La Provence* does a superb set lunch for ¥1800. The Indian food at *Spice Kingdom* (2nd floor) is praiseworthy, and there is affordable Italian fare available at *Capriciosa*, located above KFC.

Across from I-PAL, *Macous Bagel* serves fresh bagels and tasty sandwiches.

Along the shopping arcade in the entertainment district, *Kawa-Fuku* is a pleasant restaurant offering *udon* (thick, white wheat noodles), *tempura* (lightly battered seafood and vegetables) and other dishes from around ¥1000. Just beyond Kawa-Fuku is *Grill Yama*, which serves a variety of grilled meat dishes from ¥1500. Vegetarians should head over to *Café An*, a wholesome natural foods restaurant (lunch only) near the Mitsukoshi department store.

A few doors beyond the end of the Hyogo-machi arcade west of Chūō-dōri, you'll find *Tenkatsu*, a seafood restaurant where you can see your order swimming about before it's prepared.

Finally, a trip to Takamatsu would not be complete without slurping back some of the region's prized *sanuki udon* ('Sanuki' is an earlier term name of Kagawa-ken). One of the cheapest is *Sakaeda*, where you can stuff yourself for under ¥300. *Kanaizumi*, on Ferry-dōri, also specialises in sanuki udon – you may see it being made in the window. Another possibility is *Goemon*, near the Business Hotel Japan.

If you're out at Shikoku-mura, don't miss the country-style *zaigo udon* at *Waraya*, right beside the car park; the *kazoku udon* (¥2300) is a giant wooden bucket of noodles ready to feed a hungry family of four!

Cruel Cuisine

Being cruel to your food is a Japanese tradition – you know the fish is fresh if it squeals when you eat it – and Takamatsu is certainly a centre for it. A prized dish here is *sugata-zukuri* – sea bream sliced seconds before it's placed in front of you. If you're quick with the chopsticks you can get the first mouthfuls down before it dies. I ate one night at Tenkatsu, where the bar encloses a large tank of fish and other sea life. When a customer ordered octopus, the unfortunate creature was scooped out of the tank and four tentacles were hacked off. Then, still living, but less than complete, the octopus was tossed back into the tank to crawl forlornly off to a corner.

Tony Wheeler

SHIKOKU

Getting There & Away

Air Takamatsu is serviced by All Nippon Airlines (ANA), Air Nippon Koku (ANK), Japan Air System (JAS), Japan Air Commuter (JAC) and JAL (Japan Airlines). Typical one-way fares are: Fukuoka (¥17,700), Kagoshima (¥21,300), Nagoya (¥15,800), Okinawa (¥24,600), Osaka (¥11,000), Sapporo (¥33,600) and Tokyo (¥21,950).

Train The rail line crossing the Seto-ōhashi has brought Takamatsu much closer to the main island of Honshū. From Tokyo, you can take the *shinkansen* (bullet train) to Okayama, change trains and be in Takamatsu in five hours. The Okayama–Takamatsu trip takes about one hour.

From Takamatsu, the JR Kōtoku line runs south-east to Tokushima and the JR Yosan line runs west to Matsuyama. The Yosan line branches off at Tadotsu and becomes the Dosan line, turning south-west to Kotohira and Kōchi. The private Kotoden line also runs direct to Kotohira.

Bus Direct buses to/from Takamatsu operate from Tokyo, Yokohama, Nagoya and Osaka. From Tokyo the JR 'Dream Takamatsu Gō' costs ¥10,500 (10½ hours). From Nagoya, JR buses take about seven hours (¥7130), and from Osaka, the Hankyū 'Sanuki Express' takes around four hours (¥4590).

Boat Takamatsu has ferry services to several ports in the Inland Sea and Honshū, including Kōbe (¥2100, 4 hours). There is a speedboat service to Kōbe and to Osaka's Tempōzan-kō port (¥6100, 2½ hours) from the terminal near Takamatsu-jō. Slower, cheaper car/passenger ferries for Kōbe and Osaka arrive/depart at Higashi-kō port, which is 4km east of Takamatsu-jō.

Frequent boats also connect Uno, south of Okayama, with Takamatsu (¥390, one hour). Uno-Okayama trains connect with the ferry departures. Takamatsu is also the easiest jump-off point to visit Shōdo-shima.

Getting Around

Takamatsu airport is 16km from the city. Buses depart from JR Takamatsu station.

Takamatsu has local buses, but the major attractions are easily reached on the JR Kōtoku line or Kotoden line. The main Kotoden junction is Kawaramachi, although the line ends at Chikkō station, near JR Takamatsu station.

WEST OF TAKAMATSU
Sakaide 坂出

Sakaide, a port city on the JR Yosan line, has little of interest for the traveller except perhaps for the views over the Inland Sea from the southern end of the Seto-ōhashi.

Marugame 丸亀

On the JR Yosan line, just 25 minutes west of Takamatsu and close to the southern end of the Seto-ōhashi, **Marugame-jō**, dating from 1597, has one of only 12 original wooden donjon remaining of more than 5000 castles in Japan, and stepped stone walls towering over 50m high. The castle (¥50, 9 am to 4.30 pm) is about a kilometre south of the JR station.

Other attractions include the picturesque garden, **Nakazu Banshō-en** (¥1000, 9.30 am to 5 pm). The entry fee includes admission to the **Marugame Art Gallery**, which features a collection of Impressionist art. At the **Uchiwa Museum** (free, 9.30 am to 5 pm, closed Monday), there are displays and craft demonstrations of traditional Japanese *uchiwa* (paper fans). Marugame is responsible for about 90% of the country's paper fan output, making it a logical place to pick one up.

The Takamatsu tourist information centre can provide an English pamphlet on Marugame. The islands, the Shiwaku-shoto, in Western Honshū are also reached from here.

Zentsū-ji 善通寺

This temple is said to have been founded in AD 813. It is **No 75 on the 88 Temple Circuit** and boasts a magnificent five-storey pagoda and giant camphor trees. The **Mieidō Hall** is the Buddhist saint Kōbō Daishi's (Kūkai) childhood home, so it has particular importance. To get into the Buddhist spirit, for ¥500 visitors can venture

SHIKOKU

into the basement and traverse a 100m-long passageway in pitch darkness: by moving along with the left hand pressed to the wall (which is painted with mandalas, angels and lotus flowers) you are said to be safely following Buddha's way.

The same ticket allows you entrance to a small **museum** housing temple treasures, such as scrolls and a remarkable sceptre that was crafted in China by Kōbō Daishi.

Zentsū-ji is one station north of Kotohira on the JR Dosan line.

Kanonji 観音寺
pop 45,000

Kanonji is noted for **Zenigata**, the 350m-diameter outline of a square-holed coin dating from the 1600s. The coin's outline and four *kanji* (Chinese script used to write Japanese) are formed by trenches which, it is said, were dug by the local population as a warning to their feudal lord not to waste the taxes they were forced to pay him. The huge coin is beside the sea, at the foot of Kotohiki Hill in Kotohiki-kōen, 1½km north-west of Kanonji station. Also in the park is the temple, **Kanonji-jinne-in**, and the **World Coin Museum** (Sekai-no-koin-kan). The museum has coins of varying age from over 100 countries (¥300, 9 am to 5 pm, closed Monday).

Kanonji can be reached by train from JR Takamatsu station (50 minutes). If you're travelling between Takamatsu and Matsuyama you could fit in a visit to both Kanonji and Kotohira – provided you set off early enough. Buses run between Kotohira and Kanonji several times daily between 7 am and 6 pm (¥940).

Nio 仁尾

About 6km north of Kanonji is the former castle town of Nio. The surrounding coastline has good swimming beaches, a marina and is popular with water sports enthusiasts. Rates at the public *Tsuta-jima-sō* (☎ 0875-82-3351) are ¥6600 per night including two meals. The offshore islands of **Ōtsuta-jima** and **Kozuta-jima**, a short hop from Nio by ferry, also offer good beaches, walks and *camping*.

KOTOHIRA 琴平
☎ 0877

Kompira-san shrine at Kotohira is one of Shikoku's major attractions and, for anyone travelling in this part of Japan, it should not be missed (despite the huge number of pilgrims and tourists who flock here daily).

Orientation & Information

Kotohira is small enough to make orientation quite straightforward. The busy shopping arcade continues on until it reaches the shrine entranceway, lined with the inevitable souvenir shops. Those seeking to truly immerse themselves in the Japanese experience might like to buy a walking stick at one of the shops for the trek up to the shrine.

There is a tourist information centre (☎ 75-3500) in the NTT building along the main road between JR Kotohira station and Kotoden Kotohira station. Staff can provide English-language brochures, and accommodation information (9 am to 8 pm).

Kompira-san 金刀比羅宮

Kompira-san or, more formally, Kotohira-gū, was originally a temple dedicated to the Guardian of Mariners but became a shrine after the Meiji Restoration. Its hilltop position delivers superb views over the surrounding countryside, and there are some interesting reminders of its maritime connections.

An enormous fuss is made about how strenuous the climb is to the top but, if you've got this far in Japan, you've probably completed a few long ascents to shrines already. If you really blanch at the thought of climbing all those steps (nearly 800 of them) you can dish out ¥6500 and be carried up and down in a palanquin.

As you make your way up to the shrine, you might like to reflect how this is another of Japan's misplaced shrines. On Omishima in the Inland Sea, the shrine, Oyamazumi-jinja, is dedicated to a mountain god; while in this case, a hilltop shrine is venerated by seafarers!

The first notable landmark on the long climb is the **Ō-mon**, a stone gateway. Just to the right, beyond the gate, the **Hōmotsu-kan**

SHIKOKU

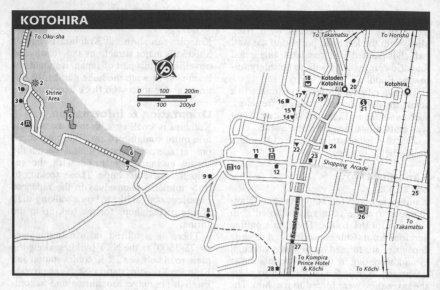

KOTOHIRA

To Oku-sha

Shrine Area

0   100   200m
0   100   200yd

To Takamatsu   To Honshū

Kotoden Kotohira   18

Kotohira

20

17   19

16   15   14

11   13   22   24
10   12   23
9

Shopping Arcade

8

25

26

To Takamatsu

27
To Kōmpira Prince Hotel & Kōchi   28   To Kōchi

---

treasure house is open daily (¥200, 8.30 am to 4.30 pm). Nearby you will find five traditional sweets vendors at tables shaded by large white parasols. A symbol of ancient times, these Gonin Byakushō (Five Farmers) are the descendants of the original families permitted to trade within the grounds of the shrine. Farther uphill is the **Shoin**, a reception hall (¥200, 8.30 am to 4.30 pm daily). Built in 1659, this National Treasure has some interesting screen paintings and a small garden.

Continuing the ascent, you eventually reach the large **Asahino Yashiro** (Shrine of the Rising Sun). The hall, built in 1837 and dedicated to the Sun Goddess Amaterasu, is noted for its ornate wood carving. From here, the short final ascent, which is the most beautiful leg of the walk, brings you to the **Gohonsha** (Gohon Hall) and the **Emadō** (Ema Pavillion); the latter is filled with maritime offerings. Exhibits range from pictures of ships, to models, modern ship engines and a one-person solar sailboat hull donated to the shrine after its around-the-world navigation. The views from this level extend right down to the coast and over the Inland Sea. Incurable climbers can continue

another 500-odd steps up to the **Oku-sha** (Inner Shrine).

Kanamaru-za 金丸座
Near the base of the steps is the Kyū Kompira Ōshibai, or Kanamaru-za, Japan's oldest **kabuki playhouse** (¥300, 9 am to 5 pm). It was built in 1835 and later became a cinema before being restored in 1976. Inside, you can wander backstage (delightfully unsupervised) and see the changing rooms and old wooden bath, and admire the revolving stage mechanism, basement trap doors and tunnel out to front-of-theatre.

Other Attractions
At the bottom of the shrine steps there's a **Marine Museum** (¥400, 9 am to 4.30 pm) with a variety of ship models and exhibits. There's also the **Kinryō-no-Sato** *sake* museum along the shrine entranceway (¥310, 9 am to 4 pm, daily). Sake tasting costs ¥100.

Note the curious **Takadōrō lantern tower** beside Kotoden Kotohira station. The 27.6m-high tower was traditionally lit in times of trouble. At the southern end of the town, just before the Kotohira Kadan Ryokan, is the wooden **Saya-bashi**, a covered bridge.

KOTOHIRA

PLACES TO STAY
9 Kotohira Grand Hotel
琴平グランドホテル
11 Shikishima-kan
敷島館
12 Bizenya Ryokan
備前屋
16 Kotohira Onsen
Kotosankaku
琴平ロイヤルホテル
23 Kotobuki Ryokan
ことぶき旅館
24 Kotohira Riverside Hotel
リバーサイドホテル
28 Kotohira Kadan Ryokan
琴平花壇旅館

PLACES TO EAT
14 Tanuki-ya Udon
狸屋
15 Murasaki Robatayaki
むらさき

17 Shōhachi Udon
将八うどん
19 Take away Mochi
お餅屋
22 Tako-zushi
たこ寿司
25 Okonomiyaki Restaurant
お好み焼き

OTHER
1 Gohonsha (Main Hall)
金刀比羅宮本殿
2 Viewpoint
3 Ema-dō Pavilion
絵馬堂
4 Asahino Yashiro
旭社
5 Shoin (Reception Hall)
書院
6 Hōmotsu-kan
(Treasure House)
宝物館

7 Ō-mon
大門
8 Kanamaru-za
金丸座
10 Marine Museum
海の科学館
13 Kinryō-no-Sato (Sake
Museum)
金陵の里
18 Post Office
琴平郵便局
20 Takadōrō (Lantern Tower)
高灯籠
21 NTT;
Tourist Information
Center
観光案内所
26 Bus Station
バス停留所
27 Saya-bashi
(Covered Bridge)
鞘橋

Places to Stay – Mid-Range

Kotobuki Ryokan (☎ 73-3872), conveniently situated by the riverside, is clean, comfortable and serves good food. The nightly cost per person with dinner and breakfast is ¥6000, which rises to ¥7000 on weekends and holidays.

The *Kompira Prince Hotel* (☎ 73-3051) has singles/doubles for ¥6620/9450. It's about 500m to the south-east of JR Kotohira station. The *Kotohira Riverside Hotel* (☎ 75-1880), just north of the shopping arcade, is at ease with foreign guests and charges ¥7100/13,650 for singles/twins.

Places to Stay – Top End

Ryokan & Onsen Kotohira has some very tasteful ryokan, particularly along the entranceway to the shrine steps. Costs per person include dinner and breakfast. On the entranceway, the *Bizenya Ryokan* (☎ 75-4131) has rooms from ¥10,000 to ¥15,000; and the classic *Shikishima-kan* (☎ 75-5111) has rooms from ¥13,000 to ¥18,000. (It dates back to 1624 and was popular with Shikoku *samurai*.) The *Kotohira Kadan Ryokan* (☎ 75-3232), costing ¥12,000 per night, is just beyond the Saya-bashi.

The elegant, Japanese-style *Kotohira Onsen Kotosankaku* (☎ 75-1000) features an excellent outdoor *onsen* (hot-spring spa bath); rates start from ¥17,000.

Hotels The luxurious *Kotohira Grand Hotel* (☎ 75-3218) near the bottom of the steps up to the shrine, will set you back about ¥30,000 a head.

Places to Eat

Many of the restaurants in Kotohira cater for day-trippers and, hence, close early. There are a couple of reasonably priced places serving udon, *katsudon* (pork cutlet served over rice) and so on across from the main post office, including *Shōhachi Udon*. Just over the bridge at the end of the shopping arcade is *Taco-zushi* (*taco* means 'octopus' in Japanese), a quaint sushi shop that won't break the budget. Look for the big red octopus painted above the door. North of here is a branch of the popular *robatayaki* (restaurant specialising in charcoal-grilled fish) chain, *Murasaki*, which has an illustrated menu.

In the far west of the town centre, over the JR tracks, there is a great, unnamed

SHIKOKU

okonomiyaki place worth seeking out; look for the blue *noren* (curtain) outside.

Up near the entrance to the shrine, many of the souvenir shops do udon lunches. They are a little expensive, but cheaper choices are available for under ¥1000. Try the *sanuki-udon teishoku* (sanuki-udon set meal) for ¥950 at **Tanuki-ya**.

If you plan to snack along the walk, there are good take-away *mochi* (pounded rice cakes) for ¥150 near the post office.

Getting There & Away

The JR Dosan line branches off the Yosan line at Tadotsu and continues through Ko-tohira and south to Kōchi. There is also a direct Takamatsu to Kotohira private Kotoden line. By either route, the journey takes around an hour from Takamatsu.

Tokushima-ken徳島県

From the vivacious Awa Odori (Awa Dance) festival and the mighty channel whirlpools of the Naruto-kaikyō, to the pristine scenery of Iya Valley and the sacred peak of Tsurugi-san, Tokushima-ken offers an array of noteworthy attractions.

TOKUSHIMA 徳島
☎ 088 • pop 270,000

Tokushima, a pleasant city on Shikoku's east coast, is the traditional starting point for pilgrims setting off on the extensive **88 Temple Circuit**. In addition to the annual Awa Odori in August and traditional Awa puppet theatre, there are several places in and around town where visitors can experience traditional crafts such as *aizome* (indigo dyeing), *washi* (paper making) and pottery.

Orientation & Information

Tokushima is neatly defined by two hills. One, with the castle ruins, rises up directly behind the station. From in front of the station, Shinmachibashi-dōri heads south-west across the Shinmachi-gawa to the ropeway station at the base of Bizan-san. The entertainment district and main shopping arcade are west of the river.

Dancing Fools

The streets of Tokushima, an otherwise placid city, play host to one of the premier good-time events in Japan, the Awa Odori (Awa Dance) festival. The event is the largest and most famous '*bon*' dance in Japan and attracts tens of thousands of people from 12–15 August every year.

Every night, over four days, the revelry continues as men, women and children don *yukata*, or light cotton kimono, and take to the streets to dance to the samba-like rhythm of the theme song *Yoshikono*, accompanied by the sounds of *shamisen* (three-stringed guitars), *taiko* (drums) and *fue* (flutes). Dancing and mayhem last into the wee hours of the morning!

As at Rio's Carnival or the Mardi Gras in New Orleans, the participants dance in *ren* (groups), waving their hands, shuffling their feet and chanting a phrase, which says it all:

The dancing fools
And the watching fools
Are foolish the same
So why not dance?

Some groups delight in having *gaijin* join their pack; staff at Tokushima Prefecture International Exchange Association (TOPIA) can provide details. And if you can't be there for the real thing in August, you can always try the dance at the local hall, the Awa Odori Kaikan (see the Bizan-san entry under Tokushima).

There's a tourist information booth outside JR Tokushima station, but the Tokushima Prefecture International Exchange Association (TOPIA; ☎ 656-3303) is a far better place to get started. There are helpful English-speaking staff and facilities include a library, satellite TV, computers and an information/message board (10 am to 6 pm daily). To reach TOPIA from inside JR Tokushima station, take the elevator to the 6th floor of Clement Plaza.

Cybercafe B (☎ 653-4856) offers Internet access for ¥10 per minute, or ¥10 per three minutes with any beverage order. It's across the river, the Suketō-gawa, on the north side of Chūō-kōen.

Bizan-san 眉山

A broad avenue with a central parade of palm trees runs south-west from the station to the foot of Bizan-san, also known as Otaki-san. There's a ropeway, otherwise known as a cable car (¥500/800 one way/ return), and a 4km toll road to the 280m-high summit. From the summit there are fine views over the city and sea. You can walk down in 15 minutes.

At the foot of the ropeway, the **Awa Odori Kaikan** (☎ 611-1611), a meeting hall, features extensive exhibits relating to the local dance, the *awa odori*. You can learn the dance here daily from 9 am to 5 pm, closed second and forth Wednesday (free).

Bizan-kōen also has a **Peace Pagoda**, erected in 1958 as a memorial to local soldiers who perished in Burma (Myanmar) during WWII, and the **Wenceslão de Morães Museum**. Morães, a Portuguese naval officer, lived in Japan from 1893 until his death in 1929, and produced a multivolume study of Japan. The museum is open from 9.30 am to 6 pm, and until 4 pm from October to March (¥200, closed second and fourth Tuesday).

Chūō-kōen 中央公園

Less than half a kilometre north-east of the train station, the ruins of Tokushima jō built in 1586, stand in Chūō-kōen. In the park you will also find the attractively landscaped **Senshūkaku-tien** (¥50), a garden dating from the Momoyama period, and the **Tokushima Castle Museum** (¥300, 9.30 am to 4.30 pm, closed Monday).

Just east of Chūō-kōen, near the Park Hotel, is Akane-an (☎ 625-8866), an excellent place to experience an authentic Japanese **tea ceremony**. For a reasonable ¥1000, you'll be served fragrant *ko-sencha* (medium grade green tea), followed by *matcha* (powdered green tea), then a sweet *yuzu* (citron) fruit juice and finally standard *o-cha* (green tea). To arrange a formal tea ceremony *(o-temae)*, reservations are required.

Awa Puppet Theatre 人形浄瑠璃

For hundreds of years, *bunraku* (puppet theatre), known in the region as *ningyō jōruri*, thrived in the farming communities in and around Tokushima as a popular form of amusement (while the wealthy were entertained with the likes of kabuki). Gradually the region's many puppet theatres dwindled and today one of the last remaining local puppet dramas can be seen at the **Awa no Jūrobei Yashiki** (☎ 665-2202).

This museum is the former residence of the samurai Jūrobei, whose tragic Edo-era life story forms the material for the drama *Keisei Awa no Naruto*. A section from this puppet drama is performed by local women. Shows take place from Monday to Saturday at 3 pm (April through November); Saturday at 3 pm (December through March); and Sunday and holidays at 10.30 am and 3 pm year-round (¥350).

A two-minute walk from here is the **Awa Deko Ningyō Kaikan** (Awa Puppet Hall), with puppet displays and demonstrations of their manufacture and use (¥400, 8.30 am to 5 pm). Take a bus from JR Tokushima station bound for Miyajima to the Jūrobei Yashiki-mae bus stop (¥290, 30 minutes).

Other Attractions

Free **boat rides** (50 minutes) can be taken on the Suketō-gawa circling Hyotan-jima, the island forming central Tokushima. Ask for a timetable at TOPIA.

There are also **rowboats** for hire on the Shinmachi-gawa. Just south of here near the entertainment district, the **dancing clock** is a curious contraption featuring figurines that perform the local Awa Odori dance; they pop out of an otherwise ordinary bus stop five times a day.

Tokushima is famed for both aizome and washi, and there are several places in and around the city where you can catch demonstrations and even try your own hand, although reservations are recommended.

For aizome, try Furushō Some Kōjō (☎ 622-3028) or the Aizumi Historical Museum (Ai no Yakata; ☎ 692-6317). For washi, head out to the Awagami Factory

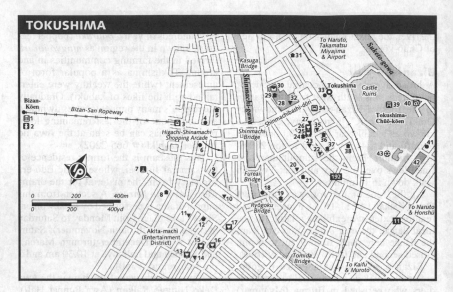

TOKUSHIMA

(☎ 0883-42-6120), near JR Awa Yama-kawa station. Pottery buffs should check into the local Ōtani-yaki wares. Detailed information on these places and more can be obtained at TOPIA.

If you don't have the time to make it out to the various factories, there is always ASTY Tokushima (☎ 624-5111), south-west of the city centre, which has potted high-lights of regional culture (including puppet drama and pottery) under one roof. At the neighbouring 'arts village' Kōgei-mura (☎ 624-5000), which is the highlight of the complex, you can observe (and for a nomi-nal fee partake in) a variety of traditional arts and crafts (9.30 am to 6 pm, closed Tuesday). Buses from JR Tokushima sta-tion reach ASTY in about 15 minutes.

Out by Tokushima airport (just off Route 11) is Awa-no-Sato, an interesting gather-ing of Japanese-style buildings recon-structed beside a giant manjū (steamed bun filled with sweet red-bean paste) factory. It's worth stopping in for samples. Entry to the compound is free, though there are charming Japanese restaurants and shops on the grounds if you do feel the urge to spend some money.

Places to Stay – Budget
Tokushima Youth Hostel (☎ 663-1505) is by the beach some distance out of town and costs ¥2800. Breakfast/dinner costs ¥600/1000.

Places to Stay – Mid-Range
Hotels close to the train station include the Dai Ichi Hotel (☎ 655-5505), with singles only from ¥5000; the Station Hotel (☎ 652-8181) and the Astoria Hotel (☎ 653-6151), both with singles/doubles at ¥6000/11,000. The Aivis Hotel has similar rates.

There are more expensive places, such as the AWA Kankō Hotel (☎ 622-5161), with rooms from ¥7200/14,000; Grand Palace Hotel (☎ 626-1111), with rooms from ¥8400/15,000; and Tōkyū Inn (☎ 626-0109), with rooms from ¥6900/12,000.

Close to Shinmachi-gawa, in a pleasant and quieter area of town, you'll find the City Hotel Hamaya (☎ 622-3411). This small business hotel is a member of the Japanese Inn Group. Singles/doubles with bathroom cost from ¥5500/9100, or from ¥4500/8100 without bathroom. Across the river, the Business Hotel New Tōyō (☎ 625-8181), has singles for ¥5100 and twins from ¥9800.

TOKUSHIMA

PLACES TO STAY

5 Business Hotel
New Tōyō
ビジネスホテルニュー東洋

8 Washington Hotel
ワシントンホテル

19 City Hotel Hamaya
シティホテルはやま

21 Marston Green Hotel
ホテルマーストングリーン

24 AWA Kankō Hotel
阿波観光ホテル

29 Tōkyū Inn
東急イン

31 Grand Palace Hotel
ホテルグランドパレス徳蕩

36 Station Hotel
ステーションホテル

37 Astoria Hotel
アストリアホテル

38 Aivis Hotel
エイヴィスホテル

42 Park Hotel
パークホテル

PLACES TO EAT

9 Nishimoto
西本

10 Hashimoto
橋本

11 Aoyagi; Basara
あおやぎ・バサラ

14 Aka Chōchin
赤ちょうちん

20 Sanuki Udon
さぬきうどん

22 Takashima
たかしま

23 Hanaya Rāmen
はなやラーメン

27 Tenkatsu
天勝

32 Mr Donut
ミスタードーナツ

35 R's Cafe
R's カフェ

OTHER

1 Wenceslão de Morães
Museum
モラエス記念館

2 Peace Pagoda
平和塔

3 Cablecar Station &
Awa Odori Kaikan
眉山ケーブルカー駅・
阿波踊り会館

4 JAS Cable Car
日本エアシステム

6 Earth Day
アースデイ

7 Zuigan-ji
端巌寺

12 Dancing Clock
阿波おどり時計

13 Paradise
パラダイス

15 Mars
マーズ

16 Warehouse
ウェアハウス

17 Dominos;
Ray Charles
ドミノス・
レイチャールズ

18 Row Boat Rental
貸しボート

25 Copa
コパ

26 Rokuemon Ichibanchō
ろくえもん

28 Sogō Department Store
そごう百貨店

30 Post Office
徳島郵便局

33 JR Tokushima; Clement
Plaza; Spice Kingdom
クレメントプラザ

34 Bus Station
バスターミナル

39 Gokoku-jinja
護国神社

40 Cybercafe B
サイバーカノエ ビー

41 Akane-an Teahouse
茜庵

43 Senshūkaku teien
旧徳島城表御殿庭園

Close to the City Hotel Hamaya is the *Marston Green Hotel* (☎ 654-1777). Singles/doubles start from ¥6800/11,500. In summer there's a *beer garden* up on the 9th floor.

Places to Stay – Top End

On the edge of the entertainment district, the *Washington Hotel* (☎ 653-7111) has singles/twins from ¥8000/17,000.

Places to Eat

If you're just passing through Tokushima, pop down to the basement of Clement Plaza (inside JR Tokushima station) and raid the expansive delicatessen area. There's also a variety of eateries on the 5th floor, including good Indian food at *Spice Kingdom*.

A two-minute walk from the station is the second-storey *R's Café* (11 am to midnight). The friendly, English-speaking owner/chef whips up pasta, including excellent lunch sets, and a wide range of fresh juices, all at reasonable prices.

Near R's Café, *Rokuemon Ichibanchō* is a basement izakaya with a decidedly country atmosphere. A few doors down (and on the 2nd floor), *Tenkatsu* is a safe bet for sushi and tempura. Lunch sets start at ¥800. Closer to Route 192, *Takashima* offers decent coffee and sandwiches. There's good, cheap *rāmen* (Chinese-style egg noodles in a broth) across the road from Takashima at *Hanaya*.

Nishimoto is a lively izakaya with reasonable prices (11.30 am to 11 pm, closed Wednesday). *Hashimoto*, a popular *soba* (buckwheat noodles) eatery, has a couple of branches, one near the 'dancing clock' and another near Shinmachi-bashi. There is tasty udon at *Sanuki Udon*, right across from the Marston Green Hotel.

In the Akita-machi entertainment district, *Aka Chōchin* is a boisterous robatayaki worth seeking out. For a more civilised Japanese meal in traditional surroundings, look into *Aoyagi* and *Basara*, which stand side by side on a narrow street near the 'dancing clock'. The food is exquisite, but expect to shell out around ¥5000 a head for lunch, and double that for dinner.

Entertainment
A short stumble from JR Tokushima station, *Copa*, formerly a popular bagel cafe, is now a woodsy little pub (from 5.30 pm, closed Sunday).

For wider nightlife variety, head to the Akita-machi area where there is an array of *gaijin*-friendly (foreigner-friendly) watering holes, with such cultured names as *Warehouse*, *Mars*, *Drug Store*, *Dominos* and *Ray Charles*. For live blues and soul music, check out *Paradise*.

Shopping
Earth Day, a short walk north of the Washington Hotel, is an attractive gallery/shop dealing in local arts and crafts. It's a good place to look for pottery.

Getting There & Away
Air JAS and ANA connect Tokushima with Tokyo's Haneda airport. JAC flies to Fukuoka and Osaka, and NAL connects Tokushima and Nagoya.

Train Tokushima is less than 1½ hours from Takamatsu by *tokkyū* (limited express). There are also train lines west to Ikeda on the JR Dosan line (which runs between Tadotsu and Kōchi) and south along the coastal Mugi line as far as Kaifu, from where you will have to take a bus to continue to Kōchi.

Bus Overnight buses to/from Tokyo depart around 9.30 pm, arriving early the next morning. Other buses connect Tokushima

with Kōbe (¥3200, two hours), Kyoto (¥4100, three hours), Matsuyama (¥4300, 3 hours), Nagoya (¥3200, six hours) and Osaka (¥3600, 3¼ hours).

Boat Ferries connect Tokushima with Tokyo, Osaka and Kōbe on Honshū, with Kokura on Kyūshū, and with various smaller ports. The hydrofoil to Kōbe, as well as the Tokushima Kanku Line between Osaka and Tokushima have both ceased to operate. Nankai Ferry (☎ 0120-732-156) has several departures daily between Wakayama in Kansai and Tokushima (express/regular, ¥3450/1730, one/two hours).

Getting Around
It's easy to get around Tokushima on foot – from JR Tokushima station to the Bizan-san cable-car station, it's only 700m. Bicycles can be rented from the underground bicycle park in front of the station.

AROUND TOKUSHIMA
Naruto Whirlpools 鳴門のうず潮
At the change of tide, sea water whisks through the narrow Naruto-kaikyō (Naruto Channel) with such velocity that ferocious whirlpools are created. Boats venture out into the channel that separates Shikoku from nearby Awaji-shima, and travel under the Naruto-ōhashi to inspect the whirlpools close up. Brochures available at JR Tokushima station information centres outline tide times (ask for *'naruto-no-uzu-shio'*) and **boat trips**. The whirls generally occur four times a day. There are views over the channel from **Naruto-kōen**, and you can save yourself the walk up to the lookout by taking a ¥200 escalator ride.

From Tokushima, take a train to JR Naruto station (¥330, 40 minutes) and a bus from there to the bridge (¥310, 20 minutes, infrequent); or take a bus directly from Tokushima bus station. Ferries also run to the park from Awaji-shima.

South of Tokushima
The JR Mugi line runs south as far as **Kaifu**, from where you can continue by bus to the cape at **Muroto-misaki** and on to Kōchi.

There are great views and **beaches** as you travel south along the Anan coast.

At **Hiwasa** in late July and early August, turtles come ashore to lay their eggs in Ohama-kōen, and there is even a local **Turtle Museum**. The beach here is one of the prettiest on Shikoku. Nakabayashi Beach looks out on some very picturesque islands, but swimming is dangerous due to rips. Swimmers should head for Kitanowaki Beach.

Submarine rides can be had on the Blue Marine (¥1400) from Shishikui, where there are **onsen** at the Riviera Hotel.

As you cross into Kōchi-ken, there is good **surfing** at Shirahama and Ikumi beaches (the overnight ferry between Osaka and Kannoura is popular with Kansai surfers), **scuba diving** around Kannoura and Muroto, and **whale-watching** tours from Sakihama-kō port.

West of Tokushima

In the mountains south-west of Tokushima, scenic Kamikatsu-chō is worth considering for the hot spring baths at **Tsukigatani Onsen**. You can *camp* here, or rent charming *wood cabins* for about ¥10,000 per night.

About 35km directly west of Tokushima is **Dochū**, where erosion has formed a large grouping of curious **sand pillars** standing about 15m high. Reached via JR Anabuki station, it is said that pillars of this height are found only in the Rocky Mountains in the USA and the European Alps.

Also worth a look is the photogenic row of **historic houses** at Minami-machi in Wakimachi, a ten-minute bus ride from JR Anabuki station.

IYA VALLEY 祖谷渓
☎ 0883

Virtually equidistant from Tokushima (via Ikeda), Takamatsu (via Kotohira), and Kōchi, the remote Iya Valley, known locally as Iya-dani, is considered one of Japan's 'three hidden regions'. It was to here that Kyoto's defeated Heike clan fled from the rival Genji clan during the civil wars of the 12th century. Iya is romanticised in Alex Kerr's award-winning book *Lost Japan* . In 1972, Kerr bought an old *kayabuki* (thatch-roofed farmhouse) in the tiny hamlet of Tsuri, and has since been restoring it to its original brilliance (see the boxed text 'Chiiori – A Rural Retreat' later in this section).

Iya draws a steady stream of travellers who come to cross the famed *kazura-bashi* (vine bridges) that span the deep river gorges. Despite their virtual disappearance (the vines comprising the bridges must be totally replaced every three years), the tourist trade has spawned a recent comeback.

At one time, rivers in the mountainous interior of Shikoku were traversed by these perilous catwalks, which, when being pursued by enemy forces, could conveniently be cut down after crossing! Even with safety cables underneath, the *feat* of crossing is not for the acrophobic or faint-hearted.

Ōboke & Koboke
大歩危・小歩危

The JR Dosan rail line follows Route 32 along the Yoshino-gawa river gorge much of the way between Ikeda and Kōchi, and the scenery is often spectacular. The *Awa Ikeda Youth Hostel* (☎ 72-5277), set away from JR Awa Ikeda station on a mountain slope, charges ¥2850 (¥500/900 for breakfast/dinner).

The gorge through Yamashiro-chō and on the 8km stretch of the Yoshino-gawa between Koboke and Ōboke is particularly spectacular. From the starting point at the Restaurant Mannaka, a 20-minute walk from Oboke station on the JR Dosan line, there are 30-minute **boat rides** down the gentle river rapids toward Koboke and back (¥1000).

Less touristy (if pricey) alternatives to boating are Yoshino-gawa **rafting** and **kayaking trips**, which run on weekends from May to October. Costs average ¥14,500 for a day excursion. For information and reservations, call (in Japanese only) Aoki Canoe (☎ 0720-40-5644), Tanken Club (☎ 0743-73-7893) or the Mont Bell Challenge (☎ 06-6538-0208).

Lapis Ōboke, a few kilometres north of JR Ōboke station (¥500, 9 am to 4.30 pm),

SHIKOKU

IYA VALLEY & TSURUGI-SAN

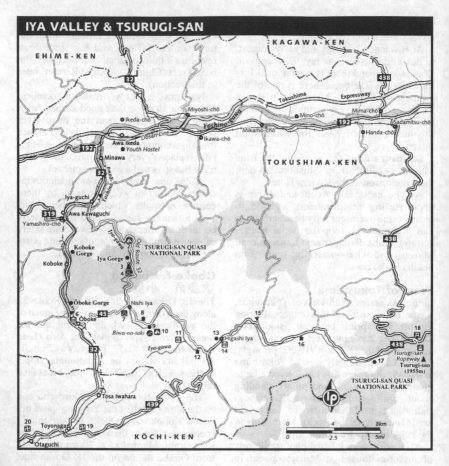

KAGAWA-KEN

EHIME-KEN

Tokushima

Expressway

438

Miyoshi-chō
Ikeda-chō
Mino-chō
Mima-chō
Sadamitsu-chō
192
Yoshino-kawa

Dosan-Line
Ikawa-chō
Mikamo-chō
Handa-chō

Awa Ikeda
Youth Hostel
192
Minawa

TOKUSHIMA-KEN

Iya-guchi

319
Awa Kawaguchi

Yamashiro-chō

Koboke
Gorge
2
Old Route 32
TSURUGI-SAN QUASI
NATIONAL PARK
438

Koboke
Iya Gorge
3
4

Ōboke Gorge
45
Nishi Iya
15

5
6
Ōboke
7
8
18

Biwa-no-taki
9
10
11
13
Higashi Iya
16
438

12
14
17
Tsurugi-san
Ropeway
Tsurugi-san
(1955m)

Iya-gawa

Tosa Iwahara

TSURUGI-SAN QUASI
NATIONAL PARK

439

20
Toyonaga
19
0   4   8km
0   2.5   5mi

Otaguchi
KŌCHI-KEN

is an architecturally-unique geology museum with a fine collection of rocks and precious stones.

There are several places to eat along Route 32, the best of which is *Woody Rest*, which serves excellent set meals for around ¥1000. The friendly owners speak English and have an English-language menu on hand.

If you are travelling south from Ikeda to Iya by private transport (bicycles included) and have time to explore, there is spectacular scenery in the deep canyons along the old Route 32. Turn east off the 'new' Route 32, over the big blue bridge near JR Iya-

guchi station (look for the sign to Deai), and follow the narrow, windy road through the gorge, Iya-kei, to the village of Icchyū in Nishi Iya. Along the way, just beyond the curious 'pissing boy' statue there are riverside hot-spring baths (¥1500) and accommodation at *Iya Onsen*.

Nishi Iya 西祖谷

Nishi (West) Iya, is best known for the extraordinary **Kazura-bashi** (Vine Bridge). There's a charge of ¥510 to walk across the bridge (sunrise to sunset, daily). Sadly, the area surrounding this beautiful bridge has

IYA VALLEY & TSURUGI-SAN

PLACES TO STAY
2 Iya-kei Camp Village
祖谷渓キャンプ村
8 Hotel Kazura-bashi;
Outdoor Bath
ホテルかずら橋
10 Kazura-bashi
Camping Ground
かずら橋キャンプ場
12 Ryūgūgake-kōen Lodge
龍宮崖公園ロッジ
16 Seishōnen Ryokō-mura
青少年旅行村

PLACES TO EAT
1 Woody Rest
渓流館

5 Restaurant Mannaka
レストラン　まんなか
15 Soba Dōjō
そば道場

OTHER
3 Pissing Boy Statue
小便小僧
4 Iya Onsen
祖谷温泉
6 Lapis Ōboke
Museum
ラピス大歩危
7 Hikyō-no-yu
秘境の湯
9 Kazura-bashi
かずら橋

11 Kimura-ke
木村家
13 Buke Yashiki
Samurai
House
武家屋敷
14 Folk Museum
民俗資料館
17 Oku Iya
Kazura-bashi
奥祖谷二重かずら橋
18 Ōtsurugi-jinja
大剣神社
19 Jōfuku-ji
常福寺
20 Buraku-ji
豊楽寺

fallen prey to an overdose of concrete, vending machines, and 'modern' architecture dominated by plastic and tin.

Hikyu-no-yu (☎ 87-2800) is a grand **onsen complex** featuring indoor and outdoor baths, a salt-filled sauna, a decent *restaurant* and *hotel*. The steep ¥1500 entry fee includes towels, toiletries and pyjamas to lounge around in after bathing. Your ticket stub will get you ¥200 off the admission price to cross Kazura-bashi, and vice-versa if you visit the bridge first. The new hotel here has rates per person from around ¥12,000 (including access to the onsen).

Rates at the upmarket *Hotel Kazura-bashi* (☎ 87-2171) are around ¥16,000 per person, including two meals. There is an excellent **rotemburo** (outdoor bath) here, which nonguests can enjoy for ¥750.

There are several cheaper *minshuku* in the Kazura-bashi area (rates average around ¥7000, including two meals), and a great *camping ground* (¥350 per person) upriver from the exit side of Kazura-bashi beyond **Biwa-no-taki**, a 50m-high waterfall.

By bus from Ōboke JR station, it's 12km to the bridge, but buses are infrequent and take an hour (¥880). Buses from Awa-Ikeda station (farther north on the Dosan line) take around 1¼ hours (¥1250).

From March to November, retro-style 'Bonnet Bus' tours to Iya leave from JR Awa Ikeda station, and cost ¥5200, which includes lunch and various entrance fees. Reserve by calling ☎ 72-1231 (in Japanese only).

Higashi Iya 東祖谷

If you want to escape the throngs of tourists around the Nishi Iya Kazura-bashi, travel another 30km west to the more remote **Oku Iya Kazura-bashi** (¥500) in Higashi (East) Iya. Set in a more pristine natural environment, the *fufu* (husband and wife) vine bridges hang side-by-side, along with a self-driven wooden monorail cart strung high over the river gorge. There is also a *camping ground* by the river's edge.

En route to the bridges are several other places of intrigue, including the **Kimura-ke**, which is a National Treasure (free), **Buke Yashiki** (¥300), a samurai house, and an interesting **folk museum** housed in the large red hall in the village centre. As Higashi Iya is a vast area spread over many kilometres of road, reaching sights by public transport is a challenge. If you cannot arrange your own wheels, hitching may be your best option.

There is reasonably-priced accommodation at *Seishōnen Ryoko-mura* (☎ 88-2975), a 'Youth Travellers' Village', near the Sugeoi bus stop, and cabins for rent at

SHIKOKU

Chiiori – A Rural Retreat

Some places in Japan appeal to us for their beauty, others for their history. Iya is pure romance. Precipitous cliffs rising from Japan's steepest gorges, swirling mists, villagers descended from 12th-century Heike courtiers. With its houses perched on hillsides high over winding roads and its air of isolation, Iya has been dubbed the 'Tibet of Japan'.

In my travels for Lonely Planet, I've rambled through vast stretches of the Japanese countryside and seen countless *minka*, or Japanese farmhouses, abandoned by families who migrated to the cities. I began 'minka hunting' in 1996 after being inspired by Alex Kerr's *Lost Japan*. In the book he writes of stumbling upon an Edo-era thatched-roof farmhouse deep in the Iya Valley, a house he later bought and named *Chiiori* (The House of the Flute). As fate would have it, I met Alex Kerr during my search and ended up his partner in the house

Chiiori has been under gradual restoration for nearly 30 years, and in 1988 underwent a complete re-thatching of the tremendous *kayabuki* roof. The task of mending and maintaining a 300-year-old wooden structure is enormous, but lately a steady stream of like-minded people have rallied around the house. In 1998 a group of them got together and founded what has become The Chiiori Project.

The ultimate goal of the Project is to bring the house and the depopulated village around it back to life, and in doing so offer people an experience like no other in Japan. We are attempting to show, in one tiny rural hamlet, that there is a way for Japan to move forward and modernise without abandoning its cultural heritage. We aim to preserve the beauty of the old and use natural materials to create a comfortable and eco-friendly retreat.

Over the past several years Chiiori has played host to hundreds of people from Japan and over 30 countries around the world. During volunteer weekends people trade their sweat for a chance to learn about Japanese crafts, such as carpentry, masonry or roof-thatching. At other times visitors attend workshops and seminars ranging from tea ceremony, indigo dyeing and lantern making to yoga, *shiatsu* and creative writing. In the evening, after a hard day's work or seminar, it's off to the local onsen. Back at Chiiori, we chat by the *irori*, or open hearth, sip sake, watch the smoke billow up into the rafters and talk of cabbages and kings until the wee hours.

You can learn more about the Chiiori Project on our Web site at www.chiiori.org.

Mason Florence

the *Ryūgūgake-kōen Lodge* (☎ 88-5001). Cabin prices start from ¥4000.

At the *Soba Dōjō* you can taste some Iya soba – and also try making your own. Farther along Route 439, past the Oku Iya Kazura-bashi, is the trailhead to sacred Tsurugi-san. Infrequent Minokoshi-bound buses run to Higashi Iya from Ikeda (via Ōboke and Nishi Iya).

Tsurugi-san 剣山

The mountain's name translates to Sword Peak, although it is actually gently rounded rather than sharp-edged. It is also known locally as 'Ken-zan'. At 1955m, it is the second highest mountain in Shikoku. A chairlift can take you to a point from which it is a leisurely 40-minute walk to the summit; but

many prefer to start the walk from **Ōtsurugi-jinja**, the summit shrine near the car park.

Upholding a long tradition of mountain worship, a **festival** is held annually on 1 August at Ōtsurugi-jinja. From April to October it is possible to stay at the *Tsurugi-jinja Lodge* (☎ 0886-67-5244) or the *Kokuminshukusha Tsurugi-sansō Lodge* (☎ 67-5150). For detailed information on hiking Tsurugi-san pick up a copy of Lonely Planet's *Hiking in Japan*.

Jōfuku-ji & Buraku-ji 定福寺・武楽寺

Farther west (in Kōchi-ken), tranquil Jōfuku-ji has a *Youth Hostel* (☎ 0887-74-0301), with nightly costs of ¥3200 (breakfast/dinner cost ¥600/1000). At JR Toyonaga station, there's a sign in English directing people to the hostel. The next stop is Ōtaguchi, from where it's a 40-minute walk to **Buraku-ji**. Its main hall dates from AD 1151.

Kōchi-ken 高知県

The largest of Shikoku's four prefectures, Kōchi-ken (formerly the land of Tosa) spans the entire Pacific coastline from the cape at Muroto-misaki to Ashizuri-misaki. Blessed with a warm southern climate, it is a popular domain for outdoor activities, from diving, surfing and whale watching to canoeing, rafting, and camping along the 192km Shimanto-gawa – the last un-dammed, naturally flowing river in Japan.

KŌCHI 高知
☎ 088 ● pop 317,000

Kōchi was the castle town of what used to be Tosa province, and the small but original castle still stands. Like Kagoshima in Kyūshū and Hagi in Western Honshū, this pleasant city lays claim to having played an important role in the Meiji Restoration.

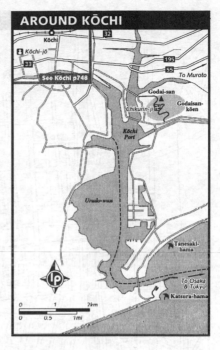

AROUND KŌCHI

Sakamoto Ryōma – Local Hero

Although it was the progressive *samurai* of Kagoshima and Hagi who played the major part in the dramatic events of the Meiji Restoration, the citizens of Kōchi claim it was their boy, Sakamoto Ryōma, who brought the two sides together.

Unhappy with the rigid class structure In-stitutionalised under Tokugawa rule, Saka-moto sought exile in Nagasaki, where he ran a trading company and helped build the pow-erful alliances that prompted the collapse of the shogunate.

His assassination in Kyoto in 1867, when he was just 32 years old, cemented his ro-mantic albeit tragic image, and he appears, looking distinctly sour, on countless post-cards and other tourist memorabilia in Kōchi. There's a notable statue of Sakamoto at Katsura-hama.

Orientation

Harimayabashi-dōri, the main street in Kōchi, runs on a north-south axis, with a tram line down the centre. The street crosses the main shopping arcade and the other main street near Harimaya-bashi. This bridge has long gone (apart from some purely decorative railings), but the citizens of Kōchi still recall a famous ditty about a bald monk buying a hair band at the bridge – presumably for a female friend.

Apart from the castle and excellent Sun-day market, most of Kōchi's other attrac-tions are some distance from the town centre. Two major festivals worth looking out for are **Yosakoi** (early-August) and **Tai Matsu Matsuri** (mid-September).

Tourist Offices The information office (☎ 882-7777) outside JR Kōchi station is open daily from 9 am to 9.30 pm. Staff can provide brochures in English, and also help to book accommodation.

SHIKOKU

KŌCHI

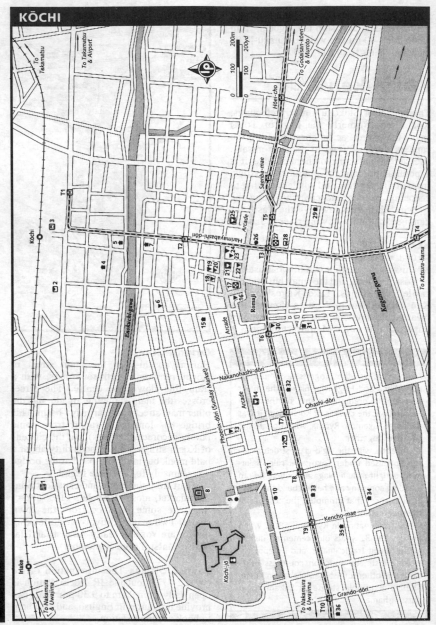

KŌCHI

PLACES TO STAY

4 Business Hotel City Kōchi
ビジネスホテルシティ
高知
5 Hotel Takasago
ホテル高砂
7 Kōchi Green Hotel
高知グリーンホテル
15 Washington Hotel
高知ワシントンホテル
29 Kōchi Business Hotel
Honkan
高知ビジネスホテル本館
31 Hotel Tosa
ホテル土佐
32 Kōchi Sunrise Hotel
高知サンライズホテル
33 Hotel New Hankyū
高知新阪急ホテル
34 Sansuien Ryokan;
Onsen Hoteru
三翠園小アル
35 Kōchi Green Kaikan
高知グリーン会館
36 Orient Hotel Kōchi
オリエントホテル高知

PLACES TO EAT

6 Mama Italia
ママイタリア
13 Hirome Market
ひろめマーケット
16 Tsukasa
料亭司
18 Murasaki
むらさき

19 Baffone
バフォネ
20 Hakobe
はこべ
22 Tsukasa
料亭司
23 Tsukasa
料亭司
24 Ninniku-ya; Cafe de Blue
にんにく屋;
カフェドブルー
30 Jungri-la
ジャングリラ

OTHER

1 Anraku-ji
安楽寺
2 Main Post Office
高知中央郵便局
3 Kōchi Bus Station (to
Katsura-hama Beach
& Matsuyama)
バスターミナル
（松山行き他）
8 Prefectural Museum-Kōchi
History Museum
高知県立文学館
9 Ote-mon
10 Kōchi International
Association (KIA)
高知インターナショナルア
ソシエーション
11 NTT
12 Post Office
郵便局

14 Bar Cake; Sunset Library
バーケーキ・
サンセットライブラリー
17 Daimaru Department Store
大丸百貨店
21 Irish Bar
アイリッシュバー
25 Get
ゲット
26 Harimaya-bashi
27 Seibu Department Store
西武デパート
28 Katsura-hama Bus Stop
かつら浜バス停

TRAM STOPS

T1 Kōchi-eki
こうちえきまえ
T2 Hasuike-machi
はすいけまち
T3 Harimaya-bashi
はりまやばし
T4 Umenotsuji
うめのつじ
T5 Dentetsu tāminaru-biru mae
デンテツターミナルビル
T6 Horizume
ほりづめ
T7 Ōhashi-dōri
おおはしどおり
18 Kochijo-mae
こうちじょうまえ
T9 Kenchō-mae
けんちょうまえ
T10 Grando-dōri
グランドどおり

Also well worth visiting for local English information and maps is the Kōchi International Association (KIA; ☎ 875-0022), located on the south side of the castle. It's open from 8.30 am to 5.15 pm, closed Sunday.

Dogs & Roosters

The Kōchi area is noted for its fighting dogs and long-tailed roosters. The mastiff-like dogs are ranked like *sumō* wrestlers and even wear similar aprons. You can see demonstration fights at the **Tosa Tōken Centre** near Katsura-hama.

Breeders have coaxed the long-tailed rooster (*onaga-dori*) to produce tail feathers up to 10m long! You can see them at the **Chōbikei Centre** in Nankoku city (¥500), out towards Kōchi airport and also at the cave, Ryūga-dō.

Kōchi-jō 高知城

Kōchi's castle may not be one of the great castles of Japan, but it is a real survivor, not a post-war concrete reconstruction, and the lovely grounds are great for a stroll. Although a building on the site dates back to the 14th century, the present castle was built between 1601–11, burnt down in 1727 and rebuilt in 1753. By this time, the peace of the Tokugawa period was well established and castles were scarcely necessary except as a symbol of a feudal lord's power.

SHIKOKU

The Kōchi lord therefore rebuilt the castle with his *kaitokukan* (living quarters) on the ground floor, with doors opening into the garden. Kōchi-jō, therefore, is not a gloomy castle, unlike those that were strongly fortified against enemy attack tended to be. The castle offers fine views over the town (¥350, 9 am to 5 pm).

At the bottom of the castle hill is the well-preserved gateway, **Ōte-mon**. Inside the castle there is a small **museum** with exhibits relating to Sakamoto Ryōma.

Godaisan-kōen & Chikurin-ji 五台山公園・竹林寺

The hilltop temple Chikurin-ji and Kōchi's botanical gardens are both in Godaisan-kōen, several kilometres from the town centre. The temple is **No 31 on the 88 Temple Circuit**, and there's an attractive five-storey pagoda at the top of the hill. The temple's Treasure House has an interesting collection of statues, some looking very Indian or Tantric.

The ¥400 entry also covers the temple garden. On the other side of the car park is the Makino Botanical Garden and greenhouse (¥500).

To get to the park and temple take a bus from the Toden Seibu bus station next to the Seibu department store at the Harimaya-bashi junction. The bus stops outside the temple steps (¥370, 20 minutes, hourly until 5 pm).

Katsura-hama 桂浜

Katsura-hama is a popular beach 13km from downtown Kōchi. Apart from the sea, sand, and a statue of Sakamoto Ryōma, there are only a handful of attractions. Dog fight demonstrations are held in the **Tosa Tōken Centre** (¥1500, 9 am to 4 pm), but you may have to wait until sufficient spectators have gathered.

A five-minute walk west of Katsura-hama is the **Sakamoto Ryōma Memorial Museum** (¥350, 9 am to 4.30 pm), which tells the local hero's life story in miniature dioramas. The **Kōchi-ken Ubusana Hakubutsu-kan** (¥500, 8.30 am to 5 pm), exhibits 4300 varieties of sea shells and coral, and runs an espresso bar if you're

craving a caffeine fix. The **Katsura-hama Aquarium** (¥1100, 8.30 am to 5.30 pm) aquarium features local *akame* fished from the bay, Tosa-wan. Local kids enjoy feeding the fish and resident sea turtles.

Buses make the run from Kōchi bus station to Katsura-hama hourly (¥610, 30 minutes); there's also a bus stop on the south-east corner of Chūō-kōn (¥560).

Sunday Market

If you're in Kōchi on Sunday, don't miss the colourful street market along Phoenix-dōri, the road leading to the castle. The market has everything from fruit, vegetables and goldfish to antiques and large garden stones.

Places to Stay – Budget

For basic accommodation, the *Kōchi Business Hotel Honkan* (☎ 883-0221) has singles/twins starting at ¥3800/7400. At the *Hotel Tosa* (☎ 825-3332), not far from the Horizume tram stop, rooms start at ¥3900.

Places to Stay – Mid-Range

Kokuminshuku-sha Out by the beach at Katsura-hama, the large green *Kokuminshuku-sha Katsura-hama Sō* (☎ 841-2201) is good value at ¥8100 per person, including two meals.

Hotels Just south of the Kencho-mae tram stop, the *Kōchi Green Kaikan* (☎ 825-2701) has singles/twins at ¥5700/10,600. Near the station, the *Business Hotel City Kōchi* (☎ 872-2121) has singles/doubles/twins from ¥5500/8200/9800. The *Kōchi Green Hotel* (☎ 822-1800) is another standard hotel that's not too far from the station. Singles cost ¥6600; twins and doubles start at ¥10,300. Also not far from the station, the *Hotel Takasago* (☎ 822-1288) offers singles/twins starting at ¥6300/12,600.

The *Washington Hotel* (☎ 823-6111), on Phoenix-dōri, is conveniently central and close to the castle. Rooms start at ¥7850/17,600 for singles/doubles. The pleasant *Orient Hotel Kōchi* (☎ 822-6565) is south of the castle and on the tram line. Rooms for one person start at ¥7700 and for two at ¥13,200.

SHIKOKU

The *Kōchi Sunrise Hotel* (☎ 822-1281) charges from ¥7200/11,100 for singles/doubles.

Places to Stay – Top End
The ryokan-style *Sansuien Hotel* (☎ 822-0131), south of the castle, includes some old buildings from the grounds of the Kōchi *daimyō* (regional lord under the shōgun) and an **onsen**. Costs per person range from ¥15,000, including meals. The onsen is open to the public between 10 am and 4 pm (¥900).

Places to Eat
Kōchi's best restaurants are clustered around the Daimaru department store, in and around the Obiyamachi shopping arcade. You'll find three branches of *Tsukasa*, a Japanese *Tosa ryori* (Tosa-cuisine) restaurant displaying plastic meals from tempura to *sashimi*. Just off the arcade there's a branch of the *Murasaki* robatayaki, easily recognisable by its thatched-house motif.

Baffone, a cosy open-air cafe, has homemade pastas and salads. *Mama Italia* has commendable brick-oven pizza, an English menu and friendly service. *Hakobe* offers excellent 'cook it yourself' okonomiyaki. Garlic lovers should try *Ninniku-ya*, with its all-garlic menu (illustrated and in English).

Jungri-la, a 2nd-floor izakaya with a jungle motif, serves out-of-the-ordinary dishes including alligator meat! Finally, *Hirome Market* boasts an interesting collection of shops and eateries that are well worth checking out.

Entertainment
Irish Bar is just what you'd expect, right down to the Guinness on tap. Quiet spots for a drink include *Bar Cake* and *Sunset Library*, while *Café de Blue* and *Get* are good places to dance.

Getting There & Away
Air ANA, JAL and JAS all connect Kōchi with Tokyo (¥23,450, 80 minutes). Other flights to/from Kōchi include Fukuoka (¥17,450, 50 minutes) and Miyazaki in Kyūshū (¥15,600, 55 minutes), Nagoya

(¥17,900, one hour), Osaka (¥12,100, 40 minutes) and Sapporo (¥35,100, two hours).

Train Kōchi is on the JR Dosan line, which runs from the north coast of Shikoku through Kotohira. It takes about 2½ hours by *tokkyū* (limited express) from Takamatsu. From Kōchi, rail services continue westward to just beyond Kubokawa where the line splits south-west to Nakamura and north-west to Uwajima. From Uwajima, you can continue north to Matsuyama.

Bus Long distance buses run between Kōchi and points on Honshū including Tokyo (¥12,500, 12 hours), Nagoya (¥9070, 10 hours), Osaka (¥6000, six to seven hours), Okayama (¥3500, 2½ hours) and Fukuoka (¥10,500, 9½ hours).

Travel between Kōchi and Matsuyama is faster by bus. These depart hourly from outside the bus station near JR Kōchi station. To travel around the south coast, either west around Ashizuri-misaki to Uwajima or east around Muroto-misaki to Tokushima, you will have to travel by bus as the train lines do not extend all the way.

Boat Kōchi is connected by overnight ferry to Osaka (¥4,610, nine hours) and Tokyo (¥10,600, 20 hours).

Getting Around
The tram service (¥180) running north-south from the station intersects the east-west tram route at the Harimaya-bashi junction. Ask for a '*norikaeken*' (transfer ticket) if you have to transfer there. You can easily reach the castle on foot, though to reach the town's other attractions you must take a bus.

AROUND KŌCHI
There are a number of other interesting places easily reached from Kōchi, including Katsura-hama.

Ino-chō 伊野町
Four stations west of Kōchi on the JR line, the **Ino-chō Paper Museum** (¥310, 9 am to 5 pm, closed Monday) is a good place to try your hand at traditional Tosa paper making.

A few hundred metres north is **Gallery Copa** (¥100), which is worth visiting to see contemporary Japanese art.

A few kilometres north of JR Ino-eki on Route 194 there is *camping* on the banks of the Niyodo-gawa; and about 8km north of the station is the **Culture Resort Ino** (☎ 088-892-1001), housing paper-making facilities, three restored *kura* (grain warehouses), a *hotel*, *restaurant* and onsen. The resort is reasonably priced, charging ¥10,000 per person, including two meals. Day-trippers can indulge in the onsen for ¥700. Ask for a pamphlet on the resort (also called Cour aux Dons) at the JR Kōchi station tourist information office.

Slightly farther afield, the **Tosa Traditional Paper and Handicraft Village** (Tosa Washi Kōgei-mura Kuraudo; ☎ 088-892-3872) offers classes and demonstrations of paper making and weaving (10.30 am to 4 pm, closed Wednesday). It's near Iwa-mura bus stop, a 15-minute bus ride from JR Ino-eki.

West of Ino-chō, **Ochi-chō** offers good hiking, riverside *camping* and has the impressive **Yokagura Natural Forest Museum** (¥500).

Ryūga-dō 龍河洞

This impressive limestone cave has characteristic stalactites and stalagmites, and traces of prehistoric habitation. You can also see the famed long-tailed roosters here. A bus bound for Odochi will get you to the cave in about an hour. Entry is ¥1000, and for an extra ¥500 you can rent a helmet and headlamp to venture deeper inside.

Aki 安芸市

Farther east is Aki, where Iwasaki Yatarō, founder of the giant Mitsubishi conglomerate, was born in 1834. His thatch-roofed house is well preserved; call ☎ 0887-34-1111 if you are would like to visit it. There are some old samurai streets around the castle remains.

Umaji 馬路村

North-east of Aki, rural Umaji is surrounded by mountains and boasts good hiking, **onsen**, and a handful of praiseworthy *eateries* serving local specialties. You can stay at the attractive *village onsen*, or *camp* in the area. Umaji is reached by bus from Kōchi (2 hours).

MUROTO-MISAKI 室戸岬

Muroto-misaki, the cape south-east of Kōchi, has a lighthouse topping its wild cliffscape. The temple **Higashi-dera** is **No 24 on the 88 Temple Circuit**. Just north of Muroto is a chain of black-sand beaches known by local surfers as **Little Hawaii**.

There's accommodation near the cape at the *Hotsumisaki-ji Youth Hostel* (☎ 0887-23-2488); nightly costs are ¥3200, plus ¥600/1000 for breakfast/dinner.

You can reach the cape by bus from Kōchi and continue right around to Tokushima on the east coast. The Tosa Dentetsu buses for Muroto-misaki run from the Harimaya-bashi intersection in central Kōchi (¥2810, 2½ hours). The JR Mugi line runs around the east coast from Tokushima as far as Kaifu.

ASHIZURI-MISAKI 足摺岬

South-west of Kōchi, Ashizuri-misaki, like Muroto-misaki, is a wild and picturesque promontory ending at a lighthouse. As well as the coastal road, there's the scenic central **Skyline Road**. The cape also has **Kongō-fuku-ji**, **No 38 on the 88 Temple Circuit**, which, like the one at Muroto-misaki, has its own *youth hostel* (☎ 0880-88-0038). Nightly costs are ¥2900 (add ¥500/900 for breakfast/dinner); call in advance. The *Ashizuri Kokuminshukusha* (☎ 0880-88-0301) costs from ¥6600 per person with two meals. Just in front is a small tourist information booth with English maps of the area and a statue of local hero John Manjirō.

The cape's main attractions, including Kongōfuku-ji and a wooded **'romance walk'**, are all within easy walking distance of the Ashizuri-misaki bus station.

From Tosashimizu, at the northern end of the cape, ferries operate to Osaka (¥6730). From Kōchi, there is a train as far as **Nakamura**. From JR Nakamura station there is a regular bus service to Ashizuri-misaki (¥1970, one hour). You can continue around the cape and on to Uwajima by bus.

Nakamura is a good place to organise trips on the beautiful **Shimanto-gawa**, proudly hailed as the last free flowing river in Japan. Staff at the tourist information office at JR Nakamura station can provide information on **river-boat trips**, camping and outdoor activities. The *Shimanto-gawa Youth Hostel* (☎ *0880-54-1352*) is most easily reached on the JR Yodo line from Uwajima (Ehime-ken) to Egawa-saki train station, from where buses take you 12km to Kuchiyanai. Beds cost ¥3150; add on ¥600/1000 for breakfast/dinner.

NORTH-WEST TO UWAJIMA

From **Tosashimizu**, the road continues around the southern coast of Shikoku to Uwajima in Ehime-ken. The scenery is particularly attractive through **Tatsukushi**, where there is a coral museum (¥300) and a shell museum (¥500). **Sightseeing boats** and glass-bottom boats operate from the town (¥850).

Sukumo has a fine harbour and the *Sukumo Youth Hostel* (☎ *0880-64-0233*) charges ¥2900, and ¥500/1000 for breakfast/dinner.

Sukumo is less than an hour by bus from Nakamura, but longer around the coast via the cape; travel on to Uwajima takes about two hours. From Sukumo, ferries make the three-hour crossing several times daily to Saeki on Kyūshū.

There are several popular **dive sites** in the area, notably at Nishi-umi and Kashiwajima; there is also good diving off Okinoshima (reached by boat from Sukumo).

Ehime-ken 愛媛県

Occupying the north-western region of Shikoku and famed for its oranges and cultured pearls, the highlights of Ehime-ken include Matsuyama-jō and Dōgo Onsen, the sacred peak Ishizuchi-san (1982m), and the pleasant towns of Uchiko and Uwajima.

MATSUYAMA 松山

☎ 089 • pop 443,000

Shikoku's largest city, Matsuyama, is a busy north-coast town and an important transport hub. Matsuyama's major attractions are its

---

Manjirō the Hero

Nearly every corner of Shikoku boasts a local hero, but perhaps most extraordinary of them all is Kōchi-born John Manjirō.

His real name was Nakahama Manjirō. In 1841, while helping out on a fishing boat, a violent storm swept 14-year-old Manjirō and four others onto the desolate shores of Tori-shima, 600km off Tokyo Bay. Five months later they were rescued by a US whaler, and granted safe passage to Hawaii.

In Hawaii the ship's captain invited Manjirō to return to his home in Massachusetts, where the boy spent four years learning English, navigation and the ways of the West, before his skills took him back to sea and around the world. In 1851, 10 years after the shipwreck, Manjirō returned to Japan, where he was interrogated (Japan's National Seclusion policy forbade overseas travel), but allowed to return to Kōchi.

When Commodore Perry's 'black ships' arrived in 1853, Manjirō was summoned to Edo to advise the Shōgun. He was later the chief translator for the Harris Treaty negotiations of 1858, and subsequently published Japan's first English-language phrase book, *Shortcut to Anglo-American Conversation*. He returned to the US in 1860 as part of a Japanese delegation, and after the Meiji Restoration in 1867 took up post at the Kaisei School for Western Learning (which later became part of Tokyo University).

Manjirō is remembered as a man whose destiny took him from the simple life of a teenage fisherman to becoming one of Japan's first true statesmen. On the cape at Ashizuri-misaki, a large statue stands in his honour, and there is a museum dedicated to his achievements. Manjirō's intrepid journey is recounted in Masuji Ibuse's *Castaways* (Kodansha International).

SHIKOKU

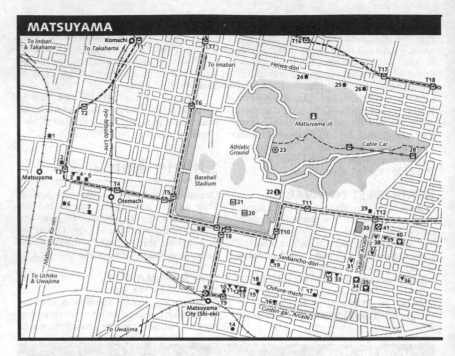

castle – one of the finest survivors from the feudal era – and the Dōgo Onsen area, with its magnificent old public baths.

Orientation & Information

JR Matsuyama station is west of the castle. The town centre is immediately south of the castle and close to Matsuyama City station (Shi-eki) on the private Iyo-tetsudō line. Dōgo Onsen is east of town, while the ferry port at Takahama is north of the town centre and the JR station.

English-language books can be found on the 4th floor of the Kinokuniya bookshop, near Matsuyama City station. Matsuyama is noted for its deep-blue textiles called *iyo-kasuri*, and *tobe-yaki* style of pottery.

There is an information counter at the ferry terminal for arrivals from Hiroshima, though the main Tourist Information Center (TIC) is the JR Matsuyama station branch (☎ 931-3914), which is open from 8.30 am to 7.30 pm daily. Dōgo Onsen also has a tourist information office near the tram terminus, at the entrance to the arcade leading to the famous public bath.

On the south side of the castle is the Ehime Prefectural Information Centre (EPIC; ☎ 943-6688), which is another good place to pick up English information.

Matsuyama-jō 松山城

Picturesquely sited atop a hill that virtually erupts in the middle of the town, Matsuyama-jō is one of Japan's finest original surviving castles. It only squeaks in with the 'original' label, however, as it was restored just before the end of the Edo period. In the early years of the Meiji Restoration, rebuilding feudal symbols was definitely not a high priority.

The castle was built in 1602–03 with five storeys; it burnt down and was rebuilt in 1642 with three storeys only. In 1784 it was struck by lightning and burnt down once again and, in those peaceful and torpid Edo

SHIKOKU

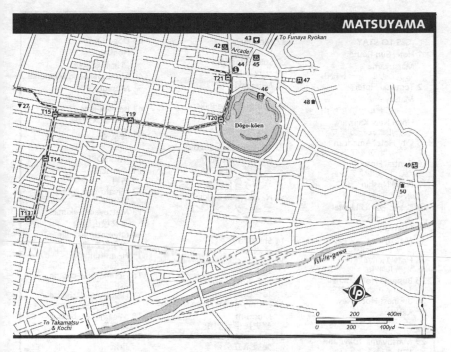

MATSUYAMA

years, it took until 1820 for a decision to be made to rebuild it and until 1854 for the reconstruction to be completed! It was completely restored between 1968–86.

You don't have to climb the steep hill up to the castle; a cable car and/or chairlift will whisk you up there for ¥400/return. Entry to the castle costs ¥350.

Consider walking down the back slopes of the castle hill to see **Ninomaru Shiseki Teien** (¥100), a garden located just north of EPIC. From the garden it's a short stroll to the **Ehime Museum of Art** (¥500, 9.40 am to 6 pm, closed Monday) and, keeping the same hours, the interesting, yet seldom-visited, **History and Folklore Museum** (free). It's on the 5th floor of the building, in view from the rear exit of the Ehime Museum of Art.

Shiki-dō 子規堂

Matsuyama claims to be the capital of *haiku* (17-syllable poems), and just south of Matsuyama City station in the temple grounds

of Shoshu-ji is a replica of the humble **house** of haiku poet Shiki Masaoka (1867–1902). The **Shiki Memorial Museum** in Dōgo-kōen is also dedicated to the poet.

Dōgo Onsen 道後温泉

This popular spa centre, 2km east of the town centre, is easily reached by the regular tram service; it terminates at the start of the spa's shopping arcade. The arcade leads to the front of Dōgo Onsen Honkan (Dōgo Spa Main Building).

Dōgo Onsen Honkan 道後温泉本館

A high priority for any visitor to Matsuyama should be a bath at this rambling old public bathhouse (6.30 am to 10 pm), which dates from 1894. Apart from the baths, there's the **Yūshinden**, a private bathing suite built for an imperial visit in 1899, and the **Botchan Room**, named for the character in the novel *Botchan* by Soseki Natsume, who was a frequent visitor to the baths.

SHIKOKU

MATSUYAMA

PLACES TO STAY
1 Hotel Sun Route
  Matsuyama
  ホテルサンルート松山
2 Terminal Hotel
  Matsuyama
  ターミナルホテル松山
4 Hotel New Kajiwara
  ホテルニューカジワラ
5 City Hotel American
  シティホテルアメリカン
6 Central Hotel
  セントラルホテル
7 Hotel Nisshin
  ホテル日進
8 Tokyo Dai Ichi Hotel
  東京第一ホテル
19 Chateau-teru
  Matsuyama
  シャトウテル松山
24 Hotel Heiwa
  ホテル平和
25 Business Hotel Taihei
  ビジネスホテル泰平
26 Business Hotel New
  Kashima
  ビジネスホテルニュー
  かしま
29 Matsuyama Tōkyū Inn
  松山東急イン
30 ANA Hotel Matsuyama
  全日空ホテル松山
48 Matsuyama Youth Hostel
  松山ユースホステル
50 Minshuku Miyoshi
  民宿みよし

PLACES TO EAT
3 Nakanoya
  中野屋
11 Atom Boy Sushi
  アトム寿司
12 a table
  アテーブル
15 Freshness Burger
  フレッシュネスバーガー
16 Charlie
  チャーリー
31 Chanoma
  茶の間
33 Goshiki
  五志喜
36 Karasu
  からす

37 Ninniku-ya
  にんにく屋
27 Spice Kingdom
  スパイス王国
38 Murasaki
  むらさき
39 Pound House Bakery
  パウンドハウス

OTHER
9 ANA & JAS & Sogō
  Department Store
  全日空／日本
  エアシステム／
  そごう百貨店蕩
10 New Grand Building
  ニューグランドビル
13 Munchen
  ミュンヘン
14 Shiki-dō
  子規堂
17 JAL
  日本航空
18 Kinokuniya Bookshop
  紀伊国屋書店
20 History and Folkore
  Museum
  歴史民俗資裏館
21 Ehime Museum of Art
  愛媛県立美術館
22 Ehime Prefectural
  Information Centre (EPIC)
  県国際交流センター
23 Ninomaru Shiseki Tei-en
  二之丸史跡庭園
28 Cable Car Station
  ケーブルカー駅
32 Post Office
  中央郵便局
34 Piccadilly Circus Bar
  ピカデリーサーカス
35 Deja vu; Club eX
  デジャブ・クラブeX
40 Bar 9 Carat
  9カラット
41 Mitsukoshi Department
  Store
  三越百貨店
42 Tsubaki-no-yu Onsen
  椿の湯
43 Dōgo Biiru-kan
  道後麦酒館
44 Dōgo Onsen Information
  Office
  道後温泉案内所

45 Dōgo Onsen
  Honkan
  道後温泉本館
46 Municipal Shiki Memorial
  Museum
  市立子規記念館
47 Isaniwa-jinja
  伊佐爾波神社
49 Ishite-ji
  石手寺

TRAM STOPS
T1 Komachi
  古町
T2 Miyato-chō
  宮田町
T3 Matsuyama-ekimae
  ＪＲ松山駅前
T4 Ōtemachi-ekimae
  大手町駅前
T5 Nishi-horibata
  西堀端
T6 Honmachi 3-chōme
  本町三丁目
T7 Honmachi 5-chōme
  本町五丁目
T8 Minami-hori bata
  南堀端
T9 Shieki-mae
  市駅前
T10 Shiyakusho-mae
  市役所前
T11 Kenchō-mae
  県庁前
T12 Ichiban-chō
  一番町
T13 Katsuyama-chō
  勝山町
T14 Keisatsusho-mae
  警察署前
T15 Kamiichiman
  上一万
T16 Shimizu-machi
  清水町
T17 Tetsubō-chō
  鉄砲町
T18 Sekijūji
  Byōin-mae
  赤十字病院前
T19 Minami-machi
  南町
T20 Dōgokōen-mae
  道後公園前
T21 Dōgo Onsen
  道後温泉

SHIKOKU

Dōgo Onsen Honkan is another place where the correct sequence of steps can be a little confusing. Pay your money outside: ¥300 for a basic bath, or ¥620 (the best overall value ticket) for a bath followed by tea and a snack, including a rental *yukata* (a light cotton kimono). For ¥980/1240 you get the *tama-no-yu* (Bath of the Spirits), followed by tea and *dango* (a sweet dumpling), and more private rest quarters.

Enter and leave your shoes in a locker. If you've paid ¥300, go to the *kami-no-yu* (Bath of the Gods) changing room (signposted in English).

If you've paid ¥620 or more, first go upstairs to get your yukata, then return to the appropriate changing room. You can leave valuables upstairs in the charge of the attendants who dispense the yukata. After your bath, those destined for upstairs can don their yukata and retire to the tatami mats and veranda to sip tea and gaze down on bath-hoppers clip-clopping by in *geta* (traditional wooden sandals).

The baths can get quite crowded, especially on weekends and holidays; dinner time is less crowded, as most Japanese tourists will be dining in their respective inns.

Tsubaki-no-yu 椿の湯 One minute on foot from the Honkan (through the arcade) is Dōgo Onsen's hot spring annexe (¥300, 6.30 am to 10.30 pm). The baths are popular with locals.

Isaniwa-jinja 伊佐爾波神社
A few minutes walk from the Dōgo Onsen bathhouse, a long flight of shrine steps leads up to the Hachiman Isaniwa-jinja, built in 1667.

Municipal Shiki Memorial Museum 市立子規記念博物館
This museum is dedicated to the memory of the local haiku master Shiki Masaoka (¥300, 9 am, to 4.30 pm, closed Monday).

Ishite-ji 石手寺
'Ishite' means 'stone hand', from a legend about a Matsuyama lord born with a stone in his hand. Dating from 1318, Ishite-ji is **No 51 on the 88 Temple Circuit** and is noted for its fine Kamakura architecture. It has a three-storey pagoda and is overlooked by a Buddha-figure high up on the hill. It's a five-minute walk east from the spa area to Ishite-ji. Matsuyama also has seven other circuit temples.

Places to Stay
Matsuyama has three accommodation areas: around the JR station (business hotels); the city centre (business hotels and more top-end hotels); and atmospheric Dōgo Onsen (youth hostels, ryokan and Japanese-style hotels).

Places to Stay – Budget
Youth Hostel Dōgo Onsen, east of the town centre, makes a pleasant area to overnight. The excellent *Matsuyama Youth Hostel* (☎ 933-6366), near Isaniwa-jinja, costs ¥3200 a night; breakfast/dinner costs ¥500/1000. Internet access is available.

Minshuku Most Japanese-style hotels and ryokan in the Dōgo Onsen area are quite pricey, but the friendly *Minshuku Miyoshi* (☎ 977-2581), behind the petrol station near Ishite-ji, is an exception at ¥4000 per person, or ¥7000 with two meals.

Places to Stay – Mid-Range
The *Central Hotel* (☎ 941-4358), close to Matsuyama station, is a business hotel with singles/twins from ¥4800/8500. Other hotels within a stone's throw of the station include the *Hotel New Kajiwara* (☎ 941-0402), with singles/twins starting at ¥5250/8820, and the *City Hotel American* (☎ 933-6660), next door. It has singles/twins from ¥4500/6000.

Hotel Sun Route Matsuyama (☎ 933-2811), has singles from ¥7300 and doubles and twins from ¥13,500. Beside the station, *Terminal Hotel Matsuyama* (☎ 947-5388) has singles/twins at ¥5775/10,500. The *Hotel Nisshin* (☎ 946-3111) is a slightly longer walk from the station, with singles/doubles starting from ¥5600/11,200.

Tokyo Dai Ichi Hotel (☎ 947-4411) is on the station side of the town centre and has

SHIKOKU

singles starting at ¥6800, and doubles and twins at ¥13,000. Rooms at *Chateau Teru Matsuyama* (☎ 946-2111), with its rooftop-garden *restaurant*, start at ¥6000/11,000 for singles/twins.

Immediately north of the castle hill is a quieter area, conveniently connected to the town centre by a tram line (Tetsubō-chō stop). Here the curiously old-fashioned *Business Hotel Taihei* (☎ 943-3560) offers singles/twins starting from ¥5500/10,000. The *Hotel Heiwa* (☎ 921-3515) has rooms starting from ¥6000/10,000, and the *Business Hotel New Kashima* (☎ 947-2100) charges ¥4510/8400.

Places to Stay – Top-End
The upmarket *ANA Hotel Matsuyama* (☎ 933-5511) near the Ichiban-chō tram stop has singles starting from ¥10,500, and twins from ¥17,500. Just across the road is the *Matsuyama Tokyū Inn* (☎ 941-0109), with singles costing from ¥8600 and twins/doubles from ¥16,000.

The *Funaya Ryokan* (☎ 947-0278) is one of the best of the onsen-ryokan, but count on around ¥25,000 upwards per person, including meals.

The tourist office near the tram terminus can provide a list of other upmarket lodgings in the area.

Places to Eat
The Ginten-gai and Okai-dō shopping arcades in central Matsuyama are the best places to seek out more interesting eating options. A few streets east of Okai-dō in the Mitsuwa 24 building, *Karasu* is a great little *yakitori-ya* (eatery specialising in charcoal-broiled chicken on skewers) worth seeking out. The talented owner/chef lived in Australia and speaks English well (5.30 pm to 2 am).

Ninniku-ya offers a wide assortment of tasty garlic-fuelled dishes, while *Chanoma* (6 pm to 2 am, closed Sunday), a friendly and *very* local traditional pub, serves hot bowls of *ocha-zuke* (tea over rice with salmon and dried seaweed) and cold beer. *Pound House*, near the *Murasaki* robatayaki, has a delicious selection of cakes.

Next to the post office in the town centre, *Restaurant Goshiki* has famed *sōmen* (very thin wheat noodles, usually served cold in summer) for ¥850, tempura and other dishes. There are plastic models in the window and an illustrated menu showing the multi-coloured noodles.

Near the Matsuyama-jō cable car pick up, *Spice Kingdom* serves authentic Indian food at reasonable prices.

Directly opposite the Matsuyama City station is *Munchen*, a pseudo-German beer hall, and also the inexpensive kaiten-zushi shop *Atom Boy*. Nearby these on Chifuna-machi, *a table* is a woodsy little bistro run by a French expat, who prepares top-notch soups, salads and tasty light meals; most dishes cost less than ¥1000. Near the Kinokuniya bookshop, *Freshness Burger* whips up good burgers and sandwiches. *Charlie*, just off the Ginten-gai arcade, has the cheapest rāmen in town (¥270).

In a pinch, there's always *gyūdon* (beef over rice) at *Nakanoka*, across from JR Matsuyama station; it's open 24 hours.

In Dōgo Onsen, just across from the main bath house, *Dōgo Biiru-kan* serves respectable micro-beer and pub grub. The arcade leading from the Dōgo Onsen tram stop to the main bathhouse also has a number of good restaurants with plastic meal replicas.

Entertainment
In and around the Okai-dō arcade are plenty of nightlife choices. *Déjà vu* and *Club eX* are Matsuyama's most infamous gaijin dives.

The basement-level *Piccadilly Circus*, a 'British antique bar', is decked out with all kinds of British paraphernalia. Cheaper and less pretentious is *Bar 9 Carat*, just down the road from the Pound House bakery.

During summer, Matsuyama has a large number of rooftop beer gardens. Try the Sogō department store, the Matsuyama ANA Hotel or the *Terrace Garden* at Chateau Teru Matsuyama.

Getting There & Away
Air ANA connects Matsuyama with Osaka, Nagoya and Tokyo (both Narita international airport and Haneda airport). JAS has

SHIKOKU

connections to Fukuoka, Miyazaki and Kagoshima, all in Kyūshū. JAL also flies to Tokyo.

Train & Bus The north coast JR Yosan line connects Matsuyama with Takamatsu and there are also services across the Seto-ōhashi to Honshū. Matsuyama to Okayama takes 3¼ hours. Another line runs southwest from Matsuyama to Uwajima and then east to Kōchi, though this is a rather circuitous route – it's faster to take a bus directly to Kōchi. There are also direct buses that run from Osaka and Tokyo.

Boat There are frequent ferry and hydrofoil connections with Hiroshima. Take the Iyo-tetsudō private train line from Matsuyama City (Shi-eki) or Ōtemachi station right to the end of the line at Takahama (¥360 from Ōtemachi). From Takahama a connecting bus whisks you the remaining distance to the port, Matsuyama Kankō-kō.

Other boats operate to/from Matsuyama and Beppu, Kokura and Oita on Kyūshū as well as Iwakuni, Kure, Mihara, Onomichi and Yanai on Honshū, but check which of the Matsuyama ports that services operate from.

Getting Around
Matsuyama has the private Iyo-tetsudō train line and a tram service costing a flat ¥170. There's a loop line and major terminus at Dōgo Onsen and outside Matsuyama City station. The Ichiban-chō stop outside the Mitsukoshi department store and ANA Hotel is a good central stopping point. Tram numbers and routes are:

Tram No	Route
1 & 2	The Loop
3	Matsuyama City station (Shi-eki)–Dōgo Onsen
5	JR Matsuyama station–Dōgo Onsen
6	Kiya-chō–Dōgo Onsen

AROUND MATSUYAMA
Kashima 鹿島
This pleasant little island, which on a hazy day is reminiscent of an idyll on the Aegean Sea, makes an easy day trip from Mat-suyama. It has resident deer, a nice **beach** that's good for *camping* on, and *minshuku* if you plan to overnight.

Trains from JR Matsuyama station reach Iyo Hōjō station in 20 minutes; from here it's a short walk to the ferry (fashioned with a plastic deer on top), and just a few minutes hop over to the island.

Ishizuchi-san 石鎚山
At 1982m, Ishizuchi-san is the highest mountain in western Japan, and is easily reached from Matsuyama. It's a holy mountain and many pilgrim climbers make the hike, particularly during the July-August climbing season. In winter it's snow-capped.

From Matsuyama, you can take a bus to Tsuchi-goya, south-east of the mountain. Or you can take a bus from JR Iyo Saijō station on the Yosan line to the Nishi-no-kawa cable car station on the northern side. This route passes through the scenic gorge, **Omogo-kei**, an attraction in its own right. Out of season, bus services to the mountain are infrequent.

You can climb up one way and down the other or even make a complete circuit from Nishi-no-kawa to the summit, down to Tsuchi-goya and then back to Nishi-no-kawa. Allow all day and an early start for the circuit.

The ropeway in Nishi-no-kawa takes five minutes (¥1000) and can be followed by a chairlift (¥300) that slightly shortens the walk to Jōju, where **Ishizuchi-jinja** offers good views of the mountain. From Jōju, it's 3½km to the top, first gently downhill through forest, then uphill through forest, across a more open area and finally up a steep and rocky ascent. Although there's a path (and often steps) all the way to the top, the fun way to make the final ascent is up a series of *kusari*, heavy chains draped down the very steep rock faces. Clambering up these chains is the approved pilgrimage method. The summit, reached by climbing along a sharp ridge, is a little beyond the mountain hut on the top.

For detailed information on hiking Ishizuchi-san, snap up a copy of Lonely Planet's *Hiking in Japan*.

SHIKOKU

Imabari 今治

This industrial port city has little of interest for the traveller except perhaps for its position at the southern end of the Kurushima Kaikyo-ōhashi (connecting Ehime-ken to Onomichi, in Hiroshima-ken). There are numerous ferry services connecting Imabari with ports on Honshū including Hiroshima, Kōbe, Mihara, Niigata, Onomichi, Takehara and islands of the Inland Sea.

Komecho Ryokan (☎ *0898-33-0843*) is 15 minutes' walk from JR Imabari station and charges around ¥5000 per person.

Imabari is noted for its tasty yakitori, particularly a variety known as *senzanki*.

Niihama 新居浜

pop 133,000

Located on Shikoku's north-central coast, Niihama sits sandwiched between the Inland Sea and a nearby mountain range. The area is known for its **parks**, **waterfalls**, and **hiking** opportunities around **Besshi-yama**, but most of all for the annual **Taiko Matsuri**, a drum festival held in mid-October. There is a **museum** attached to Niihama's 17th century Besshi Copper Mine.

UCHIKO 内子

☎ 0893

Halfway between Matsuyama and Uwajima on the JR Yosan line, the charming town of Uchiko has a photogenic street lined with traditional buildings dating from the late Edo period and early years following the Meiji Restoration. At that time, Uchiko was an important centre for the production of the vegetable wax known as *rō*, and some of the houses along Yōkaichi, the town's old street, belonged to merchants who made their fortunes from producing the wax.

The annual bamboo-decorating festival **Sasa Matsuri** (Bamboo Grass Festival), Uchiko's biggest festival is held annually in early August.

Orientation & Information

Many places on Yōkaichi are closed on Monday. There's a map with *some* English outside the JR station but very little else in Uchiko is labelled in English. Yōkaichi is a

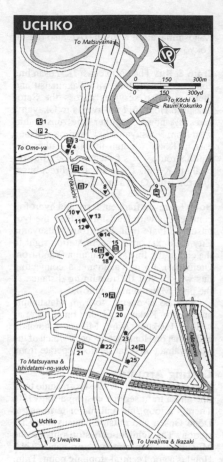

20-minute walk to the north of Uchiko station. The International Exchange Association (☎ 44-2111) on the 3rd floor of the City Hall can provide an English pamphlet on local attractions.

Yōkaichi 八日市

Uchiko's picturesque street, which extends for about 1km, has a number of interesting old buildings along with museums, souvenir and craft shops, and teahouses. At the start of the street is the Moribun Brewery, a traditional sake brewery, across from which is the **Moribun Amazake Chaya Teahouse**

UCHIKO

PLACES TO STAY

22 Matsunoya Ryokan
松乃家
23 Shin Machi-sō Ryokan
新町荘

PLACES TO EAT

8 Inariya
いなりや
10 Sōgen; Craft Shop
創玄
13 Inakappe
田舎っぺ

OTHER

1 Kōshō-Ji
高昌寺
2 Tour Bus Parking
観光バス駐車場
3 Sokō-kan Museum
素巧館

4 Traditional Umbrella
Maker
和傘製造
5 Stone Lantern
常夜灯
6 Inari romaji
稲荷神社
7 Kami-Hagi-tei Residence
上芳我邸
9 Uchiko-bashi
Bus Station
内子橋バス停留所
11 Hon-Hagi-tei
Residence
本芳我邸
12 Ōmura-tei
大村家
14 Atarashi-ya Craft Shop
あたらし屋
15 Moribun Amazake
Chaya Teahouse
森文あま酒茶屋

16 Machi-ya Shiryōkan
Museum
町屋資料館
17 Ōmori Rōsoku Candle
Maker
大森和蝋燭店
18 Moribun Brewery
森文酒醸造所
19 Hachiman-jinja
八幡神社
20 Akinai-to-Kurashi
Hakubutsu-kan Museum
商いとくらし博物館
21 Uchiko-za Theatre
内子座
24 Bus Terminal
内子バスターミナル
25 City Hall;
International Exchange
Association

(*amazake* is a sweet sake). You can sample the local brew here and visit the small 'museum' of sake and soy sauce production on the 2nd floor. A bit farther along the street, **Ōmori Rosoku** is Uchiko's sole remaining traditional candle maker. There are demonstrations of *rō* (vegetable wax) candle making, and candles and stands are for sale. Continuing up the hill, the **Machi-ya Shiryōkan** is a rustic 1790s merchant house, which was thoughtfully restored in 1987. Be sure to remove your shoes before heading up to the 2nd floor (free, 9 am to 4.30 pm).

As the road makes a slight bend, there comes into view several well-preserved Edo-era buildings such as the **Ōmura-tei** (Ōmura residence) and **Hon-Haga-tei**, a fine example of a wealthy merchant's private home (only the finely groomed garden is open for viewing). Farther down Yōkaichi is the exquisite **Kami-Haga-tei** (¥400, 9 am to 4.30 pm), a wax merchant's house within a large complex of wax-making related buildings. Towards the end of the street there is a traditional umbrella-maker's shop; and close by is the **Sokō-kan**

Museum (¥200, 9 am to 4.30 pm), which features displays of pottery and folk art.

A few minutes' walk from Yōkaichi, across from Hachiman-jinja, is the interesting Trade and Lifestyle Museum (Akinai-to-Kurashi Hakubutsu-kan; ¥200, 9 am to 4.30 pm), exhibiting historical materials, and wax figures portraying a typical merchant scene of the Taishō era (1912–26).

Uchiko-za 内子座

Uchiko za (☎ 44-2840) is a traditional kabuki theatre. It was originally built in 1915 and was restored in the mid-1980s, complete with a revolving stage. Call ahead to find out if performances are being held during your visit (¥300, 9 am to 4.30 pm).

Places to Stay

There are a couple of nice Japanese inns near the main sights in town. *Shin Machi-sō Ryokan* (☎ 44-2021) has per person rates starting from ¥4000, or from ¥8000, including dinner and breakfast. The 120-year-old *Matsunoya Ryokan* (☎ 44-2161) costs ¥12,000 with two meals, and is known for its fine cuisine.

SHIKOKU

Guests at the country-style *Raum Kokuriko* (☎ 44-2079) can experience rice planting and fruit picking, as well as periodic art exhibitions and music events. Nightly costs begin at ¥8300, with two meals. The lodge is about a 10-minute taxi ride from JR Uchiko station.

About 30 minutes north by car from JR Uchiko station, *Ishidatami-no-yado* (☎ 44-5730) is a beautifully-restored Japanese country farmhouse. Rooms begin at ¥7700 per person. You can also come here to *dine* for around ¥2500, but call ahead.

Places to Eat

There are a few small restaurants along Yōkaichi. *Sōgen*, serving good noodles and curry, is an atmospheric little spot in the back of a craft shop. Just south of it, *Inakappe* serves up country-style cooking, including skewered *tōfu* (bean curd) and mountain vegetables. *Inari-ya* is known for its sweet, jumbo-sized *inari-zushi* (sushi rice wrapped in fried tofu).

Omo-ya, housed in an old Japanese farmhouse relocated from Niigata-ken, specialises in free-range chicken dishes. It's a five-minute taxi-ride north from Uchiko station (closed Monday).

Getting There & Away

Uchiko can be reached by bus or train from Matsuyama and Uwajima. Rapid trains from Matsuyama take about 30 minutes.

Getting Around

Yōkaichi is just over 1km from JR Uchiko station; if your time is limited, consider taking a taxi. You need at least a few hours to explore Yōkaichi. The bus station is the closest transport terminus to Yōkaichi.

Ikazaki

Just over the hill from Ryūō-kōen in Uchiko is the pleasant little town of Ikazaki, a nice detour for those with extra time. There is an interesting **kite museum** and **traditional paper-making factory**, the Tenjin-san-shi Kōjō (☎ 0893-44-2002). Try your hand at the craft of paper making for ¥500; reservations are recommended (closed Sunday).

UCHIKO TO UWAJIMA

Only 20km south-west of Uchiko, there are more interesting old houses and shops near the river in Ōzu, including the impressive **Garyū-sansō** (¥500, closed Monday), a wealthy Meiji-era trader's house. Traditional cormorant river-fishing *(ukai)* takes place on the Hiji-kawa (Hija River) from 1 June to 20 September.

Ōzu Kyōdokan Youth Hostel (☎ 0893-24-2258) has nightly rates of ¥3200; breakfast/dinner costs ¥500/1000. The hostel is in the south-west of town, near the Ōzu-jō ruins. It takes 30 minutes on foot from Ōzu station, or it's a seven-minute walk from Honmachi bus stop (eight-minute ride from Ōzu station).

Kudos to the traditional surroundings at the family-run *Oyabu Onsen* (☎ 0893-34-2867). You can enjoy the cypress baths during the day (¥500, 10 am to 7 pm), or stay overnight for ¥10,000, which includes two meals (dine over an open fire pit). Oyabu Onsen is in Hiji-kawa-chō, 30 minutes by Uwajima bus from JR Ōzu station.

Ten kilometres south-west of Ōzu is **Yawatahama**, from where ferry services operate to Beppu (¥1770, 2½ hours) and Usuki (¥1320, 2¼ hours) on Kyūshū. Yawatahama-kō port, is a 10-minute bus ride north of Yawatahama station.

Sada-misaki extends about 50km towards Kyūshū, and from Misaki, near the end of the cape, car and passenger ferries make the crossing to Saganoseki (near Oita and Beppu) in just over an hour (¥610).

UWAJIMA 宇和島

☎ 0895 ● pop 68,000

Uwajima is a relatively quiet and peaceful place with a small, unreconstructed castle, the remnants of a fine garden, some pleasant temples and a notorious sex shrine! It makes a very interesting pause between Kōchi and Matsuyama, although an afternoon or a morning is long enough for a reasonable look around.

Information

There is an information office (☎ 22-3934) across the road from JR Uwajima station

(8.30 am to 5 pm). Uwajima is a centre for cultured pearls, and the helpful tourist information staff can tell you about shops dealing in them.

Uwajima-jō 宇和島城
Dating from 1601, Uwajima-jō was never a great castle, still it's an interesting little three-storey structure. It once stood by the sea and, although land reclamation has moved the water well back, it still has good views over the town.

Inside the castle grounds there are photos of its recent restoration and of other castles in Japan and overseas (¥200, 6 am to 5 pm, until 6.30 pm in summer).

Taga-jinja & Sex Museum 多賀神社
Once upon a time, many Shintō shrines had a connection to fertility rites, but this aspect was comprehensively purged when puritanism was imported from the West following the Meiji Restoration. Nevertheless, a handful survived and Uwajima's Taga-jinja is one of them – it's totally dedicated to sex. There's a tree trunk phallus and various other statues and stone carvings around the grounds, but the three-storey sex museum (¥800, 8 am to 5 pm) is the major attraction.

Inside, it's packed floor to ceiling with everything from explicit Peruvian pottery to Greek vases; from the illustrated *Kama Sutra* to Tibetan Tantric sculptures; from South Pacific fertility gods to a showcase full of leather S&M gear; and from early Japanese *shunga* (pornographic prints) to their European Victorian equivalents, not to mention modern porn magazines. Saturation soon sets in.

Temples & Shrines
In the south-eastern part of town, a number of old temples and a shrine can be found by the canal. They include Seigōzen-ji, Ryūgesan Tōkaku-ji, Kongōsan Dairyū-ji with its old tombs and Uwatsuhiko-jinja.

Bullfights 市営闘牛場
Tōgyū is a sort of bovine sumō where one animal tries to shove the other out of the ring (actually, victory is achieved when one animal forces the other to its knees, or when one forces the other to turn and flee from the ring). Fights are held occasionally at Uwajima's municipal bullfighting ring. You might be lucky enough to hook up with a tour group that has paid for a special performance; otherwise, fights are held on four dates each year: 2 January, second Sunday of April, 24 July and 14 August (¥3,000).

Other Attractions
Twenty minutes on foot from JR Uwajima station, Tensha-en is not among Japan's classic lush gardens, but it does host 14 different species of bamboo (¥300, 8.30 am to 4.30 pm).

The Municipal Date Museum has a collection that includes a portrait of Toyotomi Hideyoshi's military armour and other items connected with the Date lords (¥300, 9 am to 4.30 pm, closed Monday).

East of Uwajima there is good hiking at Yakushi-dani; while the pleasant Sagano Onsen (☎ 27-3511) has a natural setting, with a riverside bath and a good *restaurant* (¥680, 10 am to 11 pm). Take a bus from Uwajima station, or drive about 20 minutes south of Uwajima via Route 56, along the coast.

More hot spring baths are found in the nearby village of Mimaki, and farther south on Route 56 is Tsushima-cho, noted for its enormous Japanese garden, Nanraku-en, where the popular Shōbu Matsuri is held in late May/early June.

Places to Stay
The *Uwajima Youth Hostel* (☎ 22-7177) is a long walk south of the town centre: when you get to the temples overlooking the town, it's another 650m-uphill climb. From Uwatsuhiko-jinja, the hostel is a 1¼km walk, but there are fine views back down to the town. Beds cost ¥3200 per night; breakfast/dinner costs ¥600/1000.

The friendly *Minshuku Mihara* (☎ 25-5384) is good value at ¥6000 a head including two meals. At the *Shirakabe Business Hotel* (☎ 22-3585) singles cost ¥4800.

SHIKOKU

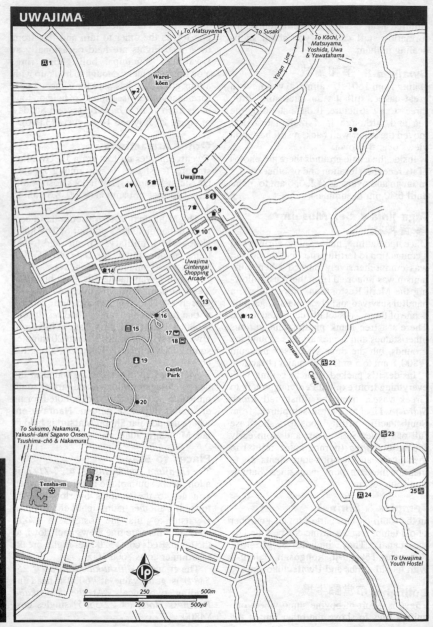

UWAJIMA

To Matsuyama

To Susaki

To Kōchi,
Matsuyama,
Yoshida, Uwa
& Yawatahama

Yosan Line

Warei-
kōen

Uwajima

Uwajima
Gintengai
Shopping
Arcade

Tatsumi Canal

Castle Park

To Sukumo, Nakamura,
Yakushi-dani Sagano Onsen,
Tsushima-chō & Nakamura

Tensha-en

To Uwajima
Youth Hostel

0   250   500m
0   250   500yd

SHIKOKU

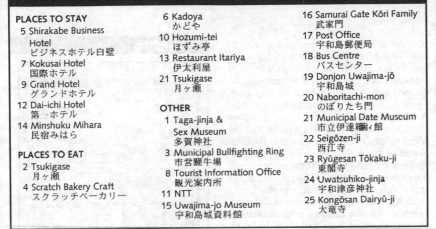

UWAJIMA

PLACES TO STAY
5 Shirakabe Business
  Hotel
  ビジネスホテル白壁
7 Kokusai Hotel
  国際ホテル
9 Grand Hotel
  グランドホテル
12 Dai-ichi Hotel
  第一ホテル
14 Minshuku Mihara
  民宿みはら

PLACES TO EAT
2 Tsukigase
  月ヶ瀬
4 Scratch Bakery Craft
  スクラッチベーカリー

6 Kadoya
  かどや
10 Hozumi-tei
  ほずみ亭
13 Restaurant Itariya
  伊太利屋
21 Tsukigase
  月ヶ瀬

OTHER
1 Taga-jinja &
  Sex Museum
  多賀神社
3 Municipal Bullfighting Ring
  市営闘牛場
8 Tourist Information Office
  観光案内所
11 NTT
15 Uwajima-jo Museum
  宇和島城資料館

16 Samurai Gate Kōri Family
  武家門
17 Post Office
  宇和島郵便局
18 Bus Centre
  バスセンター
19 Donjon Uwajima-jō
  宇和島城
20 Naboritachi-mon
  のぼりたち門
21 Municipal Date Museum
  市立伊達籍幽〈館
22 Seigōzen-ji
  西江寺
23 Ryūgesan Tōkaku-ji
  東閣寺
24 Uwatsuhiko-jinja
  宇和津彦神社
25 Kongōsan Dairyū-ji
  大竜寺

The ***Grand Hotel*** (☎ 24-3911), just south of the station, offers singles/doubles/twins from ¥5500/9200/10,500. The ***Kokusai Hotel*** (☎ 25-0111) has top-end Japanese-style rooms. Costs per-person start from ¥13,000, with two meals. The ***Dai-ichi Hotel*** (☎ 25-0001) is near the south-eastern end of the arcade and has singles/twins for ¥5700/13,500.

Places to Eat
There is an ***Andersen's Bakery*** in the JR station, and the Uwajima Gitengai shopping arcade has various places to eat. *Tai meishi* (sea bream mixed with rice) is a local delicacy on offer at ***Kadoya***, just up the main road from the station. ***Hozumi-tei*** is another good spot for seafood. It's a five-minute walk from the station (closed Sunday).

South of the station in the arcade area, drop into ***Restaurant Itariya*** for inexpensive pizza. Out by Warei-kōen, ***Tsukigase***

serves excellent tempura and local seafood; lunch sets start from ¥1500.

Finally, for a snack on your way to the Sex Museum (or you might prefer to nibble afterwards), look out for ***Scratch Bakery Craft***.

Getting There & Away
You can reach Uwajima by train from Matsuyama (via Uchiko and Uno), a one-hour and 40-minute trip by tokkyū. From Kōchi, it takes 3¾ to 4½ hours via Kubokawa. To head farther south to Ashizuri-misaki, you'll have to resort to buses as the train line from Kōchi terminates at Nakamura.

There is a ferry connection to Beppu on Kyushū via Yawatahama.

Getting Around
Uwajima is a good place to explore by bicycle as the traffic is not too bad. The tourist office rents bicycles (¥100/hour).

SHIKOKU

Kyūshū

Kyūshū is the third-largest and southern-most of the four major islands of Japan. Its population numbers 14.5 million. Although isolated from the Japanese mainstream on Central Honshū, it has been an important entry point for foreign influence and culture. Kyūshū is the closest island to Korea and China, and it was from Kyūshū that the Yamato tribe extended its power to Honshū. Some of the earliest evidence of Japanese civilisation can be seen at the archaeological excavations around Miyazaki and at the many ancient stone carvings in the Usuki area. More recently, Kyūshū was for many centuries the sole link to European civilisation. During the long period of isolation from the west, the Dutch settlement at Nagasaki in Kyūshū was Japan's only connection to the outside world.

For visitors, Nagasaki is one of Kyūshū's prime attractions, due to its European-influenced history and its atomic tragedy. In the north, Fukuoka/Hakata is a major international arrival point, a fun cosmopolitan city, and the terminus for the *shinkansen* (bullet train) line from Tokyo. In the centre of the island there is the massive volcanic caldera of Aso-san, while more volcanic activity can be witnessed in the south at Sakurajima. Larger towns like Kagoshima and Kumamoto offer fine gardens and magnificent castles, while Beppu is one of Japan's major hot-spring centres. There are some good walking opportunities, particularly along the Kirishima volcano chain.

The climate is milder than in other parts of Japan, and the people of Kyūshū are reputed to be hard drinkers (especially of *shōchu*, the local liquor) and outstandingly friendly – a visit to a local bar may provide proof of both theories.

Suggested Itineraries

If time allows, it's worth exploring the backroads of Kyūshū. If not, at least check out Fukuoka and Nagasaki. If you have three days, a Beppu-Kurokawa-Onsen-

Highlights

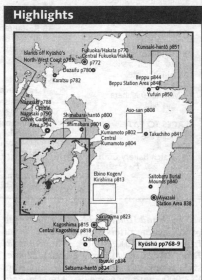

- Soak in the hidden hot-springs of onsen-crazed Beppu.
- Hike around the rim of an active volcano at Aso-san.
- Hang out in Fukuoka, a trendy Asia-aware metropolis with a thing for rāmen noodles.
- Escape to the riverside baths and unspoiled, rural hot springs of Kurokawa Onsen.
- Explore the city to which the West first exported Christianity, then nuclear holocaust – the festival-filled, easygoing Nagasaki.
- Spend time in Kagoshima, so-called Naples of the East, a vibrant port city overlooked by the smoking cone of Sakura-jima.

Kumamoto-Fukuoka loop is recommended. With an extra day take in Nagasaki and also perhaps Shimabara peninsula, or a hike up to the Aso volcano caldera. To do the island full justice, however, at least seven days is advised – do as the locals do and take it slow and easy.

Getting There & Away

Air See the introductory Getting Around chapter for details of fares and routes. There are major airports at Beppu/Ōita, Fukuoka, Kagoshima, Kumamoto, Miyazaki and Nagasaki. Fukuoka is the major international gateway for Kyūshū. There are also flights to islands off the coast of Kyūshū and to the islands south-west of Kagoshima down to Okinawa.

Train The shinkansen line from Tokyo and Osaka crosses to Kyūshū from Shimonoseki and terminates in Fukuoka/Hakata. Major cities in Kyūshū are all connected by train but not by a high-speed shinkansen service.

Road and train tunnels connect Shimonoseki at the western end of Honshū with Kitakyūshū on Kyūshū.

Boat There are numerous sea connections to Kyūshū; some of the more interesting ones are dealt with in more detail in the relevant sections of this chapter. Routes include:

Beppu or Ōita-Kōbe, Matsuyama, Osaka,
   Takamatsu, Uwajima and Yawatahama
Fukuoka/Hakata-Okinawa
Hyūga-Kawasaki and Osaka
Kagoshima-Okinawa and Osaka
Kokura-Hitakatsu, Izumiotsu, Kōbe, Matsuyama, Osaka, Pusan, Tokushima and Tokyo
Kunisaki-Tokuyama
Shibushi-Osaka
Takedazu-Tokuyama
Usuki-Yawatahama

In addition, local ferry services operate between Kyūshū and islands off the coast.

Fukuoka-ken

The northern prefecture of Fukuoka will be the arrival point for most visitors to Kyūshū, whether they cross over from Shimonoseki or fly straight into Fukuoka city's international airport.

KITAKYŪSHŪ 北九州
☎ 093 ● pop 1,018,000

Kitakyūshū, literally translated as 'North Kyūshū City', is too industrialised to top anyone's list of favourites, but it does serve as an important transport link. It actually consists of five cities – Wakamatsu, Yahata, Tobata, Kokura and Moji – which have gradually merged together.

One of these would be a familiar name today worldwide were it not for a grey, cloudy day in 1945. Kokura was set to be the world's second atomic bomb target, but cloud obscured the city and the mission was diverted – to Nagasaki.

Kitakyūshū is trying hard to attract tourists, with the development of the much-touted Space World (built in collaboration with NASA, but at times sadly resembling an early Star Trek set), and the redevelopment of the Mojiko Retro Town, the old port area. Space World (☎ 672-3600) may appeal to travellers with kids, but it's not cheap (¥4600). It's five minutes from Edamitsu station on the Japan Railways (JR) Kagoshima line. Mojiko Retro Town (JR line from Kokura to JR Mojiko) has the virtue of being free.

The reconstructed castle **Kokura-jō** is about 500m west of JR Kokura station. **Kitakyūshū Municipal Art Museum** (¥230, closed Monday) is 20 minutes by No 3 Nishitetsu bus (¥150) from the train station.

If you stay at the youth hostel or at the Hotel Town House Matsuya, consider heading out to the **Kitakyūshū Mingei Mura** (Folk Arts Village; ¥500, 9 am to 5 pm, closed Monday). Displays of folk crafts include lacquerware, furniture and paper products. From Yahata station take a Nishitetsu bus to Jizō-mae (¥430, 36 minutes).

Places to Stay

Kitakyūshū Youth Hostel (☎ 681-8142) is about a 20-minute walk uphill from JR Yahata station (or 20 minutes from Kokura on the Kagoshima line). Dorm beds cost ¥2700 and it's closed from 5 to 14 June. The Japanese Inn group's *Hotel Town House Matsuya* (☎ 661-7890) is also near Yahata station. Singles/doubles cost ¥5300/8800.

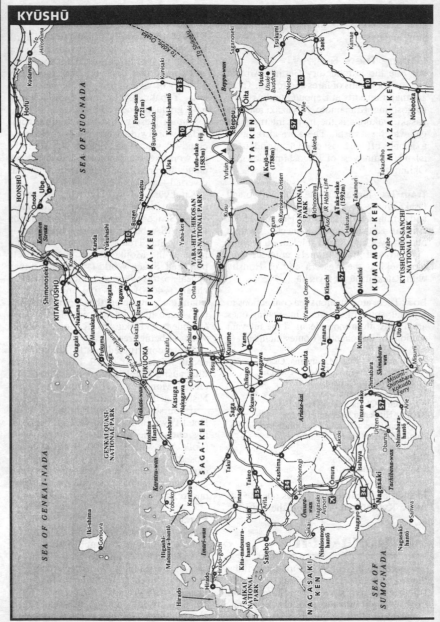

KYŪSHŪ

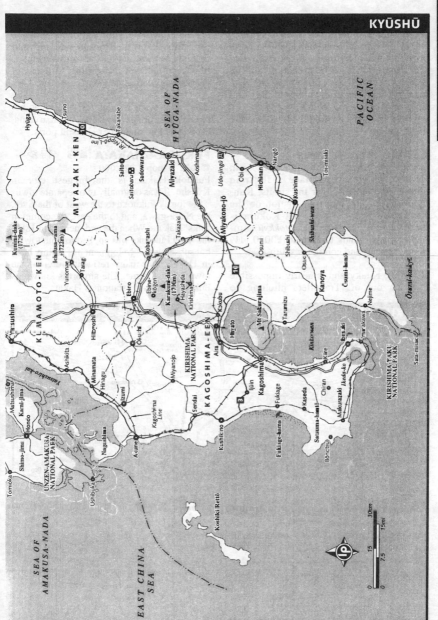

KYŪSHŪ

Behind the Sogo department store, recently built *Nishitetsu Inn Kokura* (☎ 511-5454) is comfortable enough at ¥5715, with breakfast. An older place, *Kitakyūshū Dai Ichi Hotel* (☎ 551-7331), charges ¥6500/8000. *Kokura Tōkyū Inn* (☎ 521-0109), with singles/twins from ¥6800/ 11,000, and *Kokura Washington Hotel* (☎ 531-3111), with singles/twins for ¥6200/14,000, are the other options.

Getting There & Away
Train From Kitakyūshū to Shimonoseki in Honshū, or vice versa, take a JR train through the tunnel under the straits, Kanmon-kaikyō. The first train station on the Kitakyūshū side is Moji, but Kokura is more central. The Nippō line *tokkyū* (limited express) heads to Beppu (¥3030, 1½ hours, hourly) and continues south-east.

Hitching Kitakyūshū is nearly impossible to hitch out of. Travellers hitching to

Honshū can either try the Kanmon tunnel entrance near JR Moji station or cross to Shimonoseki on the Honshū side and start from there. Hitching farther into Kyūshū is best accomplished by getting well out of Kitakyūshū before you start.

Boat There are regular ferry services between Kokura and Kōbe, Matsuyama, Osaka, Tokyo and other Honshū ports.

FUKUOKA/HAKATA 福岡・博多
☎ 092 ● pop 1,320,000
Fukuoka/Hakata is the biggest city in Kyūshū. It was originally two separate towns – the lordly Fukuoka to the west of the river, the Naka-gawa, and to the east, the common folks' Hakata. When the two merged in 1889, the label Fukuoka was applied to both towns, but subsequent development has mainly been in Hakata and many residents refer to the town by that name. The airport is known as Fukuoka, the train station as Hakata.

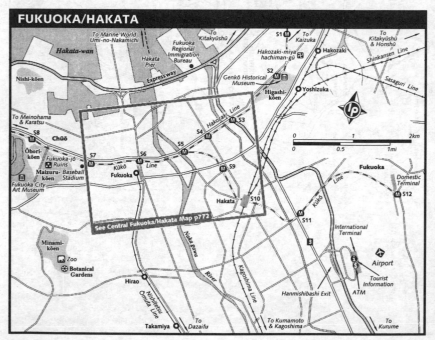

Fukuoka has transformed itself over the last decade into one of Japan's most truly cosmopolitan and internationalised cities. The local government is keenly aware of the city's proximity to the rest of Asia, and encourages international exchange. Its sightseeing attractions are contemporary rather than traditional, but they are still very much worth seeing. The new Fukuoka Asian Art Museum, and the Canal City and Hawks Town developments stand out. Fukuoka/Hakata is also renowned as a culinary centre, and its nightlife, centred around the Nakasu and Tenjin districts, is bustling.

Nearby areas of interest include the fine coastal scenery beyond Karatsu to the west and the temples and shrines of Dazaifu, a few kilometres south.

FUKUOKA/HAKATA

HAKOZAKI LINE
S1 Hakozaki-miya-mae
　　箱崎宮前
S2 Maidashi-Kyūdaibyōin-mae
　　馬出市九大病院前
S3 Chiyo-Kenchō-guchi
　　千代県庁口
S4 Gofuku-machi
　　呉服町
S5 Nakasu-Kawabata
　　中洲川端

KŪKŌ LINE
S5 Nakasu-Kawabata
　　中洲川端
S6 Tenjin
　　天神
S7 Akasaka
　　赤坂
S8 Ōhori-kōen
　　大濠公園
S9 Gion
　　祇園駅
S10 Hakata
　　博多駅
S11 Higashi-Hie
　　東比恵
S12 Fukuoka-Kūkō
　　福岡空港

Nationally the city is known for its beautiful women, known as 'Hakata *bijin*' (Hakata beautiful women), its feisty baseball team the Daiei Hawks, and, most of all, *rāmen* (Chinese-style egg noodles in a broth).

Orientation
There are two important areas in central Fukuoka – Hakata and Tenjin. JR Hakata station is the transport centre for the city and is surrounded by hotels and offices. The train station is flanked by the Fukuoka Kōtsū bus centre on one side and the Hakata post office on the other. Separating Hakata and Tenjin to the west is the Nakagawa, the site of the impressive Canal City.

Tenjin is the business and shopping centre, its focus along Watanabe-dōri. Underneath this busy street is Tenjin-chika-gai, a crowded underground shopping mall that extends for 400m. The Tenjin bus centre here is close to the terminus of the private Nishitetsu Ōmuta line. Slightly to the north, just off Shōwa-dōri, is the restaurant and entertainment district of Oyafuku-dōri.

Sandwiched between JR Hakata station and the shopping centre, on an island in the Nakagawa, is Nakasu, the entertainment centre of the city. It's a maze of restaurants, strip clubs, hostess bars, cinemas, department stores and the famed *yatai* (food stalls).

Maps The widely available *Visitors Walking Maps* for Hakata, Nakasu, Tenjin and Momochi are invaluable, as they are written in both English and *kanji*, and are free.

Information
Tourist Offices The tourist information office (☎ 431-3003) in JR Hakata station has information and maps in English (9 am to 7 pm). The office is in the centre of the ground floor. This pales into insignificance, however, beside the Fukuoka International Association Rainbow Plaza (☎ 733-2220) on the 8th floor of the futuristic IMS building in Tenjin (10 am to 8 pm). Rainbow has videos on Japan, books, magazines and a noticeboard with events, accommodation and lots of job ads. Its bilingual staff are extremely helpful.

CENTRAL FUKUOKA/HAKATA

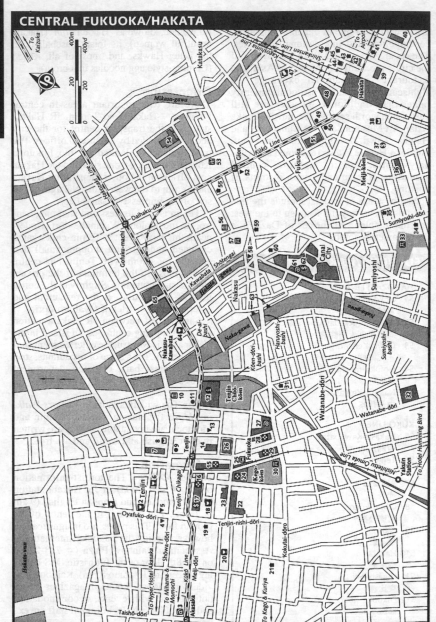

CENTRAL FUKUOKA/HAKATA

PLACES TO STAY
19 Nishitetsu Grand Hotel
西鉄グランドホテル
21 Lady's Hotel Petit Tenjin
レディースホテル
プチ天神
31 Fukuoka Arty Inn
福岡アルティイン
32 Hotel New Otani
ホテルニューオータニ
34 Hokke Club Hakata
ホテル法華クラブ博多
35 Accord Hotel
アコードホテル
36 ANA Hotel Hakata
日空ホテル博多
39 Hotel Clio Court
ホテルクリオコート
41 Sun Life Hotel 2
サンライフホテル2
42 Hotel Centraza Hakata;
Gourmet City & ATM
ホテルセントラーザ
43 Sun Life Hotel 1
サンライフホテル1
44 Green Hotel 2
グリーンホテル2
45 Green Hotel 1
グリーンホテル1
46 Hakata Grand
Suishō Hotel
博多グランド水晶ホテル
51 Hotel Nikkō
ホテル日航
55 Kashima-Honkan Ryokan
鹿島本館
59 Capsule Inn Hakata
カプセルイン博多
60 Sauna Wellbe
サウナウェルビー
66 Amenity Hotel in Hakata
アメニティホテル博多

PLACES TO EAT
4 Nanak
5 Taiwan Yatai
台湾屋台

13 Ichiran
一蘭
52 Uma-uma
うま馬
58 Menchan
めんちゃん
63 Food Stalls
屋台

OTHER
1 The Dark Room;
The Bump
2 Crazy Cock
3 Kinko's (Akasaka)
キンコーズ赤坂店
6 Off Broadway
7 Matsuya Ladies
松屋レディース
8 Fukuoka Central
Post Office
福岡中央郵便局
9 ANA
10 Former Historical
Museum
元祖長浜屋
11 JAL
12 ACROS Fukuoka
アクロス福岡
14 Tenjin Core
Building
天神コア
15 Iwataya Department
Store
天神岩田屋
16 Shintenchō Plaza
新天町プラザ
17 ATM
18 Blue Note
20 Happy Cock
22 NTT – Iwataya Z-side;
ATM; Libro
岩田屋ジーサイド；
リブロ
23 Blue Note (Jazz Bar)
24 Solaria Plaza
25 Tenjin Bus Centre
天神バスセンター

26 IMS Building – Sizzler;
Rainbow Plaza;
Maureen
IMSビル
27 El Gala
28 Daimaru Department
Store
大丸
29 Mitsukoshi
Department Store;
Yaesu Book Center
福岡三越；
八重洲ブックセンター
30 Kego-Jinja
警固神社
33 Sumiyoshi-jinja
住吉神社
37 Tokyo
Mitsubishi Bank
東京三菱銀行
38 Hakata Post Office
博多郵便局
40 NTT
47 UK Consulate
英国領事館
48 Fukuoka Kōtsū
Bus Centre
福岡交通バスセンター
49 JAS
50 ANA
53 Tōchō-ji
東長寺
54 Shōfuku-ji
聖福寺
56 Hakata Machiya
Furusato-kan
博多町屋ふるさと館
57 Kushida-jinja
櫛田神社
61 T-Zone
Dennen Kissa
62 ATM
64 Holland's
65 Fukuoka Asian Art
Museum & Hakata
Riverain
福岡アジア美術館

ACROS Fukuoka (☎ 725-9100), also in Tenjin, on the 2nd floor of its cultural centre, has information on the surrounding prefecture (9 am to 9 pm, closed Monday).

The information desk on the 1st floor of Fukuoka airport international arrivals building (☎ 483-7007) can arrange hotel accommodation and car rentals (7 am to 9.30 pm). English is spoken.

Visas The Fukuoka Regional Immigration Bureau (☎ 281-8681) is in Okihama-cho, near the International Ferry Harbour (9 am to 4 pm weekdays). Take bus 80 or 85 from Tenjin, or 19 or 84 from Hakata to Kōwankyoku Mae bus stop.

Money There is a Citibank ATM on the 1st floor of terminal No 3 at Fukuoka airport (6.30 am to 9.30 pm). Exchange facilities are available in the international arrivals customs hall (9 am to 8 pm). Elsewhere in the airport, the bureau de change close at 4 pm, and 3 pm at weekends. Travellers coming from Korea should note that there is nowhere in Fukuoka to change Korean currency.

The ATM on the 2nd floor of the Shintenchō Plaza in Tenjin accepts VISA and MasterCard, while the ATM in Canal City takes VISA and American Express cards. There is also a VISA ATM on the 1st floor of the Hotel Centraza Hakata on the east side of Hakata Station.

The Tokyo Mitsubishi bank (9 am to 3 pm weekdays), at the main (west) entrance of Hakata station, will advance cash on VISA and MasterCard, if you produce your passport.

Post Fukuoka Central Post Office, just north-east of Tenjin subway station, has full services, including poste restante. There is also a large post office next to Hakata station's west exit.

Email & Internet Access Fukuoka is a wired city. Fukuoka New Media Service, on the 7th floor of the landmark El Gala building (10 am to 5 pm weekdays) and NTT on the 7th floor, Iwataya Z-side (10 am to 8 pm) both offer free Internet access for 30 minutes. T-Zone Dennen Kissa (10 am to 8 pm) is a cybercafe in the basement of Canal City's Business Center Building.

Kinko's has 24-hour Internet access (¥200 per 10 minutes) and English-speaking assistants at its four locations around the city. The Tenjin Minami branch (☎ 722-4222), opposite Kego-jinja in Tenjin, and the Akasaka Branch (☎ 724-7177) are the most convenient.

Bookshops Kinokuniya (☎ 721-7755), on the 6th floor of the Tenjin Core building, has an excellent selection of English-language books. Other bookshops that stock English-language titles include Maruzen (☎ 731-9000), on the 6th floor of the IMS building; Yaesu Book Center (☎ 726 6128), on the 9th floor of the Mitsukoshi department store; and Libro (☎ 733-8710), on the 7th floor of the Iwataya Z-side.

Useful local English-language publications include *Fukuoka Now*, a free monthly 'what's on' guide; *The Map*, a bimonthly, bilingual guide; *Fukuoka on Foot*, which features walking courses throughout the city; and *Rainbow*, the Fukuoka International Association's newsletter. All are available at Rainbow Plaza.

Canal City Hakata

Is it a bird, is it a plane? Or is it a scheme to relieve you of all disposable income, and make you feel good about it? Fukuoka's six-building shopping mall-cum-entertainment complex verges on the sexy. The central amphitheatre looks down onto an artificial river. There are 13 cinema screens, a playhouse, two major hotels and innumerable boutiques, bars and bistros. Canal City (☎ 282-2525) is consumer heaven (10 am to 9 pm, restaurants until 11 pm).

Canal City is a few minutes' walk south of the Nakasu-Kawabata subway stop, or you can take one of the many city buses to Canal City-mae. English-language pamphlets are available.

Fukuoka Asian Art Museum

This brand-new, user-friendly museum (¥200, 10 am to 7.30 pm, closed Wednesday) on the 7th and 8th floors of the Hakata Riverain complex in Kawabata, boasts some of the finest contemporary Asian art. In particular, check out the work of Mongolian artist Tserennadmidn Tsegmed, Chinese Wang Hong Jian's almost photo-like oil paintings, and Indian Ravinder Reddy's tongue-in-cheek *Woman Holding Her Breasts*. The museum also has excellent library resources, an Art Information Corner showing videos and catalogues, and a coffee shop overlooking the atrium garden.

The museum is next to exit 6 of Nakasu-Kawabata subway station.

Hakata Machiya Furusato-kan

This folk museum, near Kushida-jinja – and a short walk from Kashima Honkan Ryokan – is well worth a visit (¥200, 10 am to 5.30 pm). It features restored merchants houses and has displays of traditional Hakata culture. You can even hear recordings of impenetrable Hakata dialect.

Momochi District

Out in the west of the city you'll find Fukuoka Tower (¥800, 9.30 am to 9 pm). The 4th floor Cafe Dart 234 (the tower is 234m tall) is a great place to view the city, especially at dusk. Next to the tower is the park, Momochi-kōen, and a beach, which is a popular spot for swimming. Access is by the Kūkō subway line to Fujisaki station.

Hawk's Town

Set on reclaimed land near Momochi-kōen, this entertainment and shopping complex is also the location of the luxury Sea Hawk Hotel. Hawk's Town is something of a seafront Canal City. The giant Fukuoka Dome (home to the local Daiei Hawks baseball team) hosts rock concerts and international sports events, as well as the regular baseball fixtures (complete with retractable roof). The highlight, though, is Sea Hawk's indoor jungle atrium, complete with waterfalls and screeching tropical bird calls.

Hawk's Town is 15 minutes' walk northwest from Kojin-machi station on the Kūkō subway line.

Fukuoka-jō, Ōhori-kōen & Fukuoka City Art Museum

Only the walls of Fukuoka-jō remain in what is now Maizuru-kōen, but the castle's hilltop site provides fine views of the city. Ōhori-kōen, adjacent to the castle grounds, has a traditional (though recently constructed) Japanese garden, Nihon-teien, on its southern side. The Fukuoka City Art Museum, also in the park, has Buddhist guardians on one floor, and works by Andy Warhol upstairs (¥200, 9.30 am to 5.30 pm, closed Monday)

Access is by bus No 13 from Tenjin, or by subway to Ōhori-kōen station.

Tenjin 天神

Shopping, or at least window shopping, in Tenjin's high-rise and underground complexes is a popular Hakata ite pastime. Tenjin-core, Mitsukoshi, Iwataya Z-side, Solaria Plaza, Daimaru, Tenjin Chikagai and IMS are all favourite spots. The latter gets bonus points for its in-elevator TVs and car-sized liquid-crystal video screens that accompany the elevators up and down the building.

Shrines & Temples

Shōfuku-ji is a Zen temple originally founded in 1195 by Eisai, who introduced Zen and tea to Japan. It's within walking distance of JR Hakata station; don't confuse it with Sōfuku-ji, a little farther away.

Other Attractions

Marine World Umi-no-Nakamichi (¥2100, 9.30 am to 5.30 pm) is a seaside amusement park and swimming pool reached by ferry across Hakata Bay from Hakata Pier. Its stars, in cute-struck Japan, are of course the sea otters.

Special Events

On 3 January at the shrine, Hakozaki-gū, young men clad in loincloths engage in a primitive kind of soccer hooliganism, raucously chasing a wooden ball in the name of good fortune. On the island, Shikano-shima, archers gather on 15 January for the festival, Kyūdō Matsuri, held at Shikaumi-jinja.

The Hakata Dontaku Matsuri on 3 and 4 May rings to the unique percussive shock of rice servers being banged together, accompanied by *shamisen* (three-stringed instrument). Further mayhem accompanies the city's main festival, Hakata Yamagasa Matsuri, held from 1 to 15 July. Seven groups of men race through the city carrying huge *mikoshi* (portable shrines). The climax comes on the evening of the 15th, when they all converge at Kushida-jinja, just north of Canal City.

The Kyūshū Bashō *sumō* tournament is held mid-November at the Fukuoka Dome, and, in early December, the Fukuoka Marathon (one of the world's most important marathons) attracts world-class runners.

Places to Stay – Budget
Fukuoka has no youth hostels, but there is one in nearby Dazaifu, within reasonable commuting distance of the city (see the Dazaifu entry later in this section). The information counters at JR Hakata station and Rainbow Plaza have lists of inexpensive hotel accommodation, and can make reservations.

If you've wanted to try a capsule hotel (see Accommodation in the Facts for the Visitor chapter), head for *Sauna Wellbe* (☎ 291-1009), next to Canal City. There's a large bath, sauna, massage room, restaurant, bar, TV room and other amenities. Capsules cost ¥3800. This hotel accepts male guests only.

Just around the corner is the older *Capsule Inn Hakata* (☎ 281-2244), with rooms for ¥3090. Some travellers have found these places to be unfriendly.

Places to Stay – Mid-Range
Fukuoka's most pleasant accommodation is at the traditional and wholly unpretentious inn, *Kashima-Honkan Ryokan*, in the Gion district just east of Nakasu and Canal City. Rooms cost ¥5500, or ¥8000 with two meals. It is built in Sukiya-zukuri style (architecture suggesting elements of the tea ceremony), has its own enclosed garden, and is nicely faded – you expect a Meiji-period (1868–1912) novelist to pop up at any moment. The meals, featuring fresh seafood, are extraordinarily good value. The owner speaks English. Kashima-Honkan Ryokan is two minutes' walk north-east of exit 2 of Gion subway station.

The city boasts a plethora of cut-price business hotels, many with rooms for ¥5000 per person or less. *Hakata Grand Suishō Hotel* (☎ 451-0101), near Hakata station, and *Amenity Hotel in Hakata* (☎ 282-0041) in Nakasu-Kawabata are recently built budget hotels within this price range.

The new *Accord Hotel* (☎ 434-1850), west of Hakata station, is equally good value, with singles/doubles for ¥4580/5720. The best bargain, however, is *Hyper Hotel Akasaka* (☎ 732-0900), with singles for ¥4800 with breakfast. If a second or third person shares a room (small, but clean and comfortable), it costs just ¥1000 extra each. The hotel is 200m west of the Taishō-dōri and Meiji-dō-ri intersection.

Hotel Humming Bird (☎ 522-4980) in Kiyokawa is conveniently located, with rooms for ¥5200. Four rooms on the 8th floor are reserved for women only.

Lady's Hotel Petit Tenjin (☎ 713-2613) is also for women only. Singles/doubles cost ¥6500/8500, while capsule rooms cost ¥3500. It's eight minutes' walk west from Tenjin station.

The charmingly named *Fukuoka Arty Inn* (☎ 724-3511) on Watanabe-dōri is right in the centre of things, seven minutes' walk east of Tenjin station. Its rooms are comfortable, its beds unusually large and the reception staff are unerringly helpful. Singles/doubles cost ¥6900/8900.

Green Hotel 1 and *Green Hotel 2* (☎ 451-4111) are typical of the dozens of cheap places directly behind the train station, with rooms from ¥6500/9700. Others include three *Sun Life* hotels (☎ 473-7112), from ¥7300/12,000.

Places to Stay – Top End
Hotel Clio Court (☎ 472-1111) is an upmarket affair, with singles from ¥12,000 and twins/doubles from ¥30,000. Facing Clio Court is the rather luxurious *Hotel Centraza Hakata* (☎ 461-0111), with singles/doubles for ¥11,000/15,000.

ANA Hotel Hakata (☎ 471-7111), on the left as you leave JR Hakata station, is one of the best places in town (from ¥14,000/24,000), but more interesting is the

Hawk's Town's **Sea Hawk** (☎ 844-8111), with singles from ¥9000 and twins/doubles from ¥18,000. Whatever you do, don't get one of the garish 'European-style' rooms; the Japanese-style ones are far better.

Places to Eat

To the vast majority of Japanese, Hakata means rāmen. In particular it means *tonkotsu-rāmen*, noodles in a distinctive, whitish broth distilled from pork bones. The Fukuoka/Hakata telephone book lists 401 rāmen shops, and there are at least twice that many yatai, or food stalls, that are not listed. Discovering your own rāmen shop (and trusting the information only to one's nearest and dearest) is all part of the fun.

The majority of the rāmen yatai are on the streets around Tenjin station, especially where Oyafuko-dōri, meets Shōwa-dōri, and along the riverbanks in Nakasu and in front of Canal City. Most open up as dusk approaches, and a bowl of noodles costs around ¥600. Fads and fashions change, but at the time of writing the unnamed stall immediately south of the east end of Haruyoshi-bashi was the city's most popular.

Menchan (☎ 281-4018) on Kokutai-dōri across from Canal City, is a friendly place (7 pm to 4 am, closed Sunday) that recently topped the honours in an online 'Rāmen Freak' questionnaire. Taking second place was **Uma-uma** (☎ 271-4025), also on Kokutai-dōri (5.30 pm to midnight, closed Saturday), west of the Gion subway station.

Ichiran (☎ 724-6766) has been serving noodles for 37 years, and is open 24 hours a day. Unusually, customers eat at individual cubicles, and fill out forms requesting precisely how they want their noodles prepared. Flavour strength, fat content, noodle tenderness, quantity of 'secret sauce' and garlic content can all be regulated. Marvellously, an English-language request form is also available. Ichiran is in a small alley to the north of Vivre 2 building.

When rāmen palls (and it does), the busy JR Hakata station offers a great number of places to eat. Behind the train station, under the Hotel Centraza Hakata, is **Gourmet City** (late morning until 11 pm), with two base-ment floors of restaurants offering Chinese, Japanese and European food and desserts. Lunch time features some excellent *teishoku* (set lunch) bargains.

Canal City has a great selection of basement restaurants, many offering excellent lunch deals. Get there early if you don't want to queue. Good places include **Nin-nikuya** (*ninniku* means garlic), which serves international cuisine; the Indian restaurant **Kohinoor**; and **Tonkatsu Wakō**. Ichiran also has a branch there. **Kirin Beer Theatre** is an *izakaya* (pub-style eatery), with the usual array of tasty offerings. Canal City has more upmarket dining in the section beneath the Washington Hotel: **La Cucina** is a superb Italian restaurant with lunch specials for around ¥800.

Sizzler (☎ 715-0650) serves Western-style steak, seafood and salads on the 13th floor of the IMS building in Tenjin (11 am to 11 pm). The salad bar lunch special for around ¥1000 is excellent (11 am to 3 pm).

A little off the beaten track in Kego, **Kuriya** (☎ 725-2203) is a trendy restaurant specialising in tofu cuisine (11.30 am to 2 pm, 5.30 to 11 pm, closed Sunday). Lunches are around ¥1000. For dinner, allow ¥3000 with drinks. The owner, Nakamura Tatsuya, speaks English. From the Kego police box, head west for three blocks on Kego Hon-dōri. Kuriya is on the 2nd floor of the Uchino 3 building.

Oyafuko-dōri, once the only chic, happening part of town, now battles it out with Canal City for the place to be seen. There are several good restaurants here, including **Taiwan Yatai**, a small but friendly place that does Taiwanese-Chinese food at very reasonable prices. Just up the road from here is **Taj**, an Indian restaurant whose Japanese sign announces *essuniku kāri senmon* (the 'ethnic curry specialist') – its prices are from ¥900. **Nanak** is an Indian chain and there is a branch on the corner of Shōwa-dōri.

Entertainment

Fukuoka-ites like to party, and the city is full of clubs, bars and pubs. Nakasu Island is one of the busiest entertainment districts in Japan, but you need to go with a Japanese

KYŪSHŪ

regular unless you're prepared to spend a fortune. Tenjin, and especially Oyafuko-dōri, are a better bet for a night out. Generally, clubs have a cover charge at weekends of around ¥2500.

The hip-hop/house-playing *Happy Cock* (☎ 734-2686), on the 9th floor of the Neo Palace building on Tenjin-nishi-dōri, heaves with partygoers (6 pm to 1 am, until 4 am weekends, closed Monday). So does its close relative *Crazy Cock* (☎ 722-3006) on Ōyafuko-dōri, which is open from 9 pm to 3 am and until 4 am weekends (closed Monday). On Half-Monty Night turn up at the Crazy Cock in underwear and you'll get free drinks. Owner Jack Holland also runs the eponymously titled, mercifully cockless *Holland's* (☎ 283-4668), in the Spoon Building in Nakasu-Kawabata, which attracts a less frenzied, slightly older clientele (7 am to 2 pm, until 4 am weekends).

Off Broadway (☎ 724-5383) is busy from start to finish, with a mixture of '60s funk, '70s pop and '90s hip-hop (7.30 pm to 2 am Sunday to Thursday, until 4 am Friday and Saturday). Beers start at ¥400, midweek beer pitchers are half-price, and every hour on the hour tequila shots are liberally donated to the crowd, ensuring a permanent party. It's a block north-east of the Oyafuko-dōri and Shōwa-dōri intersection.

The Dark Room (☎ 725-2989) is a self-styled 'urban rock bar'. It's the kind of place where your feet adhere to the floor, and the bar staff are entertainingly hyperactive (9 pm to 4 am, from 8.30 pm on weekends). Downstairs, *The Bump* (10 pm to early morning, closed Sunday) is a box-like club, cosy to the point of asphyxiation. LesGif, the Fukuoka gay and lesbian group, meets here every second and fourth Saturday. For more information, email lesgif@usa.net.

Jazz aficionados will be interested to know that Fukuoka has a *Blue Note* (☎ 715-6666). Ticket prices range from ¥8500 for international acts, but include food and drink coupons.

Shopping
Clay Hakata dolls depicting women, children, *samurai* and *geisha* are a popular

Fukuoka craft. Hakata *obi*, the silk sashes worn with a *kimono*, are another local product. Try the Mitsukoshi or Daimaru stores in Tenjin for these and other local items.

Getting There & Away
Air Fukuoka is an international gateway with flights to and from Australia, New Zealand, Hong Kong, South Korea, China, the Philippines, Thailand, Malaysia, Indonesia, Taiwan and the USA (☎ 483-7007). There are also domestic flights (☎ 621-6059) to Tokyo's Haneda airport (¥26,600, 1¾ hours, more than 50 flights daily) and to Narita international airport (four daily). Flights to Osaka (¥15,450) take just over an hour.

Japan's only independent cut-price carrier, Skymark (☎ 736-3131, Tokyo ☎ 03-3433-7670) has daily flights to Tokyo's Haneda airport for ¥16,000. If you join their 'Skyfriends' plan, you can get half-price tickets when empty seats are available.

Bus Buses depart from the Kōtsū bus centre near JR Hakata station and from the Tenjin bus centre. There are buses to Tokyo (¥15,000, 15 hours), Osaka (¥10,000, 9½ hours), Nagoya (¥10,500, 12 hours) and many destinations around Kyūshū.

Train JR Hakata station is the western terminus of the 1177km Tokyo-Osaka-Hakata shinkansen. There are services to/from Tokyo (¥21,210, five to six hours), to/from Osaka (¥14,080, 2½ to three hours) and to/from Hiroshima (¥8530, one to two hours, daily). Prices are slightly higher for the Nozomi shinkansen.

JR lines also fan out from Hakata to other centres in Kyūshū. The Nippō line runs through Hakata, Beppu, Miyazaki and Kagoshima; the Kagoshima line runs through Hakata, Kumamoto, Yatsushiro and Kagoshima; and both the Nagasaki and Sasebo lines run from Hakata to Saga and Sasebo or Hakata to Nagasaki.

From Tenjin station the Nishitetsu Ōmuta line operates through Tenjin, Dazaifu, Kurume, Yanagawa and Ōmuta. You can also travel by road or train to Karatsu and continue from there to Nagasaki by train.

Boat There are ferry services from Fukuoka to Okinawa, to Iki-shima and other islands off Kyūshū. Ferries operate between the Tokyo ferry terminal and Kokura harbour (36 hours), and also between Osaka and Shinmonshi harbour (12 hours).

Fukuoka also has an international high-speed hydrofoil service connecting the city with Pusan in Korea. The hydrofoil is run by JR Kyūshū (☎ 281-2315) and costs ¥13,000 one way (¥24,000 return, three hours, daily). The Camelia line (☎ 262-2323) also runs a ferry service to Pusan (¥9000 one way, or ¥17,100 return, 15 hours).

Getting Around

To/From the Airport Fukuoka airport is conveniently close to the city centre. Airport buses run between the international terminal and JR Hakata station (¥190, 15 minutes, every 20 minutes) and Tenjin (¥270, 30 minutes). The subway takes just five minutes to Hakata station (¥220) and 11 minutes to Tenjin station (¥220). Taxis cost from around ¥1500.

The airport has three terminals – No 3 is for international flights, No 2 is for JAL and JAS flights to Tokyo (to both Haneda and Narita airports) and to Okinawa, and No 1 is for all other domestic flights. They are connected by a free shuttle bus.

Bus City and long-distance bus services operate from the Kōtsū bus centre at JR Hakata station and the Tenjin bus centre. Nishitetsu bus has a flat ¥100 rate for city-centre rides. One-day passes cost ¥700.

Subway There are two subway lines in Fukuoka. The Kūkō (airport) line runs from Fukuoka domestic airport to Meinohama, via Hakata and Tenjin stations. The Hakozaki line runs from Nakasu-Kawabata station to Kaizuka Fares around town are ¥220 and automatic vending machines have clear English-language instructions. A one-day Free Pass costs ¥850.

Boat Buses 19 and 84 from stand E of Hakata bus station (¥200) go to the Hakata Port International Terminal.

DAZAIFU 太宰府
☎ 092 • pop 64,899

Ignore the tourist hype – Dazaifu, once the governmental centre of Kyūshū, is a nice enough place for a half-day visit, but no more, unless you happen to arrive when the Temman-gū flea market is in full swing. Once you've seen the shrine and several temples, it's deadsville. You might drop in at Futsukaichi Onsen for a dip on the way back to Fukuoka.

Information

The information office (☎ 925-1880) outside Nishitetsu-Dazaifu station, near the entrance to Temman-gū, has helpful staff and an excellent English-language brochure and map.

Temman-gū

The poet and scholar Sugawara-no-Michizane was an important personage in the Kyoto court until he fell foul of political intrigue and was exiled to distant Dazaifu, where he died two years later. Subsequent disasters that struck Kyoto were blamed on his unfair dismissal and he became deified as Temman Tenjin, or Kankō, the god of culture and scholars. His great shrine and burial place attracts countless visitors.

The brightly painted orange shrine (☎ 922-8225) is entered via a picturesque arched bridge. Behind the shrine building is the Kankō Historical Museum (¥200, closed Tuesday) with dioramas showing events in Tenjin's life. The treasure house has artefacts connected with his life and the history of the shrine. The *honden* (main hall) was rebuilt in 1583.

Once a month the shrine hosts a two-day *omoshiro-ichi* (literally, 'interesting market'), a giant flea market selling everything from antique kimono to Mickey Mouse telephones. Dates vary, so check with tourist info.

Kōmyōzen-ji

In this small temple the **Ittekikaino-niwa** (¥200, 9 am to 4.30 pm) is a beautiful example of a Zen garden and a peaceful contrast to the crowds in the nearby shrine.

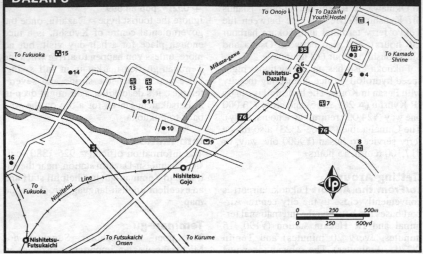

Kaidan-in & Kanzeon-ji

Kaidan-in dates from AD 761 and was one of the most important monasteries in Japan. The adjacent Kanzeon-ji dates from AD 746 but only the great AD 697 bell, said to be the oldest in Japan, remains from the original construction.

Kanzeon-ji Treasure Hall This treasure hall has a wonderful collection of statuary, most of it of wood, dating from the 10th to 12th centuries and of impressive size. The style of some of the pieces appears to be more Indian or Tibetan than Japanese. Admission is ¥500 (9 am to 4.30 pm, closed Monday).

Futsukaichi Onsen 二日市温泉

Ten minutes' walk south of Nishitetsu-Futsukaichi Station, this small hot-spring is unassuming. Its three public baths – Baden House (¥460), Gozen-yu (¥200, closed the first and third Wednesday of each month) and Hakata-yu (¥100) – are grouped together in the main street. The latter, favoured by Futsukaichi's senior citizens, is the most characteristic. All are open from 9 am to 9 pm.

Other Attractions

The **Dazaifu Exhibition Hall** (free, 9 am to 4.30 pm, closed Monday) displays finds from local archaeological excavations. Nearby are the **Tofurō ruins**, foundations of the buildings dating from when Dazaifu governed all of Kyūshū. Enoki-sha is where Sugawara-no-Michizane died. His body was transported from here to its burial place, now the shrine, on the ox cart that appears in so many local depictions. The **Kyūshū Historical Museum** (free, 9.30 am to 4 pm, closed Monday) is near the shrine.

Places to Stay

If you must stay in Dazaifu, *Dazaifu Youth Hostel* (☎ 922-8740) is an option but it's a rule-ridden place, perched on a residential hillside overlooking the city; it charges ¥2900 per night. The hostel is a 20-minute walk from the station and you must be in bed by 10 pm; 'lights' out is 30 minutes later. Check out is by 9 am.

Getting There & Away

A Nishitetsu line train connects Tenjin and Dazaifu (tokkyū, ¥390, 40 minutes) via Futsukaichi. From the Nishitetsu-Futsukaichi

DAZAIFU

1 Kankō Historical
  Museum
  観光歴史資料館
2 Temman-gū
  天満宮
3 Omoshiro-ichi
  おもしろ市
4 Treasure House
  宝物殿
5 Five-arched Bridge
  五孔橋
6 Tourist Information;
  Bicycle Rental
  レンタサイクル

7 Kōmyōzen-ji;
  Ittekikaino-niwa
  光明寺
8 Kyūshū Historical
  Museum
  九州歴史資料館
9 Post Office
  郵便局
10 Dazaifu City
  Office
  市役所
11 Kanzeon-ji
  Treasure Hall
  宝蔵

12 Kanzeon-ji
  観世音寺
13 Kaidan-in
  戒檀院
14 Dazaifu
  Exhibition Hall
  太宰府展示館
15 Tofurō Ruins
  都府楼跡
16 Enoki-sha
  榎社

station, you'll have to change for the two-station ride to Nishitetsu Dazaifu station.

Getting Around
Bicycles can be rented (¥200, one hour) from the information office outside the station.

TACHIARAI
Even the locals don't know about **Tachiarai Heiwa Kinenkan**, a tiny memorial museum established by ex-aviators and residents of Tachiarai, a small village set in farmland 40 minutes from Fukuoka. The museum commemorates Japanese killed in WWII, including kamikaze pilots and Tachiarai locals who died when 180 USAF (United States Air Force) B-52s bombed the area on 27 and 31 March 1945 (Tachiarai was the site of a military air base and aircraft factory). It's a strangely affecting place, with wartime memorabilia bundled together alongside speedometers from Phantom F-4s and Soviet Mig jets, and 24-year-old Toshihiro Watanabe's Zero-sen fighter, retrieved from the sea off Okinawa.

Take the Nishitetsu line to Ogori by *kyūkō* (ordinary express – ¥500, 30 minutes) then change to the Amagi-tetsudo line for Tachiarai (¥280, 11 minutes). The museum is in front of the station.

GENKAI QUASI-NATIONAL PARK
The Genkō fort wall at Imajuku is in the Genkai Quasi-National Park and the nearby Obaru Beach offers surprisingly good swimming. **Keya Ōto** (Great Cave of Keya) is at the western end of the peninsula. Itoshima-hantō. It's a popular tourist attraction and buses run to the nearby Keya-Ōto bus stop (¥1050, 1½ hours) and from there it's a five-minute walk to the centre.

KURUME 久留米
The town of Kurume, south of Dazaifu, is noted for its crafts, including paper making, bamboo work, lacquerware and tie-dyed textiles. Pottery is also produced in nearby towns. The **Ishibashi Bunka Center** is a Bridgestone-sponsored art museum (¥300, 10 am to 5 pm, closed Monday) and the town centre also has the Bairin-ji and the Suiten-gū. It takes about half an hour to get to Kurume from Fukuoka, either on the JR Kagoshima line or the Nishitetsu line.

YANAGAWA 柳川
Yanagawa, south-west of Kurume, is a peaceful old castle town noted for its many moats and canals. Regular canal trips are made around the waterways (¥1500). The town has some interesting old buildings, including a teahouse and a museum. Yanagawa has a range of accommodation, including *Runowaru Youth Hostel* (☎ 0944-62-2423). A train from Kurume to Yanagawa on the Nishitetsu-Ōmuta line takes about 20 minutes.

KYŪSHŪ

Saga-ken 佐賀県

KARATSU 唐津

☎ 0955 • pop 80,000

The small city of Karatsu has a reconstructed castle and a superb display of the floats used in the annual Karatsu Kunchi Matsuri. Only 50km south-west of Fukuoka, it makes a good jumping-off point for visits to the picturesque Higashi-Matsuura-hantō. Potters in Karatsu turn out primitive but well-respected pottery, with clear connections to the Korean designs first introduced into Japan. The sandy beach east of Karatsu at Niji-no-Matsubara draws crowds in summer.

Information

The information desk at Karatsu station (☎ 72-4963) has a good English-language map of the area. It can book accommodation, but no English is spoken. It is open from 9 am to 5 pm.

Karatsu-jō

Although it's a modern reconstruction, the castle (¥310, 9 am to 4.30 pm) looks great, perched on a hill overlooking the sea. Inside, there's a museum with archaeological and pottery displays.

Kunchi Matsuri Floats

The 14 floats used in the Karatsu Kunchi Matsuri are displayed in the Hikiyama Festival Float Exhibition Hall (¥200, 9 am to 5 pm) beside Karatsu-jinja. The festival is believed to have started in the 1660s. Designs include the Aka-jishi (Red Lion), a turtle, samurai helmets, a dragon and...a chicken.

Other Attractions

There are a number of kilns where you can see local potters at work, and there are also ceramic shops along the street between the train station and the town centre. The most famous kiln-gallery is that of **Nakazato Tarōemon**. It's five minutes walk south-east of Karatsu station.

A popular cycling track cuts through the pine trees planted behind the 5km-long **Niji-no-Matsubara Beach**. Each morning there is a busy *asa-ichi* (morning market) at the west end of the beach, from dawn to 9 am.

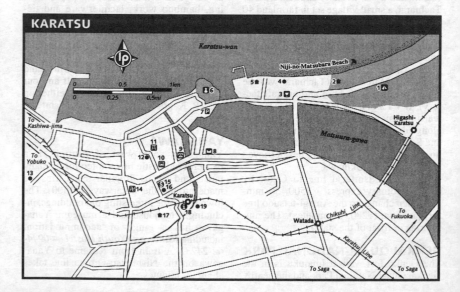

Special Events
In July and August the *doyo-yoichi* (Saturday night-market) is held in the town centre with much singing and dancing. The spectacular Karatsu Kunchi Matsuri takes place from 2 to 4 November.

Places to Stay & Eat
Karatsu City Hotel (☎ 72-1100) is a big, modern hotel right behind the train station, with singles/doubles from ¥7000/13,000. Most other accommodation is along Niji-no-Matsubara Beach and is fairly expensive. One of the cheapest is *Kokuminshukusha Niji-no-Matsubara Hotel* (☎ 73-9111), with singles/twins for ¥6000/10,000.

West of here near the beachfront, *Ryokan Yōyōkaku* (☎ 72-7181) is a beautiful Zen-like building, with rooms from ¥15,000, including two meals.

More affordable is *Niji-no-Matsubara Camp Site* (☎ 73-1785) with sites for ¥500. There are various *minshuku* (family-run guesthouses) on the island, Kashiwa-jima, which is 20 minutes by bus west of the city. Rates are around ¥6000, with two meals. There is also the *Kashiwa-jima Camp Site* (☎ 79-1218).

There are a number of cheap restaurants inside the station complex.

Entertainment
Out near the beach, *Dreadlock* (☎ 72-1207) is a fun reggae bar run by Karatsu's resident Rastafarian, Nishimura Eiji (7 pm to 2 am, closed Wednesday). Nishimura is a wealth of information about diving, surfing and ceramics, and he speaks good English.

Getting There & Away
From Fukuoka, take the Kūkō subway line from Hakata or Tenjin to the end of the line and continue on the JR Chikuhi line (¥950, one hour and 20 minutes). From Karatsu to Nagasaki take the JR Karatsu line to Saga and the JR Nagasaki line from there.

Getting Around
Bicycles can be rented from Yoshitani Cycle (¥800 for one day, 9 am to 6 pm, closed Sunday) in front of JR Karatsu station. A circuit of the Higashi-Matsuura-hantō makes a good day trip from Karatsu in a rental car. Try Eki Rent-a-Car (☎ 74-6204) in front of the station building.

HIGASHI-MATSUURA-HANTŌ 東松浦半島
Karatsu is at the base of Higashi-Matsuura-hantō with its dramatic coastline and little fishing ports.

Yobuko 呼子
This busy fishing port has a wonderful early morning market for fish and produce. A series of *ryokan*, charging from around ¥7000 per person, line a narrow lane running beside the waterfront; rooms look straight out

KARATSU

1 Niji-no-Matsubara Camp Site 虹の松原キャンプ場	7 Car Park 駐車場	14 Kinshō-ji 近松寺
2 Kokuminshukusha Niji-no-Matsubara 虹の松原	8 Main Post Office 中央郵便局	15 Saga-ginko 佐賀銀行
3 Dreadlock	9 NTT	16 Bicycle Rental レンタサイクル
4 Asa-ichi (morning market) 朝市	10 Showa Bus Station 昭和バスセンター	17 Karatsu City Hotel 唐津シティホテル
5 Ryokan Yōyōkaku 旅館洋洋閣	11 Karatsu-jinja 唐津神社	18 Tourist Information Centre 旅行案内所
6 Karatsu-jō 唐津城	12 Hikiyama Festival Float Exhibition Hall 曳山展示場	19 Nakazato Tarōemon Kiln 中里太郎右エ門窯
	13 Kojirō Kiln 小次郎窯	

KYUSHU

onto the bay. Shōwa buses run from Karatsu (¥640, 40 minutes).

Nagoya-jō
En route between Yobuko and Hatomizaki, buses stop at this now ruined castle, from which Hideyoshi launched his unsuccessful invasions of Korea.

POTTERY TOWNS
Imari and Arita are the major pottery towns of Saga-ken. From the early 17th century, pottery was produced in this area using captive Korean potters. The work was done in Arita and nearby Ōkawachiyama and the Korean experts were zealously guarded so that the secrets of their craft did not slip out. Pottery from this area, with its brightly coloured glazes, is still highly esteemed in Japan.

Imari 伊万里
☎ 0955 • pop 59,296
Although Imari is the name commonly associated with pottery from this area, it is actually produced in Ōkawachiyama and Arita. The tourist information at Imari station (☎ 22-6820) can arrange kiln visits and accommodation, but no English is spoken.

Ōkawachiyama, where 20 pottery kilns operate today, is a short bus ride (¥270, 20 minutes) from the JR Imari station. This is the cheapest place to buy the ceramics, and you can see potters at work. It is relatively untouristed. At the bottom of the village the excellent Chitōjin (☎ 22-8501) gallery is dedicated to the work of potter-genius Sawada Chitōjin, whose wonderful name means 'idiot potter person' (9 am to 5 pm).

The nearby **Nabeshima Hanyō-kōen** shows the techniques and living conditions of a feudal-era pottery.

One of Japan's most astonishing festivals takes place in the small village of Ōki, between Imari and Arita on 18 August at Ryūsen-ji. See the boxed text 'Juhachiya Matsuri' in the Matsuri Magic special colour section.

The not-so-grand *Imari Grand Hotel* (☎ 22-2811), with singles/twins for ¥5000/9600, is a business hotel 200m south-west of Imari station. *Kaneko* (☎ 22-5261), 100m west of the station, has plain but comfy rooms and a huge bath (¥5200).

Imari is connected with Karatsu by *futsū* (local train – ¥630, one hour), on the JR Chikuhi line.

Arita 有田
• pop 34,943
It was at Arita that kaolin clay was discovered in 1615 by Ri Sampei, a naturalised Korean potter, permitting the manufacture of fine porcelain for the first time. By the mid-17th century it was being exported to Europe.

Arita is a sprawling town, and less interesting than Imari. The **Kyūshū Ceramic Art Museum** (¥200) is well worth a visit if you want an overview of the development of ceramic arts in Kyūshū (9 am to 4.30 pm, closed Monday).

For the full treatment, join the Japanese package tours at **Arita Porcelain Park** (¥1500, 9 am to 4.30 pm). Shuttle buses go from Arita station (¥210, 10 minutes).

Pottery connoisseurs are sure to find **Imaizumi Imaemon Gallery** (9 am to 5 pm, closed Sunday), **Sakaida Kakiemon Kiln** (9 am to 5 pm) and **Genemon Kiln** (8 am to 5.30 pm, closed Sunday) very interesting.

China on the Park (☎ 46-3900), 5km west of Arita, on Route 202, has a restaurant, galleries and the Fukugawa china factory, where you can watch the firing process (9 am to 7 pm). A taxi from Arita station costs ¥1000.

Arita is connected with Imari on the Matsuura line (futsū, ¥400, 25 minutes). Alternatively, there are direct buses running from the Tenjin bus centre in Fukuoka (¥2000, two hours).

North-West Islands

Five large and many smaller islands lie to the north-west of Kyūshū and are accessible from Fukuoka, Sasebo and Nagasaki, but getting to them is not cheap. Tsu-shima, the largest of the group, is in the strait midway between Japan and Korea and is actually closer to Pusan than to Fukuoka. These are strictly islands for those who want to get far away from it all; foreign visitors are very rare. Some of the islands are part of Saga-ken, while other islands are part of Nagasaki-ken.

Tsu-shima also has a youth hostel and there are minshuku and ryokan on Tsu-shima, Hirado-shima and Fukue-jima.

Getting There & Away

Air There are a number of local air services to the islands. All Nippon Koku (ANK) flies between Fukuoka and Iki-shima for ¥6000, Fukuoka and Tsu-shima for ¥9080

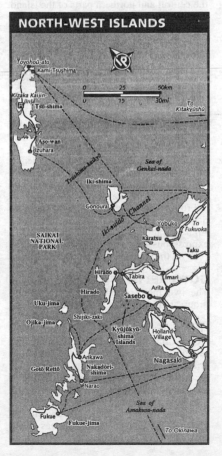

and between Nagasaki and Iki-shima for ¥8830.

Boat Jetfoil services from Hakata to Iki-shima and Tsu-shima cost ¥4600 and ¥6500 respectively, and take less than one hour. Ordinary services cost ¥3520 to Tsu-shima and ¥1890 to Iki-shima and take just over two hours.

TSU-SHIMA 対馬
☎ 09205 • pop 42,147

The mountainous island of Tsu-shima, 682 sq km in area, is actually two islands: the narrow neck of land connecting the two parts was channelled through during the 16th century. Tsu-shima has a number of small towns and a road runs most of its length.

The visitor centre (☎ 2 1566) can book accommodation and has printed information in English; however, no English is spoken.

The port of Izuhara is the island's main town and has a fort originally built by Toyotomi Hideyoshi during an expedition to Korea in 1592. The island has seen a more recent conflict when the Tzar's fleet was annihilated by the Japanese during the Russo-Japanese War in 1905, with horrific loss of life.

Sights worth seeking out include Kizaka kaijin-jinja in Mine, a shrine dedicated to the god of the sea; the remains of the Toyohōdai-ato war time battleship shelter in Kami-tsu-shima; and the Tsu-shima Yasei Seibutsu Hogo Centre wildlife park in Kami-agata. Tama no-yu Onsen on the north-east coast of the south island is popular for a quick dip.

The cheapest accommodation on the island is the 16-bed *Tsushima Seizan-ji Youth Hostel* (☎ 2-0444), which charges ¥2000 per night.

Transport can be a problem as local buses are infrequent. Cars can be hired at Yoshinaga Rent-a-Car (☎ 2-5111).

IKI-SHIMA 壱岐島
☎ 09204 • pop 34,543

Iki-shima, with an area of 138 sq km, is south-east of Tsu-shima and much closer to Fukuoka. It is an attractive island with fine beaches; it's also relatively flat and is a good place for cycling. Toyotomi Hideyoshi fortified **Gonoura**, which is the port and the main base for exploring the island. Ontake-jinja, north of Ashibe, features comical 'monkey men' carved by a local lord, while Yunomoto Onsen on the west coast is the island's only hot spring, and is the best place to stay. The *kokumin-shukusha* (people's lodge) *Iki-shima-sō* (☎ 30124) is good value.

HIRADO-SHIMA 平戸
☎ 0950 • pop 24,757

Hirado-shima's proximity to the mainland makes it easy – and cheap – to access. It hosts some interesting sights, good beaches, two noteworthy festivals, and a little-known collection of erotic drawings. Tourist information (☎ 22-4111) in the harbour terminal has English-language information and staff can book accommodation (10 am to 5 pm).

The island, close to Sasebo and actually joined to Kyūshū by a bridge from Hirado-guchi, has had an interesting European history. Portuguese ships first landed on Hirado-shima in 1549 and, a year later, St Francis Xavier paid a visit to the island (after his expulsion from Kagoshima). It was not until 1584 that the Portuguese formally established a trading post on the island, but they were soon followed by the Dutch (in 1609) and the British (in 1613). Relations between the British and Dutch became so acrimonious that, in 1618, the Japanese had to restore law and order on the island. In 1621, the British abandoned Hirado-shima and Japan, and turned their full attention to India.

The main town is small enough to navigate on foot, though rent-a-cycles are available for ¥200 an hour. **Matsuura Historical museum** (¥500, 8 am to 5.30 pm) is housed in the residence of the Matsuura, who ruled the island from the 11th to the 19th centuries. It contains the Kanun-tei *chanoyu* (tea ceremony) house, the centre for the unusual Chinshu-ryu warrior-style tea ceremony that is still practised on the island today. Hirado Tourist Museum (¥300, 8 am to 4 pm) displays items relating to the island's history, including a Maria-kannon

statue, the Buddhist goddess of compassion that the 'hidden Christians' used in the place of the Virgin Mary image.

Not mentioned in the tourist literature is the rather more earthy Issho-raku (☎ 23-3434), a small private collection of erotic drawings dating back almost 400 years. Ask the tourist information to arrange a viewing. The owners don't speak English but are very friendly. They live in Ohno-cho, 10 minutes by car from the town centre.

The island's natural scenery is most attractive. If you climb to the top of Kawachi-Toge pass, there is a magnificent view of the central and northern parts of the island. There are fine views over the islands of the Gotō Rettō from the cape, **Shijiki-zaki**, and the western coast of the island is particularly attractive. The beach, Senriga-hama, in the south is renowned for windsurfing (board rentals cost about ¥1500 an hour, ¥6000 all day).

Jangara Matsuri, a folk festival held on 18 August, is particularly colourful. It is quite different to mainland festivals and is reminiscent of Okinawa or Korea. It's held all over town, but especially by the city office. Arrive by late morning if possible, for the afternoon events. From 24 to 27 October, Okunchi Matsuri has dragon and lion dancing at Kameoka-jinja.

From Kashimae, half an hour by bus from Sasebo, regular boats operate to Hirado-shima via the islands, Kyūjūkyū-shima. An express bus runs from Hakata bus station (¥2850, three hours 40 minutes, one daily).

GOTŌ RETTŌ 五島列島

The two main islands in the Gotō Rettō group are **Fukue-jima** and **Nakadōri-shima**, but there are three other medium-sized islands plus over 100 small islands and islets. At one time, these islands were a refuge for Japanese Christians fleeing the Edo government's anti-Christian repression; today the main attraction is the natural beauty of the mountainous islands.

Fukue, the fishing port on the island of the same name, is the main town in the group. The town's **Ishida-jō** was burnt down in 1614 and rebuilt in 1849. Along with Hirado-shima and a strip of the Kyūshū coast, the Gotō Rettō islands are part of the Saikai National Park. The island's most popular beach is Taka-hama.

Jetfoils leave Nagasaki for Fukue three to five times a day (¥6080, 1½ hours).

KYŪJŪKYŪ-SHIMA 九十九島
☎ 0956

The 170-odd islands (although the name actually means '99 islands') lie between Hirado and the mainland. The calm seaways between the islands have made this Japan's sea-kayaking mecca. Try Team Umiak (☎ 28-1124) and Saikai Pearl Sea Resort (☎ 28-4187) for rentals (¥3000 a single for two hours, ¥4000 for doubles).

Buses run from Sasebo, twice daily (¥180).

Nagasaki-ken

NAGASAKI 長崎
☎ 095 • pop 450,000

Nagasaki is a busy and colourful city but its unfortunate fate as the second atomic bomb target obscures its fascinating early history of contact with the Portuguese and Dutch. Even after Commodore Perry's historic visit to Japan, Nagasaki remained one of the major contact points with the West. Despite the popular image of Nagasaki as a totally modern city rising from an atomic wasteland, there are many reminders of its earlier history and European contact. The bomb actually missed its intended target and scored a near direct hit on the largest Catholic church in Japan.

History

Nagasaki has the most varied history of any city in Japan, much of it tied up with the dramatic events of the 'Christian Century'. The accidental arrival of an off-course Portuguese ship at Tanega-shima in 1542 signalled the start of Nagasaki's long period as Japan's principal connection with the West.

The first visitors were soon followed by the great missionary St Francis Xavier in 1560 and, although his visit was brief, these Portuguese contacts were to have far-reaching effects. The primitive guns introduced by the Portuguese soon revolutionised warfare in Japan, forcing the construction of new and stronger castles and bringing to an end the anarchy and chaos of the 'Country at War' century.

Among the first Japanese to be converted to Christianity by the visitors was a minor *daimyō* (regional lord), Ōmura Sumitada, in north-western Kyūshū. Under Ōmura,

The Atomic Explosion

When the United States Air Force (USAF) B-29 bomber *Bock's Car* set off from Tinian in the Marianas on 9 August 1945 to drop the second atomic bomb on Japan, the target was Kokura on the north-eastern coast of Kyūshū. Fortunately for Kokura it was a cloudy day and, despite flying over the city three times, the bomber's crew could not sight the target, so a course was set for the secondary target, Nagasaki.

The B-29 arrived over Nagasaki at 10.58 am but again visibility was obscured by cloud. When a momentary gap appeared in the cloud cover, the Mitsubishi Arms Works, not the intended Mitsubishi shipyard, was sighted and became the target. The 4.5 ton 'Fat Man' bomb had an explosive power equivalent to 22 kilotons of TNT, far more than the 13 kilotons of Hiroshima's 'Little Boy'. Afterwards, the aircraft turned south and flew to Okinawa, arriving there with its fuel supply almost exhausted.

The explosion took place at 11.02 am, at an altitude of 500m, completely devastating the Urakami suburb of northern Nagasaki and killing 75,000 of Nagasaki's 240,000 population. Another 75,000 were injured and it is estimated that as many people again have subsequently died as a result of the blast. Anybody out in the open within 2km of the epicentre suffered severe burns from the heat of the explosion; even at 4km away exposed bare skin was burnt. Everything within a 1km radius of the explosion was destroyed and the resulting fires burnt out almost everything within a 4km radius. A third of the city was wiped out.

KYŪSHŪ

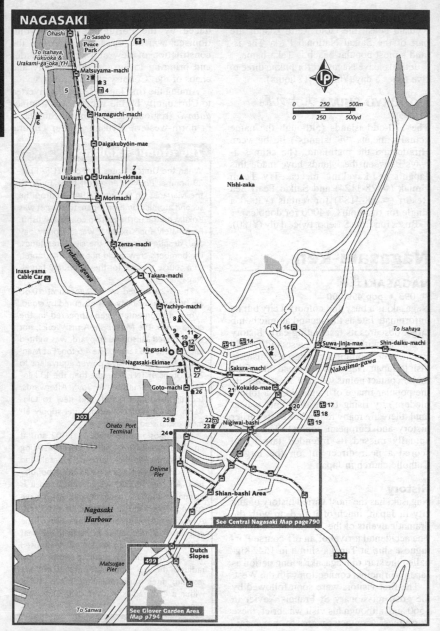

NAGASAKI

Ōhashi

To Sasebo

Peace Park

To Isahaya, Fukuoka & Urakami-ga-oka YH

1

Matsuyama-machi

2

3

4

5

6

Hamaguchi-machi

Daigakubyōin-mae

7

Urakami

Urakami-ekimae

Nishi-zaka

Morimachi

Urakami-gawa

Zenza-machi

Inasa-yama Cable Car

Takara-machi

Yachiyo-machi

8

9

10

11

12

16

To Isahaya

Nagasaki

13

14

15

Suwa-jinja-mae

Shin-daiku-machi

34

Nagasaki-Ekimae

Sakura-machi

Nakajima-gawa

28

27

Goto-machi

26

21

Kokaido-mae

20

17

18

19

202

25

24

22

23

Nigiwai-bashi

Ōhato Port Terminal

Dejima Pier

Nagasaki Harbour

Shian-bashi Area

See Central Nagasaki Map page790

Dutch Slopes

Matsugae Pier

499

324

To Sanwa

See Glover Garden Area Map p794

0   250   500m

0   250   500yd

NAGASAKI

PLACES TO STAY
2 Volks Hotel In Park
　フォルクスホテル
3 Park Side Hotel
　パークサイドホテル
6 Minshuku Tanpopo
　民宿タンポポ
9 Nishi-kyūshū Dai-Ichi
　Hotel; Capsule Inn
　Nagasaki
　西九州第1ホテル；
　カプセルイン長崎
11 Fukumatsu Ryokan
　福松旅館
15 Nagasaki Youth Hostel
　長崎ユースホステル
23 Sakamoto-ya Bekkan
　坂本屋別館
25 Newport Business
　Hotel
　ビジネスホテル
　ニューポート
26 Terada Inn
　寺田屋

28 Hotel New Nagasaki
　ホテルニュー長崎

PLACES TO EAT
21 Harbin Restaurant
　ハルビン

OTHER
1 Urakami Cathedral
　浦上天主堂
4 A-Bomb Museum
　長崎国際文化会館
5 Hypocentre
　(Epicentre) Park
　原爆落下中心地
7 One-Legged Torii
　片足鳥居
8 26 Martyrs Memorial
　二十六聖人殉教地
10 Nagasaki Prefectural
　Tourist Federation;
　Ken-ei Bus Station
　観光案内所；
　県営バスターミナル

12 Ken-ei
　Bus Station
　県営バスターミナル
13 Fukusai-ji
　福済寺
14 Shōfuku-ji
　聖福寺
16 Suwa-jinja
　諏訪神社
17 Kōfuku-ji
　興福寺
18 Ema-ji
　絵馬寺
19 Chōshō-ji
　長照寺
20 Megane-bashi
　眼鏡橋
22 NTT Dream 21
24 Harbour Cruise
　Office
　観光船大波止発着所
27 Post Office
　郵便局

Nagasaki, established in 1571, soon became the main arrival point for Portuguese trade ships. Although the Portuguese principally acted as intermediaries between China and Japan, the trade was mutually profitable, and Nagasaki quickly became a fashionable and wealthy city.

By 1587, Japanese authorities had begun to perceive the growing influence of Christianity as a threat. Jesuit missionaries were expelled and a policy of persecution was soon implemented. In 1597, 26 European and Japanese Christians were crucified in Nagasaki and in 1614 the religion was banned. Suspected Christians were rounded up, tortured and killed; the Japanese wives and children of foreigners were deported; and the Catholic Portuguese and Spanish traders were expelled in favour of the Protestant Dutch, who were perceived as being more interested in trade and less in religion.

The Shimabara peasant uprising of 1637–38 – perceived as a Christian uprising at the time – was the final chapter in the events of the 'Christian Century'. All subsequent contact with foreigners was banned and no Japanese were allowed to travel overseas. One small loophole was the closely watched Dutch enclave on the island of Dejima near Nagasaki. Through this small outpost a trickle of Western science and progress continued to filter into Japan, and from 1720, when Dutch books were once again permitted to enter the country, Nagasaki became an important scientific and artistic centre. When Nagasaki reopened to the west in 1859, it quickly re-established itself as a major economic force, particularly in shipbuilding, the industry that made it a prime target on 9 August, 1945.

Orientation

The Hamano-machi arcade and the Shianbashi entertainment area form the focus of Nagasaki's central city area, about a kilometre south of the train station. Farther south are the Chinatown, Dutch Slopes and Glover Garden areas. Nagasaki is relatively

CENTRAL NAGASAKI

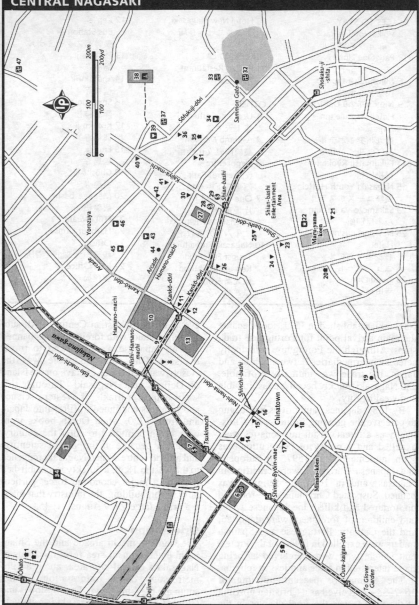

CENTRAL NAGASAKI

PLACES TO STAY
1 Harbour Inn Nagasaki
　ハーバーイン長崎
2 Hotel Ibis
　ホテルアイビス
3 Nagasaki Grand Hotel
　長崎グランドホテル
5 Fukumoto Ryokan
　福本旅館
13 Holiday Inn
　ホリデイイン長崎
14 Nagasaki Washington
　Hotel
　長崎ワシントンホテル
20 Nishiki-sō
　にしき荘
35 Miyuki-sō
　三幸荘

PLACES TO EAT
8 McDonalds
9 Lotteria
11 KFC
12 Nanaka
15 Kyōka-en
　京華園
16 Kairaku-en
　会楽園

17 Chūka-en
　中華園
18 Kōzan-rō
　江山楼
21 Kagetsu
　花月
23 Fukusaya Castella
　Cake Shop
　福砂屋
24 Akachōchin
　赤ちょうちん
25 Italian Tomato
26 Unryū-tei
　雲龍亭
30 Mr Donut
31 Bharata
36 Hamakatsu
　浜勝
40 Ginrei
　銀嶺
41 Hamakatsu
　浜勝
42 Garden Pizza House

OTHER
4 Dejima Museum
　出島資料館
6 NTT

7 Jūhachi Ginkō
　十八銀行
10 Daimaru Department
　Store
　大丸
19 Chinese Compound
22 Police Post
27 With Nagasaki
28 Shinwa Ginkō
29 Jūhachi Ginkō
　十八銀行
32 Sōfuku-ji
　崇福寺
33 Daikō-ji
　大光寺
34 Bajamut
37 Hosshin-ji
　発心寺
38 Daion-ji
　大音寺
39 JB Trick
43 10c
44 Kōbundō Bookshop
　好文堂
45 Fan Fan
46 Ayer's Rock
47 Kōtai-ji
　こうたい寺

compact and it's quite feasible to walk from the central area all the way south to Glover Garden. The atomic bomb hypocentre is in the suburb of Urakami, about 2.5km north of JR Nagasaki station.

Information

The Nagasaki Prefectural Tourist Federation (☎ 826-9407) in front of the station has detailed information on the city, and extremely helpful English-speaking staff (9 am to 5.30 pm, closed Sunday). Cross the pedestrian walkway to enter the prefectural building on the 2nd floor. The Nagasaki station tourist information office (☎ 823-3631) can assist you with finding accommodation, although you may have to be a bit persistent (8 am to 5.30 pm). No English is spoken. Chikyūkan (☎ 822-7966) in Oranda-zaka (the Dutch Slopes area), aimed at long-term

residents, has detailed information about the city and environs (and a good, cheap restaurant and Internet access). It is open from 10 am to 5 pm (closed Wednesday).

Money Amazingly, there are no ATMs that accept internationally issued cards. Shinwa Ginko will advance money on MasterCard and VISA cards, with passport proof of ID. Jūhachi Ginko will do so for VISA only.

Email & Internet Access Free Internet access is available (9 am to 4 pm weekdays) at NTT's Sakuramachi branch (near Dejima) and at its 'Dream 21' on route 34, about 10 minutes' walk from the Prefectural office. You can also get on the Net (free, 10 am to 5pm, closed Wednesday) at Chikyūkan (see Dutch Slopes in the Glover Garden area later in this section).

Urakami 浦上

A-Bomb Site Urakami, the hypocentre of the atomic explosion, is today a prosperous, peaceful suburb with modern shops, restaurants, cafes and even a couple of love hotels just a few steps from the hypocentre. Nuclear ruin seems comfortably far away. The Matsuyama-machi tram stop, the eighth stop north of JR Nagasaki station on tram routes 1 or 3, is near the site.

Hypocentre Park The park has a black stone column marking the exact point above which the bomb exploded. Nearby are bomb-blasted relics, including a section of the wall of the Urakami Cathedral and a buckled water tower.

A-Bomb Museum The Gembaku Shiryō-kan, or A-Bomb Museum (¥200, 8.30 am to 5.30 pm) opened in April 1996. As you descend the spiral walkway into the exhibit, the parallels with a descent into hell are all too obvious. It is quite a chilling experience.

Peace Park North of Hypocentre Park is Heiwa-kōen (Peace Park), presided over by the Nagasaki Peace Statue, which – good intentions aside – is a monstrosity of immense proportions. At the time of the explosion, the park was the site of the Urakami Prison and every occupant of the prison – prisoners and warders – was killed instantly. An annual antinuclear protest is held at the park on 9 August.

Urakami Cathedral The original Urakami Cathedral, the largest church in the east, was completed in 1914 and flattened in 1945. Relics from the cathedral are displayed in Hypocentre Park. The replacement cathedral was completed in 1959.

Other Relics The 'One-legged Torii' (a *torii* is an entrance gate to a Shintō shrine) is 850m south-east of the hypocentre. The blast knocked down one side of the entrance arch to the Sanno Shinto-gū but the other leg still stands to this day.

Dr Nagai Takashi devoted himself to the treatment of bomb victims until he died in 1951 from the after-effects of the bomb; his small hut is preserved as a memorial.

Nagasaki Station Area

26 Martyrs Memorial A few minutes' walk from JR Nagasaki station on Nishizaka is a memorial wall with reliefs of the 26 Christians crucified in 1597. In this, Japan's most brutal crackdown on Christianity, six of those crucified were Spanish friars, the other 20 were Japanese and the two youngest were boys aged 12 and 13. The memorial dates from 1962 and behind it is an interesting museum (¥250, 9 am to 5 pm) with displays about Christianity in the area.

Fukusai-ji Although Fukusai-ji (¥200, 9 am to 5 pm) is not on any list of architectural or cultural gems, this unique construction, also known as Nagasaki Kannon Universal Temple, shouldn't be missed. In fact, you can't miss it, since the temple is in the form of a huge turtle carrying an 18m-high figure of the goddess Kannon on its back. Inside, a Foucault pendulum (a device that demonstrates the rotation of the earth on its tilted axis) hangs from near the top of the hollow statue. Only St Petersburg and Paris have larger examples.

The original temple was built in 1628 but was completely burnt by the A-bomb fire. The replacement, totally unlike the original, was built in 1979. A bell tolls from the temple at 11.02 am daily, the exact time of the explosion.

Shōfuku-ji This temple, not to be confused with Sōfuku-ji, is near Nagasaki Youth Hostel and JR Nagasaki station. Its gardens are particularly pleasant and contain an arched stone gate dating from 1657. The gate was moved here from the old Jingū-ji outside the city in 1886. The main building, of typical Chinese style, was reconstructed in 1715. Almost adjacent to the temple is the Kanzen-ji, with the biggest camphor tree in Nagasaki.

Suwa-jinja

Between 7 and 9 October, the shrine comes to life with the dragon dance of Okunchi Matsuri, Nagasaki's most important annual celebration. Suwa-jinja was originally established in 1555 and although it is mostly new, its wooded hilltop setting is attractive. Tram lines 3, 4 and 5 run to the Suwa-jinja-mae stop, close to the shrine.

Sōfuku-ji
An Ōbaku (the third-largest Zen sect after Rinzai and Sōtō) temple, and one of Nagasaki's most important, Sōfuku-ji (¥300, 8 am to 5 pm) dates from 1629 and has a fine gateway that was built in China and brought to Japan for reassembling in 1696. Inside the temple you can admire a great bell from 1647 and a huge cauldron that was used to prepare food for victims of a famine in 1680.

Teramachi 寺町 (Temple Row)
The path between Sōfuku-ji and Kōfuku-ji is lined with a series of smaller temples. Just down the road from Sōfuku-ji, steep steps lead up to **Daijo-ji**.

At almost the bottom of the road past Daijo-ji, turn right and take a few steps to the **Hosshin-ji bell**. Cast in 1483, it's the oldest temple bell in Nagasaki. Climb up the stairs to the large Kuroganemochi tree at the entrance to **Daion-ji**. Follow the road to the left of the temple to the grave of Matsudaira Zushonokami. He had been magistrate of Nagasaki for a year when, in 1808, the British warship HMS *Phaeton* sailed into Nagasaki Harbour and seized two Dutch hostages. The British and Dutch were on opposite sides in the Napoleonic War at that time. Unable to oppose the British, Zushonokami capitulated to their demands for supplies, then promptly disembowelled himself.

A short distance further on, turn down the path to **Kotai-ji**; it's a favourite with local artists and has a notable bell dating from 1702. Continuing towards Kōfuku-ji, you come to **Chosho-ji** and **Ema-ji**, both pleasant escapes from the city hustle.

Kōfuku-ji The final temple along the temple-row walk, Kōfuku-ji (¥200, 8 am to 5 pm), dates from the 1620s and has always had strong Chinese connections. The temple is noted for its lawns and cycad palms

and for the Chinese-influenced architecture of the main hall. Like the Sōfuku-ji, it is an Ōbaku Zen temple.

Megane-bashi Parallel to the temple row is the river, the Nakajima-gawa, which is crossed by a picturesque collection of bridges. At one time, each bridge was the distinct entranceway to a separate temple. The best-known of the bridges is Megane-bashi (Spectacles Bridge), so called because if the water is at the right height, the arches and their reflection in the water come together to create a 'spectacles' effect. The double-arched stone bridge was built in 1634 but in 1982 a typhoon flood washed away all the bridges along the stream. The Megane-bashi has been meticulously rebuilt.

Shian-bashi Area 思案橋
The Shian-bashi tram stop marks the site of the bridge over which pleasure seekers would cross into the Shian-bashi quarter. The bridge and the elegant old brothels are long gone but this is still the entertainment area of Nagasaki. During Japan's long period of isolation from the west, the Dutch – cordoned off at their Dejima trading post – were only allowed contact with Japanese trading partners and courtesans. It's said that fortunes were made as much from smuggling as from the world's oldest profession.

In between the bars, restaurants and clubs, Shian-bashi still has a few reminders of those old days. A walk up from the southern tram stop on Shian-bashi-dōri to where the first road forks leads to the Fukusaya Castella Cake Shop (see Shopping later in this section). Turn left at this junction, pass the police post and you come to the driveway entrance to Kagetsu, now an elegant and expensive restaurant, but at one time an even more elegant and expensive brothel.

Dejima Museum 出島
The old Dutch trading enclave is long gone. From the mid-17th century until 1855, this small isolated community was Japan's only contact with the Western world, and fortunes were made by traders here through exchange of Japanese crafts for Western medicine and

technology. The small museum (¥100, 9 am to 5 pm, closed Monday) near the old site of Dejima has exhibits on the Dutch and other foreign contact with Nagasaki. Across the road in the museum yard is an outdoor model of Dejima. Attempts to reconstruct the trading post are slowly moving ahead.

Chinatown Area

Theoretically, during Japan's long period of seclusion, Chinese traders were just as circumscribed in their movements as the Dutch, but in practice, they were relatively free. Only a couple of buildings remain from the old area, but Nagasaki still has an energetic Chinese community that has had a great influence on Nagasaki's culture, festivals and cuisine.

Glover Garden Area

Glover Garden At the southern end of Nagasaki, some former homes of the city's pioneering Meiji period European residents have been reassembled in this hillside garden. The series of moving stairways up the hill, plus the fountains, goldfish and announcements, give it the air of a cultural Disneyland, but the houses are attractive, the history is interesting and the views across Nagasaki are superb.

The garden (¥600, 8 am to 6 pm March to November, 8.30 am to 5 pm December to February, until 9.30 pm during July and August) takes its name from Thomas Glover (1838–1911), the best known of the expat community. Glover's arms-importing operations played an important part in the Meiji Restoration; he built the first train line in Japan and he even helped establish the first modern shipyard from which Nagasaki's Mitsubishi shipyard is a direct descendant.

The best way to explore the hillside garden is to take the walkways to the top and then walk back downhill. At the top of the park is **Mitsubishi No 2 Dock building** with displays about the city's important shipyard. Going down the hill you come to **Walker House**, the **Ringer and Alt houses** and finally **Glover House**.

Halfway down the hill, above Glover House, is the renowned statue of the

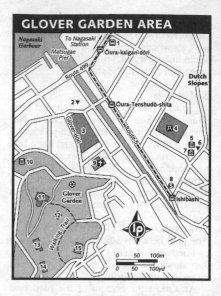

Japanese opera singer Miura Tamaki, which is often referred to as Madame Butterfly. You exit the garden through the **Nagasaki Traditional Performing Arts Museum**, which has a display of dragons and floats used in the colourful Okunchi Matsuri.

Kōshi-myō-tojinkan & Historical Museum of China Behind the gaudily coloured Kōshi-myō-tojinkan, a Confucian shrine, is the Historical Museum of China, with exhibits on loan from the Beijing Museum of History (¥525, 8.30 am to 5 pm). The original building dates from 1893 but was destroyed in the fires following the A-bomb explosion.

Ōura Catholic Church Just below Glover Garden is this attractively situated church (¥250, 8 am to 6 pm, 8.30 am to 5 pm in winter), built from 1864 to 1865 for Nagasaki's new foreign community. Soon after its opening, a group of Japanese came to the church and announced that Christianity had been maintained among the Urakami community throughout the 250 years it had been banned in Japan. Unfortunately, despite Japan's newly opened doors

GLOVER GARDEN AREA

1 Nagasaki Kōtsu Bus Office 長崎交通バス事務所	5 Woodblock Print Gallery 野口弥太郎記念美術館	11 Glover House 旧グラバー邸
2 Shikai-rō 四海楼	6 Chikyūkan 地球館	12 Walker House 旧ウォーカー邸
3 Nagasaki Tōkyū Hotel 長崎東急ホテル	7 Furushashin-kan 古写真館	13 Ringer House 旧リンガー邸
4 Kōshi-myō-tojinkan; Historical Museum of China 孔子廟; 中国歴史博物館	8 Jū-hachi-ginko 十八銀行	14 Alt House 旧オルト邸
	9 Ōura Catholic Church 大浦天主堂	15 Mitsubishi No 2 Dock Building 旧三菱第2 ドックハウス
	10 Nagasaki Traditional Performing Arts Museum 十六番館	

to the West, Christianity was still banned for the Japanese people. When this news leaked out, thousands of Urakami residents were exiled to other parts of Japan, where many of them died before Christianity was finally legalised in 1872. The church is dedicated to the 26 Christians crucified in 1597 and has beautiful stained-glass windows.

Dutch Slopes The gently inclined flag-stone streets known as Oranda-zaka (the Dutch Slopes) were once lined with wooden Dutch houses. A few have been restored, and include: Maizō Shiryō-kan, displaying Edo-period archaeological finds; Furushashin-kan, displaying old photographs – including a rare one of Meiji hero Sakamoto Ryoma; and Woodblock Print Gallery, showing the work of Tagawa Ken. An entrance ticket to all three is ¥200 (9 am to 5 pm, closed Monday). The excellent Chikyūkan is here too.

Getting There & Away Glover Garden, the Historical Museum of China and the Ōura Catholic Church are all near the end of tram Route 5; get off at Ōura-Tenshudō-shita.

To get to the Dutch Slopes, take a tram to the Shimin-Byōin-mae stop, or walk from the Dejima Museum or Glover Garden.

Inasa-yama Lookout
From the western side of the harbour, a cable car ascends to the top of 332m-high Inasa-yama, offering superb views over Nagasaki,

particularly at night (¥700/1200 one way/re-turn, 9 am to 10 pm in summer, 9 am to 5 pm in winter, every 20 minutes). Bus No 3 or 4 leave from outside JR Nagasaki station; get off at the Ropeway-mae stop. For the return trip, take a No 30 or No 40 bus.

Siebold House
Near Shin-Nakagawamachi tram stop is the site of Dr Siebold's house (¥100, 9 am to 5 pm, closed Monday). The doctor is credited with being an important force behind the introduction of Western medicine and scientific learning to Japan between 1823 and 1829.

Special Events
Colourful Peiron dragon boat races, introduced by the Chinese in the mid-1600s, still take place in Nagasaki Harbour on 24 and 25 July. On 15 August there's the beautiful Shōrō-nagashi Matsuri, where lantern-lit floats are carried down to the harbour. The best viewpoint is at O-hato.

The energetic Okunchi Matsuri, held between 7 and 9 October, features more Chinese dragons, this time dancing all around the city but especially at Suwa-jinja. O-hato is also a good viewing point.

Places to Stay
Nagasaki has a wide range of accommodation possibilities, from the love hotels clustered around the A-bomb site to the more upmarket hotels of the Glover Garden area.

KYŪSHŪ

Places to Stay – Budget

Hostels There are two youth hostels in Nagasaki. *Urakami-ga-Oka Youth Hostel* (☎ 47-8473) has beds for ¥2500. It is around 10 minutes' walk west of Ōhashi tram stop. The manager will pick you up from there if you call in advance.

Nagasaki Youth Hostel (☎ 823-5032) is within walking distance of JR Nagasaki station. It's well signposted in English. It charges ¥3150 for both members and non-members.

Minshuku & Ryokan *Miyuki-sō* (☎ 821-3487) has Japanese and Western-style rooms, and is five minutes north of the Shian-bashi entertainment district. Singles/doubles cost ¥3000/7500.

Fukumatsu Ryokan (☎ 823-3769) is a block behind the Ken-ei bus station near Nagasaki station, and charges ¥3500/7000. This is the cheapest in the area, but there are only five rooms.

Hotels For a cramped cheapie, directly behind Nishi-kyūshū Dai-Ichi Hotel is the men-only *Capsule Inn Nagasaki* (☎ 821-1099), with singles for ¥2700. Better is the similarly priced *Capsule Inn* (☎ 828-1126) directly in front of the station, which has rooms for both sexes.

Places to Stay – Mid-Range

Minshuku & Ryokan Central Nagasaki, the best place to be based, has a couple of affordable ryokan.

Pick of the pack is *Nishiki-sō* (☎ 826-6371), a delightful, creaky old building with fabulous views over Nagasaki. Rooms with bath cost ¥4500. It's close to Maru-yama-kōen. Slightly more expensive, but still a great deal, *Fukumoto Ryokan* (☎ 821-0478) has rooms for ¥4500/9000 and is clean and friendly.

Minshuku Tanpopo (☎ 861-6230), a Japanese Inn Group member, is north of JR Nagasaki station and near the A-bomb site. Singles cost ¥4000, or expect to pay ¥3500 per person in double or triple rooms. Get off at the Matsuyama-machi tram stop or JR Urakami station, cross the

river, and walk to the street with a petrol station. Follow that street, turn left at the first junction and take the right side of the fork.

Hotels The *Nishi-kyūshū Dai-Ichi Hotel* (☎ 821-1711) charges ¥5600/9600 for spartan but adequate singles/doubles.

Business Royal Hotel (☎ 827-0488) has singles/twins for ¥5600/9950 and is rather basic.

Harbour Inn Nagasaki (☎ 827-1111) is comfortable and modern, with singles/doubles for ¥6825/12,075. Next door is the economical *Hotel Ibis* (☎ 824-2171) with rooms for ¥5700/9000. Closer again to the harbour is *Newport Business Hotel* (☎ 821-0221), with singles from ¥5400 and twins and doubles from ¥9500. Reception is on the 4th floor.

Places to Stay – Top End

Ryokan South of JR Nagasaki station in the central city area, *Sakamoto-ya Bekkan* (☎ 826-8211) is an old and very well-kept place with rooms from ¥15,000 to ¥25,000, with two meals.

Hotels *Hotel New Nagasaki* (☎ 826-8000) has twins and doubles from ¥24,000 and is convenient but pricey.

Near the Shian-bashi entertainment area is the central, pleasantly appointed and good-value *Holiday Inn* (☎ 828-1234), with singles/doubles from ¥8500/16,000. *Nagasaki Grand Hotel* (☎ 823-1234) has singles from ¥9000 and twins from ¥15,000, and is also close to the central entertainment and business areas.

South of Holiday Inn, where the entertainment area merges into the Chinatown area, is the rather more upmarket *Nagasaki Washington Hotel* (☎ 828-1211), with rooms from ¥8000 to ¥15,000. The hotel is fine, but the Holiday Inn is better for this price.

Nagasaki Tōkyū Hotel (☎ 825-1501), just below Glover Garden, is little more than a tarted-up business hotel, but the location is good. Singles cost from ¥9800, and doubles from ¥20,000).

Places to Eat

Like Yokohama and Kōbe, Nagasaki has the reputation of being a culinary crossroads. The city's diverse influences come together in *shippoku-ryōri*, a banquet-style offering (generally you need at least four diners) that rolls together Chinese, Japanese and Portuguese influences. *Champon*, the local rāmen speciality, is less expensive but overrated unless you're a fan of shredded cabbage. *Sara-udon* is the stir-fried equivalent.

Hamano-machi 浜町 The best area for ferreting out restaurants is on the sidestreets that run north from the Hamano-machi arcade. *Garde Pizza House*, a block north of the arcade, has no less than 54 varieties of pizza on offer – all for ¥700/1050/1400 for small/medium/large. The restaurant has an English-language menu and generally only opens in the evening.

Around the corner from Garde Pizza is *Bharata* (☎ 824-9194), an Indian restaurant on the 2nd floor of the Yasaka St building (11.30 am to 3 pm, 5 to 10 pm, closed Monday). The name is in English outside. It offers excellent South Indian *thalis* for ¥1250 or tandoori and curry dishes from ¥800. Back on Kankō-dōri, opposite a KFC, is *Nanak* (☎ 827-7900), another fine Indian restaurant with friendly Indian staff. The Bombay Course, a combination of tandoori, curry, butter naan, salad and a drink, is a good deal at ¥2300.

Nearby, on Kajiya-machi, is *Ginrei Restaurant* (☎ 821-2073), a well-known Western-style restaurant (look for the ivy outside) that has recently been treated to a face-lift (10.30 am to 9.30 pm). It specialises in steaks, but curries and so on are also available from around ¥800.

Hamakatsu Restaurant (☎ 826-8321) serves the banquet-style shippoku cuisine for around ¥5000 per person. Around the corner, on Teramachi-dōri, the same owners run *Hamakatsu* (☎ 827-5783). It serves excellent *tonkatsu* (pork cutlets), has an illustrated menu, and is far less expensive than it looks. Try the Oranda teishoku at ¥850. It is open from 11 am to 10 pm.

Shian-bashi In among the *pachinko* (Japanese pinball) parlours and bars along Shian-bashi-dōri, you'll find an *Italian Tomato* pasta specialist (dishes from ¥1000) and the cheap and very cheerful *Aka-chōchin* (☎ 828-2930). For the latter you will need to be able to find your way around a Japanese izakaya menu (see the Food section in the Facts for the Visitor chapter), but adventurous souls will find the effort worth it. Most dishes are around ¥500 to ¥700, and it is open from 5.30 pm to 4 am.

Unryūtei (☎ 823-5971), tucked away at the end of Shian-bashi Gourmet Street, only seats six and specialises in cheap and tasty *gyoza*, or dumplings, which are excellent with a beer (open from dusk until the early hours).

At the end of Shian-bashi-dōri the road forks; turn left, walk past the police post and at the far end of the square is the entrance to *Kagetsu* (☎ 822-0191), a shippoku restaurant with a history that dates back to 1642. At one time it was a high-class brothel. Today it's still high class; count on ¥20,000 per person (noon to 2 pm, 6 to 10 pm).

Fukusaya Castella Cake Shop was established in 1624. It's in a charming traditional building, and sells its handmade cakes in gift-ready packaging. The best of the cakes – *castella ichi-gō* or *ōranda kēki ichi-gō* – cost ¥1400, but there are cheaper versions.

Chinatown During Japan's long period of isolation from the West, Nagasaki was a conduit not only for Dutch trade and culture but also for the trade and culture of the Chinese, a history reflected in the city's restaurants.

Popular Chinese restaurants around Nagasaki Washington Hotel include *Kyōka-en* (☎ 821-1507), open from 11 am to 9 pm, *Chūka-en* (☎ 822-0311) from 10.30 am to 9 pm and *Kōzan-rō* (☎ 821-3735), from 11 am to 9 pm. *Kairaku-en* (☎ 822 4261) is famed for its champon (11 am to 8.15 pm).

Other Areas The excellent *Harbin Restaurant* specialises in Russian and French cuisine. It's an atmospheric place, with white tablecloths, heavy cutlery and dark wood furniture. At lunch time you can select from a long menu offering a starter, main course, bread and tea or coffee, all for ¥1300 to ¥1600 – a real bargain. At night, main courses cost from ¥1700 to ¥5000. It has an English-language menu.

In Oranda-zaka, *Chikyukan* is a good, cheap restaurant that serves a different international cuisine each day, prepared by foreign residents (noon to 2 pm, closed Wednesday).

Entertainment

Nagasaki's nightlife is rather subdued for such a large city. In Yorozuya, *Ayer's Rock* (☎ 828-0505), by day a coffee shop, turns into a bar in the evenings. It's a friendly place, with beers for ¥500. At weekends there may be DJs spinning hip-hop and techno; the cover charge is ¥1500. The owner arranges an annual 'Summer Rave Party' at Unzen, on the third Saturday in July. Nearby, *Fan fan* (☎ 827-3976) is a jazz freak's paradise (7.30 pm to 2 am). There's a ¥500 cover charge. *10c* is a popular shot-bar on the same street. *Bajamut* (☎ 822-7734) is Nagasaki's most popular club, regularly hosting live events, with an emphasis on reggae/hip-hop. Soul bar *JB Trick* (☎ 824-9185) is a great place for an inexpensive beer on Sōfukuji-dōri (7 pm to 3 am).

Shopping

There are displays of local crafts and products directly opposite JR Nagasaki station on the same floor as the Prefectural Tourist Federation. You'll find lots of shops along the busy Hamano-machi shopping arcade. For Japanese visitors, the Portuguese-influenced sponge cake, *kasutera*, is the present to take back from Nagasaki, and Fukusaya is the place to buy it – see Shian-bashi under Places to Eat earlier in this section for details.

Please ignore Nagasaki's tortoise-shell crafts: turtles need their shells more than humans do.

Getting There & Away

Air There are flights between Nagasaki and Kagoshima, Tokyo (Haneda airport), Osaka and Okinawa as well as flights to and from a variety of other locations.

Bus Regular buses operate between Nagasaki and Kumamoto (¥3600, three hours). From the Ken-ei bus station opposite JR Nagasaki station, buses go to Unzen (¥1750, two hours) from stand No 3 (express buses from stand No 2), Shimabara (¥1850, two hours) from stand No 5, Sasebo (¥1400, 1½ hours) from stand No 2, Fukuoka (¥2900, three hours) from stand No 8, Kumamoto (¥3600, three hours) and Kokura (Kitakyūshū) from stand No 6 and sightseeing buses from stand No 12.

Night buses for Osaka (¥11,000) and Nagoya (¥12,000) leave from both the Ken-ei bus station and the Nagasaki Hwy bus station next to the Irie-machi tram stop. There are also buses running to Sasebo and Hirado from here.

Train JR lines from Nagasaki go to Fukuoka/Hakata (tokkyū, ¥1650, two hours), Kumamoto (tokkyū, ¥1650, three hours) and Beppu and Ōita (tokkyū, ¥9560, about five hours).

Getting Around

To/From the Airport Nagasaki's airport is about 40km from the city. Buses (¥1150, one hour) operate from stand No 4 in the Ken-ei bus station opposite JR Nagasaki station. If you have some spare cash a taxi will cost you around ¥11,000.

Bus Buses cover a greater area (reaching more of the sights) but the Japanese script is more difficult to decipher than the tram service.

Tram The best way of getting around Nagasaki is on the excellent and easy-to-use tram service. There are four colour-coded routes numbered 1, 3, 4 and 5 (there's no No 2 for some reason). Most stops are signposted in English. It costs ¥100 to travel anywhere in town or you can get a ¥500 all-day pass for unlimited travel. The passes are available from the shop beside the station information counter, from the Prefectural Tourist Federation across the road or from major hotels. On a one-ride ticket you can only transfer to another line at the Tsuki-machi stop. The trams stop around 11 pm.

HUIS TEN BOSCH

You'll see this 'virtual-Holland' theme-park advertised everywhere, but did you really come to Japan to spend around ¥10,000 to see a replica of another country?

Shimabara-hantō
島原半島

A popular route to or from Nagasaki is via the Shimabara-hantō using the regular car ferry service between Shimabara and Misumi, south of Kumamoto. Bus services connect with the ferry, and tour buses also operate directly between Nagasaki and Kumamoto. The major attractions on the peninsula are Unzen and Shimabara itself.

It was the uprising on the Shimabara-hantō that led to the suppression of Christianity in Japan and the country's subsequent two centuries of seclusion from the West. The peasant rebels made their final valiant stand against overwhelming odds (37,000 versus 120,000) at Hara-jō, at almost the southern tip of the peninsula. The warlords even chartered a Dutch man-of-war to bombard the hapless rebels, who held out for 80 days but were eventually slaughtered. Little remains of the castle.

In June 1991, the 1359m peak of Unzen-dake erupted after laying dormant for 199 years. The explosion left at least 38 people dead. Nearby villages were evacuated and the lava flow reached the outskirts of Shimabara.

UNZEN 雲仙
☎ 0957 • pop 1,463

Unzen is shrouded in mysterious, rather smelly gases – it is obviously a very active volcanic centre. Its walks and paths are clearly signposted and it's easy to spend several hours wandering through the town.

The bubbling and spurting *jigoku* (hells) currently boil nothing more sinister than the popular wayside snack of eggs, known as *onsen tamago*; a few centuries ago the same fate was reserved for Christians. Today you can voluntarily boil yourself at any of the resort's luxury hotels, though budget travellers will likely prefer the three public baths, all within an easy walk of the Unzen bus station: the simple Yunosato (¥100, 9 am to 10 pm); Shin-yu (¥100, 10 am to 11 pm) and, most pleasant, the recently remodelled Kojigoku (¥400, 9 am to 9 pm).

From the town there are popular walks to Kinugasa, Takaiwa-san and Ya-dake, all situated within the Unzen-Amakusa National Park, Japan's oldest national park. The screeching, geyser-like Daikyō-kan Jigoku at the top of the settlement, and the 1300-year-old temple, Mammoji, are worth seeing. Outside the town, reached via Nita Pass, is Fugen-dake, part of the Unzen-dake range, with its popular hiking trail.

Information

The visitors centre (☎ 73-2642) near the Shin-yu public bath has good information in English and excellent displays on both the national park's flora and fauna, and on hiking trails (9 am to 5 pm). The Unzen Tourist Association office (☎ 73-3434) opposite the post office also has maps and pamphlets.

Places to Stay

Unzen has numerous hotels and ryokan (most very pricey) and two kokumin-shukusha with nightly costs from around ¥7000, including dinner and breakfast. They are *Seiun-sō* (☎ 73-3273) and *Yurin-sō* (☎ 73-3355). *Unzen Kokumin Kyūka Mura* (☎ 74-9131) charges ¥7500, including two meals.

Unzen Kankō Hotel (☎ 73-3263) dates back to the 1930s, when it was a summer retreat for expat *gaijin* (foreigners). It still has character. Rates of around ¥17,000 (with meals) apply. More affordable is *Shi-rakumo-no-ike* camp site (☎ 73-2642), with sites from ¥300.

Getting There & Away

Bus Direct buses between Nagasaki and Unzen take less than 2½ hours (¥1750). Buses run more frequently from the town of Isahaya, which is 40 minutes by train (¥560) from Nagasaki on the Nagasaki line. From Isahaya to Unzen, buses take 1½ hours and cost ¥1200. From Unzen, it takes

KYŪSHŪ

SHIMABARA-HANTŌ

50 minutes by bus to Shimabara (¥730). The bus to Nita Pass, the starting point for the Fugen-dake walk, operates regularly from the Unzen bus station (¥300, 30 minutes). There's a ¥700 toll for cars. The No 262 Nagasaki-Kumamoto tour bus goes via Unzen.

FUGEN-DAKE WALK 普賢岳
Buses run from Unzen bus station to Nitatoge (20 minutes). From there take the cable car to the 1333m summit of Myōken-dake (¥1270 return, 9 am to 5.45 pm), and from there hike to Fugen-dake, via Kunimiwakare, takes just under two hours. The views of the lava flow from the summit are incredible. The walk back to Nita via the village and valley of Azami-dani takes around 70 minutes.

SHIMABARA
☎ 0957 • pop 40,222
Shimabara is the port for ferries to Misumi, south of Kumamoto. Its castle and reclining Buddha are the town's main attractions. The ferry terminal has an information desk (☎ 63-1111) that is open from 8.30 am to 5 pm.

Shimabara-jō
The castle (¥520, 8 am to 6 pm April to October, otherwise 9 am to 5 pm), originally built in 1624, played a part in the Shimabara Rebellion and was rebuilt in 1964 during Japan's nationwide spate of castle reconstruction. It houses three museums: one displaying items relating to the Christian uprising, another detailing Fugen-dake's pyrotechnic exploits (including the colossal explosion of 1792 in which 15,000 people died) and a third dedicated to works by Seibo Kitamura, who sculpted the Nagasaki Peace Statue.

Other Attractions
In the Teppo-chō area, north-west of the castle, is a *buke yashiki*, or samurai house. Just south of the town centre, near the Shimatetsu bus station, are carp streams with lots of colourful goldfish. Also south of the town centre, in Kōtō-ji, is the rather beautiful **Nehan Zō**, or 'Nirvana Statue'. It's the longest reclining Buddha statue in Japan, though by Thai or Burmese reclining-Buddha standards, it's a bit of a shorty.

Places to Stay & Eat
Shimabara Youth Hostel (☎ 62-4451) is just a few minutes' walk north of Shimabara Gaikō station, and charges ¥2950/4150 for members/nonmembers. There's also a variety of hotels. *Ajisai Inn* (☎ 64-1101) is just south of the castle and has singles/doubles for ¥5500/8000. *Sumiyoshikan* (☎ 63-0032) is a cheery small hotel opposite the City Office, south-west of Shimabara station, with rooms for ¥5700/11,000.

Shimabara's famed dishes are raw stonefish, Taira-gane crab (especially from July to September), and *guzoni*, a kind of clam stew. The latter is the speciality of *Himematsu-ya* (☎ 63-7272), open from 10 am to 8 pm, at the south-west corner of the castle.

Getting There & Away
Train JR trains on the Nagasaki line run to Isahaya (tokkyū, ¥2430, 20 minutes), where you then connect up with the private Shimabara Tetsudō line (futsū, ¥1280, one

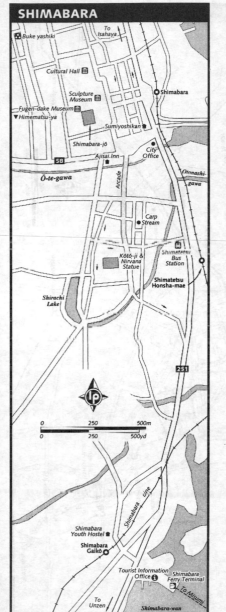

SHIMABARA

To Isahaya

Buke yashiki

Cultural Hall 🏛

Sculpture Museum 🏛

Fugen-dake Museum 🏛
▼ Himematsu-ya

Shimabara

Sumiyoshikan 🏮

Shimabara-jō

Ajisai Inn 🏯

City Office

5B

Ō-te-gawa

Arcade

Ōnoashi-gawa

Carp Stream

Shimatetsu Bus Station

Kōtō-ji & Nirvana Statue

Shimatetsu Honsha-mae

Shirachi Lake

251

0   250   500m
0   250   500yd

Shimabara line

Shimabara Youth Hostel 🏮

Shimabara Gaikō

Tourist Information Office ℹ   Shimabara Ferry Terminal

To Unzen

Shimabara-wan

To Misumi

hour) to Shimabara. Shimabara station is a few hundred metres to the east of the castle.

Boat Ferries run 13 to 17 times a day to Misumi (¥830 per person, from ¥2370 with a car, one hour). From Misumi there's a train to Kumamoto (¥720, 48 minutes, hourly). Ferries also run to the Amakusa-shotō from Shimabara.

Kumamoto-ken

KUMAMOTO 熊本
☎ 096 • pop 650,000

Kumamoto, the city that brought you the *kobori* (the art of swimming upright wearing a suit of armour; otherwise known as a 'shallow moat') has one of Japan's finest reconstructed castles, and a very fine garden. The modern city has plenty of concrete, but its brash vitality, ample nightlife and convenient location (whether you're travelling up, down or across the island) make it a very worthwhile place to visit.

Orientation & Information
The JR station is some distance south of Kumamoto's city centre. In the centre you'll find not only offices, banks, hotels, restaurants and the entertainment area but also the big Kumamoto Kōtsū bus centre, the castle and other attractions.

The tourist information office (☎ 352-3743) is in JR Kumamoto station (9 am to 5.30 pm). The English-speaking assistant is extremely helpful. Kinokuniya and Nagasaki Books are good bookshops in the central arcades. Just south of Kumamoto-jō is Kumamoto City International Center, which has CNN news, English-language magazines and Internet access – a good place to spend an afternoon if you've been out in the backwoods for a while.

Money On the north-east side of Kumamoto station, next to the photo shop, is an ATM that accepts VISA, MasterCard and Cirrus (7 am to 10 pm). Fuji Bank and Higo Bank, next to Tsuruya department store, have exchange facilities.

KUMAMOTO

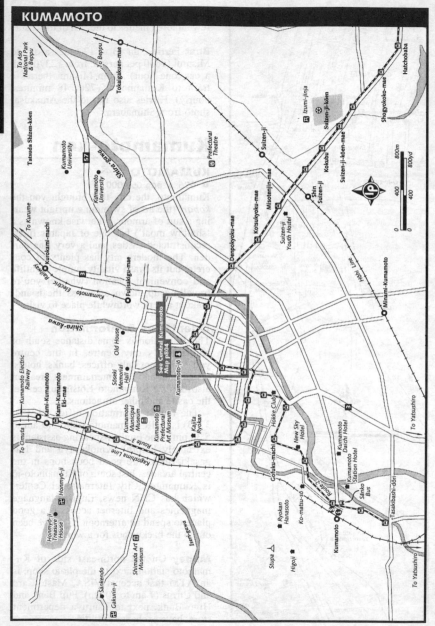

To Aso National Park & Beppu

To Beppu

To Kurume

To Omuta

Tatsuda Shizen-kōen

Kumamoto University

Kumamoto University

Shira-gawa

Shira-kawa

Kurokami-machi

Kumamoto Electric Railway

Fujisakigu-mae

Tokaigakuen-mae

Izumi-jinja

Suizen-ji-kōen

Suizen-ji-mae

Misotenjin-mae

Kotsukyoku-mae

Denpoyoku-mae

Suizen-ji-kōen-mae

Kokubu

Shin Suizen-ji

Suizen-ji

Hōhi Line

Suizen-ji Youth Hostel

Minami-Kumamoto

Shogyokōkō-mae

Hatchōbaba

800m
800yd
400
400
0
0

Prefectural Theatre

Shira-gawa

See Central Kumamoto Map p804

Kumamoto-jō

Old House

Sōseki Memorial Hall

Kumamoto Electric Railway

Kami-Kumamoto

Kami-Kumamoto Eki-mae

Kumamoto Municipal Museum

Kumamoto Prefectural Art Museum

Kajita Ryokan

Hōike Club

New Sky Hotel

Kumamoto Daichi Hotel

To Yatsushiro

Honmyō-ji

Honmyō-ji Treasure House

Shimada Art Museum

Kagoshima Line

Route 3

Iseri-gawa

Kōfuku-machi

Kumamoto Station Hotel

Route 3

Kumamoto

Ryokan Hanasato

Ko-matsu-sō

Sanko Bus

Tasakibashi-dōri

Gakurin-ji

Sankendo

Stupa

Higoji

To Yatsushiro

Post The main post office is just east of the castle, near the Tori-cho tram stop.

Email & Internet Access Kumamoto City International Center has online access (¥50 per five minutes, 9 am to 8 pm weekdays, to 7 pm weekends).

Kumamoto-jō
Kumamoto's castle (¥500, 8.30 am to 5.30 pm in summer, to 4.30 pm in winter) dominates the centre of town. A modern reproduction, its sheer size and numerous interesting exhibits make it visit-worthy. Built between 1601 and 1607, it was once one of the great castles of feudal Japan. Its architect, Katō Kiyomasa, was a master of castle design and some of his ingenious engineering, including slots for dropping stones and other missiles onto attackers, can be seen in the reconstruction.

Nevertheless, in 1877, during the turmoil of the Satsuma Rebellion, a postscript to the Meiji Restoration, the castle was besieged and burnt in one of the final stands made by samurai warriors against the new order. The rebel samurai held out for 55 days before finally being overcome. See the Kagoshima-ken section later in this chapter for more on the rebellion and its leader, Saigō Takamori.

Museums
Beyond the castle are Kumamoto Prefectural Art Museum (¥260), Kumamoto Municipal Museum (¥300) and Kumamoto Traditional Crafts Center (¥200). All are open from 9 am to 5 pm and are closed Monday. The Municipal Museum has a 3D relief map of part of southern Kyūshū. It's quite interesting to see the configuration of Fugen-dake on Shimabara-hantō, Aso-san and the many other peaks. The crafts centre has an interesting collection of odds and ends, including porcelains.

Suizen-ji-kōen
This fine, relatively extensive garden (¥200, 7.30 am to 6 pm March to October, 8.30 am to 5 pm November to February) originated with a temple in 1632. The stroll garden imitates the 53 stations of the Tōkaidō (the old road that linked Tokyo and Kyoto), and the miniature Mt Fuji is instantly recognisable. The Kokin Denju-no-Ma Teahouse (The Passing on of Knowledge Space), moved here from Kyoto in 1912, is somewhat shoddy, but the views across the ornamental lake show the garden at its finest. Turn the other way and you will see only souvenir stalls.

A Route 2 tram from JR Kumamoto station, or a Route 2 or 3 tram from the central area, goes to the garden. Get off at Suizenji-kōen-mae.

Honmyō-ji
To the north-west of the centre, on the hills sloping up from the river, is the temple and mausoleum of Katō Kiyomasa, the architect of Kumamoto's great castle. A steep flight of steps leads up to the mausoleum that was designed to be at the same height as the castle's donjon. There's a treasure house with Kiyomasa exhibits (¥300, 9 am to 4.30 pm, closed Monday).

Writers' Homes
Right in the centre of town, behind the Tsuruya department store, is the former home of writer Lafcadio Hearn (known to the Japanese as Koizumi Yakumo). Entry is free but it's not as interesting as his first Japanese residence in Matsue (see Matsue in the Western Honshū chapter). The former home of the Meiji-era novelist Sōseki Natsume is preserved as the Sōseki Memorial Hall. It's just north of the castle and the Traditional Crafts Center.

Tatsuda Shizen-kōen
Tatsuda Shizen-kōen (Tatsuda Nature Park) with the 1646 Taishō-ji and a famous teahouse, is north-east of the town centre. The grave of Hosokawa Gracia (1563–1600) is in the temple grounds. She was an early convert to Christianity but her husband arranged her death to prevent his enemies from capturing her. Take a Kusunoki-danchi-Musashigaoka-danchi line bus from platform 28 at the Kumamoto Kōtsū bus centre (¥200, 30 minutes).

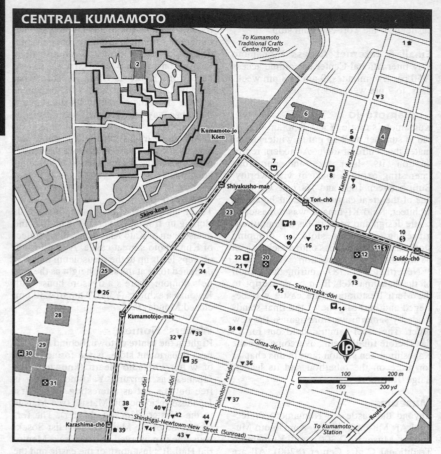

CENTRAL KUMAMOTO

The **International Folk Art Museum** is 15 minutes north-east of the Tatsuda Park and displays crafts from all over the world.

Other Attractions
Continue north up the hill beyond the cheap ryokan and minshuku near JR Kumamoto station, past the love hotels and you eventually reach the **pagoda** topping the hill. The effort of the climb is rewarded with superb views over the town. Also on this side of town, north of the pagoda and south of Honmyō-ji, is **Shimada Art Museum** (¥500, 9 am to 5 pm, closed Wednes-

day) with work pertaining to Miyamoto Musashi.

Places to Stay – Budget
Hostels The clean, welcoming *Suizen-ji Youth Hostel* (☎ 371-9193) is about halfway between the town centre and Suizen-ji-kōen. It charges ¥2800 per night. The Misotenjin-mae stop on tram Routes 2 or 3 is close by.

Minshuku & Ryokan Perched on the hill above the station is Kumamoto's best-value traditional-style accommodation,

CENTRAL KUMAMOTO

PLACES TO STAY
1 Maruko Hotel
  丸小旅館
4 Tsukasa Honten Hotel
  司本店ホテル
6 Kumamoto Castle Hotel
  熊本ホテルキャッスル
27 Kumamoto Kankō Hotel
  熊本観光ホテル
29 Kumamoto Kōtsū
  Centre Hotel
  熊本交通
  センターホテル
39 Kumamoto Tōkyū Inn
  熊本東急イン

PLACES TO EAT
3 Capricciosa
9 Mr Donut
15 Swiss Konditerei
16 KFC
21 Chai Gautama
  ちゃいゴータマ
24 Baden Baden
32 Jang Jang Go
  ジャンジャンゴー
33 Deutsche Hand-Made
  Sausage

36 Blue Seal Ice Cream
37 You & You
38 Lotteria
40 Higokko
  Robatayaki
  肥後っ子
41 Yōrōnotaki
  養老の滝
42 Kyōya Noodle Shop
  京屋そば
43 KFC
44 McDonald's

OTHER
2 Kumamoto-jō
  熊本城
5 Nagasaki Books
  長崎書店
7 Post Office
  郵便局
8 Rock Balloon
10 Higo Bank
  肥後銀行
11 Fuji Bank
  富士銀行
12 Tsuruya Department
  Store
  鶴屋

13 Lafcadio Hearn House
14 Shark Attack
17 Parco Department Store;
  Body Shop
  パルコ
18 Bar Jail
19 Tower Records
20 Daiei Department Store
  ダイエー
22 The Sharp
23 Municipal Office;
  City Hall
  市役所
25 Kumamoto City
  International Centre
  国際交流会館
26 JAL
28 NTT
30 Kumamoto Kōtsū
  Bus Centre
  熊本交通バスセンター
31 Iwataya Isetan
  Department Store
  岩田屋伊勢丹
34 Kinokuniya
  Bookshop
  紀伊国屋書店
35 Suntory Shot Bar

Higoji (☎ 352-7860), a small minshuku run by a friendly elderly gentleman. He'll pick you up from the station if you call from Kumamoto's tourist information office. English is spoken, and the night view is superb. Rooms cost ¥3500, or ¥4200 with breakfast. *Ko-matsu-so* (☎ 352-2634) is another good place five minutes north of the station, but the old lady who runs it doesn't always answer the phone! Rooms cost ¥3500.

Places to Stay – Mid-Range
Minshuku The Japanese Inn group's representative in Kumamoto, the adequate *Minshuku Kajita* (☎ 353-1546), has Japanese-style singles/double without baths for ¥4000/7600. From Kumamoto station, take a bus to the Shinmachi stop; from there it's a five-minute walk.

Hotels The 111-year-old *Maruko Hotel* (☎ 353-1241) in the town centre has an all-you-can drink special for ¥111. Rooms cost ¥6500/12,000. From JR Kumamoto station, take a Route 2 tram to Tetori-Honcho stop. There's a prominent sign from the covered arcade.

Kumamoto Station Hotel (☎ 325-2001) is about two minutes' walk from the station, just across the first small river. It's a typical modern business hotel with Japanese and Western-style rooms for ¥6000/10,600.

The plain *Hokke Club* (☎ 322-5001) is between the train station and the town centre, and has singles from ¥6300 and twins/doubles from ¥8800. *Kumamoto Kōtsū Centre Hotel* (☎ 354-1111) has singles from ¥5700 and is centrally located above the Kumamoto Kōtsū bus centre; reception on the 3rd floor. Also in the centre of town, the well-appointed *Kumamoto Tōkyū Inn* (☎ 322-0109) is part of the popular Tōkyū chain and has rooms from ¥7100/10,300.

Places to Stay – Top End
More-expensive hotels include the efficiently run and well-equipped *New Sky Hotel* (☎ 354-2111), about midway between the train station and the town centre. It has both Japanese and Western-style rooms from ¥8000/19,000. Overlooking the castle, *Kumamoto Castle Hotel* (☎ 326-3311) is perfectly sited and has singles from ¥8900 and doubles from ¥16,000.

Places to Eat
Chai Gautama (☎ 325-3125), behind the Daiei department store, has great curry and *chai* (Indian tea) teishoku for just ¥600 (11 am to 8 pm, closed Thursday). *Jang Jang Go* (☎ 323-1121) on Sakae-dōri is a trendy place serving neo-Chinese cuisine in a mock-Colonial-style building (5.30 pm to 2 am). For couples it's Kumamoto's most popular date spot. Expect to spend around ¥2500 per person.

Just off the Shinshigai arcade is *Higokko Robatayaki*, where you can sit at the bar and select from a wide range of *kushi* (assorted meat, fish and vegetables grilled on skewers). The chef will grill them right in front of you and pass them over the counter on a long paddle, rather like the one used for removing pizzas from a pizza oven. Each spit costs around ¥300 to ¥500.

Just south of this place is *Yōrōnotaki*, a link in a very successful izakaya chain. It has an excellent illustrated menu with everything from pizza to *sushi*, and prices are very reasonable.

Back down the Shimotori arcade is *Kōran-tei*, an excellent Chinese restaurant with some good teishoku deals at lunch time. Try the *chashū men* (roast-pork noodle soup) for ¥600.

For the gourmet, Kumamoto's local specialities are *ba-zashi* (raw horsemeat) and *karashi-renkon* (fried lotus root with mustard). In the Shimo-tori arcade, *You & You* (☎ 359-2929) serves ba-zashi and *Higo-gyū* (Higo beef) at a fraction of the regular price.

Rather odd, as it's run by the local Economics Federation. Budget ¥2500 per person (11 am to 10 pm, closed every second Tuesday).

Entertainment
Kumamoto has a sprinkling of gaijin haunts if you are in need of a few drinks and some conversation. Gaijin-run *The Sharp* (☎ 322-5445), behind Daiei, regularly has live bands (7.30 pm to 1 am, Friday and Saturday until 4 am). Beers cost from ¥500. *Bar Jail* (☎ 359-1814), just west of the northern end of Shimotori Arcade, is a peculiarly narrow place with an upstairs area for playing pool, and a shoebox downstairs for dancing in (7 pm to 3 am). *Rock Balloon* is a grungier establishment – graffiti and a lot of noise. Draught beers cost ¥500 and there's no cover charge. For something unusual, track down *Shark Attack*. It's the only bar we've come across that has sand (the stuff you usually find on beaches). It's on the 8th floor of the Anty Rashon building.

Shopping
Kumamoto Traditional Crafts Center (downstairs free, upstairs ¥190), just north of the Kumamoto Castle Hotel, displays local crafts and demonstrates how they're made. *Higo zōgan*, black steel with silver and gold inlaid patterns wrought into a chrysanthemum-like shape, is a renowned local craft. These items range from around ¥5000, though what you'd do with one is hard to say. Another curious local product is *obake-no-Kinta*, a tiny red head with a little red protruding tongue, the whole affair topped with a black dunce's cap – don't travel without one.

Getting There & Away
There are flights to Kumamoto from Tokyo, Osaka, Nagoya and Naha (Okinawa). The JR Kagoshima line between Hakata and Nishi-Kagoshima runs through Kumamoto and there is also a JR line to Miyazaki on the south-eastern coast. Buses depart from the Kōtsū bus centre for Hakata (¥2400, two hours).

See the earlier Shimabara-hantō section for details on travel to Nagasaki via Misumi,

Shimabara and Unzen. Kumamoto is a popular gateway to Aso-san (see Beppu later in Ōita-ken section later in this chapter for travel across Kyūshū via Aso-san to Beppu).

Train Kumamoto is connected by the JR Kagoshima line to Fukuoka/Hakata (tokkyū, ¥3940, 1½ hours) and Kagoshima (tokkyū, ¥5750, 2½ hours), and by the JR Hōhi line to Beppu (tokkyū, ¥4830, three hours).

Getting Around
To/From the Airport
The airport bus (¥670, one hour) stops at Shimo-tōri, Kumamoto Kōtsū bus centre and JR Kumamoto station.

Tram Kumamoto's tram service allows access to all the major sights. On boarding the tram, take a ticket with your starting tram stop number. When you finish your trip a display panel at the front of the tram indicates the fare for each starting point. A ¥500 one-day pass allows unlimited travel. Route 2 starts near JR Kumamoto station, runs through the town centre and out past Suizen-ji-kōen. Route 3 starts to the north, near Kami-Kumamoto station and merges with Route 2 just before the centre. Mysteriously, there is no Route 1.

YAMAGA ONSEN 山鹿温泉
☎ 0968
This is a nice enough hot-spring town, but there's really no special reason to visit here except during the spectacular **Yamaga Chōchin Matsuri** held on 15 and 16 August. The whole region seems to converge on Yamaga for these two nights, when the women of the town, clad in summer kimono, dance through the streets to the sound of shamisen, wearing lanterns on their heads. Though the sound is wholly 'Japanese', visually this is more like China or Okinawa – a reminder of Kyūshū's historical remove from 'mainland' Japanese culture.

Yamaga Cycling Terminal (☎ 43-1136) is the best place to stay, with its large communal *tatami* rooms and huge bath. Shared rooms cost ¥2940. It's a 10-minute taxi ride from the town centre. Don't try to walk back post-festival unless you've got infrared night vision – the terminal is set invisibly above pitch-black rice fields.

Buses leave the Kumamoto Kōtsū bus centre, stand 2, bound for the Yamaga bus terminal (¥860, 40 minutes, twice-hourly).

ASO-SAN AREA 阿蘇山
☎ 09676
In the centre of Kyūshū, halfway from Kumamoto to Beppu, is the gigantic Aso-san volcano caldera. There have been a series of eruptions over the past 30 million years but the explosion that formed the outer crater about 100,000 years ago must have been a big one – the crater has an 80km circumference and accommodates towns, villages and trains. And it's still active. In 1979 an eruption of Naka-dake killed a woman on her honeymoon. The last major blast was in 1993, but the summit is regularly off limits due to toxic gas emissions. Check with the Aso tourist information office for daily updates.

Orientation & Information
Highway Routes 57, 265 and 325 make a circuit of the outer caldera, and the JR Hōhi line runs across the northern section. Aso is the main town in the crater but there are other towns, including Takamori, on the southern side. All the roads running into the centre of the crater and to the five 'modern' peaks within the one huge, ancient outer peak are toll roads. There's a very helpful, informative tourist office at JR Aso station (☎ 34-0751). It's open from 9 am to 5 pm and is closed Wednesday. Rental cycles and left luggage facilities are available at the station.

Aso-gogaku
The Five Mountains of Aso are the five smaller mountains within the outer rim. They are Eboshi-dake (1337m), Kijima-dake (1270m), Naka-dake (1216m), Neko-dake (1408m) and Taka-dake (1592m). Naka-dake is currently the active volcano in this group. Neko-dake, farthest to the east, is instantly recognisable by its craggy peak but Taka-dake, between Neko-dake and Naka-dake, is the highest.

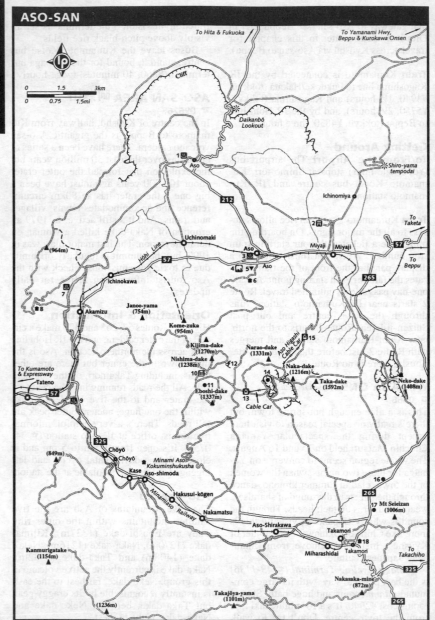

ASO-SAN

To Hita & Fukuoka

To Yamanami Hwy,
Beppu & Kurokawa Onsen

0   1.5   3km
0   0.75   1.5mi

Cliff

Daikanbō
Lookout

Shiro-yama
tempodai

1 — Aso

212

Ichinomiya

To
Taketa

2 —

Miyaji — Miyaji

57

(964m)

Uchinomaki

Hōhi Line

57

Aso
3 —
4 — 5 ▼ — Aso
6 —

265

To
Beppu

Ichinokawa

Janoo-yama
(754m)

Akamizu

7 —

8 —

Kome-zuka
(954m)

Kijima-dake
(1270m)

Narao-dake
(1331m)

15 —

Aso Higashi
Cable Car

Nishima-dake
(1238m)

12 —

10 —

Naka-dake
(1216m)

Taka-dake
(1592m)

Neko-dake
(1408m)

11 —
Eboshi-dake
(1337m)

14 —

13 —
Cable Car

To Kumamoto
& Expressway

Tateno

57

9 —

325

Chōyō
Chōyō

(849m)

Kase

Aso-shimoda

Minami Aso
Kokuminshukusha

Hakusui-kōgen

16 ●

265

Minamiaso Railway

Nakamatsu

17 ● Mt Seieizan
(1006m)

Aso-Shirakawa

Takamori

Takamori

18 —

Kanmurigatake
(1154m)

Miharashidai

To
Takachiho

Nakasaka-mine
(872m)

325

Takajōya-yama
(1101m)

(1236m)

265

ASO-SAN

Naka-dake

Naka-dake has been very active in recent years. The cable car to the summit of Naka-dake was closed from August 1989 to March 1990 due to eruptions, and it had only been opened for a few weeks when the volcano erupted again in April 1990, spewing dust and ash over a large area to the north.

In 1958, when a totally unexpected eruption killed 12 onlookers, concrete 'bomb shelters' were built around the rim for sightseers to take shelter in, in an emergency. Nevertheless, an eruption in 1979 killed three visitors over a kilometre from the cone, in an area that was thought to be safe. This eruption destroyed a cable car that used to run up the north-eastern slope of the cone, and, although the supports still stand, the cable car has never been replaced.

When Naka-dake is not misbehaving, a cable car whisks you up to the summit in just four minutes (¥410 each way). There are departures every eight minutes. The walk to the top takes less than half an hour. The 100m-deep crater varies in width from 400m to 1100m and there's a walk around the southern edge of the crater rim.

Aso-san Walks

You can hike all the way to the Aso-nishi cable car station from the Aso Youth Hostel in about three hours, but you'll be forced onto the side of the road by heavy traffic. From the top of the cable car run you can walk around the crater rim to the peak of Naka-dake and on to the top of Taka-dake. From there you can descend either to Sensui-kyō, the bottom station of the cable car run on the north-eastern side of Naka-dake, or to the road that runs between Taka-dake and Neko-dake. Either road will then take you to Miyaji, the next train station east from Aso. The direct descent to Sensui-kyō is very steep, so it's easier to continue back from Taka-dake to the Naka-dake rim and then follow the old cable car route down to Sensui-kyō.

Allow four or five hours from the Aso-nishi cable car station walking uphill to Sensui-kyō. The downhill walk takes about 1½ hours (if you're tired, a taxi costs ¥1700).

Shorter walks include the interesting ascent of Kijima-dake from the Aso Volcanic Museum. From the top of Kijima-dake you can descend to the top of the ski lift on the ski field just east of the museum. You can also climb to the top of Eboshi-dake. Any of the peaks offer superb views over the whole Aso area. The outer rim of the ancient crater also has great views. Shiroyama-tempodai, a lookout on the Yamanami Hwy as it leaves the crater, is one good point; Daikanbō near Uchinomaki Onsen is another.

Perfect after a long hike, Yume-no-yu (¥400, 10 am to 11 pm), just in front of Aso station, has small indoor and outdoor baths, and a sauna.

Helicopter Tours

Hovering over an active volcano as it belches white smoke from a turquoise-blue boiling lake is an unforgettable experience. Sagawa Kōku (☎ 34-2440), based in the horrendous and exploitative Cuddly Dominion bear park, can whisk you up and over Naka-dake – and rather swiftly back again for ¥7300 (plus ¥1580 park admission). It's a lot of money for a short flight, but how often do you get to peer down into a boiling 100,000-year-old mountain-sized cauldron? Spare a thought for the trapped animals below. Cuddly Dominion is 15 minutes' walk west of Aso station on Route 57.

Aso Volcanic Museum

Despite the usual shortage of English-language labelling, the Aso Volcanic Museum (¥840, 9 am to 5 pm) has great live footage taken inside the active crater. An entertaining selection of videos shows various volcanoes from around the world strutting their stuff.

Kusasenri 草千里 & Komezuka 米塚

In front of the museum is the Kusasenri meadow (literally, '1000km of grass'), a grassy meadow in the flattened crater of an ancient volcano. There are two lakes in the meadow. Just off the road that runs from the museum down to the town of Aso is the perfectly shaped small cone of Kome-zuka, another extinct volcano. The name means 'rice mound', presumably because that's what it looks like.

Aso-jinja

Aso-jinja is a 20-minute walk north of JR Miyaji station and is a shrine dedicated to the 12 gods of the mountain. On a Saturday in early March (dates vary) the shrine is the scene of a spectacular, highly photogenic fire festival.

Places to Stay

There are over 50 places to stay around Aso-san, including a youth hostel, a collection of places at Uchinomaki Onsen, north of Aso, and pensions at Tochinoki Onsen (to the west of the caldera) and the village of Takamori (to the south).

Places to Stay – Budget

Aso Youth Hostel (☎ 34-0804) is a 15- to 20-minute walk or a three-minute bus ride from JR Aso station. It charges ¥2400.

The newly renovated *YMCA & Youth Hostel Aso Camp* (☎ 35-0124) is near JR Akamizu station, the third stop west of JR Aso station. It charges ¥2900/3900 for members/nonmembers. *Minami Aso Koku-min-shukusha* (☎ 7-0078) is a 10-minute bus ride north of the station (¥280). Get off at the kokumin-shukusha bus stop. It charges ¥3800.

Murataya Ryokan Youth Hostel (☎ 2-0066) is right in the heart of Takamori. Beds cost ¥2700/3700 for members/nonmembers. It's conveniently located on the main street, but still quite pleasant; with only room for 30 guests it's best to book ahead in the summer months

Places to Stay – Mid-Range

Aso No Fumoto (☎ 32-0624) is a good minshuku, conveniently close to JR Aso station. Rates are ¥6000 per person with meals, ¥4000 without. The owner will pick you up. *Kokuminshukusha Aso* (☎ 34-0111) is just one minute from the station on foot and charges ¥6800 with meals, ¥3900 without. Similar rates prevail next door at *Koku-minshukusha Nakamura* (☎ 34-0317).

A national vacation village, *Kokumin Kyūkamura Minami Aso* (☎ 2-2111) is crowded in July and August. Rooms start from ¥4500.

Places to Stay – Top End

Just outside Takamori, on the southern side of the ancient crater, is a *pension mura* (pension village) with prices around ¥8000 per person, with two meals. Pensions include *Wonderland* (☎ 2-3040), *Cream House* (☎ 2-3090) and *Flower Garden* (☎ 2-3021).

Places to Eat

Towards the Kokumin Kyūkamura is *Dengaku-no-Sato* (11 am to 7 pm), an old farmhouse restaurant where you cook your own kebab-like *dengaku* (hardened mochi rice dipped in miso) on individual *hibachi* (barbecues). The teishoku is good value at ¥1680.

Entertainment

The region's nightlife centres around *Bar & Grill Crazy Glue* (☎ 34-2426) on Route 57, 10 minutes' walk south of Aso station. Look for the rear end of a Harley Davidson sticking out of the front wall. It's open from 8.30 to 1 am from Wednesday to Sunday.

Getting There & Away

The JR Hohi line operates between Kumamoto and Beppu via Aso. The Kumamoto to Aso trip on the tokkyū costs ¥1680 and takes one hour. Beppu-Aso on the tokkyū costs ¥3440 and takes two hours (three a day). To get to Takamori on the southern side of the crater, transfer from the JR Hōhi line to the Minami-aso private train line at Tateno.

From March to November the *Aso Boy* (¥1880) steam train makes a daily run from Kumamoto to Aso, terminating at Miyaji station.

From JR Aso station there are buses to the Aso-nishi cable car station.

Buses from Beppu to Aso (¥3800, 2½ to three hours) may continue to the Aso-nishi cable car station (plus ¥1550). From Takamori, buses continue on a scenic route south-east to the mountain resort of Takachiho (¥1280, 1½ hours).

Getting Around

Buses operate approximately hourly from JR Aso station via the Aso Youth Hostel to the Aso-higashi cable car station (¥420, 30 minutes up, 25 minutes down). There are less frequent services between Miyaji and Sensui-kyō on the northern side of Nakadake.

Cars can be rented at Aso and at Uchinomaki, one stop west of JR Aso station.

KUROKAWA ONSEN 黒川温泉
☎ 0967 • pop 412

This hot spring is a real treasure. A few dozen ryokan lie along a steep-sided valley beside the Kurokawa, some 6km west of the Yamanami Hwy. Though it is touristed, the development has been particularly well done, with not a karaoke bar or pachinko parlour in sight. The enlightened Onsen Association has also made it affordable. You can buy a ticket (¥1200) from the tourist information desk (☎ 44-0076) that allows you access to three ryokan baths of your choice (9 am to 6 pm). Kurokawa is especially famous for its 23 rotemburo. Yamamizuki, Kurokawa-sō and the magnificent Shimmei-kan, with its cave baths and riverside rotemburo, are among local favourites. Most places offer *konyoku* (mixed bathing) and separate male and female baths.

The piping hot Jizo-yu, overlooking the river, and Ana-yu are marvellous public baths (¥30, 24 hours). You'll need to bring your own towels.

Places to Stay

The onsen ryokan are well worth splashing out on. The countrified *Kyuhō-kan* (☎ 44-0651), charging from ¥10,000 with two meals, and *Ryokan Nishimura* (☎ 44-0753), charging ¥10,000 to ¥15,000, with two meals, are among the cheapest. However, the near-ish *Senomoto Youth Hostel* (☎ 44-0157) is one of Kyūshū's best (¥2300, nonmembers ¥3300). It has lots of information, and the friendly English-speaking manager will even pick you up from Miyaji station, a good 30 minutes' drive away, if you call in advance.

Getting There & Away

There's a late morning bus to Kurokawa from Aso Sankō bus station (one hour), but the only return bus leaves the onsen less than two hours later. The only solution is to take a taxi out to the Yamanami Hwy (¥1000) and take a bus from the Senomoto bus stop. If you're heading for Beppu there's a final bus in the late afternoon (¥3400, two hours).

If you stay at Senomoto Youth Hostel, the manager will offer you an early morning ride into Kurokawa, where he goes to pick up the newspapers.

SOUTH OF KUMAMOTO
Yatsushiro 八代
The castle town of Yatsushiro, directly south of Kumamoto, was where Hosokawa Tadoki retired. The powerful daimyō is chiefly remembered in Japan for having his Christian wife killed to stop her falling into the hands of his enemies. Near the castle ruins is the 1688 Shohinken house and garden. The town's Korean-influenced *Koda-yaki* (Koda ware) is admired by pottery experts.

Hinagu 日奈久 & Minamata 水俣
Farther south along the coast at Hinagu there are fine views out towards the Amakusa-shotō. To the north is the port of Minamata, which became infamous in the late '60s and early '70s when it was discovered that the high incidence of illness and birth defects in the town were caused by mercury poisoning. A local factory had dumped waste containing high levels of mercury into the sea and this had contaminated the fish eaten by local residents. The company's ruthless efforts to suppress the story, and W Eugene Smith's heart-rending documentary photos, focused worldwide attention on the town.

AMAKUSA-SHOTŌ 天草
South of the Shimabara-hantō are the Amakusa-shotō. The islands were a stronghold of Christianity during Japan's Christian Century and the grinding poverty here was a major factor in the Shimabara Rebellion of 1637–38. It's still one of the less-developed regions of Japan.

Hondo is the main town on the islands and has a museum relating to the Christian era. Tomioka, where Nagasaki ferries berth, has castle ruins and a museum. This west coast area is particularly interesting. *Amakusa-sō* (☎ *42-3131*) charges ¥2600 not including meals and, as this is an onsen kokumin-shukusha, it is good value.

There are ferry services from various places in Nagasaki-ken (including Mogi near Nagasaki and Shimabara on the Shimabara-hantō) and from the Kumamoto-

ken coast (including Yatsushiro and Minamata). In addition, the Amakusa Five Bridges link the island directly with Misumi, south-west of Kumamoto.

Kagoshima-ken

Kyūshū's southernmost prefecture has the large city of Kagoshima, overlooked by the ominous volcano of Sakurajima across the bay, Kinkō-wan. To the south is the Satsuma-hantō, while the north has the Kirishima National Park with its superb volcanoes.

KIRISHIMA NATIONAL PARK 霧島
The day walk from Ebino-kōgen village (the village on the Ebino plateau, not to be confused with the town of Ebino down on the plains) to the summits of a string of volcanoes is one of the finest volcanic hikes in Japan. It's about 15km from the summit of Karakuni-dake to the summit of Takachiho-no-mine and there's superb scenery all the way. If your time or energy is limited there are shorter alternatives such as a pleasant lake stroll on the plateau or a walk up and down Karakuni-dake or Takachiho-no-mine. The area is also noted for its spring wildflowers and has hot springs and the impressive 75m waterfall, Senriga-taki.

Orientation & Information
There are visitors' centres with maps and some information in English in Ebino-kōgen village (☎ 0984-35-1111) and at Takachiho-gawara, the two ends of the volcano walk. There are restaurant facilities at both ends of the walk, but Ebino-kōgen has most of the hotels and camping facilities. Kobayashi, to the north, and Hayashida, just to the south, are the main towns near Ebino-kōgen.

Ebino-kōgen Walk えびの高原
The Ebino-kōgen lake circuit is a relaxed stroll around a series of volcanic lakes – **Rokkannon Mi-ike** has the most intense colour, a deep blue-green. Across the road from the lake, Fudou-ike, at the base of Karakuni-dake, is a steaming **jigoku**. From there you can make the stiff climb to the

EBINO-KŌGEN/KIRISHIMA

Map labels:

To Ebino
Rokkannon Temple — Rokkannon-Mi-ike
Byakushi-ike
To Kobayashi & Miyazaki
Miyazaki Expressway
Ebino-kōgen Visitors Centre
Fudou-ike
Ebino-kōgen Rotenburo
Ebino-kōgen-sō
Camping Ground
Karakuni-dake (1700m)
Karakuni-dake Crater
Biwa-ike
Ōhata-ike
KAGOSHIMA-KEN
Shinshō Lookout
Onami-ike
Shinmoe-dake (1421m)
To Takaharu
Kagoshima-kōgen/Makino Line
KIRISHIMA NATIONAL PARK
MIYAZAKI-KEN
Hotel Morita Onsen
Kirishima Kokusai Hotel
Hotel Kirishima Castle
Takachiho Visitors Centre
Takachiho-no-mine (1574m)
Mi-ike
Senriga-taki
Takachiho gawara
Takachiho Crater
Ko-ike
Takaoka-san (647m)
Kirishima Golf Course
Kirishima jingu
Jingū-mae Youth Hostel, Kirishima-ji & Shimizu-sō
To Kagoshima
Takachiho Golf Course
To Miyakonojō
0 1 2 4km
0 1 2mi

1700m summit of **Karakuni-dake**, skirting the edge of the volcano's deep crater before arriving at the high point on the eastern side. There are good views back over Ebino-kōgen, but the view to the south is superb, taking in the perfectly circular caldera lake of Onami-ike, the rounded Shinmoe-dake and the perfect cone of Takachiho-no mine. On a clear day, you can see right down to Kagoshima and the smoking cone of Sakurajima.

Longer Walks

The view across the almost lunar landscape from any of the volcano summits is otherworldly. If you have time you can continue from Karakuni-dake to Shishiko, Shinmoe-dake, Naka-dake and then Takachiho-gawara, from where you can make the ascent of Takachiho-no-mine. Close up, Takachiho is a decidedly ugly volcano with a huge, gaping crater. Legends relate that Ninigi-no-mikoto, a descendant of the sun

goddess, arrived in Japan on the summit of this mountain.

Places to Stay

Ebino-kōgen village has a reasonable choice of accommodation. *Ebino-Kōgen-sō* (☎ 0984-33-0161) kokumin-shukusha is the cheapest at ¥10,190, with two meals. Check-in is at 4 pm. Just north-east of the centre is *Ebino-kōgen Rotemburo* (☎ 0984-33-0800) with basic but cheap huts for ¥1540 around a popular series of open-air hot-spring baths (bring a torch for a night bath). There's also a camping ground *Ebino-kōgen Camp Jō* (☎ 0984-33-0800). More accommodation can be found at Hayashida Onsen, between Ebino-kōgen and the shrine, Kirishima-jingū.

South-east of Kirishima-jingū, *Jingū-mae Youth Hostel* (☎/fax 0995-57-1188) is basic but adequate. It charges ¥3000 (¥4000 for nonmembers). *Kirishima-ji* (☎ 0995-57-0272) and *Shimizu-sō* (☎ 0955-57-0111)

KYŪSHŪ

both have rooms for around ¥6000 per person.

Getting There & Away

JR Kobayashi station to the north of Ebino-kōgen, and Kirishima-jinja station to the south, are the main train junctions. From Miyazaki or Kumamoto take a JR Ebino-gō tokkyū train to Kobayashi on the JR Kitto line, from where buses operate to Ebino. From Kagoshima (around one hour) or Miyazaki (1½ hours) you can take a JR Nippō tokkyū to Kirishima-jingū station. From there infrequent buses operate to Takachiho-gawara (¥550, about 45 minutes) and Ebino-kōgen (¥550, 50 minutes).

A direct bus to Ebino-kōgen is probably the best way to go. The two main approaches are Kagoshima and Miyazaki. Buses arrive and depart from Ebino-kōgen. From Nishi-Kagoshima station most buses run to Kirishima Iwasaki Hotel (one hour and 18 minutes), one stop short of Ebino-kōgen.

There are good views of the volcano scenery from buses driving along the Kobayashi Ebino-kōgen Makino Line.

KIRISHIMA-JINGŪ 霧島神社

The bright-orange Kirishima-jingū is colourful and beautifully located, with fine views down towards Kagoshima and Sakurajima. It originally dates from the 6th century, although the present shrine was built in 1715. It is dedicated to Ninigi-no-mikoto, who made his legendary landing in Japan on the summit of Takachiho-no-mine.

The shrine can be visited en route to the national park from Kagoshima or from Miyazaki. It is 15 minutes by bus from Kirishima-jingū station. The festivals of Saitan-sai on 1 January, Ota-ue-sai in mid-March and the lantern festival of Kontō-sai on 5 August are all worth seeing.

KAGOSHIMA 鹿児島

☎ 099 • pop 536,000

Known to the Japanese as the Naples of Japan, Kagoshima is the southernmost major city in Kyūshū and a warm, sunny and relaxed place – at least as long as Kagoshima's very own Vesuvius, Sakurajima, just a stone's throw across Kinkō-wan, is behaving itself. 'Dustfall' brings out the umbrellas in Kagoshima as frequently as rainfall in other parts of the world.

History

Kagoshima's history has been dominated by a single family, the Shimazu clan, who held sway there for 29 generations (nearly 700 years) until the Meiji Restoration. The Kagoshima region, known as Satsuma, was always receptive to outside contact and for many years was an important centre for trade with China. St Francis Xavier first arrived here in 1549, making Kagoshima one

KAGOSHIMA

TRAM STOPS

ROUTE 1
T1 Kōtsū-kyoku
交通局
T2 Takenohashi
竹の橋
T3 Shin-yashiki
新屋敷
T4 City Hospital
市立病院前

ROUTE 2
T5 Nakasu-dōri
中洲通り

T6 Miyako-dōri
都通り
T7 Nishi Kagoshima
Station
西鹿児島駅前
T8 Takamibashi
高見橋
T9 Kajiya-machi
鍛冶屋町

ROUTE 1 & 2
T10 Takami-baba
高見馬場
T11 Tenmonkan-dōri
天文館通り

T12 Izuro-dōri
いづろ通り
T13 Asahi-dōri
朝日通り
T14 City Hall
市役所前
T15 Prefectural
Office
県庁前
T16 Sakurajima
Sambashi-dōri
桜島桟橋通り
T17 Kagoshima Station
鹿児島駅前

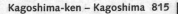

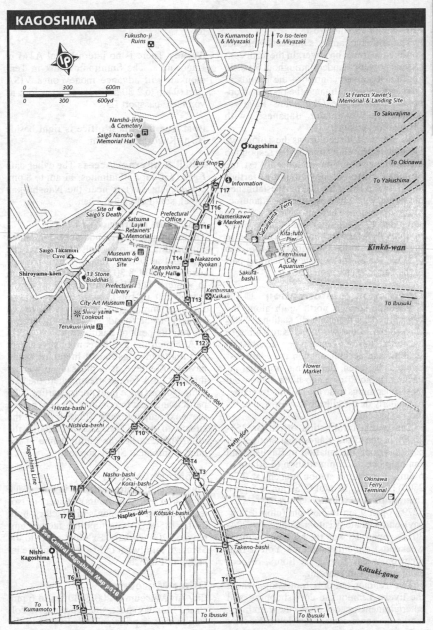

KAGOSHIMA

Fukusho-ji Ruins

To Kumamoto & Miyazaki

To Iso-teien & Miyazaki

St Francis Xavier's Memorial & Landing Site

0   300   600m
0   300   600yd

Nanshū-jinja & Cemetery

Saigō Nanshū Memorial Hall

Kagoshima

Bus Stop

To Sakurajima

To Okinawa

Information
T17

To Yakushima

Site of Saigō's Death

T16

Satsuma Loyal Retainers' Memorial

Prefectural Office

Namerikawa Market

Sakurajima Ferry

T15

Saigō Takamori Cave

Museum & Tsurumaru-jō Site

T14

Nakazono Ryokan

Kita-futo Pier

Kagoshima City Aquarium

Kinkō-wan

Shiroyama-kōen

13 Stone Buddhas

Kagoshima City Hall

Sakura-bashi

Prefectural Library

City Art Museum

Kenbussan Kaikan

T13

Shiroyama Lookout

To Ibusuki

Terukuni-jinja

T12

Kagoshima Line

Flower Market

T11

Tenmonkan-dōri

Hirata-bashi

Nishida-bashi

T10

Perth-dōri

T9

T4

Nashu-bashi

T3

Korai-bashi

Okinawa Ferry Terminal

T8

T7

Naples-dōri

Kōtsuki-bashi

T2

Takeno-bashi

Nishi-Kagoshima

See Central Kagoshima Map p818

Kōtsuki-gawa

T6

T1

To Kumamoto

T5

To Ibusuki

To Ibusuki

of Japan's earliest contact points with Christianity and the West.

The Shimazu family's interests were not confined to trade, however. In the 16th century its power extended throughout Kyūshū and it also gained control of the islands of Okinawa, where it treated the people so oppressively that the Okinawans have regarded the mainland Japanese with suspicion ever since.

During the 19th century as the Tokugawa Shogunate proved its inability to respond to the challenge of the industrialised West, the Shimazu were already looking farther afield. In the 1850s the Shimazu established the country's first Western-style manufacturing operation. Then, in 1865, the family smuggled 17 young men out of the country to study Western technology first-hand in the UK. In conjunction with the Mori clan of Hagi, the Shimazu played a leading part in the Meiji Restoration.

Orientation & Information

Kagoshima sprawls north-south along the bayside and has two major JR stations, Nishi-Kagoshima to the south and Kagoshima to the north. The town centre is between the two stations, and accommodation is evenly distributed. Iso-teien, the town's principal attraction, is north of Kagoshima station but most other things to do are around the centre, particularly on the hillside that forms a backdrop to the city.

The tourist information office (☎ 253-2500) in the Nishi-Kagoshima station car park has good information in English, and can help book accommodation (8.30 am to 6 pm). Kagoshima station branch (☎ 222-2500) is equally helpful (8.30 am to 5 pm). International Exchange Plaza (☎ 225-3279), open 9 am to 5.30 pm (closed Sunday) and Update Visitors Centre (☎ 224-8011), open 10 am to 4.30 pm (closed weekends) are other options You'll find them on the 11th and 1st floors, respectively, in the I'm Building.

The Tenmonkan-dōri tram stop, where the lively Tenmonkan-dōri shopping and entertainment arcade crosses the tram lines, marks the town centre. The Izuro Kōsoku

bus centre, for long-distance buses, is there too.

Money There is no international ATM in Kagoshima. The Sumitomo Bank in Tenmonkan will advance money on a VISA card (9 am to 2.30 pm weekdays) as long as you have passport ID.

Post The main post office is right beside Nishi-Kagoshima station.

Email & Internet Access The cyber-cafe *Eggs* (¥300 for 30 minutes, 11 am to 8 pm, closed Tuesday) is near the Nanshū-kan Hotel, south of Chū-ō-kōen.

Iso-teien (Sengan-en)

The Shimazu family not only dominated Kagoshima's history, it also left the city its principal attraction, this beautiful bayside garden (¥1000, 8.30 am to 5.30 pm, to 5 pm in winter). The 19th Shimazu lord laid the garden out in 1660, incorporating one of the most impressive pieces of 'borrowed scenery' to be found anywhere in Japan – the fuming peak of Sakurajima.

Although the garden is not as well kept and immaculate as tourist literature would have you believe, it is pleasant to wander through. Look for the stream where the 21st Shimazu lord once held poetry parties – the participants had to compose a poem before the next cup of sake floated down the stream to them. The garden contains the villa, **Shimazu-ke**, the family home of the once omnipotent Shimazu clan.

Shōko Shūseikan

This museum (entry included in the garden admission fee, same hours) adjacent to Iso-teien, is housed in Japan's first factory, built in the 1850s. At one time the factory employed 1200 workers. Exhibits relate to the Shimazu family but only a few items are labelled in English.

Other Museums

City Art Museum (¥200, 9.30 am to 6 pm, closed Monday) has a small, permanent collection that is principally dedicated to the works of local artists but also includes paintings by European impressionists. **Kagoshima Prefectural Museum of Culture** (¥260, 9 am to 4.30 pm, closed Monday) is on the former site of Tsurumaru-jō – the walls and the impressive moat are all that remain of the 1602 castle. **Kagoshima Prefectural Museum** (¥200, 9 am to 4.30 pm, closed Monday) has interesting displays on the Sakurajima volcano.

Saigō Takamori 高森

There are numerous reminders of Saigō Takamori's importance in Kagoshima, including a large statue of him near the City Art Museum. In true Japanese fashion, there's a sign showing you where to stand in order to get yourself and the statue in the same photograph. The cave where he hid and the place where he eventually committed suicide are on Shiro-yama. Farther north are Nanshū-jinja; the Saigō Nanshū Memorial Hall (¥100, closed Monday), where displays tell of the failed rebellion; and Nanshū-bochi cemetery, which contains the graves of more than 2000 of Saigō's followers.

Saigō Takamori

Although the Great Saigō had played a leading part in the Meiji Restoration in 1868, in 1877 he changed his mind – possibly because he felt the curtailment of *samurai* power and status had gone too far – and led to the ill-fated Satsuma or Seinan Rebellion. Kumamoto's magnificent castle was burnt down during the rebellion but when defeat became inevitable, Saigō eventually retreated to Kagoshima and committed *seppuku* (ritual suicide by disembowelment).

Despite his mixed status as both a hero and villain of the restoration, Saigō is still a great figure in Satsuma's history and indeed in the history of Japan. His square-headed features and bulky appearance are instantly recognisable, and Kagoshima has a famous Saigō statue (and a spooky Saigō hologram), as does Ueno-kōen in Tokyo.

Kōtsuki-gawa

Kagoshima enjoys twin-city status with Naples in Italy and Perth in Australia. The street running perpendicular to the Nishi-Kagoshima station starts as Naples-dōri and changes to Perth-dōri after it crosses Kōtsuki-gawa. There's a riverside walk starting near the station. Begin at the attractive 18th-century stone Nishida-bashi and walk south.

Here you'll find the interesting **Museum of the Meiji Restoration** (¥300, 9 am to 5 pm), complete with an hourly performance of robotic Meiji reformers, and a downright spooky-looking Saigō. Some information is in English.

Farther south is the site of Saigō's home and the 'Statue of Hat', appropriately named after the statue's only item of apparel.

Morning Market

Kagoshima's *asa ichi* (morning market; 6 am to noon, except Sunday) is just south of Nishi Kagoshima station. It's a raucous, lively event. There's another morning market up at the main JR Kagoshima station, but the Nishi-Kagoshima station market is more fun.

Other Attractions

Behind the Kagoshima Prefectural Museum is **Terukuni-jinja** dedicated to Shimazu Nari-akira, the 28th Shimazu lord who was responsible for building Japan's first factory and introducing modern Western technology. He also designed Japan's still-controversial *hinomaru* – the rising sun flag. Continue up the hillside behind the shrine and you eventually reach the lookout in **Shiroyama-kōen**.

Kagoshima boasts no less than 54 public onsen baths. Local favourite **Shin-tosō Onsen** has a good view of Sakura-jima. Take city bus No 25 from Nishi-Kagoshima station to Toso (15 minutes). Nishida Onsen is just a few minutes' walk from Nishi-Kagoshima station.

Kagoshima City Aquarium (¥1500, 9 am to 5 pm) is well done, not least the examples of local marine life, but it's very busy at weekends and holidays.

KYŪSHŪ

CENTRAL KAGOSHIMA

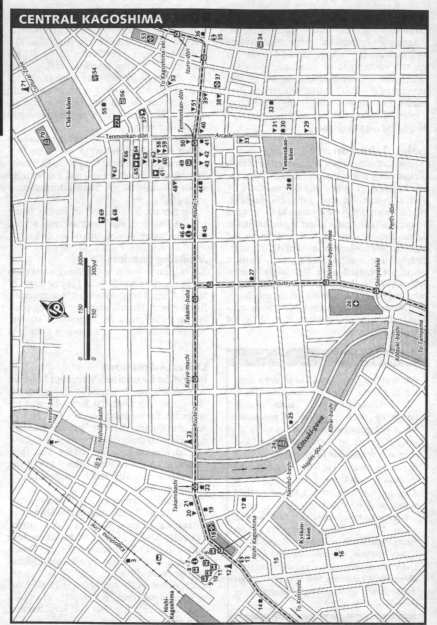

CENTRAL KAGOSHIMA

PLACES TO STAY
1 Ryokan Hyūga Bekkan
 旅館日向別館
3 City Hotel Kagoshima
 シティホテル鹿児島
14 Business Hotel Suzuya
 ビジネスホテル
 すずや
16 Silk Inn Kagoshima
 シルクイン鹿児島
17 Kagoshima Gasthof
 鹿児島ガストフ
19 Station Hotel New
 Kagoshima
 ステーションホテル
 ニューカゴシマ
21 Hotel Taisei Annexe
 ホテルタイセイ
 アネックス
22 Kagoshima Tōkyū Inn
 鹿児島東急イン
27 Hokke Club Kagoshima
 法華クラブ鹿児島
28 City Hotel Tenmonkan
 シティホテル天文館
30 Kagoshima
 Kankō Hotel
 鹿児島観光ホテル
32 Business Hotel Satsuma
 ビジネスホテル薩摩
44 New Central Hotel;
 ANA
 ニューセントラル
 ホテル
45 Kagoshima
 Washington Hotel
 ワシントンホテル

PLACES TO EAT
20 Italian Tomato
 Restaurant
29 Akachōchin
 あかちょうちん
31 Bali Bali Yakiniku
 House
 バリバリ焼肉ハウス
33 Boulangerie
38 McDonald's
39 KFC

40 Toit Vert
 天文館トワベール
42 Lotteria
43 Vie de France Bakery
48 KFC
50 Nanak
51 Mr Donut
52 Dom Dom
 Hamburgers
58 Wadaya
 和田屋本店
59 Komurasaki
 こむらさき
60 Wakana Honten
 吾愛人
62 Kuroiwa
 くろいわラーメン
63 Casa Salone
66 Kumasotei
 熊襲亭
67 Le Ciel de Paris

OTHER
2 Nishida Onsen
 西田温泉
4 Post Office
 郵便局
5 Hayashida Sangyo
 Kōtsū (Kirishima);
 Minami Kyūshū
 Kōsoku (Miyazaki)
 林田産業交通
 （至霧島）；
 南九州高速
 （至宮崎）
6 City Bus
 (Kagoshima City)
 シティバス
 （鹿児島市）
7 Tourist Information
 Office
 観光案内所
8 Kagoshima Kōtsū;
 City Bus (Sightseeing
 Buses)
 鹿児島交通
 （観光バス）
9 JR Bus (Sakurajima)
 JRバス（至桜島）

10 Hayashida Sangyo
 Kōtsū (Ebino,
 Kirishima)
 林田産業交通
 （至えびの、霧島）
11 Kagoshima Kōtsū
 (Chiran, Ibusuki)
 鹿児島交通
 （至知覧、指宿）
12 17 Young Pioneers
 Statues
 若き鹿児島の群像
13 Kagoshima Bank
 鹿児島銀行
15 Morning Market
 朝市
18 Daiei Department
 Store
 大栄
23 Statue of Ōkubo
 Toshimichi
 大久保誕生地
24 Museum of the Meiji
 Restoration
 維新ふるさと館
25 Site of Saigo House
 西郷旧居
26 Shiritsu-byōin
 市立病院
34 Izuro Kōsoku
 Bus Centre
 いづろ高速
 バスセンター
35 Sumitomo Bank
 住友銀行
36 Izuro (Stone Lantern)
 石灯籠
37 Mitsukoshi
 Department Store
 三越
41 Tower Records
46 International Exchange
 Plaza;
 Update Visitors Centre;
 I'm Building
 国際交流プラザ；
 アイムビル
47 JAL
 日本航空

CENTRAL KAGOSHIMA

49 Hayashida Bus
　林田バス
53 Yamakataya
　Department Store;
　Bus Station
　山形屋；バスセンター
54 Nishi-Honganji
　西本願寺
55 Nanshū-kan Hotel
　南州館

56 Eggs
57 T-Bone Bar
61 NAMASTE
64 Orgie
65 Kanejō
　かねじょう
68 St Francis
　Xavier
　Memorial
　ザビエル記念碑

69 St Francis Xavier
　Church
　ザビエル教会
70 Kagoshima
　Prefectural
　Museum
　県立博物館
71 Saigō Takamori
　Statue
　西郷隆盛銅像

It's near Kita-futō pier. For a hands-on aquatic experience, try **Iso-hama**, near Isoteien, the city's popular summer getaway.

Special Events
One of Kagoshima's more unusual events is the late July **Soga Don Kasayaki** (Umbrella Burning Festival). Boys burn umbrellas on the banks of Kōtsuki-gawa in honour of the Soga brothers, though why they do this isn't exactly clear.

Places to Stay – Budget
The only youth hostel close to Kagoshima is *Sakurajima Youth Hostel*. To get there you have to take the ferry across the bay (see the Sakurajima section later).

Places to Stay – Mid-Range
Ryokan The Japanese Inn Group's *Nakazono Ryokan* (☎ 226-5125), with communal bath, is a superb place to be based. Rooms cost ¥4000/7600 for singles/doubles. It's close to Kagoshima station and the Sakurajima pier, and is clearly signposted in English. *Ryokan Hyūga Bekkan* (☎ 257-3509) is good value at ¥4000/7000 and has both Japanese and Western-style rooms. It's seven minutes' walk from Nishi-Kagoshima station.

Hotels Around Nishi-Kagoshima station, the cheapest hotel (with only 22 single rooms) is *Business Hotel Suzuya* (☎ 258-2385), with rooms for ¥4800. *Silk Inn Kagoshima* (☎ 258-1221) has its own hot spring and charges ¥5800/9500. To the north-east of the station is *City Hotel Kagoshima* (☎ 258-0331), with rooms starting at ¥5500.

Just south of the Mitsukoshi department store is the cramped, dirty *Business Hotel Satsuma* (☎ 226-135), with singles with/without bath for ¥4600/3500, and twins for ¥7900/6400.

New Central Hotel (☎ 224-5551) is, as its name suggests, is in the middle of town. Singles/doubles cost from ¥5700/9300. Another central option, right in the heart of all the entertainment action, is *City Hotel Tenmonkan* (☎ 223-7181), charging ¥6000/12,000.

South of Chūō-kōen is the slightly faded but comfortable and convenient *Nanshū-kan* (☎ 226-8188), with rooms from ¥6000/8000. The water pressure in the showers is enough to knock over a horse.

More upmarket options include *Station Hotel New Kagoshima* (☎ 253-5353), charging ¥6500/12,000, and *Kagoshima Tōkyū Inn* (☎ 256-0109), with rooms from ¥7700/14,000.

Places to Eat
Most restaurants are in and around Tenmonkan. In the Tenmonkan arcade itself restaurants are few, but there are some good patisseries: *Toit Vert* and *Boulangerie*.

Akachōchin is an izakaya of wildly exaggerated cheerfulness – the welcomes are bawled out so loudly that new arrivals reel back at the door. The menu is in Japanese only, though some dishes are illustrated and most are in the ¥250 to ¥500 range. Look for the octopus over the entrance. There's another branch of this popular izakaya near Nishi-Kagoshima station.

Kumasotei (☎ 222-6356) is a favourite for its Satsuma cuisine (11 am to 2.30 pm, 5 to 10 pm). The ¥4000 dinner gives you a taste of all the most popular specialities. There is an English-language menu. *Wakasa Honten (☎ 222-5559)* has much of the same, but is rather cheaper, with all dishes around ¥700 (5.30 to 11.30 pm). One of the waiters is a moonlighting high-school English teacher!

Other places in this central area include *Casa Salone* for good-value Italian fare and *Le Ciel de Paris*, a nice little patisserie-coffee bar. For fairly ordinary Indian fare look out for *Nanak* (this is not one of the chain's best branches).

There's something of a rāmen battle going on in Tenmonkan. Word on the street says *Komurasaki* (11 am to 9 pm, closed Thursday) is good but pricey, *Kuroiwa* (10.30 am to 9 pm) – plain but tasty, and *Wadaya* (11 am to 1.50 am) – 'striking'.

Entertainment

There's a lot happening in Tenmonkan – shot bars, discos, bunny bars, peep shows, karaoke boxes and hideaway coffee shops. *Kanejyō (☎ 223-0487)* is an atmospheric jazz café and

bar, presided over by the cheery Uemura-san who waives the cover charge for gaijin guests. Next door, *Orgie (☎ 222-0902)* is a small basement dance club, swathed in pink and purple lights (8 pm to 5 am). There's a ¥500 cover charge, and cocktails start at ¥500. For a quiet, inexpensive drink try *Namaste (☎ 227-1446)*, a basement reggae bar around the corner from the Wakana restaurant. It's open from 8 am to 3 pm.

Shopping

Satsuma specialities include a variation on the *ningyō* (Japanese doll), cards printed with inks produced from Sakurajima volcanic ash, Satsuma *kiriki* (cut glass) and nifty little wooden fish on wheels. Satsuma-yaki (Satsuma ware) porcelain is also highly valued, but not as much as Kagoshima's pride and joy – *imo shochū* (potato liquor). All can be bought in the Kagoshima specialities store Kenbussan Kaikan (☎ 225-6120), north of Tenmonkan.

Getting There & Away

Air Kagoshima's airport has international connections with Hong Kong and Seoul, as well as domestic flights to Tokyo, Osaka, Nagoya and a variety of other places in Honshū and Kyūshū. Kagoshima is the major jumping-off point for flights to the South-West Islands and also has connections with the Kagoshima-ken islands and Naha on Okinawa (see the 'Domestic Airfares' chart in the Getting Around chapter for more details).

Bus Hayashida buses to Kirishima and Ebino-kōgen (¥1550, two hours) go from the Takashimaya department store in the centre. A good way of exploring Chiran and Ibusuki, south of Kagoshima, is by rented car, but you can also get there by bus from bus stop No 10 at Nishi-Kagoshima station. Buses also run from Nishi-Kagoshima station to other places near and far, including the following:

destination	bus stop	fare	duration
Miyazaki	No 8	¥2700	2½ hours
Kumamoto	No 17	¥3600	3½ hours
Fukuoka	No 16	¥5300	4½ hours
Osaka	No 8	¥12,000	12½ hours

Satsuma Ryōri

Kagoshima's cuisine speciality is known as *Satsuma ryōri* – the food of the Satsuma region. Satsuma dishes include: *tonkotsu*, which is pork ribs seasoned with *miso* (fermented soybean paste) and black sugar, then boiled until they're on the point of falling apart; *kibinago*, a sardine-like fish that is usually prepared as *sashimi* with vinegared miso sauce; *satsuma-age*, a fried fish sausage; *satsuma jiru*, a chicken miso soup; *torisashi*, raw chicken with soy sauce; *katsuo no tataki*, sliced bonito fish; *katsuo no shiokara*, those tasty salted bonito intestines; and *sakezushi*, a mixed seafood *sushi*.

Kagoshima *rāmen* (Chinese-style egg noodles in a broth) is the region's renowned noodle dish. *Imo-shōchū*, the Kagoshima firewater, is made from sweet potatoes, which the locals fiercely support against Ōita's *mugi-shōchū*, which is distilled from barley.

There are also daily tours to Ibusuki and Chiran, among other places, from bus stop No 4. As an example of what's on offer, at 10.10 am a daily bus (¥4500) heads off to Chiran, whizzes you around the sights and then does the same thing in Ibusuki, ending the day with a soak in a hot spring.

Train Both Nishi-Kagoshima and Kagoshima stations are main arrival and departure points. While Nishi-Kagoshima station is close to a greater choice of accommodation, Kagoshima station is closer to Iso-teien and the Sakurajima ferry.

Kagoshima is connected by the JR Kagoshima line to Fukuoka/Hakata (tokkyū, ¥7770, four hours) and Kumamoto (tokkyū, ¥5750, 2½ hours), and by the JR Nippō line to Miyazaki (tokkyū, ¥3790, two hours) and Beppu (tokkyū, ¥9410, six hours).

Trains also run south from Kagoshima to the popular hot-spring resort of Ibusuki (¥840, one hour and 10 minutes).

Boat Ferries shuttle across the bay to Sakurajima, and from the Kita-futō terminal farther afield to Okinawa, Ibusuki and Yakushima. Queen Coral Marikku Line (☎ 225-1551) has daily ferries to Naha (Okinawa) via Amami Ō-shima, Tokunoshima, Okino-Erabu-jima and Yoron-to (¥12,070 in 2nd class, 25 hours).

Getting Around

To/From the Airport Buses operate between Nishi-Kagoshima station (bus stop No 7) and the airport, stopping off at Tenmonkan on the way (¥1200, 50 minutes, every 20 minutes).

Bus There is a comprehensive city bus network, though trams are much simpler. For the one-day unlimited travel pass, see the following tram entry. The City View Bus (¥180 per trip, all-day pass ¥500, 9 am to 5 pm), from in front of Nishi-Kagoshima station tourist office, takes in all the major sights.

Tram The tram service in Kagoshima is easy to understand, operates frequently and

is the best way of getting around town. You can pay by the trip (¥160) or get a one-day unlimited travel pass (¥500). The pass can also be used on city buses and can be bought at the station tourist information booths.

There are two tram routes. Route 1 starts from Kagoshima station, goes through the centre and on past the suburb of Korimoto to Taniyama. Route 2 diverges at Takamibaba to Nishi-Kagoshima station and terminates at Korimoto.

SAKURAJIMA 桜島
☎ 099

Dominating the skyline from Kagoshima is the brooding cone of this decidedly overactive volcano. In fact, Sakurajima is so active that the Japanese differentiate between its mere eruptions (since 1955 there has been an almost continuous stream of smoke and ash) and real explosions, which have occurred in 1914, 1915, 1946, 1955 and 1960. The most violent eruption was in 1914, when the volcano poured out over three billion tonnes of lava, overwhelming numerous villages and converting Sakurajima from an island to a peninsula. The flow totally filled in the 400m-wide and 70m-deep strait that had separated the volcano from the mainland and extended the island farther west towards Kagoshima.

Sakurajima has three peaks: Otake-dake/Kita-dake (1117m), Naka-dake (1110m) and Minami-dake (1040m). But at present only Minami is active. While some parts of Sakurajima are covered in deep volcanic ash or crumbling lava, other places have exceptionally fertile soil. Huge *daikon* (radishes) weighing up to 35kg and tiny oranges, only 3cm in diameter but ¥500 each, are locally grown.

Sakurajima Visitors Centre

The visitors centre near the ferry terminal (☎ 293-2443) has a variety of exhibits about the volcano, its eruptions and its natural history. The working model showing the volcano's growth over the years is the centre's main attraction (9 am to 5 pm, closed Monday).

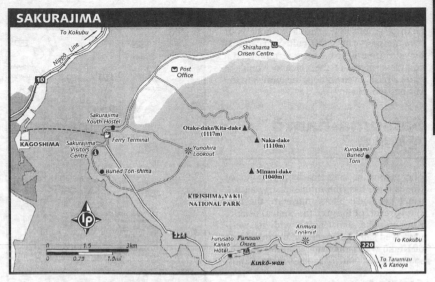

Lookouts

Although visitors are not permitted to climb the volcano, there are several good lookout points. The Yunohira lookout is high on the side of the volcano; the Arimura lava lookout is east of Furusato Onsen. There are walkways across a small corner of the immense lava flow and the lookout points offer a glimpse of the immense outpouring that linked the island to the mainland in 1914.

Other Attractions

A complete circuit of the volcano is 38km. South of the visitors centre is **Buried Tori-shima**, where the 1914 lava flow totally engulfed the small island that had been half a kilometre offshore. On the way down the mountainside the lava swallowed three villages, destroying over 1000 homes.

Continuing anticlockwise around the island, you come to the monument to writer Hayashi Fumiko, and the hot springs at Furusato Onsen. The Furusato Kankō hotel has a huge cliffside rotemburo (¥1000, closed Monday morning and Thursday). As it is also a shrine, you'll have to wear a *yukata* (light kimono for summer or indoor use) as you soak. At the **Kurokami Buried**

Torii, only the top of a torii emerges from the volcanic ash. On the north coast you can soak in the muddy waters of Shirahama Onsen Centre (¥300, 10 am to 9 pm).

Organised Tours

Sightseeing bus tours operate from the ferry terminal (¥1700, JR pass holders free, one hour, three daily). JR buses also run from the ferry terminal up to the Arimura lookout (¥330).

Places to Stay

Friendly *Sakurajima Youth Hostel* (☎ 293-2150) is near the ferry terminal and has its own onsen bath. It charges ¥2650 per night. The ferry service is very quick, so that it's possible to stay here and commute to Kagoshima.

Getting There & Away

The passenger and car ferry service shuttles back and forth between Kagoshima and Sakurajima (¥150, 15 minutes). Pay at the Sakurajima end. From Kagoshima station or the Sakurajima Sambashi-dōri tram stop, the ferry terminal is a short walk through the Namerikawa market.

KYŪSHŪ

Getting Around

Getting around Sakurajima without your own transport can be difficult. You can rent bicycles from near the ferry terminal but a complete circuit of the volcano would be quite a push, even without the climbs to the various lookouts.

Satsuma-hantō
薩摩半島

The peninsula, Satsuma-hantō, south of Kagoshima, has fine rural scenery, an unusual kamikaze pilots' museum, the hotspring resort of Ibusuki, the conical peak of Kaimon-dake, and Chiran, with its well-preserved samurai street. On the other side of Kinkō-wan is the cape, Sata-misaki, the southernmost point of Japan's main islands.

Getting Around

Using public transport around the region is time consuming, although it is possible to make a complete loop of the peninsula by train and bus through Kagoshima, Chiran, Ibusuki, Kaimon-dake, Makurazaki, Bōnotsu, Fukiage-hama and back to Kagoshima. The JR Ibusuki-Makurazaki line runs south from Kagoshima to Ibusuki then turns west to Makurazaki. You can continue on from there by bus and eventually make your way back to Kagoshima.

This is a place where renting a car can be useful. Alternatively, there are tour buses that operate from Kagoshima via Chiran to Ibusuki and then from Ibusuki back to Kagoshima via Chiran and Tarumizu on the opposite side of the bay. There is a good Yamakawa-Nejime ferry service across the southern end of the bay.

CHIRAN 知覧
☎ 0993 • pop 14,180.

South of Kagoshima, Chiran is a worthwhile place to pause en route to Ibusuki. This interesting little town has a samurai street with a fine collection of samurai houses and gardens, plus a fascinating memorial and museum to WWII's kamikaze pilots. Chiran

was one of the major bases from which the hapless pilots made their suicidal and less than totally successful attacks on Allied ships.

Samurai Street

The seven houses (¥310, 9 am to 5.30 pm) along Chiran's samurai street are noted for their formal gardens. Look for the use of 'borrowed scenery', particularly in No 6 (each is numbered on the brochure). Water is symbolised by sand or gravel, except in No 7, the Mori Shigemitsu House, where real water is used. This house is particularly well preserved and dates from 1741. Along the main road, parallel to the samurai street, is a well-stocked carp stream. In the stifling heat of mid-summer, if you're not shy, imitate the local youths and jump in the Fumoto-gawa. There's a natural pool beside an attractive bridge, 150m north-east of the Mori house.

(continued on page 833)

Matsuri Magic

FRANK CARTER

Title Page: A demon made from painted rice paper lunges from a float during the Nebuta Matsuri held in Aomori in Northern Honshū. Some theorise that Nebuta Matsuri began as a bright idea to ward off the stupor that comes with the late summer heat. And Aomori's boisterous parades with monster floats and hundreds of dancers jangling hand-held bells is enough to wake anyone up. The more historically correct theory, however, is that it commemorates a triumphant return from battle.
(Photograph by Martin Moos)

Top: Musicians perform in a mikoshi during the Gion Matsuri, Kyoto.

Bottom: A group of men carrying a giant golden chicken, one of 14 floats paraded in the Karatsu Kunchi Matsuri (Karatsu, Kyūshū). Other floats include a red lion, a turtle, samurai helmets, a dragon...

MARTIN MOOS

MATSURI MAGIC

Witnessing a *matsuri*, a traditional festival, is the high point of a trip to Japan, and offers a glimpse of the Japanese at their most uninhibited. A lively matsuri is a world unto itself – a vision of bright colours, hypnotic chanting, beating drums and swaying crowds. In addition to famous matsuri, such as Kyoto's Gion Matsuri, there are thousands of small, but spectacular local matsuri (see the boxed text 'Juhachiya Matsuri' to gain some kind of idea of the visual feast in store for you).

The Roots of Matsuri

True Shintō matsuri can be traced back to the sacred rites of Japan's rice farming peoples in the Yayoi (from 300 BC) and pre-Yayoi periods. These rites were performed to ensure a good rice harvest, to propitiate the gods and to pray for the health of the community. Although matsuri have evolved, their central meanings and patterns still reflect their agrarian roots.

In the Heian period (794–1185), Japan imported a range of Buddhist and secular rites from China and added these to native Shintō matsuri to form a full calendar of yearly events. These newer imports and other non-Shintō matsuri are properly referred to as *nenjō gyōji*. Of course, this distinction is largely academic, and these days almost any Japanese festival can be referred to as a matsuri, including modern creations, such as the Sapporo Yuki Matsuri (Sapporo Snow Festival).

Icon: Painted rice paper float, Nebuta Matsuri in Aomori, Northern Honshū. (Photograph by Martin Moos)

Right: Nebuta Matsuri, Aomori, Northern Honshū

MARTIN MOOS

Elements of Matsuri

While matsuri vary tremendously in content and form, true Shintō matsuri do contain some common elements. The first element of a Shintō matsuri is called *monomi*. This is a period of several days to a week in which the shrine priests ritually purify themselves in order to enter into communication with the *kami*, or god of the shrine. This is usually following by an offering to the kami. Typical offerings include rice, *mochi* (pounded rice cakes made of glutinous rice), *sake* or fruit and vegetables. Following this, there is ritual communication with the kami in which matsuri participants partake of these offerings, an act known as *nyorai*.

Of course, much of this happens behind closed doors, hence the most visible feature of any matsuri is a procession of *mikoshi*, or portable shrines, in which the kami is paraded around the neighbourhood on the backs of chanting young men (and occasionally women).

In some matsuri, the mikoshi may be carried down a mountainside, an act symbolic of bringing the Mountain God down to the rice fields to watch over the harvest. After the harvest is completed, another matsuri is performed in which the kami is returned to its mountaintop abode. Often accompanied by fire, these matsuri are among Japan's most spectacular; a good example being Nachi-no-Hi Matsuri.

Other matsuri may include a tug-of-war, *kyūdō* (archery), horse-racing and *sumō*, all of which were originally used to divine the will of the shrine's kami. Still other matsuri involve *gagaku* (sacred music) and lion dances.

SIMON ROWE

SIMON ROWE

Left: Every October 22 in Kyoto more than 2000 people dress in costumes ranging from the 8th to the 19th century, and parade from Kyoto Gosho to Heian-jingū for the Jidai Matsuri (Festival of the Ages).
The festival, first staged in 1895, commemorates the city's costumes down through the ages.

Right: A female archer awaits her turn during the Jidai Matsuri.

RICHARD I'ANSON

Top: Young women preparing for the Tōno Matsuri parade. The festival takes place on 14 September every year with *yabusame* (horseback archery), traditional dances and costume parades.

Bottom: A young child in Kyoto dressed in kimono for the annual Shichi-Go-San (Seven-Five-Three Festival) held in November. Traditionally, this is a festival in honour of girls who are aged three and seven and boys who are aged five. Children are dressed in their finest clothes and taken to shrines or temples where prayers are offered for their good fortune.

ERIC L WHEATER

MATSURI MAGIC

STUART WASSERMAN

MARTIN MOOS

Top: Participants in traditional costume at the Jidai Matsuri.

Bottom: Men carrying a dragon float for the Karatsu Kunchi Matsuri, Kyūshū.

Japan's Best Matsuri

There are thousands of matsuri celebrated each year in Japan. While Kyoto, Nara and Tokyo are especially famous for their matsuri, you can stumble across matsuri in every corner of Japan. For a real sensory overload, it's worth hitting one of the big ones.

Hatsumōde (First Shrine Visit) New Year's Eve, 1 & 2 January at any Shintō shrine in Japan

Yamayaki (Grass Burning Festival) 15 January in Nara, Kansai

Sapporo Yuki Matsuri (Sapporo Snow Festival) Early February in Sapporo, Hokkaidō

Kamakura Matsuri (Snow House Festival) 15 February, Yokote, Akita-ken, Northern Honshū

Omizutori (Water-Drawing Ceremony) 12–13 March at Tōdai-ji, Nara, Kansai

Takayama Matsuri (Takayama Festival) 14– 15 April at Hie-jinja, Takayama, Gifu-ken, Central Honshū

Sanja Matsuri 3rd Friday, Saturday and Sunday of May, at Sensō-ji, Tokyo

Hana Taue (Rice Planting Festival) Mid-June, Hiroshima-ken, Western Honshū

Nachi-no-Hi Matsuri (Nachi Fire Festival) 14 July at Kumano Nachi Taisha in Wakayama-ken, Kansai

Gion Matsuri (Gion Festival) 17 July, Kyoto, Kansai

Tenjin Matsuri 24–25 July, Osaka, Kansai

Kishiwada Danjiri Matsuri 14–15 September, Osaka, Kansai

Kurama-no-himatsuri (Kurama Fire Festival) 22 October, Kyoto (Kurama), Kansai

For more information on matsuri, see the Special Events sections in destination chapters, check with the JNTO or pick up a copy of their leaflet entitled *Annual Events in Japan*. If you do base a visit around festivals, remember that accommodation can be swamped by visitors from all over the country, so book well in advance.

Chris Rowthorn

Left: Masked dancer in the Tōno Matsuri.

Right: Participants in the three-day Hachiman-gū Matsuri in Kamakura.

RICHARD I'ANSON

RICHARD I'ANSON

Juhachiya Matsuri

On 18 August each year, a small roadside pit-stop of a village called Ōki in Saga-ken in Kyūshū, hosts one of Japan's most remarkable festivals – Juhachiya Matsuri. Almost everything about it is unique. The locals call it 'izayoi', and the official story is that it started life as a farmers' rain-making festival in 1576. However, even the uninitiated can see in it the origins of something far older, darker and more primitive.

The proceedings begin as night falls, with Oki's 18-year-old males parading through the village, beating with gusto on a huge gong with metal hammers. Suspended on long bamboo poles above their heads are home-made miniflares, showering them in sulphurous sparks. Flautists and drummers add to the din and smoke – it sounds like Tom Waits' percussion section falling off a cliff. Yet this is small scale – there are only about 50 men and boys – and for that reason, it's all the more striking.

The action moves to the local temple, Ryusen-ji, where a sandy arena has been prepared. The entire village is waiting, ready to witness *Ukitate Kenka,* or the Floating-Standing Fight.

The gong is moved to one side of the ring, then all hell breaks loose. The youths rush to take possession of it. However, between them and their goal are the village 'elders' – blacksmiths, firemen, truck drivers, lumberjacks – none of whom look even remotely elderly. They put up a human barricade that could teach the American Football League a thing or two. Time after time the young men attack, only to be repelled or pushed face down into the sand. One youth nearly reaches the gong, only to be dealt a stabbing right-hand jab to the cheekbone by a wiry 'elder', and he's carried off to a waiting medical crew, bleeding profusely. No one loses their temper. Finally, inevitably, the exhausted, battered youths withdraw, the gong remains in the hands of age and authority, and the temple officials rush in to set up the evening's finale, known as the *jamon.*

The jamon is a pyrotechnic catastrophe waiting to happen. All day, as the 18-year-olds have been psyching themselves up for the battle, their mothers, sisters and grandmothers have been hand-rolling miniature explosives and inserting them into the jamon, a wooden tower. At a given signal, the flame creeps slowly up the tower, the wind catches an ember, there's a glimmer of orange, and KABOOOOOOOOOOOOOM!!!

And then it's over. The villagers melt away to party at home, the country darkness floods back in, and this observer is left sharing a ghostly dark station platform with an egregiously drunken civil servant who managed to get stuck here on his way back from the town office in Arita. He asks, in all innocence, 'What was all that noise?'.

John Ashburne

(continued from page 824)

Kamikaze Peace Museum

A modern version of the samurai is commemorated in the Tokkō Heiwa Kaikan (Kamikaze Peace Museum; ¥310, 9 am to 4.30 pm), 2km west of town. There's a distinctly weird feeling to this comprehensive collection of aircraft, mementoes and photos of the young, fresh-faced pilots who were selected for the Special Attack Corps in WWII. Unfortunately, there's little English signage, apart from the dubious message that they did it for the dream of 'peace and prosperity'. There's no mention that they had little choice, and were often sent out high on Hiropon – amphetamines. Far from achieving the aim of 'a battleship for every aircraft', only minor ships were sunk at the cost of over 1000 lives.

Places to Stay & Eat

Most visitors take a day trip to Chiran or stop there on a trip between Kagoshima and Ibusuki. If you want to stay overnight, *Tomiya Ryokan* (☎ 83-4313) is on the main street opposite the bus station, and charges ¥8300. *Taki-An* on the samurai street is a traditional place with a nice garden where you can sit on tatami mats to eat a bowl of upmarket *soba* (buckwheat noodles) for ¥700.

Getting There & Away

Kagoshima Kōtsū buses to Chiran (¥860, one hour and 20 minutes) and Ibusuki run from Nishi-Kagoshima station (stand 10) or from the Yamakataya bus station in Tenmonkan.

IBUSUKI 指宿

☎ 0993 • pop 30,908

At the south-eastern end of the Satsuma-hantō, 50km from Kagoshima, is the hot-spring resort of Ibusuki. It's pretty rundown, and unless you want to stay overnight here before exploring the peninsula, it's best to make a day trip from Kagoshima.

The staff at the JR Ibusuki station information counter have some limited English-language information.

Sand Baths

On the beachfront is Ibusuki's raison d'etre, the Tennen Sunamushi Kaikan Saraku sand baths (¥900, 8.30 am to noon, 1 to 9 pm). You pay at the entrance (the fee includes a

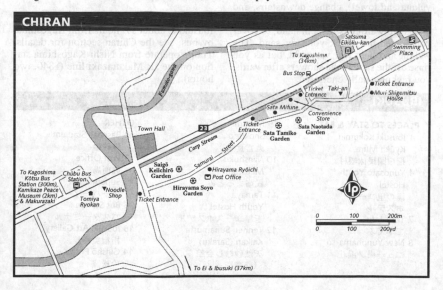

CHIRAN

KYŪSHŪ

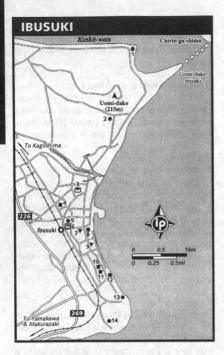

IBUSUKI

Kinkō-wan

Chirin ga-shima

Uomi-dake-misaki

Uomi-dake (215m)

To Kagoshima

226

Ibusuki

To Yamakawa & Makurazaki

269

0   0.5   1km
0   0.25   0.5mi

The sand baths are a 15-minute walk south-east of the station, or a short (¥130) bus ride.

Places to Stay & Eat

Yunosato Youth Hostel (☎ 22-5680) is just north of the station. It has its own hot spring, and rent-a-cycles (¥600 per day). Rooms cost ¥3800, or ¥6000, with two meals. The ryokan-style *Tamaya Youth Hostel (☎ 22-3553)* is near the sand baths. It charges ¥2500/3600 for members/nonmembers.

The Japanese Inn Group's *New Yunohama-sō (☎ 23-3088)* has small tatami rooms for ¥4000/3000 with/without bath. It's just 10 minutes' walk from Ibusuki station in the direction of the beach. The English sign outside announces 'New'. *Minshuku Marutomi (☎ 22-5579)* is a small but popular place, just a stone's throw from the sand baths. It charges ¥7000, with two meals.

Ibusuki is short of decent places to eat. *Marumi Shokudo (☎ 22-3424)*, a short walk east of the station, serves plain, cheap rice dishes (11 am to 9 pm, closed Tuesday). *Tefu-tefu (☎ 24-2258)* is a coffee shop and bar on the seafront (noon to midnight, closed Monday).

Getting There & Away

Ibusuki is about 1½ hours from Kagoshima by bus; see the Chiran section for details. Trains operate from Nishi-Kagoshima station on the JR Makurazaki line (¥840, two hours).

yukata and towel), change downstairs, and wander down to the beach where the burial ladies are waiting, shovel in hand, to cover you in red-hot black volcanic sand. The weight and heat feel very odd, but as you rinse off the sand in the showers afterwards, you feel unusually energised.

IBUSUKI

PLACES TO STAY & EAT

1 Ibusuki Kokumin
   Kyūka Mura
   指宿国民休暇村
4 Yunosato Youth
   Hostel
   湯の里ユース
   ホステル
7 Tefu-tefu
   てふてふ
8 New Yunohama-sō
   ニュー湯ノ浜荘

9 Marumi
   Shokudo
   丸富食堂
10 Minshuku
   Marutomi
   民宿まるとみ
11 Tamaya
   Youth Hostel
   玉屋ユースホステル
12 Tennen Sunamushi
   Kaikan (Saraku)
   天然砂むし会館
   （砂楽）

OTHER

2 Baseball Stadium
   野球場
3 Post Office
   郵便局
5 Supermarket
   スーパーマーケット
6 Bus Station
   バスターミナル
13 Ibusuki Art Gallery
   指宿美術館
14 Ginshō Pottery
   吟松窯

Other Attractions

Ikeda-ko, west of Ibusuki, is a beautiful volcanic caldera lake, inhabited by giant eels that weigh up to 15kg. Heading west along the coast, you come to **Nagasakibana-misaki**, from where the offshore islands, including Iwo-jima, can be seen on a clear day. The beautifully symmetrical 922m cone of **Kaimon-dake** can be climbed in about two hours from the Kaimon-dake bus stop.

At the south-western end of the peninsula is **Makurazaki**, a busy fishing port and the terminus for the train line from Kagoshima. Just beyond Mazurazaki is **Bōnotsu**, a pretty little fishing village that was an unofficial trading link with the outside world via Okinawa during Japan's two centuries of seclusion. North of Bōnotsu is **Fukiage-hama**, where the long beach is used for an annual summer sand-castle construction competition. *Fukiage-hama Youth Hostel* (☎ 292-3455) charges ¥2750 (nonmembers ¥3750).

The southernmost point on the main islands of Japan is marked by the oldest lighthouse in Japan. You can reach **Sata-misaki** from the Kagoshima side of Kinkō-wan either by going around the northern end of the bay, taking the ferry from Kagoshima to Sakurajima or by taking the ferry from Yamakawa, south of Ibusuki, to Nejime, near Sata-misaki. An 8km bicycle track leads down to the end of the cape.

Miyazaki-ken

OBI

Only 5km from the coast, the little castle town of Obi has some interesting buildings around its old castle site. From 1587, the wealthy Ito clan ruled from the castle for 14 generations, surviving the 'one kingdom, one castle' ruling in 1615. The clan eventually moved out in 1869 when the Meiji Restoration ended the feudal period.

Obi-jō

Although only the walls of the actual castle remain, the grounds contain a number of interesting buildings (¥500, including the entrance to Yōshōkan House just outside the castle entrance, 9.30 am to 5 pm).

The castle museum has a collection relating to the Ito clan's long rule over Obi. It includes everything from weapons and armour to clothing and household equipment.

Yōshōkan House When the Obi lord was forced to abandon his castle after the Meiji Restoration, he moved down the hill to the Yōshōkan, formerly the residence of the clan's chief retainer. It stands just outside the castle entrance and has a large garden incorporating Atago-san as 'borrowed scenery'. Beyond this house you enter the castle proper through the impressive gate, Ōte mon.

Matsuo-no-Maru Matsuo-no-Maru, the lord's private residence, has been reconstructed and there's an excellent descriptive leaflet of this quite extensive house. When the lord visited the toilet at the far end of the house, he was accompanied by three pages – one to lead the way, one to carry water for the lord to wash his hands and one to fan him during the summer months. Look for the English sign on the toilet itself that requests 'no urinating'!

Other Attractions

The hall, **Shintoku-dō**, adjacent to the castle, was established as a samurai school in 1801. Up the hill behind Shintoku-dō is the shrine, **Tanoue Hachiman-jinja**, shrouded by trees and reached by a steep flight of steps. On the western side of the river, **Ioshi-jinja** has a pleasant garden and the Ito family mausoleum. The garden, **Chikkō-en**, is on the eastern side of town, near the train station.

Places to Eat

The entranceway to the castle is flanked by *Obi-ten Kura* (9 am to 4 pm) to the right, with upmarket Japanese cooking featuring *sansai* (mountain vegetables), and *Obi-ten Jaya* (9 am to 5 pm) to the left, a friendly and unassuming noodle shop. Featured on the menu of the latter is *tsukimi soba* (literally, 'moon-viewing soba') and curry *udon* (thick, white wheat noodles).

Getting There & Away

The JR Nichinan line runs through Obi and Aoshima to Miyazaki (futsū, ¥820, one hour and 40 minutes, twice hourly). Route 222 from Miyakono-jō to Obi and Nichinan on the coast is a superb mountain road, twisting and winding as it climbs over the hills.

TOI-MISAKI & NICHINAN-KAIGAN 都井岬・日南海岸

Like Sata-misaki, the views over the ocean from Toi-misaki are superb. The cape is also famed for its herds of wild horses, although the word 'wild' has to be treated with some suspicion in Japan. There's a good beach at Ishinami-kaigan where, during the summer only, you can stay in old farmhouse minshuku. The tiny island of Kō-jima, just off the coast, has a group of monkeys that were the focus for some interesting anthropological discoveries. Farther north, the beautiful 50km stretch of coast from Nichinan to Miyazaki offers stunning views, pretty little coves, interesting stretches of 'washboard' rocks and, at holiday times, heavy traffic.

Udo-jingū

The coastal shrine of Udo-jingū is brightly painted in orange and has a wonderful setting. If you continue through the shrine to the end of the path, you'll find yourself in an open cavern overlooking some weird rock formations at the ocean's edge. A popular sport is to buy five round clay pebbles for ¥100 and try to get them into a shallow depression on top of one of the rocks. Succeeding at this task is supposed to make your wish come true. Generally wishes are concerned with marriage and childbirth, most likely because the boulders in front of the cave are said to represent Emperor Jimmu's mother's breasts! Buses connecting Nichinan and Miyazaki Kōtsu bus station stop at the shrine; the fare from Miyazaki to Udo-jingū is ¥1340 (one hour and 20 minutes).

Aoshima 青島
☎ 0985

This popular beach resort, about 10km south of Miyazaki, is a tourist trap famed for the small island covered in betel palms, fringed by washboard rock formations and connected to the mainland by a causeway. Due to the prevailing warm currents, the only place you'll find warmer water in Japan is much farther south in Okinawa.

On the island, a short walk east of the station, is the photogenic **Aoshima-jinja**, scene of two exciting festivals. Around 15 January, loin-cloth wearing locals dive into the ocean, while on 17 June there's another aquatic twist when mikoshi are carried through the shallows to the shrine.

Places to Stay Seven minutes' walk south-east of the station, *Aoshima Youth Hostel (☎ 65-1657)* charges ¥2400/3400 for members/nonmembers. *Aoshima Koku-minshukusha (☎ 65-1533)* has reasonable Japanese-style rooms from ¥7000, with two meals.

Getting There & Away Aoshima is on the JR Nichinan-Miyazaki line, a short hop from JR Miyazaki station (¥310, 25 minutes).

MIYAZAKI 宮崎
☎ 0985 • pop 290,000

Miyazaki is a reasonably large city with an important shrine and a pleasant park. Due to the warm offshore currents, the town has a balmy climate (much touted in tourist literature). The area around Miyazaki played an important part in early Japanese civilisation and some interesting excavations can be seen at Saitobaru, 27km north.

Orientation & Information

JR Miyazaki station is immediately east of the town centre. Most hotels (including the upmarket riverside ones) and the youth hostel are reasonably close to the station. The main bus station is south of the Ōyodo-gawa; the town's two principal attractions – Miyazaki-jingū and Heiwadai-kōen – are several kilometres north.

The tourist information office (☎ 22-6469) is next to JR Miyazaki station and can help find accommodation (9 am to 5 pm). English is spoken. Make sure you get the excellent *Relax and Enjoy Miyazaki* pamphlet. More-detailed information is available from the Prefectural International Centre (☎ 32-8457) on the 6th floor of the Higashi-Bekkan next to the Ken-chō Prefectural Office. It has CNN and English-language newspapers and is open from 8.30 am to 6.15 pm (closed weekends).

Money There's an ATM that accepts Visa, MasterCard and Cirrus in the Friesta shopping complex inside Miyazaki station (8.30 am to 11 pm).

Post The central post office is on the north side of Takachiho-dōri, diagonally opposite the Yamakataya department store.

Email & Internet Access NTT's Multimedia 21, on Takachiho-dōri, has Net access (free, 9 am to 4 pm, closed weekends), as does the Hotel Meridian's 3rd floor business centre (¥200 for 30 minutes).

Miyazaki-jingū & Museum

Miyazaki-jinja is dedicated to the Emperor Jimmu, the semimythical first emperor of Japan and founder of the Yamoto court. At the northern end of the shrine grounds is Miyazaki Prefectural Museum (¥200, 9 am to 4.30 pm, closed Monday), with displays relating to local history and archaeological finds. Also worth a look is Minka-en, with its four traditional-style Kyūshū homes (free, closed Monday).

The shrine is about 2.5km north of JR Miyazaki station or a 15-minute walk from Miyazaki-jingū station, one stop north. The shrine is easy to find. Just look for the big torii gate. Bus No 1 also runs to the shrine.

Heiwadai-kōen

Heiwadai-kōen (Peace Park) has as its centrepiece a 36m-high tower constructed in 1940, a time when peace in Japan was about to disappear. Standing in front of the tower and clapping your hands produces a strange echo.

Haniwa Garden in the park is dotted with reproductions of the curious clay *haniwa* (tomb guardians) that have been excavated from Saitobaru burial mounds. You can buy examples of these often rather amusing figures from a shop in the Haniwa Garden or from the park's main shopping complex. Small figures cost as little as ¥800 but the large ones cost up to ¥20,000.

Haniwa Garden is about 1.5km north of Miyazaki-jingū. Bus No 8 runs to the park from outside JR Miyazaki station (¥270).

Special Events

On 3 April there is a samurai horse riding event at Miyazaki-jingū. Mid-April's Furusato Matsuri has around 10,000 participants in traditional attire dancing to local folk songs on Tachibana-dōri. A similar event takes place in late July, with mikoshi being carried through the streets. In late July, Miyazaki is host to Kyūshū's largest fireworks show. Most locals seem to rate the Dunlop Phoenix Golf Tournament in mid-November as the major event of the year.

Places to Stay – Budget

Fujin Kaikan Youth Hostel (☎ 24-5785) is 15 minutes' walk south-west of Miyazaki station. There are only 26 beds, so it is wise to book ahead. It charges ¥2500/3500 for members/nonmembers.

The quiet and rather old *Tsurutomi-sō (☎ 22-3072)* is the only minshuku accommodation in central Miyazaki. It has just 12 rooms and a communal bath. It's off the busy shopping arcade just west of the station (from ¥3500).

Places to Stay – Mid-Range & Top End

Across the road from the station, *Miyazaki Oriental Hotel (☎ 27-3111)* is a straightforward business hotel with singles from ¥5900 and twins/doubles from ¥10,800.

Hotel Kensington (☎ 20-5500) is a cut above the average business hotel, with singles for ¥8300. It's centrally located on Tachibana-dōri. The aging *Hotel Bigman (☎ 27-2111)* – what a great name! – is farther west along the road from the youth hostel. Singles/doubles cost from ¥5400/9000.

The *Miyazaki Washington Hotel (☎ 28-9111)* has rooms from ¥6930/13,000 and is right in the middle of the entertainment area. On the riverside between Tachibana-bashi

KYŪSHŪ

MIYAZAKI STATION AREA

To Miyazaki-jingū,
Miyazaki Prefectural
Museum, Seagaia &
Heiwadai-kōen

To Saitobaru
& Beppu

Takachiho-dōri

Shopping Arcade

Miyazaki

Entertainment &
Restaurant Area

Miyazaki Eigyōsho
Bus Centre

Tachibana-dōri (Route 220)

Segashira-dōri

Nippō Line

Ōyodo-gawa

Tachibana-hashi

To Aoshima
& Nichinan

To Phoenix Hotel (100m),
Ōyodo-ōhashi (200m) &
Miyazaki Kōtsū Bus Station

0   100   200 m
0   100   200 yd

and Ōyodo-ōhashi are the *Miyazaki Kankō Hotel* (☎ *27-1212*), with singles/twins for ¥7000/11,000 and *Miyazaki Plaza Hotel* (☎ *27-1111*), with singles/twins from ¥8000/16,000.

Places to Eat

Suginoko (☎ *22-5798*) specialises in Miyazaki cuisine (11.30 am to 2 pm, 4 to 11 pm, closed Sunday). There is a brief menu in English posted downstairs. The lunchtime Kuroshio-teishoku (varying day to day) is ¥1000. At night teishoku cost from ¥4000. *Sai-en* (☎ *28-5638*) serves organic vegetarian cuisine and is open from 11.30 am to 2.30 pm and 5 to 9 pm. Teishoku cost ¥700. Sai-en in the small street full of boutiques east of Tachibana-dōri, and there's an English-language menu.

In the heart of the entertainment district, look out for *Meiji-ya* (☎ *22-6225*), a lively and inexpensive izakaya with a locomotive exterior. You'll hear it as you come down the street; speakers outside the restaurant blast out the puffing and whistling sounds of a labouring steam train.

Nearby is *Den Den*, a classy restaurant specialising in *kushiage* (deep-fried seafood

MIYAZAKI STATION AREA

PLACES TO STAY
5 Hotel Kensington
　ケンジントンホテル宮崎
9 Miyazaki Oriental Hotel
　宮崎オリエンタルホテル
10 Tsrutomi-sō
　鶴富荘
11 Business Hotel Family
　ビジネスホテル
　ファミリー
20 Miyazaki Washington
　Hotel
　宮崎ワシントンホテル
21 Hotel Meridian
　ホテルメリディアン
26 Fujin Kaikan Youth Hostel
　婦人会館ユースホステル
27 Hotel Bigman
　ホテルビッグマン
29 Miyazaki Plaza Hotel
　宮崎プラザホテル

30 Miyazaki Kankō Hotel
　宮崎観光ホテル

PLACES TO EAT
4 Italian Tomato
　Restaurant
12 Sai-en
　菜苑
13 Mr Donut
14 Tommy's
16 Meiji-ya
　明治屋
18 Den Den
　でんでん
22 Mos Burgers
23 Suginoko
　杉の子

OTHER
1 Main Post Office
　中央郵便局

2 Yamakataya
　Department Store
　山形屋
3 ANA; JAS
6 NTT Multimedia 21
　マルチメディア２１
7 Tourist Information
　Office
　観光案内所
8 ATM
15 Cannabis
17 Suntory Shot Bar;
　Time
19 Beat Clap
24 Prefectural Office
　宮崎県庁
25 Prefectural International
　Centre
28 Miyazaki City
　Office
　宮崎市役所

on skewers) that isn't as expensive as it looks. *Tommy's* is an American diner – in other words, it may be OK for a watery beer and a hamburger.

The riverside *Phoenix Hotel* has a rooftop beer garden in the summer months, with good views over the city. The Miyazaki station is known for its *shiitake ekiben*, a boxed lunch featuring mushroom.

Entertainment

Locals claim that Miyazaki has some 3500 bars. For a quiet, inexpensive beer, head over to *Suntory Shot Bar*, where a draught beer costs ¥380. The master-san speaks some English – ask him for his 'special'. *Cannabis* (9 am to 5 am) is a laid back reggae bar near the Ichibangai arcade. Great name, but don't get your hopes up. Every Saturday night the locals congregate at the barn-like club *Beat Clap* (¥1000, with one free drink).

Getting There & Away

Air Miyazaki is connected with Tokyo (¥27,050), Osaka (¥16,950), Okinawa (¥22,850) and other centres by air.

Bus Most buses originate at the Miyazaki Kōtsū city bus station south of the Oyodo-gawa in Miya-ko, near JR Minami-Miyazaki station. There is another bus station opposite Miyazaki station, which has buses to Saito-baru. Bus No 10 heads down the coast to Aoshima and Nichinan, and the Toi-misaki Express heads for Toi-misaki.

Long-distance buses (reservations ☎ 282-8851) go to Kagoshima (¥4900, 2½ hours) and Fukuoka (¥6000, 4½ hours) Buses also go to Ebino-kōgen in the Kirishima National Park (two hours and 15 minutes).

Many buses run along Tachibana-dōri, but if you don't read Japanese you're better off heading down to the south bus station.

Train The JR Nippō line runs up to Beppu (tokkyū, ¥5770, three hours) and down to Kagoshima (tokkyū, ¥3790, two hours) in the west. There are also train connections to Kumamoto (tokkyū, ¥5460, 4½ hours), Fukuoka/Hakata (tokkyū, ¥9460, six hours) and south through Obi to Nichinan.

Boat There are ferry services linking Miyazaki with Osaka (2nd class ¥8380, 16½ hours). For reservations contact Marine Express (Miyazaki ☎ 29-8311, Osaka ☎ 06-6616-4661).

Getting Around

To/From the Airport Miyazaki's airport is reached by bus from JR Miyazaki station (¥400, 25 minutes, three hourly).

Bus Although bus services start and finish at the Miya-kō bus station near JR Minami-Miyazaki station, many run along Tachibana-dōri in the centre, including Nos 1 and 2 to the Miyazaki-jingū and No 8 to Heiwadai-kōen. Miyazaki-Eigyosho, the other bus station, is near JR Miyazaki station.

Tours from the Miya-kō city bus station (around ¥5000) are operated by the Miyazaki Kōtsū bus company and cover not only the sights in town but sights along the coast to Aoshima and the Udo-jingū.

SEAGAIA シーガイヤ

The Seagaia Ocean Dome (¥4200, 9 am to 10 pm) is a miraculous thing – a kind of *Brave New World* water amusement park. It is certainly not, as the hype puts it, a 'paradise within a paradise', but the idea of putting a 140m white-sand beach and a splash of ocean under a huge dome is mind-boggling. Is putting it next to the *real* ocean a beautiful stroke of irony or a bitter reflection of our times?

Buses run from JR Miyazaki station (¥470, 25 minutes).

SAITOBARU 西都原
☎ 0983

If the haniwa pottery figures in Miyazaki piqued your interest in the region's archaeology, then head north 27km to the **Saitobaru Burial Mounds Park**, where several square kilometres of fields and forest are dotted with over 300 *kofun* (burial mounds). The mounds, dating from AD 300 to 600, range from insignificant little bumps to hillocks large enough to appear as natural creations. They also vary in shape, as do burial mounds in Korea, although Japanese scholars are reluctant to admit it. There's an interesting small mu-

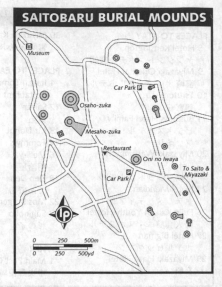

seum (¥200, 9 am to 4.30 pm, closed Monday) with displays about the burial mounds and archaeological finds that have been made, including swords, armour, jewellery, haniwa pottery figures and much more. Another exhibit shows items from the 18th century Edo period.

The park area is always open. Buses run to Saitobaru from Miyazaki station (¥950, one hour). If you want to explore the mound-dotted countryside you'll need your own transport, or you should plan to walk a lot.

Saitobaru is just outside the town of Saito, where the unique Usudaiko dance festival, with drummers wearing odd pole-like headgear, takes place in early September. The equally bizarre and mysterious **Shiromi Kagura** performances are on 14 and 15 December (☎ 43-1111).

TAKACHIHO 高千穂
☎ 0982 • pop 16,143

The mountain resort town of Takachiho is about midway between Nobeoka on the coast and Aso-san in the centre of Kyūshū. It's famed for its beautiful gorge and for a number of interesting shrines. There's a

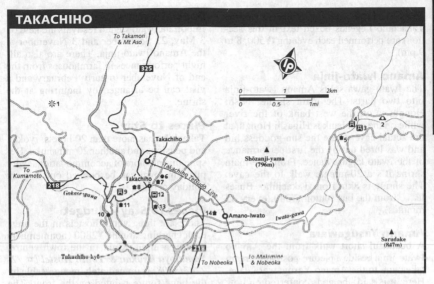

TAKACHIHO

tourist information counter (which was disastrously inept when we visited) by the tiny train station (☎ 72-4680), open 8.30 am to 5 pm.

Takachiho-kyō

Takachiho's beautiful gorge, with its waterfalls, overhanging rocks and sheer walls, is the town's major attraction. There's a 1km

walk alongside the gorge, or you can inspect it from below in a rowboat (a bit pricey at ¥1000 for 40 minutes). The gorge is about 2km from the centre (about ¥800 by taxi). You can walk it in just over half an hour.

Takachiho-jinja

Takachiho-jinja, about 1km from JR Takachiho station, is set in a grove of cryptomeria

TAKACHIHO

PLACES TO STAY
5 Iwato Furusato
  Youth Hostel
  岩戸ふるさと
  ユースホステル
7 Business Hotel Kanaya
  かなやホテル
8 Yamatoya Ryokan &
  Youth Hostel
  旅館大和屋/
  ユースホステル
11 Kokuminshukusha
  Takachiho-sō
  国民宿舎高千穂荘

13 Folkcraft Ryokan
  Kaminoya
  民芸旅館上ノ屋
14 Takachiho Youth
  Hostel
  高千穂ユース
  ホステル

OTHER
1 Kunimigaoka
  Lookout
  国見が丘
2 Amano Yasugawara
  Cave
  天安河原

3 Amano Iwato-jinja
  Higashi Hongū
  天岩戸神社東本宮
4 Amano Iwato-jinja
  Nishi Hongū
  大岩戸神社西本宮
6 City Hall
  市役所
9 Takachiho-jinja
  高千穂神社
10 Takachiho-kyō-bashi
  高千穂峡橋
12 Bus Station
  バスターミナル

pines. The local *iwato kagura* dances (see the Takachiho Legends boxed text in this section) are performed each evening (¥500, 8 to 9 pm).

Amano Iwato-jinja

The Iwato-gawa splits Amano Iwato-jinja into two parts. The main shrine, Nishi Hongū, is on the west bank of the river while on the east bank is Higashi Hongū, at the actual cave where the sun goddess hid and was lured out by the first performance of the *iwato kagura* dance. From the main shrine it's a 20-minute walk to the cave. The shrine is 8km from Takachiho. Buses leave from the bus station (¥340, every 45 minutes).

Amano Yasugawara

A beautiful short walk from the Amano Iwato-jinja beside a picture-postcard stream takes you to the Amano Yasugawara cave. Here, it is said, the gods conferred on how they could persuade the sun goddess to leave her hiding place and thus bring light back to the world. Visitors pile stones into small cairns around the cave entrance.

Takachiho Legends

Ninigi-no-mikoto, a descendant of the sun goddess Amaterasu, is said to have made landfall in Japan on top of the legendary mountain Takachiho-yama in southern Kyūshū. Or at least that's what's said in most of Japan; in Takachiho the residents insist that it was in their town that the sun goddess' grandson arrived, not atop the mountain of the same name.

The residents also lay claim to the sites for a few other important mythological events, including Ama-no-Iwato, or the boulder door of heaven. Here Amaterasu hid and night fell across the world. To lure her out, another goddess performed a dance so comically lewd that the sun goddess was soon forced to emerge from hiding to find out what was happening. That dance, the *iwato kagura*, is still performed in Takachiho today.

Special Events

Important iwato kagura festivals are held on 3 May, 23 September and 3 November at the Amano Iwato-jinja. There are also all-night performances in farmhouses from the end of November to early February and a visit can be arranged by inquiring at the shrine.

Places to Stay

Takachiho has more than 20 hotels, ryokan and pensions and another 20 minshuku. Despite this plethora of accommodation, every place in town can be booked out in peak holiday periods.

Places to Stay – Budget

There are three youth hostels in the area, each charging around ¥2800 (nonmembers ¥3800) a night. Right in the town centre, *Yamatoya Ryokan & Youth Hostel* (☎ 72-2243/3808) is immediately recognisable by the huge figure painted on the front. The owner speaks English, and he'll pick you up if you call in advance. *Takachiho Youth Hostel* (☎ 72-5192) is a couple of kilometres from the centre, near the JR Amano-Iwato station. *Iwato Furusato Youth Hostel* (☎ 74-8750) is near Amano Iwato-jinja.

Places to Stay – Mid-Range & Top End

The Japanese Inn group's *Folkcraft Ryokan Kaminoya* (☎ 72-2111) is just down from the bus station, right in the centre of Takachiho. The friendly owner speaks English well, and will also pick you up. Rooms cost from ¥4000, or from ¥6500 with two meals.

Business Hotel Kanaya (☎ 72-3261) is on the corner of the station road and the main road through town (from ¥5000). The ryokan part of *Yamatoya Ryokan & Youth Hostel* charges from ¥9500, with meals. *Iwato Furusato Youth Hostel* also has a ryokan section.

The minshuku all cost from about ¥5500 a night. A reliable one is *Kokuminshukusha Takachiho-sō* (☎ 72-3255), charging ¥6850 with two meals.

Places to Eat

Many visitors just eat at their ryokan or minshuku, but Takachiho has plenty of restaurants. Opposite the Folkcraft ryokan is *Kenchan* (5 pm to midnight, closed Sunday), a cheerful *yakitori* shop. Look out for the cave people cartoon. The yakitori (expect to spend ¥3000, with drinks) is nothing short of fabulous.

Getting There & Away

The private Takachiho Tetsudō line runs inland from Nobeoka on the coast (¥1300, just over 1½ hours). Alternatively, there are bus services to Takachiho from Kumamoto (¥2300, two hours and 40 minutes), from Fukuoka (¥3910, 3½ hours), from Nobeoka (¥1650, 1½ hours) or from Takamori (¥1280, less than an hour) near Aso-san.

Getting Around

Although you can walk to the gorge and Takachiho-jinja, the other sites are some distance from town and public transport is a problem. Regular tours leave from the bus station: the 'A Course' (¥1100) covers everything, while the 'B Course' (¥750) misses the Amano Iwato-jinja.

Ōita-ken 大分県

Ōita-ken offers Japanese onsen mania, Beppu and the once-lovely town of Yufuin. The region also bears some traces of Japan's earliest civilisations, particularly on Kunisaki-hantō and around Usuki.

BEPPU 別府

☎ 0977 • pop 125,667

At first glance, Beppu seems to be the Las Vegas of spa resort towns, a place where bad taste is almost a requisite. The secret, just as in Las Vegas, is to enjoy the kitsch and have a good time – and then get down to the serious business of bathing. Beppu's waters are first class: a sand bath to rival Ibusuki's and, best of all, hidden around the city are several wonderful hidden springs that tourists have yet to discover.

Information

In the north-east corner of JR Beppu station, housed in the Kita-Meitengai (a department store specialising in tourist goodies), is the wonderful Foreign Tourist Information Office (☎ 23-1119), open from 9 am to 5 pm. The helpful English-speaking personnel have assembled an arsenal of English-language information on Beppu and its environs, and will happily recommend accommodation, itineraries and more. Don't confuse this with the tourist information counter (☎ 24-2838) in the main station concourse, which mainly provides information in Japanese (9 am to 5 pm).

Beppu is a sprawling town and the hot-spring areas are spread out, often some distance from the town centre. The adjacent town of Ōita is virtually contiguous with Beppu, and although it lacks any notable attractions, it could be an alternative place to stay. The Hells, though mildly interesting, shouldn't distract you from the *real* hot springs.

Money There is no international ATM. The Beppu branch of the Ōita Mirai Bank will advance money on credit cards upon presentation of passport ID, at its Ekimae branch just east of the station (9 am to 3 pm, closed weekends).

Post The most convenient post office is on Ekimae-dōri next to the Cosmopia shopping centre.

Email & Internet Access NTT has free Internet access (9 am to 4 pm, closed weekends) at its branch 300m west of Beppu station.

Hot Springs

Beppu has two types of hot springs, and they pump out more than 100 million litres of hot water every day. *Jigoku* (hells) are hot springs for looking at. Onsen are hot springs for bathing in.

The Hells Beppu's most hyped attraction is the 'hells' or jigoku, a collection of hot springs where the water bubbles forth from

KYŪSHŪ

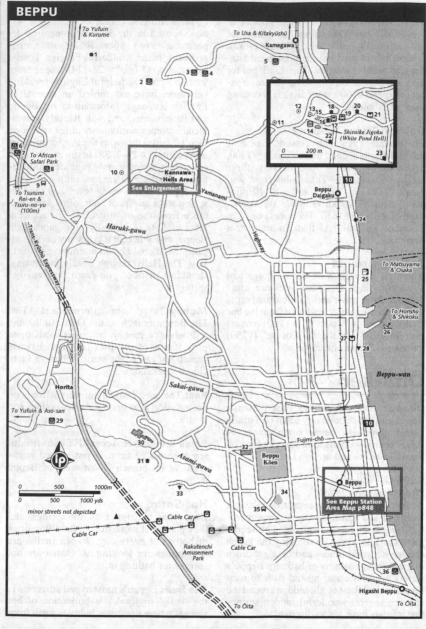

BEPPU

To Yufuin
& Kurume

● 1

To Usa & Kitakyūshū

Kamegawa

5

3 ● 4

2

12

13 15 18 20
● 11 16 17 19 21
14
22   Shiraike Jigoku
(White Pond Hell)
0   200 m   23

6
7   To African
8   Safari Park

9

10 ●
Kannawa
Hells Area
See Enlargement

Yamanami

Beppu
Daigaku

10

To Tsurumi
Rei-en &
Tsuru-no-yu
(100m)

Trans-Kyūshū Expressway

Haruki-gawa

Highway

24

To Matsuyama
& Osaka

25

To Honshū
& Shikoku

26

27   28

Beppu-wan

Horita

Sakai-gawa

To Yufuin & Aso-san

29

30

31

Asami-gawa

Fujimi-chō

32
Beppu
Kōen

34

35

Beppu

See Beppu Station
Area Map p848

10

0   500   1000m
0   500   1000 yds

minor streets not depicted

33

Cable Car

Cable Car

Cable Car

Rakutenchi
Amusement
Park

36

Higashi Beppu

To Ōita

To Ōita

BEPPU

PLACES TO STAY
16 Hotel Ashiya
   ホテルあしや
18 Rakurakuen
   Ryokan
   楽々園旅館
20 Minshuku
   Sakaeya
   民宿さかえや
22 Ōishi Hotel
   大石ホテル
23 Hyōhotan Onsen
   ひょうたん温泉
30 Suginoi Palace Hotel
   杉乃井パレス
31 Beppu Youth Hostel
   別府ユースホステル

PLACES TO EAT
28 Sunday's Sun
   Steakhouse
33 Ichinoide Kaikan

OTHER
1 Ritsumeikan Asia Pacific
   University
   立命館アジア
   太平洋大学
2 Shibaseki Onsen Area
   柴石温泉

3 Chinoike Jigoku
   (Blood Hell Pool)
   血の池地獄
4 Tatsumaki Jigoku
   (Waterspout Hell)
   竜巻地獄
5 Kamegawa
   Onsen Area
   亀川温泉
6 Myōban Onsen Area
   みょうばん温泉
7 Kakuju-sen
8 Onsen Hoyōland
   温泉保養ランド
9 Tsurumi Rei-en
   Bus Stop
   鶴見霊園バス停
10 Umi Jigoku (Sea Hell)
   海地獄
11 Yama Jigoku
   (Mountain Hell)
   山地獄
12 Kamado Jigoku
   (Oven Hell)
   かまど地獄
13 Oniyama Jigoku
   (Devil's Mountain Hell)
   鬼山地獄
14 Hihōkan Sex Museum

15 Kinryū Jigoku
   (Golden Dragon Hell)
   金龍地獄
17 Kamenoi Bus Station
   (Buses to Chinoike
   Jigoku)
   亀の井バスターミナル
   (至血の池地獄)
19 Kamenoi Bus Station
   (Buses to Beppu Station)
   亀の井バスターミナル
   (至別府駅)
21 Post Office
   郵便局
24 Shōnin-ga-hawa
   Sand Bath
   ト人ヶ浜
25 Ferry Terminal
   フェリー乗り場
26 SS Oriana
27 Main Post Office
   中央郵便局
29 Mugen-no-sato
32 B-Con Plaza
34 Baseball Stadium
   野球場
35 Kakū-jō Mae Bus Stop
36 Hamawaki Onsen Area
   浜脇温泉

underground, often with unusual results. Admission to each hell is ¥400 (a ¥2000 coupon covers all except one). Unless you like overflowing car parks and psychotically enthusiastic, flag-waving tour guides, you won't want to see them all.

The hells are in two groups – seven at Kannawa, about 4½km north-west of the station, and two more several kilometres away. In the Kannawa group, **Umi Jigoku** (Sea Hell), with its large expanse of gently steaming blue water, and **Shiraike Jigoku** (White Pond Hell) are worth a look. **Kinryū Jigoku** (Golden Dragon Hell) and **Kamado Jigoku** (Oven Hell) have dragon and demon figures overlooking the pond. Skip **Oniyama Jigoku** (Devil's Mountain Hell), where crocodiles are kept in miserable concrete pens, and **Yama Jigoku** (Mountain

Hell), where a variety of animals are kept under very bad conditions.

The smaller pair has **Chinoike Jigoku** (Blood Pool Hell), with its photogenically red water, and **Tatsumaki Jigoku** (Waterspout Hell), where a geyser performs regularly. The former is worth a visit, but the latter can be skipped (too much concrete, too little natural beauty). The final hell, and the one not included in the group's admission ticket, is **Hon Bōzu Jigoku** (Monk's Hell). It has a collection of hiccupping and belching hot-mud pools and is up the long hill from the main group of hells.

From the bus stop at JR Beppu station, bus Nos 16, 17, 41 and 43 go to the main group of hells at Kannawa. There are half a dozen buses an hour but the round trip costs virtually the same as an unlimited travel day pass. The No 26 bus continues to the smaller Chinoike/Tatsumaki pair and returns to the station in a loop.

Jigoku tour buses regularly depart from the JR Beppu station (¥4500, including admission).

Onsen Scattered around the town are eight onsen areas. Onsen enthusiasts spend their time in Beppu moving from one bath to another – experts consider at least three baths a day 'de rigeur'. Costs range from ¥60 to ¥600, though many (and two of the best) are free. Bring your own soap and towel. Try to pick up the excellent *Beppu Hot Spring Guide* from the Foreign Tourist Information Office, which explains how and where to bathe, and about the springs' health-giving properties.

The Beppu onsen area is in the town centre near JR Beppu station. **Takegawara Onsen** (¥60, sand-bath ¥630, 6.30 am to 11.30 pm) dates from the Meiji era and has a relaxing sand bath. You lie down in a shallow trench and are buried up to your neck in the Onsen-heated sand. There's a good English-language pamphlet.

In the south-eastern part of town, near the road to Ōita, is the **Hamawaki onsen area**, with the popular old Hamawaki Koto Bath (¥60, 6.30 am to 1 am). North of the town, in the **Kannawa onsen area**, near the major group of hells, is the quaint Mushiyu steam bath (¥150, 6.30 am to 8 pm). There are also many ryokan and minshuku in Kannawa.

The newly rebuilt **Shibaseki onsen** is near the smaller pair of hells. In addition to the communal baths (¥100, 7 am to 8 pm), you can rent a private *kazoku-buro* (family bath/couples bath) for ¥1050 (one hour). Also north of JR Beppu station, near Kamegawa station, is the **Kamegawa onsen area**, where the Hamada bath (¥50, 7 am to 11.30 pm) is particularly popular. The outdoor **Shōnin-ga-hama sand bath** (¥630, 9 am to 5 pm, to 4 pm November to March) is 2km south of the Kamegawa onsen area.

In the hills north-west of the town centre is the **Myōban onsen area**, where the Kakuju-sen bath (7 am to 8 pm) is free. Nearby Onsen Hoyōland (¥1050, 8.30 am to 8 pm) has wonderful giant mud baths. Bring a camera for some fun holiday snaps.

Hidden Baths

Tsuru-no-yu & Hebin-no-yu Beppu has a number of wonderful baths, tucked away out of the public eye. Locals built and maintain Tsuru-no-yu, a lovely free rotemburo up on the edge of Ogi-yama. During July and August only, a natural stream emerges to form the milky blue bath. Take a bus to Tsurumi Rei-en bus stop (40 minutes northwest from Beppu station). Turn left by the small flower shop and hike uphill till you come to **Tsurumi Rei-en** cemetery. Walk up the small road that hugs the right side of the graveyard until the road ends. Dive into the bushes to your left, and there's the bath. You could overnight in the shelter here, if you've a sleeping bag. Higher in the mountain greenery is another free rotemburo, the 'Snake Bath', Hebin-no-yu. It's impossible to describe the trail up from Tsuru-no-yu; ask another bather.

Mugen-no-Sato This is a collection of privately available small rotembura – ideal for a romantic, secluded dip. Ask for a kazoku-buro (¥500, 8 am to 10 pm). Take a bus up past Suginoi Palace Hotel to Horita. Mugen-no-sato is five minutes' walk west.

Ichinoide Kaikan This must be a first – a bath in a bentō shop! The owner of *Ichinoide Kaikan* (☎ 21-4728) is a commercial caterer, but he's also an onsen fanatic, so much so that he built three pool-sized rotemburo in his back yard. You can swim lengths, and the view, overlooking Beppu and the bay, is the city's finest. Bathing is free when you order a bentō (¥1000). The chefs prepare it while you swim. To get there, take a bus to Yakyū-jō-mae, walk 100m farther along the main road until you reach the Joyful 24-hour restaurant. Take the narrow road on the right of the restaurant and walk up, and up…and up, for about thirty minutes. A taxi (about ¥800) might be a good investment.

Hihōkan Sex Museum

Given all that sybaritic bathing, a sex museum (¥1000, 9 am to 11 pm) seems just the thing for Beppu. It's in among the Kannawa hells. Inside you'll find a bizarre collection ranging from 'positions' models and illustrations to a large collection of wooden phalluses (some very large indeed). Erotic art on display ranges from Papua New Guinean fertility figures to Tibetan Tantric figures. As you exit through a sex shop, the sales ladies (not one of them under 70) rather disconcertingly peddle the latest in vibrator technology.

Ritsumeikan Asia-Pacific University

At the time of writing, the Kyoto-based Ritsumeikan is scheduled to open its landmark college in Beppu, with more than 60% of its undergraduates drawn from other parts of Asia – a unique situation in Japan. The college is strongly supported by the city and Ōita-ken, so many of the college events will be open to the casual visitor – as will the subsidised cafeterias.

The campus overlooks the city in Jumonji-baru.

Places to Stay

Although places to stay are scattered around Beppu, they are concentrated around the south-west of town (Suginoi Palace Hotel area), around JR Beppu station and in the Kannawa hot-springs area.

Places to Stay – Budget

Beppu Youth Hostel (☎ 23-4116) is very close to Suginoi Palace Hotel, and charges ¥3000 (nonmembers ¥4000). Take a No 4 bus from Beppu station's west exit (25 minutes, hourly) or a No 14 from the station's east exit to Kankaiji-bashi (25 minutes, every 30 minutes). It's a two-minute walk to the hostel.

Shinki-ya (☎ 67-8026) in the Kannawa Jigoku area is a clean, homely place with 14 tatami rooms. It costs ¥3000 per person.

Minshuku Kokage (☎ 23-1753), a member of the Japanese Inn group, is just a few minutes walk from Beppu station. Rooms

cost from ¥3300. It's a particularly friendly minshuku, used to dealing with the vagaries of gaijin clients. There's a spacious bath downstairs and a laundry (¥100).

Places to Stay – Mid-Range & Top End

If the Kokage is full, just around the corner is the slightly down-at-heel *Kiyomizu-sō* (☎ 23-0221), with rooms from ¥4000.

Business Hotel Star (☎ 25-1188), with singles/doubles for ¥4000/7000, is right behind JR Beppu station and has very basic rooms. *Beppu Dai Ichi Hotel* (☎ 24-6311) has rooms for ¥4500/8500. About 200m south of the station, *Kamenoi Hotel* (☎ 22-3301) is excellent value at ¥5500, with breakfast, and is far more comfortable than the average business hotel.

New Hayashiya Hotel (☎ 24-5252), charging ¥3900/8400, and the *Green Hotel* (☎ 25-2244), charging ¥4725/8400 for singles/twins, are for emergency only.

Friendly *Nogami Honkan* (☎ 22-1334) is great value at ¥4500, or ¥8000 with two meals. It's near the Takegawara sand bath, and has a rotemburo. English is spoken.

There are a number of minshuku and ryokan around the Kannawa hot springs. Close to the Kannawa jigoku is *Rakurakuen Ryokan* (☎ 67-2682), which has a mixed and a women-only rotemburo (from ¥4500, or ¥6500 with two meals). Down the road from the jigoku, behind the small post office, is the tasteful *Minshuku Sakaeya* (☎ 66-6234), charging ¥4500, or ¥8000 with two meals. This popular traditional minshuku uses the heat from the local hot spring to prepare meals.

The huge *Suginoi Palace Hotel* (☎ 24-1141), priced from ¥15,000, overlooks Beppu from its hillside location but you'll pay for the view.

Places to Eat

Beppu is renowned for its freshwater fish, for its *fugu* (globefish) and for the wild vegetables grown in the mountains farther inland. If you're game for the fugu experience, you can do it in style at *Fugu Matsu* (☎ 21-1717). Expect to pay from ¥3000.

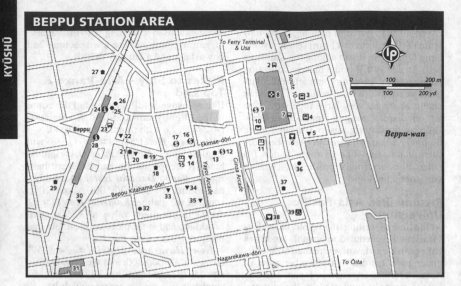

BEPPU STATION AREA

The *Jūtoku-ya* izakaya is close to the station and has an enormous range of dishes on its illustrated menu, all at very reasonable prices. It's also a good place for a couple of beers with snacks. The area around Minshuku Kokage is good for yakitori restaurants; most of them have dishes ranging from ¥200 to ¥400. *Ureshi-ya* (5.30 pm to 2 am, closed Friday) is a very popular *shokudō* (budget eatery) with donburi and noodles for around ¥700. *Kuishinbō* (☎ 21-0788) is a cheerful izakaya serving yakitori and sashimi (5 to 11 pm, closed first and third Tuesday of each month). The *katsuo tataki* (lightly grilled bonito fish) at ¥600 is a steal.

In the Yayoi arcade, *Ristorante Yayoi* (6 to 11 pm) is a collection of cafe-style street stalls serving Chinese, Italian, Japanese and Thai dishes. None cost more than ¥650. *Marui Shokudō* is a good place for inexpensive tonkatsu and *katsudon* (pork cutlet dishes).

Entertainment

Beppu's cool crowd hang out at *Speakeasy* (☎ 21-8116), a friendly shot-bar down a back alley near Takegawara onsen. Beers are from ¥500, and it's open from 8.30 pm to 3 am (closed Tuesday).

Getting There & Away

Air There are flights to Ōita airport from Tokyo, Osaka, Nagoya, Kagoshima and Okinawa. It's even possible to fly direct to Seoul.

Bus Beppu to Aso-san takes about three hours (note the routing affects price – the Kuju-go bus is ¥2950, the Aso-go/Ya-manami-go ¥3950). It's another hour from Aso-san to Kumamoto.

Train The JR Nippō line runs from Fukuoka/Hakata, via Kokura, to Beppu (tokkyū, ¥5750, 2½ hours). The line continues on down the coast to Miyazaki (tokkyū, ¥5770, three hours). The JR Hōhi line runs from Beppu to Kumamoto (¥4830, 3½ hours) via Aso-san (¥3440, 2½ hours).

Boat The Kansai Kisen ferry service (☎ 22-1311) does a daily run between Beppu and Osaka (¥7030, 17 hours), stopping en route at Kōbe (¥7030, 14 to 15 hours) and at

BEPPU STATION AREA

PLACES TO STAY
13 Green Hotel
グリーンホテル
18 Minshuku Kokage
民宿こかげ
19 Kiyomizu-sō
清水荘
21 New Hayashi Hotel
ニューハヤシホテル
27 Beppu Dai-Ichi Hotel
別府第一ホテル
29 Business Hotel
Kagetsu
ビジネスホテル花月
31 Kamenoi Hotel
亀の井ホテル
37 Nogami Honkan
野上本館

PLACES TO EAT
5 Royal Host Restaurant
14 Marui Shokudō
まるい食堂
20 Jūtoku-ya
十德屋
22 Bentō Shop
吉四六弁当
30 KFC

33 Ureshi-ya
うれしや
34 Kuishinbō
くいしん坊
35 Ristorante Yayoi
リストランテやよい

OTHER
1 Beppu Tower
別府タワー
2 Airport Bus Stop
空港バス停
3 Kamenoi Bus Station
亀の井バス停
4 Kitahama Bus Station
北浜バス停
6 Robata & Beer Pub
ろばたやきビアパブ
7 Bus Stop for Fukuoka
福岡行きバス停
8 Cosmopia Shopping
Centre; Tokiwa
Department Store
コスモピア；常盤百貨店
9 Ōita Bank
大分銀行
10 Post Office
郵便局

11 Cinema
映画館
12 Fukuoka City Bank
福岡市銀行
15 Scala-za Cinema
スカラ座
16 Beppu Shinyo Bank
別府信用金庫
17 Iyo Bank
伊予銀行
23 Beppu Station Bus Stop
別府駅バス停
24 Foreign Tourist
Information Office
外国人旅行者
観光案内所
25 JR Rent-a-Car
JRレンタカー
26 Car Rental Office
駅前レンタカー
28 Tourist Information
Counter
観光案内所
32 Laundry
36 JTB
38 Speakeasy
39 Takegawara Onsen
竹瓦温泉

Matsuyama (¥2450, 4½ hours). Late evening boats to western Honshū pass through the Inland Sea during daylight hours the next morning.

Getting Around
To/From the Airport Hovercraft run from Ōita and Beppu (¥2750) to Ōita airport, which is 40km around the bay from Beppu. The airport bus service leaves from the stop outside the Cosmopia shopping centre (¥1700, one hour).

Bus There are four local bus companies, of which Kamenoi is the largest. Most buses are numbered, but Ōita Kōtsū buses for Ōita are not. An unlimited 'My Beppu Free' travel pass for Kamenoi buses comes in two varieties: the 'mini pass' (¥900), which covers all the local attractions, including the hells; and the 'wide pass' (¥1600 for one

day, ¥2400 for two days), which goes farther afield. The passes are available at the JR Beppu station information counter and at the Beppu Youth Hostel.

A variety of bus tours operate from the Kitahama bus station including tours to the Kannawa hot springs and other attractions.

USUKI 臼杵
About 5km from Usuki is a collection of some superb 10th to 13th century **Buddha images** (¥530, 8.30 am to sunset). More than 60 images lie in a series of niches in a ravine. Some are complete statues, whereas others have only the heads remaining, but many are in wonderful condition, even with paintwork still intact. The **Dainichi Buddha head** is the most impressive and important of the Usuki images. There are various other stone Buddha images at sites around Ōita-ken, such as Motomachi, Magari and

Takase, but the Usuki images are the most numerous and most interesting. There's a choice of restaurants at the site. The town of Usuki is about 40km south-east of Beppu; trains take a little under one hour (¥1790). It's then a short bus ride (¥300, 20 minutes) to the ravine site; alternatively, you could walk the few kilometres from the Kami-Usuki station.

YUFUIN 湯布院
☎ 0977 • pop 11,548

About 25km inland from Beppu, once beautiful and quietly rustic Yufuin has suffered in the last few years from excessive tourist development. It's still worth a stop en route to Aso, but avoid weekends and holidays. It is, however, an expensive place to visit.

Information
The tourist information office in front of the train station (☎ 84-2446) has some information in English. It's open from 9 am to 7 pm. Make sure you change money in Beppu, as there's no place to do it readily in Yufuin. There is an onsen matsuri on the first Saturday and Sunday of April.

Things to See & Do
As in Beppu, making a pilgrimage from one onsen to another is a popular activity in Yufuin. **Kinrin-ko** is fed by hot springs, so it's warm all year round. Shitan-yu is a thatched bathhouse (¥100) on the northern shore of the lake. *Makiba no Yado* (¥520) has a large open-air rotemburo, and does bear and wild-boar teishoku (around ¥1500)!

The town has a number of interesting temples and shrines, including **Kozenin-ji**, **Bussan-ji** and **Bukko-ji**. Yufuin is also noted for its arts and handicrafts, which can be seen at **Mingei-mura Folk Art Village** (¥650, 8.10 am to 5.30 pm) and in a number of shops and galleries.

The double-peaked, 1583m **Yufu-dake** volcano overlooks Yufuin and takes about one hour to climb. Take a bus from the Kamenoi bus station to Yufu Tozanguchi, about 20 minutes away on the Beppu-Yufuin bus route.

Places to Stay & Eat
Yufuin has many minshuku, ryokan and pensions, including the popular *Pension Yufuin* (☎ 85-3311), which has rooms for ¥9500, with two meals. It's a typically

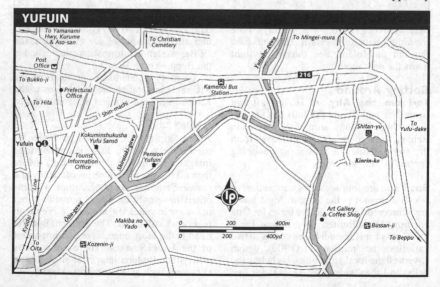

Japanese 'rural Western' guesthouse fantasy. *Kokuminshukusha Yufu Sansō* (☎ 84-2105) is next to the morning market, close to Yufuin station (¥6500, with two meals). Most of the ryokan around town are high-class places with very high costs.

Getting There & Away
Number 36 buses go to Yufuin from the JR Beppu station (¥980, one hour, hourly). The JR Kyūdai line runs to Yufuin from Ōita (¥2500, one hour and 10 minutes). Continuing beyond Yufuin is not always easy. Kyūshū Kokusai Kankō (KKC) buses go to Aso and Kumamoto but not year round.

BEPPU TO ASO-SAN
Yamanami Hwy
The picturesque Yamanami Hwy extends 63km from the Aso-san region to near Yufuin; from there, the Ōita Expressway runs to Beppu on the east coast. There's a ¥1850 toll to drive along this scenic road, however, tour buses operating between Kumamoto, Aso and Beppu, or the reverse, also use this route. The road crosses a high plateau and passes numerous mountain peaks, including Kujū-san (1788m), the highest point in Kyūshū.

Taketa 竹田
South of Yufuin, near the town of Taketa, are the Oka-jō ruins, which have a truly magnificent ridge-top position. The ruins are about 2km from JR Bungo-Taketa station; take a Taketa Kōtsū bus (¥140) there and walk back into town. Taketa has some interesting old buildings, reminders of the Christian period and a museum (no English signage). Bungo-Taketa is on the JR Hōhi line between Ōita and Aso-san. From Aso-san to Taketa, it takes just under an hour by train or bus; from there it's just over an hour by train to Ōita – a little longer by bus.

KUNISAKI-HANTŌ 国東半島
Immediately north of Beppu, Kunisaki-hantō bulges eastwards from the Kyūshū coast. The region is noted for its early Buddhist influence, including some rock-carved images that are related to the better-known images at Usuki.

Usa 宇佐
In the early post-WWII era, when 'Made in Japan' was no recommendation at all, it's said that companies would register in Usa so they could proclaim that their goods were 'Made in USA'! The town is better known for its bright orange Usa-jinja (¥300), the original of which dated back over 1000 years. The current shrine is much newer and is connected with the warrior-god Hachiman, a favourite deity of Japan's right wing. It's a 10-minute (¥240) bus ride from town. From Beppu station, the Nichirin service on the JR Nippō line runs hourly to Usa (¥1820, 35 minutes).

Other Attractions
The Kunisaki-hantō is said to have more than half of all the stone Buddhas in Japan. The 11th century Fuki-ji (¥300) in Bungotakada is the oldest wooden structure in

KUNISAKI-HANTŌ

Sea of Suo-Nada

Kakaji
Kunimi
Matama
Futago-san (721m)
213
To Nakatsu
Bungotakada
Fuki-ji
Futago-ji
Kunisaki
Usa
Usa jinja
Kunisaki-hantō
JR Nippo Line
Kumano Magaibutsu
Ōita Airport
Aki
10
Kitsuki
213
Hiji
Trans-Kyushu Expressway
10
Beppu-wan
To Ōita
Beppu

0   5   10km
0   2.5   5mi

Kyūshū and one of the oldest wooden temples in Japan. Take an Ōita Kōtsū bus from Usa station to Fuki-ji (¥770, 40 minutes).

Right in the centre of the peninsula, near the summit of Futago-san, is **Futago-ji**, dedicated to Fudō-Myō-o, the ferocious, fire-enshrouded, sword wielding deity who ensures all good Buddhists learn their Scriptures (¥200, 8.30 am to 4 pm). It's difficult to get to by public transport.

Carved into a cliff behind Taizo-ji, 2km south of **Maki Ōdō**, are two large Buddha images; a 6m-high figure of the Dainichi Buddha and an 8m-high figure of Fudō-Myō-o. These are known as the **Kumano Magaibutsu** and are the largest Buddhist images of this type in Japan. Other stone statues, thought to be from the Heian period (AD 1000–1100), can be seen in Maki Ōdō. You can get there via the bus that goes to Fuki-ji from Usa station (¥1600, two hours).

Getting Around

The easiest way to tour the peninsula is on the daily five to seven-hour bus tours from Beppu or Nakatsu. Beppu's Ōita airport is on the peninsula, about 40km from Beppu. Ōita Kōtsū buses from Usa station do a loop around the main attractions of the peninsula.

NORTHERN ŌITA-KEN
☎ 0979
Yaba-kei 耶馬溪
From Nakatsu, Route 212 turns inland and runs through the picturesque gorge, Yaba-kei. The gorge extends for about 10km, beginning about 16km from Nakatsu. **Ao-no-Dōmon** (Ao Tunnel), at the start of

the gorge, was originally cut over a 30-year period by a hard-working monk in order to make Rankan-ji more accessible.

In Yamaguni-cho's Oaza-uso village, there's a wonderfully primitive hillside rotemburo (free).

Smaller gorges join the main one, and there are frequent buses up the gorge road from Nakatsu. A 35km cycling track follows a now disused train line. You can rent bicycles (two hours for ¥360) and stay at *Yabakei Cycling Terminal* (☎ 54-2655), charging ¥5000, with two meals, or at *Yamaguniya Youth Hostel* (☎ 52-2008), charging ¥2800.

From Nakatsu station, Ōita Kōtsū buses run to Ao-no-Dōmon (¥600, 40 minutes); Ōita Kōtsu Hida-bound buses go to the cycling terminal (¥930, 50 minutes).

Hita Area 日田
Farther inland from Yaba-kei is Hita, a quiet country town and onsen resort where *ukai* (cormorant fishing) takes place in the river from May to October. Just across the prefectural border in Fukuoka-ken you can also see cormorant fishing in **Harazara**, another hot-spring resort.

North of Hita, towards Koishiwara, is **Onta**, a small village renowned for its curious pottery. The **Onta-yaki Togeikan Museum** has a display of the local product. Koishiwara also has a pottery tradition dating back to the era when Korean potters were first brought to Kyūshū.

Hita is on the JR Kyūdai line between Ōita (¥2070, two hours) and Kurume (one hour). Buses go from Hita to Onta (¥1080, 40 minutes).

Okinawa & the South-West Islands

The Nansei-shotō, or South-West Islands, usually referred to collectively as 'Okinawa', meander for more than 1000km from the southern tip of Kyūshū to Yonaguni-jima, just a strenuous stone's-throw (a little over 100km) from the east coast of Taiwan.

Okinawa-hontō is the hub of the island chain and its key role in the closing months of WWII holds a continuing fascination for visitors. But for natural beauty and deeper insights into Okinawan culture, head for the *ritō* (outer islands). Kume-jima, for example, is famed for its unspoilt beauty; Miyako-jima and Ishigaki-jima boast fine sand and coral; Taketomi-jima is a tiny island with a picture-postcard village; and rugged Iriomote-jima is cloaked in dense tropical jungle.

A warm climate, beautiful beaches, excellent diving and traces of traditional culture are the prime attractions. The chance to sample the unusually delicious Okinawan food just adds to the allure.

But don't think of these islands as forgotten backwaters with a mere handful of visitors – both All Nippon Airways (ANA) and Japan Airlines (JAL) fly tourists to Okinawa from 'mainland' Japan by the 747-load, and even the local flights from Okinawa to other islands in the chain are by 737. Despite centuries of mainland exploitation, the horrific destruction during the closing months of WWII and, more recently, the onslaught of mass tourism, many of the traditional ways of these islands live on.

Suggested Itineraries

Except when travelling to the northern Amami-shotō, which is best approached from Kagoshima (southern Kyūshū), most visitors use Naha as a point of arrival in Okinawa. From here you can explore Okinawa-hontō before heading to the outer islands.

Most islands in this chapter can be reached by both ferry and aeroplane. Your choice of transport may depend on whether you are constrained more by time or by budget.

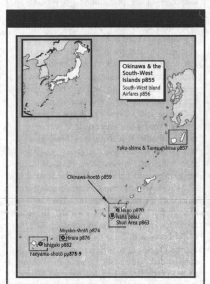

Okinawa & the South-West Islands p855
South-West Island Airfares p856

Yaku-shima & Tanegashima p857

Okinawa-hontō p859

Nago p870
Naha p862
Shuri Area p863

Miyako-shotō p874
Hirara p876
Ishigaki p882
Yaeyama-shotō pp878-9

- Hike to the giant cedar trees and high mountain peaks on Yaku-shima.
- Dive off Ishigaki-jima and its neighbouring islands.
- Explore Iriomote-jima, Japan's only pocket of jungle wilderness, on foot or by kayak.
- Visit Shuri-jō, near Naha, a beautifully executed re-creation of the traditional seat of Ryūkyū power.
- Hire a car, or take local buses, to the war-memorial sites of southern Okinawa-hontō, enjoying the rural and seaside scenery along the way.
- Explore Naha's Kokusai-dōri, a sunny, relaxed stretch of bars, steak restaurants and souvenir shops, which is great fun by day or night.

Time permitting, one popular route in the islands is to take the ferry south from Naha to the Miyako-shotō, then take a boat to the

Okinawan Cuisine

One of the real treats of visiting the southern islands is all the fine cuisine. As well as an abundance of fresh produce and seafood, prize beef cows are raised in Okinawa, and the steaks are hard to beat. Pork is also widely enjoyed, particularly in *sōki soba* – bowls of hot noodles with thick slices of tender marinated pork. Okinawan soba is justifiably famous, in particular the local varieties found in the Miyako and Yaeyama island groups.

One must-try Okinawan dish is *champuru*, a mixed stir-fry that can be made with a variety of ingredients such as *goya* (bitter gourd), *fū* (gluten), papaya, *chikinā* (pickles), *māmimā* (bean sprouts) and *numanā* (cabbage). You won't need to look far to find it.

Okinawan dishes can be washed down well with cold Orion, the local malt beverage of choice. If you fancy spirits, *awamori*, the local firewater, has an alcohol content of 30% to 60%. Drink with care! Real daredevils might want to look out for the version that comes with a small habu snake coiled in the bottom of the bottle. Most bars will have a bottle or two tucked away if you care to try a glass.

Yaeyama-shotō, where you can make jaunts from Ishigaki-jima over to Taketomi-jima, Iriomote-jima and other beautiful islands. From Ishigaki there are regular flights back to Naha and, for a price, even direct to Tokyo.

HISTORY

The islands of the Nansei-shotō chain, like stepping stones between Japan and Taiwan, have long been a bridge between Japanese and Chinese culture. As a result, the often unfortunate residents of the islands (formerly the Ryūkyū kingdom) have sometimes felt pressure from both sides. More recently, Okinawa was the scene of some of the most violent and tragic action in the closing months of WWII.

For centuries, the islands formed a border zone between Chinese and Japanese suzerainty. In 1372 an Okinawan king initiated tributes to the Chinese court, a practice that was to continue for 500 years.

In the 15th century, the whole island of Okinawa was united under the rule of the Shō dynasty, and the capital shifted from Urasoe to Shuri, where it was to remain until the early years of the Meiji Restoration (1868–1912). The period from 1477 to 1525 is remembered as a golden age of Okinawan history. By the 17th century, however, Japanese power was on the ascendancy. The Okinawans found themselves under a new ruler when the Satsuma kingdom of southern Kyūshū invaded in 1609. From this time the islands were controlled with an iron fist and taxed and exploited greedily. In 1879 the islands were formally made a prefecture under Meiji rule.

Treated as foreign subjects by the Satsuma regime, the Okinawans were subsequently pushed to become 'real' Japanese. They paid a heavy price for this new role in the closing stages of WWII, when they were trapped between the relentless US hammer and the fanatically resistant Japanese anvil.

US bombing started in October 1944. On 1 April 1945, US troops landed on the island. The Japanese made an all-out stand. It took 82 horrendous days for the island to be captured. Not until 22 June was the conquest complete, by which time 13,000 US soldiers and, according to some estimates, a quarter of a million Japanese had died. Many of the Japanese casualties were civilians; there are terrible tales of mass suicides by mothers clutching their children and leaping off clifftops to their deaths to avoid capture by the foreigners whom, they had been led to believe, were barbarians.

The Japanese commanders committed *seppuku* (ritual suicide), but a final horror remained. The underground naval headquarters were so well hidden they were not discovered until three weeks after the US victory. The underground corridors contained the bodies of 4000 naval officers and men, all of whom had committed suicide.

Okinawa became a major US military base during the Cold War. Sovereignty of the island was finally returned to Japan in 1972, but even today a strong US military presence persists on Okinawa.

OKINAWA & THE SOUTH-WEST ISLANDS

ORIENTATION

The northern half of the Nansei-shotō falls within the prefecture, Kagoshima-ken, and includes the Ōsumi-shotō and Amami-shotō. Kagoshima is the gateway to these islands.

The four island groups that form the southern half of the Nansei-shotō comprise Okinawa-ken. Of these, the main islands are in the Okinawa-shotō to the north and in the Miyako-shotō and Yaeyama-shotō to the south.

CLIMATE

The climate of the Nansei-shotō is much warmer than that of the Japanese mainland, and Okinawa is virtually a tropical getaway. November to April is considered to be the best season, May and June can bring heavy rain, July to August is not only very hot but also very crowded, and September to October is the typhoon season.

Although the winter months (November to March) are cooler, the crowds are smaller and underwater visibility for divers is at its best then.

Diving in Okinawa

Visitors interested in exploring Okinawa from a submarine perspective will find numerous opportunities to dive deep and get friendly with the fishes. Whether you're a beginner or an old hand, want to dive from a boat or from the shore, chances are there's an operator to suit you.

Little English is spoken at most of the dive outfits on the islands, which is something those who don't speak Japanese might want to consider. One exception is Fathoms Diving (☎ 090-8766-0868, fax 956-6191, email dive oki@fathoms.net), which is based at Yomitan (Okinawa-hontō) and is run by *gaijin* (foreigners). See the Okinawa City to Nago section in this chapter for details, or check out www.fathoms.net. If you're confident of your ability to go diving and speak Japanese at the same time, you'll find operator information in this chapter's Kerama-rettō, Miyako-jima, Ishigaki-jima and Iriomote-jima sections.

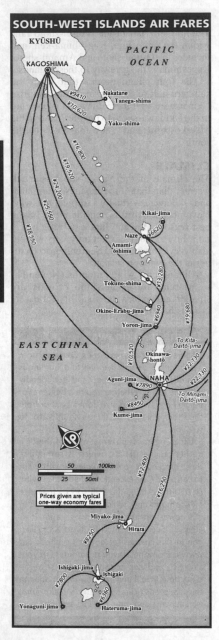

SOUTH-WEST ISLANDS AIR FARES

KYŪSHŪ

PACIFIC
OCEAN

KAGOSHIMA

¥9410

Nakatane
Tanega-shima

¥10,620

Yaku-shima

¥16,800

¥19,520

¥24,200

¥25,550

¥18,550

Kikai-jima

¥6620

Naze

Amami-
ōshima

¥13,280

Tokuno-shima

Okino-Erabu-jima   ¥6940

¥19,680

Yoron-jima

EAST CHINA
SEA

To Kita-
Daitō-jima

Okinawa-
hontō

¥10,520

¥22,130

NAHA

¥22,130

Aguni-jima   ¥7890

To Minami-
Daitō-jima

¥8450

Kume-jima

0   50   100km
0   25   50mi

Prices given are typical
one-way economy fares

¥12,400

¥16,250

Miyako-jima

Hirara

¥8250

Ishigaki-jima

Ishigaki

¥7800

¥6360

Yonaguni-jima

Hateruma-jima

OKINAWA & SW ISLANDS

Getting There & Away

There are numerous flights and ferry services to Naha, the main city on Okinawa-
hontō, from Kagoshima at the southern end
of Kyūshū and from many other cities, including Tokyo. See the Boat section and
the 'Domestic Air Fares' chart in the Getting Around chapter.

Getting Around

There are connecting flights and ships between many of the islands in the Nansei-
shotō. In this chapter, see individual
destinations' Getting There & Away sections, and the South-West Islands Air Fares
map. It's important to note that ferry schedules are particularly vulnerable to change;
it's always a good idea to check before you
plan to use these services. Information on
local transport services and vehicle rental
can be found in individual destinations'
Getting Around sections.

Ōsumi-shotō大隈諸島

The northernmost island group of the Nansei-shotō, less than 100km from Kagoshima,
is the Ōsumi-shotō. The two main islands
are Yaku-shima, an extraordinary nature-
lovers' paradise, and Tanega-shima, known
for its surf and a rocket-launch facility.
South of these islands are the smaller, scattered Tokara-rettō.

YAKU-SHIMA屋久島
☎ 09974

Just 25km in diameter, volcanic Yaku-
shima is one of Japan's most remarkable
travel destinations and justifiably was designated a Unesco World Heritage Site
(Japan's first) in 1993.

Over 75% of the island is covered with
mountains, and while the high peaks are
snowcapped in winter, the flat land around
the coastline remains subtropical. Yaku-
shima's towering terrain catches every in-
bound rain cloud, giving the island one of
the wettest climates in Japan (be prepared).

There is a 'visitors centre' (just a counter
with brochures) and restaurant (☎ 2-0091)

YAKU-SHIMA & TANEGA-SHIMA

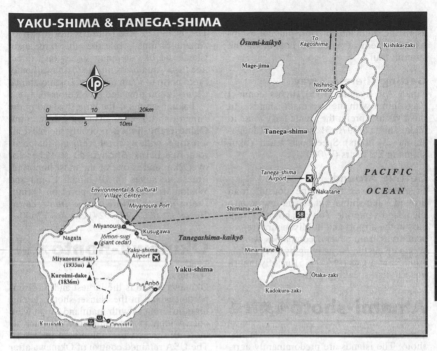

on the main road, five minutes' walk from Miyanoura-kō port, but a better place to gather information is the nearby Environmental & Cultural Village Centre (☎ 2-2900), on the access road leading from the ferry terminal.

Things to See & Do

The island offers superb hiking through ancient forests of giant *yaku-sugi (Cryptomeria japonica)*, a local cedar species. Choose a day-long outing to the 1935m summit of **Miyanoura-dake** (Mt Miyanoura), the highest point in southern Japan, or to the 7200-year-old cedar tree, **Jōmon-sugi**. Alternatively, plan a two- or three-day trek across several mountain peaks. For the complete scoop on the island's hikes, pick up a copy of Lonely Planet's *Hiking in Japan*.

Miyanoura, on the north-east coast, is the main port; a road runs around the perimeter of the island, passing through the hot-springs town of **Onoaida** in the south.

Nature Coordinated Professional (☎ 7-2364, 7-2593, email yakushima@satsuma.ne.jp) is a group that leads interpretive ecotours on the island, in English. Check out its Web site at www.satsuma.ne.jp/yakusima/jomon.htm.

Places to Stay

The woodsy ***Chinryū-an Guesthouse*** (☎/fax 7-3900, email chinryu@sa.uno.ne.jp) in Onoaida is an excellent choice. The friendly young couple here speak English well, and can provide information on hiking and other attractions on the island. Nightly costs are ¥3980 per person, and breakfast/dinner costs ¥550/1000.

Yaku-shima Youth Hostel (☎ 7-3751, fax 7-2477), a five-minute drive west of Chinryū-an, charges ¥4400 a night with two meals, ¥2800 without; nonmembers add ¥1000. ***Shiki-no-yado Onoaida*** (☎ 7-3377) is another Onoaida inn, with mountain views and nice rooms for ¥7000 including two meals.

There is camping along the coast, as well as in the highland interior, plus an established system of mountain huts along the summit trail.

Getting There & Away

Japan Air System (JAS) flights connect Kagoshima with the two main islands, but most visitors prefer the scenic ferry route to Yaku-shima (¥3970, 3¾ hours) and Tanega-shima (2¾ hours). Speedboats reach Yaku-shima in 2½ hours (¥7000).

Getting Around

Frequent buses travel the coastal road around Yaku-shima, but a scant few go into the island's interior. You can, however, rent cars at the airport and in Miyanoura (representatives from several companies wait to scoop up customers arriving by ferry). Matsuda Rent-a-Car (☎ 2-2115) in Miyanoura has English-speaking staff.

Amami-shotō 奄美諸島

There are five main islands in the Amami-shotō. The islands are predominantly agricultural and have a subtropical climate, clear water and good beaches.

Getting There & Away

There are regular flights from Kagoshima to all five main islands in the Amami group.

Ferries stop at Amami-ōshima en route from Kagoshima to Okinawa-hontō. Kagoshima to Naze (Amami-ōshima) takes about 12 hours by ferry; Ōsaka to Naze takes 25 hours.

AMAMI-ŌSHIMA 奄美大島

Amami-ōshima, the largest island in the group, is about 180km from Kagoshima. This 40km-long island, also known simply as Ōshima, has a highly convoluted coastline, with the almost enclosed strait, Ōshima-kaikyō, separating it from nearby Kakeroma-jima. Naze is the main port. The island is the northernmost place in Japan where mangoes are found.

OTHER AMAMI ISLANDS

The island of **Kikai-jima** is north-east of Amami-ōshima, while the other three main islands lie like stepping stones in a direct line from Amami-ōshima to Okinawa-hontō. From north to south they are: Tokuno-shima, Okino-Erabu-jima and tiny Yoron-tō.

Tokuno-shima is the largest island in the Amami-shotō after Amami-ōshima, but **Okino-Erabu-jima** is probably the most interesting, with its coral reefs and thatched-roof rice barns. **Shonyu-dō** stretches for over 2km and is one of the most important limestone caves in all Japan. China and Wadomari are the main ports on Okino-Erabu-jima. *Okino-Erabu-jima Youth Hostel* (☎ 0997-92-2024) charges ¥2500.

Okinawa-hontō 沖縄

☎ 098

Okinawa-hontō is the largest and most important island in the Nansei-shotō. Its cultural differences with mainland Japan were once evident in its architecture, of which almost all traces were obliterated in WWII. The USA retained control of Okinawa after the war, handing it back to Japan in 1972. The 26 years of US occupation did an effective job of wiping out what remained of the old Okinawan ways, but for good measure the Japanese have turned the island into a major tourist resort. Okinawa still has the biggest US military base in Japan, with 50,000 military and civilian personnel and dependents. See the boxed text 'The American Problem' later in this chapter.

Okinawa's wartime history may have some interest for foreign visitors, but the islands farther south probably offer a more interesting insight into the history of ancient Ryūkyū.

NAHA 那覇

☎ 098 • pop 304,000

Naha is the capital of Okinawa; it was flattened in WWII and little remains of the old Ryūkyū culture. Today Naha is chiefly a gateway to other places, but there are a number of interesting things to see and do.

OKINAWA-HONTŌ

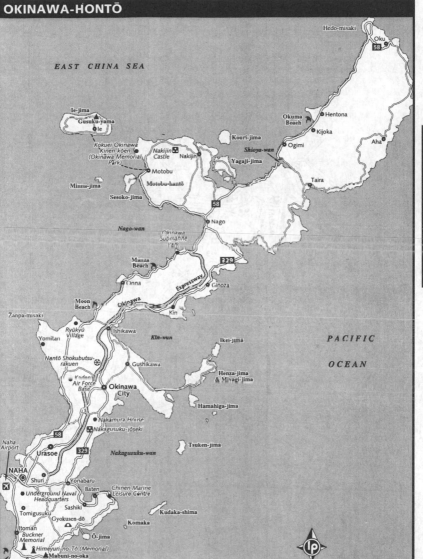

EAST CHINA SEA

Hedo-misaki

Oku
58

Ie-jima
Gusuku-yama
Ie

Okuma
Beach
Hentona

Kouri-jima
Kijoka

Aha

Kokuei Okinawa
Kinen-kōen
(Okinawa Memorial
Park)

Nakijin
Castle
Nakijin

Shioya-wan

Ogimi

Minna-jima

Motobu

Yagaji-jima

Taira

Sesoko-jima

Motobu-hantō

58

Nago-wan

Nago

Okinawa
Submarine
Park

Manza
Beach

Onna

329

Ginoza

Expressway

Moon
Beach

Okinawa

Kin

Zanpa-misaki

Ishikawa

Kin-wan

Ikei-jima

PACIFIC

Yomitan

Ryūkyū
Village

OCEAN

Nantō Shokubutsu-
rakuen

Gushikawa

Henza-jima
& Miyagi-jima

Kadena
Air Force
Base

Okinawa
City

Hamahiga-jima

Nakamura House
Nakagusuku-jōseki

Naha
Airport

58

Tsuken-jima

329

Urasoe

Nakagusuku-wan

NAHA

Shuri

Yonabaru

Chinen Marine
Leisure Centre

Underground Naval
Headquarters

Baten

Kudaka-shima

Tomigusuku

Sashiki

Gyokusen-dō

Komaka

Itoman
Buckner
Memorial

Ō-jima

Himeyuri-no-Tō (Memorial)
Mabuni-no-oka

Konpaku-no-Tō (Memorial)

Nashiro
Beach

Kiyan-misaki

0   10   20km
0   5   10mi

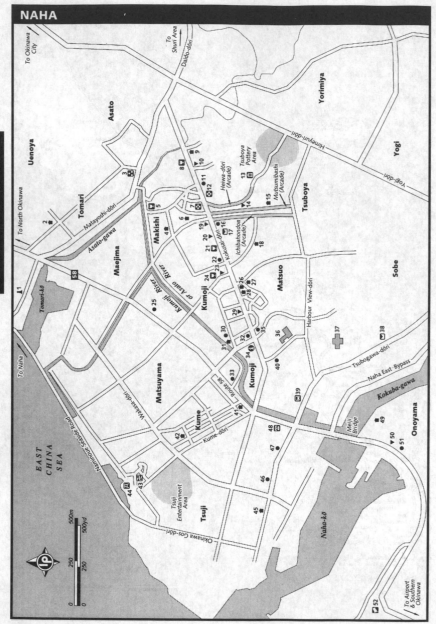

NAHA

NAHA

PLACES TO STAY

2 Harumi Youth Hostel
晴海荘ユースホステル

4 Narumi Ryokan
なるみ旅館

6 Hotel Sankyō
ホテルサンキョー

9 Nansei Kankō Hotel
南西観光ホテル

15 Domitory Okinawa
ドミトリー沖縄

18 Shinkinichi Ryokan
新金一旅館

26 Hotel Kokusai Plaza
ホテル国際プラザ

27 Naha Grand Hotel
那覇グランドホテル

28 Hotel New Okinawa
ホテルニュー沖縄

31 Hotel Maruki
ホテルまるき

37 Okinawa Harbourview
Hotel
沖縄ハーバービュー
ホテル

41 Oceanview Hotel
オーシャンビュ ホテル

42 Okiwana Washington
Hotel
沖縄ワシントンホテル

45 Okinawa Guesthousec
沖縄ゲストハウス

49 Okinawa International
Youth Hostel
沖縄国際ユース
ホステル

PLACES TO EAT

10 Rawhide; Anmā
ローハイド；
あんま一家

14 Spicy Kitchen
スパイシーキッチン

19 Grand Canyon
Steakhouse;Maui
Steakhouse
グランドキャニオン；
マウイステーキハウス

20 Jin Jin
じんじん

23 Teida Soba
ていだそば

29 Cafe Fish Pool
カフェフィッシュ
プール

50 Naha Soba
那覇そば

OTHER

1 Commodore Perry
Memorial
ペルリ提督ト陸記念碑

3 Sōgen-ji Gates
崇元寺石門

5 Kam's Jazz Bar
カムズ

7 Mitsukoshi Department
Store; Naha Tower;
Zavares
三越百貨店；
那覇タワー;ザバレス

8 Soul Brothers Club
ソウルブラザーズ
クラブ

11 Rock in Okinawa
ロックインオキナワ

12 Kokusai Shopping
Center
国際ショッピング
センター

13 Tsuboya Ceramics
Museum
壺屋焼物博物館

16 OPA; Tower Records

17 Post Office; Tacos-ya
郵便局；タコス屋

21 Helios Craft Beer Pub
クラフトビアパブ

22 Chakura & Pow Wow
チャクラ；パウワウ

24 Bar Dick
ディック

25 Nissan Rent-a-Car
ニッサンレンタカー

30 JAL
日本航空

32 JAS
日本エアシステム

33 ANA
全日空

34 Tourist Information
Office; Palette Kumoji
観光案内所；
パレットくもじ

35 Javy Building
Javyビル

36 Okinawa Prefectural
Office
沖縄県庁

38 Main Post Office
中央郵便局

39 Bus Station
那覇バスターミナル

40 Naha City Office
那覇市役所

43 Gokoku-ji
護国寺

44 Naminoue-gū
波上宮

46 Nippon Rent-a-Car
ニッポンレンタカー

47 Japaren Rent-a-Car
ジャパレンレンタカー

48 KDD (International
Telephone Office)

51 Toyota Rent-a-Car
トヨタレンタカー

52 US Consulate
アメリカ領事館

OKINAWA & SW ISLANDS

Orientation

Kokusai-dōri (International Blvd), Naha's main drag, is 1.6 busy and colourful kilometres of hotels, bars, restaurants and shops. The airport is only 3km west of Naha; a similar distance east is Shuri, the erstwhile Okinawan capital and the site of some renovated ruins.

Information

If you're looking for a source of information and news in English other than Okinawa's English print media (see Bookshops in this section), you can quickly get your fill of the US forces radio on 648 kHz AM – the ads are amazingly awful.

Tourist Offices The airport tourist information office (☎ 857-6884) is open from 9 am to 9 pm daily. The tourist information office (☎ 866-7515) in town is in the gigantic Palette Kumoji building at the southwestern end of Kokusai-dōri.

Bookshops There is a limited selection of English books and magazines in the Kokusai shopping centre, Tower Records in OPA and at the 7th-floor bookshop in the Palette Kumoji building.

Keep an eye out for the weekly *Japan Update*. Though targeted mainly at US military personnel, this English-language newspaper is excellent for keeping up on local events. Log on to its Web site at www.japanupdate.com.

Email & Internet Access Technowork (☎ 860-5757), on the 2nd floor of the Fashion Building on Kokusai-dōri (near Mitsukoshi), rents high-speed on-line connections (¥500 for 30 minutes).

Central Naha

Kokusai-dōri, with its curious mix of restaurants, army surplus stores, bars, souvenir shops and hotels, makes a colourful walk, day or night. It's very much the heart of Naha. Turning south off Kokusai-dōri opposite Mitsukoshi department store leads you down the Heiwa-dōri shopping arcade, which has the distinct flavour of an Asian market.

If you continue to the eastern end of Kokusai-dōri, a right turn takes you towards Shuri, while a left turn quickly brings you to the reconstructed temple gates of **Sōgen-ji**. These stone gates once led to the 16th-century temple of the Ryūkyū kings, but like almost everything else in Naha, it was destroyed in WWII. Continue beyond the gates and, almost at the waterfront, is the Commodore Perry Memorial, commemorating his 1853 landing in Naha. Nearby is a foreigners' cemetery.

Tsuboya Area 壺屋

Continue along the Heiwa-dōri shopping arcade, take the left fork at the first major junction, and a short walk beyond the arcade will bring you to the Tsuboya pottery area. If you miss it, ask someone for directions or simply continue in the same direction until you hit the big Himeyuri-dōri – Tsuboya is across the road from McDonald's.

About 20 traditional potteries still operate in this compact area, a centre for ceramic production since 1682. You can peer into many of the small workshops, and there are numerous shops selling popular Okinawan products such as the *shiisā* (lion roof-guardians) and the containers for serving *awamori*, the local firewater. The fascinating new **Tsuboya Ceramics Museum** (¥300, 10 am to 6 pm, closed Tuesday) features a wide range of displays and facilities.

Tsuji Area 辻

The Tsuji entertainment area was once a brothel quarter; now it features ubiquitous clubs and bars, together with a collection of colourful love hotels and US-style steakhouses. As Japanese red-light areas go, it's decidedly lacking in atmosphere.

Kume-dōri runs from Kokusai-dōri straight through Tsuji to the waterfront, where the hilltop shrine, Naminoue-gū, and Gokoku-ji and Kōshi-byō (Kōshi Ancestral Shrine) are 'picturesquely sited' overlooking the sea and the red-light district. The buildings are unexceptional modern reconstructions, and the bay they overlook has been totally ruined by litter and the highway overpass that runs straight across it.

Shuri Area 首里

In the period prior to the Meiji Restoration, Shuri was the capital of Okinawa; that title passed to Naha in 1879. Shuri's temples, shrines, tombs and castle were all destroyed in WWII. Some reconstructions and repairs have been made, but it's a pale shadow of the former city.

SHURI AREA

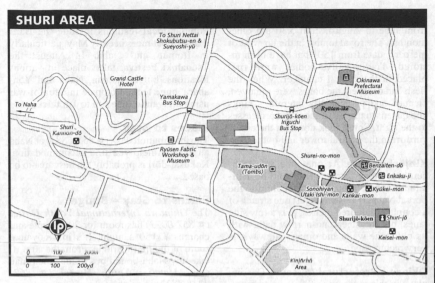

To Shuri Nettai
Shokubutsu-en &
Sueyoshi-yū

Grand Castle
Hotel

Yamakawa
Bus Stop

To Naha

Shuri
Kannon-dō

Ryūsen Fabric
Workshop &
Museum

Okinawa
Prefectural
Museum

Shurijō-kōen
Iriguchi
Bus Stop

Ryūtan-ike

Shurei-no-mon

Benzaiten-dō

Tama-udōn
(Tombs)

Enkaku-ji

Sonohiyan
Utaki Ishi-mon   Kankai-mon

Kyūkei-mon

Shurijō-kōen   Shuri-jō

Keisei-mon

0   100   200m
0   100   200yd

K'injūrhō
Area

OKINAWA & SW ISLANDS

Shuri is about 2.5km from the eastern end of Kokusai dōri. Buses (¥200) run directly to the *shurijō-kōen iriguchi* (entrance of Shurijō-kōen), a park containing most of what's left of the old Ryūkyū royal capital.

Shurijō-kōen Entry to the park itself is free, but there's a hefty charge for the castle, **Shuri-jō** (¥800, 9 am to 5 pm). The reconstructed old residence of the Okinawan royal family is just up from the entrance to the park. The original castle was destroyed in the WWII Battle of Okinawa and only reopened in early 1993. The reconstruction work was carried out with meticulous attention to detail, and there are several exhibition halls with interesting historical displays. The result is undoubtedly Naha's prime tourist attraction.

The castle's walls have numerous gates that are of minor interest. The pick of them is the Chinese-influenced gate, **Shurei-no-mon**, which appears on Japan's newly introduced ¥2000 bank note. As the ceremonial entrance to the castle, the gate was originally built some 500 years ago and rebuilt in 1958. It's considered to be *the* symbol of Okinawa, so there's a constant

stream of tour groups and school parties lining up to be photographed in front of it. Women in traditional Okinawan costume stand ready to make guest appearances in the photos, for a suitable fee.

Also worth checking out is the 15th- to 16th-century **Kankai-mon**, another gate of traditional Okinawan design. It was rebuilt right after the war. **Kyukei-mon**, built in 1508, has also been restored. Another large gate, **Keisei-mon**, was originally built in 1546.

There are a couple of temples on the park grounds, but don't expect too much from them. The temple, **Benzaiten-dō**, is in the middle of the pond, Enkan-ike, just down from Shuri-jō. The temple was originally built in 1502, then rebuilt in 1609 after being destroyed, and rebuilt once again in 1968 after being burnt out during WWII. Cross the road to the rather bedraggled remnants of **Enkaku-ji** (¥160). This temple dates from 1492, but it too was destroyed in the Battle of Okinawa. All that remains is the outer gate, a bridge leading over a lotus pond, and the steps beyond the pond leading to the main gate.

The wartime destruction also did not

spare **Tama-udon** (¥200, 8.30 am to 6 pm from June to August, until 5.30 pm other months). The royal tombs, in the far west of the park, date from 1501 but have been restored. Traditionally, bodies were first placed in the central chamber. When the flesh had decayed, the bones were removed, cleaned and permanently interred – kings and queens to the left, princes and princesses to the right. Shiisā look down on the courtyard from the central tower and both sides.

Kinjōchō Area At one time the 15th-century stone street Kinjōchō-no-Ishitatamimichi ran for 10km from Shuri to the port at Naha. Now there's just one stretch of a couple of hundred metres, plus a few side lanes, but the steep and narrow path, with its old stone walls and ornate gateways, is very picturesque.

Okinawa Prefectural Museum The displays in this museum (¥200, 9 am to 5 pm, closed Monday) are connected with Okinawan lifestyle and culture and include exhibits on the Battle of Okinawa and a large model of Shuri-jō. Ryūtan-ike, across the road, was built in 1427 and was used for dragon-boat races.

Other Attractions Shuri Kannon-dō dates from 1618; it is on the Naha side of Shuri. **Sueyoshi-gū** originally dates from the mid-15th century; the shrine is well to the north of Shuri, in Sueyoshi-kōen. **Shuri Nettai Shokubutsu-en** (Shuri Tropical Botanical Gardens), with over 400 varieties of tropical plants, may be worth a look, but the ¥1030 entry charge will no doubt deter most potential visitors.

Housed in a building brought from Ishigaki, the **Japan Folkcraft Museum** displays traditional crafts and has a collection of photographs of prewar Okinawa. The museum is closed on Tuesday. There are a number of factories in the Shuri area producing traditional *bingata* (stencil-dyed) fabrics. **Ryūsen Fabric Workshop & Museum** specialises in *ryūsen*, an expensive material similar to bingata.

Special Events

Popular local festivals include the Hārii dragon-boat races in early May, particularly in Itoman and Naha. In August the Tsunahiki Festival takes place in various locations, but in Itoman, Naha and Yonabaru, huge teams compete in a tug-of-war using a gigantic rope (up to 1m thick).

Places to Stay

The information desk (☎ 857-6884) at Naha airport can help you find accommodation. Kokusai-dōri is probably the best area to be based.

Places to Stay – Budget

The *Okinawa International Youth Hostel* (☎ 857-0073) has room for 200 people and charges ¥3150 a night. It's in Onoyama, south of the Meiji Bridge. From the airport, take any Naha-bound bus to the Kōen-mae stop. *Harumi Youth Hostel* (☎ 867-3218/4422) is north of the city, near Route 58. It accommodates 38 people and charges ¥2950 a night (¥3950 for private rooms).

At the bottom of the budget-hotel barrel, *Okinawa Guesthouse* (☎ 090-9782-9696, 090-4359-2037) is some distance west of Kokusai-dōri, but cheap as dirt at ¥1500 a bed. In the Tsuboya area, *Dormitory Okinawa* (☎ 090-7159-8741) charges ¥1800, and tea is free. Both of these places are tucked away on narrow streets and tricky to find.

Just off Kokusai-dōri, the popular *Shinkinichi Ryokan* (☎ 869-4973) has clean and comfortable rooms from ¥2800 per person (add ¥530 for breakfast). The nearby *Narumi Ryokan* (☎ 867-2138) has per-person rates from ¥3400, or ¥3700 with attached bath. In the same area, *Hotel Sankyo* (☎ 867-0105) is a low-end business hotel with singles/twins at ¥4000/7500.

Places to Stay – Mid-Range & Top End

Hotel Maruki (☎ 862-6135) is next to the JAL office, overlooking the river, Kumojigawa, near Kokusai-dōri. Singles/doubles start at ¥6500/10,000.

Along Kokusai-dōri, *Hotel Kokusai Plaza* (☎ 862-4243) has cheap singles/

Looking out over the city of Naze to the bay, Amami-Ō-shima, Kyūshū.

Carved stone Dainichi Buddha head, Usuki.

Fishing boats moored in a canal, Shimabara

The coastal shrine of Udo-jingū, near Miyazaki.

Monkey on Kō-jima, Toi-misaki

Lunar-like landscapes, Kirishima National Park.

Praying at a shrine, Kirishima National Park.

The evocatively named Chinoike Jigoku, or Blood Pool Hell – definintely not for bathing in...

doubles from ¥4800/9200 (including break-fast). Just behind it is the spiffier *Naha Grand Hotel* (☎ 862-6161), with singles/doubles/twins from ¥6500/11,000/ 12,000. Around the corner is the similar *Hotel New Okinawa* (☎ 867-7200), with singles/twins for ¥6000/11,000. The clean *Nansei Kankō Hotel* (☎ 862-7144) is right on Kokusai-dōri and has singles/twins from ¥9000/15,000.

The upmarket *Okinawa Washington Hotel* (☎ 869-2511), halfway between Kokusai-dōri and the waterfront, has singles/ doubles/twins from ¥9100/15,000/ 16,000, while on Route 58, glossy *Oceanview Hotel* (☎ 853-2112) charges from ¥9700/15,000 for singles/twins.

Places to Eat
The thing to do if you're a Japanese tourist in Naha is dine out on steak and seafood. *Rawhide* is one of the long-runners, but at *Grand Canyon Steakhouse* you can enjoy your meal in surroundings with more ambience. There are many more on Kokusai-dōri, like *Maui* (across from OPA), and also in the Tsuji area.

Seafood lovers can buy fresh fish, lobster and other, less familiar varieties of sea creature at the markets along the Heiwa-dōri arcade and have it cooked to their liking at one of several restaurants upstairs. In the same bustling arcade, *Spicy Kitchen* serves great curries.

Just next door to Rawhide, *Anma* is a rustic-looking *izakaya* (Japanese-style pub) with plastic displays in the window and a good selection of Okinawan dishes. Farther up Kokusai-dōri is *Jin-Jin*, another popular Okinawan izakaya. Tiny *Tacos-ya* puts an Okinawan twist on Mexican food: deep-fried tacos! Heading west, on the same side street as Bar Dick is *Teida*, which whips up superb vegetable *soba* (buckwheat noodles), and various other Okinawan specialities.

If you should tire of steaks and local fare, *Café Fish Pool*, a bright and trendy 2nd-storey bistro, does great continental lunch deals for under ¥1000, and also has tempting desserts.

Entertainment
Day or night, a stroll along bustling Koku-sai-dōri should be enough to keep anybody entertained, and it seems every little side street harbours a couple of hidden-away drinking spots. Most are friendly, but due to the overwhelming US military presence, don't be surprised to find signs reading 'Japanese Only' outside certain bars and clubs unwelcoming to *gaijin* (foreigners).

One place you won't have a problem entering is *Pow Wow*, a friendly 3rd-floor billiards pub with cheap drinks and good music. One floor down in the same building is *Chakura* (☎ 869-0283), a celebrated 'live house' run by local music maverick Kina Shōkichi. Kina-san and his band, Champloose, perform here nightly (when not touring), and the show should not be missed.

Other bars on, or just off, Kokusai-dōri include the curiously named *Bar Dick*, an 'American Getaway'. There are dozens more to choose from, including *Helios Craft Beer Pub*, serving commendable microbrew and light food.

Soul Brothers Club may not attract many of true African descent, but for Motown music look no further. There's a sign announcing 'Black Harlem' outside the 6th floor.

For a livelier place with room to dance in, try *Zavares* on the 7th floor of Naha Tower, just behind Mitsukoshi. *Rock in Okinawa* is a popular Kokusai-dōri live house, and there's good live jazz at *Kam's*, north of Kokusai-dōri, near the river.

Shopping
Okinawa is renowned for its fabrics, colourful Ryūkyū glassware and Tsuboya pottery. Much of the pottery is in the form of storage vessels, but look for shiisā, the guardian lion-figures that can be seen perched on the rooftops of many traditional Okinawan buildings.

Okinawa also has its own distinctive textiles, particularly the brightly coloured Bingata fabrics made in Shuri. Other fabrics made on Okinawa and other islands include Bashōfu (from northern Okinawa), Jōfu

OKINAWA & SW ISLANDS

(from Miyako), Kasuri (from southern Okinawa), Minsā (from Taketomi), Ryūsen and Tsumugi (from Kume). In Naha, these textiles can be found in some of the shops along Kokusai-dōri.

Awamori is another popular Okinawan product; the local firewater is typically sold in attractive ceramic containers.

Getting There & Away

Air There are direct flights to Okinawa from Guam, Hong Kong and Taiwan. JAL, ANA, Air Nippon Koku (ANK), JAS and Japan Transocean Air (JTA) connect Naha with major cities on the Japanese mainland, including Fukuoka (¥28,350, 1½ hours), Kagoshima (¥21,050, 1½ hours), Nagoya (¥32,750, two hours), Ōsaka (¥29,100, two hours), Hiroshima (¥26,600, two hours) and Tokyo (¥34,900, 2½ hours). See the South-West Islands Air Fares map for inter-island details.

Airlines with offices in central Naha include ANA/ANK (☎ 866-5111), JAL/JTA (☎ 862-3311) and JAS (☎ 867-8111). There are heaps of travel agencies too, particularly on Kokusai-dōri.

Boat Various operators have ferry services to Naha from Tokyo, Nagoya, Ōsaka, Kōbe, Kagoshima and other ports. The schedules are complex and there is a wide variety of fares. There are three ports in Naha, and this can be confusing. From the port, Naha-kō, ferries head north to Hakata and Yoronjima. From Naha Shin-kō (Naha New Port) there are ferries to Fukuoka/Hakata, Kagoshima, Kōbe, Ōsaka and Tokyo, and also to Miyako-jima and Ishigaki-jima. From Tomari-kō port, ferries operate to a number of the smaller islands, including Kume-jima, Aguni and the Daito-shotō.

Arimura Sangyō (☎ 869-1320; in Tokyo ☎ 03-3562-2091) operates a weekly ferry service between Okinawa and Taiwan. Some boats stop at Miyako-jima and Ishigaki-jima.

Getting Around

To/From the Airport Naha Airport is only 3km from the town centre – 10 minutes by taxi (¥1500 to ¥1800) or 20 minutes

by bus (¥200). Buses run via the main bus station and then down Kokusai-dōri. The airport has three widely spaced terminals: international, domestic 1 (for mainland Japan) and domestic 2 (for the islands).

Bus When riding on local town buses, simply dump ¥200 into the slot next to the driver as you enter. For longer trips you collect a ticket showing your starting point as you board and pay the appropriate fare as you disembark. Buses run from Naha to destinations all over the island. The bus station is near the intersection of Tsubogawa-dōri and Route 58.

There are also many bus tours around the island, particularly to the war sites in the south. Try a travel agent on Kokusai-dōri, or ask at the tourist office (☎ 866-7515) in the Palette Kumoji building.

Car & Motorcycle Okinawa is a good place to get around in a rented vehicle as the traffic is not too heavy and the northern end of the island is lightly populated and has poor public transport. There are numerous rental companies in Naha with cars from around ¥5300 per day plus ¥1500 insurance. Convertibles are popular. Try Japaren (☎ 861-3900), Nippon Rent-a-Car (☎ 868-4554) or Toyota Rent-a-Car (☎ 857-0100).

A number of places rent motor scooters and motorcycles. A 50cc motor scooter costs from ¥3300 for the day, while a 250cc motorcycle costs from ¥10,000 a day. Try Sea Rental Bikes (☎ 864-5116) or Trade (☎ 863-0908), close to Mitsukoshi department store on Kokusai-dōri.

SOUTHERN OKINAWA-HONTŌ
☎ 098
The area south of Naha was the scene of some of the heaviest fighting during the closing days of the Battle of Okinawa. There are a number of reminders of those terrible days, as well as some other places of interest in this densely populated part of the island.

The initial US landing on Okinawa took place north of Naha at Kadena and Chatan on 1 April 1945. By 20 April, US forces had captured the northern part of the island and as far south of their landing place as Naha. The rest of the island was not captured until 21 June.

Underground Naval Headquarters 旧海軍司令部壕

About 5km directly south of Naha is the underground naval headquarters (¥420, 8.30 am to 5 pm) where 4000 men committed suicide as the battle for Okinawa drew to its prolonged and bloody conclusion. Only 200m of the 1.5km of tunnels are open, but you can wander through the maze of corridors, see the commander's final words on the wall of his room and inspect the holes and scars in other walls from the grenade blasts that killed many of the men. In Japanese the headquarters are known as *kyū kaigun shireibugō*, though the sign from the main road simply reads 'Kaigungō-kōen'. To get there, take bus No 33 or 101 from the Naha bus station to the Tomigusuku-kōen-mae stop (¥240, 25 minutes), a 10-minute walk from the site.

Nearby is the Tomigusuku-jōshi-kōen (¥530), with pleasant views of Naha, though there is little trace of Tomigusuku-jō, after which the park was named.

Itoman Area 糸満

The fisherfolks' shrine, Hakugin-dō, is in this port town, 12km south of Naha. You can also check out the Kōchi family tombs here. Just south is Nashiro Beach and the Lieutenant General Buckner Memorial, in memory of the US commander who was killed here by shrapnel in the final days of the Battle of Okinawa. The site of Gushikawa-jō at the cape, Kiyan-misaki, now popular with hang-gliding enthusiasts, but in the closing days of the Battle of Okinawa many civilians jumped to their death from the cliffs. Itoman can be reached by bus No 32, 34 or 35 from Naha bus station.

War Sites

Around the southern end of the island are a series of sites connected with the final days of the Battle of Okinawa. On 19 June 1945

The American Problem

The island, Okinawa-hontō, is a tiny place, amounting to just 0.6% of Japan's total landmass. It is curious then that 75% of the nation's US military bases should be crowded onto the island. Military bases occupy over 20% of Okinawa's land.

Okinawan resentment at being a de facto US colony came to a head in September 1995, when three US soldiers abducted a 12-year-old girl, drove her to a field in a rented car and raped her. Sentencing of the soldiers to jail terms of six to seven years was widely seen as inadequate and did little to quell public anger. A protest rally in October 1995 drew a crowd of 850,000 people. US promises in late 1996 to return some 20% of military-owned land were received with little enthusiasm when the USA refused to lower the number of troops stationed on Okinawa.

Okinawan anger is directed not just at the USA but also at 'mainland' Japan, which many Okinawans claim habitually deals out losing hands to the Ryūkyū islanders. Some islanders have been heard to wonder aloud whether greater autonomy, or even complete independence, isn't the best way forward.

The issue of US bases has perhaps hastened a political awakening in a part of Japan that many see as experiencing a 'renaissance'. Okinawan music has made significant inroads into the Japanese mainstream music industry, the island's writers and artists are gaining attention, and some Japanese, tired of big-city life in mainland Japan, are starting to look south longingly at Okinawa. Many young Japanese are moving to Okinawa, where they claim life is more relaxed and relationships more intimate. It is with new-found confidence and pride that Okinawans are starting to stand up and ask the central government in Tokyo to share some of the burden if the US bases are to remain in Japan.

at **Himeyuri-no-Tō**, 200 schoolgirls and their teachers committed suicide in the school grounds rather than fall into the hands of the US military. The memorial to this event is now one of the most popular tourist attractions on Okinawa. Directly south on the coast is the **Konpaku-no-Tō**, a memorial to 35,000 unknown victims of the fighting who were subsequently buried here.

At **Mabuni-no-Oka**, the remaining Japanese forces were virtually pushed into the sea. In their underground hideaway the commanders committed seppuku on 23 June 1945, while above ground the US forces already had complete control of the island. Memorials from every prefecture in Japan dot the hillside, and the **Peace Memorial Museum** tells the gruesome story of the struggle (¥100, 9 am to 4.30 pm, closed Monday). Also at this extensive site is **Heiwa Kinen-dō** (Peace Hall; ¥520), a seven-sided tower, built in 1978, which houses a 16m-high Buddha statue. Behind the hall is a **Peace Art Museum**.

From the Naha bus station, bus Nos 32, 34, 35, 89 and 100 run to Itoman (¥500, 40 minutes), where you must change to bus No 82 or 85 to the Heiwa Kinen-kōen (Peace Park) entrance (¥400, 20 minutes).

Gyokusen-dō 玉泉洞

Japan has plenty of limestone caves, but for those who can't get enough of stalactites and stalagmites, there are more here. Nearly 1km of the cave (¥1050, 9 am to 5 pm) is open to visitors, and your ticket also gets you into Ōkoku-mura (Kingdom Village) theme park. For an extra ¥420, you can enter **Habu-kōen** and see the unfortunate 'deadly' habu, a type of snake, suffering the traditional defeat by a mongoose (see the 'Habu Snakes' boxed text). Take bus No 83 from Naha bus station (¥490, one hour).

Other Attractions

Just beyond the Mabuni-no-Oka memorials is the **Okinawa Coral Museum**. Coral is much nicer where it belongs – underwater. Continuing north on Route 15, you'll find **Himeyuri Paōku**, a park which specialises in cacti. Turn east on Route 76 to reach

Habu Snakes

Any discussion of the Nansei-shotō eventually gets around to 'deadly' habu snakes. Perhaps it's a reflection of Japan's severe shortage of real dangers, but you could easily get the impression that the poor habu is the world's most dangerous snake and that there's one waiting behind every tree, shrub, bush and bar stool on the islands. They're neither so deadly nor so prolific – in fact, the most likely place to see one is at a mongoose-versus-habu fight put on for tourists. Nevertheless, it's probably not a good idea to go barefoot when stomping through the bushes. Do stomp though – the vibrations will scare any snakes away.

Tomori-no-Ojishi, where a large stone shiisā overlooks a reservoir. This particular shiisā dates back to at least 1689; a popular image from the Battle of Okinawa shows a US soldier sheltering behind it while watching with binoculars.

Tiny **Ō-jima** is linked to the main island by bridge and has good beaches, as has Nibaru a little farther north. The island can be reached directly on bus No 53 from Naha bus station (¥580, one hour).

North of Ō-jima is the **Chinen Marine Leisure Centre**. This place is popular with Japanese tourists for the glass-bottomed-boat cruises (¥1400). There are also boats from here to **Kudaka-jima** and to minute **Komaka-jima**, which is encircled by fine beaches. You can get to the leisure centre on Bus No 38 from the Naha bus station (¥750).

CENTRAL OKINAWA-HONTŌ
☎ 098

Central Okinawa (north of Naha through Okinawa City to Ishikawa) is heavily populated, but beyond this area the island is much less crowded. The US military bases are principally in the southern part of central Okinawa-hontō, and the resorts are in the northern part. Dotted around this stretch of Okinawa are an amazing number of artificial tourist attractions where many thousands of yen could be squandered on entry fees.

Urasoe 浦添

Urasoe, 8km north of Naha, was the early
capital of the Ryūkyū kingdom, and today
its two main attractions are the **Urasoe
Yōdore** (Urasoe Royal Tombs), dating back
to the 13th century, and **Jōseki-kōen** (¥350).
The park contains the ruins of the original
castle residence of the Okinawan royal family. Bus No 56 runs from the Naha bus station to Urasoe Jōseki-kōen (¥340).

Nakagusuku-jōseki 中城城跡

North of Naha, the lovely Nakagusuku-
jōseki (Nakagusuku Castle Ruins; ¥300, 9
am to 5 pm) have a wonderful position on a
hilltop overlooking the coast. The castle was
built in 1448, predating stone construction of
this type on the mainland by 80 years. The
castle was destroyed in 1458 in a bizarre
episode of feudal manoeuvring known as the
Amawari Rebellion. When Gosamaru, the
Nakagusuku lord, heard that Amawari, another Okinawan lord, was plotting a rebellion against the king, he mobilised his troops.
The scheming Amawari then convinced the
king that it was Gosamaru who was planning
to revolt, so the hapless Nakagusuku ruler
committed suicide.

There's no sign pointing out the castle
site. Look for the entrance gate with a field
in front of it and the inevitable tourist activity. To get there by public transport from
Naha, take a bus to Futenma and from there
take bus No 58.

Nakamura House 中村家

Half a kilometre up the road from the castle is Nakamura-ke, probably the best preserved traditional Okinawan house on the
island. The Nakamura family's origins in
the area can be traced back to the 15th century, but the foundations of this house date
from around 1720. The construction is typical of a well-off farming family's residence
at that time. Originally, the roof would have
been thatched, but it was later roofed with
traditional red tiles. As you explore this interesting and surprisingly comfortable-
looking home, notice the substantial stone
pig pens, the elevated storage area (to deter
rats) and the trees grown as typhoon wind-

breaks. The house (¥300, 9 am to 5.30 pm)
is a 10-minute walk up from Nakagusuku-
jō; bus No 58 passes by.

OKINAWA CITY 沖縄市

Okinawa City is the US military centre on
Okinawa-hontō, focused around the Kadena
Air Force Base (the initial target of the US
invasion at the end of WWII). What was,
before the war, a village, has mushroomed
to boast a population of over 100,000 and
has all the hallmarks of US influence, from
pizzerias to army surplus stores. The Tuttle
Bookstore at the Plaza House shopping mall
is the best English-language bookshop on
Okinawa.

A few kilometres west of here, in Chatan,
the US-style Mihama Complex includes
movie theatres, restaurants, bars and shops.
Out on Route 58, excellent Mexican food is
available at *Obbligato Café;* upstairs is
Freedom Café, done up in an American
Southwest motif.

Attractions around Okinawa City, some
of them decidedly artificial, include the
Moromi Folkcraft Museum, the **Koza-yaki
Pottery Factory**, **Okinawa Children's Land**,
the **Nantō Shokubutsu-rakuen** (South-East
Botanical Gardens) and the **Agena-jōseki**
and **Katsuren-jō** sites. **Bullfights**, where one
bull tries to push another out of a ring, are
held on Sunday at Gushikawa. See the
'Bullfighting' boxed text.

OKINAWA & SW ISLANDS

Bullfighting

Battles between bulls, where one tries to push
the other out of the ring (rather like *sumō*
wrestling), are known as *tōgyū* in Japan. The
sport is found in a long sweep of islands all
the way from Indonesia to Japan. There are
about a dozen tōgyū stadiums in Okinawa,
the most important ones being Agena Stadium in Gushikawa and Kankō Stadium in
Okinawa City. The most important fights are
held in May and November, but they take
place a couple of times a month year round.
The bulls for Okinawa tōgyū events are bred
on Kuro-shima, near Iriomote-jima.

There are buses to Okinawa City from Naha (¥770, 1 hour and 20 minutes).

OKINAWA CITY TO NAGO
沖縄市から名護へ

Enthusiasts of castle ruins can find more of them at the **Iha-jō** site near Ishikawa and at the **Zakimi-jō** site on the west coast, north of Kadena. In Zakimi-jōseki, **Yomitan Museum** displays local farming equipment.

Fathoms Diving (☎ 090-8766-0868, fax 956-6191, email diveoki@fathoms.net), based in Yomitan, is Okinawa's only scuba outfit run by foreigners, and kindly caters to English-speaking divers. It offers classes from beginner to instructor level, rental equipment, and professional guided shore and boat dives. Go to www.fathoms.net.

The Okinawan resort strip starts from **Zampa Beach** on Zampa-misaki. The folk village, **Ryūkyū-mura** (¥600, 8.30 am to 5 pm), offers yet another opportunity for you to see a re-creation of Okinawan farming life, and yet another snake park, where, for the amusement of tourists, those 'deadly' habu lose out (once again) to plucky mongooses (see the 'Habu Snakes' boxed text earlier in this chapter).

More beach life can be found at the Ramada Renaissance Resort, Moon Beach and Manza Beach. Just before Nago is **Okinawa Submarine Park**, where you can actually descend into the ocean depths in a submarine called *Moglyn* for ¥10,000 (reserve at the Sun Marina Hotel by ringing ☎ 964-5555).

As well as the expensive resort hotels along this coast, there is *Maeda-misaki Youth Hostel* (☎ 964-2497) near Ryūkyū-mura, where dorm beds cost ¥2000. Bus No 20 from Naha runs along the west coast past all these sites to Nago. It takes about one hour and 20 minutes to get to Ryūkyū-mura or Moon Beach, one hour and 40 minutes to get to Manza Beach and two hours to get to the submarine park.

NAGO 名護
☎ 0980 • pop 51,000

Nago, site of the 2000 G8 Summit, makes a good overnight stop if you're spending a couple of days exploring Okinawa-hontō;

it's about two-thirds of the way up the island. There are fine views over the town and the coast from the castle hill, although little remains of the old castle. In spring the cherry blossoms on the hill are particularly good. A fine old banyan tree, **Himpun Gajumara**, is a useful landmark in the centre of town. You can find out all about traditional farming at the **Nago Museum** (¥150, 10 am to 6 pm, closed Monday), close to the banyan.

Places to Stay & Eat

The no-frills *Hotel Okura* (☎ 521-284) has per-person rates from ¥3500, while the similar *Business Hotel Shiroyama* (☎ 52-3111) starts at ¥4200. *Hotel Nago Castle* (☎ 52-5954) is a clean, pleasant place close to the centre of town, with singles/twins from ¥4400/7700 (breakfast ¥500). The newer *Hotel 21st Century* (☎ 53-2655) has singles/twins from ¥6500/11,000. It's farther north up Route 58. Close by, on the

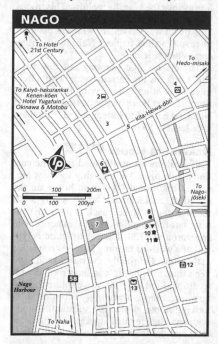

beach, is *Hotel Yugafuin Okinawa* (☎ 53-0031), where singles/doubles/twins cost ¥6500/10,000/11,000.

Shinzan Shokudō is a famous Nago soba shop that has been running for more than 60 years. For authentic Okinawan food and fresh *sushi*, head for *Izakaya Hottarakashi* (dinner only, closed Thursday). Nago's entertainment area also has the usual plethora of bars, snack bars and so on.

Getting There & Away
Nago is the junction town for buses to northern Okinawa or the peninsula, Motobu-hantō. From Okinawa City bus station, take bus No 20 or 21 (¥1740, 2½ hours).

NAGO

PLACES TO STAY & EAT
1 Hotel Nago Castle
  ホテル名護
  キャッスル
9 Shinzan Shokudō
  新山食堂
10 Hotel Ōkura
  ホテルおおくら
11 Business Hotel
  Shiroyama
  ビジネスホテル城山

OTHER
2 Bus Stop; Oki-Mart
  Supermarket
  バス停；
  おきマートスーパー
3 Market
  市場
4 NTT
5 Nago Cross Roads
  名護十字路
6 Izakaya Hottarakashi
  居酒屋ほったらかし
7 Bowling Alley
  北ボーリング場
8 Himpun Gajumara
  Banyan Tree
  バンヤンの樹
12 Nago Museum
  名護博物館
13 Post Office
  郵便局

MOTOBU-HANTŌ 本部半島
Jutting out to the north-west of Nago, the hilly Motobu-hantō has several points of interest, as well as ferry services to nearby Iejima. In Motobu town, don't miss the noodles at *Ichi Rikki Soba*.

Kokuei Okinawa Kinen-kōen 沖縄記念公園
The site of the 1975 International Ocean Exposition, Kokuei Okinawa Kinen-kōen (Okinawa Memorial Park) has a cluster of tourist attractions, most of which can be bypassed. Entry to the park itself is free, but the individual attractions charge entry fees. The **aquarium** (¥670) is claimed to be one of the largest in the world and the sharks and rays in the big tank, particularly the huge whale-shark, are indeed impressive.

Other attractions include the Oceanic Culture Museum (¥160); the Museum of Okinawa (¥150); Native Okinawan Village (free); Tropical Dream Centre (¥670), with orchid and other flower displays around the curious circular spiral tower; and a **dolphin show** (free). The park also has a beach and an amusement park.

The park is open from 9.30 am to 5.30, 6 or 7 pm depending on the season and is closed on Thursday. Individual attractions close 30 minutes earlier. Buses run to the park from Naha and Nago.

Nakijin-jōseki 今帰仁城跡
Winding over a hilltop, the 14th-century castle walls of Nakijin-jō (¥150, 8.30 am to 6.30 pm) may not be as neat as Nakagusuku-jō, but they look terrific. From the summit of the hill there are superb views out to sea. You can take bus No 66 from Nago or bus No 65 from Kokuei Okinawa Kinen-kōen.

Other Attractions
Yambaru Wildlife Park and **Pineapple Park** are other peninsula sites. There are also two islands connected to the peninsula by road. To the south is **Sesoko-jima**, which has good beaches on the western side, as well as camping facilities. Bus No 76 from Nago takes around 55 minutes. From the bus stop

it's around a 20-minute walk to the west-side beaches (the island is only eight sq km).

Three kilometres west of Sesoko-jima is tiny **Minna-jima** (0.56 sq km), with fabulous beaches. Ferries run from Motobu-kō port just south of the Sesoko-ōhashi.

IE-JIMA 伊江島

North-west of Motobu-hantō, Ie-jima offers a wonderful view from the top of the mountain, **Gusuku-yama**. It's about a 45-minute walk from the pier. The truly indolent might consider a taxi, which should cost around ¥800. Around five minutes' walk to the south of the pier is a **monument** to the US war correspondent Ernie Pyle, who was killed on the island during the early days of the Battle of Okinawa. Also possibly worth checking out is the Shimamuraya Kankō-kōen (Shimamuraya Sightseeing Park; ¥300), not far to the north of the Ernie Pyle monument.

Those planning a longer stay on the island can hire tents (¥300) at *Iejima Seishōnen Ryokō Mura* (☎ 49-5247). Alternatively, *Marco Polo Pension* (☎ 49-5242), around 300m north of the pier, has rates from ¥6500 with two meals included. *Hill Top Hotel* (☎ 49-2341), a nondescript white building, is about a 15-minute walk in the same direction and costs ¥6000 with two meals.

Ferries make the trip to the island from Motobu-kō port (¥580, 30 minutes, five times daily). Buses around the 8km-by-3km island are irregular, but bicycles, scooters and cars can be rented.

NORTHERN OKINAWA-HONTŌ 沖縄の北部

☎ 0980

The northern part of Okinawa-hontō is lightly populated and comparatively wild and rugged. A road runs around the coast, making this an interesting loop, but buses are infrequent and do not continue all the way along the east coast.

West Coast to Hedo-misaki 西海岸から平戸岬へ

Route 58 north from Nago has virtually converted the bay, Shioya-wan, into an enclosed lake. The village of **Kijoka** is noted for its traditional houses and for the production of the very rare cloth known as Bashōfu. Call ahead if you want to visit **Kijoka Bashōfu Weaving Workshop** (☎ 44-3033). Farther north, *JAL Private Resort* (☎ 41-2222) at **Okuma Beach** has pleasant cottages from ¥11,000 per person, including breakfast. The town of **Hentona** has shops, *minshuku* (Japanese B&B-style inns) and other facilities.

Hedo-misaki marks the northern end of Okinawa. The rocky point is liberally sprinkled with cigarette ends and soft-drink cans. Nevertheless, the cape is a scenic spot backed by hills, with rocks rising from the dense greenery. Bus No 67 (¥950) travels along the coast from Nago, but you have to continue north from Hentona on bus No 69 (¥660).

East Coast 東海岸

From Hedo-misaki, the road continues to **Oku**, the termination point for buses travelling up the west coast via the cape. The English sign 'Hotel' at the beginning of the village leads you, 250m farther along, to a sign which 'Wellcomes' you to *Oku Yanbaru-sō* (☎ 0980-41-8117). The per-person rate is just ¥4000 including two meals.

There are good beaches around Oku. For the next 15km the road stays very close to the coastline, with more fine-looking beaches but frequent warnings of current and tide dangers for swimmers, divers and snorkellers. **Aha** is a picturesque village that still has some traditional thatched-roof houses.

ISLANDS AROUND OKINAWA-HONTŌ 沖縄本島周辺の島々

Apart from the islands just a stone's throw from the Okinawan coast, there are other islands a little farther away.

Iheya-jima 伊平屋島 & Izena-jima 伊是名島

North of Okinawa, these two islands have good beaches and snorkelling and a number of hotels and minshuku. A daily ferry runs from Motobu's port to Izena (1½ hours) and Iheya (another 20 minutes).

Kerama-rettō 慶良間列島

There are about 20 islands in this group west of Okinawa-hontō, only four of which are inhabited.

Zamami-jima and **Aka-jima** have recently started to develop facilities to cater to the waves of tourists seeking a glimpse of the humpback whales that have recently returned to these waters. These islands have fine beaches, some good walks, camping, great lookouts and some of the best diving in Japan.

On Zamami-jima, *Shirahama Islands Resort* (☎ 098-987-2073), an eight-minute walk from the port, has rates starting at ¥7500, including two meals. You can call (in Japanese) in advance to arrange a pickup. There is also a dive shop here, Kerama Islands Club (☎ 098-987-2336).

On Aka-jima, *Resort Akajima Soadorun* (☎ 098 987 2341), a five-minute walk from the port, charges from ¥9000 with two meals. Saesir (☎ 0120-102-737) is a popular dive shop on the island.

Many dive operators on Okinawa-hontō, including the gaijin run Fathoms (☎ 0908-8766-0868, fax 098-956-6191, email diveoki@fathoms.net) run day trips to Kerama, generally returning in the afternoon (see the Okinawa to Nago section under Okinawa-hontō earlier).

Ferries from Naha take one to 1½ hours; 15-minute flights are also available.

Kume-jima 久米島

West of the Kerama-rettō is beautiful Kume-jima, with its superb scenery, excellent beaches and long, curving sweep of sandbank at **Sky Holiday Reef**, just east of the island. **Uezuke-ke** (¥300, 9 am to 6 pm) is a samurai-style home dating from 1726.

There are *ryokan* (traditional Japanese inns) and minshuku on the island, particularly near **Iifu Beach**. There are also several resort hotels, such as *Resort Kume Island* (☎ 098-985-8001), where rooms cost from ¥14,000 per person with two meals. Day trips can be made from Iifu Beach to Sky Holiday Reef.

There are ferries to the island from Naha (¥2900, four hours), and express-boat services (under two hours). JTA has regular daily flights (¥8450, 35 minutes).

You can get around the island by rented car, scooter or bicycle.

Miyako-shotō
宮古諸島

☎ 09807

About 300km south-west of Okinawa, directly en route to the Yaeyama-shotō, is the eight-island Miyako group, comprising Miyako-jima and, a few kilometres to the west, Irabu-jima and Shimoji-jima, plus a scattering of smaller islands. Each year the very low spring tide reveals the huge Yaebishi reef, north of Ikema-jima. Sadly, misguided tour operators deliver boatloads of heavy-footed sightseers directly onto the living reef! Compounding the damage done by the soles of tourists' shoes, many daytrippers come armed with crowbars and other tools of destruction to pry away coral and shellfish from the reef.

MIYAKO-JIMA 宮古島

Covered in sugar cane plantations, Miyako-jima offers fine beaches, diving and excellent deep-sea game fishing.

Japanese triathletes flock to the island in April each year for the Strongman Challenge, which involves a 3km swim, a 136km bicycle race and a 42km marathon.

Hirara 平良
- pop 34,500

Hirara, the main town on Miyako-jima, is compact and easy to get around. There are a few minor attractions here, but the operative word is indeed 'minor'. Near the waterfront, just north of the ferry terminal, is the **mausoleum** of Nakasone Toimiyā, the 15th-century Miyako hero who not only conquered the Yaeyama-shotō to the south, but also prevented an invasion from the north. There's another impressively large mausoleum cut into the hillside just beyond it.

Continuing north along the coast road you'll find the **Nintōzeiseki** (Tax Stone), a

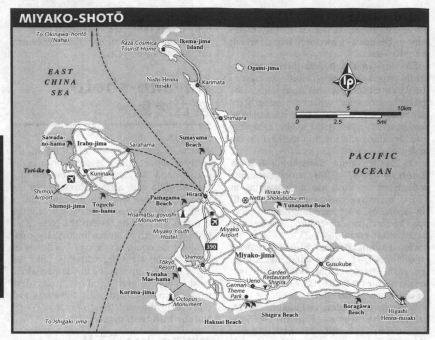

OKINAWA & SW ISLANDS

1.4m-high stone, more or less plonked down in someone's front garden. During the heavy-handed rule of the Satsuma kingdom (which invaded from Kagoshima on Kyūshū in the 15th century), anyone taller than this stone was required to pay taxes. Jōfu, Miyako-jima's traditional textile, was once used to make tax payments.

Close to the ferry terminal is **Harimizu Utaki**, a shrine devoted to two local gods. Other sights in the town include the Kaiser Wilhelm, or **Hakuai Monument**, presented to the island in 1876 as a gesture of gratitude for the rescue of the crew of a typhoon-wrecked German merchant ship in 1873. Local authorities decided to further capitalise on the historical connection by building a large, highly kitsch **German Theme Park** out on the southern coast of the island.

Beaches & Diving
Miyako-jima has its share of good beaches, surf and diving spots. Try the beaches along the south and north coasts, or Yonaha Mae-hama on the south-west coast, reputed to be the finest beach in Japan. Immediately north of Hirara is lovely Suna-yama (Sand Mountain) Beach. You can watch the sunset here through a giant stone arch on the beach.

There are also good beaches on Ikema-jima, off the northernmost point of Miyako-jima; and on Kurima-jima to the south. Both islands are linked to the main island by a bridge.

Miyako-jima is a wildly popular diving centre, and it has more than 50 dive sites and a dynamic range of underwater drop-offs and overhangs. Popular sites include Devil's Palace and Tanike, well known for cave diving. There are plenty of dive operators on the island, including Good Fellas Club (☎ 3-5483, email fellas@cosmos.ne.jp).

Higashi-Henna-misaki 東平安名岬
At the south-eastern end of the island, this long, narrow and quite spectacular peninsula

ends with a picturesquely placed lighthouse on the cape overlooking the rocky coastline.

Other Attractions

Hisamatsu-goyūshi, a monument in the village of Hisamatsu, a few kilometres southwest of Hirara, commemorates the fishermen who spotted the Russian fleet steaming north during the Russo–Japanese War of 1904–05. Admiral Tōgō was able to intercept them north of Kyūshū.

Hirara-shi Nettai Shokubutsu-en (free, 8.30 am to 5 pm) are 4km east of Hirara, in Onoyama. Just south of the botanical gardens, **Hirara-shi Sōgō Museum** (¥300, 9 am to 4.30 pm, closed Monday) has an eclectic range of items on display.

Places to Stay

Miyako Youth Hostel (☎ 3-7700), about 1km south-east of the ferry terminal, charges ¥4000 including two meals.

Hirara is chock-a-block with drab, concrete minshuku. Prices typically range from ¥5000 to ¥6000 with two meals thrown in. Try *Minshuku Shichifuku-sō* (☎ 2-3316), which has basic rooms and charges ¥5500/3500 per person with/without meals. The fragrant fumes that waft in from the awamori distillery across the road are free. *Ryokan Uruma-sō* (☎ 2-3113), up near the harbour terminal, has similar rates.

The central *Moon Hotel* (☎ 2-0003) is a clean place charging from ¥5700 per person. The in house restaurant is a good breakfast choice. At *Hotel Kyowa* (☎ 3-2288), near the waterfront overlooking Harimizu Utaki, twin rooms start at ¥11,000. The cheaper *Hotel Urizun* (☎ 2-4410) has singles from ¥3800.

The popular *New Marakatsu Hotel* (☎ 2-9936) is a rambling, slightly tatty place down an alley off the main road in Hirara. Twin rooms cost ¥10,600.

For peace and quiet in truly beautiful surroundings, book a room at *Raza Cosmica Tourist Home* (☎ 5-2020, email raza@ml.cosmos.ne.jp), located north of Miyako-jima on Ikema-jima. Run by a friendly young couple, this charming inn is eclectically decorated and sits right above a secluded little beach cove. Per-person rates

The 'Communication Drink'

The friendly people of Miyako-jima have earned a reputation for drinking, and the Izato entertainment area in the town of Hirara is said to have more bars (relative to its population) than any other town in Japan.

Miyako even has its unique local drinking custom, called *otori*. Sometimes referred to as the 'communication drink', this group drinking ritual involves making a speech, filling your own glass (usually with potent *awamori* – the local liquor) and then filling the glasses of all in the room. Everyone drinks up, the leader makes a short closing speech and picks the next victim, and the routine starts all over again.

Miyako's otori is so notorious that even hard-livered Okinawans from neighbouring islands are said to fear the ritual. If you happen to end up lured into an otori and want to sneak out before getting over-the-top plastered, one local veteran boozer advises, 'Never say goodbye. Just head for the toilet and don't come back!'.

are ¥8500, including two wholesome meals. Take a bus from the Yachiyo terminal in Hirara to the Gakko-ura bus stop (¥450), a short walk from the inn. A taxi ride from town will set you back around ¥2600.

Options farther afield on Miyako-jima include the expensive *Tōkyū Resort* (☎ 6-2109) on beautiful Yonaha Mae-hama. Prices start at ¥14,000 and reach astronomical rates.

Places to Eat

Miyako-jima is known for its local soba, and *Koja Honten* in central Hirara is as cheap and good as any restaurant in town.

Rakkii maintains a good local reputation for out-of-the-ordinary dishes you might call a taste-bud 'challenge'. Choices range from goat stew and horse sashimi to turtle soup. Rakkii is open from 11 am to 11 pm daily.

A-Dish, about 500m south-west of the ferry terminal, serves creative variations on Okinawan cuisine. Its tempting pastas feature fresh local ingredients.

Namikichi is a popular izakaya where you can eat from around ¥1000. Sample its sumptuous *tōfu* (bean curd) steak.

For the best fresh sushi and sashimi on Miyako-jima, try *Kintarō,* open 5 to 10.30 pm daily.

On the southern side of the island, near Ueno, look out for the excellent *Garden Restaurant Shigira*. The fare here is authentic Okinawan, and includes the very tasty handmade *mozoku soba* (noodles mixed with a gooey kind of local seaweed) and top-notch *goya champuru* (bitter-gourd stir-fry).

Entertainment
Jamaica-inspired *Jammin'* is a funky little reggae bar in central Hirara. *Marvin Soul Bar* plays *Soul Train* videos and Motown music, and nearby *Temps* (yes, as in *The Temptations)* is Miyako-jima's sole dance spot. In the same area, *New York, New York* has character (graffiti on the walls, and billiards), if you can tolerate hearing the same CD of 1950s love ballads being played over, and over, and over again. Upstairs from the popular A-Dish restaurant is a funky bar called *Alchemist*.

Getting There & Away
Air Direct flights on JTA cost ¥41,750 from Tokyo (Narita), or ¥34,650 from Ōsaka (KIX). JTA flies Naha–Miyako-jima about 10 times daily (¥12,400, 45 minutes) and Miyako-jima–Ishigaki-jima (¥8250, 35 minutes).

Boat There are ferries to/from Naha every two to five days (¥3880, 10 hours). Most continue to Ishigaki-jima, taking another six hours.

Getting Around
To/From the Airport A taxi from the airport into Hirara costs about ¥1000. The same journey will cost you ¥120 by bus.

Bus Miyako-jima has a comprehensive bus network. Bus Nos 1, 2, 3, 4, 7 and 8 run from Yachiyo bus station in Hirara to the north of the island, while Nos 10, 11, 12, 13 and 15 go south towards Higashi-Henna-misaki.

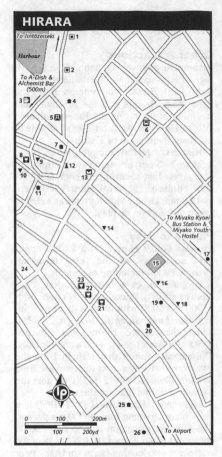

Car & Motorcycle There are a number of car- and motorcycle-rental places around town. Cars rent for as little as ¥6000 a day, motor scooters for around ¥3000 a day and motorcycles for ¥6500. Try the two Honda dealers shown on the Hirara map (Tomihama and Marutama), or Sankyū (☎ 2-2204), a dealer with a wide range of motorbikes. Bicycles can also be rented.

IRABU-JIMA & SHIMOJI-JIMA
伊良部島 · 下地島
If you fly over Shimoji-jima (between Okinawa and Ishigaki-jima), have a look at the

OKINAWA & SW ISLANDS

HIRARA

PLACES TO STAY
4 Hotel Kyōwa
　ホテル共和
7 Ryokan Uruma-sō
　旅館うるま荘
11 Hotel Urizun
　ホテルうりずん
15 New Marukatsu
　Hotel
　ホテルニュー丸勝
20 Minshuku
　Shichifuku-sō
　民宿七福荘
25 Moon Hotel
　宮古島ムーンホテル

PLACES TO EAT
9 Rakkii
　ラッキー食堂
10 Koja Honten
　古謝本店
14 Namikichi
　なみ古

16 Kintarō
　金太楼寿司
18 Nomura
　野村レストラン

OTHER
1 Chirimara Tomiyā
　Mausoleum
　和利真良豊見之墓
2 Nakasone Toimiyā
　Mausoleum
　仲宗根豊見之墓
3 Ferry Terminal
　平良港ターミナル
5 Harimizu Utaki Shrine
　張水御嶽神社
6 Yachiyo Bus Station
　八千代バスターミナル
8 Jammin' Reggae Bar
　じゃみんレゲエバー
12 Kaiser Wilhelm Hakuai
　Monument
　ドイツ皇帝博愛記念碑

13 Post Office
　郵便局
17 Sankyū
　Rent-a-Bike
　サンキューレンタ
　バイク
19 Tomihama Motorcycle
　Rental
　とみはまモーター
　サイクルレンタル
21 NewYork, NewYork Bar
　ニューヨーク
　ニューヨーク
22 Marvin Soul Bar
　マービン
23 Temps Bar
　テンプス
24 Market
　平良市公設市場
26 Marutama Motorcycle
　Rental
　丸玉モーター
　サイクルレンタル

OKINAWA & SW ISLANDS

airport runway. It seems to be out of all proportion to the size of the island and the number of flights it gets. This is because JAL and ANA use it for 747 touch-and-go training.

Irabu-jima and Shimoji-jima, linked by six bridges, are pleasantly rural islands with fields of sugar cane. **Sawada-no-hama** and **Toguchi-no-hama** are two good beaches on Irabu-jima. On Shimoji-jima, the lakes, **Tōri-ike**, are linked to the sea by hidden tunnels (a great dive-site!).

There are a few places to stay on Irabu-jima, including *Minshuku Katera-sō (☎ 8-3654)*, close to Toguchi Beach. It has rooms from ¥4500, with breakfast.

Getting There & Away
JTA has a daily flight from Naha to Shimoji-jima, but most visitors arrive on the regular ferry between Hirara on Miyako-jima and Sarahama on Irabu-jima (¥400, 15 minutes). There are two agencies in the ferry terminal selling tickets for boats.

Yaeyama-shotō
八重山諸島

At the far south-western end of the Nansei-shotō are the islands of the Yaeyama group, consisting of two main islands (Ishigaki-jima and Iriomote-jima) and a scattering of smaller islands between and beyond. There are excellent dive sites around these islands, including off Yonaguni-jima (the westernmost point in Japan) and Hateruma-jima (the southernmost point). Most visitors to the islands, in true Japanese fashion, are day-trippers.

ISHIGAKI-JIMA 石垣島
☎ 09808
Four hundred kilometres south-west of Okinawa-hontō, Ishigaki-jima is the major flight destination in the Yaeyama-shotō, and boat services fan out from its harbour to the other islands. There are several good beaches and sights on the island itself, though for

YAEYAMA-SHOTŌ

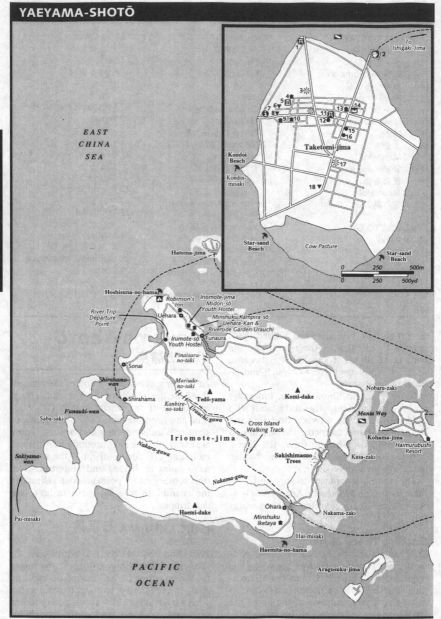

**EAST
CHINA
SEA**

Taketomi-jima

To Ishigaki-Jima

Kondoi
Beach

Kondoi-
misaki

Star-sand
Beach

Cow Pasture

Star-sand
Beach

Hatoma-jima

Hoshisuna-no-hama

Robinson's
Inn

Iriomote-jima
Midori-sō
Youth Hostel

River Trip
Departure
Point

Uehara

Minshuku Kampira-sō;
Uehara-Kan &
Riverside Garden Urauchi

Irumote-sō
Youth Hostel

Funaura

Pinaisara-
no-taki

Sonai

Mariudo-
no-taki

Nobaru-zaki

Shirahama-
wan

Tedō-yama

Komi-dake

Manta Way

Shirahama

Kanbire-
no-taki

Kohama-jima

Saba-saki

Funauki-wan

Urauchi-gawa

Cross Island
Walking Track

Haimurubushi
Resort

Sakiyama-
wan

Nakara-gawa

Iriomote-jima

Sakishimasuo
Trees

Kasa-zaki

Nakama-gawa

Pai-misaki

Haemi-dake

Ōhara

Minshuku
Iketaya

Nakama-zaki

Hai-misaki

Haemita-no-hama

**PACIFIC
OCEAN**

Aragusuku-jima

0   250   500m
0   250   500yd

OKINAWA & SW ISLANDS

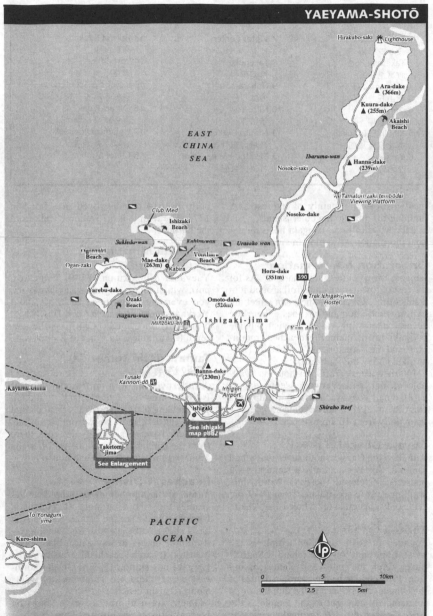

YAEYAMA-SHOTŌ

EAST
CHINA
SEA

Hirakubo-saki ☀ *Lighthouse*

▲ Ara-dake
(366m)

Kuura-dake
▲ (255m)

Akaishi
Beach

Ibaruma-wan

Nosoko-saki

▲ Hanna-dake
(239m)

⚡ Tamatori-zaki tenbōdai
Viewing Platform

Club Med

Ishizaki
Beach

Nosoko-dake

Sukieda-wan

Kabira-wan

Urasoko-wan

Ōganzaki
Beach

Mae-dake
(263m)

Yonehara
Beach

Ogan-zaki

Kabira

Hora-dake
(351m)

390

Yarebu-dake

Ōzaki
Beach

Omoto-dake
(526m)

Trek Ishigaki-jima
Hostel

Nuguru-wan

Yaeyama
Minzoku-en

I s h i g a k i - j i m a

Kam-dake

Banna-dake
(230m)

Fusaki
Kannon-dō 卍

Ishigaki
Airport ✈

Kayama-shima

Ishigaki

See Ishigaki
map p882

Miyara-wan

Shiraho Reef

Taketomi-
jima

See Enlargement

To Yonaguni-
jima

PACIFIC

Kuro-shima

OCEAN

Ip

| 0 | 5 | 10km |
| 0 | 2.5 | 5mi |

YAEYAMA-SHOTŌ

1 Misashi Utaki
  ミサシ御嶽
2 Taketomi Port
  竹富港
3 Akayamaoka
  赤山丘
4 Izumiya
  民宿泉屋
5 Kihōin Shūshūkan
  喜宝院蒐集館
6 Yarabo
  やらぼ

7 Visitor Center
  ビジターセンター
8 Takenoko
  竹の子
9 Nohara-sō
  のはら荘
10 Nitta-sō
  新田荘
11 Nishitō Utaki
  西塘御嶽神社
12 Taketomi Mingeikan
  竹富民芸館

13 Takana Ryokan
  高那旅館
14 Post Office
  郵便局
15 Bicycles & Scooters for Rent
  自転車バイクレンタル
16 Oxcart Rides
  水牛車乗り場
17 Unbufuru Lookout
  ンブフル展望台
18 Chirorin-mura

most visitors it's mainly of interest as a jumping-off point to the other islands.

Like Miyako-jima, Ishigaki hosts an annual international triathlon in spring.

Orientation & Information

Ishigaki town centres on its harbour. As for the rest of town – you can stroll around it in a short time. Parallel to the main street are two covered shopping arcades. There are several interesting places to visit outside Ishigaki town, including beaches, mountains and the Tamatorizaki-tembōdai (Tamatorizaki Viewing Platform).

Internet access (¥500 per hour) is available at Yaeyama Network Center (☎ 4-2100, email koji@yaeyama.ne.jp), upstairs from the market in the covered arcade. It's open daily from 10 am to 8 pm.

Miyara Dōnchi 宮良殿内

Although the Nansei-shotō never really had samurai, this is essentially a samurai-style house (¥200, closed Tuesday). Worthwhile strolling over to see, it dates from 1819 and is the only one left in the whole island chain.

Tōrin-ji 桃林寺

Founded in 1614, this Zen temple is the most important on the island. 'Sentry' boxes flank the gates and statues dating from 1737 (said to be the guardian deities of the islands) can be seen in the dim interiors. Immediately adjacent to the temple is the 1787 **Gongen-dō**. The original shrine was built in 1614 but destroyed in a flood in 1771. The temple is a 15-minute walk from the harbour.

Yaeyama Minzoku-en 八重山民俗園

Yaeyama Minzoku-en (¥500, 9 am to 6 pm), which faces Nagura-wan, should tell you everything you need to know about Yaeyama weaving and pottery. Bus Nos 5, 6 and 7 from Ishigaki town pass the museum (20 minutes) en route to Kabira-wan.

Tamatorizaki-tembōdai 玉取崎展望台

A little over halfway up the east coast of Ishigaki-jima is Tamatorizaki-tenbōdai. The viewing platform provides great coastal views and is a short walk from some fine, untouched beaches. Bus No 9 goes there from the Ishigaki bus station – get off at the Tamatori bus stop (¥750, one hour).

Beaches & Diving

There are a number of popular beaches around the island, notably at Yonehara, Ishizaki, Oganzaki and Ōzaki. Kabira-wan has a sheltered beach with fine sand, a collection of places to stay and a black-pearl industry. It can be reached by bus from the Ishigaki bus station (¥590). On the northeast coast, there are great coastal walks along Akaishi beach.

There are a number of dive shops on Ishigaki-jima, including Tom Sawyer

Surfers at Suna-yama, Miyako-jima, Okinawa

Sugarcane farmer, Miyako-jima

Miyako-jima is a popular surf and dive spot, with over 50 dive sites.

Carved statue of Iriomote wild cat, Iriomote-jima.

Tropical butterfly, Iriomote-jima

The Chinese-influenced Shurei-no-mon, Shurei-jō.

A replica of Shuri-jō, the former residence of the Okinawan royal family at Naha, the capital of Okinawa.

(☎ 3-4677) and Aquamarine (☎ 2-0863). Manta rays can be spotted from summer to autumn. Boat-dive trips with lunch included are around ¥12,000. Other popular beach activities, most with expensive price tags on them, include windsurfing and parasailing.

Hikes & Other Attractions

Omoto-dake (526m), in the centre of the island, is the highest point in Okinawa-ken, and there are good views from the large boulder at the top. **Fusaki Kannon-dō** dates from 1701, and from the temple's hilltop position, about 6km north-west of the town, there are good views towards Taketomi-jima and Iriomote-jima. Entry is free, but unless you hire a bicycle you'll have to take a taxi out there (around ¥1200). Close by is Tōjin-baka, a Chinese grave site. The cape at the northern end of the island, **Hirakubo-saki**, has an interesting lighthouse.

Better hiking exists on **Nosoko-dake**, the eroded core of a volcano, where a steep 45-minute trek takes you to the summit. **Mae-dake** has a moister, jungle feeling to it and, like Nosoko-dake, is steep at the top and affords great views. **Banna-dake**, 5km from town, is only 230m high but offers fine views and a botanical garden, Banna-dake Shinrin-kōen (free).

The small **Yaeyama Museum** (¥100, 9 am to 4.30 pm, closed Monday) is very close to the harbour in Ishigaki town and has displays including coffin palanquins, or gau, and dugout canoes.

Ishigaki-ke-teien (Ishigaki-ke Garden) in town follows the regular garden-construction conventions, complete with volcanic rocks. Although it is private, you should be able to see the garden if you ask politely.

Places to Stay

Ishigaki is a compact little town and there are plenty of places to stay within walking distance of the harbour. Other accommodation can be found scattered around the island.

The best budget accommodation is at **Guesthouse Rakutenya** (☎ 3-8713), an old wooden house right in the town centre. It charges ¥3000 per person. The friendly couple here, Miyako and Ren, speak English and are a great source of local information. Just next door, Ren's sparky mother runs the charming **Minshuku Ishi-gaki-jima** (☎ 2-6066), which costs from ¥6000 including two meals. You can trust the food; she has written cookbooks on local cuisine!

Yashima Ryokan Youth Hostel (☎ 2-3157) is close to the centre of town, a few minutes' walk north of the Yaeyama Museum, and costs ¥2300 per night.

The neat little **Pension Mitake** (☎ 2-4993) has per-person rates from ¥3000 (room only). Another inexpensive option worth considering is **Minshuku Yaeyama-sō** (☎ 2-3231). It's a pleasant place and its rates start at ¥4500 with two meals. Walk north from the post office for about 400m.

On the business-hotel front, **Ōhara Hotel** (☎ 2-3380) has singles for ¥6500.

More expensive hotels include **Ishigaki Grand Hotel** (☎ 2-6161), across from the harbour, with singles/doubles from ¥10,000/14,000. Nearby is **Hotel Miyahira** (☎ 2-6111), where twins cost from ¥15,500. The fancy **Hotel Nikko Yaeyama** (☎ 3-3311) is north of town, about a 25-minute walk from the harbour. Singles/twins start at ¥10,500/18,500.

Farther away from town, **Trek Ishigaki-jima Youth Hostel** (☎ 6-8257) is on the east coast of the island and charges ¥2300 per person. **Club Med** (☎ 4-4600) recently opened a plush resort north of Kabira, and there is also good **camping** at nearby Yone-hara Beach.

Places to Eat

Ishigaki has some fine eateries and several little bohemian cafes worth seeking out (the owners of Guesthouse Rakutenya are happy to make suggestions).

Yūkunumi is a cosy little place near the covered arcade serving great local soba and desserts – try kohii zenzai (¥400), shaved ice with coffee and sweet beans.

If you can brave a Japanese menu, try **Hanaki**, a delightfully cluttered place that specialises in 'country cooking' but it is

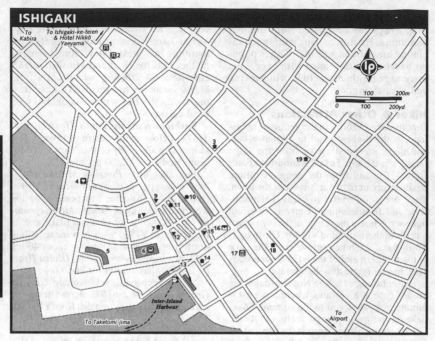

celebrated locally for its sushi. A good Chinese restaurant nearby is *Pekin Hanten*.

For drinks, check out the rooftop beer garden at the *Golden Misaki building*, a short walk north of Hotel Miyahira.

Getting There & Away

Air Direct flights on JTA cost ¥44,880 from Tokyo (Narita), or ¥30,350 from Ōsaka (KIX). JTA/ANK have more than 10 flights a day between Naha and Ishigaki-jima (¥16,250, one hour) and several between Miyako-jima and Ishigaki-jima (¥8250, 30 minutes). JTA flies from Ishigaki to the tiny Yonaguni-jima and to Hateruma-jima.

Boat Ishigaki-jima is the centre for all the Yaeyama-shotō ferries and the small harbour is a hive of activity. The two main ferry companies on the island are Yaeyama Kankō Ferry (☎ 2-5010) and Anei Kankō (☎ 3-0055). Their offices are along the two sides of the harbour; there are often several

operators servicing a given destination at varying prices.

There are services every two to five days directly between Naha and Ishigaki (¥5350, 13 hours) or via Miyako-jima. Miyako-jima-Ishigaki costs ¥1890 and takes about six hours. The Okinawa-Taiwan ferry service occasionally operates via Ishigaki (see Getting There & Away under Naha, earlier, for details).

Getting Around

There is no convenient bus service between the airport and town: a taxi costs about ¥700. The station, which is the point in Ishigaki town from which bus services fan out, is across the road from the harbour.

Rental cars are available at the airport and in town. Contact Sankyū (☎ 2-5528), an established agent with a good selection of cars/motorcycles from ¥3500/2500 per day.

Bicycles can be rented in town; the going rate is ¥500/1500 per hour/day.

ISHIGAKI

PLACES TO STAY
3 Guesthouse Rakutenya
  & Minshuku
  Ishigaki- jima
  民宿楽天屋；
  民宿石垣島
5 Hotel Miyahira
  ホテルミヤヒラ
7 Ōhara Hotel
  大原ホテル
11 Pension Mitake
  ペンション御嵩荘
14 Ishigaki Grand Hotel
  石垣グランドホテル
18 Yashima Ryokan
  Youth Hostel
  やしま旅館
  ユースホステル

19 Minshuku Yaeyama-sō
  民宿八重山荘

PLACES TO EAT
8 Pekin Hanten
  北京飯店
9 Hanaki
  はなき
12 A&W Burger
  A&W　バーガー
15 Yūkunumi
  ゆうくぬみ

OTHER
1 Tōrin-ji
  桃林寺
2 Gongen-dō
  権現堂

4 Golden Misaki;
  Beer Garden
  ゴールデンミサキ；
  ビアガーデン
6 Bus Station
  バスターミナル
10 Yaeyama Network
  Center; Market
  八重山ネットワーク
  センター：公設市場
13 Ferry Company
  Offices
  フェリー事務所
16 Post Office
  郵便局
17 Yaeyama Museum
  八重山博物館

OKINAWA & SW ISLANDS

TAKETOMI-JIMA 竹富島
☎ 09808

A 10-minute boat ride from Ishigaki is the
popular but relaxed little island, Taketomi-
jima. It's got some strong traces of Ryūkyū
culture, and plenty of traditional architecture remains (even the post office was built
Okinawan-style!).

The island is noted for its beaches and the
pretty little flower-bedecked village in its
centre. Even if you only come over for a
day trip, don't forget to bring a towel and
your bathing costume. There's excellent
swimming at Kondoi Beach, about a 20-
minute walk (or five-minute bike ride) from
the harbour area.

Orientation & Information
Taketomi-jima is a pancake-flat island with
its village in the middle. From Taketomi
Village, the (mostly) dirt roads fan out to
various places around the island's edge. A
paved road following the 10km coastline is
supposedly on the drawing board but, apart
from a section around the port and north-
western quadrant, it fortunately hasn't come
to much – paved roads would certainly de-
stroy the island's rural ambience. The visitors centre has a coral and shell display.

Taketomi Village 竹富村
The lookout on tiny Akayama Oka is atop
an even tinier hillock but, on this otherwise
flat island, it offers good views over the
red-tiled roofs. Look for the walls of coral
and rock and the angry-looking shiisā on
the rooftops. The other observation point is
the Unbufuru Tembōdai (Unbufuru Lookout; ¥100), at the northern end of the village, on top of someone's house.

Kihōin Shūshūkan (¥300) is a small private museum with a diverse collection of
local items. **Taketomi Mingei-kan** is a local
craft centre where you can see the island's
locally woven Minsā belts and other textiles
being produced. Opposite the craft centre is
Nishitō Utaki, a shrine dedicated to a 16th-
century ruler of the Yaeyama-shotō.

Beaches
Most of the island is fringed with beach, but
the water is generally very shallow. At several places you can look for *hoshisuna* (star
sand), tiny grains of star-shaped sand.
They're actually the dried skeletons of tiny
creatures. Although you are requested not to
souvenir more than a few grains, it's sold by
the bucketful at local shops. The Yayama-
shotō map shows good star-sand hunting

points on Taketomi-jima. At **Kondoi Beach**, north of Kondoi-misaki on the western side of the island, you'll find star sand and the best swimming spot on the island.

Places to Stay & Eat

Accommodation is not difficult to find on Taketomi-jima, and many of the traditional houses around the island are Japanese-style inns. *Takana Ryokan* (☎ 5-2151) is opposite the woodsy post office. The nightly cost, with two meals, is ¥7000. *Nohara-sō* (☎ 5-5252) is cheaper, with rooms for ¥5000 with two meals. Close by, *Nitta-sō* (☎ 5-2201) offers similar standards and rates, as does *Minshuku Izumiya* (☎ 5-2250) up the road.

There are several interesting restaurants and cafes scattered around the island. Woodsy little *Takenoko* serves good Yaeyama soba. *Yarabo* is another good choice for lunch or coffee. *Chirorin-mura* is a rustic little cafe-pub about 600m south of the post office.

Getting There & Away

The best deal for getting to the island is with the Yaeyama Kankō Ferry (☎ 2-5010 on Ishigaki-jima), whose boats do the 10-minute run from Ishigaki-jima (¥570) approximately every 30 minutes.

Getting Around

The island is small enough for you to be able to get around most of it on foot if the weather isn't too muggy. Otherwise, there are numerous bicycle-rental places on the island. Bikes cost ¥200/1000 an hour/day and are great for exploring the tiny island's sandy roads. You can also hire tandem bicycles, and motor scooters. For Japanese visitors, a popular activity is taking a tour of the island in a cart drawn by water buffalo (¥1000, 50 minutes – which is about what it takes to trundle around the island's points of interest).

IRIOMOTE-JIMA 西表島
☎ 09808

Dense jungle blankets much of Iriomote-jima, an island that could well qualify as Japan's last frontier. Trekking through the interior, you may find leeches, which in Japan is probably good enough to merit the 'wilderness' tag. The island's major attractions are fine beaches, rivers and waterfalls, and the Iriomote Yama-neko (Iriomote wildcat). Similar in size (and appearance) to a domestic cat, the wildcat is nocturnal and rarely seen. The picturesque road signs alerting drivers to its possible presence are, however, quite common.

Much easier to find are the curious sakishimasuo trees, with their twisting, ribbon-like root buttresses. You will find them all over the island, but particularly along the coast about 5km north of Ōhara. Iriomote National Park covers about 80% of the island, plus a number of neighbouring islands.

Orientation

Iriomote-jima has several small towns – Funaura, Uehara, Sonai and Shirahama in the north and Ōhara in the south – and a perimeter road runs about halfway around the coast from just beyond Ōhara to Shirahama. No roads run into the interior, which is virtually untouched.

River Trips

Iriomote's number-one attraction, and the principal goal for many day-trippers, is a trip up the Urauchi-gawa to the spectacular falls, **Mariudo-no-taki**. The winding brown river is indeed a lot like a tiny stretch of the Amazon, and from where the boat stops, you have about a 1½-hour round-trip walk to Mariudo-no-taki and on to the long, rapids-like **Kanbire-no-taki**. There are some good swimming holes around the falls, from which a walking track continues right across the island. Boats operate from 9 am to 4 pm, but they need a minimum of four passengers in order to set off. There is less waiting around if you arrive in the morning, when most of the day-trippers turn up.

From close to the Ōhara docks it is possible to take cruises up Iriomote's second-largest river, the **Nakama-gawa**. The cruises, through lush, jungle-like vegetation, last around an hour and 20 minutes.

Self-propelled travellers can also rent canoes and kayaks, or join one of several ecotour operators for an upriver excursion.

MaYaGuSuKu (☎/fax 5-6288) has experienced guides, and a variety of courses lasting from six hours to two days. This outfit comes highly recommended by Japanese travellers, and it's a good idea to reserve a day in advance. Kayaking/trekking tours start at ¥9000.

Walks

There are some great walks in Iriomote-jima's jungle-clad interior. **Pinaisara-no-taki**, on the hills behind the lagoon, are visible from boats coming into Funaura. To get to the falls you wade across the shallow lagoon from the causeway, plod through the mangroves behind the lagoon and then follow the river up to the base of the falls. A path branches off from the river and climbs to the top of the falls, from where there are superb views down to the coast. The walk takes 1½ to two hours and the falls are great for a cooling dip, but in summer bring salt or matches to get rid of leeches.

From Kambire-no-taki, at the end of the Urauchi-gawa trip, you can continue on the challenging cross-island trail to Ōhara. The walk takes about eight hours and is particularly popular in spring, when the many trekkers manage to lay a confusing network of false trails. All you need to know about exploring Iriomote-jima can be found in Lonely Planet's *Hiking in Japan*.

Beaches & Diving

There are some fine beaches around the island. At **Hoshisuna-no-hama** you'll find star sand. Sonai, beyond Urauchi-gawa towards Shirahama, also has a pleasant beach, and some good places to stay. **Haemita-no-hama**, south of Ōhara, is said to be the best beach on the island.

Diving around Iriomote-jima certainly isn't cheap, but there are some fine sites, like the famed **Manta Way** in the straits between Iriomote-jima and Kohama-jima, where you are almost certain to come across manta rays.

Dive operators on Iriomote-jima include Mr Sakana Diving Service (☎ 09808-5-6472) and Diving Team Unarizaki (☎ 09 808-5-6142). Both are in Uehara, and very little English is spoken at either.

Places to Stay & Eat

Iriomote-jima has many ryokan, minshuku and pensions, each of which sends a minibus to meet incoming boats at Funaura. Most places are found along the coast west of the harbour towards the beach at Hoshisuna-no-hama, and farther west near the Urauchi-gawa.

Irumote-sō Youth Hostel (☎ 5-6255) has a great hillside location near Funaura-kō port, good facilities and a dive shop. The nightly cost, including breakfast and dinner, is ¥3950. Along the coast from Funaura, *Iriomote-jima Midori-sō Youth Hostel* (☎ 5-6526, 5-6253) charges ¥3500 per night, including meals.

Also close to Funaura-kō, there's a good choice of inexpensive inns. *Minshuku Kampira-sō* (☎ 5-6526, 5-6508) charges as little as ¥3500 per person, with two meals. Not far away is *Uehara-kan* (☎ 5-6516), a white box-like building, where per-person costs with two meals are ¥5000.

Plonked in between Ōhara and Haemita-no-hama (the best-rated strip of sand on the island) is *Minshuku Iketaya* (☎ 5 5255), where rooms cost ¥5000 with two meals. There are good *camping grounds* at Hoshisuna-no-hama and Hinai Beach.

Robinson's Inn is a pleasant coffee bar on the main junction in Uehara, 1km along the road from Funaura-kō.

Close to the Minshuku Kampira-sō is *Riverside Garden Urauchi*, a rustic restaurant that looks like it has been snatched from Ko Pha-Ngan in Thailand. There are quite a few vegetarian options to choose from.

Getting There & Away

A variety of boats operate between Ishigaki-jima and Iriomote-jima, mostly to Funaura (which is the place to get the Urauchi-gawa cruise) rather than to Ōhara. Occasionally there are services to Shirahama. The trip typically takes 40 minutes to an hour on the faster craft.

Getting Around

Many minshuku and the youth hostels rent bicycles and scooters. Cars can also be rented: try Iriomote Rent-a-Car (☎ 5-5303).

OKINAWA & SW ISLANDS

There's a regular bus service between Ōhara and Shirahama, at the two ends of the island's single road. A bus from one end to the other costs ¥990 and takes nearly an hour; from Funaura-kō to Urauchi-gawa costs ¥230.

ISLANDS AROUND IRIOMOTE-JIMA 西表周辺の島々
☎ 09808

Directly north of Iriomote-jima and clearly visible from Funaura, tiny **Hatoma-jima** has a handful of minshuku and some very fine beaches and snorkelling.

Close to the east coast of Iriomote-jima, the small island of **Kohama-jima** has a sprinkling of minshuku; the rather expensive *Haimurubushi Resort* (☎ 09808-5-3111), where rates start at ¥12,200; and superb diving, particularly in Manta Way (there are boats there from Ishigaki-jima). Minshuku on the island generally charge around ¥4500 with two meals included. Clustered together in the centre of the island are three such places: *Minshuku Ufudaki-sō* (☎ 5-3243), *Kayama-sō* (☎ 5-3236), and *Nagata-sō* (☎ 5-3250). From Ishigaki-kō there are four operators, including Yaeyama Kankō Ferry (☎ 2-5010), offering seven boats to the island daily (¥1000, 25 to 30 minutes).

There are also regular services from Ishigaki-jima to the smaller **Kuro-shima**, directly south of Kohama-jima. It's renowned as the place where bulls are raised for Okinawa's *tōgyū* (bullfights; see the 'Bullfighting' boxed text in this chapter), but it also has good diving and a couple of pensions and minshuku. *Minshuku Kuroshima* (☎ 5-4251) is south-east of the harbour and has rooms from ¥4500 with two meals.

Both Yaeyama Kankō Ferry and Anei Kankō (☎ 3-0055) have ferries from Ishigaki-jima (¥1130, 40 minutes, four daily) and you can visit the island as a day trip.

YONAGUNI-JIMA 与那国島
☎ 09808

Yonaguni-jima is 100km west of Iriomote-jima and Ishigaki-jima, and only 110km from the east coast of Taiwan. The hilly island is just 11km long, and there are fine views from the top of **Urabu-dake** (231m). It's said that on a clear day you can see the mountains of Taiwan from Yonaguni. The island is renowned for its strong *sake* and its jumbo-sized moths, known as *yonagunisan*. Traditional houses on the island have thatched roofs, but tiled roofs are becoming the norm.

There's not a lot to see on Yonaguni-jima, but it has a reputation among some young Okinawans as being a mysterious place, perhaps because it's so far from the mainland and so close to Taiwan. The coastline is marked with some great rock formations, much like those on the east coast of Taiwan. The most famous of these is **Tachigami-iwa** (literally, Standing-God Rock) on the southeast coast. Another famous rock formation is **Sanninu-dai** (or Gunkan-iwa), on the southwest coast. For Japanese, this rock is famously evocative of virility (you'll see why). Of interest mainly to Japanese tourists is **Iri-saki**, a rock carved with an inscription proclaiming it the westernmost point of Japan.

Yonaguni's airport is about 10 minutes by taxi from the main town of **Sonai**. There's not a great deal of interest in town, but you might want to check out **Yonaguni Minzoku Shiryōkan** (free, 8.30 am to 6 pm), with its cluttered displays of items from Yonaguni-jima's history. Also worth checking out is the **Yonaguni Traditional Crafts Centre**, in the east of town, where you can see locals working on traditional looms.

Places to Stay
There are a few hotels and minshuku in Sonai and a couple of places over near Japan's westernmost rock. In terms of both economy and atmosphere, *Minshuku Omoro* (☎ 7-2419) makes an interesting choice, with rooms for ¥4000 with two meals. It's just south of Minzoku Shiryōkan. Just up the road is *Hotel Irifune* (☎ 7-2311), which sports a picture of a rampant marlin outside. It has rooms, with two meals included, for ¥6000.

Getting There & Away
JTA flies to Yonaguni-jima from Ishigaki (¥6400, 40 minutes, twice daily). On Wednesday and Saturday, the Fukuyama ferry service (☎ 7-2555; ☎ 09808-2-4962 on Ishigaki-jima) has boats runing from

Ishigaki-jima to Yonaguni-jima (¥3460, four hours, twice weekly). The boats return to Ishigaki-jima on Monday and Thursday. Be sure to check the schedule before you leave, as it's vulnerable to change.

Getting Around

In Sonai there are bikes for hire at about ¥1000 per day. Car and motorbike hire is available at the airport and in Sonai. A four-hour taxi romp around the island will set you back a cool ¥15,000.

HATERUMA-JIMA 波照間島

Directly south of Iriomote-jima is tiny Hateruma-jima, only 5km long and the southernmost point of Japan. In the spirit of the westernmost rock on Yonaguni-jima, Hateruma-jima sports a **southernmost rock**. There are a few minshuku on the island, but you can also visit as a day-tripper. There are four speedboats daily between Ishigaki-jima and Hateruma-jima (¥3000, 50 minutes). Slower ferries (¥2080) run once a day on Tuesday, Thursday and Saturday.

OKINAWA & SW ISLANDS

Language

It is something of a cliché that the Japanese spend years studying English and end up unable to string a coherent English sentence together. This is partly due to the language-teaching techniques employed in Japanese classrooms, but it also reflects the difficulty of translation. Structurally, Japanese and English are so different that word-for-word translations will often produce almost incomprehensible sentences.

Grammar

To English speakers, Japanese language patterns often seem to be back to front and lacking in essential information. For example, where an English speaker would say 'I'm going to the shop' a Japanese speaker would say 'shop to going', omitting the subject pronoun (I) altogether and putting the verb at the end of the sentence. To make matters worse, many moods which are indicated at the beginning of a sentence in English occur at the end of a sentence in Japanese, as in the Japanese sentence 'Japan to going if' – 'if you're going to Japan'

Fortunately for visitors to Japan, it's not all bad news. Unlike other languages in the region (Chinese, Vietnamese and Thai among others), Japanese is not tonal and the pronunciation system is fairly easy to master. In fact, with a little effort, getting together a repertoire of travellers' phrases should be no trouble – the only problem will be understanding what people say back to you.

Written Japanese

Japanese has one of the most complex writing systems in the world, using three different scripts (four if you include the increasingly used Roman script *romaji*). The most difficult of the three, for foreigners and Japanese alike, is *kanji*, the ideographic script developed by the Chinese. Not only do you have to learn a couple of thousand of them, but unlike Chinese many Japanese kanji have wildly variant pronunciations depending on context.

Because of the differences between Chinese grammar and Japanese grammar, kanji had to be supplemented with an alphabet of syllables, or a syllabary, known as *hiragana*. And there is yet another syllabary that is used largely for representing foreign loan words such as *terebi* (TV) and *biiru* (beer); this script is known as *katakana*. If you're serious about learning to read Japanese you'll have to set aside several years.

If you're thinking of tackling the Japanese writing system before you go or while you're in Japan, your best bet would be to start with hiragana or katakana. Both syllabaries have 48 characters each, and can be learned within a week — it'll take at least a month to consolidate them though. You can practise your katakana on restaurant menus, where such things as *kōhii* (coffee) and *kēki* (cake) are frequently found, and practise your hiragana on train journeys, as station names are usually indicated in hiragana (in addition to English and kanji)

Romanisation

The romaji used in this book follows the Hepburn system of romanisation. Macrons are used to indicate long vowels. In this book, common Japanese nouns like *ji* or *tera* (temple) and *jinja* or *jingū* (shrine) are written without an English translation.

Language Guides

The new edition of Lonely Planet's *Japanese Phrasebook* offers a convenient collection of survival words and phrases for your trip to Japan, plus a section on grammar and pronunciation. If you'd like to delve deeper into the intricacies of the language, we recommend *Japanese for Busy People* (Kodansha) for beginners, *Introduction to Intermediate Japanese* (Mizutani Nobuko, Bojinsha) for intermediate students, and *Kanji in Context* (Japan Times) for more advanced students.

One of the best guides to the written language, for both study and reference, is *Kanji & Kana* (Wolfgang Hadamizky and Mark Spahn, Tuttle).

The following selection of Japanese phrases will see you through some of the more common situations experienced by travellers to Japan.

Pronunciation

The following as in British pronunciation.

a   as the 'a' in 'father'
e   as the 'e' in 'get'
i   as the 'i' in 'macaroni'
o   as the 'o' in 'bone'
u   as the 'u' in 'flu'

Vowels appearing in this book with a macron (or bar) over them (ā, ē, ō, ū) are pronounced in the same way as standard vowels except that the sound is held twice as long. You need to take care with this as vowel length can change the meaning of a word, eg, *yuki* means 'snow', while *yūki* means 'bravery'.

Consonants are generally pronounced as in English, with the following exceptions:

f   this sound is produced by pursing the lips and blowing lightly
g   as the 'g' in 'goal' at the start of word; and nasalised as the 'ng' in 'sing' in the middle of a word
r   more like an 'l' than an 'r'

Basics

The all-purpose title **san** is used after a name as an honorific and is the equivalent of Mr, Miss, Mrs and Ms.

Greetings & Civilities

Good morning.
ohayō gozaimasu
おはようございます。
Good afternoon.
konnichi wa
こんにちは。
Good evening.
konban wa
こんばんは。

How are you?
o-genki desu ka?
お元気ですか。
Fine. (appropriate response)
ē, okagesamade
ええ、おかげさまで。
Goodbye.
sayōnara
さようなら。
See you later. (pol)
dewa, mata
では、また。
See you later. (inf)
ja ne
じゃ、ね。
Have a good trip.
tanoshii go-ryoko o
楽しいご旅行を。
Excuse me.
sumimasen
すみません。
I'm sorry.
gomen nasai/sumimasen
ごめんなさい／すみません。
Excuse me. (when entering a room)
o-jama shimasu/shitsurei shimasu
おじゃまします／失礼します。
Thank you.
arigatō gozaimasu
ありがとうございます。
Thank you very much.
dōmo arigatō gozaimasu
どうもありがとうございました。
It's a pleasure.
dō itashimashite
どういたしまして。
No, thank you.
iie, kekkō desu
いいえ、結構です。
Thanks for having me. (when leaving)
o-sewa ni narimashita
お世話になりました。
Please. (when offering something)
dōzo
どうぞ。
Please. (when asking for something)
onegai shimasu
お願いします。

OK.
daijōbu (desu)/ōke
大丈夫（です）／オーケー。
Yes.
hai
はい。
No.
iie
いいえ。
No. (for indicating disagreement)
chigaimasu
ちがいます。
No. (for indicating disagreement;
less emphatic)
chotto chigaimasu
ちょっとちがいます。
Cheers!
kampai!
乾杯！

Small Talk

Do you understand (English/Japanese)?
(ei-go)/(nihon-go)
wa wakarimasu ka?
（英語）／（日本語）は
わかりますか。
I don't understand.
wakarimasen
わかりません。
Please say it again more slowly.
mō ichidō, yukkuri itte kudasai
もう一度、ゆっくり言ってください。
What is this called?
kore wa nan to iimasu ka?
これはなんと言いますか。
My name is ...
watashi wa ... desu
私は、 ... です。
What's your name?
o-namae wa nan desu ka?
お名前はなんですか。
This is Mr/Mrs/Ms (Smith).
kochira wa (Sumisu) san desu
こちらは（スミス）さんです。
Pleased to meet you.
dōzo yoroshiku
どうぞよろしく。
Pleased to meet you too
kochira koso dōzo yoroshiku
こちらこそどうぞよろしく。

Where are you from?
dochira kara kimashita ka?
どちらから来ましたか。
Sorry to keep you waiting.
taihen o-matase shimashita
大変お待たせしました。
It's been a long time since I last
saw you.
o-hisashi buri desu
おひさしぶりです。
Please (also) give my regards to
Mr/Mrs/Ms Suzuki.
Suzuki san ni (mo) yoroshiku
o-tsutae kudasai
鈴木さんに（も）
よろしくお伝えください。
It's up to you.
(when asked to make a choice)
o-makase shimasu
おまかせします。
Is it OK to take a photo?
shashin o totte mo ii desu ka?
写真を撮ってもいいですか。

Requests

Excuse me please, can you help me?
sumimasen ga oshiete itadakemasu ka?
すみませんが、教えていただけますか
Please give me this/that.
(kore)/(sore) o kudasai
（これ）／（それ）をください。
Please give me a (cup of tea).
(o-cha) o kudasai
（お茶）をください。
Please wait (a while).
(shoshō) o-machi kudasai
（少々）お待ちください。
Please show me (the ticket).
(kippu o) misete kudasai
（切符を）見せてください。

Getting Around

I want to go to ...
... ni ikitai desu
... に行きたいです。
How do I get to ... ?
... e wa dō ikeba iidesu ka?
... へはどう行けばいいですか。
Where is the ... ?
... wa do chira desu ka?
... はどちらですか。

Glossary of Useful Terms

Geography

-dake/take	岳	peak
-dani/tani	谷	valley
-gawa/kawa	川	river
-hama	浜	beach
-hantō	半島	peninsula
-jima/shima	島	island
-kaikyō	海峡	channel/strait
-ko	湖	lake
-kō	港	port
-kōen	公園	park
-kōgen	高原	plateau
kokutei kōen	国定公園	quasi-national park
kokuritsu kōen	国立公園	national park
-kyō	峡	gorge
-minato	港	harbour
-misaki	岬	cape
-no-yu	の湯	hot spring
-oka	丘	hill
onsen	温泉	hot spring
-san/zan	山	mountain
-shima/jima	島	island
shokubutsu-en	植物園	botanic garden
-shotō	諸島	archipelago
-take/dake	岳	peak
-taki	滝	waterfall
-tani/dani	谷	valley
-tō	島	island
-wan	湾	bay
-yama	山	mountain
-yu	湯	hot spring
-zaki/misaki	岬	cape
-zan/san	山	mountain

Regions

-shi	市	city
-chō	町	neighbourhood or village/s
-mura	村	village
-ken	県	prefecture
-gun	郡	county
-ku	区	ward

Sights

-dera/tera	寺	temple
-dō	堂	temple or hall of a temple
-en	園・苑	garden
-in	院	temple or hall of a temple
-gū	宮	shrine
-ji	寺	temple
-jō	城	castle
-kōen	公園	park
-mon	門	gate
shokubutsu-en	植物園	botanical garden
-hori/bori	堀	moat
-jingū	神宮	shrine
-jinja	神社	shrine
-taisha	大社	shrine
-teien	庭園	garden
-tera/dera	寺	temple
-torii	鳥居	shrine gate

Do you have an English subway map?
Eigo no chikatetsu no chizu ga arimasu ka?
英語の地下鉄の地図がありますか。
How much is the fare to ...?
... made ikura desu ka?
... までいくらですか。
Does this (train, bus, etc) go to ...?
kore wa ... e ikimasu ka?
これは ... へ行きますか。

Is the next station ...?
tsugi no eki wa ... desu ka?
次の駅は ... ですか。
Please tell me when we get to ...
... ni tsuitara oshiete kudasai
... に着いたら教えてください。
Where is the ... exit?
... deguchi wa doko desu ka?
... 出口はどこですか。

How far is it to walk?
aruite dono kurai kakarimasu ka?
歩いてどのくらいかかりますか。

Where is this address please?
kono jūsho wa doko desu ka?
この住所はどこですか。

Could you write down the address for me?
jūsho o kaite itadakemasen ka?
住所を書いていただけませんか。

Can I leave my luggage here?
Nimotsu o azakatte itadakemasu ka?
荷物を預かっていただけますか。

east/west/north/south
higashi/nishi/kita/minami
東／西／南／北

Accommodation

I'd like a ... (hotel/inn).
... (hoteru)/(ryokan)
o sagashiteimasu
...（ホテル）／（旅館）を
探しています。

Do you have any vacancies?
aiteiru heya wa arimasu ka?
空いている部屋はありますか。

I don't have a reservation
yoyaku wa shiteimasen
予約はしていません。

a single room
shinguru rūmu
シングルルーム

a double room
daburu rūmu
ダブルルーム

a Japanese-style room
washitsu
和室

a room with a bathroom
basu rūmu tsuki no heya
バスルーム付きの部屋

Food

Do you have an English menu?
eigo no menyū wa arimasu ka?
英語のメニューはありますか。

I'm a vegetarian.
watashi wa bejitarian desu
私はベジタリアンです。

Do you have any vegetarian meals?
bejitarian no ryōri wa arimasu ka?
ベジタリアンの料理はありますか。

I'd like the set menu please.
setto menyū o o-negai shimasu
セットメニューをお願いします。

What do you recommend?
o-susume wa nan desu ka?
お勧めはなんですか。

Please bring the bill.
o-kanjō o onegai shimasu
お勘定をお願いします。

Shopping

How much is this?
kore wa ikura desu ka?
これはいくらですか。

It's too expensive.
taka-sugimasu
高すぎます。

I'll take this one.
kore o itadakimasu
これをいただきます。

Can I have a receipt?
ryōshūsho o
itadakemasen ka?
領収書をいただけませんか。

I'm just looking.
miteiru dake desu
見ているだけです。

Numbers

0	*zero/rei*	○
1	*ichi*	一
2	*ni*	二
3	*san*	三
4	*yon/shi*	四
5	*go*	五
6	*roku*	六
7	*nana/shichi*	七
8	*hachi*	八
9	*kyū/ku*	九
10	*jū*	十
11	*jūichi*	十一
12	*jūni*	十二
13	*jūsan*	十三
14	*jūyon*	十四
20	*nijū*	二十
21	*nijūichi*	二十一
30	*sanjū*	三十
100	*hyaku*	百
200	*nihyaku*	二百
1000	*sen*	千

5000	*gosen*	五千
10,000	*ichiman*	一万
20,000	*niman*	二万
100,000	*jūman*	十万
one million	*hyakuman*	百万

Health

How do you feel?
kibun wa
ikaga desu ka?
気分はいかがですか。

I don't feel well.
kibun ga warui desu
気分が悪いです。

It hurts here.
koko ga itai desu
ここが痛いです。

I have asthma.
watashi wa
zensoku-mochi desu
私はぜんそく持ちです。

I have diarrhoea.
geri o shiteimasu
下痢をしています。

I have a toothache.
ha ga itamimasu
歯が痛みます。

I need a doctor.
o-isha san ni mite moraitain desu
お医者さんにみてもらいたいんです。

I'm allergic to antibiotics/penicillin.
kōsei busshitsu/penishirin ni
arerugii ga arimasu
抗生物質／ペニシリンに
アレルギーがあります。

Emergencies

Help me!
tasukete!
助けて！

Watch out!
ki o tsukete!
気をつけて！

Call the police!
keisatsu o yonde kudasai!
警察を呼んでください！

Call a doctor!
isha o yonde kudasai!
医者を呼んでください！

Glossary

aimai – ambiguous and unclear way of communicating

Ainu – indigenous people of Hokkaidō and parts of northern Honshū

aka-chōchin – red lantern; a working man's pub marked by red lanterns outside

akirame – to relinquish; resignation

ama – women divers

amakudari – 'descent from heaven'; a retiring civil servant who then goes to work for a private corporation which he formerly dealt with

Amaterasu – sun goddess and link to the imperial throne

ANA – All Nippon Airlines

ANK – All Nippon Koku

annai-jo – information office

arubaito – from the German *arbeit*, meaning 'to work', adapted into Japanese to refer to part-time work; often contracted to *baito*

asa-ichi – morning market

awamori – local alcohol of Okinawa

ayu – sweetfish caught during *ukai* (cormorant fishing)

baito – a part-time job or an illegal immigrant worker (from *arbeit*, the German word for 'work')

bangasa – rain umbrella made from oiled paper

banzai – literally '10,000 years', *banzai* means 'hurrah' or 'hurray'; in the West this exclamation is, for the most part, associated with WWII, although its more modern usage is quite peaceful

bashō – sumō wrestling tournament

basho-gara – literally 'the character of a place', fitting to the particular conditions or circumstances

bentō – boxed lunch, usually of rice, a main dish and pickles or salad

bonsai – the art of growing miniature trees by careful pruning of branches and roots

boso-zoku – hot-car or motorcycle gangs, usually noisy but harmless

bottle-keep – system whereby you buy a whole bottle of liquor in a bar, which is kept for you to drink on subsequent visits

bugaku – dance pieces played by court orchestras in ancient Japan

buke yashiki – samurai residence

bunraku – classical puppet theatre using huge puppets to portray dramas similar to *kabuki*

burakumin – literally 'village people', the *burakumin* were traditionally outcasts associated with lowly occupations such as leather work

bushidō – literally 'the way of the warrior', a set of values followed by the samurai

butsudan – Buddhist altar in Japanese homes

carp – carp *(koi)* are considered to be a brave, tenacious and vigorous fish, and *koinobori* (carp windsocks) are flown in honour of sons whom it is hoped will inherit a carp's virtues. Many towns and villages have carp ponds or channels teeming with colourful ornamental *nishiki-goi* carp

chanelah – fashionable young woman with a predilection for name brands, in particular Chanel products

chaniwa – tea garden

chanoyu – tea ceremony

charm – small dish of peanuts or other snack food served with a drink at a bar – it's often not requested but is still added to your bill

chimpira – *yakuza* understudy; usually used pejoratively of a male with yakuza aspirations

chizu – map

chō – city area (for large cities) between a *ku* (ward) and *chōme* in size; also a street

chōchin – paper lantern

chōme – city area of a few blocks

chōnan – oldest son

chu – loyalty

crane – cranes *(tsuru)* are a symbol of longevity and are often reproduced in *origami* and represented in traditional gardens

GLOSSARY

daibutsu – Great Buddha

daifuku – literally 'great happiness'; sticky rice cakes filled with red bean paste and eaten on festive occasions

daimyō – regional lords under the shōguns

daira – plain

danchi – public apartments

dantai – a group

dashi – festival floats

deru kui wa utareru – 'the nail that sticks up gets hammered down'; popular Japanese proverb which is more or less the opposite of the Western 'the squeaky wheel gets the oil'

donko – name for local trains in country areas

eboshi – black, triangular samurai hat

eki – train station

ekiben – *bentō* lunch box bought at a train station

ema – small votive plaques hung in shrine precincts as petitions for assistance from the resident deities

engawa – traditional veranda of a Japanese house overlooking the garden

enka – often referred to as the Japanese equivalent of country & western music, these are folk ballads about love and human suffering that are popular among the older generation

enryō – individual restraint and reserve

ero-guro – erotic and grotesque *manga*

fu – urban prefecture

fude – brush used for calligraphy

fugu – poisonous blowfish or pufferfish

fundoshi – loincloth or breechcloth; a traditional male garment consisting of a wide belt and a cloth drawn over the genitals and between the buttocks. Usually seen only at festivals or on sumō wrestlers

furigana – Japanese script used to aid pronunciation of *kanji*

furii-kippu – one-day open ticket

fusuma – sliding screen

futon – traditional quilt-like mattress that is rolled up and stowed away during the day

futsū – literally 'ordinary'; a basic stopping-all-stations train

gagaku – music of the imperial court

gaijin – literally 'outside people'; foreigners

gaijin house – cheap accommodation for long-term foreign residents

gaman – to endure

gasshō-zukuri – 'hands in prayer' architectural style

gei-no-kai – the 'world of art and talent'; usually refers to TV where there's not much of either

geisha – a 'refined person'; a woman versed in the arts and dramas who entertains guests; not a prostitute

genkan – foyer area where shoes are removed or replaced when entering or leaving a building

geta – traditional wooden sandals

giri – social obligations

giri-ninjō – combination of social obligations and personal values; the two are often in conflict

gekijō – theatre

go – board game in which players alternately place white and black counters down, with the object of surrounding the opponent and making further moves impossible; probably originating in China, where it is known as *weiqi*

habu – a venomous snake found in Okinawa

hachimaki – headband worn as a symbol of resolve; *kamikaze* pilots wore them in WWII, students wear them to exams

haiku – 17-syllable poems

haitaku – hired taxi

hakurai – literally 'brought by ship'; foreign or imported goods

hanami – blossom viewing

haniwa – earthenware figures found in Kōfun-period tombs

hanko – stamp or seal used to authenticate any document; in Japan your *hanko* carries much more weight than your signature

hara – marshlands

harakiri – belly cutting; common name for *seppuku* or ritual suicide

hara-kyū – acupuncture

hashi – chopsticks

heiwa – peace

henrō – pilgrims on the Shikoku 88 Temple Circuit

higasa – sunshade umbrella
Hikari – express shinkansen
hiragana – phonetic syllabary used to write Japanese words
honsen – main rail line

ichi-go – square wooden sake 'cups' holding 180ml
IDC – International Digital Communications
ike-ike onna – literally 'go-go girl'; young Japanese woman who favours dyed brown hair, a boutique suntan and bright lipstick
ijime – bullying or teasing; a problem in Japanese schools
ikebana – art of flower arrangement
irezumi – a tattoo or the art of tattooing
irori – hearth or fireplace
itadakimasu – an expression used before meals; literally 'I will receive'
ITJ – International Telecom Japan
ittaikan – feeling of unity, of being one type
izakaya – Japanese version of a pub; beer and *sake* and lots of snacks available in a rustic, boisterous setting

JAC – Japan Air Commuter
JAF – Japan Automobile Federation
JAL – Japan Airlines
JAS – Japan Air System
jiage-ya – specialists used by developers to persuade recalcitrant landowners to sell up
jigoku – 'hells'; boiling mineral hot springs, which are definitely not for bathing in
jika-tabi – split-toe boots traditionally worn by Japanese carpenters and builders
jikokuhyō – the book of timetables
jitensha – bicycle
jizō – small stone statues of the Buddhist protector of travellers and children
JNTO – Japan National Tourist Organization
JR – Japan Railways
JTB – Japan Travel Bureau
jujitsu – martial art from which *judō* was derived
juku – after-school 'cram' schools
JYHA – Japan Youth Hostel Association

kabuki – a form of Japanese theatre based on popular legends, which is characterised by elaborate costumes, stylised acting and the use of male actors for all roles

kachi-gumi – the 'victory group' who refuse to believe Japan lost WWII
kaikan – hotel-style accommodation sponsored by government; literally 'meeting hall'
kaiseki – Japanese cuisine which obeys very strict rules of etiquette for every detail of the meal, including the setting
kaisha – a company, firm
kaisoku – rapid train
kaisū-ken – discount bus tickets
kaiten-zushi – sushi served at a conveyor-belt restaurant
kakizome – New Year's resolutions
kamban-musume – 'shop sign girl'; girl who stands outside a shop or business to lure customers in
kambu – management
kami – Shintō gods; spirits of natural phenomena
kamidana – Shintō altar in Japanese homes
kamikaze – 'divine wind'; typhoon that sunk Kublai Khan's 13th-century invasion fleet and the name adopted by suicide pilots in the waning days of WWII
kampai – 'Cheers!'
kampō – Chinese herbal medicines that were dominant in Japan until the 19th century, when Western pharmaceuticals were introduced
kana – the two phonetic syllabaries, *hiragana* and *katakana*
kanji – literally 'Chinese script'; Chinese ideographic script used for writing Japanese
Kannon – Buddhist goddess of mercy (Sanskrit: Avalokiteshvara)
kannushi – chief priest of a Shintō shrine
karakuri – mechanical puppets
karakasa – oiled paper umbrella
karaoke – bars where you sing along with taped music; literally 'empty orchestra'
karōshi – 'death by overwork'; the recently recognised phenomenon of over-worked businessmen falling dead on urban streets
kasa – umbrella
katakana – phonetic syllabary used to write foreign words
katamichi – one-way ticket
katana – Japanese sword
KDD – Kokusai Denshin Denwa (International Telephone & Telegraph)

keigo – honorific language used to show respect to elders

ken – prefecture

kendō – oldest martial art; literally 'the way of the sword'

ki – life force, will

kimono – brightly coloured, robe-like traditional outer garment

kin'en-sha – nonsmoking carriage

kissaten – coffee shop

kōban – police box

ko garu – 'high school girl'; in particular junior *ike-ike onna* (see earlier) wannabes

kōgen – general area, plain

koinobori – carp banners and windsocks; the colourful fish pennants which wave over countless homes in Japan in late April and early May are for Boys' Day, the final holiday of Golden Week. These days, Boys' Day has become Children's Day and the windsocks don't necessarily simply fly in honour of the household's sons

kokki – Japanese national flag

kūkō – airport

kokuminkyūka-mura – national vacation villages; a form of inexpensive accommodation set up by the government to ensure that all citizens have access to low-cost holiday accommodation

kokumin-shukusha – peoples' lodges; an inexpensive form of accommodation

kokutetsu – Japanese word for Japan Railways (JR); literally 'national iron'

Komeitō – Clean Government Party; third-largest political party

kone – personal connections

kotatsu – heated table with a quilt or cover over it to keep the legs and lower body warm

koto – 13-stringed instrument that is played flat on the floor

kuidaore – eat until you drop (Kansai)

kura – mud-walled storehouses

kyakuma – drawing room of a home, where guests are met

kyōiku mama – literally 'education mother'; a woman who pushes her kids through the Japanese education system

kyujinrui – 'old breed'; opposite of *shin-jinrui*

kyūkō – ordinary express train (faster than a *futsū*, only stopping at certain stations)

live house – nightclub or bar where live music is performed

machi – city area (for large cities) between a *ku* (ward) and *chōme* (area of a few blocks) in size; also street or area

maiko – apprentice *geisha*

mama-san – woman who manages a bar or club

maneki-neko – beckoning cat figure frequently seen in restaurants and bars; it's supposed to attract customers and trade

manga – Japanese comics

matsuri – festival

meinichi – the 'deathday' or anniversary of someone's death

meishi – business card

mentsu – face

miai-kekkon – arranged marriage

mibun – social rank

miko – shrine maidens

mikoshi – portable shrines carried during festivals

minshuku – the Japanese equivalent of a B&B; family-run budget accommodation

miso-shiru – bean-paste soup

MITI – Ministry of International Trade & Industry

mitsubachi – accommodation for motorcycle tourers

mizu-shōbai – see *water trade*

mochi – pounded rice made into cakes and eaten at festive occasions

mōfu – blanket

morning service – *mōningu sābisu*; a light breakfast served until 10 am in many *kissaten*; often simply referred to as *mōningu* by customers

mukō – 'over there'; anywhere outside Japan

mura – village

nagashi – folk singers and musicians who wander from bar to bar

nagashi-somen – flowing noodles

nengajō – New Year cards

new humans – the younger generation, brought up in more affluent times than their parents and consequently less respectful of the frugal values of the postwar generation

N'EX – Narita Express

NHK – Nihon Hōsō Kyōkai (Japan Broadcasting Corporation)
Nihon or **Nippon** – Japanese word for Japan; literally 'source of the sun'
nihonga – term for Japanese-style painting
ningyō – Japanese doll
ninja – practitioners of *ninjutsu*
ninjō – debt; fellow feeling; that which is universally right
ninjutsu – 'the art of stealth'
nō – classical Japanese drama performed on a bare stage
noren – cloth hung as a sunshade, typically carrying the name of the shop or premises; indicates that a restaurant is open for business
norikae – to change buses or trains; make a connection
norikae-ken – transfer ticket (trams and buses)
NTT – Nippon Telegraph & Telephone Corporation

o- – prefix used to show respect to anything it is applied to. See *san*
o-bāsan – grandmotherly type; an old woman
obi – sash or belt worn with a kimono
o-cha – tea
ofuku – return ticket
o-furo – traditional Japanese bath
o-jōsan – young college-age woman of conservative taste and aspirations
OL – 'office lady'; female employee of a large firm; usually a clerical worker – pronounced '*ō-eru*'
omake – an extra bonus or premium when you buy something
ombu – 'carrying on the back'; getting someone else to bear the expense, pick up the tab. Also the custom of carrying a baby strapped to the back
o-miai – arranged marriage; rare in modern Japan
o-miyage – the souvenir gifts which Japanese must bring back from any trip
on – favour
onnagata – male actor playing a woman's role (usually in *kabuki*)
onsen – mineral hot-spring spa area, usually with accommodation
origami – art of paper folding

oshibori – hot towels provided in restaurants
o-tsumami – bar snacks or *charms*
oyabun/kobun – teacher/pupil or senior/junior relationship
oyaki – wheat buns filled with pickles, squash, radish and red bean paste

pachinko – vertical pinball game which is a Japanese craze (estimated to take in over ¥6 trillion a year) and a major source of tax evasion, yakuza funds, etc
pinku saron – 'pink saloon'; seedy hostess bars
puripeido kādo – 'prepaid card'; a sort of reverse credit card: you buy a magnetically coded card for a given amount and it can be used for certain purchases until spent. The prepaid phonecards are the most widespread but there are many others such as Prepaid Highway Cards for use on toll roads

rakugo – Japanese raconteurs, stand-up comics
reien – cemetery
reisen – cold mineral spring
Rinzai – school of Zen Buddhism which places an emphasis on *kōan* (riddles)
robatayaki – *yakitori-ya* with a deliberately rustic, friendly, homey atmosphere; see also *izakaya*
romaji – Japanese roman script
rō – vegetable wax
rōnin – 'masterless samurai'; students who must resit university entrance exams
ropeway – Japanese word for a cable car or tramway
rotemburo – open-air baths
ryokan – traditional Japanese inn

sadō – tea ceremony, literally 'way of tea'
saisen-bako – offering box at Shintō shrines
sakazuki – *sake* cups
sakoku – Japan's period of national seclusion prior to the Meiji Restoration
sakura – cherry blossoms
salaryman – standard male employee of a large firm
sama – even more respectful suffix than *san* (see below); used in instances such as *o-kyaku-sama* – the 'honoured guest'

samurai – warrior class

san – suffix which shows respect to the person it is applied to; see also *o*, the equivalent honorific. Both can occasionally be used together as *o-kyaku-san*, where *kyaku* is the word for guest or customer

sansai – mountain vegetables

san-sō – mountain cottage

satori – Zen concept of enlightenment

sazen – seated meditation emphasised in the Sōtō school of Zen Buddhism

seku-hara – sexual harassment

sembei – flavoured rice crackers often sold in tourist areas

sempai – one's elder or senior at school or work

sensei – generally translates as 'teacher' but has wider reference. Politicians are *sensei* through their power rather than their teaching ability

sentō – public baths

seppuku – ritual suicide by disembowelment

setto – set meal

seza – a kneeling position

shamisen – three-stringed instrument

shi – city (to distinguish cities with prefectures of the same name)

shiken-jigoku – 'examination hell'; the enormously important and stressful entrance exams to various levels of the Japanese education system

shikki – lacquerware

shinjinrui – 'new species'; young people who do not believe in the standard pattern of Japanese life. Opposite of *kyujinrui*

shinjū – double suicide by lovers

shinkansen – ultra fast 'bullet' trains; literally 'new trunk line', since new train lines were laid for the high speed trains

shitamachi – traditionally the low-lying, less affluent parts of Tokyo

shodō – Japanese calligraphy; literally the 'way of writing'

shōgi – a version of chess in which each player has 20 pieces and the object is to capture the opponent's king

shōgun – former military ruler of Japan

shogekijō – small theatre

shōji – sliding rice-paper screens

shōjin ryōri – vegetarian meals (especially at temple lodgings)

shūji – the 'practice of letters'; a lesser form of *shodō*

shukubō – temple lodgings

shunga – explicit erotic prints; literally 'spring pictures', the season of spring being a popular Chinese and Japanese euphemism for sexuality

Shugendō – offbeat Buddhist school, which incorporates ancient Shamanistic rites, Shintō beliefs and ascetic Buddhist traditions

shuntō – spring labour offensive; an annual 'strike'

shūyū-ken – excursion train ticket

soapland – Japanese euphemism for bathhouses that offer sexual services

soba – buckwheat noodles

sōgō shōsha – integrated trading houses, like the old *zaibatsu*

sokaiya – *yakuza* who seek extortion money from companies by threatening to influence proceedings at annual general meetings

soroban – abacus

Sōtō – a school of Zen Buddhism which places emphasis on *sazen*

sukebe – lewd in thought and deed; can be a compliment in the right context (eg, among male drinking partners), but generally shouldn't be used lightly; the English equivalent would be 'sleaze bag'

sukiyaki – thin slices of beef cooked in *sake*, soy and vinegar broth

sumi-e – black-ink brush paintings

sumō – Japanese wrestling

tabi – split-toed Japanese socks used when wearing *geta*

tachi-shōben – men urinating in public are a familiar sight in Japan. It's the cause of some academic discussion over Japanese concepts of private places (strict rules apply) and public ones (anything goes)

tadaima – 'now' or 'present'; a traditional greeting called out upon returning home

tako – kite

tanin – outsider, stranger, someone not connected with the current situation

tanka – poems of 31 syllables

tanuki – racoon or dog-like folklore character frequently represented in ceramic figures

tarento – 'talent'; generally refers to musical performers
tatami – tightly woven floor matting on which shoes are never worn. Traditionally, room size is defined by the number of tatami mats
tatemae – 'face'; how you act in public, your public position
TCAT – Tokyo City Air Terminal
teiki-ken – discount commuter passes
teishoku – set meal
tekitō – suitable or appropriate
tennō – heavenly king, the emperor
TIC – Tourist Information Center
to – metropolis, eg, Tokyo-to
tosu – toilet
tokkuri – *sake* flask
tokkyū – limited express; faster than an ordinary express *(kyūkō)* train
tokonoma – alcove in a house in which flowers may be displayed or a scroll hung
torii – entrance gate to a Shintō shrine
tsukiai – after-work socialising among salarymen
tsunami – huge tidal waves caused by an earthquake

uchi – literally 'one's own house' but has other meanings relating to 'belonging' and 'being part of'
uchiwa – paper fan
ukai – fishing using trained cormorants
ukiyo-e – wood-block prints; literally 'pictures of the floating world'
umeboshi – pickled plums thought to aid digestion; often served with rice in *bentō* sets

wa – harmony, team spirit; also the old *kanji* used to denote Japan, and still used in Chinese and Japanese as a prefix to indicate things of Japanese origin; see *wafuku*
wabi – enjoyment of peace and tranquillity
wafuku – Japanese-style clothing
waka – 31-syllable poem
wanko – lacquerware bowls
waribashi – disposable wooden chopsticks
warikan – custom of sharing the bill (among good friends)
wasabi – Japanese horseradish

washi – Japanese handmade paper
water trade – entertainment, bars, prostitution, etc; called *mizu-shōbai*

yabusame – horseback archery
yakitori – charcoal-broiled chicken and other meats or vegetables, cooked on skewers
yakitori-ya – restaurant specialising in *yakitori*
yakuza – Japanese mafia
yamabushi – mountain priests (Shugendō Buddhism practitioners)
yama-goya – mountain huts
yamato – a term of much debated origins that refers to the Japanese world, particularly in contrast to things Chinese
yamato damashii – Japanese spirit, a term with parallels to the German *Volksgeist*; it was harnessed by the militarist government of the 1930s and 1940s and was identified with unquestioning loyalty to the emperor
yamato-e – traditional Japanese painting
yanqui – tastelessly dressed male, with dyed hair and a cellular phone
yatai – festival floats/hawker stalls
YCAT – Yokohama City Air Terminal
yenjoy girl – single woman with time and cash to spare
yōfuku – Western-style clothing
Yomiuri Giants – *the* Japanese baseball team; although there are 12 big league teams over 50% of the population backs the Giants
yukata – light cotton summer kimono, worn for lounging or casual use; standard issue when staying at a ryokan

zabuton – small cushions for sitting on (used in *tatami* rooms)
zaibatsu – industrial conglomerates; the term arose prior to WWII but the Japanese economy is still dominated by huge firms like Mitsui, Marubeni and Mitsubishi, which are involved in many different industries
Zen – introduced to Japan in the 12th century from China, this offshoot of Buddhism emphasises a direct, intuitive approach to enlightenment rather than rational analysis

Thanks

Many thanks to the travellers who used the last edition and wrote to us with helpful hints, useful advice and interesting anecdotes:

A Chan, A Jackson, A Vasudeu, A Yough, Aaron Quigley, Aengus Burns, Alex Black, Alex Nekrasov, Alireza Fatehi, Alison Lane, Allen Dolleris, Allison Wyndham, Amanda Phillips, Amit Luthra, Andrea Bielefeld, Andreas Strohm, Andrew Gentile, Andrew Toner, Andy Mclannahan, Anja Rohlf, Ann Saxour, Anna Trloar, Anshul Dayal, Antoine De Lattre, Arjan Klijnsma, B Cudal, Ben Benjamin, Bethan Jinkinson, Betty Gardiner, Birger Fjallman, Bjorn Burss, Blake Engelhard, Bob Aronoff, Brad Warner, Brigitte Schadow, Bug Williams, Campbell Hewston, Carelton Wesley Strub, Chao-Hui Wang, Charles Peel, Charlie Garrett, Chey Mattner, Chris Bain, Chris Sorochin, Chris Tozer, Chris White, Christian & Mayumi Masing, Christina Shankar, Christine Lutz, Christine Tanhueco, Christopher Rea, Clare Loughman, Clare Thomas, Clare Wainwright, Claudio Rosello, Colin Cha Fong, Colin Elliott, Colleen Brandrick, Corina Flaig, Craig Yanagisawa, Cyril Suszckiewicz, D Guedes, Daisuke Todoroki, Damien Sams, Dan Andrews, Darren Murdy, Dave Brown, Dave Minicola, David & Betty Odell, David Beattie, David Shih, David Todd, Dean Prenc, Deirdre Kenyon, Derek Cox, Derry McDonell, Diana Jessie, Diana Little, Didier Hia, Donald Macphee, Dorothee Retzbach, Douglas Poole, Dr A R Blythe, Dr D Johnson, Dr Paul Barret, Dr Thomas L Simmons, Dylan Brown, Einat Joseph, Eishin Joel Gerst, Elaine Davis, Elena Yap, Emma Wingqvist, Eric Meulien, Erika Kissling, Esa Aaltonen, Ethan Perk, Etienne Raynaud, Eugenia Sarsanedas, Evelyn Stein, F Rickword, Fabienne Brutt, Felix Dahm, Frank Hindle, Frank Wheby, Frank Williams, Frederic Guizot, G P Gervat, Gabriel Gonzalez Maurazos, Gail Murayama, Gary Tyerya, Gasser Christian, Geoff Bryce, Geoffrey Jackson, Geoffrey Morris, Glenn Sweitzer, Gordon Bartram, Greer Legget, Greg Sparke, Gretchen Salmon, Gustavo Zapata, H Mountain, H Yanagisawa, Hajime Hirooka, Hans ter Horst, Hayley Every, Hazel Hall, Heidi Birkbeck, Helen Tse, Henk Bekker, Herbert E Huppert, Hoi Yan Lung, Howard Reed, Hubert Chanson, Ian Walker, Inge Light, Jack Cavanagh, Jack Oso, Jackie Keating, James Best, James Hitzelberger, James Keeler, James Milling, James Saville, Jamie Reimer, Jan Rune, Janice & Brian Thorburn, Jarrod McPherson, Jason Lewis, Jay Lavergne, Jeanne C Landkamer, Jeff Taylor, Jennifer Alker, Jennifer Thompson, Jenny Bridgen, Jenny Lin, Jerome Tsu, Jo Brooks, Jo Defelice, Joan & Joe Phelan, Jody Marshall, Joel Matsuda, Joey Chen, John Charles Burdick, John Elay, John Gorick, John Gurskey, John Julian Chodacki, John Neumann, John S Germann, John, Tina & Rachel Sparks, Johnny Buckle, Jonathan Berman, Jonathan Juri Buchanan, Jordi Gernaert, Jorn Borup, Joseph Stanisic, Jouko Mahone, Julie Little, Junko Holland, Justin Brown, Kanako Sawaoka, Karen A Stafford, Karen Chou, Karene Perkins, Karl Sonnenberg, Kenneth Pechter, Kent Foster, Keri Lim, Kerrie Dodson, Kevin Dickson, Kevin Friesen, Kieran Greenhow, Kim Ey, Kirsty Hall, Kirsty Hamson, Kristin Torgerson, Krysztof Kur, Kylie Chandler, Kylie Macpherson, L Dellmann, L Lees, Lars Nilsson, Laurent Maille, Lee Woodward, Lek Wai Mun, Liisa Richardson, Linda Anika Bade, Linda Godfrey, Lisa Hirst, Liz Cunningham, Lloyd Jones, Loek Boonevamp, Louise Hirasawa, Luis Ducla Soares, Lynne Donaldson, M Greenwood, M Webber, Mae Rethers, Maria Erickson, Marie Odiel van Rhyn, Marija Minic, Mark Andrews, Mark Baker, Mark Holmes, Mark Loy, Mark Scott, Mark Watson, Markus Luczynski, Marleen Nederlof, Martin Adams, Mary McConnell, Masaru Takeuchi, Mathilde Teuben, Matt Choerton, Matthew Brown, Matthieu Grymonprez, Maumi & Eugene Orwell, Max Fette, Max McCormick, Megan Fisher, Megan Wainman, Melinda Kinnare, Menno Bangma, Meredith Lorden, Michael Bade, Michel Martin, Michelle Lum, Michiko I, Mika Tokugawa, Mike Galvin, Mike O'Loughlin, Mike Shen, Mike Steane, Mizuno Tetsuyuki, Naomi Kashiwabara, Neal Snape, Neil Atkin, Nicholas Small, Nick & Jan Wooller, Nick Clack, Nick Wagner, Nicola Hopkins, Nicola Wong, Norie Isoda, P & M Dowling, P.Sigetts, Paolo Zocchi, Patti Stratton, Paul & Lisa Ziegele, Paul Hardin, Paul Jeffs, Paul Pearce, Paul Sharkey, Paul van der Lee, Peter Andersson, Peter Aubin, Peter Boers, Peter de Jong, Peter Hayden, Peter Owens, Peter Phillips, Petter Magnusson, Phillip Nicholls, Prunella Dunn, R Brown, R Waller, Ralf Kohl, Ralph & Jan Hill, Rebecca Entwistle, Rikio Matsushita, Robert Aronoff, Robert Haden, Robert Mason, Robert Stritmatter, Robin Ward, Rochelle Kragness, Rod Campbell, Roger Lyman, Rolf Schulte, Russell Banks, Sam Dyer, Sandy Morey, Sarah Kirzinger, Saw Huay, Scott Ceremuga, Scudder Smith, Shannon Fraser, Sharon Ng, Sharon Woolley, Shelley Marsh, Shinichi Nakazono, Sibylle de Horde, Simon Gilberthorpe, Simon Merry, Starla Carpenter, Stephanie Tregaro, Stephen Lowe, Steve Bein, Steve Koerner, Steve Turner, Steven Hunter, Sue Purnell, Sue Rogala, Susan Fuhr, Susan Henderson, Suzy Okada, Tada Taku, Takashi Kubo, Tan Hwee Meing, Terry Arbaugh, Terry Gibbs, Therese Crosbie, Thomas Broggi, Tim Williams, Tomoko Yasue, Tosuke Ide, Tracy Kazunaga, Treasa Ni Mhiochain, V Griffiths, Valerie Rose, Vanessa Hayes, Vibhor Garg, Victor Sarmiento, Waiarani Eruera, Walter Bertschinger, Wendy Morton, Wilfred Aldridge, William D Cain, Y Asada, Yoshiharu Morohashi, Yota Yoshimitsu, Yuriko Aoki.

LONELY PLANET

ON THE ROAD

Travel Guides explore cities, regions and countries, and supply information on transport, restaurants and accommodation, covering all budgets. They come with reliable, easy-to-use maps, practical advice, cultural and historical facts and a rundown on attractions both on and off the beaten track. There are over 200 titles in this classic series, covering nearly every country in the world.

 Lonely Planet Upgrades extend the shelf life of existing travel guides by detailing any changes that may affect travel in a region since a book has been published. Upgrades can be downloaded for free from **www.lonelyplanet.com/upgrades**

For travellers with more time than money, **Shoestring** guides offer dependable, first-hand information with hundreds of detailed maps, plus insider tips for stretching money as far as possible. Covering entire continents in most cases, the six-volume shoestring guides are known around the world as 'backpackers bibles'.

For the discerning short-term visitor, **Condensed** guides highlight the best a destination has to offer in a full-colour, pocket-sized format designed for quick access. They include everything from top sights and walking tours to opinionated reviews of where to eat, stay, shop and have fun.

CitySync lets travellers use their Palm™ or Visor™ hand-held computers to guide them through a city with handy tips on transport, history, cultural life, major sights, and shopping and entertainment options. It can also quickly search and sort hundreds of reviews of hotels, restaurants and attractions, and pinpoint their location on scrollable street maps. CitySync can be downloaded from **www.citysync.com**

MAPS & ATLASES

Lonely Planet's **City Maps** feature downtown and metropolitan maps, as well as transit routes and walking tours. The maps come complete with an index of streets, a listing of sights and a plastic coat for extra durability.

Road Atlases are an essential navigation tool for serious travellers. Cross-referenced with the guidebooks, they also feature distance and climate charts and a complete site index.

ESSENTIALS

Read This First books help new travellers to hit the road with confidence. These invaluable predeparture guides give step-by-step advice on preparing for a trip, budgeting, arranging a visa, planning an itinerary and staying safe while still getting off the beaten track.

Healthy Travel pocket guides offer a regional rundown on disease hot spots and practical advice on predeparture health measures, staying well on the road and what to do in emergencies. The guides come with a user-friendly design and helpful diagrams and tables.

Lonely Planet's **Phrasebooks** cover the essential words and phrases travellers need when they're strangers in a strange land. They come in a pocket-sized format with colour tabs for quick reference, extensive vocabulary lists, easy-to-follow pronunciation keys and two-way dictionaries.

Miffed by blurry photos of the Taj Mahal? Tired of the classic 'top of the head cut off' shot? **Travel Photography: A Guide to Taking Better Pictures** will help you turn ordinary holiday snaps into striking images and give you the know-how to capture every scene, from frenetic festivals to peaceful beach sunrises.

Lonely Planet's **Travel Journal** is a lightweight but sturdy travel diary for jotting down all those on-the-road observations and significant travel moments. It comes with a handy time-zone wheel, world maps and useful travel information.

Lonely Planet's eKno is an all-in-one communication service developed especially for travellers. It offers low-cost international calls and free email and voicemail so that you can keep in touch while on the road. Check it out on www.ekno.lonelyplanet.com

FOOD & RESTAURANT GUIDES

Lonely Planet's **Out to Eat** guides recommend the brightest and best places to eat and drink in top international cities. These gourmet companions are arranged by neighbourhood, packed with dependable maps, garnished with scene-setting photos and served with quirky features.

For people who live to eat, drink and travel, **World Food** guides explore the culinary culture of each country. Entertaining and adventurous, each guide is packed with detail on staples and specialities, regional cuisine and local markets, as well as sumptuous recipes, comprehensive culinary dictionaries and lavish photos good enough to eat.

LONELY PLANET

OUTDOOR GUIDES

For those who believe the best way to see the world is on foot, Lonely Planet's **Walking Guides** detail everything from family strolls to difficult treks, with 'when to go and how to do it' advice supplemented by reliable maps and essential travel information.

Cycling Guides map a destination's best bike tours, long and short, in day-by-day detail. They contain all the information a cyclist needs, including advice on bike maintenance, places to eat and stay, innovative maps with detailed cues to the rides, and elevation charts.

The **Watching Wildlife** series is perfect for travellers who want authoritative information but don't want to tote a heavy field guide. Packed with advice on where, when and how to view a region's wildlife, each title features photos of over 300 species and contains engaging comments on the local flora and fauna.

With underwater colour photos throughout, **Pisces Books** explore the world's best diving and snorkelling areas. Each book contains listings of diving services and dive resorts, detailed information on depth, visibility and difficulty of dives, and a roundup of the marine life you're likely to see through your mask.

LONELY PLANET

OFF THE ROAD

Journeys, the travel literature series written by renowned travel authors, capture the spirit of a place or illuminate a culture with a journalist's attention to detail and a novelist's flair for words. These are tales to soak up while you're actually on the road or dip into as an at-home armchair indulgence.

The new range of lavishly illustrated **Pictorial** books is just the ticket for both travellers and dreamers. Off-beat tales and vivid photographs bring the adventure of travel to your doorstep long before the journey begins and long after it is over.

Lonely Planet **Videos** encourage the same independent, tough-minded approach as the guidebooks. Currently airing throughout the world, this award-winning series features innovative footage and an original soundtrack.

Yes, we know, work is tough, so do a little bit of deskside dreaming with the spiral-bound Lonely Planet **Diary,** the tearaway page-a-day **Day-to-Day Calendar** or a Lonely Planet **Wall Calendar,** filled with great photos from around the world.

TRAVELLERS NETWORK

Lonely Planet Online. Lonely Planet's award-winning Web site has insider information on hundreds of destinations, from Amsterdam to Zimbabwe, complete with interactive maps and relevant links. The site also offers the latest travel news, recent reports from travellers on the road, guidebook upgrades, a travel links site, an online book-buying option and a lively traveller's bulletin board. It can be viewed at **www.lonelyplanet.com** or AOL keyword: lp.

Planet Talk is a quarterly print newsletter, full of gossip, advice, anecdotes and author articles. It provides an antidote to the being-at-home blues and lets you plan and dream for the next trip. Contact the nearest Lonely Planet office for your free copy.

Comet, the free Lonely Planet newsletter, comes via email once a month. It's loaded with travel news, advice, dispatches from authors, travel competitions and letters from readers. To subscribe, click on the Comet subscription link on the front page of the Web site.

Guides by Region

Lonely Planet is known worldwide for publishing practical, reliable and no-nonsense travel information in our guides and on our Web site. The Lonely Planet list covers just about every accessible part of the world. Currently there are 16 series: Travel guides, Shoestring guides, Condensed guides, Phrasebooks, Read This First, Healthy Travel, Walking guides, Cycling guides, Watching Wildlife guides, Pisces Diving & Snorkeling guides, City Maps, Road Atlases, Out to Eat, World Food, Journeys travel literature and Pictorials.

AFRICA Africa on a shoestring • Cairo • Cape Town • Cape Town City Map • East Africa • Egypt • Egyptian Arabic phrasebook • Ethiopia, Eritrea & Djibouti • Ethiopian (Amharic) phrasebook • The Gambia & Senegal • Healthy Travel Africa • Kenya • Malawi • Morocco • Moroccan Arabic phrasebook • Mozambique • Read This First: Africa • South Africa, Lesotho & Swaziland • Southern Africa • Southern Africa Road Atlas • Swahili phrasebook • Tanzania, Zanzibar & Pemba • Trekking in East Africa • Tunisia • Watching Wildlife East Africa • Watching Wildlife Southern Africa • West Africa • World Food Morocco • Zimbabwe, Botswana & Namibia
Travel Literature: Mali Blues: Traveling to an African Beat • The Rainbird: A Central African Journey • Songs to an African Sunset: A Zimbabwean Story

AUSTRALIA & THE PACIFIC Auckland • Australia • Australian phrasebook • Australia Road Atlas • Bushwalking in Australia •Cycling New Zealand • Fiji • Fijian phrasebook • Healthy Travel Australia, NZ and the Pacific • Islands of Australia's Great Barrier Reef • Melbourne • Melbourne City Map • Micronesia • New Caledonia • New South Wales & the ACT • New Zealand • Northern Territory • Outback Australia • Out to Eat – Melbourne • Out to Eat – Sydney • Papua New Guinea • Pidgin phrasebook • Queensland • Rarotonga & the Cook Islands • Samoa • Solomon Islands • South Australia • South Pacific • South Pacific phrasebook • Sydney • Sydney City Map • Sydney Condensed • Tahiti & French Polynesia • Tasmania • Tonga • Tramping in New Zealand • Vanuatu • Victoria • Watching Wildlife Australia • Western Australia
Travel Literature: Islands in the Clouds: Travels in the Highlands of New Guinea • Kiwi Tracks: A New Zealand Journey • Sean & David's Long Drive

CENTRAL AMERICA & THE CARIBBEAN Bahamas, Turks & Caicos • Baja California • Bermuda • Central America on a shoestring • Costa Rica • Costa Rica Spanish phrasebook • Cuba • Dominican Republic & Haiti • Eastern Caribbean • Guatemala • Guatemala, Belize & Yucatán: La Ruta Maya • Healthy Travel Central & South America • Jamaica • Mexico • Mexico City • Panama • Puerto Rico • Read This First: Central & South America • World Food Mexico • Yucatán
Travel Literature: Green Dreams: Travels in Central America

EUROPE Amsterdam • Amsterdam City Map • Amsterdam Condensed • Andalucía • Austria • Baltic States phrasebook • Barcelona • Barcelona City Map • Berlin • Berlin City Map • Britain • British phrasebook • Brussels, Bruges & Antwerp • Budapest • Budapest City Map • Canary Islands • Central Europe • Central Europe phrasebook • Corfu & the Ionians • Corsica • Crete • Crete Condensed • Croatia • Cycling Britain • Cycling France • Cyprus • Czech & Slovak Republics • Denmark • Dublin • Dublin City Map • Eastern Europe • Eastern Europe phrasebook • Edinburgh • Estonia, Latvia & Lithuania • Europe on a shoestring • Finland • Florence • France • Frankfurt Condensed • French phrasebook • Georgia, Armenia & Azerbaijan • Germany • German phrasebook • Greece • Greek Islands • Greek phrasebook • Hungary • Iceland, Greenland & the Faroe Islands • Ireland • Istanbul • Italian phrasebook • Italy • Krakow • Lisbon • The Loire • London • London City Map • London Condensed • Madrid • Malta • Mediterranean Europe • Mediterranean Europe phrasebook • Moscow • Munich • Norway • Out to Eat – London • Paris • Paris City Map • Paris Condensed • Poland • Portugal • Portuguese phrasebook • Prague • Prague City Map • Provence & the Côte d'Azur • Read This First: Europe • Romania & Moldova • Rome • Russia, Ukraine & Belarus • Russian phrasebook • Scandinavian & Baltic Europe • Scandinavian Europe phrasebook • Scotland • Sicily • Slovenia • South-West France • Spain • Spanish phrasebook • St Petersburg • St Petersburg City Map • Sweden • Switzerland • Trekking in Spain • Tuscany • Ukrainian phrasebook • Venice • Vienna • Walking in Britain • Walking in France • Walking in Ireland • Walking in Italy • Walking in Spain • Walking in Switzerland • Western Europe • Western Europe phrasebook • World Food France • World Food Ireland • World Food Italy • World Food Spain
Travel Literature: Love and War in the Apennines • The Olive Grove: Travels in Greece • On the Shores of the Mediterranean • Round Ireland in Low Gear • A Small Place in Italy

INDIAN SUBCONTINENT Bangladesh • Bengali phrasebook • Bhutan • Delhi • Goa • Healthy Travel Asia & India • Hindi & Urdu phrasebook • India • Indian Himalaya • Karakoram Highway • Kerala • Mumbai

LONELY PLANET

Mail Order

Lonely Planet products are distributed worldwide.They are also available by mail order from Lonely Planet, so if you have difficulty finding a title please write to us. North and South American residents should write to 150 Linden St, Oakland, CA 94607, USA; European and African residents should write to 10a Spring Place, London NW5 3BH, UK; and residents of other countries to Locked Bag 1, Footscray, Victoria 3011, Australia.

(Bombay) • Nepal • Nepali phrasebook • Pakistan • Rajasthan • Read This First: Asia & India • South India • Sri Lanka • Sri Lanka phrasebook • Tibet • Tibetan phrasebook • Trekking in the Indian Himalaya • Trekking in the Karakoram & Hindukush • Trekking in the Nepal Himalaya
Travel Literature: The Age of Kali: Indian Travels and Encounters • Hello Goodnight: A Life of Goa • In Rajasthan • A Season in Heaven: True Tales from the Road to Kathmandu • Shopping for Buddhas • A Short Walk in the Hindu Kush • Slowly Down the Ganges

ISLANDS OF THE INDIAN OCEAN Madagascar & Comoros • Maldives • Mauritius, Réunion & Seychelles

MIDDLE EAST & CENTRAL ASIA Bahrain, Kuwait & Qatar • Central Asia • Central Asia phrasebook • Dubai • Hebrew phrasebook • Iran • Israel & the Palestinian Territories • Istanbul • Istanbul City Map • Istanbul to Cairo on a shoestring • Jerusalem • Jerusalem City Map • Jordan • Lebanon • Middle East • Oman & the United Arab Emirates • Syria • Turkey • Turkish phrasebook • World Food Turkey • Yemen
Travel Literature: Black on Black: Iran Revisited • The Gates of Damascus • Kingdom of the Film Stars: Journey into Jordan

NORTH AMERICA Alaska • Boston • Boston City Map • California & Nevada • California Condensed • Canada • Chicago • Chicago City Map • Deep South • Florida • Hawaii • Hiking in Alaska • Hiking in the USA • Honolulu • Las Vegas • Los Angeles • Miami • Miami City Map • New England • New Orleans • New York City • New York City City Map • New York City Condensed • New York, New Jersey & Pennsylvania • Oahu • Out to Eat – San Francisco • Pacific Northwest • Puerto Rico • Rocky Mountains • San Francisco • San Francisco City Map • Seattle • Southwest • Texas • USA • USA phrasebook • Vancouver • Virginia & the Capital Region • Washington, DC City Map • World Food Deep South, USA
Travel Literature: Caught Inside: A Surfer's Year on the California Coast • Drive Thru America

NORTH-EAST ASIA Beijing • Cantonese phrasebook • China • Hiking in Japan • Hong Kong • Hong Kong City Map • Hong Kong Condensed • Hong Kong, Macau & Guangzhou • Japan • Japanese phrasebook • Korea • Korean phrasebook • Kyoto • Mandarin phrasebook • Mongolia • Mongolian phrasebook • Seoul • South-West China • Taiwan • Tokyo
Travel Literature: In Xanadu: A Quest • Lost Japan

SOUTH AMERICA Argentina, Uruguay & Paraguay • Bolivia • Brazil • Brazilian phrasebook • Buenos Aires • Chile & Easter Island • Colombia • Ecuador & the Galapagos Islands • Healthy Travel Central & South America • Latin American Spanish phrasebook • Peru • Quechua phrasebook • Read This First: Central & South America • Rio de Janeiro • Rio de Janeiro City Map • Santiago • South America on a shoestring • Trekking in the Patagonian Andes • Venezuela
Travel Literature: Full Circle: A South American Journey

SOUTH-EAST ASIA Bali & Lombok • Bangkok • Bangkok City Map • Burmese phrasebook • Cambodia • Hanoi • Healthy Travel Asia & India • Hill Tribes phrasebook • Ho Chi Minh City • Indonesia • Indonesian phrasebook • Indonesia's Eastern Islands • Jakarta • Java • Lao phrasebook • Laos • Malay phrasebook • Malaysia, Singapore & Brunei • Myanmar (Burma) • Philippines • Pilipino (Tagalog) phrasebook • Read This First: Asia & India • Singapore • Singapore City Map • South-East Asia on a shoestring • South-East Asia phrasebook • Thailand • Thailand's Islands & Beaches • Thailand, Vietnam, Laos & Cambodia Road Atlas • Thai phrasebook • Vietnam • Vietnamese phrasebook • World Food Thailand • World Food Vietnam

ALSO AVAILABLE: Antarctica • The Arctic • The Blue Man: Tales of Travel, Love and Coffee • Brief Encounters: Stories of Love, Sex & Travel • Chasing Rickshaws • The Last Grain Race • Lonely Planet Unpacked • Not the Only Planet: Science Fiction Travel Stories • On the Edge: Extreme Travel • Sacred India • Travel with Children • Travel Photography: A Guide to Taking Better Pictures

Index

Abbreviations

Text

Bold indicates maps.

Bold indicates maps.

Bold indicates maps.

Boxed Text

Bold indicates maps.

MAP LEGEND

Freeway .... Freeway	==== ...... Unsealed Road	====== ...Tollway, Freeway	—··—··— .... International
Highway ...... Primary Road	— ...... One Way Street	====== ...... Primary Road	—··—··— .... State
Road .... Secondary Road	====== ...... Pedestrian Street	====== ..... Secondary Road	— — — .... Disputed
Street .... Street	⊓⊓⊓⊓⊓ .... Stepped Street	====== .... Minor Road	◄■━━■ .... Fortified Wall
Lane .... Lane	)= = = ... Tunnel		
.... On/Off Ramp	========== .... Footbridge		

	⊢—⊢—O⊢ .. JR Railway; Station	⊢—⊢—[▣]⊢— .. Cable Car, Chairlift
	⊢—⊢—O⊣ .. Shinkansen Railway	—————[▣] .... Ferry
⌐￣￣ .... River, Creek	⊂⊃ ...Dry Lake; Salt Lake	⊢—O— .... Local Railway	——————— .... Walking Trail
—·—·— .... Canal	⊙ ⇀ .... Spring; Rapids	⊢ + + +)· Underground Rlwy	·········· .... Walking Tour
⬭ .... Lake	❻ +⊣⬅ .... Waterfalls	—●—Ⓜ ...... Subway, Station	⌒⌒⌒ .... Path

▬▬ .... Building	⬭ .... Market	🅟 .... Beach	.... Campus
❀ .... Park, Gardens	⬭ .... Sports Ground	+ + + ... Cemetery	⎍ .... Plaza

❍ **CAPITAL** .... National Capital	● **City** .... City	● Village .... Village	
◉ **CAPITAL** .... Provincial Capital	● **Town** .... Town	▬▬ .... Urban Area	

⭑ ....Place to Stay	▼ .... Place to Eat	● ....Point of Interest

✈	.... Airport	🚲	.... Cycling	🏞	.... National Park	🅰	.... Shinto Shrine
⑤	.... Bank	ⓟ	.... Golf Course	♨	.... Onsen, Sento	⊗	..... Shopping Centre
▣	.... Bus Terminal	✛	.... Hospital	🅿	.... Parking	☎	.... Telephone
🏰	.... Castle	@	...... Internet Cafe	✚	.... Police Station	卍	...Temple, Buddhist
⌂	.... Cave	✳	.... Lookout	✉	.... Post Office	⬛	.... Tomb
⌂	.... Chalet	⚱	.... Monument	🍺	.... Pub or Bar	❶	..Tourist Information
⬛❶	.... Church	🏛	.... Museum	🏚	.... Ruins	🔲	.... Zoo

Note: not all symbols displayed above appear in this book

LONELY PLANET OFFICES

Australia
Locked Bag 1, Footscray, Victoria 3011
☎ 03 9689 4666 fax 03 9689 6833
email: talk2us@lonelyplanet.com.au

USA
150 Linden St, Oakland, CA 94607
☎ 510 893 8555 TOLL FREE: 800 275 8555
fax 510 893 8572
email: info@lonelyplanet.com

UK
10a Spring Place, London NW5 3BH
☎ 020 7428 4800 fax 020 7428 4828
email: go@lonelyplanet.co.uk

France
1 rue du Dahomey, 75011 Paris
☎ 01 55 25 33 00 fax 01 55 25 33 01
email: bip@lonelyplanet.fr
www.lonelyplanet.fr

World Wide Web: www.lonelyplanet.com *or* AOL keyword: lp
Lonely Planet Images: lpi@lonelyplanet.com.au